Sex Over Forty   Publishes information and research on sexuality and aging. www.sexualhealth.com/over40.htm

Sex Roles: A Journal of Research   Focuses on all aspects of gender roles and norms, including their interaction with sexual relationships.

Sexual Well-Being   Newsletter devoted to sexuality and health.

Sexuality and Disability   Contains information relevant to the sexual expression of persons with disabilities.

SIECUS Reports   Published by the Sex Information and Education Council of the United States. Emphasizes topics relevant to sex education but also publishes articles on all topics in the human sexuality field, as well as reviews of contemporary books and audiovisual materials. www.siecus.org/pubs

Self-Help Organizations

In many cases, you can find the service or information you are seeking by consulting either the White Pages or Yellow Pages in your local telephone book. If there is a crisis center in your area, its staff can also provide referrals. In the event that the information or service that you want is not locally available, the following sources can be helpful.

Contraception

The Planned Parenthood Federation of America, (800) 829-7732, can provide referrals to the nearest Planned Parenthood clinic or other contraception clinic for those seeking information, contraceptives, and checkups. These services may also be offered by the student health service at your college or university, or by the local public health department. www.plannedparenthood.org

Gay and Lesbian Issues

Parents and Friends of Lesbians and Gays (PFLAG), P.O. Box 27605, Central Station, Washington, DC 20038, (202) 638-4200, is a volunteer peer group whose goal is to help parents accept and understand their gay offspring. www.pflag.org/pflag.html

Association of Gay and Lesbian Psychiatrists, 1439 Pineville Rd., New Hope, PA 12938, can be a useful organization for gay individuals or couples seeking a therapist who will not operate on the assumption that their problems stem from their sexual orientation. www.members.aol.com/algpnat/homepage.html

The National Gay and Lesbian Task Force has a hotline for reporting violence against gays. Call (202) 332-6483. The Hate Crimes hotline may also be called: (800) 347-4283. www.ngltf.org

The Trevor Project has a round-the-clock national toll-free hotline for gay and questioning youth. Teens who call (800) 850-8078 can talk to trained counselors and find local resources. All calls are free and confidential. www.trevorproject.com

Intersexuality

The Intersex Society of North America (ISNA) is a peer support, education, and advocacy group founded and operated by and for intersexuals. Contact ISNA at P.O. Box 31791, San Francisco, CA 94131. www.isna.org

Sexual Dysfunctions

The American Association for Sex Educators, Counselors, and Therapists, (319) 895-8407, can provide you with the names of people in your area whom the organization has certified as sex therapists. Your county or state mental health board can also give the names of licensed therapists in your area. www.aasect.org

For those who would like information on erectile dysfunctions, the following organizations may be contacted: Impotence Information Center, Department USA, P.O. Box 9, Minneapolis, MN 55440, (800) 843-4315, or Impotents Anonymous, 119 S. Ruth St., Maryville, TN 37801, (615) 983-6092, (800) 669-1603.

Sexual Information

The Sex Information and Education Council of the United States (SIECUS), listed earlier under "Professional Organizations," also responds to phone calls from individuals with personal questions or concerns about sexuality at (212) 206-7798. www.siecus.org

Sexually Transmitted Diseases

The Public Health Service offers several AIDS hotlines. Call (800) 342-AIDS. This telephone number is staffed 24 hours a day, 7 days a week. Spanish speakers may call (800) 344-7432, from 8 a.m. to 2 a.m. daily, EST. There is a TTY number for the hearing impaired: (800) 243-7889, Monday through Friday from 10 a.m. to 10 p.m, EST.

The Herpes Resource Center, 260 Sheridan Ave., Palo Alto, CA 94306, (919) 361-2120, provides information about herpes. www.metalab.unc.edu/ASHA/herpes.hrc.html

The STD National Hotline can be consulted for information about sexually transmitted diseases and referrals to STD clinics. Call (800) 227-8922.

Erotic Products

These businesses offer a variety of products, including books about sexuality, videos, sexual toys and vibrators, massage creams, and erotic contraceptives.

Eve's Garden
119 West 57th St
New York, NY 10019
(800) 848-3837
www.evesgarden.com

Good Vibrations
1210 Valencia Street
San Francisco, CA 94110
(415) 974-8980
www.goodvibes.com

The Xandria Collection
www. xandria.com

Grand Opening
318 Harvard Street, Suite 32
Brookline, MA 02146
(617) 731-2626
www.grandopening.com

Sexual Interactions

Sexual Interactions

Fifth Edition

Elizabeth Rice Allgeier

Bowling Green State University

Albert Richard Allgeier

Allgeier and Associates, Bowling Green, Ohio

Houghton Mifflin Company   **Boston New York**

Sponsoring Editor: Kerry Baruth
Senior Associate Editor: Jane Knetzger
Senior Project Editor: Janet Young
Editorial Assistant: Nasya Laymon
Senior Designer: Henry Rachlin
Senior Production/Design Coordinator: Carol Merrigan
Senior Manufacturing Coordinator: Sally Culler
Marketing Manager: Pamela Laskey
Senior Cover Design Coordinator: Deborah Azerrad Savona

Cover image: Detail from a red-figure vase by the Dikaios Painter, with a symposium
scene, late 6th century B.C. Musées Royaux d'Art et d'Histoire, Brussels.

Credits appear following index.

Printed in the U.S.A.

Library of Congress Catalog Card Number: 98-71975

ISBN: 0-395-90925-2

123456789-DW-03 02 01 00 99

Dedication
We dedicate this book with much love to our parents,
our four children, and our five grandchildren,
Forrest, Laurel, Larkin, Maya, and Max

Brief Contents

Contents

Research on Sexuality 46

Sexual Anatomy and Physiology 66

Sexual Behavior 92

Arousal and Communication   120

Loving Sexual Interactions   146

Sexual Differentiation and Development   168

Pregnancy and Birth   196

10

Contraception   222

11

Resolving Unwanted Pregnancy   246

12

Sexuality in Childhood and Adolescence   266

Sexuality in Adulthood   294

Variations in Sexual Orientation   320

Sexual Dysfunctions and Therapy   348

Sexually Transmitted Diseases   374

17

Atypical Sexual Activity   400

18

Sexual Harassment   428

Sexual Assault and Abuse 448

Sex for Profit 472

Preface

We named our text *Sexual Interactions* because of our belief that the complexity of human sexual behavior cannot be understood by reference to just one theory or to biological, psychological, sociological, cultural, historical, medical, or religious factors alone. Instead, in most instances, an individual's sexual feelings and behaviors result from the complex interactions of these influences.

Perhaps more than any other area, the topic of human sexuality is filled with myths and misconceptions. We seek to provide readers with the most recent knowledge on sexual behavior to counter prevailing unsupported beliefs. Even accurate knowledge, however, may contribute little to the quality of people's personal and sexual experience if they lack the ability to communicate about the many sexual issues that confront individuals and couples. Thus we seek to increase readers' communication skills and comfort in sharing their feelings and desires regarding such diverse areas as birth control, sexual arousal, sexual orientation, sexually transmitted diseases, and their desire to have or to avoid sexual intimacy with a potential partner. We do this in each of the relevant chapters by presenting vignettes, dialogues, and practical advice on negotiating sexual interactions.

Awareness of the diversity in beliefs across cultures, about both the purposes of sexual activity and the causes and effects of various sexual behaviors, may broaden readers' perspectives and reduce their tendency to conclude that what is sexually normative in a particular culture is the only *right* way to conduct our sexual lives. Accordingly, throughout the text we describe cross-cultural variations regarding relationship forms (monogamy, polygamy, and so on), the abortion of fetuses because they are female, approaches to sex education, reasons for female circumcision, forms of prostitution in several different societies, and a number of other topics.

NEW PEDAGOGICAL FEATURES

We have retained the strong empirical base present in the four previous editions of *Sexual Interactions*.

To help make the knowledge generated by sex researchers more accessible to students, we have developed a number of new pedagogical features that run throughout the text.

Reality or Myth?

Each chapter now begins with five or six statements, each of which represents either a research-based finding or an unsubstantiated myth or stereotype. In reading the chapter, students learn whether each statement is indeed reality or myth. This symbol ® appears in the text by the relevant discussion. With this feature, we hope to stimulate students to think critically about their own beliefs and to evaluate them in light of scientifically gathered data.

Issues to Consider

Interpersed within the text are questions that ask students to indicate how they would handle particular situations as individuals, citizens, and parents after considering the data presented in the related section. By provoking critical thinking and values clarification, these Issues to Consider can provide the basis for engaging class discussion or small-group interactions.

Research Spotlight

Throughout the chapters we discuss significant research findings in boxes entitled "Research Spotlight." Many examine alternative sides to contemporary controversies. For example, in Chapter 3, *Research on Sexuality*, we describe the bases for initial decisions in the Tuskegee experiment to prevent the treatment of Black men with syphilis. In the chapter on sexual assault and abuse, we review the recovered memory–versus–induced memory controversy.

Highlight

An additional boxed feature running throughout the text explores special topics likely to intrigue students of human sexuality. For example, the relationship of pain to sexual arousal is described in Chapter 17. The Highlight boxes also address a number of health issues. For example, directions for doing Kegel exercises and conducting breast and testes self-exams are provided in boxed Highlights in Chapter 4. We also describe the methods available for prenatal testing (Chapter 9) and variations in response to menarche (Chapter 8), among other topics.

New Illustration Program

The book's tables, figures, and photos have all greatly benefited from their new rendering in full color. The pedagogical use of color gives diagrams greater clarity and realism, and color has given the photo program more immediacy. In addition, the sexual position drawings have been redrawn and updated for the fifth edition.

FEATURES RETAINED IN THE FIFTH EDITION

Besides adding the significant new pedagogical features described above, we have retained several basic learning tools from the previous edition.

Boldfaced Key Terms and Running Glossary

To help students master the terminology of the field, we place key terms in boldface in the text, and we provide a running glossary of these terms on the page where the terms or phrases are introduced. We also provide an end-of-text glossary for students' reference.

Summary of Major Points

At the end of each chapter, we provide a narrative review of major findings and issues described in the chapter. These summaries are intended to give students a final overview of salient information.

Sources of Information About Sexuality

On the inside front cover, readers will find the names of professional and scholarly organizations concerned with various aspects of sexuality and a list of sexuality journals. In addition, we provide the names and addresses of self-help organizations for people with questions about sexual functions and products. This information appeared in an appendix in the previous edition.

OVERVIEW OF CONTENTS

The fifth edition contains extensively updated materials, including coverage of the latest research and the use of recent examples with which students are likely to be familiar, such as President Clinton's legal difficulties with Paula Jones. In addition, it presents chapters in an almost entirely new sequence. Users of the fourth edition will find a transition guide detailing the key organizational changes between the fourth and the fifth edition in the *Instructor's Resource Manual*.

In a completely revised Chapter 1, *Sexual Interactions: Realities and Myths*, we begin with an overview of the ways in which multiple factors interact in their impact on our sexual attitudes and behaviors. We describe how uncritical acceptance of sexual myths and stereotypes may contribute to negative consequences of sexual interactions. We review myths about the effects of sexual "stimulants" on health; the nature of male versus female sexuality; the practice of female circumcision; and the effect of variations in relationship forms (e.g., monogamy, polygamy). We also feature beliefs about fertility and development and the myths and realities associated with dating and mating. We end with a Highlight describing the Valencia Declaration on Sexual Rights.

Chapter 2, *Contemporary Explanations of Sexuality*, covers major theories relevant to sexuality: evolutionary, psychoanalytic, social learning, and sociological theories. The section on sociological theory includes a description of feminist approaches to explaining sexuality.

Chapter 3, *Research on Sexuality*, provides a brief historical overview of scholarly attempts to obtain information about human sexuality. We describe the impact of cultural beliefs, political attitudes, and ethical issues on the kinds of research questions that can be addressed. We describe the process of sex research and review the methods that researchers employ when attempting to test hypotheses. We end this chapter with a focus on issues to consider when evaluating the results of sexuality studies.

In Chapter 4, *Sexual Anatomy and Physiology*, we cover anatomy, hormones, and the nervous system. We include information on breast, cervical, prostate, and testicular cancers and provide directions for self-examinations of the breasts and testes.

Chapter 5, *Sexual Behavior*, contains updated information on sexual behavior, particularly the Laumann et al. (1994) national probability survey. We emphasize safer-sex practices, given the prevalence of STDs in North America.

In Chapter 6, *Arousal and Communication,* we review sources of sexual arousal and focus heavily on communication skills. Communication issues are also discussed in other relevant chapters because of our belief that reinforcement and repetition of this crucial topic is essential for students' well-being.

For the fifth edition, we moved Chapter 7, *Loving Sexual Interactions,* from the end of the text. We also altered the organizational structure of this chapter from one based on Sternberg's triadic model of love to one that follows the current work on love and attachment styles. We review the burgeoning literature on love relationships and also describe those interactions that can be harmful even though they are initiated under the guise of love. We describe the remarkable bonobo (also called pygmy chimpanzees) who appear to resolve interpersonal conflict by engaging in sexual stimulation. We also include discussion of the differences between love, jealousy, control, and dependency.

Chapter 8, *Sexual Differentiation and Development,* contains material on typical and atypical sexual and gender differentiation from conception through puberty. We have included information on the debate over the clinical and medical treatment of intersexual infants (those with ambiguous genitals).

In Chapter 9, *Pregnancy and Birth,* recent research on the process of pregnancy and birth is presented. We cover postpartum events including the controversies surrounding breast-feeding and circumcision.

In Chapter 10, *Contraception,* we review the history of attempts to provide legal and safe methods of contraception. We cover the risks and benefits of currently available methods of contraception and describe research on future methods of birth control for men and women.

Chapter 11, *Resolving Unwanted Pregnancy,* includes a description of early abortion methods, such as using extra doses of oral contraceptives, DES, or RU-486. We present important cross-national data on the consequences of unwanted parenthood for the parent or parents and offspring.

In Chapters 12 and 13, we review sexual development across the life span. In Chapter 12, *Sexuality in Childhood and Adolescence,* we trace what is known about gender differences and similarities in sexual socialization from infancy through adolescence, ending with relationship formation that occurs during adolescence.

In Chapter 13, *Sexuality in Adulthood,* we have included recent studies suggesting that monogamy may be more prevalent among married couples and cohabiting gay or heterosexual couples than was indicated by previous research. We briefly cover studies focusing on sexual expression among aging and elderly people.

Although a number of aspects of sexual orientation are covered throughout the text, in Chapter 14, *Variations in Sexual Orientation,* we review what is known about similarities and differences in the lives and experiences of heterosexual, homosexual, and bisexual individuals. A particular emphasis is placed on cross-cultural differences in the definition of what constitutes sexual-orientation identity, and we describe the societal problems posed by those driven by antigay prejudice.

Chapter 15, *Sexual Dysfunctions and Therapy,* includes the most recent research on sexual dysfunctions and therapy. We have moved away from an emphasis on DSM-IV because of its strong medical bias.

In Chapter 16, *Sexually Transmitted Diseases,* we present the major STDs and discuss societal attitudes that may hinder treatment of STDs and efforts to impede the transmission of these diseases. The latest research on AIDS and its treatment is presented, including the protease-inhibitor cocktails. We end with practical advice on the role of communication in safer-sex practices.

In Chapter 17, *Atypical Sexual Activity,* we distinguish between noninvasive paraphilias (for instance, fetishes and transsexualism) and invasive paraphilias (such as exhibitionism and pedophilia). We also discuss the effectiveness of various treatments of the paraphilias.

In previous editions, we included the topic of Chapter 18, *Sexual Harassment,* in the sexual coercion and abuse chapter. Because of the explosion of research, legal decisions, and interest in this form of abuse of power, however, we now devote a separate chapter to harassment. We include advice on how to deal with harassment in the various settings in which it occurs.

Chapter 19, *Sexual Assault and Abuse,* covers sexual assault and child-adult sexual contact (sexual abuse). The most recent research on these violations of human dignity and consent are presented, and we describe research on ways to reduce the likelihood of dealing with the occurrence of these events. Sexual coercion is an area in which myths abound, and we review studies investigating the accuracy of a number of myths and stereotypes.

Chapter 20, *Sex for Profit*, focuses on the variety of sexual products that can be purchased; the social and legal consequences of erotica, including those materials that combine violence with sexually explicit material; and the provision of sexual services by prostitutes (sex workers).

To close, we provide a brief *Afterword*, new to this edition, in which we emphasize the complexity of sexual interactions, the importance of recognizing our sexual assumptions and beliefs, and the advantages of establishing personal sexual policies. We also reinforce points made throughout the text about the relationship of sex education to healthy, responsible sexual behavior. Finally, we end the *Afterword* with a plea for the acceptance of sexual pluralism and diversity.

ANCILLARIES

A completely revised set of supplemental materials is available with this text to enhance the teaching and learning processes.

Instructor's Resource Manual and Test Bank

The *Instructor's Resource Manual* features numerous lecture and discussion topics and classroom activities, provided by Elizabeth Rice Allgeier, and a test bank, written by Paul Yarab and Michelle Fuiman of Bowling Green State University. Each chapter of the test bank includes 100 multiple-choice questions and several essay questions. The multiple-choice questions are keyed to learning objectives and identified as factual, conceptual, or applied in nature. Factual questions have been kept to a minimum.

Computerized Test Bank

The test bank is also available on disk with software that allows instructors to add and edit questions and prepare exams.

Study Guide

Each chapter of the accompanying student *Study Guide*, written by Paul Yarab and Michelle Fuiman,

includes a chapter overview, learning objectives, a key-terms review exercise, and a multiple-choice quiz with explanations for both correct and incorrect answers.

Transparencies

A selection of several dozen full-color overhead transparencies, including images from inside and outside the text, is available.

Psychology Web Site

Houghton Mifflin's psychology web site can be reached by pointing to the Houghton Mifflin home page at http://www.hmco.com and going to the College Division Psychology page. This location provides access to additional useful and innovative teaching and learning resources.

Multimedia Policy

The Houghton Mifflin multimedia policy offers adopters a variety of videos, available through your Houghton Mifflin representative.

ACKNOWLEDGMENTS

We remain indebted to the many reviewers of the first four editions of our text. We also thank the following reviewers of this edition:

Randy D. Fisher, University of Central Florida
Norma L. McCoy, San Francisco State University
Carol L. Oyster, University of Wisconsin at LaCrosse
K. David Skinner, Valencia Community College
Jeffery Stern, University of Michigan, Dearborn

We also appreciate the suggestions that we have received from a number of professors who have used past editions of our text. In particular, we acknowledge the cogent comments (and humor) we receive from Andy Walters, Hobart and William Smith Colleges; Paul Okami, University of California, Los Angeles; and Bruce Rind, Temple University. We sought additional specialized reviews from biologist Lee Meserve, Bowling Green State University; and sociologist and STD specialist William W. Darrow, Florida International University. Psychologist Michael W. Wiederman of Ball State University read the entire manuscript and provided detailed and very helpful suggestions for improvement.

We have developed strong friendships with a number of people at Houghton Mifflin Company.

David Lee, our initial sponsoring editor, was enthusiastic and unusually involved in a number of aspects of this project, and we appreciate his strong interest. Sheralee Connors, our superb developmental editor, was particularly gifted in helping us to increase the accessibility of our book. Her sensitive and sensible editorial suggestions have been invaluable in increasing the communicability of the book without introducing the distortion that can occur with such a complex topic. For several years, we have been in almost daily contact (via e-mail) with our project editor, Janet Young. Her sense of humor, professional touches, and quick responsiveness to our questions have been very helpful. Senior Associate Editor Jane Knetzger has worked on the development of the ancillary materials and has been very much involved in advising us about the content of the book. Editorial Assistant Lou Gum also responded quickly to various questions we have had. We appreciate the work of Senior Designer Henry Rachlin, Senior Production/Design Coordinator Carol Merrigan, and Art Editor and Photo Researcher Linda Hadley. Marketing Manager Pam Laskey has demonstrated considerable interest in and commitment to keeping us aware of professors' concerns and needs in teaching college-level human sexuality courses. Although we have not had previous direct experience with editors-in-chief at other companies that have published our books, we have developed a very pleasurable relationship with Kathi Prancan, editor-in-chief for science and psychology.

E.R.A.
A.R.A.

About the Authors

Elizabeth Rice Allgeier (ALL-guy-er, rhymes with ALL-fire) earned her B.A. from the University of Oregon in 1969, her M.S. from the State University of New York at Oswego in 1973, and her Ph.D. from Purdue University in 1976. Currently Professor of Psychology at Bowling Green State University, she has won numerous teaching awards, including the BGSU Alumni Association's Master Teacher Award in 1988, and the BGSU Outstanding Con-

tributor to Graduate Education in 1992. In 1986, she was named the American Psychological Association's G. Stanley Hall Lecturer on Sexuality. She has taught human sexuality at Eastern Michigan University and at the State University of New York at Fredonia. Dr. Allgeier's interest in studying human sexual behavior began while she was living with the So, a preliterate, polygynous tribe in Uganda. Her study of this tribe resulted in a two-volume ethnography that she coauthored. Her current research interests include the societal regulation of sexual behavior, sexual coercion, and the relationship between gender-role norms and sexual interaction. Actively involved in The Society for the Scientific Study of Sex, she has served as national secretary and as president for that organization, and in 1991 was awarded its Distinguished Service Award. In 1994, she was also awarded the Alfred C. Kinsey Award for Outstanding Contributions to Sexual Science by the Midcontinent Region of The Society for the Scientific Study of Sex. She sits on the editorial board of four scholarly journals that publish sex research and was Editor of *The Journal of Sex Research* from 1993 to 1998.

Albert Richard Allgeier earned his B.A. from Gannon University in 1967, his M.A. from the American University of Beirut in Lebanon in 1969, and his Ph.D. from Purdue University in 1974. He has been Clinical Director at both the Northwest Center for Human Resources in Lima, Ohio, and Wood County Mental Health Center in Bowling Green, Ohio. He has served on the faculty of Alma College, the State University of New York at Fredonia, and Bowling Green State University. Currently, he is in private practice in Bowling Green. He has conducted research on interpersonal attraction and sexual knowledge, and has participated with Elizabeth Rice Allgeier, his wife, in a series of studies on attitudes about abortion. He is also interested in the implications of evolutionary theory for the study of human sexuality. He and Elizabeth Rice Allgeier edited (with Gary Brannigan) *The Sex Scientists* (1998). That book features the research process experienced by fifteen sexual scientists and is part of a series of books on that topic that the Allgeiers and Brannigan are developing.

The Allgeiers have four children and five grandchildren. They enjoy traveling, reading novels, and watching college athletics.

Sexual Interactions

Sexual Interactions: Realities and Myths

Reality or Myth

1. Most cultures in the world punish members of their society if they have more than one spouse at the same time.

2. The Catholic church has always prohibited abortion.

3. The practice of infanticide occurs only among nonhuman animal species.

4. In cultures in which it is expected that boys will have sexual relations with other boys, only a very small proportion grow up to engage in sex exclusively with other men.

5. Contrary to the stereotype that men do all the initiating, women also initiate romantic relationships.

6. If two people are really meant to be together, they will ultimately engage in their first intimate sexual contact with each other without the need for discussion or advance planning.

Sexual Interactions

We chose to call this book *Sexual Interactions* for several different reasons. First, at a fundamental level, throughout most of our lives, we engage in sexual interactions with ourselves (fantasy is probably the most sex-drenched venue) or others. Second, in attempting to understand the sources of our arousal and response to sexual stimulation, it is not sufficient to look *only* at psychological processes, or anatomical characteristics, *or* hormone secretion levels, *or* evolutionary processes, *or* cultural beliefs, *or* personal histories, or current health status, *or* relationship qualities. Instead, in most cases, an individual's sexual feelings and behaviors result from the complex *interactions* of all these factors and more. Further, our sexual feelings and behavior vary at different times, in different environments, and with the rewards and punishments associated with the expression of particular opinions and desires.

To add to the complexity, each of us has our own unique belief system or set of informal theories about sexuality. Thus, one person may be at the same general level on the factors listed above (e.g., similar anatomical characteristics, hormone secretion pattern, current health status) and yet have very different reactions to what appears to external observers to be a similar situation. For example, we know two women, both physically attractive, who like to play what we call "dress-up." Each will, on occasion, dress up—put on sexually appealing clothes that reveal their legs, bodily curves, and so forth—and go to a party attended by people they know, as well as by strangers. Observers might conclude that each is seeking attention and appreciation of her attractiveness. When complimented on their appearance by a stranger at the party, however, the two women react very differently. One acknowledges the compliment, smiles at the speaker, says, "Thank you," and begins a conversation with the person. The other looks scornfully at the complimenter, walks away from him, goes over to a friend of hers, and says, "Who's *that* lech?"

In the same vein, two men who seem similar along many dimensions (age, past experience, anatomical characteristics, cultural background,

and so forth) may interpret the same behavior from another person very differently. When invited to a movie or play by an attractive woman, one man may gratefully accept the invitation, feeling relief from the burden of initiating a date and the possibility of rejection. The other man, invited by the same woman, may refuse, feeling threatened and resentful that his stereotypic role of date initiation has been taken by the woman. In this book, we explore some of the reasons for these individual differences in perceptions, interpretations, and responses.

Speaking of individual differences in responses, you might want to think about how members of your human sexuality course behaved the first day of class. If you have not yet been to the first class meeting, then notice the reactions of the students around you as the professor begins to introduce the topic of human sexuality. The classroom atmosphere during the first few sessions in a human sexuality course is usually charged with tension. There is frequent laughter by some students, and in some cases, the laughter perhaps indicates anxiety. For many of the students, this may

3

be their first experience of participating in, or at least hearing, explicit discussion of sexuality and the use of various terms (*clitoris, penis, erection, orgasm,* and so forth) in a mixed-sex group of relative strangers in a brightly lit room.

Some students have even been asked by parents, roommates, or partners to justify taking the sexuality course. The queries have ranged from "Why would you want to take a class like that?" to "How can it take a whole semester just to study sex?" One woman dropped our class after her fiancé saw it listed on her schedule. She told us apologetically, "He won't let me take it. He said he'll teach me anything I need to know about sex after we get married."

 ## ealities and Myths

Despite a great many studies conducted by sex researchers in recent decades, many members of our culture continue to believe stereotypes and myths that have been demonstrated to be false. These mistaken beliefs can lead to negative results. For example, some individuals are plagued by feelings of guilt about sexuality, partially because of their adherence to various sexual myths. Although we live in a sexually charged culture where sexual images are frequently used to sell products and for various other commercial purposes (see Chapter 20), North Americans are really quite sexually restrictive compared to members of most other modern industrialized cultures (see Chapters 11 and 12).

Further, many of the potentially negative consequences of engaging in sexual contact—unwanted pregnancy, contraction of sexually transmitted diseases, experiencing various forms of sexual coercion (force)—stem from ignorance about sexuality. In the face of our relatively restrictive culture regarding sex, it is also common for young people to feel inhibited about discussing sexuality with a potential partner.

Throughout this book, we describe various stereotypes and myths and then explore what scientists have discovered based on the research they have conducted. In this chapter, we touch on a number of the beliefs and myths that have surrounded sexuality historically in North America, as well as in other cultures. We begin the book in this manner to try to

help you develop an understanding of some of the ways in which sexuality has been expressed and appreciated versus repressed and punished in human societies. We hope that discovering that many of our common sexual beliefs and behaviors have little (or no) scientific support will help you develop a questioning attitude toward many of your own preconceptions and a curiosity to learn what scientific sex research can tell us.

There are few sexual behaviors that have not been perceived as good or appropriate in some historical time or place, and bad or inappropriate in others. If history serves as any guide to the future, there is little reason to believe that the norms, values, and perceptions that prevail at the dawn of the twenty-first century in North America will be the same 300 years from now, or that people will have the same sexual beliefs and customs in the future as they do now. Economic, social, and political factors such as overpopulation, war, and sexually transmitted diseases such as AIDS will shape future sexual values and behaviors.

> ▶ **Issues to Consider:** Before reading some of the myths and realities in the rest of the chapter, list some of the myths that you remember accepting when you were younger. What led you to change your mind about each?

 ## eliefs About the Need to Control Sexual Expression

Attempts to control sexual contacts between humans have ranged from suggestions for dietary and health regimens to culturally accepted beliefs about the nature of male versus female sexuality, and the impact of the surgical removal of portions of women's genital anatomy. We describe these beliefs as well as cultural values regarding the morality of various relationship forms.

MYTHS ABOUT THE EFFECTS OF SEXUAL "STIMULANTS" ON HEALTH

The notion that sexual excesses could cause ill health was a long-held belief. In the United States in the nineteenth century, Sylvester Graham (1794–1851) found his calling as a prophet of the temperance movement, which was dedicated to encouraging abstinence from alcoholic beverages (Bullough, 1994). Graham, acclaimed as a lecturer on health and disease, maintained that health depended on avoiding all stimulants, such as alcohol, tobacco, coffee, tea, vinegar, pepper, salt, spices, meats, and rich gravies. In his view, sexual passion also constituted an excess of stimulation that led to debility and disease. Even in marriage, too many orgasms were dangerous. Graham recommended eating homemade breads to reduce stimulation and promote good health, and he

---

Kellogg's Corn Flakes were marketed as an aid for reducing sexual desire and maintaining purity. This advertisement appeared in 1907.

developed the graham cracker as an aid for those who wished to reduce their susceptibility to sexual passion. (Presumably, the addition of cinnamon to graham crackers would have deeply offended Graham, and he would probably be mystified by the development of Viagra, the drug used to aid men who have problems getting erections.)

Similarly, John Harvey Kellogg (1852–1943) invented corn flakes as a food designed to reduce sexual desire, curb masturbation, and foster good health (Money, 1991). Regarding self-stimulation, he produced a lengthy list of signs that a person was engaging in masturbation. As historian Vern Bullough (1994, p. 22) noted, however, Kellogg's list included "every form of conduct found in teenagers: fickleness, bashfulness, unnatural boldness, lassitude, and capricious appetite." Further, according to Kellogg, self-stimulation produced acne, shifty eyes, paleness, smoking, profanity, bed wetting, and fingernail biting (but for a different view, see "Highlight: Mark Twain on Masturbation" on page 6). Indeed, the general view that avoidance of sexual stimulation is important for good health has been popular throughout much of recorded history and is not limited to Western cultures.

Another myth about maladies associated with sexual expression is called Dhat syndrome. *Dhat syndrome* is the modern East Indian term for anxiety associated with the depletion of semen (Paris, 1992). The loss of this vital essence is believed to contribute to loss of health and well-being. The concept is rooted in ancient Indian medical folklore and is reported to be fairly common in India and nearby regions (Joshi & Money, 1995). Men fear that losing too much semen in sexual intercourse, masturbation, or nocturnal emission will lead to erectile dysfunction and other health problems.

Whereas Graham saw sexual intercourse as having a negative effect on health, the historian Lawrence Stone (1977), looking at the relationship between health and sexuality from a different perspective, saw poor health as having a negative effect on sexual intercourse. Stone (1977, pp. 486–487) reported that in England just 300 years ago, only a small proportion of adults were both healthy and attractive:

> [English people endured] periods of crippling illness which incapacitated them for months or years. Even when relatively well, they often suffered from disorders which made sex

Mark Twain on Masturbation

Mark Twain delivered the following musings at a private club in Paris in 1879. The material was considered so scandalous that it was not published until many years later.

> Homer in the second book of the Iliad says, with fine enthsuiasm, "Give me masturbation or give me death!" Caesar, in his Commentaries, says "To the lonely it is company; to the forsaken it is a friend; to the aged and to the impotent it is a benefactor; they that are penniless are yet rich, in that they still have this majestic diversion." In another place this experienced observer has said, "There are time when I prefer it to sodomy." Robinson Crusoe says, "I cannot describe what I owe to this gentle art." Queen Elizabeth said, "It is the bulwark of Virginity." Cetewayo, the Zulu hero, remarked, "A jerk in the hand is worth two in the bush." The immortal Franklin has said, "Masturbation is the mother of invention." He also said, "Masturbation is the best policy." Michelangelo and all the other old masters—Old Masters, I will remark, is an abbreviation, a contraction—have used similar language. Michelangelo said to Pope Julius II, "Self-negation is noble, self-culture is beneficial, self-possession is manly, but to the truly grand and inspiring soul they are poor and tame compared to self-abuse."

> painful to them or unpleasant to their partners. Women suffered from a whole series of gynecological disorders, particularly leukorrhea [vaginal infections involving smelly discharge; see Chapter 16], but also vaginal ulcers, tumors, inflammations, and hemorrhages which often made sexual intercourse disagreeable, painful, or impossible.

Stone suggested that many people in those days probably also had bad breath from inadequate dentistry and poor oral hygiene. Stomachaches, running sores, ulcers, scabs, and other unpleasant skin diseases were extremely common, and these illnesses and disorders often persisted for years. Such health problems are likely to reduce not only a person's sexual appetite but also the individual's sexual appeal to others.

In their book *Healthy Pleasures* (1989), Robert Ornstein and David Sobel maintained that pleasurable activities are linked to human health and well-being. Ornstein, a psychologist, and Sobel, a physician, studied particularly healthy and robust people. These individuals tend to ignore standard advice about exercise and diet but have a sense of optimism and an orientation toward pleasure. Ornstein and Sobel emphasized the importance to good health of engaging in enjoyable pursuits such as sex, good food, and playful behavior. They noted that 20 minutes of continuous sexual activity is not only fun but can burn 110 calories—the equivalent of about 3 miles of jogging.

Ornstein and Sobel claimed that this form of exercise is more or less universally enjoyable. Do you agree with their implication that women and men find sexual interaction equally pleasurable? We turn now to beliefs about sex differences in responses to various aspects of sexuality.

BELIEFS ABOUT THE NATURE OF MALE AND FEMALE SEXUALITY

In contemporary North American culture, it is commonly believed that males are more "sexual" than females, that they have stronger and more readily stimulated sexual appetites, and that they enjoy sex more than females do. Earlier in this century, it was believed that females were passive and uninterested in sex, but during the latter half of the century, females have begun to be perceived as willing to engage in sexual relations under certain conditions and—given a considerate partner—able to enjoy sexual stimulation. The general belief about differences

This painting reflects a common theme in Western civilization: woman as a seductive and powerful sexual temptress.

in male and female sexuality is reflected in the old phrase, "Men give love to get sex; women give sex to get love."

Current Western assumptions about men's and women's sexuality represent a relatively atypical view when seen in historical perspective. The biblical story of Eve's disastrous influence on Adam in the Garden of Eden represents a belief about the nature of female and male sexuality that has been more prevalent throughout history than is the current stereotype of men as being more sexually driven than women are. Although males have consistently held the reins of economic, political, and social power over females in the **patriarchies** characteristic of Western civilization, the dominant view has long

been that women are insatiably seductive and powerful sexual temptresses who pose danger to men, as shown in the depiction of Eve's influence on Adam in the Garden of Eden.

This view of women's sexual power as a source of peril to men is apparent in the earliest records of Western civilization. It is a theme that was frequently repeated until a couple of centuries ago, and remnants of it persist in a number of contemporary beliefs about female sexuality. Two of these include the myth that the vagina has teeth—called *vagina dentata*—that will injure the penis and the myth that the vagina can capture the penis—called *penis captivus*.

These myths appear all over the world and are reflected in certain contemporary Western fashion photography, jokes, novels, and movies (Beit-Hallahmi, 1985). Jack Nicholson, playing a man consumed with the desire for sexual conquests in the movie *Carnal Knowledge,* expressed his ambivalence about women's genitals: "When you think what a man has to dip into, he's got the right to turn soft every once in a while." And you may have heard stories about couples who claimed that they had been caught in compromising positions because the man's penis got "locked" in the woman's vagina, a variation of the penis captivus myth (Beit-Hallahmi, 1985). Although this is rare among humans, it is not uncommon among dogs, who may complete copulation in seconds but remain "locked" to each other for up to half an hour. To understand the simultaneous approach and avoidance that men have had toward women, it is instructive to consider witchcraft and beliefs that humans can be possessed by spirits.

The Diagnosis of Witchcraft. The history of witchcraft has always reflected a strong sexual element. In medieval Europe, it was believed that witches had sex with the devil. The clergy of that time blamed such ailments as erectile dysfunction (popularly, but incorrectly, called "impotence") and loss of memory on the devil and his female witch allies. Not surprisingly, given the belief that the devil was the agent responsible for disease, clergymen involved themselves in the diagnosis and treatment of witchcraft.

In 1486, the German theologians Sprenger and Kramer published *Malleus Maleficarum* ("The Witches' Hammer"). They provided a rationale for women's greater susceptibility to demonic influence to become witches. They argued that women were

patriarchy (PAY-tree-ar-kee)—A society in which men have supremacy over women, who are legally and socially dependent on them.

susceptible to witchcraft because it was rooted in sexual lust, supposedly insatiable in women:

Therefore, let us now chiefly consider women; and first, why this kind of perfidy [witchcraft] is found more in so fragile a sex than in men. . . .

Now the wickedness of women is spoken of in Ecclesiastics xxv: "There is no head above the head of a serpent, and there is no wrath above the wrath of a woman. . . . All wickedness is but little to the wickedness of a woman." What else is woman but a foe to friendship, an unescapable punishment, a necessary evil, a natural temptation, a desirable calamity, a domestic danger, a delectable detriment, an evil of nature, appointed with fair colours! . . . When a woman thinks alone, she thinks evil. . . .

For it is true that in the Old Testament the Scriptures have much that is evil to say about women, and this because of the first temptress, Eve, and her imitators. . . .

But the natural reason is that she is more carnal than a man, as is clear from her many carnal abominations. And it should be noted that there was a defect in the formation of the first woman, since she was formed from a bent rib, that is, a rib of the breast, which is bent as it were in a contrary direction to a man. And since through this defect she is an imperfect animal, she always deceives. . . . To conclude. All witchcraft comes from carnal lust, which is in women insatiable. See Proverbs xxx: "Wherefore for the sake of fulfilling their lusts they consort even with devils." More such reasons could be brought forward, but to the understanding it is sufficiently clear that there are more women than men found infected with the heresy of witchcraft. . . . And blessed be the Highest Who has So far preserved the male sex from So great a crime: for since He was willing to be born and to suffer for us, therefore He has granted to men this privilege.

The witch continues to hold the imagination of certain groups in our culture, as revealed in the report in "Highlight: Contemporary Beliefs in

After being convicted of witchcraft, people—primarily women—were burned at the stake, as shown in this German drawing of the Inquisition.

Witches." Contemporary beliefs in witches are not confined to Western cultures. In one district in India, about 200 women have been killed annually by mobs of fellow villagers who have branded them as witches (Gandhy, 1988).

Possession by Spirits. If we substitute "fox spirit" for the devil, we find a condition known as *koro*: the fear that one's sexual organs are receding into the body and that their complete retraction will result in death. It is primarily a condition reported in men, but women are also susceptible. The fear of death produces a great deal of anxiety and often a state of panic. Affected men will try to stop the shrinking, often with the assistance of relatives, by tying a string around the penis or securing it with a clamping device. Women may complain of shrinking breasts, nipples, or labia and also try to stop the retractions with anchoring devices.

Koro epidemics have been reported in a number of Asian countries. More than 3,000 persons were affected in the mid-1980s on the southern coast of China (Cheng, 1997). In the affected communities, the belief in a "fox spirit" is part of Chinese folklore.

Contemporary Beliefs in Witches

CHURCH TEENS BURN "DEMON" BOOKS, RECORDS

Blue Springs, NE (AP). Books and records have been burned by members of an independent church.

They said they were destroying the work of witches, demons and druids. The burning was organized by teenagers.

"In rock and roll, the drumbeat hypnotizes the listener, and the words are a coded spell," said Dave Kruse, one of the teenagers.

"The record production companies have witches write songs, and the companies have old druid manuscripts containing melodies and drumbeats. They hire top musicians. . . ."

About 30 members of the Gospel Fellowship Church gathered Saturday in the backyard of Doc Barton, the church leader, to burn several dozen albums and single records and about a dozen books. (Dayton Journal Herald, March 17, 1981, p. 1)

More recently, in May 1998, a student planned to sing Fleetwood Mac's "Landslide," about getting older and changing, at the Huntsville (Alabama) High School graduation ceremony. She had also planned to sing the song at a church program before graduation, but the minister of the church refused to let her sing it on the grounds that "the leader of Fleetwood Mac is a witch and Satan worshipper." The student, who said she was a Christian, said she was not trying to go against God by singing the song. Apparently, the high school still intends to allow her to sing the song at graduation.

Source: *Bowling Green Sentinel Tribune,* May 28, 1998, p. 18.

The fox spirit turns into a beautiful seductress to entice young men or women.

A man with nocturnal emissions is believed to have had sex with the fox spirit. By this act, he loses his vital energy to the spirit. He becomes weak and, if not treated, dies. Treatment often involves exorcism to drive the spirit away, after which it seeks another victim, and thus the stage is set for an epidemic.

Most koro victims have been adolescents or young adults with limited education who have been brought up in communities that believe in koro. Traditionally, Chinese cultures have not dealt with sexual issues in an open manner, which may have contributed to the anxieties associated with sexual maturation. Lacking sexual knowledge, adolescents and young adults are susceptible to sexual myths and inaccurate information.

These are just a couple of examples of the myth-driven aspects of sexuality and spirituality. Cultural beliefs about the nature of sexuality may be related to the beliefs about the impact of surgery on the genitals of females.

FEMALE CIRCUMCISION

Most North Americans consider the circumcision of male infants normal but view female circumcision as barbaric. Nevertheless, this practice, also described as female sexual mutilation, is currently performed on millions of females in about 40 nations, most of them in Africa. The surgery ranges from clipping the clitoris to cutting away the external part of the female sexual organs. In its most severe form, known as *infibulation*, the wound and vagina are sewn closed, with only a matchstick-sized hole left open for passing urine and menstrual discharge. The smaller the opening for urination and menstruation following the surgery, the greater the honor that accrues to the woman's family (Gallo & Viviani, 1992; Lightfoot-Klein, 1989).

One reason for this practice among Islamic practitioners is to reduce women's sexual desire, although Islam does not require female circumcision. However, most cultures practicing genital surgery believe that the surgery will ensure virginity at marriage and fidelity thereafter. Women are cut or forced open on

This young Egyptian girl has just undergone circumcision by a midwife.

their wedding night, endure a large surgical incision to give birth, and then are sewn up again.

Hanny Lightfoot-Klein (1989) observed and conducted interviews with Sudanese women, doctors, historians, midwives, and religious leaders in an attempt to understand the contemporary rationale for and effects of this practice. More than 90 percent of the 300 women in her sample had undergone infibulation. The exceptions were from upper-class, educated families.

Female circumcisions are generally performed on girls between 4 and 8 years old by trained midwives in cities or towns and by untrained women in villages. Of the women Lightfoot-Klein interviewed, more than half had been circumcised without any anesthesia. Immediate complications included infection, hemorrhage, shock, septicemia (bloodstream infection), tetanus (acute bacterial infection causing spasmodic muscle contractions), urine retention, trauma to adjacent tissues, and emotional trauma. No count of fatalities from the procedure could be obtained, but some Sudanese doctors estimated that in regions where antibiotics are unavailable, a third

of the girls who are circumcised die from the procedure. Nearly all women reported urinary and menstrual problems until their labia were "opened" at marriage. Circumcised virgins described taking an average of 10 to 15 minutes to urinate, and some women in Lightfoot-Klein's sample reported needing 2 hours to empty their bladders. As would be expected, urinary tract and kidney infections were common. In addition, the small opening often blocked menstrual flow almost completely, sometimes producing a buildup of clotted blood that could be removed only by surgery.

When a circumcised woman marries, her husband is expected to open the sewn-up entrance, which is usually difficult to do. The scars are often so extensive and hardened that even surgical scissors cannot cut through the tissue. The women reported going through extreme suffering during a process of gradual penetration that lasted an average of ten weeks. Tearing of surrounding tissues, hemorrhage, infections, and psychic trauma were common. Of the women Lightfoot-Klein interviewed, 15 percent reported that penetration was impossible. Other women had had midwives cut their labia with knives, but they did so secretly because of the belief that the necessity for this surgery demonstrated a husband's lack of potency. In addition, almost all Sudanese women who became pregnant required surgery during labor to permit their infant to be born because the circumcision scar prevents normal dilation. Following childbirth, almost all women had their labia sewn together again.

In view of this account, you might find it surprising that 90 percent of the women Lightfoot-Klein interviewed said that they had experienced orgasm during sexual relations. Her findings call into question the emphasis placed on the central role of the clitoris by Western experts (see Chapter 4). Despite the formidable obstacles, including removal of the clitoris and cultural prohibitions against female enjoyment of sexuality, most Sudanese women apparently retain their ability to have pleasure and orgasm during sexual relations.

In 1946, British rulers of the Sudan passed a law that made all forms of female sexual mutilation illegal. In reaction to this colonial interference, many Sudanese promptly circumcised their daughters. In the mid-1970s, the Sudanese passed a law against surgically altering the labia, but removal of the clitoris remained legal.

A 1998 ruling in Egypt outlawed female circumcision unless it is deemed necessary for a woman's health. However, implementation of the law will be difficult because it flies in the face of tradition. A 1995 government-sponsored study found that 97 percent of married Egyptian women had undergone this procedure. The World Health Organization and the United Nations Children's Fund support the view that all forms of female circumcision should be abolished.

▶ **Issues to Consider:** Do you believe that Westerners who oppose female circumcision should be allowed to impose their values on cultures that perceive such surgery as important for promoting the virtue of women? What would your reaction be if those cultures practicing female circumcision tried to import this procedure to Westerners in an attempt to protect women's chastity? What if other countries demanded that the United States ban male circumcision?

VARIATIONS IN RELATIONSHIP FORMS

Although many twentieth-century Westerners may find it difficult to believe there are groups for whom romantic love is a relatively unimportant factor in decisions about marriage, history paints a different picture. Historically and cross-culturally, religion and economics have been tied to marriage more than the bonds of romantic love.

In many cultures, families commonly arrange the marriage of their offspring to obtain economic or political benefits. Among the So of northeastern Uganda, there is no stigma attached to pregnancy before marriage; in fact, evidence that a woman is fertile enhances her value in the negotiations between her father and her prospective father-in-law. The greater her value, the more cows and goats her father's clan can demand for her betrothal. The relationship among sex, marriage, and economic relations was aptly demonstrated by the So woman who remarked that, while enduring painful intercourse, she told herself over and over: "I must do this to have babies; I must have babies to get cows."

The Mehinaku of central Brazil consider the notion of romantic love odd (Gregor, 1985). Although all romantic love is suspect, romance between spouses borders on bad taste. The Mehinaku believe that spouses should respect each other and retain a degree of separateness. Each represents a set of in-laws to whom the other owes work, gifts, and deference. Whatever potential there is for romantic attachment is diluted by living closely with many kin and by an elaborate network of extramarital affairs. Newly married couples are permitted only small expressions of affection. According to Gregor, despite the absence of romance, some spouses take an obvious pleasure in each other's company, bathing together each day and going off to their garden to have sex and converse.

For contemporary North Americans, when a partner is sexually intimate with someone other than their primary partner, the experience of jealousy can be so intense and arise so automatically that it may seem a natural or innate reaction. Some of us experience pain at the idea that our mate is interested in or aroused by someone else, even if he or she does not act on those feelings. The available evidence suggests that the value individuals place on sexual exclusivity may be related to the extent to which they enjoy sexual contact and the meaning and interpretation of such contacts. The degree to which different groups experience jealousy is tied to their beliefs about acceptable relationship forms. Contemporary laws and norms in North America support the belief that marital partners should be monogamous, that is, have sexual relations only with each other.

Within Western civilization, most groups have practiced **monogamy**. For example, ancient Egyptians were generally monogamous, and sexual expression outside marriage was unacceptable among the ancient Hebrews (Bullough, 1980). For an individual reared in a culture in which monogamy is the accepted pattern, it is easy to assume that this form of male-female relationship is natural and other forms immoral. The characteristic pattern of modern American relationships is **serial monogamy**; people are expected to confine themselves to one partner at a time, but they may have a number of sexual partners over their lifetime.

If the definition of natural or moral is determined by what the majority of cultures have practiced, then it should be noted that **polygamy**—a marital form that allows a person to have more than one lover or spouse at a time—has been permitted in more cultures than has monogamy. Usually this takes the form of **polygyny**, the marriage of one man to more than one woman. Roughly 80 percent of primate species are polygynous, a figure close to the estimates of the practice among human groups in hunter-gatherer societies (Buss, 1999). Helen Fisher (1989) studied the marital arrangements of 853 preindustrial societies and found that 84 percent permitted polygyny, but only about 10 percent of men had more than one wife at the same time.

monogamy—Having sexual contact with only one partner for a given period of time.
serial monogamy—Having sexual contact with only one partner for a given period, but if and when that relationship ends, beginning a monogamous relationship with a new partner.
polygamy (puh-LIG-uh-mee)—Relationship or marital form in which a person may have more than one partner during a period of time without violating the culture's norms.
polygyny (puh-LIH-jih-nee)—Norm in which it is acceptable for a man to have more than one wife or partner in the same time period.

Polyandry—a marital form in which a woman may have more than one lover or spouse but a man is expected to have only one partner—is rare but has been documented in several cultures. It is related to high rates of male homicide. Polygyny is strongly correlated with a *patrilineal* social organization (that is, lineage and inheritance are traced through the father) and with agricultural economies (Reiss, 1986). Monogamy is characteristic of industrialized and complex societies. In some cultures, all three patterns of relationship are still practiced. The origins and frequency of these three patterns will probably never be completely known because of a lack of historical records.

Cultures have also varied in their prohibitions against sex among relatives; that is, incest is defined differently in different cultures. In some, a relationship is considered incestuous only if an individual has sex with a member of his or her immediate family (a parent, sibling, or offspring). In others, members are barred from sexual relations with relatives with whom there is any genetic relationship, as well as with members of their clan with whom they may share no traceable genetic relationship. Although several groups, including the early Egyptians, Hawaiians, and Peruvians, have accepted marriage between brothers and sisters (at least among the ruling families), Bixler (1982) argued that marriage between siblings probably did not involve sexual intercourse. Cleopatra is probably the most famous sibling-spouse. She married her younger brother, but it is unlikely that it was a sexual union.

In another variation in beliefs about appropriate partners for sex and marriage, relatives in some groups inherit the spouses of their siblings. More than two-thirds of nonindustrialized cultures, for example, practice the *levirate*; when a woman's husband dies, his younger brother (her brother-in-law) may marry her, particularly if she is still able to reproduce. The levirate was required by ancient Hebrew law. The corresponding practice of the marriage of a widowed man to his former wife's sister—the practice of *sororate*—is much less common (Reiss, 1986).

polyandry (PAW-lee-ANN-dree)—Norm in which it is acceptable for a woman to have more than one husband or partner in the same time period.

This former Utah policeman is pictured with his two wives and six children after being fired from his job for being a polygamist.

Among the Tiwi people of Melville Island, off the coast of northern Australia, who have the levirate, a woman typically first marries a man who is much older than she. She may sequentially marry and then be widowed by several of his brothers, ending up with a husband who is younger than she. Female power in this culture comes not from having many mates but from the fact that the culture is *matrilocal*; that is, couples reside near the wife's mother, and the husband is considered to be indebted to his mother-in-law. Because their descent group consists of female offspring of the mother's line, the Tiwi are also basically a *matrilineal* group. Males, however, through their male kin, control the land, and thus can improve their economic status by arranging advantageous marriages for these male kin. The Tiwi system serves as an example of the ways in which the definition of kinship can affect the balance of power between males and females.

In patrilineal societies, biological and social inheritance are traced through paternal links; that is, all children of a married couple belong to the father's social group. In most patrilineal societies, women must leave their own relatives at marriage and spend the major part of their lives in the company of their husbands' relatives. Patrilineal societies are usually dominated by males, and in some cases women are strictly segregated from public life.

Patrilineal communities often have been associated with the development of agriculture for profit. The spread of intensive cultivation techniques led to a decrease in the number of women involved in production (capitalism). Rigid division of labor by sex developed, in which production of goods for consumption was distinguished from work connected with the home. This division of labor had the effect of isolating men and women from one another and of separating women from public life. Indeed, many agricultural societies placed a high value on restricting women to the home. This pattern is the normative one in many Islamic groups, where the segregation of women, known as **purdah**, is often a sign of wealth and status.

Some patrilineal cultures also practice the levirate system. Among the So, if a woman's husband dies, one of his brothers may marry and impregnate her. Because of the strong **reproductive bias** of the So, however, a woman whose husband dies after she has gone through menopause and is no longer able

purdah—The practice of secluding women from men.
reproductive bias—The belief that the only justification for engaging in sexual contact is to reproduce. People who adhere to this belief perceive sexual activities that cannot result in conception (e.g., mutual masturbation, oral-genital stimulation) as sinful.

This veiled woman in Afghanistan is "protected" from the eyes of males.

to have children will never be wed to her husband's brother. In view of the value that many of us place on having a partner throughout life, and our sympathy for the lonely widow or widower, we might feel sorry for the So woman who is postmenopausal. But to understand her feelings, we need to remember the potential mistake of letting our own cultural experiences bias our interpretations of the experiences of people in other historical periods or in other cultures. For So women, menopause provides a relief from the burden of engaging in sex for procreation and allows them to devote themselves to their relationships with their co-wives, sisters, and other women in their clan with whom they are closely bonded. *Reality or Myth*

Beliefs About Fertility and Development

Throughout most of recorded history, and presumably even before then, conception has been a major goal, with most cultures supporting and rewarding couples who produced large numbers of children. This goal made sense in societies with high maternal and infant mortality rates, as characterized most groups until the twentieth century. The value placed on large families was underscored by official sanctions and norms against deliberate attempts to thwart conception during sexual intercourse. Just after the middle of the twentieth century, however, the concerns that demographers and other scientists were expressing about the potential for overpopulation that led to scarcity of resources (clean water, farmable land, forested areas, etc.) began to filter down to the general population. In this section on myths and realities associated with fertility and de-velopment, we describe legal and moral positions regarding conception and contraception, the use of infanticide, and myths about practices thought to contribute to the general and sexual development in children.

ATTEMPTS TO CONTROL FERTILITY

In many contemporary cultures and across most historical periods in Western cultures, deliberate attempts to avoid conception have been illegal or against the teachings of a number of religions. Throughout most of recorded history, however, people have used a variety of methods to avoid conception (Riddle, Estes, & Russell, 1994). The availability of birth control methods, despite explicit official pronouncements against them, illustrates that sometimes what people say about the purposes of sex may not be reflected in what they do.

The ancient Egyptians, who tolerated nonprocreative sex, relied on a number of contraceptive practices, including insertion of crocodile or elephant dung into the vagina (Bullough, 1980). They also used tampons fashioned from honey and the resinous gums of acacia shrubs. These tampons may have been effective to some extent because honey reduces sperm motility and acacia gum produces lactic acid, which kills sperm. In addition, Egyptian women ingested various drinks to avoid pregnancy, but these were probably ineffective.

McLaren (1981) traced attitudes toward birth control and abortion in England from the seventeenth century on. Large numbers of herbal abortives were available in preindustrial England. At that time, neither medical nor legal authorities could determine the presence of fetal life in the first few months of pregnancy; thus, women were essentially free to end a pregnancy if they wished. The English believed that until quickening (the first movements of the fetus felt by the mother) occurred about 14 weeks after conception, ensoulment—the belief that a soul or "spirit" enters a human body—had not taken place. Even the Catholic church employed the term *ensouled fetus* until 1869. There was no specific word for the use of abortive drugs before quickening. In fact, the very books that condemned abortion contained information on using drugs to bring on menstruation. Thus, women who took such drugs prior to quickening could legitimately describe their actions as attempts to "restore the menses." Not until 1803 was abortion (after quickening) made a statutory offense in England. *Reality or Myth* 2

In the United States, attempts at birth control—except through abstinence—were illegal until the middle of the twentieth century. The fact that it is still a controversial issue reveals conflicting social beliefs about the purpose of sexual relations, as you will see in Chapters 10 and 11. Controversy also surrounds technological advances that have permitted the determination of a child's sex prior to birth.

The development of a number of procedures, described in some detail in Chapter 9, permit the identification of the sex of a fetus soon after the eighth week of pregnancy. For those who undergo one of these procedures in North America, some find this information useful for after-birth planning, whereas others prefer to wait for birth to learn the sex of their child.

In other parts of the world, this information can have dire consequences for a female fetus. China and India, for example, are both plagued by overpopulation. Government policies in China limit families to one child; in India, families are limited to two children. Because of a traditional preference for male offspring in these countries, there appears to be increasing use of sex identification procedures as early as possible and to abort the fetus if it is female (Minturn, 1995). In India more than 90 percent of abortions are sought because the fetus is female. Despite the fact that more females than males are born in most populations, more males than female fetuses survive in India.

▶ **Issues to Consider:** What do you think of abortion as a method of population control? Why not abort males as well as females? Under what conditions would you abort either?

BELIEFS ABOUT CONCEPTION

Many ancient cultures, apparently unaware of the male's role in conception, believed that pregnancy resulted from the entrance of ancestral spirits into a woman's body. Nonetheless, men and women still engaged in sex—the activity necessary for the continuation of their group into successive generations—and created other justifications for it.

Most twentieth-century North Americans understand that **coitus** is necessary for conception. In fact, some believe that conception is the only justification for sexual relations, an idea in line with the long-standing official position of the Roman Catholic church. This notion that procreation is the sole justification for having sexual relations—reproductive bias—has a lengthy history in Western cultures. Beliefs about the purposes of sex are intimately tied to the religious and ideological perspectives of cultures throughout human history.

The Mehinaku of central Brazil think of fathering children through sexual intercourse as a collective project by men. They believe that one sexual act is insufficient to conceive a child, for the semen of a

---

coitus (KOY-tus)—Penetration of the vagina by the penis; also called *sexual intercourse*.

woman's husband forms only a portion of the infant. Yet at the same time, moderation is important. A woman who produces a larger-than-normal child or bears twins is believed to have had too many lovers, and the offspring are immediately buried alive.

INFANTICIDE

In a darker vein, many species have engaged in **infanticide** to limit their number of offspring (Fisher, 1992; Buss, 1999, Wrangham & Peterson, 1996). Infanticide by adult males (not the biological father) has been observed among langur monkeys, lions, gorillas, and chimpanzees, to name just a few species that engage in this practice. From an evolutionary point of view, killing another male's offspring serves the purpose of making the mother available to become fertilized by the male who killed the infant. This often occurs when there is a change in dominance hierarchies. The new dominant male kills the offspring of a former dominant male, paving the way for the new dominant male to impregnate the female and pass his genes on to the next generation.

Humans engage in infanticide, too, but generally for reasons other than trying (unconsciously) to replicate their genes. Throughout history, infants have been left exposed to winter's ravages, drowned, and neglected in attempts to limit family size. This fate has generally fallen on baby girls because they were not considered as valuable as boys. This is not just an ancient custom. Information from India indicates that female infanticide, although now illegal, is still common (Freed & Freed, 1989; Prasad, 1993).

Infanticide also contributes to the unbalanced sex ratio in India. Female children are seen as a financial burden, because a dowry is to be paid for their marriage. Videotaped interviews about infanticide were conducted with 1,250 women in 100 randomly selected villages in India, and 111 of the women admitted to killing at least one infant. Further, 547 reported that infanticide had occurred in their families, and 837 women in the sample indicated that infanticide was common in their villages (Prasad, 1993).

It may be tempting to believe that infanticide occurs only among other species or far distant cultures.

infanticide—The killing of an infant after its birth.

However, infanticide has been practiced in the United States as well. One well-publicized recent case involved a young couple charged with placing their newborn in a dumpster. In another case, a young woman gave birth in the rest room on prom night. After disposing of the baby in the trash can in the rest room, she returned to the party and danced with her partner. There are numerous other cases of infants' being abandoned in churches, hospitals, and other places. These cases are tragic given the large number of childless couples who wish to adopt, the availability of relatively reliable and effective contraceptives, and the legal access to first-trimester abortion (see Chapters 10 and 11). *Reality or Myth* ?

BELIEFS ABOUT DEVELOPMENT

Cross-cultural research provides information about differences and similarities among groups and can help us to gain perspective on our own culture's sexual beliefs and practices. Some cultures believe that sexual intercourse is important for promoting the growth of children. For example, among the Tiwi people of Melville Island, girls go at age 7 to live with their future husbands, who are already adults. Within a year, the girls begin to have sexual intercourse because the Tiwi believe that intercourse stimulates the onset of puberty (Goodall, 1971). The Tiwi believe that young girls are incapable of beginning menstruation or developing breasts, pubic hair, and broadened hips unless they experience intercourse.

The Sambia of New Guinea hold a somewhat similar view, except that they think that boys, rather than girls, need sexual stimulation. While studying the Sambia, anthropologist Gilbert Herdt (1981, 1990) learned of secret homosexual practices among adolescent men and boys. At age 7 or 8, Sambian boys are taken from their mothers for initiation. They are told that semen is a source of life and growth, like mother's milk. The Sambians believe that to grow and mature, youngsters must consume semen by having oral sex with adolescent males. The ingestion of sperm is thought to strengthen the boys, ultimately allowing them to produce their own sperm and impregnate a wife. At about 15 years of age, the boys' roles change: they provide semen to a new generation of boys. Initially, the older boys are anxious because they fear that loss of semen is potentially dangerous, but after instruction in how to replace it "magically" by consuming tree sap, the boys accept and enjoy this form of homosexual relations.

The next phase of male sexuality, bisexuality, begins with betrothal to a preadolescent girl. When the girl matures, the couple is married. At this time the husband gives up his homosexual contracts and devotes himself exclusively to heterosexual activity. Herdt estimated that about 5 percent of the men retain a preference for homosexual activity, a proportion that is similar to estimates for North America. Thus, in Sambian society, homosexual relations constitute a normal part of the sexual life cycle for males. As we will see in Chapter 14, this view was also held by the ancient Greeks, making it part of our Western cultural heritage as well.

Reality or Myth

In contrast to the Tiwi and the Sambia, the Mehinaku of Brazil believe that the sexual stimulation of children is dangerous. Although tolerant of sexual games between young boys and girls, the Mehinaku believe that as boys approach puberty, they need to practice sexual abstinence (Gregor, 1985). When a boy is 11 or 12, his father builds a palmwood seclusion barrier behind which the youth remains for most of the next three years, taking

growth-producing medicines and following strict dietary rules. Although the Mehinaku idea that contact between boys and sexually mature women is dangerous resembles contemporary Western attitudes, it has a different rationale. The Mehinaku believe that women's menstrual blood and vaginal secretions can poison the growth medicines that boys are given and can even cause a fatal paralysis in boys. Girls are also secluded for a period of time following their first menstrual period, so that they will not "contaminate" the village boys.

In Western cultures, it is common for boys and girls to segregate themselves by sex. During late childhood, boys and girls go through what is called a *homosocial stage* in which most prefer to play and associate with others of their own sex and avoid peers of the other sex. As they enter adolescence and go through puberty, however, most girls and boys decide that peers of the other sex may have some redeeming qualities, and they take their first tenta-tive steps toward dating. We cover this shift in more detail in Chapter 12. In the next section, we jump ahead to late adolescence and early adulthood to consider some of the myths about sex differences and gender roles in the initiation of romantic relationships.

Dating and Mating

Have you ever watched a woman friend attempt to develop a relationship with a man to whom she is attracted? If so, some of the findings that we are about to report will probably be less surprising to you than if you have accepted the stereotypic belief that it is men who control the selection of partners, who "come on" to women and determine whether a relationship will develop. The long-standing myth is, of course, that women's only possible roles are to be receptive to or rejective of men's choices and advances.

PROCEPTIVITY

A woman's ability to initiate and escalate a romantic or sexual interaction is called **proceptivity**. Based on

proceptivity—The initiation and escalation of a sexual interaction with another person.

900 hours of observations in bar settings, Timothy Perper (1985) concluded that it is usually women, rather than men, who determine the onset and outcome of a casual contact in a singles' bar. Perper observed a fairly standard sequence of events between couples in their initial interaction: approach, talk, turn, touch, and synchronization of body movements and posture. Initially, synchronization involves only the matching and mimicking of each other's arm and head movements, but it progresses to complex, simultaneous movements such as drinking in unison, and it can end in full-body synchronization. Either person in a potential courtship can escalate the situation by making an overture that, if accepted, raises the level of intimacy between the two people. If the overture is not accepted or responded to, the interaction deescalates; for example, one person may look away while the other is talking.

This couple demonstrate both "gaze fixate" (extended eye contact) and synchonicity, drinking in unison, as part of their courtship encounter.

Perper observed that more than half the time the woman initiated the courtship sequence by signaling or approaching the man. Women, Perper found, have a much clearer understanding of courtship strategies than do men. He estimated that 90 percent of men cannot accurately describe the courtship sequence, even though most of them can enact it with a woman who signals her interest to him or initiates contact. In proceptive behavior, a woman must first choose a man in whom she is interested. If he responds with interest to a woman's proceptive behavior, a "power transition" may occur in which he initiates overt sexual behavior. Perper hypothesized that couples pass through a transition state that begins with proceptivity and ends with both people being sexually aroused; the man then initiates sexual foreplay.

There is further evidence that women take an active role in courtship (Moore, 1985, 1998; O'Sullivan & Byers, 1992). Monica Moore observed more than 200 women in diverse settings and coded more than 50 nonverbal signaling behaviors. For example, she described different kinds of glances that she observed women using. After entering a room—a singles' bar or party—a woman may begin with a *room-encompassing glance* in which she scans an entire room in not more than five or ten seconds without making eye contact with anyone. She does this to select a man who looks as if he may be interesting. With the *short,*

darting glance, a woman gazes at a man but looks away within three seconds. With the *gaze fixate,* a woman makes eye contact for more than three seconds; sometimes her glance is returned. Moore also frequently witnessed such behaviors as smiling and laughing, and tossing, touching, or twisting the hair; she observed coy smiles and giggles less commonly. A woman's signaling gestures included hiking her skirt slightly and touching various parts of her own body or the potential partner's body. Two behaviors involve whole-body movement: the parade and the approach. In the *parade,* a woman—supposedly going to the bar or the rest room—goes out of her way to walk by the man she has selected, and she walks across the room with an exaggerated swing of her hips, her stomach held in, her head held high, and her back arched, so that her breasts are pushed out. In the *approach,* a woman positions herself within two feet of a man, after which the two usually talk.

Moore found an unusually high correlation (.89) between the number of solicitations or displays that women gave to men and the likelihood of the targeted man's approaching the woman. Moore concluded that women are able to determine when and where they interact with potential partners by exhibiting or withholding displays and solicitations. She theorized that because women can successfully elicit numerous approaches by men, they can choose from a variety of available men. Moore also noted that sometimes it took several signals by a particular woman before a man would approach and that a man was generally reluctant to approach if he had not been signaled that the woman would accept his advances.

How do women develop their repertoire of signals? To address that question, Moore (1995) observed junior high school girls' signaling. They displayed a smaller number of signals to junior high school boys, and the signals they employed were more exaggerated than those employed by adult women. For example, the hair toss was considerably more dramatic than that displayed by women. In addition, they appeared to mimic the signaling behavior of the dominant girls in their group. Interestingly, the boys were far less likely to approach these girls than were men to approach women who engaged in the more subtle but wider range of signals. Perhaps these displays by the girls were rehearsals for later behaviors that would be more effective in eliciting men's interest.

Thus, recent research bears out what many women already know: Women use a wide repertoire of signals and displays to attract men. If a man responds to a woman's initiations, the courtship dance begins. If both partners respond to each other, there follows an escalation of intimacy and eventually perhaps a power transition in which the man assumes responsibility for initiating sexual intimacy. It is important to note that a woman's initial signals are preliminary; that is, she is not indicating that she is sexually available. Instead, she is letting the man know that she welcomes the opportunity to get to know him better. Whether she decides to participate in a romance or, eventually, a long-term commitment or marriage depends on his characteristics and, of course, his assessment of her as a suitable long-term partner.

These findings suggest that roles taken in the initial contact between men and women seem to be sex linked, with women signaling their availability to meet a potential future partner, and men responding to those signals by approaching women. If these differences in roles are sex linked, what are the implications for courtship among gays? That is, do two lesbians both signal? Who approaches the other, and on what basis do they do so? How would two men

connect with one another if they each wait for the other person to signal, as is generally the case with heterosexual men in their relationships with women? As will be seen in Chapter 14, it is clear that same-sex people do find one another for short-term relationships or long-terms commitments, just as heterosexuals do. However, there is no empirical research on the dynamic process involved in relationship initiation among gay couples of the sort provided by Perper (1985) and Moore (1985, 1998) for heterosexual couples.

Signaling potential interest in another person is just the first step in the process of mate selection. Given the central importance of the family and reproduction in all societies, it is not surprising that the selection of a mate has generated a great deal of attention. *Reality or Myth*

> ▶ **Issues to Consider:** Have you ever observed or experienced the signals and approaches described by Perper and Moore? Do you agree with their description?

MATE SELECTION

What characteristics do you think are important to women when they are selecting a partner for a long-time commitment? What about men? What do you think they seek in a partner? Do men and women place equal value on the same qualities? And what do you look for in a partner? Respond to the questions in "Research Spotlight: What Do You Look For in a Partner?" (on page 20) and then read on to see how others have responded.

Assume that you and your classmates are able to gather responses—after getting your instructor's permission, of course—from other people to the questionnaire in the "Highlight." You might assume that, compared to women, men would give higher ratings to physical attractiveness as indications of women's health and ability to reproduce. In contrast, you might hypothesize that women, compared to men, would give higher ratings to a potential partner's ability to be a good provider to her and their children, as shown by high ratings for ambitiousness, industriousness, and financial prospects.

In a study of staggering proportions designed to test these hypotheses, David Buss and his colleagues

Indicate the importance to you of the following mate characteristics by putting the number that best reflects your feelings in front of each quality

Irrelevant or
unimportant   0 ——— 1 ——— 2 ——— 3   Extremely
important

_____ 1. Dependable

_____ 2. Chaste (no previous sexual intercourse)

_____ 3. High in financial prospects

_____ 4. Intelligent

_____ 5. Good looking (physical attractiveness)

_____ 6. Sociable (outgoing, friendly)

_____ 7. Ambitious and industriousness

_____ 8. In love with the person

_____ 9. Gets along with your family

_____ 10. Considerate

(1990) studied people in 37 cultures in Africa, Asia, Europe, Canada, Australia, New Zealand, South America, and the United States. The measures consisted of 18 characteristics, including the following target items from the list in the "Highlight": physical attractiveness, good financial prospects, and ambition and industriousness. In support of Buss's hypotheses, women placed higher value on the financial prospects of potential partners than men did; differences occurred in 36 of the 37 samples. In 29 of the 37 samples, women rated a potential partner's ambition and industriousness more highly than men did, providing moderate support for that expectation. In 34 of the 37 samples, men rated the physical attractiveness of a potential partner as more important in selecting a mate than did women.

We wondered if contemporary college students still showed these sex differences in what is considered important in selecting a potential mate, so we conducted a similar project with more than 1,000 college students (Wiederman & Allgeier, 1992). Our findings were consistent with the results from the Buss et al. (1990) study. Specifically, the characteristics that were most important in differentiating men's from women's ratings were financial prospects, ambition and industriousness, and physical attractiveness. The first two were rated as more important by women than by men in selecting a partner, whereas the physical attractiveness of a potential partner was rated more highly by men than by women.

When people first become intensely attracted to one another, they tend to make their relationship with one another the major priority in their lives.

They also tend to believe that their sexual activities involve spontaneity.

▶ **Issues to Consider:** What characteristics are most important to you in choosing a mate? Do they depend on whether it will be a short-term or long-term relationship? Does your list include physical attractiveness or financial success?

SPONTANEOUS SEX: REALITY OR MYTH?

People sometimes object to the notion of negotiating—discussing with one another—their relationship and sexual activities because they think that such discussions will detract from the spontaneity ("naturalness," without premeditation) of their interactions. Thus, they do not talk about their initial intentions with one another, what to do about contraception, or how to protect themselves from giving or getting sexually transmitted diseases (STDs).

This reasoning is based on the false assumption that sexual intimacy occurs without premeditation or forewarning. We often hear people declare that an episode of sexual intimacy "just happened." In truth, although partners may behave spontaneously *during* a sexual interaction, the decision to become sexually intimate in the first place is not made without at least one partner's preparing for the event. Except in the case of acquaintance or date rape (see Chapter 19), both people in the early stages of a relationship have probably thought of the possibility of progressing to sexual intimacy—in delightful fantasies, and also perhaps with concern or anxiety.

Valencia Declaration on Sexual Rights

We, the participants of the XIII World Congress of Sexology, declare that:

Sexuality is a changing and dynamic dimension of humanity. It is constructed through the interaction between the individual and social structures. It is present throughout the life cycle harmonizing identity, and creating and/or strengthening interpersonal bonds.

Sexual pleasure, including autoeroticism, is a source of physical, psychological, intellectual, and spiritual well being. It is associated with a conflict and anxiety-free experience of sexuality, allowing, therefore, social and personal development.

We hereby urge that societies create the conditions to satisfy the needs for the full development of the individual and respect for the following sexual rights.

The right to freedom, which excludes all forms of sexual coercion, exploitation, and abuse at any time and situations in life. The struggle against violence is a social priority.

The right to autonomy, integrity, and safety of the body. This right encompasses control and enjoyment of our own bodies free from torture, mutilation, and violence of any sort.

The right to sexual equity. This refers to freedom from all forms of discrimination, paying due respect to sexual diversity, regardless of sex, gender, age, race, social class, religion, and sexual orientation.

The right to sexual health. Includes availability of all sufficient resources for development of research and necessary knowledge. HIV/AIDS and STDs require more resources for research, diagnosis, and treatment.

The right to wide, objective, and factual information on human sexuality to allow decision-making regarding sexual life.

The right to a comprehensive sexuality education from birth on and throughout the life cycle. All social institutions should be involved in this process.

The right to associate freely. This means the possibility to marry or not, to divorce, and to establish other types of sexual associations.

The right to make free and responsible choices regarding reproductive life, the number and spacing of children, and the access to means of fertility regulation. All children should be desired and loved.

The right to privacy which implies the capability of making autonomous decisions about sexual life within a context of personal and social ethics. Rational and satisfactory experience of sexuality is a requirement for human development.

SEXUAL HEALTH IS A BASIC AND FUNDAMENTAL HUMAN RIGHT. HUMAN SEXUALITY IS THE ORIGIN OF THE DEEPEST BOND BETWEEN HUMAN BEINGS, AND IS ESSENTIAL TO THE WELL-BEING OF INDIVIDUALS, COUPLES, FAMILIES, AND SOCIETY. THEREFORE THE RESPECT FOR SEXUAL RIGHTS SHOULD BE PROMOTED THROUGH ALL MEANS.

MARIA PEREZE CONCHILLO, Ph.D., President of the Congress
JUAN JOSE JOSE BORRAS-VALLS, M.D., Ph.D., President of the Scientific Committee

---

Consider the last time you had a sexual interaction with another person. It may have involved penis-in-vagina, mutual masturbation, or oral-genital contact, or it may have been as simple as a first kiss. The point is that someone, either you or your partner, had to make decisions with the intention of becoming more physically intimate. For those sexual contacts involving some form of genital contact, a number of acts necessarily precede intimate contact. You need to find a private place, there should be agreement that you and your partner want to have sex, and, of course, there is the matter of removing your clothing, so that genital intimacy can occur!

Reality or Myth

As we will see in subsequent chapters, socialization in more sexually permissive cultures is associated with fewer unintended pregnancies, STDs, and sexual episodes involving force. In these more open cultures, young people may feel more comfortable discussing these issues explicitly with a potential partner and preparing for sexual interaction in a way that enhances their mutual pleasure.

In this chapter, we have highlighted some of the myths and realities involved with sexual expression in hopes of increasing your appreciation for the relationship (or, in some cases, lack of relationship) between our cultural beliefs and what has been shown by scientific research. Considering the results of scientific research and incorporating values of equity, humane treatment of people, and rights to self-determination, participants meeting in summer 1997 in Valencia, Spain, at the Thirteenth World Congress of Sexology voted to support a declaration of sexual rights (see "Highlight: Valencia Declaration on Sexual Rights" on page 21). It contains ten sexual rights that the group declared are "inalienable, inviolable, and irreplaceable of our human condition" (June 29, 1997). The group indicated its intent to ask other international scientific and professional organizations concerned with sexuality for their discussion, elaboration, and approval of the Valencia Declaration.

We hope that after reading this chapter, you will be more cautious about evaluating variations in sexual behaviors and values. In the next chapter, we consider some of the major theories that have guided researchers in their quest for more accurate information about sexuality.

▶ **Issues to Consider:** If you were a member of one of the sexuality organizations, what would you recommend adding to, subtracting from, or otherwise changing in the Valencia Declaration on Sexual Rights, and why?

SUMMARY OF MAJOR POINTS

1. Sexual interactions: Realities and myths. Many North Americans (and members of other cultures) accept stereotypes and myths about sexual interactions that they learned during childhood and adolescence. Some of these are probably harmless, such as the myth that the ingestion of some foods will reduce sexual desire and arousal. Others, however, may lead to unrealistic expectations for ourselves or our partners, guilt for having sexual feelings in certain circumstances, or various negative consequences that can occur in the context of sexual contact such as unwanted pregnancy, STDs, or disappointment in a relationship.

2. Beliefs about the need to control sexual expression. All contemporary and past cultures for which we have records have attempted to regulate sexual expression. However, there has been a great deal of variation in the behaviors they attempt to control and their reasons for doing so. For most of the history of Western cultures, the emphasis has been on limiting the conditions under which people may interact sexually through medical advice on the dangers of masturbation and frequent sexual expression, even with one's spouse. Such attempts are still seen in a number of non-Western cultures, which practice female circumcision to increase the likelihood of women's premarital chastity and fidelity after marriage. Cultures also vary considerably in their stances regarding the acceptability of having multiple partners, with some allowing men to have several spouses at the same time and others treating such behavior as immoral and illegal.

3. Beliefs about fertility and development. The attempt to control the conditions under which people engage in sexual activity is an age-old tradition that threads its way throughout history. Many groups believe that the only legitimate reason for a couple to engage in sexual activity is to procreate, a value known as the reproductive bias. With the specter of overpopulation emerging in the past half-century, the emphasis in many Western groups has been to limit family size. However, many individuals believe that abstinence, rather than contraception and abortion, is the means by which people should do so. In some heavily overpopulated countries that have attempted to deal with the problem by curtailing the number of offspring to just one or two children, abortion and infanticide of (primarily) female children have become common. A variety of practices have been employed in different cultures to aid the general health and sexual maturation of children, ranging from segregation of children by sex to encouraging sexual contacts between same- and other-sex young people.

4. Dating and mating. The stereotype that men control the dating and mating process has been challenged by research indicating that although women do act to set limits on the speed and kinds of sexual activities, they are also very active in the selection and signaling of potential romantic partners. Studies also indicate that men and women perceive different characteristics as important in selecting a mate, with

women stressing qualities in men that are associated with being able to provide for a family, and men emphasizing the physical attractiveness of potential mates—presumably because of the association of attractiveness with health and reproductive capacity.

5. Does sex occur spontaneously? The answer of yes to this question represents one of the most common myths in our culture, particularly regarding initial contacts between partners. However, the belief that sex should be spontaneous may be related to the greater likelihood of problems resulting from sexual contact. Couples who accept the myth of spontaneity may be less likely to take steps to avoid conception unless they want to become parents (unlikely for first intercourse), remain free of sexually transmitted diseases, and experience mutually satisfying sexual interactions.

2

Contemporary Explanations of Sexuality

Reality or *Myth*?

1. *Evolutionary theorists have little to say about modern sexual behavior.*

2. *In Freud's theory, the superego is part of what most people refer to as the conscience.*

3. *The classical conditioning of female sexual responses has been demonstrated in the laboratory.*

4. *Human sexual behavior is quite similar across cultures.*

5. *Scripts are transmitted through heredity.*

6. *Feminist theory is primarily concerned with gender inequality.*

What is sex? The amount of time we spend physically engaging in it—even for the most sexually active people—is minuscule compared to the amount of time we spend eating, bathing, sleeping, working, studying, and commuting.

Although most of us do not spend more than a tiny part of our lives directly engaging in sexual stimulation and **copulation,** we spend enormous amounts of time on quasi-sexual activities. We bathe regularly, dress carefully, comb our hair, and put cologne or shaving lotion on our skin in hopes of making ourselves more appealing. We notice interesting strangers and flirt with colleagues and classmates. And we think about sex. We may indulge in elaborate fantasies and mental rehearsals of potential interactions. Maybe we visualize running into someone in whom we are interested and then engaging in conversation and in physical contact at increasingly intimate levels. Sometimes the fantasy does not go the way we want it to, so we return to an earlier point in the fantasy and alter the script to our liking.

Part of this activity—the thoughts and fantasies—is an attempt to understand and explain sexual events to ourselves. We continue this process at the most personal and practical level as we try to make sexual decisions:

"Will she think I'm not a man if I don't try to make love to her?"

"Will she think I'm interested only in sex if I do try to make love to her?"

"Will he lose interest if I don't go to bed with him?"

"Will he think I'm too 'easy' if I do have sex with him?"

We also try to understand and explain various aspects of sexuality at a more global level:

What effect would sex education beginning in kindergarten have on children?

Why does someone feel attraction toward another person?

What are the behavioral effects of viewing erotic materials?

copulation—(kop-you-LAY-shun) Sexual intercourse involving insertion of the penis into the vagina.

We develop informal theories or explanations to try to answer some of these questions for ourselves. For example, regarding the issue of early sex education, some people believe that sex is so powerful that children should be shielded from it until puberty or even marriage. Others maintain that part of the power and potential danger of sexuality comes from adults' attempt to hide it and repress children's interest in it. Essentially, the first group is theorizing that exposure to sexuality-related information will increase children's interest in engaging in sexual activity. The second group theorizes that attempts to inhibit children's interest will only stimulate their curiosity—a sort of "forbidden fruit" hypothesis.

A *theory* is essentially a model of how something works. It is a tentative explanation that is not yet accepted as fact. Ideally, a theory leads to research questions that can be tested to see whether the evidence supports or refutes the theory.

Theories can become part of the belief systems of individuals and cultures. For example, the theory that women are dangerous sexual temptresses and yet inferior to men has dominated much of the history of Western civilization. In the twentieth century, Sigmund Freud's theory about female sexuality has had a profound effect on the sex lives of millions of women and men. Accordingly, it is important to test theories whenever possible. Theories, and the research that evolves from them, provide the only reliable way of advancing knowledge.

In this chapter we examine four theoretical explanations of the function of sexuality in our lives: the evolutionary, psychoanalytic, learning, and sociological attempts to explain human sexuality. All four approaches have strengths and weaknesses. All four will undoubtedly continue to be refined and altered as we learn more. Currently, however, they provide the most useful vantage points available from which to try to understand human sexuality.

Evolutionary Approaches

Evolutionary theorists describe the period of time during which humans have existed on earth as very recent history. Our emergence over five thousand years ago constitutes a minutely thin slice of time compared to the vast stretches of the past from which humans have emerged. Give or take a billion years, the universe is about 15 billion years old. About 65 million years elapsed between the appearance of the first creatures with grasping hands, eyes at the front of their heads, and the ability to hold their bodies upright, and the subsequent appearance of a humanlike creature. It took about 5 million more years for the first identifiable **hominid** to appear. Viewed from our tiny niche of time and space, this is an immense period of time, but many scientists have been perplexed by how swiftly the longevity and intelligence of our species increased—a mere several million years from our prehominid beginnings.

Whatever the explanation of our rapid development, an evolutionary perspective gives us a far more panoramic view of sexuality than do most other theoretical frameworks. This perspective prompted an interesting statement from Alice Rossi (1978):

> *Modern society is a mere second in our evolutionary history, and it is naïve to assume that our audacious little experiments in communal living, birth control, sexual liberation and sex-role equality can overturn in a century, let alone a decade, millennia of custom and adaptation. (p.72)*

The origins of modern evolutionary theory can be traced back to the work of Charles Darwin. He proposed that living organisms evolved from one or more simple forms of life through a process he called **natural selection.** Obviously, individuals in a population differ in the number and the characteristics of offspring they produce during their lifetimes. Individuals who produce a relatively large number of children are more likely to have their **genes,** the basic units of heredity, transmitted to future generations. However, according to evolutionary theorists, the effect of the sheer number of offspring is moderated by the characteristics of those offspring. They inherit characteristics from their parents that may be more or less adaptive, or useful, in the particular environmental conditions in which they live. Some of these characteristics—for example, hunting prowess, ability to search for and store food, and skill in attracting mates—increase the likelihood that the offspring will go on to produce children of their own. Thus, adaptive characteristics are "selected" for continuation, producing **reproductive success,** a crucial concept in the theory of natural selection.

Most contemporary evolutionists assume that the characteristics of an organism exist because of their past usefulness in perpetuating the reproductive success of that organism's ancestors. Those organisms having greater reproductive success are considered to have greater **fitness.** Although some members

---

hominid—(HAW-mih-nid) Family of two-legged primates of which only humans survived.

natural selection—The process whereby species evolve genetically as a result of variations in the reproductive success of their ancestors.

genes—Complex molecules found in chromosomes of cells that are responsible for the transmission of hereditary material from parents to offspring.

reproductive success—The extent to which organisms are able to produce offspring who survive long enough to pass on their genes to successive generations.

fitness—A measure of one's success in transmitting genes to the next generation (reproductive success).

The contemporary theory of evolution is based on Charles Darwin's theory of natural selection combined with modern genetics.

ting our genes, but also through the fitness of other people who share our genes, such as our brothers and sisters. Natural selection therefore operates to make the most of **inclusive fitness**, which involves both an individual's reproductive contribution to the gene pool of the next generation and that person's contribution in aiding the survival of kin, who pass on their shared genes.

This view of natural selection has interesting ramifications for the study of social and sexual behavior (Buss & Schmidt, 1993; Caporael, 1997; Tooby & Cosmides, 1992). Evolutionary theorists are interested in the inherited psychological mechanisms underlying behavior.

PROXIMATE VERSUS ULTIMATE CAUSES OF BEHAVIOR

Evolutionary theorists suggest that we can ask two kinds of questions about the causes of behavior. Contemporary questions concern how a particular behavior came to exist; that is, they seek the *proximate cause* of a behavior. These questions require analyses of the genetic, biological, or psychological causes of a particular behavior.

In addition, evolutionary theorists are interested in why a behavior exists; that is, they seek the *ultimate cause* of a behavior. As Donald Symons (1979) put it, "Answers to questions about ultimate causation will be that the behavior functions in specific ways to maximize the animal's inclusive fitness."

of a particular species may choose not to reproduce, findings based on evolutionary predictions are consistent with data gathered since Darwin's time (Barkow, Cosmides, & Tooby, 1992; Bjorklund & Kipp, 1996). Natural selection can favor us not only through our own reproductive success in transmit-

This family group illustrates one aspect of inclusive fitness—the bonds that relatives develop for their mutual well-being.

inclusive fitness—A measure of the total contribution of genes to the next generation by oneself and those with whom one shares genes, such as siblings and cousins.

However, a problem arises:

> *Questions about the ultimate causes of be-*
> *havior thus consider primarily the species'*
> *history, and, for this reason, are difficult to*
> *answer. . . . The ancestral populations in*
> *which the behavior evolved are gone and*
> *cannot be studied. (Symons, 1979, p.8)*

Evolutionary theorists assume that sexual behaviors exist and are maintained because in the past
they served the cause of reproduction. According to
this perspective, many of our current sexual activities can be traced back to reproductive behaviors
that are believed to have existed in early hunting
and gathering groups. Scientists have used evolutionary theoretical analyses to try to explain a variety of human sexual behaviors. Two of the many
interesting hypotheses that have emerged from this
framework concern gender differences in sexuality
and courtship strategies.

GENDER DIFFERENCES IN SEXUALITY

In a major analysis of the research on the relationship of **gender** to sexual attitudes and behaviors,
Mary Beth Oliver and Janet Hyde (1993) found
a number of gender differences. One of the most
pronounced differences between men and women
emerged in attitudes toward casual sex. Compared
to women, men held considerably more permissive
attitudes regarding coitus between people in a casual
relationship or in a dating relationship that did not
involve commitment. This finding is quite consistent
with evolutionary predictions, because during the
time our species was evolving, women who conceived with uncommitted partners (i.e., single mothers) would usually have been less able to provide for
their offspring from birth to adulthood than would
women who were impregnated by men committed
to a long-term relationship with the woman and
their children. In contrast, the survival of men's
genes in successive generations would have been less
endangered by the absence of commitment to a
woman. What men might have lost in the survival of
some of their offspring would have been compen-

gender—(JEN-der) The social-psychological characteristics
associated with being a male or a female in a particular
culture.

sated for by the large numbers of offspring that they
sired.*

Focusing explicitly on the self-reported roles
taken by men and women in sexual activity, psychologist Naomi McCormick examined contemporary
sexual behaviors among college students (McCormick,
1979, 1994). In one study, aptly titled "Come-Ons
and Put-Offs" (McCormick, 1979), men reported using more strategies to initiate sexual activity than did
women; conversely, women reported employing
more strategies to avoid or limit sexual activity than
did men. *Reality or Myth* ❓ 🅘

> ▶ **Issues to Consider:** To examine gender differences
> among your peers, you could ask a few sexually inti-
> mate couples whom you know to tell you who took
> the active role in initiating the first (1) date, (2) kiss,
> (3) necking, (4) petting, and (5) sexual stimulation to
> orgasm and/or ejaculation. If you find gender differ-
> ences, how would you explain them?

PARENTAL INVESTMENT THEORY

In response to the question of gender differences, the
evolutionary perspective has yielded an intriguing
model, called the *parental-investment theory*. Specifically, Robert Trivers (1972) proposed that gender
differences in the sexual behavior of a particular
species are determined by fathers' versus mothers'
typical amount of resources, time, and energy invested in their offspring.

Your mother and father committed various resources in rearing you. Who committed more? If your
parents are typical of most in our culture, your
mother invested a lot more than did your father. After conception, she carried you for about nine months
in her uterus. After giving birth to you, she fed you
when you were too helpless to feed yourself. As you
grew up, she took care of you to a greater extent than
your father did. This does not mean that human
males are lacking in capability for parental investment. But among most humans, parental investment
by women has been greater than that by men.

According to Trivers, the average parental investment in a species influences sexual behavior in at
least three ways. Among species such as our own, in

*We have simplified our description of evolutionary theory here
because of the complexity of male-female sexual strategies (cf.
Fausto-Sterling, 1997).

which the female invests more, Trivers predicted that (1) male-male competition for female mates will be greater than female-female competition for male mates, (2) there will be a greater variation in reproductive success among males than among females, and (3) selective pressure will be greater on males than on females because of the competition among males and because some succeed in mating and some do not. This selective pressure on males should produce larger body size, greater strength, and other attributes that help some males compete successfully for mates against other males who do not have these attributes or who have them to a lesser extent. Selective pressure should also result in greater variation in hair and skin color and more aggressiveness, insofar as those male traits help males attract females.

Thus, among species in which females invest more as parents and control reproductive success, males are at a disadvantage. Males must therefore try harder to succeed in passing on their genes. Whatever strategies and attributes males have that help them to succeed will be passed on. Characteristics that may render males less successful in competing against other males in attracting females, such as passivity and physical limitations, will tend to drop out of the gene pool.

COURTSHIP STRATEGIES

At first glance, the foregoing argument might suggest that gender is destiny in determining courtship strategies. However, in a few species, the males, who are bearers of a multitude of tiny sperm, have greater parental investment than do females, who contribute a few large eggs. According to Trivers, there should be greater selective pressure on females than on males in these species, and the females in these species should demonstrate greater competitiveness, body size, and sexual aggressiveness. Observations of pipefish, sea horses, and some bird species support this theory: it is the females in these species who aggressively court males, and females are willing to mate with any male (Williams, 1966). In contrast, males in these species are more cautious and more selective about choosing a sexual partner. Symons (1979) pointed out that among those species of birds in which there is female-female competition to mate with males, the females are larger and more aggressive than the males. Evolutionary theorists, then,

view male and female sex differences as the result of different reproductive strategies.

In response to those who accuse evolutionary theorists of sexism, George Williams (1966) wrote, "The evidence strongly supports the conclusion that promiscuity, active courtship, and belligerence toward rivals are *not* inherent aspects of maleness" (p. 186, emphasis added). Williams based his argument on cross-species comparisons. In the case of a particular species—humans, for example—the impression remains that the male sexual behaviors Williams described are linked with the lesser parental investment by human males compared to females. Despite these observations, male and female sexual behaviors today appear to be strongly influenced by the current sexual climate, as we will see in later chapters.

Evolutionary analyses have been applied to a number of other human behaviors relevant to sexual behavior and gender differences. As you are undoubtedly aware if you have ever owned a dog or cat who was "in heat," the fertile period of most female mammals is readily apparent to male mammals of their species, not to mention humans in the neighborhood who are trying to sleep! In contrast, human females have what is known as *concealed ovulation*, and so men cannot tell when a woman is fertile. Evolutionary theorists have tried to explain the possible advantages for our species of concealed female fertility (Fisher, 1992; Symons, 1979). One explanation is that a female is continuously attractive to a male seeking to mate because he cannot tell when she is fertile.

The assumption that each species, including humans, evolves to enhance its reproductive success seems strange to most people. Evolutionary theorists have been attacked for **reductionism**—attempting to reduce complex social behavior to a genetic drama. They are accused of painting a picture of humans as automatons driven by genetic codes. Most evolutionary theorists, however, consider humans to be a species with an evolutionary history who are also influenced by their own environment. They emphasize the psychological mechanisms arising from evolution

reductionism—Explaining complex processes in terms of basic physical and chemical activities (for example, explaining human sexual desire only in terms of hormonal activity without reference to the particular characteristics of a desired partner).

that underlie human emotion, learning, and behavior (Allgeier & Wiederman, 1994; Bjorklund & Kipp, 1996; Tooby & Cosmides, 1992). In addition to sparking controversy over the accuracy of evolutionary explanations of gender differences in courtship strategies and other sexual behaviors, evolutionary approaches have generated a great deal of debate on political and moral grounds, a topic to which we will return.

Evolutionary theorists are concerned with how and why the early history of entire species determines what characteristics are transmitted through reproduction. Psychoanalytic theorists take a different perspective, however, emphasizing the influence of a single individual's early experience on his or her subsequent development.

sychoanalytic Approaches

The father of psychoanalytic theory, Sigmund Freud, utterly transformed prevailing beliefs about the influence of sexuality early in the life span when he argued that sexual experiences during infancy influence the development of adult personality. His ideas still shock and offend some people.

In Freud's view, sexuality is interwoven with all aspects of personality. Sexual energy is the source of all human endeavors. Because social prohibitions prevent humans from acting freely on their sexual impulses, this energy is then sublimated, or diverted into other activities. Religion, art, and culture itself result from displaced sexual energy.

Although Freud's theories were often depicted as the product of an obscene mind, the man himself was a conservative moralist. He believed that society must restrict and channel *libido*. Just as theologians had argued that all humans were tainted with original sin, Freud bestowed on them original lust. Society—and, more specifically, parents—had to bring this lust under control. His perceptions of sexuality were, to some extent, limited by the Victorian times in which he lived. Freud's major complaint against Victorian society, however, was that it too severely suppressed childhood sexuality.

FREUD'S THEORY OF PERSONALITY DEVELOPMENT

Freud developed his theory in the process of treating emotionally disturbed patients and conducting his own self-analysis. Freud read works from an extensive range of disciplines, including anthropology, sociology, psychology, medicine, and literature. Out of these influences, he fashioned a theory of personality development that revolved around sexuality.

Freud believed that all human beings have two kinds of **instincts**. One kind—*eros*, the life instinct—operates to preserve or enhance the individual and species. The other kind—*thanatos*, the death instinct—motivates the organism to return to its original state of inorganic matter and is expressed in aggressive and destructive behavior. Freud assumed that both instincts had an accompanying energy source, pushing for release or expression. As part of

Sigmund Freud, creator of psychoanalysis, emphasized the role of sexuality in personality development.

instincts—As Freud used this term, biological excitations that lead to mental activity.

the life instinct, he proposed a sexual instinct, and he named its accompanying energy source the **libido**. This instinct interested Freud the most. Unlike the need for food and water, the instinctive need for love and sex, according to Freud, can be repressed by the society or the individual. However, its energy source, the libido, remains. Freud spun his theory of personality development around the fate of the libido.

THE ID, EGO, AND SUPEREGO

Freud believed that the influence of libido on an individual's personality and behavior is determined by three subsystems in the mind: the id, ego, and superego. The **id** consists of such instincts as hunger and sex. According to Freud, the id is present at birth and is not controlled by knowledge of reality or morality. The id seeks only to gratify instinctual drives and to enjoy the pleasure that results when tension aroused by these needs is discharged. The id seeks immediate gratification without regard for moral or practical consequences.

When we feel sexual tension or desire, we may spend hours imagining an encounter with a partner, but simply wishing does not provide one. To satisfy our sexual tensions, thirst, or hunger, we must be able to perceive and solve problems, organize and store knowledge, and initiate acts to achieve these goals. According to Freud, a second subsystem of the personality, the ego, develops out of the id to perform these functions.

The **ego** is shaped by contacts with the external world. It seeks to satisfy the demands of the id in light of the constraints of the real world. In working out a realistic strategy to fulfill our needs, the ego must try to satisfy three masters. First, it must deal with the id, which wants satisfaction of needs. Then, it must take into account the demands of external reality, which prohibit many selfish behaviors. Finally, it must satisfy the last subsystem to emerge, the superego.

libido—(lih-BEE-doe) psychoanalytic term for sexual energy or drive.
id—In psychoanalysis, the source of psychic energy derived from instinctive drives.
ego—In psychoanalysis, the rational level of personality.
superego—In psychoanalysis, the level of personality corresponding to the conscience.

The **superego** develops initially from the learning of societal values, as taught by parents and other caretakers. As a child matures, the superego is also influenced by the child's own critical examination of values. The superego includes what is called the conscience, which is concerned with whether a thought or behavior is right or wrong. *Reality or Myth* ❓

In Freud's model, aspects of the ego and superego can be conscious, preconscious, or unconscious. The id always operates in the unconscious sphere. Consciousness refers to thoughts and feelings of which we are aware. The preconscious comprises mental content of which we are currently unaware but which, with effort, we can remember—for example, old addresses or childhood friends. The unconscious contains all those thoughts and feelings that are outside our awareness. We can have access to our unconscious thoughts, intentions, and desires only through indirect means, such as dreams and slips of the tongue. Freud placed great emphasis on the unconscious and believed that all our thoughts originate there. Whether these thoughts eventually come into consciousness or remain outside our awareness depends on the degree of resistance they meet. Sexual memories, images, or ideas that we find objectionable may not emerge into awareness because of their threatening nature.

PSYCHOSEXUAL STAGES

The unfolding of sexual energies from infancy on forms a central part of Freud's theory of personality development. In dealing with his patients, Freud listened to many accounts of childhood memories of sexual episodes, some of which involved parents or siblings. At one point he accepted these accounts; later he thought that his patients' memories were fantasies rooted in their own desires. We now know, of course, that many children do experience sexual approaches by family members, friends of the family, and peers (see Chapter 19). In any event, Freud concluded that, whether his patients' memories of sexual experiences were real or imagined, his patients were definitely concerned with sexual issues in childhood. He believed that early in life, libido is channeled into certain body zones, which then become the center of eroticism. These stages are shown in Table 2.1 (p. 32). Each stage of development poses demands that must be met and conflicts that must be resolved. If conflicts are not resolved, fixation occurs, in which some

TABLE 2.1   Freud's Psychosexual Stages

Age	Psychosexual Stage	Erogenous Zone	Activities	Psychoanalytic Expectations
0–1 yr.	Oral	Mouth	Sucking, biting, "taking things in"	Dependency on caretaker
2–3 yrs.	Anal	Anus	Expulsion and retention of feces	Clash of wills between child and parent; delay of gratification
4–5 yrs.	Phallic	Genitals	Playing with genitals	Oedipal complex, Electra complex, gender identity
6–12 yrs.	Latency	Genitals	Preference for same-gender playmates	Sublimation and repression of libido
13–20 yrs.	Puberty	Genitals	Dating, "practicing" for eventual mate selection	Flareup of Oedipal conflict, usually reflected in a "crush" on older person
21–? yrs.	Genital	Genitals	Sexual intercourse	Mate selection, propagation of the species

libido remains invested in that stage, to be reflected in adult behavior. For instance, Freudians see smokers as partially fixated at the oral stage. Freud believed that much of adult personality was influenced by what went on in these early developmental stages.

Of particular interest to Freud was the so-called Oedipus complex. Freud maintained that we go through a period of sexual attraction toward, and conflict with, our parents that is exemplified by the ancient myth of Oedipus. In Greek legend, Laius, king of Thebes, was warned by an oracle that his newborn son would destroy him. He decided to have his son killed and selected a herdsman to do it. The herdsman pinned the infant's feet and left him on a mountain to die of exposure. A shepherd discovered the infant and took him to another region, where he was raised by a noble family who named him Oedipus ("swollen foot").

Later, as a young man, Oedipus unknowingly slew his father after an argument. At the time, he thought his stepfather was his biological father. Eventually Oedipus became king of Thebes after solving the riddle of the sphinx and married (unknowingly) his mother, Jocasta. Ultimately, the oracle revealed the truth about the royal couple. Jocasta hung herself and Oedipus blinded himself and went into exile from Thebes.

According to Freud, boys and girls develop love and jealousy relationships with their parents. Children initially identify with their mothers. However, boys must shift their identification to their fathers. Around the ages of 3 to 5, the young boy develops a sexual desire for his mother. Simultaneously, he fears that his father will punish him and cut off his penis. At this age, according to Freud, the penis is the center of a boy's sexual energy, and it is where the boy feels most vulnerable.

This castration anxiety leads the boy to repress his desire for his mother and to begin to identify with his father. By identifying with his father, he strives to become as strong and invulnerable as his father appears, and to be able to possess a woman just as his father does. Boys thereby resolve the Oedipus complex at about 6 years of age by developing an intense identification with their fathers' values and behaviors.

The female Oedipal complex, which some of Freud's students called the Electra complex, refers to the desire of a young girl for her father. Penis envy plays basically the same role in the development of girls that castration anxiety does in the development of boys. The girl, having no penis, assumes that she has been castrated. Blaming her mother for this loss, she shifts her love to her father. It does not take long, however, for her to find that she cannot compete with her mother for her father's affection, so she continues to identify with her mother and develops a feminine identity. Eventu-

During early childhood, most daughters are very affectionate toward their fathers. Freud attributed the attachment to the Electra complex—a daughter's desire to take the place of her mother in gaining her father's attention.

ally, she finds an appropriate love object in an adult male.

Freud's theories were primarily masculine in orientation, reflecting his Victorian upbringing. For him, females were essentially inferior to males, burdened by an envy of the male penis. This masculine bias was roundly attacked and revised by some later psychoanalysts, among them Karen Horney and Clara Thompson. Horney, in particular, did not think much of Freud's concept of penis envy. She claimed that envy of the penis could be explained by looking at the dominant role of men in Western societies, which created a subservient role for women. The "envy" that women feel arises from the desire for the autonomy and freedom that men have rather than from the wish for a penis specifically.

Critics have also attacked Freud for placing too much emphasis on the role of sex in human behavior, being unduly pessimistic about human nature, paying minimal attention to female personality, and neglecting to supply adequate scientific evidence for many of his assumptions. Other researchers have tested many of Freud's ideas and found some supported by data, whereas others have not been supported (Baumeister, Goldberg, & Fisher, 1996; Bornstein & Masling, 1998; Greenberg & Fisher,

1996). We will present these findings in appropriate chapters.

▶ **Issues to Consider:** Do you think that the behavior of young children is motivated by sexual energy (libido), as Freud maintained?

RECENT PSYCHOANALYTIC DEVELOPMENTS

Psychoanalytic theorists have taken many new directions since Freud did his original work. Some of these theorists, Wilhelm Reich, Herbert Marcuse, and Geza Roheim among them, stressed the importance of sex in human affairs to an even greater extent than Freud did. Reich, for example, took libido theory to the ultimate extreme by claiming that almost all maladaptive behavior is tied to dammed-up sexual energy. For Reich, the extent of orgasmic release became a measure of health. The unhealthy person was one who was unable to experience a full orgasm and the release of sexual energy.

In contrast to Reich's approach, most refinements of psychoanalytic theory, some of which are called *object-relations theory,* have stressed the adaptiveness of the ego and how we interact with others. Margaret Mahler, W. R. D. Fairbairn, Heinz Kohut, Nancy Chodorow, and Erik Erikson are a few of the major names in these relatively recent developments.

For example, Nancy Chodorow (1978) pointed out that because infants—both boys and girls—generally have the most contact with their mothers, they initially identify and form intense relationships with their mothers. For girls, this identification is never completely severed, but boys must relinquish their identification with their mothers as they take on masculine roles. Chodorow maintained that this differing experience produces distinct coping strategies for males and females in dealing with the world. Specifically, women emphasize relationships *with* others, whereas men focus on their own individualism and independence *from* others.

We agree with Carol Gilligan (1982), who wrote an insightful and very readable book, *In a Different Voice.* We believe that an exclusive focus on either way of dealing with the world may restrict both men and women. The woman (or, for that matter, man) who views herself only in relationship to others (wife, mother, but not an individual in her own right) may limit her own independent development. The man (or woman) who views himself only in terms of his own achievements and independence (boss, owner, director, sole author) may handicap his capacity for intimate connection with others.

Erik Erikson (1982) accepted Freud's idea that sexual impulses and experiences have their onset in infancy. He also adopted Freud's notion that much of the child's developing personality is influenced by biological drives focused first on the mouth, and then on the anus and genitals.

Erikson departed from Freud, however, in a number of important ways. Although he agreed that early experiences are extremely influential in personality development, he gave far more weight to the power of experiences throughout life to modify both positive and negative early events. Erikson thought that the development of a trusting nature was extremely important for a one-year-old, but he also suggested that positive experiences later in life could offset a less-than-desirable set of early-life circumstances. Similarly, optimal experiences during infancy could be overshadowed by the impact of negative events later in life.

Perhaps Erikson's needs were consistently and affectionately met during his first year of life. In any event, he is one of the most optimistic of personality theorists. He was also well ahead of his time in being concerned with the interaction of biological, psychological, and environmental factors in the development of the individual. We cover his assumptions in more detail in the chapters on life-span development.

Learning Approaches

The evolutionary and psychoanalytic theories that we have just described emphasize biological explanations of human sexual behavior. We turn now to an approach that focuses on the relationship of learning to our sexual behavior. The research presented throughout this book demonstrates that much of our sexual behavior—what we do; with whom we do it; when, where, and how we do it—is influenced by learning processes.

Learning theorists assume that most behavior, including sexual behavior, is strongly affected by learning processes. Many of the processes or "laws" of learning were formulated in the first half of the twentieth century when a brand of psychology called behaviorism was developing. The early behaviorists, among them John Watson (1878–1958), maintained that to be scientific, researchers must focus only on what is observable and measurable. Thus, the early behaviorists studied overt behavior and disregarded mental events—thoughts, ideas, beliefs, and attitudes.

Watson studied sexual response by connecting measuring instruments to himself and his lab assistant while they had sexual intercourse. (He collected several boxes of data before his wife discovered the reason for her husband's long hours in the laboratory!) He not only was forced to resign from his university position but was divorced by his wife. During his divorce trial, the judge called him an expert in *mis*behavior (Magoun, 1981).

Despite his misfortunes, Watson was instrumental in initiating a school of research that has yielded several important principles that have become part of most contemporary theories of learning. Behavioral research has been conducted on both common behavior (that related to heterosexual attraction, for instance) and uncommon behavior (that related to shoe fetishes, for example). Two basic principles central to learning theory are classical conditioning and operant conditioning.

CONDITIONING

Most students who have taken an introductory psychology course have learned about the concept of classical conditioning developed by Russian physiologist Ivan Pavlov (1849–1936). In the classic experiment, Pavlov presented dogs with food, an unconditioned stimulus (UCS), which yielded an unconditioned response (UCR): the dogs salivated. Pavlov sounded a buzzer at the same time that he

---

behaviorism—A theoretical approach that emphasizes the importance of studying observable activity.

unconditioned stimulus (UCS)—A stimulus that evokes a response that is not dependent on prior learning.
unconditioned response (UCR)—A stimulus-evoked response that is not dependent on experience or learning.

gave the dogs the food; he repeated the conditioning until eventually the dogs would salivate at the sound of the buzzer alone. In terms of classical conditioning, the buzzer was a **conditioned stimulus (CS)**, and the salivation in response to it was a **conditioned response (CR)**. The dogs learned to salivate in response to a stimulus that previously had not elicited this response.

Researchers have employed classical conditioning to explain how people can come to be sexually aroused by a wide range of stimuli. The way in which a neutral object can acquire sexual significance was suggested by a study involving three male graduate students (Rachman, 1966). The students were asked to judge a series of photos of nude females. The photographs they judged to be sexually stimulating were then paired with slides of women's high black boots. The students were repeatedly shown slides of women's high black boots followed by the photos of the nude women they had rated as sexually stimulating. After repeated pairings of the nudes and the boots, the students were shown the boots alone, to which the males responded with sexual arousal, as measured by changes in penile blood volume. Gradually, arousal was produced in response to other types of women's shoes as well. In short, the pairing of previously neutral stimuli with sexual stimuli led to the neutral stimuli acquiring erotic significance.* Although male sexual arousal may be influenced by classical conditioning, there is no formal evidence that female sexual arousal can be classically conditioned (Letourneau & O'Donahue, 1997). *Reality or Myth*

You have undoubtedly experienced some classical conditioning of your own sexual arousal without fully recognizing it at the time. Have you ever felt arousal when smelling a particular cologne or perfume? If you have an erotic interest in someone who wears a specific brand, you may have noticed that the smell arouses you; perhaps you shake, you feel short of breath, your pulse races, and your heart beats faster when you smell a scent that you associate with the person who attracts you.

OPERANT CONDITIONING

Besides learning to respond to one stimulus because of its association with another stimulus to which we already have an unconditioned response, humans also learn to behave in particular ways as a function of whether their behaviors are rewarded, ignored, or punished. This form of learning is called *operant conditioning* or *instrumental conditioning*. Its principles were first described by E. L. Thorndike and developed into an influential theory by B. F. Skinner.

In the most general form, this theory maintains that behavior is influenced by its consequences. Behavior followed by pleasurable consequences (posi-

B. F. Skinner (1904–1990) was an American behavioral psychologist whose theory of operant conditioning maintains that behavior is influenced by its consequences.

---

*Subsequent attempts to replicate Rachman's study of the classical conditioning of atypical sexual arousal have not been successful. However, Rachman's research does provide a clear example of how we expect this type of conditioning to occur.

conditioned stimulus (CS)—In classical conditioning, a stimulus that is paired with an unconditioned stimulus until it evokes a response that was previously associated with the unconditioned stimulus.
conditioned response (CR)—An acquired response to a stimulus that did not originally evoke such a response.

An enjoyable date may be a rewarding experience that provides pleasure and influences attraction.

eral factors may serve as reinforcers for higher frequency of sex as well (exchange of sex for attention, giving in to pressure, or mercenary [economic gain] motives). (p. 106)

We learn many kinds of behavior through being rewarded, ignored, or punished for it. Positive sexual experiences are certainly rewarding, but in both laboratory and field experiments, other, less physically rewarding experiences have been shown to provide pleasure or reinforcement and to influence attraction (Byrne & Schulte, 1990). We are more likely to feel attraction to, and to want contact with, people who praise and compliment us, who demonstrate attitudes similar to ours, and whom we perceive as physically appealing. That is, we are attracted toward those who reward us in some way. In contrast, we are less likely to feel attracted toward those who put us down (but see Chapter 6 for exceptions to this generalization), who hold very different attitudes from ours, or toward whom we are not physically attracted.

We are less likely to repeat experiences that are not particularly pleasant or are punishing. Punishment tends to work best when it is immediate, intense, and unavoidable. In the short run, mild punishments have mild effects. And in the long run, people adapt to punishment if its intensity is gradually increased, so ultimately it loses its power to change behavior.

Although research has demonstrated that punishment reduces the frequency of undesirable sexual behavior, it has also shown that harmful side effects may occur. The child or adolescent who is yelled at, scolded, or physically punished may cry, cringe, or feel suppressed anger. These responses are incompatible with the punished behavior and thus replace it, but only for the moment. The child or adolescent may engage in the punished behavior again, although he or she may feel guilty while doing it.

In general, punishment may produce aggressive behavior by the person who is punished, thus undermining the impact of the attempt to alter the person's behavior (Catania, 1992). Punishment can be useful when the immediate suppression of behavior is necessary, such as when a child runs into the street. However, it is difficult to think of any sexual behavior for which the positive effects of punishment would be worth the cost of the negative effects. Even

tive reinforcement) is likely to recur and increase in frequency. Behavior associated with the removal of an aversive (unpleasant) stimulus is also likely to recur and increase in frequency (negative reinforcement). Conversely, behavior that is not rewarded or is associated with an aversive stimulus (punishment) occurs at a diminished frequency or not at all. Upon removal of the aversive stimulus, the behavior may reappear or increase in frequency.

One of the simplest models for frequency of sexual activity is operant. We are most likely to repeat a behavior that has been reinforcing—that is, it is pleasurable, or at least relieves unpleasant states. Those people who experience the most pleasure or reduction of discomfort from sexual stimulation are likely to seek it frequently. Stuart Brody (1997) elaborated on this principle:

Some of the pleasure associated with sexual activity may stem from anticipation and excitation before initiating a given coital event, and therefore, factors that affect this arousal may play a role in the reinforcement value (in addition, the absence of sexual prohibitions at both a societal and interpersonal level may enhance the degree of pleasure). More periph-

in the case of rape, punishment has not been particularly effective in eliminating a rapist's tendency to assault others. In fact, it may increase the aggression and anger that most scholars today believe is part of the motivation of some rapists, as we shall see in Chapter 19.

Other techniques—such as removing rewards in cases of undesirable behavior and rewarding responses that are incompatible with undesirable behavior—are more effective. In the case of children playing with their genitals, for example, parents can encourage a son or daughter to engage in that pleasurable activity in the privacy of the bedroom or at least not in the presence of people who might object, such as grandparents or neighbors. Interestingly, the work of many learning theorists supports some religious teachings stressing that acts of love (positive reinforcement) influence behavior more than does punishment.

Many researchers in this area have written little about the social context in which people were punished or what the punished people thought about it. Many students of sexual behavior consider these factors to be as important as conditioning principles. Concern with the influence of social and **cognitive** factors has led to extensions and revisions of the basic learning theories just outlined.

SOCIAL LEARNING THEORY

We learn most of our behavior in the context of our interactions with others. People need other people from the beginning of life to the end of it. Most of us can look at our own histories and see the central place of our interactions with particular people and the importance of our thoughts about them. In an early fervor to be scientific and to isolate behavior in the laboratory, behaviorists overlooked the significance of such social interactions and thoughts. Gradually, some behavioral scientists, known as social learning theorists, began to examine the influence of other people and of cognitions—observations, perceptions, ideas, beliefs, and attitudes—on sexual behavior.

cognitive—Related to the act or process of engaging in mental activity (thoughts).

Albert Bandura is one of the most influential of the social learning theorists. He argued that sex-related behavior can be learned, without the learner's receiving any direct reinforcement, through observation of other people and events. This process is called **modeling.** Bandura (1986) would suggest, for example, that if we observed someone being rewarded or reinforced for engaging in premarital sex, we would be more likely to engage in this behavior. Similarly, if we observed someone being punished for practicing premarital sex, we would be less likely to have sex before marriage. In support of this hypothesis, Scott Christopher, Diane Johnson, and Mark Roosa (1993) found that perceived peer sexual behavior was a strong predictor of early sexual involvement.

The principles of social learning theory have been applied to the widespread problem of sexual assault. A common concern among those who conduct research on eroticized film and magazine depictions of sexual aggression against females is that victimized females are portrayed as ultimately enjoying violations of their bodies. During exposure to such depictions, viewers may be incorrectly "learning" that women are sexually aroused by sexually assaultive approaches (see Chapters 19 and 20).

Social learning theorists place significant emphasis on cognitions (Hogben & Byrne, 1998). Many current investigators of sexuality are guided by the general philosophy of social learning theory: that some combination of learning and cognitive principles will best explain sexual behavior. In attempting to explain sexual attitudes and behaviors in terms of cognition and complex social events, contemporary learning theorists have taken an approach similar to that of sex researchers trained in the discipline of sociology.

▶ **Issues to Consider:** John has been forbidden by his parents to use "dirty" words. However, he has seen his father laugh affectionately when his mother occasionally uses them. Based on learning principles, what is your expectation regarding John's future use of "taboo" words?

modeling—Learning through observation of others.

Sociological Approaches

In contrast to scientists who take the evolutionary and psychoanalytic approaches, most sociologists concerned with sexuality believe that human sexual behavior is more readily understood through examination of **socialization** processes and cultural beliefs and norms rather than by studying biological development or individual learning experiences. According to John Gagnon and William Simon (1973), without the complex psychosocial process of development experienced by humans, the physical acts involved in sexual activity would not be possible: "The very experience of excitement that seems to originate from hidden internal sources is in fact a learned process, and it is only our insistence on the myth of naturalness that hides these social components from us." (Gagnon & Simon, 1973, p. 9).

The sociological perspective is similar to that taken by social learning theorists. However, social learning theorists tend to examine the socialization and conditioning of the individual; in contrast, sociologists take a broader view, looking at the relationship between beliefs and norms shared by members of a society to understand the sexual interactions of members of that group.

In addition, sociologists maintain that these individual learning experiences do not allow an adequate explanation for why people in one society differ so much in their sexual lifestyles from people in another society. Sociologist Ira Reiss examined research from a variety of sources, including descriptions of 186 nonindustrialized cultures. From his review of studies of these societies, Reiss (1986) concluded that although biological and psychological factors are crucial in comparing individuals, they are not of major importance in comparing societies.

For example, although all human females are capable biologically of experiencing great pleasure during sexual interaction, whether they do enjoy sexual relations varies from one culture to another and is related to the culture's perception of the importance of female sexual pleasure and of the purpose of sex.

socialization—The process of developing the skills needed to interact with others in one's culture.

As discussed in "Highlight: A Polygynous African Tribe," (p. 40) the So women of Uganda do not enjoy sex but endure it because they want to conceive. In their culture, genital touching is taboo, and orgasm is assumed to occur only in males (Allgeier, 1992). In contrast, the Mangaian people of Polynesia are encouraged from childhood on to learn as much as they can about how to give and receive sexual pleasure. Mangaian girls learn that women should be sexually active and responsive and should experience sexual relations with a number of men to find a spouse with whom they enjoy sex. Donald Marshall (1971) estimated that women in Mangaian culture have three times as many orgasms as do men. *Reality or Myth*

Ira Reiss is well known for his research on changes in premarital sexual standards during the 1950s and 1960s. He subsequently developed a theory of the ways in which society influences our sexual attitudes and behavior.

Reiss (1986) hypothesized that, in almost all societies (the So are an exception), genital stimulation and response usually lead to physical pleasure and self-disclosure. No matter how permissive most societies are about sexuality, they place importance on the potential for development of an interpersonal bond through the pleasure and disclosure characteristics of sexuality. Interpersonal bonding is universally emphasized because it is the basis of stable social relationships, the structural foundation of societies. Reiss (1986, p. 210) elaborates:

> *Societies organize the bonding power of sexuality so as to enhance socially desired relationships and avoid socially undesired relationships. To illustrate: sexual bonding is encouraged in marital relations that tie together individuals from different social groups, whereas sexual bonding is discouraged in parent-child relationships to avoid role conflict and jealousy and also to encourage young people to seek mates from other groups and thereby build alliances that can be helpful.*

SCRIPTS

To develop social stability, groups attempt to define what is proper behavior for a specific situation. Members of a particular society then have a set of social guidelines, or **scripts,** that they can adopt or alter to suit their purposes. On the individual level, scripts are cognitive plans that enable us to behave in an organized and predictable fashion.

Reality or Myth

Our individual scripts are part of the cultural expectations about interactions between people. Just as actors have scripts to guide them through a play, we have our own scripts to guide us through various interactions. Just as actors learn their parts so thoroughly that they perform their roles without being conscious of the script, so do we perform much of our own scripted behavior as if it were second nature.

John Gagnon (1990) described three levels of sexual scripts. In addition to the societal scripts or cultural scenarios previously mentioned, we can also examine interpersonal and intrapsychic scripts. *Interpersonal scripts* refer to our social interactions

Organized dances are one way that young people learn scripts about how to behave romantically.

scripts—Largely unconscious, culturally determined mental plans that individuals use to organize and guide their behavior.

H I G H L I G H T

A Polygynous African Tribe

In 1969–1970 the anthropologist Charles Laughlin and I spent a year living with the So tribe in the semiarid mountains of northeastern Uganda in Africa (Allgeier, 1992; Laughlin & Allgeier, 1979). In this polygynous tribe, the number of cows and goats owned by a man is a measure of his wealth, and it is in cows and goats that he pays for his wives.

We spent several months informally observing the So, learning their language, and taking a census. I then conducted a series of interviews with a random sample of the tribal members to attempt to understand their sexual attitudes and behavior.

Following a general principle for studying sensitive topics, in the first interview I asked relatively innocuous questions to give the informant and me some time to become acquainted and feel at ease. In constructing the most intimate questions, I tried to avoid wording that would imply any value judgment.

There were some topics for which there were no So words. For instance, there was no term for *masturbation*, and although I was able to get the idea across to males through appropriate gestur-ing, the practice seemed to be totally unimaginable to females. Although adolescent males occasionally masturbated, it was taboo for married adult males to masturbate, because doing so constituted a "wasting of seed."

Love was another word for which no So term existed. There was *apudori* (sexual intercourse), and there were words for friendship, but no word for *love* per se. The So did not practice homosexuality, which fell into a category of behaviors (including adult masturbation, intercourse during menstruation, and bestiality) that they considered evidence of witchcraft. In addition, contraception was totally unknown to the So. My question "What can you do if you don't want to have any more children?" was greeted with the same sort of astonishment that you might express if someone asked, "What can you do if you no longer want your legs?"

The attitudes and experiences of men and women regarding intercourse differed strikingly. For men, intercourse was positive, both because they valued procreation highly and because they enjoyed the activity itself. Those men who were married to more than one woman spent an equal

---

with others. The expectations that we perceive others to have of us may influence the way in which we behave or act out our role.

The patient-doctor relationship illustrates the power of interpersonal scripts. There is no other circumstance under which we would allow, and in fact pay, a relative stranger to probe intimate parts of our bodies, occasionally inflicting some discomfort in the process. Further, most people do not perceive a gynecological or urological exam as sexual, even when the exam includes breast or testicle "fondling" to check for lumps and manual penetration of the vagina and anus. Small variations in context can make huge differences in the probability of a person's perceiving a situation as sexual.

Intrapsychic scripts refer to those ideas, images, and plans we think about in the privacy of our minds. Thus, we can rehearse various scenarios using our imagination before deciding on a plan of action, or we can decide not to act at all. It is in this sphere that we attempt to integrate cultural scripts and interpersonal scripts. For example, think of times when you have rehearsed in your mind the sequence of events as you hoped they might happen during an upcoming date. Your fantasies about what you might or might not do may be influenced by cultural scripts

amount of time with each wife, but they avoided a particular wife when she was menstruating. During intercourse they did not engage in any foreplay. Female breasts, which So women left exposed, had no erotic significance. And except for the incidental contact that occurs during vaginal penetration, to touch any portion of the vulva was forbidden.

In the absence of precoital stimulation, the negative attitude of So women toward sexual intercourse was not particularly surprising. I still have a vivid memory of one very beautiful middle-aged woman, with clenched teeth and hands, describing her first experience with intercourse. She said that it hurt badly—it burned—but that she got through it by telling herself repeatedly that she had to do this to get a baby and that she had to have a baby to get cows. When asked how she felt about sex now, she said that she wished her husband had enough cows to take a "little wife" but that it did not hurt as much now as it had at first. In no instance did a woman indicate ever having an orgasm; in fact, the So viewed orgasm as synonymous with ejaculation and as exclusively a male phenomenon. In exploring the total absence of female orgasm, I attempted to find out if So women were aware of having a clitoris. I described it and drew pictures of vulvas, but to no avail.

Over the years, I have considered at length these gender differences in sexual attitudes, attempting to find explanations. Perhaps the tribe's survival depended to some extent on these attitudes. In the face of disease and constant warfare with neighboring tribes, the tribe was in danger of extinction. Because females outnumbered males, the population could be maintained as long as women gave birth to as many children as possible. If women enjoyed sex, they might not want to share their husbands with other women. As it was, however, co-wives tended to have rather close relationships with one another. They did not compete for men; rather, they shared the responsibilities of raising their husband's children and providing him with food from their gardens. Were wives to value sexual intercourse other than for reproduction, they might resent the time their husbands spent with the others— three weeks out of four in the case of a man with four wives.

Source: E.R.A.

regarding what is "appropriate" behavior on a date and how much you adhere personally to these scripts. You may allow yourself a range of fantasies as to what might happen, but decide not to act on any of them.

From the standpoint of script theory, there is little sexual interaction (or other behavior) that can truly be called spontaneous. Members of each culture share learned patterns that facilitate their sexual interaction. Inherent in script theory is the notion that scripts allow a sexual encounter to take place by providing the participants with a program for action. The script defines the situation, names the actors, and plots the sequence of events in a sexual interaction. For example, at a heterosexual party when a person (typically, a man) wants to "cut in" to take over the position of another person's dancing partner, he taps the other man on the shoulder rather than simply grabbing the woman away from the current dancing partner.

On the societal level, sexual scripts are the beliefs that people in a particular group share about what are good and bad sexual thoughts, feelings, and behaviors. These sexual scripts function as guideposts, describing the proper social circumstances in which sexual responses may occur. In a large and complex society such as our own, sexual scripts vary somewhat depending on social class and age group, but there is still much similarity in the sexual scripts across these groups. One such similarity has been the male control of resources in most cultures.

▶ **Issues to Consider:** Why do you think men have controlled the resources in most societies throughout history?

POWER, GENDER, AND THE RISE OF FEMINIST APPROACHES

According to Reiss (1986), power is the ability to influence others and achieve one's objectives despite the opposition of others. Powerful people seek to obtain and retain their control over the valuable resources in their society. Insofar as sexuality is considered a valuable resource, powerful people seek to gain control of it. Men generally have had more power than women have had in almost all cultures. So, according to Reiss, powerful men seek not only to obtain sexual satisfaction for themselves but also to control sexual access to those who are important to them, such as wives, daughters, and sisters. In his view, differences between the roles of men and women stem not from biological differences but from the degree of male control of key societal institutions.

Partly in response to this male dominance, Betty Friedan's (1963) book *The Feminine Mystique* and Germaine Greer's (1971) *The Female Eunuch* addressed issues that had largely been ignored by theorists and researchers—the role of female experience and thought. Their arguments have given rise to a larger number of scholars who view themselves as feminist theorists. If there is a common theme among feminists, it is the belief in the full social, political, and economic equality for women (Steinem, 1994). Much of feminist theory is guided by the idea that gender is a **social construction**. According to this view, there are few aspects of gender,

social construction—Theoretical framework that emphasizes the importance of cognitions (thoughts) in creating a shared reality.

sex, and reproduction that are not governed by social stereotypes and expectations. Many of these stereotypes put women in an inferior or unequal position relative to men. As noted by Jean Kilbourne in her frequently humorous presentation, "Killing Us Softly," many contemporary advertisements reflect men's dominance over women, although there have been some recent exceptions in which women are portrayed as powerful and equal to men. Efforts to enhance women's power to make it equivalent to that of men has led to a great deal of diversity and divisiveness among feminists.

Reality or Myth **6**

Naomi McCormick (1994) summarized the complexity of the range of feminist positions and their implications for how we view gender and sexuality. She described two groups that she labeled "liberal feminists" and "radical feminists." The liberal approach emphasizes women's sexual pleasure and their freedom to explore beyond restrictive gender-role norms, whereas radical feminism concentrates on protecting women from danger and coercion. Radical feminism targets men and masculinity as the culprits in the subjugation (dominance) of women. Radical feminists believe that pornography is directly linked to male sexual violence and should be restricted.

In contrast, liberal feminists see motivation, rather than gender, as the major factor in antisocial sexual behavior. They do not support the suppression of pornography. Instead, woman-affirming erotica is proposed as an antidote to violent pornography. Liberal feminists perceive the sexual landscape as skewed toward a male, or patriarchal, direction that can be changed to produce more gender equality.

We will include feminist perspectives in appropriate chapters in the book, as we do with other theories. Our guiding principle is best stated by McCormick's (1994, p. 33) approach:

> *As we move into the twenty-first century, it is time to make sexology holistic and woman-affirming. Too many years have been devoted to sexual bookkeeping, recording the frequency and variety of people's genital experiences. This distracts us from the more*

important aspects of sexuality, how we think and feel about intimacy.

Political and moral reactions to particular theories can sometimes impede scientific understanding

of human sexual behavior. As we'll see, all four approaches to sex have caused political and moral controversy.

heories, Politics, and Morality

Confusion about the purpose of a theory is common among laypersons and not unknown among scientists. The goal of a theory is to present a tentative model of the causes of human behavior. A theory is not intended to be a blueprint or set of directions for how we should behave, but rather a picture of why we do behave in particular ways. When Freud theorized that humans are capable of sexual feelings and motives from infancy on, the public and many of Freud's scientific colleagues were deeply offended. Some of their reactions resulted from a confusion of theory with advocacy. Freud was not advocating sexual experience for infants and children; instead, he was trying to understand factors that influence personality development, and he theorized that sexual energy was one of these factors that was present from birth onward.

This same confusion of theory and advocacy is apparent today in the passionate controversy surrounding evolutionary theory. Questions of free will versus determinism (do we freely choose our behavior, or are we genetically programmed to respond in particular ways?), racial and gender discrimination, and religion are among the issues that have been raised by those who reject evolutionary approaches. Again, scientists who propose evolutionary theories as explanations of human sexual behavior are not advocating superiority of males over females or of one racial group over another. Instead, these scientists are trying to understand how a widespread phenomenon—for example, that men generally *do* dominate women in most cultures—could have developed. Evolutionary theorists are also not suggesting that humans are forced by "inherited" characteristics to behave like robots responding to genetic programs. Evolutionary approaches explicitly recognize the ability to learn as an adaptive capacity. It is what enables us to evaluate the likely

consequences of our behavioral choices.

People with political motives use bits and pieces of a theory to justify their beliefs and prejudices, just as they select one biblical passage and reject another when they want to support a particular argument. But in doing so, they are merely displaying their ignorance of the purpose of theory, which is to try to understand human behavior rather than to advocate particular policies. The validity and usefulness of theories should be determined on the basis of research results that support or refute their tenets, not on the basis of anyone's beliefs.

Some of the criticisms of learning theory and sociological approaches also stem from a misunderstanding of the nature of a theory. The issue, again, is one of free will versus determinism. Most of us prefer to believe that we freely choose our behaviors. We may, by gaining knowledge, increase our ability to enhance our freedom of choice. But the research described throughout this book also demonstrates that our individual experiences and cultural beliefs are quite predictive of how we behave. In subscribing to learning theories and sociological theories, researchers are not suggesting that we *should* be influenced by our individual reinforcement histories or by societal norms and beliefs, only that most of us *are* so influenced.

Another problem that has confronted scientists is opposition from those who see scientific theories as conflicting with religious morality. Religious and moral thinking is quite different, however, from scientific reasoning. Modern science is not a set of absolute truths; it is a method of inquiry—of testing hypotheses and building theories on the basis of data collected and verified according to standard procedures. Scientific theories are always tentative and subject to modification or rejection if they do not fit observable data. Religions, in contrast, consist of absolute beliefs, which are not subject to empirical tests in scientific terms. As such, science and religion operate in different spheres of human experience.

Rather than judging theories in terms of politics, morality, or even the elusive quality of accuracy, scientists judge on the basis of usefulness. All four theories that we have reviewed, as well as the findings of research conducted to test them, have contributed to our understanding of human sexual behavior. We are all affected by our ancestral history (evolutionary theory), our childhood experiences (psychoanalytic theories), our socialization and conditioning (social learning theories), and our cultural expectations and beliefs (sociological theories). Rather than competing with one another, the four theories generally complement one another. The questions that arise from each theory demand analysis at different levels of abstraction. In other words, which theory is most useful in a particular case may depend on the level that interests the investigator—biological, psychological, or social. At present, it appears that the factors emphasized by each of the theoretical approaches combine to produce the complexities that are involved in our sexual interactions.

SUMMARY OF MAJOR POINTS

1. The role of theory in understanding sexual behavior. Sexual theories are explanatory models of the causes and consequences of various facets of sexual attitudes and behaviors. Theories lead to predictions about particular responses under specific conditions. Such predictions can then be tested by research. Research findings may support a theory or, if they do not, can lead to modification of the theory in an attempt to increase its accuracy.

2. Evolutionary approaches. Evolutionary approaches trace the causes of much of contemporary sexual behavior back thousands of years to our distant ancestors. According to this view, modern sexual behaviors exist because they served the cause of reproductive success in the past. The characteristics of contemporary men and women, as well as their courtship patterns, evolved because they led to the reproductive success of their ancestors.

3. Psychoanalytic approaches. To explain sexual behavior, the creator of psychoanalytic theory, Sigmund Freud, examined the history of the individual rather than the history of our species. Psychoanalytic theory has undergone many revisions and changes since Freud's day, but it still places heavy emphasis on early experience as a determinant of adult sexuality and personality.

4. Learning approaches. Social learning theories, as the name implies, assume that most, if not all, sexual behavior is learned. Learning theorists have applied the principles of learning to the conditioning, maintenance, and elimination of sexual behaviors. Social learning theorists have been able to increase, reduce, or eliminate the performance of some sexual acts by manipulating the reinforcements for those particular acts.

5. Sociological approaches. Sociologists have attempted to explain how social institutions affect our sexual behavior. Because sexuality is a potent resource, the power structure of a society determines how male and female gender roles are defined. Inherent in the sociological approach is the idea that we must learn a complicated sequence of behaviors before a sexual or nonsexual interaction takes place. Thus, sexual interaction is not spontaneous but rather is the result of scripts that we learn so thoroughly that we do not usually even think about them.

6. Feminist approaches. Growing to some extent out of social learning and sociological approaches are a number of different feminist models that have been proposed to account for gender differences and similarities in gender roles and sexual behavior. The two most prominent—liberal feminism and radical feminism—have rather different underlying assumptions. Liberal feminists emphasize women's sexual pleasure and capacity for exploration beyond restrictive gender-role norms. In contrast, radical feminists focus on strategies for protecting women from danger and sexual coercion and assume that men are inherently sexually aggressive.

7. The role of theories in society. A theory is an attempt to build a model or picture of what we do and why we do it. A theory of some aspect of sexual behavior is not a recommendation to engage in or avoid that behavior. Nor is it an attempt to promote or advocate any particular moral or political stance. Each of the theoretical perspectives in this chapter is useful because each provides hypotheses about hu-

man sexual behavior, which researchers can test. People may argue about which theoretical approach is most accurate, but such arguments will probably never be resolved because each type of theory attempts to explain human sexual behavior from a different level of abstraction. In the real world, the multiple factors considered by multiple theories appear to interact in their impact on our sexual attitudes and behaviors.

Research on Sexuality

Reality or Myth ?

1. *Alfred Kinsey and his colleagues' research has been generally dismissed because of Kinsey's personal behavior.*

2. *Since the pioneering work of the Kinsey group and Masters and Johnson, opposition to sex research has almost disappeared.*

3. *Changes in dependent variables are assumed to depend on variations in the independent variable.*

4. *Participants in sex research almost always report accurately about their sexual behavior.*

5. *Research indicates that vitamin E has no effect on sexual activity.*

6. *"Participation observation" means taking part in the activities of the people being studied.*

ow frequently do people engage in sexual activity? How many sexual partners does the average person have in a lifetime? Are relationship satisfaction and sexual satisfaction related? These are just a few of the many questions about sexuality that researchers attempt to answer.

When we make decisions that affect our lives, it is helpful to have information about the potential consequences of the available choices. Sexual decisions can have major consequences in terms of costs and benefits, but in this area, many of us make decisions in the dark, so to speak. With relatively little knowledge, we make judgments as voters for or against sex education, as parents giving advice about nonmarital sex, or as consumers of contraceptives or products to promote fertility. One goal of sex researchers is to increase knowledge about the causes, correlates, and consequences of sexual attitudes and behaviors. The outcome of their work can have a direct effect on our lives, so it is important for us to have some idea about how they go about their work and the extent to which we can have confidence in their conclusions.

In this chapter, we first look at the movement away from religious doctrines and toward empirical research as bases for reaching conclusions about various sexual issues. Next we consider contemporary political and social barriers to sex research and the risks that several pioneering twentieth-century sex researchers took.

We discuss a number of ethical considerations that arise in conducting research on sexual and nonsexual topics. We then turn to the process of sex research in a discussion designed to help you evaluate the findings of sex researchers as you make sexual decisions in the coming years.

The Rise of Science

For several centuries prior to 1900, religious influence and interpretations were on the decline in intellectual circles as scientific explanations of the world and human behavior became increasingly influential. In their response to sexuality, however, scientists were not much more tolerant than clergymen had been. As the devil and his disciples were held less accountable for the world's misfortunes, a new scapegoat had to be found. Insanity was the choice, and its alleged cause was not a pact with the devil, but masturbation. From the eighteenth century until the end of the nineteenth century, this new "illness" was known as masturbatory insanity (Szasz, 1990).

The assumption that masturbation caused various maladies continued well into the twentieth century. In fact, it represented a transformation of the religious equation of sexual pleasure with sin into the medical idea that losing sperm is disease producing. Perhaps the most influential medical proponent of these ideas was Richard von Krafft-Ebing.

RICHARD VON KRAFFT-EBING

Krafft-Ebing (1840–1902), considered one of the world's leading psychiatrists during his lifetime, is an appropriate symbol for Victorian sexual attitudes. His

This 19th-century picture shows the supposed fate of a masturbator. In addition to insanity, masturbation was thought to cause a variety of physical disorders, among them epilepsy, poor eyesight, and loss of memory.

Some 18th-century boys wore spiked rings around the penis at night. If the wearer experienced a nocturnal erection, the spikes in the ring would cause pain that would awaken him, deterring him from the temptation of masturbation.

major work, *Psychopathia Sexualis* (1882), reflected the dominant theme of the time—sex as disease. It catalogued many types of sexual variations, illustrated with more than 200 case histories. Krafft-Ebing emphasized bizarre cases of sexual expression, and the thread running through all the variations he documented was masturbation and hereditary degeneracy.

Krafft-Ebing's work reflected the concern of the times about "deviant" sexuality, which included all sexual acts that did not have reproduction as their goal. He helped to spread the fear of most forms of eroticism by lending a scientific cast to these beliefs. Krafft-Ebing was a leading figure in the linking of non-reproductive sexual activity with disease. In contrast to this rather dismal view of sexuality, a less medical and more optimistic perspective was developed by a pioneer whose life overlapped Krafft-Ebing's.

HENRY HAVELOCK ELLIS

Henry Havelock Ellis (1859–1939) was perhaps the central figure in the emergence of the modern study

of sexuality. The historian Paul Robinson (1976) has contended that Ellis was to modern sexual theory what Albert Einstein was to modern physics because Ellis established a framework that has influenced all

Henry Havelock Ellis was a key figure in the modern study of sexuality. His writings on sexual deviance contradicted prevailing Victorian views.

subsequent theories about sexuality. The first six volumes of Ellis's *Studies in the Psychology of Sex* were published between 1897 and 1910. His initial volume, *Sexual Inversion*, was an attempt to broaden the spectrum of normal sexual behavior to include homosexuality. He argued that homosexuality is congenital (that is, existing at or before birth) and thus is not a vice or a moral choice. It is simply a variation from a statistical norm, heterosexuality.

In his second volume, *Auto-Eroticism*, Ellis attacked the nineteenth-century theories that linked masturbation with insanity. His work transformed masturbation from "a malignant vice into a benign inevitability" (Robinson, 1976, p. 13). Elsewhere, Ellis argued that most of the major forms of sexual deviation are congenital and related to some aspect of normal sexual life. Ellis fostered an acceptance of sexual variation that stood in marked contrast to the Victorian atmosphere of his lifetime. He, along with Sigmund Freud (described in Chapter 2), helped to open the subject of sexuality to serious research and began the assault on the barriers of prudery that had blocked public and scientific discussion of sexuality. Many societal barriers remain, however.

The Impact of Societal Beliefs, Political Attitudes, and Ethical Issues on Research

The questions researchers ask about sexuality and the methods they use to search for answers are intimately related to societal values and beliefs plus ethical considerations, as well as to their own beliefs. Sometimes it is hard to see the difference between these influences. For example, sex research with children is contrary to the ethical values held by the scientific community because it violates the principle of informed consent; that is, a child is not considered mature enough to consent to participate in sex research. Such research also violates the societal belief that sex research with children is immoral. In this instance, then, ethical values and societal beliefs are in agreement regarding the moral inappropriateness of such research. Here we separate the discussion of these influences on research, however, because sometimes societal beliefs conflict with ethical views of appropriate topics for sex research.

POLITICAL AND SOCIETAL BARRIERS TO RESEARCH

When a few nineteenth-century physicians attempted to institute training or research procedures related to sexuality, they suffered dire consequences. In the mid-nineteenth century, for example, Dr. James Platt White allowed 20 medical students to do vaginal exams on a consenting pregnant woman prior to and during childbirth as part of their training for obstetrics. Responding to objections from other physicians, who believed that it was wrong for a doctor to see women's genitals even when delivering babies, the American Medical Association expelled White in 1851 and passed a resolution against such training (Bullough, 1983).

You might assume that such extreme reactions and beliefs are relics of the nineteenth century, but even scientists who have studied sexual behavior in the mid-twentieth century have paid a price, both professionally and personally, for doing so. To illustrate the risks taken by sex-research pioneers, we focus on a select group of sex investigators who experienced many obstacles in their endeavors.

The Kinsey Group.   In the mid-1930s, Alfred Kinsey and some other Indiana University faculty members were asked to teach a course on marriage and the family. In preparing for the course, Kinsey discovered that there was little scientific information about the sexual aspects of marriage, so he decided to do his own research. Initially, he administered questionnaires to his students about their sexual experiences. By 1938, he had established a research group at Indiana, and they began the first of their interviews

---

informed consent—The ethical principle of informing potential research participants, before their consent to participate, of any aspects of the research that might be embarrassing or harmful.

In a meeting at the Institute for Sex Research in Bloomington, Indiana, Kinsey and his colleagues discuss some of their statistical analyses. From left to right are Alfred C. Kinsey, Clyde E. Martin, Paul H. Gebhard, and Wardell B. Pomeroy.

with thousands of Americans about their sexual experiences and behaviors. Kinsey and his colleagues, Wardell Pomeroy, Clyde Martin, and Paul Gebhard, undertook the task of describing the sexual behavior of typical Americans throughout the life span by using a combination of intensive interviews and questionnaires.

For the first several years of this project, Kinsey and his colleagues were repeatedly warned about the dangers of collecting sex histories, and they experienced some organized opposition. The harassment was not limited to the scientists on the project; a high school teacher who helped the Kinsey group find volunteers outside the school but in the same city was dismissed by his school board. In addition, there were attempts to persuade Indiana University to stop the study, censor or prevent publication of the results, and fire Kinsey. But the university's administration defended the Kinsey group's right to do scientific research. By the time the group published *Sexual Behavior in the Human Male* (1948) and its sequel, *Sexual Behavior in the Human Female* (1953), the United States was in the grip of the McCarthy era involving years of intense political repression. Under pressure from a congressional committee, the Rockefeller Foundation withdrew its

financial support of the project. Kinsey died three years later.

Even today, Kinsey's integrity has been questioned. James Jones has written a biography that intensely probes Kinsey's private life. According to Jones's book *Alfred C. Kinsey: A Public/Private Life,* Kinsey was both a homosexual and a masochist. Jones sought almost everyone he could find who knew Kinsey, or thought they knew something about him, and spread their memories across almost a thousand pages. Jones questioned Kinsey's motives and his research (he was not the first). Kinsey's interest in human sexuality was depicted as the outcome of his "perversions," and his research was portrayed as an attempt to liberalize American sexual mores. *Reality or Myth*

It is obvious that Jones had little empathy for Kinsey, and his sources are primarily anonymous. Even if Jones's accusations are true, what are the implications for the Kinsey group's research finding? Probably none. The work of Kinsey and his colleagues has undergone intense scientific scrutiny over almost half a century, and its shortcomings have been known. Jones's book adds nothing new. What he does add is a rather scurrilous attack on Kinsey's private life that landed him on the television talk-show circuit.

The Kinsey group's findings benefited the general public by providing a basis for social comparison that previously had not existed. For instance, we now know that the majority of people report masturbating at various times, a fact unknown before the publication of the Kinsey group's two major books. Presumably, people who realize that masturbation or other sexual behavior is typical of most people in our culture do not suffer the pangs of remorse and guilt that previous generations endured—or that may still afflict those people who are unaware that most people masturbate.

Kinsey and his associates helped pave the way for subsequent researchers to investigate sexual attitudes and behavior. "Without their original foot in the door," said William Masters, "we would never have been allowed to work. . . . These people broke the ice. When I went to the powers that be at Washington University in 1953, the [Kinsey] male book was out and the female book was just being published. I asked for permission to work in human sexuality. Well, obviously, there was a precedent set." (quoted in Allgeier, 1984).

> ▶ **Issues to Consider:** Why do you believe there has been so much opposition to sex research in the United States?

William Masters and Virginia Johnson. In 1966 William Masters and Virginia Johnson published their first major book on sexuality, *Human Sexual Response*. Instead of interviewing people about their sexual practices, as the Kinsey group had done, Masters and Johnson directly observed sexual stimulation in a laboratory. They studied volunteers through one-way glass as they masturbated, had oral sex, or engaged in coitus. The two researchers measured sexual responsiveness with the use of devices that fit around the penis or were inserted into the vagina. Their work is responsible for the popularization of the finding that—contrary to Freud (see Chapter 15)—the clitoris is involved in most women's sexual responsiveness.

In 1983 Masters recounted some of the difficulties that he and Johnson experienced as they developed what became known as the Masters and Johnson Institute in St. Louis. Despite the Kinsey group's precedent-setting work, when Masters asked the Washington University authorities for permission to do sex research, "they were terrified . . . but had they known what we were going to do, they'd have been even more so." In 1954 Masters finally obtained approval from the university's board of trustees to begin his work. He ran into problems right away, however, because his interest in the basic physiology of human sexual functioning was taking him into uncharted waters. At the outset, he could rely for previous research on only one book—Dickinson's *Atlas of Human Sexual Anatomy*—and the library would not let Masters have the book. (Only full professors could check it out, and Masters was an associate professor at the time.) His department's chairperson checked it out for him, but it had little information relevant to his interests. Undaunted, Masters spent a year working with a group who might know something about the physiology of sexual response: prostitutes. When he sought permission from the chancellor of his university to set up a laboratory, "the man turned deathly pale." Masters ulti-

mately obtained permission, however, although his work was supervised by a review board headed by the chancellor, a newspaper publisher, the chief of police, and a member of the clergy (Allgeier, 1984).

One prostitute with whom Masters worked ("a most attractive prostitute who had a Ph.D. in sociology and had hit upon a uniquely tax-free method of enhancing her university salary") told him that to understand the subjective aspects of female sexual functioning, he would need a female colleague. After interviewing many candidates, he found Virginia Johnson. "She met the following criteria," he later explained: "(a) good with people, because I'm not; (b) had to work; (c) married and divorced, and at least one child . . .; (d) intelligent; and (e) no postgraduate degree." Masters included the last criterion because he did not want the responsibility of exposing a woman to the risk of losing her degree (women with advanced degrees were rare in the mid-1950s), although he was well aware that he himself "had a good chance of losing an M.D." (Allgeier, 1984).

Masters and Johnson began working in their laboratory in 1957 with two different populations: one group they observed in the research laboratory (to gain information about normal sexual response) and one group they studied in a clinical setting (to gain information about—and treat—sexual and reproductive problems). In the late 1950s, the team ex-

William Masters and Virginia Johnson were pioneering researchers on physiological aspects of human sexual response.

perienced sabotage: some of their equipment disappeared, and then they were the targets of personal attacks. According to Masters: "What we didn't expect was how they were done: They were fundamentally carried out against our children, [who] were socially ostracized [and] bitterly attacked as being sex-mongers. I had to move my daughter from St. Louis and send her to prep school." After publication of *Human Sexual Response* (1966), "the hate mail was unbelievable. . . . The drop dead category was about 90–95% of the mail." Despite this early harassment, Masters and Johnson persevered, and we know of no books dealing with human sexual response that do not reference Masters and Johnson's work—a testament to their important contributions to the field.

Vern Bullough. Historian Vern Bullough also endured his share of professional difficulties resulting from his work on sexuality. Bullough obtained his Ph.D. in history from the University of Chicago in 1954 and began his career with historical analyses of nonsexual topics. In 1957 the Wolfenden Report, a study of prostitution and homosexuality in Britain, was published, and Bullough wrote a review of it. Repeatedly invited by a publisher to write a book on either of these topics, Bullough eventually consented to examine the history of prostitution: "I did not consent to write about homosexuality because, at that time, I was very concerned about being labeled a homosexual. I didn't mind being labeled a prostitute. I also took great care to publish research on a number of other topics so that I would not be labeled as a sexologist" (Bullough, 1983).

Bullough has described himself (personal communication, June 6, 1986) as a historian of science and medicine, not a sexologist, but he has not completely succeeded in avoiding that label. In introducing Bullough's presentation on medieval universities and professionalism at a conference of the American Historical Association, the session's moderator described him as a "historian who specializes in whores, queers, and perverts, but who occasionally could do some real research if he put his mind to it." In fact, of the more than 50 books that he has written, half of them coauthored with his wife, Dr. Bonnie Bullough, fewer than half have focused on sexual topics.

Bullough learned in the 1970s that the FBI was investigating him. In 1976, under the provisions of

Vern and Bonnie Bullough lean on some of the books they have written individually and in collaboration with one another. Fewer than half of their books have focused on sexuality. Nonetheless, known for his historical analyses of sexual attitudes and behavior, Vern Bullough was once classified as a dangerous subversive by the FBI, presumably because of his sex research. Bonnie died in 1996.

the Freedom of Information Act, he requested his FBI file. It took him almost a year to get the file, which exceeded 100 pages, and its contents "shocked and horrified" him. He learned that the FBI had classified him as a security risk, meaning that he could be imprisoned in the event of a national crisis. He earned this classification during the years that J. Edgar Hoover, the long-time director of the FBI, was in office. Ironically, rumors had long circulated that Mr. Hoover was gay and occasionally dressed in women's attire. His "tough cop" image may have been, at least in part, an attempt to counteract the rumors of his homosexuality (Gentry, 1991). In the late 1960s, when Bullough received a Fulbright scholarship (one of the nation's most prestigious awards) to do research in Egypt, overseas agencies of the United States were alerted to keep a watch on him and his family because they were regarded as "dangerous subversives." It is not clear how or why a dangerous subversive would receive a Fulbright, but as Bullough put it, "Sometimes, one wing of the government doesn't know what the other wing does."

In this section we have considered some of the barriers and risks faced by pioneering sex researchers, but as the Kinsey group wrote in 1953, sex researchers are not alone in experiencing such barriers:

> There was a day when the organization of the universe, and the place of the earth, the sun, the moon, and the stars in it, were considered of such theologic import that the scientific investigation of these matters was bitterly opposed by the ruling forces of the day. The scientists who first attempted to explore the nature of matter, and the physical laws affecting the relationships of matter were similarly condemned. . . . We do not believe that the happiness of individual men, and the good of the total social organization, is ever furthered by the perpetuation of ignorance. (p. 19)

Having read this review of the harassment experienced by several sex research pioneers, you may be left with the mistaken impression that hostility to sex research is behind us. In fact, contemporary efforts to gather data still face uphill battles. For example, a study that became known as the National Health and Social Life Survey was initially designed in 1988 by contract with the National Institute for Child Health and Human Development (Laumann, Gagnon, Michael, & Michaels, 1994). The study was to be the first to question a nationally representative sample of American adults about their sexual attitudes and behaviors. Funding for pilot research was awarded in July 1988, and interviews were planned with about 20,000 people.

Reality or Myth

Then conservative politicians such as Senator Jesse Helms of North Carolina got wind of the proposed study and were able to create a political atmosphere that led to the withdrawal of funding for the project. A flavor of the Helms opposition is revealed in the following remarks he made before the U.S. Senate:

> *The real purpose . . . is not to stop the spread of AIDS. . . . These sex surveys have not— have not—been concerned with legitimate scientific inquiry as much as they have been concerned with a blatant attempt to sway public attitudes in order to liberalize opinions and laws regarding homosexuality, pedophilia, anal and oral sex, sex education, teenage pregnancy and all down the line. (Congressional Record, September 12, 1991, pp. S12861—S12862)*

Fortunately, the investigators were able to obtain private funding, although they had to scale back the number of respondents to 3,432. Ironically, their findings, many of which we report in this book, revealed a more conservative sexual atmosphere in the United States than had most previous studies!

ETHICAL ISSUES

In addition to the limitations that societal attitudes and beliefs impose on the kinds of questions that can be investigated, scientists must also be concerned with the rights, safety, and well-being of those who participate in their research. Over the years, several principles have been developed to safeguard the rights of volunteers for research.

The principle of *informed consent* stipulates that participants be informed of any aspects of a study that might be embarrassing or damaging to them, including all the procedures they will undergo, before they consent to participate. Prisoners, psychiatric patients, developmentally disabled adults, and children are not considered capable of giving informed consent. When children are the population of interest for a particular study, researchers must obtain the informed consent of their parents.

The principle of *freedom from coercion* requires that potential volunteers be free of undue pressure to participate in research. In the past, prison inmates have been induced by offers of shortened sentences to participate in drug research, and college students have been required to "volunteer" for research or accept an incomplete grade in particular courses. Such practices are now viewed as coercive.

RESEARCH SPOTLIGHT   Ethical Principles and the Tuskegee Study

In 1932 the U.S. Health Service sponsored a research program in Tuskegee, Alabama, to study the long-term effects of untreated syphilis—a research project that exemplifies the violation of all four ethical principles of research (Jones, 1993). Syphilis is now easily cured in its early stages, but it can lead to mental and physical disability and death if left untreated.

In the 1930s mercury and two arsenic compounds were known to be effective in killing the bacteria that cause syphilis. Unfortunately, these drugs are also highly toxic, and patients experienced serious and occasionally fatal, reactions to the drugs. When the study began, therefore, the treatments may have been worse than the disease, at least in the short term. The Tuskegee study, however, involved no treatment; its goal was to examine the long-term effects of untreated syphilis in Blacks (Jones, 1993).

To obtain research participants, the Public Health Service held meetings at Black schools and churches in Macon County, Alabama, at which it was announced that "government doctors" were giving free blood tests. As residents of one of the poorest counties in the South, most of the citizens had never even seen a doctor, much less been treated by one. The response to announcement was overwhelmingly positive, and thus began one of the most tragic human studies of the twentieth century. Between 1932 and 1972, approximately 625 Black males in the county who were identified as having syphilis received blood tests and underwent physical examinations to determine the progression of the disease. This study may have had some ethical justification during the 1930s, when the treatment for syphilis was dangerous. But the withholding of treatment after 1943, the year in which it was discovered that penicillin could kill the bacteria without killing the victim, represented a serious violation of the risk-benefit principle.

The lack of ethical principles of the researchers became clear when the men visited local clinics for checkups for other disorders. The public Health Service informed the attending physicians that the men were not to be treated for syphilis because they were part of an experiment; World War II military authorities dealing with draftees got similar instructions. The denial of effective treatment not only endangered the lives of the men being studied without their informed consent, but also resulted in the transmission of syphilis to their wives and congenital syphilis to their children. The principle of informed consent was also seriously violated because the men did not even realize that effective treatment for syphilis was being withheld from them. They were told that they had "bad blood" and that they were being studied by the government.

Only 120 in the group were known to be still alive in 1974. Most of the remaining 500 or so syphilis victims could not be located and were presumed dead. In 1997, President Clinton formally apologized for the government's abuse to the eight people who were still alive. An award-winning HBO film, *Miss Evers' Boys*, depicts the events surrounding the Tuskegee study and is available on video.

The principle of *protection from physical or psychological harm* deals with a particularly thorny ethical problem. If we knew all the potential effects of a sex therapy treatment, medical procedure, or contraceptive drug, there would be no reason to conduct research to determine these effects. But not knowing what the effects may be, researchers risk negatively affecting the physical or psychological health of research participants. This ethical principle requires that researchers be aware of this danger and design their study to minimize it. Specifically, volunteers should encounter no more risk to their physical or psychological health during the course of a research project than they would in their normal daily lives.

To test the hypothesis that being questioned about their sexual behavior may encourage adolescents to increase their level of sexual activity, Carolyn Halpern, Richard Udry, and Chirayath Suchindran (1994) compared students who were questioned twice with those who were questioned up to 5 times about their age at first intercourse, number of sexual partners, and so forth. At the end of the study, they found that the groups did not differ on any of the measured variables. Thus, it appears that being questioned about sexual behavior does not alter the sexual behavior of respondents.

Protecting the anonymity of volunteers and the confidentiality of their responses is an important part of the research principle of protecting participants from harm. If, for example, we were interested in the relationship between women's responses to first intercourse and the duration of involvement with their current partner, the behavior of their partner during the experience, or the amount of prior experience with necking and petting with other partners, we would need to ask a number of sensitive questions. Some women in the sample might not wish to share this information with their parents or current partners; thus their participation in the study and their responses would need to be held confidential. In keeping with the principle of protection from physical or psychological harm, most informed-consent statements explicitly indicate that anonymity and confidentiality will be maintained.

Research on some topics poses dilemmas that cannot be adequately resolved by reference to the principle of protection from physical or psychological harm. We evaluate testing in these and similar areas on the basis of the *risk-benefit principle*. For example, after the birth control pill had been developed and tested with animals, it could not be marketed until its effects on humans had been measured (Reed, 1983). Because the researchers were trying to determine whether the pill produced serious side effects, they obviously could not give unconditional guarantees of protection from harm to volunteers for the testing program. Pregnancy itself poses a health risk, however, and the mortality rates for women and babies were known to be higher when pregnancies occurred less than two years apart than when they occurred at longer intervals. Thus, development of a highly reliable contraceptive appeared to offer great potential benefits when testing began in the 1950s. In support of the application of the risk-benefit principle to this case, the maternal mortality rate from pregnancy and childbirth, as we now know, is higher than that from any form of contraception. Therefore, when the potential benefits of research outweigh the

potential risks, research is considered permissible, provided the principle of informed consent is maintained.

To make sure that scientists adhere to these four ethical principles, ethics boards review research proposals. The goals of scientific research are to increase our understanding of how variables are related, and ultimately to augment our general well-being. The need to prepare proposals for review by ethics boards adds an extra step to the research process, and a study is sometimes blocked or slowed down even when it adheres to the four ethical principles just described (Wiederman, 1999). Nonetheless, some research procedures used in past studies demonstrate the critical importance of adhering to ethical guidelines in conducting scientific studies. A case in point is the Tuskegee study, which James Jones (1993) documented in the book *Bad Blood* (see "Research Spotlight: Ethical Principles and the Tuskegee Study").

If an ethics review board approves a research proposal, scientists can begin their study. The results of their research may be presented at professional meetings and published in scholarly journals (see Appendix) and subsequently reported in the popular press. At that point, you may become aware of the research and wonder to what extent you should make personal decisions on the basis of it. The remainder of this chapter is aimed at providing you with skills to make an educated judgment regarding the applicability of research findings to you as an individual.

Understanding the Process of Sex Research

Initial attempts to understand the research process are a bit like making bread or making love for the first time. It is one thing to read about evaluating research in a textbook, kneading dough in a cookbook, or caressing genitals in a sex manual, and quite another to engage in these processes. Initially, you are likely to feel unsure of exactly what to do. How do you knead dough, anyway? Are you supposed to push it or squeeze it? How hard are you supposed to knead it, and for how long? Similarly, how do you caress genitals? In regard to understanding research, what are the relevant questions, and how do you get the answers?

DEFINITION OF RESEARCH TERMS

When researchers seek scientific evidence relevant to issues in any discipline or field, they generally begin by stating their question as a **hypothesis**, which is a statement of a specific relationship between two or more variables. Put another way, a hypothesis is an educated guess stated in such a way that it can be accepted or rejected on the basis of research results. A **variable** is anything that can vary or change. For in-

hypothesis—(hy-PAW-theh-sis) Statement of a specific relationship between or among two or more variables.
variable—Any situation or behavior capable of change or variation.

Figure 3.1 Degree of Nudity as an Independent Variable
Although the degree of nudity varies in these photos, other factors vary as well. Thus responses to the photos may differ not only because of the degree of nudity but also because of the extent of body contact.

stance, our levels of hunger, happiness, sexual arousal, and time spent studying can all change, so these can all be defined as variables.

To formulate a testable hypothesis, a scientist must operationally define the variables. An **operational definition** is a description of each variable, so that it can be measured or counted and people can agree on the definition. Given these criteria, some variables cannot be operationally defined. For example, consider the classic question, "How many angels can dance on the head of a pin?" Although we could probably agree on what we mean by "head of a pin" and "dance," we might hit a snag with the term *angel*. Counting or measuring the angels is even more difficult. If we cannot operationally define a variable, we cannot study it.

Kinds of Variables.   There are three kinds of variables: independent, dependent, and control. **Independent variables** are those that can be manipulated or varied by an experimenter. For instance, to investi-

gate the effect of nudity on sexual arousal, we might vary the degree of nudity (the independent variable) in a series of photos, such as those in Figure 3.1.

Dependent variables are those that are measured. Changes in dependent variables are assumed to depend on variations in the independent variable. For instance, after exposure to one of the photos in Figure 3.1, volunteers could be asked to indicate their level of arousal. Their response—their reported level of arousal—would then be the dependent variable. Independent variables are sometimes called *stimulus variables*, and dependent variables can also be called *response variables*.

Experimenters try to keep all factors other than independent variables from changing. **Control variables** are factors that could vary but are controlled or held constant. Because in our example we are interested in the effect of nudity on arousal, we want to hold all other variables constant if we can. A number of variables were controlled through the use of the same couple in all three photos in Figure 3.1.

operational definition—Description of a variable in such a way that it can be measured.
independent variables—Variables that are manipulated or varied by an experimenter.

dependent variables—Variables that are measured or observed.
control variables—Variables that are held constant or controlled to reduce their influence on the dependent variable.

Otherwise, differences in reported arousal might be confounded—that is, unintentionally influenced—by responses to variations in the age, attractiveness, and so forth of each couple rather than to the degree of nudity per se. *Reality or Myth* ?

OBTAINING RESEARCH PARTICIPANTS: PROBLEMS IN SAMPLING

The last time a lab technician pricked your finger to draw some blood, you were participating in a **sampling** process. When physicians order a blood sample, of course, they are not particularly interested in the properties of the small amount of blood that is drawn. Rather, they assume that the properties of that sample are the same as those of the person's entire blood supply.

Scientists conducting sex research would be delighted if they could place as much confidence in their sampling procedures as the lab technician can in blood-sampling procedures. Obtaining accurate results in the sampling of most aspects of human sexuality, however, is considerably more difficult. Most characteristics of sexual behavior are not evenly distributed throughout whatever population we might wish to sample. Further, because all potential sources of **bias** have not been identified, it is difficult to obtain a representative sample. Among the most persistent sources of sampling bias that have been identified are volunteer bias and self-report bias.

Volunteer bias refers to the differences between those who volunteer and those who refuse to participate in research. Studies of volunteer bias have indicated that although volunteers for sex research do not differ from nonvolunteers in most personality characteristics or in level of presonal adjustment, systematic differences do appear in their attitudes toward sexuality and in their experience with various sexual activities (Bogaert, 1996; Strassberg & Lowe, 1995 Trivedi & Sabini, 1998). Specifically, compared to nonvolunteers, volunteers are more sexually liberal, more positive toward sexuality, more sexually curious, and more supportive of sex research. Gener-

ally volunteers are more sexually experienced and report having had a greater number of sexual partners than do nonvolunteers. Men are more likely than women to volunteer for research on sexuality and other "unusual" topics.

After volunteers have been obtained for sex research, another kind of bias, self-report bias, can restrict **generalizability.** **Self-report bias** can result from participants' reluctance to provide honest answers or an inability to give accurate answers. Fearing that they will appear deviant in their sexual feelings and behavior, volunteers may either fail to report or underreport (or in some cases overreport) their behavior. They may respond with what they believe is the socially desirable behavior rather than with their actual behavior (Wiederman, 1993; Wiederman, Weis, & Allgeier, 1994). *Reality or Myth* ?

Even when volunteers want to report accurately, they may have difficulty recalling some past events. For example, you can probably remember quite accurately the first time you kissed someone erotically. But can you give as accurate an account if you are asked how many times you have kissed someone or how many different people you have kissed?

These sources of bias do not eliminate the usefulness of sex research, nor are they unique to sex research. They simply limit the extent to which we can assume that all people feel or behave precisely the way that research volunteers do. With these potential limitations in mind, let us turn to the two major methods used to gather information about sexual attitudes and behavior.

▶ **Issues to Consider:** According to a college newspaper, 20 percent of students at that college have a sexually transmitted disease. The reporter based these results on data from students who were treated at the local health center. Is there a problem with the reporter's conclusions?

▶ **Issues to Consider:** Would you volunteer to participate in a research project to (1) respond to a questionnaire about your sexual attitudes and behavior, (2) observe erotic films, (3) be observed engaging in sexual behavior? Why or why not?

---

sampling—The process of selecting a representative part of a population.

bias—An attitude for or against a particular theory or hypothesis that influences one's judgment.

volunteer bias—Bias introduced into the results of a study stemming from systematic differences between those who volunteer for research and those who avoid participation.

generalizability—The extent to which findings from a particular sample study can be described as representing wider populations and situations.

self-report bias—Bias introduced into the results of a study stemming either from participants' desire to appear "normal" or from memory lapses.

RESEARCH METHODS

In gathering evidence relevant to the testing of a hypothesis, researchers generally rely on one of two methods: the **correlational method** and the **experimental method**. With both methods, researchers pay close attention to the bases for selection of samples of the organisms under study, whether they are people, monkeys, rats, or germ cells.

Correlational Methods.   An idea that students have brought to class for the past several decades is that vitamin E increases sexual desire and performance. How would you test this belief? Using a correlational approach, you could give a questionnaire to a large group of people regarding the frequency and quality of their sexual experiences. You could also ask them about the kinds and amounts of vitamins they take. Assume that people who take large dosages of vitamin E also report engaging in more sexual activity than those who take little or no vitamin E. This correlation between taking vitamin E and engaging in more sexual activity indicates that the two are related, but it does not tell us that vitamin E *causes* greater levels of sexual activity or higher levels of performance.

Experimental Methods.   The hypothesis that vitamin E enhances sexual performance was tested with an experimental approach by Edward Herold and his colleagues several decades ago (Herold, Mottin, & Sabry, 1979). Specifically, volunteer couples were randomly assigned to one of two groups. One group received capsules containing vitamin E. The other group received capsules that were identical in appearance but, unknown to them, did not contain vitamin E. Thus the presence or absence of vitamin E—the independent variable—was manipulated. The volunteers also completed questionnaires reporting both their sexual and nonsexual feelings—the dependent variables.

The random assignment of the couples to the vitamin or nonvitamin groups provided a means to

control the influence of other, irrelevant variables. We can assume that through random assignment, the average level of reported sexual activity prior to participation in the study would have been about the same in both groups.

Before we reveal the results of the study, note that if Herold and coworkers found, using an experimental method, that the vitamin E group had greater levels of sexual desire and performance than the nonvitamin E group, we could conclude that vitamin E *enhances* (a causal inference) sexual performance. In fact, these researchers found that the vitamin E group reported increased energy and more other positive effects than did the nonvitamin E group. However, the two groups did not differ in reported levels of sexual activity. *Reality or Myth*

Differences Between Correlational and Experimental Methods.   Both methods require careful and consistent measurement of the relevant variables. The two methods vary in the following ways: (1) control of variables, (2) artificiality, (3) generalizability, and (4) conclusions that may be drawn. Correlational and experimental methods differ in the extent to which the variables of interest are controlled. With the correlational method, researchers simply measure the level of variables (in our example, vitamin E and levels of sexual activity). With the experimental method, the independent variable (vitamin E) is manipulated or varied, and the dependent variables (sexual desire and performance) are measured. Researchers thus have much more control over the amount and frequency of the independent variable in the experimental than in the correlational method.

A second difference between the two approaches is the extent of **artificiality**. In general, correlational methods involve more natural settings and processes than do experimental methods. Experimental methods can produce what is known as **reactivity;** that is, volunteers may react to the knowledge that they are being studied. This circumstance may make their responses somewhat less spontaneous and natural than if they did not know that they would be asked to report their behavior.

correlational method—A research method involving the measurement of two or more variables to determine the extent of their relationship.
experimental method—A research method involving the manipulation of one or more independent variables to determine their influence on dependent variables.

artificiality—The extent to which a research setting differs from one's normal living environment.
reactivity—The tendency of a measurement instrument (or observer) to influence the behavior under observation.

Third, partly because of the artificiality typically present in the experimental method, the results obtained sometimes have less generalizability. Thus, although it is probably safe to assume that other groups of volunteers who might participate in the same experimental procedures would behave in about the same way, we do not know the extent to which the knowledge that they are taking part in an experiment alters their normal behavior.

The issues of artificiality, reactivity, and generalizability pose particular difficulties in studies with psychological or behavioral variables. You perhaps volunteered for an experiment while taking an introductory psychology course. If so, you may have had a number of motives for responding in ways other than the way you would respond normally. To begin with, most people prefer to be evaluated positively rather than negatively. Thus, they attempt to figure out the researcher's hypothesis. Once they have an idea, they may choose one of three alternatives instead of reporting their actual responses. First, they may respond in a way that will put them in a favorable light, creating what is known as *social-desirability bias*. Second, they may try to help confirm what they believe to be the experimental hypothesis. This is referred to as *complying with the demand characteristics of an experiment* (or, informally, as the "help the experimenter" effect). Third, volunteers may be irritated at feeling forced to participate in research as part of a course requirement and may respond inaccurately in an attempt to refute what they believe to be the hypothesis (known informally as the "screw you!" effect). These kinds of influences limit the extent to which we can generalize findings from experiments to the real world.

The two methods also differ regarding the conclusions that may be drawn. With correlational methods, finding an association between two variables does not permit the conclusion that there is a cause-and-effect relationship. A causal connection can be established through the use of experimental methods, however, by controlling nonrelevant variables—through random assignment of volunteers to groups, as in the vitamin E example—or by holding other variables constant. If there is a systematic difference in the level of the dependent variable between the two groups, then there is support for the hypothesis that variations in the independent variable have caused the change in response—the dependent variable.

To sum up, there are advantages and disadvantages to the correlational and experimental methods. Therefore, it is desirable to use both methods in trying to answer a particular question. If the findings from both correlational and experimental methods yield the same results, we can have greater confidence in the conclusions.

Other Methodological Variations. Beyond using correlational and experimental methods, researchers also select the location of research and the length of time needed to collect information. Research may be conducted in a laboratory or in a field setting. By the terms *lab* and *field*, we do not mean that the researcher takes the participants either to a gleaming white sterile laboratory or to the middle of a grassy, sunlit meadow. *Lab* refers to a specific location of the researcher's choice in which to observe participants' behavior. *Field* generally means the participants' own environment—wherever they normally live. Field research, then, can refer to studies that are conducted in people's homes, to observations of baboons in their natural environment, or to observations of flirting in singles bars.

Research on a particular topic sometimes begins in lab settings and then moves to field settings so that the researcher can see whether results from the lab are consistent with those from the field. In other cases, initial studies are begun in field settings and then repeated in lab settings.

Cross-Sectional and Longitudinal Research. Research also varies in terms of whether it is cross-sectional or longitudinal. Imagine that we are interested in determining the effects of oral contraceptives on fertility. Using a **cross-sectional** approach, we might try to find a large group of women who used the pill for five years and then stopped two years ago in an attempt to become pregnant. We could then compare the pregnancy rate of this group with that of another group of women who were similar to the first group except that they relied on a contraceptive method not involving hormones, such as the diaphragm or condom. Although it might take some time to locate two equivalent groups of women, the comparison in fertility rates could be made for the same time period.

cross-sectional research—Comparisons of distinct but similar groups at the same point in time.

The participant at left is taking part in laboratory research, in the form of responding to test stimuli. At right is an example of field research—observing the behavior of women in singles bars.

A **longitudinal** approach may also be used to examine the relationship between oral-contraceptive use and later fertility. In a longitudinal design, researchers study the same group over a period of time. An example is research that compared the offspring of mothers who did not want the children with those whose mothers did (David, 1992). The children in both groups were compared on a number of measures of adjustment up to ages 21 to 23 (see Chapter 11).

Relatively few researchers rely on longitudinal approaches because they are time-consuming and therefore more expensive than cross-sectional research. Further, a relatively high proportion of the initial volunteers in a longitudinal study may be lost through relocation, death, or decisions that automatically remove them from the sample. Nonetheless, longitudinal studies offer some distinct advantages over cross-sectional approaches. Instead of relying on participants' memories of events that occurred a long time ago, researchers can ask that each of these events be reported at the time, and that feature provides greater accuracy. Just as experimental or correlational methods may be used in laboratory or field settings, either of these methods may be applied in conducting cross-sectional or longitudinal research.

▶ **Issues to Consider:** Do you think we can develop an accurate understanding of human sexual behavior without longitudinal research?

Measurement in Sex Research

Methods of measuring sexual responses include self-administered measures, interviews, direct observation, physiological and biochemical measures, case studies, and focus groups. When researchers are designing or choosing research measures, they must determine the **reliability** and **validity** of the measures. If a measure is reliable, then individuals will respond the same way over a period of weeks or months (test-

longitudinal research—Comparisons of the same groups across time.

reliability—The extent to which a measure elicits the same response at different times.
validity—The extent to which something measures what it was designed to measure.

retest reliability). A measure is valid to the extent that scores on it accurately reflect the variable in question. If, for example, you created a self-report measure of sexual arousal in response to erotic stimuli, you might test its validity by comparing responses on physiological measures of arousal (for example, erection and vaginal lubrication). If physiological measures reflect greater levels of arousal as self-reported ratings of arousal increase, then confidence in the validity of your self-report measure increases.

SELF-ADMINISTERED QUESTIONNAIRES, SURVEYS, AND SCALES

Hundreds of measures have been developed to record attitudinal and behavioral responses to various aspects of sexuality (Davis, Yarber, Bauserman, Schreer, & Davis, 1998). By comparing responses to these measures across samples from different populations, researchers can get an idea of how different groups of people (for example, men versus women, adolescents versus adults, sexually experienced versus sexually inexperienced people) differ in their attitudes, knowledge, and behavior regarding such matters as contraception, abortion, homosexuality, and rape. By comparing the survey responses from samples of the same population across different time periods, researchers can get an idea of what changes over time.

Interviews. Researchers also obtain information about sexual attitudes and behavior by interviewing people. This method is usually more expensive and time-consuming than pencil-and-paper measures, but it allows for greater flexibility in acquiring in-depth information.

Although it has been more than half a century since Alfred Kinsey and his colleagues conducted the classic interview studies of the sexual behavior of American males (Kinsey et al., 1948) and females (Kinsey et al., 1953), the Kinsey-group research is still the largest interview study of sexual behavior ever done in North America. They interviewed more than 10,000 people and amassed an incredible amount of information. Both the quantity and the quality of the interviews earned the group a great deal of respect.

Kinsey and his colleagues did not attempt to select a random or representative sample of the U.S.

population. Instead, they selected various organizations and tried to interview all members. This strategy produced a sample in which the responses of middle-class, relatively well-educated Whites were overrepresented. For example, about 75 percent of the women who responded had attended college. On the other hand, given the paucity of information at the time on the sexual practices of normal or typical Americans, and the difficulty of getting agreement from a representative sample of people to participate in sex research, the Kinsey group did obtain valuable data by sampling groups that were likely to represent diverse patterns of sexual behavior.

There is also the problem of the accuracy of participants' reports of their behavior. The Kinsey group attempted to assess the accuracy of these reports in a number of ways. They reinterviewed some of the volunteers 18 months after the first interview. This procedure, similar to a test-retest check for reliability, is known as a take-retake interview. They also compared the reports of husbands and wives on questions about which these partners should have had the same answers, such as their frequency of marital sex. Correlations for the take-retake and husband-wife comparisons were generally high on such items as extent of education, number of children, and occupation of the father, but they were much lower for frequencies of sexual activity. Memory errors probably account for much of this variability, but Kinsey did not take this factor into account statistically. He gave as much weight to reports based on memories of events that took place many years earlier as he did to reports of current activities.

Finally, demographic and personality differences among interviewers can influence volunteers' responses and thus also constitute a potential source of bias. However, checks on reliability of responses to one interviewer versus another in the Kinsey studies indicated few differences.

Although there are obvious limits to the extent to which the Kinsey results were generalizable to all Americans at that time, most sex researchers remain impressed with the broad and thorough description of **normative** sexual behavior contributed by the Kinsey group.

normative—The average or typical response of members of a sample.

DIRECT OBSERVATION

Direct observation involves exactly what its name implies: the behavior of interest is directly observed. For example, researchers have directly observed such sexual behaviors as flirtation in bars (Moore, 1998) and the sexual activity of heterosexual and homosexual couples (Masters & Johnson, 1966, 1979). This approach is also useful with nonhuman species because they cannot respond to questionnaires or interviews.

A problem with direct observation is that the presence of an observer may alter the behavior of the organisms being observed. Many of us have experienced this phenomenon when under observation while we were learning to drive or type. The problem of potential bias introduced by the presence of observers may be magnified when humans are the object of study. You might ask 10 of your sexually experienced friends how willingly they would volunteer for a sexual-behavior study requiring (1) responding to a questionnaire, (2) participating in an interview, or (3) being observed during sexual activity. Many of them would probably be more willing to participate in the first two alternatives than in the last. Volunteer bias, then, may be a greater problem when researchers use direct observation than when they rely on self-reported behavior for information about sexuality (Strassberg & Lowe, 1995).

One way in which a researcher may reduce volunteer bias in direct observation is to participate in the behavior being studied. This method is known as **participant observation.** For example, Marilyn Story (1993) described the benefits of her being a social nudist and conducting research on the attitudes and behaviors of social nudists compared to people who did not engage in social nudism. *Reality or Myth* 6

PHYSIOLOGICAL RESPONSE MEASURES

Some other approaches that are used to record changes resulting from sexual arousal are measures of general responses, such as heart rate and dilation of the pupils, measures of genital responses, and analysis of blood or saliva samples to measure sex hormones such as testosterone. The general measures

participant observation—Conducting research while simultaneously engaging in the behavior with the group being studied.

do provide information about arousal; however, they do not indicate whether sexual or nonsexual stimulation is the source of the observed arousal. For example, when Hoon, Wincze, and Hoon (1976) showed videotapes containing neutral material, erotic material, or Nazi war atrocities, the participants' arousal, as measured by heart rate and other general measures of bodily arousal, did not differ according to whether they were watching the erotic tape or the one depicting war atrocities. Genital responses, however, did vary according to the content of the films.

Among the devices for measuring male genital response are the penile plethysmograph, the mercury-in-rubber strain gauge, and the metal-band gauge. All three devices fit partially or totally around the

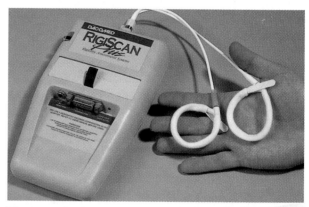

The Rigiscan Plus monitor measures the circumference and rigidity of the penis.

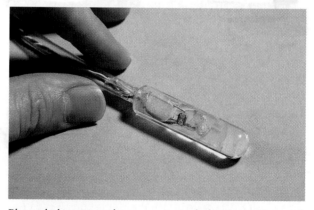

Photoplethysmography uses a vaginal photometer inserted into the vagina to measure changes in blood volume in the vaginal tissues.

penis and are designed to measure changes in its circumference.

Some devices currently used to measure female genital response are the vaginal myograph and the rectal myograph. Both devices monitor the muscular activity of the pelvic floor. Another measure, vaginal photoplethysmography, measures changes in blood flow in the vagina. The most widely used type of vaginal photoplethysmography is a menstrual tampon–sized device containing an infrared light-emitting diode as a light source and photo transister as a light detector (Laan & Everaerd, 1995).

These genital measures have advantages over more general measures. However, their use reflects an unintended bias: that sexual response is primarily a genital, rather than a total body-and-mind, process.

CASE STUDIES AND FOCUS GROUP RESEARCH

When a researcher studies a single person, family, or small group without the intention of comparing that person, family, or group with others in the same study, the approach is known as the case study or focus group research. With the case study, a single individual is studied extensively using one or more of the methods (e.g., scales, interviews, biochemical measures). This approach does not permit cause-and-effect inferences, nor can the responses from a single person be generalized beyond that person. On the other hand, the case study of one individual can disprove an assertion containing "always" or "never"—for example, "women never ejaculate" or "men always ejaculate." Researchers also use case studies to generate hypotheses for larger correlational or experimental studies.

Researchers using focus groups obtain samples of people who share some common characteristics and interview the participants in groups. For example, Offir, Fisher, Williams, and Fisher (1993) were interested in studying inconsistencies in the use of safer-sex practices by gay men. Their work indicated that although most men in their samples had modified their sexual behaviors in an effort to reduce the risk of transmission of the human immunodeficiency virus (HIV), the men reported that there were circumstances in which they engaged in unsafe sex.

One purpose of focus groups is to permit group members to generate their own questions and issues.

When researchers select questions without giving volunteers the opportunity to indicate the issues relevant to a particular topic that they consider important, the researchers may miss important variables that potentially influence sexual decisions. For example, if you were asked on a questionnaire whether you had asked a potential partner to discuss contraception with you, or to tell you his or her number of previous partners, you might indicate that you had asked neither of these questions. The researcher might then conclude that, in making sexual decisions, you were unconcerned about contraception or about the potential risk of contracting a sexually transmitted disease from a partner who had had many sexual partners in the recent past. In the context of a focus group discussion, however, you might say that although you did not explicitly ask these questions or discuss these issues aloud, your (potential) partner had placed a packet of condoms on the coffee table while you were making out and that you had checked with friends who knew a lot about your potential partner before agreeing to date him or her. Thus, an advantage of this approach is that it can allow participants to express information that the researchers who designed the questions overlooked. The understanding that can emerge from such focus groups can help health care professionals target educational programs to try to increase the likelihood that people will engage in healthier sexual behaviors.

As with case studies of individuals, focus group research is aimed at hypothesis generation rather than hypothesis testing. The hypotheses that develop from case studies and focus groups can then be tested with larger samples using correlational or experimental designs.

COMPARING METHODS OF MEASUREMENT

Six ways to obtain information about sexuality have been described: self-administered measures, interviews, direct observation, physiological and biochemical measures, case studies, and focus groups. Pencil-and-paper tests, interviews, and case studies or focus groups may be regarded as relatively subjective in that they rely on volunteers' self-reports. Direct observation, physiological measures, and biochemical measures are more objective because they assess the response directly rather than relying on volunteers to report their responses.

Because self-report measures are the easiest to use, researchers have tried to see whether responses obtained from self-reports are consistent with those obtained from physiological measures. To compare self-reports with results from physiological measures, Julia Heiman (1977) exposed college students to a series of erotic audiotapes. Physiological arousal was assessed using the mercury-in-rubber strain gauge for men and the photoplethysmograph for women. The great majority of participants reported arousal and responded physiologically to the erotic tapes. In general, there was a strong relationship between the physiological and the self-report measures of arousal for both men and women; that is, when the physiological records of their responses suggested that they were sexually excited, they also reported that they were aroused. This relationship, however, was considerably stronger for men than for women. As Heiman put it in describing male responses, "Ex-

actly zero percent were able to ignore an erection—the male approximation of genital blood volume change" (1975, p. 94).

Women reported arousal when the physiological measure of vaginal pressure pulse suggested that they were highly aroused, but they were less likely to report any arousal when the photoplethysmograph recorded moderate levels of arousal. It is probable that biological and sociological factors are jointly responsible for this difference in men and women. In any event, the fact that women appear to make more "errors" in their subjective recognition of physiological arousal does discourage reliance solely on self-reports of sexual excitement, at least in work with women volunteers.

▶ **Issues to Consider:** Do you think that self-reports of sexual arousal are more accurate than physiological measures? Why or why not?

Evaluating Results of Studies of Sexuality

In the desire to improve our lives and relationships, we tend to be receptive to new information. In making decisions about whether to act on new information, we are wise to consider several issues. At the least, such factors as generalizability, potential side effects, temporary versus lasting effects, and **replication** of the results should be considered before we embrace a new discovery.

GENERALIZABILITY AND POTENTIAL SIDE EFFECTS

In evaluating a treatment, whether it involves a drug, psychotherapy, or other interventions, we should ask whether it applies to everyone under all conditions—that is, to what extent we can generalize the findings. A related issue is the extent to which we can generalize the results of research on animals to human populations. Researchers commonly test new drugs on nonhuman species such as rats and monkeys. Although many drugs have similar effects on humans and nonhumans, occasionally a drug will have a different effect on humans than it does on animals.

We should also investigate the possible side effects of a treatment, particularly those that may not appear right away. For example, millions of women adopted the birth control pill within the first decade after it was marketed. Before making it widely available, the developers tested it and found that the immediate side effects were relatively minor and temporary. Unfortunately, it took far longer to discover that the pill could have more serious long-term effects for a small percentage of women, primarily those who were already at risk for cardiovascular illness (see Chapter 10). Thus, in making a decision about the use of a treatment, consumers should attempt to determine what is known about its short- and long-term risks.

Will a treatment that appears to solve a particular problem continue to be effective, or are there other factors responsible for a "quick fix" that may disappear in time? Central to this question are two phenomena: the effect of **placebos** and the effect of novelty.

replication—The practice of repeating a study with a different group of research participants to determine whether the results of previous research are reliable.

placebos—Usually an inert substance or treatment that exerts an effect because of an individual's psychological beliefs.

In a variety of situations, a belief that something will help appears to contribute to a cure, known as the *placebo effect*. For example, when two partners spend time and money to avail themselves of a sex therapist to improve their sexual relationship, simply making a joint decision and setting aside time to focus on their relationship may be responsible for much of the benefit that they experience. If the couple's mutual commitment is the cause of the high cure rate reported by sex therapists, thousands of dollars could be saved, at least by some clients.

Novelty may also produce temporary effects. A person who has had various problems in a relationship may decide that the appropriate "treatment" is to find a new partner. In the new relationship, the person may describe the success of this solution:

"Oh, he [she] is so warm and so much more capable of intimacy than my previous partner. I didn't realize how great a relationship could be." The "treatment" (leaving the former partner and entering a new relationship) appears to be effective. Sometimes a conversation with this person six months later indicates, however, that the problems that riddled the previous relationship have reemerged in this one. The "treatment" had only a temporary effect. Before investing in a new treatment, then, we should determine whether its effect is likely to be temporary or long lasting.

In evaluating treatments for sexual problems, it is important to understand the anatomy and physiology upon which sexual functioning rests. This topic is the focus of the next chapter.

SUMMARY OF MAJOR POINTS

1. The emergence of the scientific study of sexuality. During the first half of the twentieth century, scientists began to conduct research on sexual attitudes and behaviors. Their pioneering efforts met with considerable opposition and harassment from those who believed that research on sexuality was immoral or unnecessary. Nevertheless, their courageous work laid the groundwork for what is now an active research field.

2. Ethical issues in research. In an attempt to eliminate abusive practices in the conduct of research on sexual and nonsexual topics, the scientific community has made adherence to specific ethical principles an indispensable part of research procedures. These principles are informed consent, freedom from coercion, protection from physical or psychological harm, and risk-benefit considerations.

3. The research process. Research involves testing hypotheses about the relationship between operationally defined variables. A population is sampled, and members of the sample volunteer for research in which stimuli are manipulated or measured. The volunteers' responses are obtained and analyzed.

4. Research methods. In testing hypotheses about sexuality, researchers rely on one or more of the following approaches: surveys, interviews, direct observation, physiological measures, and case histories and focus groups. Each method has advantages and disadvantages. More confidence may be placed in research results if the same findings are obtained with more than one of these methods.

5. Evaluating research results. When experimental research involves the manipulation of the variables of interest and adequate control of other variables, it is possible to infer a cause-effect relationship between variables. When stimuli are measured but not manipulated, as in correlational research, causal inferences cannot be made. In making decisions based on research results, we should know the situations and populations to which results can be generalized. Before research results can be considered valid, they should be replicated with a variety of samples, locations, situations, and researchers.

Sexual Anatomy and Physiology

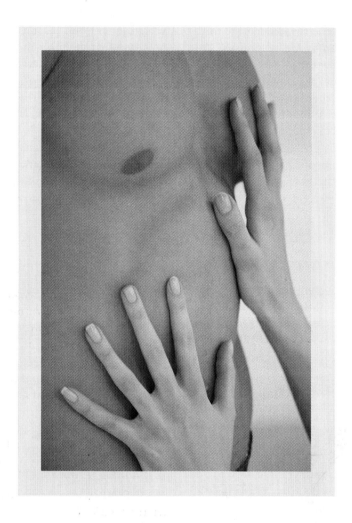

Reality or Myth

1. *Cancer of a testicle usually results in erectile dysfunction.*

2. *Male circumcision is now common in all societies that have been studied.*

3. *The area most sensitive to sexual stimulation in women is the clitoris.*

4. *The ovaries are the only source of estrogen in females.*

5. *Ejaculation or orgasm can be influenced by our thoughts.*

Sexual arousal involves the body in a concert of responses that usually culminates in a coordinated climax far more intricate than that achieved by the conductor and members of an orchestra. Sexual response is influenced by the interactions of the sexual organs, the endocrine system, the brain and the nervous system, childhood socialization processes, previous sexual experience, and the immediate situation. In this chapter we focus on the first three variables: the sexual organs, the endocrine system, and the nervous system. We also explore the effects of certain illnesses on sexual functioning.

Sexual Anatomy

The entire body participates in sexual response. In this section we describe the anatomy of the genitals—those parts of the body most closely identified with sexual response.

THE MALE SEXUAL SYSTEM

The male sexual system consists of a pair of testes, which produce sperm and sex hormones; a network of ducts that transport sperm from the testes to the outside world; a number of glands that produce seminal fluid; and the penis, which delivers the semen (see Figure 4.1 on page 68).

The Testes. The word **testes** (singular, *testis*) comes from the Latin word for "to testify" or "to witness." Instead of placing hands on a Bible, as is customary today, the early Romans placed their hands over their testes when taking an oath. The fact that women do not have testes did not pose a problem because Roman women were not considered important enough to take oaths.

A popular slang term for the testes, *balls,* suggests that they are round in shape. Actually they are

testes—(TES-tees) Two small, oval organs located in the scrotum that produce mature sperm and sex hormones.

oval, or egg-shaped, organs, located in a saclike structure called the **scrotum.** The scrotum helps to maintain the temperature necessary for the production of viable sperm. Normal scrotal temperature is about five and a half degrees lower than normal core body temperature. Within the scrotum, each testis is suspended at the end of a cord called the **spermatic cord.** The cord contains blood vessels, nerves, a sperm duct called the vas deferens, and the thin **cremaster muscle,** which encircles each testis and raises it closer to the body in response to cold, fear, anger, or sexual arousal.

Each testis contains **seminiferous tubules** and **interstitial cells** (also called Leydig cells). Sperm are produced within the seminiferous ("seed-bearing") tubules. Hundreds of these tubules lie tightly coiled

scrotum—(SCROH-tum) Sac that contains the testes.
spermatic cord—(spur-MAH-tik) Cord that suspends the testes and contains the vas deferens, blood vessels, nerves, and cremaster muscle.
cremaster muscle—(CRE-mah-ster) Muscle that runs from the testes into the spermatic cord and controls the proximity of the testes to the body.
seminiferous tubules—(sem-ih-NIF-er-us) Long, thin, tightly coiled tubes, located in the testes, that produce sperm.
interstitial cells—(in-ter-STIH-shul) Cells in the spaces between the seminiferous tubules that secrete hormones.

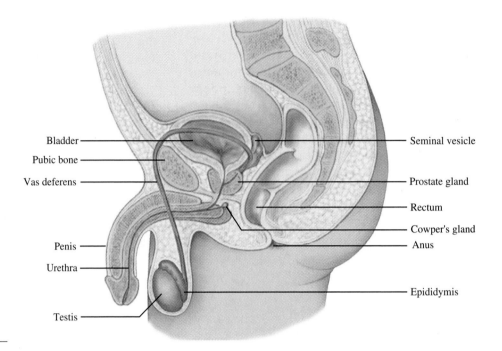

Figure 4.1   The Male Genital System

within each testis, and each tubule is between 1 and 3 feet long (see Figure 4.2). The interstitial cells, which are located in the connective tissue between the seminiferous tubules, synthesize and secrete sex hormones. About 95 percent of the testosterone manufactured by the body comes from testicular interstitial cells; the remainder comes from the adrenal glands. Interstitial cells also produce small amounts of estrogen, a feminizing hormone. In addition, each testis produces **inhibin,** a hormone involved in regulating sperm production. When sperm count rises, inhibin signals the brain to inhibit further production of sperm. When sperm count decreases, inhibin secretion decreases and sperm production begins again.

About 4 of every 100,000 U.S. men develop cancer of the testes. Testicular cancer strikes at a younger age than do most other cancers, usually afflicting men between the ages of 20 and 35. The American Cancer Society estimated that 7,000 new cases of testicular cancer would develop in 1999, but expected only 400 deaths. Risk of developing this cancer increases to 11 to 15 percent in men whose

> **inhibin** —(in-HIB-in) A hormone produced by the testes that regulates sperm production by reducing the pituitary gland's secretion of follicle-stimulating hormone.

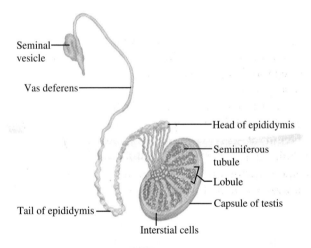

Figure 4.2   Cross-Section of the Internal Structure of a Testis

testes either do not descend or descend after the age of 6.

Because self-examination is helpful in detecting testicular cancer, men should examine their testes monthly. (See "Highlight: Testes Self-Examination.") In this procedure, each testis is rolled between the thumb, which is placed on the top of the testis, and the index and middle fingers, which are positioned on the underside of the testis (see Figure 4.3).

Testes Self-Examination

Because self-examination is helpful in detecting testicular cancer, men should examine themselves monthly. In this procedure, each testis is rolled between the thumb, which is placed on the top of the testis, and the index and middle fingers, which are positioned on the underside of the testes.

If a man discovers a hard lump, he should see a doctor immediately, even though the lump may not be cancerous. With early detection and treatment, testicular cancer is highly curable. Delayed treatment, however, increases the risk of the cancer spreading to other parts of the body.

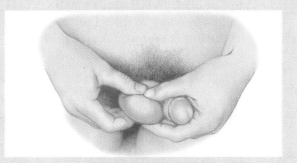

Figure 4.3   Self-Examination of the Testes

With early detection and treatment, testicular cancer is highly curable. If a man discovers a hard lump, he should see a doctor immediately, even though the lump may not be cancerous. Treatment generally involves removal of the diseased testis. Sexual functioning and fertility usually remain unimpaired because the other testis can manufacture enough androgen and sperm to compensate for the missing testis. *Reality or Myth* 2

Sperm pass out of the seminiferous tubules and into the **epididymis,** which lies adjacent to the back portion of each testis. It is in the tightly coiled tubules that make up the epididymis that sperm become functionally mature and then are stored until they are ejaculated from the body. The smooth muscle of the wall of the epididymal tubules contracts when a male ejaculates. These contractions move the sperm out of the epididymis and into the vas deferens for transport to the urethra.

The Male Genital Ducts.   The ducts of the male genital organs are the vasa deferentia, the ejaculatory ducts, and the urethra. The *vasa deferentia* (singular, **vas deferens**) consist of two slender ducts or tubes,

one from each epididymis. These run from the epididymis into the abdominal cavity and join with the duct from the seminal vesicles at the back of the urinary bladder to form the ejaculatory ducts. Sperm travel through each vas deferens to the ejaculatory duct, where they receive fluid from the seminal vesicles.

The **ejaculatory ducts** enter the **prostate gland,** where fluid from the prostate and the seminal vesicles combines with sperm to produce the semen that enters the urethra. The **urethra** has two functions in the male: it conveys both urine and semen.

Glands Producing Seminal Fluid.   Despite the presence of 200 million to 400 million sperm in the average ejaculate, sperm account for only about 1 percent of the total volume of **semen.** Secretions from the epididymis contribute a small amount of fluid, but most of the teaspoonful of semen in the

epididymis—(ep-ih-DIH-dih-mis) Tightly coiled tubules, located at the top of the testes, in which sperm are stored.
vas deferens—(VAS DEH-fur-renz) Slender duct through which sperm are transported from each testis to the ejaculatory duct at the base of the urethra.

ejaculatory ducts—(ee-JAK-u-la-TOR-ee) Tubelike passageways that carry semen from the prostate gland to the urethra.
prostate gland—Gland located at the base of the male bladder that supplies most of the seminal fluid.
urethra—(ur-REE-thrah) Duct or tube through which urine and ejaculate leave the body.
semen—(SEE-men) Milky-white alkaline fluid containing sperm; a product of fluids from the epididymis, seminal vesicles, prostate, and Cowper's glands, combined with sperm from the testes.

69

average ejaculate comes from the seminal vesicles, the prostate gland, and the Cowper's glands.

In 1991, Niels Skakkebaeh, a Danish endocrinologist, reported that sperm counts of men in the United States and 20 other countries have plunged by an average of 50 percent since 1938. A possible culprit in this decline may be environmental chemicals that resemble estrogen and fit into the same cell "receptors." Pesticides, PCBs (used in the manufacture of electronics), and chlorine compounds used to bleach paper are just a few of the hundreds of chemicals that can mimic estrogen. Men may be exposed to estrogen-like chemicals in their mother's blood as fetuses and her milk as infants. These chemicals could fit into the estrogen receptors and trick the body into turning off or turning up certain biochemical pathways, particularly those in the reproductive systems.

The **seminal vesicles** are two saclike structures on either side of the bladder. At their base are two straight, narrow ducts that enter into the ejaculatory duct. The seminal vesicles secrete a fluid that not only provides sperm with energy in the form of fructose (a sugar) but also neutralizes the normal acidity of the female's vagina, which can be fatal to sperm. Thus, the neutralizing elements in semen increase the likelihood that sperm will survive to penetrate the egg.

The prostate gland, which surrounds the urethra at the base of the urinary bladder, is about the size of a large walnut. At the moment of ejaculation, it expels its alkaline fluid into the urethra just below the urinary bladder. During ejaculation, the nervous system coordinates the closing of sphincter muscles where the urethra leaves the urinary bladder, allowing semen to pass through the urethra without mixing with urine.

The majority of men beyond their mid-40s experience an enlargement of the prostate that can cause problems with urination. Frequent urination, particularly at night, is a common symptom of prostate enlargement. Enlargement may also lead to difficulty in urinating and in emptying the bladder, because the enlargement sometimes partly blocks the urethra.

---

seminal vesicles—(SEM-ih-nal VES-ih-kelz) Two saclike organs lying on either side of the prostate that deposit fluid into the ejaculatory ducts to contribute to semen.

This condition is usually benign, but it can be cancerous. In 1999, 320,000 new cases of prostate cancer were expected to be diagnosed, and in that same year 42,000 men were predicted to die from the disease (American Cancer Society, 1999). Prostate cancer deaths have increased since 1973.

Prostate cancer may be detected through laboratory tests and rectal exams involving palpation (examination through touching) of the prostate. Men over age 40 are advised by the American Cancer Society to have prostate examinations annually. Transrectal ultrasound, a newly developed technique that uses sound waves to reflect the prostate on a video console, can reveal cancers too small to be detected through palpation. The prostate-specific antigen (PSA) test can detect elevations in a blood substance that are associated with diseases of the prostate, including cancer. The PSA reportedly has been able to detect in about 80 percent of prostate cancers and is twice as effective as the digital rectal exam.

Black American men have the highest rate of prostate cancer in the world, and a 40 percent higher risk than do White American men, but it is not known whether this incidence stems from genetic or environmental influences. It is unusual for males to develop prostate cancer before the age of 50. In fact, 80 percent of all prostate cancers are diagnosed in men who are age 65 or older.

During the initial stages of prostate cancer, men may experience an increase in sexual interest and frequency of erection, but later there is a reduction in sexual functioning. Prostate cancer may be treated with estrogen (feminizing hormones), which retard its growth. Because androgens tend to accelerate the growth of the cancer, treatment may also include castration of the testes to eliminate the major source of androgens (masculinizing hormones). The cancerous prostate may also be surgically removed. Of all prostate cancers, 60 percent are diagnosed while still localized, and the five-year survival rates for these men are 98 percent. For all stages combined, the survival rate has increased steadily in the past three decades from 50 percent to 85 percent (American Cancer Society, 1999).

A radical surgery called prostatectomy, used to treat prostate cancer, frequently results in the loss of erectile capacity. Learning that he has prostate cancer can be very unsettling for a man, partially because of the equation of masculinity with the capacity to have erections. Of patients treated with more recent surgical techniques, however, 65 percent have been reported to have had erections sufficient for vaginal penetration within nine months after surgery (Graber, 1993).

An experimental technique for treating prostate cancer with thin beams of radiation has produced survival rates equal to other treatments and leaves some men with the capacity for penile erection. Standard radiation is not very precise, but this new technique, called proton-beam therapy, is quite accurate, affecting little tissue around the prostate. Another technique is to implant radioactive "seeds" into the cancerous cells of the prostate gland.

The **Cowper's glands,** each about the size of a pea, flank the urethra and empty into it through tiny ducts. During sexual arousal, these glands secrete a clear, slippery fluid, a drop of which usually appears at the tip of the penis prior to ejaculation. This alkaline fluid helps to neutralize the acidic effects of urine in the urethra, making the urethra more hospitable to the passage of sperm. The fluid sometimes contains small numbers of sperm, particularly when a couple engages in coitus a second time without the male's having urinated. In such a case, any sperm remaining in the urethra from the previous ejaculation are likely to be carried out of the penis in the fluid secreted from the Cowper's glands during sexual arousal. People who have been practicing withdrawal to avoid conception may be surprised to learn that sperm can be carried into the vagina by this fluid before ejaculation, sometimes causing pregnancy to occur even if the man avoids ejaculating into the woman's vagina.

People vary in their attitudes toward coming into contact with semen during the process of oral-genital stimulation. Although there is no evidence that healthy semen harms the mouth or digestive system, some people find the idea of having semen in their mouths distasteful, perhaps because of their association of the genitals with the products of elimination, and thus they are not enthusiastic about oral

sex. As one of our students wrote:

I like to have oral sex with him because I know he really likes it. But one time, he came before he meant to, and getting his semen in my mouth made me kind of sick. I got right up and went to the bathroom to spit it out and rinse my mouth with mouthwash. Since then, I've always been kind of nervous when we're having oral sex.

Other people respond positively to ejaculation during oral sex. Another student reported:

His semen tastes extremely clean, with the flavor a little different from one time to the next. Sometimes, it is very sweet, and almost tasteless. Other times, it has a stronger flavor. When we're kissing each other and I'm holding his penis in my hand, I can feel the pulsing at the bottom of his penis just before he comes. That makes me more excited, and then his semen spurts into my mouth and that pushes me into orgasm and it feels like I'm him and he's me, and we're coming everywhere.

The Penis.   The male sexual organ, the **penis,** seems to have evolved when organisms developed reproductive strategies leading to internal rather than external fertilization. Internal fertilization has the advantage of placing sperm deep inside a female's body. External fertilization is not as economical because many sperm are lost before they reach their destination. External fertilization is exhibited by most species of fish, which release eggs and sperm into the water, where they may become fertilized. The males of many mammalian species have a bone that runs the length of the penis. Humans and whales are two exceptions: their penises do not contain bones.

The human penis consists of three parallel cylinders of spongy tissue that provide the penis with its capacity to become erect (see Figure 4.4 on page 72) Two of these cylinders are on both sides of the penis laterally and are called the cavernous bodies, or **corpora cavernosa.** If the penis is held straight out, the

---

Cowper's glands—(COW-perz) Two small glands that secrete a clear alkaline fluid into the urethra during sexual arousal.

penis—(PEE-nis) The male sexual organ.
corpora cavernosa—(COR-por-uh kah-vur-NOH-sah) Two columns within the penis that contain small cavities capable of filling with blood to produce an erection.

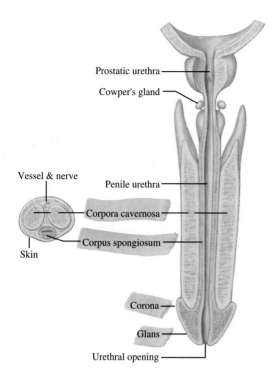

Figure 4.4   The Internal Structure of the Penis A cross-section and a longitudinal section are shown.

Labels in Figure 4.4:
- Prostatic urethra
- Cowper's gland
- Vessel & nerve
- Penile urethra
- Corpora cavernosa
- Corpus spongiosum
- Skin
- Corona
- Glans
- Urethral opening

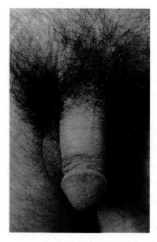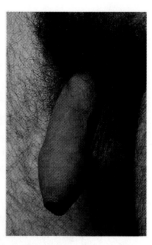

Penises vary considerably in appearance. The penis on the left has been circumcised. The penis on the right has not.

third cylinder, the **corpus spongiosum,** can be felt on the underside of the penis. It surrounds the urethra.

Each of these cylinders contains tissue with irregular cavities, or spaces. These spaces do not have much blood in them when the penis is flaccid, or soft. When a male becomes sexually aroused, however, the blood vessels dilate, and the cavities become engorged with blood. This engorgement produces the rigidity and stiffness of an erection, known in slang as a "hard-on" or "boner."

The end of the corpus spongiosum enters the **glans** at the tip of the penis. The glans is more sensitive to stimulation than the rest of the penis because it contains abundant sensory receptors to pressure and touch. The most sensitive parts of the glans are

corpus spongiosum—(COR-puhs spun-jee-OH-sum) A column of spongy tissue within the penis that surrounds the urethra and is capable of blood engorgement during sexual arousal.
glans—The sensitive tip of the penis or clitoris.
corona—(cor-OH-nah) The sensitive rim of the glans.

the **corona,** or rim, and the **frenulum,** a strip of skin on the underside, where the glans meets the body of the penis. At the time of birth, the penis has a fold of skin called the foreskin, or prepuce. More than 60 percent of American males and about 50 percent of Canadian males have their foreskin surgically removed through circumcision within a few days of birth (Niku, Stock, & Kaplan, 1995). This practice is very uncommon in northern Europe, Central and South America, and Asia. *Reality or Myth* ❓

▶**Issues to Consider:** Why do you think there are such large differences in the rates of male circumcision in different countries?

When flaccid, the average penis is about 9 cm (3.5 in.) in length and about 9.5 cm (3.75 in.) in circumference. An erect penis is about 16 cm (6.3 in.) in length and about 12 cm (4.85 in.) in circumference (Jamison & Gebhard, 1988; Masters & Johnson, 1966). Wardell Pomeroy (1972) reported that the largest penis he and his associates encountered in their research was 10 inches long when erect. The smallest erect penis was 1 inch long. Medical literature contains reports of men whose penises do not exceed 1 cm when erect. This condition, some-

frenulum—(FREN-yu-lum) A small piece of skin on the underside of the male glans where the glans meets the body of the penis.

times called *micropenis*, usually results from inadequate levels of masculinizing hormones during early development.

Penis size tends to be of great concern to many people because size is commonly equated with sexual prowess. Among adolescent women, rumors circulate that you can tell the length of a man's penis by his height or by the length of his foot, nose, or thumb. Research has not demonstrated a relationship between penis length and the proportions of any other part of a man's body. In addition, smaller flaccid penises undergo greater increases in size during erection than do larger flaccid penises (Jamison & Gebhard, 1988).

As far as the issue of sexual prowess is concerned, it is important to realize that various characteristics of female sexual anatomy make penis length irrelevant to the physiological arousal of most women. For many women, stimulation of the vagina is less effective for sexual arousal than is stimulation of the clitoris. Furthermore, the vagina is an extraordinarily elastic organ. Although it expands to accommodate the passage of babies, which are far larger than the biggest penis, it is quite small in its usual state.

Some people have speculated that long penises may be more psychologically arousing than shorter penises. So far, only one research group has examined the influence of penis length on erotic arousal (Fisher, Branscombe, & Lemery, 1983). Although volunteers were clearly aroused by the erotic stories they were given to read, their arousal did not vary as a function of the length of the penises described in the stories. The answer to the question posed by the researchers in the title of their study—"The Bigger the Better?"—seems to be no.

THE FEMALE SEXUAL SYSTEM

The female sexual system consists of a pair of ovaries, a pair of Fallopian tubes, a uterus (or womb), a vagina, a clitoris, and a vulva (see Figure 4.5). The female has at least two areas of intense erotic sensation. One area is the clitoris, located externally at the top of the vulva, where the inner lips meet. The inner lips and the entrance to the vagina are also sensitive in some women, as are the breasts and nipples. A second area, known as the Gräfenberg spot, is located at the base of the bladder and can be accessed by stimulation of the anterior wall (the top wall if the woman is lying on her back) of the vagina. *Reality or Myth* ?

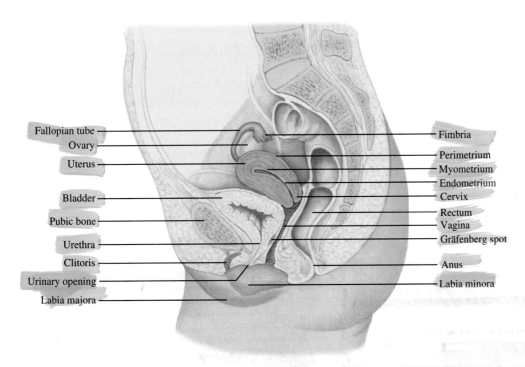

Figure 4.5
The Female Genital System

The Ovaries.   The **ovaries** are flattened, egg-shaped organs located in the pelvic cavity. They lie nestled in the curve of the Fallopian tubes. The ovaries are similar to the testes: both develop from similar tissue within a few months after conception, both produce reproductive cells (eggs or sperm), and both secrete hormones. The principal hormones secreted by the ovaries are the feminizing estrogens and progesterone. The ovaries also secrete smaller amounts of masculinizing hormones, one of which is testosterone.

The ova (singular, *ovum*), or eggs, are found near the surface of the ovary. Each ovum is encircled by clusters of nutrients and hormone-secreting cells. These bundles (ovum, nutrients, and hormone-secreting cells) are called ovarian **follicles.** The number of ovarian follicles present in both ovaries at birth ranges from 400,000 to 500,000. During a woman's lifetime, however, no more than 400 to 500 ova are released through ovulation. Generally, one ovum is discharged from its follicle every month from puberty until menopause, except during pregnancy or in some women while they are breast-feeding.

The Fallopian Tubes.   Each **Fallopian tube** is about 4 inches long. The end of the Fallopian tube nearest the ovary is not directly connected to the ovary but opens into the abdominal cavity. The other end of each tube is connected to the uterus.

When an ovum is released from an ovary, it is propelled into the near Fallopian tube by thin, hairlike structures (called *fimbriae* from the Latin word for "fringe") that line the opening of the Fallopian tube. After the ovum is in the Fallopian tube, tiny hairlike structures called *cilia* help transport it toward the uterus. The cilia sweep in the direction of the uterus, acting as tiny fingers that aid the ovum in its movement. Contractions of the Fallopian tube itself also help to propel the ovum. The upper third of the Fallopian tube is typically the site of the union between egg and sperm if fertilization occurs.

The Uterus.   The **uterus,** or womb, resembles an upside-down pear (see Figure 4.6). In contrast to the thin-skinned pear, however, the uterus has thick, muscular walls. It is suspended in the pelvic cavity by a collection of ligaments, which allow it to shift and contract in response to sexual tension, pregnancy, and the filling of the urinary bladder or rectum. The uterine walls are composed of three layers of tissue. The most internal layer—the one that lines the uterine cavity—is the **endometrium.** The inner two-thirds of the endometrium are shed during menstruation. The middle layer of the uterine wall is the **myometrium,** a thick layer of smooth muscle. The myometrium is responsible for the contractions of the uterus that occur during sexual tension, orgasm, childbirth, and menstruation. The external surface of the uterus is covered by a thin layer of connective tissue, the **perimetrium.**

The lower end of the uterus extends into the vagina and is called the **cervix** (neck). It contains glands that secrete varying amounts of mucus. The presence of this mucus, which plugs the opening into the uterus, may explain why male ejaculate contains millions of sperm. Despite the action of enzymes in the semen that digest the cervical mucus, the cervix still creates a formidable barrier. It is more likely to be penetrated by sperm at ovulation, when the mucus is thinner.

Cervical cancer occurs most frequently in women who begin having sexual intercourse at a young age, who have a large number of sexual partners, and who have particular sexually transmitted diseases. The reason for the relationship among cervical cancer, age, and number of partners is not known, but it is possible that the more partners a woman has, the greater her risk of exposure is to various infections that irritate the cervix and vagina. Although genital herpes has been a prime suspect in cervical cancer, recent research has implicated the

ovaries—(OH-vah-rees) Two small organs that produce eggs and hormones, located above and to each side of the uterus.

follicles—(FALL-ih-kulz) In the ovary, sacs of estrogen-secreting cells that contain an egg.

Fallopian tubes—(fah-low-pee-an) Tubes through which eggs (ova) are transported from the ovaries to the uterus.

uterus—(YOU-tur-us) The place where a fertilized egg is implanted and the fetus develops during gestation.

endometrium—(en-doe-MEE-tree-um) The lining of the uterus, part of which is shed during menstruation.

myometrium—(MY-oh-MEE-tree-um) The smooth muscle layer of the uterine wall.

perimetrium—(pehr-ih-MEE-tree-um) The thin connective tissue membrane covering the outside of the uterus.

cervix—(SIR-vix) The lower end of the uterus that opens into the vagina.

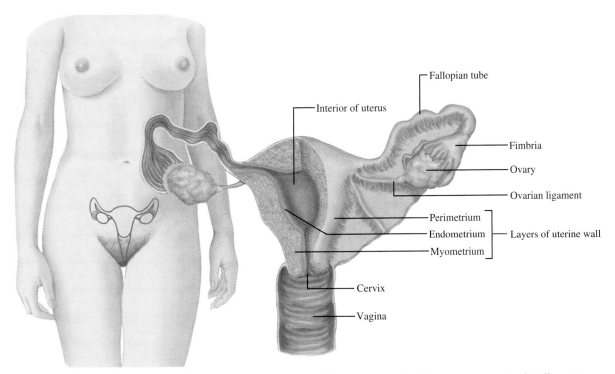

Fallopian tube

Interior of uterus

Fimbria

Ovary

Ovarian ligament

Perimetrium
Endometrium
Myometrium
Layers of uterine wall

Cervix

Vagina

Figure 4.6 The Internal Female Reproductive System   Parts of the uterus and vagina are cut away in this illustration.

papilloma virus as a causative agent. This virus, which causes genital warts (see Chapter 16), has been present in 90 percent of cases of cervical cancer that have been studied (Koutsky et al., 1992). Most investigators believe that if the papilloma virus is the culprit, it does not act alone. Cervical cancer is also more common among women who smoke, are obese, and were exposed prenatally to diethylstilbestrol (DES), a powerful estrogen. Research is under way to identify other factors that contribute to the risk of cervical cancer.

To improve the chances of early detection of cancer of the cervix, women should get a Pap test done at least once a year beginning in their late teens or at the point when they become sexually active. The Pap test is named for its originator, George Papanicolaou. Overall, the death rate for uterine cancer has decreased more than 70 percent in the past 40 years. This dramatic decline is attributable to early detection through the Pap test and regular checkups (American Cancer Society, 1999). If cervical cancer is diagnosed and treated early, before it has spread beyond the cervix, the five-year survival rate is 90 percent, and if it is noninvasive, the rate is almost

100 percent (American Cancer Society, 1999). Treatment depends on the stage at which the cancer is discovered. It may involve **hysterectomy** followed by radiation or, if the disease is detected early, destruction of the cancerous cells through extreme cold (cryotherapy) or extreme heat (electrocoagulation).

Endometrial cancer may also be detected by the Pap test and primarily afflicts women beyond the age of 50. As with cervical cancer, treatment is a hysterectomy and radiation therapy. The five-year survival rate after treatment is about 83 percent overall, and 94 percent when it is detected at an early stage (American Cancer Society, 1999). Regardless of the type of cancer and treatment, almost 70 percent of women are able to have a satisfactory sexual life (Schultz et al., 1992).

The Vagina.   The **vagina** is a thin-walled muscular tube that extends from the uterus to the external opening in the vulva. The vagina increases in length

hysterectomy—Surgical removal of the uterus.
vagina—(vah-JYE-nah) The muscular tube that extends from the uterus to the vulva.

and width during sexual arousal and childbirth. The vaginal walls contain many small blood vessels that become engorged with blood during sexual excitement, in a process similar to that leading to erection in the male. The pressure from this congestion causes small droplets of the colorless, fluid portion of the blood to ooze through the vaginal walls. These droplets appear as beads on the internal surface of the vaginal walls, and they coalesce into a layer of shiny **lubricant** that coats the walls.

The walls of the vagina, particularly the inner two-thirds, contain few touch and pressure receptors, making it relatively insensitive to erotic stimulation. If the vagina were more sexually sensitive, childbirth would be more painful than it is for the delivering mother.

The Gräfenberg Spot. The Gräfenberg spot, or G spot, provides the exception to the general rule that the vagina is erotically insensitive. The Gräfenberg spot is accessed through the anterior wall (the upper

wall nearest the urethra) of the vagina, about halfway between the pubic bone and the cervix (see Figure 4.7). It varies from about the size of a dime to a half dollar. Coital positions in which the penis hits the spot, such as woman above or rear entry, as well as stimulation of the spot with the fingers, may produce intense erotic pleasure, although initial stimulation may result in a sense that one needs to urinate (Perry & Whipple, 1982). Thus, women who desire this form of stimulation should urinate just before engaging in sexual contact.

There is conflicting evidence on the location of the Gräfenberg spot. As discussed in Chapter 5, some researchers maintain that the entire front wall of the vagina, not just a single spot, is erotically sensitive. We should also note that not all women who have been studied report erotic feelings in response to stimulation in this area (Whipple, 1994).

The Vulva. The **vulva**, which includes all the external genitals of the female, is shown in Figure 4.8. The major external female genitals are the mons pubis, the outer and inner lips, the clitoris, and the vaginal opening.

Figure 4.7 The Gräfenberg Spot

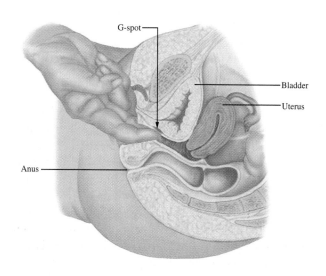

lubricant—A shiny, slippery fluid secreted through the walls of the vagina during sexual arousal.
Gräfenberg spot—(GRAY-fen-berg) An area of sensitivity accessed through the upper wall of the vagina. Also known as the G-spot.

Figure 4.8 The Vulva The external genitals of the female, collectively referred to as the vulva, are shown.

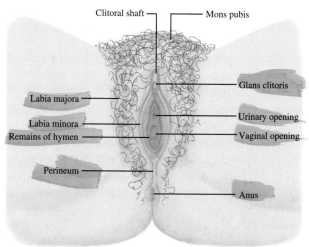

vulva—(VULL-vah) External female genitals: the mons pubis, outer and inner lips, clitoris, and vaginal opening.

 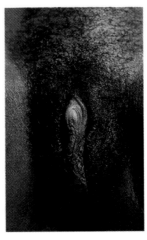

No two women's vulvas are identical. The inner lips of the vulva of the woman on the left are parted to expose the opening of her vagina. The inner lips of the vulva of the woman on the right touch one another as is common with women in their nonaroused state.

The **mons pubis,** or mons veneris ("mound of Venus"), is essentially a cushion of fatty tissue covered by pubic hair. The mons has more touch receptors than does the clitoris, but fewer pressure receptors. Stimulation of the mons can produce intense sexual excitement and can even trigger orgasm in some women.

The outer lips (*labia majora*) are the outermost, hair-covered folds of skin that envelop the external genitals. They merge with the other body skin in the back, near the anus. In the front, they come together a small distance above the clitoris. The outer lips are similar to the skin of the scrotum in the male. During sexual stimulation, the outer lips flatten and expose the inner lips as well as the vaginal opening.

The inner lips (*labia minora*) are the second, inner covering of the vaginal opening. The minor (inner) lips are thinner than the major (outer) lips and are hairless. During sexual stimulation, these layers of skin become engorged with blood and turn from their customary pink to a dark red. The minor lips enclose both the vaginal and urethral openings, as well as the ducts of the Bartholin's glands. The Bartholin's glands correspond to the Cowper's glands in the male, but their function is not known.

mons pubis—In adult females, the cushion of fatty tissue above the labia that is covered by pubic hair.

The **clitoris** is the only part of the human external sexual anatomy that appears to have purely a pleasure function; all of the other structures also have reproductive functions. At the top of the vulva, the inner lips come together to form the clitoral hood, also known as the prepuce or foreskin of the clitoris. Anatomically, the hood is similar to the foreskin of the penis. The minor lips, which closely surround the vagina, are stretched back and forth during intercourse as the penis thrusts in and out. They in turn tug on the clitoral hood, providing stimulation that may elicit orgasm. Alternatively, the clitoris may be stimulated manually or orally.

The clitoris develops out of tissue similar to that which forms the penis in the male. Like the penis, the clitoris contains two corpora cavernosa. Unlike the penis, the clitoris is physically separated from the urethra and does not contain the corpus spongiosum. It does, however, have a swelling at its tip—the glans—similar to the male penile glans. During sexual excitement, the clitoris becomes engorged with blood, increasing in diameter and remaining enlarged during sexual stimulation. The clitoris is permeated with sensory receptors and has more pressure receptors than the penis does (Levin, 1992).

▶ **Issues to Consider:** Why do you think the clitoris is the only external sexual organ that has a purely erotic function?

Just as most North Americans consider the circumcision of male infants normal, about forty countries, mostly in Africa, consider female circumcision natural. This practice, as described in Chapter 1, can involve removal of the clitoris and sometimes the inner vaginal lips.

Most newborn girls have a ring or fold of connective tissue at the vaginal opening. This tissue is the **hymen,** commonly called the "cherry" in slang. The hymen varies in size, shape, and the extent to which it blocks the vaginal opening. Some females

clitoris—(CLIH-tor-iss) Small, highly sensitive erectile tissue located just above the point where the minor lips converge at the top of the vulva; the only known function is to provide female sexual pleasure.
hymen—(HYE-men) Layer of tissue that partially covers the vaginal entrance of most females at birth.

are born without hymens. Contrary to popular belief, the presence or absence of the hymen is not a reliable indicator of whether a woman has had sexual intercourse. The hymen may be ruptured during bicycle or horseback riding, vigorous exercise, or insertion of menstrual tampons. And the hymens of some sexually active women remain intact until they go through childbirth.

Another common belief is that first intercourse for a woman is painful because of the rupture of the hymen. This may be the case for a woman with a particularly thick hymen that blocks most of the vaginal entrance. Other women, however, experience first intercourse and the rupturing of the hymen, if it is intact, without any pain. The example of one of our students is rather typical:

> *After he came, the man I had sex with for the first time accused me of lying about being a virgin. He said that if I were a virgin, it would have hurt and there would have been some bleeding when my cherry was broken. Actually, I didn't feel much of anything physically— no pain, and no particular pleasure. What I did feel was disappointment that sex wasn't any big deal, and anger over his accusation.*

Because of the myth that an intact hymen indicates virginity, many men have attached a lot of importance to the tissue, and many women have expended a lot of energy to demonstrate its existence. To this day, physicians are asked to sew in hymens for women without them. Some of these women are hymenless virgins, whereas others are sexually experienced women who wish to convince a future partner that they are inexperienced. Despite all the concern about this little piece of tissue, its purpose or function is not known.

Although the pelvic muscles and breasts are not part of the female genitals, both are important in sexual arousal. We therefore turn to a description of their sexual functions.

The Pelvic Muscles. A ring of muscles surrounds the vaginal opening. One of these muscles, the **pubococcygeus muscle (PC muscle)**, is important in female

pubococcygeus muscle (PC muscle)—(pew-bow-cawk-SEE-gee-us) The muscle that surrounds the vaginal entrance and walls.

orgasmic response. The PC muscle is a slinglike band of muscle fibers that forms part of the floor of the pelvic cavity and partially supports the uterus, part of the vagina, the urinary bladder, the urethra, and the rectum. If this muscle is not taut, the uterus and vagina can sag, allowing leaking of urine from the urethra (that is, urinary incontinence). Some time ago, Arnold Kegel (1952) suggested that sexual responsiveness could be increased through exercise of this muscle. See "Highlight: Kegel Exercises," for directions for doing these exercises.

The Breasts. The breasts are fatty appendages that play an important role in sexual arousal for many women and men. A few women have orgasm solely through stimulation of their nipples and breasts, and some can experience arousal while breast-feeding.

Embedded in the fatty breast tissue are secreting glands that have the potential to produce milk. The nipples contain erectile tissue and can become erect in response to sexual stimulation or cool temperatures. The sensitivity of the nerve fibers in the breasts is associated with hormonal levels that fluctuate with pregnancy and the menstrual cycle.

Just as men experience concern over penis size, many women worry about the shape and size of their breasts. The fact that the number of nerve endings does not vary with breast size suggests that small-breasted women would be more erotically stimulated by the fondling of a particular amount of breast tissue than would large-breasted women. However, responsiveness to the stimulation of breasts—by both the receiver and the giver—is generally related far more to learning than to the size or shape of the breasts.

There is perhaps no more profound demonstration of the value we attach to breasts as symbolic of female attractiveness than the reaction of many women to the diagnosis of breast cancer. The discovery of any cancerous condition is frightening, and the source of terror is typically fear of impending death. With breast cancer, however, fear of breast loss and mutilation often outweighs fear of remaining malignancy and death. As one writer observed, "It is an outrage to have one's breast turn cancerous. The change in breast tissue from life-giving to life-threatening is a betrayal, a form of somatic treason" (Gates, 1988, p. 148). For a poignant account of one woman's reaction to the diagnosis of breast cancer, see Betty Rollin's book *First You Cry* (1976).

Kegel Exercises

Kegel exercises, named for the physician, Arnold Kegel (1952), who devised them, promote healthy muscle tone in the vagina and urethra and can be practiced by both men and women. In addition to increasing awareness of the location of the pubococcygeal (PC) muscle, which is active during orgasm, exercise for the purpose of toning this muscle may also reduce stress incontinence (involuntary passage of urine upon, for example, sneezing or being tickled), aid women who have recently given birth to restore the vagina to its former tone, and benefit men following surgery for prostate cancer.

You are probably already aware of your PC muscle, although you may not have consciously thought about it. If you have ever urgently needed to urinate or defecate while in the midst of a phone call, you perhaps recall contracting your PC muscle until you could get to a bathroom. The next time you are urinating, you can identify your PC muscle by stopping the flow of urine midstream. The muscle you contracted to halt the urination is the PC muscle. Having identified it, you can exercise it in a variety of ways—even in such public situations as sitting in class or waiting in a grocery store line.

One exercise requires contracting the PC muscle for three seconds, then relaxing it for three seconds, and finally contracting it again. Barbach (1976) suggested doing 10 three-second squeezes at three different times daily. Although the "workout" sounds simple (you can try it as you read this), initially it may be difficult to hold the contraction for three whole seconds, so you may want to start with one or two seconds and gradually lengthen the contraction time as your PC muscle gets stronger.

Another exercise consists of contracting and releasing the PC muscle as quickly as possible, aiming for a sequence of 10 contraction-release cycles three times a day. A woman may also exercise her PC muscle by pretending that she is trying to pull something into and then push something out of her vagina, again holding each effort for three seconds. Barbach (1976) recommended slowly increasing the number in each series of exercises until you can do 20 repeats of every exercise in succession three times a day. As with any other exercise that you are just beginning, you may feel some tightness or stiffness at first, but with continued practice, the exercise will feel comfortable and can be done with ease.

One in eight U.S. women gets breast cancer by the time she is 85 years old, and 185,000 new cases were estimated for 1999, with 1,000 of these expected in men. Killing 46,000 women (and 300 men) in 1998, breast cancer is the second leading cause of cancer deaths among women. With early detection and treatment, 94 percent of women with localized breast cancer survive for at least five years after treatment (American Cancer Society, 1999). If the cancer is noninvasive, the survival rate is almost 100 percent. Even when the cancer is invasive and has spread to the region around the breast, the survival rate is 71 percent.

At age 20, women should begin engaging in monthly breast self-examinations (BSE; see "Highlight: Breast Self-Examination" on page 80 and 81). Self-examination increases the likelihood that women will detect cancerous lumps before they have spread beyond the readily treatable stage. Nevertheless, 80 percent of breast lumps are nonmalignant. Because most breast lumps are painless, some time may elapse before a woman detects a lump, unless she performs BSE routinely. More than 90 percent of all breast cancers are self-diagnosed. Early detection of a lump through monthly BSEs improves one's chance of survival.

When they reach age 40, women are advised to obtain a baseline mammogram, which involves an X-ray technique called **mammography**. In their 40s, women should have a mammogram every other year unless they are in one of the high-risk groups, in which case a mammogram should be obtained each year. Beginning at age 50, an annual mammogram is recommended (American Cancer Society, 1999).

---

mammography—An x-ray technique for the detection of breast tumors before they can be seen or felt.

Breast Self-Examination

1. Before a Mirror

Facing the mirror, inspect your breasts with arms at your sides. Next, raise your arms high overhead. Look for changes in the contour of each breast: a swelling, dimpling of skin, or changes in the nipple. Left and right breast will not exactly match; few woman's breasts do. Then rest your palms on your hips and press down firmly to flex your chest muscles. Again, look for changes and irregularities. Regular inspection reveals what is normal for you and will give you confidence in your examination.

2. In the Shower

Examine your breasts during your bath or shower because your hands will glide more easily over wet than dry skin. Hold your fingers flat, and move them gently over every part of each breast. Use the right hand to examine the left breast and the left hand for the right breast. Check for any lump, hard knot, or thickening.

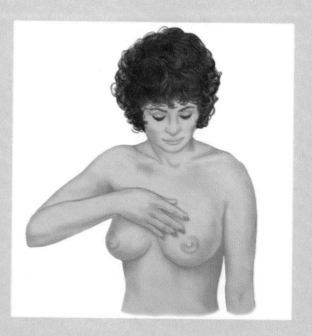

3. Lying Down

To examine your right breast, put a pillow or folded towel under your right shoulder. Place your right hand behind your back; adopting this position distributes breast tissue more evenly on the chest. With the left hand, fingers flat, press gently in small circular motions around an imaginary clock face. Begin at the outermost top of your right breast for twelve o'clock, then move to one o'clock and so on around the circle back to twelve. (A ridge of firm tissue in the lower curve of each breast is normal.) Then move one inch inward, toward the nipple. Keep circling to examine every part of your breast, including the nipple. A thorough inspection will require at least three more circles. Now slowly repeat the procedure on your left breast with a pillow under your left hand behind your head. Notice how your breast struc-

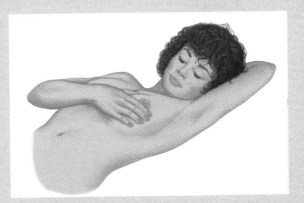

ture feels. Finally, squeeze the nipple of each breast gently between the thumb and index finger. Immediately report any discharge, clear or bloody, to your doctor.

Some women avoid mammograms because they believe that the procedure is painful. The mammogram involves placing the breast on a clear plastic surface; another sheet of plastic is then placed on top of the breast, which is then X-rayed. The breast is then positioned between two vertical plastic surfaces and again X-rayed. The pressure on the breast is sometimes a bit uncomfortable for the several seconds needed to take the diagnostic photograph, but the discomfort—if any—disappears immediately when the plastic surfaces are removed. If cancer is present, early detection allows for far less invasive (and less painful) treatment than if the cancer spreads beyond the early stages.

If a breast lump is discovered, the person should immediately see a physician. Often the presence or absence of cancer can be determined simply by insertion of a hollow needle into the lump to obtain a sample of the tissue for laboratory analysis. Or the physician may **biopsy** a suspicious lump—that is, remove it from the breast in a surgical operation requiring anesthesia.

Women should be aware that there is a high rate of false-positive results for mammograms—that is, their results suggested the possibility of cancer when no breast cancer was present. A woman who gets a mammogram every year for 10 years has almost a 50-50 chance of experiencing a breast cancer false

alarm. (Elmore, et al., 1998). Mammograms are an important, if imperfect, tool, and more reliable tests for breast cancer are needed. Knowing that this technique is far from foolproof may help reduce some of the anxiety associated with obtaining a false-positive result.

If a biopsy reveals signs of a **malignancy**, treatment almost always involves surgery to remove the affected area. The traditional treatment for breast cancer has been radical **mastectomy**. This procedure involves the surgical removal of the entire breast, the underlying tissue and muscle, and the lymph nodes under the arms. But this extreme surgical approach is no longer the preferred treatment for breast cancer, except in rare cases. The most common contemporary treatment is the modified radical mastectomy, which does not involve removing all of the underlying muscles or all of the lymph nodes. **Radiation**

---

biopsy—The removal of bits of living tissue from the body for diagnostic examination.
malignancy—Very dangerous or deadly tissue.
mastectomy—The surgical removal of a breast.
radiation—The process in which energy is dispersed in the form of rays of light, heat, etc.

therapy, **chemotherapy**, or hormone therapy (or some combination of these) may also be recommended.

If there is no evidence that the cancer has spread beyond the tumor, a **lumpectomy** may be performed. In this procedure, the breast is left intact, and the surgery is confined to the removal of the malignant tumor and some surrounding tissue.

In considering whether to have a mastectomy or the less invasive lumpectomy, the patient should seek the opinions of more than one physician. In recognition of the appropriateness of obtaining a second opinion, many insurance policies now cover this additional expense. Comparative studies of mastectomy and lumpectomy treatments found that the less invasive method was associated with fewer adverse effects on body image, fewer fears of disfigurement, and a less impaired sense of femininity (Schultz et al., 1992).

Regardless of the type of treatment, two-thirds of women with breast cancer are able to master the crisis and resume sexual activity. Psychological factors are assumed to play a major role for those who do not adjust sexually (Schultz et al., 1992).

Recent developments in breast reconstruction have increased the choices for women who have been treated for breast cancer. Researchers have found that the sooner after treatment that breast cancer reconstruction begins, the less psychological distress and sexual dissatisfaction (Schultz et al., 1992).

We have now described those body structures that most people identify as sexual. These organs and tissues could not develop or be maintained, however, without hormones.

Hormones and the Endocrine System

The body has two kinds of glands: **endocrine,** or ductless, **glands,** which secrete hormones directly into the bloodstream, and exocrine glands, which secrete substances into ducts that empty into body cavities and onto other body surfaces. Sweat glands, salivary glands, mammary glands, and digestive glands are examples of exocrine glands.

THE ENDOCRINE GLANDS

The term **hormone** derives from the Greek word meaning "to activate." Hormones are carried by the blood throughout the entire body. The internal organs, the glands, and the central nervous system (CNS) can be affected by any hormones for which they have receptors. Six endocrine glands are directly involved in sexual functioning: the adrenal glands, the pituitary gland, the hypothalamus, the testes, the ovaries, and, when pregnancy occurs, the placenta.

The Adrenal Glands. The adrenal glands lie on top of the kidneys and are composed of two sections, the outer cortex and the inner medulla. The outer cortex secretes androgens (masculinizing hormones) and estrogens (feminizing hormones), along with other steroid hormones that are only indirectly related to sexual function. *Reality or Myth*

The Pituitary Gland. The pituitary is a pea-sized gland attached to the base of the brain and functionally connected to the hypothalamus by a system of blood vessels and nerve fibers. The pituitary gland is largely controlled by the hypothalamus. It secretes many different hormones, some of which stimulate the other endocrine glands to produce their hormones.

One of the pituitary hormones, growth hormone, stimulates the growth of long bones and the development and maturation of various body tissues. Two other pituitary hormones, **gonadotropins** (which means "gonad changers"), stimulate the gonads (ovaries and testes). One of the gonadotropins

---

chemotherapy—Prevention or treatment of disease by the administration of drugs.

lumpectomy—The surgical removal of a breast tumor with minimal removal of adjacent normal tissues.

endocrine glands—(EN-doe-crin) Ductless glands that discharge their products directly into the bloodstream.

hormone—(HOR-mohn) Internal secretion of an endocrine gland that is distributed via the bloodstream.

gonadotropins—(goh-NAH-doe-TROE-pinz) Chemicals produced by the pituitary gland that stimulate the gonads.

is **follicle-stimulating hormone (FSH)**, which induces the ovarian follicles to mature. In the male, FSH stimulates sperm production in the testes beginning at puberty. The other gonadotropin is **luteinizing hormone (LH)**, which stimulates the female to ovulate and the male to secrete androgen from his testes.

Prolactin and oxytocin are two other hormones that come from the pituitary gland. Both are important in the production of breast milk. Prolactin stimulates the mammary glands in the breasts to manufacture milk, and oxytocin causes the release of milk from the glands, so that it is available to the sucking infant.

Oxytocin is also released by males and females during the orgasmic phase of sexual response and appears to contribute to "social bonding" (strengthening the relationship between sexual partners) in some species (Uvnas-Moberg, 1998; Uvnas-Moberg and Carter, 1998). Oxytocin may play a role in sperm transport in males as it contracts smooth muscles. In females, it stimulates uterine contractions that may also facilitate sperm transport (Carter, 1998).

The Hypothalamus. The functioning of the pituitary gland is under the direct control of the central nervous system through a network of blood vessels that links the hypothalamus with the pituitary. Some of the cells of the hypothalamus secrete substances that directly control the secretions of pituitary hormones. For example, cells of the hypothalamus secrete **gonadotropin-releasing hormone (GnRH)** through the system of blood vessels, prompting the pituitary to release gonadotropins, which in turn affect the activities of the gonads and their discharge of sex hormones.

Two of the other endocrine glands directly involved in sexual functioning, the ovaries and the testes, reach maturity during puberty through the action of the sex hormones. In addition, fat tissue converts androstenedione into estrone, an estrogen. This conversion accounts for about half of males' estrogens. Because estrone is carcinogenic, overweight people (of both sexes) with more fat tissue are at increased risk of some forms of cancer.

THE EFFECTS OF HORMONES

The hypothalamus, pituitary, and gonads operate in continuous feedback loops in which specific glands monitor levels of hormones and secrete substances that regulate the release of hormones from other glands. For example, the hypothalamus is sensitive to varying levels of circulating sex hormones. It monitors the levels of various hormones in the blood and responds by either increasing or decreasing the rate of secretion of hormones or releasing factors. If the level of a particular hormone becomes too low, gonadotropins are discharged by the pituitary until the gonads produce enough sex hormone to signal a stop to gonadotropin secretion. Thus, the brain, the pituitary, and gonads interact continuously. Changes in one system lead to alterations in the other systems. By way of analogy, just as a decrease in temperature signals a thermostat to turn on the heat or air conditioning, a drop in the level of estrogen in a woman's system at the time of uterine bleeding signals the hypothalamus to secrete Gn-RH. In turn, Gn-RH prompts the pituitary to secrete FSH and LH. The FSH then brings about the growth of the follicle, and the LH signals the follicle to produce estrogen and secrete it into the bloodstream. The rise in the estrogen level in the bloodstream directs the pituitary to stop releasing FSH, just as an increase in the temperature in a home signals a thermostat to turn off the furnace.

Hormones also affect the sex centers of the brain. In most female mammals, estrogen influences sexual attraction and receptivity, but in human females, the estrogen level, if within the normal range, does not appear to affect sexual desire. Excessive estrogen, however, seems to reduce sexual desire in both men and women. Testosterone is evidently the hormone that plays the major role in the sexual desire of both males and females. When it is not present, there is little sexual desire. However, research indicates that GnRH may boost sexual desire in the absence of testosterone or in cases where testosterone is ineffective (Dornan & Malsbury, 1989).

The major difference between male and female sex-hormone secretion lies in the pattern of secretion. Females secrete estrogen in a cyclic pattern, re-

> **follicle-stimulating hormone (FSH)**—A gonadotropin that induces maturation of ovarian follicles in females and sperm production in males.
> **luteinizing hormone (LH)**—A gonadotropin that stimulates female ovulation and male androgen secretion.

sulting in the monthly rhythm of the menstrual cycle. Males secrete testosterone in a daily cycle, with the level rising during the night and reaching its peak in the early morning hours (Hoyenga & Hoyenga, 1993).

▶ **Issues to Consider:** Do you believe there is any significance to male testosterone reaching its peak in the morning?

THE MENSTRUAL CYCLE

Most of the time, we go about our lives unaware of the efficient performance of our endocrine glands and the effects of the hormones they secrete. One of the most dramatic demonstrations of the complex relationships between the activities of these glands, however, appears with the onset of the menstrual cycle in females. Most women can describe where they were and what they were doing at **menarche**.

The menstrual cycle involves a highly intricate set of interactions of physiological processes, some of the details of which are beyond the scope of this book. The menstrual cycle can be conceptualized as a series of five overlapping processes: the **follicular phase, ovulation,** the **luteal phase,** the **premenstrual phase,** and **menstruation**. The complete cycle generally ranges from 23 to 32 days in length. A cycle longer than 32 days or shorter than 23 days is considered irregular. Each phase of the cycle is controlled by fluctuations in the kind and amount of hormones secreted into the bloodstream from the ovaries, the pituitary, and the brain (see Figure 4.9). The menstrual cycle of a nonpregnant woman can be seen from the standpoint of ovarian activity (follicu-

lar phase, ovulation, luteal phase) or uterine activity (menstrual, proliferative or growth, and secretory phases).

The fact that a woman produces only about 2 tablespoons of estrogen and progesterone over her entire life span reveals the potency of the sex hormones. These hormones are primarily responsible for the development of the uterine lining, which nurtures an egg in the event that it is fertilized; if the egg is not fertilized, the subsequent drop in the levels of these hormones results in the disintegration and discharge of the uterine lining (menstruation). FSH stimulates the growth of the follicle that contains the ovum; the cells of this follicle secrete estrogen as they grow. LH then triggers the release of the ovum (ovulation) from the follicle, the conversion of the ruptured follicle into a corpus luteum, and the secretion of progesterone.

The Follicular Phase. The follicular phase lasts from 7 to 19 days and is controlled by sensitivity of the ovary to FSH. Just before the time menstruation (uterine discharge) begins, the production of estrogen and progesterone drops. The low levels of these hormones bring about an increase in ovarian sensitivity to FSH. The FSH causes 6 to 12 follicles to start growing within the ovaries—the phenomenon from which the follicular phase gets its name. Normally, only one of these follicles reaches the mature stage.

As the follicle grows, its cells secrete estrogen. After several days, the estrogen level in the blood reaches the point of creating a relative insensitivity of the ovary to FSH. High levels of estrogen prompt the hypothalamus to release GnRH, which stimulates a surge in production of LH, shown in Figure 4.9.

Ovulation. About 18 hours after the LH surge, the mature follicle in the ovary ruptures and releases the developing ovum. This process is called *ovulation*. The ovum enters the Fallopian tube, where it may be fertilized by a sperm, but most of the time, it is not. Some women are able to feel the rupturing of the follicle releasing the ovum from the ovary as a sharp twinge known as *mittelschmerz* (German for "middle pain"). But most women must rely on other methods to determine the date of ovulation (see Chapter 10).

---

menarche—(MEN-ark) The first menstrual period.

follicular phase—Menstrual-cycle phase during which follicle-stimulating hormone stimulates the growth of the ovarian follicles.

ovulation—The release of a mature egg from an ovary.

luteal phase—Menstrual-cycle stage following ovulation during which growth of the uterine lining is stimulated by secretion of progesterone from the corpus luteum.

premenstrual phase—The 6 days prior to menstruation, when the corpus luteum begins to disintegrate if the egg has not been fertilized.

menstruation—The sloughing of the uterus's endometrial lining, which is discharged through the vaginal opening.

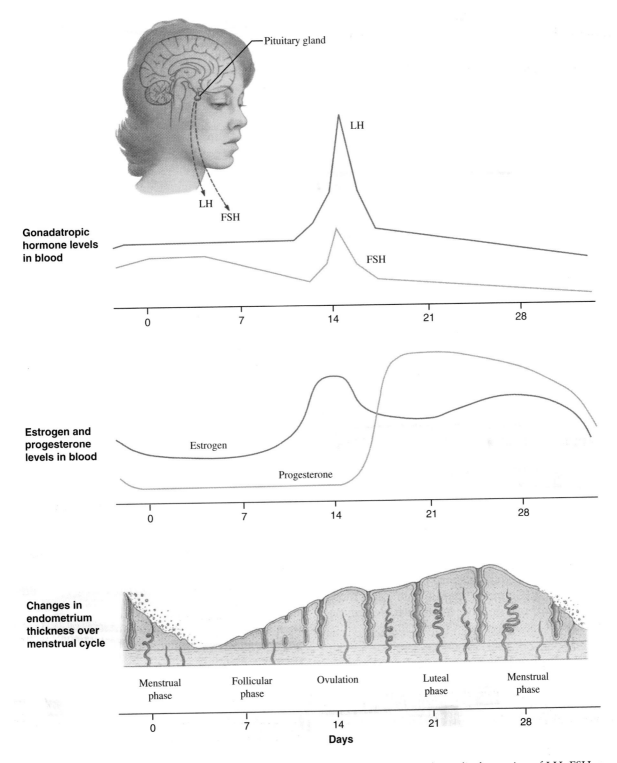

Figure 4.9 The Menstrual Cycle and Hormonal Fluctuations This figure shows the cyclical secretion of LH, FSH, estrogen, and progesterone during the menstrual cycle. Changes in the endometrial thickness are also shown.

The Luteal Phase. The luteal phase lasts from 8 to 10 days. Following ovulation, the ruptured follicle, known in its empty state as the **corpus luteum** ("yellow body"), secretes progesterone, starting the luteal phase. Progesterone stimulates the growth of glands in the endometrium (uterine lining) in preparation for the egg if it is fertilized.

The Premenstrual Phase. In the absence of fertilization, the corpus luteum begins to disintegrate, producing a decrease in the levels of both progesterone and estrogen. Women vary in their awareness of the premenstrual phase, which lasts approximately from 4 to 6 days. Some experience a sense of heaviness, cramps, or aching in the pelvic area and at times some depression. In a month-long study of the relationship of menstrual cycle phase to sexual interest, Stephanie Van Goozen and her colleagues (1997) found that women who had no symptoms during the premenstrual phase reported a peak in sexual interest during this phase. In contrast, women who had premenstrual-phase complaints reported a peak in sexual interest at ovulation.

Menstruation. The disintegration and discharge of part of the endometrium—menstruation—goes on for about 3 to 7 days. This part of the menstrual cycle results from a decrease in progesterone and estrogen. The lining of the uterus, containing blood, nutrients, and mucus, is discharged through the cervix and vagina to the vaginal opening.

In describing the menstrual cycle, we started with the follicular phase, as if the menstrual cycle proceeded in a linear fashion, with the follicular phase representing the first phase and menstruation representing the last phase. The menstrual cycle is continuous, however, and thus is more accurately represented by a set of overlapping circles than by a line with a beginning and an end. For instance, before the end of the premenstrual phase, the follicular phase begins again, with prompting of the growth of follicles in the ovary opposite the one that released a follicle the previous month.

Although the menstrual cycle does not really begin with any one phase, the first day on which menstrual blood appears is counted as day 1 of the cycle, simply because this is the easiest way to keep track of the phases. Monitoring the menstrual cycle is useful for purposes of becoming pregnant, avoiding pregnancy, or determining whether one's cycle has suddenly changed (a circumstance that might indicate either pregnancy or disease).

The complex relationship between the sexual organs and the endocrine system cannot be fully understood without considering the nervous system. It coordinates the menstrual cycle, as well as other sexual and reproductive events.

The Nervous System

As you read this textbook, you are probably not paying much attention to such life-sustaining activities as your breathing, the pumping of blood by your heart, and the activity of your digestive system. Such bodily functions are controlled by nerves that extend to every organ in the body.

We can divide the nervous system into two major components: the *peripheral nervous system* and the *central nervous system*. The central nervous system, discussed in the next section, includes the brain and spinal cord. The peripheral nervous system includes the nerves that provide input to and output from the sense organs, muscles, glands, and internal organs outside the central nervous system.

The peripheral nervous system itself can be conceptualized into two subclassifications, with the names of each based on its functioning: *autonomic* and *voluntary*. The voluntary activities are the ones we are generally aware of, such as those needed to turn the pages of your book. The autonomic portion of the peripheral nervous system derives its name from its control of involuntary activities. Many bodily functions, including sexual functioning, are di-

---

corpus luteum—(COR-pus LOO-tee-um) The cell mass that remains after a follicle has released an egg; it secretes progesterone and estrogen.

rected by the autonomic nervous system, which itself can be divided into two subdivisions: the *sympathetic* and the *parasympathetic*.

THE SYMPATHETIC AND PARASYMPATHETIC NERVOUS SYSTEM

These two systems differ from each other in both structure and function. Although they affect many of the same organs, they usually act in an antagonistic, or oppositional, manner.

The sympathetic nervous system prepares the body to deal with emergency situations. It prepares us for "fight or flight" by speeding up the heart, sending blood to the muscles, and releasing sugar from the liver for quick energy. It can be activated by threat or sexual arousal.

In contrast, the parasympathetic nervous system predominates when we are relaxed and inactive or when an emergency has passed. The parasympathetic system carries out a variety of maintenance needs. It promotes digestion, provides for the elimination of wastes, directs tissue repair, and generally restores the supply of body energy.

In sexual arousal, the two systems take turns in influencing sexual response. The system primarily involved in periods of relaxation is also responsible for initial sexual arousal. In males, for example, initial arousal and penile erection primarily result from the firing of the parasympathetic nerves, which causes the arteries in the penis to dilate, so that blood can rush in. The sympathetic nervous system, which figures in intense arousal, then becomes dominant. It appears likely that sympathetic nerve fibers close off valves in the penis, thus reducing the flow of blood out of the penis.

Ejaculation is also carried out primarily by the sympathetic nervous system, with some help from nerve fibers that are partially under voluntary control. Ejaculation of semen consists of two phases: emission and expulsion. During the emission phase, seminal fluid and the glandular secretions of the prostate are moved by muscular contractions from the epididymis, through the vas deferens, to the base of the penis. This movement is under the control of the sympathetic nervous system. After emission, nerves more responsive to voluntary control produce the muscular contractions that propel semen out of the penis. This event, known as the *expulsion phase*, also involves movements of the pelvic muscles and other portions of the body. Shortly after ejaculation, the penis begins to become flaccid. The action of the sympathetic nerves accompanying ejaculation constricts the arteries—vessels that carry blood *from* the heart—in the penis. The accumulated blood then flows out of the penis through veins—vessels that carry blood *to* the heart.

Little research has centered on the working of the sympathetic and parasympathetic nervous systems in female sexual arousal. It has been assumed that the swelling of various parts of the female vulva and vagina and subsequent lubrication lie primarily under the control of the parasympathetic nervous system. The sympathetic nervous system becomes more active at orgasm (Levin, 1992).

The fact that anxiety or fear is common to most sexual dysfunctions can be explained in terms of the different roles of the sympathetic and parasympathetic nervous systems. Anxiety or fear activates the sympathetic nervous system, which can interfere with the functioning of the parasympathetic nervous system by blocking the relaxation needed for initial sexual arousal (erection, lubrication).

THE CENTRAL NERVOUS SYSTEM

The central nervous system (CNS) coordinates all bodily functions and behavior. It is the processing unit for all components of the nervous system.

Networks of nerves within the CNS are organized into hierarchical schemes to serve certain functions; that is, higher centers exert control over lower ones. Such human sexual responses as ejaculation, erection, and vaginal lubrication are influenced by reflex centers located in the lower centers. These reflexes generally operate on an involuntary basis. For instance, we usually cannot decide to produce an erection of the nipples or penis. Nor can we choose to make our genitals fill with blood (vasocongestion) to produce erection or vaginal lubrication. Anatomically, these functions are controlled by nerves located toward the lower end of the spinal column. These reflex centers controlled the same processes in our primate vertebrate ancestors (animals with segmented spinal columns).

As the human brain evolved, these reflex centers were influenced and modified by higher centers located in the brain. The result is that many "higher brain" centers affect lower reflex functions, and thus can influence sexual response, regardless of whether the particular response is voluntary or involuntary. For example, reflexes such as ejaculation and orgasm can be influenced by our thought processes and can therefore be brought under some degree of voluntary control. *Reality or Myth*

Alternatively, sexual response can be inhibited by thoughts of pregnancy, punishment, or interruption. In fact, one of the strategies used by some men who ejaculate sooner than they want to is to focus on nonerotic thoughts or tasks (for example, mental arithmetic or unpleasant situations) to try forestalling ejaculation.

The Spinal Cord. The spinal cord is crucial in sexual response. It is a thick cable of nerves that extends through the interior of the bony spinal column to and from the brain. The spinal cord carries nerve fibers in both directions—up the cord to the brain, where sensations are actually felt, and down the cord to muscles and other organs, where actions are carried out. The brain and spinal cord thus work together as an integrated unit.

The spinal cord is divided into segments and numbered relative to the spinal vertebrae (see Figure 4.10). Different segments are associated with specific functions. For instance, when a man's genitals are touched erotically, spinal cord segments S2, S3, and S4 (the S stands for "sacral segment") produce a reflexive response.

A second penile erection center is located higher in the spinal cord, in segments T11 through L2 (T stands for "thoracic," and L stands for "lumbar"), which are part of the sympathetic nervous system. This center is affected by brain activity such as thinking or fantasizing about sex.

Responses involved in ejaculation also have dual locations on the spinal cord. The first phase of ejaculation, seminal emission, is triggered by the sympathetic segment of the spinal cord (segments T11 through L2). The second phase of ejaculation, expulsion, is triggered by segments S2 through S4 and can be voluntarily controlled. Men whose spinal cords have been severed may be able to respond to stimulation of the penis with ejaculation, although they feel no genital sensation when it occurs; that is, ejac-

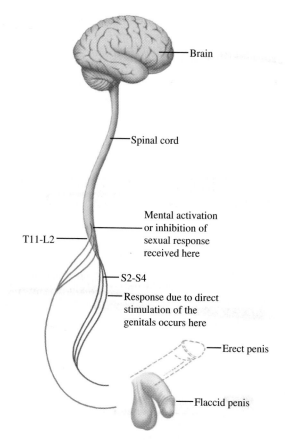

Figure 4.10   The Spinal Cord and Sexual Response
The spinal cord is intimately involved in sexual response. Different portions of the spine transmit sensory and mental stimulation.

ulation can occur without erection, just as erection can occur without ejaculation.

In the erotic response of males, two nerves running from the genitals to segments S2 through S4 of the spinal cord appear to be important. One of these, the **pudendal nerve**, transmits sensations arising from stimulation of the surface of the penis. The other, the **pelvic nerve**, relays sensations of sexual tension from within the corpora cavernosa and corpus spongiosum inside the penis. Because a reflex center higher up in the spinal cord mediates these

pudendal nerve—(poo-DEN-dal) Nerve that passes from the external genitals through spinal cord segments S2 through S4 and transmits sensations from the genitals.
pelvic nerve—The parasympathetic nerve involved in involuntary sexual responses of the genitals.

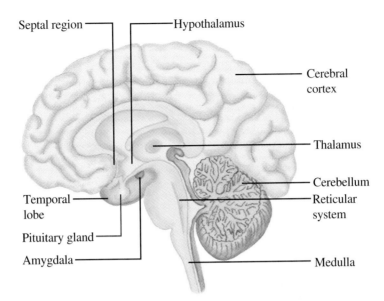

Septal region — Hypothalamus

Cerebral cortex

Thalamus

Temporal lobe

Cerebellum

Reticular system

Pituitary gland

Amygdala — Medulla

**Figure 4.11
Side View of
the Human
Brain**

sexual responses and transmits them to the brain, these involuntary reflexes may be modified by specific learned experiences or emotional states.

The Brain.   Some people have been taught that sexual response involves animalistic drives. All levels of the brain, however, from the lower centers that we share with our animal ancestors to the distinctly human portions, are involved in human sexual behavior. We focus here on those shown to have the most direct effects on sexual behavior. The major portions of the brain are the hindbrain, the midbrain, and the forebrain (see Figure 4.11).

The hindbrain is believed to be the earliest part of the brain to have evolved because it is found in even the most primitive vertebrates. In humans it is located at the base of the skull, where the spinal cord emerges from the spinal column, and it forms the lower part of the brain.

The midbrain, as the name implies, lies between the base of the brain and the top of the brain (forebrain). It contains cell bodies that either trigger immediate responses or relay information to more complex parts of the brain.

The forebrain contains a number of structures that are important for sexual functioning, including the thalamus, the amygdala, the hypothalamus, and the cerebrum. The **thalamus** acts as a relay station, sending incoming messages from the sense organs to the outer layer of the cerebrum. The nerve pathways involved in transmitting and relaying tactile information to the forebrain are also involved in ejaculation. Stimulation of certain areas in the thalamus, and along a nerve tract that enters the thalamus, produces ejaculation.

The **amygdala** is a complex collection of cell groups adjacent to the temporal lobe. The amygdala is thought to play an important role in the regulation of a number of primary emotional states, including sexual arousal. Among these roles, it appears that the amygdala interprets sensory information for its emotional significance. Is the stimulus punishing or rewarding? Damage to the amygdala is associated with reduced sexual activity, which results from the inability to appreciate the meaning of sensory stimulation (LeVay, 1993).

The hypothalamus, about the size of a marble, contains cells that regulate body temperature, eating,

thalamus—(THAL-uh-mas) The major brain center involved in the transmission of sensory impulses to the cerebral cortex.

amygdala—(uh-MIG-duh-luh) Brain center involved in the regulation of sexual motivation.

drinking, and sexual behavior. Parts of the hypothalamus are important in the control of milk production and the reproductive cycles in females and can affect the manufacture of masculinizing hormones. As noted earlier, the hypothalamus is connected to the pituitary gland, which is involved in the production of sex hormones. The hypothalamus also plays a role in erection and in orgasmic response. The fact that damage to the hypothalamic regions of the human brain can produce either extreme sexual desire or loss of interest in sex suggests the existence of a region that regulates sexual behavior.

The hypothalamus contains both pleasure and pain centers that are probably intimately connected with sexual response. Experiments with the pleasure centers in the brain were first described by James Olds and Peter M. Milner in 1954. Rats were given access to a lever that could deliver a brief pulse of electric current to a thin wire electrode implanted in the brain. If the electrode tip was in one of the so-called pleasure centers of the brain, the rats repeatedly pressed the lever. They chose to stimulate their brains in preference to eating, drinking, and other activities. One rat pressed the lever as often as 5,000 times an hour.

Research has indicated that the cells of the pleasure center respond to *endorphins*, a special class of molecules manufactured by brain cells. These molecules act on brain cells in much the same way as do morphine and other opiates, producing euphoria and alleviating pain.

Close to these pleasure centers are systems that, if stimulated, produce unpleasant feelings. These pain centers are crucial to our survival, and it makes evolutionary sense that they take priority over areas associated with pleasure. Attending to sexual desire, rather than to a threat, would leave us vulnerable. Thus, the pain centers of the brain inhibit sexual desire when we experience physical harm, anticipate danger, or undergo severe stress.

The most recently evolved and physically prominent part of the human brain is the **cerebrum**, which balloons out over the rest of the brain. The surface layer of the cerebrum is called the cerebral cortex. The cerebrum is divided into two nearly symmetrical

halves, called the cerebral hemispheres. Each of the cerebral hemispheres is, in turn, divided into four sections, or lobes.

The cerebral cortex, at the top of the hierarchical scheme of the nervous system, is involved in the complex functions of perception, learning, thinking, and language. Thus, it can facilitate or inhibit the sexual response systems found lower in the CNS. Erotic fantasies, daydreams, and memories of pleasant sexual experiences are processed by the cortex and can produce arousal.

Some systems are not limited to one area of the brain, such as the hindbrain, midbrain, and forebrain. One such system is called the **reticular activating system (RAS)**, which is the arousal center of the brain. Beginning in the hindbrain, the RAS extends through the midbrain and sends its fibers up to the forebrain. When the RAS is stimulated, a person seems to become receptive to sexual stimulation. People have reported experiencing relatively long periods of sexual stimulation under the influence of drugs such as cocaine and amphetamines, which affect the RAS (Rosen, 1991).

The **limbic system** is another example of a functional entity within the brain that is not confined to just one area. It consists of a ring of structures in the center of each cerebral hemisphere. The limbic system includes the amygdala, hypothalamus, part of the thalamus, and several other forebrain structures that lie inside the cortex. The limbic system also contains nerve fibers that connect it to the hindbrain. Stimulation of parts of the limbic system in male animals produces erection, mounting, and grooming behavior; pleasure centers have been found near these sites. Stimulation of other parts of the limbic system provokes aggressive behavior.

In Chapter 4 we have emphasized the biological bases of sexual development and function. Although our biological capacities are crucial for human sexual activity, they are interwoven with the texture of human experience. We turn to this experience in Chapter 5 as we explore the many ways in which humans engage in sexual behavior.

---

reticular activating system—(RAS) The system of nerve paths within the brain that is involved in arousal.

limbic system— The set of structures around the midbrain involved in regulating emotional and motivational behaviors.

cerebrum—(sare-REE-brum) The surface layer of cell bodies that constitutes the bulk of the human brain.

SUMMARY OF MAJOR POINTS

1. The structural similarity of males and females. Both females and males have gonads (ovaries or testes, respectively) that secrete sex hormones and produce reproductive cells (eggs or sperm). The hormones are released into the bloodstream, and the reproductive cells are transported through a system of ducts: the Fallopian tubes in the female and the vasa deferentia in the male. For females, stimulation of the clitoris and of the Gräfenberg spot produces intense arousal. For males, penile stimulation triggers the most intense sexual arousal.

2. Hormones and sexuality. The hormone-secreting endocrine glands also influence sexual behavior. These glands—the adrenals, pituitary, ovaries, and testes—secrete hormones into the bloodstream. The hormones, in turn, affect the nervous system and influence the secretion of hormones from other endocrine glands. Hormone secretion in females of reproductive age fluctuates in a monthly cycle. Testosterone levels fluctuate daily in males.

3. The menstrual cycle. One effect of the cyclical pattern of hormone secretion in females is the menstrual cycle. This cycle consists of a continuous series of overlapping processes. During the follicular phase, ovarian follicles ripen and mature. At ovulation, a follicle ruptures from the ovary, and an egg is released from the follicle. The ruptured follicle, known in its empty state as the corpus luteum, secretes the progesterone that stimulates the growth of the uterine lining during the luteal phase. In the absence of fertilization, the egg fails to implant in the uterine lining, which then begins to disintegrate during the premenstrual phase. The uterine lining is discharged from the body during menstruation.

4. Sexual response and the nervous system. The responsiveness of the genitals to sexual stimulation is mediated by the nervous system. The parasympathetic nervous system is predominant in initial arousal: erection in males and vaginal lubrication in females. The sympathetic nervous system is more active during emission in males and during orgasm in females. Psychological responses such as fear, anxiety, stress, and fatigue can inhibit nervous system responses and thus inhibit sexual feelings and processes.

5. The contribution of the brain and spinal cord to sexual response. Some people believe that sexuality stems from animalistic drives. The entire brain, however, from those centers that we share with our animal ancestors to the distinctly human portions, is involved in human sexual behavior. Supplementing the roles played by the thalamus, hypothalamus, and limbic system, the cerebrum can aid sexual response through erotic fantasies and pleasant memories, or it can inhibit response through negative learning and painful memories. Arousal can occur through genital stimulation and is transmitted via the spinal cord to the brain. Conversely, erotic or painful mental events processed by the brain can result in the transmission through the spinal cord of messages that either enhance or inhibit genital response.

Sexual Behavior

Reality or Myth

1 Nocturnal emissions, or "wet dreams," often are a sign of sexual problems.

2 Masturbation by a married person is almost always related to marital problems.

3 Oral-genital sex is illegal in a number of states in the United States.

4 There have been no consistent differences among ethnic groups in reported frequency of sex or in numbers of sexual partners.

5 If two people are engaging in effective sexual stimulation, they should experience simultaneous orgasm.

6 Although women occasionally pretend to have an orgasm, men never do so.

Because we can't live together right now and are often separated, we masturbate together by talking on the telephone, which is just out of sight! We talk to each other late in the evening because both of us are very busy during the day and sometimes we'll be on the phone almost all night talking each other into coming, . . . and then we become more intimate and feel closer.

To me, good sex means being able to give and also being able to take. When I'm with a man who doesn't like to take, who's unwilling to just lie back and let me give to him, a man who needs to be in charge all the time, I lose interest.

The most important breakthrough in my sex life was when I learned it was all right for me to touch my own clitoris during intercourse. Since I've started doing that, I almost always have orgasms, and I have come to believe that this is just the way I am and that there's nothing wrong with it. Because I believe that, my partners have accepted it without any difficulty.

The relationship is what has always mattered to me. I never went to bed just to be going to bed or because he was "Joe Blow." It had to be with a person who had some depth and warmth. I didn't have to be in love necessarily, but we had to be able to communicate well. For me, good sex comes from good communication.
(Barbach & Levine, 1980, pp. 11, 91-92)

As these quotations of different individuals from the book *Shared Intimacies* illustrate, there is a great deal of diversity in what people find sexually pleasurable. In our culture, however, the popular perception is that in heterosexual intercourse, the woman lies on her back and the man lies on top of her. After they have engaged in enough foreplay to elicit vaginal lubrication, he inserts his erect penis into her vagina and moves it in and out until he is stimulated to ejaculation. She may or may not have an orgasm. This

method works well for purposes of procreation, but it represents a rather rigid, stereotyped view of sexual intimacy, and the extent to which it provides sexual pleasure varies from one person to the next and, for some individuals, from one sexual encounter to the next.

In this chapter we consider what humans do sexually to stimulate themselves and others. Effective sexual stimulation evokes a relatively predictable pattern of bodily responses, which we review. We also examine researchers' varying views on what actually happens in the human sexual response cycle, and we examine the similarities and differences in male and female orgasmic patterns.

ources of Sexual Pleasure

Our focus in examining what humans do to produce sexual sensation and response is behaviorally oriented. As we will see however, in the next chapter, people's sexual actions and responses also are

strongly associated with their thoughts, feelings, and fantasies.

Sexual behavior among the majority of heterosexual Americans follows a general script (DeLamater & MacCorquodale, 1979; Laumann et al., 1994; Simon & Gagnon, 1987). Gay people engage in the same general activities, with the obvious exception of vaginal intercourse. The scenario starts with kissing and eventually leads to the man's touching the woman's breast while covered by clothing and then under clothing. The next step in the script involves caressing of the woman's genitals by the man, followed by the woman's fondling of the man's penis. This is usually followed by genital contact and vaginal intercourse, although some couples engage in oral-genital stimulation prior to or instead of vaginal intercourse. Various factors may slightly alter the script, but the order of events usually unfolds in this manner. Before focusing on sexual activities involving a partner, we begin with solitary sexual experiences.

Nocturnal Orgasm

Nocturnal orgasm refers to the sexual arousal and response that occur while a person is sleeping.* It is experienced by both males and females and is often accompanied by erotic dreams—thus the popular term **wet dream** for ejaculation during sleep. Almost all men and 70 percent of women who participated in the Kinsey et al. (1948, 1953) studies reported having sexual dreams. Nocturnal orgasms were reported by 90 percent of the men but by less than 40 percent of the women. This gender difference may stem from differences in anatomy. The extension of the male penis allows for the possibility of more stimulation by movement against sheets or a mattress than does the less exposed clitoris of the female. In addition, evidence of male orgasm with ejaculation is available upon awakening, whereas confirmation of nocturnal orgasm is far less detectable among females. Alternatively, men may simply be more likely than women to experience nocturnal orgasm. *Reality or Myth* ❓

---

*Sexual activity performed by a sleeping person is a rare but reported occurrence (Rosenfeld & Elhajjar, 1998). An individual (usually male) may engage in a variety of erotic behaviors with a partner or alone and not be aware of such activity.

---

wet dream—Slang phrase for orgasm and/or ejaculation while asleep.

The Kinsey group (1948, 1953) found that men reported the highest frequency of nocturnal orgasm during their late adolescence and early 20s. In contrast, women reported the highest frequency of nocturnal orgasm during their 40s. Among women who experienced nocturnal orgasm, the frequency was about three or four per year, whereas men reported having three to eleven nocturnal orgasms a year. About 5 percent of men and 1 percent of women averaged one nocturnal orgasm a week.

Barbara Wells (1986) found evidence that the percentage of young women reporting nocturnal orgasms may be increasing. Of 245 undergraduate and graduate women she surveyed, 37 percent had experienced nocturnal orgasms. In contrast, only 8 percent of the women in the Kinsey group sample (1953) had nocturnal orgasm by the time they were 20 years old. Liberal sexual attitudes as well as positive feelings about and knowledge of nocturnal orgasm were strongly related to experiencing orgasm while sleeping (Wells, 1986).

Why do people have orgasms while they sleep? One common belief is that nocturnal orgasm fulfills a compensatory function; that is, if sexually mature adults have a decrease in sexual outlets during their waking hours, they will experience a corresponding increase in nocturnal orgasms. This hypothesis has not been supported, however; the available research has found no relationship between the frequency of sexual release while people were awake and the frequency of nocturnal orgasm (Burg, 1988; Kinsey et al., 1948). Whatever the function of nocturnal orgasms, they should be enjoyed as much as other sexual activities because for most of us, they are few and far between.

Masturbation by Yourself

Masturbation is sometimes called **autoeroticism,** or the seeking of pleasure with oneself. In this section, we focus on masturbation by yourself—stimulation of the genitals when no one else is present. A person also may engage in self-stimulation in the presence of a partner, or partners may masturbate each other.

Masturbation is a common form of sexual outlet for the majority of North Americans and Europeans

---

autoeroticism—Sexual self-stimulation.

(Breakwell & Fife-Schaw, 1992; Clement, 1990; Leitenberg, Detzer, & Srebnik, 1993) (see Table 5.1). Ulrich Clement, Gunter Schmidt, and Margaret Kruse (1984) found masturbation to be the first sexual experience among the majority of a sample of German students (66 percent of women and 90 percent of men). More men than women report masturbating, and of those who do, men masturbate more frequently than do women (Laumann et al., 1994; Oliver & Hyde, 1993). In one study of U.S. university students, nearly twice as many men as women reported ever having masturbated. Of those who masturbated, men reported doing so almost three times more frequently than did women (Leitenberg, Detzer, & Srebnik, et al., 1993).

▶ **Issues to Consider:** Why do you think that men masturbate more frequently than women?

The more formal education that people have, the more likely they are to masturbate frequently. They are also more likely to report pleasure from masturbation (Laumann et al., 1994). There is also an interaction between education and ethnicity, with Black men and women reporting less masturbation than do Whites. For example, Black men were almost twice as likely to report not masturbating in the past year than were White men (Laumann et al., 1994).

Throughout history, attitudes toward the pleasurable practice of masturbation have been riddled with misconceptions, guilt, and fear. These traditional biases continue to have an impact on many people. In the eighteenth century, Simon André Tissot (1728–1797) continued the long tradition of "vital fluids." He theorized that semen was important for healthy bodily functioning and that wasting it through sexual activity would weaken the body and produce illness. This "vital liquid" was supposed to be carefully monitored, and semen was to be "spent" only when there was a reasonable chance of conception.

Building on this theory, nineteenth-century physicians developed a catalog of illnesses that they traced to the waste of semen through "unprofitable" sexual activity, including masturbation. Fear of masturbation and of its supposed harmful effects was widespread in the nineteenth century. According to the physician W. H. Walling (1904), the effects of masturbation included

TABLE 5.1   Prevalence of Self-Stimulation

Results of surveys by the Kinsey group and Hunt and research conducted by Janus and Janus (1993) show that the proportion of people who report engaging in masturbation has remained about the same for males and females, with slight variations that probably stem from methodological differences.*

	Kinsey Group (1938–1949)	Hunt (1972)	Janus & Janus (1988–1992)
Males	92%	94%	81%
Females	62	63	72

*In a national probability sample of Americans, more than 60 percent of men and almost 50 percent of women reported masturbating in the past year (Laumann et al., 1994).

loss of memory and intelligence, morose and unequal disposition, aversion, or indifference to legitimate pleasures and sports, mental abstractions, stupid stolidity, etc.

Additionally, Walling cited the observations of a distinguished German physician that

the masturbator gradually loses his moral faculties, he acquires a dull, silly, listless, embarrassed, sad, effeminate exterior. He becomes indolent; averse to and incapable of all intellectual exertion; all presence of mind deserts him; he is discountenanced, troubled, inquiet whenever he finds himself in company; he is taken by surprise and even alarmed if required simply to reply to a child's question; . . . previously acquired knowledge is forgotten; the most exquisite intelligence becomes naught, and no longer bears fruit. (pp. 37–38)

Some nineteenth-century commentators considered people who masturbated dangerous to society and believed that their lives were shortened by the practice. The catastrophic consequences of self-stimulation could not, according to T. W. Shannon (1913), be avoided by having someone else stimulate the genitals. He wrote that married people who manually brought each other to orgasm risked all the same physical and mental afflictions as solitary masturbators, and thereby shortened their lives. These writers would probably be terribly concerned about the threat to our species posed by such contemporary books as Betty Dodson's *Sex for One: The Joy of Self-Loving* (1987), which encourage self-stimulation as part of healthy sexuality. Furthermore, masturbation training has become part of the therapeutic techniques used in treating certain sexual dysfunctions. The more often people masturbate, the more likely they are to experience orgasm during this activity (Laumann et al., 1994).

Beginning in the twentieth century, the connection between masturbation and illness became more difficult to defend. Concern shifted to particular aspects of masturbation. One controversy centered on the definition of "excessive" masturbation. Unfortunately for the masturbator, these "authorities" never concretely defined what was too much, normal, or too little. Leitenberg et al. (1993) found that the university men in their sample reported masturbating once a week and the women reported doing so once a month on average.

Conventional religious doctrine has denounced the practice of masturbation throughout the twentieth century. The Roman Catholic church still condemns masturbation as a mortal sin, although many Catholics ignore this dictum. Barraged by such pronouncements from secular and religious authorities, a person who masturbated could easily conclude that he or she was on the road to weak character development from a medical point of view or on the road to hell from a religious point of view. Roughly half of men and women who reported masturbating said that they felt guilty afterward (Laumann et al., 1994).

Contemporary parental views on masturbation were investigated by John Gagnon (1985). A majority (86 percent) of a sample of 1,482 parents thought that their preadolescent children masturbated. About 60 percent of the parents thought that masturbation was acceptable, but only about one-third wanted their children to have a positive attitude toward masturbation. The latter finding is puzzling; one would think that parents would wish their adolescents to see masturbation as a positive alternative to engaging in sexual activity with others, which would expose the youths to the risks of pregnancy and sexually transmitted diseases. Perhaps many parents simply prefer that their children remain asexual for as long as possible. Alternatively, parents may fear possible social embarrassment if their children, particularly younger offspring, publicly express positive attitudes toward masturbation. Maybe it is acceptable to the parents as long as masturbation is practiced privately and not talked about openly. Whatever their motivation, parents can rest assured, because early masturbation experience appears to be unrelated to sexual adjustment in young adulthood (Leitenberg et al., 1993).

The conditions under which masturbation occurs also affect attitudes about self-stimulation. For example, masturbation may be condoned when a person has no partner but considered inappropriate if a person has a spouse or regular partner. Although cohabiting individuals and young married respondents reported comparatively high rates of both partnered and solitary sexual stimulation, these beliefs persist (Laumann et al., 1994). Perhaps they are maintained by our culture's view that a person's sexuality belongs to his or her sexual partner. From this perspective, to masturbate when an appropriate partner is available is to violate that partner's property rights. Or perhaps people assume that something is lacking in a couple's sexual relationship if one or both partners engage in solitary masturbation. There do appear to be gender differences in response to partner's masturbation (Clark & Wiederman, 1998); college men have more positive reactions than do women, and men were more likely to attribute partner masturbation to curiosity/sex drive. However, there was no gender difference in attributions regarding being appealing to one's partner. Both men and women had more negative reactions to the use of erotica by a partner than to a partner's masturbation. Also, women were more likely than men to rate a partner's use of erotica to the partner's dissatisfaction with the relationship. In a study of married women, those who reported having masturbated to orgasm had higher self-esteem, more orgasms with their spouses, greater sexual desire, and greater marital and sexual satisfaction than married women who did not masturbate to orgasm (Hurlbert & Whittaker, 1991). *Reality or Myth* ❓

▶ **Issues to Consider:** If you learned that your steady partner engaged in masturbation, how would you react? Why?

The age at which humans discover that playing with particular parts of the body produces strong pleasure varies from one person to another. Some young people inadvertently stumble on sexual arousal and orgasm in the course of engaging in some other physical activity. The result can be surprising, and sometimes distressing, if the child or adolescent has received no prior information. Other youngsters purposefully stimulate themselves, goaded by curiosity after getting suggestions or advice from friends. These initial explorations can be both clumsy and ineffective. We have a friend, for example, who told us that when he was 12 years old, he hung out with a group of older boys who frequently discussed masturbation as something that "grown" boys did. These discussions never dealt with the specifics of self-stimulation; that is, no one explained exactly how to do it. Our friend, who was less interested in masturbating than he was in being accepted as a full member of the group, tried to masturbate but experienced no success. He finally gave up in despair, convinced either that he was not old enough or that something was wrong with him. About six months later, he woke up with an erection and began to move up and down against his sheet, finally experiencing orgasm. He said that he realized only then that an erection was necessary, his previous attempts having been made when his penis was flaccid.

The most frequent reasons that both men and women say they masturbate are to relieve sexual tension, achieve physical pleasure, enjoy sexual stimulation in the absence of an available partner, and relaxation (Laumann et al., 1994). Thus, self-stimulation can provide sexual release when a partner is not available or when you are feeling sexually aroused by someone with whom sexual intimacy is impossible or inappropriate. It is also pleasurable. You can be good to yourself physically after having a bad day or reward yourself for spending hours on chores. Finally, knowing how to make yourself feel good gives you self-knowledge—information that you can share with a partner.

Male Methods.   When masturbating, men tend to focus on stimulation of the penis. It may be rubbed against the body with one or both hands, or it may be rolled between the palms of the hands as they move up and down the shaft of the penis. Some men reach orgasm by lying on a pillow and thrusting

against it. However, the majority of the 312 men who masturbated while being observed by William Masters and Virginia Johnson (1966) moved their hands up and down the shaft of their penises (see Figure 5.1 on page 98). The stroking of the penis can vary from a light touch to a strong grip, as well as from a leisurely speed to a more rapid movement. As males approach ejaculation, they tend to increase the speed of stimulation to the penis. When they begin to ejaculate, however, most men decrease or stop penile stimulation abruptly, reporting that continued intense stimulation of the glans is unpleasant (Masters & Johnson, 1966).

Aside from a minute amount of fluid, produced by the Cowper's glands, that appears at the opening of the urethra, there is no natural lubrication of the external skin of the penis. Therefore, some men use saliva, oil, cream, or soap (during a shower or bath) to allow the hand to glide smoothly over their penises. A vibrator may also be used to stimulate the penis. Some men stimulate their nipples or anus with one hand while rubbing their penis with the other hand.

Many males are completely oriented toward orgasm in their masturbatory techniques. The average man reported to the Kinsey group (1948) that he ejaculated after stimulating himself for 2 or 3 minutes. Some men reported a more leisurely pattern of self-stimulation; a few men reported ejaculating within 30 seconds of the onset of masturbation. This efficiency is useful if one has an appointment to keep, but it may be poor preparation for shared sex; racing through one's sexual response is not generally conducive to mutual pleasure.

This speed of ejaculation also seems to hold if someone else is doing the masturbation. In a "no-frills" approach, 29 Japanese men aged 18 to 25 were masturbated by a masseuse in a laboratory setting (Kameya, Deguchi, & Yokota, 1997). The participants blindfolded themselves and lay down on a bed after entering the laboratory room. A female masseuse then applied oil to her hand and applied a localized massage. This procedure was performed four times at one-week intervals with the same participants and the same masseuse. Ejaculation time was measured as the interval of time between obtaining an erection and ejaculation. The average ejaculation time in this study was 2 minutes, 36 seconds with a range from 45 seconds to almost 8 minutes,

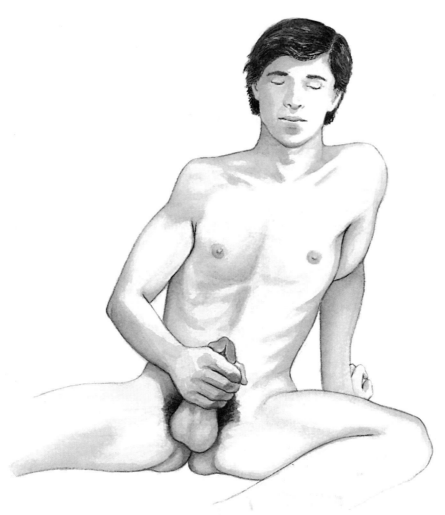

Figure 5.1   Male Masturbation Although we are all unique in what pleases us sexually, there are some general differences between the self-stimulation methods used by males and those used by females.

which is quite similar to the male self-reports in the Kinsey group study.

Female Methods.   In contrast to males, females vary considerably in the methods they use to stimulate themselves. Masters and Johnson (1966) found that no two female research volunteers masturbated in quite the same way. Stimulation of the clitoral shaft, clitoral area, and mons with a hand or an object is the method that women most commonly employ (see Figure 5.2). For direct stimulation, making a circular motion around the clitoral shaft and glans and rubbing up and down one side of the clitoris are popular methods. Pulling on the inner lips causes the loose skin covering the clitoral glans to slide back and forth, creating a sensation that can be quite sexually arousing. Clitoral stimulation can also be accompanied by moving the fingers in and out of the vagina. Vaginal penetration alone, however, is not a frequently used masturbatory technique. Masters and Johnson (1966) reported that most women in their research preferred to stimulate the entire mons area rather than concentrate exclusively on the clitoris. The clitoral glans is sensitive, and direct stimulation for an extended period of time can be irritating.

Some women also masturbate by using a vibrator. Vibrators, which may be purchased in a variety of sizes and shapes, are usually battery operated or electric. Some vibrator kits have a number of differ-

Figure 5.2   Female Masturbation

ent accessories and provide a choice of several vi-
bration speeds. Vibrators should not be loaned to
other people because of the potential for passing on
infections and sexually transmitted diseases.

Other masturbatory techniques that women
use include pelvic thrusting, squeezing and contracting the thigh muscles, inserting objects into
the vagina, stimulating the breasts, and fantasizing.
Pelvic thrusting of the genitals against a bed, pillow, clothing, or other objects produces direct
stimulation of the vulval area, as well as increasing
muscular tension through contraction of the thigh
and gluteal muscles. This technique spreads stimulation over a wide area. For some women, pressing
the thigh muscles together, usually with their legs

crossed, applies steady, rhythmic pressure on the
genitals.

A small percentage of women report that they
can reach orgasm through breast or nipple stimulation alone (Kinsey et al., 1953; Masters & Johnson,
1966). Usually, however, women who stimulate
their breasts during masturbation (about one in ten
of Kinsey's respondents) do so in combination with
stimulation of the clitoral area. About 2 percent of
Kinsey's respondents claimed that they could reach
orgasm through erotic fantasy with no direct stimulation of the genitals—a real tribute to the powers
of the mind. This phenomenon has been measured
by self-report and physiological indicies in laboratory settings where seven out of ten women had

Nearly all the vibrators in this photo support the male notion that women use vibrators as surrogate penises. Although this is true for some women, most others use a smaller device intended not for insertion in the vagina but for stimulation of the clitoris. The small device at the top-center (beside the red-and-white vibrator) appears to be one of the latter type.

orgasm relying only on fantasy (Whipple, Ogden, & Komisaruk, 1992). Breast stimulation or fantasy alone is rarely used by women, however, and even less commonly by men.

Masters and Johnson (1966) observed an interesting gender difference in the process of self-stimulation. Most women prefer continued stimulation of the clitoral shaft or mons area during orgasm. In contrast, men typically slow down or stop manual stimulation during orgasm. This gender difference appears to be true of coital orgasm as well, and thus has implications for sexual interaction.

Female sexual response is not much slower than male response during masturbation: a little less than 4 minutes after the beginning of self-stimulation (Kinsey et al., 1953). Some women have an orgasm in less than 30 seconds. The relatively small difference between male and female patterns of response becomes larger during stimulation through sexual intercourse. It takes the average woman

longer than the average man to have orgasm during coitus because there is usually not as much direct stimulation of the clitoral area as there is during masturbation.

MUTUAL MASTURBATION

Mutual caressing of the breasts and genitals is widely practiced in North America. More than 90 percent of men and women report manually stimulating the genitals of their sexual partners (Breakwell & Fife-Schaw, 1992; Kinsey et al., 1948, 1953). Manual stimulation of a partner's genitals can serve as a prelude to oral sex or sexual intercourse, or it can be the means of achieving orgasm for one or both partners. Couples who have considerable experience with solitary masturbation can give each other information and guidance about what techniques are most pleasing.

Mutual masturbation provides a satisfying and pleasurable form of sexual intimacy and release for

Figure 5.3   Mutual Masturbation by a Gay Male Couple

many couples. If birth control is unavailable and a heterosexual couple wants to have sex, it offers one of several enjoyable alternatives to sexual intercourse. Mutual masturbation is also one of the most common techniques that gay and lesbian couples use during sexual intimacy (see Figure 5.3). The two women shown in Figure 5.4 on page 102 are engaging in **tribadism**. They are rubbing against one another for clitoral stimulation.

ORAL SEX

Kissing.   Kissing—mouth-to-mouth contact—is usually the first step in sexual interactions in Western cultures. Among other cultures and species, however, deep kissing (putting a tongue in another person's mouth; also "french" kissing) for the purpose of erotic arousal is relatively rare. Although all human

tribadism—Sexual activity in which one woman lies on top of another and moves rhythmically for clitoral stimulation.

cultures use some form of mouth or nose contact to indicate greeting and affection, in many societies people do not include kissing in their erotic interactions. Traditional Chinese did not kiss for any reason. Until about three decades ago, there was no word for *kiss* in Japanese. In their survey of a variety of cultures, Clellan Ford and Frank Beach (1951) found that kissing was mentioned in only 21 cultures and accompanied sexual intercourse in only 13 cultures. Around the world, the deep kiss is less often a part of sexual intimacy than are other forms of mouth or nose contact. The Tinguians of Micronesia (in the western Pacific Ocean) place their lips near their partner's face and suddenly inhale. Balinese (Indonesia) lovers simply bring their faces close enough to sense each other's perfume and skin.

Human kisses are probably related to the olfactory investigations that mammals make on greeting. Most mammals rely on their sense of smell to recognize friends or enemies and to determine each other's state of sexual arousal. The popularity of the kiss in

Figure 5.4   Tribadism

many cultures may be traced back to the infant-mother bond. Infants are lavishly touched, cuddled, and kissed all over their bodies, not only by their mothers but also by relatives and friends. Because the mouth conveys positive feelings between infant and adult, the infant may learn that touching something soft with the mouth provides a calming and pleasurable sensation.

The pleasure that lovers obtain from kissing may be partially due to the fact that all the senses can be stimulated during that activity. The lips, mouth, and tongue are among the most exquisitely sensitive parts of the body. Indeed, 5 of the 12 cranial nerves that affect brain functions are involved in a kiss. Kissing also involves our senses of hearing and sight. We may be aroused by the associated sounds of sucking and licking, and we may be affected by the sight of a partner's lips and tongue.

Although deep kissing is relatively uncommon across cultures, kissing or licking of other parts of the body, including the genitals, is widely documented in many societies. Historically, North Americans have held negative attitudes toward oral-genital

sex. It has been, and remains, illegal in a number of states. **_Reality or Myth_** 🠂

Oral-Genital Sex.   Current views of oral sex vary widely. Some people see it as a way of expressing deeply intimate feelings; others react with disgust to the mere idea of oral-genital contact. Negative feelings about the odor, texture, and appearance of the genitals may inhibit some people from participation in oral sex. Because urination and defecation are associated with the genitals, some may feel that oral contact with the genitals will expose them to excrement and germs. In addition, some people may not like the idea of taking semen or vaginal secretions into their mouths or may dislike the taste. And some perceive oral sex as less intimate than sexual intercourse because it precludes extensive body-to-body and face-to-face contact. Others, feeling that oral sex is more personal than sexual intercourse, believe that only couples within a committed relationship should engage in it.

Attitudes toward oral-genital sex have changed rapidly in this century. Acceptance of oral sex has increased significantly among married couples and for some is a favored means to orgasm (Hurlbert & Whittaker, 1991; Janus & Janus, 1993) (see Table 5.2). The incidence of oral sex is also common among adolescents and single adults in North America, England, and France (Billy, Tanfer, Grady, & Klepinger, 1993; Giami & Schlitz, 1996; Wellings, Field, Johnson & Wadsworth, 1994). It is particularly popular among those with coital experience, partly because it eliminates worries about birth control for heterosexuals.

There appear to be ethnic differences in giving and receiving oral sex in the U.S. In a nationally representative sample, more White men performed (81 percent) and received (81 percent) oral sex than did Black men (50 percent performed and 66 percent received oral sex) (Laumann et al., 1994). More White women performed (68 percent) and received (73 percent) oral sex than did Black women (34 percent performing and 49 percent receiving). Hispanic men and women engaging in oral sex fell roughly midway between the percentages reported by Blacks and Whites. As we saw with masturbation, the higher the educational level was, the more likely it was that a person had engaged in oral sex (Laumann et al., 1994).

> ▶ **Issues to Consider:** The higher the educational level, the more likely it is that a person has engaged in oral sex. How would you explain this relationship?

There are many ways of having oral sex. Partners may stimulate each other's genitals with their mouths before sexual intercourse or orally caress each other to mutual orgasm. Depending on preference, a person can swallow the semen or stop orally stimulating the penis just before ejaculation and move slightly away.

Partners can perform **cunnilingus** and **fellatio** using a variety of positions. Some partners like to take turns, bringing each other to orgasm in sequence. Others prefer to stimulate each other orally at the same time (see Figure 5.5 on page 104). Simultaneous

cunnilingus—(KUN-nih-LING-gus) Oral stimulation of the female genitals.
fellatio—(fell-LAY-she-oh) Oral stimulation of the male genitals.

TABLE 5.2 Prevalence of Oral Sex

The proportion of people who reported engaging in oral sex increased from the 1930s to the 1990s.

	Kinsey* group (1938–1949)	Hunt* (1972)	Laumann et al. (1992)
Fellatio			
Males	59–61%	54–61%	78%
Females	46–52	52–72	68
Cunnilingus			
Males	16–51	55–66	77
Females	50–58	58–72	73

*The Kinsey and Hunt figures included only married people.

oral stimulation is known popularly as "69." Many couples enjoy having various parts of their bodies kissed and licked during sexual intimacy. For some partners, the sexual repertoire includes **analingus,** the oral stimulation of the sensitive tissue around the anus. It is important for both heterosexual and homosexual couples to realize, however, that HIV can be transmitted during oral stimulation of the genitals (see Chapter 16). Small fissures in the gums, genitals, or anus may permit transmission of the virus from an infected person to the bloodstream of a noninfected person. Thus, unless a couple is monogamous, partners should make sure that they are both free of HIV before engaging in oral sex or analingus.

In cunnilingus, a woman's partner can caress and separate her vaginal lips with the hands or tongue. The clitoris can be licked, sucked, or gently nibbled, although too much direct stimulation may be uncomfortable, because the clitoris is extremely sensitive. Having the side of the clitoral shaft massaged or rapidly flicked by the tongue is generally quite pleasurable for women.

Oral stimulation of a man's genitals can also provide deep pleasure. The most sensitive parts of the penis are the glans, or tip, and the frenulum on the underside of the glans. Having these areas licked or sucked is quite pleasurable. The testes can also be

analingus—(a-nil-LING-gus) Oral stimulation of the tissues surrounding the anus.

Figure 5.5   Mutual Oral-Genital Stimulation

taken gently into the mouth and sucked or licked. The head and shaft of the penis can be sucked slowly or rapidly while the penis is held and the scrotum is caressed.

These are some of the more common means of oral stimulation. As with other forms of sexual intimacy, people need to be sensitive to the likes and dislikes of their partners when giving and receiving oral stimulation.

"FOREPLAY" AND COITUS

The term **foreplay** usually refers to activities that are seen as a prelude to intercourse, such as kissing, manual caressing of the genitals, and oral sex. The term reflects the long-ingrained belief in our culture that "having sex" is an experience that must culminate in coitus and male orgasm, or else it isn't really sex. Rather than being viewed as pleasures and ends in themselves, mutual caressing, kissing, and oral sex are often seen as necessary tasks on the way to achieving coital orgasm.

Given this belief, how much time do partners spend in stimulating each other before and during sexual intercourse? The average duration of foreplay

foreplay—Term used by some people to refer to sexual behavior occurring before intercourse.

appears to be about 12 to 15 minutes (Fisher, 1973; Hunt, 1974). In more recent research, women indicated that they preferred an average of about 17 minutes of foreplay prior to penile penetration (Darling, Davidson, & Cox, 1991). Thus there may be a discrepancy of 2 to 5 minutes between what women desire on the average and what they get.

After penile insertion, women seem to require an average of about 8 minutes to experience orgasm, although their preferred length of intercourse after penile insertion was about 11 minutes (Darling et al., 1991; Fisher, 1973). It should be noted that there was a wide range in the length of time women needed to experience orgasm, with some requiring just 1 minute and others needing about 30 minutes.

For men, the average time from insertion to orgasm was about 10 to 11 minutes (Darling et al., 1991; Hunt, 1974). This longer duration to orgasm for men than for women is interesting, in that women in the Fisher study estimated that it took them 40 percent to 80 percent more time to attain orgasm than it did their partners. Some of this discrepancy is undoubtedly due to different sampling and methodological techniques used in these studies. However, women who experienced orgasm after their partner reported less sexual satisfaction than did women who had orgasm before or simultaneously with their partner (Darling et al., 1991). Although women prefer more time spent in sexual fore-play and in sexual intercourse, research on men's preferences is lacking.

Having reported these data on time spent in foreplay and intercourse, we want to caution readers not to focus too heavily on timing as an index of sexual pleasure. We know one couple who ended up in therapy because the husband was experiencing difficulty getting an erection. It turned out that his wife—a very busy woman—was in the habit of keeping a stopwatch by their bed to time how long it took him to reach orgasm!

COITUS AND COITAL POSITIONS

Nonhuman species rely almost entirely on rear entry as their main position during sexual interaction, although the bonobo use a variety of positions (see Chapter 7) and porpoises use a face-to-face position while swimming. In contrast, humans employ a wide range of positions during sexual activity, and the popularity of various positions differs from one culture to another.

The typical coital position used in a particular culture appears to be correlated with the social status of females. For example, among several American Indian tribes and among groups in the South Pacific, where females enjoy high status, the woman-above position is most popular, and sexual satisfaction is considered at least as important for women as it is for men. The cross-cultural association between female status and coital position is especially interesting in the light of two studies in our own culture. Although Masters and Johnson (1966) found that the woman's sexual response develops more rapidly and with greater intensity in the face-to-face, woman-above position than in any other coital position, the Kinsey group (1948, p. 578) concluded that "nearly all coitus in our English-American culture occurs with the partners lying face to face, with the male above the female. There may be as much as 70 percent of the population which has never attempted to use any other position in intercourse."

This man-above position remains quite popular, but many couples vary the positions they use during sexual intercourse (see Table 5.3). Although different coital positions can produce different physical sensations, any position in which the penis penetrates the vagina can result in conception, so couples who do

TABLE 5.3 Prevalence of Coital Positions		
The Kinsey and Hunt surveys showed the following trends among married people in use of coital positions.		
	Kinsey Group (1938–1949)	Hunt Study (1972)
Female-above position	33%	75%
Side-by-side position	25	50
Rear-entry (vaginally) position	10	40
Sitting position	8	25

not want to conceive should use a reliable contraceptive when they have coitus of any kind.

Face to Face, Man Above. In the face-to-face, man-above position, a woman usually lies on her back with her legs apart and her knees slightly bent (see Figure 5.6 on page 106). A man lies on top of her with his legs between hers, and he supports most of his weight with his elbows and knees.

Because the partners are face to face, they can communicate feelings by continued erotic kissing, eye contact, and facial expressions. The penis can be inserted into the vagina as the partners move their bodies together, or it can be directed by hand. After insertion of the penis, the man has more control of body movement than does the woman, whose pelvic movements are restricted by the pressure of his weight. Limitation of the woman's pelvic movement can be a drawback of this position. When a man is considerably heavier than a woman, another coital position may permit greater participation from the woman. In the man-above position, however, a woman can enhance her capacity to move in pleasurable ways by pulling her legs up toward her shoulders or by placing them on the man's shoulders. She can also entwine her legs around his back and lock her feet together. These actions can be supplemented by placement of a pillow under her lower back, which increases the contact between her clitoris and her partner's body. By changing the position of her legs, she can then more easily coordinate the movement of her pelvis with the man's coital thrusts, as well as maintain the kind of stimulation to her clitoral area that will result in orgasm.

Figure 5.6   Face-to-Face, Man-Above Coital

A disadvantage of the face-to-face, man-above position is that the man's hands are not free to stimulate his partner. For couples who desire this pleasure, the coital position that follows is recommended.

Face to Face, Woman Above.   In the face-to-face, woman-above position, a man lies on his back with a woman kneeling over him, her knees positioned on either side of his body. She can lean her upper body forward and guide his penis into her vagina as she moves down on it. She can then either sit upright or lie on top of her partner, depending on how much body contact she wants (see Figure 5.7). If she remains sitting or kneeling, he can readily caress her breasts and face.

The advantages of this position for women are similar to the advantages of the man-above position for men. Positioned above her partner, a woman has better control over coital movement and depth of penetration, and either she or her partner can manually stimulate her clitoris. Men often experience less sexual intensity in this position, and this may be desirable if the woman is typically slower to respond than the man or if the man ejaculates more quickly than he wishes. Furthermore, when a man wants to prolong the pleasure of arousal, leisurely lovemaking may be easier for him in this position than in the

man-above position, in which he is likely to reach orgasm faster.

The woman-above position is not desirable when a man wants to take primary responsibility for sexual movement. In addition, the position may put some men in a passive or subordinate role, which can make them psychologically uncomfortable. Thus, a person who wishes to try the woman-above or any other coital position should ask his or her partner's feelings about it rather than simply assume that the partner has the same desires.

Face to Face, Side by Side.   The side-by-side variation of the face-to-face position offers both partners the opportunity to control their own body movements during coitus (see Figure 5.8). The partners can lie in several different positions, all of which eliminate weight on either partner. These positions allow a lot of body contact and free the hands for caressing and touching. The side-by-side positions are particularly useful for overweight people and for women in the later stages of pregnancy, when man-above and woman-above positions may be uncomfortable because of the woman's enlarged abdomen.

Partners may begin in the man-above position and then roll onto their sides with the penis inserted in the vagina. In this position, penetration tends to

Figure 5.7   Face-to-Face, Woman-Above Coital

Figure 5.8   Face-to-Face, Side-by-Side Coital

Rear-entry coitus is the most prevalent coital position among nonhuman species.

Rear Entry.   This approach involves vaginal intercourse in which the male positions himself behind the woman. Rear-entry coitus does not mean anal sex, with which it is sometimes confused. Because rear entry is the most prevalent coital position among nonhuman species, some people believe that the position is degrading or animalistic. This idea is unfortunate because there are advantages to rear-entry positions. For example, they allow a man more access to a woman's body. If both of them are lying on their sides, the man can caress the woman's breasts, most of her upper body, and her abdomen, clitoris, buttocks, and back. In fact, stimulation of the clitoris is easier in rear-entry than in any other coital position. In addition, stimulation of the Gräfenberg spot by the thrusting of the penis against the anterior wall of the vagina is more likely in rear-entry than in the face-to-face positions.

Rear entry can be accomplished with a woman lying on her stomach or kneeling. The man faces her back and inserts his penis into her vagina. Alternatively, the woman can sit on the man's lap, facing away, or the man can enter the woman while both are standing up, although it may be necessary for the woman to stand on a stool if the man is considerably taller than she is.

be shallow, and movements may be somewhat restricted or less vigorous. Depending on partners' preferences at a particular time, the more gentle movement can be an advantage or a disadvantage. They might choose this position, for example, when they want to prolong playful and intimate sexual relations before orgasm.

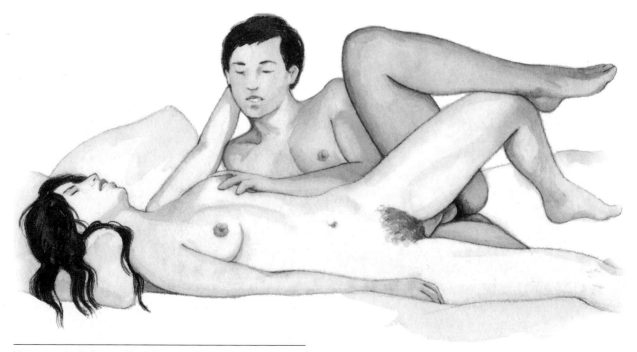

Figure 5.9   Scissors Position

A variation of this position, known as the scissors position, permits a woman to vary her pelvic thrusting with more ease while allowing a man greater ejaculatory control. To use the scissors position, the partners may begin with both the woman and the man lying on their left sides, with the woman's back to the man. She then rolls partially onto her back, putting her right leg over the man's legs, so that his penis can enter her vagina. For ease of entry, their heads and upper bodies should be at some distance from each other so that their bodies resemble a pair of open scissors. This position allows the man to caress the woman's genitals or breasts easily. The ease with which the partners may caress and look at each other contributes to the intimacy of this position (see Figure 5.9).

Rear-entry positions can be less physically demanding than other positions. They can be used during the third trimester of pregnancy or during illnesses that limit physical activity.

ANAL SEX

Anal sex involves the stimulation of the anus by a partner. The stimulation may involve fingers, the tongue, a penis, or an object. The anus is rich in nerve endings and is involved in sexual response regardless of whether it is directly or indirectly stimulated. The anus does not produce much lubrication, but lubrication can be supplied through the use of a sterile, water-soluble product such as K-Y jelly. Vaseline and other petroleum-based lubricants should not be used in the anus or the vagina because they tend to accumulate and are not as easily discharged as are water-soluble lubricants.

The anal sphincter muscle responds to initial penetration with a contraction that may be uncomfortable. The spasm usually relaxes within 15 to 30 seconds in a person who is familiar with anal intercourse (Masters & Johnson, 1979). In a tense, inexperienced person, the spasm may last for a minute or longer, but the discomfort usually disappears.

Like masturbation, oral stimulation, and coital position variations, anal sex apparently became more prevalent in the past 50 years. Even with the advent of AIDS and the urgent need for safer-sex practices, there has not been a marked decline in anal sex in the United States, as can be seen in Table 5.4.

As with oral sex, there appear to be ethnic differences in the likelihood of people's engaging in anal

TABLE 5.4 Prevalence of Anal Intercourse

These studies of percentage of people engaging in anal intercourse are difficult to compare because researchers asked questions in different ways.

Kinsey Group (1938–1949)	Hunt (1972)	Laumann et al. (1992)
Never tried: 89%	Under age 25: 25%	
Tried unsuccessfully: 3%	At ages 25–34: 25%	Males 18–59: 26%
Have experienced: 8%	At ages 35–44: 14%	Females 18–59: 20%

sex (Laumann et al., 1994). The patterns are complicated among men and women. Hispanic men report the most experience with anal intercourse (34 percent), and Black women report the least experience (10 percent).

If partners choose to engage in anal sex despite the risk of AIDS, a lubricated condom should be worn, and penile penetration of the anus should be carried out gradually and gently. The penis should never be inserted into the vagina or mouth after anal penetration unless it has been washed. The anus contains bacteria that can cause infection.

FREQUENCY OF COITUS AND NUMBER OF SEXUAL PARTNERS

Concern about what is a "normal" or average number of sexual contacts often surfaces in classes on human sexuality. Most of these questions focus on sexual intercourse. In addition to frequency, the number of sexual partners people have has become a mounting concern with the threat of AIDS as well as other sexually transmitted diseases.

The average American couple has coitus about one to three times a week in their early 20s, with the frequency declining to about once a week or less for those aged 45 and older (Blumstein & Schwartz, 1983; Hunt, 1974; Smith, 1991). These figures provide rough estimates for the total sample but do not give a true notion of the variability in sexual activity among Americans. For example, 22 percent of Tom Smith's (1991) national sample reported total abstinence in the previous year, whereas John Billy et al. (1993) found a few men in their national sample who reported having vaginal intercourse more than 22 times a week! Thus, there is no "gold standard" against which we can measure the "appropriate" frequency of sexual activity. There is simply a great deal of variability among couples and for a given couple over different time periods. As we discuss in Chapter 13, however, lack of, or very little, sexual activity is often associated with relationships characterized by friction and strain.

Regarding the number of sexual partners, Smith (1991) found an average of 7 partners since age 18, although men reported considerably more partners (12) than did women (3), which he believed stemmed from men's overreporting and women underreporting. When the 12 to 18 months prior to data collection were considered, the number of partners was a little over 1. As might be expected from the decrease in frequency of sexual activity with age, the number of sexual partners also declined with age. As with frequency of sexual activity, there is a great deal of variability among individuals in their reported number of sexual partners. In the Laumann et al. (1994) and Billy et al. (1993) studies, 17 percent and 23 percent, respectively, of the men had 20 or more coital partners, and a few men reported more than 900 lifetime coital sex partners. Only 3 percent of women reported 21 or more partners since age 18 (Laumann et al., 1994). No consistent ethnic or social differences emerged in self-reported frequency of sex or numbers of sexual partners (Billy et al., 1993; Laumann et al., 1994; Smith, 1991). *Reality or Myth*

SEXUAL SATISFACTION AND ENJOYMENT

The preceding descriptions of the various types of sexual stimulation are by no means exhaustive. The possibilities are limited only by imagination, body build, energy level, and agility. Some couples may find a particular position or stimulation technique so satisfying that they have little interest in exploring others. If they do not find their pattern monotonous, there is no compelling reason that they should experiment. Partners who feel that their sexual interaction has become automatic may be able to add zest and intensity to their lovemaking by trying alternative ways of giving pleasure to each other.

It is important to keep in mind that the physical expression of our sexuality takes place in the context of daily life. Sexual intimacy can provide a break from a demanding schedule in the form of experiences ranging from simple physical release to the communication of intensely felt affection and connection. Perhaps the ultimate measure of sexual satisfaction is the quality of the period of time following orgasm. At its best, it is a time of mutual relaxation and shared intimacy, a time when we may be more open than usual to new ideas and suggestions. This aftermath can provide an opportunity to talk about and reflect on matters not directly related to mundane daily tasks. At other times, we may feel energized by sexual interaction, ready to return to work or other activities with renewed vigor.

Sexual intimacy, then, can have different purposes. Release from tension, the sense of intense union, or the expression of affection can be part of any sexual contact that is more than just momentary. Sometimes a source of ecstasy, sometimes mediocre or rather disappointing, the experience of sexual contact can fluctuate a great deal. If we accept these variations and do not focus on any one episode as the main determinant of the quality of our sexuality, we can enjoy the diversity.

SIMULTANEOUS ORGASM: A NOTE

In the section on masturbation, we noted that most men slow down or stop manual stimulation of the penis during orgasm. In contrast, women generally prefer continued stimulation of the clitoris or mons during orgasm. This difference is consistent with the observation that most men attempt deep vaginal penetration with little further thrusting at the onset of ejaculation during coitus, whereas the typical woman prefers continued male thrusting during her orgasm (Masters & Johnson, 1966). Because of this difference in the typical response styles of men and women, simultaneous orgasm can be difficult to obtain. In a study of female nurses, only 17 percent of the sample experienced orgasm at about the same time as their partner (Darling et al., 1991).

Preoccupation with the attempt to achieve simultaneous orgasm can detract from what might otherwise be a pleasurable experience. An exception to this generalization is when a couple is "swept away" with the emotional intensity of the interaction, a typical situation during the early stages of a sexual relationship or during the periodic renewal of intensely passionate feelings that can occur in long-term relationships. These conditions can lead to simultaneous orgasm that has little to do with sexual technique.

Because women can continue coitus indefinitely before and/or after orgasm, whereas men's erections generally subside after ejaculation, an approach to orgasm that emphasizes "ladies first" may be most satisfying for many couples. For example, if a woman finds it easier to have an orgasm in the woman-above position, a couple can employ this position until the woman has orgasm. At that point, the couple can move into whatever position the man finds most stimulating. *Reality or Myth*

Another kind of satisfying experience may provide a useful model for many couples: a massage. Having your body massaged allows another person to give you pleasure, while you simply relax and let your feelings emerge. It can also be rewarding to take the active role, arousing great pleasure in your partner. Regardless of what positions and techniques couples use in their sexual interaction, their bodies tend to respond in one of just a few relatively predictable patterns of physical response.

▶ **Issues to Consider:** How would you deal with a partner who insisted on having simultaneous orgasms in all your sexual encounters?

Sexual Responses

Prior to Masters and Johnson's (1966) work, men and women were believed to have different sexual responses. Common wisdom held that men had easily triggered sexual drives, whereas women's responses needed careful nurturing through long periods of courtship and foreplay. In addition, men were thought to reach orgasm readily and quickly. In contrast, orgasm for women was perceived by those who believed in its existence as a highly elusive response. Furthermore, it was thought that men could ejaculate and that women could not. The extent to which these perceived differences resulted from differences in cultural training rather than (or in addition to) differences in physiology was seldom considered.

In focusing on biological capacities, Masters and Johnson emphasized the similarities, rather than the differences, in the sexual responses of men and women. They found that most of the bodily changes that occurred in the sexual response cycles of both men and women were attributable to two major alterations in the genital organs: vasocongestion and muscle tension.

Vasocongestion, or blood engorgement, is the process by which various parts of the body (primarily the genitals and breasts) become filled with blood

during sexual excitement. **Muscle tension** refers to involuntary contractions of muscles during sexual response. Masters and Johnson's physiological recordings of the contractions of orgasm showed that one occurred every eight-tenths of a second in men—precisely the same interval as was recorded between the orgasmic contractions in women.

Masters and Johnson concluded that there were only two major differences between the sexual responses of men and women. First, men could ejaculate, and women could not. Second, women were capable of having a series of orgasms within a short period of time, and men were not. More recent research has suggested that even these differences may not be absolute. As you will see later, some men are capable of multiple orgasms, and some women appear to ejaculate a fluid at orgasm.

We turn now to the phases of the sexual response cycle (desire, excitement, orgasm) as described by Helen Singer Kaplan (1974, 1979) and Masters and Johnson (1966). A summary of responses during this cycle is presented in "Highlight: Physical Reactions During Sexual Response" on page 113. Remember that these are descriptions of typical physiological

vasocongestion—Engorgement with blood.

muscle tension—Involuntary contractions of muscles during sexual response.

changes, with little attention paid to the psychological states that accompany them.

SEXUAL DESIRE

Kaplan (1974, 1979) was one of the first sexual scientists who emphasized the importance of sexual desire in the sexual response cycle (SRC). She believed that desire is interconnected with the other phases of sexual response but also separate in terms of the biological systems that underlie them. Most of us have a pretty good understanding of the subjective experience of sexual desire.

Distinguishing sexual desire as a separate phase in the SRC has important implications for sexual dysfunctions and their treatment, discussed in Chapter 15. For now, we will simply let Kaplan (1979) describe the desire phase of sexual response:

> *Sexual desire or libido is experienced as specific sensations which move the individual to seek out, or become receptive to, sexual experiences. These sensations are produced by the physical activation of a specific neural system in the brain. When this system is active a person is "horny"; he may feel genital sensations or he may feel vaguely sexy, interested in sex, open to sex, or even just restless. These sensations cease after sexual gratification, i.e., orgasm. (p. 10)*

EXCITEMENT/PLATEAU

In the excitement phase, the penis begins to become erect. This swelling is due entirely to vasocongestion—the filling of the three spongy columns of the penis (the two corpora cavernosa and the corpus spongiosum) with blood. Arteries carrying blood into the penis dilate, allowing blood to engorge the spongy tissues.

During the plateau phase, the erection of the penis becomes more stable; that is, a man is less likely to lose his erection in the face of such distractions as ringing telephones or nonerotic thoughts. This stability may be related to a further engorgement of the penis with blood, which has the effect of constricting the three veins that carry blood out of the penis. In addition to swelling the penis, vasocongestion affects the testes, increasing their size by about 50 percent. Because of the tightness of the capsule surrounding each testis, most men can feel the sensations associated with this swelling. Contraction of the muscles surrounding the vas deferens pulls the testes up during excitement, so that they press against the body. When men become sexually aroused but do not ejaculate, the swollen testes can become painful, a condition popularly known as "blue balls" or "lover's nuts." There are women (see Chapter 19) who have consented to unwanted intercourse to relieve their partners of such pain (O'Sullivan & Allgeier, 1998). No one has ever died of swollen testes, however, and if a woman does not want to engage in further sexual activity, a man can readily reduce the swelling in his testes by masturbating.

Erotic excitement produces vasocongestion in the female genitals, as it does in the male genitals. Whereas engorgement of the penis results in erection, engorgement of the inner lips, clitoris, and vaginal walls with blood produces a slippery, clear fluid—vaginal lubrication—on the vaginal walls. As the vaginal walls swell with blood, the inner two-thirds of the vagina widens and lengthens in what is called the *tenting effect* (see Figure 5.10). The clitoris becomes congested with blood and increases in diameter. It remains enlarged during the plateau and orgasm phases. The outer lips, which touch when the woman is not aroused, now flatten and move apart to leave the swollen inner lips, clitoris, and vaginal entrance exposed.

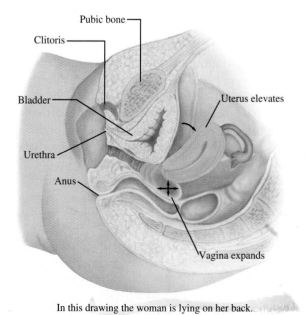

In this drawing the woman is lying on her back.

Figure 5.10 Muscular Contractions of Female Orgasm

Physical Reactions During Sexual Response

Excitement/Plateau

Engorgement of penis with blood

Increase in length and diameter of penis

Engorgement of vaginal walls and inner lips with blood

Onset of vaginal lubrication

Flattening of outer lips and their retraction from the vaginal entrance

Lengthening and expansion of inner two-thirds of the vagina

Initial slight swelling of the clitoris followed by retraction of the clitoris until it is completely covered by the clitoral hood and decreases about 50 percent in length

Swelling, elevation, and rotation of testes

Erection of nipples (less common among males)

Size increase of female breasts

Appearance of a "sex flush," a rosy, measles-like rash over the chest, neck, face, shoulders, arms, and thighs

Increase in heart rate and blood pressure

Increase in muscle tension

Secretion of fluid by Cowper's glands

Increase in respiration

Orgasm

Contractions beginning as far back as the testes and continuing through the epididymis, vas deferens, seminal vesicles, prostate gland, urethra, and penis

Beginning of strong muscle contractions in outer third of vagina, with first contractions lasting for 2 to 4 seconds and later contractions lasting from 3 to 15 seconds, occurring at 0.8-second intervals

Contraction of uterus

Occurrence of three or four powerful ejaculatory contractions at 0.8-second intervals, followed by two to four slower contractions of the anal sphincter

Slight expansion of inner two-thirds of the vagina

Testes at their maximum elevation

Sex flush at its peak

Heart rate up to 160–180 beats a minute

Respiration up to 40 breaths a minute

General loss of voluntary muscle or motor control

The enlarged clitoris retracts beneath the clitoral hood during the plateau phase and cannot be seen again until after orgasm. However, it can continue to receive stimulation through manual or oral movements on the clitoral hood. Thrusting of the penis in the vagina can also stimulate the clitoris, as pressure of the penis on the inner lips pulls the clitoral hood back and forth.

ORGASM

The orgasm phase actually occurs in two stages for the male, both of which involve contractions of the muscles associated with the internal sex organs. The first stage, **emission**, takes 2 or 3 seconds. During emission sperm and fluid are expelled from the vas deferens, seminal vesicles, and prostate gland into the base of the urethra near the prostate. As seminal fluid collects there and the urethra expands, men have the feeling that they are about to ejaculate ("ejaculatory inevitability"), but semen is not yet expelled from the urethra.

The second stage, **ejaculation**, involves expulsion of the semen by means of muscle contractions. There is also a contraction of the neck of the bladder, which prevents semen from flowing into the bladder. The semen is propelled by the muscular contractions of orgasm into the portion of the urethra within the penis and then expelled from the urethral opening in the glans (see Figure 5.11). These orgasmic contractions occur four or five times, at intervals of eight-

---

emission—Propulsion of sperm and fluid to the base of the urethra during orgasm.

ejaculation—Expulsion of seminal fluid out of the urethra during orgasm.

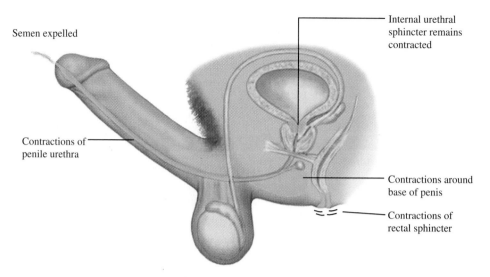

Semen expelled

Internal urethral
sphincter remains
contracted

Contractions of
penile urethra

Contractions around
base of penis

Contractions of
rectal sphincter

Figure 5.11   Ejaculation Stage of Male Orgasm

tenths of a second. Simultaneously, muscles within the anus contract because both sets of muscles share a common nerve supply.

As a woman approaches orgasm, the outer third of the vagina becomes constricted through blood engorgement. This constriction forms a narrow tube. The muscular contractions associated with orgasm occur in the vagina, uterus, and Fallopian tubes (refer to Figure 5.10 on page 112). Most women, however, subjectively experience the contractions in the outer third of the vagina as the most intense. Muscular contractions often occur in many other parts of the body as well.

RESOLUTION

After ejaculation, the resolution phase begins in the male. This process restores the genital organs and tissues to their preexcitement phase as the blood that filled the penis flows back into the veins. After this phase, most men experience a **refractory period**—a period of time following ejaculation during which nerves cannot respond to further stimulation. Most of us have experienced refractory periods in other contexts. For example, when a flashbulb is used to take our picture, most of us are momentarily blinded

refractory period—Period of time following ejaculation during which nerves cannot respond to further stimulation.

because the nerves in our eyes are temporarily unable to respond to the stimulation of light. Similarly, for many men, further erotic stimulation for a period of time following ejaculation provokes no response and may even be unpleasant. Masters and Johnson (1966) described the male refractory period as lasting between 30 and 90 minutes. However, some men are not able to become erect again for a considerably longer interval. Other men can have multiple orgasms; that is, they do not experience the typical refractory period.

During the resolution phase, the female body returns to its preexcitement state. With continued stimulation, however, some women have additional orgasms with little intervening time; females do not have the refractory period characteristic of males. In about 30 to 40 percent of men and women, a sweating reaction occurs during resolution.

PATTERNS OF SEXUAL RESPONSE

Major differences in the patterns of sexual response among men mainly involve the length of various phases rather than the intensity of response. In contrast, among women, Masters and Johnson (1966) concluded that there is a wide range of intensity. Also, a particular woman may respond with different patterns at various times, depending on her past experiences and the effectiveness of stimulation.

Some of the following descriptions of excitement and orgasm were written by women and some by men (Vance & Wagner, 1976). Can you tell the gender of the author of each description? For the answers, see page 116.

1. I think that there are a variety of orgasms that I experience. I have noted a shallow "orgasm" which consists of a brief period that is characterized by an urge to thrust but which passes quickly. On the other hand, I have also experienced what I call a hard climax, characterized by a mounting, building tension and strong thrusting movements which increase in strength and frequency until the tension is relieved.

2. It is a very pleasurable sensation. All my tensions have really built to a peak and are suddenly released. It feels like a great upheaval; like all of the organs in the stomach area have turned over. It is extremely pleasurable.

3. Tension builds to an extremely high level—muscles are tense, etc. There is a sudden expanding feeling in the pelvis and muscle spasms throughout the body followed by release of tension. Muscles relax and consciousness returns.

4. Orgasm gives me a feeling of unobstructed intensity of satisfaction. Accompanied with the emotional feeling and love one has for another, the reality of the sex drive, and our culturally conditioned status on sex, an orgasm is the only experience that sends my whole body and mind into a state of beautiful oblivion.

5. Physical tension and excitement climaxing and then a feeling of sighing, a release of tension-like feeling.

6. An orgasm is a very quick release of sexual tension which results in a kind of flash of pleasure.

Masters and Johnson observed three typical patterns of sexual response in their female volunteers. In pattern A, a female proceeds through the entire response cycle into one or more orgasms without interruption. This pattern is the typical multiple-orgasm response, with orgasms occurring far enough apart that they are distinguishable from one another. In pattern B, there is a gradual increase in arousal and a fluctuating plateau phase, with small surges toward orgasm followed by a relatively slow return to the physiological state of prearousal. This pattern seems to occur in young or sexually inexperienced women, who may not be sure that they have experienced orgasm. In pattern C, there is a single orgasm of extreme intensity, with little time spent in the plateau phase. Women report feelings of great release and gratification with this pattern. Despite sex differences at the physiological level, the subjective feelings of men and women during intense sexual response may be similar (see "Research Spotlight: Whose Is It?").

NORMAL VARIATIONS

In examining the patterns of sexual response, we must remember that they represent the typical patterns that Masters and Johnson found in their volunteers. Some people are tempted to measure themselves against such patterns. If their own responses do not generally match one of these patterns, they may conclude that there is something wrong with them, ignoring the fact that there are variations from one person to the next and from one sexual episode to the next. There are two reasons that we may be tempted to place undue importance on such patterns in evaluating our own sexual responses.

First, until recently there was little research on sexual response. We had no authorities to provide information or bases for comparing our own feelings and responses to those of other people. Second, although we are encouraged to ask parents, friends, and teachers about a variety of matters, including facts pertaining to reproduction, a cultural taboo has prevailed against "comparing notes" or seeking information about sexual pleasure, a circumstance that may make us overly receptive to recent research and information on the topic. It is fascinating, for instance, that each of the volumes by Masters and Johnson (1966, 1970) has sold well, even though the writing is quite technical and thus difficult for the average person to understand.

These two factors—the absence of research on sexual response until recently and the taboo against sharing information with relatives and friends—have conspired to make us overly vulnerable and insecure about our own sexual feelings and responses. In our eating habits, we do not generally worry that we sometimes enjoy wolfing down a hamburger but at other times love the ritual of a seven-course meal.

Nor are we upset when we have no appetite for either potato chips or chateaubriand. We realize that what is important is whether we feel good while having a particular meal, not whether we conform to the average American's typical pattern of eating an average of 700 calories per meal in an average of 17.3 minutes. Yet we may become overly concerned about going from the sexual excitement phase through plateau to orgasm in the space of 5 minutes or less or responding slowly during sexual intimacy, lingering over each phase. At times like this, we should remember that the measure of sexual health is not the extent to which we conform to some average pattern, but whether the process feels good and is satisfying to us and to our partners.

Orgasm consistently draws more attention, rightly or wrongly, than any other sexual response, by both the public and the sex-research community. In the following section, we present some of the current research on this human phenomenon.

▶ **Issues to Consider:** How do you know whether your sexual life is "normal"? How could you find out?

# **V**arieties of Orgasm

Females show greater variability in their sexual response patterns than do males. It appears, however, that the personal or subjective experience of orgasm does not differ between men and women. Look again at the descriptions of orgasm written by men and women in "Research Spotlight: Whose Is It?" on page 115 (Vance & Wagner, 1976). The researchers conducting the study obtained 48 such descriptions. After removing obvious gender cues, they presented these descriptions to physicians, psychologists, and medical students and asked them to judge whether each had been written by a male or a female. The fact that these professionals could not accurately identify the samples suggests that the experience of orgasm is quite similar for women and men. How did you do? The first three quotes in "Research Spotlight" on page 115 were written by women and the last three by men.

FEMALE ORGASM: DIFFERENT TYPES?

For decades, psychoanalysts believed that adult women should respond orgasmically to penile thrusting in the vagina. They described women who obtained orgasm primarily from clitoral stimulation as being fixated at the phallic stage of childhood, as suffering from penis envy, and as having failed to develop "normal" adult female patterns of sexual response. It was in an atmosphere of general acceptance of that point of view that Masters and Johnson (1966) published one of their most influential findings. Specifically, they reported that for a woman, the site of effective stimulation for orgasm is the clitoris, with orgasmic contractions then occurring in the vagina. Their conclusion helped deal the death blow to the idea that there was a clitoral orgasm distinct from a vaginal orgasm. Their physiological recordings of responses at the outer portion of the vagina indicated that the same orgasmic response occurred regardless of the site of stimulation.

Masters and Johnson did not focus on psychological reactions to orgasms or compare orgasms produced during coitus with those produced by clitoral stimulation alone. Other studies, however, have indicated that women do make subjective distinctions between masturbatory and coital orgasms (Bentler & Peeler, 1979; Singer & Singer, 1978). Women in one study described vaginally induced orgasms as "more internal," "fuller, but not stronger," and "more subtle" than orgasms resulting from clitoral stimulation (Butler, 1976).

Perhaps the most well-developed criticism of Masters and Johnson's work on orgasm came from the Singers (1978). They took issue with the conclusion that all orgasms are physiologically the same regardless of the type or site of stimulation. The Singers favored a broader definition of orgasm that includes emotional satisfaction as well as physiological changes. Accordingly, they described three types of female orgasm.

The first type is the vulval orgasm, which can be induced by coital or noncoital stimulation and does not have a refractory period following it. This orgasm is the type that Masters and Johnson measured (1966). It is characterized by involuntary rhythmic contractions of the outer third of the vagina. In contrast, a uterine orgasm is characterized by a gasping type of breathing that culminates in involuntary breath-holding. The breath is explosively exhaled at orgasm, and the orgasm is followed by a feeling of relaxation and sexual satiation. This response seems to occur upon repeated deep stimulation involving penis-cervix contact that displaces the uterus and causes stimulation of the membrane lining the abdominal cavity. This type of orgasm is followed by a refractory period. The third type of orgasm, which combines elements of the other two types, is called a blended orgasm. It is felt as being deeper than a vulval orgasm and is characterized by both breath-holding and contractions of the orgasmic platform.

It is possible that orgasm resulting from clitoral stimulation corresponds to what Singer and Singer (1978) call vulval orgasm. The uterine orgasm they described may correspond to orgasm produced by vaginal wall stimulation. Finally, the blended orgasm they describe may result from simultaneous stimulation of the clitoris and the vaginal wall. Researchers continue to study possible variations in female orgasm, as well as the physical response systems associated with them. In addition to watching for the results of their findings, you may want to note interpretations of the significance of different kinds of orgasms. We hope that there will be no return to the practice of attributing moral and emotional superiority to any particular orgasmic pattern.

RESEARCH ON FEMALE EJACULATION

References to women's expelling a fluid at orgasm have appeared in such fictional works as *Lady Chatterley's Lover* (Lawrence, 1930), in marriage manuals (van de Velde, 1930), and in the professional literature. Ernest Gräfenberg (1950) observed:

> *This convulsory expulsion of fluids occurs always at the acme of the orgasm and simultaneously with it. If there is the opportunity to observe the orgasm of such women, one can see that large quantities of a clear, transparent fluid are expelled not from the vulva, but out of the urethra in gushes. (p. 147)*

Some have interpreted women's ejaculation of fluid as a normal, if atypical, response to sexual stimulation. Others have assumed that women who experienced ejaculation were simply suffering from incontinence—the inability to control urination—and developed a number of surgical, chemical, and electrical procedures to correct what they believed

was a pathological condition. In 1982, however, a book that dealt with female ejaculation and the Gräfenberg spot (*The G Spot*, by Ladas, Whipple, & Perry) was published, followed by scores of reviews and articles.

Some women have reported that stimulation of the anterior wall of the vagina produces enlargement of the Gräfenberg spot at the base of the bladder. A number of these women described expulsion of a clear to milky-white fluid from the urethra at orgasm (Belzer, 1981). A number of researchers have conducted chemical comparisons of urine with samples of this fluid (Zaviacic & Whipple, 1993). The ejaculate differed from urine in a number of respects, the most notable of which was that the ejaculate was high in prostatic acid phosphatase (PAP), a chemical believed to be secreted only by the male prostate gland. However, other analyses of the fluid expelled from the urethra by women at the height of sexual excitement indicated no differences between this fluid and urine for some women in the sample (Zaviacic & Whipple, 1993). At present, it appears that some women expel a fluid similar to urine from the urethra during sexual release, others expel a urethral fluid different from urine, and still others expel no fluid from the urethra at all during orgasm.

On the basis of their work with volunteers, Perry and Whipple (1982) concluded that perhaps 10 percent of women ejaculate. In a study of professional women, almost 40 percent reported experiencing ejaculation at the moment of orgasm (Davidson et al., 1989). But those women who believe themselves to be ejaculators would be more likely to participate in lab research, and to complete questionnaires, than would those women who do not believe themselves to be ejaculators or who believe that research on sexual response is immoral.

At this time there is no basis for accurately estimating the incidence of female ejaculation. Nor do we know the source of the ejaculate, although some researchers have suggested the presence of a rudimentary prostate gland at the base of the bladder (Sevely & Bennett, 1978; Zaviacic & Whipple, 1993). Considerably more investigation is needed before researchers can reach firm conclusions about the function of female ejaculation.

prostatic acid phosphatase (PAP)—a fluid secreted by the prostate gland.

THE CONSISTENCY OF ORGASM

Although most women are capable of experiencing orgasm, some women do so inconsistently, and others do not have orgasms at all. Kinsey et al. (1953) reported that 10 percent of married American women and 30 percent of sexually active unmarried women had never experienced orgasm.

In the Laumann et al. (1994) study, only 29 percent of the women reported that they always had an orgasm during sexual activity with a partner. Nevertheless, 40 percent claimed to be extremely physically satisfied with their partner, and 39 percent were extremely emotionally satisfied with their partner. It should be noted that some women who did not experience orgasm nevertheless reported their sexual activity as quite pleasurable.

Many women who do not experience orgasm consistently may feel pressured to meet their partner's and society's expectations that people should have at least one orgasm during each sexual encounter. Some pretend to have orgasms in their desire to please their partners. In a sample of 805 professional nurses, 58 percent reported that they had pretended at some point to have orgasm during sexual intercourse (Darling & Davidson, 1986). In a study of more than 200 college women, about one-quarter had not yet experienced intercourse (Wiederman, 1997). Of those women who had had coitus, slightly more than half reported having pretended having orgasm. How do you think the pretenders differed from the nonpretenders? It may surprise you to learn that compared to the nonpretenders, the pretenders had more liberal sexual attitudes, higher sexual esteem, began coitus at a younger age and perceived themselves to be more facially attractive. The pretenders also reported a greater number of intercourse and oral sex partners. In a subsequent study, Wiederman (personal communication 1998) found that about a quarter of coitally experienced college men had pretended to have orgasm, so faking is not just a female phenomenon. **Reality or Myth** 6

Although some women may attempt to soothe the egos of their partners by pretending orgasm, they may actually be providing misleading feedback and disrupted sexual communication to their partners. This sexual deception could lead the partner into thinking everything is going well in the couple's love making rather than looking for other approaches that might be more satisfying to the woman.

The Kinsey group (1948) did not present detailed data on the consistency of male orgasm because they assumed that married men had orgasms almost 100 percent of the time. However, 25 percent of men in the Laumann et al. (1994) study indicated that they did not always have an orgasm during sexual activity with their partner.

MULTIPLE ORGASMS

One of the most frequently quoted findings of Masters and Johnson (1966) is their report of multi-orgasmic responses among some of their female volunteers. More recently, Carol Darling, J. Kenneth Davidson, and Donna Jennings's (1991) survey of nurses indicated that almost 43 percent usually experienced multiple orgasms during some form of sexual activity. However, it was Masters and Johnson's (1966) report of physiological recordings of multiple orgasm in women that prompted contemporary interest in the phenomenon. Their research indicated that most women are capable of having multiple orgasms if they are adequately stimulated.

Some writers have interpreted women's capacity for multiple orgasm as an indication that women are "more sexual" than men (Sherfey, 1972). Others have assumed that multiorgasmic women are sexually superior to women who have one orgasm or who do not have orgasms at all. Most of this reasoning could be dismissed as downright silly if it did not adversely affect the sexual lives of many women and men. The multiple-orgasm response is not the zenith of sexual activity. Many women who are able to have multiple orgasms often prefer to experience just one intense uterine orgasm (Singer & Singer, 1978). Some women enjoy alternating their sexual patterns, experiencing multiple orgasms some of the time and one orgasm at other times. Sometimes they may experience no orgasm at all during lovemaking.

In one study of college women, no clear preference for multiple or single orgasms appeared (Clifford, 1978). Most of the women who experienced multiple orgasms found them no more satisfying than single ones. Thus, it appears that the quality of sexual interaction is more important than the quantity.

Masters and Johnson (1966) found a few men below age 30 who experienced repeated orgasm and ejaculation without the refractory period that is characteristic of most men. These individuals were called multiejaculatory because each of the repeated orgasms was accompanied by ejaculation.

More recently, there have been reports that some men can experience two or more orgasms before or following ejaculation (Dunn & Trost, 1989; Robbins & Jensen, 1978). These men reported having an average of 2 to 16 orgasms per sexual encounter, and one of the individuals in Mina Robbins and Gordon Jensen's study reported as many as 30 orgasms over the course of 1 hour (confirmed by physiological measures). After an orgasm, the degree of penile engorgement decreased, but his penis remained fully erect, and the resolution phase did not occur.

Some of the men in the Marian Dunn and Jan Trost (1989) study thought that they had always been multiorgasmic and that their experience was "natural," whereas others reported learning to inhibit or control ejaculation until the final orgasm. It is widely believed that men are capable of only a single orgasm and ejaculation. As men become more aware of the possibility of multiple orgasm, it will be interesting to see whether the percentage of men experiencing it, which is presumably small, increases. For those who are interested, William Hartman and Marilyn Fithian's (1984) book, *Any Man Can*, provides detailed instructions for learning how to have multiple orgasms.

The techniques that elicit sexual responses obviously do not develop in a social vacuum. Our personal histories and the social situations in which we interact are strongly related to our patterns of sexual arousal. In Chapter 6 we examine some ways in which learning and feelings may interfere with or enhance sexual arousal and response.

SUMMARY OF MAJOR POINTS

1. Autoeroticism and sexual learning. Self-stimulation can provide useful training for sexual interaction with a partner, as well as being pleasurable in its own right. Women show more variety in the kinds of stimulation they use during masturbation than do men. Women tend to prefer continued self-stimulation during orgasm, whereas men usually stop stimulation or move their hands more slowly as they begin to have an orgasm.

2. Mutual sexual stimulation. Almost any part of the body can be employed in stimulating another person, but the hands, mouth, genitals, and, to a lesser extent, the anus generally are used most often during sexual interaction. A couple can engage in coitus in a variety of positions, each of which provides somewhat different possibilities for stimulation. The choice of positions and stimulation techniques during sexual interaction should be guided by personal preference and pleasure; no one way is necessarily superior or inferior to any other.

3. Response of the body during sexual stimulation. The sexual response cycle encompasses desire, excitement, and orgasm. Desire involves awareness of wanting sexual stimulation. During excitement, vasocongestion produces erection and vaginal lubrication accompanied by mounting muscle tension. Orgasm involves spasm contractions and tension reduction and is followed by resolution—a return to the preexcitement state.

4. Varieties of orgasmic experience in women. Recent evidence indicates that women are capable of having diverse orgasmic experiences, depending on the site of stimulation. Both clitoral stimulation and deep pressure on the vaginal walls can produce intense pleasure for women. Preliminary data suggest that some women ejaculate fluid from the urethra. The range of responses to sexual stimulation from one woman to the next is quite large, and individual women respond differently from one sexual encounter to the next. Some women rarely have an orgasm, others have a series of orgasms during sexual stimulation, and still others experience a single, intense orgasmic release.

5. Varieties of orgasmic experience in men. Compared with women, men appear to show fewer individual differences in response to sexual stimulation. In general, sexual contact leads quite reliably to a single orgasm, followed by a refractory period during which the nerves do not respond to further stimulation. A few men, however, have trained themselves to have multiple orgasms by preventing full ejaculation until the final time they have orgasm in a particular sexual encounter.

Arousal and Communication

Reality or Myth

1. *Women are interested in sex primarily when they are fertile.*

2. *There are few gender differences in sexual fantasies.*

3. *Women who feel guilty about sexuality are more likely to use contraception than are those who do not feel guilty.*

4. *Children typically receive the majority of their sex education from their parents.*

5. *Initially saying no when one is willing to become sexually intimate is known as the "token no."*

*M*aybe I'll see him at the party Friday night and be able to talk to him. . . . Maybe I'll ask him what his summer was like. . . . No, that's dumb. . . . Let's see, maybe we'll be at the party and a snowstorm will close everything down, and we'll be marooned. Well, no, there will be a lot of people there. . . . We'll get into a good conversation, get hungry for pizza, and decide to go pick up some, and then get stuck and have to leave the car. And then we'll walk back to my apartment. He'll come in and take off his coat, and I'll put some music on. He'll say, "Do you want to dance?"—I wonder if he likes to dance?—We'll start dancing, and he'll nuzzle my neck. We'll kiss, and then sit down on the couch. He'll start to play with my breasts slowly and gently, and. . . . No, let's see, I'll put some music on, but I'll say I'm really freezing and want to take a nice warm bath. So I'll go turn on the water, and then when I come out, he'll ask me if I want to dance. He'll start nuzzling my neck, and we'll kiss, and then I'll say I have to turn off the water. When I come back, he'll be sitting on the couch, so I'll sit down too, and we'll start kissing again. He'll start to take my clothes off and ask me if I want him to wash my back, and I'll ask him if he wants to take a bath, too, and . . .

During the second decade of life, we typically begin to have sexual **fantasies** and feel sexual arousal. We mentally construct sequences of events leading to romantic and sexual interaction, such as the fantasy in the preceding vignette, and we experience sexual arousal in connection with our fantasies. Before we can decide whether to express some of our fantasies and feelings with a potential partner, we first need to be able to communicate, both verbally and nonverbally, with other people.

In this chapter we describe the process by which we learn to feel sexually aroused and the purposes of sexual arousal. The impact of our senses and our thoughts on sexual arousal is examined. We then turn to the interpersonal communication of arousal and consider individual differences in reactions to arousal. For example, some people respond to feelings of arousal with happiness and pleasure, whereas others feel embarrassment and guilt. Finally, we discuss the importance of being able to communicate clearly with each other to have satisfying relationships, and we consider some practical issues relevant to the management of fantasy and arousal.

*L*earning to Be Aroused

The capacities for language and sexual arousal are both innate; however, just as the specific language that we speak is learned, the specific objects and acts that we find sexually arousing appear to be—for the most part—conditioned by our culture and our own experiences. For example, if a man or woman with a nickel-sized hole in the lower lip, out of which tobacco juice and saliva were dribbling, walked up to you enticingly, would you feel sexual attraction? You

fantasies—Usually pleasant mental images unrestrained by the realities of the external world.

What is considered sexually attractive varies across cultures, subcultures, and historical periods.

might if you had been reared among the So of northeastern Uganda. And within a culture, the specific stimuli that are paired with arousal vary from one time period to the next. For example, sometimes big breasts are fashionable, whereas at other times in the same culture, people may respond erotically to small, delicately formed breasts.

Both of these examples demonstrate culturally shared ideas about what is arousing. When everyone around us seems to share the same general perceptions about what is attractive, it is easy to assume that there is something natural about being attracted

to particular types of stimuli. Our own unique experiences, however, can lead us to respond sexually to particular experiences that do not have any erotic significance for our friends.

What would happen if you showed the drawing in Figure 6.1 to a 2- or 3-year-old child? A child that age would be unlikely to perceive the picture as either erotic or disgusting. (We are *not* suggesting that you show this picture to young children.) The point is that we learn to interpret certain pictures, objects, and parts of people's bodies as sexually arousing. We go through a long period of training during child-

Figure 6.1   What Is Your Response?
Most of our erotic responses are learned. Depending on training, adults might respond to this drawing with arousal, indifference, or disgust, but it would be meaningless to a 3-year-old.

hood and adolescence. Depending on our generation, culture, socioeconomic status, unique experiences, and momentary feelings, we learn to feel aroused, unaffected, or disgusted by particular body types, pictures, objects, sensations, and situations.

MODELS OF AROUSAL

If you have ever felt intense erotic attraction toward someone, the experience probably defied easy explanation. Sexual arousal is a complex set of responses by an individual. Even something that is commonly assumed to evoke unconditioned (that is, unlearned or involuntary) responses, such as having our genitals stroked, does not necessarily elicit sexual arousal.

> ▶ **Issues to Consider:** How would you explain your sexual arousal to another person?

Looking back on your own experiences, you may recall feeling arousal and attraction toward people who rewarded you (operant conditioning) and toward stimuli associated with those people (classical conditioning). You may have had other experiences, however, that do not fit neatly into the classical and operant conditioning models. What about the situation in which you feel respect and admiration for one person who is good to you, yet your sexual arousal and attraction are directed toward someone not nearly so kind or admirable? In fact, you may be most aware of your arousal and desire

for this person at times when you are feeling jealousy, an emotion that is not pleasant or rewarding. How does this kind of feeling develop?

THE TWO-STAGE MODEL OF SEXUAL AROUSAL

Noting that people sometimes feel attracted to and aroused by others who apparently provide them with more pain than pleasure, Ellen Berscheid and Elaine Walster (1974; Walster's last name is now Hatfield) proposed that simple conditioning models may not be adequate to explain all instances of intense attraction. They argued that the experience of love—perhaps **lust** would be a more accurate word—may result from a two-stage process. First, we feel physiological arousal and the responses that accompany it, such as a racing heart and pulse, sweating palms, and heavy breathing. Second, in our desire to understand the source of the arousal, we search for an explanation—a label—for the arousal.

Berscheid and Walster (1974) proposed that, under some conditions, we may experience physiological arousal and conclude that we are feeling love or sexual attraction. If the arousal occurs in the context of sexual intimacy with an appropriate object of our love, this conclusion seems logical. However, Berscheid and Walster suggested that under certain conditions, *any* source of arousal can increase the likelihood that we will label our feelings love or attraction. For example, physical arousal from such sources as exercise could be mistaken for attraction to another person.

This hypothesis was tested by Donald Dutton and Arthur Aron (1974) in a somewhat unusual setting—two bridges overlooking the Capilano River in British Columbia, Canada. One of the bridges was 5 feet wide, 450 feet long, and made out of wooden boards attached to wire cables. As the researchers put it,

> *The bridge has many arousal-inducing features such as 1) a tendency to tilt, sway, and wobble, creating the impression that one is about to fall over the side; 2) very low handrails of wire cable which contribute to this impression; and 3) a 230-ft. drop to rocks and shallow rapids below the bridge. The*

lust—Intense sexual desire.

"control" bridge was a solid wood bridge far-ther upriver. Constructed of heavy cedar, this bridge was wider and firmer than the experimental bridge, was only 10 ft. above a small, shallow rivulet which ran into the main river, had high handrails, and did not tilt or sway. (p. 511)

After walking over either the arousal-inducing bridge or the control bridge, men were approached by either a male or a female interviewer and asked to respond to a short questionnaire, then to write a short story based on a picture of a young woman covering her face with one hand and reaching with the other.

Two measures were used to assess the volunteers' sexual arousal. First, the volunteers' stories were examined for sexual content. When the interviewers were women, the stories from volunteers who were on the arousing bridge contained significantly more sexual content than did those from volunteers on the control bridge. When the interviewer was male, sexual content did not vary according to which bridge the volunteers were on. Second, after the volunteers had completed the questionnaire, they were offered the interviewer's name and telephone number in case they wanted to have the experiment explained in more detail. The researchers hypothesized that volunteers on the arousing bridge would be more likely to call the female interviewer than would volunteers on the control bridge. As Table 6.1 shows, 50 percent of the males from the arousing bridge did call the female interviewer. This percentage was higher than both the percentage from the control bridge who called the female interviewer and the percentage from either bridge who called the male interviewer.

Other research has also provided evidence that misattribution of arousal may affect romantic attraction. For example, in a laboratory study, Gregory White and Thomas Kight (1984) asked men to run for 15 seconds (low physiological arousal) or for 2 minutes (high physiological arousal). Regardless of whether they ran for 15 seconds or 2 minutes, the importance of the physical activity in the experiment was either minimized or emphasized. The men were then shown a videotape of a female college sophomore in "appealing, form-fitting clothes talking energetically about a variety of topics including . . . favorite dating activities. . . . She also mentioned that

TABLE 6.1 Attraction and Sexuality on Anxiety-Arousing Bridge and on Safe Bridge	
	Percentage of Subjects Telephoning Interviewer
Female interviewer	
Safe bridge	12.5
Anxiety-arousing bridge	50.0
Male interviewer	
Safe bridge	16.7
Anxiety-arousing bridge	28.6

Source: Adapted from Dutton and Aron, 1974 (Table 7-3), p. 516.

she was looking forward to meeting people in general and the subject if possible and that she had no current boyfriend" (p. 58). Some of the men were told that they would meet the woman, whereas others were told that they would not meet her. The men were more attracted to the woman when they were more physiologically aroused, when they expected to meet her, and when the importance of the source of initial arousal was minimized.

In general, then, the less able we are to identify the source of our physiological feelings of arousal and the more likely we are to have the chance to interact with a person, the more romantically attracted we feel toward that person. Strictly speaking, this finding appeals only to the romantic attraction of a man to a woman, because these studies of arousal have used only heterosexual men. Although it may seem reasonable to assume that women and homosexuals respond similarly, research with women and with gay people is needed to determine whether these findings generalize beyond young heterosexual men.

On the basis of experiments examining the influences of arousal on attraction, Berscheid and Walster (1974) concluded that, under the appropriate circumstances, arousal, regardless of its source, increases the likelihood that one person will be attracted to another. Their analysis may help to explain why someone is attracted to another person when outside observers can see no logical reason for the attraction.

A related point, which we discuss in more detail in Chapter 7, is the importance of distinguishing be-

This couple's behavior reflects the consuming connection that often accompanies the beginning of a relationship.

tween anxiety-related arousal and lasting attraction. During the initial stages of a relationship, the arousal from sexual attraction is likely to be laced heavily with anxiety, which increases the level of **epinephrine** in our bodies. We wonder: How interested in me is she? Is she just being nice, or does she really care about me? Do I look attractive to her? If the relationship blossoms and endures, there is usually a decrease in arousal, associated with the lessening of anxiety. A couple may interpret this change as a diminishing of love if they have defined love as intense arousal. Labeling feelings of sexual attraction, euphoria, and anxiety as *love* may evoke disappointment when these sources of physiological arousal subside.

THE PURPOSES OF SEXUAL AROUSAL

Cultural beliefs about the goodness or badness of sexual feelings affect individuals' responses to sexual stimulation. From childhood on, some people are taught that sexual arousal is bad or sinful and should

epinephrine—A hormone secreted by the adrenal gland that is involved in emotional excitement; sometimes called adrenaline.

be avoided or controlled except for purposes of reproduction. Others learn that their capacity for sexual arousal and expression is an enjoyable, healthy, and positive aspect of being alive. Most people receive mixed messages about sexuality, leading to confusion and doubts about their own sexual experiences and desires.

Comparing our species with others helps us to understand the functions of human sexual arousal. If the only purpose of sexual arousal is to reproduce, it would make more sense for human females to be uninterested in sexual interaction except when they are fertile. In fact, the females of most species are receptive to sexual interaction only when they are fertile. In contrast, human females, though fertile only one-seventh of the time, are continuously capable of strong sexual interest and arousal (Regan, 1996). Indeed, most human females report sexual arousal and behavior long after they cease menstruating and are no longer able to reproduce. *Reality or Myth*

The fact that human females eagerly engage in sexual intimacy at times when they are not fertile leads to an enhancement and lengthening of the period of sexual attraction. This was an evolutionary adaptation that made sense for the survival of our early ancestors' offspring. A human fetus takes nine months to mature in the uterus and the infant then takes many more years to develop to the point of self-sufficiency and reproductive maturity. Presumably, until recently in our evolution, it would have been difficult for a single parent to rear offspring to the point of reproductive maturity; forming a strong bond with a companion who would help to provide sustenance and support for the offspring would improve the child's chances of survival. The offspring of those early humans who felt continuing attraction toward each other may therefore have been more likely to survive than those whose parents were less sexually attached to each other.

Sexual arousal, then, can form the basis of a continuing bond. It can be disruptive of bonding, however, when it promotes attraction to persons outside the bond. Sexual arousal can lead to short-term, pleasure-oriented encounters or to nothing at all. The many purposes of sexual arousal depend on how the individual has learned to interpret and perceive his or her arousal and the sources of that arousal.

Sources of Arousal

Our senses are an intimate part of our sexuality. Touch, smell, sight, and hearing can all be sources of erotic arousal as a wide variety of sensory stimuli come to be associated with the pleasure of sexual experience. In this section we examine the role of the senses in arousal.

TOUCH

Our tactile capacities (that is, our ability to receive sensory stimulation from touch and pressure receptors) are intricately involved in sexual arousal. Our bodies—particularly our genitals—are richly endowed with receptors for touch and pressure. Because these receptors are distributed unevenly, some parts of the body are more sensitive than others. The most erotically sensitive areas are called **erogenous zones.** Many areas besides the genitals can be erotically sensitive to touch: the mouth, ears, buttocks, palms of the hands, fingers, abdomen, inner thighs, soles of the feet, and toes, for example.

Touch is the only type of stimulation that can elicit a reflexive response that is independent of higher-brain centers. For example, men with spinal cord injuries that prevent impulses from reaching the brain but leave the sexual centers in the lower spinal cord intact are able to respond with an erection when their genitals or inner thighs are touched.

The erotic aspects of touching must be understood in the broader context of the fundamental human need for bodily contact, a need that is apparent from infancy. Of all our senses, neural pathways underlying skin sensation and responses to body stimulation are the first to develop. Touch is crucial in the fulfillment of the basic needs for affection, security, and love and in the development of our capacity to give affection (Hatfield, 1994). The detrimental effects of depriving infants of adequate sensory stimulation by withholding touching, caressing, and cuddling are examined in Chapters 7 and 12.

SMELL

Many species rely heavily on chemical attractants in their sexual interactions. Such attractants are loosely categorized as pheromones. There are numerous examples of the importance of pheromones in regulating the behavior of nonhuman organisms (Kohl & Francoeur, 1995).

Among insects, for instance, pheromones seem to have an irresistible and predictable effect on behavior. Female moths have special abdominal glands that manufacture pheromones capable of attracting males from far away. The automatic response to pheromones shown by male insects does not appear to characterize species closer to humans on the evolutionary scale.

Pheromones also function as sex attractants, territorial markers, and orientation signals in a number of higher species, but these species appear to be less

---

erogenous zones—Areas of the body that are erotically sensitive to tactile stimulation.

impelled to respond to the chemical substances. Male dogs, for example, mark their territory by urinating on the boundaries. Primates signal sexual availability to potential mates through both the release of odors and the use of such visual signals as swollen, reddish genitals.

Interest in searching for human pheromones has grown since it was discovered that female rhesus monkeys secrete fatty acids called copulins, which seem to have an aphrodisiac effect on males. It appears, too, that human females vaginally secrete copulins, which may have some effect on sexual desire. Smelling copulins may stimulate the desire for sexual activity among some couples, although for other couples, sexual desire seems to be unaffected by copulins (Udry, 1998). Likewise, a purported human male pheromone has been reported to increase the frequency of sexual intercourse for some men (Cutler, Friedmann & McCoy, 1998).

It is interesting in this regard that most people in our culture believe that the secretory odors of bodily areas as diverse as the mouth, underarms, genitals, and feet are unpleasant or downright disgusting. Adolescents use the comment, "He sniffs bicycle seats," as an insult, implying that someone who would deliberately expose himself to such an odor is perverted. You too may think that an aversion to the odor of bodily secretions is natural. The deodorant industry spends millions of dollars attempting to convince us so. Young children, however, do not appear to be troubled by the smell of bodily secretions, and cross-cultural data suggest that not all adults characterize bodily odors as offensive. Thus, in all likelihood our response to such smells has a healthy dose of learning. Advertisers assure us that if we buy underarm and vaginal deodorants, we will be free of worries about these unpleasant and embarrassing smells. These products are unnecessary; regular bathing with soap and water is sufficient to eliminate old bacteria that produce strong odors. Furthermore, many vaginal deodorants on the market are harmful to the delicate genital tissues.

SIGHT

As with the sense of smell, the extent to which our sexual responses are affected by inborn versus learned reactions to what we see is not clear. We do know that what we consider visually attractive is heavily influenced by experience. What we do not know is whether humans as a species have any innate preferences for specific visual sights as erotic stimuli.

You may have noticed the swollen red genitals of some female primates at the zoo. Their genitals are most brightly colored when they are fertile and sexually receptive. This pattern of swollen red skin may signal the females' fertility and sexual receptivity to males, who typically approach from the rear to mate.

Evolutionary theorists have suggested that humans are inherently attracted by a clear complexion. This is seen as an indicator of general health and reproductive fitness.

Body symmetry, in which the body can be divided into similar halves (left and right half of the body, face, and so forth), also appears to be an important determinant of attractiveness and mate choice (Buss, 1999; Gangestad & Thornhill, 1997; Shackelford & Larsen, 1997). Because asymmetry has been associated with a wide range of illnesses and disabilities, evolutionary theorists think that symmetry reflects a robust physiology and high probability of being fertile. Presumably a preference for symmetrical features developed in small hunter-gatherer groups, which many anthropologists believe is where 99 percent of human evolution occurred.

What other features do humans find attractive? Attractiveness may be based, in part, on development of facial characteristics that appear to be relatively similar across cultures. High levels of testosterone in males beyond puberty lead to the growth of the lower face and jaw, and projection of the central face between the brow and bottom of the nose. Both chin length and chin width contribute to perceptions of male attractiveness. On average, males have bushier eyebrows set closer to the eyes, a more pronounced brow ridge, and sunken eyes. Males' noses and mouths are wider on average than is seen in the average female face, and the lower jaw is both wider and longer.

Relatively high levels of estrogen and lower androgen levels of the pubescent female lead to increased lip size. Victor Johnston and Juan Oliver-Rodriguez (1997) proposed that shorter-than-average lower face proportions and fuller-than-average lips in women can serve as indicators of fertility. But this is not the whole story. In keeping with our emphasis on sexual

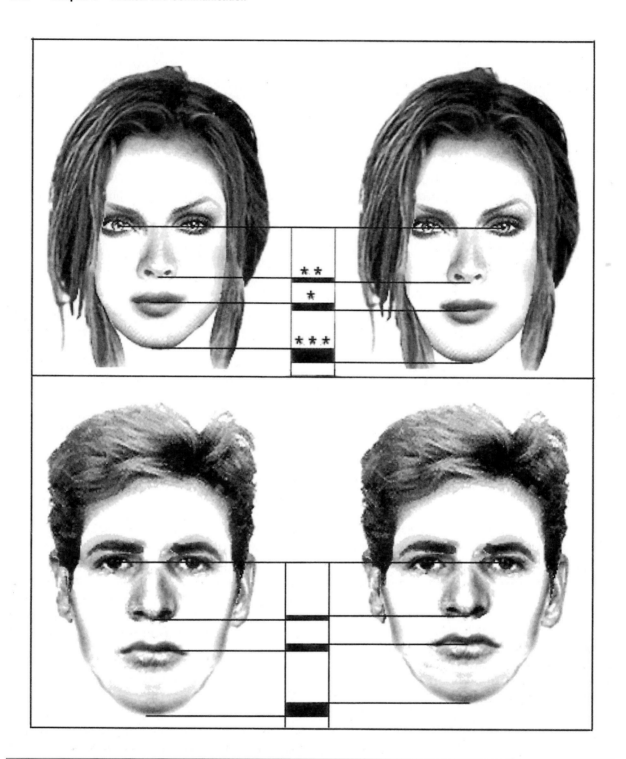

Figure 6.2   Characteristics of Facial Attractiveness

Women with full lips and shorter-than-average lower face proportions (panel a) are judged by people in many cultures to be more attractive than those with smaller lips or larger lower face proportions (panel b). Men with larger chins, measured in both width and length, (panel c) are judged more attractive than those with smaller chins (panel d). In addition, men typically have bushier eyebrows and a more pronounced brow ridge than women.

The smaller a female's waist is in relation to her hips, the more sexually attractive males perceive her to be.

interactions, these physical attributes can be modified by interpersonal characteristics. Looking at Figure 6.2, would your attraction be altered by modifiers "cruel" or "kind"? A whole host of psychosocial factors can alter our initial perceptions of what and who is attractive. Short-term mating strategies (having sex in a "one-night-stand" situation) may be heavily influenced by physical attraction, but long-term strategies (getting along over a long period of time) may be more influenced by a partner's personal characteristics.

Another indicator of reproductive fitness is a woman's waist-to-hip ratio (WHR). The lower the female WHR (waist is smaller than hips), the more attractive both men and women rate female figures (Singh, 1994). Females may place more importance on males' physical stamina, which might serve as an indication that a male may be a good provider. In an examination of what college students rate as important in judging male and female physical attractiveness, Stephen Franzoi and Mary Herzog (1987) found generally that men stressed those parts of women's bodies directly related to sexuality and women emphasized men's physical condition or en-

durance. These authors suggested that men are "socialized to perceive women as sexual providers, whereas women may be taught to perceive men as material providers" (p. 29). David Buss and his colleagues (1989) also found that across cultures, men placed more stress on a potential mate's physical attractiveness than did women, whereas women rated financial prospects, ambitiousness, and industriousness as more central in their choice of a mate than did men. Thus sight seems to play a more central role for men than for women in the evaluation of attractiveness.

HEARING

Touch, smell, and sight are the senses most strongly implicated in sexual arousal, but hearing can also come into play. The sensuous rhythms associated with certain types of music and poetry can raise our level of sexual arousal and thus are often associated with romance. We may also learn to respond sexually to the tone and rhythm of a person's voice or to the kind of language a partner uses. The particular terms or phrases that arouse us vary from one person to another. For example, some individuals are turned on by explicit sexual words, whereas others are excited by gentle, romantic whispers of endearment.

Generating sounds during sexual interaction is widespread among primates and humans, but little attention has been paid to its significance. Groans, moans, sighs, and screams and logical, directive vocalizations can provide information about pleasure, reactions to sexual stimulation, and orgasm (Wiederman, Allgeier, & Weiner, 1992). Many of these sounds can be highly arousing to men and women and may facilitate orgasm. Commercial telephone sex, produced mainly for the male market, relies exclusively on sounds and vocalization to arouse the listener sexually.

FANTASY AND SEXUAL AROUSAL

One of the most intriguing aspects of being human is the ability to fantasize. In our minds we can recall and refashion past experiences, anticipate and rehearse future events, and create unique scenes that are neither likely nor necessarily desired in reality. People may imagine receiving recognition for scholastic or athletic achievements or appreciation for their acts of generosity. They may imagine failing, perhaps on tests or in job interviews.

Similarly, sexual fantasies may involve either pleasant events, such as sexual or romantic interest from a person toward whom we are attracted, or unpleasant occurrences, such as rejection by a desired partner. Erotic fantasies can give both intensity and direction to sexual goals, and they may be a major influence on sexual identity and orientation. Many scholars believe that early adolescence is a critical period in the formation of sexual attitudes and behavior (Byrne, 1977; Money, 1991). Surveys on adolescent sexual fantasies indicate that they begin shortly after the onset of sexual arousal. For boys, this is around 11½ years and for girls about one to two years later (Gold & Gold, 1991; Leitenberg & Henning, 1995). At first, these fantasies tend to be about familiar persons, such as a teacher or an older acquaintance, or situations, such as dates. By late adolescence, most people have developed fantasies with well-defined, specific, erotic scripts that often involve daring, unconventional themes such as engaging in group sex, being caught or observed having sex, and having sex with strangers.

Gender differences are present from the beginning of sexual fantasy life. In general, males' fantasies contain visual images, physical characteristics, active and explicit sexual behavior, and interchangeable partners. Compared to males, females' fantasies are more concerned with emotional involvement, romance, committed partners in a caring relationship, and touching. Females' fantasies are also more complex and vivid (Alfonso, Allison, & Dunn, 1992; Gold & Gold, 1991; Leitenberg & Henning, 1995). Males tend to report more frequent sexual fantasies than do females. These gender differences in sexual fantasy are consistent with traditional societal definitions of gender roles in Western cultures.

Reality or Myth ❓

People can fantasize when they are engaged in nonsexual activities such as washing dishes or mowing the law. The majority of individuals report employing sexual fantasies while they are masturbating or involved in sexual interactions with others (Cado & Leitenberg, 1990; Leitenberg & Henning, 1995). For both men and women, sexual fantasies decrease in frequency but do not disappear as they advance from adolescence to old age (Purifoy, Grodsky, & Giambra, 1992).

Fantasies: Healthy or Deviant? Sigmund Freud theorized that sexual fantasies represent wishes or unfilled needs. Basically, he believed that sexual fantasies are signs of sexual frustration and emotional immaturity. In the beginning of the twentieth century, his perspective was reflected in the beliefs of many clinicians and psychoanalytic theorists.

More recently, researchers have emphasized the positive contributions of fantasy to sexual interaction (Heiman & LoPiccolo, 1988; Leitenberg & Henning, 1995). This change may be welcome news to the majority of North Americans who fantasize during masturbation and coitus and may experience guilt over their thoughts.

Guilt reactions to fantasies, particularly when they occur during intercourse, are related to beliefs that such fantasies are deviant and negatively related to sexual adjustment. In fact, Suzana Cado and Harold Leitenberg (1990) found that people who reported feeling most guilty about having fantasies during intercourse were more sexually dissatisfied and had more frequent sexual problems than did those individuals who felt less guilty.

Perhaps the reason that sexual fantasies have been regarded historically with fear and guilt lies in the Christian belief that thinking about something is the same as doing it. According to this view, thinking about having sex with someone other than a primary partner is as much a sin as actually having sex with the person. This lack of distinction between thought and behavior continues to color opinion about sexual fantasy. Much of the contemporary concern about pornography is based on the assumption that fantasies derived from erotic material are eventually put into action. Such a progression of thinking to behavior among those who view erotic material has not been demonstrated (see Chapter 20).

Fantasizing about socially unacceptable behavior, however, is not the same as engaging in it. We may have numerous fantasies in the course of a day that we never act out. Although relatively little research is available on the various functions that fantasy can fulfill, some of the more common of these functions can be identified.

The Functions of Fantasy. At different times and at different stages in a relationship, the same person can have fantasies for different reasons. Many of us have felt attraction to someone with whom we have been casually acquainted. In the desire to change the relationship from a platonic friendship to a romance, one or both people may imagine conversations and interactions leading to increasingly intimate emotional and physical contact. An example of such an extended fantasy appeared at the beginning of this chapter. These imaginary encounters permit us to rehearse ways of approaching the other person, consider his or her likely responses, and even make ourselves aware of the long-term consequences of the various behaviors that we envision ourselves trying. The utility of such rehearsal fantasies is that we can select the one that feels most comfortable and seems most likely to lead to the outcome we desire.

Fantasies and daydreams can be a source of entertainment, transporting us to exciting places and allowing us to mingle with celebrities and embark on exciting erotic adventures. Such fantasies can relieve the monotony of driving on a tedious stretch of road or sitting in a boring class or meeting. Sexual reveries also permit us to indulge in thinking about that we would not consider doing in reality, and to imagine

having partners who are unavailable to us. Alternatively, our fantasies can be built around the memories of previously rewarding sexual experiences.

Some fantasies involve imagined events that the person has no desire to experience in reality, such as sadomasochistic activities or rape. Such fantasies may be either solitary or shared with a partner. It is particularly important to realize that this kind of fantasy does not in and of itself indicate that the fantasizer actually wants to be the helpless victim of an aggressor. For example, Steven Gold, Bill Balzano, and Robin Stamey (1991) asked college women to report their sexual fantasies and describe their feelings following the fantasy. Those women who reported fantasies involving force, compared to those who did not, reported more fear, guilt, and disgust, and less happiness and less likelihood to act on their fantasy. Women with childhood sexual abuse experiences were also likely to report more fantasies containing images of force (Gold & Gold, 1991).

In contrast to the findings of Gold and his colleagues, college women who participated in research conducted by Donald Strassberg and Lisa Lockerd (1998) reporting force fantasies, compared to those who did not, were lower in sex guilt, higher in erotophilia, and also reported more nonforce fantasies and more sexual experience. Histories of being sexually abused or coerced were unrelated to the likelihood of having force fantasies. Given the conflicting findings in research on the relationship of force fantasies to women's sexual experiences and personality characteristics, we must conclude that we do not know the sources or causes of such fantasies.

As noted earlier, men and women in our culture are socialized to play different roles in their sexual interactions: women to play a passive sexual role and men to be sexual initiators. As the active partner, the man not only has the responsibility for selecting and carrying out a sexual script, but also regularly risks rejection. Moreover, the initiator of sexual interactions misses the pleasure of being pursued.

Accordingly, some women may have difficulty allowing themselves to be desirous and responsive unless they imagine themselves as unable to control a partner's advances. This fantasy is reflected in such common expressions as, "He swept me off my feet," and, "He hypnotized me with his eyes" (Cassell, 1984). Fantasies about being raped, tied down, or made love to while sleeping may also have the effect of releasing the fantasizer from responsibility for her (or his) own arousal (Cramer & Hewitt, 1998).

Finally, individuals may use fantasy either to improve or intensify sexual intimacy in a relationship of long duration. For example, in numerous studies a majority of the women reported having fantasies during sexual intercourse with their husbands or partners (Crepault, Abraham, Porto, & Couture, 1977; Lunde, Larsen, Fog, and Garde, 1991; Pelletier & Herold, 1988). They often employed these fantasies to enhance their sexual arousal and help to trigger orgasm (Davidson & Hoffman, 1986; Lunde et al., 1991). The use of fantasies for this purpose appears to be positively related to orgasmic capacity and sexual satisfaction for women, but this relationship is less clear in men (Alfonso et al., 1992; Arndt, Foehl, & Good, 1985; Purifoy et al., 1992). In other words, fantasies are not necessarily compensations for an unrewarding sexual existence. Such fantasies may be enjoyed without the knowledge of the other partner, or they may be shared and enacted with a partner, as described in Barbach and Levine's book *Shared Intimacies* (1980, pp. 85–86).

Once we were traveling out of the country and we decided to act out a fantasy of mine. I went down to the hotel bookstore and Murray came down and acted as if we were strangers and picked me up. We just started talking, asking each other our names and where we were from. Then he invited me back to the room and it was as if we hardly knew each other and were having sex for the first time.

We decided to act out our own fantasy, to make up our own film, so to speak. . . . It was weird because when we walked in the door, we felt like these other people. . . . Then it became obvious to both of us, these two new people, that there was an interest and a desire to continue from that point on. We undressed each other and explored each other's bodies and the whole time it was nonverbal. . . . We made love to each other, and held each other afterward. Then we just went to sleep. The next morning, we were back to ourselves.

These two fantasies, the first by a thirty-five-year-old woman and her husband, and the second by a thirty-four-year-old woman and her female lover, show how sharing fantasies can provide both partners with pleasure. But a word of caution is in order. When two people know each other well, are secure in their relationship, and have agreed that the sharing of fantasies is fun and a source of pleasure, mutual disclosures can enrich a relationship. The disclosure of fantasies under other conditions can evoke pain in a mate, who may conclude that the partner finds him or her unsatisfying or may come to feel inadequate in the face of a lover's desires that he or she can never fulfill. In deciding whether to share fantasies with a loved partner, consider your reasons as well as the potential effect of doing so.

▶ **Issues to Consider:** How would you react to the revelation from a steady sexual partner that he or she often has fantasies while you were having sex together?

ATTITUDES TOWARD SEXUALITY

Other sources of arousal, both positive and negative, involve our attitudes about sexuality. Our attitudes toward sexual activity may enhance, or be associated with difficulties in, relationships in both sexual and the nonsexual realms. Several measures have been developed to assess attitudes about sexuality, including the Sexual Opinion Survey and the Sex Guilt Scale.

Erotophilia and Erotophobia. To measure emotional responses to sexuality, Byrne and his colleagues (Byrne, Fisher, Lamberth, & Mitchell, 1974) developed the twenty-one-item Sexual Opinion Survey (SOS). Responses to the survey can range from primarily negative (when a respondent is **erotophobic**) to primarily positive (when a respondent is **erotophilic**). Items in the survey include the following:

erotophobic—Having a negative emotional response to sexual feelings and experiences.
erotophilic—Having a positive emotional response to sexual feelings and experiences.

The following statements are a sample of items from Mosher's (1988) revised measure of sex guilt. Respondents are instructed to rate each item on a 7-point scale from 0 (not at all true) to 6 (extremely true).

Masturbation

1. is wrong and will ruin you.
2. helps you feel eased and relaxed.

Sex relations before marriage

3. should be permitted.
4. are wrong and immoral.

When I have sexual desires

5. I enjoy them like all healthy human beings.
6. I fight them, for I must have complete control of my body.

In my childhood, sex play

7. was considered immature and ridiculous.
8. was indulged in.

Unusual sex practices

9. are awful and unthinkable.
10. are all right if both partners agree.

"Swimming in the nude with a member of the opposite sex would be an exciting experience" (positive); "If people knew that I was interested in oral sex, I would be embarrassed" (negative); "Thoughts that I may have homosexual tendencies would not worry me at all" (positive). Erotophilia-erotophobia is thought to be learned in childhood and adolescence through experiences associating sexual cues with positive or negative emotional states.

In most studies females have tended to be more erotophobic than are males. This gender difference may stem from females' greater exposure to negative messages about sexuality. As might be expected, erotophobic students reported more parental strictness about sex than did erotophilic students. Compared to erotophilic parents, erotophobic parents reported having given their children less information about sex. And the college students' early experiences appear to be related to differences in their sexual and contraceptive behaviors. Erotophilic college students reported more past sexual experience, more frequent masturbation, and more sexual partners than did erotophobic students. Furthermore, use of contraception was both more common and more consistent among erotophilic students than among their erotophobic peers. SOS scores have been shown to be predictive of a wide range of sexual attitudes and behaviors across a number of different cultures, including India and Hong Kong.

A number of other behaviors are associated with erotophilia-erotophobia. Erotophilic people, compared to those who are erotophobic, have more positive reactions to erotic material, think about sex more often, draw more explicit and more detailed nude figures, and create more explicit and positively toned erotic fantasies (Byrne & Schulte, 1990; Garcia & Carrigan, 1998).

Sex Guilt.   Among the emotions that can become associated with sexual arousal is guilt. **Sex guilt is the expectation that we will feel badly if we violate or think we will violate standards of proper sexual conduct** (Mosher, 1966, 1988). Psychologist Donald Mosher constructed a measure of sex guilt in 1966 that was revised in 1988. The measure has been widely used in the investigation of various sexual issues. For a sample of the items in the revised Mosher Guilt Inventory, see "Research Spotlight: Do You Feel Guilty About Your Sexual Feelings?" Mosher assumed that individuals who feel guilty about their sexual responses were scolded and punished during their childhood for interest in sexual matters to a greater extent than were people who respond to their sexual feelings with acceptance and enjoyment.

For example, imagine a three-year-old girl playing idly with her vulva while watching *Sesame Street* on television. Her parents might scold her, slap her hand, or order her to stop. One isolated incident would probably have little effect on the extent to which the child will associate guilt and anxiety with sexuality in her adulthood. The parent who spanks a three-year-old for casually playing with herself,

sex guilt—Sense of guilt resulting from the violation of personal standards of proper sexual behavior.

Although many parents take a dim view of their toddlers' self-exploration and genital stimulation, this mother grins while watching her son playing with his genitals.

however, is probably also likely to punish the girl when she is older for other activities that the parent interprets as sexual—for example, playing doctor, asking questions about genitals, or telling sexual jokes. Over time the child absorbs the message that sex is bad, dirty, and sinful and the person who shows too much curiosity or interest about sexuality is equally bad, dirty, and sinful.

To protect children from the unwanted consequences of sexual intimacy, such as unintended pregnancy and sexually transmitted diseases (STDs), parents may discourage children from having anything to do with sex. The problem with such discouragement is that long-term association of sex with anxiety and guilt is linked to the development of certain undesirable characteristics. Indeed, several studies have found that people high in sex guilt operate at lower levels of moral reasoning than do people with less sex guilt. For example, Meg Gerrard (Gerrard & Gibbons, 1982) studied the relationship among sexual experience (not necessarily intercourse), sex guilt, and sexual moral reasoning. The findings indicated

that experience is important in the development of sexual morality and that people high in sex guilt tend to avoid sexual experience, thus hindering their development of sexual morality. Based on research with female college students, Gerrard (1987) concluded that although sex guilt did not necessarily keep women from having sexual intercourse, it did appear to inhibit the use of effective contraceptives. *Reality or Myth* ⬛

Extensive research on sex guilt after childhood demonstrates the influence of conditioned or learned responses on our capacity for sexual arousal and pleasure. Dennis Cannon (1987, p. 9) summarized the research on the relationship of sex guilt to other variables. Based on these studies, he characterized a "sexually guilty" person as

devout and constant in religious beliefs, who subscribes to higher authority, believes in myths about sex, may use denial in dealing with feelings about sex, is less sexually active, is more offended and disgusted by explicit sexual material, less tolerant of variations in others' sexual behavior, at a lower level in Kohlberg's stages of moral reasoning, and who holds traditional views of what males' and females' sexual roles should be.

Rather than rearing offspring to feel guilty about sex, parents might emphasize effective communication skills and the importance of open discussion about sexual functions and feelings. Building children's sexual knowledge and confidence will more adequately prepare them for dealing with their emerging sexual feelings in a healthy manner than will instilling guilt.

Studies of sex guilt have consistently yielded the finding that females score higher on measures of sex guilt than do males. Is there something in the biology of females that makes them more susceptible than males to anxiety and guilt over sexuality? Probably not. The explanation probably lies in the fact that daughters, not sons, can become pregnant, and so parents may be more restrictive in training their daughters than in training their sons.

GENDER DIFFERENCES AND SIMILARITIES IN AROUSAL

As we saw in Chapter 5, females are less likely to engage in self-stimulation than are males, and they generally respond more slowly during sexual interaction. An examination of research on the conditions under which males and females respond to erotic material suggests that different cultural expectations for men and women contribute heavily to the observed gender differences.

A great deal of survey research has supported the assumption that men are more interested in, and more responsive to, sexual cues than are women. However, experimental studies conducted during the past decade have indicated that men and women respond similarly to erotic stimuli such as sexually explicit stories and pictures and X-rated films (see Chapter 20). Why does survey research find gender differences that experimental research does not?

In the survey method, men and women are asked to report their past and present levels of arousal to erotic material, how often they seek or purchase such material, and so forth. In our culture, interest in sex is considered more appropriate for men than for women. Thus in responding to surveys, men may ac-

curately estimate, or even overestimate, their interest in erotica, whereas women may underestimate theirs in an attempt to present themselves in a socially desirable light.

How have the experimental studies differed from the survey methods? Volunteers for experimental research on erotica are exposed to sexual stimuli. Their responses are then measured through self-reports, physiological recordings of their genital responses, or both. These physiological measures generally demonstrate little or no difference in arousal between men and women when they are exposed to erotica. As William Fisher (1983) pointed out, compared with men, women have been trained over a long period of time to avoid erotic material and show less interest in sex. But when men and women are exposed to sexual stimuli, women are as capable of arousal as are men.

The differences produced by the two research approaches are exemplified by Julia Heiman's (1975) classic study of responses to erotic audiotapes. She found that males and females did not differ when their arousal was assessed by physiologic measures. When self-reports of arousal were compared, however, several male-female differences emerged. First, on average, males reported greater arousal than did females. Second, whereas the arousal reported by males matched the arousal indicated by their physiologic recordings, females' reports did not always reflect the physiologically measured arousal. In fact, in about half the cases, females reported either no arousal at all or less arousal than was indicated by the devices attached to their bodies.

Why did many of the women in Heiman's study fail to perceive their own arousal? When we first read her study, that question intrigued us, so we asked students in our human sexuality classes to recall the first time they could remember having the kind of feeling that they would now label as sexual arousal. We asked them to write down their thoughts on the reasons for their physical responses at that time.

In general, the men attributed their erections, preejaculatory emissions, and so forth to having been aroused either by their thoughts about, or their interaction with, another person. About half the women drew similar conclusions about their vaginal lubrication and "tingling" genital feelings. But the other half of the women gave various other explanations. Many thought the vaginal lubrication had been just another variation in their menstrual cycle that they had not noticed before. Several women attributed the lubrication to a "clear period," and a sizable number reported that they thought they might have had a vaginal infection. One woman wrote that she had asked her mother whether she should see a doctor or get some medicine.

Biological differences in the extent to which physical changes associated with sexual arousal are readily observable may also account for some of these gender differences. Although arousal produces vasocongestion (blood engorgement) in both men and women, women are sometimes unaware of the lubrication of their vaginas, whereas erect penises call attention to themselves.

This biological difference in the effects of vasocongestion is enhanced, in turn, by cultural expectations. Men are encouraged to be sexually active, whereas women are generally discouraged from seeking sexual stimulation and satisfaction. Men are trained to be sexual responders, and women learn to be sexual stimuli. In summary, anatomical differences and learned psychological differences between males and females may interact to produce differences in the tendencies of men and women to report arousal. When physiological arousal is directly measured, however, the gender differences are reduced or eliminated (Heiman, 1977). Some stereotypes about gender differences in sexual behavior may be less accurate than is commonly believed.

Communication About Sexuality

Communicating sexual feelings to a potential or actual partner requires care and practice. For people who have learned to associate their sexual feelings with shame or sin, sharing sexual feelings can also take courage. In this section, we discuss socialization practices that increase or reduce the likelihood that we can communicate our sexual feelings effectively. Traditionally, males and females are given different messages about discussing their feelings, and we examine how that may relate to communication. Finally, we focus on methods of improving interpersonal communication, especially relating to sexual issues.

SOCIALIZATION FOR COMMUNICATING ABOUT SEX

We are constantly bombarded with the message that sexiness is an attractive quality; indeed, media stars get a great deal of money and adulation for projecting sexy images. But just like the rest of us, stars have private lives in which they need to communicate and negotiate their desires with their partners. Unfortunately, many of us—private citizens and media stars alike—are given little training in communication skills.

Few members of our culture are given labels for sexual feelings during infancy, childhood, or adolescence. Furthermore, if we fondled our genitals during infancy and childhood, most of us not only learned no label for that activity but also may have

been punished for our behavior. If, instead, we were taught sexual labels and encouraged to communicate our feelings, such training might reduce or prevent sexual problems later in life.

Although students enrolled in a human sexuality course tend to be more liberal and knowledgeable about sex—even when they begin the class—than those enrolled in other classes at the same academic level, these well-informed students typically received little of their information from their parents. For example, only 14 percent of students enrolled in our sexuality course in 1994 had heard the word *clitoris* from their mothers; when we surveyed the class again in 1998, the figure had dropped to less than 1 percent. Only 3 percent (all men) had heard the word from their fathers in 1994 (less than half of 1 percent in 1998). A slight majority of students had heard the word *vagina* from their mothers (52 percent in 1994; 54 percent in 1998). But only 14 percent of the students reported hearing the word *vagina* from their fathers in both years. The word *penis* had been used by 20 percent of the students' mothers and 55 percent of their fathers in 1994, and by 57 percent of the mothers and 23 percent of the fathers in 1998.

This discrepancy in the likelihood of hearing the word *clitoris* versus the words *penis* and *vagina* from parents might be partially explained by the fact that the penis can be seen more easily than the clitoris.

TABLE 6.2   Sources of Information About Sexuality

Source of Information	Reproductive Aspects (percent)		Passionate Aspects (percent)	
	1994	*1998*	*1994*	*1998*
Mother/stepmother	22	44	0	29
Father/stepfather	1	7	0	3
Sibling	1	7	5	5
Friends	7	26	25	46
Boyfriend/girlfriend	0	8	22	39
Books/magazines	11	22	32	22
School	47	50	11	50
Doctor	3	1	0	1
Church/synagogue	0	1	0	1

Use of Term*	Mother to Daughter	Mother to Son	Father to Daughter	Father to Son
Vagina	10 (3–16)	10 (1–16)	11 (4–18)	10 (1–15)
Penis	10 (3–18)	11 (1–16)	12 (4–18)	8 (1–14)
Clitoris	14 (10–17)	11 (10–12)	16 (16)	12 (8–18)
Erection	12 (8–18)	11 (4–15)	14 (10–18)	10 (4–16)
Vaginal lubrication (getting wet)	14 (8–17)	12 (12)	16 (16)	13 (8–18)
Orgasm	14 (10–19)	12 (8–16)	14 (8–18)	11 (8–16)
Ejaculation	13 (8–18)	11 (8–16)	14 (12–18)	12 (8–16)

*The first number is the average age at which students first heard the term; the set of numbers within the parentheses is the range of ages.

Another possible explanation is that every other organ of the body can be described as having some separate, societally approved function. To describe clitoral function, however, parents or teachers must introduce the concept of sexual arousal and pleasure. Other parts of the body (nose, mouth, penis, rectum, vagina) may also be associated with sexual pleasure, but parents can provide an explanation of what those organs do without ever mentioning sexual pleasure. Parental reluctance to acknowledge the pleasurable sensations that many children experience may explain parents' failure to discuss the clitoris when describing sexual anatomy to children.

Not only do we often ignore the function of the clitoris, but we also have few ways of referring to it. Although we have many slang terms for the penis (*prick, bone, dick, tool, peter, schlong, dong, salami,* and *thing,* to name just a few), there are few slang terms for the clitoris beyond the shortened form, *clit.* A colleague of ours pointed out two synonyms, *pearl* and *hooded lady,* that had been used in erotic litera-

ture (Commons, 1984). However, in our search among students, friends, and colleagues, we have encountered only three other slang terms for the clitoris that are used in actual speech: *joy button, magic button,* and (ironically, given that the clitoris is part of the female anatomy) *little man in a boat.* There is a similar discrepancy in the number of slang terms for male ejaculate and vaginal lubrication. How many expressions have you heard for each?

We have also asked our students to indicate their most accurate source of information regarding the reproductive and passionate aspects of sexuality. Opponents of public school sex education assert that children should receive information about sexuality from their families rather than from teachers. As Table 6.2 shows, however, fewer than half the students we asked in our large (more than 200 students each semester) sexuality course perceived their parents as providing accurate information about the reproductive aspects of sex and even fewer about its passionate aspects. These findings are consistent with other research in the past two decades. **Reality or Myth**

> ▶ **Issues to Consider:** Where did you first get information about the reproductive aspects of sexuality? The passionate aspects of sexuality?

Two aspects of Table 6.2 (on page 137) are particularly noteworthy. First, in most cases, there has been a considerable jump in the percentage of students rating the various sources of information as accurate in the four years since 1994. Apparently students are locating more sources of information—before entrance in college—that they perceive as accurate sources. Notice the large jump in the rating of the accuracy of schools in providing information about the passionate aspects of sexuality between 1994 and 1998.

Second, very small percentages of parents are reportedly providing their children with a sexual vocabulary in 1998. Note, for example, that only one mother ever used the phrase "vaginal lubrication" or "getting wet" to her son. Only two fathers used that phrase with their daughters, and only two used the word *clitoris*. However inspection of Table 6.2 (on page 137) shows that of those parents who do provide sexual terms to their offspring, the majority do so before their children, on average, were likely to have reached puberty. Of the 28 comparisons, 18 provided sexual vocabulary before age 13; in the other 10 comparisons, vocabulary was provided at age 13 or older, but in general, it was not much later than that. Children need to be given accurate information and a sexual vocabulary before they begin to become sexually intimate with others so that they can communicate with one another about the risks and benefits of potential sexual activity.

What if our parents did acknowledge that we have sexual feelings and that there are words—labels—for these feelings: *arousal, interest, curiosity?* We might then be given permission to talk freely about our own sexual feelings. But that parental acknowledgment rarely occurs in most cultures. So we enter adolescence with an inadequate vocabulary and, in most cases, without an environment conducive to open discussions with our parents. Thus, the people who presumably care about us the most avoid giving us the opportunity to rehearse later discussion of sexual feelings.

Parents who avoid discussion of sexual topics may do so because of fears that such conversations will encourage their offspring to engage in early sexual exploration. To examine the relationship of parental attitudes, extent of family communication, and adolescent sexual activity, Terri Fisher (1993) conducted a series of studies that gathered data from adolescents and their parents. She found that among parents with relatively permissive attitudes, family discussions of sex were related to a greater likelihood of females' engaging in premarital sexual behavior. One could argue that permissive families produce more sexually active adolescents. It is also plausible, however, that sexually active young women find it easier to discuss their sexual experiences and feelings with relatively permissive parents than do sexually active women with more restrictive parents. Fisher also found that males who had discussed sex with their parents, and males with sexually liberal parents, had more accurate sexual information and were more likely to report using contraception.

GENDER DIFFERENCES IN THE COMMUNICATION OF FEELINGS

In addition to overall societal restrictions on parent-child communication about sex, there are differences in the extent to which it is acceptable for males versus females to talk about feelings versus sex. In most families, it is more acceptable for girls than for boys to talk about their positive or depressed emotions (the so-called tender feelings), and more acceptable for boys than for girls to talk about hostile feelings, such as anger and aggression, and sexual interests.

We are not suggesting that these differences in communication styles are inherent aspects of being male or female. Instead, the tendency in our culture for males to suppress their feelings or to give only minimal information about their emotions, and for females to provide more detail than males about their fears and hopes, presumably stems from the differences in training to become a "man" or a "woman." When people subsequently attempt to establish heterosexual relationships, these gender differences in the content and style of communication of feelings may magnify the difficulty of resolving the inevitable problems that emerge in ongoing relationships (Michaud & Warner, 1997; Tannen, 1990).

When the focus is on *sexual* feelings, the gender-role expectations are different. A stereotypic part of being masculine in our culture involves intense interest in obtaining sexual experience, for example, "scoring." In contrast, many adolescent women fear that communicating about their sexual desires in general, or their preferences for specific kinds of stimulation in particular, signals that they are immoral, "dirty," or "experienced." Another concern that women may have is that sexual requests may threaten their partners' feelings of prowess. Regardless of the source, such reluctance to communicate may result in sexual dysfunctions or date rape (see Chapters 15 and 19).

OVERCOMING BARRIERS TO INTERPERSONAL COMMUNICATION

During infancy and early childhood, we are provided with labels to help us distinguish and communicate our desires for hunger versus holding. Many of us, however, are not given labels to help us distinguish, as we advance into adolescence and adulthood, between desire for cuddling and desire for coitus or for cunnilingus or fellatio (oral stimulation of the female or male genitals, respectively). Negative cultural connotations associated with desire for various forms of sexual stimulation, or the fear that specific sexual requests will upset a partner, can make it difficult for us to say to a mate, "You know, I'd really enjoy giving [or receiving] oral sex," or to say, "Right now, I'm feeling very tense about my final exams, and I'd just like you to cuddle me."

How can we improve interpersonal communication about our personal and sexual feelings? What can we do to increase the likelihood of honestly relating our feelings to potential or actual partners? At the outset, we need a sexual vocabulary and permission to use it from those whom we admire: our parents, teachers, peers, and partners. After we have a sexual vocabulary and feel free to use it, we need to communicate, verbally and nonverbally, what we want from potential or actual sexual partners.

Even with the best intentions, it is sometimes difficult for a man to interpret a woman's signals, and vice versa, in the complex world of sexual interactions. Men's difficulties in evaluating a woman's desire may be magnified by the fact that in our soci-

ety, it is still considered the man's prerogative to initiate sexual intimacy, whereas women are expected to be the "gatekeepers"—that is, to take responsibility for setting the limits on the extent of sexual intimacy. In several surveys of students' misperceptions in natural settings, 72 percent of women and 60 percent of men reported having had their friendliness misperceived as a sexual invitation (Abbey, 1987). Misperceptions were most common by casual friends or acquaintances and less common by strangers or close friends. When students in Antonia Abbey's (1987) surveys were asked to describe their experiences with misperceiving the intentions of potential partners, men and women were equally likely to report having misperceived someone else's friendliness as indicating sexual interest (40 percent). For example, one woman wrote: "Since I liked him I took everything he did as a hint, and he was very attentive and nice to me. However, the next day he acted as though he had never seen me before in my life" (pp. 189–190).

▶ **Issues to Consider:** What are the consequences of men's traditional role in Western culture as the initiators of sexual intimacy? What social, cultural, religious, and biological factors might account for this role. What conditions might change it?

We have noted in Chapter 1 that women appear to select men and signal their interest in getting to know them better. A signaling of interest is simply that; it does not necessarily mean that a woman is ready to have sex with the man. Women appear to be signaling a desire to get to know the man better and then deciding whether they want to develop a relationship with him; that is, women may perceive the process as involving a series of steps, with each decision dependent on previous interactions.

Misperceptions may occur because the behaviors that are misperceived can have ambiguous meanings. You may engage in a smiling conversation with someone and leave a party with him or her because you feel sexually attracted or merely because you are interested in the topic being discussed and are tired of the smoke and noise at the party.

Thus, difficulties may arise in an individual's interpretations of others' intentions and behavior. Because of women's socialization in our culture, and perhaps because of the gender differences in mate-selection strategies, most women want to spend some time getting to know a man before deciding whether to become sexually intimate. Even if a woman desires intimacy fairly early in the relationship, she risks the stereotype that a woman who does so is "easy" or has "rocking-chair heels" (that is, if a man pushes her slightly, she will immediately lie down for him). *Reality or Myth* ?

If the woman is interested in further interaction with the man, she is confronted with a dilemma: She needs to communicate interest but probably wants to avoid giving him the impression that she is sexually available to anyone who approaches her. If the man is interested in pursuing the relationship, he faces the problem of deciphering her intentions.

The man's difficulties in trying to infer the woman's intentions are also increased by the woman's use of what is known as the "token no"—initially saying no when she is actually willing to become sexually intimate. In one study (Muehlenhard & Hollabaugh, 1988), almost 40 percent of the college women reported at least one instance of refusing sexual intercourse when they wanted to have coitus.

Women's explanations for saying no when they really meant yes are instructive. Charlene Muehlenhard and L. C. Hollabaugh (1988) isolated three major categories of reasons for the use of the token no. The first involved "practical reasons," which included the fear of appearing promiscuous, the belief that sex was inappropriate in the relationship (because he was a boss or coworker or because she or the man was involved in another relationship), uncertainty about the potential partner's feelings for her, fear of getting pregnant or contracting a sexually transmitted disease, and inappropriateness of the physical setting for a sexual interaction. The second category, labeled "inhibition-related reasons," included emotional, religious, and moral reasons; the woman's fear of physical discomfort; and self-consciousness or embarrassment about her body. The third category, "manipulative reasons," included game playing, anger with the partner, and a desire to be in control.

Individual differences among the women were also related to the probability of their use of the token no. Those who say no when they want to say yes to sex are at intermediate levels of traditionalism in their sexual attitudes. They are more likely to believe that token resistance is a common behavior among women, that male-female relationships are adversarial, that it is acceptable for men to use physical force in obtaining sex, and that women enjoy sex more when men resort to force in sexual relationships. These findings do not sit well with those who endorse egalitarian relationships between men and women or between sexual partners of the same gender, but use of the token no—at least on one occasion—is common among heterosexual women and men (Muehlenhard & Rodgers, 1998; O'Sullivan & Allgeier, 1994; Shotland & Hunter, 1995).

INFORMED CONSENT AND SEXUAL INTIMACY

Clearly, men and women have difficulty communicating their sexual intentions to each other, in part because of their fear of what their potential partners will think about them (for example, a man's worries that he will not be seen as masculine if he refuses an opportunity for sex, or a woman's apprehensions that she will be perceived as easy if she agrees to have sex too readily). In this section we propose what should not be a radical model of communication but nevertheless is, given contemporary stereotypes about sexual communication. We recommend that people be direct with each other about what they want. This directness should apply equally to the initial phases of courtship and specific acts and timing after two people have become sexually involved. In Chapter 3 we introduced the concept of informed consent in the context of research. This concept is also useful for couples who are negotiating their sexual relationships.

The process of obtaining informed consent for sexual intimacy involves several steps. Until you have tried the technique, you may react to what follows with, "Aargh! This will ruin the spontaneity and turn off my partner." Nothing could be further from the truth. Regardless of your ultimate decision to have or to avoid sex with a potential partner, the *process* of engaging in informed consent is arousing and fun. "Highlight: Negotiating a Sexual Relationship" (on page 142) sets out a sample interaction.

Here are some of the issues to consider in seeking to obtain informed consent for sexual intimacy:

1. What are the conditions under which you and your partner are comfortable with increased sexual intimacy? How well do you believe you should know each other? What level of relationship is needed before you become sexually intimate? Mutual attraction? Dating each other exclusively? Engagement? Marriage? Two partners may view each other as an "S.O.," but "S.O." may stand for "significant other" to one and "sex object" to the other. This is not to suggest that sex is appropriate only under conditions of strong commitment. Instead, it is important that each person understand his or her own motivations for the sexual interaction.

2. If you do not wish to conceive a child, how will you reduce the likelihood of conception, especially given that no contraceptive is 100 percent effective? What will you do in the event that pregnancy occurs?

3. How will you reduce the risk of contracting or transmitting a sexually transmitted disease? If one or both of you have had sexual partners in the past, have you been screened to confirm that you do not currently have an STD? Testing is important because STDs do not necessarily have symptoms in their early, most treatable stages; one of you may have an STD without being aware of it (see Chapter 16).

4. What are your beliefs about sexual exclusivity? Two people may assume that if they become sexually intimate with each other, they will not engage in sex with others until or unless the current relationship ends. Based on responses from our students, many do not even discuss the issue. If both assume that they will be sexually exclusive, fine. But if that is not the case, then both people need to be aware of their potential differences in beliefs about exclusivity before making a decision to become intimate.

Several other issues come into play in the process of obtaining informed consent, and these are discussed throughout the text. The main point is that it is important to discuss your intentions, feelings, and motives with a partner *before* becoming physically intimate. Such discussions will reduce the likelihood of disappointment and feelings of degradation or abuse.

In a couple's discussions prior to or after sexual intimacy, a general format taught in communication skills classes can be helpful in clarifying feelings, resolving problems, and preventing arguments. The format centers on taking responsibility for your own feelings and behavior and realizing that neither you nor your partner can read minds. At the practical level, people who are skilled in this method of communicating use what are called "I feel" messages and then describe the other person's behavior, while avoiding the attribution of motives or intentions to the other person.

For example, assume that Kim and Chris are lovers but have not discussed the issue of sexual exclusivity. Kim is upset with Chris after discovering that Chris is having sexual relations with someone else. Kim assumed that they would have sex only with each other. In the attempt to resolve the issue, Kim has the following discussion with Chris:

KIM: Chris, I'm feeling really hurt that you had sex with Pat. I thought that when we got involved, you wouldn't be intimate with anyone else. [Note that Kim avoids words like *cheating* and makes no attributions about Chris's motives—for example, "You don't love me."]

CHRIS: Oh, Kim, I'm sorry that you're feeling hurt. Because we never discussed it, I didn't realize that you assumed we'd see only each other. I guess we'd better talk about this; I really care about you. [Note that Chris does not put Kim down or make accusations about control issues.]

KIM: I really care about you, too, and I want us to give our relationship a chance to see where it goes. If you want to see other people, that's your right, but I want us to date just each other. [Note that while Kim acknowledges Chris's freedom to make choices, Kim's own desires are also valued.]

Chris may have assumed all along that Kim was also seeing other people. Chris may in fact be quite happy to agree to a monogamous relationship with Kim. Alternatively, Chris may not want to be confined to one person at this point. In any event, if each partner can communicate using "I feel . . . about your behavior, and I want . . ." without making attributions about the other's motives, the two of them are more likely to be able to resolve differences or,

Negotiating a Sexual Relationship

Tom and Becky were introduced to each other by a mutual friend at a party about two weeks before the beginning of summer vacation. They talked for about half an hour, but Becky said that she needed to leave the party early because she had to finish a term paper. Tom asked if he could give her a call, and Becky gave him her telephone number.

They went out several times before the end of the semester and discovered that they had a lot in common, including the fact that they were both enrolled in the same class on human sexuality. One evening they stayed up very late talking at Becky's place. It turned out that they each had relationships with partners back in their home towns, and despite their mutual attraction, they avoided any physical intimacy. But when Tom got ready to go, Becky walked him to the door, and they embraced. Both acknowledged that they were sorry that vacation was beginning after finals the next week because their homes were several hundred miles apart and both had summer jobs back home.

Over the summer they had several long-distance telephone conversations, and both eagerly anticipated their reunion in the fall. As soon as Tom arrived back at college, he called Becky to invite her out. She agreed, and he picked her up late that afternoon. They greeted each other rather shyly and went to a local bar. They each ordered a beer and compared notes on their course schedules.

BECKY: You know, it's hard to believe that we knew each other for only two weeks before summer break.

TOM: Yeah, I've really been looking forward to seeing you again. What happened with your boyfriend back home?

BECKY: Uh, well, I went out with him off and on, but I don't have the same feelings about him. We just don't seem to have that much in common anymore.

TOM: I have to admit that I'm glad to hear that. I saw my girlfriend just before I came back to college to break off my relationship with her. After meeting you, she just didn't seem that interesting.

BECKY (smiling and reaching out for his hand): Well, it's been an eventful summer for both of us!

TOM (grinning): Yeah! I think we should go out for dinner to celebrate. (They go to a Mexican restaurant, order dinner, and then sit just gazing at each other.)

TOM: Boy, you know I'd just like to take you back to my apartment right now. My roommate won't be coming in for a few days yet.

conversely, to discover that their desires are so different that they perhaps should not continue their intimate relationship.

THE MANAGEMENT OF SEXUAL FEELINGS AND BEHAVIOR

Regardless of whether we are single or involved in an ongoing, committed relationship, most of us feel sexually attracted to different people throughout our lives. Attraction and sexual arousal are feelings, and as such they do not necessarily require any action or guilt. If we decide not to act on them, we can simply enjoy them. These feelings can be intense, however,

and if we are moved to express them, we are wise to rely on rationality in our decision making.

Women, to a greater extent than men, have been socialized to be sexual gatekeepers. Societal expectations may be such a source of emotional conflict that a woman will justify an affair with the claim that she could not resist her feelings of attraction to a particular person. The tendency to attribute one's behavior to a force greater than one's will—"I just couldn't help myself"—is not unique to women. Both men and women indulge in rationalizations of helplessness in a sexual encounter, such as "I got carried away," "I was drunk," "I thought I was in love," "I thought she/he

BECKY: I'd love to go, but I think we should talk about some things over dinner. Sounds like you aren't involved with anyone right now.

TOM (with a big smile): Well, present company excepted.

BECKY (smiling and tracing a circle on the back of Tom's hand): Well, yeah. Uhhh . . . did you and your old girlfriend get together this summer? I mean . . .

TOM: You mean did we have sex?

BECKY: Well, yeah.

TOM: No. I guess after I met you, I just wasn't interested in her or anyone else.

BECKY: Well, gee. The same thing happened to me. We kissed and stuff, but I didn't feel about him the way I used to, so I didn't want to make love. Also, the previous summer I'd been on the pill, but I went off it last fall and haven't started taking it again.

TOM: Yeah, I was wondering about that—birth control, I mean.

BECKY: You know, after taking that sex class, I wonder if condoms might be better? The prof said we should all get ourselves tested for STDs. I've had only two partners, Bob and then—real briefly (she smiled)—a guy I went to senior prom with in high school, and I don't think I've got anything. But I don't know how many people you've been with.

TOM: Uh, I . . . fooled around quite a bit in high school until I got involved with my girlfriend, but I haven't been with anyone since her. But if you want to go get tested, we could go together. The prof said that Planned Parenthood gives screening tests for both guys and girls.

BECKY (gazing at Tom): Yeah, that would be good. But I'd also like to go back to your apartment as long as your roommate isn't in yet. Do you have any condoms? I don't think I want to rely on them for long for contraception, but . . . well, just in case we get carried away.

TOM (with a big grin on his face): No, I don't have any, but there's a drugstore down the street from my place. How about we go shopping after dinner? We don't have to use them tonight if we decide we aren't ready to make love yet, but it might take awhile to get an appointment at PP and then get the results.

BECKY: Hey, I like shopping! (She smiles warmly at him.)

Their dinners arrived. They weren't particularly hungry at that point—for dinner, anyway—so they ate a bit and then asked their server to bring them boxes so that they could take their dinner home with them. They went shopping, then back to Tom's apartment. Later that evening they reheated their food and had a midnight snack. They congratulated each other on their responsible behavior, and they had every right to be proud of themselves!

loved me." The fact is that humans generally *are* capable of controlling their behavior. People who truly cannot help acting on "irresistible" impulses tend to end up in institutions—jails or mental hospitals.

In the next section we focus on people who are committed to a primary relationship but feel attraction to someone outside the relationship. It is wise for people who feel commitment to a primary relationship, marital or otherwise, to reach agreements on how they will handle the (inevitable) attraction to people who are outside the relationship. Keep in mind that there is no guarantee that either partner will be able to live up to any agreement.

HONORING AGREEMENTS

Regardless of what agreements you and your partner make, there will be times when you feel sexual arousal toward someone outside your primary relationship. Let us assume that the feelings you experience are ones that you believe you should not actualize (express behaviorally) with the other person. The trick is to give yourself time to think about the strong attraction you feel and what you are comfortable doing and not doing about it. That is not always easy; a chance meeting, a long-term friendship, or an effective working relationship with a classmate or a colleague can suddenly (sometimes it seems as if it takes only a few seconds) turn into a potential romance. There you are, minding your own business, having a conversation with a person whom we will call Tracy. All of a sudden, you see Tracy differently. You may start shaking or perspiring, and you may wonder what is wrong. The situation can be particularly difficult if the shift in feelings is reciprocal, that is, if Tracy also sees you in a new light. What do you do?

First, get away from Tracy as quickly as you can to give yourself time to think. Then try to decide whether increased involvement with Tracy is consistent with, or a violation of, your agreement with your primary partner. If an affair with Tracy would be acceptable in the context of your agreements with your partner, and if you feel comfortable with your partner and see Tracy as primarily a supplement rather than as a potential replacement, then, provided that you and Tracy are each aware of the other's motives and goals, an affair might be mutually satisfying.

If you decide that you are not going to get involved in an affair with Tracy, with whom you already have a friendship, what do you do about your feelings of sexual arousal? You can enjoy the feelings and fantasies, but your behavior must be consistent with your decision rather than with your fantasies. From a practical standpoint, here are three guide-

lines that you might apply to your situation with Tracy:

1. Avoid any location (your apartments, a hotel room, a classroom) where only the two of you will be present.
2. Avoid drinking alcohol or using other intoxicants when you are with Tracy.
3. Learn from your feelings and fantasies.

Are there some aspects of your relationship with Tracy that you could infuse into your primary relationship? Revitalizing your primary relationship may reduce the intensity of your attraction to Tracy, so that you can resume the pleasure of your friendship without fear that you will violate your decisions about sexual intimacy.

> ▶ **Issues to Consider:** Assume that you are in a committed relationship but are feeling attracted to someone else. Based on advice given in this chapter, how would you handle the situation?

In this chapter we have examined sexual fantasies, arousal, and communication and their roles in sexual intimacy. In Chapter 7 we explore the role of love in sexual interactions. Although love and sex have different meanings to most people, they can overlap considerably as we shall see. We also examine other forms of love, such as that between a parent and child.

SUMMARY OF MAJOR POINTS

1. The conditioning of arousal.   Our capacity for sexual arousal is part of our biological heritage, but the specific objects, acts, situations, and people we find arousing are influenced by societal norms and our own unique experiences. We learn to respond sexually to particular external stimuli through association of those stimuli with arousal (classical conditioning) and through sexually rewarding or punishing experiences involving those stimuli (operant conditioning). Some evidence supports the hypothesis that any source of arousal, positive or negative, can lead to heightened attraction to a person who is associated with that arousal.

2. Sexual arousal and our sensory capabilities. Almost all of our senses come into play when we are sexually stimulated. Touch, smell, sight, and hearing are all important in sexual arousal. We learn to consider particular kinds or locations of tactile contact, particular smells, and certain sights to be erotic. Because these associations are unique to each individual, the specific touches, sights, smells, and sounds that arouse one person do not necessarily arouse another.

3. Variations in response to sexual arousal.   Just as we learn to associate sexual responses with different stimuli, we learn different attitudes toward the process of sexual arousal. Some of us are taught that sexual arousal is a healthy, normal, enjoyable process, whereas others learn to feel guilty about feeling sexy. These attitudes are instilled from an early age, and are consistently related to our capacity to respond sexually in a variety of situations. Females are more frequently taught to view their sexuality negatively than are males, and the average female feels guiltier about sexual feelings and behavior than does the average male. When responses are physiologically measured, however, males and females do not differ in their arousal by erotic material.

4. Fantasy and sexual arousal. Just as learned attitudes toward sexual arousal vary, so do reactions to the capacity to have fantasies. Fantasies provide a way to rehearse future events and try out different alternatives in our minds. They can also embellish our own experiences, improve our relationships, and entertain us. Imagination and reality are not the same thing; only when an individual confuses them, or uses fantasy as a substitute for relations with others, can any problem with fantasy arise. Fantasies of arousal can be acted out with a willing partner under certain conditions.

5. Communication and sexual feelings. When we experience sexual arousal that we would rather not act on, we must take practical steps to manage our behavior. In making wise decisions about whether to act on sexual feelings, we should be aware of, and discuss, our sexual policies with potential partners. Open communication enhances the likelihood that our interactions with others will be pleasurable and satisfying.

7

Loving Sexual Interactions

Reality **?** or Myth

1 *People who love themselves are more able to be loving with other people.*

2 *Men make a stronger distinction between love and sex than do women.*

3 *Infatuation is not considered real love by most researchers.*

4 *Limerence is a form of love that describes same-gender friendship.*

5 *Men's jealousy is one of the primary reasons for marital murder in North America.*

6 *After a person has formed a romantic relationship with someone, he or she will not be sexually attracted to or have fantasies about anyone else.*

Sexual stimulation can be fun, relaxing, and physically rewarding. And sexual interactions, in the context of strong attachment, mutual respect, and concern for a partner's feelings and well-being, can allow us to realize our potential to take part in one of the most remarkable experiences available to human beings. A loving sexual relationship can provide what Abraham Maslow (1962) called a **peak experience.**

What is love? It can be a momentary feeling or attitude that results in a loving act, such as helping a hurt person. It can be a more enduring feeling or attitude directed toward a specific person over a long period of time. Love can take a variety of forms, which we consider later in the chapter. For now, we rely on science-fiction writer Robert Heinlein's (1961) definition: love is the feeling that someone else's needs and well-being are as important to you as your own.

How we develop the capacity to participate in a loving sexual relationship is the topic of this chapter. First, we look at the relationship between being loved during infancy and childhood and the capacity to love others during adulthood. We then examine models of the development of love relationships. Finally, we turn to some of the problems that couples need to resolve

to develop enduring relationships characterized by loving sexual expression.

Being Loved: Early Experience

What does a child need to grow into a mature, loving person? We cannot systematically vary the environment in which children are raised to examine, experimentally, the effects of different kinds of child rearing on personality development. However, observations of abused and neglected children, experimental research with primates, and cross-cultural correlational studies offer clues to the importance of early experience in creating our capacity to grow physically and emotionally, love ourselves, and form loving bonds with others.

THE PRIMATE STUDIES

Erik Erikson's (1982) contention that consistent loving care during infancy and childhood is necessary

for the development of basic trust is supported by experimental research with primates (Harlow & Mears, 1979). Young monkeys undergo a relatively lengthy period of dependence on adult care that is somewhat similar to that of human children. Rhesus monkey mothers are protective and typically nurse their infants for a year or more. The kind of care that the monkey receives profoundly affects its later behavior, as does its contact with other infant and juvenile monkeys.

In one famous study, monkeys were separated from their mothers shortly after birth and reared in a laboratory. The infants were put into cages with one of two surrogate mothers. One surrogate was a plain wire-mesh cylinder from which the monkeys could receive milk from a bottle. The other was a terrycloth-covered form, but no milk was available from that surrogate. When the monkeys were allowed to choose between the two surrogate mothers, even

peak experience—Maslow's term for a personal experience that generates feelings of ecstasy, peace, and unity with the universe.

That infant monkeys need contact comfort is revealed by their choosing a cloth-covered surrogate more frequently than a wire surrogate that provides milk.

those who got their milk from the wire mother spent more time clinging to the cloth mother. The cloth "mother" seemed to provide more comfort to the infant monkeys (Harlow & Harlow, 1962).

In another series of studies, young rhesus monkeys were brought up in isolation. Lighting, temperature, cage cleaning, food, and water were provided by remote control; the totally isolated monkeys saw no other living beings. The longer the monkeys were isolated, the more abnormal and maladjusted they became. Monkeys reared in isolation for six months were described as social misfits; monkeys isolated for the first year of life appeared to be little more than "semi-animated vegetables" (Suomi & Harlow, 1971). Despite subsequent socialization, these monkeys, as they advanced into childhood and adolescence, were still social misfits compared with those who were reared with their mothers and peers. The monkeys who had been isolated for six months had

biologically normal reproductive systems but were sexually incompetent, as the researchers noted:

Their gymnastic qualifications are only quaint and cursory as compared with sexual achievement customary at these ages. Isolates may grasp other monkeys of either sex by the head and throat aimlessly, a semi-erotic exercise without amorous achievements. . . . The exercise leaves the totally isolated monkey working at cross purposes with reality. (Harlow & Novak, 1973, p. 468)

Those monkeys isolated for a year did not even approximate the botched sexual behavior of the six-month isolates; they attempted no sexual contact at all. The lack of successful mating on the part of these isolates may have been fortunate, for isolated females who had been impregnated accidentally or artificially were generally rejecting or incompetent mothers. Early deprivation thus has devastating effects on monkeys' sexual and parenting behavior in adolescence and adulthood.

An intriguing series of studies nevertheless has demonstrated that these maladjustments may not be permanent or irreversible. In a kind of sex-therapy procedure, isolated monkeys were paired with younger normal monkeys for specific periods of time, such as two hours a day for three days a week. The individual therapy sessions were augmented with group therapy involving two isolates and two "therapists" (normal monkeys). After six months of therapy, the isolates showed remarkable improvement in their behavior. By adolescence, the isolates' sexual behavior was normal for their age (Novak & Harlow, 1975; Suomi, Harlow, & McKinney, 1972).

Harry Harlow postulated that if the infant experiences a severe lack or loss of contact comfort from the parents, normal body contact will be extremely difficult to accept when the time arrives for social play and peer love:

It is this knowledge of learning what the body as a whole can do, in air and sea, on land and snow, that reinforces the first pleasure in mastery and also gives the first confidence in self. . . . The basis for self-esteem is a prerequisite for the love of living and loving, no matter what love at what age or stage. (Harlow & Mears, 1979, p. 170)

DEPRIVATION OR ENHANCEMENT?

Human infants reared in an orphanage or an institution where they receive only rudimentary care come closest to experiencing the deprivation encountered by the monkeys in the Harlow studies. In the past, institutionalized babies were kept in individual cubicles separated from other infants, and their adult contact was brief and hurried. For example, in one case, eight infants had to share one nurse (Spitz, 1947). These children were thus deprived of the range of sensory stimulation that a child normally receives from being picked up, cuddled, talked to, played with, and rocked. An impoverished environment of this kind was associated with major disturbances in interpersonal relationships and with emotional problems during childhood and adolescence (Casler, 1968).

▶ **Issues to Consider:** How would you try to help an adult who was deprived of adequate human contact and affection during childhood?

Because of the remarkable similarities between human infants and other primate infants, John Bowlby (1973) hypothesized that the attachment between infant and caregiver forms the basis for later attachments in adulthood. Mary Ainsworth and her colleagues (Ainsworth, 1989; Ainsworth, Blehar, Waters, & Wall, 1978) made a major contribution to understanding how differences in early caregiving are related to personality differences in young children. They observed mother-infant pairs at home and then in a laboratory in the so-called strange situation.

In the home visit, observers recorded how mothers treated their infants. In the next step, observers recorded infants' reactions in the strange-situation procedures in the laboratory. Mothers would play with their children until the children had settled down and then leave the room for a few minutes while a stranger remained there. Based on the infants' response to the departure and return of the mother, they were classified as securely attached, anxious-avoidant, or anxious-resistant:

1. *Secure.* This pattern is marked by the mother's noticing, understanding, and responding to infant needs. These children showed signs of distress when the mother left the laboratory, but when she returned, the child was easily comforted and quickly settled down to play.

2. *Anxious-avoidant.* Some mothers consistently neglected their infants' need for comfort and close body contact. These children acted as if they expected to be rejected and so tried to make do without love and support. When these infants' mothers left the room, they showed little reaction, and when the mothers returned, they generally avoided her and paid attention to the toys.

3. *Anxious-ambivalent.* Some mothers were inconsistent in their response to their infants' needs. Sometimes they "over-responded" by mothering the child, and at other times they ignored their infants' signals. Because of this inconsistency, these children tended to be clinging and distressed. In the laboratory situation, these infants were angry and anxious when their mothers left the room. When she returned, they would display their ambivalence by clinging to her and then pushing her away.

More recently researchers using the same techniques as Ainsworth and self-report have identified a fourth pattern of attachment (Main & Hesse, 1990; Main & Solomon, 1990):

4. *Disorganized/disoriented.* Mothers of these infants were often depressed and/or verbally or physically abusive. These infants did not appear to have developed the skills to deal with distress. In the strange-situation procedure, they engaged in a mixture of anxious-avoidant and ambivalent behaviors when their mothers left.

Although early researchers of attachment were concerned with mother-infant interactions, more recent work has also included fathers (van Ijzendoorn, 1995). In general, a child's attachment style follows the style of the primary attachment figure. An infant of 12 months can display different attachment styles with different parents.

Attachment behaviors that are assessed at age 1 appear to be good predictors of later childhood social behaviors. Securely attached children are more socially competent, have higher self-esteem, and have more satisfying relationships than do other children (Elicker, Englund, & Sroufe, 1992).

Children who receive physical affection during childhood are likely to become trusting and affectionate adults.

Researchers of infants and parents in other cultures have found differences in the kinds of attachment they form compared to North Americans. There are differences in the percentage of children who fit into the four attachment categories. For instance, secure attachment occurs less frequently in countries that have been studied outside the United States (Nakagawa, Lamb, & Miaki, 1992; Sternberg & Lamb, 1992). This should not be surprising given cultural differences in child-rearing practices. It does suggest that the attachment process is more complicated from a global perspective.

Attachment styles have been found to be related to romantic relationships in adults (Aron, Aron &

Allen, 1998; Hatfield & Rapson, 1996; Shaver & Hazan, 1994). Although there is a need for more research tracing attachment styles from infancy through adulthood, the available evidence indicates that attachment classifications are fairly stable over extended periods of time. Main and her colleagues (1990) found that current parents' reports about interactions with their own parents years earlier could predict their children's strange situation classifications with about 80 percent accuracy, a finding that has been replicated several times (van Ijzendoorn, 1995). We will go into more detail on the implications of attachment styles for adult love scripts later in the chapter.

Children enjoy the pleasure of physical intimacy without thinking of it as sexual.

Many researchers have examined the self-reported childhood experiences of adults who sexually assault others (see Chapter 19). These studies indicate that a high proportion of sexually violent adults were themselves physically and sexually abused during childhood. Just as abuse breeds violence, caring breeds love. At first the child is a passive recipient of the care and affection of the parents, but before long, a loved child becomes a loving child. From a very early age, loved children derive a great deal of pleasure from displaying affection toward their parents and others.

Sigmund Freud contended that this love contains a sexual component. Children's love clearly includes the sensual pleasure derived from intimate body contact with members of the family. The idea that the child desires sexual intercourse, however, depends on whether the child can understand this activity. At this point we have no evidence that young children have such a concept, and research strongly indicates that they do not (Goldman & Goldman, 1982). In fact, many preadolescent children, upon hearing about the activity leading to conception, express revulsion. Children's occasional expression of the desire to marry one or both of their parents probably stems not from copulatory urges but from their love of their parents, their observation of the pleasure that their parents take in their marriage, and a desire to maintain ongoing connection with their parents.

CROSS-CULTURAL OBSERVATIONS

In some cultures, infants and children are given minimal physical affection and body contact in the belief that the withholding of physical intimacy makes them grow up to be independent and self-reliant. In other cultures, adults take great pleasure in holding, caressing, stroking, and playing with babies (Hatfield, 1994; Thayer, 1987). James Prescott (1975) examined the relationship between the treatment of infants and the level of adult violence in 49 cultures. Those cultures in which infants are reared with a great deal of physical affection tend to display little physical violence; conversely, those cultures in which infants are deprived of physical affection display relatively high levels of physical violence among adults.

▶ **Issues to Consider:** Why do cultures who rear children with physical affection tend to display little physical violence?

On the basis of these observations, Prescott (1975) suggested that affection and aggression are, to some extent, mutually exclusive. That is, children reared with physical affection are likely to be affectionate and nonviolent as adults. Prescott believed that in the absence of physical affection during infancy and childhood, brain development is restricted, with the result that adult aggressiveness becomes more likely. Social learning theorists suggest a modeling effect: children learn affectionate or aggressive behavior from affectionate or aggressive parents and peers. Whether the mechanisms producing affectionate or aggressive adults are due to structural alterations in the brain or social learning experiences, or both, it is clear that children who receive love and physical affection are more likely to give love and respect themselves.

Self-Love

Most of us have heard exhortations against selfishness from our parents, religious leaders, and teachers all our lives. In stressing that one of the factors most consistently associated with healthy psychological functioning and adjustment is self-esteem, are we advocating selfishness? Not at all; there is a world of difference between self-esteem, or self-love, and selfishness.

SELF-LOVE VERSUS SELFISHNESS

Answering the following questions illuminates the enormous gulf between self-love and selfishness:

1. When was the last time you felt unhappy with yourself (insecure, hassled, irritable)?

2. When did you last feel very happy with yourself (proud of yourself, pleased with some of your personal qualities)?

3. How did you behave toward others on those two occasions? On which occasion were you kinder, more generous, more sensitive to others' feelings, and more willing to go out of your way to help other people?

In all probability, you were more selfish when you were unhappy with yourself. When we dislike ourselves, our energies are directed toward protecting and helping ourselves, not toward protecting and helping others. It is when we love ourselves that we are most capable of giving to and loving others. Similarly, when we are insecure and ashamed of our bodies, our energies are concentrated on hiding and protecting ourselves. It is difficult to make love to another person when we are ashamed or embarrassed about our own feelings and our own bodies.

Reality or Myth

Love for oneself, then, is intricately connected with love for any other being. According to Erich Fromm (who can be forgiven for his sexist language, given the time when he wrote this!),

> *The affirmation of one's own life, happiness, growth, freedom is rooted in one's capacity to love. . . . If an individual is able to love productively, he loves himself too; if he can love only others, he cannot love at all.*
> *(1956, p. 60)*

Loving Others

Writers throughout history have tried to describe love's elusive qualities:

Love is patient and kind; love is not jealous or boastful;
> *It is not arrogant or rude. Love does not insist on its own way; it is not irritable or resentful;*
> *It does not rejoice at wrong, but rejoices in the right.*

Love bears all things, believes all things, hopes all things, endures all things.
(St. Paul, I Corinthians 13:4–7)

Tell me whom you love and I will tell you who you are, and more especially, who you want to be. (Theodore Reik, 1949, p. 46)

Love is aim-inhibited sexuality.
(Sigmund Freud, 1955, p. 142)

Although love has fascinated philosophers, theologians, writers, poets, and artists for ages, only recently have scientists attempted to describe and measure it.

CONSTRUCTIONS OF LOVE

The scientific investigation of love has increased markedly since the mid-1960s. Researchers have explored the relationship between love and friendship (Hendrick & Hendrick, 1992; Sternberg, 1991), passionate and companionate love (Hatfield & Rapson, 1993), and attachment and love (Shaver & Hazan, 1993). The components and forms of love have also been probed (Fehr, 1993; Hendrick & Hendrick, 1995; Lee, 1998; Sternberg, 1991). Many recent studies have focused on romantic love, at least in part owing to researchers' reliance on college students as volunteers. Although romantic love is thought to be in full bloom during late adolescence, it remains to be seen whether the results obtained from this age group are characteristic of other stages in the life span.

Many scales employed to measure love reflect a stereotypically feminine perspective that emphasizes emotional expression and shared feelings. These measures have resulted in what Francesca Cancian (1986) has called the feminization of love and may yield an incomplete conception of it. For example, in one study, some of the behaviors described as love were "communicating without words," "sharing someone's feelings," and "letting someone know all about you" (Foa et al., 1987). Generally these are the expressive aspects of love, and women tend to have more expressive skill than do men. Instrumental behaviors, more stereotypical of men than of women, are usually neglected in measures of love. Practical help, shared physical activities, and emphasis on physical sex are some of the characteristics associated with men. Because many of our measures of love reflect the stereotypically feminine ideal, it is not surprising that women emerge as more capable of love than do men. For example, a woman would be perceived as showing love if, at the end of a long day, she shares her feelings about a hassle at work or asks about her partner's feelings (expressive behaviors). If, on that same evening, her partner noticed that her tire was flat and decided to change it for her (an instrumental behavior), this would not necessarily be perceived as showing love.

Rather than trying to make men become more "loving" by becoming more stereotypically feminine, Cancian (1986, p. 709) argued for a more androgynous conception of love that is both expressive and instrumental. As she put it:

> *Who is more loving: a couple who confide most of their experiences to each other but rarely cooperate or give each other practical help, or a couple who help each other through many crises and cooperate in running a household but rarely discuss their personal experiences? Both relationships are limited. Most people would probably choose a combination: A relationship that integrates both feminine and masculine styles of loving, an androgynous love.*

Given the foregoing analysis, and in the light of gender differences in attitudes about sex described throughout this book, it should come as no surprise that there are also gender differences in attitudes about love. Men tend to differentiate love and sex more strongly than do women (Hendrick & Hendrick, 1995; Regan & Berscheid, 1995). Gender differences in attitudes about love are strongest for homosexuals, less strong for single heterosexuals, and least strong for married heterosexuals. This pattern of results is also found in Sweden, although the differences are not as pronounced, indicating a greater likelihood of fusing sex and love in that culture. There is also evidence that the tendency to differentiate between love and sex decreases as people grow older (Foa et al., 1987; Sprague & Quadagno, 1989). *Reality or Myth* [?]

Men are more likely than women to view love as a game to be played out with a number of partners (Hendrick & Hendrick, 1995; Hensley, 1996). This orientation can lead to the manipulation of others and to sexual aggression, and men who perceive love as a game may be wary of emotional investment. But overall, this style of love is one of the least frequently endorsed by both men and women. Women are more likely than men to merge love and friendship. Perhaps because women have been socialized to view sex as a precious commodity that must be guarded, they are also more pragmatic about love than are males. That is, they emphasize "love planning" based on the potential of a lover to meet particular criteria.

> ▶ **Issues to Consider:** Why do you think women are more likely to merge love and friendship than are men?

FORMS OF LOVE

If you think about the many ways that we use the word *love,* you quickly realize that it is a multipurpose term with many meanings. We can love our parents, our country, and our dog, to name just a few of the possibilities. In this chapter, we are primarily concerned with love between individuals after childhood.

Friendship. The first type of love that most of us experience outside our families is a close friendship with a person of the same gender. Friendship, or liking, is reserved for close friends; passing acquaintances do not inspire it. Also known as **philia** and **platonic love**, friendship is a form of love in which we are as concerned with the well-being of our friend as we are with our own well-being. Friendships can evolve into relationships characterized by passionate arousal and long-term commitment; when this occurs, the friendship goes beyond liking and becomes another form of love.

Most people view friendship as a relationship between equals that is characterized by sharing and caring (Blieszner & Adams, 1992). It is interesting that throughout most of history, the experience of this kind of love between a man and a woman was seen as unlikely or impossible. Among the early Greeks, the deepest love was believed to exist in the friendship of two men, who might also be involved in an erotic love relationship.

With the movement toward equality for men and women in the twentieth century, intense friendship is no longer confined to partners of the same gender. Nonetheless, 75 percent of the respondents in a magazine survey (*Psychology Today,* 1979) saw same-gender friendships as different from other-gender friendships. Friendships between men and women were seen as more difficult and complicated because of potential sexual tensions, the lack of social support for male-female friendships, and the belief that men and women have less in common than do friends of the same gender. There are still challenges to friendships between men and women in that they, or other observers, may assume that the couple are secretly sexually involved. However, such concerns do not seem to be as important to today's college students (Monsour, Harris, & Kurzweil, & Beard, 1994).

Infatuation or Passionate Love.   One dictionary defines *infatuate* as "to inspire with a foolish or extravagant love or admiration." **Infatuation**, or passionate love, involves a high degree of physiological arousal and an intense desire to be united with the loved person. It can be seen in the experience of "love at first sight." It is essentially the same kind of love that Dorothy Tennov (1979) called **limerence**—a love characterized by preoccupation, acute longing, exaggeration of the other's good qualities, seesawing emotion, and aching in the chest. These characteristics can be experienced as either intensely pleasurable or painful, depending on the response of the loved one, or "limerent object." *Reality or Myth* ❓

Unlike other forms of love, limerence is an all-or-nothing state that men and women experience in similar ways. Based on several hundred descriptions of limerence obtained through personal interviews, Tennov (1979; 1999) outlined a number of characteristics of this state:

1. *Preoccupation with the limerent object.* You are unable to think about anything else but the object of your affection. Everything you do is calculated in terms of how the limerent object would respond—whether he or she would like or dislike it. You may feel happy or sad depending on the degree of attention you get from your limerent object.

2. *Intrusive or unintentional thinking about the limerent object.* In addition to spending a great

---

philia—Love involving concern with the well-being of a friend.

platonic love—Nonsexual love for another person; often referred to as spiritual love.

---

infatuation—Foolish and irrational love.

limerence—(LIH-mer-ence) Love marked by obsession and preoccupation with the loved one.

deal of time intentionally fantasizing about the limerent object, you find that thoughts about your beloved intrude and interfere with other mental activity in an apparently involuntary way. You may be working on a paper or performing some task at work when thoughts and fantasies of the love object come to the fore.

3. *Desire for exclusivity with the limerent object.* You crave the limerent object and no one else. You want commitment to ensure exclusivity even when it is premature or inappropriate. This can lead you to smother the object of your affection with attention and pressure rather than allowing the relationship to develop gradually.

Tennov proposed that limerence develops in stages, the first being admiration for another person who possesses valued qualities and for whom one feels a basic liking. This stage is followed by an awareness of sexual attraction. Once admiration and sexual attraction are present, the next step is to undergo an experience that raises the possibility that these feelings might be reciprocated. This experience could be something as simple as observing a look or gesture or being asked to go to dinner or a party. *Reality or Myth* At this point in the development of limerence, the first "crystallization" occurs: one begins to focus on the good qualities of the limerent object and to disregard his or her bad qualities. After the first crystallization, if the two people develop a mutual attraction, the intensity of the romantic involvement is relatively mild. Doubt about the limerent object's commitment, however, can evoke extreme, or "crazy," limerence. Tennov maintained that full-blown limerence cannot develop without an element of uncertainty. The interaction between hopefulness and uncertainty leads to the second crystallization, which results in feeling an intense attraction to the other person.

Limerence is a tantalizing state that promises great things that never can be fully realized. In the beginning it can also be devastating, especially if the limerent object is lost abruptly. Tennov outlines three ways in which limerent attraction can end:

1. The development of a deeper relationship, which evolves if one is able to withstand the major disappointments and emptiness of fading limerence.

2. Abandonment owing to a lack of reciprocity on the part of the limerent object.

3. The transfer of attention to another limerent object—a continuation of the limerent state.

Romantic Love. The deeper relationship that may blossom out of limerent love, or infatuation, is characterized by romantic love. Romantic love comprises intimacy as well as passion. It is the "Romeo and Juliet" type of love: liking with the added excitement of physical attraction and arousal but lacking commitment.

Humans' first experience of romantic love can occur during infancy and childhood. Infants normally display a passionate attachment to their parents (Shaver, Hazan, & Bradshaw, 1988). Much like adolescent and young adult lovers, they get intense pleasure in parental attention and approval, and they express distress when separated and affection when reunited. Five-year-olds often display passionate love for others by reporting that there is another child they cannot stop thinking about, whom they want to be near, and whom they would like to touch and be touched by (Carlson & Hatfield, 1992). The Greeks called this form of love **eros.**

Many people wonder whether it is possible to have a romantic love relationship with more than one person in a lifetime. When an intense romantic relationship ends, it is common to feel that you will never again experience romantic love. Yet as people who find another mate after separation, divorce, or the death of a beloved partner discover, it is possible to form a romantic bond with more than one person.

Some researchers, unlike Tennov, maintain that romantic love does not differ from infatuation. For example, as described in Chapter 6, Ellen Berscheid and Elaine Walster (1978) contended that defining our feelings as love depends on a two-stage process: we first become physiologically aroused, and then cognitive labeling takes place.

Prior to the development of Berscheid and Walster's model, many researchers assumed that loving is an intense form of liking, governed by the same principles. Voluminous research by Donn Byrne (1971) and others had indicated that we like those who share our values and attitudes and who evaluate us

eros—Erotic love.

positively. We find associating with someone who shares our beliefs and attitudes rewarding because he or she affirms our perceptions of the world. And obviously, we find compliments or positive evaluations rewarding.

Berscheid and Walster cited two other reasons for their rejection of the idea that loving is simply a more intense form of liking, explained by the same principles: **unrequited love** and jealousy. In unrequited love you feel or express, or both, intense feelings for another person, but the object of your desire behaves as if you do not exist or, worse, appears to be repelled by you. Unrequited love appears to be very common, at least among American college students. In one study, 85 percent of college men and women reported rejecting someone who loved them and 93 percent reported being rejected by someone they loved (Baumeister, Wotman, & Stillwell, 1993). Surprisingly, they did not remember the experience of a "broken heart" with bitterness and hatred. Instead, the experience was seen as reflecting both positive and negative feelings. Jealousy is not an emotion that most of us find rewarding, and yet many of us have experienced heightened feelings of desire for a person after thinking that he or she was attracted to someone else.

Based on these and other similar observations, Berscheid and Walster proposed that we are more likely to label our feelings toward someone as love when we are physiologically aroused. An obvious source of physiological arousal, of course, is sexual arousal. But as we noted in Chapter 6 in the discussion of the experiment involving two bridges, Berscheid and Walster argued that *any* source of physiological arousal—for example, fear, euphoria, or anxiety—can increase the likelihood of our defining our feeling as love.

The second step, cognitive labeling, occurs because we seek an explanation for our feelings. Most of us are conditioned over a long period to associate feelings of arousal with romantic attraction. Berscheid and Walster's two-stage theory of love (or infatuation) helps to explain why we may perceive punishing sources of arousal, such as jealousy and

unrequited love—Intense romantic/erotic attraction toward another person who does not have the same feelings toward you.

Based on their facial expressions and posture, this couple seems to have developed the friendship, mutual trust, and reliance characteristic of companionate love.

anxiety, as indicators of the strength of our feelings for others.

Companionate Love.   Companionate love involves intimacy and commitment but no passion. It is essentially a long-term friendship such as often develops in marriage after a couple's passion has died down.

Strongly connected couples past the surging emotions of passion usually develop a system of shared values. The extent of support and interplay is often unspoken and habitual, and only upon death or divorce do they become aware of how much they have lost. Having been concerned with what was not working well, they may have failed to realize fully how many of their joint pursuits were successful.

LOVE SCHEMAS

Earlier in the chapter, we discussed the importance of attachment in infancy and childhood, and we suggested that attachment styles have implications for adult relationships. The basic concept driving this research is that infants and children construct mental

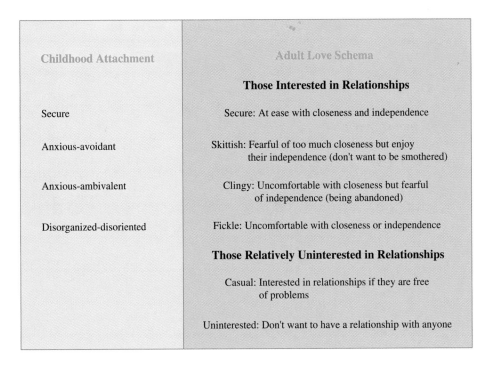

Childhood Attachment	Adult Love Schema
	Those Interested in Relationships
Secure	Secure: At ease with closeness and independence
Anxious-avoidant	Skittish: Fearful of too much closeness but enjoy their independence (don't want to be smothered)
Anxious-ambivalent	Clingy: Uncomfortable with closeness but fearful of independence (being abandoned)
Disorganized-disoriented	Fickle: Uncomfortable with closeness or independence
	Those Relatively Uninterested in Relationships
	Casual: Interested in relationships if they are free of problems
	Uninterested: Don't want to have a relationship with anyone

Figure 7.1 Love Schemas

models (also referred to as maps, schemas, or scripts) of themselves and their caretakers that affect relationships throughout their lives.

Stage theorists such as Erik Erikson (1982) pointed out, however, that infancy is just one, albeit a very important, stage in the life cycle. We face a continuing series of developmental challenges throughout our lives that may alter or change our earlier scripts.

In an attempt to integrate attachment theory and stage theory, Elaine Hatfield and Richard Rapson (1996) have developed a model of how people develop love **schemas** and the subsequent influence of these schemas on thought and behavior. Hatfield and Rapson proposed that people's love schemas depend on (1) how comfortable they are with closeness and/or independence and (2) how eager they are to be involved in romantic relationships.

Those interested in romantic relationships are thought to fall into four categories that parallel the four categories of childhood attachment that we described earlier in the chapter (see Figure 7.1). In addition, there are two other categories of people who are not very interested in becoming involved in relationships. Love schemas are thought to start developing during children's early experiences and become more complex as the individual matures.*

The Secure. People with secure attachment report that they seldom worry about being abandoned by a partner. They believe other people have good intentions and are trustworthy. They place high value on, and derive the most pleasure from, relationships rather than work. If a relationship does not work out, secure people may be upset, but they tend to rebound fairly quickly compared to people in the other attachment categories. Because they value themselves, they feel confident in their ability to attract

---

schemas—Cognitive plans or structures that serve as guides for interpreting information and planning behavior. Basically the same as scripts as discussed in Chapter 2.

---

*Many of the following descriptions of attachment styles are based on the following sources: Bachman, Levine, Muto, and Hatfield, 1994; Brennan and Shaver, 1995; Choo, Levine, and Hatfield, 1995; Feeney and Noller, 1990; Hatfield and Rapson, 1996; Hazan and Shaver, 1990; Shaver and Hazan, 1993; Singelis, Choo, and Hatfield, 1995; Singelis et al., 1997.

other secure people. They tend to be calm and confident in the face of impending commitments.

The Skittish.   These folks tend to describe themselves as wary of intimacy and are uncomfortable being close to others. A skittish person is afraid of becoming dependent on another, and expects love relationships to fail. Skittish people report frequent emotional fluctuation and high degrees of jealousy when in a relationship. In the face of impending commitments, they tend to feel fearful and trapped. Not surprisingly, the skittish tend to prefer work over love relationships. A good example of the skittish is George Costanza, played by Jason Alexander on the recently ended TV series *Seinfeld*. (If you happened to miss the original shows, it will probably continue to be in reruns for years.)

The Clingy.   The clingy desire a great deal of closeness and often worry that their partners do not love them or will leave them. They tend to fear being on their own or "abandoned." The clingy feel that it is easy to fall in love but when they do, they experience high degrees of sexual attraction and jealousy. Riding an emotional roller-coaster, they have difficulty establishing a stable relationship. In the face of a pending commitment, they often feel anxious and insecure. The clingy are more likely to experience obsessive love than are people in the other attachment categories. They report that they often worry about love's interfering with work.

The clingy style is often seen in people who cohabit or marry at a young age to escape their families of origin. Before they have a change to develop their own identities fully, they become enmeshed in a relationship characterized by insecurity. They develop little interest in outside social relationships. Their existence is marked by fear of abandonment. Unsure of their own value in the world, they are consumed by measuring themselves by the judgment of one other person—a perilous gamble.

The Fickle.   The fickle are uncomfortable with both closeness and independence. As such, they are unlucky enough to have the problems of both the skittish and the clingy. They are never comfortable with what they have. If they fall in love and the love is reciprocated, they tend to get anxious and make an exit. Later they may decide that splitting up was a mistake and try to renew the relationship. If successful, they soon become dissatisfied again. Similar to the skittish, they are suspicious of commitment, fearing entrapment.

I (Rick) once saw a couple in therapy who were on their fourth marriage to each other. That is, they kept divorcing, and then remarrying each other. Using his powers of persuasion, this fickle man would convince this clingy woman that "things would be different," and they would marry again, only to have him once again become dissatisfied with the relationship. The husband could be a charming suitor when they were unmarried and he wanted her back, particularly if she became interested in another man. In therapy, the wife urged me to make him promise that he would not leave her again, while he sat there with a bemused smile. After several irritating sessions, I advised them either to separate for good or learn to enjoy wallowing in their misery.

The Casual.   A casual love affair can be a lot of fun if that is the intention of both partners. However, if one of them wants a more serious relationship, that person is in for some painful times. The person who is apparently not capable of more than casual attachment probably represents the zenith of the "fear of intimacy" that has been ascribed to men more frequently than to women. The lack of commitment or investment on the part of the casual can lead to a lonely old age when one's own attractiveness is decreasing. I (Rick) once saw a male artist in his 70s after he had attempted suicide following a breakup with his 27-year-old lover. His whole life had been a series of casual affairs, and he was terrified that he could no longer attract another woman to participate in his temporary romances.

The Uninterested.   These rare folks just are not interested in relationships. If they do somehow end up in a relationship, they seem to get little pleasure out of it. And when it ends, which it usually does, they typically experience relief. The Unabomber, Theodore Kaczinski, is an example of this orientation, albeit a pathological one. Living pretty much as a hermit, apparently he never had a romantic relationship (that we know of) before he was arrested and convicted.

Based on these descriptions, where would you place yourself? In their study, Theodore Singelis,

Patricia Choo, and Elaine Hatfield (1995) asked college students from a variety of ethnic backgrounds to rate their feelings and experiences to these forms of attachment. Approximately 62 percent described themselves as fairly secure, 10 percent were skittish, 8 percent were clingy, 12 percent were fickle, 7 percent were casual, and fewer than 1 percent were disinterested. Thus the majority of these students placed themselves into the secure attachment category.

LOVE VERSUS LUST

One dictionary defines *lust* as "an intense longing" and "sexual desire often to an intense or unrestrained degree." In Robert Sternberg's (1986) theory, lust is the passionate component of love. Lust or passion can be so strong as to elicit the feelings and behaviors often associated with emotional disturbance. Infatuated people may be distracted by obsessional thoughts about the object of their affection. Normally poised and well coordinated, they may find themselves speechless and clumsy in the presence of the person to whom they are attracted. Mood swings from euphoria to depression are common, and a person's priorities may be drastically altered, at least temporarily. For some people, the experience of falling in love bears a striking resemblance to temporary insanity. Perhaps this similarity underlies the expression, "I'm crazy about you."

Feelings Versus Behaviors.   Like fear, hunger, happiness, and anxiety, lust is a human feeling. You cannot choose to experience or to avoid feelings, but you can control your responses to them. If you are dieting, you may choose to have just one egg at breakfast rather than two, even though you may still be hungry after eating the single egg. If you experience irritation with your partner while at a party, you may choose to scream and yell publicly, or you may opt to postpone your reaction until the two of you are alone. Similarly, if you are feeling lust, you may deal with it in various ways, including having sex with the nearest willing person, masturbating, running around the block, or taking a cold shower. We are responsible for the specific acts and behaviors we choose, but because we do not choose the specific feelings we have, guilt (or pride) over our feelings is inappropriate. Feelings are neither good nor bad, moral nor immoral, although some feelings are more pleasant than others.

Confusing Lust and Love.   Lust is a normal, healthy human emotion that can be very pleasurable for two people when they both desire sexual expression with one another. It is reasonable for two adults who are sexually attracted to each other to choose to express their lust by becoming sexually intimate. If the two people do not deal honestly with their feelings prior to engaging in sexual activity, however, these feelings can lead to considerable pain and guilt.

As we mentioned in Chapter 6, differences in the sexual socialization of males and females in North American culture contribute to the difficulties that adolescents in particular have in communicating their feelings. Specifically, females are traditionally taught to look for a partner for an enduring romantic relationship, whereas males are culturally conditioned to seek sexual experience per se. Feeling lust (but not love), a young man may attempt sexual activity with a young woman. She may interpret his sexual attentions as love, and indeed he may say, "I love you," to persuade her to agree to sexual intimacy. If his acts are based primarily on feelings of lust, he attains his goal when he has an orgasm.

The young woman's objectives and expectations may be quite different. For her, sexual intimacy may be a means to the goal of an enduring relationship rather than an end in itself. There is no reason that a young man and woman (or any other couple, for that matter) should not have sexual relations based on lust, but honest communication and agreement about expectations must occur prior to sexual intimacy if they are to avoid using others or feeling used. In the absence of the honest disclosure of feelings and goals, prospective sex partners may exploit one another.

There is an old cliché suggesting that men use love to get sex and women use sex to get love. With North American culture's progress toward gender equality in recent decades, some men complain that women exploit them sexually, and women may protest that "just because I went to bed with him, he thinks he owns me." There is evidence to suggest, however, that young women are still more likely than young men to find sex acceptable only in a love relationship (Buss, 1999).

A striking example of this gender difference is reflected in two studies by Russell Clark and Elaine Hatfield (1989). In these experiments, male and female confederates of average attractiveness approached students on a college campus and said, "I have been noticing you around campus. I find you to be very attractive." The confederate then asked the students one of three questions: (1) Would you go out with me tonight? (2) Would you come over to my apartment tonight? or (3) Would you go to bed with me tonight? None of the women who were approached agreed to go to bed with the male confederate, whereas more than two-thirds of the males agreed to such a proposal. These studies illustrate the pronounced difference between men and women in willingness to engage in sexual intimacy outside the context of a committed or loving relationship. Clark and Hatfield collected their data prior to highly publicized information that unprotected sex (without condoms) could lead to contracting HIV. However, Clark (1990) conducted a similar study in 1989, and obtained the same general gender differences. Are you as surprised by his finding as we are?

People also differ in the meanings that they attach to the word *love,* and we turn now to this issue.

Love as Dependency, Jealousy, and Other Unlovely Feelings

Even when two people sincerely believe that they love each other, problems may arise because of differences in their interpretations of the word *love.* As we have seen, love can take many different forms. It may connote both passion and a commitment so strong that a temporary absence of sexual pleasure is cheerfully accepted. It may carry the message that "I will sacrifice for you and you should sacrifice for me." It may mean, "I have the right to control you," or it may sometimes be used to express a state of tension. At other times, love can communicate a sense of peacefulness.

DEPENDENCY AND CONTROL

It has been proposed that humans have a fundamental need for social attachment that is conditioned in particular ways by specific cultures (Baumeister & Leary, 1995; Shaver et al., 1988). One way that North American adolescents and adults satisfy this need is through romantic love. Dependency has been seen as a central component of romantic love by a number of researchers (Dion & Dion, 1988).

North Americans tend to prepare their offspring to seek security through emotional attachment to other people. In its extreme form, the association of security with attachment can lead to exaggerated expectations about what another person in a relationship can provide. Some people seek security and self-gratification through one other person, who provides a buffer against an often tumultuous and threatening world. Just as people can become dependent on drugs, work, or (as we will see in Chapter 17) atypi-

cal sexual practices, they can also become desperately attached to another person. Such an attachment may lead to what Stanley Peele and Archie Brodsky (1975) called *interpersonal addiction,* a classic syndrome involving both tolerance and withdrawal.

You are probably familiar with the concepts of tolerance and withdrawal as applied to substance abuse. As people's dependency on a particular drug grows, they acquire a tolerance for it, and their bodies require more and more of the substance to provide a reassuring "high." Over time, most addicted people become increasingly unable to cope with the problems and uncertainties that first attracted them to the drug. They cannot envision everyday life without the drug and feel unable to free themselves from its grip. When the drug is not available, their bodies react to withdrawal with fever, sweating, shivering, and alternating patterns of insomnia and drowsiness. Addicts even experience anxiety over the potential unavailability of the drug.

Just as drug addicts seek security in chemicals, some individuals seek comfort and security in an emotional attachment to another person. They can become so addicted to another that they let go of all other interests and activities. (We should note that many scholars do not agree with addiction models as an explanation of complex social behaviors.) According to Peele and Brodsky (1974, p. 25),

As an addictive relationship unfolds, the lovers may seem to be seeing each other for the pleasure and excitement of it, but this doesn't last. After a while, the lovers are just

Some individuals feel that they cannot live without their lover, regardless of how that lover treats them in return. *Dependency* is a more accurate word for such feelings than *love*.

there for each other, not for mutual growth or self-expression, but for comfort and familiarity. They reach a tolerance for each other. As for withdrawal, we have all seen the emotional and physical havoc that follows in the wake of some breakups, and the desperate ploys a jilted lover will try in order to get another "shot" of his or her beloved.

Lovers sometimes talk as if their love were unconditional. This outlook is reinforced in traditional North American marriage vows, by which the couple pledge to love one another in sickness and in health, for richer or for poorer, and so forth. Certainly a marital commitment should not be severed because of changes in a partner's health or wealth. The concept of unconditional love applied to a relationship between adults, however, often masks dependency. Adults who value themselves do not unconditionally accept a relationship with a partner who abuses them. For example, an unhappy woman who puts up with a continuing pattern of physical or emotional abuse from her partner may be remaining in the rela-

tionship out of dependency, not love. The man who fails to assert his rights as an adult to determine his own activities and time schedules may do so not from love but from the inability or unwillingness to function as an independent adult.

JEALOUSY

Just as we may confuse love with dependency, we may define an emotion as love when it is actually jealousy. Of all the feelings we experience, jealousy is among the most unpleasant. In the grip of this painful emotion, the most poised, self-confident, attractive person can disintegrate into a frightened, hostile, suspicious, defensive, complaining being.

One of the potential drawbacks of becoming attached to another person is that the bond can make us vulnerable to jealousy. Feelings of jealousy can be so intense and unpleasant as to provoke us to attempt to control and possess the sexual thoughts, feelings, and expression of the person to whom we are attached. There is evidence that men and women differ in their perceptions of the behaviors that indicate infidelity and elicit jealousy (see "Research Spotlight: Dating Infidelity" on page 162).

Because jealousy, or at least competition for mates, is apparent among mammals, Kinsey, as well as many contemporary evolutionary theorists (Buss, 1999; Fisher, 1992; Symons, 1979), considered jealousy and competition to be a part of our evolutionary inheritance. Male jealousy is a common motive in the murder of married women in North America (Buss, 1999; Fisher, 1992). Reiss (1986) also believed jealousy to be a universal emotion, but he did not link it to our genetic heritage. Instead, he maintained that all societies set boundaries for important relationships, particularly marriage. When the boundaries of a relationship are violated, jealousy arises.

Reality or Myth ?

The observation that not everyone experiences jealousy upon learning of a mate's sexual interaction with another person suggests that the capacity for jealousy can be affected by psychological and social experiences. In cultures that permit polygamous marriages, husbands and wives do not associate outside sexual activity with anger and with fear of rejection

Before a serious commitment exists between two people, it is common for each of them to go out with other people. Difficulties can arise, of course, if one member of a couple believes that he or she is at a later stage in the dating relationship than the other partner does, or if he or she had different values about the extent of dating and sexual exclusivity that should exist between them at a specific dating stage. To examine a phenomenon that they labeled dating infidelity, Roscoe, Cavanaugh, and Kennedy (1988) gathered the responses of 247 unmarried college students to the following questions:

1. What behaviors do you think constitute being "unfaithful" to a dating partner provided the couple is in a serious dating relationship (in other words, they have assumed that they are to date only each other)?

2. What are some reasons a person in a serious dating relationship would be "unfaithful" to a dating partner?

3. What would you do if you learned that your dating partner was "unfaithful" to you? (p. 37)

If you are currently in what you consider to be a serious dating relationship, you and your partner might want to discuss these questions with one another. In general, students in the Roscoe et al. study described three major behaviors as constituting infidelity if done with someone else: dating or spending time; having sexual intercourse; and engaging in other sexual interactions, such as flirting, kissing, necking, and petting. Men and women differed in their views of infidelity, however, with more women than men listing dating or spending time with another and keeping secrets from the primary partner. In contrast, men were more likely than women to state that having sexual interactions with another person constituted unfaithfulness.

The top three reasons that students thought infidelity would occur were dissatisfaction with the relationship; boredom; and revenge, anger, or jealousy. More women than men listed relationship dissatisfaction as a reason, and more men than women listed sexual incompatibility and lack of communication or understanding as a potential cause for infidelity. If they learned that their dating partner had been unfaithful, 44 percent of the students said that they would terminate the relationship, with women more likely than men to indicate that they would first discuss the situation with the partner.

A final interesting set of findings from Roscoe et al.'s research concerned their examination of students' attitudes as a function of whether they reported always having been faithful. A slight majority of both men and women stated that they had not always been faithful in a dating relationship. Those who had engaged in dating infidelity at some time, compared to those who had always been faithful, were more likely to give the following reasons for a person's dating infidelity: dissatisfaction with the relationship, sexual incompatibility, and being insecure or unsure about the relationship.

and loss to the same degree that North Americans do (Allgeier, 1992). Sexual jealousy may be related to economic systems that involve accumulation and ownership of property. Jealousy may be most intense and dangerous for women in cultures where woman and children are viewed as men's property.

Some researchers have concluded that the extent to which jealousy dominates and overwhelms an individual's sense of well-being is related to such individual characteristics as insecurity, inadequacy, and dependency (Buss, 1999; Fisher, 1992). On the basis of his longitudinal research, Gregory White (1981; White & Helbick, 1988) concluded that feelings of inadequacy evoke jealousy, as least among women. In men, he believed, the relationship is reversed: men become aware of jealousy and then begin to feel inadequate.

There is evidence that some people deliberately provoke jealousy in their partners (Sheets, Fredendall, & Claypool, 1997), with women more likely than men to report this behavior. The most common method of piquing jealousy reported by White's respondents was talking to the mate about how appealing someone else was, and the most common motive was to get more attention from the mate. Other methods included flirting, dating others, pretending to be attached to someone else, and talking about a former partner.

We know a woman who has had a number of extramarital affairs and characterizes them all as a form of revenge. Whenever she learned of another of her husband's affairs, she sought an extramarital relationship to even the score. Women's general response to jealousy, however, is to increase efforts to make themselves attractive to the primary partner. In contrast, men are more likely to seek outside relationships for solace and retribution. Jealousy is more common among younger than older people and among less educated than more educated people, and it is more intense in new relationships than in those of longer duration. Finally, people who report overall dissatisfaction with their lives have more frequent bouts of jealousy than do happier people (Wiederman & Allgeier, 1993).

Jealousy is a fact of life for most Americans. Some researchers maintain that jealousy is inevitable in the context of Western norms that revere pairing, family orientation, ownership, private property, competition, and the ideal of the perfect relationship (Reiss, 1986; Wiederman & Allgeier, 1993).

Most researchers studying jealousy have examined people's reactions to the idea of their spouse's engaging in extramarital sexual contact, or their committed partner's having extradyadic (or "ED," *dyad* meaning "pair") sexual relationships. However, in a series of studies, Yarab and Allgeier (1997; see also Yarab, Sensibaugh, & Allgeier, 1997) asked a large number of undergraduates to describe behaviors by their partners that they would judge as unfaithful and likely to make them feel jealous. This procedure yielded a large number of behaviors (e.g., having lunch with a member of the other sex) that did not necessarily involve sexual activity. The researchers retained the behaviors mentioned most commonly and administered the list to a new group of volunteers. One of the most surprising findings was that respondents perceived their partner's having sexual fantasies about someone else as unfaithful, jealousy inducing, and threatening to the primary relationship. Even more interesting was that many respondents reported ED behaviors with others and having fantasies toward others. However, they perceived their own ED behaviors and fantasies as not indicative of unfaithfulness and not as a threat to their primary relationship! That is, respondents exhibited a double standard. The phrase *double standard* is usually used in the context of gender differences. In this case, however, double standard refers to the finding that we judge the same behaviors, including fantasy, as more threatening to our primary relationship when our partners engage in them than when we engage in them. We seem to believe that we can handle such experiences without their threatening our primary relationship, but our partner cannot engage in the same behaviors and fantasies without endangering the primary relationship with us. *Reality or Myth* ⍰

▶ **Issues to Consider:** Have you ever felt jealousy in a relationship? If so, how did you cope with the feeling, and what advice would you have for others who experience jealousy?

How can one cope with the painful feelings of jealousy and minimize the destructive behaviors that those feelings sometimes elicit? Persons who feel threatened by jealousy in a relationship commonly withdraw from their partner or go on the attack. Either response can stimulate a similar reaction—withdrawal or counterattack—in the partner. These responses may be perceived by the jealous partner as further evidence that his or her fears are justified. An alternative reaction to feelings of jealousy is to acknowledge one's feelings and describe their source: "Paul, I'm feeling jealous and afraid that you've lost interest in me because of the time you spent talking with Michelle at the party." Because this reaction is not an attack or a withdrawal, Paul may be more disposed to provide reassurance and a hug than he would be if his partner stomped off angrily, muttering, "Well, you certainly have the hots for Michelle, don't you?" If one partner continually punishes the other partner by attacking or withdrawing when there has been no real violation of their relationship agreement, the accusations may produce the violation that the jealous partner fears.

Sometimes one partner *has* violated the agreement between the couple, and so the other partner's jealousy and anger are justified. In that case, too, successful resolution is more likely if the partner presents an honest, direct description of his or her feelings about the other person's behavior.

Finally, some couples have problems in negotiating their differences because of their desire for control or power over their partner. In his intriguing book, *Intimate Terrorism*, the psychotherapist Michael Vincent Miller (1995) eloquently described some of the difficulties inherent in intimate relationships overshadowed by the struggle for power.

▶ **Issues to Consider:** Why would intimate relationships be as much about power as about love?

Miller's work with couples experiencing this kind of contention is described in "Highlight: Intimate Terrorism" on page 164. Miller maintained that power is just as dominant a factor as love when couples become close. He described this dynamic (1995, pp. 31–32):

> If these power struggles rarely show up at first, it is because infatuation and courtship

Intimate Terrorism

Psychotherapist Michael Vincent Miller has described the process of "intimate terrorism" between partners. He suggested (1995, p. 40) that we spend much of our lives

> caught in the tension between the push for autonomy and the pull for intimacy. We want to be independent, self-reliant, in command of ourselves, but at the same time deeply attached to someone else. The needs for separate identity and intimate attachment often seem to be at odds and yet they are really aspects of each other.

Miller asserted that the partners in healthy relationships make use of their personality differences by learning from one another, so that each partner's repertoire is expanded. In contrast, Miller observed a polarization in many of the troubled couples with whom he has worked: each partner takes the opposite approach with respect to rationality and emotionality, for example (1995, p. 28):

> Each feels deprived and is trying to control the other in a different way: she by pressing claims for more intimacy; he by demanding more freedom. . . . They paint each other

into separate corners from which neither can escape to reach the other in a fulfilling way. He interprets her demands for more emotional communication as attempts to destroy his spontaneity and independence. She interprets his attempts to guard his freedom as a denial of love for her and of responsibility for their marriage. She feels neglected and taken for granted; he feels imprisoned and punished unjustly. Blame has replaced desire, and the role of lover has been exchanged for that of victim.

Miller saw the fears of abandonment and engulfment among some of the couples whom he treated as having originated in early childhood. He suggested that some parents may use childhood fears of abandonment and loss of love to control their children's behavior. Through this kind of experience, the child learns to perceive love as hard to get, something that must be earned and, once acquired, held onto tightly. Parents who smother a child with too much intimacy and attention can threaten the child's identity as a separate being. For people to make good contact, Miller wrote, a delicate balance is needed between sharing and privacy.

are so mutually satisfying, but they often surface once the relationship becomes a matter of daily living. When two people begin to fail at making each other feel powerful through appreciating and affirming each other, each may soon seek to gain power for the sake of self-protection at the other's expense. The ensuing conflict leads them to employ increasingly drastic means of bringing psychological pressure against one another.

Loving Sexual Interactions

Earlier we described Peele and Brodsky's (1975) concept of addiction. By way of contrast, they also described some of the characteristics of mature love, and the following five questions are based on their work:

1. Have you continued to maintain individual interests, including meaningful personal relationships with people other than your partner?

2. Are you and your lover friends? If your erotic involvement ended, would you continue to see one another as friends?

3. Have you maintained a secure belief in your own value as an independent person?

4. Is your relationship integrated with the rest of your life rather than set off or isolated from your other activities?

5. Do you feel improved by the relationship? Have you become stronger, more attractive, more accomplished, and more sensitive since becoming involved with your partner?

If you are part of a loving sexual relationship, you and your partner might want to answer these questions individually and then discuss your responses. If either of you believes that the answer to two or more of these questions is a sad no, you may want to discuss the possibility of making some changes in your relationship. Note, of course, that few of us can give an unqualified and enthusiastic yes in response to all five questions. And, in any case, relationships, especially good ones, are always changing, and thus your answers may differ from one month or year to the next.

The quality of a relationship is not appropriately measured by its complete absence of problems. There is no such thing as a perfect relationship that is always problem free. The qualities that are important in a loving sexual (or, for that matter, nonsexual) relationship are honesty, integrity, and concern for resolving problems in such a way as to meet the needs of *both* partners.

A couple can have a richly satisfying relationship without seeing eye to eye on everything. In fact, if they are both healthy, independent adults, differences of opinion are inevitable. (For an example of how differences and disagreements are handled in another species, see "Highlight: Make Love, Not War" on page 166.) Disagreements about fundamental aspects of the relationship, however, may make the couple's long-term investment in the union inadvisable. For example, before making a long-term commitment, a couple should discuss their feelings regarding whether they should be sexually exclusive or free to have other sexual relationships, whether they want children, and whether their relationship will be characterized by highly traditional or egalitarian roles. There are many other areas in which agreement is not at all necessary. For example, whereas a woman who believes that a couple should share all activities may feel deserted as a result of her mate's solo interest in gardening or golf, people with well-developed avocations may welcome the fact that their spouses also have independent interests and hobbies. In fact, the combination of taking part in some activities independently of one another and cultivating common interests is related to the satisfaction of partners in a long-term relationship.

VITALITY IN LONG-TERM RELATIONSHIPS

At the beginning of a relationship, there is a great deal of arousal that is not purely sexual. Uncertainty about how the relationship will turn out generates its own excitement or arousal. Not knowing how the other person feels, and wondering about our own attractiveness and sexual performance, lend a dimension of vulnerability and risk to initial involvement with another person.

After a relationship has existed for a while, the sexual arousal may be as strong as it was initially, but if the relationship is characterized by mutual trust and commitment, the other contributions to the feelings of arousal may fade. In any good ongoing relationship—whether with parents, children, siblings, friends, roommates, or coworkers—there are cycles. Different points in the cycle are characterized by periods of intense connection, irritation, indifference, and dislike. In some couples, people fall into rigid ways of relating to each other socially and sexually. Reliance on inflexible and highly predictable schedules, social activities, and patterns of sexual interaction can deaden the sense of passion and excitement in the relationship and lead to automatic rather than spontaneous interaction.

Even among couples who have relatively flexible relationships, expectations based on the dizzying feelings that occur during courtship can cause difficulties. We have some recently married friends who are now going through the normal adjustment process associated with marriage. At times during their premarital affair, they would ignore work or other obligations in favor of romantic time alone together. Now they have integrated their relationship into the rest of their activities, but in their busy lives, time for sex no longer "spontaneously" occurs. Of course, it never did. It is simply the case that earlier, the couple gave sexual intimacy the highest priority in their hierarchy of activities, whereas now it has taken its place as one of numerous other important commitments. For them and for all of us who value the pleasure and intimacy shared during loving sexual interactions, it is essential to set aside periods of leisure time for emotional and sexual bonding.

Make Love, Not War

Imagine a society in which there is minimal violence, no warfare, and disputes are settled by engaging in sexual behavior. Don't look for such a group among humans, but among a close relative with whom we share more than 98 percent of our genetic characteristics: the bonobo (buh-NO-boh). Once known as the pygmy chimpanzee, these elegant primates are believed to have split off from our human ancestors and other chimpanzees about eight million years ago.

The bonobo have woven sexuality into the fabric of their social life. They engage in many forms of sexual stimulation that are not limited to adult male-female interaction. Tongue kissing, oral sex, genital massage, and face-to-face coitus are just part of their sexual repertoire (de Waal, 1995).

The bonobo often engage in sexual activities when they are in competition for attention, food, or some other object. Their sexual activities appear to ease tension. For example, when I (Rick) was visiting the San Diego zoo in 1996, I watched a bonobo mother nursing her infant. While attempting to nurse, the mother was being annoyed by her adolescent son. The mother put up with his irritating behavior for several minutes, but when he persisted, she seemed to shrug in resignation. She set down her infant, then chased and caught the adolescent. She lay on top of him and rubbed her genitals against his for about 10 seconds. After dismounting, she resumed feeding her baby. The adolescent wandered off in apparent contentment and did not bother her again while I was observing.

You might think that my observation of the way in which the bonobo use sexual activity to reduce conflict stems from the fact that the group I observed were in captivity in a zoo. However, Frans de Waal (1995) reported that bonobo observed in their natural habitats in Africa engage in the same pattern of using sex to defuse disagreements.

Some of the bonobo's interesting use of sexual activity has to do with their social structure, which has been described as female-centered and egalitarian. The strongest social bonds are formed among females, although the females also bond with males. The status of a male depends on the position of his mother, to whom he remains closely bonded for her entire life. If a male gets "out of hand," the smaller females band together to discourage him.

The net result is that bonobo substitute sex for aggression. Or perhaps the bonobo might see humans as peculiar creatures who substitute aggression for sex! Is there a lesson for us in the way in which the bonobo handle conflict?

Another trap that busy people should avoid is viewing sex as one more task in the roster of daily chores. People who typically view participation in sexual interaction with their partner as just another of their many duties are more likely to develop sexual problems in response to stresses from work or other sources. A sexual relationship that is vulnerable to stress often follows a conventional but unrealistic script in which the partners feel compelled to play their respective roles. Heavy breathing, erections, lubrication, and orgasm are the criteria. It is the type of sex you have to be up for, and the kind of sex you avoid if you have a headache rather than the kind that relieves headaches; the kind that risks coronaries rather than the kind that relaxes; the kind that is just another duty rather than the kind that is a break from daily responsibilities.

In contrast, sexual intimacy can be viewed as a relief from life's chores and responsibilities. The partners involve themselves sexually for reassurance and support rather than to try to live out some media depiction. They can be genuinely irresponsible. Free to express insecurities, worries, and doubts, they can obtain relief from such feelings, with orgasm being a secondary goal. Individuals who view their sexual relationship in this way are less likely to develop sexual problems when they are under stress, depressed, or suffering from midlife crisis or physical pain.

People who like themselves and take pleasure in life are exciting to be around. Thus it is important for each of us to do things that enhance both our self-regard and our daily pleasure if we wish to have vital and loving sexual interactions with our partners.

In addition, it is essential that we give ourselves the time and leisure to share feelings about our experiences and about each other. At times, engaging in honest sharing can be painful and exhausting, and leaving ourselves vulnerable can be threatening. If we develop our own capacities to love and choose our partner wisely, however, we can share our vulnerability with another independent adult. Making the commitment to nourish our relationships with mutual giving and receiving can provide us with one of life's greatest rewards: loving sexual interactions.

SUMMARY OF MAJOR POINTS

1. Early experiences and the capacity to love. Experimental studies with primates, correlational research in a number of cultures, and observations of the development of neglected and abused children all suggest that the young need physical and emotional affection to become well-adjusted adults.

2. Self-love versus selfishness. Although sometimes confused, these two characteristics have different sources and consequences. When we feel competent and pleased with ourselves, we are far kinder to others than when the reverse is true. At those times when we do not love and respect ourselves, we withdraw and act selfishly. Self-love and appreciation, then, are related to loving and appreciating others.

3. Love schemas. Adult romantic attachments appear to be strongly related by the schemas or mental models that we develop early in life. These schemas become more complex as we move through the developmental challenges of the life cycle. We describe six different love styles (secure, skittish, clingy, fickle, casual, and uninterested). The development of these styles depends on (1) how comfortable we are with closeness and/or independence and (2) how willing we are to be involved in romantic relationships.

4. Love versus lust. Initially, erotic lovers typically feel enormous arousal from a number of sources, including sexual desire and anxiety over rejection. Whether they are experiencing lust, infatuation, or the beginning stages of an enduring romantic love, an obsessional preoccupation with the other person is common. A mutual lustful attraction can be highly, if briefly, pleasurable to some couples, but difficulties can arise if one partner is motivated by lust and the other by a commitment to developing an enduring romantic bond. The sharing of feelings and intentions by both partners can minimize the feelings of guilt and exploitation that can arise when two people have conflicting motivations for a relationship.

5. Dependency and jealousy. These two arousal-laden emotions are frequently confused with the arousal associated with erotic love. Dependency and jealousy are more commonly and intensely experienced by people who lack self-confidence and self-esteem, and both can result in manipulative, exploitive, and nonloving behavior. Most of us feel these painful emotions at some point. Communicating feelings instead of accusing and attacking one's partner reduces the destructive effects of dependency and jealousy.

6. Loving sexual interactions. Independent, mature, self-confident adults have the greatest capacity for healthy, mutually enhancing, loving sexual interactions. When two such adults form an erotic bond, they can enjoy their similarities and yet be comfortable with their differences. Making another person the exclusive focus of one's life can reduce the vitality of a relationship. If, instead, each partner develops his or her own potential, each is better able to contribute his or her unique qualities to a mutually satisfying and stimulating relationship. This ideal is not easily attained or constantly maintained, but striving toward it contributes to the hope, pride, and pleasure that characterize enduring and loving sexual interactions.

Sexual Differentiation and Development

Reality or Myth?

1. The genetic sex of a child is determined by its mother.

2. A fetus born five months after conception can survive outside its mother's uterus.

3. By the eighth week of prenatal development, an embryo has a pair of gonads that will later become testes or ovaries.

4. Intersexuality refers to conditions caused by an inconsistency in sexual differentiation.

5. On average, males go through puberty at a later age than females do.

How can anyone know if a newborn baby is a boy or a girl? These are the responses of children aged 5 and older to this question, asked by Ronald and Juliette Goldman (1982, pp. 194–196) in their cross-cultural study of children's thinking about sexuality:

> "Because mum dressed her in a dress. There's no other way to tell."
>
> "We began as girls and a penis grew later."
>
> "You can see it by the face, and if it cries a lot it's a boy."
>
> "Girls don't have dicky birds."

In this chapter we describe the process of fertilization and the intricacies of genetic inheritance. We examine conception and prenatal development and conclude the chapter with an overview of sexual differentiation.

Fertilization

Although the origins of life on earth are still shrouded in mystery, we know a great deal about how individual humans begin life. Much of this knowledge is quite recent. As late as the eighteenth century, the scientific community was engaged in vigorous debate about whether a female's ovaries contain tiny embryos that are activated by male sperm or whether sperm contain preformed miniature human beings that begin to grow after they are deposited in a fertile womb (see Figure 8.1 on page 170).

In 1677 Anton van Leeuwenhoek reported his observation of live sperm cells to the Royal Society of London. About five years earlier, Reanier de Graaf had viewed embryonic cells removed from the reproductive tubes of a female rabbit. The contemporaries of these two men did not fully appreciate the significance of their discoveries. Gradually, however, this information about the nature of sperm and egg cells became part of our general knowledge.

Nevertheless, even in this century, some groups are unsure about how reproduction occurs. Some Australian Aborigine groups, for example, do not consider sexual intercourse to be particularly important in producing pregnancy. Rather, they see intercourse as an act of preparation for the reception of a spirit baby (Montagu, 1969). The Mehinaku of Brazil believe that pregnancy develops through repeated acts of intercourse that accumulate enough semen to form a baby (Gregor, 1985). The Wari' of the Amazonian basin have a similar belief: that it takes multiple sexual encounters with at least two and possibly more partners to make a baby incrementally over the course of a pregnancy (Conklin & Morgan, 1996). They believe that a baby is produced

Figure 8.1 An Early Theory of Conception
This drawing is from a seventeenth-century representation of a little man (homunculus) in the head of a sperm. At that time, some people believed that small, preformed humans were ejaculated from the penis into the womb, where they were housed and nourished until birth.

not from one act of fertilization but from the maternal accumulation of semen and maternal blood.

MEETING OF SPERM AND EGG

We now know that one of a woman's two ovaries releases an egg (ovum) about halfway through her monthly reproductive cycle in the process known as **ovulation**. The egg, about one-fourth the size of this dot (.), is the human body's largest type of cell. After its release, the egg usually makes its way to the funnel-shaped end of the nearer Fallopian tube.

Sperm are among the smallest cells in the body: Each sperm is only 1/600th of an inch from its head to its tail. Before reaching the upper third of the Fallopian tube, where fertilization usually occurs (see Figure 8.2), sperm must make a lengthy journey, and most of them die en route.

The semen of fertile men who have not ejaculated in the previous twenty-four hours or so contains about 100 million to 400 million sperm. Only

ovulation—Release of an egg from the ovary.

one of these sperm normally penetrates an egg, however. Only 50 to 60 percent of the average man's sperm are **motile**, and some of these may be destroyed by the normally acidic secretions of the vagina. Others fail to get through the cervical mucus to enter the uterus. Of those entering the uterus, some are propelled toward the Fallopian tube that contains no egg. Each of these factors reduces the number of sperm that meet the egg.

About 2,000 sperm actually reach the egg, and they attach themselves to the membrane surrounding it. While affixed to the membrane, the sperm release enzymes that eliminate the extracellular material on the outside of the egg. As soon as one sperm has entered the egg, penetration by other sperm is generally impossible.

For fertilization to take place, the meeting of the egg and sperm generally must occur between 2 and 48 hours after sexual intercourse. Although it appears that sperm can live as long as five days, most do not live longer than 48 hours after ejaculation, about the same length of time the egg is fertilizable (Wilcox, Weinberg, & Baird, 1995).

The now-fertilized ovum contains in its genes all the information needed to produce the estimated 100 trillion cells of an adult human. To understand what happens after fertilization, we must first know something about the cellular structure of the human body.

CELL DIVISION

The human body is composed of two structurally and functionally different types of cells. The sperm and ova are gametes, or **germ cells.** All other cells are **body cells** (somatic cells). Germ cells and body cells differ not only in function but also in the way they divide and in the number of **chromosomes** they contain.

motile—Exhibiting or demonstrating the power of motion.
germ cells—Sperm or egg cells.
body cells—All the cells in the body except germ cells. Also called somatic cells.
chromosomes—The strands of deoxyribonucleic acid (DNA) and protein in the nucleus of each cell. They contain the genes that provide information vital for the duplication of cells and the transmission of inherited characteristics.

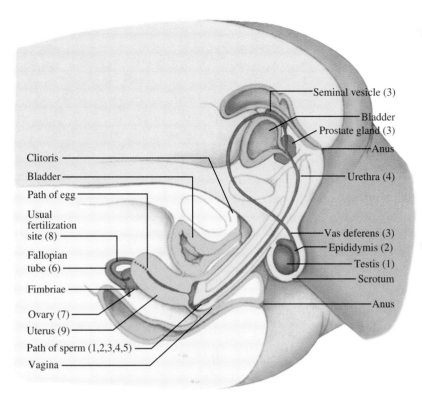

Sperm:

1. produced in the seminiferous tubules of the testes.
2. stored in epididymis.
3. during sexual arousal, travel through the vas and mix with seminal fluid from seminal vesicles and prostate.
4. released through urethra of penis during ejaculation.
5. deposited in the seminal pool of vagina, near cervix.
6. pass through cervix into uterus and Fallopian tubes.

Egg:

7. produced by one of the ovaries.
8. fertilization site in upper third of Fallopian tube.
9. site of implantation for developing zygote around 6th day.

Figure 8.2   Fertilization
This drawing illustrates the journey of egg and sperm toward fertilization, which generally occurs in the upper third of the Fallopian tube.

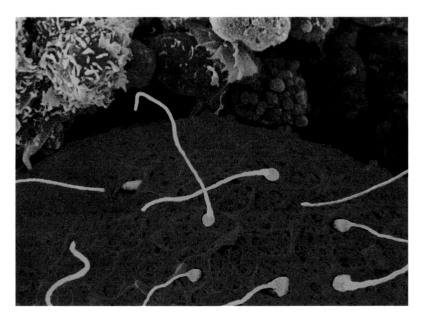

Although numerous sperm surround an egg, only one sperm is able to penetrate it, at which point the egg is impenetrable to other sperm.

Chromosomes—literally, "colored bodies"—are complex, threadlike bodies made up of two kinds of chemical material: deoxyribonucleic acid (DNA) and protein. They are found in the nucleus of every cell. All organisms possess chromosomes, which contain the genetic material that is passed on from generation to generation. Chromosomes were discovered in 1842, but the exact number contained in human cells was not clarified until 1956, when Tijo and Levin reported finding 46 chromosomes in embryonic cells.

The human body develops and repairs itself through a complex process of cell division. Division of the somatic, or body, cells occurs through **mitosis**, a process that creates two new, identical cells. The replication process leads to two new cells, called *daughter cells*, that are exactly like the original parent cell. Through mitosis, the single cell that is the fertilized ovum divides into the trillions of cells that make up every adult human.

The gametes, or germ cells, divide by a different process, called **meiosis**. This results in the production of sperm in males and ova in females. In each case, however, the process produces daughter cells having half the number of chromosomes contained in the parent cell. That is, in the testes and ovaries, a body cell with 46 chromosomes—23 pairs—divides in such a way that each daughter cell contains only one member of each pair of chromosomes. Thus, mature egg and sperm cells contain only 23 single chromosomes rather than 23 chromosome pairs. When a sperm and an egg cell unite, the resulting **embryo** contains 46 chromosomes, arranged in two sets of 23: one set from the mother and the other set from the father. This process ensures that the amount of genetic material will not double with each generation, producing embryos whose cell division becomes logistically impossible.

Chromosomes carry the information that determines a person's inherited characteristics. Strung along the length of each chromosome like beads are thousands of segments called **genes,** the basic units of hereditary information. Genes are made up of the complex chemical **deoxyribonucleic acid (DNA),** which is the information-containing molecule that forms part of every organism. DNA acts as a blueprint for all cellular activity. It determines the makeup of every cell in our bodies, each of which contains an estimated 100,000 genes that determine our inherited characteristics.

Through a microscope, chromosomes can be distinguished as either **sex chromosomes** (chromosomes that determine whether an individual is female or male) or **autosomes** (chromosomes that do not determine a person's genetic sex). The 22 pairs of autosomes are responsible for the differentiation of cells that results in various characteristics of the body.

SEX CHROMOSOMES AND GENETIC SEX

The twenty-third pair of chromosomes in each cell of the human body is composed of the sex chromosomes, X and Y. The X chromosome is about five times longer than the Y chromosome and contains at least 100 genes. A female has two X chromosomes in each body cell; a male has an X and a Y chromosome in each body cell. Therefore all eggs carry X chromosomes, whereas a sperm may carry either an X or a Y. If a sperm with an X chromosome fertilizes an egg, the offspring will be female (XX). If a sperm with a Y chromosome fertilizes an egg, the offspring will be male (XY). The genetic sex of a child is thus determined by the father. The gene sequence that determines male sexual differentiation exists on the Y chromosome (Lukusa, Fryns, & van den Berghe, 1992). *Reality or Myth* ❓

Our understanding of the genetic sex of an individual received a major boost in 1949 when Murray

---

mitosis—(my-TOE-sis) A form of cell division in which the nucleus divides into two daughter cells, each of which receives one nucleus and is an exact duplicate of the parent cell.

meiosis—(my-OH-sis) Cell division leading to the formation of gametes in which the number of chromosomes is reduced by half.

embryo—The unborn organism from the second to about the eighth week of pregnancy.

genes—Part of DNA molecules, found in chromosomes of cells, that are responsible for the transmission of hereditary material from parents to offspring.

deoxyribonucleic acid (DNA)—(dee-OX-see-RYE-boh-new-KLAY-ik) A chemically complex nucleic acid that is a principal element of genes.

sex chromosomes—The pair of chromosomes that determines whether an individual is female or male.

autosomes—The 22 pairs of chromosomes that are involved in general body development in humans.

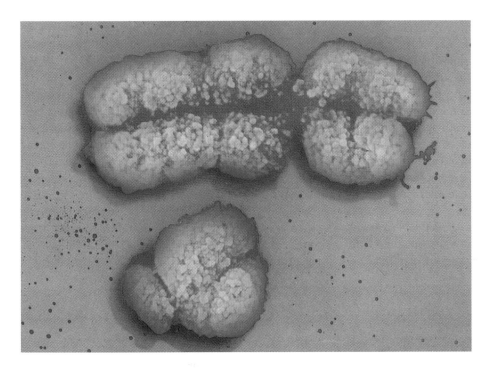

The Y chromosome can be detected by its fluorescence when it is stained, as the top picture shows.

L. Barr and E. G. Bertram reported that a well-defined mass of **chromatin**, the substance from which chromosomes form, is absent from the body cells of males but can be observed in the nuclei of female body cells at a certain phase in cell division. Through a microscope, the chromatin body appears as a dense clump of heavily stained material. It is called a **Barr body** in honor of the scientist who discovered it.

The Barr body does not appear in cells with only one X chromosome, for there is always less Barr body than there are X chromosomes. Thus, the cells of normal males, who have only one X chromosome, lack the Barr body, and the cells of normal females, who have two X chromosomes, have one Barr body. Because the presence or absence of the Barr body is an indication of the genetic status of XX or XY, respectively, it has been used to establish the genetic sex of athletes in the Olympics: cells are scraped from the lining of the cheek inside the mouth and examined with a microscope.

Part of the Y chromosome, when stained, appears as a small, brightly fluorescent body in the nuclei of male cells. This portion of the Y chromosome, called the *Y-body*, can also be used to determine genetic sex.

In addition to carrying the genes that determine genetic sex and sex characteristics, the X and Y chromosomes carry a variety of other genes. All the genes located on these sex chromosomes are called *sex-linked genes* because inheritance of these genes is connected to inheritance of the sex of the individual. Studies of patterns of inheritance are based on this concept of **sex linkage**: that a person who inherits a chromosome also inherits the genes it carries. Thus males, who always inherit a Y chromosome, inherit other Y-linked characteristics, such as testes formation. Males also inherit an X chromosome, however, and they inherit with it characteristics that

chromatin—(CROW-mah-tin) The substance in the nucleus of a cell from which chromosomes form during mitosis.
Barr body—Condensed, inactive X chromosome that distinguishes female cells from male cells. It appears as a dense clump when it is stained and examined under a microscope.

sex linkage—The connection between the sex chromosomes and the genes one inherits. When a person inherits a sex chromosome, he or she also inherits the genes it carries.

are X linked, some of which are not related to sex characteristics.

One of these conditions is color blindness, caused by a recessive gene. It usually occurs in males because only when a person's sex chromosomes are X and Y (as in a male) does a chromosome normally lack an identical paired chromosome. In females, both X chromosomes must carry a recessive gene before the characteristic controlled by the recessive gene is displayed. Because males can inherit recessive X-linked traits with only one recessive gene, they have more recessive X-linked traits. Thus, males are more susceptible than females to a number of disorders carried by recessive genes, such as hemophilia and color blindness, even though the transmitters of such disorders

are always females. There is evidence for more than 150 X-linked traits in humans, many of them disease related and recessive (McKusick & Amberger, 1993). Y-linked traits are comparatively few.

Because we inherit a set of genes from each parent, our two sets of genes do not contain identical genetic information. One gene in each set is usually dominant over the other, and it is the dominant gene that determines the person's inherited characteristic. For recessive genes to determine a person's characteristics, he or she must have either two recessive genes—one from each parent—or one recessive gene without a corresponding dominant gene. We now consider the remarkable process of prenatal development following conception.

Prenatal Development

The nine months of pregnancy, called **gestation**, are conventionally described in terms of three trimesters. The first trimester covers the first through the third month, the second spans the fourth through the sixth month, and the third extends from the seventh through the ninth month.

FIRST TRIMESTER

After fertilization has occurred but before a woman knows that she is pregnant, the embryo begins a period of rapid cell division. It has entered the *germinal stage*, a period of time encompassing the first two weeks following conception. Within 30 hours of conception, the embryo divides into two cells. Within three days, continuing cell division produces a solid ball of cells. Meanwhile, the embryo has been moving down the Fallopian tube toward the uterus and enters it at approximately this time (see Figure 8.3).

On about the fourth day, after entering the uterine cavity, the mass of cells separates into two parts. The outer cell mass develops into the major part of the **placenta**. On roughly the sixth day, the entire cell mass attaches itself to the uterine wall, and by the end of the first week, it is loosely implanted in the upper part of the uterus. By the end of the second week, the embryo is usually firmly implanted in the uterus. The outer layer of the embryo, call the *ectoderm*, will become the skin, sense organs, and nervous systems. The middle layer, the *mesoderm*, will develop into the heart, blood vessels, muscles, and skeleton. The inner layer, the *endoderm*, will form the respiratory system, the digestive system, and such related organs as the liver, pancreas, and salivary glands.

Meanwhile, the outer mass is developing into structures that nurture and protect the organism during its stay in the uterus: the chorion, the umbilical cord, and the amniotic sac. The **chorion**, which surrounds the embryo, thickens on one side to become the fetal portion of the placenta, and the placenta and the embryo remain connected by the umbilical cord. Through the **umbilical cord**, the embryo receives oxygen and nourishment from the mother's bloodstream and delivers its body wastes to the mother. The placenta protects the embryo

---

gestation—The entire period of prenatal development, from conception to birth.
placenta—The organ formed by the joining of the tissue of the uterine wall with that of the developing fetus; a major source of hormones during pregnancy.

chorion—The outermost of the two membranes that completely envelop a fetus.
umbilical cord—The connection of the fetus to the placenta, through which the fetus is nourished.

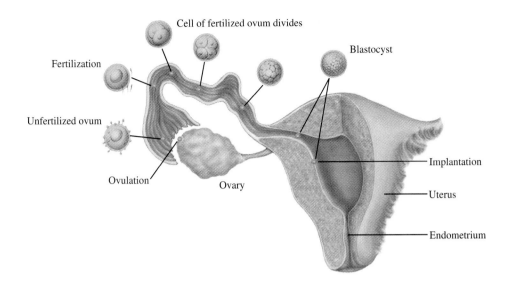

Cell of fertilized ovum divides

Blastocyst

Fertilization

Unfertilized ovum

Ovulation

Ovary

Implantation

Uterus

Endometrium

Figure 8.3
Fertilization and
Migration
The ovum is fertilized
typically in the upper
third of the Fallopian
tube, and numerous
cell divisions take
place before it im-
plants in the uterine
wall approximately
five days later.

from microbes, although small viruses such as rubella (responsible for German measles) can pass through to the embryo. The placenta produces the hormones that support pregnancy and that later assist in preparation of the mother's breasts for *lactation,* the manufacture and secretion of milk. The **amniotic sac** is a fluid-filled space bounded by the amniotic membrane that encases the developing organism, cushioning it, giving it room to move, and ensuring that it does not permanently adhere to the uterine wall.

A critical embryonic stage begins with full implantation of the cell mass at the beginning of the second week of pregnancy and lasts until the end of the eighth week. It is a period of remarkable growth, during which the embryo develops its major organs, among them the eyes, which begin to form by 21 days.

At the sixth or seventh week, about 100 embryonic cells become the material from which sperm or ova are produced 10 to 15 years later. This process is called *sexual differentiation*, and we return to it later in this chapter.

At eight weeks, the embryo is about 1 inch long. It has a recognizable brain and a heart that pumps blood through tiny arteries and veins. It has an intestinal system that produces digestive juices and a liver that manufactures blood cells. Its kidneys have

already begun to function, and it has an endocrine system. The embryo now has limbs and a disproportionately large head with eyes, nose, ears, and mouth, although its eyelids have not yet formed.

At the end of the eighth week, the head constitutes about half the length of the embryo. It has fingernails, toenails, lips, vocal cords, and a prominent nose. The arms have almost reached their final relative lengths, but the legs are not yet well developed.

From the ninth week on, beginning with the development of bone cells, the embryo becomes known as a **fetus**. These bone cells gradually begin to replace the cartilage cells that formed the initial embryonic skeleton, although cartilage continues to make up the soft parts of the nose and ears of an adult.

By the end of the twelfth week, the external genitals of the fetus are distinguishable. At this point, the fetus has also developed basic reflexes. If an aborted 12-week-old fetus has its lips stroked, it responds with a sucking reflex; if its eyelids are stroked, it squints. If its palm is touched, the fetus makes a partial fist.

Development during the first trimester illustrates a rule from evolutionary theory that **ontogeny** repeats the major stages of **phylogeny**. That is, during

fetus—The unborn organism from the ninth week until birth.
ontogeny—(on-JOF-en-ee) The history of the development of an individual organism.
phylogeny—(fu-LOJ-en-ee) The evolutionary history of a species or group.

amniotic sac—The pouch containing a watery fluid that envelops a developing fetus in the uterus.

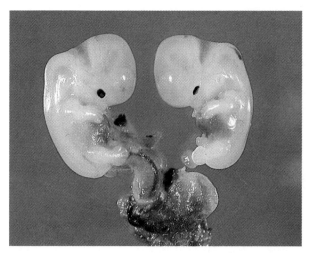

At eight weeks the embryo has the beginnings of both internal and external genitals. Fingernails, toenails, lips, nose, and ears have also begun to develop.

prenatal development, we briefly display characteristics of our evolutionary past. The embryo passes through a stage during which it has gill slits like those of our fish ancestors. These gill slits develop into the chin, cheek, jaw, and outer ear. We also have tails at one point during prenatal development. The tail develops into a small triangular bone—the coccyx, or tailbone—at the base of the spine.

Only a few new structures appear during the fetal period. Development primarily involves the growth and maturation of tissues and organs that began to form during the embryonic stage. This delicate growth continues as the fetus moves month by month toward the point of birth.

Second Trimester

The fourth month begins a period characterized by rapid body growth. The umbilical cord is as long as the fetus and continues to grow with it. Skeletal bones are hardening; X-rays (taken only for diagnostic reasons) clearly show skeletal bones by the beginning of the sixteenth week. The legs are well developed, and the ears stand out from the head. A fetus at this age can suck its thumb.

By the time a fetus is 5 months old, it appears in many ways to be a fully developed human being. If it were to be taken from its protective environment, however, it would not survive. Only about 10 inches long and weighing about half a pound, its lungs,

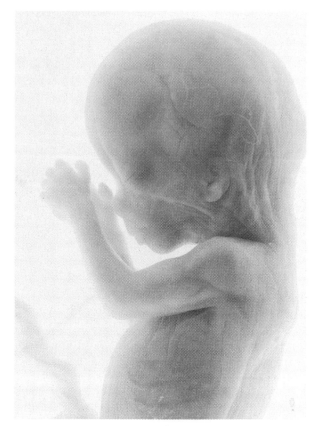

Weighing only about half a pound, this fetus could not survive outside the uterine environment.

though well formed, are not ready to function, and its digestive system cannot yet process food.

Reality or Myth ❓

The fetal skin is now covered by a greasy substance, the **vernix caseosa,** which protects it from abrasions and chapping as a result of being enveloped in the amniotic fluid. The 20-week-old fetus is usually covered with a fine, downy hair called **lanugo,** which may, among other things, help to hold the vernix on the skin. The fetus has now found its favorite position in the uterus and is stretching, squirming, and hiccuping.

At 6 months the fetus has begun to develop a padding of fat beneath its skin. Its skin is somewhat wrinkled and is pink-to-red in color because blood in

---

vernix caseosa—(VUR-nix kah-see-OH-sah) A greasy substance that protects the skin of the fetus.
lanugo—(lah-NEW-goh) Fine hair that appears on the developing fetus during the fifth or sixth month.

the capillaries has become visible. It can cry and make a fist with a strong grip, and all organs are fairly well developed. The fetus that is born prematurely at this point, however, often dies within a few days because of the functional immaturity of its respiratory system.

THIRD TRIMESTER

At 7 months a prematurely born fetus could live. Its potential for survival, however, is low because of the continuing likelihood of respiratory difficulties. A premature infant weighing at least 3½ pounds has a fairly good chance of survival if intensive medical care is provided. A fetus born at this point would probably have to live in an incubator until its weight increased to 5 pounds.

Lanugo may disappear around this time, or it may remain until shortly before birth. The skin is slightly wrinkled, but the fetus is filling out as fat forms under the skin. The nervous system has developed to the point that the fetus can sustain rhythmic breathing movements and control its body temperature. Eyes are open, and eyelashes are present. From this point on, the fetus is aware of events outside its mother's body. It responds to loud sounds as well as to the reaction of its mother's heart to such sounds.

At 8 months, layers of fat continue to develop and smooth out the skin. The fat helps the fetus adjust to the temperature variations that it will experience after leaving the uterus. The fetus is 18 to 20 inches long, and it weighs between 5 and 7 pounds.

At 9 months most fetuses are plump and crowd the uterus. The reddish color of the skin is fading. The chest is prominent, and the mammary glands protrude in both males and females because they are affected by the hormones that are preparing the mother's breasts to secrete milk. In males the testes have usually descended from the abdominal cavity into the scrotum.

During the ninth month the fetus usually acquires some antibodies from its mother's bloodstream. These provide the fetus with temporary immunity against bacteria and viruses from which its mother is protected. This is important because the newborn's immune system is not yet fully functional. It is now ready for birth, but we will save the description of that remarkable event until Chapter 9.

We now return to a point shortly after the sixth week of pregnancy to describe the remarkable series of changes that result in our genital appearance as males or females (at least most of the time) when we are born.

Typical Sexual Differentiation

The process by which we differentiate into either males or females occurs in a series of stages. The early stages take place during the development of the embryo and fetus, but differentiation is not completed until puberty (see Table 8.1 on page 178). Although the steps are usually predictable, errors occasionally occur. We look first at the normal processes.

As described earlier, your genetic sex was determined at conception as a result of whether the sperm that your father contributed contained an X or a Y chromosome. If someone with X-ray vision had peered at you in your mother's womb six weeks after you were conceived, they could have seen your eyes and your major organs, but they would have been unable to tell whether you were a male or a female. Shortly after the sixth week, however, the process of sexual differentiation began, and it continued until about the twelfth or thirteenth week of gestation.

GONADAL SEX

At 8 weeks the embryo, whether it is genetically male (XY) or female (XX), has a pair of gonads (which will become testes or ovaries). It also contains tissues that may eventually develop into female or male structures. The tissue that develops into female structures (the Fallopian tubes, the uterus, and the upper part of the vagina), is called the **Müllerian-duct system.** The lower two-thirds of the vagina forms from the same tissue that gives rise to the urinary bladder and

---

Müllerian-duct system—Fetal tissue that develops into the internal female reproductive structures if the fetus is genetically female.

TABLE 8.1   Chronology of Sexual Differentiation

Prenatal Development

Characteristic	Source	Male Development	Female Development
Gonadal	Y chromosome	Testes	Ovaries
Internal sex organs	Androgens and Müllerian-inhibiting substance	Wolffian structures develop into ejaculatory duct and other reproductive structures; Müllerian structures degenerate	Wolffian structures degenerate; Müllerian structures develop into uterus, Fallopian tubes, and other reproductive structures
External sex organs	Level of androgens	Scrotal sacs and penis	Labia and clitoris
Brain	Level of androgens	Masculine organization	Feminine organization

Pubescent Development

Characteristic	Source	Male Development	Female Development
Breasts	Pituitary growth hormone, estrogens, progestins		Growth of breasts (8–13 years)
Genitals	Pituitary growth hormone, testosterone, estrogen	Growth of testes, scrotal sac (10–14 years); penis (11–15 years)	Growth of vagina and clitoris, enlargement of uterus, increase in length and width of Fallopian tubes (8–14 yrs.)
Pubic hair	Testosterone in males; adrenal androgens in females	Growth of pubic hair (10–15 years)	Growth of pubic hair (8–14 years)
Menarche	Gonadotropin-releasing hormones, FSH, LH, estrogens, progestins		Onset of menstrual cycle (10–17 years)
Voice change	Testosterone	Growth of larynx, deepening of voice (11–15 years)	
Body hair	Testosterone in males; adrenal androgens in females	Growth of underarm and facial hair (12–17 years)	Growth of underarm hair (10–16 years)
Oil and sweat glands	Testosterone in males; adrenal androgens in females	Development of oil- and sweat-producing glands; acne (12–17 years)	Development of oil- and sweat-producing glands; acne when glands blocked (10–16 years)

urethra. The embryonic tissue that develops into male structures become the epididymis, vas deferens, seminal vesicles, and ejaculatory duct and is called the **Wolffian-duct system.** If no Y chromosome is present, the embryo continues to grow for another few weeks before the outer part of the primitive gonads develops into ovaries packed with immature egg cells (see Figure 8.4). *Reality or Myth*

HORMONAL SEX

The early development of the testes appears to be related to another embryonic phenomenon that provides a clue to how the process of sexual differentia-

Wolffian-duct system—Fetal tissue that develops into the internal male reproductive structures if the fetus is genetically male.

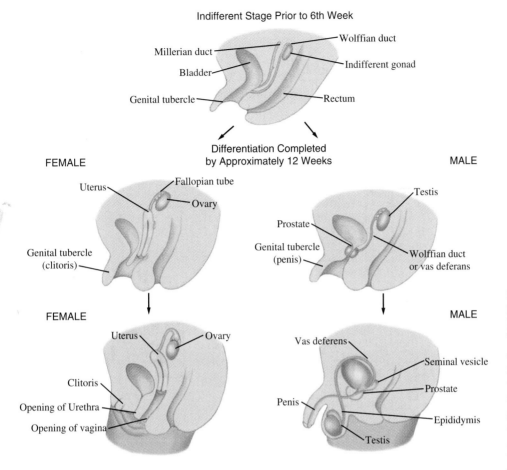

Indifferent Stage Prior to 6th Week

Millerian duct
Bladder
Genital tubercle
Wolffian duct
Indifferent gonad
Rectum

Differentiation Completed
by Approximately 12 Weeks

FEMALE

Uterus
Fallopian tube
Ovary
Genital tubercle
(clitoris)

MALE

Testis
Prostate
Genital tubercle
(penis)
Wolffian duct
or vas deferans

FEMALE

Uterus
Ovary
Clitoris
Opening of Urethra
Opening of vagina

MALE

Vas deferens
Seminal vesicle
Prostate
Penis
Epididymis
Testis

Figure 8.4
Internal Gender Differentiation
This diagram shows differentiation of the internal sexual structures in a male or female direction. This gender differentiation occurs during the latter part of the first trimester of pregnancy.

tion works. If the gonads are removed during the critical embryonic period, the embryo develops as a female, even if it is genetically (XY) male. Therefore, as John Money and Anke Ehrhardt (1972, p. 7) put it, "Nature's rule is, it would appear, that to masculinize, something must be added." This extra something consists of **testosterone** and **Müllerian-inhibiting substance (MIS)**. When the primitive gonads differentiate as testes in the male, they begin to manufacture these two substances.

▶ **Issues to Consider:** In describing fetal sex differentiation, Money and Ehrhardt concluded that "nature's rule is, it would appear, that to masculinize, something must be added." What is the evidence for their conclusion?

testosterone—The major natural androgen.
Müllerian-inhibiting substance (MIS)—A hormone secreted by the fetal testes that inhibits the growth and development of the Müllerian-duct system.

Testosterone promotes the development of the Wolffian ducts into the internal male reproductive structures, whereas MIS is responsible for curbing the growth of the Müllerian-duct system. Both of these substances must be present for normal development of the internal reproductive structures of the male. In normal male anatomical development, only one of the duct systems expands and develops. The development of the other system regresses, so that only traces of it remain in the body.

Because of the popular definition of **androgens** as "masculinizing hormones" and **estrogens** as "feminizing hormones," many people mistakenly assume that we produce one or the other, depending on whether we are male or female. In fact, both males

androgens—Generic term for hormones that promote the development and functioning of the male reproductive system.
estrogens—Generic term for hormones that promote development and functioning of the female reproductive system.

The Major Sex Hormones

Androgens The general name for masculinizing sex hormones; the two most common are testosterone and androstenedione. In males most of the androgen is produced in the testes; a small portion (about 5 percent) is produced by the adrenal glands. In females the ovaries and adrenal glands manufacture small amounts of androgen. Testosterone is considered to be the major biological determinant of sexual desire in men and women.

Estrogens The general name for feminizing hormones that are secreted in the ovaries, testes, and placenta. Of the three major estrogens in humans, the most potent and abundant is estradiol. In both males and females, estradiol is synthesized within the body from progesterone of which the source is the steroidal substance cholesterol, from which the body derives all of its steroidal hormones. In females estrogens are important in maintaining the elasticity of the vagina and the texture and function of the breasts. They also contribute to the production of vaginal lubricant. In males the function of estrogens is unknown. Too much estrogen in males can result in diminished sexual desire, enlargement of the breasts, and difficulties with erection.

Progestagens The general name for hormones that prepare the reproductive organs for pregnancy. The most abundant, progesterone, is produced by the corpus luteum of an ovary. Generally, progestagens are active only in females because the hormones' effect is dependent on the previous action of estrogen. Males who receive estrogen and progesterone sequentially develop functional mammary glands. Progesterone inhibits the flow of cervical mucus that occurs during ovulation, and it diminishes the thickness of the vaginal lining.

Follicle-stimulating hormone (FSH) One of the gonadotropins (gonad changers) secreted by the pituitary gland. Beginning at puberty, FSH stimulates the production of sperm cells in the testes in males and prepares the ovary for ovulation in females.

Luteinizing hormone (LH) Another gonadotropin that is produced by the pituitary. In females LH triggers ovulation, the release of an egg from the ovary. In males it is sometimes referred to as interstitial cell stimulating hormone because it stimulates the interstitial (Leydig) cells of the testes to manufacture testosterone.

Prolactin A hormone produced by the pituitary gland that stimulates the production of milk in the breasts.

Oxytocin A pituitary hormone that causes milk to flow from the glandular tissue of the breast to the nipple in response to a baby's sucking and induces strong uterine contractions during childbirth. It is also released by males and females during the orgasmic phase of sexual response.

Vasoactive intestinal polypeptide A peptide hormone involved in erection of the penis and vaginal blood flow during sexual arousal.

Gonadotropin-releasing hormone (GnRH) A hormone produced by the hypothalamus that regulates the secretion of both follicle-stimulating hormone and luteinizing hormone by the pituitary. GnRH is also called luteinizing hormone-releasing factor.

Inhibin A hormone produced by the testes that regulates sperm production by reducing the pituitary gland's secretion of FSH. It is also produced by ovaries. It feeds back to inhibit FSH release in females too.

---

and females secrete the same three kinds of sex hormones. In males the testes synthesize progesterone, one of a general class of feminizing hormones called **progestagens** (pregnancy promoting); testosterone (an androgen); and **estradiol** (an estrogen). Similarly, in females the ovaries secrete progesterone, androgens, and estrogen. Both males and females also secrete small amounts of all these hormones from the outer portion (cortex) of their adrenal glands (see "Highlight: The Major Sex Hormones").

progestagens—Generic term for hormones that prepare the female reproductive system for pregnancy.
estradiol—The major natural estrogen, secreted by the ovaries, testes, and placenta.

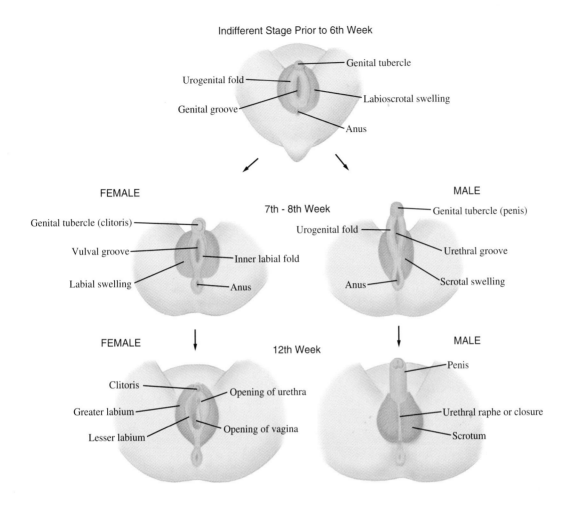

Indifferent Stage Prior to 6th Week

Figure 8.5 Differentiation of External Genitals
After the internal reproductive structures of the fetus have differentiated, the external genitals differentiate in a male or female direction, as this figure shows.

Sexual differentiation depends on the relative amounts of these hormones in much the same way that the products of baking depend on the amounts of flour, sugar, salt, leavening, shortening, eggs, and liquid. Just as a cake is generally made with larger proportions of sugar and shortening, and bread results from higher proportions of flour and salt, the development of sexual anatomy is influenced by the relative proportions of androgens and estrogens secreted, as well as the numbers of cells that are responsive to these hormones. The proportion of androgens and estrogens varies somewhat among individuals, but as long as this variation falls within

normal limits, it does not seem to affect the individual's gender identity or sexual functioning. The effects of differences in the levels of masculinizing and feminizing hormones on the developing brain are a subject of controversy.

GENITAL SEX

Several weeks after the internal structures of the embryo have differentiated, with one set of potential reproductive organs beginning to develop and the other set failing to do so, the external genitals start to differentiate (see Figure 8.5). Our external genitals are created from a small, protruding bud of tissue called a **genital tubercle,** an opening with two small swellings called the **labioscrotal swellings,** and folds or strips of skin called the **urogenital folds** on each side of the tubercle. If testes are developing, testosterone begins circulating in the bloodstream. As we have seen, testosterone acts directly on the Wolffian ducts to cause differentiation of the vas deferens, epididymis, and seminal vesicles. For the development of the external male genitals, however, **dihydrotestosterone (DHT),** produced by the metabolism of testosterone in cells within and outside the testes, is needed. DHT causes the elongation of the genital tubercle into the **phallus.** As the phallus grows, it pulls the urogenital folds forward, and they fuse with each other on the underside of the penis to form a urethral tube. The urethra connects to the bladder, prostate gland, and vas deferens. The two labioscrotal swellings fuse together to form a scrotum, which houses the testes when they eventually descend from the abdominal cavity, about eight months after conception.

The development of female external genitals needs no hormonal prompting; it occurs in the absence of androgens. In females, the genital tubercle remains relatively small and becomes a clitoris. Instead of fusing, the urogenital folds of skin remain distinct and form the two inner vaginal lips and the clitoral hood. The two labioscrotal swellings also remain separate, forming the two outer vaginal lips. The opening develops a dividing wall of tissue that separates the vaginal entrance to the uterus from the urethra, which connects to the bladder.

We have been discussing normal development and sexual differentiation. However, much of our understanding of those normal processes has been produced by studies of atypical development, the topic to which we turn now.

Atypical Sexual Differentiation

Variations in the process of sexual differentiation can occur at any stage of development. Abnormalities can be caused by defects in chromosomes, environmental threats to fetal development, inheritance of atypical sex chromosomes, abnormal differentiation of gonads, or alterations in the secretion or metabolism of sex hormones. Although there are many types of autosomal defects, we focus only on sex chromosome abnormalities.

Sex Chromosome Abnormalities

So far, more than 70 irregularities of the sex chromosomes have been identified (Hoyenga & Hoyenga,

1993). Many of these result from abnormal combinations of sex chromosomes that cause a person to be neither an XX female nor an XY male. Some of the more common sex chromosome abnormalities are presented in Table 8.2.

The X chromosome appears to be crucial for survival. The genes on the Y chromosome are coded for "maleness" and little else (Lukasa, Bryns, & van den Berghe, 1992). The presence of a single Y chromosome generally results in an individual's having a male appearance, no matter how many X chromosomes that person has in his chromosomal makeup. Female development can occur without the presence of a second X, as in Turner's syndrome (see Table 8.2). But the absence of the second X reduces the likelihood of ovarian development and fertility.

In general, extra X chromosomes make no difference in females, but they may make males more like females. An extra Y chromosome, however, may increase height. In addition, the presence of extra X and Y chromosomes appears to be related to below-normal intelligence in some people, although the intelligence of individuals with an extra Y chromosome is not as limited as that of persons with extra X chromosomes (Hoyenga & Hoyenga, 1993).

---

genital tubercle—A small, protruding bud of fetal tissue that develops into either a penis or a clitoris.

labioscrotal swellings—The fetal tissue that develops into either the scrotum in a male or the two outer vaginal lips in a female.

urogenital folds—Folds or strips on each side of the genital tubercle of the fetus that fuse to form the urethral tube in a male or the inner vaginal lips in a female.

dihydrotestosterone (DHT)—A hormone produced from testosterone that is responsible for the development of the external genitals of the male fetus.

phallus—The penis.

TABLE 8.2   Common Sex Chromosome Abnormalities

Syndrome	Makeup of Chromosomes	Incidence per Live Births	Characteristics	Treatment
Klinefelter's Syndrome	XXY; in rare cases an additional X occurs (XXXY).	1 in 1,000	Shrunken testes, breast development (gynecomastia) in about one-half of all cases, disproportionate arms and legs, elevated urinary gonadotropins, infertility in most cases, low levels of testosterone sometimes, increased likelihood of mental retardation	Administration of testosterone during adolescence often produces more masculine body contours and sexual characteristics in addition to increasing sexual drive.
XYY Syndrome	XYY	1 in 1,000	Genital irregularities, decreased fertility, increased likelihood of mental retardation	None
Turner's Syndrome	XO	1 in 5,000*	Short stature (4 to 5 ft), loose or weblike skin around the neck, a broad and "shieldlike" chest with the nipples widely spaced, nonfunctional ovaries, no menstruation or development of adult breasts, infertility in almost all cases	Administration of estrogen and progesterone can induce menstruation and development of the breasts, external genitals, and pubic hair. Androgen administered during puberty can help the child attain a greater adult height.
Triple-X Syndrome	XXX	1 in 1,000	Almost no major abnormalities, though these women are likely to be less fertile than XX females; higher incidence of mental disturbance than among XX females	None

*This figure is not an accurate indicator of the incidence of the condition. About one-tenth of all pregnancies that end in spontaneous abortion are XO—although this is a conservative estimate because many embryos with Turner's syndrome and other atypical chromosomal patterns are spontaneously aborted, at times before the woman is even aware she is pregnant.

INCONSISTENCIES IN SEXUAL DIFFERENTIATION

In addition to atypical sex chromosome patterns, another cause of atypical sexual differentiation is an error in the differentiation process during prenatal development. A discrepancy may occur between genetic sex and gonadal, hormonal, or genital sex. An inconsistency in the process of sexual differentiation results in a condition known as **intersexuality**. Inter-sex conditions also include birth defects of sex organs, accidents, and atypical changes in body structure at puberty. *Reality or Myth* 🔲

intersexuality—A condition in which a person is born with both male and female characteristics, such as an ovary on one side and a testis on the other, with an ova-testis on each side, or with ambiguous genitals. Also called *hermaphroditism*.

One source of potential variations in sexual differentiation is exposure to excessive levels of sex hormones during prenatal development. Exposure of genetic males to excessive levels of androgen appears to have no effect on the development of their internal and external genitals, but it may affect behavior. Ehrhardt (1975) compared nine boys who were prenatally exposed to higher-than-normal levels of androgens to their unaffected siblings. The androgen-exposed boys differed from their brothers only in their greater interest in sports and rough outdoor activities.

Prenatal exposure to elevated levels of estrogen and progestagens does not affect anatomical development and has little effect on the gender-related behavior of human males (Reinisch, Ziemba-Davis, & Sanders, 1991). The effects of excess estrogen on human genetic females are not clear. There appear to be no effects on sexual differentiation of the genitals and little or no effect on gender-role behavior (Lish, Meyer-Bahlburg, Ehrhardt, Travis, & Veridian, 1992).

Sexual Differentiation in Genetic Males. As we have seen, hormones are important in the determination of early sexual differentiation. Thus, it may be reasonable to assume that atypical patterns of exposure to sex hormones might lead to atypical sexual differentiation. Numerous researchers have investigated this hypothesis.

Some XY people have a condition known as **androgen insensitivity syndrome** (AIS, sometimes called testicular feminization). The male secretes normal amounts of androgen, but the normal target cells are unresponsive to it. These males do not have an androgen receptor gene on the X chromosome.

The Wolffian structures of an AIS fetus fail to develop into normal internal male structures (prostate, seminal vesicles, and vas deferens) because they are insensitive to androgen. MIS, however, is usually produced, so the Müllerian structures do not develop either. Thus, the baby is born without a complete set of either male or female internal genital organs.

AIS individuals develop a normal clitoris and a short vagina. The vagina generally does not lead to a

---

androgen insensitivity syndrome—Condition in which males secrete normal levels of androgen but lack a normal androgen receptor gene on the X chromosome and are thus unresponsive to androgen.

---

functional uterus, but occasionally a small structure regarded as a rudimentary uterus is present. Testes do not usually descend; if they do, they appear only as small lumps near the labia. (These small lumps are often misdiagnosed as hernias.) The undescended gonads (testes) do not produce viable sperm. Because people with this syndrome respond to the presence of female hormones, breast development and female pelvic changes occur at the onset of puberty. Menstruation does not occur, however, and the person with AIS cannot reproduce.

AIS individuals can engage in sexual activity and reach orgasm. Because their genitals appear to be female, they are typically reared as females from birth, and they develop feminine identities. Surgery is sometimes conducted to lengthen the upper vagina for satisfactory sexual intercourse, but this intervention is controversial (Chase, personal communication, 1997). Insertion of elongated devices into the vagina to increase its capacity to expand during arousal is an alternative to surgery for some people. If testes are discovered, they are generally surgically removed during childhood or adolescence because leaving the testes in place increases the risk of cancer. These individuals then take estrogen supplements to replace the estrogen formerly secreted by the testes.

John Money and his colleagues studied 14 males with AIS who were reared as females. In attitude and behavior, they resembled traditional females, exhibiting well-developed maternal desires. The research group described them as excellent adoptive mothers (Money & Ehrhardt, 1972). Because they were socialized as females, of course, it is difficult to separate the effects of their insensitivity to androgen from the effects of their being brought up as females.

People with a condition known as *partial androgen insensitivity syndrome* can make partial use of testosterone. The infant is born with a "penis" only slightly larger than a clitoris and a urethra located in the peritoneal area rather than in the penis. His scrotum is partially unfused, and the testes can be felt as lumps in the groin. The usual treatment has been to rear this child as a female. Surgery can reduce the size of the penis and separate the scrotum to open and deepen the vagina. The Intersex Society of North America (ISNA), a peer support group for intersexual people and their families, has challenged the need for this type of surgery in infancy or childhood be-

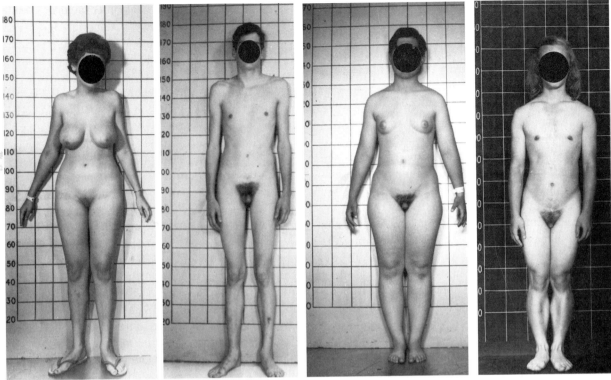

As you can see from these clinical photos of two genetic males with AIS (left) and also those of two females with CAH (right), the effects of these conditions on the persons who have them can vary considerably. Clinical photos of such intersexed individuals typically block out their faces as is shown here. However, as Cheryl Chase, Executive Director of Intersex Society of North America (ISNA) has pointed out, such portrayals tend to dehumanize intersexed people.

cause the outcome is often unsatisfactory, and the children are not given the opportunity to provide informed consent. Estrogens can be administered to produce the development of breasts and other feminine characteristics.

Occasionally an individual with AIS has a phallus large enough to cause him to be identified as a male at birth. When he reaches puberty, however, he begins to develop breasts and lacks masculine body traits. His penis may not have the ability to become erect, and his prostate gland may not produce ejaculatory fluid. Surgery can complete the fusion of his scrotum and bring his sterile testes down into it, but it cannot make his penis grow. His pubescent breasts can be surgically removed, but masculine secondary sexual characteristics cannot be created. Giving him extra doses of testosterone is useless. He is already producing all that he needs; the problem is that his body cells cannot use it. People with AIS or partial AIS tend to have bodies that appear female, and they

have difficult sex lives. For individuals with AIS, then, the possession of an XY chromosome pattern and testes does not always mean being "male."

▶ **Issues to Consider:** If you were (or are) a parent, how would you respond to the news that physicians have determined that your son has androgen insensitivity syndrome (AIS) or partial AIS?

In a condition known as **hypospadias**, some boys are born with an atypical position of the opening of the urethra through which urine passes (Mureau, Slijper, Slob, & Verhulst, 1995). Hypospadias can result when testosterone is insufficiently converted to dihydrotestosterone to produce normal penile fusion

hypospadias (HY-poe-SPAY-dee-us)—A condition in which the urethral opening is located somewhere other than at the tip of the penis.

during prenatal development. The urethral opening may be located on the glans (but not at the end of the glans, as is typical for most males), on the corona, at some point along the shaft of the penis, at the junction of the penis and scrotum, or on the perineum—the area between the anus and the scrotal sac. Depending on the distance of the urethral opening from the glans, surgical reconstruction may be performed to improve males' ability to urinate while standing and to engage in unhampered sexual and reproductive functioning in adulthood. The penis is often circumcised as part of the reconstruction.

According to a study sponsored by the Centers for Disease Control (Paulozzi, Erickson, & Jackson, 1997), the rates for hypospadias nearly doubled between 1968 and 1993, now supposedly affecting nearly 1 per 100 boys nationwide. However, it is not clear whether this increase stems from an actual increase in the anomaly, or merely from an increase in reporting.

As you can see from the definition given, the extremity of the distance from the tip of the penis and the urethral opening can vary widely. It is possible that some babies now diagnosed as having a condition needing medical intervention were previously perceived as simply having a slight variation in the location of their urethral opening. Similar to the increase in the reported number of hypospadia, Alice Dreger (1998) described a dramatic increase in the reported number of cases of intersexuality. This author cited a 1995 study (Fichtner, Filipas, Mottrie, Voges, & Hohenfellner) in which 45 percent of a random sample of men were diagnosed as hypospadic, but all but 6 of the 225 men given this diagnosis were unaware of any penile "abnormality." Dreger expressed concern about the possibility of an increase in hypospadias surgeries' producing an increase in "hypospadias cripples"—men made miserable and dysfunctional by surgeries designed to "correct" a merely "cosmetic" problem (*ISNA News*, 1997).

In an intriguing interaction between cultural attitudes toward circumcision and medical diagnoses and treatments, Marc Mureau et al. (1995), working with a sample of Dutch men operated on for hypospadias, noted that the men's perceptions of their genitals postsurgically were significantly more negative when they viewed their penises as different from those of other males, and when men were dissatisfied

with their circumcised status that occurred as a result of surgery. (Circumcision is uncommon among Dutch males.) In North America, where circumcision is the norm rather than the exception, presumably having a circumcised penis would not increase negative reactions to the surgery. Mureau et al. recommended that treatments for hypospadias that save the foreskin should be offered as an alternative in countries where circumcision is uncommon.

Dihydrotestosterone-deficiency (DHT) syndrome is a genetic disorder that prevents the prenatal conversion of testosterone into DHT. Males with DHT-deficiency syndrome lack an enzyme (5-alpha reductase) that is necessary for this conversion. As described earlier, DHT stimulates the development of the external male genitals. Thus, at birth, males with DHT-deficiency syndrome do not have identifiably male genitals.

Researchers studied 33 genetically male inhabitants of an isolated village in the Dominican Republic who had the enzyme deficiency (Imperato-McGinley, Guerrero, Gautier, & Peterson, 1974; Imperato-McGinley et al., 1982). At birth these males had genitals that either were ambiguous or resembled those of females. At puberty, however, they experienced an increase in muscle mass, growth of the phallus and scrotum, and deepening of the voice. Nineteen of the males studied by the researchers had been brought up as females to the age of puberty. Of these, adequate information could be obtained on 18. The research team reported that of the 18, 16 gradually adopted a masculine gender identity and an erotic interest in women. These observations have been questioned, however, by others who found that about two-thirds of the 19 DHT males adopted a male gender role (Herdt, 1994).

Julio Imperato-McGinley and her colleagues hypothesized that the increase in testosterone at puberty masculinized not only the body but also the mind, including the sex drive. Thus nature seems to have triumphed over nurture among these boys. As you might expect, however, this explanation is over-

---

dihydrotestosterone-deficiency (DHT) syndrome—Genetic disorder that prevents the prenatal conversion of testosterone into DHT because of the absence of an enzyme (5-alpha reductase) that is necessary for this conversion. At birth, males with DHT-deficiency syndrome do not have identifiably male genitals.

simplified and underestimates some important psychosocial factors. Although these males lived as girls, they had been stigmatized as freaks. At age 12, they were called *huevodoces*, which translates literally as "eggs [balls] at twelve." They were also known as *machihembra*, which translates roughly to "macho miss," with the implication that they were half-girl, half-boy freaks. In their traditional village culture, there was no possibility of their becoming wives or mothers, nor was there any other feminine role for them that would not make them an economic liability to their families. The only real alternative was for them to adapt as best they could to being males.

Further implicating the role of psychosocial variables in DHT-deficiency syndrome, Gilbert Herdt and Julian Davidson (1988) described five males in New Guinea who were reared as females until puberty, at which point they changed to a male role. The researchers reported that these individuals suffered considerable social trauma in making the gender switch. Because they live in a male-dominant society, however, their gender switching was a practical adaptation in that it potentially elevated their status.

Clearly gender identity and sexual orientation cannot be ascribed to any one nature or nurture variable. Rather, it is an example of the sexual interactions that occur during the development of biological and psychological characteristics. The "females" would not have changed to "males" if their bodies had not changed so dramatically at puberty. After their bodies no longer supported a feminine identity, cultural expectations and social conditions helped to create their gender-identity change.

Sexual Differentiation in Genetic Females. Prenatal exposure to excess androgen has the effect of masculinizing genetic females. Research has identified three sources of such masculinization: (1) malfunction of fetal adrenal glands, (2) administration of hormones to pregnant women, and (3) ovarian tumors during pregnancy.

A condition known as **congenital adrenal hyperplasia (CAH)** is a genetically transmitted malfunction of the adrenal glands. The fetus with this condition secretes too much adrenal androgen. Normally the adrenal glands secrete both cortisol and androgens (cortisol is related to androgen levels in the body). The adrenal glands of CAH females, however, fail to synthesize cortisol and instead secrete excess androgens (Diamond, 1996a).*

The release of extra androgens during the critical period for differentiation of the external genitals (about three months after conception) leads to masculinization of the external genitals. The vagina may not be open, and the clitoris is often enlarged. The surge in androgen comes too late in development to affect the internal organs, so the ovaries, Fallopian tubes, and uterus are normal (Zucker & Bradley, 1995). If it is realized at birth that the masculinized baby is really a female, her external genitals can be surgically altered shortly after birth, but this practice has been questioned (Reiner, 1997). For example, surgical reduction of an enlarged clitoris can reduce sensation and thus interfere with genital pleasure. The CAH female can be given cortisone to reduce the output of androgens from the adrenal glands. Under these conditions, the child usually will be relatively well adjusted and undergo the typical sexual differentiation associated with puberty (Zucker, 1996). If the problem is not corrected by cortisone injections from infancy onward, however, the excessive androgen secretion continues to masculinize the child after birth and at puberty.

In a comparison of CAH women with their unaffected sisters or cousins, CAH women had lower rates of heterosexual fantasies and fewer sexual experiences with men. However, they did not have more sexual experience with women. CAH women recalled more cross-gender role behavior and less comfort with their sense of femininity during childhood than did the control group women. There was no difference in gender dysphoria (discomfort with one's biological sex or assigned gender) between the two groups (Zucker et al., 1996). Although intervention specialists have invariably emphasized that CAH females should be assigned the feminine role, many of these people eventually take on a male role (Meyer-Bahlburg et al., 1996).

congenital adrenal hyperplasia (CAH)—Genetic malfunction of the adrenal glands resulting in secretion of too much adrenal androgen during prenatal development, leading to masculinization of genetic females.

---

*Males can also inherit CAH, but it is not detected except for illnesses that some males experience from malfunctioning of the adrenal glands.

Cheryl Chase and a number of her intersexed colleagues have attempted to halt the traditional practice of performing clitoral surgery on intersexed infants before they can give their informed consent. Seen in this photo before the U.S. Capitol Building where they lobbied Congress to extend protection against clitordectomies to intersexed infants are, from left to right, Heidi Walcutt, OR; Martha Coventry, MN; Cheryl Chase, CA; and Kiira Triea, MD. They are conferring with Nancy Buermeyer of the Human Rights Campaign.

Changes in maternal hormone levels may masculinize the external genitals of genetic females. Hormone levels can change because of ovarian tumors that secrete hormones that masculinize the fetus, or because the mother receives synthetic progestins during pregnancy (Ehrhardt, Meyer-Bahlburg, Feldman, & Ince, 1984; Reinisch, Ziemba-Davis, & Sanders, 1991). At one time progestins were given to women who were at risk of miscarriage to help them maintain their pregnancies. Progestagens, whether natural or synthetic (progestins), are biochemically similar to androgens and may be metabolized to androgens, acting on the body in similar ways. Follow-up studies of baby girls born to women who took progestagens during their pregnancies have shown that the masculinizing effects of the hormones were limited to the prenatal period. After the babies were born, the masculinizing influence ended.

At birth the appearance of babies' genitals affected by progestins varied, depending on the strength of the masculinizing hormone. Some looked female, some looked male, and some looked ambiguous. Their internal reproductive organs, however, developed normally. Thus, babies recognized as females and given adequate surgical and hormonal treatment developed normally and were capable of reproduction.

The fate of genetic females with progestin-induced masculinized external genitals provides another example of the interaction of biological, psychological, and social factors in the formation of gender identity. When the effect of the progestin is pronounced, females may be born with a clitoris the size of a penis and with labia that have fused and give the appearance of a scrotum. The "penis" may even contain the urethral tube. Under these circumstances, the pronouncement at birth that "it's a boy" is quite understandable. The fact that the newborn's "scrotum" is empty would not necessarily raise questions, because in 2 percent of all males, the testes do not descend into the scrotum until after birth. At puberty, however, the child's ovaries secrete normal amounts of estrogen, which elicits menarche (first menstruation) and the beginnings of female body contours. By this time, of course, the genetic female has lived 12 or more years under the assumption that she is a male, and the discovery of her internal femininity, not to mention the enlargement of breasts, can be a shock. After living so many years with a male gender identity, the person may choose to have the female internal organs (ovaries and uterus) removed surgically. At the same time, administration of androgen helps to masculinize the body, and artificial testes can be inserted into the scrotum, although no sperm will be produced.

ASSIGNED SEX VERSUS GENETIC SEX

Money and Ehrhardt (1972) made an intriguing comparison among genetic females with (1) progestin-induced masculinization, (2) congenital adrenal hyperplasia (CAH), and (3) normal sexual differentiation. Individuals in all three groups were perceived as female at birth and were reared with no ambiguity regarding their gender. The 10 girls in the first group were exposed to progestin prenatally but to no masculinizing agents after birth. The 15 girls in the second group were immediately recognized as having CAH and placed on cortisone therapy to correct the condition.

Comparisons of the childhood behavior of the girls in the first two groups with that of the 25 normal girls in the third group indicated that the prenatally masculinized girls were more likely to display a number of stereotypically male interests and behaviors while developing a female gender identity. They liked strenuous physical activity and were not concerned about "feminine" attire. They tended to join boys in rough games such as football. Girls in the first two groups were more likely to be described as tomboys throughout their childhood. Although some of the girls in the normal control group also engaged in episodes of tomboyish behavior—a stage that is typical for most girls in our culture—the consistency of the behavior in the first two groups led Money and Ehrhardt to speculate that the masculine childhood behavior was linked to the presence of progestin or androgen during prenatal development. The behavioral differences between the CAH girls and the normal girls could derive from genetic factors or from some alteration in the uterine environment other than the excess androgen. The girls who were prenatally masculinized by the artificial progestins, however, showed many of the same masculine childhood behaviors.

The dosage level appears to be a crucial factor in the effect of progestin. With the use of lower dosages of progestin, the masculinizing effect Money and Ehrhardt saw does not appear (Freund, 1985). In fact, Ehrhardt et al. (1984) reported that young girls who had been exposed to low dosages of progestin prenatally exhibited slightly more female-stereotyped behavior than did normal girls.

Secondary Sexual Characteristics

After the period from the sixth to the twelfth week of gestation, sexual differentiation remains relatively inactive until around the age of 9 or 10, when the first signs of **puberty** occur: the growth of pubic hair and the formation of breast buds. Puberty represents another major biological event in our development as a male or a female. The age at which puberty begins varies from one person to the next. Menstruation starts for some girls at the age of 10

> **puberty**—The onset of reproductive maturity, occurring at age 12 to 13 for females and usually a few years later for males.

or 11 but not for others until they are 15 or 16. Similarly, although the onset of sexual maturation occurs on the average a couple of years later in boys than it does in girls, boys vary considerably in the age at which the process of sexual maturation begins. *Reality or Myth*

Puberty is triggered by the maturation of the hypothalamus. The mature hypothalamus starts to synthesize and secrete Gonadotropin-Releasing Hormone (GnRH). At puberty both males and females begin to grow hair around their genitals and, somewhat later, under the arms. Both discover that their developing sweat glands emit relatively strong

Meanings of Menarche

My mother had described menstruation to me and had bought me some sanitary napkins and a belt, and from the time I was about 12, I waited in anticipation for it to appear. Finally, in the middle of my thirteenth year (I can still remember the exact date), I went to the bathroom and discovered, to my surprise, some blood on the toilet paper. I went racing out of the bathroom, yelling, "I'm a woman, I'm a woman!" at the top of my lungs, only to discover, much to my embarrassment, that my mother had gone out. In response to my father's inquiries, I muttered "Never mind" and waited impatiently for my mother to return so that I could tell her the wonderful news. My irrational sense of pride with myself each month my period began didn't finally diminish until after I'd had several children.

I was in the eighth grade when I got my first period. Some of my friends had already started their period, and I was kind of apprehensively awaiting mine. The day it started, my mom was flat on her back with a bad case of the flu, and my dad and brother were avidly watching a football game.

I can remember trying to figure out how the pad fit on the sanitary napkin belt. I was so scared I almost cried. I wanted to talk to my mom, but I was afraid to because she was sick. So I put on the bulky pad, and I remember being very self-conscious, thinking that everyone noticed.

Mom asked me the next day if I had my period. She had noticed a napkin as she emptied the trash. She started telling me horror stories of the bad cases of cramps she used to get. I wondered if the dull aches I felt were cramps. I don't think I thought even once that they were cramps before that.

I was bitter for probably about a year because I couldn't understand why women had to go through this torture. I couldn't understand why I had to tell my friends that I couldn't go swimming because I was "ragging it." Finally, I said, "Mom, will you please let me try tampons?" She was a rough case, but I finally convinced her. She thought tampons were nothing but trouble. It

---

odors. For the first time, both become capable of releasing mature germ cells (eggs or sperm). And both discover themselves suddenly, and involuntarily, emitting fluid from their bodies—menstrual flow in the case of females and semen in the case of males.

Offsetting these developmental similarities are a number of differences. First, whereas males are totally unaware of the reproductive processes of sperm production and maturation taking place in their bodies, females are dramatically reminded of their reproductive capacity through the regular appearance of their menstrual periods.

Second, prior to the onset of puberty, equal levels of estrogen (secreted by the adrenal glands) are found in the urine of boys and girls. One of the first indicators of puberty in females is an increase in the production of estrogen. From puberty on, the reproductive capacities of women are influenced by the interactions and fluctuations of these major hormones, which, together with other hormones secreted by the brain and the adrenal glands, produce women's characteristic monthly cycle. In contrast, the reproductive capacity of men is relatively acyclic (stable). The extent to which men experience cycles is a matter of debate, but any cycles that men may experience are less obvious and dramatic and are timed differently than are the cycles of women.

FEMALE MATURATION

Between the ages of 8 and 14, the ovaries begin to secrete estrogen, the follicles in the ovaries grow, and the uterus enlarges. The formerly convoluted Fallopian tubes mature and increase in both length and width, becoming straighter in the process. The vagina and clitoris also grow, and the fine, downy hair on the vulva is gradually replaced with a few coarse little hairs. At about the same time, the breasts start to protrude a bit, mainly right around

turned out that they made all the difference in the world. That dreaded five days was now just like the rest of the month.

It was Thanksgiving Day and I was only 10½ years old. No one expected my periods to start so soon, so when I first realized I was bleeding, I couldn't even imagine that what was happening to me might be normal. I thought there was something terribly wrong, at least until my mother checked with the doctor, getting him at home because of the holiday. Once she realized what was happening to me, she took me aside and gave me a quick refresher on what she had already taught me about women's bodies and what happens to girls when they become women. Then she made an announcement to all our guests and dedicated that Thanksgiving to me and my emerging womanhood. I still have a special feeling about that holiday, and—in spite of fairly difficult periods with severe bloating, painful cramps, heavy PMS, and so on—have never felt anything but pride in that emblem of womanhood.

The feelings I had the day I got my first period are clear to me. When I saw the blood on my underpants while in the bathroom at school, I felt scared. Then a surge of warmth ran all through me, and I caught myself smiling alone in the bathroom stall. I went to find my best friend. She went with me to the nurse's office. The nurse's scratchy voice seemed extra loud that day when she asked me if I wore tampons or napkins. I said quietly, "I don't know, this is my first time." She got me a belted napkin and went on explaining how to use it for what seemed like an eternity while I turned crimson. After that, I called my mom and said, "Guess what? I got my period!"

She shared and even increased my enthusiasm as she congratulated me and said, "We'll have to celebrate tonight!" When my family was all seated around the dinner table that night, mom brought out a bottle of champagne and toasted me, saying, "You're a woman. Congratulations!" I felt a little embarrassed and I'm sure I blushed, but more than that I felt special, as if in that day I had matured years. I am especially thankful for my mother's response of delight and enthusiasm, which made my coming into womanhood as special and wonderful as it should be.

Source: Authors' files.

the nipples. The areolae and labia also increase in size. Estrogen plays an extremely important role in most of these specific changes, as well as in the spurt of general body growth and the widening of the pelvic girdle. Many other hormones, in interaction with estrogen or on their own, also stimulate the differentiation and growth of the pubescent female.

Several years after the onset of these initial, relatively subtle signs of puberty, menarche—the first menstrual period—occurs (see "Highlight: Meanings of Menarche"). Adolescent girls tend to be shy about this event, often using euphemisms for menstruation. Although the average age of menarche is 12½, the point at which the first menstruation begins ranges widely, from about 9 to 17 years. Biologically, puberty is considered to be precocious (unusually early) if its presence is detected before age 8 in females and is considered to be delayed if no breast growth has occurred by age 14 or no skeletal growth spurt has appeared by age 15.

Menstruation can be quite erratic after the first period. Within a few years, however, the interval tends to become fairly regular, with menstruation appearing every 23 to 32 days or so. Over the course of approximately 35 years of reproductive capacity, women will menstruate about 420 times, minus 9 or 10 menstrual periods per completed birth. Such a repetitive event becomes routine for most women, and they take menstrual periods in stride.

MALE MATURATION

For males, the onset of puberty arrives later on average than for females. Male puberty is considered to be precocious if it occurs before age 10 and delayed if it has not begun by age 15. The pituitary gland begins secreting follicle-stimulating hormone (FSH) and luteinizing hormone (LH) (sometimes called interstitial-cell stimulating hormone) under regulation of the hypothalamus just as it is in females. The LH stimulates the interstitial cells in the testicles to manufacture increased levels of testosterone. FSH elicits the production of sperm cells in the seminiferous tubules and causes the various other sexual structures to increase in size (see Chapter 4).

Externally, the testes and penis begin to grow, pubic hair gradually replaces the softer body hair around the genitals, and height and muscular strength increase. Several years later, hair grows under the arms and on the face, although the coarse hair that characterizes the adult beard is not in evidence until several years after soft, downy hair first appears on the upper lip. Although a young man may take pleasure in these effects of testosterone, he does not welcome another common symptom of male pubescence, acne. These skin eruptions are partially the result of the influence of testosterone. Secretion of that hormone elicits a dramatic increase in the production of oil-releasing glands in the skin. Sebum, the oil manufactured by these glands, acts as a lubricant and can irritate and block the hair follicles, causing redness and blackheads. Because acne results

primarily from the pubescent rise in adrenal androgens, it is less common in females, who secrete lower levels of these androgens. Testosterone also stimulates the growth of the larynx; the adolescent boy's voice begins to break unpredictably at about age 13 or 14, becoming the reliably deeper voice of an adult male at about age 15 or 16. The areolae double in diameter, and marked breast enlargement occurs in the majority of boys, diminishing within a year or so.

Pubescent boys start to experience nocturnal emissions; that is, while asleep, they expel semen containing sperm. Although boys are capable of orgasm from birth on, the ability to ejaculate semen does not develop until the testes enlarge at puberty.

▶ **Issues to Consider:** Do you believe that puberty is easier or more difficult for girls than for boys? Why?

All of these changes produce the capacity for normal anatomical and physiological sexual functioning. But what is the experience of development for those who are intersexual?

Sexual Differentiation and Gender Identity

The earlier overview of the disorders associated with atypical hormone exposure indicates that the sex hormones, particularly the androgens, have an enormous influence on anatomical differentiation in a male or a female direction during prenatal development. However, as we discussed, the development of gender identity stems from the interaction of physiological factors and environmental influences. Milton Diamond (1997) has reviewed a number of cases in which individuals, because of accidents to their genitals or because they were born with ambiguous genitals, were assigned a gender they later rejected.

A GENITAL ACCIDENT

In the early 1960s, two male (XY) twins were circumcised when they were 8 months old. The circumcision (removal of the foreskin of the penis) went fine with one of the twins. However, the other twin, John (pseudonym), had his penis badly burned during his circumcision. The parents and local medical personnel consulted with specialists and ended up taking the advice of medical psychologist John Money and his associates at Johns Hopkins University. Believing that people are psychosexually neutral at birth, Money and his colleagues recommended that John be raised as a girl. When John was 17 months old, he was surgically reassigned as a female. His testes were removed, and physicians began to construct a vulva. John, now Joan (pseudonym), was treated as a girl by her parents, family, and all professionals associated with the case. Her reassignment as a girl was described as highly successful (Money & Ehrhardt, 1972; Money & Tucker, 1975).

In the late 1970s the British Broadcasting Company (BBC) decided to produce a follow-up documentary on Joan's life. As described by Diamond (1982, 1997), independent psychiatrists obtained by the BBC to interview Joan reached a very different conclusion. In spite of Joan's rearing from infancy on as a girl, she did not feel like a girl. She preferred to play with boys and to engage in typical boys' activities. She avoided the usual activities and interests of girls. She had been given estrogen therapy by her physician, which produced breast development and rounded hips. Her preference for male behaviors continued, however, and when she was 14, she rebelled against living as a girl, although she was unaware of her history. She told her physician, "I suspected I was a boy since the second grade" (Diamond, 1997, p. 200).

Subsequently, Joan, the clinical team overseeing her treatment, and her family discussed Joan's desire to live as a male. Finally learning about her history provided him with relief, as it confirmed what she had believed all along. She switched to living as John. John's parents felt guilty about their participation in the original sex reassignment, but they and John have reconciled. John subsequently obtained a mastectomy and surgically created penis, and lives as a man. Although he had been approached romantically by boys and men when he was living as a girl, he had always rejected them. In contrast, he was erotically interested in girls and women. At age 25 he married a woman several years older than he and adopted her children.

AMBIGUOUS GENITALS

Working with members of the ISNA, Diamond (1997) described several cases of individuals born with both male and female characteristics.

Samantha (pseudonym) was described as a girl at birth, but began to grow the bud of a penis at the age of 5. She was raised as a girl but failed to begin menstruation or show breast development. During puberty her voice deepened, she began growing thicker body hair, and she was shaving by age 15. Her physician prescribed oral contraceptives to counteract hair growth and stimulate menstruation and breast growth. Samantha (now Sam) noted that the physician did not give her a physical examination or discuss her situation with her. The oral contraceptives did stimulate cyclic bleeding, but she was disgusted by menstruation.

When she was 18, she had her first (brief) sexual experience with another person. Her male partner "found the vagina she herself never previously investigated. The session was brief, and her partner did not mention anything notable. Sam recalled enjoying the

reification of her female self and her ability to attract a man she found handsome but reported feeling it was actually more of what she imagined a homosexual encounter might be like" (Diamond, 1997, p. 201).

Sam left home to live by herself for the first time when she was 23 and sought a medical examination to resolve the male-female questions she had. She was diagnosed an XX true **hermaphrodite** with ambiguous genitals. At age 28 she discussed the situation with a counselor, who suggested that Samantha might be happier living as a male. Sam, now in his late 40s, said:

> After years spent wandering in an emotional quagmire and living an agonizing lie, I made the mammoth switch to becoming a man. I did it cold turkey, almost overnight. I just stopped taking the estrogens and let my beard grow in. I immediately gave away everything that was female. And I never looked back. . . . And when I got my brand new male birth certificate from the court (after prolonged legal wrangling) it was the happiest moment of my life. Now I don't think of how to behave. My maleness just comes naturally. (Diamond, 1997, p. 202)

Sam now describes himself as a bisexual male seeking another person with whom to share his life. To prevent any possibility of getting pregnant, Sam had a tubal ligation (female sterilization). He takes androgens and believes his decision to live as a male was correct and psychologically necessary.

In another case with a similar diagnosis, Bill (pseudonym) was born with an enlarged clitoris and apparently normal genitals and reproductive organs. He was initially diagnosed as a male pseudohermaphrodite and assigned to be raised as a boy. However, at 18 months of age he was diagnosed as a true hermaphrodite and reassigned as a girl. Billie's clitoris and inner vaginal lips were removed. Although she was not told why, the testicular portions of her gonads were surgically removed at age 8. When Billie was about 10, her mother told her that her clitoris had been removed but not why or what her clitoris

---

hermaphrodite—A person with both male and female characteristics, such as an ovary on one side and a testis on the other.

was. She was taken to a psychiatrist because she was supposedly "incorrigible." The psychiatrist reinforced her femaleness (with no discussion of doubt), and Billie entered adolescence no longer doubting her assignment as a female, although her interests were more stereotypically masculine (e.g., electronics, construction) than feminine (e.g., cooking, dresses).

She began normal menstruation and breast development during puberty, but did not date while she was a teenager. She spent time with boys because of shared interests, not because of erotic attraction. She tried to masturbate during puberty, but her genitals were not sensitive to touch. When she was 22, she convinced a physician to obtain her old hospital records and finally learned her true diagnosis.

Billie went through many years of great emotional crisis before finally coming to terms with her situation:

She continued to live as a woman reinforced by a female body with breasts and menstruation. Moreover, she now took pride in her differences. She found strength in identifying as an intersexed person with male and female aspects that meld in ways that she felt appropriate. This acceptance of her hermaphroditism, however, has not come easily. It required coming to grips with feelings of shame and inadequacy. It still requires living with a great deal of anger over the surgical loss of her clitoris and associated erotic sensitivity. Billie would have preferred the opportunity to participate in deciding her future as a male or fe-

male. . . . Angry over loss of her genital sensitivity, Billie is adamantly against the nonconsensual enforcement of either gender with accompanying genital surgery on infants. Billie is now a professional woman active in the Intersex Society of North America (ISNA). (Diamond, 1997, p. 203).

There is intense disagreement among researchers and health care professionals regarding how to respond to intersexed infants. Some, following the lead of John Money, adhere to the belief that intersexed infants should be unambiguously assigned to one or the other gender at as early an age as possible, preferably before the emergence of gender identity in the second year of life. This is also the position taken by ISNA, although it does not recommend performing genital surgery on infants and children, who are too young to give their informed consent. Surgery invades their rights as humans to make such decisions when they are old enough to consider the costs and benefits of such interventions, or to choose to remain as intersexed individuals with their own identity.

▶**Issues to Consider:** ISNA members and Milton Diamond (1997) have argued that surgery should not be done on intersex children until they are old enough to understand the possible risks and benefits and give informed consent. What do you think about this position?

For the sake of those dealing with ambiguous genitals, we hope that considerably more is learned about these conditions. See the Appendix for the address of ISNA.

SUMMARY OF MAJOR POINTS

1. Fertilization. Fertilization depends on the depositing of a large number of viable sperm in the vagina around the time of ovulation. Many sperm are lost in the journey from the vagina to the Fallopian tube containing the mature egg (ovum). For fertilization to occur, a large number of sperm must attach themselves to the egg, where they secrete an enzyme that helps to dissolve cellular material on the outside of the ovum, permitting one sperm to penetrate it.

2. Creation of an embryo. The genetic sex of the fetus is determined immediately upon fertilization. The egg contains 22 autosomes (chromosomes that determine body characteristics) and one X chromosome. The sperm contains 22 autosomes and either one X chromosome or one Y chromosome. The combination of the X chromosome from the egg and an X chromosome from the sperm results in a genetic female (XX); the combination of the X chromosome from the egg and a Y chromosome from the sperm results in a genetic male (XY).

3. Development during the fetal stage. The developing human is called a fetus when its bone cells begin to appear, replacing cartilage cells, approximately two months after conception. From this point on, development consists primarily of the growth and maturation of organs and structures that appeared during the embryonic stage.

4. Sexual differentiation. Sexual differentiation of the male fetus begins about two months after conception, at the onset of the fetal stage. If the fetus carries a Y chromosome, this chromosome signals the development of gonads into testes rather than into ovaries. The testes then secrete testosterone, which masculinizes first the internal and then the external genital organs. The testes also secrete Müllerian-inhibiting substance (MIS), which inhibits the development of female sexual and reproductive structures. In the absence of testosterone or MIS, the fetus differentiates in a female direction, regardless of genetic gender. This finding suggests that the basic human form is female and that substances must be added to produce a male.

5. Atypical sexual differentiation. Observations of individuals who have experienced atypical sexual differentiation have contributed to our understanding of fetal differentiation into male or female. Possession of at least one X chromosome appears to be crucial for survival, whereas possession of the Y chromosome seems to be important for maleness but not for life itself. Regardless of genetic sex, exposure to androgens during the early fetal period masculinizes a fetus. In the absence of androgens, or if the fetus is unable to respond to them, it differentiates in a feminine direction.

6. Sexual and reproductive maturation. As young people move into their second decade, hormonal processes within their bodies stimulate the changes associated with puberty. Females generally enter puberty at an earlier age than do males. The most obvious physical sign of maturation is menarche for girls and nocturnal emission for boys.

7. Sexual differentiation and gender identity. For those born with ambiguous genitals or experience a genital accident, the course of development to adulthood can be considerably more difficult than it is for those with unambiguously male or female genital and reproductive organs. We do not know to what extent the difficulties experienced by such intersexual people stem from interventions performed by well-meaning caretakers and professionals rather than from the intersexual condition itself.

Pregnancy and Birth

Reality or Myth

1. Most pregnancy tests are based on the detection of human chorionic gonadotropin (HCG) in women's blood or urine.

2. The average woman gains 20 to 30 pounds during pregnancy.

3. Shaving of the laboring mother's pubic hair is required in all North American hospitals.

4. Women can become sexually aroused while breast-feeding an infant.

5. Most women experience health problems in the first two weeks after giving birth.

6. Most couples begin engaging in sexual intercourse again in the first month after birth.

o impregnate and to become pregnant signify to the individual a kind of categorical maturity as human beings; the natural consequence of sexual intercourse fixes more permanently and obviously the private experience of love-making and the status of adulthood, of being grown up. (Rainwater & Weinstein, 1960, pp. 81–82)

In this chapter we present the processes of pregnancy and birth. Sexual intercourse during pregnancy, preparation for childbirth, normal birth, and some of the controversies regarding medical and hospital childbirth policies are reviewed. We discuss such **postpartum** issues as depression, breast-feeding, circumcision, and sexual intimacy between the new parents.

regnancy

Millions of women give birth each year, yet there is a tendency for women, particularly with their first pregnancies, to feel that they are doing something uniquely remarkable—and indeed they are.

EARLY SYMPTOMS OF PREGNANCY

A few women, especially those who have been pregnant before and those who are actively trying to conceive, suspect pregnancy within ten days or so of conceiving. They may recognize heaviness in the abdomen and breasts, and the nipples may feel a bit irritated. For most women, however, the first real indication of pregnancy is the absence of menstruation about two weeks after conception.

As soon as a woman believes that she is pregnant, she should obtain a pregnancy test. Early diagnosis of pregnancy is important for a number of reasons. First, pregnant women should avoid most drugs and exposure to certain diseases (see Table 9.1 on page 198). Second, some potentially dangerous medical conditions can be corrected if they are identified early, drastically improving the chances of a positive outcome for both the mother and the baby. Third, occasionally a woman can have symptoms of pregnancy, including amenorrhea (absence of expected menstrual bleeding), abdominal swelling, or nausea, yet not be pregnant.

Most pregnancy tests are based on detection of **human chorionic gonadotropin (HCG)** in a woman's blood or urine. After conception, the placenta, which connects the uterus to the developing fetus, begins to produce HCG at rapidly increasing levels. HCG secretion reaches its maximum level about nine weeks after conception and then stabilizes at a lower level. The presence of HCG in a woman's bloodstream may be detected in a blood sample within a week after conception. Analysis of urine for the presence of HCG is highly accurate as early as the first day of the expected (but missed) menstrual period.

Reality or Myth 1

Home pregnancy test kits also work by detecting HCG in urine and are highly reliable if a woman

---

postpartum—(post-PAR-tum) Relating to the time immediately following birth.

---

human chorionic gonadotropin (HCG)—(CORE-ee-ON-ik goh-NAH-doe-TROE-pin) A hormone produced by the placenta.

TABLE 9.1   Factors That May Affect the Fetus

Drugs

Alcohol	Small head size, defective joints, congenital heart defects, mental retardation
Nicotine	Spontaneous abortion, prematurity, low birth weight, stillbirth, nicotine dependency at birth
Vitamin A (excessive doses)	Cleft palate, neural tube defects
Aspirin (moderate use)	Relatively safe until third trimester; use then may prolong labor and lengthen clotting time for both mother and baby, increasing the risk of hemorrhage
Tetracycline	Bone and tooth damage, discolored teeth
Heroin	Spontaneous abortion, low birth weight, fetal addiction and withdrawal, respiratory depression
Methadone	Low birth weight, respiratory depression, mild degrees of mental retardation
Marijuana	Reduced fetal growth rate, overall risk of congenital malformations, limb deficiencies
Cocaine	Neonatal intoxication

Diseases or Medical Conditions

Rubella virus	Infant deafness, blindness, cataracts, heart malformations
Diabetes	Spontaneous abortion, maternal toxemia, stillbirths, abnormally large fetus, respiratory difficulties
Chlamydia	Premature birth, inflammation of the eye (conjunctivitis), and pneumonia
Syphilis	Spontaneous abortion, prematurity, stillbirth, syphilitic infant
Herpes, type II	Spontaneous abortion, prematurity, stillbirth, neonatal herpes infection, congenital abnormalities
AIDS	Postnatal death from opportunistic infections
Radiation	Microcephaly, mental retardation, skeletal malformations

Hormones

Androgens	Female offspring: masculinization of internal and/or external genitals
Estrogens	Female offspring: clitoral enlargement, labial fusion, congenital anomalies
Progestagens	Cardiovascular anomalies
DES	Male offspring: semen and testicular abnormalities, reduced fertility; female offspring: abnormal vaginal or cervical growth, masculinization, reproductive organ cancers
Oral contraceptives	Suspected but unconfirmed reports of physiological difficulties, among them anal, cardiac, kidney, and limb abnormalities

SOURCES: Andres (1999); Jones (1999); Ness et al. (1999)

adheres precisely to the directions for their administration. They are useful for early screening if a woman suspects that she is pregnant and cannot obtain an immediate appointment with a health care provider. However, such test kits should always be followed by a visit to a health care provider if the result is positive, indicating that the woman is pregnant. If the result is negative but the conditions that led a woman to believe that she was pregnant persist for the next week, she should also see a health care provider.

One dangerous medical condition that can be checked is **ectopic pregnancy.** In an ectopic pregnancy, the fertilized egg implants outside the uterus, usually in a fallopian tube. Such pregnancies are often aborted spontaneously, but if they are not, the growing embryo can rupture the fallopian tube within about six weeks. If a woman with a ruptured tube does not receive treatment for the internal bleeding within about 30 minutes, she may die. A woman with one ectopic pregnancy who loses one of her fallopian tubes can have subsequent pregnancies. However, after one ectopic pregnancy, a woman has a 25 percent chance of experiencing a second ectopic pregnancy, in which case she will be unable to conceive.

Approximately 15 percent of people of childbearing age in the United States experience involuntary childlessness or infertility (Leiblum, 1993). Infertility is related to a wide range of negative emotional experiences. An increase in marital conflict and decreases in sexual self-esteem, satisfaction with one's sexual performance, and frequency of sexual intercourse have been reported (Honea-Fleming & Blackwell, 1998; Lukse and Vacc, 1999). Research has supported the idea that infertility leads to these psychological problems rather than the psychological problems' causing infertility.

Sterility can result from genetic factors, damage to the reproductive organs, drugs and environmental pollutants, and a variety of other sources. Possible causes of infertility in women include tumors and cysts, which may be benign or malignant. There are a number of procedures available for the treatment of male and female infertility. Artificial insemination from a donor, surrogate motherhood, and in vitro fertilization or embryo transfer are just a few of the techniques.

THREATS TO FETAL DEVELOPMENT

Spontaneous abortion (miscarriage) can occur at any point in pregnancy. The later it occurs, the more dangerous it is for the mother. Signs of impending miscarriage include vaginal bleeding, abdominal cramping, and lower backache. Women experiencing these symptoms should contact a health care provider. Sometimes a miscarriage and the expulsion of the fetus are relatively painless and physically nontraumatic. Nevertheless, both the woman and the fetal remains should be examined by a doctor. Tissue left in the uterus can be a source of maternal infection, so if the aborted fetus does not appear to be intact, the physician should check for and remove any remaining fetal tissue to reduce the risk of later infections or other difficulties.

Genetic testing or ultrasonography may be ordered for pregnant women over age 35, those with family histories of genetic disorders, or those who are susceptible to any other potential difficulties. (See "Highlight: Tests for Identifying Fetal Abnormalities" on page 200.)

There are several conditions that can cause miscarriage or, if the fetus survives, problems after birth. The specific cause is not known in most cases, but it can result from the genetic or chromosomal conditions described in Chapter 8 or from some of the drugs or diseases listed in Table 9.1. The damage done by exposure to drugs and diseases is greatest during the first three months of pregnancy.

A pregnant woman must consider dosage levels when deciding whether to ingest drugs; a proper dose for a woman weighing, say, 125 pounds may be a large overdose for a 1- or 2-pound fetus. The livers of infants do not begin functioning until a week after they are born, and the liver is not fully functioning for several more months. When a fetus is exposed to drugs taken by the mother, its liver is incapable of breaking them down as efficiently as an adult's liver would.

Heavy alcohol use during pregnancy is the leading environmental cause of mental retardation in infants, with 40 percent of chronically alcoholic women producing an infant with symptoms of **fetal alcohol syndrome (FAS):** a short upturned nose, small and underdeveloped midface, short eye slits, and missing or minimal ridges between the nose and the mouth. Mental retardation, poor motor development, and retarded physical growth also occur. There are no reports of pregnant women who drank less than 2 ounces of alcohol a day giving birth to babies with FAS characteristics (Andres, 1999); however, no

---

ectopic pregnancy—A pregnancy that occurs when a fertilized egg implants itself outside the uterus, usually in a Fallopian tube.

fetal alcohol syndrome (FAS)—A disorder found in the offspring of heavy drinkers that causes a group of specific symptoms, including mental retardation.

Tests for Identifying Fetal Abnormalities

Three procedures are used to check the fetus for the presence of genetic and other disorders: ultrasonography, amniocentesis, and chorionic villi sampling (CVS).

Ultrasonography is the least invasive of the procedures, because it relies on the use of sound waves and a computer to create a visual image of a fetus. Ultrasound scans help resolve questions about the due date by determining fetal size and development. They can also be used to detect fetal abnormalities, twins, ectopic pregnancies, or tumors.

Amniocentesis is a diagnostic procedure in which amniotic fluid is extracted from the uterus and fetal cells are analyzed for chromosome defects. It is the traditional method for identifying fetal chromosomal defects. In this procedure, an ultrasound scan shows the fetus and its location. With the location of the fetus known, a clinician inserts a needle into the woman's abdomen until it penetrates the uterus (but avoids the fetus). A small amount of amniotic fluid surrounding the fetus is removed through the needle, as shown in Figure 9.1. Cells from the fluid are cultured (grown) for several weeks, and photos of the chromosomes are examined for abnormalities. Amniocentesis is useful for diagnoses only after the first trimester.

Analysis of the fetal chromosomes can detect chromosomal defects such as Down's syndrome, as well as the gender of the fetus. In addition, biochemical tests of the cultured cells can detect many

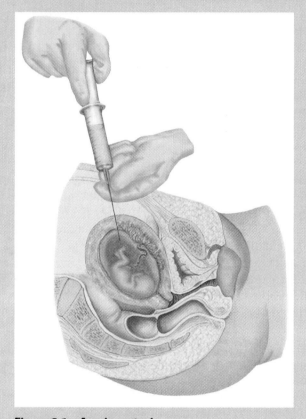

Figure 9.1   Amniocentesis
In this procedure, fluid and loose fetal cells are withdrawn from the amniotic sac. The cells are then cultured and examined for abnormalities.

absolutely safe levels have been established, and most health care providers now advise their patients to abstain from alcohol during pregnancy.

Fetal health is also seriously jeopardized when the mother is infected with a sexually transmitted disease. Chlamydia is a sexually transmitted bacterial infection (see Chapter 16) that can be passed from mother to fetus during pregnancy or to the baby during vaginal delivery. Although it is readily treated, many women are asymptomatic (without symptoms) and thus do not seek treatment. Women who have chlamydia during the first trimester of pregnancy have a greater incidence of premature births. All pregnant women

should be tested and treated for chlamydia rather than waiting for their babies to get sick with conjunctivitis (eye inflammation, which occurs in up to 50 percent of exposed babies) or pneumonia (which is seen in up to 15 percent of exposed babies) (Cates, 1998).

Another major sexually transmitted infection, which cannot be cured, is genital herpes (see Chapter 16). A woman infected with genital herpes is more likely to have a spontaneous abortion, a stillbirth (that is, the baby is dead when born), or an infant born with congenital abnormalities. If a woman has an active outbreak of herpes at the time of delivery, a cesarean section should be performed to protect the

problems from genetic abnormalities that cause no visible changes in chromosomes, such as spina bifida (opening in the spine) and cleft palate.

Another genetic test, *chorionic villi sampling,* involves insertion of a thin tube through the cervix into the placenta to obtain a sample of chorionic villi. The villi are fingerlike projections of tissue that transfer oxygen, nutrients, and waste between mother and embryo. The villi are composed of the same cells as the fetus.

The advantages of CVS over amniocentesis are that it can be performed from the ninth to the twelfth week of pregnancy, it is a less invasive procedure, and results are available within 24 hours. The risk of miscarriage following CVS is slightly higher than with amniocentesis. Some of this increased risk, however, may be due to the greater risk of miscarriage during the first trimester that exists regardless of whether prenatal diagnostic tests are performed. Furthermore, if a woman elects to terminate the pregnancy based on the results of CVS analysis, she faces relatively low risk because she is still in her first trimester. Like amniocentesis, CVS can help detect Down's syndrome, Tay-Sachs disease, sickle-cell anemia, hemophilia, and about ninety other genetic diseases.

baby from potential contact with the virus during the delivery (Cates, 1998). Finally, there is an increase in the number of babies being born with HIV, the virus that causes AIDS. As noted in Chapter 16, there are interventions that can reduce the risk that an HIV-positive woman will transmit HIV to her fetus, but only if she knows she is pregnant.

▶ **Issues to Consider:** Do you think society should regulate the behavior of alcoholic women who become pregnant?

STAGES OF PREGNANCY

Paralleling the stages in fetal development and growth described in Chapter 8 is a series of remarkable physiological and psychological changes that women undergo during the nine months of pregnancy. Pregnancy is conventionally divided into three trimesters. Each stage of pregnancy brings characteristic alterations in the woman's body and in her feelings about herself and her role as a mother. For the first-time mother, each sensation is a new experience.

The gestation period lasts approximately 266 days from conception to birth; the expected delivery date is normally calculated by subtracting three months from the first day of the last menstrual period and then adding 53 weeks to that figure. This method is not foolproof because some women continue to menstruate for a month or more after becoming pregnant. A friend of ours was undergoing a final check before going into surgery for a tumor

when it was discovered that the "tumor" was a 4-month-old fetus. She had not suspected that she was pregnant because she had continued to have normal menstrual periods. Five months later, she gave birth to a healthy baby girl. Most women stop menstruating when they are pregnant, however, and most babies are born within a week of the date calculated by the method just described.

Pregnancy has an enormous impact on a woman's body and emotions. In many cases, the emotions of an expectant father are also strongly affected. Impending parenthood alters women's and men's definitions of themselves and their relationships. It changes their status among their relatives and in society as a whole, as the quotation at the beginning of this chapter conveys.

It is important that couples be aware of the physical, emotional, social, and financial challenges imposed by pregnancy, impending birth, and the responsibilities of parenthood. If a couple has been experiencing serious marital problems, it is a good idea to consider marital counseling to try resolving the conflicts before the child is born. As Kenneth Reamy and Susan White (1987, p. 178) pointed out, "The idea that a child will bring harmony and intimacy into a dysfunctional marriage is erroneous, if not ludicrous." Difficulties in a couple's relationship that existed prior to pregnancy usually remain or intensify, and new problems may emerge. Among cou-

▶ **Issues to Consider:** What do you think the effects are on two people of having a child when they are experiencing problems in their relationship?

The first trimester of pregnancy does not produce major physical changes in most women. Compare this photo with the changes illustrated in the subsequent two photos.

ples who have a stable and mutually satisfying relationship, the decision to have a baby and the sharing of feelings about the pregnancy may add to their sense of commitment and intimacy, two factors that are important for the experience of love (see Chapter 7).

First Trimester. Most women do not realize that they are pregnant for several weeks or even a month or more following conception. Although women should record the dates of their periods on a calendar, not all do. Those who do not are sometimes unaware that they have skipped a period.

In addition to ceasing menstruation, many women experience swelling in their breasts. Their nipples may become temporarily sensitive, so that manual stimulation or even contact with clothing is uncomfortable. In a first pregnancy, the areolae of some women darken early in the first trimester. During pregnancy, estrogens aid in the development of the milk ducts, and progestagen stimulates the completion of the development of these ducts and **alveoli.**

About six weeks after conception, noticeable changes occur in a woman's cervix. Normally the cervix has a hardness and resiliency similar to those of the end of the nose or the top of the ear. About a

alveoli—(AL-vee-OH-lee) Milk-secreting cells in the breast.

month after the first missed menstrual period, however, the cervix feels relatively soft and malleable, a difference that can be detected by a woman who is familiar with the feeling of her cervix, as well as by a health care provider during manual inspection.

During the first trimester, about half of all pregnant women have periodic bouts of nausea as a result of elevated levels of HCG and changed carbohydrate metabolism. This condition is called "morning sickness" because it is usually most severe in the morning. For some women, the nausea is relatively mild and can be controlled by eating dry crackers before getting up in the morning; eating small, frequent meals; and avoiding spicy foods. For other women, the nausea is considerably more severe and is accompanied by vomiting. A few women must be hospitalized to control the potential dehydration from constant vomiting.

Increased fatigue and sleepiness are common during the first trimester. Many women also report feeling more irritable, vulnerable, and dependent than they did prior to conception. The changes in the shapes of their bodies depress some women. At this stage they are not yet "showing" the pregnancy enough to justify wearing maternity clothes, but they may have trouble buttoning slacks or skirts toward the end of the first trimester.

Pregnancy is commonly depicted as a time of calm and radiance, but women often feel ambivalent in the first trimester. Even in a planned pregnancy, a woman is frequently surprised that conception has actually occurred. Women who need to make changes in career plans and commitments or feel financially stressed are most likely to feel ambivalence. Some women also express fears about pregnancy, labor, and delivery. Such worries are likely to be the most intense when the pregnancy is unwanted or unplanned.

A pregnant woman tends to look for physical signs to prove to herself that she is truly pregnant. She becomes conscious of small changes in her body. She watches for thickening of her waist, weight gain, and breast development. Even morning sickness, however unpleasant, is confirmation that she is in fact pregnant. Usually by the end of the first trimester, she has resolved any ambivalence and has accepted the developing fetus as a temporary part of herself.

Like the expectant mother, the father also needs to adjust to the pregnancy and the coming changes in his life. Most men feel pride that conception has occurred; at the same time, many express ambivalence. The extent of the ambivalence is related to a variety of factors, such as his relationship with the mother, his age, their financial status, and whether the pregnancy was planned.

After the initial excitement and announcement of the pregnancy, many fathers feel left out. Attention becomes focused on the mother, who may act differently than she did prior to her pregnancy. Her mood changes and fatigue may confuse the expectant father. He may experience her focus on herself as a kind of rejection of him. Many men worry about their ability to be a good father and spend much time thinking about their own fathers.

Some men develop symptoms similar to those of pregnant women: fatigue, sleeping difficulties, backaches, and nausea. The term **couvade** refers to the phenomenon in which men develop symptoms similar to those of their pregnant partners. Perhaps these symptoms provide a way for a man to identify with his partner and to participate in the pregnancy.

▶ **Issues to Consider:** Why do you think some men develop symptoms that mimic those of their pregnant partners (couvade)?

Second Trimester. For most women, the second trimester is characterized by a sense of well-being and pleasure. The sometimes unpleasant symptoms of the first trimester diminish or disappear entirely, and, because they may take better care of themselves during pregnancy, some women report having more energy and feeling healthier in their second trimester than they did before they became pregnant.

Small amounts of **colostrum**, a thin, yellowish fluid high in proteins and antibodies, may be expelled from the nipples during the second trimester. Colostrum production continues throughout pregnancy. The abdomen increases in fullness, particularly in women who have been pregnant before. The pressure of the enlarging uterus on the bladder interferes with women's activities, as well as their

couvade—(ku-VAHD) Phenomenon in which some men develop symptoms similar to those of their pregnant partner.
colostrum—(cuh-LAWS-trum) A thin, yellowish fluid secreted from the nipples before and around the time of birth.

This photo shows physical changes during the second trimester of pregnancy.

sleep, by increasing the frequency of their need to urinate.

Most health care providers schedule monthly prenatal checkups for women who have reached the beginning of the second trimester. These checkups are extremely important to detect any problems that might threaten the life or well-being of the mother or fetus. During these visits, the woman's weight, blood pressure, and urine are checked. Some appointments also include a pelvic examination to determine the position and development of the fetus.

Expectant parents generally are very excited by two events that occur around the middle of the second trimester. One is **quickening,** the woman's first awareness of fetal movement. The other is detection of the fetal heartbeat, amplified with a device known as a Doppler. Some health care providers invite women to bring their partners with them to their next checkup after the heartbeat is detected, so that both expectant parents can hear the fetal heartbeat.

By the middle of the second trimester, women usually have to replace most of their regular clothing with loose slacks and dresses to allow for the expansion of the uterus. Having adjusted to these changes in appearance, the woman usually takes pleasure in

quickening—The first fetal movements felt by the mother.

This expectant father is obviously enjoying listening to and feeling his baby in his partner's uterus.

the sensations of pregnancy and begins to picture the fetus as a real person. Quickening gives a woman a sense of "knowing" the baby. Many women are eager to learn about childbirth and child care during this time.

The changes of early pregnancy also prompt a woman to think about her relationship with her partner and her status as a new mother. Many women feel anxiety about their partners, especially if their mates respond to the pregnancy by withdrawing. Like the mother, an expectant father needs to resolve any mixed feelings he has about the pregnancy. An expectant father may feel ambivalent about his partner's changing appearance; some men experience a diminished interest in sex, although others have the opposite reaction. The expectant father's involvement in preparing for the baby, hearing the baby's heartbeat, and feeling fetal movements usually help him adjust to his new situation.

Third Trimester.   During the last three months of pregnancy, most women have an awkward gait and feel rather blimplike. The average weight for a full-term baby is 7½ pounds but, as shown in Figure 9.2, the average woman gains 20 to 30 pounds during pregnancy. Increased fluid retention and fat are responsible for much of the gain. *Reality or Myth*

The baby's kicking and movement, initially a source of great pleasure and interest, may become downright irritating in the third trimester, particularly during the mother's attempts to sleep. Occasionally the fetus gets hiccups, and the regular spasms can be as distracting as a slowly dripping faucet. An expectant father may feel the kicking and movement readily with his hands or occasionally in the small of his back when the woman snuggles against him in bed. Many women have difficulty finding a comfortable position in which to sleep. The need for frequent urination returns, requiring several trips to the bathroom at night to release the small amount of urine because of the pressure as the bladder is being crowded by the growing fetus.

During the third trimester, a pregnant woman generally feels a sense of pride combined with anxi-

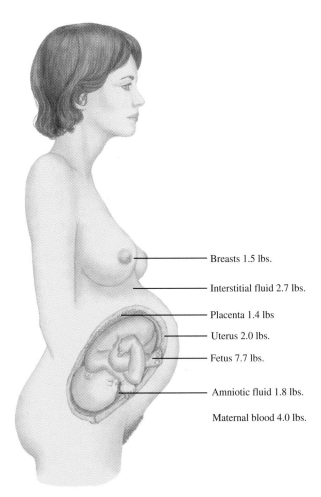

This photo shows physical changes during the last trimester of pregnancy.

Figure 9.2   Weight Gain in Pregnancy
The weight of the full-term baby contributes only about one-third of the 20 to 30 pounds gained by the average woman during pregnancy.

Breasts 1.5 lbs.
Interstitial fluid 2.7 lbs.
Placenta 1.4 lbs
Uterus 2.0 lbs.
Fetus 7.7 lbs.
Amniotic fluid 1.8 lbs.
Maternal blood 4.0 lbs.

ety about the future. Many women simultaneously experience an intense desire for the pregnancy to be over and anxiety about labor and birth. Fears about the baby's health and possible birth defects tend to surface in the last trimester. With increased girth, the woman may need help with some tasks. For example, if she is somewhat short, she may find that she has to move the driver's seat of her car so far back to accommodate her swollen abdomen that she can no longer reach the pedals to drive. Toward the end of this period, the woman usually experiences a burst of energy and a need to prepare a "nest" for the baby. She makes final arrangements for the baby's needs and plans for the first few months after the birth.

If the couple has communicated effectively and resolved any problems, the third trimester is likely to be the most peaceful one. The father usually has adjusted to the pregnancy and is ready to become involved in preparing for the baby. He may participate in prepared-childbirth classes and become increasingly supportive of the mother.

If the father has remained detached, however, his early anxieties about the pregnancy may recur. For example, he may worry about family finances or about his ability to be a good father. Even a detached father-to-be may feel an increased sense of responsibility as the birth approaches.

SEX DURING PREGNANCY

Sexual expression during pregnancy varies widely across cultures and among couples. Depending on the culture, pregnancy provides a rationale either for or against sexual intercourse. In some cultures, sexual intercourse ceases for most couples as soon as a woman knows that she is pregnant. When asked about intercourse during pregnancy, the So of northeastern Uganda asked, "Why would you want to do that? There is already someone in there."

Coital positions and sites of sexual stimulation generally shift during pregnancy. After the first part of pregnancy, use of the man-above coital position tends to be replaced with a preference for positions that place less pressure on the woman's abdomen, such as the position shown in Figure 9.3.

Many couples find that the frequency of coitus declines during the last three months of pregnancy. The reasons vary from woman to woman, but physical discomfort is probably the most frequent. Other reasons expectant mothers cite include fear of injuring the baby, lack of interest, feelings of awkwardness or unattractiveness, and health care providers' advice (Lowdermilk, Perry and Bobok, 1997).

Couples' fears notwithstanding, in a healthy pregnancy there is no reason to limit sexual activity. In fact, in a study of 14,000 pregnant women, Read and Klebanoff (1993) found that women who reported having engaged in coitus one to four times a week during weeks 23 to 26 (the end of the second and beginning of the third trimesters) were about one-third less likely to have a premature birth than were women who had coitus less frequently. This finding certainly does not indicate that frequent coitus causes full-term delivery, but it does suggest that coitus is unlikely to produce premature delivery. If a woman in her third trimester is uncomfortable with coitus for whatever reason, she and her partner can engage in such noncoital forms of sexual intimacy as manual and oral stimulation of the genitals. Cuddling, kissing, and holding each other can often meet the needs of a pregnant woman and her partner.

Two sexual practices should be avoided during pregnancy. One of these is blowing air into the vagina during cunnilingus as this may cause air **embolisms**. In addition, pregnant women should avoid sexual contact with a partner who may have a sexually transmitted disease. If a woman becomes infected, the disease may be transmitted to her baby during the pregnancy or during vaginal delivery.

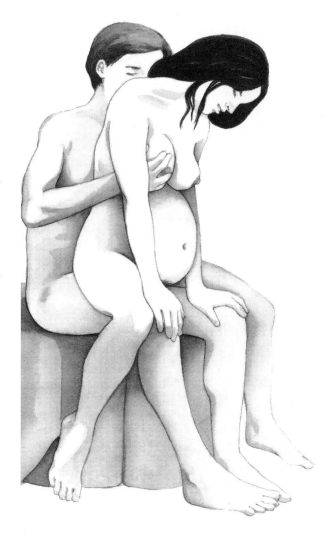

Figure 9.3 Sex During Late Pregnancy
During the third trimester, a couple often shifts to coital positions that place less pressure on the woman's abdomen.

Labor and Birth

As the end of pregnancy draws near, a woman may be reluctant to make appointments or start new projects because the birth process could begin at any moment. This waiting game, with its persistent telephone calls from relatives and friends, can get tedious.

Expectant parents become increasingly eager to see their baby. In addition to preparing the household for the new arrival, many parents spend the last weeks of pregnancy actively preparing for childbirth. In giving birth, the average woman engages in about

embolism—Any foreign matter such as a blood clot or air bubble that causes the obstruction of a blood vessel.

H I G H L I G H T

A Personal Account of Childbirth

Pregnant women generally receive a great deal of advice and information from other women who have experienced childbirth. Here is mine.— E.R.A.

I have given birth in a hospital and at home, with and without anesthesia, with and without the help of my husband, with and without the benefit of prepared-childbirth instruction. In my experience, the ideal birth takes place at home, without anesthesia, and with the assistance of the expectant father, who has also participated in prepared-childbirth classes. The most important of these four conditions are the help of a mate and the classes. I would avoid anesthesia unless it is really needed, both for the baby's well-being and for the quality of the birth process. Because an unusually prolonged or complicated labor will mar the experience for the mother, however, anesthesia should be used when necessary.

Second-stage labor has been compared to a particularly prolonged bowel movement and to orgasm, but neither approaches the intensity of childbirth. Given my druthers on a Sunday afternoon, I'd prefer orgasm to childbirth. However, the exhaustion produced by the labor of childbirth is followed by exhilaration at birth and a period of euphoria following birth that is unique in my experience.

My advice to expectant parents is to get as much information about pregnancy and birth as possible. The more they know about it, the more fascinating the process. Prepared-childbirth classes and diligent practice of childbirth exercises are invaluable.

Amid the rhetoric regarding women's and men's liberation, childbirth provides an extraordinarily liberating opportunity for a woman. It presents her with the opportunity to experience the union of her voluntary and involuntary processes in an event that wholly claims her—the expression of life force through her with her utter cooperation.

15 hours of increasingly strenuous work—hence the term **labor** for the stages directly leading to and including birth.

PREPARATION FOR CHILDBIRTH

During much of the twentieth century in Western countries, preparing for childbirth meant packing a suitcase with clothes for the hospital stay of the mother and newborn baby. Few expectant parents actually prepared for childbirth, and most women received little education about labor and giving birth. After admission to a hospital, they went through labor and birth in a sort of solitary confinement, attended only by hospital personnel who gave pelvic exams, checked vital signs, shaved pubic hair, and administered enemas. Despite having contributed half

labor—The process of childbirth, consisting of contractions, thinning out and expansion of the cervix, delivery of the baby, and expulsion of the placenta.

the genetic heritage of the baby, the father rarely participated in the delivery, much less witnessed the emergence of his child into the outside world (see "Highlight: A Personal Account of Childbirth").

In contrast, most health care providers and hospitals now encourage expectant parents to enroll in prepared-childbirth classes and to work as a team during labor and childbirth. Expectant parents usually enroll in these classes at the beginning of the third trimester. Instructors typically provide information about pregnancy and the stages of childbirth, in an effort to dispel fears and myths about birth. The course also generally includes a tour of the hospital's birthing center or maternity ward unless the couple plans to give birth at home with the help of a midwife. Finally, expectant parents learn exercises and procedures designed to facilitate childbirth. Expectant fathers master massage techniques to help relieve the lower back pain that sometimes accompanies labor contractions. Expectant mothers learn procedures to help them relax and work with contractions instead of bracing against them. They are taught breathing techniques that are useful during different stages of labor. Participants in these courses have reported that this preparation reduced their anxieties.

The idea of active participation by both the mother and the father became popular only in the late 1960s, partly stemming from changing attitudes toward the use of anesthesia. Anesthesia was not used for childbirth until 1847, at least in part because the Bible held that "children should be brought forth in pain and sorrow." After anesthesia was introduced, however, it quickly became routine in hospital deliveries.

> ▶ **Issues to Consider:** Why would anyone write that "children should be brought forth in pain and sorrow? Do you think the author was a man or a woman?

In the book *Childbirth Without Fear* (1932), English physician Grantly Dick-Read questioned the use of anesthetics during labor. His objections were based on the potential danger to the baby and mother. He maintained that the pain stemming from labor contractions could be eliminated or at least reduced through the kind of education and training for relaxation that are now a routine part of prepared-childbirth classes.

French obstetrician Bernard Lamaze also contributed to our contemporary approach to birth. After observing women in Russia undergoing labor with little pain, he began to train pregnant women and their husbands (or other "coaches") in muscle relaxation and breathing techniques. One technique he introduced, called *effleurage*, consists of light, circular stroking of the abdomen with the fingertips to help a woman relax. Lamaze students today also are strongly encouraged to be in top physical condition for labor. Exercises to strengthen the leg muscles are taught because the legs undergo considerable strain during childbirth.

The repertoire of techniques used in prepared childbirth is similar to that employed in hypnosis. For example, a woman is told to concentrate on an object—a bead in a necklace, for example, or a picture on a wall—to aid her in relaxing during labor. She learns to control her breathing and is reassured that she can manage the stress of childbirth.

The assistance of a familiar, supportive person is of great benefit to a woman giving birth. During labor and delivery, a woman's coach not only times her contractions, but also supports and encourages her in relaxation and proper breathing. The use of these

Hockey forward Lisa Brown-Miller was six weeks pregnant when she won a gold medal at the 1998 Winter Olympics.

techniques is associated with fewer birth complications, less use of anesthesia, and shorter labor than are typical with more traditional approaches to childbirth. Mothers using prepared childbirth also have more positive attitudes following birth, higher self-esteem, and a greater sense of self-control.

LABOR FOR CHILDBIRTH

Although childbirth may be the most concentrated physical effort that a woman experiences in her life, women who have carried a growing baby for nine months are generally ready for labor to begin. Sometimes they experience **Braxton-Hicks contractions** for weeks prior to the onset of labor. Some women

Braxton-Hicks contractions—Irregular contractions of the uterus that are often mistaken for the onset of labor.

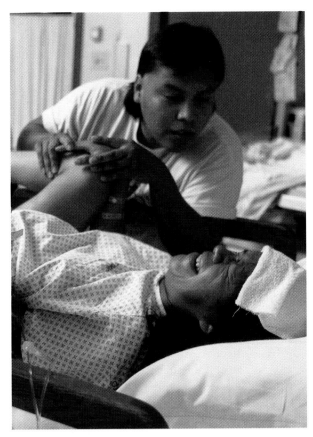

The participation of a partner who provides encouragement, times contractions, and gives lower-back massages can be very helpful to a woman in labor.

also undergo false labor—periodic contractions that seem to signal the beginning of labor but eventually stop, rather than increase in frequency and intensity.

The Onset of Labor. As the due date approaches, pregnant women begin watching for signs of the onset of labor. It is thought that labor begins when the fetus's adrenal glands produce hormones that are secreted into the placenta and uterus. These secretions stimulate the release of prostaglandins that induce contractions in the uterus. The gradual awareness of these contractions is the first symptom of labor for many women. Initially, the contractions may be so mild and infrequent (30 minutes or more apart) that women are unsure that they are actually experiencing them. The contractions gradually increase in frequency, duration, and intensity. Most women are instructed to call their doctors or midwives when the contractions occur at five-minute intervals.

Other symptoms of impending labor that can occur before or after the onset of contractions include a pinkish discharge from the vagina and/or varying amounts of a watery discharge ("breaking waters") from the vagina. The discharge comes from the rupture of the amniotic sac. During pregnancy, the fetus is protected by a cushion of almost 2 pounds of amniotic fluid. With the onset of labor, the fluid is generally released in varying amounts, from a trickle to a gush. After the release of the amniotic fluid, contractions usually increase in frequency and intensity, although some women go through most of labor or even childbirth without the amniotic sac breaking. An Irish myth suggests that a baby born "in a caul"—that is, in the unruptured amniotic sac—is lucky. Such a baby, somewhat protected from the contractions of labor, may experience a relatively easy time during birth.

Location of Labor and Birth. In 1900 more than 95 percent of American women delivered their babies at home rather than in hospitals. Now the figures are reversed, with only a small percentage of women giving birth at home. Some of these home deliveries are unplanned, but many families who deliver at home choose to do so, with the aid of a physician or midwife. Today's midwives may be nurses, who can be certified as nurse-midwives in most states, or laypersons who are trained by experienced midwives.

The advantages of home birth are the greater familiarity and comfort of the environment to the mother, the greater accessibility of family and friends who wish to be present at the birth, and the reduced expense. Home birth can be a safe option for women who have a low risk of obstetric complications. An overview of four northern European studies indicated that a planned at-home delivery had as good an outcome as a planned hospital delivery (Springer & van Weel, 1996). The most obvious disadvantage of home birth is the reduced access to equipment and trained personnel in the event that an emergency develops during labor or delivery.

Although home birth is gaining in popularity, most couples in North America go to a hospital or birthing center for childbirth. Birthing centers—health care facilities usually affiliated with hospitals but physically separated from them—generally allow a woman and her family more control over the experience of childbirth than they are likely to have in a hospital.

Birthing centers are typically less expensive than are hospitals and are designed for early discharge from the center, generally within a day of the birth. They are supplied with emergency equipment for medical problems and have advance arrangements for transferring a woman to a hospital if an emergency occurs. Research indicates that delivery at birthing centers is associated with a low cesarean section rate and low or no neonatal mortality (Eakins, 1989). Nurses and nurse-midwives usually staff the facilities. Physicians often attend the deliveries, but some centers are staffed entirely by nurses affiliated with a particular hospital.

Labor is divided into three stages. During first-stage labor, the cervix gradually opens enough to permit passage of the baby. Birth occurs during second-stage labor. The placenta, or afterbirth, is expelled during third-stage labor.

First-Stage Labor.   At the beginning of first-stage labor, a woman is given a checkup and a pelvic exam. Her blood pressure is measured and blood and urine samples are collected. These samples are analyzed for any signs of abnormality that might affect the process or outcome of birth.

The position of the fetus is checked to see whether **engagement** has occurred. With engagement, the fetus drops several inches lower in the abdominal cavity, and when the head has gone past the mother's pelvic bone structure, it is said to be engaged. Engagement may happen at any time from a week before birth to several hours after the onset of labor.

During the pelvic exam, some labor contractions are monitored. The uterus becomes very firm, almost rigid, during each uterine contraction. This firmness can be felt by placing a hand on the abdomen; the characteristic hardness is absent during a false labor contraction. The extent of **effacement** and **dilation**—thinning out and opening up of the cervix—is also checked. If one or more of these signs indicates that the woman is in labor or if the amniotic sac has rup-

tured and released some amniotic fluid, the woman is prepared ("prepped") for childbirth.

In some cases, little effacement or dilation may have occurred. At this point many women, particularly those with a first pregnancy, experience one of the two most frustrating events associated with normal childbirth.[1] They are sent home! They may have been having regular contractions five or fewer minutes apart, only to have the contractions abruptly halt after they reach the hospital or birthing center. In recognition of this phenomenon, many hospitals do not admit maternity patients until after the initial checkup and pelvic exam. If the amniotic sac has not ruptured and the cervix is completely undilated, hours or even a few days may elapse before effective labor begins. In this event, it makes no sense to keep a woman in the hospital or birthing center. Nonetheless, after notifying relatives that the baby's birth is imminent, a woman who must return home still pregnant can be disappointed to tears.

Once effective labor is in progress, women are prepared for childbirth. The abdomen, vulva, and thighs are washed with an antiseptic solution to reduce the chances that infection will be transmitted to the baby during birth. Traditionally, women were given enemas and had all their pubic hair shaved, but some researchers have questioned the necessity of both practices.

Shaving the pubic hair was done to facilitate sterilization of the area. In contemporary obstetric practice, however, shaving is recommended only if an **episiotomy**—a surgical incision at the opening of the vagina—is planned. Otherwise, shaving of the pubic hair is unnecessary, and the irritation of the vulva that women feel as the hair grows back adds to their postpartum discomfort. *Reality or Myth* ⑫

The rationale for the enema was twofold: The bowels should be empty so that feces are not pushed out during birth, and the enema might speed labor. Because women are given no solid foods after labor

---

[1]The other source of frustration for a woman is learning that her cervix has dilated only a few centimeters after she has been in labor for several hours and is sure that delivery is near.

engagement—Movement of the fetus into a lower position in the mother's abdominal cavity, with its head past her pelvic bone structure.

effacement—Flattening and thinning of the cervix that occurs before and during childbirth.

dilation—(die-LAY-shun) Expansion or opening up of the cervix prior to birth.

episiotomy—(eh-PEE-zee-AW-tuh-mee) A surgical incision made from the bottom of the entrance to the vagina down off to the side of the anus to prevent vaginal and anal tissues from injury during childbirth.

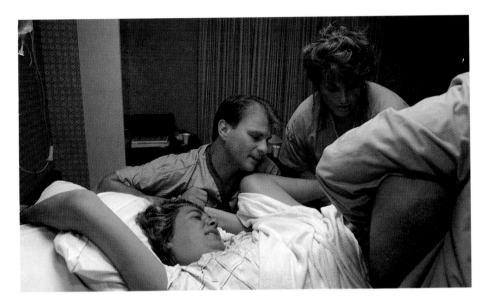

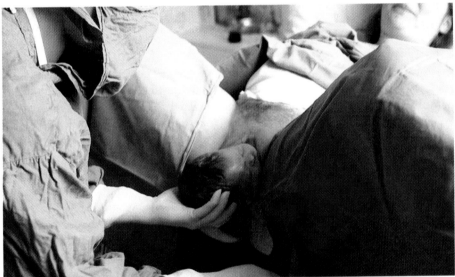

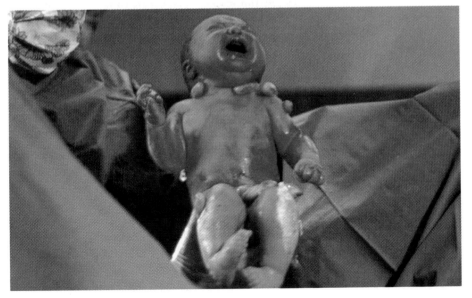

In the top photo, this woman holds onto a rail behind her to help her respond to the urge to bear down to expel the baby. Her partner coaches her during delivery. In the middle photo, the baby's head has emerged from the woman's vagina. After the shoulders have come out, the rest of the baby readily emerges. In the bottom photo, the newly born baby utters its first cry. When it is clear that the baby can breathe on its own, the umbilical cord attaching it to its mother (her placenta) is cut.

begins, however, any food that they have eaten previously has already been digested and expelled unless labor is very rapid, in which case the enema does not eliminate the food farther up in the intestines. Enemas are currently recommended only if the woman has a large amount of hard stool in the rectum.

After the preliminary pelvic exam and checkup, the woman is taken to a labor room or birthing room, accompanied by the expectant father or another birth coach, where her contractions prepare her body to expel the baby. The contractions of early first-stage labor feel like a tightening of the abdomen and are generally not uncomfortable. As labor progresses, the tight feeling is accompanied by a sense of pressure, sometimes in the lower back and sometimes inside the abdomen just above the line of the pubic hair. The feelings grow in intensity, particularly after the release of amniotic fluid, but there are usually resting periods of a minute or two between each contraction. The breathing exercises taught in prepared-childbirth classes help a woman to avoid tensing her muscles in opposition to the work of the contractions. Fear and tension may create or heighten the intensity of a contraction.

After the cervix has dilated 5 or 6 centimeters (about 2 inches, or the width of three fingers), the hormone oxytocin is secreted by the pituitary, and the frequency and intensity of the contractions increase considerably. The end of first-stage labor is signaled by a relatively short period of highly intense and seemingly incessant contractions known as **transition.** The transitional contractions complete the dilation of the cervix to 10 centimeters (4 inches), so that the baby's head can pass through it.

After the baby's head appears in the vagina, doctors often perform an episiotomy. The supposed purpose of the episiotomy is to decrease the likelihood of vaginal tearing when the baby's head and shoulders pass out of the woman's body. The surgery is performed in more than 60 percent of U.S. deliveries (Olds et al., 1992). However, except in cases in which a woman is delivering an exceptionally large baby or has an exceptionally small vaginal opening, the episiotomy is unnecessary. Furthermore, there is

---

transition—A short period of intense and very frequent contractions that complete dilation of the cervix to 10 centimeters.

---

no reduction in rates of tearing among women given episiotomies compared to those who deliver without the surgery (Lowdermilk, Perry and Bobak, 1997). Even if some slight tearing does occur, the wound tends to mend quite readily without any postpartum stitching, whereas a surgical cut requires stitches, although they usually dissolve within a few days.

Second-Stage Labor.   In the second stage of labor, the intense and constant contractions of transition are replaced by an extremely strong urge to "bear down"—that is, to push the baby out—with each contraction. Contractions at this stage are strong, but compared to the contractions of transition, they are not particularly uncomfortable, and they are less frequent. Any discomfort is relieved when the woman does push, but depending on the position of the baby, the woman may need to control the urge to bear down, so that the baby's position may be altered by the doctor or midwife to decrease the likelihood of tearing of the cervical or vaginal opening. Rapid panting, a breathing pattern learned in prepared-childbirth classes, can be helpful at this time. As seen in Figure 9.4, when the baby is positioned correctly, a woman is told that she may bear down at the next contraction.

Within a period of time that varies from a few minutes to more than an hour, the woman succeeds in pushing the baby out. After the baby's head has emerged, a woman may feel a heady combination of relief, exhaustion, and exhilaration. Controlling the urge to bear down at this point is considerably easier. When the baby's shoulders have emerged, the rest of the baby's body usually slides out readily. Thus ends second-stage labor for normal birth.

After a normal birth and a quick inspection of the baby's genitals, the midwife or doctor proclaims, "It's a girl!" or "It's a boy!" Depending on the policies of the doctor and hospital and the wishes of the mother, the baby may be given to her immediately to hold and nurse.

When it is clear that the baby is able to rely on its own lungs to obtain oxygen and the umbilical cord has ceased pulsating, the cord is clamped in two places and cut. Sometimes the father is allowed to perform this procedure, which is painless for both mother and baby. If the woman has had an episiotomy, the health care provider stitches up the incision.

Third-Stage Labor and Recovery.   After the baby is born, a woman continues to have a few contractions,

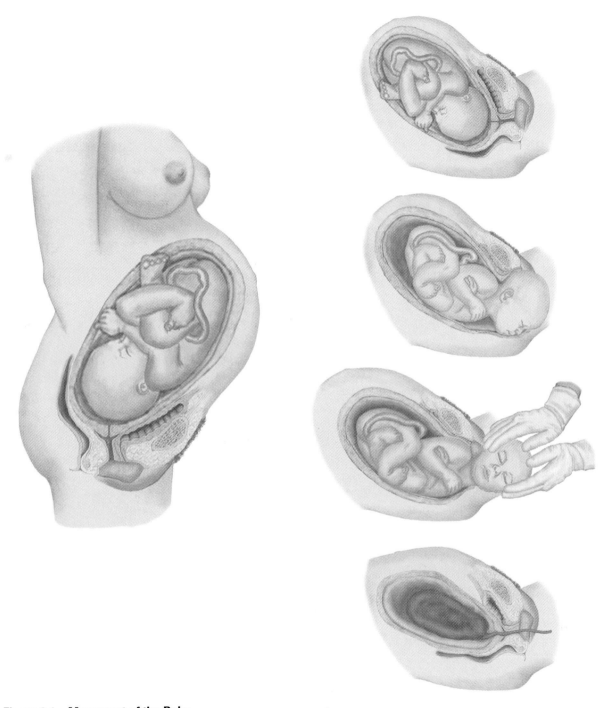

Figure 9.4 Movement of the Baby
Labor contractions help to move the baby from the uterus to the outside world.

usually quite mild, that aid her in expelling the placenta, or so-called afterbirth. Third-stage labor ends with the expulsion of the placenta. It is this process that poses the greatest risk for the mother. As the placenta is expelled, the blood vessels formerly attaching the placenta to the uterus generally close off. If they do not, hemorrhage and shock are possible. To avoid this danger, the woman's vital signs are monitored for an hour or so to ensure that blood vessels close properly.

The baby is bathed, and an antibiotic solution is placed in its eyes to minimize the chances of infection. Having abstained from solid food for ten hours or more, many women are ravenous and are given a meal. New mothers are generally encouraged to get up and walk around, use the bathroom, or go to the windows of the nursery to peer at their babies as soon as they feel comfortable doing so.

Some hospitals and birthing centers provide the option of "rooming in" for the mother: the baby is housed in a bassinet next to the mother's bed. This option is particularly convenient for the mother who wishes to breast-feed her baby because she can respond much more quickly to the baby's cry or restlessness than can nursery room staff.

In a day or two, if all is well with the mother and baby, they are released from the hospital or birthing center to go home. The lives of couples who are parents for the first time enter a different stage, with a host of new joys and responsibilities. We will delay a description of these until after we describe difficulties that can emerge in later pregnancy and during birth.

POSSIBLE PREGNANCY AND BIRTH COMPLICATIONS

Reading about potential difficulties that can occur during pregnancy and childbirth can be alarming, particularly for the couple expecting their first child. With effective prenatal care and a nutritionally balanced maternal diet, however, most couples have little need to worry about their expected baby. About 99 percent of U.S. babies are born healthy and normal (Creasy and Resnik, 1999).

Several factors can complicate the pregnancy and birth process, however—among them eclampsia, atypical fetal positioning, the need for a cesarean section, multiple births, and variations in the length of gestation.

Preeclampsia and Eclampsia. Up to 10 percent of American women develop preeclampsia (also called toxemia) during pregnancy. Symptoms include retention of toxic body wastes, high blood pressure, protein in the urine, swelling, and fluid retention. Preeclampsia generally develops in the third trimester and is more common during first pregnancies than in subsequent ones (Roberts, 1999). It is also

associated with excessive weight gain, which is one of the reasons that pregnant women are advised to avoid gaining more than 30 to 35 pounds during pregnancy. There are several hypotheses regarding the cause of preeclampsia—perhaps an abnormal response to hormone changes during pregnancy or an abnormal immune reaction to the fetus—but its cause or causes have not been determined.

About 5 percent of toxemic women suffer from *eclampsia,* a condition that can bring on convulsions and coma. The mortality rate for women who develop eclampsia is about 15 percent. The only real "cure" is termination of the pregnancy, so if the symptoms reach danger levels, preterm delivery may be recommended as soon as tests indicate that the fetus is mature enough to have a good chance of surviving. Treatment includes various measures to control the symptoms, including a diet designed to control weight gain, fluid retention, and blood pressure.

Birth Position. Atypical fetal positioning is one source of childbirth complications that can endanger the baby's or the mother's life. Most babies spend the first two trimesters of pregnancy upright in the mother's uterus. During the third trimester, the fetus generally reverses its position, so that its head is near the cervix and its buttocks and feet are at the top of the uterus, like the baby shown in Figure 9.4 on page 213. About 90 percent of babies are born head first, the safest and easiest position for birth.

A small number of babies, however, do not reverse their direction before the onset of labor. Instead, they may present the buttocks first (breech presentation) or a shoulder or side first (transverse presentation). In many cases, the doctor or midwife can alter the position, so that the baby emerges head first. If attempts at repositioning are unsuccessful and if the mother is very small or the baby is very large, a cesarean section may be necessary.

Cesarean Section. About 21 percent of U.S. babies are delivered by **cesarean section (C-section)** rather than through the vagina (Sachs, Kobelin, Castro & Frigoletto, 1999). In a C-section the woman is given

cesarean section (C-section)—An incision made through the mother's abdomen, under a general or local anesthetic, so that the baby can be removed.

general or local anesthesia, and an incision is made through the abdomen and uterus, so that the baby can be removed. Because a C-section is a surgical procedure requiring anesthesia, women tend to be more uncomfortable following this kind of delivery than they are after a vaginal delivery. Typically, women who have a C-section remain hospitalized for four days (MMWR, 1995). They may resume coitus within the usual length of time. Women undergoing a C-section because of problems with the baby's presentation or size, lengthy labor, or other medical emergencies can usually deliver subsequent babies vaginally. But if small pelvic size is the reason for the C-section, then future births may also require this method unless the subsequent babies are small.

Premature Birth, Low Birth Weight, and Delayed Birth. The chances of a baby's surviving birth and infancy are reduced by premature birth, low birth weight, and delayed birth. Babies are considered premature when they are born before 37 weeks from the first day of the last menstrual period. In a study of 14,000 pregnant women, Read and Klebanoff (1993) found that more than 11 percent of the mothers delivered their babies prematurely. Almost no infants delivered at or before 23 weeks of gestation survive (Creasey and Iams, 1999). A baby has more than 90 percent chance of survival if it is born at 30 weeks' gestation.

Factors associated with premature birth include complications during pregnancy, ingestion of drugs, maternal malnutrition, inadequate prenatal care, multiple pregnancies, and some infectious and non-infectious illnesses. Women having a first baby after age 40 and those having a series of babies during adolescence are more likely to have premature babies than are women giving birth during their 20s and 30s. Premature babies tend to develop somewhat slowly at first, but if they are given adequate treatment, they generally show normal physical development by the time they are 3 years old.

About 12 percent of babies are born two weeks after they were expected, and 4 percent are born at least three weeks late. Late babies have a mortality rate three times that of babies born when expected. Causes of death include cerebral hemorrhage and suffocation. Although some late babies are heavier than average, others may be underweight because the placenta stopped functioning after the due date. When the symptoms of labor have not appeared several weeks after the due date or when medical problems indicate that birth should be accomplished as quickly as possible, a woman may be given synthetic oxytocin to speed the labor. Oxytocin is the hormone associated with the intense contractions of transition. Labor-inducing drugs should be used only when the risks of prolonged labor outweigh the risks of administering the drug (Resnik and Calder, 1999).

Early knowledge of pregnancy and regular prenatal checkups reduce the likelihood of parents' experiencing these complications of pregnancy and childbirth. Awareness of, and avoidance of, potential risks can increase the chances that expectant parents will experience a happy and satisfying pregnancy and childbirth.

Postpartum Events and Decisions

Within hours of their child's birth, the mother and father turn their attention to the innumerable decisions they have considered over the course of the pregnancy. Two of these are the method of feeding and, if the infant is a male, the question of circumcision.

FEEDING

All mammals, including humans, have the capacity to suckle their offspring. Just prior to birth, the woman's estrogen and progesterone levels fall. This hormonal decline stimulates the pituitary to secrete prolactin, a hormone that aids in milk production and stimulates the alveoli to secrete milk. The release of oxytocin, another pituitary hormone, is activated by the baby's sucking. Just as oxytocin stimulates contractions of the smooth muscles of the uterus during birth, it stimulates contractions of the cells that surround the alveoli, and these contractions eject the milk into the ducts, so that the baby can

This year-old baby nurses to obtain nutrition, but breast-feeding also provides the baby and mother with an opportunity to cuddle and play. Notice the hand-holding in both photos.

easily obtain the milk by sucking. Colostrum provides the newborn with its first liquid food. The colostrum is replaced by milk about 48 hours after birth.

Throughout most of our history, human mothers have breast-fed their babies. During the earlier part of the twentieth century, the popularity of breast-feeding declined throughout the world in favor of the use of bottled milk, or formula. Breast-feeding was perceived as "lower class," and bottled formula was thought to be antiseptic and scientific.

About 60 percent of women in the United States today either breast-feed exclusively or in combination with formula at the time they are discharged from the hospital. However, only about 22 percent had continued to nurse at six months (Ryan, 1997). Research in North America and Europe provides strong evidence that breast-feeding decreases the incidence and severity of diarrhea, respiratory infections, ear infections, certain bacterial infections, botulism, and urinary tract infections (American Academy of Pediatrics, 1997). Breast-fed babies acquire **passive immunity** from their mothers. Because breast milk contains antibodies from the mother's immune system, breast-fed babies are temporarily immune to a variety of diseases, including viruses and respiratory and gastrointestinal infections.

Breast milk is usually better than cow's milk or commercial formulas for the infant's physical well-being. Babies can digest human milk more easily than they can other animals' milk or vegetable-based formulas such as those made from soybeans. The American Academy of Pediatrics (AAP, 1997) recommends that breast-feeding begin as soon as possible after birth, usually within the first hour. Newborns should be nursed 8 to 12 times a day each time until they are full. Furthermore, the AAP suggests that breast-feeding continue for at least 12 months and for as long thereafter as mutually desired. Following these recommendations can be difficult for mothers employed outside the home because feeding could take up to 6 hours a day. Women who are employed outside the home can use breast pumps to obtain and refrigerate their milk for others to provide to their infants. Also, for women who cannot or do not wish to breast-feed their babies (or cannot do so full time), but who want them to have the nutritional advantages of human milk, milk banks are now available in many areas.

The average baby takes in approximately 1,000 calories per day from its mother's breast milk, a circumstance that benefits a woman who gained more weight than she wished during pregnancy. A woman can generally shed pounds steadily without denying

passive immunity—A kind of immunity to certain diseases or conditions acquired by a baby when it receives its mother's antibodies through her breast milk.

herself food if she nurses for six months or so. The oxytocin secretion stimulated by the baby's sucking also stimulates the smooth muscles of the uterus, providing another major benefit to a nursing mother. The resulting involuntary "exercise" of the uterus helps it to return to its normal size more quickly than it would if the woman did not breast-feed. The introduction of solid foods to supplement breast milk should be implemented by the fourth to the sixth month (Campbell et al., 1990).

Breast-feeding is particularly pleasant when the baby gets older and becomes active and playful. Some mothers find the sucking of their nipples sexually arousing, and a few experience orgasm during breast-feeding (Reamy & White, 1987). Depending on a woman's sexual attitudes, such arousal can be either extremely disconcerting or an additional pleasure associated with breast-feeding. *Reality or Myth*

Some women begin to breast-feed but terminate the process within a few days because of tender nipples and the engorgement of their breasts with milk, characteristics of the early weeks of breast-feeding. The duration and frequency of breast-feeding appear to be related to nipple discomfort. For women who experience nipple tenderness from breast-feeding, the discomfort is slight to moderate; it usually peaks at the third day and then decreases rapidly thereafter (Rebar, 1999). The woman can reduce or eliminate nipple tenderness by allowing the breast milk to dry on the nipples. She can reduce breast engorgement by nursing the baby and taking a warm shower to release some of the milk.

Just as some drugs and medications taken by a pregnant woman can transfer through the placenta to the fetus, so can they also be received by a baby through breast milk. A nursing mother should check with her health care provider before taking any medications.

▶ **Issues to Consider:** What are the advantages and disadvantages of breast-feeding an infant? Why do you think so many women give up breast-feeding after the infant reaches 6 months of age?

Although feeding an infant presents a number of decisions for parents, there is another decision that parents have in some cultures: whether to allow surgery on their infant's sex organs.

CIRCUMCISION

Throughout history, diverse operations have been performed on the sex organs of infants, as well as children and young adults. Boys have had their foreskins removed (circumcision) and slits made in the entire length of their penises (subincision). As noted in Chapter 1, sometimes girls have their clitorises, their clitoral hoods, and their labia removed. Some women have their labia sewn together. These operations have been performed in compliance with religious, ritual, hygienic, or sexual beliefs in various cultures. At present these practices remain common only in some parts of the Middle East, Africa, and Australia, as well as in the United States. More than 1 million baby boys are circumcised each year in the United States, and circumcision is the most common surgery performed on children (Lannon et al., 1999).

Many contemporary American parents support circumcision, because their religion prescribes it, because they mistakenly think that it is legally required, or because they believe that the presence of the foreskin causes cancer later in life. Recent research indicates that circumcision is associated with a slightly reduced risk of penile cancer (Niku et al., 1995). Since 1930 about 60,000 men have been diagnosed with this rare form of cancer. Almost all were uncircumcised. However, the incidence of penile cancer may be related to personal hygiene. Evidence linking cervical cancer to sexual intercourse with uncircumcised men is inconclusive (Niku et al., 1995). A task force of the American Academy of Pediatrics (AAP) reviewed the data and concluded that the surgery is not essential to the infant's well-being (Lannon et al., 1999). Also, for the first time, AAP recommended that circumcision should be done only on babies who have received analgesic pain relief. Newborn circumcision has potential medical benefits and advantages as well as disadvantages and risks. When circumcision is being considered, the benefits and risks should be explained to the parents but the AAP does not recommend the surgery be done routinely (Lannon, et al., 1999).

Another common belief is that circumcision affects sexual arousal. Some have argued that the removal of the foreskin reduces sensitivity because constant contact with clothing toughens the glans. In earlier times, this assumed reduction in sensitivity was considered an advantage in curbing masturbation. More recently, the assumed decrease in sensitivity was believed to delay orgasm in men, thereby enhancing their desirability as sexual partners because women tend to become aroused more slowly than do men. These long-held ideas notwithstanding, the presence or absence of the foreskin is not related to sexual sensitivity, the tendency to masturbate, or the speed of orgasm. As K. E. Paige (1978, p. 45) put it, "Sexual sensitivity appears to be in the mind of a man, not in his foreskin."

Depending on the area in North America, circumcision is done without an analgesic or anesthesia (painkillers) in 64 percent to 96 percent of the surgeries (Lander et al., 1997). Research has revealed that infants who receive a painkiller showed less distress and pain than infants who did not (Taddio et al, 1997). Various surgical techniques are used, and the complication rate is about 4 percent, which translates into more than 50,000 complicated circumcisions each year. Hemorrhage, mutilation, infection, and surgical trauma are the most serious complications. Furthermore, evidence suggests that for a short time after the operation, circumcised babies not only have increased heart rates and hormone-release patterns but also manifest greater levels of irritability than do uncircumcised babies (Niku et al., 1995).

A growing number of insurance companies and state Medicare agencies in the United States refuse to cover the cost of circumcision unless it is medically indicated. For example, in rare cases of phimosis (a condition in which the foreskin is so tight that it cannot be retracted from the glans), circumcision is considered medically appropriate. The proportion of newborn U.S. boys who are circumcised has been dropping. In Canada, after an examination of research on the effects of circumcision to determine if the government should continue to pay for the procedure, Cadman, Gafini, and McNamee (1984) concluded that the operation constitutes cosmetic surgery and thus should be paid for by parents who desire it for their sons.

▶ **Issues to Consider:** If you had (or have) a boy, would you (did you) have him circumcised? Why or why not?

Making decisions about feeding or circumcision are some of the factors that can contribute to the stress of new parenthood.

POSTPARTUM ADJUSTMENT

Because giving birth involves both physiological and psychological adjustment, the six weeks following childbirth are inherently stressful. First, the new mother experiences a rapid decline in estrogen and progesterone levels. High levels of estrogen during the menstrual cycle are associated with a general sense of well-being, whereas the low levels that precede the onset of menstruation are often accompanied by unwanted premenstrual symptoms. The decrease in estrogen associated with birth might also be expected to be related to such symptoms as fatigue, depressed mood, and edginess.

Second, both parents may get little sleep because most infants awaken frequently at night. The resulting fatigue can be particularly taxing for the mother, who may still be tired from lack of sleep in the final weeks of pregnancy and from the strenuous activity of giving birth. In addition, the deep sleep phase is reduced in women prior to delivery and typically does not return to normal until the second week following birth (Creasey and Resnik, 1999).

Third, for first-time parents, the loss of freedom and the number of tasks involved in caring for a helpless infant can be overwhelming. For couples who were accustomed to accepting last-minute invitations to parties or requests to work overtime, the realization that they cannot act as spontaneously as before can lead to a sense of being trapped, even when the pregnancy was planned. The opportunity for uninterrupted conversation or lovemaking may be sharply curtailed for months (or years!) after the birth, leaving the mother or father, or both of them, feeling neglected, jealous, or resentful of the baby. Some new parents suspect that their seemingly helpless infants are considerably more aware of the surrounding environment than is commonly thought. As one young father put it, "That damn kid has ESP. Every time I get his mother alone for a few minutes, he wakes up and starts wailing!"

Although women are generally expected to be elated, even if exhausted, by the arrival of the "blessed event," 87 percent of new mothers experience health problems in the first two months postpartum, such as tiredness, backaches, anemia, breast problems associated with breast-feeding, and depression (Glazener et al., 1995). In the light of these factors—changes in hormone levels, loss of sleep, and reduced freedom—it is surprising that "postpartum blues" are not universal. *Reality or Myth*

When these symptoms continue beyond a few weeks, a woman may be diagnosed as experiencing **postpartum depression,** including prolonged dysphoria (absence of enjoyment of life) and loss of concentration and self-esteem. Severe and lengthy symptoms of depression affect only about 1 or 2 women per 1,000 births (Lowdermilk, 1997).

POSTPARTUM SEXUAL EXPRESSION

Many physicians have routinely banned coitus for six weeks following birth. This ban may be linked more to societal or religious taboos based on beliefs about women's "uncleanliness" during menstruation and the immediate postpartum period than to empirical data indicating medical risks (Reamy & White, 1987). Yet for the first few weeks after birth, coitus may be the furthest thing from a new mother's mind. Tenderness in the vaginal area (particularly after an episiotomy), general fatigue, diminished levels of estrogen, and the vaginal discharge that occurs in the days following birth all may contribute to temporarily diminished sexual desire. Gradually these symptoms decline. The original discharge is replaced by **lochia,** a discharge consisting of a smaller amount of red or brown blood that may continue for two to four weeks or more following birth. This discharge need not interfere with intercourse, however, if the woman begins to feel the familiar stirrings of desire.

If a woman has not had an episiotomy or if the episiotomy has healed quickly, the couple may resume coitus within three or four weeks after birth. In a study of more than 1,000 women and their spouses or partners during pregnancy and the year postpartum, Hyde, DeLamater, Plant, and Byrd (1996) found that about 90 percent of couples reported having intercourse during the fourth and twelfth month

postpartum, but only about 19 percent reported coitus in the month immediately following birth. Nevertheless, the majority of couples did report petting during the first month postpartum. At all three times postpartum, women and men in the study were above the midpoint in their ratings of their satisfaction with their sexual relationship, including the first month postpartum. For most women, first postpartum coitus occurs between the first and second month following birth, with the fifth week being the most common time for resumption of coitus (Reamy & White, 1987). *Reality or Myth*

It is normal for women to feel apprehensive when they contemplate resuming coital relations; many fear a renewal of the vaginal discomfort that they experienced during childbirth and recovery. But new mothers have other concerns as well, about birth control, vaginal tenderness, harm to internal organs, infections, waking the baby, and decreased vaginal lubrication.

The issues of effective contraception and waking of the baby can be handled with some preplanning. However, if a woman is experiencing perineal tenderness from the birth or from an episiotomy, the couple should postpone coitus until she is more comfortable. A temporary reduction in vaginal lubrication for a short time following childbirth is normal; water-soluble lubricants can be used until the woman begins to secrete adequate amounts of vaginal lubrication.

Some new mothers also worry about their sexual attractiveness. Stretch marks, extra weight, and loose skin in their abdomens, all remnants of the pregnancy, may contribute to their self-doubt. But the stretch marks lose their reddish color and fade with time, and weight reduction and the firming of abdominal skin and muscles can be accomplished with appropriate diet and exercise. Of additional concern to some women are the shape, size, and tone of the vagina after birth. One of the remarkable features of the vagina, however, is its elasticity. Although it stretches to permit the birth of a baby, the vaginal muscles tighten again fairly soon after birth. The new mother can speed the process by which these muscles regain their tone and strength by doing Kegel exercises (see Chapter 4). Henderson (1983) instructed a group of new mothers to perform these exercises and found that they had greater muscle

---

postpartum depression—Intense sadness or general letdown some women experience following childbirth.
lochia—(LOH-kee-ah) Dark-colored vaginal discharge that follows childbirth for several weeks.

Even as couples carry out their roles as parents, it is important that they maintain their relationship as a couple.

tone at their first postpartum checkup than did a control group of women.

Although the physical changes following childbirth temporarily require substantial adjustment, psychological and social changes may pose greater challenges for both parents. First-time parents may find that it takes time to integrate their new roles as parents with their former roles as companions and lovers. A candlelit dinner away from home, a walk in the woods, or any other activity that gives a couple time away from the baby, may help to speed that integration.

SUMMARY OF MAJOR POINTS

1. Symptoms of pregnancy. A missed menstrual period is generally, but not always, the first indication that a woman is pregnant. Most lab tests for pregnancy are based on the detection of the hormone HCG in a blood or urine sample. Reliable test results can be obtained as early as a week after conception. Home pregnancy test kits administered as early as the first day of the expected menstrual period are also highly reliable when done correctly. Although these home tests may be a convenient preliminary indicator of pregnancy, they should not be used as a substitute for a laboratory test because conditions other than pregnancy can affect test results.

2. The experience of pregnancy. Although each pregnancy is unique, women commonly experience some fatigue and occasional nausea during the first trimester and lose some interest in sexual interaction. In contrast, during the second trimester, most women feel healthy and energetic. By the third trimester, pregnant women tend to feel increasingly bulky as the fetus gains in weight and size, and fatigue and discomfort are common. For healthy women so inclined, sexual interaction appears to have no negative effects on the fetus during the third trimester. Fathers also experience pregnancy in stages, with responses ranging from ambivalence to a heightened sense of responsibility.

3. The onset of labor. Various events signal the onset of labor, including uterine contractions and release of the amniotic fluid. The extent of prepping a woman undergoes depends on the policies of the physician or midwife and the hospital or birthing center.

4. The process of labor. During first-stage labor, increasingly frequent and intense contractions efface and dilate the cervix to widen it for the baby's passage. The most frequent and intense contractions occur during transition, at the end of first-stage labor. During second-stage labor, a woman bears down at the height of the birth contractions to help push the baby out of the uterus and vagina. During third-stage labor, the placenta and the umbilical cord are delivered.

5. Postpartum parental decisions. One issue that must be decided shortly after the birth of a baby is whether to breast-feed. Breast milk is nutritionally superior to bottled milk or formula. Another decision that new parents must make is whether to circumcise a baby boy. This practice of removing the foreskins of infant boys is the subject of considerable controversy.

6. Postpartum adjustment. New parents, and particularly new mothers, normally experience fatigue and bouts of depression from a combination of abrupt hormonal changes, loss of sleep, and loss of freedom brought on by the responsibility of caring for a helpless new human. Those who experience these problems can reduce their severity considerably by reserving some time for their own needs as individuals and as a couple. Although emotional intimacy can be maintained throughout pregnancy and the postpartum period, sexual intercourse is generally not resumed for three to six weeks following birth. For new parents, the weeks following the birth of a first baby are devoted to adding the new role of parents to their former roles as lovers and spouses, and this process has both its stresses and its joys.

Contraception

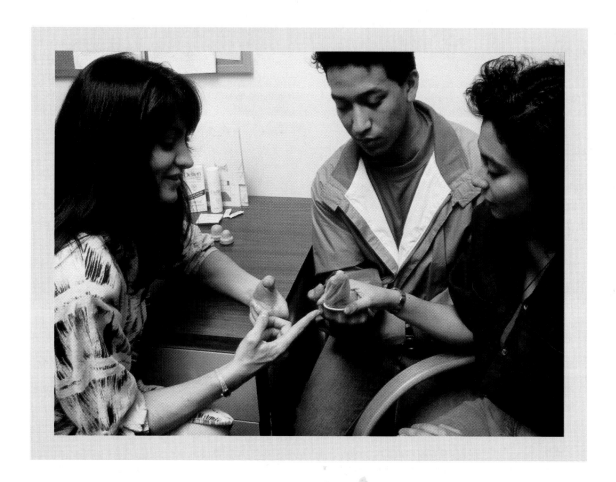

Reality or Myth

1. *Young women are at greater risk of death from pregnancy and birth than they are from any form of contraception.*

2. *The rhythm method is just as effective as other contraceptive methods in preventing pregnancy.*

3. *The condom is the only reliable temporary method of male contraception.*

4. *Female condoms have a lower breakage rate than male condoms.*

5. *Low-dose oral contraceptives reduce a woman's risk of contracting uterine and ovarian cancers.*

6. *Following vasectomy, a man may begin engaging in intercourse as soon as he recovers from the minor surgery, without fear of impregnating his partner.*

How many humans can the earth support? Control of the growth of the earth's population is one of the most fundamental problems facing our species. Our planet's air, land, and water resources are being overwhelmed by population growth. The world's population now surpasses 5 billion, and it is expected to reach 6 billion very soon. In the minute that it takes you to read this paragraph, more than 175 babies will have been added to our population, and many are unplanned or unwanted.

In this chapter we describe **contraceptives** and the major political and social factors that influenced their development and legal acceptance. We also examine some of the reasons that people engage in unprotected intercourse. We consider the advantages and disadvantages of each of the temporary and permanent methods of **birth control** currently available, along with some that are now being developed.

The Development and Use of Modern Contraceptives

Despite the age-old belief that *the* purpose of sexual interaction is to reproduce, people have attempted to practice birth control for thousands of years. In Europe large segments of the population began to use birth control in the latter part of the eighteenth century. They employed such methods as withdrawal, absorbents placed in the vagina, postcoital douching, abortion, and even infanticide (the killing of newborns). With the obvious exception of the last two, these methods were not highly reliable, but they did lower the birthrate.

During the nineteenth century, the widespread desire for more effective methods of birth control re-

contraceptives—Any techniques, drugs, or devices that prevent conception.
birth control—The regulation of conception, pregnancy, or birth with preventive devices or methods.

sulted in the development of the forerunners of modern diaphragms, spermicidal agents, cervical caps, condoms, and methods of female sterilization. The early twentieth century witnessed the development of the intrauterine device (IUD), modern methods of sterilization, and new techniques for abortion. One of the latest widely available methods of birth control—oral contraception, or "the pill"—was first marketed in 1960.

The notion that people should have the right to control the number of children they produce, independent of the frequency of their sexual intimacy, continues to be a topic of controversy. When the reproductive-rights pioneer Margaret Sanger devoted much of her life to facilitating the development and distribution of reliable methods of birth control, she did so as a staunch advocate of women's right to control their own reproductive capacity. In her

Margaret Sanger (1883–1966) was a pioneer in the birth control movement.

career as a nurse, Sanger, who was one of 11 children, personally saw the problems associated with uncontrolled fertility, illegal abortions, and unwanted children. After her husband's death, she used her personal and financial resources to provide support for research on female contraceptives. She founded the National Birth Control League in the United States in 1914, and published the magazines *Birth Control Review* and *Woman Rebel*. She also opened a birth control clinic in Brooklyn, New York, that police closed after a mere two weeks. Despite jail sentences and a two-year exile from the United States to escape a 45-year prison term (later overturned), she continued to support the birth control movement, providing funding for various scientists, including the so-called father of the pill, Gregory Pincus (Watkins, 1998).

In 1965 the U.S. Supreme Court overturned state laws prohibiting the dissemination of contraceptive information and devices. Such laws were judged to be unconstitutional because they interfered with a couple's right to privacy. With the marketing of the pill and the IUD in the 1960s, and the Supreme Court's removal in 1973 of any legal barriers to a woman's decision to obtain an abortion during the first three months of pregnancy, the goal of greater control over reproduction was realized. (But see "Highlight: Sponge-Worthy?")

These achievements made an important contribution to the reproductive freedom of women. Women, however, continue to bear the major burden of contraception. All recently developed contraceptive methods are for women. Although the only contraceptive for men—the condom—does not have side effects, the most effective methods for women—the pill, the IUD, and hormonal injections and implants—have negative side effects for some women. The fact that many women want contraceptive control over their bodies during certain periods of their fertile years does not mean that all women want total responsibility for contraception throughout their entire reproductive life span.

Another major contraception-related controversy centers on the marketing and advertising of contraceptives. Although North Americans are exposed to thousands of sexual scenes on television each year, in daytime soap operas as well as prime-time programming, the major television networks have not aired advertisements for contraceptives. This practice obviously has not been applied to vaginal douches, hemorrhoid medication, or pregnancy tests. In 1994, the U.S. government sponsored a relatively direct advertising campaign for television and radio media aimed at young Americans, with the message: Use condoms or abstain from sex; above all, protect yourself from AIDS. The use of condoms for contraceptive protection was not mentioned. In contrast, cable channels such as MTV regularly air contraceptive commercials.

SELECTING A CONTRACEPTIVE

One of the most important considerations in the selection of a birth control method is its effectiveness. We often think of a word such as *effective* in an absolute sense: Either something works, or it does not. But in the realm of birth control, such certainty is impossible. On rare occasions, babies have even been born following attempted abortions or sterilizations. Birth control methods are therefore evaluated in terms of their probability of failure. This probability is calculated by determining the number of sexually active women out of one hundred who become pregnant in the course of a year while relying on a particular method (see Table 10.1 on page 226).

Contraceptive effectiveness is measured in terms of both the perfect and the typical failure rate. The

Sponge-Worthy?

"Today," the contraceptive sponge, was approved by the FDA in 1983, but survived in the contraceptive market for only about a decade. Although relatively expensive, it had a number of advantages. Women (or their partners) could buy it without a prescription. After insertion in the vagina, it was effective for 24 hours, it contained spermicide with nonoxynol-9 (effective at killing a number of STDs), and additional spermicide did not need to be added if the woman's partner ejaculated more than once in her vagina during the 24-hour period. However, the pharmaceutical company that manufactured the sponge withdrew it from the market, saying that it would be too expensive to upgrade the plant where the sponge was made to meet new FDA safety rules (Ingrassia, Springen, & Rosenberg, 1995).

In addition, pharmaceutical companies have become increasingly concerned with the possibility of being sued. Apparently some teenage girls responded to written instructions to "wet the sponge before inserting" (meaning to moisten it with water prior to insertion) by using saliva or Coca-Cola. Further, the use of the sponge was associated with a slightly increased risk of bacterial infection, but the risk was reduced if women remembered to remove the sponge within 30 hours of insertion and not to use it during their menstrual periods. Nonetheless, the manufacturer feared lawsuits.

The removal of the Today sponge from the market inspired a hilarious episode of the television show *Seinfeld*, and it continues to be aired in reruns. The character Elaine was portrayed as relying on the sponge for contraception, and when she discovered it was no longer being manufactured, she bought as many remaining cases of the sponge as she could find. Even so, given the finite number of sponges she was able to obtain, she began to evaluate potential lovers regarding whether they were "sponge-worthy"!

George's girlfriend at the time, Susan, also relied on the sponge, and she had run out of them before discovering that they were no longer being produced. She suggested that she and George use condoms, but he maintained that they were too difficult to use. In one scene, they are in bed, both aroused and ready to engage in intercourse. However, George was unable to figure out how to get the condom packet open before losing his erection. He subsequently pleaded with Elaine to give away some of her sponges to Susan, but to no avail.

As those of you who have seen it may agree, this episode of *Seinfeld* was very funny. What is not so funny is the absence of greater governmental and pharmaceutical support for the development of a range of contraceptive options for women—and men. During the 1960s, nine major American pharmaceutical companies were doing research on the development of contraceptives. By the late-1990s, only one remained committed to this endeavor. What steps would you take to try to resolve the conflict between fears of lawsuits, the profit motive, and the need for a range of contraceptives to meet the differing situations of people living in an increasingly overpopulated world?

One of the people credited with helping to develop oral contraceptives, Stanford chemist Carl Djerassi, stated, "The pharmaceutical industry has washed its hands of birth control. . . . If we can put a man on the moon, why can't we come up with decent birth control?" (Ingrassia et al., 1995, p. 61).

---

perfect failure rate is the number of failures that occur when the method is used consistently and correctly. In those cases, conception results from the failure of the method itself. The **typical failure rate** is the number of failures that occur as a result of either

perfect failure rate—The failure rate of a contraceptive method when it is used consistently and correctly.
typical failure rate—The failure rate of a contraceptive method that takes into account both failure of the method and human failure to use it correctly.

TABLE 10.1 Effectiveness of Various Birth Control Methods Used in U.S.

This table shows the failure rate during the first year of typical use and the first year of perfect use of contraception; and the percentage continuing use at the end of the first year.

Method (1)	% of Women Experiencing an Unintended Pregnancy within the First Year of Use		% of Women Continuing Use at One Year
	Typical Use (2)	Perfect Use (3)	(4)
Chance	85	85	
Spermicides	26	6	40
Periodic Abstinence	25		63
Calendar		9	
Ovulation Method		3	
Symptothermal		2	
Post-ovulation		1	
Cap			
Women who have given birth	40	26	42
Women who have not given birth	20	9	56
Sponge			
Women who have given birth	40	20	42
Women who have not given birth	20	9	56
Diaphragm	20	6	56
Withdrawal	19	4	
Condom			
Female (Reality)	21	5	56
Male	14	3	61
Pill	5		71
Progestin only		0.5	
Combined		0.1	
IUD			
Progesterone T	2.0	1.5	81
Copper T 380A	0.8	0.6	78
LNg 20	0.1	0.1	81
Depo-Provera	0.3	0.3	70
Norplant and Norplant-2	0.05	0.05	88
Female Sterilization	0.5	0.5	100
Male Sterilization	0.15	0.10	100

SOURCES: Hatcher et al. (1998); Trussell and Kowal (1998).

failure of the method or failure to use a method correctly and consistently.

In choosing a birth control method, you are wise to consider both the advantages and the disadvantages. The advantages include relative effectiveness and convenience. Possible disadvantages include health risks, other undesirable side effects, or the po-

tential need to interrupt lovemaking (for example, to use the condom or diaphragm).

Although the health risks associated with the use of various contraceptives receive much media publicity, the greatest mortality risk for sexually active women comes from dangers associated with pregnancy and childbirth, which kill 1 in 10,000 women each year. In contrast, the lowest mortality rates are associated with the use of a barrier method of contraception, such as a diaphragm or a condom, in combination with legal abortion during the first nine weeks if the barrier method fails and a pregnancy occurs: 1 in 400,000 sexually active women dies from this combination of methods (see Table 10.2). We cover the advantages and disadvantages of the methods when we describe each. *Reality or Myth* ❓

CORRELATES OF CONTRACEPTIVE USE

Because of the relatively large proportion of adolescents and young adults who engage in sex without contraception, many subsequently experience an unwanted pregnancy (most research has been conducted with this age group). There are four necessary conditions for the use of contraceptives: (1) the existence of legal and reliable contraceptives, (2) contraceptive education, (3) easy access to contraceptives, and (4) motivation to employ contraception. In the case of most U.S. teenagers, only one condition—the existence of legal and reliable contraceptives—has been met. In 1977 the Supreme Court struck down a New York State statute that had prohibited the sale or distribution of nonprescription contraceptives to minors under age 16. This decision, combined with several other rulings, eliminated all legal barriers to the acquisition of *nonprescription* contraception by adolescents. However, access to contraceptives requiring a doctor's prescription has become more difficult for minors wishing to obtain them without having their parents notified or providing consent in those states requiring parental notification or consent.

The lack of contraceptive education also remains a major barrier to contraceptive use. Exposure to formal contraceptive programs increases by about one-third the likelihood that a teenage woman will use a contraceptive method at first intercourse. If contraceptive education occurs in the *same year* that a teenager becomes sexually active, the odds of using some method of contraception are increased by 70 to 80 percent. Jane Mauldon and Kristin Luker (1996) suggested that with greater educational efforts, the proportion of teens using no method might decrease by 8 percent.

What about the belief that easy access to contraception leads to promiscuity? Ironically, the evidence

TABLE 10.2 Voluntary Risks in Perspective

Activity	Chance of Death in a Year
Risks per year for men and women of all ages who participate in:	
Motorcycling	1 in 1,000
Automobile driving	1 in 5,900
Power boating	1 in 5,900
Rock climbing	1 in 7,200
Playing football	1 in 25,000
Canoeing	1 in 100,000
Risks per year for women aged 15 to 44 years:	
Using tampons	1 in 350,000
Having sexual intercourse (PID)	1 in 50,000
Risks for women preventing pregnancy:	
Using oral contraceptives (per year)	
Non smoker	1 in 66,700
Age less than 35	1 in 200,000
Age 35–44	1 in 28,600
Heavy smoker (25 or more cigarettes per day)	1 in 1,700
Age less than 35	1 in 5,300
Age 35–44	1 in 700
Using IUDs (per year)	1 in 10,000,000
Using diaphragm, condom, or spermicides	None
Using fertility awareness methods	None
Undergoing sterilization:	
Laparoscopic tubal ligation	1 in 38,500
Hysterectomy	1 in 1,600
Vasectomy	1 in 1,000,000
Risk per pregnancy from continuing pregnancy	1 in 10,000
Risk from terminating pregnancy:	
Legal abortion	
Before 9 weeks	1 in 262,800
Between 9 and 12 weeks	1 in 100,100
Between 13 and 15 weeks	1 in 34,400
After 15 weeks	1 in 10,200

SOURCE: Trussell and Kowal, 1998, p. 230.

▶ **Issues to Consider:** Assume that you have a child who is about to reach puberty. What education would you have already provided about contraception? What information would you want to give as he or she enters puberty?

This playful ad shows an erotophilic attitude towards contraception.

shows that use of reliable contraceptives is associated with strong commitment to one partner rather than with promiscuous sexual activity involving a number of different partners (Adler & Hendrick, 1991; Zlokovich & Snell, 1997). Even for first intercourse, there is greater use of reliable contraception among partners who are in love or planning to marry than among partners who are less involved with each other. The greater the degree of involvement is between two partners the first time they have sex, the more likely they are to use a reliable contraceptive.

Adolescent females who consistently use reliable contraceptives differ from those who do not in background, knowledge, attitudes, and personality. On the basis of research, it is possible to draw a general picture of teenagers from each of these two groups. The socioeconomic status of teenage women who consistently use contraception tends to be higher than that of women who are less conscientious. Moreover, the older, and presumably the more ma-

ture, a woman is when she first has intercourse, the greater is the likelihood that she will use birth control (Mauldon & Luker, 1996).

Although religious affiliation was related to contraceptive use in the past, research suggests that this is no longer the case (Tanfer, Grady, Klepinger, & Billy, 1993). Catholics, for example, are now as likely as Protestants to use contraception.

Attitudes toward sex are also strongly associated with contraceptive behavior. Consistent use of contraception is more likely among men and women with positive (erotophilic) attitudes and openness toward sex in general and toward their own sexual activity in particular (Fisher et al., 1988). People who cannot acknowledge that they are planning to be sexually active, however, are unlikely to obtain and employ contraception.

Some students who discover that they are pregnant come to us seeking information about various community resources. They cannot deny, of course, that they have been sexually intimate, but many of them describe the occurrence of intercourse as somehow accidental or unintentional, using versions of the claim that "the devil made me do it." They blame arousal ("We got carried away"), intoxication ("I got drunk"), or their partner ("He made me do it"; "She should have stopped me"). As discussed in Chapter 1, some people inaccurately think that sex somehow just occurs spontaneously.

Given the obvious association between sexuality and contraception, it is not surprising that guilt about sex affects attitudes and behavior regarding contraception. In fact, sex guilt may even interfere with a person's ability to learn about contraception. Schwartz (1973) found that when college students heard a lecture containing birth control information that is not commonly known, those who felt guilty about sex received lower scores on a test of their retention of the information than did those who felt less guilty.

If the rearing of children to feel guilty about their sexual feelings were effective in preventing premarital intercourse, then the negative effect of sex guilt on teenagers' use of contraceptives would not be of great concern. But research involving sexually active college students indicates that sex guilt may be more effective in blocking contraceptive use than in preventing premarital intercourse (Strassberg & Mahoney, 1988).

Our culture's assumptions about men's and women's differing motivations for intercourse and the possible outcome—pregnancy—have affected the development of contraceptives. The bulk of the blame and responsibility for unwanted pregnancy falls on women. Despite men's apparent willingness to use contraceptives, their use is less likely when a man initiates intercourse than when a woman is the initiator (Harvey & Scrimshaw, 1988). Thus most efforts to increase contraceptive use have targeted women.

Various lines of evidence suggest, however, that men are willing to take contraceptive responsibility, although there is currently only one effective temporary method that men can use: the condom. For example, several cross-cultural studies conducted by the World Health Organization (1980, 1982) found that a considerable proportion of men reported willingness to use hormonal contraceptives. In the past few decades, researchers and family planning agencies have shown increased interest in male contraceptive behavior.

Methods of Contraception

We now discuss current methods of birth control and their potential advantages and disadvantages, benefits, and impact on sexual response.[1] Because new information about birth control becomes available each year, you should consult a health care provider before making contraceptive choices. You and your health care provider should take into account your age, lifestyle, personality, and medical history in choosing a good method for you.

RHYTHM

We begin with the so-called **rhythm method,** mainly because the knowledge a couple needs to make this technique effective can be useful in increasing the effectiveness of almost all other birth control methods. About 4 percent of women report using this method as a contraceptive technique (Forrest & Fordyce, 1993). Essentially it means abstaining from coitus for at least a week around the time of ovulation. The date of ovulation must therefore be determined.

Knowledge of the time of ovulation is useful to women for several reasons. First, pinpointing the date of ovulation and engaging in intercourse at that time can improve the woman's chances of beginning a wanted pregnancy. Second, the more that women

know about the cycles and functioning of their own bodies, the more likely they are to recognize potential medical difficulties. The currently available methods of detecting ovulation involve the use of a calendar, the recording of one's daily temperature, the monitoring of cervical mucus, and the use of ovulation detection kits, which are available in drugstores. This test, which monitors the presence of an enzyme associated with ovulation, can only confirm, not predict, ovulation (Jennings, Lamprecht, and Kowal, 1998).

The Calendar Method.   The calendar method of determining ovulation is based on the law of averages. The average menstrual cycle is about 28 days long, with ovulation occurring, on average, 14 days *prior* to the onset of the menstrual period. To determine when ovulation occurs, a woman must be able to predict accurately the day she will begin her next period. Such forecasting can pose a problem because emotional and biological factors such as illness, fatigue, rigorous exercise, and stress can alter the cycle interval. Menstrual regularity is also rare in the first few and last few years of a woman's reproductive span. Furthermore, women occasionally release more than one egg in a particular cycle, which can throw off the timing.

The Symptothermal Method.   To determine the time of ovulation by the **symptothermal method,** a woman takes her temperature each morning before

---

rhythm method—A birth control technique based on avoidance of sexual intercourse during a woman's fertile period each month

symptothermal method—A way of determining the date of ovulation based on changes in a woman's basal body temperature and the stretchability of her cervical mucus.

---

[1]Unless otherwise noted, statistics on effectiveness are based on Hatcher et al. (1998).

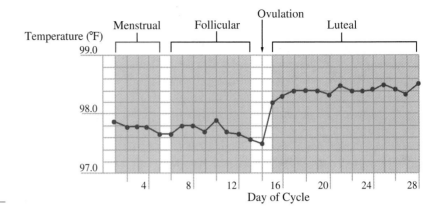

Figure 10.1 Basal Body Temperature (BBT) Chart
Note that the temperature pattern for this average woman includes a sharp rise in BBT on day 15, indicating the point of ovulation as day 14.

she gets out of bed with a basal body temperature (BBT) thermometer (an ordinary thermometer is not sensitive enough) and examines her cervical mucus. Generally low during the first part of the menstrual cycle, the BBT tends to drop a bit further on the day of ovulation, as shown in Figure 10.1.

The BBT then rises on the day after ovulation and remains relatively high throughout the rest of the cycle. Because the most definite indication of ovulation, the rise in BBT, occurs the day *after* ovulation, successful use of this method depends on a woman's keeping track of her cycle for up to six months *and* having a regular cycle. A woman can predict the day she will ovulate only if both conditions are met.

A woman can confirm the information she ob-

tains from the BBT by examining her cervical mucus. The amount and characteristics of the mucus vary at different points in the menstrual cycle. During most of the menstrual cycle, the cervical mucus does not stretch at all. During ovulation, however, the mucus stretches and resembles the consistency of unbeaten raw egg whites. To check the extent of stretchiness, a woman first inserts her finger into her vagina to obtain a sample of cervical mucus. After withdrawing her finger, she touches it to her thumb and then slowly pulls her thumb and index finger apart. If ovulation is occurring, she will observe a thin, connecting thread of mucus up to an inch long.

Effective use of the symptothermal method depends on the woman's accurately pinpointing the time of ovulation and avoiding unprotected coitus during the fertile period (from five days preceding ovulation until three days following ovulation). For a graphic representation of the symptothermal rhythm method, see Figure 10.2. The symptothermal method is not as effective as other methods to be described, but it involves far less risk than no method at all. The effectiveness of the method is greatest when a couple engages in coitus only after ovulation. This practice yields a perfect failure rate of about 2 pregnancies per 100 women who engage in coitus on a fairly regular basis for a year. *Reality or Myth*

Drawbacks of the symptothermal method include the fact that accurately determining the date of ovulation takes a minimum of six months. Second, although the symptothermal method has no direct physical effect on sexuality, it may have psychological effects for some couples. This method requires couples to abstain from coitus for one to three weeks

At ovulation a woman's cervical mucus stretches to form a connecting thread up to an inch long, as this photo shows.

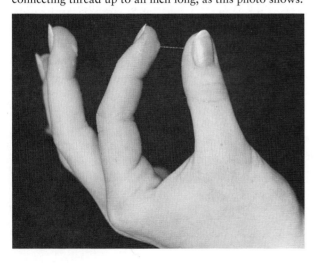

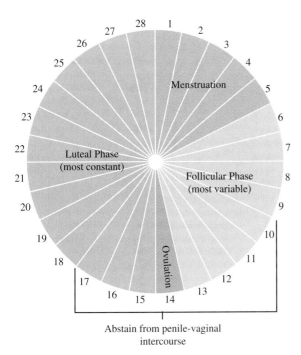

Figure 10.2 Hypothetical Menstrual Cycle Illustrating the Use of the Rhythm Method of Contraception

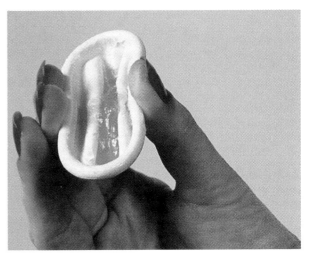

Diaphragm and spermicide

out of each cycle depending on the regularity (and thus the predictability) of a woman's menstrual cycle. The periods of abstinence may result in considerable frustration for some couples. The temporary ban on coitus need not be a great disadvantage, however, because couples can engage in oral or manual stimulation without fear of conception during those times when a woman is fertile. The major benefit of the symptothermal method is that it does not interfere with the woman's reproductive system in any way; therefore, she need not be concerned about potential side effects.

DIAPHRAGM AND SPERMICIDE

The **diaphragm** is a dome-shaped cap made of soft rubber that is designed to fit inside the vagina and cover the cervix. It was the first widely available con-

> **diaphragm**—(DYE-uh-fram) A dome-shaped rubber contraceptive device inserted into the vagina to block the cervical opening. The diaphragm should always be used with a spermicide.

traceptive for women. Many women abandoned it in favor of the pill during the 1960s, and only about 4 percent of women currently use it as a contraceptive (Forrest & Fordyce, 1993). All diaphragms should be used with a **spermicide**. Spermicides designed to be used with a diaphragm come in tubes of cream or jelly and are available at drugstores without a prescription. Diaphragms may be obtained only by prescription from a physician because they must be fitted to the size of the user.

To use a diaphragm (see Figure 10.3 on page 232), the user places spermicidal jelly or cream in the center and around the rim of the device. Either the woman or her partner inserts the diaphragm into the vagina with an applicator or with the fingers, positioning the diaphragm so that the side containing the spermicide is next to the cervix. A well-fitted, properly placed diaphragm is not felt by either man or woman; in fact, some women have been known to forget that they are wearing a diaphragm. A diaphragm should be refitted after any changes that might alter vaginal size, such as pregnancy, childbirth, and weight increases or decreases of 10 pounds or more. It should also be inspected regularly for holes or tears. This examination may be done by holding the diaphragm up to a light or filling it with water to see whether there are any leaks.

> **spermicide**—A chemical that kills or immobilizes sperm.

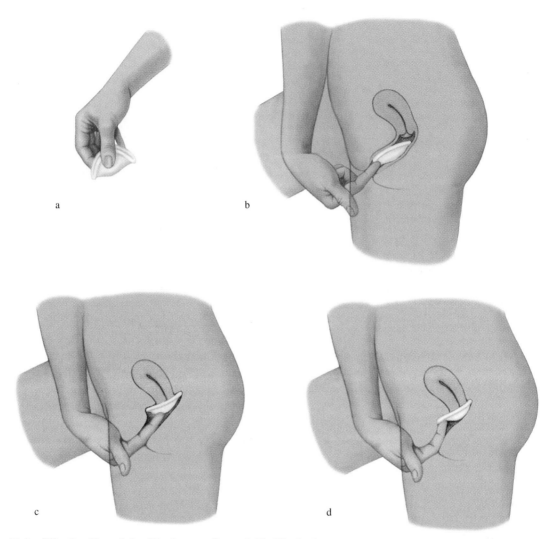

Figure 10.3   Effective Use of the Diaphragm-Spermicide Method
To use this method effectively, a woman should place about a tablespoon of spermicide in the center of the diaphragm and a little spermicide around the rim. The diaphragm is then (a) pinched between the thumb and fingers and (b) inserted lengthwise into the vagina, so that it covers the cervix. The woman should then check to make sure that (c) the diaphragm is covering her cervix and (d) the edge of the diaphragm closest to the vaginal entrance is lodged behind the pubic bone. To remove the device, she inserts a finger under the rim and pulls the diaphragm forward.

The diaphragm-spermicide method works in two ways. First, the diaphragm provides a physical barrier across the entrance to the uterus, reducing the likelihood that sperm will reach the egg. Second, the thick spermicide kills or immobilizes the sperm. The diaphragm should be inserted no more than two hours prior to intercourse. It should be left undisturbed for six to eight hours following ejaculation because it takes spermicide that long to be effective.

The failure rate for the diaphragm-spermicide method ranges from the perfect yearly rate of 6 per 100 women to the typical failure rate of 20 (Trussell & Kowal, 1998). Failure of the spermicide is generally caused by leakage. The spermicide is most potent if the diaphragm and spermicide are inserted just prior to penile penetration. A couple can thus increase the effectiveness of the method by making insertion of the spermicide-coated diaphragm part of lovemaking.

Diaphragm failure is usually associated with the shifting of the device as a result of particularly vigorous intercourse, changes in the size of the vagina during sexual arousal, or use of the woman-above coital position (Stewart, 1998). Therefore, if conception must be avoided, it is wise to use an additional method of contraception, such as a condom, during ovulation.

The diaphragm is used only when needed and has no influence on subsequent fertility. In rare cases, an individual may be allergic to the latex in the diaphragm or to the spermicide, but this problem can usually be solved by switching to a different brand. The contraceptive effect of the diaphragm is immediately reversible: The partners can simply abandon diaphragm use when they wish to conceive.

A potential drawback of the diaphragm-spermicide method is that it may limit the range of sexual behavior for some couples. For example, the spermicide may inhibit the desire for cunnilingus. Most spermicides are safe and nontoxic, but the odor and the taste of the standard spermicides are not particularly appealing. Tasteless and odorless spermicides are now available, and fruit-flavored spermicides can be purchased in specialty shops or through mail order catalogs (see the Appendix).

CERVICAL CAP

The **cervical cap** is a rubber dome that is available in four sizes to fit a woman's cervix. It differs from the diaphragm in that it is smaller and can be inserted earlier. After placing spermicide inside the cap, the woman or her partner may insert it up to six hours before coitus; like the diaphragm, the cervical cap should not be removed for at least six hours after ejaculation.

The Food and Drug Administration (FDA) has concluded that the cervical cap may remain in place without additional applications of spermicide for 48 hours. It advised that the cap be prescribed only to women with normal PAP test results and that users should have a follow-up PAP test three months after beginning use of the device. At a failure rate ranging from 9 to 40 per 100 women, the cap is not quite as

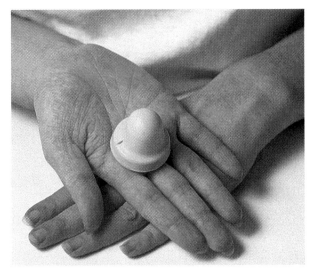

The Prentif cavity rim cervical cap is a soft rubber cup that is inserted into the vagina and pressed onto the cervix. Spermicide is used to fill one-third of the dome prior to insertion of the cap.

effective as the diaphragm (Trussell & Kowal, 1998). The most frequently cited reason for failure is incorrect or inconsistent use. Reported side effects include unpleasant odor, partner discomfort, and a slightly increased risk of toxic shock syndrome. It is used by less than 1 percent of contracepting women (Forrest & Fordyce, 1993).

CONDOM

The **condom** is the only available method of male contraception and can be purchased without a prescription. When unrolled, the rubber or cecum (skin) condom resembles a long, thin balloon. Designed to envelop a man's erect penis, it is put on prior to penetration and intercourse (see Figure 10.4 on page 234). About half an inch of space should be left at the condom's tip, so that there is room for the ejaculated semen; some condoms come with a protruding tip designed to catch the ejaculate. After intercourse, the rim of the condom should be held against the base of the penis as it is withdrawn from the woman's vagina so that the condom does not

cervical cap—A contraceptive rubber dome that is fitted to a woman's cervix; spermicide is placed inside the cap before it is pressed onto the cervix.

condom—A sheath placed over the erect penis for prevention of pregnancy and protection against disease.

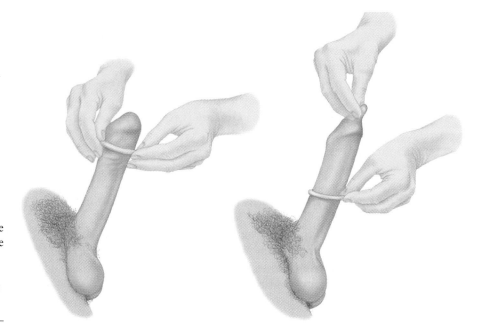

Figure 10.4   Putting on the Condom
The condom is placed over the head of the penis, with a space left at the tip to hold semen. The condom is then rolled all the way down the shaft of the erect penis.

come off. After withdrawal the condom should be taken off and discarded. *Reality or Myth*

The condom works by preventing sperm from entering the vagina. Many condoms come with spermicidal lubricants, such as nonoxynol-9, that boost the condom's effectiveness further. The failure rate for condom users ranges between 3 percent and 12 percent per year. Because condom manufacture in the United States is supervised by the FDA, breakage due to defect is rare. However, improper treatment of the condom by the purchaser can reduce its effectiveness. Condoms should be kept away from heat; for example, a condom should not be kept in a wallet in one's back pocket.

A nationally representative sample of men aged 17 to 22 reported a condom breakage rate in the past year of 2.5 percent (Lindberg, Sonenstein, Ku, & Levine, 1997). Recent sex education was associated with almost an 80 percent decrease in risk of breakage among young men who used condoms infrequently, suggesting that increasing access to such education could reduce failure rates from condom use.

To increase a condom's effectiveness, a man should wear it during any vaginal penetration, and he should hold on to it firmly while withdrawing. Some men engage in penetration for some time prior to ejaculation and put the condom on only when they intend to ejaculate. This practice raises the fail-

ure rate for a couple of reasons. First, the droplet of fluid that appears on a man's penis during arousal but prior to ejaculation sometimes contains sperm (see Chapter 4).

Second, ejaculation may occur before a man can withdraw to put on the condom. Psychological factors may influence the unintentional ejaculation. A man may feel that his "loss of control" is a compliment to his partner. Moreover, a woman may get some pleasure out of encouraging a man to demonstrate his loss of rationality in the heat of passion for her. Whatever psychological satisfactions come into play at the moment of ejaculation, they are quickly replaced by far more negative feelings as the couple anxiously await the arrival of the woman's menstrual period later in the month. Thus, a couple who is relying on the condom should make sure that it is always worn prior to *any* vaginal penetration.

For additional lubrication, a couple can choose lubricated condoms or employ a water-soluble product such as surgical jelly (K-Y jelly, for example) or saliva. Petroleum jelly (such as Vaseline) should be avoided for two reasons: It may damage the condom, and it is not easily discharged from the vagina.

Aside from those who are allergic to latex, no negative side effects are associated with condom use, and condoms can prevent the spread of many sexually transmitted diseases (STDs) (see Chapter 16).

Lubricated condoms now come in such flavors as banana, lime, licorice, peppermint, and strawberry. They also allow a man to take contraceptive responsibility, although one company markets a condom contained in a plastic cup for women to carry in their purses. Almost 75 percent of men in a national survey agreed with the statement that the use of a condom shows that the man is a concerned and caring person (Grady, Klepinger, Billy, & Tanfer, 1993).

Most men (75 percent) using condoms report a reduction in sensation to the penis (Grady et al., 1993). According to an old saying, wearing a condom is like taking a shower with a raincoat on. However, a man who ejaculates very quickly may appreciate a slight decrease in sensation, as may his partner, if it prolongs intercourse. About 32 percent of the men in the Grady et al. study reported that condom use made sex last longer. Latex condoms inhibit the transfer of heat to some degree. The more expensive cecum condoms, made from the intestinal tissue of lambs, allow transmission of changes in temperature and result in a more natural sensation for the couple. However, in addition to being at least three times more costly, cecum condoms provide less protection from sexually transmitted diseases (Warner & Hatcher, 1998). In laboratory trials, virus particles pass through cecum condoms because of the size of the pores in the lambskin relative to the size of such viruses as HIV and hepatitis B.

> ▶ **Issues to Consider:** Regardless of whether you are male or female, how would you respond to a potential partner who wants to have sex with you but does not want to use a condom because it reduces the physical sensation?

In 1994, the first male polyurethane condom was introduced in the United States. It is stronger and thinner than latex, and it is usually odorless and transparent. In a study comparing the effectiveness of polyurethane and latex condoms, the breakage rate of the polyurethane condom was significantly higher (7 percent) than for the latex condom (1 percent). However, nearly half the men preferred the polyurethane condom because of the greater sensitivity it provided (Frezieres, Walsh, Nelson, Clark, & Coulson, 1998).

Some couples see the act of putting on the condom as an interruption of their sexual expression. Others incorporate the activity into their pattern of erotic stimulation. Attitudes toward condom use are important. If a couple uses condoms in an erotic fashion (she helps put it on in a sensual way, for example), there tends to be more sexual pleasure (Tanner & Pollack, 1988).

FEMALE CONDOMS

Several intravaginal pouches, or "female" condoms, have been developed. The **female condom** is generally made of polyurethane or latex and lines the vagina. It can be a highly effective contraceptive method if used correctly (Farr, Gabelnick, Sturgen, & Dorflinger, 1994). The female condom is almost twice as thick as most male condoms. Female and male condoms should not be used at the same time as they can adhere to each other causing slippage or displacement of one or both contraceptives. (Stewart, 1998) Female condoms are more expensive and generally less acceptable to users than are male condoms. For example, only about half of a group of British women who used the female condom for at least three months had a positive attitude toward the method (Ford & Mathie, 1993). Obstacles to the use of the female condom resemble those posed by the male condom. That is, they may be viewed as interfering with the pleasure of the sexual experience (Sly et al., 1997). *Reality or Myth* ?

FOAMS AND SUPPOSITORIES

Contraceptive foams and **contraceptive suppositories** may be purchased without a prescription. These products should be kept cool because heat can decompose them, reducing their effectiveness. Contraceptive foam must be shaken before it is placed in an applicator and inserted in the vagina prior to intercourse. It should remain in the vagina for six to eight hours after ejaculation. More foam must be injected before each succeeding ejaculation.

> **female condom**—A pouch placed inside the vagina to line the vaginal walls for prevention of pregnancy and protection against disease.
> **contraceptive foams**—Spermicidal foams that are injected into the vagina prior to coitus.
> **contraceptive suppositories**—Solid contraceptive substances containing a spermicide, inserted in the vagina prior to coitus, and that melt in a matter of minutes.

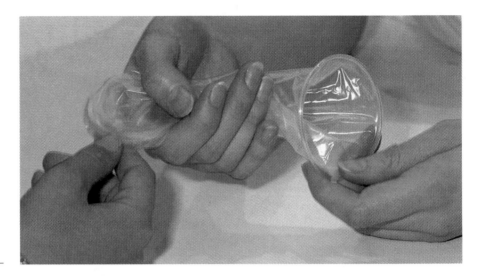

The FDA's approval of the female condom in 1992 gave women an opportunity to use a method that provides a woman with protection from both conception and sexually transmitted diseases.

A contraceptive suppository should be placed in the vagina at least 10 minutes and no more than two hours before ejaculation. After insertion, the suppository melts, filling the vagina with a spermicidal foam. Another suppository must be inserted for each subsequent act of intercourse, and a woman should avoid douching or bathing for at least two hours following intercourse.

The chemical components of spermicides kill or immobilize sperm, and their thick consistency provides a physical barrier to the entrance to the cervix. Used alone, spermicides have a relatively high failure rate: up to 26 per 100 women. Errors in the timing of insertion, as well as coital positions (such as the woman-above position) that allow the foam to move away from the cervix, contribute to the failure rate. Couples can increase the contraceptive effectiveness of spermicides, however, by using them in combination with a condom (Cates & Raymond, 1998). From 1 to 3 percent of women use only foams or suppositories for contraception (Forrest & Fordyce, 1993).

The relatively high failure rates of foams and suppositories when used alone are one of their disadvantages. In addition, they are irritating to the genital tissues of some people, which is their only physical side effect. They do not interfere with the reproductive system, and their effects are completely and immediately reversible. In combination with barrier methods, they are also effective in reducing the likelihood of contracting sexually transmitted diseases.

Although spermicides have no direct physical effects on sexual response, they may have some psychological disadvantages. Some couples object to the noise produced by the extra liquid during thrusting of the penis into the vagina. Furthermore, some women dislike having to wait several hours after coitus before bathing.

ORAL CONTRACEPTIVES

When "the pill" was first marketed in the early 1960s, it was the first widely available, coitus-independent method of birth control; that is, for the first time, a couple could reduce the chances of conception without having to remember in the midst of lovemaking to insert a diaphragm and spermicide, put on a condom, and so forth. About 40 percent of sexually active U.S. women aged 15 to 44 use the pill for contraception (Forrest & Fordyce, 1993). "The pill" actually refers to about 30 different oral contraceptive products available in the United States, all of which contain synthetic forms of the hormones estrogen and/or progestagen/progestin (Hatcher & Guillebaud, 1998).[2] When **oral contraceptives** first received FDA approval in 1960, they contained relatively high doses of progestin and estrogen. Today

[2]There are various terms for the class of synthetic and naturally secreted progestational (pregnancy-supporting) hormones. For simplicity, we use the generic term *progestin* for synthetic progesterone.

oral contraceptives—Pills containing hormones that inhibit ovulation.

the average combination pill contains much lower levels of both hormones.

Oral contraceptives require a prescription from a physician. To use the pill, a woman takes one each day for 21 days, stops for 7 days to permit menstrual bleeding, and then begins a new cycle. With some brands, the woman takes a pill during the 7 menstrual days as well; however, those 7 pills are placebos and contain no hormones. Oral contraceptives are highly effective, with a maximum failure rate of 3 percent. Of all the oral contraceptives, the "combination pill," which acts in several ways, is the most effective. It contains both an estrogen and a progestin. The estrogen and progestin prevent ovulation. In addition, the progestin appears to interfere with the development of the normal lining of the uterus so that, should ovulation and fertilization occur, implantation is inhibited. The progestin also acts to thicken the cervical mucus, with the result that sperm have a difficult time getting through it.

Another kind of oral contraceptive, the mini-pill, contains very small doses of a potent progestin, which has the effects just described. Although the mini-pill usually does not interfere with ovulation, because it contains no estrogen, it has a very low failure rate—just slightly higher than that of the combination pill. With all of these oral contraceptives, a woman should use a backup method of contraception during the first month she is using the pill.

In contrast, with the **triphasic oral contraceptive,** a woman begins to take the pills on the first day of her menstrual cycle and need not use a backup contraceptive. Like other pills, the triphasic pills contain both estrogen and progestin. The difference between triphasics and other oral contraceptives is that the level of progestin (and in some cases, the level of estrogen) in triphasics varies over the month. This variation permits the use of very low levels of hormones—levels that reduce the risk of negative side effects.

Aside from remembering to take the pill at the same time each day, a woman does not have to do anything more to increase the effectiveness of the oral contraceptives, provided that she has the correct dosage. Physicians normally attempt to prescribe the

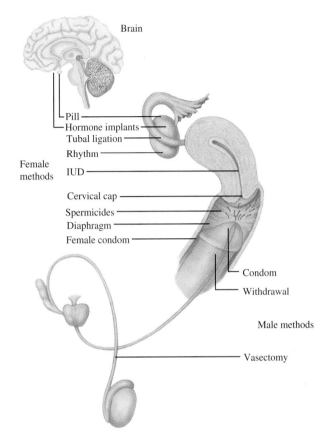

Figure 10.5 Location of Contraceptive Effects
This drawing indicates the sites of effectiveness for male and female contraceptives.

lowest possible effective levels of estrogen and progestin for each woman; sometimes it takes a bit of trial and error to determine the proper dosage.

If a woman forgets to take the pill for one day, she may take two the following day with no measurable rise in the risk of conception. If she forgets the pill for several days, the risk of conception increases. In that case, she should stop taking the pills for seven days and then begin a new pill cycle. In the meantime, she should rely on another method of contraception until she has completed at least seven pills in the new cycle.

Because hormones in the pill interact with a woman's system, the side effects of pill use are highly individual, depending on a woman's medical history, age, and personal habits. In general, the side effects are minor and tend to stabilize after a few cycles. They mimic some of the symptoms of early pregnancy, including weight gain, slight breast enlargement and tenderness, reduction in the amount of

---

triphasic oral contraceptives—Low-dose birth control pill in which the levels of hormones are varied over the menstrual cycle.

menstrual discharge during a woman's period, breakthrough bleeding (that is, bleeding not associated with menstruation), emotional depression, and nausea. Headaches, nausea, and dizziness may be a sign that the dosage is too high. Although occasional "spotting" of blood is not unusual, persistent breakthrough bleeding may indicate that the dosage is too low. If any of these conditions arises, a woman should notify her health care provider.

Major side effects from the pill are less common. Involving mainly the cardiovascular (heart and blood vessel) system, they include hemorrhaging and blood clotting, which can be fatal. These cardiovascular problems, although rare, have prompted the FDA to urge the lowest dose pill possible.

The FDA has estimated that from 30 to 40 percent of the 8 to 10 million women who take the pill smoke. The health risks of pill use rise with age and with heavy smoking (15 or more cigarettes a day). In short, cigarette smokers should not use the pill.

A possible association also exists between pill use and cancer. This link, however, is complicated and has been difficult to evaluate. It is unfortunate that, although some women have avoided the pill because of fear of cancer, actuarial data suggest that low-dose contraceptives may actually *reduce* the likelihood of women contracting some forms of cancer and may slow the growth of others (Hatcher & Guillebaud, 1998). For example, the risk of a woman's contracting the most common form of uterine cancer, endometrial cancer, is lower for women who take the pill than for women who do not (Hatcher & Guillebaud, 1998). A similar relationship has been found between pill use and ovarian cancer. In addition, research indicates that pill users have no increased risk of cervical cancer (Hatcher & Guillebaud, 1998). The pill's risks and benefits with regard to breast cancer are less clear. Because the body of evidence on the association between pill use and breast cancer is contradictory, potential users should obtain the latest information about potential risks from their health care providers. *Reality or Myth*

The pill appears to be a safe, highly effective contraceptive for most women. Oral contraceptives are not messy and are taken independent of coitus. For couples who place a high premium on unplanned coitus, the pill is a highly desirable method. For women with very heavy or lengthy menstrual periods, the pill has the added advantage of decreasing the menstrual flow. Furthermore, for some women, pill use eliminates, or reduces the severity of, menstrual cramps, and consistent pill use almost eliminates unwanted pregnancy.

HORMONE IMPLANTS AND INJECTIONS

In 1990 the FDA approved an implantable slow-release contraceptive for use by U.S. women. Known as **Norplant**, it consists of six thin, flexible capsules, less than 1.5 inches long, that are inserted just under the skin of a woman's upper arm. Over a period of five years, these capsules slowly and continuously release a synthetic progestin into the user's bloodstream. The method may be relied on for contraception within 24 hours following insertion. A variation of the method, Norplant-2, consists of implanting two rods in the upper arm. Both methods are highly effective, with a failure rate of less than 1 percent. Clinical trials with women with contraceptive implants also show a reduced incidence of ectopic pregnancy compared to that occurring among noncontraceptive users and about equivalent to that observed among IUD users (Darney, 1994).

Similar to oral contraceptives, the implants work by suppressing ovulation and thickening cervical mucus, which inhibits the ability of sperm to enter the uterus. The most common side effects of the method are changes in menstrual symptoms, such as irregular bleeding, spotting, and increases and decreases in menstrual flow, especially during the first year (Forrest & Kaeser, 1993). Other possible side effects are headaches, nervousness, nausea, and dizziness.

From 76 percent to 90 percent of women continue to rely on implants after the first year (Darney, 1994). For women who wish to have Norplant removed, either because of side effects or because of a desire to become pregnant, removal, accompanied by a local anesthetic, is done by a physician. The most common reasons for removal in a sample of women ranging in age from 13 to 46 included irregular bleeding, weight gain, headaches, and desire for pregnancy (Cullins, et al. 1994).

In one study, 30 percent of women reported an improvement in their sex lives after having Norplant

---

Norplant—A contraceptive implant, inserted into a woman's upper arm, that slowly releases hormones to inhibit ovulation.

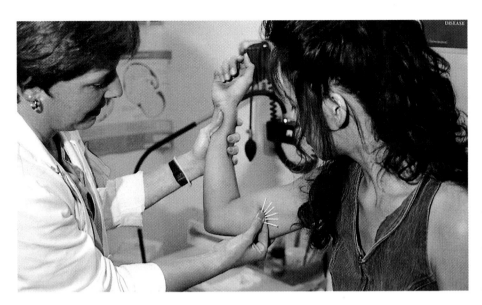

Norplant capsules inserted into a woman's arm provide contraceptive protection by releasing progestin over a five-year period.

inserted, primarily because they were less concerned about pregnancy and thought that sex could be more spontaneous (Darney et al., 1990). About 25 percent of the women reported a decrease in frequency of intercourse because of menstrual changes or, for a very small number of women, decreased libido.

As Heather Kuiper and her colleagues (Kuiper, Miller, Martinez, Loeb, & Darney, 1997) pointed out, highly effective contraceptive methods that, once administered, require no further contraceptive responsibility on the part of the user (at least for a five-year period) could dramatically reduce the high rates of unintended, unwanted pregnancy among adolescents and young women. Despite its initial promise, however, current use of hormonal implants is low (Hatcher, 1998).

Kuiper et al. (1997) conducted focus groups aimed at exploring reasons for the reduction in the popularity of implants among teenagers. Concerns about peer and potential partner perceptions of them were associated with disinclinations to rely on implants for contraceptive protection. Most young women worried that their friends would see the implants in their arms and think them "gross," "stupid," or "crazy" to allow doctors to cut them up. Also, almost all implant users, and some nonusers, in their sample worried about or experienced sexual harassment as a result of wearing the implants. One implant user reported that "[One guy said to me,] 'Hey hey, baby, you have Norplant. Wanna fuck?'" (p. 169). A possible solution to concerns about the use of Nor-plant's being apparent to casual observers (at least in warm weather) would be to find another bodily site for placement of the implants that is less readily seen.

Over the years, judges have occasionally ordered women who have been convicted of abusing or killing their offspring to use contraceptive implants. For example, a California woman pregnant with her fifth child was convicted of child abuse after beating two of her children severely enough to leave permanent scars was ordered by the judge to have Norplant implanted after her release from prison. Opponents of such decisions have argued that even women guilty of child abuse should not be prevented from making their own reproductive decisions.

▶ **Issues to Consider:** Do you believe that women who have been convicted of child abuse should be forced to have compulsory contraceptives such as Norplant implanted? What about the mandatory sterilization of men or women who have been convicted of abusing their children?

Depo-Provera (medroxyprogesterone acetate) is a long-acting progestin that was approved in 1992 for contraceptive use in the United States. A single injection is given every three months for contraceptive purposes. The first-year probability of failure is less than 1 percent (Hatcher, 1998).

Depo-Provera—A contraceptive with a long-acting progestin that is injected every three months.

INTRAUTERINE DEVICES

The **intrauterine device (IUD)** is a small plastic or metal device that is placed inside the woman's uterus. The IUD must be inserted by a trained health service provider. An inserter is pushed gently through the cervical opening. Then the compressed IUD is released from the inserter into the uterus, where the IUD regains its original shape. A string attached to the IUD hangs from the cervix into the vagina, so that a woman can check it periodically to see that the IUD is still in place. The string also facilitates the removal of the IUD by a physician.

The IUD appears to work by preventing sperm from fertilizing ova (Stewart, 1998). The low failure rates, ranging from 0.1 to 2.0 per 100 women annually, underscore its effectiveness. The mildly irritating effect of the IUD on the uterine wall may stimulate the release of extra amounts of prostaglandins that may in turn trigger spotting or a menstrual period. Thus, the IUD may prevent normal development of the uterine lining, so that when a fertilized egg makes its way down the Fallopian tube, it cannot implant in the uterus.

IUD insertion involves varying amounts of discomfort, depending on a woman's history and the diameter of the particular IUD inserter. A rare but potentially fatal risk associated with IUD insertion is perforation or puncturing of the uterus. This risk is lessened when experienced professionals perform the insertion. Other adverse side effects of the IUD include cramping, an increase in the amount and duration of menstrual flow, pelvic inflammatory disease (PID; see Chapter 16), expulsion of the IUD, and ectopic pregnancy (see Chapter 9). These side effects are most pronounced during the initial months of use.

The history of the use of the IUD for birth control provides a classic example of why risks and benefits should be weighed carefully by those making contraceptive choices. In 1977, 15 percent of all married women using reversible methods of contraception were wearing IUDs. But by 1986 all but one IUD (Progestasert) had been withdrawn from the market by their manufacturers. Because the string hanging out of the cervix into the vagina makes it easier for bacteria to travel into the uterus, IUD users were as

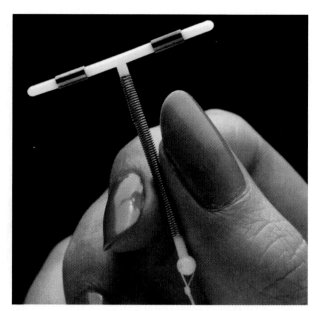

The copper T IUD is a plastic T-shaped device with copper collars on the arms, copper wound around the stem, and Progestasert, which contains progestin. Highly effective, it has an annual failure rate of less than 1 per 100 women.

much as six times more likely to develop PID (and subsequent infertility because of scar tissue in the fallopian tubes) than were women who used other contraceptive methods (Daling, Weiss, Voight, McKnight, & Moore, 1992). The longer these early IUDs were used, the greater was the risk of PID and infertility.

The two contemporary IUDs—the Copper T and Progestasert—are highly effective. If users carefully follow instructions regarding safer-sex practices, check to make sure that the IUD is in place, and have annual pelvic exams, these two IUDs are relatively free of health risks, but are still used by only 1 percent of sexually active women (Forrest & Fordyce, 1993).

RELATIVELY INEFFECTIVE METHODS

Each of the contraceptive methods just described is more effective than is withdrawal, postcoital douching, or breast-feeding to prevent ovulation. Still, because millions of people regularly use these three methods, we discuss them briefly.

Withdrawal. Referred to as *coitus interruptus* in early sex manuals, **withdrawal** involves removing the penis from the vagina prior to ejaculation. Although the failure rate of this method is as high as 19 per-

---

intrauterine device (IUD)—A small plastic device that is inserted into the uterus for contraception.

cent, it is still lower than the 85 percent pregnancy rate of sexually active women who use no method.

There are two problems with withdrawal. One arises from the vast difference between intentions and actions. As described in the section on condom use, two people engaged in lovemaking may intend to disengage their genitals before the man ejaculates, but they may not always achieve this goal, for a variety of psychological and physical reasons. The other problem centers on the secretions of the Cowper's glands. When a man becomes aroused, these glands release clear, slippery droplets at the opening of the penis, and sometimes this fluid contains sperm.

Postcoital Douching. More than one-third of U.S. women douche regularly, with 18 percent doing so at least once a week (Aral, Mosher, & Cates, 1992). About 3 percent of sexually active women may engage in the practice because of the popular (but inaccurate) belief that **postcoital douching** has contraceptive benefits (Forrest & Fordyce, 1993).

Some women douche with carbonated beverages following coitus in a vain attempt to prevent conception. Such acidic solutions do kill sperm, but they must be in contact with the sperm to do so. Therein lies the problem. Sperm start moving through the cervix and into the uterus in a matter of seconds after ejaculation. Therefore, even if a woman has an acidic douche ready to insert into her vagina right after ejaculation, many sperm may have already escaped to the safety of her uterus. Furthermore, the carbonation in these drinks may even help propel the sperm toward the cervical entrance.

Breast-Feeding. Physicians and laypeople have claimed for years that breast-feeding acts as a natural contraceptive. This claim is based on several observations. First, breast-feeding does appear to delay the return of menstruation following childbirth in some women, although women who rely on the return of menstruation to begin contraceptive use should know that ovulation can occur prior to the resumption of menstruation. Second, cross-cultural comparisons indicate that breast-feeding women take longer to conceive another child than do women who do not breast-feed (Ellison, 1991). It appears that prolactin, a hormone secreted in response to suckling the nipples, is closely related to the mechanism that suppresses ovulation. However, the frequency of nursing appears to be crucial in delaying ovulation. For example, !Kung women, hunter-gatherers in southern Africa, nurse about every 15 minutes during the day and much of the night. In contrast, U.S. women usually nurse about every three or four hours for about 20 minutes each time, and they attempt to eliminate night feedings as soon as possible. In addition, in the absence of a sufficient level of calories (a circumstance more likely in nomadic hunter-gatherer groups than among contemporary North American women), ovulation and menstruation are disrupted. The reasons for differences in the return of ovulation and menstruation in various populations are still being investigated. At present, the available data suggest that breast-feeding in and of itself is not a reliable form of contraception.

Moving from these ineffective contraceptive methods, we turn to an extremely effective and permanent form of birth control.

Sterilization

Sterilization—the use of surgical procedures to block an egg's passage through the Fallopian tube or the sperm's passage through the vas deferens—has been

rapidly gaining in worldwide popularity. Almost 5 million Americans and 120 million couples throughout the world rely on sterilization for birth control (Stewart & Carignan, 1998). With more than a million sterilizations performed annually, it has become

---

withdrawal—Removal of the penis from the vagina before ejaculation.
postcoital douching—(DOO-shing) Insertion of chemical solutions into the vagina after coitus in the usually vain attempt to kill sperm.

sterilization—A surgical procedure performed to make a person incapable of reproduction.

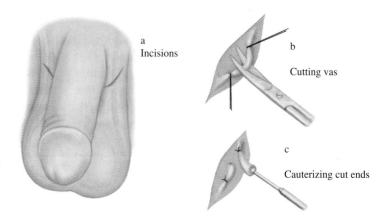

Figure 10.6   Vasectomy
A vasectomy prevents sperm from traveling out of the scrotum. Drawing *a* shows the site of the incisions in the scrotum. Drawing *b* illustrates the cutting of the vas deferens with surgical scissors, and *c* shows the blocking of the cut ends of the vas deferens to reduce the chances of their growing back together.

the most widely used form of birth control for married couples over 30 years of age.

▶ **Issues to Consider:** At what point in your life, if ever, would you (or did you) consider sterilization to avoid having a child or more children?

VASECTOMY

For males, sterilization means a **vasectomy,** a surgical procedure in which the vas deferentia are cut. First performed more than 300 years ago, the operation has been carried out routinely since 1925. About half a million vasectomies are performed annually in the United States (Stewart & Carignan, 1998). Because the effects of a vasectomy can be permanent, it is important for a man or a couple to consider the decision carefully.

The operation, usually performed on an outpatient basis, requires only a local anesthetic. An incision less than 1 inch long is made either in the middle or on each side of the scrotum. The vas deferens is cut and blocked, and then the incision is sewn up (see Figure 10.6). Because a vasectomy prevents sperm from traveling beyond the point of incision into the upper part of the vas deferens to join the semen, it is an extremely effective birth control technique, with a failure rate of less than 1 percent. In rare cases, however, the cut ends of the vas deferens manage to reconnect themselves, and additional surgery is required. Vasectomy appears unlikely to raise men's chances of developing either prostate or testicular cancer (Rosenberg et al., 1994).

After surgery, a contraceptive should be used until two successive semen analyses have confirmed the

absence of sperm. It takes about four to six weeks and 6 to 36 ejaculations to clear remaining sperm from the vas deferens (Stewart & Carignan, 1998).
Reality or Myth ?

A "no-scalpel" procedure that was developed in China in 1974 is now being used in some places in North America as well as in other countries around the world (Stewart & Carignan, 1998). After an anesthetic is administered, a dissecting forceps punctures and stretches a small opening in the skin and vas sheath. The vas is lifted out and clamped or tied off. No sutures are needed to close the small wound. The no-scalpel method appears to have lower complication rates than the scalpel procedure.

Vasectomized men who change their minds after having a vasectomy may have the procedure reversed through a microsurgery procedure called **vasovasectomy.** Across studies, rates of conception following vasovasectomy have ranged from 16 percent to 79 percent (Stewart & Carignan, 1998). Because vasovasectomy is not 100 percent successful, men should not have vasectomies unless they are quite sure that they do not want to father more children. If a man does change his mind after being sterilized, however, he should undergo vasovasectomy as soon as possible.

The major benefit of a vasectomy is that after all sperm have been eliminated from the ejaculate, impregnation is impossible. Vasectomy does not alter hormone production or the ability to ejaculate because 95 percent of the volume of semen is made up of fluids produced by glands located above the point

vasectomy—Male sterilization involving cutting or tying of the vas deferentia.
vasovasectomy—Surgical reversal of vasectomy.

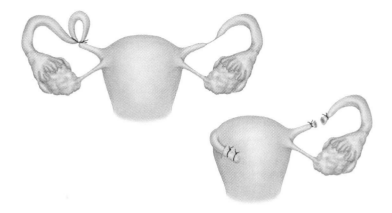

Figure 10.7 Tubal Ligation
In the Pomeroy technique (top drawing), the Fallopian tube is grasped by its midsection and tied to make a loop, which is then cut. The severed ends scar over, leaving a gap of half an inch or more between the ends of the tube. The lower drawing shows the Irving technique, in which the Fallopian tubes are cut rather than tied.

of incision. Moreover, because vasectomy does not influence the production of testosterone or other hormones, no physiologically based effects on sexual desire or responsiveness would be expected. A wide range of psychological responses may occur, however. Most vasectomized men report either no effect on their sexuality or an improvement in their desire and responsiveness.

TUBAL LIGATION

Women are sterilized by having their Fallopian tubes cut or tied (ligated), effectively blocking the route normally taken by a mature egg to its potential meeting with sperm. **Tubal ligation** is considerably more complicated and expensive than vasectomy, generally requiring hospitalization, more extensive anesthesia, and a longer recovery period (see Figure 10.7). Nevertheless, more than half a million U.S. women undergo the procedure annually (Stewart & Carignan, 1998).

There are a number of variations in female sterilization procedures. One that has been gaining in popularity is known as the Band-aid operation. This method is performed with a **laparoscope,** a device that is inserted into the abdomen through an incision below the navel after the woman receives anesthesia. Gas is then pumped into the abdominal cavity, which inflates her abdomen, allowing access to the Fallopian tubes. A portion of the tube is grasped and is usually clipped or banded. After the procedure is repeated on the other tube, the gas is released from the abdomen. Finally, the incision is closed with an absorbable suture and covered with a Band-aid. Complications from female sterilization procedures

include possible bowel perforation, infection, hemorrhage, and adverse effects from anesthesia.

Unlike a vasectomized man, a sterilized woman may engage in coitus without any additional contraception as soon as she wants to, although she may have a day or two of slight discomfort following the procedure. Hormone production and the menstrual cycle are unaffected by tubal ligation, and the operation appears to have no physiological effect on sexual desire or response. Psychological effects range from none to positive, with the latter presumably resulting from the elimination of fears of pregnancy. This confidence is well founded; the failure rate of tubal ligation is less than 1 percent. However, there is a very small chance, less than 1 percent, that some women will develop an ectopic pregnancy after sterilization (Stewart & Carignan, 1998).

Just a decade ago, fewer than 25 percent of women who obtained reversals of tubal ligation were subsequently able to conceive. Recent advances in sophisticated microsurgery techniques have led to much higher rates of success in restoring fertility. The overall rate of live births following reversals ranges from 43 percent to 88 percent (Stewart and Carignan, 1998). Like men, however, women should not seek sterilization unless they are quite sure that they do not want (more) children. Women face higher risks than do men when they undergo sterilization and subsequent reversal surgery.

tubal ligation—Cutting or tying the Fallopian tubes to block sperm from reaching the egg.
laparoscope—(LAP-ar-oh-SCOPE) A long, hollow instrument inserted into the abdominal cavity through a small incision directly below the navel.

Contraceptive Techniques of the Future

It should be abundantly clear by now that most of the currently available, effective methods of contraception are designed to be used by women. Moreover, each poses various problems, although any one of them is preferable to unprotected intercourse followed by an unintended pregnancy. We turn now to current research on methods to control male fertility.

RESEARCH ON FUTURE METHODS OF CONTRACEPTION FOR MEN

It is unlikely that an effective male method of contraception aside from the condom and sterilization will be available in the next few years (Gabelnick, 1998). Even after effective methods are found, a number of years will be needed to study the possible long-term side effects before FDA approval can be obtained.

One promising approach for men involves developing vaccines against sperm using either follicle-stimulating hormone (FSH) or luteinizing hormone-releasing factor (LHRH). The FSH vaccine has eliminated sperm while maintaining normal testosterone levels in monkeys (Gabelnick, 1998). Alternatively, a vaccine using LHRH shuts down both testosterone and sperm production; to maintain sex drive, men would have to supplement this vaccine with testosterone.

There are a number of hormones currently under study. One testosterone derivative suppresses sperm production enough to provide reliable protection (Gabelnick, 1998). However, because weekly injections of testosterone are required, many men would find this an impractical solution. In addition, there is a relatively lengthy period from the beginning of testosterone injections and effective sperm suppression (roughly, four months), so couples would need to use another method of contraception until sperm suppression is achieved (World Health Organization Task Force, 1996; Wu, Farley, Peregoudov, & Waites, 1996). Hormone delivery systems that can deliver testosterone for two to three months and testosterone-derivative implants that are effective for up to a year are being studied.

RESEARCH ON FUTURE METHODS OF CONTRACEPTION FOR WOMEN

Most of the research on new contraceptives for women focuses on extensions or modifications of methods that are already available.

The vaginal ring, developed by the World Health Organization, is a plastic ring that releases progestin or both progestin and estrogen (Gabelnick, 1998). It is worn around the cervix for three weeks each month and then is removed during menstruation. The vaginal ring has only a 3 percent failure rate.

Cyclo-Provera is a monthly-injectable contraceptive containing both estrogen and progestin. It has been tested in clinical studies by the World Health Organization in more than 10,000 women. It is currently being evaluated at 42 different sites in the United States for safety and ease of use. Cyclo-Provera differs from Depo-Provera in that it is injected once a month instead of once every three months. Women generally have normal periods each month and, if conception is sought, Cyclo can be discontinued more quickly than is the case with Depo, which tends to remain in the woman's body for a longer period of time (Planned Parenthood Today, 1997). This shorter duration might be particularly desirable for the many women who experience a miscarriage and are advised to avoid trying to conceive for several months following the miscarriage, but who want to conceive as soon as possible following recovery from the miscarriage.

▶ **Issues to Consider:** If Cyclo-Provera is approved by the FDA, and you (or your partner) wanted to use an injectable contraceptive, would you be more likely to choose Cyclo- or Depo-Provera? Why?

Focus on an antipregnancy vaccine for women has involved the hormone human chorionic gonadotropin (HCG). However, because the vaccine also can be used to induce abortion, it is unlikely that American companies will pursue this form of birth control within the near future.

Although these birth control methods appear promising, the speed with which they become generally available will be influenced by the amount of money that is devoted to research. An increase in annual expenditures for research and development of new, safe, and effective methods of birth control would accelerate progress, although as we saw in the Highlight at the beginning of this chapter, such an increase is unlikely.

Sometimes, even when a couple uses contraception regularly, an unwanted pregnancy may occur. This is even more likely if a couple uses contraception inconsistently or not at all. We turn to methods of revolving unwanted pregnancies in Chapter 11.

SUMMARY OF MAJOR POINTS

1. The development and acceptance of contraceptives. Although contraceptive techniques have been used throughout history, their use was illegal in the United States well into the twentieth century. Legal barriers were slowly eliminated, and, in the 1960s, the pill and the intrauterine device joined the less reliable barrier methods as popular contraceptives. In subsequent years, these methods were followed by the availability of injected and implanted contraceptives. For various reasons, the focus has been on the development of female, rather than male, contraceptives.

2. The evaluation of contraceptive methods. The prospective contraceptive user should consider the effectiveness and potential side effects of each method, as well as his or her own habits and preferences. Contraceptive effectiveness and risks depend on the lifestyle and medical history of the user, as well as on the likelihood that a method is employed during every act of coitus. For most women, the greatest risk of illness and death is associated with engaging in unprotected intercourse. In the absence of birth control, about 85 of every 100 sexually active women become pregnant within a year.

3. Barriers to contraceptive use. Reluctance to obtain and use contraception is associated with certain psychological and social factors. Those who feel guilty about sexuality and those who are less emotionally committed to their partners are less likely to use contraception. Contraceptive knowledge is related to the likelihood of people's use of birth control, but ready access to contraceptives and emotional factors appear to be more important than information in determining contraceptive use.

4. Temporary methods of contraception. The safest methods of contraception are the barrier methods: the diaphragm and spermicide, the cervical cap and spermicide, the condom, and spermicidal foams and suppositories. These methods are less effective, however, in preventing conception than are the pill, the IUD, and hormonal implants and injections. The effectiveness of the rhythm method may be increased by use of several means of determining the date of ovulation. Although withdrawal, postcoital douching, and breast-feeding may reduce the risk of conception somewhat, these three attempts at birth control are not nearly as effective as the barrier or hormonal methods.

5. Permanent methods of contraception. Sterilization has become the most popular method of contraception among those above age 30. Vasectomy, the severing of the two vasa deferentia, is highly effective and entails little risk of side effects for most men. Female sterilization methods are somewhat more complicated than is the vasectomy, because an abdominal incision must be made to expose the Fallopian tubes. These methods are highly effective and do not interfere with sexual response. Although physicians report increasing success with sterilization reversals, people should not undergo sterilization unless they are certain that they do not wish to conceive.

Resolving Unwanted Pregnancy

Reality or Myth ?

1. Some countries facing major overpopulation force women to undergo abortions after they have had one child.

2. The majority of Americans support legal abortion under at least some circumstances.

3. To reduce medical risks for the woman with an unwanted pregnancy who chooses to abort, it is important that she obtain an abortion as soon as possible after discovering the pregnancy.

4. Most women experience intense sadness, guilt, and regret for a number of years following an abortion.

*T*he four women sat waiting for their turn with the lab technician. Each offered resolutions and bargains.

TRACY: If I'm not pregnant, I'll never forget to take the pill again.

MICHELLE: I'll never, ever go to another party without first putting in my diaphragm.

THERESA: How on earth are we going to feed another one? So much for his promises that he'll pull out in time. I'm never going to let him anywhere near me again unless he already has his rubber on!

SONI: If only I'm not pregnant, I'll study twice as hard and stay away from men. I faithfully took the pill every day!

After discovering an unwanted pregnancy, a woman has three options: obtaining an abortion; continuing the pregnancy, keeping the baby, and rearing the child with or without the help of its father; or placing the baby for adoption. We examine the available abortion methods, the legal status of this option, and the short-term and long-term effects of choosing this alternative. If an unmarried woman decides against abortion, she is far more likely now than in the past to raise the baby rather than to place him or her for adoption. Recent re-search suggests, however, that without considerable social and economic support, the mother and her off-spring face numerous difficulties.

Unintended Pregnancy

Defining the phrase *unintended and unwanted pregnancy* is tricky because the individual words do not necessarily fit together. A conception may be unintended, but confirmation of the pregnancy may lead a couple to celebrate. Or a pregnancy may be carefully planned but later not wanted for a variety of reasons: the end of a marriage or other relationship, a pregnant woman's exposure to **teratogenic** drugs or disease early in pregnancy, or financial setbacks such as loss of a job. Finally, of course, conception may be both unplanned and unwanted.

About half of all pregnancies in the United States are unintended (Henshaw, 1998; Mosher & Bachrach, 1996). The rate of unintended pregnancies is higher for teenagers (73 percent) than for women aged 20 to 24 (46 percent) and for women aged 25 to 29 (32 percent).

The number of **abortions** performed annually in the United States—about 1.2 million—provides a minimum estimate of the number of unintended pregnancies (Henshaw, 1998). In addition, well over 1 million babies are born annually to women who did not intend to conceive. Thus we might conclude that there are more than 2 million unwanted conceptions per year. Two million is a conservative estimate, however, because this figure does not include the number of unwanted pregnancies that end in spontaneous abortion or stillbirth. We discuss the fate of these unintended pregnancies that result in birth later in the chapter. First, we consider the most

---

teratogenic (tare-AH-toe-JEN-ik)—causing birth defects.

abortion—spontaneous or medical terminations of pregnancies before fetuses can survive outside the uterus.

frequently used method of resolving unwanted pregnancy: abortion.

Unintended pregnancy is linked to income and ethnic background. The closer to poverty the woman is, the higher the unintended pregnancy rate is. The pregnancy rate for Black women is almost three times that of White women, with the pregnancy rates of women of other ethnic backgrounds falling between these two groups (Henshaw, 1998). However, because of the relationship of minority status and poverty, it is not clear whether it is poverty or ethnic background that is more predictive of unintended pregnancy.

Abortion: A Human Dilemma

Deliberate abortion is one of the oldest medical procedures known to humans, practiced throughout history since well before the time of Christ and across Western and non-Western cultures (Bullough, 1994). Attitudes toward the practice have varied greatly. Even the Catholic church, which currently condemns abortion, has taken an antiabortion stance for only the past 150 years.

During the past decade, slightly under one-third of all pregnant American women obtained abortions each year (Henshaw & Kost, 1996). The majority were performed on White, unmarried women under age 25 in the first eight weeks of pregnancy.

THE MORAL DEBATE OVER ABORTION

One dictionary defines *murder* as "the unlawful killing of one human being by another, esp. with premeditated malice." Lobbyists for a congressional or constitutional ban on abortion make their case on the grounds that abortion is murder. In contrast, supporters of legalized abortion argue that the practice is not murder because the fetus is not a human being with the legal rights of a person. Actually, both arguments seem faulty to us. If abortion is legal, then pregnancy termination is not unlawful, and there is no evidence to suggest that women seeking abortion feel "premeditated malice" toward the fetus. Biologically, the fetus is clearly alive in the uterus (as were the sperm and egg that contributed to conception), so there is life. However, the fetus is not viable—capable of survival outside the uterus—until late in the second trimester, and more than 90 percent of abortions are performed during the first trimester.

viable—able to live and continue normal development outside the uterus.

Participants in the ongoing abortion debate often talk as if there were only two possible positions: proabortion and antiabortion. Yet these two stances represent only the extremes. At one end of the continuum are those who believe that after conception has occurred, a woman should be compelled to give birth, regardless of the woman's life circumstances or the viability of the fetus. A doctor who used to perform abortions now believes that a fetus is entitled to protection from the time of implantation in the uterus (Nathanson, 1979). Garrett Hardin (1974) referred to proponents of this position as advocates of "mandatory motherhood."

At the other extreme are the small minority who favor compulsory abortion. Those who advocate compulsory abortion do so with two different goals in mind: to prevent overpopulation and to block reproduction by developmentally disabled or emotionally disturbed individuals or those with genetically transmitted diseases. In their program to control the growth of their population, the Chinese do not physically compel abortion, but they punish couples who already have one child and refuse to abort subsequent pregnancies. Punishment may include pay cuts or job demotions. *Reality or Myth*

▶ **Issues to Consider:** Do you think that it is ethical for countries faced with massive overpopulation to punish people for having more than one or two children? What alternative methods could you suggest for governments trying to control population growth?

Between these two extreme positions—compulsory motherhood versus pressure to abort—there is a third position: that decisions regarding conception, pregnancy, and birth are best left to the woman or couple involved. Supporters of this position generally

Attitudes toward abortion vary widely among North Americans—and are sometimes fervently demonstrated.

express great concern for babies' well-being, arguing that it is wrong to bring unwanted infants into the world, particularly if they are likely to be badly deformed because of prenatal exposure to disease or drugs. In his testimony several decades ago at a Senate Judiciary Subcommittee hearing on a "human life" bill that would ban abortion, Dr. George Ryan, then the president of the American College of Obstetricians and Gynecologists, spoke against the bill:

> *The same people who want to "save" babies are unwilling to give them food stamps. They don't care if the babies live in roach-infested houses. They don't care if they get adequate schooling. It's a strange contradiction that the people who say they want to save lives have so little compassion for people after they are born.*

Scientists can do little to resolve differences in the moral values of those who disagree over abortion rights. Nathanson (1979) suggested one solution: transplanting an embryo from the uterus of a woman who does not wish to maintain pregnancy to the uterus of a woman desiring a baby. But embryo-transfer procedures are unlikely to eliminate the demand for abortion. For example, in cases in which a pregnant woman's desire for abortion is based on fears that she is carrying a defective embryo, another woman would be unlikely to want the embryo.

Recent research reveals little support for an absolute ban on abortion. Even those generally opposed to it support the procedure under some circumstances, such as if the mother's health is endangered or if the pregnancy resulted from rape or incest. A Gallup poll conducted in 1998 revealed that 23 percent of respondents supported no restrictions on abortion, 58 percent supported abortion in some circumstances, and 17 percent wanted abortion banned regardless of the circumstances (*Gallup Poll Monthly,* 1998). *Reality or Myth* 2

Compared to previous polls, this one shows a shift away from favoring unrestricted access to abortion. From 1975 through 1995, Gallup polls showed a steady increase in support for legal abortion under

"It is better to have an only child," says the poster outside this Chinese family-planning clinic.

any circumstances, reaching a peak of 31 percent in 1995. Since then, the number has declined to roughly a quarter of those polled. However, the wording and order in which items assessing attitudes toward legal availability of abortion affect people's responses to abortion. For example, when a first-trimester pregnancy is specified, 55 percent of respondents agree that a woman should be able to obtain an abortion for any reason, compared with 44 percent when no pregnancy duration is specified (Bumpass, 1997).

Attitudes toward abortion vary according to socioeconomic status, race, religious affiliation, and age. Catholics and Mormons hold more negative attitudes toward abortions than do Protestants, agnostics, and atheists (Bowers & Weaver, 1979; Granberg, 1985; Marsiglio & Shehan, 1993). The degree of guilt that a person feels about sex—a factor related to religion—also is associated with abortion attitudes. People with high levels of sex guilt are less accepting of abortions for women who desire them than are those with lower levels of sex guilt (Allgeier et al., 1981, 1982). Blacks feel more negatively about legalized abortion than do Whites (Hall

& Ferree, 1986), although race was not a strong predictor among a nationally representative sample of males aged 15 to 19 when other background factors were controlled (Marsiglio & Shehan, 1993). Not surprisingly, unmarried women between menarche and menopause (that is, capable of reproduction) are more supportive of legalized abortion than are other-aged females or males (Betzig & Lombardo, 1992). However, research reviewed and conducted by Marsiglio and Shehan (1993) indicated that North American men under age 30 were less supportive of abortion than were men aged 30 and older. Finally, college-educated Americans, as well as those with higher incomes, are more supportive of legalized abortion than are their less educated and less affluent counterparts (Gallup, 1998).

Some people may consider a woman's sexual behavior in making judgments about the appropriateness of abortion. When asked to evaluate a series of fictitious case histories, college students approved of abortion for women who had become pregnant despite the conscientious use of a reliable contraceptive. (See "Research Spotlight: Abortion Case Histories.")

RESEARCH SPOTLIGHT   **Abortion Case Histories**

These are the fictitious descriptions used in the Allgeier et al. studies (1979, 1982) of unmarried women applying for abortion. Volunteers were asked to indicate the extent to which they favored or were against abortion in each case. How do you feel?

Gloria C. has been dating a variety of men over the past several years. She has had sexual intercourse with some of them and has always used a diaphragm for contraception. She has become pregnant despite her use of the diaphragm and does not know which man is the father.

Jill K. recently discovered that she is pregnant. She has been going with Steve for almost a year. Over the past three months, they have engaged in sexual intercourse about five times. In each instance, they had not planned it, but got carried away and ended up having intercourse without any contraception.

Sue T. has had several love affairs in the past two years. She was convinced that premarital pregnancy was something that would never happen to her, so she never worried about birth control. She discovered that she was pregnant several weeks ago but is not sure who the father is.

Betty P. has dated a number of different men over the past year and a half. She has had sexual intercourse with some of them, but only during her "safe" time because she wanted to avoid any possibility of getting pregnant. Despite her precautions, she has become pregnant.

Ruth D. got a prescription for the pill when she and Greg, her boyfriend for the past year and a half, began having intercourse. Ruth forgot to take her pills with her on a camping trip they went on over a long weekend, and she's now pregnant.

Debra N. has no regular boyfriend, but has several friends with whom she occasionally has intercourse. She usually tries to keep track of her menstrual cycle and to avoid having intercourse except when she's safe, but she forgot to write down the date of her last period and recently had intercourse even though she wasn't sure whether she was fertile.

Kathy B. usually uses a diaphragm when having sexual intercourse. She went to a party thrown by her cousin, who wanted to fix her up with a friend of hers from work. She didn't have her diaphragm with her, and now she is six weeks pregnant.

These students were also more supportive of abortion for women who had become pregnant with a steady partner rather than during a casual sexual encounter (Allgeier, Allgeier, & Rywick, 1979). Participants in the study made a number of revealing comments when describing their reasoning. For instance, one person who approved of abortion for "Ruth" said that if Ruth and her boyfriend "are really close, I could see granting it. She did take precautionary measures." This same person denied "Sue's" abortion request, saying, "If Sue had sexual intercourse with other men, I don't think she should be granted an abortion, especially since she doesn't know who the father is."

Such reasoning ignores both the argument for fetal rights advanced by the antiabortion faction and the argument for women's rights offered by the prochoice faction. The reasoning observed in this research has the effect of "rewarding" conscientious women by granting them abortions and "punishing" less responsible women by conferring motherhood

on them, or at least full-term pregnancy and birth. Presumably, however, less responsible women are less desirable candidates for motherhood, at least at this point in their lives, than are more responsible women.

Ten years after our series of studies with college students on abortion policies, we were intrigued to learn that a state legislative coordinator for the National Right to Life Committee said that his organization was considering proposals to ban abortions in those cases in which a couple failed to use contraception. Such a law would presumably be difficult to enforce in the absence of witnesses observing the couple at the time of conception!

REASONS FOR ABORTION

Women usually cite several concurrent reasons for seeking abortion; only 7 percent of women in a study of almost two thousand abortion patients reported that one factor alone influenced their decision

(Russo, Horn, & Schwartz, 1992). More than 75 percent of unmarried minors in the Russo et al. study reported that they were not mature enough to raise a child, with only 5 percent reporting that they sought to avoid single parenthood as a reason for abortion. External reasons to these adolescents were also important: a desire to complete their education, the inability to afford a child, concern about social disapproval, and their partner's reaction to the pregnancy were the most common factors influencing their decision to have an abortion.

Among the adults, more than one-third indicated they could not afford to have a baby now. Nonmothers who were unmarried were more likely to say that they were not mature enough to have a child than were unmarried mothers, married mothers, or married nonmothers. Married mothers were more likely to give health-related reasons for abortion. Married nonmothers were more concerned with effects of prescription medications, worries having to do with the fetus, and diagnosed fetal defects as reasons. Furthermore, in another study of women who decided to abort, more than half (52 percent) of married women aged 15 to 17 and most of those aged 18 to 19 (60 percent) already had children (Powell-Griner, 1987). The results from these studies indicate that a woman's reasons for seeking an abortion are multiple and vary with life circumstances.

Abortion: An Individual and Family Dilemma.

In 1997, in a remarkable revelation for a member of Congress, Representative Elizabeth Furse, a Democrat from Oregon, said that in 1961, when abortion was still illegal, she underwent a hysterectomy rather than give birth to a baby who was likely to be blind, deaf, and severely brain damaged. At the time, Furse was only 25 years old. She already had two children when she and her husband conceived a third child, and they were thrilled. But shortly before the end of the first trimester, Furse contracted measles. Testing revealed that the fetus had been badly damaged. Her physician sympathized, but said he could not help because abortion was illegal. Furse ruled out illegal abortion because her husband was a physician and had seen the damage created by illegal abortions. Instead, she was advised to have a hysterectomy, which was legal, but would leave her unable to have any

U.S. Rep. Elizabeth Furse (D–Ore.) revealed that she had a hysterectomy to avoid delivering a severely impaired child.

more children, although she and her husband wanted to have a larger family (Baum, 1997).

The Abortion-as-Birth-Control Hypothesis.

In 1977 President Jimmy Carter justified his opposition to the federal funding of abortions for poor women on the grounds that such funding might encourage women to use abortion rather than contraception for birth control. How much support exists for this hypothesis? To begin with, there is no 100 percent effective temporary method of contraception. Although the risk of conception can be dramatically reduced by consistent use of reliable contraceptives, it cannot be totally eliminated by any of the available contraceptive methods. Thus, the fact that women get pregnant is not, in and of itself, evidence that they are relying on abortion rather than contraception for birth control. In fact, more than half of all abortion patients in 1995 reported that they had been using contraception during the month in which they conceived (Henshaw, 1998).

Second, as we have seen, many adolescents do not use contraceptives. Among adolescents with unintended pregnancies, however, those choosing abortion are more likely to have used contraception than those opting to maintain the pregnancy (Zelnik & Kantner, 1978).

Third, most investigators of repeat abortion find little evidence that repeaters fail to use contraception because legal abortion is available (Abrams, 1985). Scientists have compared the contraceptive behavior of women after abortion with that of women after giving birth (Shulman & Merritt, 1976) and women with no prior abortions (Kurstin & Oskamp, 1979). These studies revealed no differences among the groups in contraceptive behavior; in fact, contraceptive usage rates tend to improve following abortion (Miller, 1992).

Despite these data, some would argue that President Carter's point is supported by the abortion recidivism rate (that is, the incidence of a woman having two or more abortions), which is increasing. In 1974 approximately 15 percent of all legal abortions were repeat abortions. The percentage of repeat abortions climbed to 23 percent in 1976 and reached 42 percent in 1987 (Henshaw, 1987; Millar, Wadhera and Henshaw, 1997). But this rise did not necessarily result from the abandonment of contraceptives. Indeed, Tietze (1978) maintained that increasing numbers of repeat abortions would result from the greater number of women having a *first* abortion. Because undergoing one abortion has no impact on subsequent contraceptive failure, sexually active women risk having a second unwanted pregnancy as time goes on. In addition, having resolved the first unintended pregnancy through abortion, these women may be more likely than women with no prior abortions to rely again on medical termination of pregnancy when contraception fails.

In the light of these and other factors, Tietze concluded that a high repeat-abortion rate is "to be expected without any decline—indeed, even in the face of improvement—in contraceptive practice"

(p. 288). Data from nations with a history of legal abortion longer than that of the United States suggest that the percentage of repeat abortions increases for a few years following legalization and then levels off (Millar, Wadhera & Henshaw, 1997).

ABORTION AND THE LAW

An estimated 36 million to 53 million abortions are performed every year throughout the world. Between 26 million and 31 million of these are legal (Henshaw & Van Vort, 1992). Three-quarters of humans live in countries where abortion is legal at least when the woman's health is at risk, and more than half of these people reside in areas where abortion can be obtained on request for any reason.

The movement toward liberalized abortion laws in many nations has been rooted in three humanitarian principles: (1) the recognition that illegal abortion poses a threat to public health, (2) the belief that social justice requires equal access to abortion for rich and poor alike, and (3) support for a woman's right to control her own body.

In evaluating the issue of legalized abortion, it is important to take the alternatives into account. If legal abortion is unavailable, many women will die from self-administered abortions, abortions performed by others who lack formal training in abortion procedures, or the complications of unwanted pregnancy and childbirth. In 1965, eight years before the decision in *Roe* v. *Wade* (see "Highlight: The Legal Status of Abortion in the United States" on page 254), an estimated 20 percent of all deaths related to pregnancy and childbirth stemmed from illegal abortions (Adler et al., 1992). Further, the legalization of abortion has brought about a decrease in the mortality rate of women from pregnancy and childbirth, partly because some women who may be at risk of death from full-term pregnancies are having first-trimester abortions. Maternal mortality is down to an average level of 6 deaths per 100,000 legal abortions worldwide and 1 death per 100,000 procedures in the United States (Henshaw & Van Vort, 1992; Koonin, et al., 1997).

For the past few decades, efforts to make abortion readily available figured prominently in the movement to protect women's rights. However, there has been a

The Legal Status of Abortion in the United States

In the past three decades, laws have proliferated, liberalizing and then restricting the conditions under which pregnancy could be terminated. In 1970 the New York State legislature ruled that physicians could provide an abortion for any woman requesting it who was less than 24 weeks pregnant. In January 1973 the U.S. Supreme Court ruling in *Roe* v. *Wade* prohibited states from interfering in decisions reached by a woman and her doctor during the first three months of pregnancy. During the second trimester, states could regulate abortion in ways that are reasonably related to maternal health, by requiring, for example, that an abortion be performed in a hospital. The states' right to regulate abortion to protect the fetus during the last trimester remained intact, except if abortion was necessary to protect a woman's life or health.

The U.S. Supreme Court reaffirmed support of *Roe* v. *Wade* in 1983 and again in 1992, but the general trend in the U.S. courts and legislatures has been to restrict access to abortion. For example, the access of a minor to abortion has been increasingly regulated, through the requirement that a parent be notified and/or give consent for a minor to have an abortion. Public funds such as Medicaid have been drastically restricted for women seeking abortion. Federal and state laws remain confusing and, at times, contradictory.

With violence and murder of abortion clinic personnel escalating, President Clinton signed the Freedom of Access to Clinic Entrances Act (FACE) in 1994. FACE made it a federal crime to use force, threat of force, or physical obstruction to interfere with abortion providers or reproductive health care services or their patients.

In 1996, President Clinton vetoed the so-called partial birth abortion ban (PBAB) on the grounds that it would deny safe, legal abortion to women faced with threats to their health and life. In 1997, the House and Senate again passed the PBAB; Clinton again vetoed it.

fervent movement in this country to ban abortion and protect the fetus. In support of this latter position, activists have backed various federal antiabortion bills, including one that would outlaw almost all abortions by declaring that life begins at conception. One law, in effect for five years, suppressed even the dissemination of information about abortion.

Antiabortion laws include restrictions on minors' access to abortion. Most states have parental notification laws for minors who are seeking abortion, as well as judicial bypass laws through which minors who fear their parents' reactions can seek a judge's opinion that they are sufficiently mature to make medical decisions for themselves. In responding to an applicant's request for judicial bypass, juvenile court judges vary greatly in their decisions (Sensibaugh & Allgeier, 1996). This variation has led to "shopping" for judges who are known to be sympathetic to the adolescents' requests. One associated problem is that the time involved in seeking a court decision increases the duration of pregnancy, thus increasing the risks of medical complications involved in the abortion procedure.

▶ **Issues to Consider:** If you were a juvenile court judge, under what conditions would you approve a minor's request for judicial bypass in making an abortion decision?

In 1988, just prior to the end of his presidency, Ronald Reagan enacted the Gag Rule, a law that forbade any institution receiving federal funds from providing pregnant women information about abortion. Violators risked loss of their federal funding. This ban extended to physicians, even if a patient specifically requested such information or if withholding the information would endanger her health.

Challenges to the Gag Rule worked their way through the courts up to the Supreme Court, which in May 1991 *upheld* the Gag Rule in a five-to-four decision. It was not until 1993 that the gag rule was overturned by a newly elected President Bill Clinton.

Antiabortion activists have never before been more vocal and visible than in the 1990s. Indeed, militant prolife activists, apparently motivated by their belief that abortion is murder, have used arson, fire bombings, and blockades as weapons of intimidation and obstruction. For example, in 1998, Dr. Barnett Slepian, a New York physician, was murdered for performing legal abortions. And in 1998 a bomb explosion at a Birmingham, Alabama, clinic killed a security guard (an off-duty policeman) and critically injured a nurse. Although the major prolife organizations have condemned such violence, occasionally individuals associated with these organizations have engaged in violence.

R. N. Emily Lyons speaks of surviving the 1998 bombing of a Birmingham, Alabama, abortion clinic.

Abortion: The Process

The debate about abortion is complicated by the fact that some methods of contraception can also function as abortives. The intrauterine device, emergency contraceptive pills, and RU-486 can be used as methods of early abortion. Most books listing methods of birth control classify these with contraceptives rather than with abortion methods, presumably because any abortions they cause may occur before a woman knows that she is pregnant.

ABORTION METHODS EARLY IN PREGNANCY

Several early methods exist for women who have engaged in unprotected intercourse and wish to terminate a potential pregnancy: administration of extra doses of birth control pills, DES (diethylstilbestrol), or RU-486 and menstrual extraction. These methods can be used before the woman knows if she has conceived.

Various hormone preparations are capable of terminating a pregnancy. Extra doses of emergency contraceptive pills (ECPs) involving common oral contraceptives have been shown to reduce the likelihood of conception or implantation of a fertilized egg. In 1996 the Food and Drug Administration (FDA) concluded that ECPs could be used safely and effectively to avoid pregnancy as late as 72 hours after exposure to sperm. The pills are most effective if begun within 12 to 24 hours of unprotected intercourse. Analyses of results from eight published studies involving 2,839 women indicated that such emergency use of oral contraceptives reduced the risk of pregnancy by about 75 percent (Trussell, 1998). Students interested in ECPs that can be used in emergencies should consult Hatcher et al.'s *Contraceptive Technology* (1998). Women with health problems that make the use of oral contraceptives inadvisable should not use ECPs. As soon as possible, the woman should obtain a reliable method of contraception that she can use on a regular basis. ECPs should be used only in emergencies, and they are not as effective as other methods.

The best known of the hormones for abortion—and the only one approved by the FDA—is DES. Taken in what is popularly called the morning-after pill, DES is a highly potent synthetic estrogen. To end a potential pregnancy, a woman must begin taking 25 mg of DES twice a day within 72 hours of unprotected intercourse and continue to do so for five days. In general, DES is recommended only in an emergency such as rape. Although it is highly effective in interrupting pregnancy, the side effects are quite uncomfortable for many women who use it and should not be taken by women for whom estrogen poses a medical hazard.

DES's low cost and effectiveness are its main advantages. It is also advantageous for women who wish to avoid knowing whether they are pregnant, because DES is used before a pregnancy is confirmed. Taken later in pregnancy, DES has been associated with genital cancers and other problems in both male and female offspring. Used as an abortive, however, it has not been associated with any long-term side effects. Nonetheless, caution is advised because the hormone has not been used as an abortive agent for a long enough period of time for researchers to confirm that effects will not emerge.

Another hormonal abortion procedure is RU-486 (mifepristone). Taken orally, this drug blocks the action of progesterone, the hormone that prepares the uterine lining for the implantation of a fertilized egg. RU-486 is most effective if taken within 49 days of the last menstrual period. Women who have not aborted within about 48 hours of taking the drug return to the clinic to receive prostaglandins. These hormones make the uterus contract and bleed and are accompanied by mild to severe cramping. This procedure is reportedly 95 percent to 99 percent effective in inducing abortion (Cates and Ellertson, 1998). The major side effect is prolonged uterine bleeding, but this usually does not require transfusion or curettage (surgical scraping of the uterus).

RU-486 was approved for use in France in 1988 and is also available in China and Great Britain. Tests of RU-486 began in the United States in 1994; in fall 1996, the FDA announced that it considered RU-486 "approvable," but it still had not been made available as of January 1999. Because RU-486 holds promise for treating breast cancer, endometriosis, Cushing's disease, forms of leukemia, malaria, advanced anemia, other cancers, and perhaps AIDS, groups concerned with the treatment of these conditions have argued for lifting the ban on RU-486 in the United States.

In a third early abortion method, menstrual extraction, menstrual blood and tissue are removed from the uterus with a cannula and sometimes a suction machine. This method is generally employed when a woman's period is late by a week or two. A positive pregnancy test is not needed prior to a woman's undergoing menstrual extraction; in fact, some women have used the technique to shorten the length of their menstrual periods. Casual use of menstrual extraction is not recommended, however, because of the risk of hemorrhage and of introduction of bacteria into the uterus.

The advantages of menstrual extraction are that it is less expensive than a suction abortion (described later) and requires less dilation of the cervix than methods used later in pregnancy. Another advantage of the procedure for some women is that it can be performed before the woman knows whether she is pregnant.

FIRST-TRIMESTER ABORTION METHODS

More than 90 percent of the abortions performed in the United States occur during the first trimester (Henshaw & Kost, 1996). Methods include suction abortion and dilation and curettage (D&C).

Suction abortion, also called vacuum aspiration, is usually done on an outpatient basis under local

---

prostaglandins—hormones that stimulate muscle contractions as well as help regulate ovulation and the release of prolactin from the ovaries.

cannula (CAN-u-luh)—a tube inserted into the body through which liquid or tissue may be removed.
suction abortion—removal of the contents of the uterus through use of a suction machine.

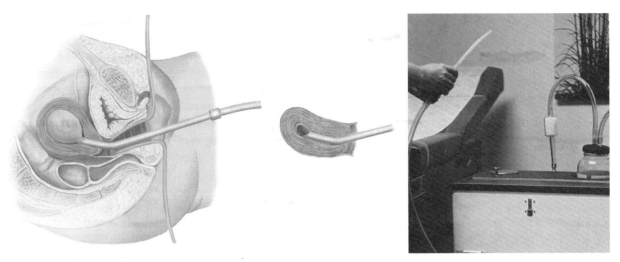

Figure 11.1   Vacuum Curette
In abortion by vacuum aspiration, a vacuum curette that is connected by rubber tubing to a suction machine is inserted through the cervix into the uterus. The vacuum-aspiration machine (right) is used to suction the uterine contents into a jar on top of the machine.

anesthesia. It accounts for more than 95 percent of the first-trimester abortions in most Western countries (Cates and Ellertson, 1998). A local anesthetic is injected into the woman's cervix, which is then dilated. A cannula is introduced into the uterus through the cervix. The suction machine draws the blood, fetal tissue, and mucus from the uterus and out through the cannula. This part of the procedure generally takes less than five minutes. A doctor may scrape the uterus with a **curette** to ensure that all fetal material has been removed (see Figure 11.1).

Bleeding similar to that experienced during menstruation may continue for several days following a suction abortion. The majority of women ovulate within three or four weeks following the abortion, and so a couple should resume intercourse only with a reliable contraceptive. Normal menstrual periods typically return within a month or two of the abortion.

Complications of suction abortion may include hemorrhage, uterine perforation (puncturing of the uterus), and infection. The most common complication, hemorrhage, afflicts fewer than 1 of every 100 women and is rarely severe enough to require blood transfusions. Perforation of the uterine wall with the

dilator or currette is a far more dangerous complication, often requiring surgical repair of the perforation. In rare cases, a hysterectomy may be the only effective method for stopping hemorrhaging from the perforation. The third possible complication, abortion-related infection, is suspected when fever, abdominal pain, or a yellowish vaginal discharge develops. The infection is usually eliminated with antibiotics.

Suction abortion has a number of advantages over the dilation and curettage (D&C) and second-trimester methods described later. The time required for the procedure is shorter, recovery is quicker, and complications are fewer because a woman does not have to recover from the effects of general anesthesia. Suction abortion is also considerably less expensive than a D&C, which involves hospital costs. Furthermore, the risks associated with a suction abortion are fewer than those associated with pregnancy or childbirth. Most women report little or no pain with suction abortion.

The other first-trimester abortion method is **dilation and curettage**. (D&Cs are also performed for various medical reasons on nonpregnant women.)

curette (cure-RET)—a scooplike instrument used for scraping bodily tissue.

dilation and curettage (D&C) (die-LAY-shun and CURE-eh-taj)—dilation of the cervix followed by scraping of the interior of the uterus with a curette.

This procedure is similar to the suction abortion except that a doctor often administers general, rather than local, anesthesia and uses a curette to scrape out the contents of the uterus instead of suctioning them out. This procedure is still common in developing countries where abortion is legally restricted (Cates and Ellertson, 1998), and it is preferable to suction abortion when the pregnancy has progressed to the end of the first trimester.

Possible complications from a D&C include those listed for suction abortion (hemorrhage, perforation, and infection), as well as complications associated with general anesthesia.

SECOND-TRIMESTER ABORTION METHODS

Fewer than 10 percent of the women who have abortions do so after the first trimester, and many of these women seek abortion only after learning of major fetal defects. (Cates and Ellertson, 1998). The maternal mortality rate for abortions performed during the second trimester is much greater than that for abortions performed during the first trimester, increasing by about 50 percent for each week beyond the first trimester. *Reality or Myth* ?

The **dilation and evacuation (D&E)** method, which combines elements of the D&C and vacuum-aspiration methods, is generally used early in the second trimester in a hospital or clinic setting. After administration of local or general anesthesia, the cervix is dilated to a greater extent than with a D&C to allow passage of a larger fetus. Because of fetal skeletal development, special instruments must be used to crush the fetus in the uterus prior to its extraction with a large vacuum curette. The fetal remains are then reassembled to make sure that all the contents of the uterus have been removed. Until the sixteenth week of pregnancy, the D&E is the safest of the second-trimester methods and takes the shortest time to perform. Starting at the sixteenth week, it has complication and mortality rates equivalent to those of the other methods. Possible complications include infection, perforation of the uterus, and reactions to the anesthesia.

> **dilation and evacuation (D&E)**—an abortion method, generally used in the second trimester, in which the fetus is crushed within the uterus and then extracted through a vacuum curette.

Abortion by means of an **intra-amniotic injection** is another alternative and accounts for about 1 percent of all abortions in the United States (Cates and Ellertson, 1998). With this method, saline (salt) solution, which causes fetal circulatory arrest, is injected into the amniotic sac. The drug pitocin is also administered to induce labor contractions and expulsion of the fetus and placenta. In some cases, prostaglandins are used instead of the saline solution.

Major complications occur more frequently from intra-amniotic injections than from D&Es. Complications from saline abortions primarily stem from three factors: (1) accidental injection into the uterine muscle, blood vessels, or abdominal cavity; (2) infection; and (3) absorption of some of the saline solution into the bloodstream. When prostaglandins are used instead of a saline solution, complications may include vomiting, nausea, diarrhea, cervical tearing, and asthma-like symptoms. This method should not be used with asthmatic women. Abortion via intra-amniotic injection can also be quite painful for some women.

The only major advantage of intra-amniotic abortion is that it is preferable to the alternative of giving birth to a fetus that is likely to be deformed or dead.

LATE-PREGNANCY ABORTION

Hysterotomy is used only when medical conditions contraindicate a D&E or intra-amniotic injection and when the pregnancy threatens the woman's life. An incision is made in the abdomen through the uterine muscle, and the fetus is removed. Only about 0.1 percent of abortions require uterine surgery (Cates and Ellertson, 1998).

In another late-term abortion method, a doctor partly delivers a late-term fetus who is not developed enough to be able to survive. The doctor uses a suction device to extract brain tissue before removing the rest of the body through the vagina.

> **intra-amniotic injection**—replacement of amniotic fluid with either prostaglandins or a salt solution, causing fetal circulatory arrest; occasionally used in second-trimester abortions.
> **hysterotomy** (HIS-ter-AW-tuh-mee)—surgical incision into the uterus; when used for abortion, the fetus is removed through the incision.

Abortion opponents use the term "partial-birth abortion" to describe this procedure, which has been the subject of intense political debates. In 1997, President Clinton vetoed a bill that would have banned the procedure. In response, antiabortion activists have turned their attention to state legislatures. By 1998, 15 states had outlawed the rarely used procedure.

PSYCHOLOGICAL RESPONSES TO ABORTION

Numerous studies conducted since the 1970s have examined the reactions of women to their discovery of an unintentional pregnancy and subsequent decision to obtain an abortion. An overview of this research indicates that the greatest distress occurs before the abortion and that severe negative reactions after an abortion are rare (Adler et al., 1992; Russo & Dabus, 1997). For most women, a legal abortion is followed by a mixture of emotions, with positive feelings predominating over negative feelings. This pattern has been found immediately after and up to eight years after abortion. The most important predictor of a woman's sense of well-being after having an abortion is her level of self-esteem before the pregnancy (Russo & Dabul, 1997). *Reality or Myth*

The small minority of women who do experience emotional distress within three weeks after abortion are more likely to report that (1) the pregnancy was intended and meaningful; (2) there was lack of support from their parents or partner for the abortion; (3) they felt in conflict and less certain of their decision and coping abilities before the abortion; (4) they blamed themselves for the pregnancy; and (5) they delayed the abortion until the second trimester (Lewis, 1997; Major & Cozzarelli, 1992).

As in other stressful situations, the more support and encouragement that women receive, the more positive they are about their ability to cope with an abortion. Thus, events that impair women's expectations for coping with an abortion, such as receiving counseling that emphasizes the negative effects of abortion or being confronted by individuals picketing abortion clinics, may make it more difficult for such women to adjust to an abortion experience.

THE MALE ROLE IN ABORTION

Our informal contacts with unmarried student couples who are dealing with unplanned pregnancy suggest that young men's reactions to the pregnancy of their lovers vary from strong advocacy of abortion to passionate pleas that the woman maintain the pregnancy. As one young man in the latter group put it, "I don't want her killing my baby." In this case, the young woman chose to abort the fetus after ending the relationship. She said with considerable agitation that it was all well and good for him to "lay guilt trips" on her regarding abortion, but because he apparently did not intend to stay around to help with the emotional and physical support of the child for the next 18 years, he could not have anything to say about the decision.

It is not known whether men whose partners seek abortions experience guilt over their part in conception, anger, relief that the woman has chosen to abort, or some combination of emotions.

Research is needed on the reactions of male partners before and after decisions about unwanted pregnancy are made. Researchers' neglect of abortion applicants' sexual partners was aptly described two decades ago in terms that remain accurate today:

> *Men are almost ephemeral objects who, once they've done their share in the conception of the fetus, are rarely seen again; or at least they're not very visible in the pages of journal articles on problem pregnancy or on abortion.* (Lees, 1975, p. 2)

Interested in exploring the male role in abortion, Lees interviewed 73 men who accompanied their unmarried partners to a Detroit abortion clinic. He found that the more emotional involvement the men reported with their partners, the greater was their anxiety during the pregnancy termination. Lees hypothesized that the higher anxiety of these involved men was probably rooted in empathy and a willingness to share the burden of responsibility for the pregnancy and abortion with their partners.

Most college students believe that in making a decision about an unwanted pregnancy, a woman should consider her partner, although the majority also think that ultimately the decision rests with the woman (Rosenwasser, Wright, & Barber, 1987). Shusterman (1979) studied the reactions of male partners using reports that were given by abortion clients. The overwhelming majority of women reported that their partners supported the abortion decision, regardless of the length of the relationship.

Planned Parenthood has figured in landmark rulings about a father's role in the abortion decision.

In 1976, the U.S. Supreme Court ruled in *Planned Parenthood* v. *Danforth* that the wife should have the final decision when a married couple disagrees about the resolution of a pregnancy. This ruling was based on the argument that because she is the one who must bear the child and thus is most affected by the pregnancy, she should control the decision regarding abortion. Despite that decision, about 10 states enacted laws requiring that women notify or obtain the consent of their husbands before obtaining abortions. However, in 1992, the U.S. Supreme Court ruled in *Planned Parenthood* v. *Casey* that a Pennsylvania law requiring notification of a husband prior to abortion was unconstitutional.

Some men believe that their legal exclusion from the decision is unfair and denies them a voice in the decision about whether to become a parent. They are right in feeling that the process is unfair. Biologically, they cannot become pregnant, and no amount of legislation can change that fact. However, if a woman is to have control over her body, she must make the final decision about whether to carry a pregnancy to term. Nevertheless, men may not be as powerless as their legal status suggests, for a man's emotional response generally has a substantial impact on his partner. The more involved and supportive the male partner is, the greater are the self-esteem and self-worth of the woman who has had an abortion (Major & Cozzarelli, 1992; Russo & Dabul, 1997).

> ▶ **Issues to Consider:** To what extent, and under what conditions, do you believe that a man who impregnated his partner should have a legal right to require that she maintain a pregnancy that she doesn't want? What if she does want to give birth and raise the child, but the man wants her to abort?

*U*nintended Parenthood

Just as we have relatively little information about men's roles in and reactions to abortion, we have little but anecdotal information about the proportion of men favoring the maintenance of an unplanned pregnancy versus the proportion favoring abortion. We do know that recourse to marriage as a solution is less prevalent than it used to be. With legal abortion unavailable, a pregnant unwed teenager in the 1950s would often acquire a spouse through a "shotgun" wedding, and nearly 25 percent of 18- and 19- year-old women were married. In the 1950s, about two-thirds of unmarried pregnant women married their partners, whereas only one-third did so following the legalization of abortion (Baldwin, 1976). The teenage birthrate was also higher in 1957 than it was following the legalization of abortion in 1973.

The decrease in the popularity of forced marriage and adoption as alternatives for women who maintain pregnancy has resulted in a rise in the number of unmarried mothers. Single parenthood has

TABLE 11.1	Numbers of Pregnancies, Legal Abortions, and Births for Adolescent Women		
	1975	1985	1994
Under Age 15			
Pregnancies	31,950	30,930	25,100
Legal abortions	15,260	16,970	12,170
Births	12,642	10,220	12,930
Age 15 to 19			
Pregnancies	1,056,120	1,000,110	781,900
Legal abortions	324,930	339,200	276,010
Births	582,252	467,485	505,980

Note: The total number of abortions and births does not add up to the number of pregnancies because some of the pregnancies ended in miscarriages Henshaw (1997, 1998; Henshaw & Van Vort, 1992).

been increasing for all ages of women who bear children and is particularly high among adolescents. Although the birthrate among unmarried teenagers has remained high, only about 3 percent of unmarried mothers currently elect to place their children for adoption (Mosher & Bachrach, 1996).

ADOLESCENT PARENTS

Between 1973 and 1991 there were more than 1 million teenage pregnancies every year in the United States (Henshaw, 1993, 1998). Teenage pregnancies fell below 1 million in 1992 and continue to decline, as have the number of teenage abortions. As Table 11.1 shows, however, a greater proportion of pregnant women aged 15 to 19 chose to maintain the pregnancy than to have an abortion. More than half of the teenagers who chose to become mothers were unmarried (Henshaw, 1998; Mosher & Bachrach, 1996).

▶ **Issues to Consider:** What would your advice be to a 16-year-old pregnant female who does not know who impregnated her?

Pregnancy among adolescents carries more risk than it does among older women. Teenage mothers are more likely than adult mothers to get inadequate prenatal care, gain insufficient weight during pregnancy, have labor and delivery problems, end their education prematurely, have decreased earning po-

tential, and live in poverty (Alan Guttmacher Institute, 1994; Mosher & Bachrach, 1996).

In the most extensive longitudinal study of the effects of early motherhood, Frank Furstenberg and his colleagues (Furstenberg, 1976; Furstenberg, Brooks-Gunn, & Morgan, 1987) found that early parenthood creates many disadvantages for young women and their children. These young mothers consistently experienced greater difficulty in realizing their life plans than did a control group of their nonpregnant classmates. As Furstenberg (1976, p. 219) observed:

Their prospects of achieving a stable marriage were damaged by the early pregnancy, and they were having great difficulty supporting a family on their own. Poorly educated, unskilled, often burdened by several small children, many of these women at age 20 or 21 had become resigned to a life of economic deprivation.

Seventeen years later, the picture was not as grim for a substantial number of these women (Furstenberg et al., 1987). Although 70 percent of them had received welfare at some time during the 17 years, two-thirds of them had managed to get off welfare and were employed. Another 9 percent of the women were actively seeking employment. One-quarter of the women had annual family incomes in excess of $25,000, well above the poverty level at that time. Obviously, adolescent pregnancy presents formidable

Financial setbacks and increased risk of divorce may face these adolescent parents.

obstacles, and many women in the study remained mired in poverty. But a number rebounded from their adversity and established adequate lives for themselves.

Adolescent mothers who marry are twice as likely to separate or divorce as are married women who have a first child in their 20s. In one study, one-third of the 15- to 19-year-old mothers who had married before giving birth were found to have separated or divorced by the time their children were 6 years old (Presser, 1980).

What happens to the children of adolescent mothers? When tested at various ages up to their seventh year, the offspring of adolescents were found to be somewhat lower in IQ and cognitive development than the children of older women. Children whose mothers were employed or in school scored higher than those whose mothers were at home full time. Some studies have shown deficits in the social and emotional development of the children of adolescent

mothers, but others have not (Baldwin & Cain, 1980). Many children in the Furstenberg et al. (1987) study appeared destined to experience their own struggles. The children were characterized generally as having high rates of school failure. Adolescent pregnancy by the daughters and juvenile delinquency by the sons were common. Other research also indicates that the children of adolescent mothers are more likely than the children of older mothers to become adolescent mothers themselves (Manlove, 1997). In fact, the best predictor of the age that a girl or woman first becomes a mother is that age at which *her* mother gave birth to her first child.

Occasionally television commentators and print media columnists blame the welfare system for the illegitimacy rate. Some have even gone so far as to suggest that poor mothers deliberately become pregnant as a way to get more money from federal social support programs. Cutright (1971) tested this hypothesis several decades ago by examining the relationship between illegitimacy rates and the existence or size of welfare benefits across a large number of countries. He found no relationship between these variables. Studies in the United States also have failed to confirm any relationship between illegitimacy rates and potential welfare benefits (Moore & Caldwell, 1977; Presser, 1974).

The fate of most adolescent fathers is similar to that of teenage mothers. Generally having come from poor, relatively uneducated backgrounds, they experience serious social and economic disadvantages when compared with young men who postpone fatherhood until a later age (Hardy, Duggan, Masnyk, & Pearson, 1989; Marsiglio, 1987). Gradually many of these fathers decrease their contact with their child. Most of the fathers lack the necessary skills to provide a stable home environment for their families, even if they want to do so. In short, poverty is the tie that binds most adolescent fathers and mothers, and although some manage to cope with their situation and succeed, the odds are stacked against them.

Two variables are strongly associated with the development and life experiences of adolescent parents and their offspring in the various samples: the single parent's economic level and the extent of social support received by the single-parent family. The disadvantages experienced by adolescent mothers and their offspring are either reduced or nonexistent when adolescent mothers receive strong social support from older people or have above-average economic resources.

KEEPING AN UNWANTED CHILD

What about the offspring of women who are unable to obtain wanted abortions? Because of restrictive abortion legislation in effect in several European countries, researchers have had a chance to compare unwanted and wanted children (David, Dytrych, Matejcek, & Schuller, 1988; David, 1992). The children have been studied up through ages 26 to 28.

Comparisons of the unwanted children with the wanted offspring showed that, as a group, those who had been unwanted were less well adjusted at age 9 and at ages 14 to 16, and had greater psychosocial instability at ages 21 to 23. David et al. (1988, p. 124) reported that their adult relationships "with their families of origin, friends, coworkers, supervisors,

and especially with their sexual or marital partners are dogged by serious difficulties." Research on the marital partners of unwanted children (now aged 26 to 28) found that they were similar to their spouses. These families had more difficulties or were more problem prone than families founded by individuals wanted or accepted in early pregnancy (David, 1992). Even so, David et al. (1988, p. 124) observed that the unwanted offspring were not so much overrepresented on the very negative indicators as they were underrepresented on the positive measures:

> They are rarely observed on any indicator of excellence. . . . Insufficient gratification of basic social and emotional needs (which accompanies many UP [unwanted pregnancy] children from early childhood) tends to create an unfavorable social environment with negative effects in personality development, social relations, and self-realization. Whether or not this tendency will affect the next generation, only time will tell.

These results strongly suggest that in the interests of children's well-being, prospective parents should delay parenthood until they want to have children. Educating adolescents about sexuality and contraception is one way to help them postpone parenthood.

UNWANTED PREGNANCY IN ADOLESCENCE: ETHICS AND EDUCATION?

We might usefully compare our culture's approach to adolescents' sex education with the ways in which we deal with their wishes to learn to drive. Adults might have various responses to young people's desire to drive. They might (1) prohibit adolescents from driving; (2) hand them the car keys with little instruction in safe and responsible driving; (3) wring their hands and mutter, "Tsk, tsk," at the incidence of car accidents among untrained and unlicensed drivers; or (4) provide extensive classroom instruction and practical tutoring in driving and encourage enrollment in these courses by giving course credit, reduced insurance premiums, and the like. In general, our society has taken the fourth of these alternatives regarding driving.

In contrast, we have used all but the fourth alternative to deal with adolescents' capacity for sexual interaction. First, we discourage sexual expression by adolescents. Second, although adolescents already have the keys, so to speak, we try to keep them from realizing that they possess those keys rather than showing them how to use them. When they discover the keys anyway, they use them, with minimal instruction on safe and responsible sexual expression. Third, we complain about the incidence of "accidents" (unintended conceptions) among adolescents untrained in responsible sexual interactions.

Taking the fourth approach—providing extensive instruction to prospective drivers—does not totally eliminate car accidents, and we cannot expect that offering thorough sex education would eliminate unplanned pregnancies either. However, following the model used for driver education would be a step in the right direction when dealing with adolescent sexuality; that is, adolescents could be given extensive classroom instruction on responsible sexual expression. This instruction could include practical tutoring in techniques for inserting diaphragms or putting on condoms (using plastic models of the body), as well as information about obtaining contraception, discussing sexual feelings and responsibilities with another person, and recognizing the difference between sexual feelings and sexual actions. Emphasis on the enormous responsibility of child care and the emotional and financial investment involved in rearing a child for at least two decades could be provided as well. Explicit discussion of these issues in the classroom might furnish a much-needed model for explicit discussion of issues between adolescents when they decide to become sexually involved.

Unfortunately, our society has largely chosen to avoid discussion of contraceptive use with adolescents. Thus, it is hardly surprising that the majority of them follow our example and do not discuss the issue among themselves, with fairly predictable results: unintended pregnancies, abortions, and unprepared parenthood.

▶ **Issues to Consider:** What do you think is the best way to decrease the number of unintended or unwanted pregnancies?

SUMMARY OF MAJOR POINTS

1. Unintended and/or unwanted pregnancy. More than 2 million unwanted conceptions occur every year in the United States. About 1.2 million women a year end their pregnancies through abortion, terminating roughly 30 percent of all confirmed conceptions. The number of single women who choose to maintain their pregnancies and take on the responsibilities of parenthood, however, has been increasing dramatically.

2. Access to abortion. In the historic *Roe* v. *Wade* decision of 1973, the Supreme Court eliminated legal barriers to women's right to abortion during the first two trimesters of pregnancy. Citizens have continued to debate the morality of the procedure, however, and those who oppose abortion have succeeded in getting Congress to pass legislation preventing the use of federal funds for abortions. Those who favor legal abortion maintain that women should have the sole decision regarding the use of their bodies.

3. Abortion procedures. Most abortions are performed during the first trimester through either the suction or the D&C method, or through a combination of the two. Legal first-trimester abortions are among the safest of all medical procedures. Second-trimester abortions are considerably more complicated. They are performed through injection of saline solution into the amniotic fluid, injection of prostaglandins, or a D&E. Clearly, first-trimester abortion is preferable, but sometimes situations that occur after the first trimester, such as exposure to teratogenic diseases or conditions, prompt women to seek abortion. Late-term abortion is rare but has been the center of a great deal of political controversy.

4. Emotional responses to abortion. Relatively little is known about the psychological reactions of women and men while they are reaching decisions about unwanted pregnancy. However, the vast majority of women who choose abortion subsequently report that positive feelings predominate over negative feelings. Few experience guilt, sorrow, or severe distress.

5. Unintended parenthood. Compared with women who first give birth in their 20s, teenage mothers (and their offspring) generally suffer a number of long-term disadvantages. Whether particular women and their children experience problems is strongly associated with two factors: financial status and social support. Relatively little is known about the men who are faced with an unwanted pregnancy.

Sexuality in Childhood and Adolescence

Reality or Myth

1. At birth, boys are capable of having erections and girls are capable of vaginal lubrication.

2. All gender stereotypes are inaccurate.

3. Males are not able to have an orgasm until they reach puberty (adolescence).

4. In North America, some homosexual behavior is often a normal part of growing up.

5. Sex education programs emphasizing postponement and protection appear to be more effective in delaying sexual initiation than are abstinence-only programs.

6. Men and women report more anxiety and pleasure, and less guilt, about their first coital experience in a voluntary, close relationship than in a casual encounter.

Most people in our culture assume that humans are asexual for many years after birth. Infants are the epitome of innocence, and at least in North America, sexuality represents the opposite of innocence. In fact, first coitus is sometimes referred to as the "end of innocence."

In this chapter we explore childhood and adolescent sexuality and gender. We begin by considering researchers' persistent difficulties in obtaining information about sexual behavior in childhood and early adolescence—difficulties that are associated with our culture's attitudes toward sexuality. We then examine theories about the influence of early relationships with family members on personality development. The biological, psychological, and social aspects of gender identity and sexual development are considered, as well as the role of sexual play as a rehearsal for adult interactions and a source of information about sexuality. Next, we evaluate the quality of sex education at home and in school and its association with sexual attitudes and knowledge from infancy through adulthood. Then we explore the process of sexual maturation that marks the end of childhood and the exploration of sexual behaviors and personal identities through which most adolescents pass. Finally, we consider some of the behaviors involved in initial experiences of sexual intimacy with a partner.

Understanding Childhood Sexuality

Our cultural assumption that the innocence of infancy and childhood is the opposite of sexuality has a number of effects. One is that few investigators have dared to delve into sexual feelings and experiences early in the life span because of the taboos that surround childhood eroticism. Even after children reach school age, researchers have difficulty obtaining permission to ask questions about what youngsters know about sex, and it is extremely unlikely that researchers would be allowed to ask children what they do sexually (see "Research Spotlight: Children's Sexual Knowledge: An Immoral Research Topic?" on page 268).

Just as conducting research on childhood sexuality tends to be forbidden in North American culture, the exploration and expression of childhood sexuality tend to be prohibited or discouraged by parents and other caretakers. In many respects, scientists encounter

Most people make assumptions about infants that influence treatment of and expectations about them.

the same set of problems that children face in their search for sexual information. Children with an active curiosity about sexuality may elicit concern, anxiety, and reprimands from parents and other adults. Similarly, investigators of childhood sexuality and advocates of sexuality education programs are confronted with suspicion and, at times, public outcry.

Theories About the Development of Gender and Sexuality

Why do some people find sexual feeling and expression a source of deep pleasure, whereas others feel relatively little interest in this area of life, and still others experience shame, embarrassment, or fear that inhibits their ability to interact sexually with a person whom they love dearly? Such questions have stimulated theorists to devise models of how we acquire variations in our personalities (see Table 12.1).

When we turn to the issues of sexual orientations, attitudes about masturbation, masturbatory behavior, necking, petting, and stimulation to orgasm, we find many individual variations. Your own sexual attitudes and behaviors may seem natural and normal to you. Consider, however, the attitudes and behavior of others whom you know well. It is quite likely that you cannot name two other people who

hold identical points of view. What is the source of these variations? In this section we focus primarily on theorists' attempts to account for the similarities and differences in males' and females' development and expression of sexuality.

As was pointed out in Chapter 2, Sigmund Freud, the founder of psychoanalysis, believed that personality variations result from individuals' experiences as they attempt to cope with sexual energy during successive stages of childhood. Three aspects of Freud's model are relevant to our discussion. One is his hypothesis that children compete with the parent of the same sex for a sexual relationship with the parent of the other sex: respectively, the Oedipus complex and the Electra complex. The second involves the ideas that boys relinquish their desire for

TABLE 12.1   Models of Development and Sexual Capacities

Stages	Ages	Freud's Stages	Erikson's Crises	Capacities
Infancy	Birth to 18 months	Oral stage	Basic trust vs. mistrust	Sensuality via sucking, touching, holding, bodily contact Genital exploration, erection of penis, lubrication of vagina, and capacity for orgasm
Early childhood	18 months to 3 years	Anal stage	Autonomy vs. doubt, shame	Development of sphincter control; ability in males to produce erections Awareness of nongenital gender differences and gender identity Development of language and potential to begin to acquire sexual vocabulary (names of body parts, processes)
Preschool years	3 to 5 years	Phallic stage (Oedipus/Electra complexes)	Initiative vs. guilt	Deliberate pleasurable self-stimulation Curiosity about sexual and reproductive processes Well-developed gender identity
Late childhood	5 to 11 years	Latency	Industry vs. inferiority	Active sexual exploration with both same- and other-gender friends Active desire for sex information Prepubescent surge in hormones, growth of internal and external sexual organs
Adolescence	12 to 20 years	Genital stage	Identity vs. role confusion	Development of capacities to ejaculate and to menstruate; sexual maturation Increasingly intense romantic attachments Absorption in questions regarding self and identity

Oedipus complex (EH-dih-pus)—in Freudian theory, a son's sexual desire for his mother.

Electra complex—in Freudian theory, a daughter's sexual desire for her father.

castration anxiety—fear of losing the penis, thought by psychoanalysts to result from the child's fear of retaliation for forbidden sexual desire toward one's mother.

penis envy—in psychoanalytic theory, a woman's wish to possess a penis.

latency—in psychoanalytic theory, a stage lasting from about 6 years of age until puberty, in which there is supposedly little observable interest in sexual activity.

their mother because of fear of losing their penis, and that girls give up desire for their father from an awareness of having already lost their penis: the concepts, respectively, of **castration anxiety** and **penis envy.** The third aspect of Freud's model of psychosexual development is his belief that after a sexually active first five years of life, children enter a period of repressed sexual interest and activity, which lasts until about age 11. He called this period **latency.** Freud theorized that if development went awry during these early years, psychotherapy could help a

RESEARCH SPOTLIGHT   Children's Sexual Knowledge—An Immoral Research Topic?

Ronald and Juliette Goldman (1982) have described some of the difficulties faced by those who attempt to investigate children's sexuality. The Goldmans interviewed 838 children in Australia, Britain, the United States, Canada, and Sweden, at the ages of 5, 7, 9, 11, 13, and 15. To understand children's thinking about sexuality, they asked each of these children 63 questions.

After examining previous research in the area in the course of designing the study, the Goldmans wrote, "The paucity of published articles reinforced our conviction for the need to undertake what was to prove a difficult and demanding project for the next two years" (1982, pp. xvi–xvii). In selecting the specific topics to be investigated, the Goldmans noted that gathering information on a number of sexual behaviors, including childhood masturbation, would have been

extremely valuable, but we judged from trial responses that to have included such items would have gone beyond the limits set by social taboos in home, school, and community. . . . Operating within the constraints evident within the public school systems the content had to be adjusted to what was realistically possible and acceptable. The influence of these and other sexual taboos, preventing discussion, exploration or research in certain areas, is in itself an indication of the need for research into sexual thinking. (pp. 62–63)

The Goldmans carefully designed their interviews to avoid offending school boards and parents, who had to read a description of the research and sign consent forms before children could participate. The researchers experienced no difficulties in obtaining their samples from three of the five countries. The exceptions were the United States and Canada—specifically, the cities of Buffalo and Niagara Falls, New York, and the province of Ontario, Canada:

On both sides of the Canadian-USA border, despite the continuous efforts of university colleagues to help us make contacts and gain access to schools, we encountered widespread negative attitudes, and considerable opposition. This was so pronounced that after more than a month of fruitless effort, we almost gave up and returned to Britain.

The overall reason for these difficulties would appear to be the direct political control exercised by elected Boards of Education in the USA, to whom area superintendents of schools are responsible. These Boards are usually composed of lay persons who act as watchdogs, if not leaders, of the community. . . . By a misfortune of timing, we were trying to gain entry to schools in New York State only a few weeks before the local Boards of Education elections. Administrators were plainly anxious that our project might provide political ammunition during those elections and leave them exposed to public criticism. . . . One superintendent said to us that he didn't want his home bombed, and another, due to retire shortly, reported that he would not put his pension at risk. (pp. 73–74)

---

person to understand, but not necessarily eliminate, the effects of destructive early experiences.

Erik Erikson, a psychoanalytic scholar who also proposed that humans go through stages of personality development, was considerably more optimistic than Freud about an individual's chances of surviving a difficult early childhood if positive experiences followed during later stages. Erikson (1982) saw development as a process in which the person must resolve successive dilemmas. He described eight stages of life, each of which poses a crisis or opportunity for the individual. Successful resolution of life crises enables us to become healthier, more well-developed, integrated, and mature human beings. Like many other theorists, Erikson perceived the first years of life as extremely important to personality development. Unlike Freud, he thought that although the development of a trusting nature is crucial for the 1-year-old, positive experiences later in life can offset less-than-desirable early life experiences. Similarly, the effect of positive experiences and development during infancy can be overwhelmed by the negative effects of crises arising later in life.

A rather different perspective on the development of sexual behavior and sex differences is held by evolutionary theorists, who view differences between males and females as the result of natural selection (Buss, 1999; Buss & Schmitt, 1993; Symons, 1979). Evolutionary theorists assume that sex differences emerged over time and stem from the reproductive success of individuals with adaptive traits. Pointing out that we have been a hunting-gathering species for all but a tiny fraction of our past, they argue that those men who had the skills to acquire needed resources (food, shelter) would have had greater reproductive success than their less skillful counterparts. Selective pressure, then, favored the evolution of such hunting assets as visual and spatial skills in men, including the ability to calculate distances and directions. Well-developed gross motor skills and aggressiveness in males would also have been valuable.

In contrast, attachment bonds, sociability, and interpersonal sensitivity would have been favored in women because of the usefulness of these traits for the survival and development of children. According to this view, the offspring of women lacking these attributes would have been less likely to survive. Interpersonal sensitivity and the ability to form intense bonds, then, may be part of women's psychobiological structure, developed over hundreds of thousands of years and inherited from our ancestors.

Finally, social learning theorists, as their name implies, attribute similarities and differences in gender roles, sexual attitudes, and sexual behavior to human learning in social contexts. These theorists believe that sexual attitudes and behavior are influenced throughout the life span by rewards, expectations, and punishments associated with sexual activities, as well as by observations of these activities. For example, the first time you heard of deep or "french" kissing, you may have found the concept revolting. Later, in the context of a romantic relationship, you may have responded differently to this behavior. Social learning theorists might attribute your initial attitude to early punishment for sharing food—and thus saliva—with others, and your subsequent reward to your association of deep kissing with pleasurable arousal. Similarly, we learn to exhibit certain traditionally expected behaviors for our gender while visiting an elderly relative, whereas in the company of peers, we often feel freer to behave in a more "unisex" fashion. A social learning theorist would explain these variations in sexual attitudes and gender-role behaviors as stemming from the differential rewards and punishments associated with them at different times and in varying situations.

As we describe development from infancy into adolescence, we will return to one or more of these theoretical approaches as appropriate.

▶ **Issues to Consider:** Which theory of sexual development in childhood most closely resembles your own ideas?

nfancy

After nine months in the protective uterine environment, an infant emerges into the outside world and is immediately assigned a sex: "It's a girl [boy]!" Research shows that the behavior of adults toward the child varies according to whether they believe an infant is male or female, regardless of its actual gender (see Figure 12.1). In a study first conducted in the 1970s (Will, Self, & Datan, 1976) and recently replicated (Katz, 1996), adults were found to be more uncomfortable when they interacted with an infant without knowledge of its sex. When the investigators gave the baby a name, in situational interactions with the infant, the adults chose a football when they thought the baby was Johnny and a doll when they thought the baby was named Jane. In actuality, Jane and Johnny were the same baby! These and other findings demonstrate that adults apply their expectations of gender-linked interests in children beginning in infancy. Such gender stereotyping of infants is more prevalent among children, adolescents, and young adults than it is among older adults (Stern & Karraker, Maccoby, 1998; Vogel, Lake, Evans, & Karraker, 1991).

PARENT-CHILD ATTACHMENT

Women display a number of unlearned responses to their infants that probably strengthen the bond between them. An infant's crying stimulates the secretion of oxytocin in its mother, which erects the nip-

Figure 12.1 The Innocent Infant Adults respond differently to an infant, depending on whether they are told that the baby is a boy or a girl.

ples for nursing and releases the milk. Further, most mothers carry their infants in their left arm without being aware of it while engaging in various chores (Hoyenga & Hoyenga, 1993; Whiting & Edwards, 1988). In this position, an infant is soothed by the sound of the familiar maternal heartbeat. New mothers also appear to have a relatively predictable sequence of reactions to their babies (Rossi, 1978, p. 75):

> *The new mother touches the baby's fingers and toes with her own fingertips, puts her palm on the baby's torso, and then wraps the baby in her arms. All the while she maintains full eye contact with the infant and her tension mounts until the baby opens its eyes and returns the gaze. Finally, when mothers talk to their babies, they also share a set of actions—wide-open eyes, raised eyebrows, sustained facial expression and baby talk— a shift in speech that elongates the vowels.*

This predisposition among women to form an intense attachment to their young makes evolutionary sense. Humans are much more immature at birth than are infants of other primate species. If they are to survive and prosper, they need prolonged care, which is ensured by the intense physical and emotional attachment of the mother to the infant.

Until recently, men in almost all cultures contributed little to the direct caregiving of infants

(Hoyenga & Hoyenga, 1993). Now that notions about the natures and roles of men and women have begun to change, however, many fathers take a much more active role in infant care. Expectant mothers and fathers holding egalitarian views toward women's roles anticipate more father involvement in infant care than do those holding more traditional perspectives (Fishbein, 1989). Following the birth of a child, fathers who are given the opportunity to have contact with their new babies touch, hold, and kiss them just as much as the infant's mothers do (Parke & O'Leary, 1976). When Parke and Sawin (1976) compared the feeding skills of fathers and mothers, they found both equally adept at responding sensitively to infants' cues.

Regardless of the extent of their contact with their infants, fathers tend to differ from mothers in the kinds of interactions that they have with babies. Initially, the contribution of fathers tends to involve physical assistance: taking care of the infant when the mother is tired, playing with the baby while the mother makes dinner, and taking over some of the routine chores of maintaining the household (Maccoby, 1998). Fathers usually do not become heavily invested in their parental role until the child begins to walk and talk (Rossi, 1985). Thus mothers are much more involved than fathers in child care during infancy in most cultures (Hoyenga & Hoyenga, 1993). However, when men assume full responsibility for child care, as in the case of single parenthood, they employ strategies that are considered stereotypically feminine in providing adequate care for their children (Silverstein, 1996).

In general, fathers tend to emphasize physical games with their infants, whereas mothers are more likely to engage in verbal games (McDonald & Parke, 1986; Ross & Taylor, 1989). Even among monkeys, physical play is the primary mode of interaction between fathers and their offspring. Possibly because fathers initiate more unusual and physically arousing games, children are more likely to choose their fathers than their mothers as play partners by the time they are 18 months old (Clarke-Stewart, 1978; Whiting & Edwards, 1988). These gender-based interactions appear to be culture bound. Among families of the hunter-gatherer Aka Pygmy tribe, both fathers and mothers were equally responsible for their infants (Hewlett, 1991). As researchers study the active and close relationships ba-

bies can form with their fathers, they are beginning to realize fathers' important role in child rearing.

SENSUALITY DURING INFANCY

In discussing early development, we must be careful not to define children's activities by adult standards. By the time we reach adulthood, most of us have learned to differentiate—in fact, to segregate—our sexual feelings and experiences from our other sensations and activities. Young children do not appear to make these distinctions, however. With this in mind, let us consider biosexual development before birth and eroticism during infancy.

Before birth, the fetus absorbs hormones secreted by the mother, and these effects do not disappear immediately after birth. Thus, newborn infants

It is clear that mammals become attached to each other relatively easily. Is our capacity for attachment a genetic predisposition?

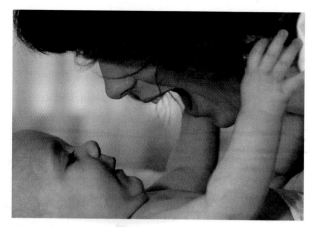

This mother and baby reflect the beauty of intense bonding.

briefly show several signs associated with reproductive maturity. The genitals and breasts of baby boys and girls are typically large and prominent. A milky substance is secreted from the nipples of breast-fed infants, who continue to receive some hormones through their mother's milk. Prolactin, responsible for the production of the mother's milk, is found in these infants' urine. Infant girls also may have slight vaginal bleeding suggestive of menstruation. All of these symptoms gradually disappear well before the end of a baby's fourth month.

The ovaries of baby girls have a ribbon-like appearance at birth. They increase quite slowly in size and weight until puberty, when they develop dramatically. Until that time, estrogen secretion is slight and constant; the adrenal glands are thought to be the source of the estrogen. The uterus of a baby girl is tiny, and the fallopian tubes have a coiled appearance.

The structure of the testes and epididymis of baby boys is established by the middle of the gestation period. Some interstitial cells, which produce testosterone, are present at birth. After some fluctuation in testosterone levels in the first seven months of an infant boy's development, testosterone levels remain fairly similar to those in infant girls from the third month until the onset of puberty. Adrenal androgen levels, however, rise a few years before puberty begins, which may influence skeletal maturation (Vermeulen, 1986). Like girls, boys ex-

perience little development in their sexual and reproductive structures until the onset of puberty.

Before a baby begins to acquire language, communication between the infant and the outer world takes place largely through physical sensations. The ways in which adults hold and caress the infant, as well as their responses to the child's discomfort, affect a child's emerging concept of his or her own body and developing sensuality (Field, 1998).

In the uterus, the fetus's basic needs are satisfied automatically and continuously through the umbilical cord. After birth, an infant must depend on the responsiveness of adults for its nourishment. Cuddling within the womb is replaced by cuddling with caretakers. An infant whose needs are satisfied in a loving and consistent way develops a trusting stance toward others. If caretakers are unloving or react inconsistently to the infant's needs, the child may form an attitude of generalized mistrust. An infant who lacks a trusting stance toward life is unlikely to have an optimistic, hopeful approach toward the future.

Compared with the contact that mothers have with their children, the contact that fathers have with their children often involves more physical activity.

Instead, according to Erikson, the infant will worry constantly about the satisfaction of current needs and will therefore be tied to the present (Belsky, 1991; Shaver & Hazan, 1994). Thus, the quality of the attachment between an infant and caretakers is a critical aspect of the infant's development (see Chapter 7).

Human infants are able to decipher body language before they can understand the content of words. Well-intentioned caretakers who are extremely tense and nervous in their attempts to calm a distressed infant tend to do just the opposite. Conversely, the pleasure and contentment of a nursing mother are mirrored in the pleasure of her infant. A nursing infant sometimes even shows body tension and release similar to that observed during erotic interaction between adults. The important factors in the infant's sensual development are probably the body contact, cuddling, and caressing that accompany feeding rather than the actual source of nourishment (breast or bottle).

From birth on, male babies are capable of erections, and female babies are capable of vaginal lubrication. If erections are not observed during waking hours, they may be seen during the stage of sleep accompanied by rapid eye movement (REM). REM sleep is associated with dream states in children and adults, and erections in males frequently appear during these periods of dreaming. *Reality or Myth*

The signs of infant eroticism—erections and lubrication—are primarily reflexive during the first year of life; that is, touching or brushing the genital area may bring about a "sexual" reflex. The infant does not, as far as we know, fantasize or purposely try to bring about erection or lubrication. Yet there are exceptions. According to one report (Kinsey et al., 1953), six infants under 1 year of age were observed masturbating. In general, however, genital fondling by infants is not goal directed, as is adult masturbation. For infants and young children, touching or rubbing the penis or vulva is a generally pleasurable activity like many other sensuous pursuits,

Cuddling and hugging between adults may have its roots in early contacts between parents and their babies.

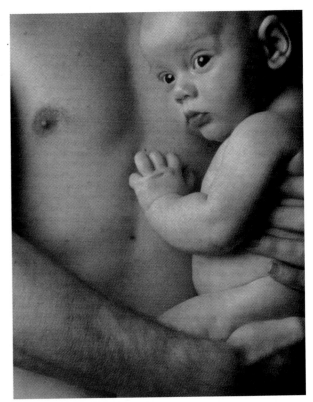

such as sucking their fingers and playing with their toes. Only as they mature do children start to masturbate with the intent to have orgasm. Some preliminary reports of children in their first year suggested little or no difference between boys and girls in the frequency of autoerotic play (Roiphe & Galenson, 1981).

PARENTAL REACTIONS TO EARLY SENSUALITY

Our cultural norm of segregating the sexual from the rest of our experience begins during infancy. Most parents make a happy fuss over their infant's discovery of his or her own toes, ears, and fingers. But if they make a fuss over the discovery of the penis or the vulva, it is not likely to be a happy or positive fuss. Parents either ignore the discovery, or they actively discourage genital exploration by moving the little fingers or covering the genitals with a diaper. What significance do infants attach to the fact that when they suck on their toes, their parents imitate their behavior and also suck on their infants' toes, but when they pull on the labia or penis, parents do not laughingly join in?

Assumptions that humans naturally differentiate between the genital and nongenital explorations of their infants and naturally avoid any genital contact with infants are not supported by evidence from other cultures (Frayser, 1994). Not only are self-exploration and stimulation accepted in many societies, but in some cultures adults use genital fondling as a method of soothing cranky babies. Mothers in Trinidad, for example, massage their infant's genitals to calm them and induce sleep.

Certain learning experiences during infancy may be important for developing the capacity to give and receive erotic pleasure in adulthood. Many expressions of tenderness between parents and their offspring—snuggling, hugging, stroking, and caressing—are similar to intimate behaviors between adults. People who receive little sensual contact during infancy and childhood often have difficulty in accepting and giving tenderness when they grow up. Many of the techniques that sex therapists employ can be viewed as attempts to teach inhibited adults how to recapture the pleasure of sensual interaction.

Early Childhood

During the first year of life, children are highly dependent. At some point before the end of their first year or shortly into the beginning of their second, however, babies demonstrate rapidly rising levels of physical and verbal competency. The early childhood stage covers the ages of 18 months to 3 years.

Erikson (1982) described the challenge of this second stage as the conflict of autonomy versus shame and doubt. The child's task at this developmental stage is to form a sense of autonomy and a balance between it and feelings of shame and doubt. Children who are encouraged to develop their competencies in a protective environment begin to acquire a sense of autonomy, or the ability to direct and control themselves. Too much protectiveness and interference thwart the toddler's developing sense of competency; too little protection may cause a toddler to experience the world as a painful and unsafe place. In the first case, the child experiences shame, and in the other, doubt.

LANGUAGE, GENDER, AND SEXUALITY

A baby quickly acquires a sense of being either male or female through interaction with adults and older children. By the time children begin to talk (generally between the first and third years), they can apply the appropriate gender label to themselves. By recogniz-

gender identity—the feeling or conviction that one is a male or a female.
gender roles—the traits and behaviors expected of males and females in a particular culture.
gender-role identification—the process by which individuals incorporate behaviors and characteristics of a culturally defined gender role into their own personalities.

ing basic differences between genders, children begin to grasp the concept of **gender identity.**

A baby girl assigned a female gender at birth will perceive and describe herself as a girl, thereby developing a female gender identity by the time she is 3 years old. She learns the behaviors that are expected of females in her culture and incorporates these behaviors into her personality. As she learns about becoming a female, she is learning about **gender roles.** As she gradually assumes the characteristics of this role, she is acquiring a **gender-role identification.**

By this time, children may have already learned to differentiate between their sexual anatomy and other parts of the body. When such differentiation begins to occur, parents are likely to bolster a child's impression that there is something mysteriously taboo about the genital regions. Children may note that whereas parents are willing to provide such labels as "nose" and "eyes," they consistently appear reluctant to say "penis" and "vagina." Some parents give minimal information, labeling the entire genital area "your bottom," "your privates," or "down there." Others refuse to provide any label, saying instead, "Never mind."

TOILET TRAINING AND GENDER: DIFFERENCES IN SEXUAL ASSOCIATIONS

Within a few months of their second birthday, toddlers begin to demonstrate some rudimentary control of their sphincter muscles, so they are able to deposit their urine and feces in whatever place the culture deems appropriate. Parents employ a variety of toilet-training techniques, but a common theme in parental instruction in our culture is an emphasis on the dirtiness of feces and urine. Long after children have learned appropriate places to eliminate bodily wastes, they may retain the accompanying lesson that the genital area is bad, dirty, and not to be touched for fear of contact with smelly and filthy bodily discharges. This association can be seen in our culture's labeling of sexual stories, allusions, or jokes as "dirty."

Both boys and girls are taught the association between dirt and the genitals, but two differences may account for different sexual attitudes and behaviors of boys and girls.

In general, little boys are dressed in more rugged

and easily washed clothing than little girls are, and as they play, little boys are expected to get "dirty" to a greater extent than are little girls. The phrase "dirty little boy" does not have as negative a connotation as the phrase "dirty little girl." Ironically, the association of gender and dirt changes later in the life span; rarely are elderly women referred to as "dirty old women," but a "dirty old man" is someone to avoid.

Although the genitals often are linked with dirtiness for both boys and girls, having the characteristic of dirtiness is traditionally a far more serious offense for girls than for boys. The vaginal douche and deodorant industries thrive on the concerns of adolescent and adult women about the cleanliness and odor of their vaginas. In most grocery stores, signs alert customers to the location of the shelves devoted to products for "feminine hygiene." One searches in vain for corresponding "masculine hygiene" sections; there is no parallel marketing of products for hygiene of the penis or scrotum. Thus it would seem that whereas women need chemical aids to be hygienic and clean, men do not have such problems!

Typically, boys are taught to wipe themselves with toilet paper after they defecate but not after they urinate. The fact that a few drops of urine may get on their son's clothing is not a matter of great concern to most parents. In fact, the tolerance of males' urine was immortalized in the old saying

You can shake it, you can break it,
you can bang it on the wall,
but when you put it in your pants,
that last drop is sure to fall!

▶ **Issues to Consider:** Do you think there are ways of minimizing the association between "dirty" and the genitals that arises during childhood?

Conversely, little girls are taught always to wipe themselves after using the toilet. Because differentiating the urethra from the clitoris and the vagina from the anus is considerably more difficult than differentiating the penis from the anus, girls may assume that the urethra, clitoris, and vagina are all dirty. When they reach puberty, many girls are taught that menstrual bleeding is unclean, an idea further reinforcing

Some parents insist that their young children be clothed at all times, whereas others consider nudity acceptable under certain conditions. These children have the opportunity to observe other children nude and therefore may have healthier and more positive attitudes about the human body.

the connection between the genitals and dirt for females. The association of dirtiness with the reproductive organs can lead to significant problems with sexual expression later in life.

AWARENESS OF GENDER DIFFERENCES

Toddlers can label accurately the gender of others, apparently based on external appearances stemming from gender-role norms, such as hair styles and clothing (Fagot, 1995; Katz, 1996). In their interview study with children, Ronald and Juliette Goldman (1982) found that most children under the age of 9 were unable to give an accurate description of how to tell whether a newborn baby was a boy or a girl.

There is, however, considerable difference from one culture to another and from one child to another in awareness of genital differences. This variation suggests that such awareness is at least partially due to differences in the opportunities children have to observe males and females. One little boy we know had apparently been oblivious to any anatomical difference among his sisters, his parents, and himself, despite the fact that he had been taking baths with one or another family member since birth. One day shortly before his second birthday, when he and his mother were taking a bath, he began to stare at her vulva. A look of great consternation came over his face, and he asked, "Where penis?"

 **reschool Years**

According to Erikson, the crisis and opportunity of ages 3 to 5 involves the conflict of initiative versus guilt. Whether children emerge from this stage with their sense of initiative favorably outbalancing their sense of guilt depends largely on how adults respond to the children's self-initiated activities.

Both Erikson and Freud believed that during this stage, the child begins to internalize reprimands and prohibitions from authorities. Thus authority figures are no longer necessary to evoke shame over the youngster's wrongdoing. The child's own internal sense of right and wrong becomes important in guiding behavior.

Freud believed that boys' internalization of parental moral values was more complete than was girls'.

He thought that this supposedly greater morality in boys resulted from their higher anxiety, arising from fear of castration by their fathers as punishment for boys' intense attraction to their mothers—the Oedipus complex. To resolve the conflict between their attraction to their mother and fear of their father, boys internalize their father's beliefs and values by the time they are about 5 years old. Although Freud wrote that girls also feel attraction to their fathers—the Electra complex—they have less to fear, because they had supposedly already been punished by castration. Thus, they internalize their mother's values with less intensity and develop less of a conscience.

In contrast with Freud's theory about the development of values and morality, however, females appear to be more controlled by societal dictates than do males, a gender difference that social learning theorists attribute to the different ways in which they are socialized rather than to the possession of a penis or a clitoris. Social learning theorists believe that children continue throughout their development to build associations of positive and negative consequences to their behavior; thus, they learn to engage in some acts and avoid others.

GENDER-ROLE SOCIALIZATION

The process of **gender-role socialization** occurs throughout childhood and adolescence as the child is influenced by the family, peer group, and school system. The behavior and traits seen as characteristic of masculinity or femininity are culturally defined.

The specific traits and behaviors expected of males and females vary from one culture to the next. In our culture, males have been expected to be active, aggressive, athletic, and unemotional. Females have been expected to be passive, nurturant, yielding, emotional, and gentle. In New Guinea, though, among the Mundugamor, aggressiveness is expected and observed in both men and women. In contrast, the mountain-dwelling Arapesh women and men of New Guinea both behave in ways that are traditionally associated with feminine gender-role expectations in our culture. Among the lake-dwelling Tchambuli of that island, the traditional roles of our culture are reversed, with females being aggressive and males being gentle and nurturant (Mead, 1935). Although Margaret Mead's research has been criticized for inaccuracies and oversimplification (Freeman, 1983), it still remains an important work on the interplay between culture and gender.

Both parents usually engage in differentiation based on the gender of their offspring, but distinctions that fathers make are more pronounced than those that mothers make. Fathers rate their sons as being better coordinated, hardier, and stronger than their daughters. In their observations of groups of 3-year-old boys and girls and their parents, Jacklin, DiPietro, and Maccoby (1984) found

that father-son pairs displayed higher levels of rough-and-tumble play than any other parent-child combination. They concluded that fathers assume more of a role than do mothers in socializing their children to play according to traditional gender roles (Maccoby, 1998).

If you have observed parents interacting with their children, you may wonder about the effectiveness of such gender-role training. To the casual observer, some 4-year-old girls appear to be quite resistant to parental attempts to encourage them to remain neat and clean, a stereotypically feminine behavior. Similarly, it may seem to you that the crying howl of the frustrated or hurt little boy is so loud that he could not possibly hear his parents' admonition that "big boys don't cry." Nonetheless, such parental efforts to push little boys and girls into gender-stereotypic attitudes and behaviors are not only effective but also begin to show their effects early in life.

GENDER SIMILARITIES AND DIFFERENCES VERSUS GENDER STEREOTYPES

Some additional concepts are important to understanding gender similarities and differences. A **gender difference** is a reliable difference between the average male and the average female that has been scientifically observed when large groups of males and females have been studied. For example, the average female reports lower levels of interest in sexuality than does the average male. It is important to realize, however, that even where gender differences exist, the groups generally overlap. For example, the distribution of sexual interest and outlets in females overlaps the distribution of these variables in males. Some females report greater interest in sexuality than do the average male, and some males report lower levels of interest than do the average female (Baldwin & Baldwin, 1997). So knowledge of someone's sex does not allow us to predict his or her level of sexual interest.

gender-role socialization—the training of children by parents and other caretakers to behave in ways considered appropriate for their sex.

gender differences—differences in physique, ability, attitude, or behavior found between large groups of males and females.

overlapping distribution—a statistical term describing situations in which the levels of a variable for some members of two groups are the same, although a difference exists between the average levels of the particular variable for the two groups.

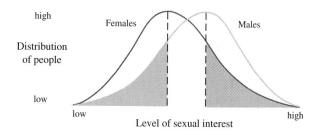

Figure 12.2   Overlapping Distribution in Sexual Interest

Such **overlapping distributions** (see Figure 12.2) characterize many aspects of gender and sexual behaviors as well, including sexual appetite, speed of arousal and orgasm, frequency of masturbation, and desire for sexual variety. Nonetheless, it is commonly believed that males have larger sexual appetites than do females. Such a belief about the characteristics of a person based on his or her gender is a **gender stereotype.** A gender stereotype may be accurate or inaccurate. For example, the stereotype that females are less likely to masturbate than males, or at least to report masturbating, has been supported by research (Laumann et al., 1994; Leitenberg et al., 1993). In contrast, the gender stereotype that females are less

aroused by explicit sexual material has not been supported by contemporary research (Laan & Everaerd, 1995). Regardless of the accuracy or inaccuracy of a given gender stereotype, we cannot use it as a basis for predicting the behavior of a particular male or female because of the overlapping distribution of gender characteristics and sexual behavior in males and females. *Reality or Myth* ❓

SEXUAL LEARNING

Just as they display a keen interest in learning about how to be a boy or girl in their culture, most children also reveal a marked curiosity about sexuality during their preschool years. Discouraging and punishing their sexual exploration will lead children to feel guilty about sex. Acknowledging children's curiosity without ridiculing or inhibiting fantasy activity fosters a sense of competence and encourages assertiveness.

The capacity for self-stimulation and orgasm seems to be potentially available to most children by the age of 5. Kinsey and his colleagues (1953) estimated that almost all boys could have orgasm, but without ejaculation, three to five years before reaching puberty, and more than half could reach orgasm

Young children cuddle and hug in imitation of adult affection.

by 3 to 4 years of age. Equivalent systematic research is lacking for girls. *Reality or Myth* 3

During the preschool years, children's sexuality becomes more social. Children kiss, hug, or hold hands in obvious imitation of adults. Much of their curiosity about sexuality is woven into their play. This play facilitates their intellectual and social development, permitting them to explore their environment, learn about objects, and solve problems. Through acting out roles in fantasy play, children learn to understand others and practice roles they will assume as they grow older. They can test without fear the outer limits of what is acceptable. In our culture, much of children's curiosity about their own and others' bodies is expressed through such well-known games as "playing house" and "playing doctor."

THE PRIMAL SCENE: PSYCHOSEXUAL TRAUMA OR SEX EDUCATION?

A child's witnessing of parental lovemaking is referred to as the **primal scene.** Many psychoanalytic therapists believe that this experience can have traumatic effects on a child's psychosexual development. This belief stems, in part, from reports of therapy patients who said that they were shocked and horrified during childhood when they stumbled on their parents having sexual intercourse. Inferences were then made about an association between such exposure and the problems that brought these patients into therapy. However, there is no empirical evidence linking accidental observation of parental lovemaking with subsequent psychological harm (Okami, 1995; Okami, Olmstead, Abramson and Pendleton, 1998). Although they were not directly investigating the impact of the observation of parental lovemaking on offspring, Lewis and Janda (1988) found that the current sexual adjustment of college students was unrelated to the extent of their childhood memories of parental nudity, exposure to nudity in general, and sleeping in the parents' bed.

Given these results, we speculate that the effects of observing parental sexual activity depend on the general family environment. If parents tend to be extremely private about their affection, avoiding any touching, hugging, or kissing except when they are alone; if they avoid any nudity; and if they punish their child's interest in and exploration of his or her

primal scene—a child's observations of parental coitus.

own body, children who observe their parents making love witness a host of new experiences: nudity and parental contact plus the specific behaviors associated with sexual activity. Children raised in such a household could have even more difficulty interpreting the primal scene if parents scold them and angrily send them out of the room, or if they avoid giving any sort of explanation. It would seem reasonable for such children to have fearful reactions, perhaps interpreting the event as a violent one in which the parents are hurting each other.

In contrast, a child reared in a generally less restrictive atmosphere has fewer new experiences to interpret. Upon discovering his or her parents having intercourse, the child might be likely to ask a question already posed in numerous other circumstances: "What're you doing?" If the parents respond with something like, "We're cuddling; do you want to come cuddle for a few minutes before you go back to bed?" the child's reaction will probably not be much different from his or her response if the parents were snuggling fully clothed on the couch while watching television when the child wandered in. Parents who opt for this alternative need not worry about the child's seeing the father's erection, because loss of erection is notoriously rapid when a man is startled or interrupted. Thus, the father's penis would probably be quite flaccid long before the child could climb into bed.

CHILDREN'S SEXUAL KNOWLEDGE

A major study by Ronald and Juliette Goldman (1982) yielded some fascinating information about children's developing understanding of sexuality. The Goldmans interviewed 838 children in Australia, Britain, Canada, Sweden, and the United States whose ages ranged from 5 to 15 years. Among the 63 questions the Goldmans asked was, "How can anyone know a newborn baby is a boy or a girl?" They also asked how boys and girls grow differently as they get older. The Goldmans suggested that if Freud's hypotheses are correct regarding the Oedipal conflict, its resolution at about age 5, and latency (the subsequent period of so-called sexual disinterest and inactivity),

one would expect many 5-year-olds to be aware of sexual differences and to show relatively little embarrassment when asked the question about newborn babies, and for inhibitions to occur strongly at 7 years with recognition of differences being repressed until about 10 or 11 years of age. A similar observation might be made about castration fears, but there is little evidence for these in the responses of the sample. (p. 194)

Presumably children who were afraid of being castrated or believed themselves to be already castrated would be aware of the physical differences between males and females. However, at the age of 5, a large majority of the children in the four English-speaking countries gave responses that demonstrated no awareness of genital differences, whereas less than half (43 percent) of the Swedish children did so. Thus, there is little evidence for the occurrence of the Oedipal or Electra complexes among children in this study. Nor

▶ **Issues to Consider:** How does the Goldmans' study on children's sexual knowledge cast doubt on Freud's theory of the Oedipal and Electra complexes?

do these findings support Freud's idea that genital anxieties or envies motivate children to accept as their own the values and attitudes of their same-sex parents.

This variation between the English-speaking children and the Swedish children may stem from differences in the educational policies of these cultures. In 1956 Sweden instituted mandatory sex education in school from kindergarten on and also emphasized gender-role egalitarianism in its educational system. In contrast, more than four decades later, the English-speaking countries are still debating the content of sex education programs beginning in elementary or middle school. Thus, it should not be surprising that the majority of children are unaware of genital differences between males and females until the age of 9.

PHYSICAL ATTRACTIVENESS

Although preschool children may be unaware of genital differences between males and females, they do ap-

This little girl is learning that wearing makeup is part of the Western idea of female sexual appeal.

pear to notice physical attractiveness. The strong connection in most cultures between physical attractiveness and sexual desirability may have its roots in early childhood. This link, which is exploited in our culture in most communications media and especially in advertising, equates "sex appeal" with our cultural standards of physical attractiveness (see Chapter 20). According to social learning theorists, such learned associations explain the relationship of physical appearance to sexual attraction. In contrast, evolutionary theorists believe that tendencies to evaluate and choose people on the basis of their physical appearance and characteristics have an evolutionary basis. Specifically, ancestors who mated with persons possessing physical characteristics such as smooth skin and shiny hair may have had greater reproductive success than those who chose partners without such characteristics (Buss, 1999; Symons, 1979). According to this perspective, these characteristics are associated with general physical health and thus greater fitness for reproduction. As mentioned in Chapter 6, attractive people who possess average, symmetrical bodies have been found to be fairly resistant to parasites and various diseases (Gangestad, Thornhill, & Yeo, 1994).

Children as young as 2 months old differentiate between slides of attractive and unattractive female faces (Langlois et al., 1987). These infants spent more time looking at the attractive faces than they did the unattractive faces. Because these slides were rated as to their attractiveness by college students, it appears that infants and adults use similar standards in evaluating others' attractiveness. Children as young as 3 to 5 years old attribute positive qualities and abilities to attractive individuals and negative qualities and abilities to unattractive individuals, just as adults do (Ecker & Weinstein, 1983; Langlois & Roggman, 1990). Because preferences for physically attractive faces emerge so early in development, evolutionary theorists have suggested that recognition of correlates of health such as facial and body symmetry—how closely each side of the face and body matches the other—may be part of our genetic heritage (see Chapter 6).

Furthermore, the ways in which others treat and respond to children are influenced by the attractiveness of the children. Some research has suggested that children with unattractive body builds or faces may indeed develop the undesirable characteristics attributed to them because of their looks (Langlois & Casey, 1984). In other words, these children may learn to behave in a manner that is consistent with others' expectations. As they become older, they may generalize these negative feelings about themselves to include their sexuality. Misled by the cultural myth that only the physically attractive are sexually appealing, they may doubt their desirability as sexual beings.

Middle to Late Childhood

In modern industrialized societies, the child's world expands dramatically with entrance into school. By the sixth year of life, children spend a large portion of their day in the company of peers rather than with family members.

The developmental task of late childhood (ages 5 to 11 years), according to Erikson, is to strike a balance within the personality by resolving the conflict of industry versus inferiority. For children who are essentially trusting, autonomous, and able to take initiative, there is now the opportunity to be responsible for schoolwork and other school-related activities. If parents and other caretakers respond positively to the child's work, his or her self-confidence continues to develop. Conversely, sarcastic and derogatory responses undermine the child's sense of industry, lead-

ing to a feeling of inferiority instead. If children doubt their skill or status among their peers, they may become discouraged from pursuing further learning.

Freud described the ages of 6 to 11 as a period of latency, that is, a time of disinterest and inactivity regarding sexuality. However, the empirical evidence has not supported this idea. Let us examine children's behavior during this stage.

SEXUAL REHEARSAL

Childhood sexual play among many of the primates—the order of mammals that includes monkeys, apes, and humans—appears to serve as a rehearsal for adult sexual behavior. Such play has been observed among the young of many cultures in situations where it was not inhibited by adults (Ford & Beach, 1951; Frayser, 1994). The aborigines of Australia's northern coast, for example, had no taboo against infantile sexuality until they came into contact with Western ideas. Aborigine children aged 5 or 6 engaged in coital-positioning play. Adults responded to these childhood rehearsals with amusement: "Isn't it cute? They will know how to do it right when they grow up" (Money, 1976, p. 13).

We do not know why some children engage in such rehearsal of adult sexual interaction. Perhaps it is a natural developmental stage that all children would act out if they were not inhibited. Of the Kinsey group's (1948, 1953) sample, 57 percent of the men and 48 percent of the women reported memories of some sex play, mostly between ages 8 and 13.

Even with cultural prohibitions against children's sex play, almost half of the children in a longitudinal study were reported by their parents in interviews to have engaged in interactive sex play before age 7 (Okami, Olmstead, & Abramson, 1997). There was no association between engaging in sex play in childhood and psychological adjustment at ages 17 to 18.

I (E.R.A.) have asked students in my large undergraduate human sexuality course about their experiences in "playing doctor" or engaging in exploratory sex play with other children when they were young. Responding anonymously, about a fifth of the men and a little more than a third of the women reported having engaged in such play during childhood with others of the same sex. Of the students who reported such experiences, men had their first experience at about an average age of 11; women's average age was about 8. Sex play was more common with children of the other sex: about two-thirds of the men (average age, about 10) and half of the women (average age, about 8.5) reported these activities.

Interest in these games and discussions may be fueled to some extent by parents' failure to provide children with explicit information about sexual anatomy, the absence of opportunities in traditional families for casual observations of parents and siblings when they are nude, and children's feeling inhibited about asking family members for information about sexuality. These percentages may represent an upper estimate of such play and discussions in that students who elect to take human sexuality courses may be more likely to feel comfortable in reporting these experiences. Most sexual activity in childhood tends to cen-

ter around discovering and playing with one's own body or those of peers. For example, 61 percent of college students in one study reported that they had had some sexual experience with another child before the age of 13 (Leitenberg, Greenwald, & Tarran, 1989). When these students were compared to students who reported no sexual experience with another child before age 13, there were no differences between the two groups in sexual adjustment during young adulthood. In general, the occurrence or nonoccurrence of sexual activity with another child has little association with later sexual behavior. Even when the sexual activity involved a sibling, as happened in 17 percent of the cases, there was no apparent connection to sexual adjustment in young adulthood (Greenwald & Leitenberg, 1989).

▶ **Issues to Consider:** What would you do if you discovered that your 8-year-old-child was engaging in sex play with another child?

Perhaps because the threat or use of force was almost nonexistent in the reports of students in this research, negative outcomes were minimal. Other studies have shown negative reactions to preadolescent sexual activity with siblings when there were larger age differences between the siblings and if force was used to obtain sexual contact (Finkelhor, 1980). Despite our cultural beliefs about the detrimental effects of such preadolescent contacts, current research indicates little relationship between these experiences and the sexual adjustment of young adults, provided that force was not involved.

HOMOSOCIALITY

Young people begin to broaden their social contacts as they move into seventh grade and beyond. Cliques—small groups of intimate friends—become important. These tend to be same-sex groups in late childhood and early adolescence, becoming heterosexual in the later stages of adolescence, although many teenagers belong to both kinds of groups. Sharp differentiation of masculine and feminine gender roles, and the development of competence in interpersonal relationships, are facili-

homosociality—a period in middle and late childhood in which social and personal activities are centered around members of the same sex.

During preadolescence, Western children tend to confine their social relationships to others of the same gender.

tated by close association with same-sex peers. This sex segregation is called **homosociality**. It usually begins around age 8 and peaks in late childhood, at about ages 10 to 13. During this time, children may express considerable distaste for children of the other sex.

Because children play almost exclusively with members of their own sex, it is not surprising to find that homosexual behavior is more common during this period than later in adolescence (Leitenberg et al., 1989). Homosexual activities are a common element in sexual development in our culture, and such experiences seldom determine one's orientation toward sexual partners of the same or other sex in adulthood (Bell, Weinberg, & Hammersmith, 1981; Van Wyk & Geist, 1984). Fearing this possibility, however, parents who find their children in sexual exploration with other children of the same sex may attach adult meanings to the activity. Inappropriate overreactions by parents may be one of the sources of the widespread negativity toward same-sex contacts and homosexuality, an attitude known as anti-gay prejudice. *Reality or Myth* ❓

Some of this same-sex (and other-sex) exploration play stems from an intrinsic curiosity about sexuality. Unfortunately for young children, the rela-

tive neglect of sex education in North America may increase such exploration, producing guilt and secretiveness about sexuality.

SEX EDUCATION

The arguments advanced by those who oppose sex education reflect an unstated assumption: that we can choose whether children and adolescents receive sex education. It should be amply clear from the evidence discussed so far that children learn about sex from birth on, although the accuracy of their knowledge varies considerably as a function of the source and goals of that education.

During childhood, some information and many attitudes about sex are acquired in the course of learning sexual slang. Children's informal learning of a sexual vocabulary often takes place without their associating the words with sexual activity. A host of other meanings and associations may be linked to formal sexual terms. Children learn and use sexual slang terms, such as *fuck* and *queer*, for example, without a sense of their sexual meanings or the physical activities they entail.

Their use of these words, however, is charged with emotion that is often hostile or aggressive in nature. Slang phrases for such concepts as coitus and fellatio, for example, are frequently used to indicate dislike and verbal hostility. "Screw you!" and "cocksucker," for instance, are seldom used publicly as expressions of endearment. The hostile associations with sex words may influence the child's perception of sexuality far into adulthood.

It is difficult for many children to make sense of sexuality, and many wonder why it is so important and yet so shrouded in secrecy. Most children hear about sexual intercourse and its connection to pregnancy by the age of 8 or 9. Many of them associate the processes of coitus and birth with the anus. This natural association is reflected in a statement by St. Augustine: *Inter faeces et urinam nascimur* ("We are born between feces and urine"). Children's reaction to coitus as they perceive it may be one of shock, disbelief, and disgust. A friend of ours overheard his son discussing sex and reproduction with another boy, who explained that babies were caused by daddies' sticking their things into mommies' bottoms to plant seed, and a year later "the mommy poops out a baby." Our friend's son's reaction was, "Yuck!"

Another idea that children sometimes form about pregnancy is the "digestive fallacy." The Goldmans (1982, p. 49) described it in this way: "Mother eats food and she becomes fat. The food is the baby and it comes out where food normally comes out, through the anus." Such inaccurate explanations were given by the majority of North American children in the Goldmans' study until around the age of 11. At that age, 50 percent gave accurate descriptions, and at age

13, 79 percent did so. It is clear from this research that in the absence of information about sex and reproduction, children devise their own explanations.

Various studies have shown that the majority of respondents would choose to get their sex education from their parents. However, in samples of people ranging in age from 9 to over 50 years of age, only 10 percent of males and 16 percent of females listed "parent" as their primary source of information about sexuality (Ansuini, Fiddler-Woite, & Woite, 1996). Because parents do not provide sufficient details about sex, most young people seek information elsewhere.

When parents and children communicate about sexuality, it appears that attitudes and values rather than facts are generally conveyed. The sexual knowledge of children who learned about sex at home has not been found to be superior to that of children who learned about sex from other sources (Fisher, 1986).

When sex education courses are offered in the public schools, fewer than 3 percent of parents refuse to let their children participate, and Gallup polls indicate widespread support among both teachers and the general public for such courses (Caron, 1998). As of 1999, only twenty states, plus the District of Columbia, had mandated school-based sexuality education. In contrast, the majority of states (35 states and the District of Columbia) have mandated the provision of education on sexually transmitted diseases and human immunodeficiency virus (STD/HIV). We find this difference ironic, in that it is difficult to imagine how anyone could provide good STD/HIV education without covering various topics relevant

Most young people seek sex information from sources other than their parents, such as their friends and magazines.

to sexual activity, specific sexual acts, ways to reduce risk, and so forth. Several studies of the effects of these courses indicate that they improve the accuracy of students' knowledge about sex but do not necessarily produce major changes in sexual attitudes and values (Kirby, Barth, Leland, & Fetro, 1991). The importance of sex education, whether at home or school, has been underlined by statistics on adolescent sexual activity and contraceptive use.

Much has been written, particularly in the popular press, about high levels of sexual permissiveness among adolescents today. The attention is understandable, for research consistently shows that by age 16, the majority of North American adolescents have engaged in coitus and a variety of other sexual activities (Coley & Chase-Lansdale, 1998; Day, 1992; King et al., 1988; Laumann et al., 1994). Higher proportions of boys than of girls initiate early intercourse (see Table 12.2). Predictors of having first sex by age 14 are having a mother who began having sex at an early age and who has worked extensively outside the house (Mott, Fondell, Hu, Kowaleski-Jones, & Menaghan, 1996).

Scientific and societal interpretations of increased adolescent sexual activity vary considerably. Some people consider increases in adolescent sexual expression, including masturbation, to be symptomatic of a decadent society; they voice concern that such early "self-indulgence" leads to promiscuity, an inability to form permanent relationships, and soaring divorce rates. Taking a different view, others maintain that because the onset of sexual maturity (from a biological perspective) occurs in early adolescence, cultural restrictiveness regarding masturbation and nonmarital sexual interaction is unrealistic.

TABLE 12.2	Cumulative Percentages of Adolescents Who Have Become Sexually Active by a Given Age		
Age	Boys	Girls	Total
13	14.7	2.7	8.6
14	24.6	10.8	17.7
15	35.0	27.3	31.2
16	63.1	47.1	54.9
17	72.1	65.8	68.6

Source: Mott et al. (1996)

Adolescents are usually anxious and awkward during their initial experiences with sexual and quasi-sexual contact. Many of their early dates may be seen as practice for the more serious pairing that occurs later in adolescence. Through self-stimulation, experimentation with same-gender friends, behavioral scripts provided by the culture (for example, through peers and the media), and increasingly intimate sexual interactions, adolescents gradually learn to express their sexual feelings.

In response to these trends toward early onset of sexual activity, hundreds of sexuality education curricula have been implemented in middle and high schools in the United States in the past two decades (Kirby et al., 1991). They can be broadly characterized as employing one of two approaches. One teaches sexual abstinence until marriage and avoids discussing methods for responsible nonmarital (or even marital) sexual activity, including contraception for couples who do not wish to conceive and use of condoms to reduce the risk of disease. The other approach emphasizes postponement of early sexual involvement but provides education for responsible sexual contacts when couples decide they are ready to have sex.

Abstinence-Only Programs. The abstinence-only approach in the United States has received political backing and major funding from the federal govern-

Quasisexual contact is a rehearsal for later activity.

RESEARCH SPOTLIGHT | **The Relationship Between the Provision of Sex and Contraceptive Education and Unwanted Pregnancies in Western Nations**

The quality of sex and contraceptive education and the timing of its provision vary dramatically among Western nations. Elise Jones and her colleagues (1986, 1988) examined teenage pregnancy rates in 37 developed countries to isolate variables that might explain why teenage pregnancy rates are so much higher in the United States than in other Western nations (see the accompanying figure).

A culture's openness about sex is related to low rates of teenage pregnancy. Despite the soaring U.S. teen pregnancy statistics, the authors not only found the United States far less open about sex than most of the other countries, but also described the United States as having "an ambivalent, sometimes puritanical attitude about sex" (Jones et al., 1986, p. 230).

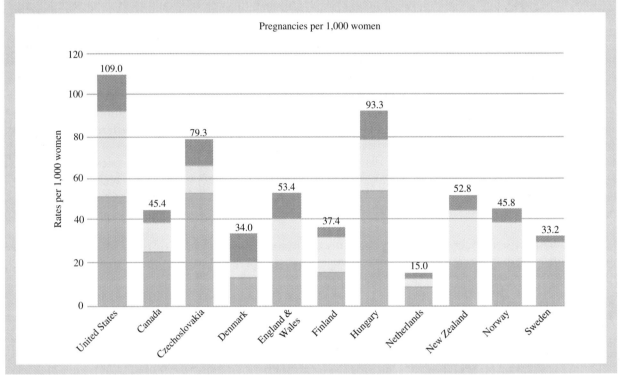

Pregnancies per 1,000 women

ment. This approach does not differentiate between those circumstances that promote pleasuring, bonding, and wanted procreation from those circumstances that expose persons to disease, coercion, and unwanted pregnancy.

Sex education foe Phyllis Schlafly, backed by her Eagle Forum organization, has appeared frequently on television to argue against sex education programs, claiming that the high levels of unintended adolescent pregnancy in the United States have been *caused* by school-based sex education. This stance is clearly contradicted by the cross-national study done by Elise Jones and her colleagues (1986; see "Research Spotlight: The Relationship Between the Provision of Sex and Contraceptive Education and Unwanted Pregnancies in West-

ern Nations") and by U.S. studies comparing the sexual behaviors and pregnancy rates of adolescents who have and have not received education about sex and contraception (Howard & McCabe, 1990; Kirby et al., 1991).

Unfortunately, the U.S. government has promoted abstinence to the exclusion of sex and contraceptive education. The Adolescent Family Life Act, passed in 1981, permitted the Office of Adolescent Pregnancy Programs to provide millions of dollars annually to fund projects for promoting abstinence from sexual interaction until marriage (Goodheart, 1992).

There has not been much systematic evaluation of the effectiveness of abstinence-only programs. What research does exist suggests that these programs are not only ineffective in delaying sexual initiation, but actually may be associated with earlier sexual initiation—the reverse effect from that intended (Christopher & Roosa, 1990; Roosa & Christopher, 1990).

Postponement and Protection Programs. Fortunately, there are other programs that include more thorough sex and contraceptive education. Outcome evaluations of these programs show considerably more promise, although they need to be refined and presented in more depth (Cagampang, Barth, Korpi, & Kirby, 1997; Kirby, Korpi, Barth, & Cagampang, 1997).

The longitudinal Reducing the Risk (RTR) program of Douglas Kirby and his colleagues (1997) is among the most well developed of the existing U.S. programs. This program directs instructors to describe social pressures to have sex, describing common "lines" that are used in the attempt to obtain sexual access, and to teach students to develop strategies and skills in response to social pressures to have sex. Students have opportunities to practice talking to one another about abstinence and contraception. The situations they are given to role-play increase in difficulty over the course of the program. The RTR program also gives students practice in obtaining contraceptive information from stores and clinics.

Kirby et al. (1997) found that this program, delivered in five sessions, each lasting about 45 to 60 minutes, produced changes in sexual attitudes and behaviors among seventh and eighth graders in California lasting three months after the presentations. Unfortunately, seven months after the program, none of the effects were sustained. Their results suggest that the program needs to carried out for more than five sessions if it is to have a lasting impact on young people's sexual behavior.

Other postponement and protection programs have shown the ability to delay sexual initiation, increase contraceptive use, and decrease pregnancy rates among adolescents (Frost & Forrest, 1995). These programs were most successful when aimed at younger people, before they had begun to engage in sexual activity with a partner. *Reality or Myth*

Regardless of their education for handling their emerging sexual feelings as they enter puberty, pubescent development occurs—and with it comes the capacity for procreation. We turn now to this stage in the life cycle.

> ► **Issues to Consider:** If you were on your local school board, what type of sex education, if any, would you support for your schools?

Adolescence

In the light of the fact that adolescence (roughly the years from ages 12 to 20) has been characterized as a time of turbulence, rebelliousness, and stress, the responses of young teenagers to two questions asked by the Goldmans (1982) are somewhat surprising. The Goldmans inquired, "What is the best time to be alive?" and then asked for reasons for the choices. Prior to age 13, children's responses were quite variable, but the majority of 13-year-old respondents chose the teenage years. Some of their reasons: "As a teenager, you're at your physical peak. It's a crucial time which decides what happens [to you] later. You've got your head together more. You know more about life than when you were younger. Your brain works better. You know what to expect" (p. 119).

The responses suggest that these teenagers were well on their way to achieving the solid self-concept that Erikson (1982) proposed is the developmental goal of this period: identity versus role confusion.

Erikson noted that the biological events of puberty bring on a physiological revolution (see Chapter 8), and he pointed out that the adolescent must contend with playing a variety of roles. One of the most profound is the acquisition of gender-role identification and its interaction with sexual roles.

If you have children or younger brothers and sisters at around puberty, you may remember with amusement one conspicuous aspect of their transition from childhood into adolescence. After years of relative unconcern about appearance, teenagers monopolize bathrooms and mirrors with astounding obsessiveness. Other family members may have difficulty obtaining even a few moments of privacy in the bathroom, let alone the opportunity for a bath, because the adolescent's third shower of the day has used up all the hot water.

The adolescent experiments with different roles and fantasies, just as he or she tries out clothing and hair styles. At this stage, the adolescent runs the risk of developing a fragmented identity: too much freedom may result in confusion about personal identity, but too little does not permit an exploration of role possibilities and may leave the adolescent ill equipped to deal with adult life. Erikson suggested that moderate levels of freedom, accompanied by structure and advice from parents and other caretakers, can help the adolescent to integrate his or her exploration of various roles into a coherent identity.

In contrast to Erikson, Freud emphasized the biological and genital changes of puberty. Freud called this period—in his framework, the last step in psychosexual development—the genital stage. He hypothesized a resurgence of sexual energy and activity with the onset of puberty. Freud also believed that adolescents experience renewed sexual interest in the parent of the other gender, which generally expresses itself in adolescent crushes on older people.

An emphasis on learned sexual behavior characterizes the approaches taken by such sociological theorists as Gagnon and Simon (1973; Gagnon, 1990). In their view, basic sexual roles and scripts gradually emerge during adolescence. Sexual fantasies develop, serving as rehearsals for eventual interactions and as ways of exploring different sexual scripts. Out of a relatively chaotic approach to sociosexual transactions, complicated sexual scripts emerge. The body parts that can be touched and the circumstances under which they can be caressed, as well as all the subtleties of dating, are incorporated into the adolescent's behavioral repertoire.

GENDER-ROLE IDENTIFICATION IN ADOLESCENCE

Attitudes and beliefs about appropriate behavior for males and females as a function of gender have changed remarkably in the past few decades, and as we will see, these changes are associated with attitudes about acceptable sexual behavior for men and women. Just three decades ago, behavioral scientists and mental health professionals alike assumed that mentally healthy women were quite different in their personality traits from mentally healthy men. Take a minute to rank yourself on the scale shown in Table 12.3 to get an idea of how gender-role identification was measured.

The developers of measures of gender-role identification made two major assumptions. First, they assumed that the checkmarks of a healthy woman should fall fairly close to the items on the left-hand side

of the scales, and those of a healthy adult man close to the right-hand side. Second, they presupposed that identification with masculine characteristics was the opposite of identification with feminine characteristics; that is, a person was either passive or active, yielding or stubborn. In reality, of course, most of us are yielding under some conditions and stubborn under others.

Armed with these measures, many therapists labeled men "psychologically disturbed" if some of their checkmarks fell to the left-hand side. Similarly, a woman ranking herself as "aggressive," "taking leadership roles," and so forth was considered to be in need of therapy. These people then might have undergone psychotherapy for "gender-role confusion" or "inappropriate gender-role identity." Although use of these labels represented an improvement over such phrases as "penis envy" to describe women who felt constrained by traditional gender roles, the concept that men and women are—or should be—distinctly different psychologically was still accepted without question.

Sandra Bem developed a gender-identity measure, the Bem Sex Role Inventory (1974), that treats identification with masculine traits as independent of identification with feminine traits. In Bem's scoring system, people who describe themselves as having masculine and feminine traits and behaviors in equal measure are called **androgynous.** Those who endorse characteristics traditionally associated with their biological sex are called **sex-typed** or **gender-typed.** Bem's both/and concept of psychological identification quickly replaced the either/or notion that had dominated earlier personality measures.

Bem and others using the scale found that androgynous people, regardless of their anatomical sex, responded more flexibly to a variety of situations. They could be nurturant when dealing with people in need and assertive when their rights were in danger of being violated. Sex-typed persons were more limited. Although they could respond readily with behaviors stereotypic of their gender, when a behavior

---

androgyny (ann-DRAW-jih-nee)—the ability of a person to express both stereotypically masculine and stereotypically feminine traits and behaviors; from the Greek *andro*, meaning "male," and *gyn*, meaning "female."

sex-typed identification (also called **gender-typed identification**)—incorporation into the personality of the behaviors and characteristics expected for one's sex in a particular culture, with avoidance of those characteristics expected of the other sex.

TABLE 12.3   Feminine or Masculine?

To use this scale, place a checkmark on each line at the point along the scale that most closely represents your personality.*

Passive	Active
Dependent	Independent
Like to take care of others	Don't like to take care of others
Yielding	Stubborn
Nonaggressive	Aggressive
Soft-spoken	Use harsh language

*We have placed the so-called masculine traits on one side and feminine traits on the other to make it easy to see the configuration of traits supposedly attributable to the "healthy" man or woman. In practice, the masculine and feminine traits are usually reversed on about half the scales so that they are counterbalanced.

or trait traditionally displayed by the other gender was more appropriate (for instance, nurturance in men, assertiveness in women), they were constrained and uncomfortable (Bem, 1975; Bem & Lenney, 1976; Bem, Martyna, & Watson, 1976).

▶ **Issues to Consider:** What are the advantages and disadvantages of being androgynous?

THE SEXUAL DOUBLE STANDARD

Although an enormous shift has occurred in attitudes toward premarital sexual expression in the past two decades, North Americans must still contend with a **sexual double standard**. Early studies indicated that both men and women accepted the idea of premarital sexual experience for men but not for women. Some more recent studies have found equal levels of approval for premarital sex for men and women (DeLamater & MacCorquodale, 1979), but other evidence suggests that it may be too soon to dismiss the double standard totally. Although it has become socially acceptable for both men and women to engage in premarital intercourse, men and women are stereotypically expected to play different roles in those encounters. Specifically, men are supposed to be the initiators of sexual interaction, whereas women set limits on the extent of the sexual contact.

Naomi McCormick (1979) studied the strategies that men and women use both to initiate and avoid

sexual intimacy. She asked students to imagine that they were alone with an attractive person with whom they had "necked" but not yet had sexual intercourse. The respondents indicated how they might influence that person to have sexual intercourse, as well as what strategies they would use to avoid having sex. When McCormick presented these same strategies to another group of volunteers, these participants rated the strategies for seeking intercourse as primarily employed by men and the strategies for avoiding sex as predominantly used by women. These differences appear to be due to different motivational systems. Men's motives for sexual intercourse more often include pleasure, fun, and physical reasons, whereas women's motives are more often based on love, commitment, and emotions (Buss, 1999; Carroll, Volk, & Hyde, 1985).

Do these beliefs accurately reflect gender-role behavior in sexual interactions today? Research results on this question are mixed, suggesting that we are in a state of transition regarding the influence of traditional gender-role stereotypes in sexual interactions. Men tend to hold more positive attitudes toward the idea of women's taking the initiative in dating and sexual intimacy than do women. Ilsa Lottes (1993) found that initiating sexual activity was becoming more common among college women.

Before they come to the end of adolescence, most people have begun having sexual intercourse. The

▶ **Issues to Consider:** Do you think a sexual double standard still exists in North America? Explain your answer.

sexual double standard—the belief that a particular behavior is acceptable for one sex but not for the other.

In the past, men were more likely to have first intercourse with a prostitute or casual partner, whereas contemporary adolescents, both males and females, generally have first coitus with a steady partner with whom they feel an emotional bond.

majority of adolescents today describe their first sexual partner as someone toward whom they felt emotional attachment or love (Miller, Christopherson, & King, 1993). In contrast, four decades ago men were more likely than they are currently to have first intercourse with a casual acquaintance or a prostitute. In reviewing research regarding the degree of commitment that people report toward their first sexual partner, DeLamater and MacCorquodale (1979) concluded that women have become more permissive. They engage in intercourse with men toward whom they feel affection rather than waiting until a love relationship develops or until they become engaged to marry. Conversely, men are becoming less permissive. They are more likely than they were formerly to have first intercourse with a person toward whom they feel emotional attachment or love. The net effect of these shifts is a reduction in

gender differences regarding the kind of relationship with the first coital partner.

The emotional responses of people to their first coital experience vary considerably (Abma, Driscoll, & Moore, 1998; Sprecher, Barbee, & Schwartz, 1995). Both men and women reported more anxiety, more pleasure, and less guilt when sex occurred in a voluntary, close relationship rather than in a casual one. What factors were associated with their positive or negative feelings about first intercourse? David Weis (1983) found that women were more likely to have positive feelings if they described their partner as loving, tender, and considerate than if they did not. Further, women who had had more dating partners and more noncoital sexual experience (necking, petting) prior to first coitus and those who were older at first intercourse were more likely to experience pleasure and less likely to experience anxiety during first coitus than were younger women with fewer dates and less noncoital sexual experience. Finally, there is one other finding from Weis's research that the sexually inexperienced may appreciate: the extent to which women perceived their partners as sexually experienced was *not* related to the women's pleasure, guilt, or anxiety. *Reality or Myth*

The motives for and experience of first intercourse are related to subsequent sexual behavior and current and future relationships (Cate, Long, Angera, & Draper, 1993). We will have more to say about gender roles and their relationship to sexual attitudes and behavior as we continue our examination of the development of sexuality across the life span. In the next chapter, we consider sexual intimacy during the adult life span, beginning with a discussion of the relationship between sexual and emotional intimacy.

SUMMARY OF MAJOR POINTS

1. Barriers to knowledge and theoretical perspectives. Information about sexuality early in the life span has been difficult to obtain, partly because of the belief that children are not sexual and partly because of taboos against asking children about their sexual feelings and behaviors.

2. Infantile sexuality. Infants are capable of responses that adults label as sexual, including erection and vaginal lubrication. But these responses are primarily reflexive, not intentional. Experiencing cuddling and sensual contact as an infant seems to be important in developing healthy adult sexuality.

3. Early childhood (18 months to 3 years). Parents convey attitudes about sexuality as they help their offspring develop language skills and bodily control of elimination. Casual genital stimulation occurs among children, but apparently without the goal of reaching orgasm. During early childhood, children learn their own gender and begin to demonstrate some awareness of gender differences, although they use such cues as hair and clothing styles rather than anatomical differences to determine whether others are male or female.

4. Preschool years (3 years to 5 years). At this stage, children show increasing independence and self-direction. Although they continue to need protection, their movement toward initiative must also be supported. During this period, children begin to internalize parental and societal expectations about "right" and "wrong" behavior.

5. Gender stereotypes versus gender differences. Research has demonstrated that males and females are more similar than they are different. Most attributes exist on overlapping distributions. Before accepting a cultural belief about a supposed gender difference, it is important to determine whether the difference exists and whether the difference characterizes all males and females or typifies the average male versus the average female.

6. Sexual exploration in childhood. During early childhood, children explore their environment, and their curiosity about sexuality is evident. They play quasi-sexual games and act out adult roles, but the majority do not connect differences in genital anatomy with maleness or femaleness. Variations in physical attractiveness, important in determining adult evaluations of others, begin to influence children in early childhood.

7. School-age children. During the elementary school years, sexual exploration with others may be stimulated more by curiosity than by arousal. Friendships at this age are primarily homosocial, and sexual play with children of the same sex is common. Freud's theory of latency—that children between ages 6 and 11 are uninterested in sex and are sexually inactive—is not supported by research. Instead, children appear to become increasingly interested in and curious about sexuality as they get older.

8. Sex education. Although children want to obtain information about human sexuality and reproduction, relatively few North American children enter puberty with accurate information about sexuality in general or about the changes occurring in their own bodies. Comparisons of abstinence-only programs with postponement and contraceptive protection programs suggest that the latter are more effective in encouraging young people to postpone sexual activity and to use contraceptives when they do become sexually intimate.

9. Adolescence. A primary task of adolescence is to begin the development of a coherent identity as a person. One aspect of this developmental stage involves people's acceptance of their society's gender roles—that is, gender-role identification. Research in the past few decades has suggested that androgyny—the incorporation of characteristics stereotypic of both masculinity and femininity into one's identity—may be beneficial for personality development.

10. The sexual double standard. The sexual double standard—the idea that premarital sex is acceptable for males but not for females—has been diminishing over the past several decades. Nonetheless, men are still expected to initiate initial sexual contact, and women are expected to set limits on the extent of sexual intimacy.

13

Sexuality in Adulthood

Reality or Myth?

1. *Cohabiting couples have sex more frequently than do married couples.*

2. *Married couples who are both employed have sex less frequently than do married couples in which only one partner works outside the home.*

3. *In countries that have been studied, financial problems are the most common reason for couples to divorce.*

4. *In general, women experience more severe emotional problems following the breakup of a relationship than do men.*

5. *Hormone replacement therapy alleviates the symptoms of male menopause.*

6. *Young married couples who have an active sex life are more likely to maintain regular sexual activity in their old age than are less sexually active young couples.*

The passage from adolescence to adulthood is often subtle and poorly marked, leaving the person concerned and sometimes confused about his or her identity and proper behavior. In this chapter, we examine the phases of exploring sexual behaviors and developing personal identities through which most adults pass. We also look at how sexuality in young adulthood relates to the eventual development of emotional intimacy and the commitment to a long-term relationship. Several lifestyle options are available to young heterosexual adults: marrying early, postponing marriage, cohabiting, and remaining single. Homosexual and bisexual persons also face the task of selecting among these lifestyle options, although homosexual marriage still faces imposing legal obstacles. We discuss what is known about the costs and benefits of each of these alternatives.

As is true in all societies, the vast majority of North Americans eventually marry, and many of those who do not marry form long-lasting intimate bonds in the absence of a marriage license (Buss, 1999; Laumann et al., 1994). Thus, the relationship of marriage to the level of sexual activity and satisfaction is also considered. We review research on extramarital affairs and examine how the quality of sexual expression bears on a couple's decision to separate and divorce. Factors related to postseparation adjustment are also discussed. Finally, we explore the relationship of sexual pleasure to biological, social, and psychological changes among middle-aged and elderly people.

Young Adulthood

The age at which adolescence ends and adulthood begins is not always clear. Is a 24-year-old graduate student who still depends on his parents for financial support an adult? Is an 18-year-old factory worker who supports herself and has her own apartment an adolescent? Becoming independent of one's parents usually signals the transition from adolescence to adulthood. People achieve such independence at different ages, depending in part on their educational and vocational aspirations.

Regardless of the exact age at which it begins, young adulthood brings new challenges. Erik Erikson described three stages of adulthood (see Table 13.1 on page 296). Erikson (1982) proposed that the major task young adults face is developing their capacity to be intimate. Having shaped a firm sense of identity during adolescence, the individual is now able to risk forming close bonds with other people.

Although long-term relationships, between married or unmarried partners, can enrich life and increase the individual's sense of purpose and value, such associations can also be experienced as threatening. A close attachment to another person provides someone with whom to celebrate successes and recover from disappointments. But for some people, the vulnerability that accompanies a close bond is

By late adolescence, most people have begun to establish relatively stable, if not necessarily permanent, emotional and sexual relationships.

too great a risk; another person can smother you, reject you, or let you down. Some individuals deal with the uncertainty by maintaining shallow levels of intimacy, either because they perceive close relationships as a source of entrapment or because they fear loss and rejection. Erikson described these persons as resolving the developmental crisis by maintaining iso-

lation. However, those who resolve the crisis through marriage are not necessarily any happier, as we discuss later.

The process of getting to know a potential partner for a long-term relationship is variously known as dating, going out, going together, or seeing someone. The phenomenon of dating as a means of selecting a marriage partner is a relatively recent social invention in the United States (circa 1920). Current trends in premarital sexual behavior and their related expectations seem to depend on the stage of development in the dating relationship as well as on gender-role stereotypes. John Roche (1986; see also Roche & Ramsby, 1993) conceptualized the progress of a dating relationship as a progression through five stages:

Stage 1: Couple dates without affection.

Stage 2: Couple dates with affection but not love.

Stage 3: Dating individuals consider themselves to be "in love."

Stage 4: Each individual dates the loved person exclusively.

Stage 5: Couple becomes engaged to marry.

Roche asked heterosexual college students and young adults to indicate what they considered to be proper sexual behavior, ranging from no physical contact to sexual intercourse, during these five stages. During the first three stages, men condoned greater permissiveness and reported that they engaged in significantly more sexual behavior than did women. In the last two stages, these gender differences diminished. Men and women agreed about the appropriateness of genital fondling and intercourse

TABLE 13.1   Erikson's Stages of Development During Adulthood

Age	Crisis or Stage	Sexual Expression and Capacities
Young adulthood (20–39)	Intimacy versus isolation	Sexual intimacy, capacity for reproduction[a]
Middle age (40–64)	Generativity versus stagnation	Parenting, adapting to the aging of the body
Old age (65→)	Ego integrity versus despair	Loss of many attributes considered attractive and sexual

[a] A person acquires the capacity for reproduction during puberty, but does not generally attain the emotional maturity and economic resources important for the process until young adulthood.

during stages 4 and 5, and large numbers of both sexes reported engaging in sexual intercourse during those stages. A substantially higher proportion of men reported receiving oral-genital stimulation at each dating stage.

A large majority of the students in Roche's study thought that sexual intercourse was acceptable for a couple who were "in love" and dating each other exclusively. It is important to note that both men and women reported greater permissiveness in their actual behavior than in their definitions of proper behavior (Laumann et al., 1994). DeBuono, Zinner, Daamen, and McCormack (1990) compared the prevalence of sexual intercourse among college women during 1975, 1986, and 1989 and found that in all years, 87 percent to 88 percent of the women had had coitus. Although AIDS has apparently not reduced the likelihood of premarital coitus, condom use had increased at each time period: 12 percent in 1975, 21 percent in 1986, and 41 percent in 1989. No differences were found, however, in the number of sexual partners or the likelihood of engaging in fellatio, cunnilingus, or anal sex.

The Relationship Between Sexual Intimacy and Emotional Intimacy

Although nonmarital sexual intimacy has become almost universal in North American culture, attitudes about this practice vary widely. Some individuals believe that early sexual intercourse is an effective and acceptable means by which couples can develop intimacy. Others assert that engaging in intercourse early in a relationship can hinder greater closeness and commitment.

Generally we lack the **longitudinal research** needed to answer questions about the role of early emotional and sexual intimacy in relationships. However, Letitia Anne Peplau, Zick Rubin, and Charles Hill (1977) examined dating couples over a two-year period during their sophomore and junior years of college. At the beginning of the study, the couples had been dating for an average of about eight months. Few of the 231 couples had made defi-

longitudinal research—research carried out with the same sample of people over a period of months or years.

nite plans to marry, although about a fifth of them were living together. On the basis of the couples' responses, the researchers identified three patterns of sexual behavior and emotional intimacy: sexually liberal (had coitus within a month of their first date), sexually moderate (waited to engage in coitus until later in their relationship), and sexually traditional (planned to avoid coitus until marriage).

The Peplau group (1977) was interested in the association between the timing of first coitus and the outcome of the relationship. At the end of two years, the researchers were able to obtain information about 221 of the original 231 couples. They found that 20 percent of them had married, and 34 percent of them were still dating. The remaining 46 percent of the couples had broken up. It may surprise you to learn that there was no association between the pattern of their sexual behavior when first contacted (coitus within a month, later coitus, or abstention) and the outcome of their relationship (marriage, dating, or separation) two years later. Peplau et al. found no evidence that sexual intimacy early in a relationship either short-circuits or encourages a long-term commitment. Similarly, abstinence was unrelated to the likelihood of developing a lasting relationship.

To what extent are norms shifting in other areas relevant to sexuality, relationship and family formation, and other lifestyle issues? We now turn to the available research on these questions.

▶ **Issues to Consider:** Based on what you know about these groups so far, which group do you expect to have the highest proportion of couples who ultimately married one another?

Lifestyle Choices and Shifting Norms

Young adults face major decisions regarding lifestyles, jobs or careers, and relationships. Their choices can have far-reaching consequences for structuring their lives throughout adulthood.

Until recently, most individuals reaching adulthood perceived their main tasks to be finding gainful employment and selecting a mate with whom to have children. If marriage was postponed, the delay was due more to economic conditions than to personal choice. Those who did not take religious vows were expected to take marital vows, and those who did not marry were frequently the objects of pity. It was assumed that permanently single people were atypical with respect to physical attractiveness, sexual feeling, or emotional adjustment. Such judgments applied particularly to unmarried women, who were commonly referred to as old maids or spinsters.

Choices for men and women today are considerably more diverse. Instead of the issue of whom to marry, the question centers on whether to marry and, if so, when. Instead of discussing how many children to have, it has become acceptable, at least among some segments of society, to talk about whether to have any children at all. In addition, most people begin engaging in sexual intercourse before they reach the end of adolescence, and well before they marry.

Women have made significant progress toward achieving economic and social equality, but is there any evidence of corresponding changes in women's roles in romantic and marital relationships? If attitudes are changing, what is the influence of new attitudes on contemporary choices regarding lifestyles?

Single Lifestyles.   When we think of a household, we usually assume that it consists of at least two people. The proportion of households that contain only one person, however, is rising rapidly. Almost 25 percent of households are composed of a single occupant, compared to 7 percent in 1949. The growing incidence of one-person households has stemmed primarily from an increase in the number of never-married persons who either do not intend to marry or are postponing marriage.

With the median age at first marriage gradually rising to the mid-20s in the 1990s (27 years for men, 25 years for women in 1997), more people than in the past are single during part or all of their young adulthood (U.S. Bureau of the Census, 1999). Even among those who marry, more than half return to single status through separation or divorce, and many others return to single status as the result of a spouse's death. The rise in the number of one-person households consisting of divorced or separated men under age 35 has been particularly notable. Among women, the number of widows continues to grow, but not so much as the numbers of never-married, divorced, and separated women (U.S. Bureau of the Census, 1999).

Remaining single is a fulfilling lifestyle for many men and women.

Although there is no particular type of person who remains single, women with graduate school training and women with little education (fewer than five years) contribute disproportionately to the ranks of the never married (Saluter, 1992). Women with graduate training may perceive marriage as interfering with their career plans. Those with little education may be seen as undesirable partners, especially if their lack of education stems from problems such as low income and mental or physical disabilities.

Singles, particularly those over 25 years old, are the victims of a number of misconceptions. One of the most common is that they are "swingers." The stereotype of the promiscuous and carefree bed-hopper pursuing endless amorous adventures is an enduring fantasy. It is interesting that the alleged swinging lifestyle of an unattached man is often viewed with envy or fascination, whereas single women are often seen as threatening, particularly by their married counterparts. Another misconception about singles is that they are not married because they have been unable to find anyone willing to marry them. Emotional instability, physical unattractiveness, and low intelligence may be attributed to individuals to explain why they are unmarried. The underlying assumption appears to be that all normal people marry. In addition, singles must often endure insinuations that they are homosexual. Fear of homosexuality is so pervasive in our culture that any deviation from marriage leaves one vulnerable to the charge. The conclusion that an unmarried person must be promiscuous, unattractive, or gay, however, reflects ignorance about single lifestyles.

In departing from the conventional choice of marriage, at least for a period of time, single men and women must develop an alternative network of relationships that provide support and intimacy. Many form friendships in the workplace, in school, at parties, and through hobbies and sports. Remaining single has become a workable and satisfying alternative to marriage for many men and women, one that can last for a few years or a lifetime. A form of legal, if not emotional, singleness that has become popular is cohabitation.

▶ **Issues to Consider:** In what ways do you think the trend toward later marriages affects men and women who wish to marry at younger ages?

Cohabitation. The practice of sharing a residence with a sexual partner before marriage or instead of marriage—**cohabitation**—has rapidly increased in popularity in the past three decades. About 25 percent of college students report having cohabited (Newcomb, 1986; Thornton, 1988). In the United States as a whole, the proportion of persons who lived with a partner before marrying for the first time increased from 11 percent in 1970 to nearly half for recent first marriages (Bumpass, Sweet, & Cherlin, 1991). The actual number of people cohabiting is higher because about 20 percent of cohabitors do not ever expect to marry or marry again. Although most cohabitors plan to marry at some point, they do not necessarily intend to marry the person with whom they are living.

The majority of cohabiting relationships break up or end in marriage within two years (Brown & Booth, 1996; Laumann et al., 1994). Only about 20 percent of cohabiting couples live together for more than five years, and roughly half of these couples end their relationships before marriage. Marriages that are preceded by cohabitation have higher dissolution rates than marriages without previous cohabitation (Horwitz & White, 1998; Laumann et al., 1994).

The mention of cohabiting usually elicits a stereotyped image of two young people adjusting to living together, but 40 percent of cohabiting households include children. Most cohabitors report that their lives would be pretty much the same if they were married (Bumpass et al., 1991). The quality of the relationship between cohabitors who intend to marry is the same as for their married counterparts (Brown & Booth, 1996). In fact, cohabitors report more frequent interaction with their partners than do married couples.

Cohabitors and noncohabitors have been compared on a variety of demographic and personality measures (Byers & Heinlein, 1989; DeMaris & Rao, 1992; Laumann et al., 1994). In general, cohabitation is more prevalent in large urban centers than in rural areas. Cohabitors tend to have higher expectations for marriage than do their noncohabiting counterparts. Moreover, cohabitors are more experienced sexually and become intimately involved at younger ages than noncohabitors do. Both groups reported similar levels of sexual satisfaction, although cohabiting couples report having sex more frequently than do married couples (Laumann et al., 1994; Sprecher & McKinney, 1994).

Couples who cohabit in part to avoid legal hassles may find some recent court cases sobering. In contrast to laws governing marital relationships, laws concerning cohabitation and the ending of cohabiting relationships have not been particularly well defined. As a result, the potential is high for lengthy and expensive legal battles if long-term cohabitants decide to separate. Many attorneys advise a couple intending to cohabit to sign a contract regarding the division of property and income acquired during the relationship to clarify the situation should the individuals decide to separate.

cohabitation—an arrangement in which an unmarried couple live together.

Whether they want to make a contract, all gay or straight couples who decide to live together—regardless of their marital status—can benefit from considering various material and emotional issues. Therapists working with couples having relationship difficulties often hear such statements as, "Well, I thought I could change him [her]" and "I didn't think it was important" in response to questions about whether the client was aware of particular preferences, behaviors, or personality characteristics of his or her partner before making a commitment to live with the person. About 40 percent of cohabiting couples go on to marry one another (Laumann et al., 1994). *Reality or Myth* **?** **1**

> ▶ **Issues to Consider:**   Is cohabiting part of a developmental sequence that begins with romantic attraction and proceeds to sexual intimacy, then cohabitation, and finally marriage? Or does the increase in the practice of cohabitation indicate vast changes in our society, from which a new family form is emerging?

EXTRADYADIC SEXUAL RELATIONS: BACK BURNERS?

What about extradyadic (ED) involvement by partners prior to marriage? Michael Wiederman and Catherine Hurd (1998) found that dating and sexual activity with people other than one's steady partner while engaged in a "serious" or "exclusive" dating relationship was quite common among college students. They sampled almost 700 students, but 11 percent could not be included because they had never been in a serious relationship. Of the 89 percent who had been in a serious relationship and potentially could have had an ED partner, 75 percent of the men and 68 percent of the women reported engaging in some form of ED dating or sexual activity. With the exception of romantic kissing, more men than women reported having engaged in ED sexual activity and were also more likely to have had multiple ED partners. Almost half (49 percent) of the men compared to less than a third (31 percent) of the women reported ED sexual intercourse. Similarly, more men reported indicating performing (47 percent) and receiving (53 percent) oral sex than did women (29 percent and 31 percent, respectively).

Although researchers have traditionally limited their concepts of "unfaithfulness" to activities involving genital contact with a third party, college students have a broader definition of unfaithfulness. Paul Yarab and others (Yarab, Sensibaugh, & Allgeier, 1998) investigated perceptions of what constituted unfaithfulness among college students. In addition to activities involving genital stimulation, students listed sexual and nonsexual fantasies involving no actual contact with a third person. The sexual fantasies involved coital activity, oral sex, and sex play. The nonsexual fantasies involved falling in love with a third person. Other activities listed involving a person outside the primary relationship included flirting, romantic attraction, dancing, dating, going out to lunch, and even behaviors in groups that included members of the other sex such as studying, having lunch or dinner, going to a movie, and fast dancing.

Yarab et al. then provided the list to a second group of students and asked them to indicate if they had engaged in the behaviors. Large proportions of the students reported having engaged in many of the activities with a person outside their primary relationship, and relatively few sex differences emerged. The few that did occur were in the realm of fantasy. For example, 84 percent of men, compared to 52 percent of women, reported fantasies of coitus with someone other than their primary partner—a solitary activity that students in the first group listed as unfaithful. In the realm of behavior, 78 percent of the men versus 58 percent of women reported having "hit on" a third person.

Christine Cregan Sensibaugh and her colleagues (Sensibaugh, Yarab, & Allgeier, 1996) discovered a phenomenon that they termed "back-burner relationships": a practice in which one is in an ongoing committed relationship but engages in activities to attain or maintain the romantic interest of a third person. These activities may or may not include genital contact. Other phrases used for the retention of a person on the back burner are "stringing someone along" and "keeping someone on the line." In their survey of 350 heterosexual college students, Sensibaugh et al. found that more than 75 percent of the respondents reported having been involved in a back-burner relationship as the person keeping a back burner (the control position), the primary partner, or the back burner. About half the sample indicated being in the control position and in the back-burner position, but only a quarter reported having been the primary partner of someone who kept a back burner, although many primary partners may be unaware of their partners' activities with others. The most commonly reported motive for having a back burner by both men and women was to obtain additional attention. Men and women differed in other motives, however. Men were more likely than women to indicate the desire for additional access to sex, whereas women were more likely than men to indicate that they wanted the additional attention that they got from the back burner.

It would be intriguing to learn what proportion of those who engage in ED relationships while in a serious primary relationship go on to engage in extramarital sex. No researchers have examined this question yet.

Marriage and Long-Term Commitments

Marriage has traditionally been portrayed in countless movie and TV scripts as a climactic event, after which a couple live "happily ever after." Many people retain an image of a young couple who, after finishing their educations, getting satisfying jobs, and spending a period of time engaged to each other, exchange wedding vows. Within a few years, they greet the first of several babies, who are brought up to expect the same idealized future.

How accurate is this depiction of families today? Recent census data provide extensive information about the characteristics of contemporary U.S. families. The contrast between the dream and the reality of U.S. marriages may be seen by inspecting Table 13.2.

Some elements of the cultural dream are based on the assumption that there are certain prerequisites for rearing emotionally healthy children. Biases against single-parent or gay-parent families, for example, may rest on the assumption that without both a mother and a father present throughout childhood, a child will become maladjusted. There is no evidence, however, to suggest that the offspring of single or gay parents are generally more poorly adjusted

---

TABLE 13.2   Contemporary American Families: Dreams and Reality

Cultural Dream	Cultural Reality
1. Couples get married and live with one another.	1. More than 15 million unmarried couples share a household.
2. Pair bonding takes place between one man and one woman.	2. Approximately 3 percent of the population live in two-person, same-gender households.
3. "Normal" people marry in their early 20s.	3. About 45 million people aged 25 or older are unmarried.
4. A couple's first baby is conceived after the wedding.	4. About a third of all first births are to unmarried women.
5. Marriages continue until the death of one spouse.	5. More than half of all first marriages end in divorce or separation.
6. Children live with both biological parents.	6. Fewer than half of children live with both parents until age 18.
7. Children are raised by both a mother and a father.	7. About 15 percent of all family groups with children under age 18 are headed by a single parent.
8. After a child is born, its mother ceases employment until the child has left home.	8. More than half of women with children under 3 years old are in the labor force.

Sources: Ahlburg & DeVita (1992); Henshaw (1998); Saluter (1992); U.S. Bureau of the Census (1997).

than are their counterparts from intact heterosexual families (Feltey, 1995; Tasker & Golombok, 1997).

In fact, heterosexual partners who stay in their marriages in the face of being dissatisfied do not necessarily provide the best environment for children. Some people have unhappy childhoods spent in tension-filled homes with parents who constantly bicker and say hurtful things to one another. Maintaining such marriages because of religious convictions, economic restrictions, or concern for the children may be of dubious benefit to those sons and daughters. The children might be far better off living with one parent, if that parent could create a happier and more positive environment in the absence of the other parent.

WORK, TIME, PARENTHOOD, AND SEX

High levels of passion are characteristic of the initial stages of a sexual relationship. Research conducted over the past 50 years has consistently shown that married couples engage in sexual intercourse two or three times a week during the early years of marriage, with the frequency of intercourse declining over time. The drop in sexual activity over the duration of a relationship also holds true for couples who cohabit and for gay and lesbian couples (Laumann et al., 1994; Sprecher & McKinney, 1994).

Parenthood is one factor in the reduced frequency of heterosexual couples' sexual contact (Call, Sprecher, & Schwartz, 1995). When they are parents, a couple who formerly made love in the middle of the afternoon find themselves faced with fussing babies and demanding children. By the time the children go to sleep for the night, the ardor that the couple may have felt while making dinner may have faded to a wistful, "Well, honey, maybe tomorrow."

Further, the assumption that there *is* a tomorrow may decrease a couple's sense of urgency about expressing their sexual feelings immediately. For many couples, the reduced level of sexual activity may be merely a practical response: The presence of children decreases the opportunity for sexual expression. There has been a considerable drop in the number of married couples with children under age 18. About half of married couples had children in the home in 1967, but the percentage had dropped to about a third by 1997. During roughly the same period, the percentage of single-parent families doubled. In 1970, 6 percent of families were headed by a single parent; the percentage had climbed to 14 by 1997.

Some people assume that opportunities for sexual intimacy are further reduced if both partners are employed outside the home. This hypothesis is referred to as the DINS (double income, no sex) dilemma. However, employment of both spouses does not appear to affect the frequency of marital sexual intercourse (Call et al., 1995; Hyde, Hewitt, & DeLamater, 1998; Olson & DeFrain, 1994). It appears that couples who want to have sex make the time for it, rendering the DINS hypothesis inaccurate.

Even if both spouses were employed prior to pregnancy, women tend to cease or limit their outside employment for varying lengths of time after giving birth. The length of time women remain at home after giving birth has decreased in recent years. By 1995, about two out of three mothers with children under 1 year old were employed outside the home (U.S. Bureau of the Census, 1997).

If one spouse is gone all day (typically the husband) and the other one remains in the house with the baby (typically the wife, at least for a while), the homebound spouse may begin to take most of the responsibility for such family tasks as house cleaning, grocery shopping, child care, and meal preparation. The spouse at home may begin to feel dependent on the employed spouse for stimulation and contact with the outside world. But the employed spouse, preoccupied with tasks, relationships, and issues taking place outside the house, may view home as a place to relax and withdraw from work and relationship pressures. This difference in expectations can strain a formerly egalitarian relationship.

Further, when the wife does return to work, she typically continues to take responsibility for the bulk of household and parenting tasks. The division in household labor between men and women was investigated by analyses of diaries kept by married couples in a national sample of more than 500 American couples (Pleck, 1983). These couples recorded all their daily activities for one year. Employed husbands spent fewer than 14 hours a week on all family work, compared to 28 hours for employed wives and almost 49 hours for wives not employed outside the house. Husbands performed about 32 percent of the couple's total family work if the wife was employed and 21 percent of the family work if the wife was not employed. Such overloads on women have also been found in Canadian samples (Douthitt, 1989). Although men's contribution to housework has increased, the average working woman still does two to three times as much family work as does her husband (Major, 1993; Silverstein, 1996).

Women with multiple and time-consuming roles have little time for leisure or intimacy. Working couples who desire more time for sexual intimacy could discuss the possibility of the husband's expanding his contribution to household chores and the wife's reducing her time spent on housework. If each partner assumes responsibility for about half the housework, the couple has additional time to spend on their relationship. In Pleck's (1983) study, there were about 42 hours a week of housework, of which the wife was responsible for 28 hours and the husband for 14 hours. A husband who increases his share to 21 hours could give the couple 7 hours a week to devote to pleasurable pursuits.

Pepper Schwartz (1994) studied 56 dual-career couples who had an egalitarian division of labor.

Characteristics of these peer marriages included a division of household labor that was close to equal (within a 40/60 split), equal influence in decision making and economic resources, and each partner's vacation being given equal weight in the couple's life plans. According to Schwartz, the major reward for this lifestyle is the primacy of the relationship: The relationship take precedence over everything else. These couples are best friends and find each other irreplaceable. The downside of this relationship form is that there is little social support for it, particularly for men. Those whose job advancement depends on extensive travel or overtime may face an insoluble conflict between the demands of job and home, particularly if the couple has young children. The spouse whose job requires that he or she be out of town half the time has less ability to contribute to the many tasks involved with caring for the children.

In the next section we examine the association of long-term relationships with the quality and frequency of sexual expression. *Reality or Myth* ?

▶ **Issues to Consider:** Would you want to be in a peer relationship as defined by Schwartz? Why or why not?

ong-Term Relationships

The phrase "until death do us part," included in most marriage vows, had a far more literal meaning for most of human history than it does today. In nineteenth-century America, marriage lasted an average of only 12 years before one of the partners died. Today, extended human longevity allows for much longer relationships, which may be complicated by the intrusion of some of the problems common to middle and old age. Most of our examination of long-term relationships focuses on marriage because there is little information about extended relationships among unmarried people.

ATTRACTION VERSUS ATTACHMENT IN LONG-TERM RELATIONSHIPS

Marital satisfaction is positively related to how often a couple has sex (Blumstein & Schwartz, 1983; Call

et al., 1995). Specifically, the more often that sexual intimacy occurs, the more satisfied couples are with their marriage. However, as the length of a relationship continues, frequent sex becomes less crucial for marital satisfaction (Call et al., 1995). Over the course of a long-term relationship, many people begin to value personal attachment more highly than sexual attraction.

The decreasing importance of sexuality in a marriage over time, at least in the successful long-term relationships that have been studied, has been examined in terms of sexual attraction and attachment. Troll and Smith (1976) suggested that there is an inverse relationship between these two factors: Sexual attraction is high in the beginning of a new relationship, but attachment is low; over the years, sexual attraction diminishes as novelty wanes, but attachment increases. If marital satisfaction or happiness is measured in terms of sexual attraction, a steady decrease over time is inevitable, with perhaps a temporary rise when the children's departure creates a new domestic situation for husband and wife. If marital satisfaction is measured in terms of attachment, security, and loyalty, however, couples' marital happiness tends to increase over time.

As we have seen, the initial phases of most romantic relationships are characterized by passion and sexual intimacy. The experience of being swept away does not last long, however, as many parents have advised their unheeding offspring over the years. After couples begin to see each other regularly, passion typically lasts approximately 18 months to 3 years (Fisher, 1992). In short, passion and sexual intimacy appear to be more important to loving relationships in early adulthood, whereas tender feelings of affection and loyalty are more important to loving relationships in the second half of life (Byrne & Murnen, 1988; Fisher, 1992).

But many people feel some conflict between their needs for security and a stable relationship on the one hand, and a desire for excitement and novelty on the other. The simultaneous yearning for the sexual novelty of a new partner and for the comfort of a familiar partner creates a dilemma that many people have difficulty resolving. These reactions to sexual novelty are not confined to humans. The response to a familiar versus a new partner has been reported in a number of mammalian species. A male will readily copulate and ejaculate several times with a sexually receptive female and then stop. Confronted by a new sexually receptive female, the male becomes sexually active again immediately. Such male rearousal by a new female is called the Coolidge effect, based on this story:

> One day the President and Mrs. Coolidge were visiting a government farm. Soon after their arrival they were taken off on separate tours. When Mrs. Coolidge passed the chicken pens she paused to ask the man in charge if the rooster copulates more than once each day. "Dozens of times," was the reply. "Please tell that to the President," Mrs. Coolidge requested. When the President passed the pens and was told about the roosters, he asked "Same hen every time?" "Oh no, Mr. President, a different one each time." The President nodded slowly, then said, "Tell that to Mrs. Coolidge." Bermant, 1976, pp. 76–77)

Partially because of the inherent tension between the desires for new sexual experiences versus those for continuity and comfort, monogamous relationships are perhaps the most difficult of all human

Passion and the desire to be close to one another characterize the beginning of most romantic relationships.

Couples in lengthy relationships can slip into monotonous routines that dull their attraction to one another. Developing shared interests such as travel and physical fitness can increase pleasurable time spent together away from everyday household rituals.

contracts. Additional strain may stem from the fact that such relationships are expected to satisfy so many varied needs for the individuals. The needs for passion, security, and play, to name a few, are channeled into monogamous marriages that are typically strained by concerns about children, vocations, and economics. Slowly and often imperceptibly, these relationships can drift toward dispassionate companionship. As a relationship becomes habitual, the partners become limited to a constricted range of experiences because it is difficult to preserve the excitement of a relationship when one is enmeshed in the rituals of security. Some people have attempted to resolve this dilemma by continuing their primary relationship while simultaneously having sexual relations with others outside the marriage.

EXTRAMARITAL SEXUAL RELATIONS

Extramarital sex can be covert or overt. Covert activities encompass all extramarital sexual relations that occur without the spouse's knowledge. Overt extramarital sex may take several different forms: open marriage, swinging, mate swapping, and group marriage. In these agreed-on arrangements, both marital partners engage in extramarital sexual activity with others.

A majority of respondents in Western societies disapprove of extramarital relationships in any form (Bringle & Buunk, 1991; Wiederman, 1997). Still, in Laumann et al.'s (1994) national sample, about 25 percent of men and 16 percent of women reported having had an extramarital affair. In Tom Smith's (1991) national sample, about 21 percent of men and 13 percent of women indicated that they had had an extramarital affair. These findings are in contrast to previous estimates that at least half of married people have had extramarital sex (Blumstein & Schwartz, 1983; Buss & Schmitt, 1993). This difference probably stems from the fact that the earlier research employed groups that were not representative of the U.S. population (Wiederman, 1998).

There is a strong relationship between an individual's sexual attitudes and his or her behavior with respect to premarital sex (Reiss, Anderson, & Sponaugle, 1980). The more tolerant or permissive one's attitudes toward sex before marriage are, the more likely it is that one will engage in that activity. For extramarital sex, however, the relationship between attitudes and behavior may be considerably weaker (Glass & Wright, 1992), in part because of "stronger cultural norms [against extramarital sex] which may not stop the behavior but will produce guilt" (Reiss et al., 1980, p. 398).

Why do people have extramarital sex? The old line, "My wife [husband] doesn't understand me," reflects a pervasive cultural belief that a person strays from the marital bed because of marital discontent or dissatisfaction with the quality of the couple's sex life (Wiederman & Allgeier, 1996). Research indicates associations between the likelihood of having affairs and unhappy marriages, but some studies also indicate that happily married people sometimes have extramarital affairs (Bringle & Buunk, 1991). Factors other than marital happiness may be responsible for the associations found. For example, the belief that one's marriage should fulfill all one's interpersonal needs may be unrealistic.

Some people may choose to have extramarital relationships not just because of the sexual variety but because of other shared interests. Friendships between men and women may also provide a strong inducement for extramarital affairs. Anxiety over waning attractiveness, particularly among men, has been implicated as another motivation for extramarital sex, which provides a way for the man to prove to himself that he is still sexually attractive and virile. Although husbands are more likely to be involved in extramarital affairs than are wives (Buss, 1999; Laumann et al., 1994), they are also more likely to perceive affairs as destructive—*if* their wives are "unfaithful"! Like men, women often start affairs in their late 30s or early 40s seeking passion, a reaffirmation of their sexual attractiveness, and the excitement of courtship and love (Bringle & Buunk, 1991; Lawson, 1988). Sexual relationships outside marriage are not limited to middle age, of course. They can and do occur at any time during a marriage. Teenagers and grandparents have affairs and give a variety of reasons for doing so.

To determine under what conditions people perceive extramarital sex as justified, Glass and Wright (1992) distributed questionnaires to adults at an airport and during the lunch hour in downtown Baltimore. Based on the responses of married people in their sample, four factors or reasons emerged: (1) sexual factors (excitement, enjoyment, curiosity, and novelty), (2) emotional intimacy, (3) extrinsic motivation (career advancement, revenge on spouse), and (4) love. Men were more likely to endorse sex as a justification, and women were more likely to see love as a justification for extramarital involvement.

An interesting aspect of Glass and Wright's work is that they went beyond much of the earlier research that defined extramarital involvement as having sexual intercourse. They broadened the definition of extramarital involvement to include sexual involvement without intercourse or some type of nonsexual emotional involvement. In their sample, 25 percent of the women and 44 percent of the men had experienced extramarital coitus; the figures for extramarital involvement rose to 47 percent of women and 63 percent of men when sexual involvement without coitus was included.

Sometimes a marital imbalance leads a husband or wife to feel justified in seeking an extramarital relationship. Walster, Walster, and Berscheid (1978) have distinguished two kinds of imbalance. First, we may feel overbenefited when our marital rewards are greater than our costs. Second, we may experience deprivation when we perceive our investment as greater than our rewards. Finally, **equity** exists when we perceive our rewards as being roughly equal to our investment in the marriage.

Rewards and investments can be defined in various ways. People bring diverse contributions to a relationship—financial assets, practical know-how, or physical appeal, for example. Walster et al. found some support for their hypothesis that spouses who perceive themselves to be overbenefited or in an equitable relationship are less likely to become involved in extramarital affairs than spouses who see themselves as deprived. To test this hypothesis, the researchers used a survey published by *Psychology Today*. To measure perceived equity, they analyzed responses to an item in which each volunteer was asked to describe his or her partner's desirability on a scale ranging from "much more desirable than I" through "as desirable as I" to "much less desirable than I."

Walster et al. believed that spouses would see the relationship as inequitable if they perceived themselves as more desirable than their mates. Consequently, they assumed that these people would engage in affairs earlier in their relationship and with

equity—in a personal relationship, a perceived balance between the benefits the relationship provides and the personal investment it requires.

RESEARCH SPOTLIGHT   The Relationship of Equity to Likelihood of Having Extramarital Sex

In a study of married Dutch persons, 30 percent of whom had been involved in extramarital affairs, Prins, Buunk, and VanYperen (1993) examined the relationship of equity to the likelihood of such extramarital liaisons. Women who felt deprived *or* advantaged in their marital relationships were more likely to have extramarital relations than were those women who reported equity in their marital relations. In contrast, men's likelihood of engaging in extramarital sex was less related to their relative sense of equity in their marital relationships. Prins et al. also found that although men reported stronger desires to engage in extramarital sex, there were no differences in the percentage of men and women reporting involvement in such affairs.

more partners than would those who perceived themselves to be either in an equitable relationship or overbenefited. Their results supported this assumption. Although frequency of extramarital relationships did not vary according to gender or length of the primary relationship, it did vary according to perceptions of the equity of the primary relationship. It was particularly interesting that among couples who had been together for 15 years or longer, there was little difference between the behavior of deprived men and deprived women. Deprived men reported having had an average of 3.3 partners outside the relationship, as compared with 2.6 partners for deprived women. It is possible, of course, that guilt over these affairs cultivated a tendency in volunteers to deprecate their marital relationships; that is, by lamenting the state of their marriage, they might have been seeking to justify their socially disapproved behavior and thus reduce their guilt (see "Research Spotlight: The Relationship of Equity to Likelihood of Having Extramarital Sex").

Consensual Extramarital Sex.   Some couples reach an agreement that permits each spouse to be sexually active with persons outside their marriage under certain circumstances. Consensual extramarital sex can take various forms. A couple can agree that each partner individually may have intimate relationships with other people. Alternatively, a couple may engage in recreational sex with people who are relative strangers and with whom they tend not to be otherwise involved, an arrangement known as "swinging." Or two or more couples may switch partners for purposes of sexual and emotional intercourse, called mate exchange or mate swapping. Finally, in group marriage, couples may share each other's partners, a residence, incomes, child care, and household responsibilities. In group marriage, as in traditional marriage, participants are typically expected to confine their sexual expression to members of the marriage.

Advocates of consensual extramarital sex have argued that the institution of marriage, with its normative requirement of sexual exclusiveness, results in sexual monotony, boredom, and sexual jealousy. They maintain that it is far preferable for a couple to inject variety into their marriage by having extramarital relations openly than to engage in secret and guilt-producing relationships (Gilmartin, 1974; Palson & Palson, 1972). In contrast to these idealistic viewpoints, Buunk (1991), in a five-year follow-up study of open marriages, found a trend for jealousy to increase over this time period. He also reported that over the five years, the quality of the marital relationship deteriorated and sexual satisfaction in the marriage declined. He could not determine whether this was typical of marriages in general or stemmed from the extramarital relationships. Conflicting results were reported from another study in which Rubin and Adams (1986) compared sexually open couples with sexually exclusive couples. They found no difference in marital stability over a five-year period. Obviously, these differing results can be used to support divergent views of the stability of open marriages.

In research on nonswingers' views of swingers (Jenks, 1985), nonswingers judged swingers' attitudes and behavior to be quite different from their own and thus saw practically everything about them as odd or immoral. In fact, swingers generally have been found to differ from nonswingers only in the practice of swinging. Brian Gilmartin (1974) conducted one of the more systematic studies of swingers, comparing 100 swinging couples with 100 control group couples. All participants were legally married, middle-class couples living in suburban residential areas. Compared with nonswingers, swingers reported less gratifying relationships with their parents during childhood and adolescence, viewed their parents and relatives as less important in their lives, and interacted with their parents and other relatives less frequently. Gilmartin found many more areas where swingers and nonswingers did not differ, however, and the similarities that he reported are in some ways more interesting than the differences. The two groups did not differ, for example, in reported personal happiness, marital contentment, drinking habits, boredom, or likelihood of seeking therapy.

One additional finding from the Gilmartin study is intriguing. Although the control group couples were not involved in consensual extramarital sex, 31 percent of the husbands and 8 percent of the wives did report having had secret extramarital affairs. In contrast to the earlier hypothesis that extramarital sex occurs because of unhappy marriages, control group spouses who had had secret affairs perceived their marriages as no less happy than those who reported having been sexually faithful to their spouses. The vast majority of swingers and nonswingers rated their marriages as happy or very happy.

Aside from their sexual behavior, many open couples are conservative in both their political and their social attitudes, and their average educational level is higher than that of the general population (Bell et al., 1975; Gilmartin, 1976; Jenks, 1998). Research with other samples of swingers, however, has shown them to be relatively liberal and nonreligious (Gilmartin, 1974). Obviously, swingers vary in their political and social attitudes just as people in general do.

You may notice the absence of citations to research conducted and published in the 1990s and conclude that the phenomenon of swinging and consensual extramarital sex is another casualty of HIV/AIDS. Although empirical research on the topic has dwindled, there are numerous groups and clubs devoted to swinging. One swingers organization, called In Touch, holds annual meetings in various cities. For one of their recent meetings, members of the group rented all the rooms in a four-story hotel in St. Louis, Missouri, for a long weekend. A number of other swinger organizations also hold periodic meetings, and there are numerous swingers groups with web pages on the Internet (James W. Howell, personal communication, June 5, 1998).

SEPARATION AND DIVORCE

The U.S. divorce rate has been on the rise since the Industrial Revolution. This increase started to level off in the early 1980s, although more than half of recent first marriages still end in separation or divorce (Sprecher & Fehr, 1998). Most industrialized nations have experienced similar patterns, although divorce is more common in the United States than elsewhere (Ahlburg & DeVita, 1992).

Pessimists point to these statistics as reflections of widespread instability, the decline of the family, and moral decay in contemporary society. This concern about the demise of the family is not new, as the following quotation shows: "The family in its old sense is disappearing from our land, and not only our free institutions are threatened but the very existence of our society is endangered" (Cherlin, 1981, pp. 2–3). This appeared in the Boston *Quarterly Review* in 1859!

Optimists take a different view, suggesting that the numbers simply underscore high expectations for the quality of marital relationships. We are, they say, unwilling to settle for the "lives of quiet desperation" that have characterized the many marriages held together for the sake of children or religious or financial considerations in previous generations. Optimists cite another statistic to support their point: 60 percent to 80 percent of divorced people, depending on the group studied, marry a second partner (Ahlburg & DeVita, 1992; Sprecher & Fehr, 1998). It seems that these people are rejecting a particular spouse but not the institution of marriage.

Some sex differences appear in patterns of divorce and remarriage. Women, at almost all ages, are more likely to initiate divorce proceedings (Buckle, Gallup, & Rodd, 1996). After divorce, however, women are less likely to remarry, particularly if they have children, than are formerly married men.

How is it that two people can enter marriage full of love, hope, and commitment, only to have the relationship dissolve? Although the causes of divorce are complex and there is not enough evidence to answer this question definitively, certain conditions are associated with the longevity of relationships. Age at marriage and educational level are two of the most consistent (White, 1991). Teenage marriages are more than twice as likely to end than are unions of people in their 20s, with the most stable first marriages occurring among women who wed after the age of 30 (Martin & Bumpass, 1989; Norton & Moorman, 1987). Divorce peaks between the ages of 20 and 24 for both sexes in the United States, which is slightly younger than for other societies for which data are available (Fisher, 1992). The proportion of divorces is highest at around the fourth year of marriage in most of the 24 societies that anthropologist Helen Fisher studied. In the United States, the peak is found somewhat earlier, occurring around the third year of marriage (Fisher, 1992; Kurdek, 1993). Divorce then becomes less likely over the course of the marriage.

An analysis of 160 societies indicated that infidelity, particularly by the wife, was the most common reason given for divorce (Betzig, 1989). Infertility was the next most commonly mentioned reason. Cruelty, especially by the husband, ranked third worldwide among reasons for divorce. Although these reasons are closely related to sex and reproduction, divorce in the contemporary United States seems to be less tied to sex and reproductive reasons. Individuals' accounts of their own divorces implicate such factors as substance abuse, infidelity, personal incompatibility, sexual incompatibility, physical and emotional abuse, financial problems, and gender-role disagreements (White, 1991).

Kinsey et al. (1953) did note that a decrease in women's orgasm rates frequently preceded divorce and separation, but the meaning of this change was unclear. Did the marital problems leading to divorce affect wives' sexual responsiveness? Or did the decline in responsiveness lead to increased marital distance and ultimately divorce? Several studies of married couples indicate that happy marriages can exist between couples whose sexual encounters are not particularly frequent or earthshaking (Blumstein & Schwartz, 1983; Laumann et al., 1994). Sexual incompatibility, however, has been found to be associated with breakups of relationships among dating, married, and homosexual couples (Call et al., 1995; Hatfield & Rapson, 1996; Laumann et al., 1994; Sprecher & McKinney, 1994).

On the interpersonal level, longitudinal and observational studies have found a number of behavioral patterns that are predictive of marital instability and divorce (Gottman, 1994; Gottman, Coan, Carrere, & Swanson, 1998). Contempt, criticism, defensiveness, and "stonewalling" (listener withdrawal) during conflict were the most predictive factors of divorce. It may surprise you that anger during marital conflicts was *not* predictive of divorce.

Most conflict begins with the woman indicating that she is usually given the task of being the emotional caretaker of the relationship. If the start-up is negative and the husband withdraws, there is often an escalation of negativity. However, if the wife is able to soften the start-up and the husband acknowledges her concerns, there is a good chance that the conflict will deescalate. The greater the ratio of positive affect (agreement, approval, humor, smiling, pleasant physical contact) to negative affect (contempt, defensiveness, withdrawal, belligerence), the better the chance is that the conflict will be resolved to the satisfaction of both partners.

One intriguing observation by John Gottman (1994) is that, in some ways, men are more physiologically reactive to stress than are women. Because of the aversive nature of this physiological arousal, men may be more likely to try to withdraw from the conflict. Gottman suggested that physiologically soothing the man with positive physical contact, humor, and appreciation may forestall his withdrawal. Obviously, women also react physiologically to conflict, and this is predictive of illness. They also need physiological soothing.

Finally, there is growing realization that spouses who accept their partner as they are rather than demand change may contribute to marital stability (Jacobson & Christensen, 1996). Paradoxically, acceptance often leads to desired behavioral change. **_Reality or Myth_** ⬛

ADJUSTMENT TO SEPARATION: WHO SUFFERS MOST?

Women are stereotypically portrayed as far more dependent on love and marital relationships than are men, and thus more devastated by separation and divorce. The evidence suggests, however, that the responses of men and women to separation and divorce are somewhat more complicated than usually portrayed.

Men are more likely than women to experience depression and illnesses requiring hospitalization following divorce. Women's reactions are less severe but more frequent and long-lasting; they include mild depression and anxiety about living alone (Hatfield & Rapson, 1996; Kitson & Morgan, 1991). In addition, some divorced women feel helpless, unattractive, isolated, and concerned about loss of status.

These gender differences may have roots in many factors, including the fact that a woman's financial resources are reduced by about 30 percent after divorce (Pollock & Stroup, 1998). Related to their standard of living is the greater difficulty that women may experience in finding employment that provides sufficient income following the loss of the husband's paycheck. In divorce settlements, the custody of children is still generally awarded to women, and the responsibility for rearing children single-handedly may restrict the ability of women to pursue new social relationships.

In research designed to identify variables that correlate with positive adjustment to divorce, Clarke-Stewart and Bailey (1989) interviewed divorced women and men who had custody of their school-age children. Three years following divorce, the men were generally better adjusted psychologically, had more stable and satisfying jobs, and were more financially successful than were the women. Those women who were better adjusted felt that they had received more social support from their friends and family, were more likely to have moved away following the divorce, and experienced less financial stress.

Other research that has examined the relationship of gender-role attitudes and gender identification to a person's adjustment to divorce has consistently shown more positive adjustment among women with egalitarian gender-role attitudes and with androgynous or masculine identities than among more traditional women. Women with identities that incorporated some typically masculine traits were more likely to see divorce as partly the product of their own needs and behaviors than were more feminine women. As might be expected, divorced women with fewer children, a college degree, a comfortable income, and greater levels of ambition were happier than were divorced women with more children and less money, education, and ambition (Granvold et al., 1979; Hansson et al., 1984; Stroup & Pollock, 1999).

In general, postdivorce adjustment is probably less related to sex differences per se than to the extent to which the divorcing couple want the divorce, have a sense of control over their lives, and have access to personal, social, and economic resources. As women become more independent and gain greater access to resources and satisfying careers, the gender differences in adjustment to divorce may disappear.

After divorce, men and women usually do not become celibate. Even when concerns about contracting AIDS became widespread, only 20 percent of the separated and 26 percent of the divorced people in Tom Smith's (1991) nationally representative sample reported abstinence during the previous 12 months. Further, the number of partners since age 18 for the currently separated was about 12 and for the currently divorced was about 13—higher numbers of partners than for single, married, or widowed people. As might be expected, divorced men were more sexually active than were divorced women, and younger divorced people were more sexually active than were older divorced people (Stack & Gundlach, 1992).

Regardless of marital status, at some point during their 40s or 50s, as they come to grips with the fact that they no longer have as much time remaining in their lives as they had during young adulthood, people begin to assess what they have done with their lives so far. *Reality or Myth* 🔲

Midlife Sexuality

Most sex research has focused on individuals in late adolescence or early adulthood. The fact that people beyond early adulthood have received only limited research attention is probably due to several factors, including our species' relative inexperience with aging, traditional beliefs about the purposes of sex, and the greater ease of obtaining samples of college students than of older adults.

For most of human existence, relatively few individuals lived to advanced ages. Even in the United States, which in terms of human history has existed for an extremely brief period, it is only in the twentieth century that living beyond age 40 has become commonplace. Because life was short and seldom sweet, it was crucial for our ancestors to reproduce as early and as frequently as possible. The historical equation of reproduction with sexuality, strengthened by thousands of years of struggling to survive as a species, may still affect our vision of sexuality. The identification of sexuality with fertility perpetuates the idea that people beyond their reproductive years are sexless. Decreases in reproductive capacity, however, need not eliminate sexual feelings and responsiveness.

Nonetheless, in North America, sexuality is generally treated as a quality and activity limited to the young. Many older members of society accept this stereotype, and some of them welcome the release from what they perceive to be a burdensome obligation. Other people, however, find that age brings a different kind of release. As one woman put it,

The older I get, the more I enjoy sex. When I was in my teens and 20s, I spent a lot of time thinking about how I should act and I felt shy about my body. I know that, objectively, I was a lot more attractive then than I am now in my late 40s. But I feel so much freer and prettier now that I don't worry about what I'm supposed to do or how I'm supposed to look. Instead of thinking about what my partner thinks of my body, I'm appreciating my body for the pleasure it gives me. (Authors' files)

MENOPAUSE

The average woman experiences **menopause**, the gradual ending of ovulation, menstruation, and reproductive capacity, at around age 51, although it can occur any time between the ages of 35 and 60. There is usually a seven-year transitional period, known as the perimenopausal stage, characterized by increasing irregularity of menstrual cycle length and bleeding pattern.

One of the most common changes associated with menopause is the decline in sex hormones. This decline is the source of the "hot flashes" and sudden sweating that many menopausal women report. Fatigue, depression, and headaches are also common, and some women experience reductions in vaginal lubrication. These symptoms, linked to decreases in estrogen secretion, can persist for several years. The administration of hormone replacement therapy (HRT)—usually low dosages of estrogen and progesterone—reduces unwanted symptoms associated with menopause. Estrogen suppositories or creams placed in the vagina several times a week may also reduce problems associated with estrogen deficiency.

Although medical experts once widely agreed that menopausal women experience a declining level of sexual response in correspondence with declining levels of estrogen, more recent studies have found a great deal of variation in sexual response during this period (Cutler, Garcia, & McCoy, 1987; Mansfield, Koch & Voda, 1998). Although very low estrogen levels are associated with infrequent sexual activity, no one knows whether low levels of estrogen cause or are the result of low levels of sexual activity. However, research does indicate that menopause need not bring women's sexual responsiveness to an end.

The continuance or decline of sexual responsiveness at menopause may be related to a woman's social class. In Hallstrom's (1977) study of 800 women, upper-social-class menopausal women showed less decline in sexual interest, capacity for orgasm, and coital frequency than did menopausal women of lower social classes, who revealed age-related deficits in their sexual responses.

What about "male menopause"? A review of the male menopause literature indicated that a significant number of men experience psychological and social difficulties in middle age, but these appear to stem from cultural and lifestyle changes rather than from hormonal changes (Metz & Miner, 1998). **Reality or Myth**

THE DOUBLE STANDARD OF AGING

In our culture, aging is more of a challenge for women than for men, for two reasons. First, because

---

menopause—the end of menstruation, ovulation, and a woman's reproductive capacity.

Actor Sean Connery continues to be a box-office draw despite being in his 60s. In contrast, aging actresses often find it difficult to obtain leading roles. Yet singer and actress Tina Turner demonstrates that aging women can be sensuous and vibrant.

female reproductive capacity terminates at menopause, whereas male reproductive capacity wanes gradually, women beyond the age of menopause are more likely to be stereotyped as sexless. (If this stereotype were accurate, there would be little reason to study the sexuality of older women.) Second, the physical characteristics regarded as attractive in females—smooth skin, slim physique, firm breasts—tend to decline earlier than the physical qualities considered sexy in men. A man's gray or white hair is often described as distinguished, and the lines on his face, increasing and becoming more deeply etched with age, as bestowing character. His sexual value is defined more by power and status than by physical characteristics. In contrast, a woman's youthful physical appearance has traditionally defined her attractiveness (Buss, 1999).

The visual media not only perpetuate such stereotypes, but they also help to create unrealistic fantasies. Hollywood generally rejects women of 40 as vital sexual beings but hands many romantic leads to men of that age or older. Actress Joanne Woodward, in a television interview, compared herself to her husband, actor Paul Newman, as follows: "He gets prettier; I get older." But there are signs that this double standard is gradually changing with the aging

of the general population. Recent television programs such as *Murphy Brown*, starring Candice Bergen, and *Cybill*, staring Cybill Shepard, featured women in their 40s and 50s who were depicted as quite interested in sex. These shows may have contributed to the portrayal of older women as intelligent, attractive, and sexy. Older actresses who continue to enjoy popularity include Sophia Loren, Goldie Hawn, Bette Midler, Cher, and Susan Sarandon.

▶ **Issues to Consider:**   Do you think there is still a double standard of aging and sexuality for men and women?

MIDLIFE CHALLENGES AND GENDER ROLES

Erikson (1982) described the developmental challenge of this period as involving the conflict of generativity versus stagnation. Generativity is a concern for the future of our species, expressed not only in involvement with our own children, if we have them, but with children in general. Successful resolution of this stage requires looking beyond our own goals of personal gratification and yields a sense of intense connection to the well-being of others in our family, community, and nation and to humanity in general. People who do not resolve the crisis of this stage feel little connection with anything beyond their own personal gratification. For such persons, the aging process involves stagnation. Failing to form a deep connection with others, these people experience aging simply as an inevitable movement toward loss of physical and personal power and death. Embedded in this period are the biological changes associated with aging.

There is evidence that traditional gender roles become less important from middle age onward and that people take on personality attributes typically defined as characteristic of the other gender; that is, as men become older, they tend to express their affiliative and nurturant feelings, whereas women become more responsive to and less guilty about their egocentric and assertive impulses. In traditional societies, women become more assertive as they become older and often more influential in their social groups. Fisher (1992) suggested that biology may play a role. Levels of estrogen decline with menopause, allowing testosterone, which has been linked with assertiveness, to exert greater influence. Psychologically, there is a counterbalancing of personality traits between men and women, and more complex conceptions of what it means to be male and female develop (Hatfield & Rapson, 1996). Although many adults experience a time during which they question the value of what they have done and are doing, such soul searching is by no means automatic.

For both men and women, the average frequency of intercourse declines as they advance into old age (Call et al., 1995; Laumann et al., 1994). However, there is considerable variation in the sexual practices of older people.

ld Age

Erikson maintained that the challenge of the last stage of life is to resolve the conflict of integrity versus despair. During self-assessment at this stage, the emphasis is on evaluating the kind of person one has been and the meaning that one's life has had. This evaluative process can produce a sense of satisfaction and integrity. People who have been relatively successful in resolving earlier crises can view their lives as having been purposeful, and the resultant sense of integrity can soften the fear of death. Conversely, the realization that there is not enough time left to try to improve or alter what has been done with one's life may engender a sense of pointlessness and despair. In addition to various psychological changes, advancing age brings some inevitable physiological changes.

Physiological Changes

Aging males in species ranging from rodents to humans experience declining levels of testosterone (Hoyenga & Hoyenga, 1993). With the decline in testosterone secretion, several physiological changes occur. The amount of seminal fluid is reduced, it becomes thinner, and ejaculatory pressure decreases. The prostate gland often enlarges, and its contractions during orgasm weaken. After age 70, the size of the testes begins to decline, as does their firmness, so

Actor Kirk Douglas, as a role model for two sons, demonstrates a positive resolution of midlife changes. Son Michael is an actor, and both sons are producers.

Gender differences peak in the reproductive years and gradually diminish as males and females advance into their later years.

they do not elevate to the same degree during sexual activity. This decline appears to result from a reduction in the number and size of the interstitial (Leydig) cells, which synthesize and secrete sex hormones (Schiavi, 1990). The seminiferous tubules, on the other hand, which are the site of sperm production, hold up quite well throughout the aging process. Sperm production is relatively unchanged in older men. There are many cases in which men of advanced age have fathered children. Senator Strom Thurmond of South Carolina, for example, fathered his fourth child at the age of 74.

Changes occur in the phases of the sexual response cycle (Rowland, Greenleaf, Dorfman, & Davidson, 1993). This is particularly true after the age of 60. Masters and Johnson (1966) studied changes in the sexual responses of people from late adolescence to the age of 89.

Aging men tend to take longer to attain an erection during sexual stimulation. On the other hand, they may remain erect for a longer period of time after tumescence than was typical when they were younger. Some men whose penis has been erect for a relatively lengthy period during coitus may experience ejaculation as a seeping out of semen rather than a forceful expulsion of seminal fluid. The penis may become flaccid more quickly following ejaculation rather than remaining erect for a number of

minutes. There tends to be an increase in the length of the refractory period, which may last from 12 to 24 hours.

Estrogen production in women usually begins to decline after age 40, and the decrease continues until about age 60. With the reduction in estrogen secretion, the vaginal walls of postmenopausal women generally become thinner and lose some of their elasticity, although these phenomena and the amount of vaginal lubrication produced by women during sexual stimulation vary. These changes may be reduced by the use of HRT, which also reduces the risk of osteoporosis (bone loss). It is particularly important to realize that there is a great deal of variation from one person to another in the extent of experience with changes in sexual response associated with aging.

Social Stereotypes and Self-Image

Social and psychological factors can either diminish or emphasize the effects of aging. As our elderly population increases and we learn more about sexuality among the aged, social recognition and acceptance of the sensual appeal of older people may become more common.

In the early 1990s, several groups of older women were featured in talk shows and live performances around the United States, including the Sensuous Seniors and the Dancing Grannies, who dressed in body suits and performed aerobic dancing to popular music. Ranging in age from their 50s to their 70s, these women appeared to be more agile than many adolescents and young adults. In addition to altering stereotypes about aging women, the vigorous exercise regimen followed by the Dancing Grannies probably has beneficial effects on their self-esteem and physical health. They were not seeking to portray themselves as young women. Instead, their goal was to demonstrate that elderly women can be sensuous, healthy, and vibrant.

In sum, our culture has traditionally propagated stereotypes suggesting that individuals become sexually inactive in their older years. The persistence of such ideas may make people feel guilt or worry if they continue to have sexual feelings as they advance into and beyond middle age. But just how widespread is termination of sexual expression during old age?

DECREASING SEXUAL ACTIVITY: AGING OR OTHER FACTORS?

In the general population, there is a steady decline in frequency of sexual activity with age, although this pattern varies considerably from one person to the next. The average man's sexual interest diminishes as he ages. No other factor affects men's frequency of total sexual outlet as much as age (Kinsey et al., 1948; Laumann et al., 1994). It is more difficult to assess women's than men's sexual expression over the life cycle, for several reasons. First, for unmarried women, societal restrictions tend to inhibit coital activity. Second, for married women, coital activity is likely to be influenced by a husband's sexual inclinations, which show a decline over time. A third complication in measuring female sexuality through the years is that women generally tend to have orgasm less consistently than do men.

The largest survey to date on sexuality and the elderly relied on responses to a questionnaire appearing in *Consumer Reports* (Brecher, 1984). Among the many findings was the fact that 59 percent of the men and 65 percent of the women 70 years or older still engage in sexual intercourse, and half of those make love at least once a week. Some of the other findings are presented in Table 13.3 on page 317. It

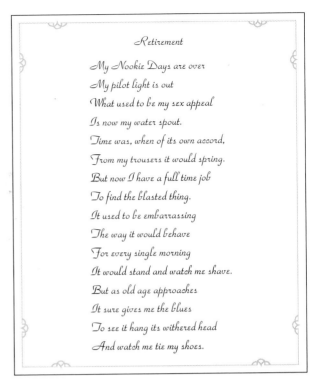

Retirement

My Nookie Days are over
My pilot light is out
What used to be my sex appeal
Is now my water spout.
Time was, when of its own accord,
From my trousers it would spring.
But now I have a full time job
To find the blasted thing.
It used to be embarrassing
The way it would behave
For every single morning
It would stand and watch me shave.
But as old age approaches
It sure gives me the blues
To see it hang its withered head
And watch me tie my shoes.

Figure 13.1 Assumptions about aging men's sexuality

is apparent that many people in this age range remain sexually active. Sexual activity was not limited to the marital relationship. Almost 25 percent of the husbands and 8 percent of the wives reported that they had engaged in extramarital sex at least once after age 50.

People tend to assume that aging persons lose their capacity for sexual arousal and response as a result of the physiological changes. However, because the quality and frequency of sexual expression vary greatly over the later years, researchers have suggested that several other factors may also determine whether sexual expression continues.

One difficulty with research demonstrating a decline in sexual activity over the course of middle and late adulthood is that it is generally cross-sectional; that is, different age groups are surveyed or interviewed at the same point in time. Variations in sexual interest and activity between 30-year-olds and 60-year-olds are then often assumed to be a function of age. These differences, however, may be a function of the time periods during which the groups received

Dear Ann Landers:

I read the various letters you printed in response to "Sexless in Canada," who found sex unhygienic and degrading. A woman from Virginia said that, in her opinion, there is no connection between love and sex.

I am 78 years old, and my wife is 61. Making love is a very important part of our relationship. To me, it is a demonstration of the love and affection I feel for my spouse. I call her "my spouse" because she is much more than a wife. She is my mate, my comforter, my companion, and my lover. While walking alone or in a crowd, we hold hands or lock arms. It's obvious to anyone who sees us that we belong to each other. Even while sitting on the couch and watching TV, we search for each other's hand.

To the lady from Virginia who thinks there is no connection between love and sex, I can only say it's a shame for a person to have to go through life denying herself the tremendous pleasures and spiritual warmth one derives from a complete relationship.

I know this may sound like something out of a "B" movie, but it's not. To look at us, you would see two over-the-hill, middle-class senior citizens—a tall, skinny guy and a dumpy little gal. But we have found something very special in each other. We have cast aside religious hang-ups and do what comes naturally, as God created us. The rewards have been enormous. We are not just "going through life," we have life flowing through us.

HARVEY IN ORLANDO

Figure 13.2 One couple's experience of sexuality in later years

their early socialization and value orientations. For example, women growing up in the 1930s were socialized to show little sexual interest or enjoyment, and therefore their frequency of sexual activity may always have been low. In contrast, women reared in the 1960s were exposed to much more permissive attitudes concerning sexuality and may feel freer to respond to their own sexual desires; thus, their frequency of sexual activity may be higher. If we compared these two groups of women in the 1990s, we might be inclined to attribute their differences in frequency of sexual activity to age rather than to their having been brought up in different historical periods.

A group of Duke University scientists reported that the decline in sexual interest and activity over the second half of life is at least partially a reflection of variations in the patterns of different generations rather than just an age-related decline. A longitudinal study of married couples ranging in age from 60 to 94 indicated that patterns of sexual activity remained more stable in middle and later life than was previously thought (George & Weiler, 1981; Newman & Nichols, 1960; Pfeiffer, Verwoerdt, & Wang, 1968; Verwoerdt, Pfeiffer, & Wang, 1969). Only about 8 percent of the men and 15 percent of the women reported a cessation of sexual activities.

Although the Duke scientists found a progressive decline in the frequency of sexual expression with advancing age, they also discovered great variations in sexual capacity among their older volunteers. The ability to engage in sexual activity has been reported among 70-, 80-, and 90-year-old people (Brecher, 1984; Karlen, 1994; Weizman & Hart, 1987). After age 80, the most common sexual activity for both men and women was touching and caressing without sexual intercourse, followed in popularity by masturbation and then sexual intercourse (Bretschneider & McCoy, 1988). Sexual activity appears to be associated with two other factors in addition to physiological capability: past sexual activity and opportunity. Older people's sexual activity generally follows the patterns established in younger years. If sex has been a source of caring and comfort, it can provide warmth and security in advanced years. But if sex has caused conflict or pain or if a person has seldom been interested in or rewarded by sexual activity, old age

TABLE 13.3   Sexual Activity in Those 50 Years of Age and Older

	In Their 50s	In Their 60s	70 and Over
Men who masturbate	66%	50%	43%
Frequency of masturbation per week for these men	1.2	0.8	0.7
Husbands who have sex with their wives	87%	78%	59%
Frequency of sex per week for these men	1.3	1.0	0.6
Women who masturbate	47%	37%	33%
Frequency of masturbation per week for these women	0.7	0.6	0.7
Wives who have sex with their husbands	88%	76%	65%
Frequency of sex per week for these women	1.3	1.0	0.6

Source: Brecher (1984).

Although still relatively rare, some older women share a mutual attraction with somewhat younger men. This woman, age 78, and man, 71, are shown at their wedding.

can represent a welcome opportunity to end sexual relations. The advice that one should maintain a regular program of physical exercise to be physically fit in later years ("use it or lose it") appears to apply to sexual capacities as well. Volunteers who engaged in sexual activity relatively frequently during early adulthood and middle age were more sexually active during old age than were volunteers who were less sexually active during their youth and middle age. For some elderly people, sexual interactions end simply because they lack a partner. There are almost six times as many widowed women as widowed men in the United States (U.S. Bureau of the Census, 1997). The ratio of unattached older women to unattached older men is further unbalanced by the tendency of men in our society to marry younger women. **Reality or Myth**

> ▶ **Issues to Consider:** Would you feel comfortable talking about sexuality with an elderly person such as a grandparent or a neighbor? Why or why not? Would the sex of the older person matter?

TRANSITIONS

The death of a spouse can be devastating for the remaining partner. Interviews conducted with more than 700 widowed Americans revealed that the levels of depression of widowed men were greater than those of widowed women (Umberson, Wortman, & Kessler, 1992). However, the researchers concluded that gender was probably a less important predictor of depression following the death of a spouse than were the different ways in which men and women are affected by widowhood. Specifically, women's depression was primarily associated with financial strain, whereas men's depression was related to problems with household management.

Men have an easier time than women in establishing a relationship with a new partner because of the gender differences in mortality rates. There are approximately 14 million widowed persons in the United States, 12 million of them women (U.S. Bureau of the Census, 1997). The median age for widowhood was 49. In view of the preponderance of widows, many elderly women who wish to be sexually active must either have affairs with married men or masturbate if they are unwilling to be a part of a polygynous relationship or unable to change their sexual orientation. Although older women are increasingly open to masturbation as a sexual outlet, masturbation cannot satisfy the need for sexual intimacy in widows who experienced close sexual relations in their marriages. More attention should be devoted to the question of satisfying the needs of the three out of four wives who eventually become widows.

Until recently, little attention had been paid to the sexual needs of the approximately 5 percent of Americans over 65 who are confined to convalescent homes and other institutions (Ahlburg & DeVita, 1992). Institutionalized people often encounter regimented environments in which they are assumed to possess the judgment of young children. Institutional design and planning seem to be based on the belief that the institutionalized aged have no interest in sexual activity. Residents who attempt to express sexual needs often are characterized as "acting out" or "suffering from senile psychosis." However, many residents of convalescent homes retain their interest in intimacy and sexual activity (Bullard-Poe, Powell, & Mulligan, 1994; Spector & Fremeth, 1996). Typically, staff members have little knowledge of the sexuality of aging, and their ignorance leads to prohibitions or constraints on the most moderate forms of sexual expression. Even tactile comfort is unavailable to many nursing home residents. Genevay (1975), who observed residents and staff in a nursing home for three months, saw only one incident in which one resident touched another in an affectionate way.

Touching can provide a sense of connection and pleasure with other people across the lifespan.

The elderly have the right to a living arrangement that allows for the possibility of sexual interaction. Whether an individual chooses to take advantage of the possibility of sexual interaction is, of course, up to him or her. But for those who do, the interaction may be beneficial; one study showed that a gender-integrated living arrangement in a New York City nursing home was associated with increased sexual contacts, a more cheerful atmosphere, and improved self-care (Silverstone & Wynter, 1975).

More than the sum of biological drives, the erotic impulse is an expression of basic desires for human contact, love, and life itself. The erotic impulse may be a fundamental expression of an appetite for life; starvation of this appetite through premature denial of our continuing erotic impulses may contribute to feelings of isolation and despair. Correlational data support this speculation: Older persons who have intimate relationships are more likely to enjoy high levels of both objective and self-perceived well-being than those who do not. These findings suggest that sexual feelings and expression should be nurtured rather than suppressed. Healthful activities during their younger years may help individuals who wish to be sexy, sensuous seniors to increase their likelihood of achieving that goal.

SUMMARY OF MAJOR POINTS

1. Young adulthood and sexual lifestyle choices. The decision to remain single for varying lengths of time, or permanently, has become more acceptable. Choosing singleness does not necessarily mean choosing celibacy. In general, cohabiting individuals do not differ greatly from people who opt to marry before living together. The primary differences appear to be a greater likelihood of flexibility in gender roles and more sexual experience beginning at an earlier age among those who cohabit. As seen later in the life cycle, a substantial proportion of young people involved in serious relationships report having extradyadic sexual contacts.

2. Work, parenthood, and sexuality. Although children can provide immense satisfaction to a couple, they also appear to have a rather dampening effect on the flexibility of a husband's and wife's timing of sexual expression and the frequency of their sexual interaction. Contrary to cultural myths regarding the timing of and the roles involved in marriage and parenthood, the majority of contemporary women, regardless of whether they have children, are employed outside the home. The decades since the 1960s have been a period of transition in social attitudes about the tasks and roles of spouses, although women still do the majority of housework.

3. Long-term relationships. Sexual satisfaction appears to be less important to perceptions of marital satisfaction as people get older. Sexual boredom can be problematic in long-term relationships if couples develop rigid and highly predictable patterns of relating to each other.

4. Extramarital relations. Disapproval of extramarital sex remains high in the United States. There is evidence, however, that substantial numbers of men and women have been sexually intimate with people other than their spouses. Most married people who have extramarital encounters do so without the agreement, approval, or knowledge of their spouses. Research conducted at the end of the 1980s and early 1990s indicates that earlier studies may have overestimated the frequency of extramarital affairs.

5. Separation and divorce. More than half of contemporary first marriages end in separation or divorce. A small proportion of divorced men tend to have serious reactions that are more severe than those experienced by women. However, a larger proportion of women than men suffer minor adjustment problems, many linked to access to economic resources and control over their lives. Most men and women are sexually active after divorce, and the majority eventually remarry.

6. Cultural attitudes toward aging. Our society is youth oriented in its views of what constitutes eroticism, and we tend to equate sexual functioning with reproductive ability, particularly in women. A double standard of aging has led postmenopausal women to be viewed as having lost their erotic appeal, whereas men are considered sexy as they gain status and power with age.

7. Sexual expression among the elderly. There is considerable variation in the frequency of sexual expression among elderly people. Longitudinal research indicates that people who enjoy frequent sexual stimulation and interaction during middle age show relatively little decline in sexual expression as they age. There is some reduction in the speed of arousal and orgasmic response, but the frequency of sexual contact among elderly people who remain sexually active is quite stable. Correlational data indicate greater health, life satisfaction, and general well-being among elderly people who are sexually active and have intimate relationships than among those who do not engage in sexual or sensual activity.

Variations in Sexual Orientation

Reality or Myth?

1. *Homosexual behavior occurs among many species.*

2. *Researchers have found that lesbians slightly outnumber gay men in the United States.*

3. *An imbalance of sex hormones is the most frequent cause of homosexuality.*

4. *Nearly all homosexuals can be identified by their physical characteristics.*

5. *Homosexuals are allowed in the United States military as long as they are not public about their sexual orientation.*

6. *Many people who have had sexual experience with both sexes do not consider themselves bisexual.*

We each have a sexual orientation. Some of us feel sexual arousal toward individuals of the same sex; others are attracted to people of the other sex. Some of us find people of both sexes sexually appealing.

In this chapter, we survey research on human sexual orientation. Most of this research has focused on attraction to people of the same sex—that is, homosexuality—and our coverage will reflect that bias. Studies of heterosexual orientation have been neglected, perhaps because funding agencies and researchers have perceived heterosexuality as being "natural" or "normal" and thus needing no explanation. We look at homosexuality in other species and cultures, and we also examine the relationship of gender-role identity to sexual orientation. We discuss what is known about the incidence of homosexual behavior and the typical characteristics of gay lifestyles, and we review current explanations of the development of sexual orientation. Antigay prejudice, sometimes called **homophobia**, has captured the attention of researchers, and we discuss what their studies have shown about it and its consequences. We examine the assumption that people who have an erotic orientation toward others of the same sex are in need of psychotherapy, and we describe attempts to alter sexual orientation. The legal and social treatment of gay people within our culture and the emergence of the gay liberation movement are considered. Finally, we consider bisexuals—people for whom gender is not an influence in erotic attraction to others—and we consider whether this identity is transitional or stable.

▶ **Issues to Consider**   Why would anyone study sexual orientation?

What Is Sexual Orientation?

The labels that we apply to varying sexual orientations, such as *gay*, *bisexual*, or *straight*, are relatively recent concepts in Western culture (Katz, 1995). Most North Americans reserve the label *heterosexual* for people who have had sexual interactions only with members of the other gender. All others, regardless of how many homosexual or heterosexual interactions they have had, are lumped into the *homosexual* category. How accurate is the common assumption that a heterosexual has sexual contacts exclusively with members of the other sex and that a homosexual is anyone who has ever had sex with a person of the same sex? Although we noted in Chapter 3 that the Kinsey group's sample was not representative of the U.S. population, Kinsey et al. (1948) found that 37 percent of men and 13 percent of women in their sample had had at least one homosexual encounter. Kinsey and his colleagues introduced an orientation rating scale that subsequent researchers have used

homophobia—Negative attitudes toward homosexuality.

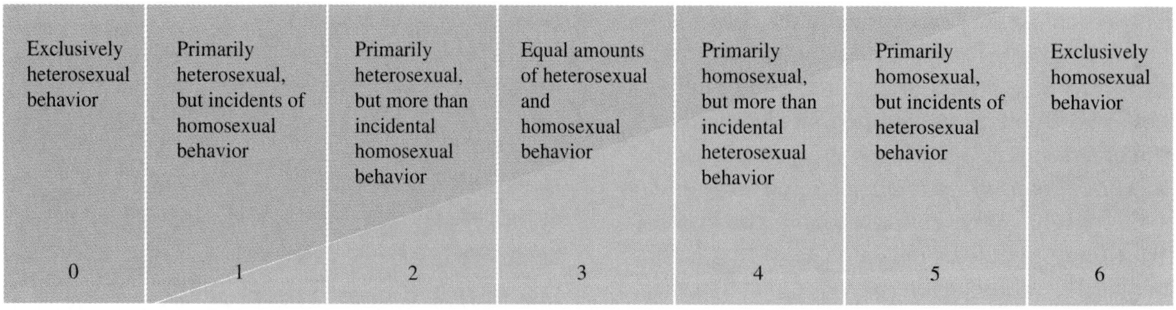

Exclusively heterosexual behavior	Primarily heterosexual, but incidents of homosexual behavior	Primarily heterosexual, but more than incidental homosexual behavior	Equal amounts of heterosexual and homosexual behavior	Primarily homosexual, but more than incidental heterosexual behavior	Primarily homosexual, but incidents of heterosexual behavior	Exclusively homosexual behavior
0	1	2	3	4	5	6

Figure 14.1   Heterosexual-Homosexual Rating Scale
Rather than treating people as either heterosexual or homosexual, the Kinsey group placed individuals along a continuum divided into seven categories, as this figure shows. (From "Heterosexual-Homosexual Rating Scale, The Kinsey Continuum." Reprinted by permission of The Kinsey Institute for Research in Sex, Gender, and Reproduction, Inc.)

extensively. Based on their sexual behaviors and erotic feelings, individuals are assigned a place or number on Kinsey's seven-point continuum from exclusive heterosexuality to exclusive homosexuality.

Although the Kinsey group did take psychological reactions to people of the same and other sex into account in classifying sexual orientation—that is, fantasies and feelings about same-sex people by individuals who did not have homosexual contacts— they emphasized behavioral criteria. In contrast, other social scientists (Storms, 1980, 1981; Hogben & Byrne, 1998) have presented evidence that an individual's erotic fantasies and feelings are central to the development of sexual orientation. These erotic fantasies motivate and give direction to sexual behavior and to the selection of partners. In using the terms *gay*, *homosexual*, and **lesbian** in this chapter, we are referring to people who are motivated by a definite erotic desire for members of the same sex and who usually (but not necessarily) engage in overt sexual relations with them.

Many people confuse gender identity with sexual orientation; that is, they assume that homosexual orientation occurs because of inappropriate gender identification. Consequently, men who prefer male sexual partners are frequently portrayed in the media as highly effeminate—"swishy" in slang terms. In fact, the gender-role identities of gay men and lesbians are often consistent with their biological sex. Later in the chapter, we will examine several possible

lesbian—A woman who is attracted to or has sex with other women.

explanations for variations in orientation, but for now we can say that the stereotypes of gay men as effeminate and lesbian women as masculine are, more often than not, inaccurate. For example, both Mary and Susan may be quite stereotypically feminine in their gender identities, yet they may be involved in a lesbian love affair with each other. There is also a tendency to confuse transvestism and transsexuality with sexual orientation. See "Highlight: Variations in Sexual Orientation and Gender Identity" for definitions of some key terms.

CROSS-SPECIES AND CROSS-CULTURAL PERSPECTIVES

Homosexual behavior is fairly common among non-human mammals. Mounting of one male by another has been observed among rodents and primates. Among nonhuman primates, same-sex sexual behavior appears to occur most often in times of stress or when social relations are unresolved. Male-male mountings are much more likely to occur when one of the males displays feminine behavior, although this behavior is not necessarily a sexual act. For example, among some types of monkeys, a male adopts a "receptive" posture as a gesture of appeasement after an argument with a more dominant male (de Waal, 1995). Dominance per se, however, is not central to nonhuman primate same-sex sexual behavior (Wallen & Parsons, 1997). It may reflect a developmental stage for juvenile males such as observed among baboons where they mount other males more frequently than they do females, although this behavior does not seem to occur among juvenile fe-

Variations in Sexual Orientation and Gender Identity

Heterosexuals. People who have sexual relationships primarily or exclusively with members of the other gender.

Homosexuals. People who have sexual relationships primarily or exclusively with members of their own gender.

Bisexuals. People who have sexual relationships with members of either gender, although not necessarily at the same time.

Transsexuals. People who appear biologically to be members of one gender but who feel psychologically as if they were members of the other gender.

Transvestites. People who become sexually aroused when wearing clothing stereotypical of the other gender. (Most contemporary transvestites are heterosexual males.)

males. Female-female mounting is also common among mammals. Female same-sex sexual behavior is more common when females reach reproductive age. There is no evidence of preferential or exclusive same-sex sexual behavior in nonhuman primates (Wallen & Parsons, 1997).

In summary, homosexual interaction has been observed in many species that researchers have studied (Pavelka, 1995). Animal studies have given us little insight, however, into human homosexual behavior, so it is advisable to keep in mind Frank Beach's (1976, p. 298) warning:

The fact that some animals engage in homosexual behavior has often been mentioned in discussions of human sexuality, with the implication that the mere existence of the similarity proves something or other about homosexuality in man; e.g., that homosexuality is "biologically normal." The conclusion may or may not be correct but the empirical evidence is irrelevant and neither supports nor denies the deduction. **Reality or Myth** ?

Our information about homosexual expression among humans in other cultures is primarily based on anthropologists' observations. In *Patterns of Sexual Behavior* (1951), Cleland Ford and Frank Beach reviewed studies of about 76 (of 190) societies for which information about homosexual behavior was available and reported that homosexual behavior

was not found to be a predominant sexual activity among adults in any of these groups. In the majority of these societies, same-sex sexual relations were considered to be normal and socially acceptable, at least for certain members of the community. In 37 percent of these societies, adult homosexual behavior was reported to be rare, absent, or carried on only in secrecy.

As described in Chapter 1, the Sambia of New Guinea is an example of a culture that prescribes a period of ritualized homosexuality for young males. In fact, up to 20 percent of the distinct cultures in New Guinea practice some form of ritualized homosexuality (Herdt, 1984). In these cultures, semen is believed to be a precious resource that must be transferred to a young male to enable him to reach maturity. Techniques for achieving this transfer include oral intercourse, anal intercourse, and masturbation, followed by a smearing of semen over the body. Most of these young males become heterosexual, marry, and father children.

Davenport (1965) provided an excellent account of a group of Melanesian people living on a Pacific island, where adult male homosexual relations with adolescents and homosexual relations between two adolescents were completely acceptable and openly discussed. Mutual masturbation and anal intercourse were considered normal within these relationships, although oral-genital activity was unknown. When a man was about 20 years old, he married a woman,

Rigid Versus Fluid Definitions of Orientation

Psychologist Michael Stevenson (1997) received a Fulbright scholarship to study in Indonesia. He described an experience on the flight to Jakarta in which he was sitting next to a middle-aged married Indonesian man. The man asked Stevenson a variety of increasingly personal questions (including inquiring about whether Stevenson had been circumcised!) and made it quite clear that he was interested in a sexual liaison with him. Stevenson indicated a number of times that he was not interested, but the man insisted on giving Stevenson his telephone number. After arriving in Jakarta, Stevenson asked if the behavior of his fellow passenger was commonplace. He was told that it was not typical, but it also was not unusual.

Stevenson wrote that because of the diversity in cultures in Indonesia, it was inappropriate to make many generalizations about sexual orientation. However, one generalization that can be made is that the whole definition of sexual orientation appears to be more fluid in Indonesia than characterizes how North Americans perceive orientation. Specifically, it appears that the use of the rigid labels *heterosexual* or *homosexual* that is common in North America to refer to both behavior and identity is not applied in most Indonesian cultures. Indonesians recognize that a heterosexually married man may have recreational sex with another man; he is not then labeled as homosexual or bisexual.

but he could still engage in extramarital homosexual relations. Thus, men in this society demonstrated either heterosexual or bisexual behavior. Davenport found no adult males who were exclusively homosexual.

These societies that have an institutional phase of homosexuality for males during their youth offer a rather striking contrast to Western expectations regarding adolescent sexuality. Popular Western stereotypes suggest that homosexuals adopt either male (the butch) or female (the femme) roles. A homosexual man who inserts his penis during fellatio or anal intercourse is considered to be active and masculine, whereas a man who receives the penis is seen as passive or feminine. Based on his preference in sexual activities, each "type" supposedly exhibits stereotypically masculine or feminine attributes in nonsexual areas. Much of North American and British research, however, does not support this rigid stereotyping. A substantial proportion of male homosexuals show a wide variety of traits associated with both masculine and feminine roles and engage in all forms of, and positions in, homosexual activity. Further, most homosexual men are attracted to masculine rather than to effeminate male partners. Similarly, lesbians are typically attracted to each

other on the basis of their femininity (Bailey, Kim, Hills, & Linsenmeier, 1997; Blumstein & Schwartz, 1983; Schreurs, 1993).

Most of this research has focused on middle- and upper-class Western males in developed countries (Carrier, 1980). In contrast, substantial numbers of males in Mexico, Brazil, Greece, and Turkey express a clear preference for playing either the active or the passive role when engaging in homosexual relations. These cultures have rigidly defined gender roles that shape heterosexual as well as homosexual interaction. Apparently there is little stigma attached to the active, inserter role in homosexual contacts in these groups because this role is considered to be masculine. A man's penetration of another man is viewed as an accomplishment of sorts, like sexual penetration of a woman. But a person who takes the submissive, receptive role is ridiculed and stigmatized as effeminate. In Brazil, for example, the average person does not perceive the man who takes the active sexual role as homosexual (Parker, 1991). When two men engage in sex, only the receptive or feminine man is labeled as homosexual. In East Asian societies, as in South American cultures, the crucial issue is who is the penetrator. Insertion is in keeping with the masculine role, whereas the person who is penetrated is ascribed female-like qualities, regardless of biological sex (Matteson, 1997).

It seems, then, that in cultures or subcultures where rigid gender-role stereotypes prevail, cultural expectations lead to narrowly prescribed sexual relationships. In predominantly middle- and upper-class North America, where gender roles are more flexible, we find greater variation in sexual expression among both heterosexuals and homosexuals, and less pressure to engage exclusively in sexual activities associated with stereotypically masculine or feminine roles. For example, fellatio appears to be more common among Americans than among, say, Mexicans (Carrier, 1980). Homosexual Mexican males, reflecting their societal values, are expected to achieve sexual satisfaction through anal intercourse rather than fellatio, just as heterosexual Mexicans are expected to prefer sexual intercourse to fellatio (see "Highlight: Rigid Versus Fluid Definitions of Orientation").

There has been little cross-cultural research on lesbianism until recently. A comparison of lesbian and heterosexual women in Brazil, Peru, the Philippines, and the United States found similarities in the development of lesbian sexuality and differences between lesbian and heterosexual women across these cultures (Whitam, Daskalos, Sobolewski, & Padilla, 1998). Compared to heterosexual women, lesbian women were more sexually active as children and had earlier sexual experiences. Interestingly, the first sexual contact for lesbians was split roughly evenly between males and females, whereas heterosexual women's first sexual contact was almost exclusively with males. Lesbians also defined themselves as such at a later age than heterosexual women defined themselves as heterosexual. Thus, regardless of the culture, lesbian sexuality and identity emerge despite the obstacles created by the dominant heterosexual ethos.

Homosexual Behavior and Gay Identity

Since the Kinsey group's research, in which they found that more than a third of men and about 13 percent of women had same-sex sexual encounters, there have been a number of efforts to assess sexual orientation in the United States and other countries. Some of these studies have used national probability sampling, tapping a more representative group than did the Kinsey group (Billy et al., 1993; Laumann et al., 1994). These researchers have come up with markedly lower estimates of the prevalence of homosexuality among Americans. For example, Sell, Wells, and Wypij (1995) compared the prevalence of homosexuality in the United States, Britain, and France (see Table 14.1).

It is difficult to determine whether the lower numbers reflect more representative sampling techniques or a failure to elicit honest answers from the respondents. Most recent researchers have employed interviewers with only limited training in sexual interviewing, as compared to the extensive experience of the researchers associated with the Kinsey group. For example, in the Smith (1991) study, the interviewers were primarily middle-aged women, most of whom had no college degrees. Gebhard (1993, p. 64) also pointed out that random probability samples

are problematic in trying to determine the incidence of homosexuality:

Homosexuals migrate from rural communities where it is hard to conceal their orientation,

TABLE 14.1 Homosexual Attraction and Behavior Across Cultures

	United States	Britain	France
Percentage reporting homosexual attraction but no homosexual behavior since age 15			
Males	8.7	7.9	8.5
Females	11.1	8.6	11.7
Percentage reporting some sexual contact with someone of the same sex in the previous five years			
Males	6.2	4.5	10.7
Females	3.6	2.1	3.3
Percentage reporting homosexual attraction and homosexual behavior since age 15			
Males	20.8	16.3	18.5
Females	17.7	18.6	18.5

Source: Adapted from Sell, Wells, and Wypij (1995).

to the anonymity of large cities, so rural samples will be largely devoid of them. In the cities the homosexuals congregate in gay communities. These are usually relatively small and therefore easily missed in random sampling. Worse yet, the custom of interviewing only one member of a household is disastrous in a gay community, where everyone in a household is apt to be homosexual.

Given these complications, the best estimate seems to be that about 4 percent to 6 percent of men and 2 percent to 4 percent of women are predominantly homosexual for a large part of their lives (Diamond, 1993; LeVay, 1996).

A substantial number of people who engage in homosexual behavior do not become exclusively homosexual. The typical male pattern is homosexual contact during preadolescence and the teens, followed by little or no further homosexual activity. This finding raises an intriguing question about sexual orientation: Why do a large number of males who engage in youthful homosexual activity eventually indulge primarily in heterosexual relations and presumably maintain a heterosexual identity, whereas others adopt a homosexual identity? On a more concrete level, how do people who have had one or more homosexual contacts know whether they are homosexual or heterosexual? Or, if they have developed a strong emotional attachment to a member of the same sex, how do they decide whether this attachment should be classified as a homosexual orientation or a deep friendship that includes sexual expression? These questions all involve our identities and self-definitions as sexual beings. **Reality or Myth** ?

SELF-DEFINITION

The search for meaning and self-definition is at no other time more pressing than during adolescence. During childhood and adolescence, most people experience a great deal of confusion and ambiguity about sexual thoughts, feelings, and behavior. What is normal, they wonder, and what is deviant or abnormal? What is the appropriate role to choose in relationships with others? In moving awkwardly through this complicated process, a person begins to construct a sexual identity. For most people, one aspect of that identity is heterosexual, but for some it is homosexual or, more rarely, bisexual. The many paths that lead to a homosexual identity are far more difficult to travel because of the sanctions against homosexual behavior.

Adults who define themselves as homosexual often experience a sense of being "different" in childhood and adolescence (Telljohann & Price, 1993). One study of 1,000 gay people indicated that "homosexual feelings" occurred typically at age 14 among boys and about age 16 among girls. For both sexes, the feelings had arisen at least two years before they ever made genital contact with a person of the same gender (Bell et al., 1981).

Acquiring a gay identity is a gradual process. The emergence of homosexual feelings is usually followed by an individual's adoption of the label *gay*, association with other gay individuals, and a first homosexual love relationship (Harry, 1993; Rust, 1993a). There is evidence that young men identify themselves as gay at an earlier age if they are able to meet openly with gay men in a supportive environment where homosexuality is considered normal (Boxer & Cohler, 1989). This sort of environment is most likely to be found in large cities, where there are well-developed support systems for gays.

After individuals define themselves as gay, the stage is set for a number of other important decisions. Should they remain "in the closet," keeping their sexual orientation as private as possible? If they decide to "come out"—that is, to acknowledge their gay identity to others—how publicly should they express their orientation? Should they tell their family and friends? What about employers and strangers? Coming out is a complex phase in the individual's life, during which he or she adopts a gay identity and explores the homosexual community. Most men come out at about age 19 or 20; women tend to come out somewhat later, in their early 20s (Harry, 1993; Rust, 1993a).

This coming-out process may have unintended positive consequences for gay men and lesbians. The best predictor of heterosexuals' attitudes toward gay men is personal contact with a gay man or lesbian. Of the respondents in a national survey, 35 percent of those who had a friend, acquaintance, or relative who was homosexual had more positive attitudes toward gay men than did those who had no such contact (Herek & Glunt, 1993). Heterosexuals who know two or more gay people have more positive attitudes toward gays than those who had less or no contact (Herek & Capitanio, 1996). Thus, acknowledging one's homosexual orientation to close associates may lead to more positive attitudes among the general population toward homosexuals. An alternative interpretation of the conclusions of Herek and his colleagues is that gays are more likely to reveal their orientation to others who have positive attitudes toward homosexuality.

Faced with the intolerance of conventional heterosexual society, some gay people nevertheless openly exhibit their affection to their partner, while others carefully shroud their sexual orientation in secrecy. Most choose a position somewhere between these two extremes (Cox & Gallois, 1996; Harry, 1993). Gays who tend to be overt about their orientation are most likely to volunteer for research on the topic. Therefore, we know more about the lifestyles of those people than we do about less openly gay persons.

SEXUAL EXPRESSION

Homosexuals use the same methods of sexual expression as heterosexuals, with the obvious exception of coitus. For lesbians, the most common sexual activities are hugging, snuggling and kissing, cunnilingus, mutual masturbation, and **tribadism** (Fassinger & Morrow, 1995; Schreuers, 1993). To perform the last, one woman lies on top of the other and makes rhythmic thrusting movements to stimulate their clitorises. The use of dildos and the practice of analingus (stimulation of the anal area with the [aka rim job] tongue) appear to be relatively rare among lesbians (Schreurs, 1993), despite their popularity in erotic films and books. Gay men most frequently engage in fellatio, mutual masturbation (shown in Chapter 5), anal intercourse, and interfemoral intercourse (rubbing the penis between the partner's legs until orgasm) (Bell & Weinberg, 1978; Weinrich, 1994).

In their comparison of heterosexual and homosexual physiological responses, Masters and Johnson (1979) found no differences between the two groups in patterns of sexual arousal and orgasm. In other words, a human body responds to sexual stimulation in the same predictable ways whether the arousal

tribadism—Sexual activity in which one woman lies on top of another and moves rhythmically for clitoral stimulation.

Gay men who openly express their affection toward their partners are often criticized for "flaunting" their homosexuality. In contrast, heterosexual couples who hug in public are rarely condemned for flaunting their sexuality.

Masters and Johnson (1979) claimed that gay couples may have a more relaxed and less goal-oriented approach to sexual intimacy than do heterosexual couples. However, the degree of relaxation is probably a function of the length of a relationship and level of commitment, regardless of people's sexual orientation.

comes from males, females, or objects. The application of sexual stimulation, however, may be somewhat different in homosexual lovemaking than in heterosexual lovemaking. Masters and Johnson reported that gay people are more relaxed than heterosexuals, tending to adopt a slower and less demanding sexual approach with each other. They seemed to be more wholeheartedly involved in their sexual activity and demonstrated greater communication than the heterosexual couples whom Masters and Johnson studied. The heterosexual couples were described as being more performance oriented; that is, they spent less time giving sensual pleasure to each other as they pursued orgasm: "At times, they created the impression that the objective of goal attainment was valued almost as much as the subjective experience of orgasmic release" (Masters & Johnson, 1979, p. 65).

Masters and Johnson (1979) attempted to explain these differences by suggesting that it is easier for women to know what pleases women and for men to know what pleases men. Consequently, homosexuals have an intuitive understanding of their partners' sexual wants. Masters and Johnson maintained that a pattern in which partners take turns giving and receiving stimulation reduces fears about sexual performance. They believe that heterosexual interactions involve more dependence on and respon-

sibility for the partner, a pattern that distracts each partner from his or her own subjective experience.

If Masters and Johnson's (1979) findings are generalizable to the larger proportion of sexually proficient and psychologically adjusted homosexuals, then these gay couples may have something to teach heterosexuals about sensuality. The relaxed and less goal-oriented approach of the homosexual couples that Masters and Johnson observed epitomizes the advice that most sex therapists give to both heterosexuals and homosexuals for enhanced sexual enjoyment.

In contrast to Masters and Johnson's conclusions, Jay and Young (1979) reported that 42 percent of the 1,000 lesbians in their study complained of frequent difficulty in sexual communication with their partners. Further, in Bell and Weinberg's (1978) study, between 43 percent and 61 percent of the gay men and women reported that lack of orgasm for themselves or their partner was sometimes a problem.

Almost all gay men and lesbian women have been involved at some point in a relatively steady relationship with a same-sex partner (McWhirter & Mattison, 1984; Schreurs, 1993). In Bell and Weinberg's (1978) study, more than 50 percent of the men and approximately 70 percent of the women were currently in a steady relationship.

Comparisons of the values of gay and heterosexual men and women have yielded great similarities in

Having successfully sued the state of New Jersey for the right to adopt children, partners Jon Holden and Michael Galluccio added legal parenthood to their stable relationship.

the groups' rankings of the values (described later) that they considered important in a relationship. Their romantic view of love, degree of commitment, and satisfaction with their relationships were also similar (Fowlkes, 1994). But gay men differed from heterosexuals in that they attached less importance to sexual exclusivity in a relationship. In terms of psychological adjustment and measures of satisfaction and commitment, there appear to be no differences between monogamous and nonmonogamous gay male couples (Blasband & Peplau, 1985; Kurdek & Schmitt, 1985/1986). Apparently both types of relationships can be satisfying for gay men.

Researchers have also found differences between dependent or traditional women involved in lesbian relationships and independent, feminist lesbians (Peplau & Gordon, 1983). Mirroring the tendency of traditional heterosexual women, traditional lesbian women were especially dependent on their partners for fulfilling their needs. In contrast, the independent, feminist lesbians sought satisfaction from professional and community involvement, not just from their love relationships.

Gender Differences.   Most of the differences that have been found between gay men and lesbian women are those that might be expected from the different socialization experiences of males and females (Leigh, 1989; Schreurs & Buunk, 1995). For example, women, regardless of sexual orientation, rank emotional expressiveness and equality in their love relationships as more important than do gay and straight men. And in contrast to many gay male relationships, lesbian love affairs are relatively long-lasting ones in which the couples show a considerable degree of fidelity to each other (Kurdek & Schmitt, 1987; Schreurs & Buunk, 1995). Perhaps for this reason, public **cruising** is much less frequent among lesbians than among gay men. When the women did cruise, the activity was almost entirely limited to bars and private parties. Only 17 percent of lesbians had actively sought sexual encounters during the year previous to the research (Bell &

cruising—Socializing in a variety of locations in the attempt to find a partner.

Hawaii is the only state that recognizes homosexual marriage. The state has appealed Circuit Court Judge Kevin S. C. Chang's decision to the Hawaiian Supreme Court. Chang has ruled that the state had failed to prove that same-sex marriages would harm children or anyone else.

Weinberg, 1978). In contrast, about 85 percent of men reported cruising about once a month. We might expect the frequency of cruising to have diminished with the advent of HIV/AIDS, but current data are not available.

One of the most striking differences between homosexual men and women lies in their number of sexual partners. Almost half the homosexual men in the Bell and Weinberg (1978) study said that they had had at least 50 different sexual partners during their lives, and 28 percent claimed 1,000 or more partners. None of the lesbians in the total sample reported having had this many partners, and more than half had been involved with fewer than 10 sexual partners. One of the unfortunate consequences of the men's pattern is that about two out of three reported having had a sexually transmitted disease

(STD) at one time or another, whereas only 1 of the 293 women in this study had ever contracted an STD from homosexual activity.

Symons (1979) argued that lesbian and gay male sexual behavior represents a pure form of female and male sexuality. Homosexual men, in many respects, show more extremely stereotypical "masculine" sexual behavior than do their heterosexual counterparts; that is, they tend to seek a variety of partners and to engage in impersonal and frequent sexual activity to a greater extent than do heterosexual men. Lesbians tend to form stable, intimate relationships in which sexual relations are generally associated with enduring emotion and a loving partner.

Both gay men and heterosexual men report similar levels of sexual interest. Gay and heterosexual women also have similar levels of sexual interest, but it is lower than that of gay and heterosexual men. However, gay men come closer to fulfilling their desires by having sex more frequently and with more partners than do heterosexual men, perhaps because they are not constrained by the unwillingness of women to have sex with them (Bailey, Gauling, Agyei, & Gladue, 1994).

▶ **Issues to Consider**   In what ways are gay males more like heterosexual males than they are like lesbians?

Aging.   There is no particular reason to believe that the biological effects of aging on sexual response are any different for homosexuals than for heterosexuals. Masters and Johnson (1979) demonstrated that sexual response does not differ according to sexual orientation, and it is difficult to imagine factors that would alter this fact in the second half of life.

Most studies (Bell & Weinberg, 1978; Kinsey et al., 1948, 1953; McWhirter & Mattison, 1984) indicate that homosexuals experience the same general age-related changes in their sexual behavior as do their heterosexual counterparts. Linda Wolf (1979) nevertheless found that although the aging gay people whom she interviewed experienced many of the life changes that are characteristic of our culture at large, their sexual orientation did produce different challenges as they dealt with the effects of menopause, the changes of midlife, and plans for retirement activities. For gay men, psychological adjustment in later life is associated with a strong commitment to homosexuality, integration into the gay community, low concern with concealment of sexual orientation, and a satisfactory sex life, usually within an exclusive relationship (Berger, 1996).

There is a stereotype in Western societies of the aging homosexual as fearful and lonely. This stereotype has not been supported by research (Berger, 1996; Kye, 1995). In fact, Weinberg and Williams (1975) found that older respondents tended to have better self-concepts and to be more stable than younger gays. Among older respondents, more women than men tended to be sexually active, but men who were still sexually active did not differ from the women in frequency of sexual expression. Women showed more interest than men did in long-term relationships. One difference that emerged from this research was that lesbians were less anxious

about growing old than were gay men. The reverse has been found to be true among heterosexuals. Perhaps this is a reflection of the gender of the person one wishes to attract. Because men value youth and beauty in a partner, people who wish to be sexually attractive to men—heterosexual women and gay men—may become overly concerned about their own youth and beauty, a fact that might make them more vulnerable to eating disorders, for example, in their efforts to remain thin and attractive (Gettelman & Thompson, 1993).

Homosexuals who are open about their lifestyles may not experience the midlife crisis that many heterosexuals encounter (Kye, 1995). Relatively early in life, most homosexuals go through a crisis that heterosexuals do not: they must face and manage a conventionally nonaccepted sexual lifestyle. It may be that if they successfully resolve this challenge, their ability to cope with the changes of aging is strengthened. In addition, the majority of homosexuals do not face family responsibilities and changes in family involvement that often confront heterosexuals as they age.

Kimmel (1978) pointed out that because of the stigma associated with a homosexual orientation, aging gays are deprived of many of the social supports that benefit their heterosexual age peers. For example, when a heterosexual loses his or her mate through divorce or death, friends and relatives tend to be supportive through a grieving period. But when a homosexual bond ends, friends and relatives may be relieved; when a gay person's mate dies, bereavement may be a solitary experience unless the survivor has a close support network in the gay community.

The renowned social psychologist Roger Brown (1996, p. 2) described how he coped with the aftermath of the death of his partner of 40 years in this insightful and poignant view of aging and loss:

> *Old gay men in stable same-sex unions are not very different from old men in straight unions unless they lose a spouse. Then the difference is great. The elderly widower is a social prize who can be introduced to a different prospective bride every evening if he so chooses—and many do. Not infrequently he will have picked out a potential successor from among his*

wife's friends before her demise. For me the case proved quite otherwise, and so it does, I think, for most gay widowers.

Situational Same-Gender Contacts: Prisons.   In sex-segregated institutions such as prisons, homosexual relations are fairly common. Homosexual behavior under these conditions is frequently spurred by the lack of opportunity for heterosexual contact and is known as *transient* or *situational homosexuality.* In one early study of prison life, about 40 percent of the convict population was found to have engaged in homosexual activity (Clemmer, 1958). Of these, only about 10 percent had engaged in such behavior before they went to jail.

Same-sex sexual interactions in men's prisons are often based on the wish to dominate those perceived as weaker or possessing "feminine" characteristics (Long & Sultan, 1987; Struckman-Johnson, Struckman-Johnson, Rucker, Bumby, & Donaldson, 1996).

In a situation similar to those reported in the earlier discussion of cross-cultural research on homosexuality, the dominant man does not view himself as homosexual, and seldom is the sex reciprocal. That is, the dominant man uses the "weaker" man for sexual release but does not in turn provide sexual pleasure for the subordinate man (see "Highlight: Male Rape" on page 454 of Chapter 19).

There has been little research on sexuality in female prisons. In one study of several midwestern state prisons, only 7 percent of women prisoners reported experiencing sexual coercion, compared to 22 percent of men prisoners (Struckman-Johnson et al., 1996). As might be expected from the previous discussion of lesbian relationships, women prisoners usually integrate sexuality into an ongoing relationship. Most of the women who engage in same-gender relations in prison do not think of themselves as homosexuals, and they usually return to heterosexual behavior when they are released.

Explanations of Sexual Orientation

Until recently, most hypotheses advanced to explain sexual orientation have included the notion that people are gay because of defects: inherited disorders, deviant hormonal exposure, harmful family patterns, early sexual experiences, or gender-role nonconformity. If not for negative influences, it was thought, the individual would be heterosexual. We consider this assumption after reviewing the data relevant to each hypothesis.

BIOLOGICAL CORRELATES

Historically, scientists have tended to look to biological or genetic factors to account for behavioral phenomena that they did not understand, including homosexual behavior. Conclusions based on such influences, even when inaccurate, seem to resolve complex and elusive questions in an orderly way.

Interest in a hereditary basis for homosexuality dates back to the eighteenth century, when all sexual variations were assumed to be a sign of a degenerate family tree. Not surprisingly, most theorizing regarding homosexuality and heredity has portrayed homo-

sexuality as maladaptive. For example, an early investigator of homosexuality wrote:

> *The urgency of [research] with respect to the genetic aspects of homosexual behavior is underscored by the ominous fact that* adult homosexuality continues to be an inexhaustible source of unhappiness, discontent, and a distorted sense of human values. *(Kallmann, 1952, p. 296, emphasis added)*

As this statement demonstrates, Kallmann was not the most objective observer of homosexuality. In 1952, he published an extensive study of sexual orientation in twins, in which he examined **concordance rates.** Kallmann reported that the concordance rate was nearly 100 percent for monozygotic (genetically identical) twins and about 10 percent for dizygotic (not genetically identical) twins. This work was

---

concordance rate—The likelihood that if one person manifests a certain trait, a relative (twin, sibling, uncle, etc.) will manifest that same trait.

criticized because many of the men in his study came from prisons and psychiatric institutions and because there was no information about how Kallmann judged whether the twins were monozygotic (MZ) or dizygotic (DZ).

More recent twin studies have shown concordance rates for homosexual orientation in males to be as high as 66 percent for MZ twins and 30 percent for DZ twins (Bailey & Pillard, 1991; Whitam, Diamond, & Martin, 1993). For lesbian women, 48 percent of the MZ twins were lesbian or bisexual compared to 16 percent of DZ twins and 6 percent of adoptive sisters (Bailey, Pillard, Neale, & Agyei, 1993). These findings suggest a genetic contribution to homosexual orientation.

The idea of a genetic or biological basis for some male homosexuals is reinforced by the report by Hamer, Hu, Magnusen, Hu, and Pattatucci (1993). They found a region on the X chromosome that appears to contain a gene or genes for homosexual orientation. Thirty-three of the 40 pairs of homosexual brothers had similar genetic markers and appear to have inherited the chromosome responsible for the trait from their mothers. Figure 14.2 presents data from their study showing the relationship of the maternal connection to homosexual orientation in men. For example, in Family A, Generation I, the woman's brother is gay. The woman (let's call her Sally) has one daughter and four sons, one of whom is gay. Sally's daughter then produces a daughter and a son who is gay. It should be noted that Hamer and his colleagues think that homosexuality arises from a variety of causes, both genetic and environmental.

In keeping with this emphasis on biology, there have been reports of differences between the brains of homosexual and heterosexual men (LeVay, 1991, 1996; Swaab, Gooren, & Hofman, 1995). One of the four regions in the hypothalamus of the brain, the

---

Figure 14.2   Family Trees of Homosexual Males
Samples of homosexual males and their families were asked by Hamer et al. (1993) to identify, if possible, other family members who were or are gay. (The filled triangles represent gay members.) Families A and B both have a single gay man in each of three maternally related generations. In Family C two gay brothers have a maternally related gay uncle and nephew. Family D, for whom information was obtained about six generations, contains seven (known) gay males. These gay men are all related through the sequential marriage of two sisters to the same husband in generation II. As Hamer et al. put it, in addition to evidence of transmission of gay male orientation through the maternal line, the striking aspect of these genealogies "is the absence of transmission through the paternal line and the paucity of female homosexuals" (p. 323).

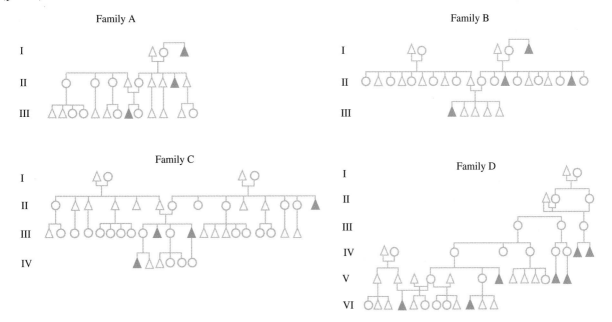

INAH-3, is generally larger in men than in women. Based on research with animals, the region appears to be involved in male-typical sexual behavior.

In an intriguing study, Simon LeVay (1991) hypothesized that the volume of INAH-3 would show a size difference not just with biological sex, but with sexual orientation. LeVay obtained statistically significant differences in the volume of the INAH-3 region between the three groups in his sample. As predicted, heterosexual men had a higher volume in that region of the hypothalamus than did homosexual men. Homosexual men were intermediate between heterosexual men and heterosexual women in the INAH-3 volume, with women having the lowest volume. We must emphasize that these results are preliminary and have been questioned as to their relevance to sexual orientation (De Cecco & Parker, 1995). Further, LeVay could not obtain enough deceased lesbian women to include in his sample of relatively young people, as lesbians tend to be quite healthy.

Consistent with beliefs in the 1930s and 1940s in the biological origins of homosexuality, several attempts were made to treat gay men with androgens. This approach was based on the idea that gay men were not masculine enough, so they needed the boost of masculinizing hormones. Although the androgen administration usually succeeded in increasing sexual interest and activity, partner attraction remained unchanged.

The vast majority of homosexual males appear to have testosterone levels within the normal range (Banks & Gartrell, 1995). Research on sex hormones is even more difficult in women than in men because of the fluctuation in women's hormone levels over the course of the menstrual and life cycle. Past studies indicate that the majority of lesbians appear to have testosterone and estrogen levels within the normal range (Banks & Gartrell, 1995; LeVay, 1996).

Anthony Bogaert and Ray Blanchard (1996) hypothesized that differences in sexual differentiation in the brain during prenatal development might result in differences in the height, weight, and age of puberty in homosexual versus heterosexual men. With a sample of more than 600 men, half of whom described themselves as homosexual and the other half as heterosexual, the authors found that on average, the gay men were shorter, weighed less, and reported earlier onset of puberty than did the heterosexual men. Their findings confirmed those of earlier researchers. Given these differences, Bogaert and Hershberger's (1998) findings are somewhat surprising from a secondary analysis of the penis size of more than 5,000 men from the Kinsey group's samples (4,187 heterosexuals, 935 gay men). The men estimated (and also measured) the length and circumferences of their penises in both the flaccid and erect states. The average size of gay men's penises exceeded those of heterosexual men, although the differences were small. For example, the average (self-measured) length of the erect penises of gay men was 6.46 versus 6.14 inches for the heterosexual men. Thus, the average gay man is physically smaller than the average heterosexual man, except for erect-penis length.

To our knowledge, no one has made comparisons of physical (or genital) characteristics of samples of lesbian versus heterosexual women. If differences in prenatal brain differentiation are associated with one's orientation, however, then lesbian women, compared to heterosexual women, should be heavier, taller, and have later onset of puberty.

There is growing interest in the possible prenatal hormonal contribution to sexual orientation, but we are probably decades away from adequately testing this theoretical link. Even if such a prenatal contribution exists, whether it is overtly expressed would probably depend on many other lifetime experiences. *Reality or Myth*

FAMILY EXPERIENCES

Several researchers influenced by psychoanalytic theory have explored the role of early family influences in the development of sexual orientation. In one such study, Bieber, Dane, and Prince (1962) described a **triangular family system** to account for the development of male homosexuality. According to this hypothesis, a homosexual is typically the child of an overly intimate, controlling mother and a detached, hostile, rejecting father. Bieber and coworkers based

> **triangular family system**—In psychoanalytic theory, the notion that a male homosexual's mother is intimate and controlling and his father is detached and rejecting.

their system on the differences they found between a group of homosexual men and a group of heterosexual men in psychoanalysis. Even so, 38 percent of the homosexuals did not come from a triangular family system, and 32 percent of the heterosexuals reported such a family background. At best, this research suggests that many people in therapy, regardless of their sexual orientation, may be the products of a triangular system.

Some conflicting results emerging from studies of homosexuals' family backgrounds can be attributed to variations in the populations from which the homosexual samples were drawn. In some studies, these populations consisted of patients or prisoners. Marvin Siegelman (1972a, 1972b) attempted to reduce the potential bias introduced with such samples by administering questionnaires, including one that measured neuroticism, to groups of "normal" (nonclinical) homosexuals and heterosexuals. When he compared homosexual and heterosexual men who were low in neuroticism, there were *no* differences in the parental backgrounds of the two groups. The same was true of women who scored low in neuroticism. Other research has not supported the hypothesis that orientation toward same-sex partners stems from being raised in a triangular family system (Milic & Crowne, 1986; Newcomb, 1985; Siegelman, 1987).

Overall, this research supports the idea that parental characteristics may correlate with tendencies toward neuroticism in *both* homosexuals and heterosexuals but are not related to sexual orientation per se. Therefore, the evidence on family background and sexual orientation supports the position that Evelyn Hooker (1969) took about three decades ago that disturbed parental relations are neither necessary nor sufficient conditions for the development of homosexuality.

GENDER-ROLE NONCONFORMITY DURING CHILDHOOD

A growing body of evidence indicates that one pathway to becoming a homosexual in adulthood is nonconformity to societal expectations for one's gender in early childhood. Researchers have reported that "feminine" boys have a much higher probability of becoming adults with a homosexual orientation than do more "masculine" boys (Bailey, Miller, & Willerman, 1993; Green, 1987; Phillips & Over, 1992).

Homosexual men were more likely to characterize their childhoods as having involved interest in toys stereotypic for girls, cross-dressing, preference for girls' games and activities, preference for the company of women, being regarded as a sissy, and preference for boys in childhood sex play (Whitam, 1977). Similarly, lesbians recalled more male-stereotypic behaviors in childhood than did heterosexual women in the United States, Brazil, Peru, and the Philippines (Phillips & Over, 1995; Whitam & Mathy, 1991).

Adult gay men who have a strong preference for receptive anal intercourse have the strongest recollections of gender-role nonconformity in childhood (Weinrich et al., 1992). If this finding is replicated, it suggests that there may be a distinct subgroup of gay men whose preferred erotic behavior is a continuation of a lifelong gender-atypical pattern. Gay men who do not have a strong preference for receptive anal sex have a childhood history that is more conventional regarding gender-role conformity and has a substantial overlap with the history typical for heterosexual men.

Not all homosexuals display traits or interests atypical of their gender in childhood. About half the homosexual men in the Bell et al. (1981) research appeared to have masculine identities, interests, and activities in childhood, compared to about three-fourths of heterosexual men. About one-fifth of lesbian women, compared to one-third of heterosexual women, reported being highly "feminine" while growing up.

The link between homosexuality and gender nonconformity in childhood has been questioned because of the way in which it was established. In the Bell group's study, individuals were asked to describe their childhoods. Beyond the usual difficulties associated with remembering events long past, this population may have introduced an additional bias. Having already accepted a gay identity and a set of beliefs about homosexuality, they may have unintentionally edited their memories to make those memories consistent with their current belief systems. Such a bias may be particularly problematic when the sample is recruited from members of the gay liberation movement.

Richard Green (1987) avoided the problem of inaccurate memories by conducting a longitudinal study in which boys who were effeminate during childhood were compared to a control group of conventional boys. Following these boys into adolescence, he found that the gender nonconformists were more likely to become homosexual than were members of the control group.

Michael Ross (1980) suggested that researchers would find less rigid gender stereotyping in less traditional countries. Studies in Sweden and Australia support his hypothesis. Swedish homosexuals, reared in a society in which adopting nontraditional gender roles is acceptable, recalled less feminine childhood play than did Australian homosexuals, who typically were reared to adopt traditional gender roles. Thus early atypical gender-conforming interests and activities may be related to homosexuality in cultures that emphasize rigid distinctions between masculinity and femininity.

Of the factors that we have considered thus far, only gender-role nonconformity in childhood appears to have a fairly solid link to homosexual orientation, at least for some people. Sexual orientation appears to be fairly well established in males around age 18 and in females around age 21. Masturbatory fantasies may reinforce these sexual orientations through sexual arousal and orgasm (Storms, 1980, 1981; Van Wyk & Geist, 1984). With increasing social acceptance and social support, we expect that same-sex sexual orientation would become established at an earlier age. McClintock and Herdt (1996) reported that both men and women reported their first awareness of attraction to people of the same or other sex as occurring when they were 10 or 10½ years old.

In his Exotic Becomes Erotic (EBE) model (summarized in Figure 14.3), which subsumes a number of the proposed explanations for orientation that we have already described, Daryl Bem (1996) hypothesized that biological variables (genes, prenatal hormones, brain neuroanatomy) do not directly cause a particular orientation. Instead, these factors result in childhood temperaments that may influence a child's preferences for gender-typical or -atypical activities and peers. According to Bem, such preferences then lead children to feel different from their peers of the same or other sex and to see the peers from whom they feel different as dissimilar, unfamiliar, and exotic. This perception stimulates heightened physiological arousal that is erotically responsive to (some)

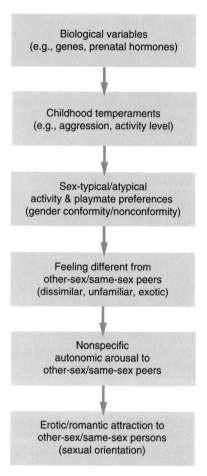

Figure 14.3   Bem's Model of the Development of Sexual Orientation
Daryl Bem has hypothesized a temporal sequence of events leading to sexual orientation for most men and women.

members of the sex they perceive as different from themselves in terms of interests and activities. Thus, the exotic (different) becomes erotic.

Bem's model incorporates the findings we previously discussed regarding the correlation between gender-role nonconformity during childhood and subsequent development of homosexual orientation. It also has the advantage of explaining the correlation between gender-role conformity and subsequent development of heterosexual orientation.

Bem's hypotheses need to be investigated empirically, and we hope that his model will stimulate research on the sources of sexual orientation. The model has already been challenged. Letitia Anne Peplau and her colleagues (Peplau, Garnets, Spalding, Conley, & Veniegas, 1998) faulted the model on two major bases (as well as some minor ones). First, they argued that the evidence does not support Bem's hypothesis that all or most adults are erotically attracted to the class of people (men or women) from whom they felt different during childhood. Second, they questioned Bem's assertion that EBE theory accounts equally well for the development of orientation in both men and women. Calling the model "androcentric" (male centered), Peplau et al. argued that the model neglects or misrepresents women's developmental and sexual experiences.

Regarding the first charge, Bem (1998) retorted that he had not claimed that EBE theory could explain the path to adult sexual orientation of *all* people; instead, he maintained that the EBE model described the modal (most common) path to adult orientation. In response to the claim that EBE theory is androcentric, Bem conceded that there are some important sex differences between men and women regardless of their sexual orientation. For example, men's sexuality may be more driven by lust, whereas women's sexuality may be characterized by greater emphasis on limerance (see Chapter 7). However, he contended that this sex difference is irrelevant to the path leading to adult orientation. He also described women's sexual orientation as more fluid than that of men, with women more likely to be bisexual than men, and men more likely to be exclusively homosexual than women. In addition, he asserted that if our society becomes less gender polarized, people may be less likely to use sex (male or female) as a necessary condition for attraction and may place greater value on a diversity of other attributes (e.g., personality characteristics). Under that condition, he expected that his model would have less explanatory power.

In summary, there appear to be many different paths to the development of erotic orientation that vary by culture and historical period. Earlier, we mentioned the historical claim that gays are maladjusted, a topic to which we turn now.

Sexual Orientation and Adjustment

Over the years, homosexuals in North America have been accused of being mentally ill or maladjusted. Mental health professionals have tried to "cure" homosexuals, and researchers have attempted to measure emotional health and adjustment as a function of a person's sexual orientation. However, many gay people experience adjustment problems because of the prejudice against homosexuality that they face in their daily lives.

ANTIGAY PREJUDICE

At the outset, it is important to understand the difference between *prejudice* and *discrimination*. Most of us have prejudices—negative (or positive) attitudes and stereotypes about particular groups—but we do not necessarily act on these prejudices in ways that interfere with the rights of people who belong to those groups. When our prejudices are expressed in behaviors that harm others, our actions constitute discrimination, a topic we will discuss later in this chapter. Although evidence is lacking to support most contemporary North American stereotypes about homosexuals, such as the idea that all gays are maladjusted, negative attitudes against homosexuals remain widespread (Kite & Whitley, 1998; Weinrich, 1994).

For many people, aversion to homosexuals approaches a true phobia—that is, a persistent and irrational fear. National surveys measuring attitudes toward homosexual relations between adults found that a majority of those questioned believed that such relations were wrong (Davis & Smith, 1984; Herek & Glunt, 1993). In their worst forms, homophobia and antigay discrimination are responsible for the verbal and physical abuse of gays. In recent surveys, as many as 92 percent of lesbian women and gay men reported that they have been verbally abused or threatened because they were gay. As many as 40 percent report experiencing physical attacks because of their sexual orientation (D'Augelli, 1998; Otis & Skinner, 1996). Antigay hate crimes may have increased as part of the public reaction to the AIDS epidemic, and the response of government and public health officials to the AIDS crisis may have lagged because most of the early victims of AIDS in North America were gay men.

Like their heterosexual counterparts, gays and lesbians tend to learn and internalize the social norms of their culture. Thus, some gays may have to struggle with an internalized homophobia that has been linked to depression, suicide, substance abuse, and eating disorders (DiPlacido, 1998).

Negative attitudes toward gay men are more prevalent among heterosexual men than among heterosexual women, although heterosexual men and women do not differ in their attitudes toward lesbian women. Heterosexual men's less negative attitudes toward lesbians may partially stem from the erotic value they attribute to lesbianism. If the erotic value is experimentally controlled, heterosexual men's attitudes toward lesbians are similar to their attitudes toward gay men (Louderback & Whitley, 1997; Whitley, Wiederman, & Wryobek, 1998). In addition, compared with people who are tolerant of others' sexual orientation, antigays attend church more frequently and are more likely to be affiliated with fundamentalist religions and to come from rural areas. Moreover, they tend to be more authoritarian, feel guiltier about sex, display greater gender-role rigidity, and are more likely to view sex as primarily for procreative purposes than do those who are tolerant of gays (Herek & Capitanio, 1995; Herek & Glunt, 1993; Simon, 1998).

Although sexual orientation is just one aspect of identity, our society tends to view the sexual orientation of homosexuals as an extremely important, if not the most important, aspect of their identity. Regardless of their occupations, accomplishments, personalities, and the myriad other factors that make up the complexities of being human, people who express their sexuality with others of the same sex are culturally defined, first and foremost, as homosexuals; this definition affects the ways in which others interpret all their actions.

This link between homosexual orientation and other personal characteristics and behaviors is even more problematic when we consider that most homosexuals and heterosexuals cannot easily identify the sexual orientation of other individuals. In one study, students observed videotapes of interviews of heterosexual and homosexual men and women (Berger, Hank, Rauzi, & Simkins, 1987). Nearly 80 percent of the students were unable to identify the sexual orientation of those shown in the videotapes beyond chance expectations. The difference that is so emphasized in our society is not readily apparent to most of us.

Implicit in many negative attitudes toward gays and lesbians is the fear that homosexuality is contagious. Perhaps the most damaging myth about homosexuals is that they are abusers of impressionable young children, whom they will seduce and lure into a gay lifestyle. Despite the fact that research has not supported it, this belief has caused overwhelming hardships for teachers who are homosexual and gay parents seeking child custody. Most teenagers have their first homosexual experiences with other adolescents rather than with adults. Furthermore, most child sexual abuse is committed by heterosexual men, not gays.

On a related note, the fact that the vast majority of homosexuals are reared in homes with heterosexual role models indicates that it is unlikely that the offspring of gay parents would become homosexual as a result of the early childhood models they encountered. In fact, research has shown that lesbian mothers' sexual orientation does not produce homosexuality in their children or have damaging consequences for their offspring's development (Coleman, 1990; Golombok & Tasker, 1996; Tasker & Golombok, 1997).

One of the possible explanations of homophobia dates back to Freud, who speculated that a fear of homosexuality was a defensive reaction against one's own erotic feelings toward someone of the same sex. In an interesting probe of this idea, Adams, Wright, and Lohr (1996) divided a group of college student men into homophobic and nonhomophobic groups on the basis of their scores on a measure of homophobia. Both groups were exposed to sexually explicit videotapes of heterosexual, gay male, and lesbian sexual interactions. More homophobic men (54 percent) displayed an increase in penile erection to the gay male tapes than did nonhomophobic men (24 percent). When questioned later, the homophobic men significantly underreported their arousal, suggesting that they were unaware of it or denying it. Thus, it may be that some of the dislike of homosexuals is a fear that they might be vulnerable to their own erotic feelings toward men and demean these feelings because they are incongruent with their image of themselves as heterosexual.

These lesbian parents are helping their son with an art project. There is no evidence that the offspring of lesbian parents are more likely to become homosexual or maladjusted than are children raised by heterosexual parents.

A literary example of the idea of defensive homophobia appears in Patricia Cornwell's (1998) best-selling novel, *Hornet's Nest*. A character called Bubba becomes convinced that a handsome reporter is homosexual. Bubba ruminates (p. 110):

> *Bubba could see it now. The pretty boy getting what he deserved, from the rear, from a manly man like Bubba, whose favorite movie was Deliverance. Bubba would teach the little asshole, oh yes he would. Bubba hated fags so intensely that he was on the lookout for them in every sports bar and truck stop and in all vehicles he passed on life's highways and in politics and the entertainment industry.*

Despite research to the contrary, many people find it difficult to accept the idea that homosexual lifestyles offer legitimate and productive alternatives for some individuals. By treating homosexuals as perverted or diseased, others can affirm their own normalcy. Thus a sense of "rightness" is maintained by dwelling on the "wrongness" of homosexual lifestyles. Faced with such discriminatory attitudes and behavior on the part of some public officials, it is to be expected that some homosexuals have grown more militant. It is also not surprising, then, that "queer" studies have developed on many college campuses. Emphasizing a difference between gay, lesbian, bisexual, and transgendered people versus the normative heterosexual culture, the "queer" studies articulate and elaborate those aspects of sexual diversity that distinguish variations in sexual orientations from normative sexuality. *Reality or Myth*

▶ **Issues to Consider**   What are the potential benefits and risks to children raised by gay parents?

CHANGING VIEWS OF MENTAL HEALTH

Homosexuals have had to deal with the predominant view that they are "sick" and cope with the knowledge that the behaviors associated with their "illness" were illegal.

HIGHLIGHT

Turning the Tables

The popular press has frequently linked homosexual orientation to various undesirable characteristics. In the following eample, the "pathology" associated with heterosexuality is satirically described.

In January 1972, the *Los Angeles Advocate*, the respected nationally distributed gay newspaper, devoted an entire page, including an editorial, to serious questions about the majority culture. The editor asked, "Is *Heterosexuality* an illness?" Most of the page was taken up with abstracts of items—35 of them—found in the pages of the *Los Angeles Times* in the space of five weeks. Here are three of them, and not necessarily the worst.

CINCINNATI, Jan. 5—Mrs. Eulalia Fuchs, 44, pleaded guilty to manslaughter in the fatal shooting of her husband, Sept. 19, during an argument over whether to watch football on television or listen to music.

WASHINGTON, Jan. 6—A 57-year-old woman teacher was shot to death in front of her fifth-grade class after an argument with her estranged husband.

GARDEN GROVE, CALIF., Dec. 28—A Stanton man was burned to death early Monday as he was apparently attempting to set fire to the home of his ex-wife and her (new) husband—his brother—police reported.

The accompanying editorial, "Don't jail heteros; they need help!" read:

The problem of the violence-prone heterosexual community is alarming to most homosexuals. Some dismiss the problem as an abnormality deeply rooted in heterosexual history; others advocate extreme oppression that has never worked in the past.

One gay extremist, for example, regards all heterosexuals as being sick and will have nothing to do with them. He would seize on any pretext he could to put them in jail. He attempted to justify his rigid attitude in a recent interview:

"Now someone who's unfortunate enough to be heterosexual and doesn't get into any trouble . . . has nothing to worry about. . . . But the vicious, violent, aggressive, recruiting-type heterosexual is a problem. . . ."

We share this individual's concern, but we think that his solution is no solution at all. Jails have been filled with heterosexuals since jails were invented, and heterosexual violence has increased steadily to frightening proportions.

So there is overwhelming evidence of a tragic defect in the heterosexual personality. Rather than jail them, however, we think it would be far more valuable to confine heterosexuals to hospitals at some stage in their early development so that those who are most afflicted with the virus of violence can be isolated and treated. Those who are no danger to themselves and others can be released to procreate the nonviolent human beings of the future, while the experts study those who are sick in a serious, all-out attempt to develop a cure.

Only when we find such a cure for this heterosexual madness will we achieve that long-sought goal: peace on earth.

Source: Abbot & Love (1985, pp. 198–199).

It was not until 1974 that members of the American Psychiatric Association ratified a resolution that "homosexuality per se implies no impairment in judgment, stability, reliability or general social or vocational capabilities," thus removing homosexuality from the list of official mental disorders. This removal was due partly to research conducted over the past four decades that failed to establish any direct connection between homosexual orientation and mental or emotional disorders. To some extent, it was also a response to the growing social and political influence of gay people who fought against psychiatric labeling and criminal prosecution.

Early research on the psychological adjustment of homosexuals relied on clinical reports of homosexuals in therapy. The investigators, who were usually therapists, tended to assume that homosexuals were maladjusted. Why else would they be in therapy? In another research approach, homosexuals in therapy were compared with control groups of heterosexuals who were usually not in therapy. This design too provided evidence that homosexuals were maladjusted. The results of these studies then tended to be generalized to all homosexuals. For an unusual description of this kind of reasoning applied to heterosexuals, see "Highlight: Turning the Tables." Assumptions that homosexuals are maladjusted started changing when researchers began to draw samples from populations of homosexuals who were not in therapy. One strategy used in this kind of research is to administer various psychological tests to see whether there are differences between homosexuals and heterosexuals. Such comparisons should be made only between groups that are matched with respect to criteria such as age, religious beliefs, education, economic level, and relationship status. If such demographic factors are not controlled, it is impossible to know whether it is the influence of these factors or the effect of sexual orientation that is responsible for any differences in psychological adjustment. Unfortunately, many of these studies did not carefully match heterosexual and homosexual samples and thus yielded inconsistent results. In general, however, there is no evidence of major differences in adjustment between homosexuals and heterosexuals (Gonsiorek, 1991; Weinrich, 1994).

Some research has indicated that "masculine" homosexual males are better adjusted than are "feminine" homosexual males (Siegelman, 1987). Other work has suggested that this difference in adjustment also appears to hold true for heterosexual males (Jones et al., 1978). In keeping with this "genderized" effect, people who engage in behaviors and display characteristics of the other sex are negatively evaluated (Kite & Whitley, 1998). This may be even more true for groups who are stereotypically perceived as exhibiting cross-gender traits and behavior.

In North American culture, where antigay discrimination and gender-role stereotypes are common,

a homosexual man who displays some feminine characteristics often has difficulty keeping his psychological balance (Walters & Hayes, 1998). Heterosexuals and homosexuals who display gender-reversed patterns of behavior are both likely to experience adjustment problems. These problems will probably be more severe for the homosexual because she or he violates gender-role norms in a more public and visible way through erotic attachment to persons of the same sex.

A small proportion of homosexuals have been found to have significant problems with adjustment. For example, Bell and Weinberg (1978) reported that about 12 percent of the gay men and 5 percent of the lesbian women in their total sample could be classified as dysfunctional. These individuals experienced numerous problems in their day-to-day lives and appeared to fit society's stereotype of the maladjusted homosexual. What is remarkable, however, is that most gays function as well as their heterosexual counterparts despite society's negative sanctions. Their adjustment in the face of overwhelming societal burdens is testimony to the adaptiveness and resourcefulness of the human being.

▶ **Issues to Consider**   Why do you think homosexuality was once considered a mental illness?

THERAPY

In the past, clinicians who treated homosexuals widely assumed that their clients' sexual orientation, rather than the social oppression they experienced because of their orientation, was the crux of their problems. In fact, the psychoanalyst Kenneth Lewes (1988) has suggested how conservative psychoanalytic thought attributed difficulties of both homosexual men and heterosexual women to individual defects rather than to societal expectations. For example, until recently, a woman at home with young children who went to a psychoanalyst and complained of depression was thought to be maladjusted. Similarly, a homosexual who sought therapy because of feelings of alienation from his family was assumed to be neurotic, with "conversion" to heterosexual orientation the recommended treatment. In contrast, many therapists today explore whether a woman's depression stems from feeling trapped all day without adult companionship and whether a gay man's alienation is rooted in fear of familial rejection if he acknowledges his orientation.

In addition to being ethically questionable, the use of psychoanalysis and behavior therapy to change sexual orientation has been ineffective (Davison, 1991). Most therapists report a "cure" rate ranging from 10 percent to 30 percent, depending on the length of client follow-up. An exception is Masters and Johnson's report (1979) that 67 percent of the gay men and 60 percent of the gay women in their therapy program had "achieved" heterosexual behavior. All of these individuals had sought therapy because of sexual dissatisfaction. Nearly 25 percent of the applicants to the therapy program were denied admission for a variety of reasons, however, including insufficient motivation. More than half the clients selected were in heterosexual marriages, and

only 12 of the 67 men and women were predominantly or exclusively homosexual. Most of the clients fit Kinsey category 3 or 4 (bisexual). Thus, reports of Masters and Johnson's success at "changing" homosexuals' orientation should be viewed skeptically. In all likelihood, the impetus among clinicians to change or "cure" homosexuals stems from the difficulties of recognizing a difference without labeling it as psychologically abnormal.

Despite bias among some clinicians, many therapists now concentrate on helping their clients to accept their sexual orientation and develop their potential to survive in an antigay society rather than on attempting to change sexual orientation—unless such a change is the client's own goal (Gonsiorek, 1995; Lewes, 1995).

Discrimination and Gay Liberation

The discrimination against people who are, or are thought to be, homosexuals has a long and far-reaching history. Gays' civil rights have been limited by discrimination in such areas as housing, employment, immigration, naturalization, child custody, and military service. In response to this bias, gays and lesbians have organized various groups collectively known as the gay-liberation movement to press for equal rights under the law.

DISCRIMINATION

Discrimination can range from being snubbed or derided while shopping (Walters & Curran, 1996) to being incarcerated for breaking "sexual" laws that are almost never used to prosecute heterosexuals. By 1998, only six states had passed legislation protecting lesbian and gay people against discrimination based on sexual orientation (the first was Wisconsin) (Caron, 1998).

In contrast, in 1996, the U.S. Congress passed, and President Clinton signed, the Defense of Marriage Act (DOMA), which prohibited federal recognition of marriage between gays. Passage of this legislation was ironic given the belief of some

DOMA supporters that all gays are promiscuous. Such people presumably would wish to support the legalization of marital vows for gays.

U.S. criminal law has contributed more than its fair share of discrimination against individuals who engage in homosexual acts. In general, homosexuals have been prosecuted under state sodomy laws, which generally outlaw "unnatural acts"—nonprocreative activity such as oral sex and anal intercourse. As of 1998, six states (Arkansas, Kansas, Maryland, Missouri, Oklahoma, and Texas) ban these sexual acts exclusively between people of the same sex. Another 15 states ban these sexual acts for people of any sexual orientation (these are Alabama, Arizona, Georgia, Idaho, Louisiana, Michigan, Massachusetts, Minnesota, Mississippi, North Carolina, Rhode Island, South Carolina, Utah, and Virginia). The remaining 29 states no longer consider sodomy a crime. Sodomy laws are out of step with what most Americans believe, but the trend toward their elimination may have ended in 1986. In a 5-to-4 decision, the Supreme Court upheld a Georgia law that makes sodomy (oral or anal sex) a felony, punishing consenting adults with up to 20 years in prison. The Gallup Organization conducted a poll of a nationally representative sample of U.S. adults shortly after the Court decision. Of those surveyed, 57 percent thought that states should not prohibit private homosexual practices between consenting adults, and 74 percent said that states should not prohibit non-coital (that is, oral or anal) heterosexual activity (*Newsweek*, July 14, 1986).

In Canada sodomy is known as buggery and includes having sexual relations with animals. An individual can be charged with the offense only if a participant is under age 21, or if the act takes place publicly or involves an animal (*Pocket Criminal Code*, 1987).

Cross-culturally, homosexual behavior is illegal in many countries, including Chile, Israel, and Kenya. In Iran, too, homosexuality is illegal, and under Islamic law, gays and lesbians can be executed.

In the military, a person who engages in homosexual behavior faces grave penalties regardless of whether the behavior is because of orientation or the lack of heterosexual opportunity. He or she is in con-

flict with a Pentagon rule stating that "persons who engage in homosexual conduct" or "demonstrate a propensity" to do so "adversely affect the ability of the armed forces to maintain discipline, good order, and morale."

The ban on gays in the military provoked sharp debate in the 1990s (Shilts, 1993). President Clinton initially pledged to end the military's ban on homosexuals, but in the ensuing furor, he accepted a compromise proposal in 1994: "Don't ask, don't tell, don't pursue." Theoretically, this would permit gays in the military as long as they make no public declarations of their orientation. But in 1996, a man was discharged after a colleague, charged with homosexual rape, was offered a plea bargain if he would name other gays (Komarow, 1997). In addition, in 1993, when the policy was zero tolerance for homosexuals, 682 gays were discharged; in 1994, the number dropped slightly to 617. But in 1997, while the "Don't ask. . ." policy was still in effect and the military was smaller, almost a thousand (997) people

Political demonstrations by homosexuals have brought attention to the pervasive discrimination they experience at the hands of the heterosexual majority.

were discharged for being homosexual (*Time*, April 20, 1998, p. 19). Until gays are fully accepted in the U.S. military and elsewhere, they will continue to face stigma and potential extortion.

Among the countries that do not discriminate against gays in the military are Australia, Austria, Belgium, Canada, Denmark, Finland, Italy, the Netherlands, Norway, Spain, and Sweden (Caron, 1998). *Reality or Myth*

THE GAY LIBERATION MOVEMENT

Spiraling concerns about homosexual rights in the 1980s and 1990s resulted from gays' efforts to organize and influence the political process in the time-honored American tradition of participatory democracy. These strategies have their roots in the older civil rights movement of the 1950s and 1960s. The beginning of the gay liberation movement in the United States is usually traced back to an incident on June 27, 1969, when police raided the Stonewall Inn, a gay bar in New York City. The angry patrons pelted the officers with bottles and stones until police reinforcements arrived and the crowd dispersed. For the next five nights, crowds of homosexuals, joined by heterosexual sympathizers, gathered in the vicinity of the inn to protest the vice squad raid and to confront the police. Within a month after the Stonewall riots, the Gay Liberation Front had been organized in New York City. Although groups concerned with gay rights such as the Mattachine Society, One, and Daughters of Bilitis had existed since the 1950s, it was the Stonewall riots that marked the emergence of homosexuals' open political activism. In 1973 the National Gay Task Force (now the National Gay and Lesbian Task Force) was created, and it joined a number of other organizations actively working to end discrimination and change the negative stereotypes of lesbian women and gay men.

Much recent gay activism has been channeled into obtaining increased funding for AIDS research and education. With the growth of gay liberation, a wide variety of support systems for gay individuals has evolved in urban areas. Friends or partners can be found in gay social clubs, churches, political organizations, and discussion groups. Large cities have easily identifiable gay neighborhoods with bookstores, physicians, realtors, clothing stores, lawyers, and many other resources that cater to a gay clientele.

We hope that homosexuals will someday be treated as ordinary people and that sexual orientation will become strictly a private issue. This can happen only when society accepts and protects all its variations.

Bisexuality

Sandra Bem, famous for her studies of gender-role identification, denied being **bisexual**, but like many other bisexuals, she considers biological sex to be irrelevant in what attracts her to other people:

> *I am not now and never have been a "heterosexual." But neither have I ever been a "lesbian" or a "bisexual." . . . . The sex-of-partner dimension implicit in the three categories . . . seems irrelevant to my own particular pattern of erotic attractions and sexual experiences. Although some of the (very few) individuals to whom I have been attracted . . . have been men and some have been women, what those individuals have in common has nothing to do with either their biological sex or mine—from which I conclude, not that I am attracted to both sexes, but that my sexuality is organized around dimensions other than sex. (1993, p. vii)*

Bisexuality, or sexual attraction to both men and women, has received little scientific or social attention in a world polarized into homosexual and heterosexual camps (Firestein, 1996). The homosexual subculture often views the bisexual as someone who is going through a phase of heterosexual encounters because he or she is unwilling to come to grips with being homosexual (Rust, 1993b, 1995; Weinberg, Williams, & Pryor, 1994). The heterosexual community, for its part, tends to lump bisexuals into the general category of homosexuals or views them as

bisexual—The capacity to feel erotic attraction toward or to engage in sexual interaction with both men and women.

confused heterosexuals who need guidance. Researchers have reported, however, that a substantial number of men report bisexual attraction and engage in sex with both men and women during adulthood (Doll et al., 1992; Lever, Kanouse, Rogers, Carson, & Hertz, 1992; Stokes, Damon, & McKirnan, 1997).

Michele Eliason (1997) found a relatively high degree of **biphobia** among heterosexual undergraduates. Half the students rated bisexual women as unacceptable, and 61 percent found bisexual men unacceptable. Acceptance was defined as "deserve equal protection and the same rights as homosexuals" (p. 320). They were less likely to rate lesbians (38 percent) or gay men (43 percent) as unacceptable. Heterosexual men rated bisexual men as very unacceptable, but were more tolerant of bisexuality in women, consistent with findings that heterosexual men tend to eroticize women regardless of their orientation (Kite & Whitley, 1998).

Biphobia appears to be related to homophobia, although one of the major differences is that many homosexuals also have negative attitudes toward bisexuality (Rust, 1995). Perhaps the negative light in which bisexuals are viewed will change as we learn more about this orientation.

INCIDENCE

How many people can be classified as bisexual? As with other classifications, the number depends on the definition of the term. If the criterion is at least one overt sexual experience with a member of each sex, then a third of the Kinsey group's (1948) males fell into the bisexual category. If the additional 13 percent who reported having had erotic feelings toward both sexes but overt experience with only one of them are added, the total was 46 percent of the sample. Although comparable figures for the Kinsey group's (1953) females are difficult to report, about a third as many females as males reported overt experience with both sexes, and about half as many females as males reported erotic responses to both sexes. Looking at this question from another standpoint, 52 percent of the exclusively homosexual and 93 percent of the predominantly homosexual males

biphobia—Negative attitudes toward bisexuality.

in Bell and Weinberg's (1978) study reported engaging in heterosexual coitus at least once. The comparable figures for lesbian women were 77 percent and 93 percent, respectively.

These statistics indicate that substantial numbers of people who consider themselves to be either heterosexual or homosexual have the capacity to engage in sexual activity with members of both sexes. Many of these individuals engage in same-sex sexual activity only once or a few times, usually in adolescence, and therefore do not really qualify as bisexuals.

Many people who have experienced a sexual relationship with both sexes do not think of themselves as bisexual. Lever et al. (1992) found that more than two-thirds of bisexually experienced men labeled themselves as heterosexual. One of the most prominent characteristics of whether a bisexually active man identified himself as bisexual was adolescent homosexual experience. The greater the amount of adolescent homosexual experience, the more likely the men were to label themselves as bisexual (Lever et al., 1992). However, many men engage in sexual activities with both sexes and continue to consider themselves heterosexuals (Weinberg et al., 1994). Many of these men engage in same-sex sexual activity only once or a few times, usually in adolescence, and therefore do not really qualify as bisexuals.

Reality or Myth 6

CHARACTERISTICS

Although we all have the potential to respond erotically to both sexes, only some of us do so. What factors lead some people to interact sexually with both men and women?

Answers to that question and many others about bisexuality must be tentative because few studies have investigated people describing themselves as bisexual. In one such study, Blumstein and Schwartz (1976) interviewed 156 bisexuals and found three themes to be particularly prevalent among the respondents. The first of these was sexual experimentation in the context of friendship. Some of the individuals had progressed from intense emotional attachment to sexual involvement with a friend, although they had never previously had an erotic attraction to a person of that sex. The second theme was interaction in group sex. This pathway to bisexuality is quite common for women who are involved in swinging and who are often encouraged by their husbands or friends to engage in same-sex sexual activity (Weinberg et al., 1994). In this situation, Blumstein and Schwartz's respondents focused on the pleasurable feelings of these encounters rather than on the sex of the person providing the pleasure. The third theme was the presence of a belief system in which bisexuality was seen as a normal state. Some respondents in the study had embraced bisexual identification because they believed that a truly free person should be able to love both sexes. Although some respondents had not actually engaged in bisexual relations, many agreed intellectually with the idea of inborn bisexuality.

Bisexuals tend to display higher levels of eroticism in their fantasy and behavior than do their heterosexual counterparts. They report more heterosexual fantasies, begin heterosexual activity sooner and engage in it more frequently, masturbate more, report stronger orgasms, and are more sexually adventurous than are heterosexuals (Van Wyk & Geist, 1984).

Bisexually experienced men, compared to heterosexual men, report engaging in more high-risk behaviors (multiple partners, anal sex) and are more likely to report having had an STD in the past five years. However, the frequency of these risk characteristics among bisexual men is less than that found among homosexual men (Lever et al., 1992).

Particularly disturbing is that many bisexually active men do not tell their women partners about their homosexual contacts. In a study of 350 behaviorally bisexual men, 71 percent did not reveal their sexual activity with men to the women with whom they had sex, and 59 percent did not disclose to their steady female partner in the previous six months (Stokes, McKirnan, Doll, & Burzette, 1996). Thus, these women are unknowingly at risk for contracting sexually transmitted diseases, including HIV.

Comparisons of bisexual men and women who have been heterosexually married show several gender differences. Bisexual women tend to marry at an early age, and they are more likely than bisexual men to become aware of their homosexual feelings after they wed. Bisexual women are also more likely than bisexual men to terminate their marriages early because of conflicts arising from their bisexuality and sexual dissatisfaction (Bell & Weinberg, 1978; Coleman, 1987). The fact that the marriages of bisexual women are shorter than the marriages of bisexual men may stem from the differing socialization of males and females. Like lesbians, bisexual women seem less inclined to engage in multiple sexual relationships than bisexual or homosexual men. The conflict generated by their feelings for a woman in the face of their desire for monogamy may prompt some bisexual women to end their marriages. Bisexuals have begun to develop broad social networks. The first international conference was held in Amsterdam in 1991 (Rust, 1993b).

▶ **Issues to Consider**   Do you think most people could be bisexual under certain circumstances?

BISEXUAL IDENTITY: STABLE OR TRANSITIONAL?

One question that people who engage in sexual activity with both sexes face concerns whether their dual attraction is a stable identity, simply a "phase" out of which they will grow, or a transition to homosexuality. Paula Rust (1993b), who interviewed lesbian women about their beliefs concerning bisexual women, found that most lesbian women believed that bisexuality was more likely than lesbian identity to be a phase or a way of denying one's true sexuality. They also believed that bisexual women are less personally and politically loyal and more able and willing to "pass" as heterosexuals than are lesbians. However, Rust found that most lesbians were not particularly hostile toward bisexual women. More than half of a small sample of men and women who currently considered themselves as bisexual or gay reported having identified with the other orientation (gay or bisexual, respectively) in the past (Rosario et al., 1996).

In their interviews with more than 500 Black and White bisexually active men, Joseph Stokes and his colleagues (Stokes, Damon, & McKirnan, 1997) found that bisexual behavior appeared to be relatively stable, and 60 percent of the respondents had bisexual sexual contacts in the past six months. More than half the men had begun bisexual activity at least five years prior to the study. However, Stokes et al. (1997), found that over the period of a year, men who initially identified themselves as bisexual were more likely to change toward a homosexual (34 percent) than a heterosexual identity (17 percent), although about half remained stable in their identification as bisexual—at least over the period of a year.

Other researchers have found that over a five-year period, 33 percent of men and 40 percent of women retained a bisexual identity, whereas others moved toward either a more homosexual or heterosexual identity (Weinberg et al., 1994). Despite these variations in the permanence of bisexual orientation, bisexuals as a group appear to be as well adjusted psychologically as the heterosexuals and homosexuals who have been studied (Firestein, 1996).

Perhaps as wider recognition is accorded bisexual orientation, more people will claim this label. It may soften the hard edges of the homosexual and heterosexual categories, which ignore many people who do not fit neatly into either. If Freud, Kinsey, and the behaviorists are correct about the human potential for bisexual responses, then recognition of this possibility, regardless of whether a person acts on them, may be the way out of an illusory heterosexual-homosexual dichotomy.

▶ **Issues to Consider**   Having read the chapter, what do you believe is the cause of your own sexual orientation?

SUMMARY OF MAJOR POINTS

1. Sexual orientation. Most individuals confine their sexual interactions to the other gender, although many people who define themselves as heterosexuals have also experienced erotic attraction to members of their own gender. Homosexuals feel attraction toward and interact sexually with people of the same gender. Aside from sexual orientation toward individuals of the same gender, research has uncovered few reliable differences between heterosexuals and homosexuals.

2. Gender differences and sexual orientation. Gay males tend to seek variety and relatively impersonal sex in a pattern more similar to that of heterosexual males than to that of heterosexual females. Lesbian relationships and values resemble those of heterosexual females. These gender differences are consistent with variations in the ways in which males and females are socialized. It is not known, however, whether socialization is entirely responsible for these differences.

3. Explanations of sexual orientation. The assumption that homosexual orientation stems from either genetic or hormonal conditions or a social situation such as a disturbed family relationship dominated early research into the causes of homosexuality. Although there is little evidence to support most of these assumptions, preliminary data suggest a biological contribution to at least some types of homosexuality. Gender-role nonconformity in young boys and sexual experiences in late childhood and adolescence have also been associated with adult homosexuality.

4. Sexual orientation and adjustment. Many early studies of the psychological adjustment of homosexuals compared gays in therapy with heterosexuals not in therapy. This research led to the conclusion that gays were maladjusted. More appropriate comparisons have failed to identify reliable differences in people as a function of their sexual orientation.

5. Discrimination and gay liberation. Fear, hatred, and discrimination toward homosexuals characterize the attitudes of many people in our culture. In the United States, the civil rights of homosexuals have been limited in such areas as housing, military service, and the enforcement of certain laws regulating sexual behavior. In response to this history, gays have organized politically to pursue equal protection under the law.

6. Bisexuality. Bisexuals are capable of feeling erotic attraction toward and engaging in sexual intimacy with individuals of both genders. They present an interesting question for future research: Why do some people restrict their range of potential partners to one gender (either the same or the other gender), and other people (bisexuals) consider gender unimportant in selecting partners? From this standpoint, exclusive heterosexuals are similar to exclusive homosexuals. Bisexuality appears to be a stable identity and behavior for some people, whereas for others, it represents a transitory phase, usually to homosexual identity and behavior.

Sexual Dysfunctions and Therapy

Reality or Myth ?

1. Low sexual desire is caused by abnormally low levels of testosterone.

2. Nymphomania is the most common female sexual dysfunction.

3. Premature ejaculation refers to ejaculation before the man wants it to occur.

4. Masters and Johnson developed the most successful approach to sex therapy.

5. In sex therapy, one therapist (of either sex) working alone is as effective as two (a man and a woman) working together.

6. Before sex therapists advertise their services, they must obtain licenses certifying their competence.

ob and Elaine have been cuddling on the couch, drinking wine, and watching the late movie on television. Elaine starts fondling Bob's penis, but it does not get erect, although Bob wants to have intercourse. Across town, Sally and Don returned from the ball game more than an hour ago and immediately took off their clothes and went to bed. They have been kissing and caressing pretty much steadily since then, but Sally's vagina has remained dry. Next door, their neighbors Mary and Lisa are both excited and wet, and Mary has come several times. Lisa wants badly to have an orgasm, too, but no matter what she and Mary do, she cannot quite come.

Does Bob have erectile dysfunction? Is Sally the victim of inhibited sexual excitement? Does Lisa have orgasmic dysfunction? Yes. All three are sexually dysfunctional for the moment; that is, they are not responding sexually in the way that they want. Whether they would be clinically diagnosed as having sexual dysfunctions would depend on the frequency of their inability to respond sexually and how they feel about it.

The diagnoses would also depend greatly on the beliefs of the particular clinicians whom they saw if they decided to seek help. Professionals do not always agree with one another on the sources of and solutions to sexual problems, as you will see. In this chapter we examine common dysfunctions and some

factors associated with them. We also look at various therapeutic approaches and controversies regarding their use. Then we consider the issue of sexual interaction between therapist and client and some other sources of controversy among therapists who treat sexual dysfunction.

Sexual Dysfunction: Contributing Factors

There was little systematic survey information on the frequency of sexual dysfunction in this country until the Laumann et al. (1994) research. In this study, the proportion of respondents indicating that they had experienced a sexual problem in the past year varied from 5 percent to roughly 25 percent, depending on the disorder, with the exception that about one-third of women reported lacking interest in sex for several months or more (see Table 15.1 on page 350).

Most factors that impair sexual functioning are classified as either biological or psychosocial in origin. Although we too make use of this convenient division, it does not reflect the complex interactions of biological, psychological, and social factors that pro-

duce sexual dysfunctions, a fact that we discuss further at the end of this section.

PAST EXPERIENCES AND SEXUAL DYSFUNCTIONS

Our experiences with our bodies and with sexuality begin in infancy. Deprivation of physical contact and love can blunt our emotional growth and our potential for sexual expression (Hatfield, 1994). Those professionals influenced by psychoanalytic theory look to critical childhood experiences to explain sexual dysfunction. The underlying assumption is that specific childhood incidents exert a subconscious influence on one's adult behavior. In contrast, other

TABLE 15.1   Estimates of Sexual Dysfunctions (in percentages)

	National Probability Sample[a]	Clinical Samples[b]
Sexual Dysfunctions of Men		
Climax too early	28	15–46
Anxiety about performance	17	—
Lacked interest in sex	16	32–60
Unable to keep an erection	10	36–53
Unable to have orgasm	8	3–8
Sex not pleasurable	8	—
Pain during sex	3	—
Sexual Dysfunctions of Women		
Lacked interest in sex	33	37–70
Unable to have orgasm	24	18–76
Sex not pleasurable	21	—
Had trouble lubricating	19	14–62
Pain during sex	14	5–18
Anxiety about performance	12	—
Climax too early	10	—

[a]Proportion reporting experience in the previous twelve months (Laumann et al., 1994).
[b]Proportion reporting problem in clinical settings (Spector & Carey, 1990).

therapists and researchers believe that the causes of sexual problems can be found in a couple's immediate situation. Communication difficulties, sexual misinformation, conflicted relationships, and faulty learning are some of the immediate factors seen as crucial in the development of dysfunctions.

Although most of our early experiences take place within a family, the nature and quality of those experiences can also depend on the larger social context that encompasses a family. For example, some cultures are extremely restrictive about eroticism; others are relatively permissive. The restrictiveness of a culture is linked to the incidence of difficulties in a man's getting or maintaining an erection. In an examination of 30 preindustrial and industrializing countries, Welch and Kartub (1978) found that the more restrictive a society was regarding such behaviors as premarital, marital, and extramarital sex, the greater was the number of reported problems with erectile functioning. Within Western cultures, there are many

examples of societal beliefs that were later shown to be erroneous that contributed to sexual problems.

Sigmund Freud's theory of female sexuality provides a prime example of a widely held belief that has interfered with women's ability to be sexually responsive. Freud (1905) described young girls' source of sexual pleasure as masculine because they obtain pleasure from stimulation of the clitoris, just as young boys do from stimulation of the penis. Freud claimed that as women become healthy adults, the source of pleasure and orgasm shifts from the clitoris to the vagina. Some psychoanalytic writers took this idea at face value and asserted that orgasm from clitoral stimulation is an expression of immaturity, neuroticism, masculinity, and frigidity. In *The Power of Sexual Surrender* (1959), Marie Robinson claimed that the truly mature woman always experiences vaginal orgasms; the woman who has only clitoral orgasms is suffering from a form of frigidity. Interestingly, Robinson acknowledged that scores of women find clitoral stimulation and orgasm so gratifying that they are not motivated to achieve what was thought of as sexual maturity.

Some Freudian theorists advocated what could be called "psychological circumcision"; that is, they called the woman immature or neurotic, or both, who did not reject clitoral stimulation. Thus, many women who experienced sexual pleasure and orgasm through clitoral stimulation but did not have orgasms from penile thrusting in the vagina without clitoral stimulation were left with doubts, guilt, and feelings of inadequacy about their sexuality. Rather than physically obliterating a source of sexual pleasure, Freudian ideas psychologically blocked many women's enjoyment of clitoral stimulation. As you saw in Chapter 5, there is no evidence to indicate that women who receive pleasure and orgasm from clitoral stimulation are immature or emotionally disturbed. Nonetheless, because of the Freudians' theories, many women sought therapy for a source of pleasure that they were led to believe was a problem.

Many psychoanalytic writers disagreed with the position that healthy adult women should experience pleasure solely from stimulation of the vagina rather than from the clitoris (Benedek, 1959; Horney, 1933; Marmor, 1954), but they were not as influential as the doctrinaire Freudians. Their lack of influence probably can be attributed to the predominant cultural belief that the sole purpose of sexuality is reproduction. Ideas change slowly, and it is humbling to ponder how many of our current beliefs about sexuality will be shown to have as little substance as the Freudian view on clitoral versus vaginal orgasms.

In addition to the sexual restrictiveness and beliefs of members of a specific culture, traumatic childhood events have been implicated in sexual dysfunction (Beitchman et al., 1992). Rape, parental discovery of sexual activity, and incestuous experiences are examples of events that can bring about a sexual dysfunction.

Many sexual problems originate in myths and misinformation that individuals are exposed to at a fairly young age. These mistaken ideas can lead to misguided or ineffective attempts at sexual interaction that leave the individual feeling depressed and incompetent. Several botched sexual experiences can result in the avoidance of future sexual contact.

The differences between the backgrounds of people with healthy sexual responses and those of people with sexual dysfunctions should not lead you to believe that being brought up in a sexually restrictive environment is sufficient by itself to cause sexual dysfunction. Many people with adequate sexual functioning have family and cultural backgrounds that are similar to those of people with sexual dysfunctions (Heiman, Gladue, Roberts, & LoPiccolo, 1986). Factors such as the ones described in the next section are also related to the development of dysfunctions and may interact with the more remote factors that we have just discussed.

CURRENT SOURCES OF SEXUAL DYSFUNCTION

In general, any disease or surgery that affects the reflex centers in the spinal cord and the nerves that serve them can result in sexual impairment. Many of the drugs used to treat particular mental and physical conditions can reduce responsiveness. A variety of medical conditions that can influence sexual functioning are summarized in "Highlight: Disorders, Diseases, and Other Factors That Can Affect Sexual Functioning" on page 352.

Many sexual difficulties result from psychosocial factors, but there is little consensus on the nature of these factors (Wiederman, 1998). Sexual dysfunctions can be related to both recent experiences *and*

childhood events. Although we categorize factors related to dysfunction as either past or current, keep in mind that recent and remote factors often interact to produce sexual difficulties.

The most frequent psychosocial contributors to current sources of dysfunction are (1) anxiety, perhaps over sexual performance, and ideas that interfere with sexual arousal; (2) inadequate information about sexuality that leads to ineffective sexual behavior; (3) failures in communication; and (4) stress (Cranston-Cuebas & Barlow, 1990; Masters & Johnson, 1970; Morokoff & Gillilland, 1993). Anxiety and thoughts about sex can interact in complex ways.

Anxiety. Helen Singer Kaplan (1974) and William Masters and Virginia Johnson (1970) concluded that anxiety about sexual performance is the most important immediate cause of sexual dysfunction. Concerns about performance consist of an emotional component (performance anxiety) and a cognitive component (a person's evaluation of his or her sexual performance). Anxiety over sexual performance usually involves the fear of failure. After a person has experienced the inability to have or maintain an erection or vaginal lubrication, he or she may become obsessed with failing again. This fear of failure can start a vicious cycle in which the person does fail again because of fear.

Spectatoring refers to a person's inspecting and monitoring his or her own sexual activity and the partner's response rather than becoming immersed in the sexual experience. The person becomes a spectator rather than a participant. A man may worry: "Is my erection firm enough?" "Is my partner being satisfied?" A woman may engage in the same sort of judgmental viewing: "Am I wet enough for him?" "Is my partner getting tired of rubbing my clitoris?" "Should I change the rhythm of my movement?" "Will I come?" People who become absorbed in self-questioning have difficulty suspending distracting thoughts and losing themselves in the erotic experience. Such interruption of the unfolding of sexual feeling leads to problems with arousal and/or

spectatoring—Evaluating one's own sexual performance rather than involving oneself in the sexual experience with one's partner.

Disorders, Diseases, and Other Factors That Can Affect Sexual Functioning

Neurological disorders affect the sex centers of the brain and the spinal cord structures that serve the genital reflexes. Head injuries, strokes, multiple sclerosis, and tumors are examples of such disorders.

Endocrine disorders affect the body's hormonal balance. Any problem that results in lowered testosterone levels may alter sexual response. Diabetes, thyroid disorders, and kidney disease are examples of endocrine disorders.

Cardiovascular disorders affect the circulatory system. Cardiac disease, hypertension, and atherosclerosis are some vascular disorders that can impair sexual functioning.

Debilitating illnesses, such as lung disease and advanced stages of cancer, produce general ill health that can reduce sexual responsiveness.

Drugs, such as tranquilizers, antipsychotics, and antidepressants, used to treat emotional problems can cause sexual dysfunction. Alcohol, heroin, and barbiturate abuse can have the same result. Drugs that are frequently prescribed for the treatment of high blood pressure may periodically cause sexual dysfunction.

Source: Schiavi (1994).

---

orgasm. Not paying attention to one's own sexual feelings and responses is a foolproof method for obtaining minimal sexual gratification.

The relationship between anxiety and sexual dysfunction is not simple, however, because in some circumstances, anxiety appears to facilitate sexual response. In a series of carefully designed experiments, David Barlow and his colleagues (summarized in Cranston-Cuebas & Barlow, 1990) compared men who were functioning well sexually ("functional") to men who had sexual difficulties—in particular, inability to develop and maintain an erection ("dysfunctional"). They found that these two groups responded very differently while watching erotic films. Anxiety produced by the threat of being given a painful electric shock often *increased* the sexual response of functional men but *decreased* the sexual response of dysfunctional men.

Functional men and dysfunctional men react differently to their motivational states and use different cognitive processes to understand them. In laboratory studies, functional men respond to performance demands with heightened arousal. In contrast, dysfunctional men perceive a performance demand in sexual situations, which causes them to feel anxiety.

This anxiety leads them to become preoccupied with nonerotic thoughts—for example, "Am I losing my erection?" In addition, dysfunctional men experience this anxiety as negative arousal. Functional men perceive their increased arousal as sexual excitement.

This analysis of sexual dysfunction is promising, but it has been done primarily with men. It also does not tell us how these men developed different ways of perceiving emotional states or why they interpreted their arousal in different ways.

Misinformation. Some couples who seek help for sexual dysfunctions reveal a lack of knowledge about their bodies and sexual functioning that leads to ineffective sexual behavior. They may not know where the clitoris is, for example, or may not be aware of its erotic potential. If ignorant of a woman's sexual response, a man may not engage in sufficient stimulation to arouse his partner. Because of her own socialization, the woman may be too naive or embarrassed to tell him what feels good. Thus, she may be inadequately lubricated for intercourse and consequently may experience it as painful.

The abundance of sexual misinformation in our culture can also contribute to sexual problems. Men may succumb to the myth that they should always be ready to engage in genital sex with regularity, enthusiasm, and efficiency, regardless of their mood and the situation. When they experience temporary fluctuations in desire or their sexual response is diminished by fatigue, they may react with great alarm and subsequently become obsessed with "failing" again. Some men are also unaware of the refractory period most men experience following ejaculation (see Chapter 5). They become concerned when they cannot immediately respond to further stimulation rather than recognizing that they are simply experiencing a normal physiological phenomenon. Women may succumb to the myth that they should be interested in sex only when their partners are or that they should reach orgasm only through stimulation of the vagina in intercourse—and then they wonder why they experience difficulties with orgasm.

Communication Difficulties.   A substantial number of sexual problems could be resolved if people felt free to communicate with their sexual partners or friends about their sexual feelings. The notion that sex is something people do not and should not talk about is directly associated with sexual problems. This belief is based on the assumption that we are mind readers and should know our partner's sexual feelings. At an initial therapy session, one or both members of a sexually troubled couple often make such statements as, "Gee, I never knew you felt that way," or "I never tried to do that because I thought you wouldn't like it." Some of these couples might have saved themselves time and money if they had learned to communicate effectively by giving information about their sexual feelings and asking about their partner's feelings. Many people have difficulty telling their sex partner directly about their feelings and responses, but they must learn to do so if the other person is to find out whether he or she is providing pleasure. Talking about sex involves revealing our innermost private feelings; taking this risk can lead to more intimate and satisfying sexual relationships (MacNeil & Byers, 1997).

▶ **Issues to Consider:** Why is there so much sexual dysfunction in our culture?

Couples may avoid sexual problems by sharing information about their sexual feelings.

Open communication can also develop a sense of trust, which is central to any personal relationship, particularly one that involves sexuality. A couple's progression into intimate behavior can be a complicated ritual as each person tries to determine the other's intentions and trustworthiness. Traditionally, the complications have often revolved around women's feelings of being used as sexual objects. However, being used can be a concern for men as well. Uncertainty about commitment to a relationship, whether heterosexual or homosexual, can lead to mixed sexual feelings and behavior that fosters sexual problems. Fear of sexually transmitted diseases and concerns about birth control and pregnancy can also inhibit pleasurable sexual relations.

Sexual dysfunctions are often related to nonsexual problems that are not discussed openly in a relationship—for example, money worries, conflicts involving dominance, decision-making controversies, or problems in expressing affection. Women who feel that their partners are not affectionate except when making love may express their resentment by not becoming aroused or orgasmic. Their partners then cannot have the satisfaction of bringing them sexual pleasure.

The problem of inadequate communication can increase a couple's difficulties in resolving some of the problems associated with sexual dysfunction. Overall sexual satisfaction for these partners is likely to improve if their communication about the frequency and nature of sexual activities improves. Such openness presumably increases a couple's abilities to address constructively the inevitable differences in opinions and feelings that occur in any relationship and to avoid using sex as a weapon.

Many romantic relationships are as much about power and control as they are about love and sex. Some people believe that their partner dominates the relationship and makes most of the important decisions. Their resentment toward the partner may result in an inability to release themselves to the pleasure of sex, because doing so would be seen as another sign of dependency. Similarly, they may make themselves sexually unavailable to demonstrate that they have the power to control sexual activity in the relationship. Thus, the bed can become a battleground on which combatants vie for the upper hand in a relationship.

Stress. The diagnosis of causes of sexual dysfunction as biological *or* psychosocial obscures the complex interactions between mind and body. Sexual dysfunctions are almost always the result of **stress** originating from biological and psychosocial sources. Whatever the cause(s), stress can disrupt sexual functioning, decrease testosterone and luteinizing hormone levels, and lower sexual drive (Herbert, 1996).

Some diseases or psychological factors may be severe enough to disrupt sexual functioning directly. In other cases, a physical illness may make an individual vulnerable to psychological factors, such as depression and anxiety, that result in sexual dysfunction. Schumacher and Lloyd (1981, p. 49) postulated the following relationship between stress and sexual dysfunction:

stress—Physical, emotional, or mental strain or tension.

Financial worries and other stressors may inhibit the sex drive while the mind and body seek to prioritize needs.

In the hierarchy of systems of the body, sexual function has a low status since it does not appear essential for the individual's life or health. Therefore when the body is under threat from physical and/or psychological stress, sexual functions may be sacrificed to foster the systems that are more important for survival or health.

A severe emotional state such as clinical depression brought about by a psychosocial factor (rejection or loss of a job or partner, for example) can impair sexual functioning by affecting the nervous and endocrine systems. Thus, biology and psychology are delicately intertwined, influencing each other in many ways. To arrive at a complete understanding of a sexual dysfunction, we must attempt to understand the relative contribution of these factors to the different types of sexual dysfunctions.

Types of Sexual Dysfunction

Psychosexual disorders were listed for the first time in 1980, in the third edition of the American Psychiatric Association's *Diagnostic and Statistical Manual of Mental Disorders (DSM)*, a handbook almost all mental health professionals use. This listing has led to an increasing medicalization of sexual problems that can allow individuals to avoid examining their own attitudes and experiences that could have contributed to their dysfunction (Tiefer, 1996). If the source of the problem is "medical," then individuals may not see the need to take responsibility for their problems. If the problem is a lack of desire, the medical diagnosis can be used as a rationale to continue to avoid sexual activity.

The *DSM-IV* (that is, the fourth edition of the *DSM*, published in 1994) classifies sexual dysfunctions as primary or secondary. A *primary dysfunction* occurs when an individual has never experienced one of the phases of the sexual response cycle. A *secondary dysfunction* refers to a situation in which a person has been able to respond in the past to one of the phases but is not responsive at the current time, or can experience one of the phases only in certain circumstances.

It is important to remember that many people do not fit neatly into any of the diagnostic categories we are about to describe. In one study, almost half the patients seeking treatment had a sexual problem in more than one area. Thus, in many cases, problems with desire, excitement, and orgasm overlap (Segraves & Segraves, 1991).

SEXUAL DESIRE DISORDERS

Deciding whether a given response should be considered a dysfunction is particularly problematic in the case of desire disorders, where the variable is the amount of sexual interest. What is a "normal" level of sexual desire? In our culture, men are expected to want sex more frequently than are women. Thus, gender-role expectations are related to our beliefs about what constitutes "normal" levels of sexual desire.

Hypoactive Sexual Desire and Sexual Aversion.
The *DSM-IV* divides desire disorders into two categories: hypoactive sexual desire disorders and sexual aversion disorders. The first of these, **hypoactive sexual desire disorder,** is defined as deficient or absent sexual fantasies and desire for sexual activity with anyone. The judgment of deficiency or absence is made by the clinician, taking into account factors that affect sexual functioning such as age, sex, and the context of the person's life. The deficiency may be selective: a person may experience erection or lubrication and orgasm but derive little pleasure from the physical feelings and thus have little interest in sexual activity. In other cases, the individual's desire is at such a low ebb that he or she has no interest in self-stimulation or in participation in sexual interaction that might even lead to arousal. For example, a young man we know told us about his strong romantic attraction to another man but said that he felt inhibited about trying to develop the relationship; although his feelings of love had previously been directed toward men rather than women, he experienced very little desire for sexual interaction. Some people can be described as asexual; that is, they do not experience desire for any kind of sexual activity. This is not considered a dysfunction if the individual is satisfied with not engaging in sexual activity.

The sources of sexual desire disorders have not been well clarified. Most current knowledge of the causes of low sexual desire is based on clients who are seen in therapy and thus must be viewed with caution until more objective research has been conducted using nonclinical samples. With that caveat in mind, low sexual desire has been associated with such factors as anxiety, religious orthodoxy, depression, **habituation** to a sexual partner, fear of loss of control over sexual urges, sexual assault, medication side effects, marital conflict, and fear of closeness (Letourneau & O'Donohue, 1993; LoPiccolo & Friedman, 1988).

Comparisons of women experiencing inhibited sexual desire with women expressing normal sexual desire revealed no differences in psychological

---

hypoactive sexual desire disorder—Deficient or absent sexual fantasies and desire for sexual activity with anyone.
habituation—Responding to someone or something out of habit rather than out of current feelings.

adjustment or hormonal levels (Letourneau & O'Donohue, 1993; Stuart, Hammond, & Pett, 1987). Women with inhibited sexual desire did report significantly greater dissatisfaction with their marital relationship than did other women. Depression may play a crucial role in hypoactive sexual desire; women with inhibited sexual desire reported twice as many depressive episodes as did women with normal sexual desire (Schreiner-Engel & Schiavi, 1986). Additional research is needed, however, to determine whether depression leads to low sexual desire, low desire produces depression, or other factors mediate this relationship.

In the general population, 16 percent of men and 33 percent of women aged 18 to 59 (refer to Table 15.1) reported that they lacked interest in sex for a period of several months or more in the year before they were interviewed (Laumann et al., 1994). The suppression of sexual desire is, of course, not dysfunctional in and of itself. Most of us learn scripts to suppress sexual desire for inappropriate partners, such as parents, close relatives, and children, and in inappropriate situations.

Before they learn to suppress their sexual feelings in public situations, some young men experience quite a bit of discomfort and embarrassment. Trying to hide an erection when one is asked to come to the front of a classroom can be difficult. Researchers have demonstrated that men can suppress their erections in the presence of erotic stimuli (Adams, Motsinger, McAnulty, & Moore, 1992; Cranston-Cuebas & Barlow, 1990). They accomplish this by concentrating on nonsexual thoughts, such as arithmetic computations. Women have the advantage in this case, because their signs of arousal are less obvious. Many people also learn to suppress sexual desire for individuals of a particular sex. Persons with a strong heterosexual identity may have learned to suppress sexual desire for people of the same sex. Those with a strong homosexual identity may use the same mechanism to keep their desires channeled only toward people of the same sex and to suppress sexual desire for individuals of the other sex. People who feel sexual desire for both men and women (bisexuals) have apparently learned not to suppress desire toward either sex.

Alcohol and marijuana may act to release suppressed sexual desire, but this release is usually only

Alcohol and other drugs may lubricate social situations, but taken in excess they can disrupt a relationship.

temporary. A person who experiences an intense sexual desire for someone after drinking alcohol or smoking marijuana—a situation colloquially called "beer goggles"—may not feel the same way after the drug wears off. Awakening in the morning with their inhibitions back, some people who have acted on the desires unleashed while they were "high" then wonder how they ever found the other person sexually desirable.

Sexual aversion disorder is a persistent aversion to almost all genital sexual contact with a partner. Whereas individuals displaying hypoactive sexual desire are often indifferent about sexual interaction, sexual aversion reflects fear, disgust, or anxiety about sexual contact with a partner. An individual

---

sexual aversion disorder—Extreme dislike and avoidance of genital sexual contact with a partner.

with sexual aversion disorder may still engage in autosexual behaviors such as masturbation and fantasy, while avoiding interpersonal sexual behavior.

People with sexual aversion disorder tend to experience anxiety and sometimes hostility toward their partners. When they anticipate sex with their partners, their feelings of anxiety or hostility suppress any initial stirrings of erotic sensation. Eventually they block sexual arousal at its earliest stage and avoid the anxiety associated with sexual expression. Childhood sexual abuse and adult rape have been found to be significantly related to sexual aversion (Gold & Gold, 1993). *Reality or Myth* 🔲

Excessive Sexual Desire. Excessive sexual desire, which has also been called hyperactive desire, sexual compulsion, and sexual addiction, has received considerable publicity in the popular media. Despite this attention, clinicians and therapists seldom encounter individuals with excessive sexual desire. Although people with enormous sexual appetites are fairly common in erotic literature and films, **nymphomania** in women and **satyriasis** in men appear to be rare. Symons (1979, p. 92) suggested that the "sexually insatiable woman is to be found primarily, if not exclusively, in the ideology of feminism, the hopes of boys and the fears of men."

Excessive sexual desire is often associated with paraphilias (see Chapter 17) and/or with an **obsessive-compulsive reaction.** For example, A.R.A. treated a 26-year-old man who was referred for therapy by his parole officer. The client was living in a halfway house after having been released from prison following conviction for automobile theft. While in prison, he had been raped many times and had been involved in several stabbing incidents, one of which had led to another inmate's death. His sexual behavior was problematic. Staff at the halfway house reported that he often masturbated in public and had been accused of exhibitionism. The homosexual prison rapes had traumatized him, and he felt his

sexual behavior had changed drastically. He had had several sexual experiences with different women since his release from prison and was steadily dating a woman 15 years older than he was. All of his sexual episodes involved rather long bouts of intercourse in which he had orgasm 10 or 15 times. He reported that the women all commented positively on his sexual prowess. The man experienced little relief or relaxation after orgasm. He reported masturbating from 8 to 20 times a day—whenever he began to feel tense. The client had an obsessive-compulsive reaction. His short stature (five feet three inches) and the prison rapes had led to obsessive fears that he was not masculine and was possibly gay. This fear created anxiety that he could reduce temporarily by compulsive sexual behavior, which reassured him. Without the ritual of sex, his anxieties would overwhelm him and drive him "crazy."

Preliminary evidence indicates that men with paraphilic disorders are two to three times more sexually active than men in the general population (Kafka, 1997). In obsessive-compulsive states, the individual becomes preoccupied with sexuality and may masturbate or engage in sexual interaction with a partner five or ten times a day. The sexual activity is used to reduce the anxiety and tension resulting from obsessive thoughts about sex or other aspects of the person's life. *Reality or Myth* 🔲

SEXUAL AROUSAL DISORDERS

Some people feel deep sexual desire and want to make love with their partners but experience little or no physical response (erection or vaginal lubrication and swelling) to sexual stimulation. **Sexual arousal disorders** are diagnosed when there is recurrent or persistent failure by a woman to attain or maintain the lubrication and swelling response or failure by a man to attain erection during sexual activity. Such a diagnosis is made only when the clinician is sure that the difficulty does not stem from physical disorders or medication and when the amount of sexual stimulation provided should be adequate to produce

nymphomania—Excessive and uncontrollable sexual desire in women.
satyriasis (SAH-ter-RYE-uh-sis)—Excessive and uncontrollable sexual desire in men.
obsessive-compulsive reaction—Engaging in compulsive behaviors in reaction to persistent or obsessive thoughts.

sexual arousal disorders—Failures to attain or maintain erection or vaginal lubrication and swelling despite adequate stimulation.

vasocongestion. Sometimes failure to respond results from insufficient stimulation rather than from inhibition of excitement.

Sexual arousal disorders were formerly called *frigidity* in women and *impotency* in men. Both terms are degrading and sound more like complaints than clinical disorders. They suggest rigid and distant women and ineffectual and helpless men. We have known men who employ the term *frigid* to describe any woman who refuses to have sex with them. In contrast, the phrase *sexual arousal disorder* is descriptive without being demeaning.

It is important to realize that occasional nonresponsiveness during sexual interaction is common. Many men have experienced sexual arousal and a desire for interaction when they have had too much to drink, only to find that although the mind was willing, the genitals were unresponsive. Women who smoke marijuana may also notice a diminishing of vaginal lubrication (along with a sense of dryness in the mouth and nose). Similarly, fatigue, stress, and minor irritations with one's partner can temporarily interfere with sexual response. Such occasional nonresponsiveness can become problematic if people fear that they may not be able to respond sexually in the future. This fear of failure can create anxiety about sexual performance, which can lead to future problems in responding. If the individual instead accepts the fact that occasional inability to respond sexually is normal, dysfunctions are less likely to arise.

Women's reactions to an inability to respond to erotic stimulation show much greater variation than do men's. Most men react to **erectile dysfunction** as if it were a disaster, whereas women's responses range from anxiety or distress to casual acceptance of the difficulty. To some extent, cultural expectations are responsible for these differences. In most cultures, men are expected to be sexually active and to perform satisfactorily. Women are not generally subjected to the same performance pressures and, in some cultures, are not expected to be sexually responsive. In addition, differences in anatomy and physiology make it more difficult for men to cover up and compensate for a dysfunction. A limp penis is difficult to hide and to use in a sexual interaction, whereas a dry vagina is more easily hidden and, with the aid of a lubricant, can even accommodate sexual intercourse.

Erectile dysfunction is generally the most common complaint among men who seek sex therapy. In more representative samples, however, about 10 percent of men report experiencing erectile dysfunction (Laumann et al., 1994). Some men with erectile dysfunction never have more than a partial erection during sexual activity. Others become erect, only to lose firmness when they attempt to have intercourse. Some men have erection problems with one partner but not with another.

Ruling out medical difficulties as a major cause is easier with erectile dysfunction than with most other dysfunctions. During an average night, a man will have three to five erections during rapid eye movement (REM) sleep, which is highly correlated with dreaming. If a procedure called the nocturnal penile tumescence test in a sophisticated sleep laboratory reveals that a man does not have these erections or that they are impaired, the source of his problem is likely to be physical. But simply asking men whether they have early-morning erections—the so-called "piss hard-on"—is just as predictive of biological impairment as are the fairly sophisticated and expensive biological measures. Men who report that they do not have morning erections usually have biological or medical problems (Gordon & Carey, 1995; Segraves, Segraves, & Schoenberg, 1987).

Most men who experience problems with erection after a period of normal responsiveness respond well to treatment. The prognosis is not so good for men who have never been able to attain or maintain an erection with a partner (Hawton, 1992).

A rare condition that seems to be the opposite condition of erectile dysfunction is **priapism**, or prolonged erection without sexual desire. This condition can result from damage to the valves in the corpus cavernosa that regulate the flow of blood, as well as from infection, tumors, cocaine and heroin use, and some medications. Untreated, it can lead to destruc-

---

erectile dysfunction—Recurrent and persistent inability to attain or maintain a firm erection despite adequate stimulation.

priapism (PRE-uh-PIZ-um)—Prolonged and painful erection without sexual desire.

tion of the spongy tissue of the penis from the co-agulation of blood, resulting in permanent erectile dysfunction.

About 20 percent of women aged 18 to 59 in the general population reported trouble lubricating in the past year (Laumann et al., 1994). Often the problem stems from the combination of widespread ignorance in our culture regarding women's sexual anatomy and the socialization of women to attend more to others' needs than to their own. We consider the issue of women's difficulties with orgasm in the next section.

ORGASM DISORDERS

Some people have orgasms within minutes of sexual interaction. Others engage in sexual stimulation for an hour or more before having orgasm. And some people never have orgasm. Nowhere else is the problem of defining sexual dysfunction more evident. In fact, except in extreme cases involving orgasm within seconds or no orgasm at all, the main difficulty is a difference in the speed of the partner's responsiveness rather than any dysfunction.

The fact that one person responds quickly and his or her partner responds more slowly does not necessarily imply that either is dysfunctional. As noted in Chapter 5, orgasm need not and generally does not occur simultaneously for a couple. Although orgasmic and ejaculatory dysfunctions do exist in some people, simple differences between partners in the timing of orgasmic release are not necessarily problematic or indicative of sexual dysfunction.

Premature Ejaculation. Perhaps the most useful definition of **premature ejaculation** is ejaculation before the man wants it to occur. Speed of ejaculation is related to age (older men have fewer problems with ejaculatory control than do younger men, particularly adolescents), sexual inexperience, and novelty of the sexual partner.

The diagnosis of premature ejaculation is not appropriate unless the speed of a man's ejaculation be-

---

premature ejaculation—Ejaculation before the man wants it to occur.

comes a regular, unwanted aspect of a couple's sexual activity. Ejaculation is a reflex that is difficult to control once it has been activated. The key to learning control is to recognize the signals that occur just before ejaculation, an awareness that can be difficult for young, inexperienced men. Roughly 30 percent of men report that they ejaculate more rapidly than they would like. Some men who continue to have problems with premature ejaculation after they have become sexually experienced may be hypersensitive to penile arousal and predisposed to early ejaculation (Grenier & Byers, 1995; Strassberg, Mahoney, Schangaard, & Hale, 1990). *Reality or Myth* ?

Inhibited Male Orgasm. In clinical studies, inhibited male orgasm (also known as *retarded ejaculation* or *ejaculatory incompetence*) accounts for about 3 to 8 percent of men seeking treatment, and this rarer form of sexual dysfunction has been found to occur in about 3 to 10 percent of men in nonclinical samples (Laumann et al., 1994; Spector & Carey, 1990; refer to Table 15.1). The inhibition of orgasm may include delayed ejaculation or a total inability to ejaculate despite adequate periods of sexual excitement. As with the other dysfunctions, a diagnosis of inhibited male orgasm is not made when the problem stems from medication side effects or some physical disorder.

Interestingly, many men diagnosed as having inhibited ejaculation sustain erections far beyond the ordinary range during coitus, and their wives are often multiorgasmic (Apfelbaum, 1989). Many of these men say that they prefer masturbation over intercourse, even though they continue to produce an erect penis for coitus with their partner. It also appears that some men may condition themselves to patterns of stimulation and ejaculation that are different from the stimulation provided by coitus. Mann (1977) reported examples of masturbation techniques that include stroking the urethral opening with a throat swab and striking the shaft of the penis forcefully with the heel of the hand. It is understandable that men accustomed to such stimulation might not be able to have orgasm during coitus.

Clinicians have identified various factors associated with inhibited orgasm: religious orthodoxy, fear of creating a pregnancy, negative feelings toward the sexual partner, maternal dominance, hostility, aggression, and fears of abandonment (Dekker, 1993). Men who have lost the capacity to ejaculate after a period of normal functioning often report that a stressful event preceded the problem. Further, discovery of attraction to other men or development of a paraphilia may also impede the ease of engaging in genital stimulation to orgasm with their usual partner.

In a physical condition known as **retrograde ejaculation**, the usual expulsion of ejaculate through the urethra is reversed. The neck of the bladder does not contract, so the semen is expelled into the bladder rather than out through the urethral opening in the penis. The condition usually results from surgery involving the genitourinary system or can be a side effect of some medications.

Inhibited Female Orgasm. Some women suffer from inhibited orgasm, a condition that prevents them from having orgasm despite adequate sexual stimulation. Difficulty with orgasm is one of the most common sexual concerns among women (refer to Table 15.1 on page 350).

Women with this dysfunction may look forward to sex, and many experience high levels of sexual excitement with vaginal swelling and lubrication, but they are usually unable to have orgasm. Sexual arousal causes congestion of the pelvic blood vessels, and without orgasm, the congested blood remains for a while (analogous to the congestion in the testes associated with the absence of orgasmic release in highly aroused men). Consistent arousal in women without orgasmic release can result in cramps, backache, and irritation.

Inhibited female orgasm may arise from guilt-producing thoughts. Kelly, Strassberg, and Kircher (1990) compared the sexual activities that orgasmic women reported with the sexual experiences of women who seldom had orgasms. The relatively nonorgasmic women described more negative attitudes toward masturbation, greater sex guilt and endorsement of sex myths, and more discomfort over communicating with their partners about sexual activities involving direct clitoral stimulation than did the women who experienced orgasm more consistently.

retrograde ejaculation—A condition in which the base of the bladder does not contract during ejaculation, resulting in semen discharging into the man's bladder.

In keeping with the view that sexual dysfunction is a problem only when it persistently interferes with personal satisfaction, only women who wish to have orgasm during coitus but cannot do so should seek treatment. It is debatable whether a dysfunction exists when a woman does not have orgasm during coitus but does climax during other kinds of stimulation—oral or manual stimulation, for example. Calling this pattern a sexual dysfunction and assuming that it requires sex therapy would dictate treatment for a large number of women, given that fewer than 50 percent of women consistently have orgasm during coitus, as discussed in Chapter 5. Darling, Davidson, and Cox (1991) asked more than 700 nurses to report the factors they believed inhibited them from having orgasm during coitus; the women's responses are shown in Table 15.2. Many therapists no longer consider a woman dysfunctional unless she suffers from primary orgasmic dysfunction and then only if she perceives it as a problem.

▶ **Issues to Consider:** If a woman does not consistently experience orgasm during sexual intercourse, should she seek sex therapy?

TABLE 15.2   Factors Inhibiting Women's Orgasm During Coitus

Factors	Percent
Lack of foreplay	63.8
Fatigue	53.6
Preoccupation with nonsexual thoughts	45.5
Ejaculation too soon after intromission*	43.1
Conflicts between partners unrelated to intromission	34.6
Lack of interest or foreplay by partner	24.3
Lack of adequate vaginal lubrication	23.7
Lack of tenderness by partner	22.7
Lack of privacy for intromission	20.3
Overindulgence in alcohol	16.3
Desire to perform well after intromission	14.9
Difficulty with sexual arousal with partner	14.3
Painful sexual intercourse	12.0
Overeating	10.3

*Insertion of the penis into the vagina
Source: Adapted from Darling et al.'s (1991) study of more than 700 nurses, p. 11.

Sexual pain disorders include dyspareunia, which males and females can experience, and vaginismus, which is exclusively a female complaint.

Painful Intercourse. **Dyspareunia** is the technical term for recurrent and persistent genital pain in a man or woman before, during, or after sexual intercourse. They may experience the pain as repeated, intense discomfort; momentary sharp sensations of varying intensity; or intermittent twinges and/or aching sensations. Dyspareunia in men, who may experience the pain in the testes and/or the glans after ejaculation, appears to be much less common than painful intercourse in women (see Table 15.1, page 350).

A wide variety of diseases and disorders of the external and internal sex organs and their surrounding structures can make intercourse painful for men and women. When physical disorders have been ruled out, psychological factors are assumed to be the cause. Lazarus (1989) reviewed 20 cases of painful intercourse in women he had treated and noted that almost half these women reported they were involved in unhappy relationships. He speculated that after ruling out biological factors, he would not be surprised if "about half the women who suffer from dyspareunia are simply having sexual intercourse with the wrong man!" (p. 91).

Vaginismus. **Vaginismus** refers to the involuntary spasm of the pelvic muscles surrounding the outer third of the vagina. Women who experience these spasms of the pubococcygeus (PC) and related muscles may be quite capable of becoming sexually aroused, lubricating, and experiencing orgasm but cannot have intercourse (Beck, 1993). The partner of a woman with this dysfunction who tries to have intercourse with her may have the sensation that his penis is hitting a rigid wall about an inch inside her vagina. Vaginismus rates have ranged from 12 to 17

percent of the women treated at sex-therapy clinics (Spector & Carey, 1990).

The vaginismus spasm can be triggered by anticipated penetration of the vagina. Vaginismus can be a source of dyspareunia, just as recurrent dyspareunia can precede vaginismus.

Among the events triggering vaginismus are rape, abortion, painful gynecological exams, pelvic inflammatory disease, and accidents producing vaginal injury. Other factors in women's histories related to vaginismus include vaginal surgery, problems stemming from episiotomies (surgical incision of the vagina in preparation for childbirth; see Chapter 9), vaginal infections, constipation, and pelvic congestion (Beck, 1993). Imagined rapes and general fears about men and vaginal penetration are sometimes associated with vaginismus. Regardless of the source of the difficulty, the woman cannot control the contractions of vaginismus. Attempts at vaginal penetration produce pain and anxiety, and the woman may try to avoid the possibility of such pain by avoiding sexual encounters.

Treatment ranges from the medical correction of physical problems to the use of psychotherapy, although it is sometimes difficult to determine the precise source(s) of the vaginismus (Beck, 1993; Hawton, 1992). Relaxation training and gradual insertion of successively bigger dilators into the vagina appear to be highly effective in curing vaginismus. It is very important, however, that the woman (rather than a therapist or her partner) control the pace of treatment and the size of the dilator (Heiman & Meston, 1997).

From this review of sexual dysfunctions, it should be clear that whatever the original source (biological, psychosocial, or both) of a person's inability to respond as he or she wishes, the problem may be aggravated by the development of fear of failure in future sexual contacts. Such fear can produce self-fulfilling prophecies; that is, an intense focus on whether a person will respond adequately can reduce the likelihood that healthy sexual feelings and responses will unfold. No matter what particular treatment procedures sex therapists use, they should also identify and attempt to eliminate both clients' fears of sexual inadequacy and their tendency to engage in distracting and maladaptive thoughts during sexual intimacy.

---

dyspareunia (DIS-par-OO-nee-ah)—Recurrent and persistent pain associated with intercourse for a woman or man.
vaginismus (VAH-jih-NIS-mus)—Involuntary spasms of the pelvic muscles surrounding the outer third of the vagina.

Sex Therapy

Although sexual dysfunctions have been treated by a wide array of different therapies, in this section we concentrate on the most commonly used techniques in sex therapy. Until the 1960s, the predominant approach to the treatment of sexual dysfunction was psychoanalysis. Sexual problems were viewed as symptoms of emotional conflict originating in childhood. The sexual difficulties or symptoms would persist, the analysts claimed, unless the conflict could be resolved and the personality of the individual restructured. The trouble with this approach is that the sexual difficulties may persist even after the client understands or gains insight into the origin of the problem. In addition, psychoanalytic therapy can be time-consuming and expensive.

Cognitive-behavioral psychologists have long taken issue with the psychoanalytic approach. They believe that a person can be emotionally healthy and still have sexual difficulties. Maladaptive sexual functioning is learned, they believe, and it can be unlearned without extensive probing into a client's past. Cognitive-behavioral approaches deal directly with sexual dysfunction by using techniques designed to overcome anxiety and to change self-defeating thought patterns. Behavioral therapies were first applied to sexual problems in the 1950s. The behavioral approach was later used by Masters and Johnson (1970).

MASTERS AND JOHNSON'S APPROACH

The treatment program that Masters and Johnson developed is a two-week process, conducted by a man and a woman. Both partners in the couple seeking treatment are given a thorough medical examination and interviewed by the therapist of the same sex, followed by an interview with the other therapist. All four people (the couple and the two therapists) then discuss treatment goals.

Masters and Johnson recommended the use of both a male and a female therapist to provide a "friend-in-court" for the client of the same sex. They stressed the treatment of specific symptoms rather than extensive psychotherapy aimed at determining potential underlying, unconscious sources of difficulty.

Effectiveness of Masters and Johnson's Sex Therapy Approach.

One of the most impressive aspects of Masters and Johnson's (1970) therapeutic approach with almost 800 persons with sexual problems was that they reported success in treating more than 80 percent of their clients who experienced various types of sexual dysfunction. Of the successful clients who could be found five years later (313 couples), only 5 percent reported recurrence of the dysfunctions for which they had obtained treatment. The therapeutic community was quite impressed with the success of Masters and Johnson's approach, and for years other therapists used modified versions of many of their methods.

Gradually, however, outcome statistics reported from clinical practice revealed overall improvement in only about two-thirds of cases. The improvements obtained from controlled treatment studies have all been more modest than the proportions Masters and Johnson reported (Grenier & Byers, 1995; Wiederman, 1998). Do these findings indicate that the only reliable source of sex therapy is Masters and Johnson? Probably not. Instead, differences between the failure rates that Masters and Johnson reported and those that other sex therapists and researchers reported probably stem from a combination of factors other than Masters and Johnson's skill as therapists. Among these factors are methodological problems, increasing sexual knowledge among North Americans, and changing characteristics of clients.

Bernard Zilbergeld and Michael Evans (1980) noted that Masters and Johnson's research methodology was quite vague and that they may have been lenient in their judgments of what constituted a successful outcome. Another factor in Masters and Johnson's reported success rates may have been that 90 percent of their clients traveled to St. Louis from other parts of the country. Having left behind the routine and cares of their daily lives and made the commitment of time and money to improve their relationships, these highly motivated couples were likely candidates for rekindling sexual interest and changing their sexual attitudes and behavior.

In addition, many of the problems that Masters and Johnson's clients experienced stemmed from misinformation and ignorance. People in the 1950s and 1960s did not have the easy access to information about sexuality that we have today. Clients today whose problems stem from a lack of information may be "curing" themselves instead of seeking professional treatment. The caseloads of sex therapists today may include a greater proportion of clients with sexual difficulties resulting from deeply rooted emotional problems or from conflicts within their relationships—sexual problems that are often difficult to treat. This factor would, of course, result in lower success rates and higher relapse rates.

Another question that must be addressed in the evaluation of any sex therapy is whether the treatment yields sustained change over the years. There is very little available research on this subject. Summarizing what is known, Hawton (1992) reported that the successful short-term results of sex therapy for erectile dysfunction were maintained in the long term (one to six years), whereas those for premature ejaculation were less permanent. Men with low sexual desire had a fairly poor response to treatment in the short and long terms. Sex therapy for vaginismus was highly effective in the short and long terms, whereas the long-term results of treatment for low sexual desire in women were fairly poor. Interestingly, there was improvement in the way a number of clients *felt* about their sexuality, despite the fact that some had returned to pretreatment dysfunctions in sexual behavior. If these clients had received occasional clinical "booster" sessions over the years, their posttreatment improvement would perhaps have been maintained through preventive measures (McCarthy, 1993). *Reality or Myth*

KAPLAN'S APPROACH

Helen Singer Kaplan developed an approach to sex therapy that combined some of the insights and techniques of psychoanalysis with behavioral methods. Her approach begins at the "surface," or behavioral, level and probes more deeply into emotional conflicts only if necessary.

Helen Singer Kaplan (1929–1995) has described a pattern of sexual desire, arousal, and response that is probably closer to the sequence of feelings that most of us experience than is that described by Masters and Johnson on the basis of their physiological recordings of sexual responding.

Many sexual difficulties stem from superficial causes. If a sexual difficulty is rooted in a lack of knowledge, for example, information and instruction may be all that are needed to treat it. If the trouble is of recent origin, a series of guided sexual tasks may be enough to change patterns of response. If deep-seated emotional problems exist, the therapist may use more analytic approaches to help clients obtain insight into the less conscious aspects of their personality. This last approach has been designated as psychosexual therapy to distinguish it from sex therapy.

Kaplan questioned Masters and Johnson's use of two therapists. Research, too, has suggested that treatment is not more effective if two therapists instead of one are assigned or if the therapist is of the same sex as the dysfunctional member of the couple being treated (Hawton, 1992; LoPiccolo et al., 1985). The involvement of two trained professionals is, of course, also twice as expensive as the use of one. *Reality or Myth*

Treatment of Sexual Dysfunctions

In this section we consider some of the more common treatments used in sex therapy. Caird and Wincze (1977) described most behavioral treatment programs as including three general components:

Education: The client and/or partner receives instruction in communication skills, sexual techniques, and the anatomy and physiology of sexual functioning.

Redirection of sexual behavior: The client's focus of attention is redirected from self-monitoring to giving pleasure to the partner.

Graded sexual exposure: Anxiety about sexual performance is reduced through gradual exposure to the anxiety-evoking situation. Exposure may be brought about through a series of relaxation exercises or through homework exercises with a partner.

When problems are based on relationship conflicts or serious individual disturbances, behavioral approaches may not be effective because they require both partners' active cooperation. Individual psychotherapy may be more likely to resolve individual disturbances, and communication skills training may be helpful for relationship conflicts. This is the case for gay, lesbian, and heterosexual couples.

Nondemand Pleasuring and Sensate Focus. In exercises involving nondemand sensate focus, the clients initially avoid sexual intercourse. In fact, couples are forbidden to engage in any sexual activity until the therapist instructs them to do so. Over the course of treatment, they receive homework assignments that gradually increase their range of sexual behaviors. Initially, only kissing, hugging, and body massage may be allowed.

The partners are instructed to take turns in the roles of giver and receiver as they touch and caress each other's body. When playing the role of giver, the person explores, touches, and caresses the receiver's body. In applying this technique, called **nondemand**

pleasuring, the giver does not attempt to arouse the receiver sexually. In an exercise called **sensate focus,** the receiver concentrates on the sensations evoked by the giver's touch on various parts of the body. In these exercises, the giver's responsibility is to provide pleasure and to be aware of his or her own pleasure in touching. The receiver's role is to prevent or end any stimulation that is uncomfortable or irritating by either telling or showing the partner his or her feelings.

Men and women with sexual excitement difficulties may find that taking a turn as the receiver helps to counteract any guilt they have learned about receiving sexual attention. Because they are not expected to do anything but receive the pleasure and give feedback when appropriate, the exercise may help them focus on their own erotic sensations.

The next step is to engage in nondemand breast and genital caressing while avoiding orgasm-oriented stimulation. Masters and Johnson (1970) recommended the position shown in Figure 15.1 for this phase because it allows easy access to the breasts and vulva when the woman is in the receiving role. It also allows the receiver to place his or her hand over the partner's hand to provide guidance to the kind of stimulation that is most pleasurable. If the partner of the person who is experiencing sexual difficulty becomes highly aroused during this exercise, that partner may be brought to orgasm orally or manually *after* completion of the exercise.

Other sexual behaviors are gradually added to the clients' homework. Successive assignments may include nongenital body massage, breast and genital touching, simultaneous masturbation, penile insertion with no movement, mutual genital manipulation to orgasm, and, finally, intercourse.

After the partners reach a sufficient level of arousal through sensate focus and nondemand pleasuring, they proceed to nondemand coitus. If the woman has had problems involving either excitement or orgasm, she is instructed to initiate sexual intercourse when she feels ready. Masters and Johnson (1970) recommended the woman-above position because it gives the woman more control over both insertion of the penis and intensity and frequency of

---

nondemand pleasuring—Partners' taking turns in exploring and caressing each other's bodies without attempting to arouse their partner sexually.

sensate focus—Concentration on sensations produced by touching.

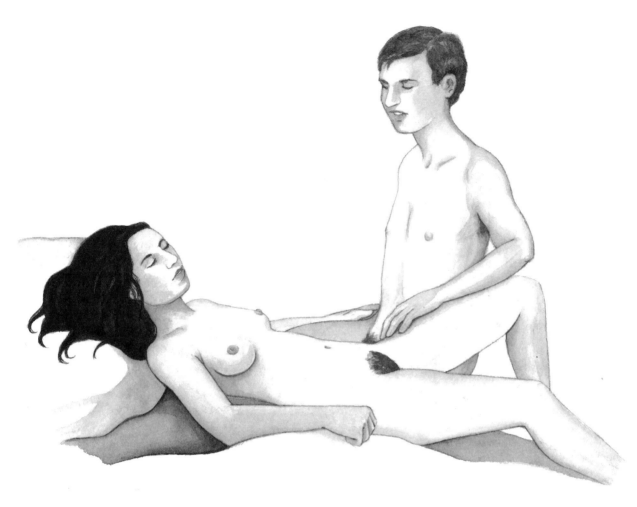

Figure 15.1   Nondemand Pleasuring
This position, which allows easy access to the breasts and vulva,
is often used in exercises designed to relieve sexual problems.

thrusting. Her partner is typically advised to thrust slowly rather than forcefully. Usually the couple is counseled to disengage several times during coitus and to perform the nondemand genital stimulation exercises. Throughout these exercises, the woman is encouraged to remain relaxed and to indulge in arousing fantasies. The couple can thus learn to enjoy sexual pleasure without worrying about performing later.

Masturbation Training. Most treatment programs for orgasmically inhibited women include training in masturbation, particularly if the woman has never had an orgasm. A treatment program for such women is presented in "Research Spotlight: A Treatment Pro-

gram for Orgasmically Inhibited Women", page 366. This approach is used mainly in cases of primary orgasmic dysfunction and female hypoactive sexual desire (Hurlbert, 1993; McVey, 1997). In this approach, women are encouraged to learn about their bodies and relax to the point where they can experience orgasm.

Women with secondary orgasmic dysfunction have not responded as well to this approach. Nondemand sensate focus exercises combined with techniques to heighten arousal, however, are often effective in treating secondary inhibited orgasm. Kaplan (1974) claimed that sexual arousal can be enhanced by having a man penetrate his partner slowly and then withdraw after a brief period, engaging in

RESEARCH SPOTLIGHT   A Treatment Program for Orgasmically Inhibited Women

The psychologist Joseph LoPiccolo and his colleagues (Heiman & LoPiccolo, 1988; LoPiccolo & Lobitz, 1972) developed a treatment program for orgasmically inhibited women that involves four major components.

1. Masturbation Training
   a. The woman is instructed to take a warm bath and examine her genitals with a mirror. Diagrams are used to aid her in identifying her muscles and genital organs. Pubococcygeal muscle exercises are begun.
   b. The client is instructed to explore her genitals by touch.
   c. The client continues tactile and visual exploration in an effort to locate pleasure-sensitive areas.
   d. The woman manually stimulates the pleasure-producing areas while using a sterile lubricant.
   e. If orgasm has not occurred by this time, the client is instructed to purchase a vibrator and use it to reach orgasm, placing it on her mons pubis near her clitoris.

2. Skill Training for the Partner
   a. The partner observes the woman's masturbation to learn what is pleasurable for her. Various aspects of sensate focus exercises are begun.
   b. The partner masturbates the woman to orgasm.
   c. Manual stimulation is combined with intercourse.

3. Disinhibition of Arousal: Some women may not be able to reach orgasm with their partner because they are embarrassed about showing intense arousal or fear losing self-control. These women are asked to role-play a grossly exaggerated orgasm, with violent convulsions, screaming, and other extreme behavior. Repeated performances in the company of the partner usually result in amusement and, eventually, boredom.

4. Practice of Orgasmic Behaviors: Actions such as pelvic thrusting, pointing the toes, tensing the thigh muscles, holding the breath, pushing down with the diaphragm, and throwing back the head often occur involuntarily during intense orgasm. If the woman practices these behaviors voluntarily when she is experiencing sexual arousal, they may trigger orgasm.

---

sexual foreplay before reentering with slow, teasing thrusts.

The Squeeze Technique.   The approach most commonly employed for premature ejaculation is the **squeeze technique** (Masters & Johnson, 1970). The partner circles the tip of the penis with the hand, as shown in Figure 15.2. The thumb is placed against the frenulum on the underside of the penis, while the fingers are placed on either side of the corona ridge on the upper side of the penis. When the man signals that he is approaching ejaculation, his partner applies fairly strong pressure for 3 to 5 seconds and then stops with a sudden release. The partner stimulates his penis again after the sensations of impending ejaculation diminish, usually within 20 to 30 seconds. Typically, the man is told that he should not try to control his ejaculation but should rely instead on the squeeze technique. The entire process is usually repeated twice per session before ejaculation is allowed.

Some couples prefer to apply the squeeze technique as close as possible to the base of the penis rather than the tip. This variation has the advantage of being easier to do during intercourse, but for some couples it does not work.

The next step is to apply a water-soluble lubricant, such as K-Y jelly, to the hand and then stimulate the penis to approximate more closely the sensations experienced during vaginal intercourse. The squeeze technique is then applied again. If this step is successfully completed, the couple proceeds to intercourse using the woman-above position. The woman guides the penis into her vagina while remaining motionless. If the man does not feel close to

squeeze technique—A treatment for premature ejaculation in which a man signals his partner to apply manual pressure to his penis to delay ejaculation.

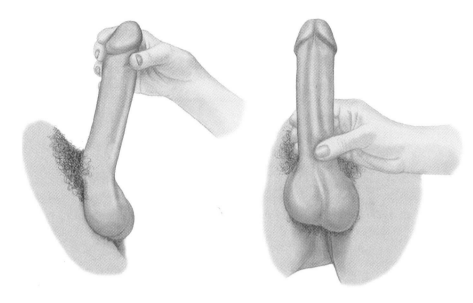

Figure 15.2 The Squeeze Technique
The squeeze technique, which can be applied at either the corona (left) or the base of the penis (right), is useful for the treatment of premature ejaculation.

orgasm, the woman can start to lift her body slowly on and off her partner's body. The man can place his hands on her hips to guide the pace of intercourse. When he signals that he feels the sensations of impending orgasm, his partner withdraws from contact and applies the squeeze technique. The process is repeated after the urge to ejaculate diminishes. The man is usually not permitted to ejaculate until the squeeze technique has been applied twice or until the woman experiences orgasm.

If the partners are successful with this position, they most often proceed to side-by-side intercourse, employing the squeeze technique as needed. The final step is to have coitus in the man-above position. After the partners have attained satisfactory intercourse with the man on top, the choice of sexual positions and techniques is left up to them. Having tried the side-by-side position, couples whom Masters and Johnson (1970) treated continued to use it 75 percent of the time, even after having had success with the man-above position. Success in gaining ejaculatory control using the squeeze technique is around 60 percent (Grenier & Byers, 1995).

Group Therapy and Systematic Desensitization.
Numerous other therapy formats and techniques are sometimes used in conjunction with the foregoing approaches to treatment of sexual dysfunctions. For example, for women who have primary or secondary orgasmic dysfunction, group therapy is effective and

less expensive than individual therapy (LoPiccolo & Stock, 1986; McCabe & Delany, 1992).

Systematic desensitization involves learning a series of muscle relaxation exercises. The client and therapist then construct a set of imaginative anxiety-provoking scenes that go from the least to the most anxiety producing. Gradually the client attempts to replace anxiety to the imagined scene with a relaxation response.

The client starts by imagining the least anxiety-laden scene. If the client feels anxiety, he or she is told to stop imagining and to employ relaxation procedures. The person repeats this exercise until he or she can imagine the scene without feeling anxiety. The client then imagines the next scene, practicing relaxation techniques if necessary. This process continues until the last scene can be imagined without anxiety. The process can take from a few sessions to 15 or more. For an abbreviated example, see "Highlight: Systematic Desensitization Hierarchy for Inhibited Ejaculation" on page 368.

A problem with the use of systematic desensitization lies in its lack of generalizability to real-life situations. For example, if a man experiencing inhibited orgasm is successful in completing the hier-

---

systematic desensitization—A behavioral therapy in which deep relaxation is used to reduce anxiety associated with certain situations.

H I G H L I G H T

Systematic Desensitization Hierarchy for Inhibited Ejaculation

1. You and your partner have turned out the lights and are lying in bed talking before going to sleep.

2. You feel close to her at this moment as you begin to kiss her.

3. You feel your penis becoming erect as you continue kissing and begin to fondle her breasts.

4. She responds warmly to your caresses by rubbing your inner thigh.

5. You now feel your penis becoming hard and elongated as you manually stimulate her genitals.

6. You reach to the bedside table and take out the electronic vibrator you know gives her pleasure and begin to stimulate her genitals as she massages your penis.

7. She moves her body to you and presses your penis against her stomach while whispering how much she wants you.

8. You remove her gown and position yourself between her legs.

9. As your penis penetrates your partner's vagina, you experience very pleasurable sexual sensations.

10. You both begin thrusting, gradually at first, enjoying the sensations of intercourse.

11. As you continue thrusting, you notice your partner increasing the tempo of thrusting as she nears orgasm.

12. As you meet the tempo of your partner's thrusting, she reaches orgasm while holding you tightly.

13. You feel your muscles tensing as you continue thrusting while your partner verbally encourages you toward ejaculation.

14. Your muscles tighten and you feel a wave of sensations radiating through your body as you ejaculate into your partner's vagina.

Source: Abridged from Tollison and Adams (1979, p. 133).

archy described in the Highlight, he can now imagine ejaculating into his partner's vagina without anxiety. But the fact that he can imagine a behavior does not necessarily mean that he can engage in the behavior with his partner. To overcome this problem, some clinicians use in vivo desensitization, which involves actual sexual experiences rather than imaginary ones. For example, if a person learns that it is acceptable to tell his or her partner about feelings of nervousness and does so, the partner can pull back from sexual activity while the tense person relaxes. The procedure gives the nervous partner a sense of personal control and may also encourage both partners to communicate their feelings more openly.

Sexual Surrogates.   Most sexual therapies include homework assignments that require a cooperative partner. In attempting to meet the needs of the dys-

functional client who has no steady partner, some therapists have used "bodywork therapy" in which the client and a **sexual surrogate,** with the direction of a therapist, may engage in private sexual activity as part of the treatment (Apfelbaum, 1980).

Most professionals view sexual contact between clients and therapists as unethical. Masters and Johnson (1970) attempted to solve this problem by employing a therapy partner for clients who did not have one. They reported that the participation of a cooperative and skilled surrogate who had no prior association with the client was as effective as the participation of marital partners in the treatment of

sexual surrogate—A member of a sex therapy team whose role is to provide education and direction as well as to have sexual interactions with a client as part of the therapy.

sexual difficulties. But Masters and Johnson discontinued the controversial practice, as have many other therapists, because the use of sexual surrogates is highly controversial. Critics have contended that the use of surrogates is thinly disguised prostitution, with potentially damaging consequences. Defenders of the practice claim that surrogates are carefully screened and taught to be sensitive to the therapeutic nature of their task. That is, they are trained to help the client learn skills that he or she can use with a regular partner.

In an ideal world, the employment of sexual surrogates would depend solely on their effectiveness in attaining treatment goals. A comparison of the progress of clients treated by therapists employing surrogates with that of clients treated without surrogates would aid in determining their usefulness. But in the world in which we live, no such study has been conducted or is likely to be done in the near future, because of legal and ethical concerns. In most clinics that treat sexual dysfunctions, the use of sexual surrogates has been abandoned (Leiblum & Rosen, 1989).

▶ **Issues to Consider:** If you had a history of sexual difficulties and were currently without a partner, how would you respond to a therapist who suggested employment of a sexual surrogate? Do you think men would respond differently from women?

OTHER TREATMENT APPROACHES

Various approaches involving surgery and mechanical approaches, hormones, and drugs have been used in the attempt to treat sexual dysfunctions. The fact that most of these treatments have been developed for male sexual difficulties probably reflects our culture's emphasis on male sexual performance. In general, before permitting these kinds of treatments, the client should make sure that no other type of treatment is effective for him and obtain a second opinion.

Surgical and Mechanical Approaches. Surgical procedures, including implants, have been used in the treatment of erectile dysfunction. There are two basic types of plastic or silicone implants. One is a semirigid rod that keeps the penis in a constant state of erection but can be bent for concealment under clothing. The

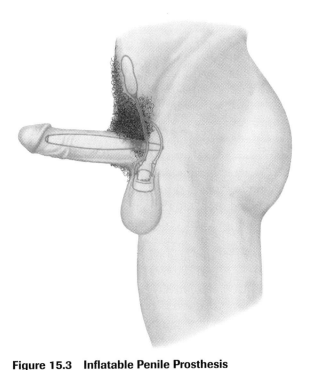

Figure 15.3　Inflatable Penile Prosthesis
This drawing shows an inflatable penile prosthesis. With most inflatable penile prostheses, a reservoir of fluid is implanted under the abdominal muscles, and an attached pump is embedded in either the abdominal cavity or the scrotum. A man presses the pump to force fluid into cylinders in his prosthesis when he wishes to have an erection. A release valve allows the fluid to return to the abdominal reservoir.

other type of silicone or plastic (polyurethane) implant, an inflatable device, is surgically implanted under the skin of the penis; to achieve erection, the man presses a pump implanted in the scrotum. The pump forces fluid from a reservoir put under the abdominal muscles into cylinders implanted in the penis. Complications of this method include infection and mechanical failure. Follow-up studies of **prosthesis** recipients and their partners have indicated that they were generally satisfied with the choice to have the surgery (Graber, 1993). Partner satisfaction of men who received the inflatable prosthesis was higher than that of partners of men who had the semirigid rod implanted. However, no differences in satisfaction have been reported between men who received the

prosthesis—Artificial replacement for a body part.

inflatable versus the semirigid prostheses (Tiefer & Melman, 1989). Most men who have implants can experience ejaculation and orgasm unless there has been previous neurological damage (Krane, 1986; McCarthy & McMillan, 1990).

A diversity of surgical techniques, including microsurgery, have been developed to increase blood flow to the penises of men with erectile dysfunction. The surgery is similar in principle to bypass surgery for heart patients with blocked arteries. The blocked arteries are bypassed through grafts that allow for a greater blood supply to the penis. This procedure appears promising, but results so far have been quite variable, and the procedure appears suited for only a small percentage of men who have erectile dysfunction (Graber, 1993).

The vacuum pump has been used as a nonsurgical method to treat erectile difficulties. The penis is inserted into an acrylic tube while a hand-held vacuum pump draws blood into erectile tissue. A rubber band holds the blood in place for up to 30 minutes.

Hormones. Hormone administration, principally testosterone, has been used for years to treat erectile dysfunction. If the problem is not due to hormone deficiency, however, hormones can increase sexual arousability without improving performance, which can result in further deterioration of the client's condition (Rosen & Ashton, 1993; Segraves, 1988). Testosterone treatment also increases the risk of coronary thrombosis, atherosclerosis, and cancer of the prostate.

Susan Rako, a psychiatrist in private practice in Boston, published a book called *The Hormone of Desire: The Truth About Sexuality, Menopause, and Testosterone* (1997) in which she advocated women's use of testosterone to increase their sexual desire. This approach involves the use of combination testosterone-estrogen pills, creams, and gels. It is unlikely that these medications are helpful except, perhaps, for women with abnormally low levels of testosterone and without other complicating factors (e.g., anxiety, stress, guilt, anger at partner) that are inhibiting their sexual response. Research is badly needed on the effectiveness of this approach as well as possible side effects. For example, the dosage level is presumably important; high levels of testosterone might increase sexual desire in some women, but

they also would tend to masculinize the woman, producing unwanted body hair and the like. The manufacturer of the testosterone patch, Theratech, is conducting research on the effects of testosterone-based products on the sexual desire of women.

Drugs. Drugs are sometimes used to alleviate some of the symptoms associated with sexual dysfunctions. As noted earlier, anxiety plays a large role in the development of sexual dysfunction in both women and men. Physicians may attempt to treat some dysfunctions through the prescription of minor tranquilizers, such as Librium or Valium, that reduce anxiety. Some individuals with sexual dysfunctions have reported improvement after treatment with antidepressant medications (Crenshaw & Goldberg, 1996). Although their frequency of sexual behavior did not increase significantly, their satisfaction with their own sexuality did.

A number of drugs can create pharmacological erection through injection into the penis by relaxing the smooth muscle of the corpora cavernosa (Heiman & Meston, 1997). They appear to be most useful for men with irreversible biological erectile dysfunction. The client can be taught to inject the drug himself. Erection usually occurs within 10 minutes and lasts about 2 hours. There is some risk with this treatment, which has a number of side effects, such as penile scarring, priapism, cardiac irregularities, and changes in the liver with long-term use.

A new drug, sildenafil citrate, approved by the Food and Drug Administration in 1998, is taken orally as a pill. Sildenafil is marketed as **Viagra** (rhymes with Niagara, as in the Falls). Used by men who have erectile difficulties, it is taken 1 hour before the man wants to have an erection, and the erection can last for up to 4 hours following administration. Unlike other treatments, Viagra does not work unless the person is experiencing sexual arousal (Rosen, 1996). It works by blocking an enzyme that allows blood to flow out of the penis.

The marketing of Viagra in the spring of 1998 received an enormous amount of attention in

Viagra (vy-AG-ra)—A drug that increases the likelihood of erection by blocking an enzyme that allows blood to flow out of the penis.

the press, on talk shows, and on late-night-TV monologues. Research reported in the *New England Journal of Medicine* by Irwin Goldstein and his colleagues (1998) involving a **double-blind study** with 532 men showed that about 70 percent of all attempts at coitus with an erect penis were successful for men when they were taking Viagra, whereas only 22 percent of attempts were successful when men were administered a placebo. Despite its expense (each pill costs about $10), at the time we went to press, 20,000 prescriptions for Viagra were being filled *every day*. A typical prescription contains six pills. The immediate and immense popularity of Viagra might suggest that a very large number of men experience erectile difficulties. Presumably, however, some prescriptions are sought by men without erectile dysfunction who wish to improve their performance. But they are wasting their money, because Viagra does not enhance normal sexual function.

The cost of prescription drugs is covered by many health insurance policies. In the case of Viagra, however, it was reported on the network evening news programs at the end of April 1998 that Blue Cross/Blue Shield of California had ruled that men covered under their plan could receive coverage for a maximum of six pills per month. That doesn't necessarily mean that these men can enjoy half a dozen episodes of coitus and orgasm per *month*, because Viagra works only about 70 percent of the time, as noted earlier.

Although Viagra may have improved the sex lives of thousands of men and their partners, scattered reports have appeared of women seeking divorces after they found some of their husband's Viagra tablets missing from their medicine chest. In a satirical essay, John Perry (personal communication, May 1, 1998) summed up the responses of such women: "I don't know who got the benefits," the wife said, "but I know I didn't get screwed, I got stiffed!"

In addition, Viagra users may face serious health risks. As of August 1998, more than 100 men who took Viagra had died. It is not clear that Viagra was responsible for their deaths, but almost half of these

men had taken nitroglycerin for heart problems. Also, the use of Viagra by men taking medications to lower their blood pressure appears to be a risk factor. These are, of course, correlational data, but we strongly recommend that men with cardiovascular problems consult their physicians before taking Viagra or other similar medications that are being developed.

Clinical tests of the effectiveness of Viagra for women with arousal difficulties are under way in Canada and the United States. Pfizer, the pharmaceutical company that manufactures the drug, recently completed an international study with 700 premenopausal women. The success rate was somewhat lower than that with men: 50 percent of the women given Viagra reported satisfactory results, but 20 percent of women given a placebo also responded favorably. As with men, Viagra would presumably enhance sexual response (e.g., vaginal swelling, lubrication) among those women who desired their partners but were experiencing problems with blood flow to their genitals. It would not be expected to enhance the performance of women with normal blood flow to the genitals during sexual stimulation (Hospital Testing Viagra for Use on Women, Hamilton [Canada] Daily News, June 16, 1998).

▶ **Issues to Consider:** Why do you think there are more treatments for men than for women who experience sexual dysfunctions?

QUALIFICATIONS AND ETHICS OF THERAPISTS

One of the challenges for individuals who are experiencing sexual problems is finding a qualified therapist. There are a considerable number of people who call themselves sex therapists but have little training or competence.

Most qualified sex therapists make themselves and their credentials known to other professionals in the community. There is no legislative control of the title "sex therapist" in many states, and so the appearance of the title in the telephone book does not testify to an individual's skills. In all states, however, licensing laws control who can be listed as a psychologist or physician. The American Association for Sex Educators, Counselors, and Therapists (AASECT) certifies individual sex therapists (see Appendix).

double blind study—A research design in which neither the participants nor the experimenters know which treatment is being applied until the research is over.

Reality or Myth 6

Before expending a lot of time and money in therapy, people seeking help should try to identify their goals, and discuss these with a potential sex therapist to see if they are in general agreement. For example, gay or lesbian couples who experience sexual difficulties may seek help from a therapist, only to discover that the therapist has an implicit belief that the "problem" is that they are trying to have a committed sexual relationship with a person of the same sex and the "solution" is for them to separate and find a partner of the other sex. A therapist with this value system in not likely to be able to provide the help that the gay or lesbian couple needs in resolving sexual difficulties. The same problems can emerge if a couple (or individual) differs from a therapist regarding appropriate roles for men versus women. Thus, people should ask a potential therapist about his or her values and assumptions.

There are certain practices that we believe are not appropriate in sex therapy regardless of the therapist's qualifications. Unless a therapist is a licensed physician who recommends a physical examination, he or she should not ask clients to take off their clothes. And although the conversation, material, and assignments are explicitly sexual, overt sexual activities should not occur in the therapist's presence. Not all therapists share our sentiments on this subject. From 2 percent to 7 percent of psychologists have reported sexual contact with their clients (Pope, Sonne, & Holroyd, 1993; Stake & Oliver, 1991). A few therapists have even advocated therapist-client sexual intimacy as part of sex therapy. However, sexual contact between clients and therapists is generally considered unethical and destructive to the therapeutic relationship. One study indicated that 90 percent of the clients who had been sexually intimate with their therapists reported some negative effects, such as feeling guilty or exploited (Bouhoutsos, 1981).

Our opposition to therapist-client sexual intimacy is based on the ethical and emotional problems inherent in the practice. First, the purpose of therapy is to aid individuals who are distressed about some aspect of sexual functioning. These people seek professional help for problems they have been unable to resolve themselves. Therapists and their clients are not equal; therapists, as professionals, are in a position of greater power stemming from their expertise in the area, and clients are vulnerable to exploitation because of their position of need. A therapist-client sexual relationship ultimately exploits (and potentially harms) rather than aids the client.

Second, the purpose of seeing a therapist is to receive help in identifying feelings and resolving conflicts without having another person's desires imposed on oneself. In cases in which the therapist believes that sexual interaction during treatment is necessary or useful but the client has no partner, the use of a surrogate minimizes the likelihood that a conflict of interest will develop between the therapist and client, although its controversial nature raises problems of its own.

Third, as we have emphasized, sexual difficulties often include conflicts about relationships and anxiety about sex rather than simple problems of technique. The problems typical of persons seeking sex therapy are not likely to be solved through sexual relations with a therapist and may, in fact, be worsened.

▶ **Issues to Consider:** Your best friend is seeking a sex therapist, knows that you're taking a human sexuality course, and asks your opinion on finding a qualified professional. What advice would you give?

It is not uncommon for therapists to experience attraction toward clients. In one study of more than 500 psychologists, 95 percent of the men and 76 percent of the women reported sexual attraction toward some of their clients (Pope, Keith-Spiegel, & Tabachnick, 1986). Only 9 percent felt that they had received sufficient training for dealing with potential attraction toward clients. Many student therapists refrained from discussing this issue with their supervisors for fear of being perceived as having "problems." Clearly, graduate school and medical school courses must give greater attention to the management of therapists' sexual feelings toward clients. Just as people must develop ways to manage their sexual feelings and behavior in social situations, prospective therapists need training to deal with these emotions in the clinical environment. In their national survey of graduate students in clinical and counseling psychology who were in their fourth or fifth year of training and about to go on their internships, Devine and Allgeier (1997) found that although more than three-quarters reported having had sexual feelings toward at least one client during their supervised training, 43 percent of the students thought that their training in classes and by supervisors on how to handle such feelings was less than adequate.

More adequate therapist training aimed at preventing therapist-client sexual interaction might avert the problems that can arise when therapists and clients become sexually intimate. Such training might also be very helpful to therapists dealing with clients who are experiencing a sexually transmitted disease, the topic of the next chapter.

SUMMARY OF MAJOR POINTS

1. Stress and sexual dysfunctions. Problems in sexual response are associated with a variety of physical and psychological stresses, including long- or short-term medical conditions, fatigue or illness, anxiety, a disproportionately heavy focus on performance evaluation, ignorance about sexuality, and relationships dominated by conflict or inadequate communication.

2. Specific types of sexual dysfunction. Levels of desire and responsiveness normally vary from one individual to the next and from one time to the next. When an individual is bothered by consistent failure to respond in the way he or she wishes, it may be appropriate to seek professional help. A person can experience difficulty during any phase of a sexual interaction. The individual may feel little or no desire for sexual relations or may be obsessed with the desire for sexual stimulation. If a person's level of desire is consistently different from that of his or her partner, therapy can be used to resolve the discrepancy. Alternatively, an individual may feel deep desire for sexual relations but have difficulty becoming excited or aroused. Finally, an individual may respond quickly or slowly to sexual stimulation. When a person's pattern of desires is consistently different from that of his or her partner and from the way the person wishes to respond, sex therapy may help the couple.

3. Major approaches to sex therapy. Masters and Johnson's behavioral approach, which stresses the learned nature of many sexual responses, focuses on the development of more satisfying patterns of response. Kaplan included a similar approach in her therapeutic treatment but distinguished between specific maladaptive sexual responses and more general sources of difficulty, including personal conflicts and unresolved problems between a couple, which may require more prolonged and in-depth treatment.

4. Effectiveness of sex therapy. Masters and Johnson reported higher success rates than many other contemporary sex therapists typically experience. Although it is possible that they employed superior techniques, it is likely that several other factors explain this difference.

5. Treatment of sexual dysfunctions. Sex therapists use various techniques to help people have more satisfying sexual experiences. These include systematic desensitization, nondemand pleasuring, sensate focus, masturbation training, and the squeeze technique, in addition to psychotherapy. Medical treatments include hormone therapy, prosthetic devices, and drugs that are used primarily to treat erectile dysfunction.

6. Controversies surrounding sex therapy. The use of client-therapist sexual contact, the employment of sexual surrogates, and the basis for providing sex therapists with credentials to practice are among the issues that therapists are currently debating. Sexual contact between therapist and client is unethical and usually has negative effects on the client. There is no evidence regarding the effectiveness of sexual surrogates in treating sexual dysfunction, and few therapists employ them because of the additional expense. Most sex therapists have licenses to practice as psychologists, physicians, social workers, or counselors.

Sexually Transmitted Diseases

Reality or Myth

1. *People are more knowledgeable about HIV/AIDS than they are about other sexually transmitted diseases (STDs).*

2. *Most cases of gonorrhea take several years to disappear after medical treatment.*

3. *Brain damage can be one of the results of untreated syphilis.*

4. *Most babies born from mothers infected with HIV/AIDS contract HIV/AIDS themselves.*

5. *Blood transfusions are responsible for causing about half of all AIDS cases in the United States.*

6. *There is a highly effective vaccine for hepatitis B virus.*

exual intimacy can be a source of ecstatic pleasure, but it also carries the risk of exposure to infection from sexually transmitted diseases (STDs). *STD* is the term used to describe more than 25 infectious organisms that are transmitted through sexual activity, as well as the many disorders that they cause. More than 15 million Americans contract an STD each year. Two-thirds of STD cases afflict persons under 25 years old, and 3 million teenagers become infected each year with STDs (Fact Sheet, 1997). If left untreated, many STDs result in severe consequences, including infertility, ectopic pregnancy, cancer, and even death.

We begin this chapter by examining how attitudes about sexuality and morality may increase the likelihood of contracting and transmitting STDs. Then we review the common STDs and genital infections and discuss measures that reduce the risk of contracting or transmitting an STD.

Attitudes Toward Sexually Transmitted Diseases

Some years ago, an anthropologist (Miner, 1956) wrote a description of a people called the Nacirema. These people were notable for their obsessive rituals and their worship at altars made of large white bowls on pedestals of varying heights. Each Nacirema family owned at least three of these bowls, sometimes as many as ten, and they engaged in rituals in front of them half a dozen or more times a day. The cleanliness rituals they performed were thought to bring moral goodness.

Nacirema is *American* spelled backward. Indeed, our culture places a high premium on cleanliness, health, and physical beauty. From childhood on, hygiene and health are linked to moral goodness, and dirtiness is linked to disease. Although the emphasis on hygienic practices is valuable in reducing sickness and increasing longevity, some negative side effects are associated with our national obsession with cleanliness and health. Among these are the counterproductive personal and societal responses to STDs, which usually originate in our childhood learning to link dirt and disease with sin and sexuality (see Chapter 12).

When a person contracts an STD (formerly called a venereal disease, or VD), the rational response is to have it diagnosed and treated immediately and to notify partners so that they may do the same. However, people who associate diseases, especially STDs, with sin and "dirtiness" may become embarrassed and ashamed to admit they contracted an STD. This shame and embarrassment often inhibit reasonable and healthy responses to dealing with these infections and infestations.

It is important for sexually active people to obtain diagnosis and treatment of any suspicious symptoms because most STDs are readily cured in their early stages. Further, the partners of a person with an STD must be informed that they have been exposed because as many as 80 percent of women and many men may be **asymptomatic** with some of the STDs. Because of the high proportion of asymptomatic infections, sexually active people should be tested for STDs during annual pelvic (female) or urologic (male) examinations.

Many people who are diagnosed as having an STD are reluctant to name their partners to physicians or clinic personnel. On one level, it is quite understandable that they would rather deliver the bad news themselves. Instead of informing their partner, however, these individuals may surreptitiously attempt to discover whether the partner has any symptoms of the particular disease. If the partner appears to be healthy, they may decide to avoid disclosing their own infection, on the assumption that the partner did not catch it. In the case of a partner who contracts an STD during extradyadic or extramarital relations, fear of seriously disrupting or even destroying the primary relationship may dissuade him or her from informing an apparently healthy partner.

The absence of recognizable symptoms does not mean that the partner does not have the genital infection, because many people are asymptomatic. Gonorrhea, for example, is notoriously silent in women, with only about 20 percent having recognizable symptoms during the early, and readily treatable, stages of the infection. Many men are also asymptomatic (Fleming et al., 1997).

ATTITUDES TOWARD PEOPLE WITH STDs

In addition to dealing with the medical consequences of STDs, infected persons may experience difficult psychological reactions. They may have lowered self-esteem, feelings of isolation and loss of control, and a negative body image (Catotti, Clarke, & Catoe, 1993; Perlow & Perlow, 1983). Some of the negative psychological reactions and feelings of psychological isolation that infected persons experience may stem from expectations that others will reject them—a fear that may be realistic.

All sexually active people can be at risk of contracting STDs, however, and extensive education of the general public and complete reporting by STD patients are important for controlling the spread of these diseases. Sexually active people can also take responsibility for controlling STDs by getting themselves screened annually or whenever changing sexual partners. A person who contracts an STD should tell his or her sexual partners so that they can be tested and, if necessary, treated. After treatment for a curable STD, patients should be retested to be sure that they no longer have the STD.

Some STDs are not curable; the most notable contemporary example, of course, is AIDS. The deaths of such public figures as actor Rock Hudson and pianist Liberace and the spread of AIDS among highly visible heterosexuals such as basketball star Magic Johnson have done what the deaths of thousands of anonymous AIDS victims were not able to do: spurred governmental and public response to the epidemic (Moskowitz, Binson, & Catania, 1997; Shilts, 1987). For example, people who reported being influenced by Magic Johnson's announcement in 1991 that he was HIV-positive were more likely to increase their condom use (Moskowitz et al., 1997). *And the Band Played On*, a movie based on Randy Shilts's gripping and well-documented book of the same title, was released on video in 1993, and we highly recommend it, especially for students interested in the competition

---

asymptomatic (A-symp-toe-MAH-tik)—Without recognizable symptoms.

H I G H L I G H T

How Accurate Is Your Knowledge of HIV/AIDS?

In responding to these questions, put a T (true) or F (false) in front of each statement.

1. AIDS is caused by bacteria.

2. AIDS can be inherited.

3. A healthy person who is HIV-positive can transmit HIV to another person.

4. HIV can be transmitted through semen.

5. Unlike the common cold, HIV cannot be transmitted through the open air.

6. AIDS can be treated in its earliest stage with penicillin.

7. A pregnant woman who has HIV can give it to her baby.

8. Most people can tell by someone's physical appearance if that person is HIV infected.

9. Using latex condoms properly reduces the risk of getting HIV/AIDS.

10. A vaccine for AIDS will be available for the general population within a year.

---

among public health researchers within the United States and internationally as they attempted to deal with the spread of AIDS. Shilts died of complications from AIDS-related disease in 1994.

THE RELATIONSHIP OF AIDS KNOWLEDGE AND ATTITUDES

STD research recently has primarily focused on students' attitudes and knowledge about AIDS, undoubtedly due to the devastating impact of this infection compared to infection with other STDs. However, much of what we have learned about the social dimensions of AIDS is also applicable to other STDs. Before reading further, you may wish to take the test on AIDS knowledge (see "Highlight: How Accurate Is Your Knowledge of HIV/AIDS?" above) to see how well informed you are. After you have finished reading the chapter, go back to the test to see how accurate your knowledge was.

Studies of Americans, from teenagers through the elderly, show that people are more knowledgeable about HIV and AIDS than they are about other STDs (Benton, Mintzes, Kendrick, & Solomon, 1993; Sweat & Lein, 1995). Younger people are generally more knowledgeable about AIDS than are older people. There are few ethnic or racial differences in HIV/AIDS knowledge when socioeconomic status (SES) is controlled. That is, people of lower SES have less knowledge about HIV/AIDS than do people of higher SES

regardless of their ethnic or racial background (Sweat & Lein, 1995). Nevertheless, researchers have shown that HIV/AIDS knowledge is only modestly related to behavior change and lower rates of unsafe sexual activity (Caron, Davis, Wynn, & Roberts, 1992; Fisher & Fisher, 1992; Zagumny & Brady, 1998).

College students are generally knowledgeable about AIDS and HIV, but most report that they take no special precautions against HIV infection. Although

Randy Shilts was an investigative reporter whose book, *And the Band Played On*, documented the search for the cause of AIDS.

TABLE 16.1   Symptoms of Sexually Transmitted Diseases and Genital Infections

Bacterial Infections	Annual Estimated Incidence	Symptoms
Gonorrhea	800,000	*In males:* painful urination; smelly, thick, yellow urethral discharge, appearing 2 to 10 days after sex with infected person. *In females:* vaginal discharge; some pain during urination; mild pelvic discomfort and/or abnormal menstruation (but most women are asymptomatic).
Syphilis	101,000	Hard, round, painless sore or chancre with raised edges that appears 2 weeks to a month after contact.
Chlamydia and nongonococcal urethritis (NGU)	4,000,000	*In females:* mild irritation in the genitals; itching and burning during urination; some cervical swelling (but most women are asymptomatic). *In males:* thin, relatively clear, whitish discharge; mild discomfort during urination 1 to 3 weeks after contact.
Cystitis		Painful urination; lower back pain; constant urge to urinate.
Prostatitis		Groin and lower back pain; fever; burning sensation during and following ejaculation; thin mucous discharge from urethra before first morning urination. Prostatitis can be either congestive (from infrequent ejaculation) or infectious (from *E. coli* bacteria).

this does not mean that knowledge is unimportant, it highlights the need for HIV/AIDS education to do more than simply promote information and dispel myths. To address this issue, education programs have been developed to increase student involvement and motivation and to teach them the necessary behavioral skills designed to reduce unsafe sexual behaviors. Peer counseling, group discussions, role playing, sexual assertiveness training, and safer-sex communication skills training have been used successfully to reduce risky sexual behaviors (Kelly, 1995; Ploem & Byers, 1997; Smith & Katner, 1995; Weisse, Turbiasz, & Witney, 1995). Effective AIDS education appears to be best served by programs that combine these strategies with providing accurate information. **Reality or Myth**

ATTEMPTS TO REDUCE STD TRANSMISSION

In addition to education programs, public health authorities have employed numerous approaches to try to alter sexual practices and thereby reduce the spread

▶ **Issues to Consider:** What would you include in the design of an educational program to prevent unsafe sexual activities?

of AIDS and other STDs. However, behavior change among sexually active heterosexual adolescents and young adults has been difficult to achieve (Fisher & Fisher, 1992; Melnick et al., 1993). For example, a national survey of college students revealed that nearly 50 percent of the heterosexual respondents reported multiple sexual partners and that approximately 60 percent used condoms less than half the time when they engaged in sexual intercourse (DiClemente, Forrest, & Mickler, 1990).

Surveys of adolescents indicate that they have made moderate changes in their sexual practices or use of contraceptives in response to the AIDS epidemic. For example, condom use has increased among high school and college students (Ashcraft & Schlueter, 1996; Shew et al., 1997; Tanfer, Cubbins, & Billy, 1995).

When behavior changes are made, the most commonly reported are reducing the number of sex partners and being more careful in partner selection (Melnick et al., 1993). Taking care in partner selection is no guarantee of freedom from risk, however (Misovich, Fisher, & Fisher, 1996). Most people lie some of the time in both their casual and close relationships (DePaulo & Kashy, 1998). In their study of college students, Cochran and Mays (1990) found

Bacterial Infections	Annual Estimated Incidence	Symptoms
Gardnerella vaginalis		Leukorrhea and unpleasant odor.
Shigellosis	24,000	Pain; fever; diarrhea; inflammation of the mucous membranes of the large intestines; sometimes vomiting and a burning sensation in the anus.
Pelvic inflammatory disease (PID)	1,000,000	Intense lower abdominal and/or back pain; tenderness and fever; pain when cervix is moved from side to side. Symptoms usually develop within weeks after the STD that causes PID is contracted.

Viral Infections	Annual Estimated Incidence	Symptoms
Acquired immunodeficiency syndrome (AIDS)	840,000	Swollen lymph nodes; unexplained weight loss; loss of appetite; persistent fevers or night sweats; chronic fatigue; unexplained diarrhea; bloody stools; unexplained bleeding from any body opening; skin rashes; easy bruising; persistent, severe headaches; chronic, dry cough not caused by smoking or a cold; chronic, whitish coating on the tongue or throat.
Herpes simplex type II (genital herpes)	200,000–500,000	Small blisters on the genitals or vulva, developing 3 to 7 days after contact. After tingling, itching, and creating a burning sensation, they break open and spread.
Genital warts (HPV)	500,000–1,000,000	Soft, pink, painless single or multiple growths resembling cauliflowers on the genitals or vulva.
Hepatitis B	200,000	Nausea; vomiting; fatigue; mental depression; jaundice; dark urine.

that 34 percent of men and 10 percent of women had lied in order to have sex. Further, about 20 percent of the men said that, to get sex, they would lie about having tested negative for HIV antibodies.

Surveys of adolescents and adults in the United States and Holland have found that a perception of susceptibility to HIV infection is associated with a reduction in high-risk sexual behaviors (DiClemente, 1989; Buunk et al., 1998). In Fisher's (1988) study of potential factors affecting condom use among adolescents, however, perceived peer-group behavior was the only factor that differentiated adolescents who used condoms from those who did not. Those who viewed their peers as supporting condom use were almost twice as likely to report using condoms.

In a longitudinal study of gay men, Joseph and coworkers (1987) reported that, even among adults, the belief that one's friends were adopting recommended behavior changes was positively and consistently related

to adopting safer-sex practices, becoming monogamous, and reducing the number of partners and the frequency of sexual activity. The authors suggested that "the norms shared within a network . . . may be the most important in influencing the adoption of behaviors consistent with risk reduction" (p. 86).

Despite all efforts to reduce the spread of STDs, people still contract them. We turn now to the symptoms, consequences, and treatment of specific STDs (see Table 16.1), including diseases and infections caused by bacteria, viruses, and parasites. Of these, viral infections are the most problematic because they cannot be killed by antibiotics.

▶ **Issues to Consider:** Given the percentages of people who report having lied to obtain sex, what steps would you take to determine the truthfulness of a potential sexual partner about the person's STD status?

Bacterial Infections

Bacteria are one-celled organisms that can be seen only through a microscope. STDs caused by bacteria are generally curable, and include gonorrhea, syphilis, chlamydia, nongonococcal urethritis, cystitis, prostatitis, gardnerella vaginalis, shigellosis, and chancroid.

GONORRHEA

Gonorrhea (also called "clap" and "drip") infection is caused by gonococcus bacteria (*Neisseria gonorrhoeae*), which thrive on mucous membranes in the mouth, vagina, cervix, urethra, and anus. The bacteria can be acquired by kissing or engaging in oral, anal, or vaginal sex with an infected person. Although the bacteria from urethral discharge can survive for up to 24 hours on towels and toilet seats (Neinstein, Goldering, & Carpenter, 1984), transmission from these sources has not been demonstrated. The probability of contracting gonorrhea from having intercourse once with an infected partner is about 50 percent for women and 20 percent for men, and the risk increases with each additional sexual contact. In their national sample, Laumann et al. (1994) found that the self-reported lifetime incidence (the number of people who said that they had the disease at least once) of gonorrhea among participants was almost 6 percent.

There is little need to worry about the effects of gonorrhea *if* it is diagnosed and treated quickly. Gonorrhea symptoms usually appear within 2 to 10 days after intimate contact with an infected person. Symptoms in men include painful urination and a smelly urethral discharge that is thick and yellow. Some men experience no symptoms or discomfort, however. Of women who contract gonorrhea, 80 percent have mild symptoms or no symptoms at all. Symptoms in the remaining 20 percent of women in-

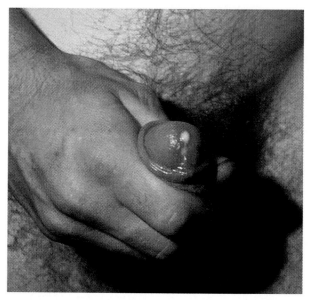

Symptoms of gonorrhea include a yellowish discharge from the urethra and painful urination.

clude altered vaginal discharge, some pain during urination, mild pelvic discomfort, and/or abnormal menstruation.

In North America and most other developed countries, gonorrhea is treated with antibiotics, which usually kill the bacteria efficiently. However, the situation is quite different in developing countries, where there is often limited access to diagnostic tests and treatment. In addition, the inappropriate use of antibiotics has led to high rates of gonococcal infections that are antibiotic resistant. Gonorrhea strains that are resistant to antibiotics appear to be increasing and now account for more than 5 percent of all gonorrhea cases (Alary, 1997; Aral & Holmes, 1991). Thus, a follow-up test should be performed to ensure that the person is completely free of the bacteria. People who have been cured are not immune to future infection. Thus, another reason that a sexual partner with gonorrhea should be examined and treated is to avoid reinfecting a partner who has been cured.

gonorrhea—For those with symptoms, an STD accompanied by painful urination. In males, smelly, thick, yellow urethral discharge. In females, vaginal discharge and mild pelvic discomfort.

If not diagnosed and treated within a few weeks, gonorrhea can have serious complications. In males, these may include infection of the prostate, testes, and epididymis, potentially causing sterility. The bladder, kidneys, and rectum of males and females may also be infected with gonorrhea. In females, untreated gonorrhea and other infections may produce pelvic inflammatory disease. Furthermore, women may pass untreated gonorrhea to a baby during childbirth, possibly causing blindness in the infant. *Reality or Myth*

SYPHILIS

Syphilis is caused by a spirochete, a tiny, corkscrew-shaped bacterium named *Treponema pallidum*. Primary (first-stage) syphilis is transmitted through intimate sexual contact with an infected person. Syphilis first produces a usually painless **chancre**, a hard, round, dull-red sore or ulcer with raised edges. A chancre can form in the mouth, vagina, urethra, or rectum, or on the anus, external genitals, or nipples, so almost any act of sexual intimacy with a person who has primary syphilis can allow the microorganism to invade the uninfected person. The probability of infection from one sexual contact with a syphilis carrier is about 30 percent. Fewer than 1 percent of Laumann et al.'s (1994) national sample reported having been diagnosed with syphilis during their lifetime.

The chancre typically appears 10 to 90 days after exposure to an infectious case of syphilis (Romanoski, 1997). Because it is usually painless, a woman may not realize that she has the chancre if it breaks out in the vagina, on the cervix, or in the rectum. Similarly, if the chancre erupts within a male's urethra or rectum, he may be unaware of it. After several weeks, the chancre spontaneously disappears, often leaving syphilis patients with the false impression that they have no infection.

Syphilis is usually diagnosed through examination of a blood sample for antibodies. If syphilis is

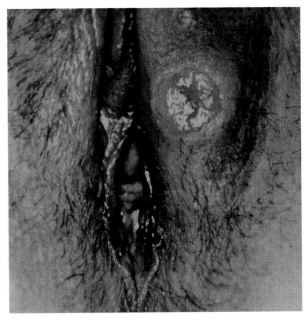

The syphilis chancre is a painless sore that appears where the spirochete entered the body.

present, it is readily treated with a long-acting antibiotic different from those used to treat gonorrhea. Just as with gonorrhea, exposure to syphilis does not ensure future immunity, so a treated person can be reinfected during subsequent sexual contact with a syphilis carrier.

If not treated, syphilis goes into a second stage, called secondary syphilis, about 4 to 10 weeks after the initial signs of the primary infection. Secondary syphilis is characterized by a generalized body rash, sometimes accompanied by headache, fever, indigestion, sore throat, and pain in the joints or muscles. Primary and secondary syphilis are jointly referred to as early symptomatic syphilis and are highly contagious during these stages.

Following the secondary stage, a latent stage begins when no external symptoms are observable, but the spirochetes are nonetheless burrowing their way into internal organs such as the brain, spinal cord, bones, and bodily tissues. After syphilis has been latent for about a year, an untreated person is no longer infectious.

syphilis—An STD that may be accompanied by painless sores called chancres among those with symptoms.
chancre (SHANG-ker)—A dull-red, painless, hard, round ulcer with raised edges that forms where the spirochete causing syphilis enters a person's body.

Third-stage, or late, syphilis is reached by about 15 percent of all untreated victims, typically 10 to 30 years after infection. Treatment even at this advanced stage can cure syphilis, but heart failure, loss of muscle control, blindness, deafness, brain damage, and other complications may have already occurred (refer to "Research Spotlight: Ethical Principles and the Tuskegee Study" in Chapter 3).

Untreated syphilis can infect a fetus, as well an infected woman's sexual partner, because the spirochetes can cross the placental barrier after the sixteenth to eighteenth week of pregnancy. Thus, all pregnant women should be tested for syphilis at the time of the first prenatal visit. Infected pregnant women are administered the same regimen of antibiotics as are infected nonpregnant women. After birth, their infants are also treated. In 90 percent of the cases in which a pregnant woman's syphilis is not treated during early pregnancy, the fetus is miscarried, stillborn, or born with congenital syphilis. The newborn can be treated to prevent further damage, but treatment will not undo the damage that has already been done, which may include partial blindness, deafness, and deformities of the bones and teeth. *Reality or Myth* ?

CHLAMYDIA AND NONGONOCOCCAL URETHRITIS

Chlamydia, the source of many vaginal and urethral infections in women and men, is caused by *Chlamydia trachomatis* or T-strain *Mycoplasma*, which are both bacterial microorganisms. These bacteria were not isolated until the 1970s. Before that time, infections that did not result from the gonococcus bacterium or other known organisms were diagnosed as **nongonococcal urethritis (NGU)** in men and as **vaginitis** in women. Chlamydia in men is still frequently referred to as NGU, and about 40 percent of NGU cases are due to chlamydia infection (CDC, 1998). The lifetime incidence of both chlamydia and NGU is 3.2 percent

chlamydia (clah-MID-ee-uh)—For the minority of those with symptoms, an STD accompanied by discomfort during urination and in men, a thin, whitish discharge.

nongonococcal urethritis (NGU) (non-GON-ohj-KOK-al yur-ree-THRY-tis)—A term for urethral infections in men that are usually caused by the chlamydia bacterium.

vaginitis (VAH-jih-NYE-tis)—A general term for any inflammation of the vagina.

(Laumann et al., 1994). With more than 4 million chlamydia infections reported annually, it is the most prevalent bacterial STD in North America (DeLisle, 1997; Patrick, 1997). As with gonorrhea, the risk for acquiring chlamydia from having intercourse once with an infected partner is greater for women (40 percent) than it is for men (20 percent).

Chlamydia is transmitted primarily through sexual contact, but it can be spread from one body site to another (e.g., by touching urethral discharge and then the eyes). It can also be transmitted nonsexually, through contact with the fingers or feces of an infected person. Symptoms generally appear 1 to 3 weeks after contact with the infection.

In males, chlamydia symptoms include a thin, relatively clear, whitish discharge. NGU may also trigger inflammation of the urethra and mild discomfort during urination. However, approximately 50 percent of men have no symptoms or such mild ones that they do not seek treatment (DeLisle, 1997).

Symptoms among the approximately 20 percent of women who have them include mild irritation in the genitals, as well as itching and burning during urination. The paucity of symptoms among females was dramatically demonstrated by the screening of 3,202 sexually active women aged 12 through 19 years during 5,360 visits to five school-based clinics, two family planning clinics, and two STD clinics in Baltimore, Maryland, over a 33-month period ending in September 1996 (Burstein et al., 1998). In this research program, the females were asked their reason for visiting the clinic. Only 20 percent reported the presence of STD symptoms, although 75 percent reported inconsistent condom use and 60 percent simply wanted to get themselves screened. Many of the females who were diagnosed and treated for chlamydia returned for subsequent visits more than a month later and had recontracted the disease.

Chlamydia and NGU can be treated effectively with antibiotics. If left undiagnosed and untreated, both can profoundly affect health and fertility. Infection of the epididymis in men and the Fallopian tubes in women can create scar tissue that blocks the passage of sperm or egg, causing permanent sterility. Of infants born to women with untreated chlamydia, up to 20 percent become infected with chlamydia pneumonia, and up to 50 percent develop conjunctivitis, a serious eye infection. In fact, chlamydia is one of the leading causes of preventable blindness in the world.

CYSTITIS

Cystitis is sometimes called honeymoon cystitis because it is often brought on by frequent or vigorous intercourse. This condition can occur in both men and women but is more common among women. It is caused by various bacteria, including *Escherichia (E.) coli*, which can be transmitted nonsexually or sexually. Wiping from the anus toward the urethra (rather than the reverse) after a bowel movement may carry *E. coli* from the rectum to the urethral opening. Also, engaging in anal sex and then switching to vaginal penetration without first thoroughly washing the penis can bring on infection. Strenuous intercourse may have the same effect.

Within a day or two after bacteria are introduced into the urethra, the person may experience a more or less constant urge to urinate, burning during urination, and pain in the lower back or abdomen. Sulfa drugs are usually effective in curing the condition, and drinking large quantities of fluids, including cranberry juice, helps to eliminate the infection.

For some unfortunate people, 90 percent of them women, cystitis becomes chronic and is called interstitial cystitis (IC) (Webster, 1996). Almost half a million Americans suffer from IC. In addition to low back pain and the burning sensation associated with very frequent urination, many people with IC also must contend with painful intercourse. A variety of treatment approaches have been used to attempt to relieve the symptoms of IC, but no effective cure has been developed.

PROSTATITIS

Prostatitis refers to any infection or inflammation of the prostate gland. Prostatitis affects between 30 percent and 40 percent of U.S. men between ages 20 and 40. There are two major types: infectious prostatitis, caused by *E. coli* bacteria, and congestive prostatitis.

Infectious prostatitis can result from the transmission of bacteria during sexual contact. Celibate men can be afflicted with congestive prostatitis (technically not an STD), which may stem from infrequent ejaculation or abstention from sexual activity. Some men are asymptomatic, but when symptoms are present, they include pain in the groin and lower back, fever, and a burning sensation during and following ejaculation. Another symptom is a thin, watery discharge from the urethra in the morning before urinating. Infectious prostatitis is commonly treated with antibiotics, and the inflammation of the prostate can be reduced by palpating (manipulating) that organ.

OTHER BACTERIAL INFECTIONS

Three other STDs caused by various bacteria are gardnerella vaginalis, shigellosis, and chancroid. **Gardnerella vaginalis** is sometimes referred to as vaginitis; however, this term is misleading. As with some other bacterial infections that are diagnosed as "vaginitis," both males and females may contract and transmit these infections, although it is more prevalent among women during their reproductive years.

Gardnerella vaginalis results in thin **leukorrhea,** which ranges in color from gray to greenish-yellow and has an unpleasant odor. It is treated by oral administration of the prescription drug Flagyl (metronidazole) to the infected woman and her partner. Men infected with gardnerella vaginalis are typically asymptomatic, but some men do develop symptoms, which include urethritis and inflammation of the foreskin or glans.

Shigellosis is an acute diarrheal disease that can be contracted through sexual contact or contact with feces carrying the bacteria. In the 1990s, approximately 17,000 to 24,000 cases of shigellosis were reported annually in the United States (CDC, 1998). Oral stimulation of the anus of an individual with shigellosis exposes the stimulator to the disease. Pain, fever, diarrhea, and inflammation of the mucous membranes of the large intestine are among the

---

cystitis (sis-TYE-tis)—A general term for any inflammation of the urinary bladder marked by frequent urination accompanied by pain.

prostatitis (praw-stay-TYE-tis)—Inflammation of the prostate gland accompanied by burning pain during and after ejaculation.

gardnerella vaginalis—Infection producing a thin, smelly discharge; afflicts both men and women.

leukorrhea (LOO-kor-EE-ah)—A whitish discharge from the vagina, often caused by a fungus infection.

shigellosis (SHIH-geh-LOW-sis)—A form of dysentery (diarrhea) that can be transmitted by sexual contact.

symptoms of shigellosis. Shigellosis is diagnosed by culturing a stool specimen. It can be treated with ampicillin or tetracycline, although *Shigella* bacteria rapidly develop resistance to antibiotics.

The number of reported **chancroid** cases in the United States has been rising since the 1980s (CDC, 1998). About 3 to 5 days after contact, a small pimple surrounded by a reddened area appears at the site of infection, usually on the genitals. Within a day or two, it becomes filled with pus and breaks open to form irregular, soft ulcerations. The softness of the chancroid sores and their painfulness distinguish them from the hard and painless chancres of syphilis. In more than half of chancroid cases, the lymph nodes on the infected side of the groin become inflamed and swollen. These enlarged lymph nodes, called buboes, can rupture and ooze thick, creamy pus. Diagnosis is made through physical examination. Treatment by antibiotics is highly effective.

Pelvic Inflammatory Disease

The most common serious complication of untreated gonorrhea, chlamydia, and other genital infections
in females is **pelvic inflammatory disease (PID)**. PID develops when the chlamydia, gonorrhea, or other infection moves through the cervix to infect the uterine lining or Fallopian tubes. PID can develop within weeks after a woman contracts the STD.

About 2 percent of U.S. women aged 18 to 59 report having been diagnosed with PID (Laumann et al., 1994). This translates into more than 2 million cases of PID annually in the United States. In addition to the expense of diagnostic tests, doctors' office visits, medicine, hospitalization, surgical fees, and time lost from work, there are costs to PID sufferers that cannot be measured in dollars: pain, anxiety, and the elevated risk of ectopic pregnancy and sterility.

Sexually active women who use oral contraceptives are half as likely to be hospitalized for PID as women who do not use this form of contraceptive (Cates & Stone, 1992b). Smoking cigarettes and douching are associated with an increased risk of contracting PID (Scholes et al., 1993).

Some women with acute PID experience intense lower abdominal pain, tenderness, and fever. These women are fortunate because their symptoms at least make it likely that the PID will be discovered and treated before permanent damage is done. Many women with acute PID, however, have less well-defined symptoms and thus may not seek treatment. The vast majority of patients with acute PID respond quickly to treatment with antibiotics (DeLisle, 1997).

The STDs discussed so far are caused by bacteria and are treated relatively easily. Scientists have not been as successful in finding cures for infections caused by viruses. In the next section we consider AIDS, the most deadly of these viral diseases.

*A*cquired Immunodeficiency Syndrome (AIDS)

In the past two decades, we have witnessed the rapid spread throughout the world of **human immunodeficiency virus (HIV)**, the virus that can lead to

acquired immunodeficiency syndrome (AIDS). AIDS has been devastating not only in terms of its impact on patients and the family members and friends who love them, but also in terms of the increase in antigay discrimination that it has spawned (see "Highlight: An Epidemic of Stigma"). The fact that it first gained

---

chancroid (CANE-kroid)—An STD characterized by soft, painful genital sores.
pelvic inflammatory disease (PID)—Swelling and inflammation of the uterine tissues, Fallopian tubes, and sometimes the ovaries.
human immunodeficiency virus (HIV)—The retrovirus that causes AIDS.

---

acquired immunodeficiency syndrome (AIDS)—A virally caused condition in which severe suppression of the immune system reduces the body's ability to fight diseases.

An Epidemic of Stigma

As we will see in Chapter 18, Sexual Harassment, some of us have a tendency to blame the victim. This victim-blaming phenomenon has been seen in the responses of some people to other members of our society who have contracted HIV. Proposition 64, a referendum to quarantine people found to be HIV+ (positive), was placed on the ballot in the 1986 California election. Voters defeated the proposal, but the fact that many people favored such a quarantine—despite no evidence indicating that AIDS could be spread through casual contact—provides a vivid example of the way in which society sometimes blames the victim.

In an article from which we have taken the title for this box, researchers Gregory Herek and Eric Glunt (1988) quoted several instances in which discriminatory behavior appeared to be stimulated by the stigma associated with AIDS.

In White Plains, New York, a mail carrier refused to deliver mail to an AIDS Task Force office for two weeks because he feared catching the disease ("Mail Service Ordered to AIDS Center," 1987).

In Arcadia, Florida, three brothers tested positive for HIV. After word spread of their infection, their barber refused to cut the boys' hair, and the family's minister suggested that they stay away from Sunday church services. Eventually, the family's house was burned down (Robinson, 1987).

In a 1986 [article] in the New York Times, *William F. Buckley, Jr., proposed that "everyone detected with AIDS should be tattooed on the upper forearm, to protect common-needle users, and on the buttocks, to prevent the victimization of other homosexuals" (p. A27).*

In the American Spectator, *Christopher Monckton (1987) wrote: "Every member of the population should be blood tested every month to detect the presence of antibodies against [AIDS], and all those found to be infected with the virus, even if only as carriers, should be isolated compulsorily, immediately, and permanently" (p. 30).*

After you read the section on AIDS, you may want to return to this Highlight to consider whether the available data on the disease support the attitudes and policies described here.

---

publicity in North America primarily among homosexual men in the United States led some to call AIDS the "gay plague"; however, AIDS is caused by a virus, not by a person's sexual orientation. Data from Haiti and Africa underscore the fact that it is intimate contact with an infected person rather than an individual's sexual orientation that places one at risk of contracting HIV. In Central Africa, AIDS is far more prevalent among heterosexuals than among homosexual men, and antibodies to HIV are as common in women as in men.

AIDS first captured the attention of physicians in 1981, but the syndrome had existed for some time prior to the 1980s. In 1952, a 28-year-old Tennessee man known as R.G. was admitted to a hospital in Memphis, gasping for air. Over the next few months, he suffered one debilitating infection after another, until his overwhelmed body could not cope any longer, and he died. Although not recognized at the time as AIDS, it ran a course typical of this illness, and was later identified, earning R.G. a place in medical history (Ewald, 1994).

Several cases of a condition later to be known as HIV/AIDS were identified in the United States at the beginning of the 1980s, but it took a great deal of detective work to pin down the cause and the means of transmission. In *The Sex Scientists* (Brannigan, Allgeier, & Allgeier, 1998), William W. Darrow, formerly at the Centers for Disease Control and Prevention (CDC), has provided a highly readable account of the process that he and his colleagues engaged in to attempt to trace the source of HIV infection, a process that led to the location of an airline pilot designated as Patient 0. After interviewing Patient 0, Darrow tried to find some of Patient 0's estimated 2,500 sexual partners all over the world to see what the men had in common. Darrow's role in trying to unravel this mystery is portrayed in the previously mentioned book and film, *And the Band Played On.*

The origin of AIDS has yet to be determined, although most scientists agree that the HIV viruses are basically ape or monkey viruses because of their genetic similarities. Humans have hunted and handled other primates for thousands of years. Anyone who was bitten, scratched, or cut himself or herself while handling a primate could have become infected.

Other lines of investigation of the sources of HIV have included Africans, Haitians, mosquitoes, and pigs (Biggar, 1986; Norman, 1986). The fact that the vast majority of people who are stricken with AIDS in the United States, Europe, and Africa are in the sexually active age range and/or are the recipients of blood products from other infected people makes mosquitoes an unlikely source. Mosquitoes bite people of all ages, but there are relatively few AIDS patients who are 5 to 13 years old, and those who are infected in that age group were born to HIV-infected mothers or received HIV-infected blood or plasma. In other words, if mosquitoes were a source, the prevalence of AIDS among children—indeed, people of all ages—would be much higher. Antibodies to HIV have been found in analyses of blood samples that were collected in the 1960s and 1970s in Central and East Africa, lending some support to the hypothesis that AIDS originated there (Epstein et al., 1985; Ewald, 1994; Nahmias et al., 1986). That hypothesis is weakened somewhat by the fact that only since 1980 have African medical records contained descriptions consistent with a diagnosis of AIDS (Biggar, 1986). If the origin of HIV is ultimately determined, that knowledge may contribute to finding a vaccine and a cure.

PREVALENCE

Before 1981, only 92 people in the United States were diagnosed as having the symptoms later to be called AIDS. From 1981 through December 1998, state and territorial health departments reported more than 600,000 cases of AIDS among men, women, and children. More than 400,000 AIDS-related deaths have occurred (CDC, 1998). Because of reporting delays and other factors (e.g., physicians may not keep track of their patients who move away), these numbers are minimal estimates. Reporting by states of AIDS cases to the Centers for Disease Control is about 85 percent complete, and reports of deaths are about 90 percent complete (CDC, 1998). In 1996, AIDS-related deaths decreased by 15 percent, to 36,000 deaths and in 1997 dropped to less than 17,000 deaths.

Minority group members have been disproportionately represented among U.S. citizens infected with HIV (CDC, 1998). However, members of ethnic minorities in the United States are also overrepresented among the least educated and poorest segments of American society, and it may be that their poverty and lack of education are more predictive of their greater risk of HIV infection than their ethnic minority status. Intravenous (IV) drug use rather than homosexual activity appears to be the source of most HIV infection among minorities.

AIDS is most prevalent in large, urban centers, but an increasing proportion of all cases is being reported from smaller cities and rural areas (CDC, 1998). The rates of AIDS cases among men who have sex with men have been dropping and now account for fewer than half of all new cases.

▶ **Issues to Consider:** Why do you think that HIV/AIDS is more prevalent among the poor and less educated?

Children with AIDS.   HIV can pass from an infected mother to her fetus during pregnancy and to a baby through breast milk. About one-fourth of all babies born to mothers with HIV become infected with the virus. However, if their HIV-infected mothers are treated with zidovudine (AZT) during their pregnancies, the rate of HIV infection among the children is reduced by two-thirds, to about 7 percent of babies (Ungvarski, 1997). Among children diagnosed as having AIDS, 88 percent had at least one parent with AIDS or with increased risk of developing AIDS. Another 7 percent had contracted AIDS during blood transfusions. ***Reality or Myth*** ❓

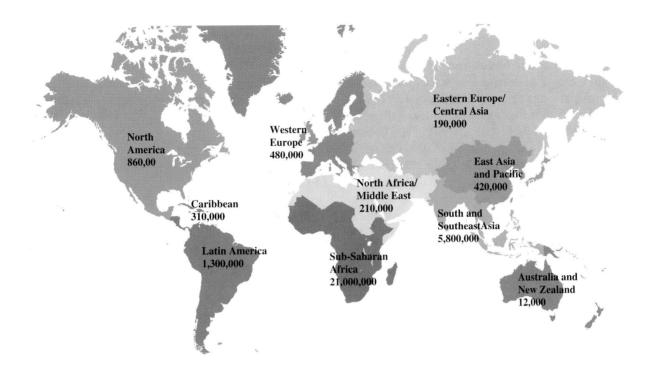

Figure 16.1   Living with HIV/AIDS
Worldwide, more than 42 million people have been infected with HIV. Of those, almost 12 million have died, but more than 30 million are living with HIV/AIDS. Although considerable progress has been made in identifying treatments to slow the infection, these medicines have limited availability and are very expensive. Most infected people (90 percent) live in developing countries and are unable to afford the new antiviral drugs (Sternberg, 1998). (Copyright 1998, *USA Today*. Reprinted with permission.)

CAUSES

The **retrovirus** that causes AIDS was identified in 1983 in France and in 1984 in the United States and given the name human immunodeficiency virus (HIV) (Shilts, 1987). There are at least 10 subtypes of HIV (Ungvarski, 1997). The two most prominent are HIV-I, found primarily in the West and responsible for the vast majority of the world's AIDS cases, and HIV-II, most commonly found in Africa.

HIV must make copies of its own structure before it can reproduce inside a host cell. Many people experience flulike symptoms within days after the virus has entered the body. At this time, HIV particles are reproducing in their favorite target, specialized white blood cells called helper T-cells (also called CD4 cells), which are vital to the functioning

retrovirus—A form of virus that cannot reproduce inside a host cell until it has made copies of its own structure.

of the immune system. When the helper T-cells are attacked, the body uses all its resources to protect these cells.

After the body has swept the virus from the blood and trapped it in the lymph nodes, HIV continues to churn out copies of itself. The immune system reacts with two strategies that initially limit damage. First, it activates antibodies to neutralize HIV particles. Then specialized white blood cells, called killer T-cells, attack and digest infected tissue. This is the stage during which most people who have themselves tested for HIV antibodies discover they are HIV-positive.

This asymptomatic stage can last from 5 to 12 years. Each year, however, more HIV escapes from the lymph nodes into the blood. The immune system becomes progressively weaker as more and more helper T-cells die. Eventually HIV destroys the ability of the body's immune system to fight diseases.

RISK FACTORS

HIV has been found in blood, semen, vaginal secretions, and breast milk and less frequently in the saliva, tears, and urine of infected people. The risk of contracting AIDS from the saliva, tears, or urine of an infected person is believed to be extremely low.

In descending order of risk, behaviors that increase the risk of contracting HIV infection from an infected partner are receptive anal sex; needle sharing during injecting drug use; heterosexual contact; receiving a blood transfusion; receipt of transplanted tissues, organs, or artificial insemination from an HIV-positive donor; and hemophilia/coagulation disorder (CDC, 1997).

The risk of acquiring HIV and developing AIDS appears to be highest among individuals with large numbers of sexual partners and frequent sexual contacts: the more partners a person has, the more likely he or she is to encounter someone carrying the virus (Tanfer et al., 1995). Engaging in sexual practices with an HIV-infected partner that expose one to blood or semen increases the likelihood of contracting HIV. Sexual practices that cause fissures or tears in an orifice generate higher risk—by providing HIV with access to the bloodstream—than do practices that are unlikely to damage sensitive bodily tissues. Thus, HIV is most prevalent in people who engage in unprotected receptive fisting (insertion of the fist into the anus, which produces fissures that leave receivers vulnerable to contraction of HIV if they engage in anal sex), receptive anal coitus, and receptive vaginal intercourse. Heterosexual anal intercourse has been thought to play a minor role in the spread of HIV. However, Bruce Voeller (1991) argued that underestimating the incidence and riskiness of heterosexual anal intercourse is dangerous in view of the fact that receptive anal intercourse carries the greatest relative risk of HIV infection for homosexual men. Voeller's review of surveys of sexual practices indicated that more than 10 percent of U.S. women in the samples engaged in anal intercourse with some regularity. Standard medical or field interviews are unlikely to reveal such activity because of the reluctance of women to admit it except under conditions in which an interviewer is skilled at conveying a nonjudgmental attitude. For example, Laumann et al. (1994) reported that only 6 percent of women in their sample said they engaged in

anal sex. Voeller concluded that heterosexual anal sex should be carefully monitored by sensitive and skilled researchers who can conduct nonjudgmental interviews. In other countries with high levels of AIDS infection (for example, Brazil), heterosexual anal intercourse, practiced for contraception or for the preservation of virginity, is common (Voeller, 1991).

People with a history of other STDs such as gonorrhea, chlamydia, and syphilis are also at higher risk of contracting AIDS than are individuals who have never been infected with these agents (Fisher & Fisher, 1992; Institute for Medicine, 1997). Scientists do not know the precise reasons for this correlation, but it is possible that a person who has had other STDs has a weakened skin area where the infection occurred, making the area more vulnerable to HIV infection. Another possible reason for this relationship is that both treatable STDs and HIV infection are more likely to occur among persons with multiple partners.

Sharing needles during intravenous drug use places people at risk of exposure to HIV-infected blood. In rare cases, individuals have contracted AIDS from contaminated blood products received during medical treatment, but this risk has been greatly reduced with improvements in the screening procedures for HIV infection. About 1 percent of the U.S. cases of AIDS have resulted from receiving transfusions of contaminated blood (CDC, 1998). There is no risk in giving blood, for which sterile, disposable needles are used. AIDS rarely results from casual contact, and then only if contact with the body fluids of infected persons occurs. Casual contacts with AIDS patients that do not involve the exchange of body products, such as shaking hands, hugging, or providing health care, are not risk factors. *Reality or Myth*

DIAGNOSIS AND SYMPTOMS

Acquired immunodeficiency syndrome is called a syndrome because a variety of life-threatening conditions are associated with it. AIDS patients suffer from severe **immunosuppression.** Normally, our im-

---

immunosuppression—The suppression of natural immunologic responses, which produces lowered resistance to disease.

mune systems protect us from various diseases to which we are exposed, but HIV, perhaps in combination with other physiological factors, cripples the immune system. Patients are then vulnerable to numerous opportunistic infections—that is, infections that take hold because the impairment of the body's immune system gives them the opportunity to flourish. People are diagnosed as having AIDS when they develop one of the opportunistic infections or diseases associated with AIDS and when they receive a positive result from tests for HIV. Common early signs of AIDS are lymphadenopathy, unexplained weight loss, loss of appetite, persistent fevers or night sweats, chronic fatigue, unexplained diarrhea or bloody stools, unexplained bleeding from any body opening, skin rashes, easy bruising, persistent severe headaches, chronic dry cough not caused by smoking or a cold, and a chronic whitish coating on the tongue or throat. All of these symptoms result from the opportunistic infections that accompany AIDS.

It is important to note, however, that some of the same symptoms are also associated with other diseases and infections, such as the flu and colds, or with physical and psychological stress. The presence of one of these symptoms, such as swollen lymph nodes, does not necessarily indicate that a person has contracted HIV, particularly if he or she is not engaging in risky behaviors and is not the partner of someone who is infected with HIV. A positive blood test for HIV antibodies is needed to make a diagnosis of AIDS.

Although the CDC concluded that the available blood tests for HIV antibodies, such as the ELISA test, are highly accurate, they are not perfect. That is, occasionally a person receives a false-positive result (erroneously indicating HIV antibodies when there are none) or a false-negative result (incorrectly indicating no HIV antibodies when they are in fact present). (See "Highlight: Being Tested for HIV Antibodies" on page 390.) In addition, there may be as long as a six-month period between contracting the infection and testing positive for HIV. For further accuracy, follow-up testing can be done using the Western blot test.

In 1996, the Food and Drug Administration (FDA) approved an HIV test that can be taken at home. By calling a toll-free number and punching in a code number, the user gets a recorded message if the result is negative. With a positive result, a trained counselor answers the call and refers the consumer to a local clinic for further testing. HIV home tests have been shown to be as accurate as tests provided through clinics or doctors' offices (Frank et al., 1997).

▶ **Issues to Consider:** Would you be more willing to take a home test than a test at a health care clinic to determine your HIV status? Why or why not?

The opportunistic infections most commonly suffered by AIDS patients are pneumocystis carinii pneumonia (PCP), Kaposi's sarcoma (KS), and cytomegalovirus infection. In 1993, three other infections were added: pulmonary tuberculosis, recurrent pneumonia, and invasive cervical cancer. Other opportunistic infections attacking AIDS patients without KS or PCP account for only a small proportion of cases. In 1993, the definition of AIDS infection was expanded to include a laboratory measure of severe immunosuppression (CD4+ T-lymphocyte count of fewer than 200 cells or less than 14 percent of total lymphocytes) (CDC, 1998).

PCP used to be a rare parasitic infection of the lungs usually observed only in cancer patients who were undergoing chemotherapy or in organ-transplant patients who were given drugs to suppress their immune systems. PCP is now the most common opportunistic disease associated with AIDS.

Kaposi's sarcoma (KS) is a rare form of cancer of the skin and connective tissues (bones, fats, and muscles), which in the past mainly affected elderly men in Western societies. In some parts of Africa, KS now accounts for 9 percent of all cancers detected in men. Some KS patients develop lesions on their palate (roof of the mouth), face, arms, and other skin areas. Men who develop KS have a shorter interval from the time they are diagnosed with HIV to the development of AIDS than do men without KS (Lifson et al., 1990). In contrast, non-AIDS-related KS (also called classical KS) progresses slowly, first appearing in the form of lesions on the limbs.

Cytomegalovirus (CMV) infections, caused by a group of herpes viruses, result in enlargement of the cells in various parts of the body, including the lungs, intestines, and central nervous system. CMV

H I G H L I G H T

Being Tested for HIV Antibodies

As I sit here dispassionately describing the testing process for HIV antibodies, I vividly remember my own experience of being tested. I realized that the hepatitis that my husband and I had contracted while in Africa is one of the infections associated with AIDS. A local hospital had a free and anonymous AIDS testing program, and one of my students asked whether I thought it really was confidential. He is gay, and he was afraid that if he were tested, his parents, potential employers, and others might find out. I was willing to be tested with him because I thought that it might be beneficial to find out firsthand about the procedures and the extent of anonymity. We made appointments, and on a snowy Monday evening we drove to the hospital to have the ELISA test done.

When we arrived at the hospital's testing site, the receptionist gave us each a slip with a four-digit number on it and told us to have a seat. Soon a volunteer counselor came out and called my number. He gave me a short questionnaire to fill out anonymously, on which I was to indicate such details as my age, gender, sexual orientation, marital status, number of sexual partners in the recent past, and drug use patterns. When I returned the questionnaire, he read it over and asked why I wanted to be tested because I did not seem to fit any of the high-risk groups. I explained about Africa and related my other reasons. He then competently obtained my informed consent regarding the blood test and the hospital's procedures to guarantee anonymity.

I was shown a videotape reviewing much of the same material that the counselor had presented. A nurse took a blood sample, wrote my number on the vial, and directed me back to the receptionist, who scheduled my appointment for the following week. I found my friend, and we drove home, comparing notes on the way. He was worried, and we talked about his potential risk. After I dropped him at his dorm, I began to feel anxious about my own test results. I talked with my husband, Rick, about it, and during the next week I thought a great deal about what I might do if the test result were positive.

I was relieved when told that my test was negative, and I was delighted to see the huge grin on my friend's face when he returned to the waiting room. On the drive home, we talked about our anxiety during the past week, which was nothing compared to the fear, anguish, and eventual physical pain of those who get positive test results and go on to develop AIDS.—E.R.A.

symptoms include fever, blindness, pneumonia, colitis, and low blood-cell counts.

AIDS patients are understandably depressed when their disease is diagnosed. In some cases, the depression may be a response to the impact of HIV on the spinal cord and brain, which can produce neurological deficits called AIDS dementia complex. Brains of infected persons decrease in size through the atrophy (wasting away) of some nerve cells. In the early stages of AIDS dementia, patients may experience forgetfulness, withdrawal, and difficulty concentrating. Then problems with walking and talking develop, and response time in visual and motor tasks becomes impaired. Later, AIDS dementia patients experience seizures and spasms.

TREATMENT

A cure for AIDS will probably not be found in the foreseeable future, but there are treatments for some of the opportunistic infections that attack people with impaired immune systems, and some drugs slow the effects of the AIDS virus. Zidovudine (AZT) is more effective than placebos in extending the lives of AIDS patients and was licensed by the FDA in 1987. Despite AZT's effectiveness in reducing the severity of illness and extending the lives of AIDS patients, the drug has potentially severe side effects. Another problem with AZT is that HIV can become resistant to the drug with long-term treatment. However, the combination of several other drugs with AZT ap-

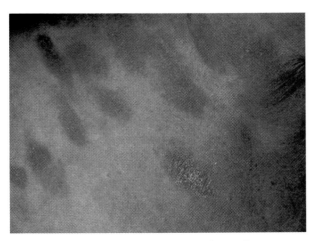

Kaposi's sarcoma (KS) was once a rare form of cancer. A virulent variety of the disease afflicts some AIDS patients, often appearing first as a lesion on the palate. This patient has lesions on his neck.

study raised ethical concerns about continuing to provide testosterone injection therapy to the few men who reported having engaged in unsafe sexual behavior (W. A. Fisher, 1997).

Scientists are working on vaccines for HIV. In 1987 the first AIDS vaccine entered clinical trials in the United States (Hochhauser & Rothenberger, 1992). At this point, the results of research with this vaccine are ambiguous. Other experimental vaccines have emerged since 1987, but research on HIV vaccines must be conducted with humans, and that raises controversial ethical problems. Furthermore, there are many strains of HIV, and the virus is constantly mutating. In 1996, Liu et al. reported that approximately 1 percent of people have a "defective" gene that renders them immune to the effects of HIV. Further research with that gene may lead to the development of a treatment or vaccine for HIV/AIDS.

pears to increase its effectiveness. Newer drugs called protease inhibitors have been shown to extend the lives of people infected with AIDS. These drug "cocktails" block production of a key enzyme, protease, that the virus needs to replicate itself. Ritonavir, indinavir, helfinavir, and saquinavir are the four approved protease inhibitors (Flexner, 1998). These medications are quite expensive, however, and are unlikely to be available to the poor, particularly in the developing world.

Noting that HIV/AIDS infections are associated with depression, reduced sexual desire, and sexual dysfunction, Wagner, Rapkin, and Rapkin (1997) conducted a study with a group of AIDS patients in which they provided testosterone injection therapy. Compared to a control group of AIDS patients (who subsequently received the testosterone treatment), those receiving the therapy showed increased pleasure with life, sexual desire, and sexual functioning. Some of the men engaged in masturbation, some had sex with partners and used condoms, but a few of the men engaged in unprotected insertive sex with a partner who was unaware of the patient's AIDS status. Testosterone treatment could improve the quality of life for AIDS patients (Tiefer, 1997), but this

▶ **Issues to Consider:** If you were a member of a research team providing testosterone injection therapy, what would you do about the few men who subsequently reported engaging in unsafe sexual behavior? Remember that research participants are generally guaranteed confidentiality, and refusing to provide further therapy to those few men who reported engaging in risky sexual behavior would reduce the likelihood that they or other men in the study would report honestly their sexual behaviors.

PROTECTION AGAINST AIDS

Unless a person is celibate or involved with an uninfected partner in a monogamous relationship, he or she should take direct steps to reduce the risk of HIV infection. Methods of lowering one's risk of contracting STDs, including HIV/AIDS, are described at the end of this chapter.

The relationship between having a history of other STDs and contracting AIDS may simply be evidence of the fact that people with AIDS and those with other STDs share certain risk factors. For example, they may have unprotected sex with a large number of partners, not use a barrier contraceptive method (the condom, the diaphragm, or the female condom), or engage in sexual practices that increase the likelihood of infection if they have sex with an infected partner.

One of the reasons that AIDS initially may have been more prevalent among homosexuals than among U.S. heterosexuals is that homosexuals do not use contraceptives. Barrier methods of contraception reduce the risk of HIV transmission when used properly.

The protective effect of barrier methods is supported by the fact that AIDS is as prevalent among females as males in some African populations, most of whom do not use these contraceptives. Asking about the health and sexual risk-taking behaviors of potential partners is crucial in slowing the spread of AIDS, but it is also important in reducing the incidence of other viral STDs, a topic to which we turn now.

ther Viral STDs

Like AIDS, the other sexually transmitted viruses are incurable at present. They can be treated, but no methods are yet available to purge the virus from the body and thus prevent recurrent episodes of these diseases. These virally produced STDs include genital herpes, genital warts, and hepatitis B.

HERPES SIMPLEX TYPE II

Many people have experienced the episodic, mildly painful, and unsightly fever blisters or cold sores of herpes simplex type I. Although most people do not welcome the irritating sores, herpes I is not worrisome after the lesions have healed.

A related virus, **herpes simplex type II** (called herpes II or genital herpes and abbreviated HSV-II), causes most genital herpes infections, although herpes I may also appear on the genitals if they are orally stimulated by a partner with an active outbreak of herpes I around the mouth. Conversely, herpes II may develop in the mouth if an individual orally stimulates the genitals of a partner who has an active infection of herpes II.

The CDC estimates that there are about half a million new cases of herpes II each year, with several million people experiencing recurrent episodes annually. About 45 million Americans are believed to have herpes II (Fleming et al., 1997).

Genital herpes is most often contracted through physical contact with the open herpes II sores of an infected person. In its dormant phase, the disease is

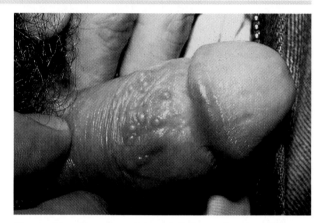

Herpes II patients experience periodic outbreaks of these sores.

less contagious, but people who are shedding the virus without visibly obvious lesions and/or without even knowing that they are infected can infect their partners. The symptoms, which include small blisters similar to those created by herpes I, generally appear at the site of the infection 3 to 7 days after infection. They may tingle and itch, or they may produce a burning sensation. When the blisters break open, the infection can spread to other parts of the body. The open wounds are also susceptible to secondary infections from skin bacteria. Other symptoms of genital herpes include fever and swollen lymph glands. In women, herpes II blisters commonly break out on the outer and inner lips of the vagina, the clitoral hood, and the cervix. In men, the blisters tend to erupt on the glans or foreskin of the penis. Primary, or initial, herpes infections produce open sores that last for an average of 16 to 21 days in men and 10 to 16 days in women. In general, symptoms and complications of

---

herpes simplex type II—A viral infection contracted through physical contact with an infected person during an active outbreak of the sores.

recurrent outbreaks are milder than those associated with the primary outbreak of herpes.

In a cross-sectional sample in the United States, less than 10 percent of all those whose blood tested positive for genital herpes were aware that they were infected (Fleming et al., 1997). Presumably people with mild or no symptoms may be more likely to transmit herpes to others because they do not realize that they have the virus. The percentage of women with HSV-II was higher for women than for men (26 percent versus 18 percent, respectively). There was also a higher percentage of HSV-II–positive tests for Blacks (46 percent) than for Mexican Americans (22 percent) or Whites (18 percent) (Fleming et al., 1997).

Laboratory studies reveal that some contraceptives are effective in reducing the risk of transmitting or contracting herpes II. Spermicides containing nonoxynol-9 have been shown to deactivate the herpes virus on contact. Condoms also block the passage of the virus in laboratory tests. Although sexual contact should be avoided during active herpes II outbreaks, laboratory studies suggest that sexual intercourse is probably safe during remission of herpes II. Remission can occur for years after the initial episode, and during this time there are no outbreaks of the symptoms. Nonetheless, couples engaging in sex should use condoms with liberal amounts of spermicide.

Pregnant women with genital herpes can transmit the disease to a fetus. A woman who has an active case of primary genital herpes has about a 50 percent risk of transmitting it to the baby during vaginal delivery. Women who have visible lesions during labor or have recently tested positive for herpes II should deliver by cesarean section (Kroon & Whitley, 1994; Steben & Sacks, 1997).

Accurate diagnosis of genital herpes is enhanced by obtaining samples of the infected tissue early in the infection and subjecting them to laboratory analysis. Although researchers are working on a cure, current treatments only reduce the discomfort of the symptoms; they do not eliminate the virus. The drug acyclovir, taken orally, relieves pain, shortens the time required for the healing of herpes lesions, and can suppress recurrent outbreaks in some patients. Other methods for treating the symptoms of genital herpes are available or under development, so genital herpes patients should check with their health care providers for the latest information.

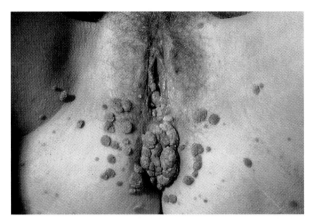

The common genital wart is a soft pink lesion that can be sexually transmitted.

Many people experience intense emotional reactions when they are initially diagnosed as having genital herpes. Herpes patients can receive counseling about ways of reducing or avoiding stressful factors in their lives and of coping with recurrent outbreaks. Herpes II patients have banded together to form the Herpes Resource Center, which disseminates information about recent research and sources of emotional support for those with herpes II. (Consult the Appendix for further information.)

GENITAL WARTS/HUMAN PAPILLOMA VIRUS

Genital warts are caused by the human papilloma virus (HPV). They are soft, pink, painless, single or multiple growths resembling a small cauliflower. The virus is transmitted through direct contact with the warts during vaginal, oral, or anal intercourse, but it may also be contracted through nonsexual contact. The warts, which are highly contagious, begin to appear one to three months after contact and are diagnosed visually. They may be removed by freezing (cryotherapy), burning, dehydration with an electrical needle, or surgery. If the warts are unusual or persistent, they should be biopsied to determine whether they are precancerous. There are more than 70 types of human papilloma viruses and of these, more than 20 can be sexually transmitted (Lytwyn & Sellors, 1997). A number of these have

genital warts—An STD that can also be contracted nonsexually; caused by the human papilloma virus.

been implicated in the development of cancers of the anus, cervix, vagina, and vulva. If they are on the penis or in the vagina, abstinence from intercourse or the use of a condom until the warts have been removed can lessen the likelihood of transmitting the virus.

More than a million cases of genital warts requiring treatment have been reported each year in the United States (Fact Sheet, 1997). Most male partners of women with genital warts or HPV have no visible genital warts, and there is no screening test for the presence of the HPV in men without visible warts.

Although genital warts sometimes regress without treatment, they may spread and grow to the point where they block the vaginal or rectal opening. Further, the virus can be transmitted to a baby during vaginal delivery if the warts are located on the cervix or in the vagina.

HEPATITIS B

There are different types of hepatitis, each thought to be caused by a different virus. In all forms of hepatitis, the virus attacks the liver. Our main concern here is with **hepatitis B,** because it can be transmitted through exposure to the blood, saliva, or semen of infectious carriers, although saliva and semen tend to have lower concentrations of the virus than does blood. The causative agent is the hepatitis B virus (HBV).

The World Health Organization estimates that there are currently more than 2 billion people infected with HBV (Teppers & Gully, 1997). In the United States, approximately 300,000 people, most of them young adults, are infected each year. About 10,000 require hospitalization, and about 250 of the patients die annually, usually of liver cancer (Institute of Medicine, 1996). Up to 10 percent of young adults with HBV infections become carriers, and the United States has an estimated pool of half a million to one million carriers. People who are carriers are generally symptom free, but carry the virus and can pass it on to others.

HBV infection usually begins within 45 to 180 days after exposure to an infectious carrier. The most common symptoms are mild fever, fatigue, sore muscles, headache, upset stomach, skin rash, joint pains, and dark urine. The characteristic external sign is a yellowing of the whites of the eyes. The skin may also become yellow, or jaundiced. The disease is diagnosed by a specific blood test, the hepatitis B surface-antigen test.

We are happy to end this sobering section on the effects of sexually transmitted viral infections by reporting that an effective vaccine against HBV was licensed in 1981, making hepatitis B the one viral STD that can be prevented by a vaccine. The CDC reported that people who develop adequate antibody levels after vaccination have almost complete protection against HBV. In some states, hepatitis B vaccination is now required or highly recommended for newborns. *Reality or Myth* 6

Parasitic Infections

We now turn to some of the sexually transmitted infections caused by parasites, fungi, protozoa, and yeasts.

CANDIDIASIS

The yeastlike fungus *Candida albicans* (also known as moniliasis, and commonly called a yeast infection) normally lives in the mouth, the digestive tract, and the vagina. Growth of the fungus is usually restricted

by the presence of other bacteria. When these controlling bacteria are reduced in number by antibiotics, frequent douching, pregnancy, diabetes, or other conditions that reduce the acidity of the vaginal environment, such as oral contraceptive use, the unrestricted growth of the fungus in the vagina can result in infection.

Candidiasis produces a thick, white vaginal discharge resembling the curd of cottage cheese, an un-

---

hepatitis B—A virus that attacks the liver; often sexually transmitted.

candidiasis (KAN-dih-DYE-ah-sis)—An infection of the vulva and vagina caused by the excess growth of a fungus that occurs normally in the body.

pleasant yeasty odor, and severe itching. The vaginal walls may be inflamed, the labia sometimes swell, and intercourse may be painful. Candidiasis is diagnosed by visually examining a fresh specimen of discharge or by growing the fungus in a culture. It is treated with antibiotic-antifungal compounds in suppositories or ointments, many of which are available without a prescription. During treatment, couples should abstain from coitus or use a condom to avoid infection or reinfection of the partners.

TRICHOMONIASIS

Trichomoniasis is an infection with an estimated annual incidence of 3 million cases (Fact Sheet, 1997; Institute of Medicine, 1996). It is caused by a protozoan (a one-celled animal) called *Trichomonas vaginalis*. It can be transmitted through sexual interaction, but infection can also result from contact with infected wet towels and wet bathing suits.

The incubation period ranges from 4 days to a month. A minority of women with this infection produce a frothy yellow-green or white vaginal discharge with a strong odor, and some men have an inflamed urethra (urethritis). The majority of people with trichomoniasis, however, are asymptomatic.

A diagnosis is made by examining a sample of the discharge for trichomonads (the protozoa) under a microscope. Both the person who has been diagnosed as having trichomoniasis and his or her partner(s) are usually given medronidazole (Flagyl) to eliminate the infection.

OTHER PARASITIC INFECTIONS

Amebiasis, also known as amebic dysentery, is caused by a one-celled animal, *Entamoeba histolytica*. Amebiasis is transmitted through both sexual contact and exposure to contaminated water and food. Analingus and fellatio following anal sex can transmit the parasite. Amebic infection is treated by a variety of medications, including Flagyl.

Scabies is a highly contagious infestation by tiny, eight-legged parasitic mites called *Sarcoptes scabiei*. These creatures travel quickly and can be transmitted both sexually and nonsexually. When the eggs deposited by the mites hatch, they cause red, itchy, pimple-like bumps on the skin. Scabies can be diagnosed through microscopic inspection of infected skin. It is treated with the nonprescription drug Kwell (called Kwellada in Canada), which is applied as a shampoo from the neck down. In addition, scabies sufferers must wash all bedding and clothing to get rid of the eggs.

Pediculosis pubis, or crabs, is an infestation of six-legged lice about the size of a pinhead. They inhabit hairy areas of the pubic region, anus, underarms, and eyelashes. Eggs, or nits, are laid by the female. These nits mature in 2 or 3 weeks and begin feeding on blood, producing inflammation of the skin and itching. They may be transmitted sexually or nonsexually through contact with infected bedding, towels, or clothing. Like scabies, crabs can be eliminated by shampooing the infected areas with nonprescription medicines such as Kwell.

Safer-Sex Practices: Reducing the Risk of Contracting STDs

There has been a lot of discussion about "safe sex" in the media, but you may have noticed that we have consistently used the phrase "safer sex" in this book. The reason is that, from the standpoint of wanting to avoid an STD (or, for that matter, an unwanted pregnancy), there is no such thing as completely safe sex if genital contact is involved. There are, however, practices that reduce risk: abstinence, avoiding

anonymous "one-night stands," communicating clearly about your sexual policies with a person prior to deciding whether to become sexually intimate with him or her, limiting sexual activities to contacts

amebiasis (ah-ME-BYE-uh-sis)—A parasitic infection of the colon that results in frequent diarrhea.
scabies—A contagious skin condition caused by an insect that burrows under the skin.
pediculosis pubis (peh-DIK-you-LOW-sis PYOU-bis)—A lice infestation of the pubic hair; commonly referred to as crabs.

trichomoniasis (TRIK-uh-muh-NYE-ah-sis)—An inflammation of the vagina characterized by a whitish discharge.

that do not involve bodily penetration, and using condoms during any sexual intimacy.

For many couples, one of the most difficult steps in deciding whether to become more sexually intimate and engage in safer-sex practices is discussing the matter with each other. But frank and open dialogue is absolutely essential if you are to make wise decisions about developing a relationship that may affect your physical and psychological well-being for the rest of your life. To make sexual decisions in the dark, so to speak, is like driving with your eyes closed. In addition, one benefit of the discussions you have prior to making that decision is that they may ultimately enhance your emotional and physical intimacy as a couple.

RELATIONSHIP NEGOTIATION

Most of us are sexually attracted to many different people in our lives, but we generally go through a screening process (although we may not think of it that way) as we try to decide whether to act on our feelings. Some people choose not to act on their attraction to an individual because they wish to wait until they are in a relationship involving serious commitment, engagement, or marriage before becoming sexually intimate. Others may avoid acting on sexual attraction because they are already in a monogamous relationship with another person. People who are unattached or who are not in a monogamous relationship may feel attracted to someone on the basis of his or her looks, but after a few conversations, they may realize that the person's physical appearance is all that they find attractive.

Assuming that you are a terrific human being with a wide range of attractive and valuable attributes, you can afford to be selective about your choice of sexual partners and practices. Being selective, however, requires that you devote some time to deciding your sexual policies. "Sexual policies" and "selective" may sound abstract and vague, but determining sexual policies so that you can be selective involves a series of concrete steps:

1. *Clarify your sexual policies.* Make decisions about your sexual policies when you are calm and able to think clearly, not when you are sexually aroused and have to make an instant decision about a particular person. In forming your policies, ask yourself questions about the conditions under which you wish to become physically and emotionally intimate with another person:

   a. Do I want to select partners who are capable of valuing others as much as they value themselves?

   b. What kind of relationship am I seeking, with what level of mutual commitment?

   We know two students—one a heterosexual woman and the other a gay man—who, for different reasons, plan to avoid serious commitments for a couple of years. Neither of them is averse to casual relationships, but both make it clear to potential partners that they are not emotionally available for any intense or long-term relationship.

2. *Communicate your policies to a potential partner.* After you become aware that you and another person are interested in each other, it is important to spend some time getting to know one another before deciding to become sexually intimate. Your prospective partner may appear to meet the criteria that you established in your sexual policies, but first impressions are not always accurate. In addition, there is a tendency to ascribe motives and characteristics to another person whom we find attractive without explicitly verbalizing our own motives and policies or asking the other person about his or hers.

3. *Identify the extent to which your own past sexual behaviors pose a potential risk to the person in whom you are interested.* If you have been sexually active with others, have you been tested for STDs to make sure that you will not transmit an STD to this new person? You should be able to give this new person that information, although you need not deliver a litany of names and specific episodes, but if, for example, you were sexually involved with someone and broke off the relationship because you discovered that your former partner was also having sex with someone else, then you are at risk of having contracted an STD. Until you have been tested and found to be free of any STDs, you risk transmitting an STD to a new sexual partner.

By bathing or showering together, you can enjoy erotic play and have an opportunity to see each other's bodies.

4. *Ask about your potential partner's risk of having contracted an STD.* If that person cares about you, she or he should willingly provide you with the same information that you provide. If the person refuses to tell you about the frequency of past sexual experiences with different partners, perhaps your criteria for an intimate sexual relationship have not been met. Remember that some people who are currently healthy may be engaging in sexual practices that put them at risk of transmitting an STD. For example, we know a woman who was approached for a sexual encounter by a man whom she liked very much. She was aware, however—and he frankly acknowledged—that he frequently engaged in group sex. She conceded her fondness and attraction for him but told him that, although she accepted his sexual lifestyle, it involved more risk than she was willing to take. He accepted her rejection of a sexual relationship gracefully, and they remained good friends.

5. *Postpone physical intimacy involving the exchange of body fluids until laboratory tests have verified that you are both free of STDs.* You may perceive our emphasis on getting yourself tested before entering a new relationship as an expensive practice that kills sexual spontaneity. But keep in mind that it is not nearly so expensive as contracting an STD, particularly one of the incurable viral diseases. In addition, a clinic in your area may provide testing services free or on a sliding scale based on income.

   If, after considering your own values and establishing open communication, you and the other person decide that you feel sufficiently committed to each other to have sex, both of you can reduce the risk of infection by incorporating safer-sex practices into your lovemaking. If a couple approaches the situation with some imagination and humor, these practices can be both erotic and romantic as well as safer. They need not resemble a medical examination or a police body search. If you care enough about your partner to want to be sexually intimate with him or her, you should also want to protect that person—as well as yourself—against possible disease.

6. *Shower or bathe together before becoming sexually intimate.* Washing yourselves and each other can be highly erotic. It also gives you both the opportunity to observe each other's bodies.

7. *Learn about each other's bodies.* You may want to invest in some light bulbs that provide soft light for your bedroom (or wherever you choose to have sex). If you notice anything unusual about your partner's body (for example, bumps or discharge), you should ask about them. If you suspect that one of you has symptoms of an STD, you should delay further physical intimacy.

8. *Use latex condoms and spermicides together.* The combination can be highly effective in reducing the likelihood of transmitting most STDs. If you find the usual spermicides less than aesthetically pleasing, you may want to obtain one of the flavored spermicides. In the event that you and your partner decide to make a long-term, monogamous commitment to one another and neither of you is infected, condom and spermicide use can be abandoned (and will have to be at some point if your long-term commitment includes plans for children!).

▶ **Issues to Consider:** Have you developed your own set of sexual policies? Why do you think it is necessary (or not necessary) to do so?

OTHER PRACTICES THAT REDUCE RISK

Our intention in providing the following list of practices is not to be moralistic but to help you avoid contracting AIDS or any of the other STDs:

1. Do not use intravenous drugs, iso-butyl, or poppers (amyl nitrate).

2. Do not share needles or any other IV drug equipment.

3. Do not use the belongings of others that contain any of their body fluids (blood, saliva, urine, semen, and so forth).

4. Avoid unprotected sexual intimacy with IV drug users. Many of the new AIDS cases result from people who inject drugs and share needles or have had unprotected sexual contact with IV drug users.

5. Remain abstinent until you are confident that sexual activity between you and a desired partner will not pose health risks for either of you.

If you are sexually active and nonmonogamous, following these safer-sex and general health practices is extremely important. You may also want to change your sexual lifestyle until vaccines against viral STDs become available. Our capacities to provide one another with sexual pleasure can be seriously jeopardized by AIDS or other STDs. If one does not practice abstinence, there is no absolute guarantee that a sexual contact will not result in an STD. Although those who wish to remain sexually active and healthy may not be thrilled about altering their sexual practices to avoid disease, for most people, survival is more important than high-risk sexual encounters with a variety of partners.

Note: AIDS information is available from the following sources. *United States:* For a tape recording of the latest information, call, toll free, 1-800-342-AIDS. AIDS information is available (although not always toll free) from the Department of Health in each state and the District of Columbia. To inquire about a toll-free number in your locale, call 1-800-555-1212. *Canada:* National AIDS Centre, Ottawa, 1-613-957-1772. Toronto Area Gay Hotline, 1-416-964-6600.

SUMMARY OF MAJOR POINTS

1. Attitudes, knowledge, and diagnosis of STDs. Unfortunately, inadequate knowledge, negative attitudes, and shame about STDs often interfere with responsible health practices. Early diagnosis and treatment of STDs are necessary to avoid the dangerous long-term effects of undetected STDs that can readily be cured. In addition, knowledge of our STD status is important so that we do not spread them, particularly when they involve the currently incurable viral STDs.

2. Categories of STDs. STDs can be classified into three major categories: bacterial infections, viral diseases, and parasitic infestations. Except for viral STDs, these can be readily cured in their early stages. Contracting an STD in the past may increase one's chances of contracting HIV; thus sexually active people should take preventive measures to avoid any STD.

3. Bacterial STDs. The bacterial infections include gonorrhea, syphilis, chlamydia, nongonococcal urethritis, (cystitis, prostatitis, gardnerella vaginalis, shigellosis, and chancroid). The most common serious complication of untreated bacterial genital infections in women is pelvic inflammatory diseases. A variety of medications are successful in treating these conditions, particularly if they are used in the early stages of the infection.

4. Viral STDs. The viral STDs include AIDS, herpes II, genital warts, and hepatitis B. Although there are treatments for the symptoms and for some complications of these diseases, none can be cured. There is a vaccine for hepatitis B, however, and people at risk of contracting it should be vaccinated.

5. Parasitic STDs. Infections caused by parasites, fungi, protozoa, and yeasts include candidiasis, trichomoniasis, amebiasis, scabies, and pediculosis pubis. Antibiotic and antifungal compounds are generally effective in treating these infections.

6. Safer-sex practices. Except for celibacy, there is no way to eliminate the risk of contracting STDs. But sexually active people can sharply reduce the likelihood of contracting AIDS and other STDs by refraining from IV drug use, avoiding contact with others' body fluids (including blood and semen), and adopting safer-sex practices. Reducing exposure to STDs involves careful selection of partners and the correct and consistent use of latex condoms and ample amounts of spermicide. Condoms reduce the likelihood of transmitting or contracting most STDs, and spermicides are effective in killing many of the organisms that cause STDs, including herpes.

Atypical Sexual Activity

Reality or Myth?

1. Transvestites experience sexual pleasure from dressing in the clothes of the other sex.

2. Female-to-male sex-reassignment surgery (SRS) is usually less successful than male-to-female SRS.

3. Most transsexuals describe first experiencing gender cross-identification when they are in their early 30s.

4. Women show little sexual interest in watching partners undress.

5. Men who expose themselves in public (exhibitionists) or "peep" (voyeurs) are seldom dangerous.

6. Pedophiles tend to be older and use lower levels of violence with children than do men who rape adult women.

Y ou pervert!

High school students commonly use this epithet, usually jokingly, to label someone who engages in a quasi-sexual behavior deviating slightly from the norm. What does the word **perversion** mean? One dictionary defines it as a maladjustment involving aberrant or deviant ways of seeking sexual satisfaction. A problem with this label and other similar terms, such as deviation, is that what is considered aberrant or deviant at one time and place might be considered normal at other times and places.

Some of the atypical behaviors we will cover do not involve or victimize others and so are considered to be more curious or annoying than dangerous. Other paraphilias are invasive of others' rights and thus can be seen as coercive sexual behavior. In considering societal responses to paraphilias, it is important to differentiate between those that are simply variations from normal or typical behavior and those that infringe on the lives of other people.

In this chapter we examine noninvasive fetishes, transvestism, and transsexuality. We also review the characteristics and possible motivations of those who engage in uncommon and invasive practices, including people who are sexually attracted to children. The various

treatments given to those who have strayed from what North American culture considers normal sexual behavior are examined.

The Paraphilias

Because beliefs change with respect to what sexual activities are normal, many professionals prefer to avoid the terms *perversion* or *sexual deviance*. Someone who practices an atypical sexual activity is not necessarily dangerous or in need of therapy. **Paraphilia** (the love of unusual, or atypical, sexual activ-

perversion—Deviance from the normal in sexual activities or desires.
paraphilia (par-rah-FIL-ee-ah)—Love of the unusual; the term now used to describe sexual activities that were formerly labeled deviance (*para*: "beside or amiss"; *philia*: "love").

ity) is the term now used for a restricted group of sexual behaviors that are considered unusual by the society to which the person performing them belongs.

The current view of paraphilias differs from earlier definitions of sexual deviance. For example, the second edition of the American Psychiatric Association's *Diagnostic and Statistical Manual of Mental Disorders (DSM-II,* 1968) classified sexual behavior as abnormal if it "deviated from a defined norm of heterosexual coitus between adults under nonbizarre circumstances." According to this definition, homosexuality was automatically classified as a deviation. More recently, clinicians have labeled an atypical pattern of sexual behavior as a variation rather than a deviation, and this approach "implies neither health nor illness, goodness nor badness, usefulness nor uselessness" (Stoller, 1977, p. 192). Such labeling describes rather than evaluates the behavior. Although many experts find descriptive labeling a useful approach to discussing the paraphilias, some people have difficulty separating description from evaluation.

Because of social and legal restrictions, reliable data on the frequency of paraphilic behaviors are limited. Most of our information about the paraphilias comes from people who have been arrested or are in therapy. However, it is likely that most people who engage in paraphilias do not fall into either of these two categories, so our ability to generalize most research findings is limited.

One solidly supported generalization about paraphilias, however, does appear to be appropriate:

males are far more likely than females to engage in them. More than 90 percent of people who are arrested for sexual offenses other than prostitution in the United States are males (Uniform Crime Reports, 1997).

Atypical sexual patterns can coexist with emotional disorders. People who confine their sexual outlets to strange and occasionally bizarre activities sometimes have trouble relating to other adults in a meaningful way. Yet many individuals who engage in paraphilic acts are also able to take part in "normal" sexual behavior with adult partners without relying on paraphilic fantasies or behaviors to generate sexual excitement.

▶ **Issues to Consider:** How would you define "abnormal" sexual behavior?

The Noninvasive Consensual Paraphilias

Many types of atypical sexual behavior involve consensual adults: people who mutually agree to observe, participate in, or just tolerate the behavior in question. No one's rights are violated, and the vast majority of society's members are unaware that the behaviors even exist, except for those who watch daytime talk shows.

FETISHES

The term *fetish* is derived from the Portuguese word *fetico*, meaning "charmed" or "obsessive fascination." In current clinical terms, **fetishism** refers to the use of objects as a "preferred" or "exclusive" means of inducing sexual arousal. In other words, some object comes to symbolize or embody the sexual arousal value usually reserved for human beings. To some extent, we are all fetishists, in that various objects can sexually arouse us. We may associate items

fetishism—Obtaining sexual excitement primarily or exclusively from an inanimate object or a particular part of the body.

of clothing with specific body parts or with a particular person. Bras, underpants, and jock straps have definite associations with specific body parts and may acquire the capacity to arouse us sexually by themselves. Similarly, cars, colognes, or hairstyles that we associate with a loved one can arouse us.

Fetishism is thought to be primarily a male characteristic. There have been very few documented cases of female fetishism. Most frequently, fetish objects are used in connection with fantasy and masturbation. Sometimes they are employed to build arousal during sexual intercourse or in combination with other forms of sexual expression. Fetishism usually develops around puberty (Weinberg, Williams, & Calhan, 1995). In one study of 100 people with rubber fetishes, the average age at which they first experienced attraction toward rubber objects or material was just under 11 (Gosselin, 1978).

Although the list of possible fetish objects is inexhaustible, certain items are more likely than others to be associated with sexual arousal, perhaps because they are more similar in texture or appearance to the genitals. Shoes, boots, and undergarments are frequent objects of fetishistic interest. In addition, items made of leather, rubber, fur, or silk seem to be particularly popular fetishes in North American culture.

Feet and their coverings have been used as symbols for sex in many cultures throughout history, and the foot has been one of the most common phallic symbols. In Slovene, a language spoken in Eastern Europe, the penis is called *tretja noga,* or "third foot." On the feast day of St. Cosimo in the area around Naples, Italy, a large phallic object called "the big toe of St. Cosimo" is offered to the saint (Rossi, 1976). The practice of binding the feet of young Chinese girls persisted for more than 1,000 years because small feet were considered erotic. Known as the lotus or lily foot, the bound foot came to have almost as much erogenous importance as the vagina itself. And as Rossi (1976, p. 15) noted:

> *The romantic and sexual magic of the shoe flourishes in many forms. In Sicily, young women sleep with a shoe under their pillow to improve their chances of getting a husband. In rural Greece, the woman believes that a lost lover can be retrieved by burning an old shoe. In Spain and Mexico, admiring women toss a slipper into the bullring to applaud the matador. He picks up the shoes gently as kittens, kisses them, and tosses them back into the crowd.*

In North American culture, the erotic symbolism of the foot is much more subtle. Shoes are still tied to the back of the car of a newly married couple, however. Perhaps the foot has been erotically significant because it is one of the body's most sensitive tactile organs, possessing a heavy concentration of nerve endings. The feet also participate reflexively during orgasm in what are called carpopedal spasms. Whatever the reasons for eroticizing feet, since ancient times there has been a nearly universal relationship between the foot as a male sexual symbol and the shoe as a female sexual symbol.

Shoes are generally made of leather, which is animal skin. Perhaps it is this juxtaposition of skin against skin that gives objects like shoes their erotic appeal. Aromas are an important source of arousal for many people, and leather has a distinctive odor. An evolutionary theorist might suggest that the shoe or leather fetishist may only be carrying to an extreme a general human attraction toward these objects.

Freud believed that in childhood, fetishists develop the idea that their mother possesses a penis, and then in adulthood they persist in believing that their mother has some kind of mysterious penis for which the fetish object is a substitute. A typical psychoanalytic case study involved a shoe fetishist who became fixated after seeing his governess expose her foot when he was a young boy (Fenichel, 1945). The psychoanalytic view holds that the boy equated the foot with the penis, and so the boy concluded, "My governess has a penis." The shoe supposedly stimulated sexual arousal because viewing it quieted the boy's castration anxiety. The Freudian theorist Otto Fenichel imagined the reasoning process to be something like the following: The idea that there are human beings without a penis and that I might myself be one of them makes it difficult for me to become sexually aroused. But now I see a symbol of a penis in a woman; that helps me quiet my fear, and I can allow myself to be sexually aroused (Fenichel, 1945).

Learning theories stress the association between the fetishistic object and sexual arousal. Sexual arousal and orgasm, both reflexive responses, may be inadvertently elicited by a strong emotional experience that happens to involve some particular object or body part. This initial conditioning experience may be reinforced through masturbation and orgasm.

TRANSVESTISM

A man who has strong urges to dress in women's clothing and becomes sexually aroused while wearing feminine apparel is called a **transvestite,** or TV. For most transvestites, cross-dressing is *not* an attempt to reject their biological gender. Although transvestism can be seen as a mild expression of discontent with one's biological sex and gender roles, it seldom entails the extreme rejection of one's biological sex seen in transsexualism (the belief that one is psychologically a member of the other sex). Both gay and straight men can be transvestites (Bullough & Bullough, 1997). In addition, some gay men cross-dress to

transvestite—A person sexually stimulated or gratified by wearing the clothes stereotypic of the other gender.

Cross-dressing can take many forms, from the elaborate attire of glamorous drag performer RuPaul, on the left, to the more practical attire of the man on the right.

attract a partner, but wearing clothes of the other gender does not in and of itself sexually arouse most homosexuals.

Cross-dressing was reported in Greek legend and among Roman emperors. It existed during the Middle Ages, and it is recognized and accepted today in many cultures (Bullough & Bullough, 1997; Stevenson, 1998). Although in both industrialized and nonindustrialized cultures, it is usually men who practice transvestism, Bullough and Bullough (1997) noted that prior to the twentieth century, there were more reports of female than of male cross-dressers. One of the major charges against Joan of Arc in her trial for heresy was her preference for male hairstyles and attire.

Until the late 1960s, most information about transvestites came from the reports of clinicians working with men who wished to be rid of their desire to cross-dress. Since that time, several research teams have sampled groups of transvestites from the general population.

Several aspects of research on nonclinical samples tend to contradict commonly held stereotypes about transvestites. For example, respondents generally described themselves as heterosexual; only a small percentage considered themselves exclusively homosexual. Most reported having been treated as boys—not as girls—during childhood, and although very few reported being cross-dressed by their parents, most began cross-dressing before puberty (Bullough & Bullough, 1997; Schott, 1995). Most studies have yielded no evidence that transvestism is associated with any major psychiatric symptoms (Beatrice, 1985; Bentler, Sherman, & Prince, 1970).

Cross-dressing is usually done at periodic intervals of a little more than once a month. Masturbation may take place during the cross-dressing episode, but often the cross-dressing itself produces orgasm. Although most transvestites report that they feel like women when cross-dressed, they say that they feel like men when nude, as well as when dressed in their usual attire. When transvestites were exposed to films of nude women, their erotic responses, as measured by penile volume, were within the normal range for heterosexual males (Buhrich & McConaghy, 1977; Buhrich, Theile, Yaw, & Crawford, 1979).

As might be expected, given the strength of attitudes in our own culture regarding gender roles, the desire to cross-dress introduces some novel problems into transvestites' relationships (Hunt & Main, 1997). Most transvestites who have participated in studies either had been or still were married. The majority of the transvestites in Buhrich's (1976) sample thought that their desire to cross-dress would disappear with marriage, so they did not tell their partner about it before the wedding. Some wives were unaware of their husbands' cross-dressing, even after they had been married for years. When wives did find out, their responses ran the gamut from complete disapproval and antagonism to acceptance and cooperation, the latter to the point of the wives' lending their husbands their own clothing. Wives sometimes accompany their husbands when they appear in public in feminine attire (Brown & Collier, 1989), and many wives report having sex with their husbands when their husband is cross-dressed (Bullough & Weinberg, 1988). *Reality or Myth*

Explanations of Transvestism. We have no conclusive explanation of the urge to cross-dress. Male hormone deficiency has been suggested as one cause, but comparisons of transvestites with nontransvestites have found no differences between the groups in testosterone levels (Buhrich et al., 1979).

One particularly puzzling aspect of transvestism is its apparent absence among contemporary Western women. Some scholars have argued that female transvestism is rare because norms with respect to what one may wear are far less restrictive for females than they are for males. For example, if you caught your aunt foraging in the kitchen for a midnight snack dressed in your uncle's pajama top, you might think she looked cute. Your reaction would probably be quite different, however, if you were to find your uncle rummaging through the refrigerator with your aunt's negligee on.

Several factors argue against this difference in restrictiveness as the cause of gender differences in the incidence of transvestism. First, most women who wear men's garb do not appear to derive the sexual satisfaction that men experience when they cross-dress. Second, Buhrich's (1976) research suggested that transvestites' urge to cross-dress is not satisfied by wearing ambiguous or unisex attire. Instead, they tend to desire apparel that is exclusively for females—for example, lacy bras, slips, and garter belts. (Similar behavior on the part of a female might be to don a pair of jockey shorts.) Third, transvestism most frequently appears in cultures with relaxed rather than restrictive gender-role norms. In all probability, then, the restrictiveness of norms for male clothing styles is not responsible for the incidence of male transvestism and the absence of female transvestism in the twentieth century.

The anthropologist Robert Munroe and his colleagues (Munroe & Munroe, 1977; Munroe, Whiting, & Hally, 1969) reviewed cross-cultural research on transvestism to explore whether any social or economic factors were associated with the practice. They found transvestism most likely to be prevalent in cultures having two characteristics: relaxed gender-role norms and greater pressure on men than on women to ensure the family's economic survival. In contrast to cultures with rigid gender-role norms and a lower status for women, cultures with relaxed norms grant women many of the privileges accorded to men. At the same time, women in most cultures do not have as much pressure and responsibility for economic survival placed on them as men do. Men's economic burdens may perhaps lead some males to take a "vacation" by temporarily abandoning their role as provider and symbolically adopting women's roles, behaviors, and attire. Even if this speculation is eventually supported by evidence, it still leaves many questions unanswered, including why the urge to cross-dress begins so early in life and why it is associated with arousal.

Whatever the explanation of the desire to cross-dress, it is clear that transvestites are not rejecting their biological sex. Instead, they find pleasure in occasionally donning the intimate attire that members of the other sex in their society typically wear. In contrast, transsexuals dislike the anatomical attributes of their biological sex, and many of them seek the anatomical characteristics of the other gender. We turn now to that phenomenon.

TRANSSEXUALITY

As members of a culture that is fascinated by sexual symbols of manhood (for example, penis size and functioning) and womanhood (such as breast size), many of us cannot comprehend the feelings of a person consumed with the desire to be rid of the physical attributes of his or her sex. Indeed, most people in our culture who are dissatisfied with their sexual organs seek to enhance rather than to eliminate them.

For some men, however, their male sexual organs are in conflict with their feminine psychological identity. These men are male-to-female (M-F) transsexuals. Similarly, for the female-to-male (F-M) transsexual, the physical symbols of the female biological sex are at odds with their masculine identification.

Definition and Incidence. A transsexual is a biologically normal male or female who feels that he or she is a member of the other sex. The term *transsexualism* was first used in 1910 by Magnus Hirschfeld and later by David O. Cauldwell (1949) in his diagnosis of psychopathia transsexualism for a genetic female who believed himself to be a male. A few years later, in 1953, Harry Benjamin described the syndrome more fully (Bullough & Bullough, 1993). Although transsexualism has only recently been defined, historical records describe a number of individuals who managed to live as members of the other gender (Bullough & Bullough, 1993). Classical mythology also contains repeated references to people who wished they were of the other sex.

It is easy to become confused if you try to categorize a transsexual's sexual orientation. From a genetic standpoint, we could conclude that many transsexuals have homosexual orientations because they are genetic males who are attracted to men or genetic females who are attracted to women. On the

transsexual—A person whose gender identity is different from his or her anatomical sex.

other hand, from a psychological standpoint, most M-F transsexuals feel as if they are really women and perceive their attraction to men as demonstrating heterosexual orientation. In various studies of transsexuals, up to a third of transsexuals reported little or no sexual activity before surgery and were classified as asexual (Blanchard, 1989; Freund, Steiner, & Chan, 1982).

It is estimated that one in every 50,000 persons over the age of 15 is likely to be transsexual. In most cultures, it appears that transsexualism is distributed evenly among males and females (Pauly, 1990).

▶**Issues to Consider:** Do you think transsexualism stems more from psychological or biological factors?

M-F Transsexualism. Although not the first to seek and obtain surgery, George Jorgensen, in the early 1950s, was the first American whose sex reassignment was widely publicized. His childhood and adolescence were similar in many ways to those of other

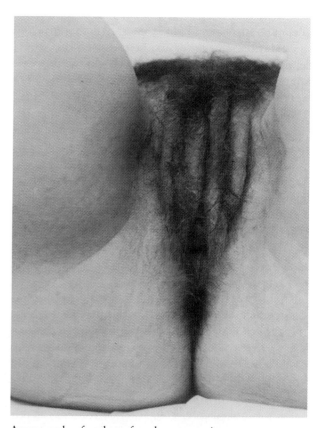

An example of male-to-female sex reassignment surgery.

transsexuals. He remembered wishing for a pretty doll with long golden hair for Christmas when he was 5 years old; he was disappointed to get a red model train instead (Jorgensen, 1967). He avoided rough-and-tumble games and fistfights and described himself as having been frail and introverted as a child. At the age of 19, he was drafted into the military service. He weighed 98 pounds and had underdeveloped genitals and almost no beard.

He experienced emotional feelings for several men but did not view these attachments as homosexual. He felt himself to be a woman. He wanted to relate to men and to the world at large as a woman, and he read everything that he could find about sex hormones. He moved to Copenhagen, Denmark, in 1950 after hearing that surgery for his condition might be available. In 1952, after taking estrogen on a regular basis, he underwent a series of three operations. Two months later, at the age of 26, she returned to the United States as Christine Jorgensen.

Jorgensen's parents were unaware of her decision to seek sex reassignment until after the surgery was performed. They initially reacted with anguish but later accepted the decision. Jorgensen never regretted her decision, and she felt that she might not have survived if she had not been able to get the surgery. Christine Jorgensen never married but was engaged twice and reported having been in love with several men. She died in 1989.

Subsequent research involving transsexuals who have undergone sex reassignment in the United States over the past few decades suggests that Jorgensen's feelings are quite representative. Some transsexuals, lacking access to sex-reassignment surgery, have been so desperate that they have attempted self-castration.

For most M-F transsexuals, identification with females and a preference for girl's clothing, or crossdressing, begin at an early age. On psychological inventories, the scores of feminine boys are very similar to those of girls of the same age (Bullough & Bullough, 1993). In adolescence and adulthood, some transsexuals engage in hyperfeminine behavior, characterized by "an overwhelming aroma of perfume, seductive behavior, and attire which is inappropriate to the occasion" (Pauly, 1974, p. 510).

In a study of behavioral differences between M-F transsexuals and women, Barlow et al. (1980) pointed out that typical men and women differ in the way they sit, stand, and walk. For example, women generally sit with their buttocks against the back of the chair, whereas men sit with their buttocks away from the chair back. Women tend to stand as if keeping their feet on a line, whereas men stand as if straddling a line. Observing these and other behaviors in a sample of presurgical transsexuals, Barlow found that they engaged in more stereotypically feminine behaviors than did a control group of women who had been selected because of their highly stereotypical feminine appearance. In their desire for a feminine identity, some transsexuals may overdo the associated behaviors. Researchers have also noted tendencies among transsexuals to give responses on psychological inventories that are more stereotypically feminine than those given by control groups of women (McCauley & Ehrhardt, 1977).

The sexual practices of those who believe that their biological sex is the wrong one reflect their convictions about their true identities. M-F transsexuals who marry women tend to visualize themselves as women during coitus with their wives (Blanchard, 1993). Transsexuals who have anal intercourse with men do not view the act as homosexual because they believe themselves to be female, regardless of whether they have undergone surgery.

For people who experience no conflict between their anatomy and their gender identity, the desire for sex-reassignment surgery may be the most difficult aspect of transsexualism to comprehend. For many transsexuals, however, the elimination of the penis as well as other reminders of their genetic gender provides a welcome relief.

More than 40 hospitals and clinics in North America have provided transsexuals with therapy and surgery since the first sex-reassignment operation was performed at the Johns Hopkins University Hospital in Baltimore in 1966. Applicants for surgery are first evaluated psychologically; individuals who appear to be suffering from disturbances other than a conflict of gender identity are not accepted for surgery.

Those who are accepted for sex-reassignment surgery are instructed to live as women by adopting women's clothing and a feminine lifestyle for a year or two if they had not already been doing so. If they successfully accommodate to this lifestyle, they are given an estrogenic compound to increase the soft-ness of their skin, the size of their breasts, and the fat deposits on their hips. The growth of facial and body hair is reduced by this hormone, and pubic hair begins to grow in a typically female pattern. Muscle strength and libido diminish, and a gradual reduction takes place in the frequency of erection and ejaculation and the amount of semen. The estrogen treatment does not alter voice pitch, so M-F transsexuals often take lessons to change their voice. The hormonal therapy has little effect on penis length but does reduce the size of the testicles. These effects can be accentuated by administration of drugs that lower testosterone levels (Futterweit, 1998).

If, after a year or more, the person still wishes sex-reassignment surgery, a series of operations is performed. The testes and penis are removed, and silicone may be implanted in the breasts. Labia and a facsimile of a vagina are constructed. The skin of the penis, with its sensitive nerve endings, is laid inside the vagina, and a form is placed within the vagina for several hours each day to keep the grafted skin from growing together. Body and facial hair may be removed by electrolysis or laser light treatment, and plastic surgery may be performed to feminize the person's appearance. With the removal of the testes, the source of sperm and most of the masculinizing hormones is eliminated, and sterility results. M-F transsexuals may engage in sexual intercourse, however, and many report erotic feelings and orgasm after their operations (Rehman, Lazer, Benet, Schaefer and Melman, 1999).

F-M Transsexualism. Although there are some similarities between male and female transsexuals, several studies suggest intriguing differences in both overt behavior and certain aspects of sex-reassignment surgery.

Most F-M transsexuals report having thought of themselves as boys for as long as they can remember, with cross-identification first occurring at about 3 or 4 years of age (Pauly, 1985). Cross-dressing, a preference for boys instead of girls as close friends, and a dislike for dolls and other stereotypically feminine toys during childhood are typical of girls who become transsexuals. If they play house, these girls volunteer for the father role, and their interest in parenthood is confined to fantasies of being a hus-

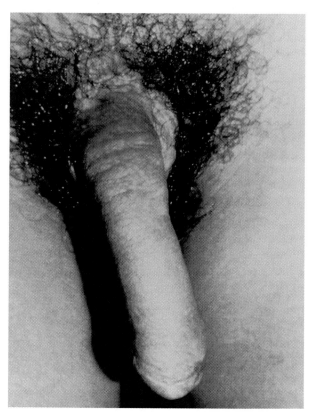

An example of female-to-male sex reassignment surgery.

band and father. In general, they report no interest in handling babies (Ehrhardt et al., 1979).

Most young girls without gender-identity conflicts go through normal transitory periods wherein they express the desire to be a boy and so may be labeled tomboys. Parents need not necessarily be concerned if their daughters engage in tomboyish behavior. For F-M transsexuals, however, the preference for masculine activities and attire persists for years and is coupled with a strong rejection of the feminine role. Their sense of being male despite having anatomical and assigned roles as females is a source of pain and confusion for them (Bullough & Bullough, 1993).

Puberty is an especially difficult time for female transsexuals. Although many girls express fear or disgust upon first experiencing menstruation, particularly when sex education is inadequate, menarche is usually a source of pleasure for them as a symbol of their emerging womanhood. However, F-M transsexuals feel intense revulsion toward menarche and other aspects of female development. Moreover, although girls in our culture commonly exaggerate their developing breasts with the aid of tissues, wadded-up stockings, and the like—understandable behavior, given our society's obsessive interest in breasts—transsexuals commonly report having hidden or bound their developing breasts (Ehrhardt et al., 1979; Steiner, 1985).

Many F-M transsexuals report an awareness of having been attracted to females during early adolescence, but they generally do not begin having sexual relations with women until about five years later, at about the age of 18. Their sexual partners are often markedly feminine, heterosexual women, although some report relationships with gay men (Devor, 1993). During sexual relations, many F-M transsexuals do not allow their partners to see them nude, penetrate their vaginas, or touch their breasts and genitals (McCauley & Ehrhardt, 1980). Of those who do permit touching, most limit the contact to clitoral stimulation. Transsexuals whose clitorises have been enlarged through androgenic compounds often imagine their clitorises to be penises. Pauly's (1985) research suggested that F-M transsexuals take on the masculine role more believably than their M-F counterparts take on the feminine role. The responses of most F-M transsexuals on diagnostic inventories indicate no severe psychological disturbance other than gender-identity conflict (Coleman, Bockting, & Gooren, 1993).

After psychological screening, applicants for F-M sex-reassignment surgery are asked to live as males for a year or more. If they are successful in this adaptation, they are given androgenic compounds. These masculinizing compounds stimulate the growth of facial and body hair, slightly decrease breast size, increase the size of the clitoris, suppress menstruation, and deepen the voice (Asscheman & Gooren, 1992).

If the person still desires surgery after having lived as a male for a year or so, a series of operations is performed. Because it is easier to remove than to add body parts, F-M sex-reassignment surgery is more complex (Lief & Hubschman, 1993) and frequently less successful than surgery for their M-F counterparts.

For some F-M transsexuals, the lack of success with constructing an artificial penis leads them to avoid this surgery, as shown in this excerpt (Brame, Brame, & Jacobs, 1993, p. 424):

> *If you have the female-to-male surgery and get a constructed penis, they take out all the internals, the uterus and ovaries, and they close up the vagina, and they reroute the urethra, which can cause problems later. There's a lot of reconstruction. The male-to-female stuff is peanuts by comparison. Female-to-male is also more expensive than the male-to-female. I was quoted a cost [of] around $60,000. There are other things I can think of to buy with $60,000 than a dick that doesn't work.*

For those who choose to have this surgery, skin from the labia and abdomen is used to fashion a penis and scrotum. An artificial testis may be placed in each side of the scrotum. The penis looks quite realistic, but no surgical procedure at present can create a penis that becomes erect in response to sexual stimulation. Several techniques are available for providing a rigid penis for purposes of sexual penetration. One of these is to make a skin tube on the underside of the penis into which a rigid silicone may be inserted. Although the artificial penis does not respond to physical stimulation, erotic feelings and orgasm remain if the clitoris has been left embedded at the base of the penis. Additional surgery can involve removing the breasts, uterus, and ovaries and sealing off the vagina. Removing the ovaries eliminates eggs and the primary source of estrogen, so, like the M-F transsexual, the F-M transsexual can no longer reproduce.

Ideally, a postsurgical transsexual continues to receive medical follow-up and counseling. Such therapy can also be beneficial to a transsexual's family and lover. Unfortunately, these postoperative practices are not always followed. *Reality or Myth* ?

Controversies About Transsexualism.   Some individuals function in a psychologically healthy fashion except for a deeply felt conflict between anatomical features and psychological gender identity; for them, the use of the term *transsexual* may be appropriate. Sometimes, however, people may mistake other situations for transsexualism. They may blame their inability to deal effectively with various life challenges on a gender-identity conflict. Further, researchers' estimates (Pauly & Edgerton, 1986) indicate that about a third of applicants for sex-reassignment surgery are homosexuals who cannot accept their sexual orientation and apply for reassignment surgery mainly in the hope of bringing their practices into compliance with a heterosexually oriented society. Still other people may view the painful surgery as a method of punishing themselves for real or imagined "sins." None of these individuals fits the definition of a transsexual.

Explanations of Transsexualism.

There is no agreement as to why some people feel an intense conflict over gender identity. Some studies have reported abnormal brain wave patterns in about one-third of transsexuals, but the significance of these findings is still not known (Hoenig, 1985; Pauly, 1974). Postmortem study of the brains of transsexuals has not shown differences between them and "normal" brains (Emory, Williams, Cole, Amparo, & Meyer, 1991).

Hormonal explanations of transsexualism have fared no better. Most adult transsexuals have hormone levels that fall within the normal range for their genetic gender (Jones, 1974; Goodman et al., 1985).

Because gender identity is learned very early in life and most transsexuals report cross-identification well before puberty, the dynamics within the family might be linked to the development of transsexuality. However, no systematic patterns have emerged with respect to parents (Devor, 1997).

Until further research has been done focusing on large samples of transsexuals, the most honest answer we can give to the question of what causes transsexualism is that we do not know. *Reality or Myth* ❓

Treatment: Surgery or Psychotherapy?

Until the 1960s, the U.S. medical profession was generally opposed to sex-reassignment surgery, defining the problem of transsexualism as psychological rather than medical in nature.

To some extent, people's attitudes regarding the appropriateness of surgery depend on what they view as the source of the problem. Virginia Prince (1977) suggested that surgical solutions to conflicts of gender identity represent a confusion between biology and psychology. In her succinctly stated opinion, surgery "is only a painful, expensive, dangerous

and misguided attempt to achieve between the legs what must eventually and inevitably be achieved between the ears." Physicians who are faced with a desperate plea for surgery on the part of a transsexual whose conflict is a source of great pain and who may have contemplated or even attempted suicide obviously have a difficult choice.

Most transsexuals claim to be happier following surgery than prior to it and report that they would go through the procedure again (Lief & Hubschman, 1993; van Kesteren, Gooren, & Megens, 1996). There appear to be sex differences in postsurgical adjustment, however. F-M transsexuals more often have stable relationships with a partner and appear more socially adjusted than M-F transsexuals do (Kockott & Fahrner, 1988; Verschoor & Poortinga, 1988). Psychological adjustment has also been found to be greater in postsurgical transsexuals than in presurgical transsexuals. The quality of the surgery too may affect postsurgical adjustment (Rehman, Lazer, Benet, Schaefer, Melman, 1999).

One study, however, indicates that surgery is not necessarily essential to a transsexual's psychosocial adjustment. A comparison of the social and psychological adjustment of 34 postsurgical transsexuals with the adjustment of 66 transsexuals who did not receive surgery revealed improvements in both groups (Meyer & Reter, 1979). For example, both experienced a 70 percent decrease in the number of visits to psychiatrists over a six-year period.

There is a need for further research to determine whether the operation makes enough of a difference to justify the pain, expense, and drastic anatomical and hormonal alterations. The evidence does clearly suggest, however, that sex-reassignment surgery can alleviate the emotional distress associated with feeling that one is of a different gender than one's anatomy indicates (Green & Fleming, 1990; Pfäfflin, 1992).

Research on transsexualism holds the promise of helping us to unfold the mysteries surrounding the development of sexual and gender identity. As Robert Stoller (1975) pointed out, transsexual surgery is an experiment that researchers would never dare to perform on those with consistent biological sex and psychological gender identities.

Earlier, we alluded to hypotheses that some individuals seeking reassignment surgery may be motivated by the desire to punish themselves for real or imagined "sins." Such a connection between sexuality and the infliction of real or symbolic pain is a theme for those engaging in sadomasochistic activities, a topic to which we turn now.

> ▶ **Issues to Consider:**   Assume that you have a sibling or close friend who is convinced that he or she is really a member of the other gender and is living in the wrong body. Based on what you have read, what advice would you give?

SEXUAL SADISM AND SEXUAL MASOCHISM

Sexual sadism refers to the infliction of physical or psychological pain on another living creature to produce sexual excitement for both partners. In this section, our consideration is limited to consenting partners, for sadism performed on an unwilling victim is sexual assault.

Only pain-inflicting acts that sexually excite the inflictor can be classified as sadistic. In mild forms of sadism, the administering of pain can be primarily symbolic, such as beating someone with a soft object that is designed to resemble a hard club. In these cases, the partner just pretends to be in pain. At the other end of the continuum is the sadist who can become aroused only if the partner is savagely attacked or even murdered. In this case, it is not the corpse that excites the sadist but the victim's suffering and dying. Sadism has traditionally been associated exclusively with men, although we shall see that that stereotype is not supported by the data.

Sexual masochism refers to experiencing sexual arousal by suffering physical or psychological pain that is produced in specific ways. The individual may be aroused by being whipped, cut, pricked, bound, spanked, or verbally humiliated. A masochist responds sexually only to particular sorts of pain. A masochist who becomes sexually aroused while being whipped, for example, does not respond with erection or vaginal lubrication if a car door is slammed on his or her finger. The masochist usually has specific requirements with respect to the manner

sexual sadism—The intentional infliction of pain or humiliation on another person for sexual excitement.
sexual masochism—Sexual gratification through experiencing pain and humiliation.

in which pain is inflicted, the area of the body assaulted, and the person who inflicts the pain. If the pattern is not followed, the pain will lose its arousal power. See "Highlight: Pain and Sexual Arousal" on page 412.

Most information about sadism and masochism comes from clinical case reports, but another source is several questionnaire studies that have been conducted with individuals located through sadomasochistic magazines and clubs (Breslow, Evans, & Langley, 1985; Spengler, 1977). More than half the respondents indicated that they played both dominant and submissive roles within the sadomasochistic context. This finding suggests that many people who participate in sexual activities involving the intentional infliction of pain are more accurately described by the compound term *sadomasochist* than by the single word *sadist* or *masochist*. In one study, 25 percent of respondents were women who were not prostitutes (Breslow et al., 1985). This percentage is surprising in the light of an earlier research conclusion that most women who participate in sadomasochism are prostitutes doing so for financial reasons (Spengler, 1977).

Men indicated that they first became aware of their sadomasochistic interests at around age 15, whereas women reported that they became interested in sadomasochism at about age 22. Men seemed to discover sadomasochism on their own, whereas women tended to be introduced to it by a sexual partner. Both men and women viewed sadomasochism as primarily sexual foreplay. There appear to be more men than women involved in the sadomasochistic subculture, but women respondents who did participate had sadomasochistic sex more often and with more different partners than did men. Table 17.1 (on page 413) shows the respondents' behavioral preferences. The more extreme forms of sexual activity associated with sadomasochism, such as torture and use of excrement, were relatively rare.

The most popular sadomasochistic sexual activities, which include spanking and master-slave relationships, are featured in sadomasochistic magazines and movies. Sadomasochists may belong to special clubs, contact like-minded others on the Internet, or visit prostitutes who indulge their fantasies (Ernulf & Innala, 1995; Chivers & Blanchard, 1996). For many years, Monique von Cleef operated a "House of Torture" in a luxurious 16-room home in Newark, New

Pain and Sexual Arousal

One of the unusual relationships that can exist between the perception of pain and sexual arousal is illustrated in the following excerpt from Brame, Brame, and Jacob's (1993) book, *Different Loving: An Exploration of the World of Sexual Dominance and Submission*:

The real nature of S&M was driven home to me about 15 years ago. I was doing a movie called House of Sin. *There was an S&M scene [with] a mistress and her slave, who were, in real life, living together. She had him on the floor, with his hands tied behind him. She had a dog chain wrapped around his cock and balls and was lifting him off the floor by his cock and balls and smacking him across the nuts, hard enough so that*

every guy in the room had his legs crossed. Two things stuck in my mind: First, that while this was happening, this guy had an incredible erection, and two, as soon as I yelled, "Cut!" he immediately started to bitch and moan about the fact that he was lying on a hardwood floor and didn't have a pillow behind his head. At that moment I realized that what she was doing to his genitals was not painful; the little bit of pressure on the back of his head, that's what his brain was interpreting as pain. But the hard pressure of her hand coming in contact with his nuts was erotically stimulating. I realized that in S&M, if it's painful, you're doing it wrong. (pp. 42–43)

The bondage apparel displayed in this sex-specialty shop is designed for sadomasochistic activities.

TABLE 17.1 A Comparison of the Sadomasochistic Preferences of Females and Males[a]

Interest	Male (%)	Female (%)
Spanking	79	80
Master-slave relationships	79	76
Oral sex	77	90
Masturbation	70	73
Bondage	67	88
Humiliation	65	61
Erotic lingerie	63	88
Restraint	60	83
Anal sex	58	51
Pain	51	34
Whipping	47	39
Rubber/leather	42	42
Boots/shoes	40	49
Verbal abuse	40	51
Stringent bondage	39	54
Enemas	33	22
Torture	32	32
Golden showers	30	37
Transvestism	28	20
Petticoat punishment	25	20
Toilet activities	19	12

[a]Some of these activities are part of the usual sex play of couples; these same activities (e.g., required oral sex, golden showers, erotic lingerie) are considered part of a sadomasochistic pattern when the dominant "demands" it or the submissive "pleads" for it. "Golden showers" refers to urophilia—obtaining erotic pleasure from incorporation of urination in erotic play. "Petticoat punishment" is a form of tranvestism in which the male is made to look ridiculous instead of feminine.

Source: Based on responses to questionnaires completed by people located through sadomasochistic magazines and clubs, by Breslow, Evans, and Langley (1985). *Archives of Sexual Behavior, 14,* p. 315. Copyright 1985 by Plenum Publishing Company. Reprinted by permission.

Jersey. She specialized in sadomasochistic services for men with a sexual affinity for leather. Her employees, whom she called "leather social workers," wore knee-high or hip-high leather boots and leather clothing. When the police raided her establishment, they found card files on more than 15,000 patrons.

Sadomasochistic sexual practices may also include bondage and discipline, a pattern in which a sexual partner is tied up and then sexually stimulated. The exchange may involve dog collars, leashes, and chains but usually follows predetermined patterns and stops short of physical harm.

What seems to be central to sadomasochistic activities is a master-slave relationship. The partner playing the master can exercise complete control over the other person for a time, and the partner playing the slave can give up all personal responsibility. Sexual expression is controlled and predictable in these carefully structured situations (Moser, 1998; Weinberg, 1994), and it is common for couples to engage in elaborate negotiations about their specific roles before beginning sadomasochistic play.

Sadomasochism and Beliefs About Gender Differences. Richard von Krafft-Ebing, the nineteenth-century chronicler of atypical sexuality, believed that sadism was a pathological exaggeration of the normal psychology of men and that masochism was a distorted extension of normal women's sexual inclinations. He saw sadism as an essentially masculine disorder and masochism as a feminine disorder. Krafft-Ebing was apparently unconcerned that the Austrian novelist after whom he named the syndrome of masochism, Leopold von Sacher-Masoch, was a man. Sadism takes its name from the eighteenth-century French writer, the Marquis de Sade.

Like Krafft-Ebing, some psychoanalytic authors also stressed a gender difference in sadomasochism. For example, psychoanalyst Helene Deutsch, in her book *The Psychology of Women* (1944), advanced the belief that human survival depended to some extent on women associating pain with pleasure. She devoted an entire chapter to the topic. However, men and women both engage in sadism, and their masochistic partners are both men and women.

Research on normal populations suggests that there is a *slight* difference in the proportion of men and women who enjoy sadomasochism in some form. For example, Kinsey et al. (1953) found that 22 percent of men and 12 percent of women reported some sexual arousal from sadistic stories. A large number of women and men also reported erotic responses to being bitten, as Table 17.2 (on page 414) shows. Of those who enjoyed being bitten, a little more than half reported that biting frequently accompanied their sexual activities.

There appear to be gender differences, however, in how men and women approach masochism. Male masochism appears to be an escape strategy from the traditional male role (Baumeister, 1988a). Being humiliated and degraded, and sacrificing or postponing

TABLE 17.2   Normal Sadomasochism

Erotic responses to being bitten	By Females (%)	By Males (%)
Definite and/or frequent	26	26
Some response	29	24
Never	45	50
Number of people interviewed	2,200	567
Erotic arousal from sadomasochistic stories		
Definite and/or frequent	3	10
Some response	9	12
Never	88	78
Number of people interviewed	2,800	1,016

Source: Adapted from Kinsey, A.C., Pomeroy, W., Martin, C., Gebhard, P. *Sexual Behavior in the Human Female*, pp. 677–678. Philadelphia: Saunders, 1953. By permission of the Kinsey Institute for Research in Sex, Gender, and Reproduction, Inc.

one's own sexual pleasure, contradict the masculine archetype. This escape from self may reduce high levels of self-awareness and intensify a focus on the immediate present and bodily sensations. Female masochism follows a different route in escaping from one's everyday self by exaggerating the female stereotype. The woman devotes herself to her partner's pleasure, and her role is transformed to "remove responsibility, insecurity, and sexual inhibition" (Baumeister, 1988b, p. 497). Again, we emphasize the difference between consensual sadomasochistic activities versus invasive sadism in which one person attempts to, or does, exert complete control over another person against that person's will.

▶ **Issues to Consider:**   Do you think that men's masochism might be associated with *withdrawal* (escape) from the traditional male role and women's masochism might be associated with an *exaggeration* of the female stereotype? If so, why?

The Invasive Paraphilias

Invasive paraphilias involve behaviors that violate other people's personal space. That is, few people would consent to unexpectedly encountering someone exposing his genitalia to them. Similarly, while undressing or making love in our homes, most of us would not welcome the idea that someone was observing us with binoculars from behind a tree in our backyard. For clinicians to consider a diagnosis of paraphilia, a person must display recurring, intense sexual urges and fantasies—carried out behaviorally—that can disrupt other people's lives. Many people who are arrested for invasive paraphilic behaviors do not qualify for a clinical diagnosis because they do not meet these criteria. They may resort to the paraphilia for lack of a socially appropriate sex partner, because of an unusual opportunity, or out of a desire to experiment. As we consider the major paraphilias, it is important to remember that personal or subjective considerations often play a greater role in labeling a person as sexually atypical than do objective, scientific facts (Levine & Troiden, 1988).

VOYEURISM

Voyeurism refers to obtaining sexual gratification by observing others without their consent who are un-

voyeurism (VOY-yer-ism)—Obtaining sexual arousal by observing people without their consent when they are undressed or engaging in sexual activity.

These waitresses most likely consider the male looking they encounter on the job "normal" rather than voyeuristic.

dressing, naked, or participating in sexual activity. Many people enjoy observing nudity and sexual activity, as the popularity of erotic literature and X-rated movies and videotapes demonstrates. You may therefore wonder where the dividing line is between "normal" looking and voyeurism. After all, in our culture, watching women has been as accepted a male pastime as watching the Super Bowl, and it is certainly a component of courtship behavior. In their national sample, Laumann et al. (1994) found that, for men, watching their partners undress was a more popular sexual activity than receiving oral sex.

Although women traditionally have been assumed to possess little interest in the uncovered bodies of men, the popularity of male strip shows, male go-go dancers, and photos of men in women's magazines such as *Cosmopolitan* is evidence to the contrary. Like girl watching, women's interest in these phenomena is considered normal rather than voyeuristic. In Laumann et al.'s (1994) national sample,

women rated watching their partners undress as just slightly less appealing than receiving oral sex.

Looking becomes voyeurism, a criminal offense, when the voyeur observes people who are unaware that they are being watched or are unwilling to be observed. Because only a few states prohibit voyeurism, voyeurs are often prosecuted under antiloitering and disorderly conduct laws. For the voyeur, the viewing of strangers without consent is the primary or preferred sexual activity.

Convicted voyeurs are almost always men. Many women enjoy observing nude men, but women seldom invest the energy required to seek out unsuspecting men for observation. This sex difference may stem from cultural constraints against women's actively seeking out sexual stimuli. Alternatively, the difference may be due to men's greater receptivity or sensitivity to visual sexual stimuli. One hypothesis holds that men's keener interest in visual sexual stimuli is rooted in our evolutionary past. That is, women's physical attractiveness may have symbolized general health and therefore reproductive fitness. Male sexual arousal at the sight of nude or partially nude females was therefore a critical part of the process leading to reproduction (Symons, 1979).

Ford and Beach's (1951) review of cross-cultural studies showed that no group in the sample allowed women to expose their genitals except under restricted circumstances. This prohibition prevents accidental exposure under conditions that might provoke unwanted sexual advances by men toward women, thus preserving women's opportunity to choose a mate with qualities of reproductive fitness. Margaret Mead (1967) pointed out that girls are permanently clothed before boys are in all societies that have been studied. She maintained that because older boys and men find young girls attractive, the bodies of young girls, as well as of their older sisters and mothers, must be guarded from the male eye.

It is also possible that there are more women voyeurs than arrest and conviction records indicate. A man out for a walk who stops to view a nude woman in a window may be arrested for voyeurism. But if a man undresses in front of a window and a woman stops to look, the man may be as likely to be arrested for exhibitionism as the woman for voyeurism. Police and court records may reflect this bias. *Reality or Myth*

Characteristics of Voyeurs. Voyeurs tend to be young and male, with the average age at first conviction being 24 (Gebhard, Gagnon, Pomeroy, & Christenson, 1965). Paul Gebhard and his associates found that few voyeurs had serious mental disorders, and alcohol or drugs were seldom involved in their "peeping." Some voyeurs resemble other sex offenders in that they display deficient sexual relationships, but others are able to interact sexually with consenting partners with no evidence of dysfunction.

The voyeur derives sexual arousal from the notion that he is violating the privacy of his victims. Like practitioners of other criminal sexual variations, the "peeping tom" may be stimulated by the danger of apprehension. The willingness to run risks is what distinguishes the voyeur from the average woman watcher. The voyeur may scale high fences, bore holes in bedroom walls, risk injury from watchdogs, and endure terrible weather conditions to observe what excites him. The act of looking is usually accompanied by sexual excitement, and frequently by orgasm. Sometimes the voyeur masturbates while he is gazing at unsuspecting targets, or he may do so later when remembering the scene.

As with other paraphilias, the cause of voyeurism is not known. Behaviorists emphasize that the initial association of sexual arousal with peeping may be accidental. If a male masturbates while peeping or later while recalling the act in fantasy, the association is strengthened. Repeated incidents can lead to reliance on peeping as the main source of sexual arousal.

Some psychoanalysts trace the disorder back to childhood episodes in which the child witnessed his parents having intercourse, but there is no research that supports this hypothesis. For persons who have poorly developed social and sexual skills, voyeurism provides a means of sexual gratification that avoids the potential threat of sexual interaction. Taking the risk of being caught may bolster the voyeur's often deficient sense of masculinity, just as it does for the exhibitionist.

Exhibitionism

Exhibitionism refers to obtaining erotic gratification from displaying one's genitals. The public display of

exhibitionism—Obtaining sexual gratification by exposing one's genitals to an unwilling observer.

the genitals, or indecent exposure, is illegal in every state. Exposing one's genitals to another person in private is, of course, a normal part of sexual interaction. It is only when this activity becomes the primary or preferred source of sexual gratification and involves unwilling or unsuspecting victims that it becomes problematic.

As with most other paraphilias, exhibitionism is almost exclusively a male activity. There are only three published cases of exhibitionism in women who were not retarded, epileptic, or schizophrenic (Arndt, 1991). Whereas exhibitionism by a man is seen as threatening, a woman's partial or full exposure of her breasts or genitals is usually perceived as seductive, even though it is technically criminal if done publicly. Because strippers and nude models—both men and women—shed their clothes primarily for economic gain rather than for sexual pleasure, they are not considered exhibitionists.

Exhibitionism is the most common sexual offense, accounting for about a third of all sex-crime arrests (Arndt, 1991). Generally, indecent exposure is a misdemeanor unless it is committed under "aggravating" circumstances, which include having minors as victims or having a number of previous convictions for indecent exposure. Exhibitionism occurs primarily during warm weather (May to September), in the middle of the week, between 3:00 P.M. and 6:00 P.M., and in public settings (Arndt, 1991; MacDonald, 1973). Contrary to the American Psychiatric Association's definition of exhibitionism as involving the baring of the genitals to strangers, a study of college women found that 36 percent of the reported exposure episodes involved men whom the victims knew (Cox, 1988). A change in the psychiatric definition of exhibitionism therefore may be appropriate.

It is common for the exhibitionist to have an erection when he exposes himself. About half of one sample of 130 exhibitionists reported always or almost always having erections when exhibiting (Langevin et al., 1979). Almost half this group reported masturbating when exposing themselves.

Many exhibitionists use the episode as a source of fantasy for later masturbation. There is evidence to suggest that indulging in such fantasies during masturbation may be critical in the development and maintenance of exhibitionist behavior (Blair & Lanyon, 1981).

This stripper is not an exhibitionist if her exposure does not excite her sexually.

▶ **Issues to Consider:**   Why do you think that the exposure of men's genitals is a crime and women's exposure of their genitals is usually commercial entertainment?

Characteristics of Exhibitionists. Exhibitionistic men are typically in their 20s the first time they expose themselves (Arndt, 1991). The most frequent targets of these displays are 16- to 30-year-old women (Langevin et al., 1979). A substantial number of men in the Langevin et al. study (1979) wanted the women to whom they exposed themselves to be impressed by the size of their penises. They described the desire for sexual relationships with their victims as a secondary motivation.

Exhibitionists generally score in the normal range on measures of intelligence, personality, and psychological adjustment (Arndt, 1991; Levin & Stava,

1987). Although no difference in testosterone levels has been found between exhibitionists and other men, certain biological conditions may contribute to exhibitionism. Some developmentally disabled individuals may not be fully aware of the social disapproval associated with the exposure of their genitals at inappropriate times and places. Similarly, older men may suffer from senility that can lead to decreased self-control.

All definitions of exhibitionism include the association of exposure with sexual excitement. The sexual arousal may be generated by the response of the women to whom men expose themselves. However, nearly half the 130 exhibitionists whom Langevin et al. (1979) studied reported that they exposed themselves without physical gratification. These men may be as motivated by the thrill-seeking aspect of risking arrest for their exhibitionism as they are by its overt

What is shown in this photo—voyeurism, exhibitionism, or self-expression?

deter them from subsequent "flashing." One-third of the convicted offenders in one study had four to six previous convictions, and another 10 percent had been convicted seven times or more (Gebhard et al., 1965). This recidivism rate may reflect the fact that many exhibitionists display themselves repeatedly in the same place and at the same time of day with seeming disregard of the danger of being rearrested.

Many exhibitionists expose themselves even when they have opportunities for consensual sexual contact. A wife or lover can admire an exhibitionist's penis for only so long. Perhaps "the exhibitionist may be like an actor on the stage who wants an audience but does not want it to participate in his act" (Langevin et al., 1979, p. 328).

Although most experts consider exhibitionism and voyeurism to be distinct syndromes, many individuals indulge in both activities and a number of other invasive sexual behaviors as well, including rape. Using interviews and guaranteeing confidentiality, Gene Abel and Jeanne Rouleau (1990) found that a group of 142 men incarcerated for exhibitionism had committed a total of 71,696 invasive paraphilic acts, only a quarter of which were exhibitionism. Some of these men reported 10 different kinds of invasive paraphilias, including rape. Of a group of more than 600 men referred to a clinic for sexual offenses, all those who had engaged in voyeurism also had committed other sexual offenses (Langevin, Paitich, & Russon, 1985). Exhibitionism and voyeurism are almost always related to other paraphilias. Thus, targets of these paraphilias should not treat them as harmless. Instead, they should get away from the perpetrator as quickly as they can and report the behavior to police. *Reality or Myth* ?

sexual aspects. For many exhibitionists, self-exposure may be a way of compensating for timidity and lack of assertiveness. The exhibitionistic act may make them feel like powerful men, and the danger of being apprehended and prosecuted as criminals may contribute to this feeling. The psychoanalytic view of exhibitionism fits with this general picture: it is thought that by displaying the penis, exhibitionists seek to prove to the world and, most important, to adult women that they are indeed men.

The association of masculinity with exposing must be extremely powerful, because being convicted of a sex offense can result in social and professional ruin. Once ruined, many exhibitionists have little to

Obscene Telephone Calls. People who describe sexual activities to a listener over the telephone can be thought of as exhibitionists who "exhibit" verbally. Like the man who exposes his genitals, the obscene caller enjoys the frightened or startled response of the victim. Masturbation during or shortly after making the call is common, and almost all obscene calls are made by men rather than women. In one study, 61 percent of women had received obscene phone calls (Herold, Mantle, & Zemitis, 1979).

The recipient of such telephone calls can be unnerved if the calls are made repeatedly by someone who breathes heavily or describes sexual acts. Nevertheless, a person who receives an obscene telephone call should try to react in a calm manner and get off the telephone as quickly as possible. A man recently called our house purportedly wanting to do a survey on female lingerie, and he has called many of our women students with the same ploy. When I (E.R.A.) answered the phone and heard his pitch, I said, "Certainly. Just let me turn on the speaker phone so that my husband can hear." The caller immediately hung up. Anyone who is the recipient of such repeated calls should report them to the telephone company and the police (even if that person has caller ID). Persistent obscene calls can sometimes be traced.

FROTTEURISM

Frotteurism is characterized by touching or rubbing one's body against a nonconsenting person, usually a woman. The frotteur typically rubs his penis, usually covered, against a woman to achieve sexual arousal and/or orgasm. Subways, buses, and other crowded situations provide opportunities for such gratification, which typically elicits either little notice or only minor annoyance from the target.

Frotteurism often occurs in conjunction with other paraphilias. In one study, almost 70 percent of men referred for frotteurism were also found to have been involved in voyeurism, exhibitionism, or rape (Freund & Blanchard, 1986).

The paraphilias that we have described—voyeurism, exhibitionism, and frotteurism—are also behaviors that pedophiles, people who are sexually attracted to children, may practice.

PEDOPHILIA

The term **pedophilia** has its origin in Greek and literally means "love of children." The pedophile, or sexual abuser of children, is usually envisioned as a dirty old man who lures an innocent young girl into

a dark alley or the woods, where he rapes her. Men incarcerated for child sexual abuse tend to be the prisoners whom guards and other prisoners most despise, and are regarded with even more disgust and rage than are rapists of adult women. How accurate is this stereotype of pedophiles as "dirty old men"? At the outset, we should note that people who sexually approach children (primarily men) are usually either related to or acquaintances of the youngsters.

Those convicted of sexual offenses against minors tend to be older than other convicted sex offenders. Their average age at conviction is 35, and about a quarter are over age 45 (Arndt, 1991; Gebhard et al., 1965). Past clinical and survey literature has described the pedophile as conservative, socially inadequate, psychosexually immature, and psychologically disturbed, but in their review of the literature, Paul Okami and Amy Goldberg (1992) found no evidence to support these assumptions. Even if we consider only convicted child sex offenders, clear-cut psychiatric disturbance is not generally apparent, although many child offenders tend toward shyness, loneliness, low self-esteem, isolation, and sensitivity to the evaluations of others (Okami & Goldberg, 1992). In general, the younger the victim is, the more likely it is that the sexual offender exhibits psychopathology (Kalichman, 1991). Similar to sexually coercive college men (see Chapter 19), convicted offenders of sexual crimes against children do not appear to lack appropriate social skills (Koralewski & Conger, 1992; Okami & Goldberg, 1992). Further, an anonymous survey of almost 200 college men indicated that about a fifth felt sexual attraction toward some small children, and 7 percent indicated some likelihood of having sex with a child if they would not be caught or punished (Briere & Runtz, 1989). Although attraction to children was associated with a number of negative attitudes toward women and with negative early sexual experiences, men in Briere and Runtz's sample reporting attraction and fantasies about young children did not differ from other men in levels of sexual repression or impulse control.

There is some evidence that men who attempt to have sexual contact with children adjust their sexual behaviors to the age level of their partner or victim (Okami & Goldberg, 1992). That is, they will engage in the early stages of a normal courtship

---

frotteurism—Obtaining sexual arousal by touching or rubbing one's body against the body of an unsuspecting or nonconsenting person.

pedophilia (PEH-doe-FIL-ee-ah)—Sexual contact between an adult and a child.

sequence, looking and touching, but they generally avoid more intimate forms of sexual contact. In only 4 percent of cases that Finkelhor (1979) studied did the prepubescent girls report that coitus had occurred between them and the offender. The contact was confined to exhibitionism in 20 percent of the episodes and to touching and fondling of the genitals in another 38 percent of child-adult sexual interactions.

A primary and relatively permanent sexual interest in children (true pedophilia) actually characterizes only a quarter to a third of imprisoned child molesters. The rest of those convicted of the offense appear to have made advances to a child for situational reasons; that is, the contact occurred during periods of stress, frustration, or lack of other sexual outlets or during an unusual opportunity (Arndt, 1991; Gebhard et al., 1965).

If a person develops a sexual interest in children, how is this interest translated into behavior? From time to time, all of us experience arousal under inappropriate conditions or toward inappropriate people, and we choose not to act on our arousal. You may feel attracted to your best friend's partner, or you may get inexplicably "turned on" while sitting in class one day, but you inhibit your feelings to avoid hurting your friends or embarrassing yourself. The sexual abuser, however, may be disinhibited as a result of various factors, a major one being alcohol.

Cognitive distortions or unusual thought processes are also thought to allow the offender to bypass his normal inhibitions. In a study of 101 child sex offenders undergoing treatment, the following cognitive distortions were the most frequently mentioned when the men were asked to report what they were thinking at the time of the offense (Neidigh & Krop, 1992, p. 212):

> *"She enjoyed it."*
>
> *"This won't hurt her or affect her in any way."*
>
> *"This is not so bad, it's not really wrong."*
>
> *"I was high on alcohol or drugs at the time."*
>
> *"I wasn't thinking at all or I wouldn't have done it."*
>
> *"No one will ever find out so I won't get caught."*
>
> *"She is flirting and teasing me, she wants me to do it."*

It has also been suggested that the exposure of pedophiles to child pornography may incite them to act on their sexual fantasies about children (Russell, 1984). Experimental research relevant to this hypothesis is not available because no one has yet been able to design ethically acceptable research to test it. It is apparent that we know very little about pedophilia beyond clinical observations. We hope that knowledge about this behavior will improve in the near future.

We have several more paraphilias to describe, but before proceeding to them, we address the extent to which societal responses to adult attempts to use children sexually are likely to alter the behavior of the adult. *Reality or Myth* ⁉️

SEXUAL PREDATOR LAWS

A number of jurisdictions in North America have passed laws requiring public notification when incarcerated sex offenders have completed their sentences and are released back into society. In the United States, six states have enacted sexual predator laws,

A completed prison sentence, therapy, and statements of remorse do not deter neighbors of this Massachusetts man convicted of child abuse from harassing him.

and an additional 30 states are likely to do so in the near future (Collins, 1997). How effective are such public notification laws likely to be?

In a thought-provoking analysis of the potential impact of such laws, Paul Fedoroff and Beverly Moran (1997) suggest five reasons why such laws may have the opposite effect of what is intended. First, the most common form of adult-child sexual contact involves a parent or stepparent of the child. The other parent and child, of course, are already aware of the former offender's past behavior. Second, many sex offenders tend to be very adept at deceiving children, rendering public notification relatively ineffective for the specific children the adult may target. Third, as a group, adults who sexually approach children are not typically competent at establishing stable relationships with appropriate adult partners; public notification is likely to impede their ability to do so further. Fourth, such laws may increase the difficulty that former offenders have in seeking therapy—therapy that they should have received while in prison but generally did not. Fifth, public notification laws about adults after they have completed their prison terms may lead many offenders to believe that it is the community's responsibility, rather than their own, to monitor and control their behavior.

To their list, we add a sixth reason: the phenomenon of the self-fulfilling prophecy. That is, our behavior tends to be influenced by the expectations of others. In the presence of others who expect us to be, say, honorable and competent, the likelihood of our performing in those ways increases. In contrast, when faced with a person or persons who thinks we will try to cheat, or are incapable of particular tasks, we are likely to perform more poorly. For a simple example of this, think about when you were learning to drive. Did your performance vary as a function of whether you were being accompanied by a highly critical person versus someone who behaved on the assumption that you would be able to maneuver the car competently? If former sex offenders have received some therapy or treatment and have resolved to control their sexual interest in children, they are probably less likely to be successful if everyone in their environment expects them to approach children sexually.

Fedoroff and Moran (1997) were not questioning the need for mandatory reporting laws that require mental health care professionals to report ongoing or imminent sexual abuse or assault to authorities. They argued that such reporting laws are needed to protect those at risk of attack; reporting could be helpful in providing therapy for the offender by communicating to the adult that illegal sexual approaches are not acceptable.

Some of the more controversial sexual predator laws include not only requirements for community notification regarding offenders who are being released, but also are designed to make it more difficult for offenders to be released directly into the community from prison. Although these offenders are supposed to receive treatment while in prison, most do not. Leroy Hendricks, for example, was sentenced to 10 years in prison for taking "indecent liberties" with two 13-year-old boys. He completed his term in 1994 but, according to a report in *Time* (July 7, 1997), as soon as he left prison in Hutchinson, Kansas, he was taken to a "correctional mental health facility," where he remains locked up. In the year of his release from prison, Kansas had passed the Sexually Violent Predator Act, which allows judges to order offenders like Hendricks to be confined indefinitely. The judge had ruled that Hendricks's "mental abnormality" rendered him likely to offend again. Although Hendricks and his lawyers challenged the constitutionality of a law that allows incarceration on the basis of what someone might do in the future, the U.S. Supreme Court upheld the law in a 5-to-4 decision in the summer of 1997. Speaking for the majority, Justice Clarence Thomas was quoted as saying, "It cannot be said that the involuntary civil confinement of a limited subclass of dangerous persons is contrary to our understanding of ordered liberty" (Collins, 1997, p. 29). We found this rather contorted sentence ironic in the face of Thomas's experience during his confirmation hearings when Anita Hill alleged that he had engaged in sexual harassment (see Chapter 18).

Although we share the concerns that Fedoroff and Moran (1997) expressed and Collins (1997) reported about the effectiveness and constitutionality of some of the sexual predator laws, current research

▶ **Issues to Consider:** What steps would you recommend to protect children's safety while also guarding the civil rights of adult offenders who have completed their sentences?

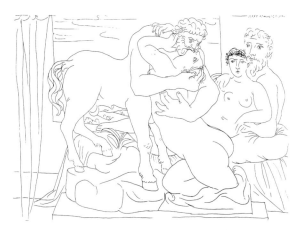

Picasso's etching of the centaur and a woman. Artistic depictions of sexual contact between humans and animals stretch back to the beginnings of recorded history.

clearly indicates that, in the absence of therapeutic interventions, the best predictor of future behavior is past behavior. The implication of that robust finding is not repressive sexual predator laws but the need for effective treatment approaches, a topic to which we shall return at the end of this chapter.

ZOOPHILIA

A human's sexual interaction with a member of another species—a dog, horse, or sheep, for example—is known as **zoophilia**, or bestiality. The use of animals as the preferred or exclusive means of obtaining erotic pleasure is relatively rare; most often an animal is employed sexually because the person currently lacks a human partner.

References to sexual contact between animals and humans appear throughout recorded history. Such contact is depicted often in ancient mythology and classical art. Some modern pornography also contains depictions of sexual relations between humans (usually women) and animals. It has been suggested that devotees of this kind of pornography are excited by the degradation of the woman rather than by the sexual activity itself.

Incidence and Characteristics. About 8 percent of men and 4 percent of women in the Kinsey group's (1948, 1953) samples reported having had sexual experience with animals, with considerably higher rates among boys raised on farms. About 17 percent of farm boys experienced sexual arousal to the point of orgasm as a result of contact with animals. The same percentage of boys had animal contacts that did not result in orgasm. Coitus with animals such as calves and sheep was the most common form of sexual interaction reported by the Kinsey group's adolescent male volunteers. In another common pattern, reported especially among residents of urban areas, household pets—most often dogs and sometimes cats—stimulated their owners' genitals.

The great majority of animal contacts that the Kinsey group's male volunteers reported occurred during adolescence, prior to the beginning of sexual relations with other people. By adulthood, most of the men had abandoned their sexual contacts with animals.

It appears that substantial numbers of people find observation of animals in coitus to be sexually arousing (see Table 17.3). Almost a third of the men and 16 percent of the women in the Kinsey (1953) group reported that they had experienced an erotic response when observing copulating animals.

In addition to arguing that sexual contact with animals per se was not aberrant, Kinsey expressed concern over the fact that the laws in most states treat bestiality as a crime and punish it with stiff prison terms. Kinsey suggested that the incidence of sex with animals closely paralleled that of prostitution and homosexuality, and thus he questioned whether zoophilia should even be classified as a paraphilia.

NECROPHILIA AND MISCELLANEOUS "PHILIAS"

Having sexual relations with a corpse is called **necrophilia**. Clinically, necrophilia differs from extreme sadism in that the source of sexual excitement appears to have nothing to do with the pain or death of the sex object. Instead, the excitement is associated with the corpse.

Despite jokes about morticians who enjoy sex with corpses, necrophilia appears to be extremely

zoophilia (ZOO-oh-FIL-ee-ah)—Sexual activity with animals.

necrophilia—Sexual arousal and/or activity with a corpse.

TABLE 17.3 Erotic Responses to Observing Animals in Coitus

Erotic Response	By Females (%)	By Males (%)
Definite and/or frequent	5	11
Some	11	21
Never	84	68
Number of people interviewed	5,250	4,082

Source: Adapted from Kinsey, A.C., Pomeroy, W., Martin, C., Gebhard, P. *Sexual Behavior in the Human Female*, p. 663. Philadelphia: Saunders, 1953. By permission of the Kinsey Institute for Research in Sex, Gender, and Reproduction, Inc.

rare. Those few persons who have reported necrophilic behavior typically have had severe emotional problems. After a man was discovered fondling a woman's corpse in an Iowa funeral home, legislators were unable to find any law banning such behavior, so they passed a bill to outlaw sexual abuse of a corpse in 1996.

One of the more bizarre "philias" involves using a rope, belt, or something similar to apply pressure to one's neck, thus decreasing the oxygen supply to the brain and elevating the carbon-dioxide level in the blood. This produces a state of euphoria that enhances the pleasure derived from masturbation to orgasm. Tragically, this practice, called **asphyxiophilia,** often leads to death by hanging even though the victim may have tried to use safety mechanisms to avoid death (Innala & Ernulf, 1989). Estimates are that between 500 and 1,000 deaths occur yearly in the United States as a result of asphyxiophilia (McAnulty, 1995).

See "Highlight: Uncommon Paraphilias" (on page 424) for a listing of other such practices.

COMPULSIVE SEXUAL BEHAVIOR

Many individuals who engage in paraphilic behaviors would be described by psychologist Patrick Carnes (1983, 1991) as "sexual addicts." Just as alcoholism or drug dependency involves an obsessive

asphyxiophilia—Elevation of carbon dioxide in the blood via reduction of oxygen to the brain by applying pressure to the neck with a rope or belt during arousal and orgasm. Supposedly enhances the intensity of orgasm but sometimes results in accidental death.

relationship with a mood-altering chemical, so "sexual addiction" supposedly involves a pathological relationship with mood-altering sexual experiences. According to Carnes, who was instrumental in developing a new disorder and then providing a "treatment," sexual addiction progresses through a four-step cycle that intensifies with each repetition:

1. *Preoccupation*—a trancelike engrossment in thoughts of sex, which creates a compulsive search for sexual stimulation.

2. *Ritualization*—special routines that precede sexual behavior and intensify sexual arousal and excitement.

3. *Compulsive sexual behavior*—the sexual act itself, which addicts are unable to control or stop.

4. *Despair*—the feeling of utter hopelessness that addicts of every kind have about their behavior.

Trancelike states are often a part of intense sexual encounters in normal relationships. The despair that the person experiences after the sexual act can be numbed or alleviated by sexual preoccupation, which begins the cycle anew. Taken to the extreme, the individual is preoccupied with sex and intensifies this preoccupation through rituals. For example, the exhibitionist may develop a number of regular routes that he ritualistically follows at certain times when he wants to expose himself. Eventually the compulsive sexual behavior begins to be noticed because the person can no longer control it. Carnes advocates treatment based on family therapy and the Alcoholics Anonymous program's 12-step treatment model. Adequate information is lacking about the effectiveness of this approach for reducing compulsive sexual behavior.

H I G H L I G H T

Uncommon Paraphilias

In addition to the paraphilias that we have already described in some detail, some people are aroused by other objects that most people do not find sexually stimulating. *Partialism* refers to an exclusive focus on a particular part of the body for arousal. *Coprophilia* is arousal associated with feces, either depositing them on the partner or having them deposited on oneself. *Urophilia* is similar, except that the arousal stems from urine instead of feces. *Klismaphilia* refers to arousal from receiving enemas.

A person occasionally experiencing arousal from one of these sources might not be diagnosed as having a paraphilia needing treatment unless the person is very distressed by it. The *DSM-IV* differentiates between persons with mild (has fantasies or urges but has never acted on them), moderate (has occasionally acted on them), and severe (has repeatedly acted on them) paraphilic urges.

The concept of sexual addiction or compulsion is highly controversial (Coleman, 1991; Levine & Troiden, 1988). As John Money (1988) suggested, the notion of addiction to sex is not logical. In the context of sexual arousal, there can only be addiction to some*thing* or some*one*. Observing that an alcoholic is not addicted to thirst but to alcohol, Money noted that the logical treatment outcome for sexual "addiction" would be sexual abstinence. Levine and Troiden (1988) expressed concern about the invention of a new "disease" that could threaten the liberties of sexually variant people. These criticisms of the notion of sexual addiction are especially revealing when we consider that the medical establishment defined masturbation, oral sex, homosexuality, and high numbers of sexual partners ("promiscuity") as forms of mental illness in the first edition of the *DSM* in 1952. The fact that these behaviors are no longer considered pathological reflects altered social values rather than advances in clinical research.

Treatment of the Invasive Paraphilias

The public's widespread sense of moral outrage toward paraphiliacs is reflected in many of the painful and dubious treatments administered to individuals who engage in paraphilias. Electroconvulsive therapy or shock treatment, castration, and mood-altering drugs have all been used at one time or another to treat sexual offenders.

PSYCHOTHERAPY

Conventional counseling or psychotherapy has not been very effective in modifying paraphiliacs' behavior. Success rates in this area compare with those of standard psychotherapy treating drug addiction or alcoholism. The reasons for the poor track record of traditional treatments are unclear. Some researchers have speculated that the unusual behavior is crucial for paraphiliacs' mental stability (Stoller, 1977). According to this view, without their paraphilia, patients would undergo severe mental deterioration.

Another view is that although people are punished for sexual deviance, they also experience rewards. For example, paraphiliacs whose activities make them vulnerable to arrest, such as exhibitionists, voyeurs, and pedophiliacs, seem to have a strong need to run great risks. The constant danger of arrest may become as arousing as the sexual activity itself.

The difficulties encountered in treating paraphiliacs may be related to the restrictive and often emotionally impoverished environments that many of them experienced as children and adolescents. It is difficult to undo the effects of years of conditioning in one or two hours of therapy per week. Convicted sex offenders report more physical and sexual abuse in their childhood than do those convicted of nonsexual crimes (Barbaree, Hudson, & Seto, 1993), but there is little scientific evidence for the abuse-to-abuser hypothesis (Fedoroff & Moran, 1997). That is, many people who were abused during childhood do not engage in the abuse of others when they become adults, and many adults convicted of sex offenses did not experience abuse during their own childhoods.

All explanations of the paraphilias are still speculative. Attempts to treat these problems, however, have not been deterred by the scarcity of information about them.

SURGICAL CASTRATION

"It is evident that castration turns the clock back to medieval times, when amputation of the hands was practiced as a means of curing thievery" (Heim & Hursch, 1979, p. 303). We would amend the "medieval" by noting that in some Islamic countries (e.g., Afghanistan, Iran, and Saudi Arabia), this is still a common practice. In the past, castration was used for many reasons: to prevent procreation by those who were judged undesirable, to punish certain crimes, and, more recently, to treat violent sexual offenders. Castration was recommended as a treatment for "sexual overexcitement" in the late eighteenth century and was first used as a therapy in 1889 (Karpman, 1954). Castration can involve removal of the testes or the entire external genital system, including the penis. Castration for "therapeutic" purposes involves removal of the testes only.

Although the surgical castration of incarcerated sexual offenders is not unknown in North America, it has been practiced on a much wider scale in some northern European countries. The appeal of castration as a treatment for sexual offenders lies in the belief that testosterone, produced by the testes, is necessary for sexual behavior.

This reasoning has a straightforward appeal, but we hope by now you are convinced that the causes of sexual behavior are far more complicated than this surgical treatment suggests. Reducing the amount of testosterone in the blood system does not always change sexual behavior. Contrary to the prevalent myth that the sex offender has an abnormally strong sex drive, many sex offenders have little sexual desire or are sexually dysfunctional (Gebhard et al., 1965; Groth & Burgess, 1977). Presumably castration would not have a marked effect on the behavior of an offender who already had a weak sex drive.

There is substantial evidence that the effect of castration on male sex drive is strongly influenced by an individual's psychological attitude toward castration. As Ford and Beach (1951, p. 232) stated:

We consider it more probable that some men, being convinced in advance that the operation will deprive them of potency, actually experience a lessening of sexual ability. Other individuals unprejudiced by such anticipatory effects are able to copulate frequently despite loss of hormonal support.

The diverse effects of castration on sex offenders were illustrated in West Germany (Heim, 1981). Questionnaires were mailed to a group of sex criminals who had been castrated before release from prison. These individuals had been out of jail for periods ranging from 4 months to 13 years. They reported sharp reductions in the frequency of coitus, masturbation, sexual thoughts, sex drive, and sexual arousability. Almost a third of the men, however, could still have sexual intercourse.

CHEMICAL TREATMENT

Some treatments involve the administration of chemicals to inhibit desire in sex offenders. Chemical treatment has the same goal as surgical castration, but with a major advantage for the offender: he keeps his testes.

Estrogens have been found to reduce sex drive in paraphilic men, but they are no longer used because they can have feminizing effects on the male physique, including enlargement of the breasts (Bradford & Greenberg, 1996). In contrast, there are antiandrogenic drugs that interfere with the action of testosterone but do not feminize the body. Medroxyprogesterone (MPA; trade name, Depo-Provera) and cyproterone acetate (CPA), the most commonly used antiandrogens in North America, block the effects of testosterone on the target organs. This treatment does not affect the direction of sexual behavior, but it does reduce or inhibit sexual response. In 1996, California passed a law requiring repeat child sex offenders to undergo weekly injections of Depo-Provera. Clinical studies indicate that these antiandrogens are fairly effective in suppressing sexual fantasy, desire, and arousal in men (Bradford & Bradford, 1996). When used in conjunction with counseling, they benefit some sex offenders. The best candidates for this treatment are self-referred, highly motivated men with good social support (Cooper, 1986).

Antidepressant medications have also been used successfully to treat paraphilias (Kafka, 1997). The theory is that many paraphilic disorders stem from an underlying imbalance of brain chemicals, particularly serotonin, and administering the antidepressants restores the balance.

These chemicals offer considerable promise in treating sex offenders. Nevertheless, adequate empirical studies of the effects of these chemicals on sexual behavior are still needed, and side effects and short- and long-term behavior changes need to be assessed. Chemical treatments are often combined with cognitive-behavior therapies.

▶ **Issues to Consider**   Do you believe that the government has the right to require surgical or chemical treatment for sex offenders?

COGNITIVE-BEHAVIOR THERAPIES

Cognitive-behavior therapists teach techniques to decrease or control paraphiliac sexual motivation and behavior. The cognitive component involves modifying distorted beliefs or cognitions that paraphiliacs use to justify their behavior. Most comprehensive cognitive-behavior therapy programs generally include the following components (Abel, Osborn, Anthony, & Gardos, 1992, p. 256):

1. Behavior therapy to reduce inappropriate sexual arousal and to enhance or maintain appropriate sexual arousal.

2. Training to develop or to enhance prosocial skills.

3. Modification of distorted cognitions and development of victim empathy.

4. Relapse prevention.

An example of a comprehensive cognitive-behavior approach to the treatment of exhibitionism was reported by Marshall, Eccles, and Barbaree (1991). They instructed exhibitionists to carry smelling salts (which have an unpleasant odor) to inhale whenever they felt the urge to expose themselves. This helped the offender to develop control over his thoughts by associating aversive smell with deviant fantasies. Additional aspects of this program include training in assertiveness and stress management, changing cognitive distortions through role playing, and training in relationship skills. Recent cognitive-behavioral therapies have been shown to be effective in treating paraphilias and reducing repeat offenses (Abel et al., 1992; Pithers, 1993).

OTHER APPROACHES

In addition to the medical and cognitive-behavior therapies, a wide range of other therapeutic techniques can help clients develop more socially approved sexual arousal patterns and skills. For example, in directed masturbation therapy, the client is instructed to masturbate to socially acceptable sexual fantasies and to cease masturbating to paraphilic themes (Laws & Marshall, 1991). As the client learns that he can successfully masturbate to nondeviant themes, he gradually changes his self-definition from sexually deviant to normal. Other approaches include family or systems psychotherapy, group therapy, psychoanalysis, and systematic desensitization.

A factor complicating the effective treatment of convicted sex offenders is the reality that therapy typically is conducted while the offenders are incarcerated, in either psychiatric hospitals or prison environments. Prisons tend to have small numbers of therapists, and, given their caseloads, they often can offer only minimal treatment. In addition, prisons lack appropriate partners with whom sex offenders might try to initiate consenting sexual behaviors.

Despite these problems, cognitive-behavior therapies and chemical approaches appear to be effective in treating sex offenders. The question facing society is whether to opt for treatment or to incarcerate offenders without therapy. The latter option is the one more commonly adopted, and it is associated with recidivism and, eventually, more victims.

SUMMARY OF MAJOR POINTS

1. Fetishism.   A fetishist requires the presence of an inanimate object to become sexually aroused. To the extent that we learn to associate inanimate objects such as clothing with arousal, we all have minor fetishes.

2. Transvestism.   Often confused with homosexuality or transsexuality, transvestism, or cross-dressing, usually is practiced by individuals who are biologically and psychologically masculine but who derive erotic pleasure from wearing stereotypically feminine attire.

3. Transsexualism.   Some people whose genetic, gonadal, hormonal, and genital gender development all coincide nevertheless believe themselves to be members of the other gender. The causes of transsexuality are unknown. Many transsexuals who undergo surgical sex reassignment report greater happiness and adjustment in their new status.

4. Sadomasochism.   Sadists are aroused by inflicting pain on others, and masochists are erotically stimulated by receiving pain. Sadomasochism differs from sexual assault in that both participants consent to the activity. A variant of this fetish, bondage and discipline, involves symbolic dominance and submission more than it involves physical pain.

5. Voyeurism and exhibitionism.   Voyeurism involves observing others without their consent who are nude and/or sexually involved, and exhibitionism is showing others one's genitals without being invited to do so. As far as is known, voyeurs and exhibitionists are almost exclusively men. Targets of voyeurs and exhibitionists may be startled or frightened by the intrusion, but a calm response is generally effective in discouraging the behavior and is least likely to reward the perpetrator.

6. Pedophilia.   Adults convicted of sexual contacts with children resemble convicted rapists with respect to feelings of inadequacy, although they are generally not as aggressive as rapists. Factors that impair judgment, such as alcohol and emotional disturbance, are quite common among those convicted of sexual relations with children.

7. Zoophilia.   Most individuals who report engaging in sex with animals do not describe it as a preferred or exclusive mode of sexual interaction. When zoophilia occurs, it usually takes place during adolescence and is abandoned in adulthood.

8. Compulsive sexual behavior.   Many paraphilias seem similar to addictions to alcohol or drugs in that the individual engages in the behavior to alter his or her mood and seems unable to control the behavior. The concept of addiction to sex has received considerable criticism.

9. Treatment of the invasive paraphilias.   Numerous approaches are used to treat paraphiliacs. Many early treatments resembled punishments more than therapies. Cognitive-behavior therapies and pharmacological treatments appear to be effective in treating paraphilias. Whether these treatments are employed depends on whether society emphasizes rehabilitation and treatment or incarceration and punishment.

Sexual Harassment

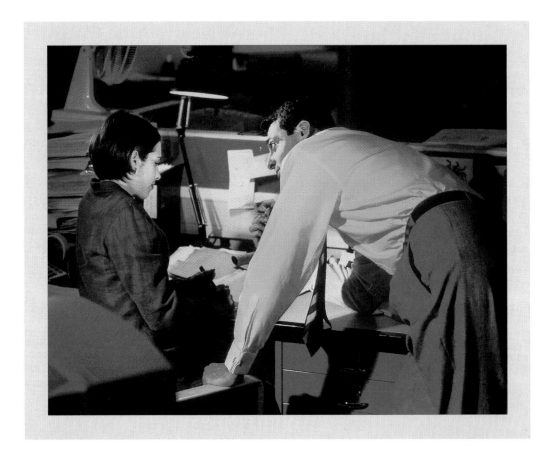

Reality or Myth?

1 *Most cases of sexual harassment in colleges and universities are reported to authorities.*

2 *Men who are likely to harass sexually tend to score high on measures of traditional masculinity.*

3 *Male-dominated workplaces are more likely to foster sexual harassment of females.*

4 *Most therapists report feeling sexual attraction toward some clients.*

5 *Sexual harassment by the clergy is usually directed at adult women.*

Several high-profile cases in corporations, government, and the military have brought greater attention to the issue of sexual harassment. This chapter seeks to define such behavior and to give you helpful information on how to identify and avoid sexual harassment and how to respond to it when it does occur.

Sexual Harassment: What Is It?

The reasons for engaging in sexual behaviors are complex and not well understood. At the most basic level, sex can be for pure physical pleasure, but even this is not straightforward. Even in the most egalitarian relationship, the desire and motives for sex at particular times may sharply differ between two people. Sometimes we may consent to sex to give pleasure to our partner even though we feel little desire at the moment (O'Sullivan & Allgeier, 1994). We can also engage in sex with the hope of conception, obtaining status through association with a powerful person, establishing dominance over another person, or obtaining gifts or money. Understanding sexual behavior becomes even more complicated when the interaction takes place between individuals having unequal status. If the individual with greater economic, evaluative, or psychological power employs that advantage to obtain sexual gratification from an individual who is in a subordinate position, it shades into the arena of sexual harassment and has potential legal repercussions, as we shall see.

Sexual harassment appears in diverse forms and in many different environments. For example, an employer may use the power to hire, promote, and fire to force an employee into having sexual relations. An instructor may use the power to grade to coerce sexual intimacy. Harassment can take place between health care providers and clients, between clergy and parishioners, and between those of different ranks in the military. Most of these situations involve interactions between two people who are not equal in power.

Vern Bullough's (1990) historical review suggests that sexual harassment in the nursing profession is not a recent phenomenon. He reported that Florence Nightingale took steps in her training of nurses to prevent them from being harassed by establishing separate residence areas for nurses. She also wrote

sexual harassment—The use of status and/or power to coerce or attempt to coerce a person into having sex; also, suggestive or lewd comments directed at a person in occupational, educational, or therapeutic settings.

regularly to hospital authorities about her concerns, as Bullough describes:

> *In fact, the danger of dark stairwells is a recurring theme in her letters. She was also concerned with the treatment of nurses by male physicians and surgeons and mentioned some of the offenders by name. Somehow nurses needed to be protected from this.* (p. 6)

The legal system has had great difficulty in trying to develop a clear picture of sexual harassment. In 1988, the Equal Employment Opportunity Commission (EEOC) issued the following guidelines to clarify the legal definition of sexual harassment:

> *Unwelcome sexual advances, requests for sexual favors, and other verbal or physical conduct of a sexual nature constitute sexual harassment when: submission to such conduct is made explicitly or implicitly a term or condition of an individual's employment; submission to, or rejection of, such conduct . . . is used as a basis for employment decisions . . . ; or such conduct has the purpose or effect of unreasonably interfering with an individual's work performance or creating an intimidating, hostile, or offensive working environment.* (Tamminen, 1994, p. 44)

In 1991, Congress amended Title VII of the Civil Rights Act to allow plaintiffs in sexual harassment cases the right to jury trials with the possibility of collecting monetary damages.

There are, legally speaking, two kinds of sexual harassment. The first, and less controversial, of the EEOC guidelines is the **quid pro quo** (literally, "something for something") element. At its most basic level, this type of harassment involves requiring sexual relations for such things as a job promotion, a pay raise, or a high grade. This kind of exchange violates the integrity of individuals who believe they must provide sex to get ahead. It also violates the integrity of the organization in which such behavior occurs. At the individual level, requiring sex as a condition of advancement—even simply to avoid a

demotion and keep a job—can negate the need for achievement that is a crucial element of the personalities of most people. Employees may come to feel that no matter how competent one is at a job, it will have little meaning if sex is the only means by which one gets rewarded. At the organizational level, it invites cynicism as to how effort is rewarded. The more widely known the harassment is, the more likely it is that the organizational goals and the organization's credibility will be questioned (Fitzgerald, Drasgow, Hulin, Gelfland, & Magley, 1997).

One famous example of an allegation of quid pro quo sexual harassment was made in 1994 by Paula Jones against Bill Clinton, the president of the United States. Jones, an Arkansas state employee, claimed that while Clinton was governor of Arkansas, he exposed himself to her and asked for oral sex. No sex took place, and Clinton denied the allegation. Jones claimed that her supervisors mistreated her after she rejected Clinton's advances. For example, she maintained that her coworkers received bigger raises and that her job became a dead end. Later, Jones said that Clinton tried to kiss her and grab her crotch, and briefly he blocked her from leaving the room. The judge dismissed Jones's case, but she subsequently appealed the dismissal. Eventually the case was settled out of court with Ms. Jones receiving $850,000.

The second, and more controversial, kind of sexual harassment is known as "hostile environment." In 1986, in its first ruling on sexual harassment, the U.S. Supreme Court held that speech or conduct can in itself create a hostile environment, which violates the Civil Rights Act. According to the justices, unwelcome verbal or physical behavior, if severe or pervasive, is discrimination even when there is no quid pro quo. This expansion of the concept of sexual harassment has been a source of heated debate among legal scholars. Depending on who is defining the terms, just about anything could be viewed as a hostile environment. See "Highlight: Examples of Sexual Harassment?"

Quid pro quo cases are difficult to win in court because it is often one person's word against another's. As such, most sexual harassment cases are based on the vaguer principle of "hostile environment."

We have presented an overview of the legal development of sexual harassment laws. It is an area that will undoubtedly change as more cases wind their way through the court system. We now exam-

---

quid pro quo—Requiring something in exchange for something else, for example requiring sex from a student in exchange for a better grade.

H I G H L I G H T

Examples of Sexual Harassment?

Do you agree or disagree that the following examples of interactions between people involve harassment?

- A first-grader in Lexington, North Carolina, was given a day's suspension from school and excluded from an ice cream party for kissing a classmate on the cheek. Although the girl had asked the boy to kiss her, the teacher reported the event to the principal, who concluded that the boy had violated a school policy on "student-to-student sexual harassment" (Klatt, 1998, p. 53).

- A waitress refused to serve a journalist in Berkeley, California, because he was reading a *Playboy* article (ironically, on the Bill of Rights). She was so upset by the sight of the magazine that she felt sexually harassed, raped, and in danger of losing her self-esteem. She maintained that the *Playboy* was pornography that constituted hate literature and threatened women's health. Thus, "hate literature," even when privately read, was construed as sexually harassing (Klatt, 1998, p. 51).

- During her master's degree program, a woman's major professor approached her a number of times for "emotional support," professed his love for her, and began to pressure her for increasingly intimate physical contact. When she discovered that he was behaving similarly with other women students, she attempted to lodge a complaint. He then claimed to his colleagues that she was mentally disturbed. The student was distraught when her student colleagues who had also been harassed by the professor would not publicly support her claim for fear of academic reprisals. Ultimately, she felt that she could not trust any man to be her major professor (Allgeier, Travis, Zeller, & Royster, 1990).

- A graduate student who was serving as an instructor described his affairs with some of his women undergraduate students. Although he had not disclosed his marital status to them, some discovered that he was married and informed his wife. She was upset and divorced him, and ultimately, he was dismissed from his doctoral training program. He said that his main problem was that he had to seek admission elsewhere, but felt no remorse or guilt over the affairs with the students (Allgeier et al., 1990).

- In *Fair* v. *Guiding Eyes for the Blind,* a heterosexual woman who was the associate director of a nonprofit organization claimed her gay male supervisor had created an offensive environment by making gossipy conversation and political remarks concerning homosexuality. The court ruled that the supervisor's conduct did not constitute sexual harassment.

---

ine what the research has indicated about these complicated social issues.

PREVALENCE OF SEXUAL HARASSMENT

An overview of studies on sexual harassment in a variety of settings suggests that employees or students have at least a 40 percent chance of encountering sexual harassment in their place of work or study (Barak, Fisher, & Houston, 1992). It is difficult for researchers to arrive at a single estimate of sexual harassment, however, because of methodological problems that range from using different definitions of sexual harassment to ways in which potentially affected populations are sampled.

Part of the problem with determining the extent of sexual harassment is that different researchers use different definitions. Some use a very broad definition that encompasses such behavior as unwanted looks or suggestions, whereas others limit their definitions to coercive sexual touching, genital stimulation, and sexual intercourse.

Amanda Henderson of South Carolina claimed her male coach's attention escalated into harassment. His firing earned her the ire of teammates.

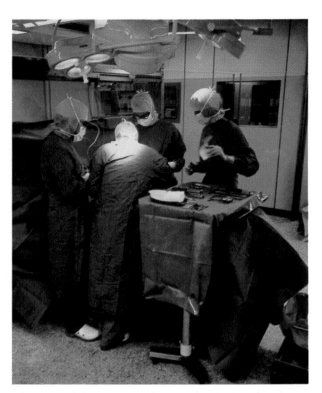

The surgical theater is a male stronghold where female colleagues have sometimes been made unwelcome.

A catalogue (not exhaustive) of some of the items that constitute one view of sexual harassment can be found in Bernice Sandler and Robert Shoop's (1997) edited book: "sexual innuendoes, comments or bantering" through "humor or jokes about sex or females in general," "asking for sexual behavior," "touching a person," "giving a neck or shoulder massage," "leering or ogling such as 'elevator eyes,'" calling women "'hot stuff' or 'cutie pie,'" "sexual graffiti," "laughing or not taking seriously someone who experiences sexual harassment," right up to "attempted or actual sexual assault or abuse" (quoted in Patai, 1998, p. 229).

▶ **Issues to Consider:** What behaviors do you think should be classified as sexual harassment?

One of the difficulties that has plagued sexual harassment researchers concerns differences in the behaviors that recipients find objectionable. For example, very few college students label inappropriate sexual behaviors as sexual harassment (Shepela &

Levesque, 1998). See "Research Spotlight: Variations in Judgments of Sexual Harassment," for examples of behaviors on which people may differ as indicating harassment.

A frequently used measure of sexual harassment is the Sexual Experiences Questionnaire (SEQ, Fitzgerald, Weitzman, Gold, & Ormerod, 1988), which was revised in 1995 (Fitzgerald, Gelfland, & Drasgow, 1995). The SEQ is used to measure three types of sexual harassment:

1. *Gender harassment*–generally sexist behavior, behavior that disparages the sex of the target or conveys hostility toward women, sexist jokes and remarks, and so forth.

2. *Unwanted sexual attention*–unwanted touching, hugging, stroking, or repeated unwanted requests or pressure for dates.

3. *Sexual coercion*–subtle or direct demands for sexual favors through the threat of negative job-related consequences or the promise of job-related rewards.

RESEARCH SPOTLIGHT   Variations in Judgments of Sexual Harassment

Rate the following behaviors on a scale of 1 (not at all harassing) to 10 (extremely harassing) to indicate the extent to which you think each should be considered sexual harassment if done by (a) a professor to a student and (b) a fellow student.

Sexual jokes	(a)_____	(b)_____
Stereotyped jokes about men	(a)_____	(b)_____
Stereotyped jokes about women	(a)_____	(b)_____
Sexual graffiti	(a)_____	(b)_____
Suggestive looking or leering	(a)_____	(b)_____
Sexual letters or calls	(a)_____	(b)_____
Leaning over or cornering	(a)_____	(b)_____
Pressure for dates	(a)_____	(b)_____
Touching on "nonprivate" places (e.g., shoulders, waist)	(a)_____	(b)_____
Touching on "private" places (e.g., breasts, buttocks, genitals)	(a)_____	(b)_____
Asking for sexual activity	(a)_____	(b)_____
Attempted sexual activity with person who has indicated nonwillingness	(a)_____	(b)_____
Actual sexual assault	(a)_____	(b)_____
Laughing or otherwise not taking seriously someone who feels sexually harassed	(a)_____	(b)_____

Some of the social-sexual behaviors that occur at work, such as compliments, hugging, putting an arm around another person's shoulder, requests for dates delivered in a joking manner, and sexual jokes or comments not directed to any single individual, are not considered harassing by most people (Gutek, 1992). Thus, boundaries are often blurred between sexual harassment and "normal" romantic and sexual behavior.

Researchers have come up with prevalence rates of sexual harassment of college students that range from 9 percent to 60 percent (de Albuquerque, 1998; Gruber, 1990). In one survey of 431 employed women who had received the degree of Master of Business Administration from the University of Pittsburgh, 222 (52 percent) reported experiencing discrimination in their work. Of these, only 8 women (4 percent) mentioned situations that could be regarded as sexual harassment (Murrell, Olson, & Frieze, 1995). This suggests that women in the workplace are more likely to experience other forms of discrimination that are not sexual in nature. In contrast, however, Schneider, Swan, and Fitzgerald (1997) found that 68 percent of women employed at a large company reported that they had experienced at least one SEQ item (there are 18 items) during the previous two years.

In a much different approach that sought to arrive at a realistic estimate of sexual harassment on college campuses, Klaus de Albuquerque (1998) examined actual harassment complaints. He obtained data on sexual harassment complaints filed against professors at a number of college and universities. It has been estimated that only one of ten students who think they have experienced an incident of sexual harassment makes a formal complaint (Dziech & Weiner, 1984). de Albuquerque multiplied the actual number of complaints by a factor of 100, rather than 10, and arrived at what is probably an inflated estimate of 2 to 3 percent of students annually reporting harassment from professors. *Reality or Myth* []

Just as our obsession with sexual misconduct obscures many other forms of harassment facing women, it also leads us to overlook some distressing harassment confronting men on the job. Hostility is not uncommon from male coworkers seeking to deprecate or drive away men who threaten the masculine image of the workplace. If a job is thought to confer manliness, it must be held by those who project the desired masculinity. In some work settings, men are threatened by the presence of any man perceived to be gay or perceived to lack the "manly competence" considered suitable for those who hold the job. Surveys by the U.S. Merit Systems Protection Board (1981, 1988, 1994) revealed that 14 to 19 percent of male federal workers reported being sexually harassed at work.

The Effects of Sexual Harassment

Harassment victims report various reactions to the unwanted approaches, including nervousness, loss of motivation, sleeplessness, uncontrolled anger or crying, weight loss, decreased job satisfaction, and self-reported decrements in job performance (Fitzgerald et al., 1997). The threat to penalize a woman who does not submit to a supervisor's sexual advances causes as much harm to her as if the woman were actually threatened and subsequently punished (Schneider, Swan, & Fitzgerald, 1997). Nonetheless, women are unlikely to report the episode(s) to authorities out of fear of losing their jobs and sabotaging their careers (Gutek, 1985; Schneider et al., 1997). Awareness of the problem has increased recently because of demonstrations by women's groups to call attention to the issue and because of some well-publicized lawsuits.

The fact that large numbers of both men and women report harassment suggests that the phenomenon is common, although women are the predominant target of harassment in the workplace (Berdahl, Magley, & Waldo, 1996). Cindy Struckman-Johnson and David Struckman-Johnson (1994) found that most men who had personally experienced an incident of unwanted sexual contact with a woman did not differ from noncoerced men in overall self-esteem and depression. The researchers concluded that most men had few negative reactions to the undesired sexual incident. However, one-fifth of the men who reported unwanted sexual contact expressed negative reactions, including fear and confusion, embarrassment, concern about their heterosexuality if they resisted the advance, and fear of telling others because they might not be believed. The extent to which men report a negative reaction to an unwanted female sexual contact is probably affected by gender-role norms. That is, it may be culturally unacceptable for a man to seek help after an attempted or completed episode of sexual harassment.

Gender Differences in Sexual Harassment

A number of differences have been found between men's and women's likelihood to harass others. Men and women also differ in their reasons for sexually harassing behavior and their reactions when they are recipients of unwanted sexual attention.

▶ **Issues to Consider:** Why do you think men are more likely than women to engage in sexual harassment?

Men have significantly higher propensities to harass members of the other sex than do women (Perry, Schimtke, & Kulik, 1998). As we saw in Chapter 6, there is a traditional belief or sexual script that men pursue and women resist sexual interaction. This stereotype, however, is open to debate; women often initiate sex, and a substantial proportion of men report that they have experienced women's attempts to have sex with them through nonphysical coercive strategies (Lottes, 1992). Comparatively little attention has been paid to women's beliefs and their use of pressure tactics to obtain sex (Struckman-Johnson & Struckman-Johnson, 1994). Michele Clements-Schreiber, John Rempel, and Serge Desmarais (1998) reported that employed women's likelihood of using overt ("undo his belt or pants") or covert ("get him a little drunk") pressure tactics with reluctant or uninterested men was related to their attitudes about male sexuality. Married women who believed that men are easily accessible sexually ("the truth is that most men will not pass up a sexual opportunity even if it means being unfaithful") were more likely to report using overt and covert sexual pressure strategies. For unmarried women, the likelihood of using overt and covert pressure on reluctant or uninterested men was associated with the belief that men and women do not differ in their need for or enjoyment of sex.

Men and women appear to attend to different facets of harassment situations. Women are more sensitive to power issues, whereas men are more likely to attend to the sexual aspects of the situation (Berdahal et al., 1996). Student men are more likely to interpret unwanted sexual attention from female professors as relatively benign—expressions of nurturing rather than sexual behaviors (Katz, Hannon, & Whitten, 1996). Additionally, male students are likely to be flattered by the sexual attention of a female professor and, if offended, be more embarrassed or ashamed about reporting it (Marks & Nelson, 1993). A common stereotype is that a man is abnormal if he reacts to a sexual opportunity with anything less than enthusiasm. A man's negative reaction to an unwanted sexual encounter may fly in the face of his own normative belief that men always want sex, regardless of the circumstances. To resolve the difference between his beliefs and his reaction to the incident, he might alter his perception of the event in a more benign direction. Following this line of reasoning, men may minimize or underreport the negative aspects of their reactions to unwanted sexual pressure.

An overview of the research on sex differences in the perception of sexual harassment (mostly conducted with undergraduates) reveals that when there are differences, women are more likely to rate behaviors as sexually harassing, although these differences are not large (Frazier, Cochran, & Olson, 1995). In general, men and women students have been more likely to differ in their perceptions of more ambiguous or less severe behaviors such as crude language, sexual jokes, suggestive looks, flirting, and nonsexual touching. Certain behaviors such as sexual bribery, explicit sexual propositions, and sexual touching are perceived by almost all men and women as sexual harassment. In addition, behaviors engaged in by people with higher status or greater authority are more likely to be perceived as harassment. For example, behaviors engaged in by a faculty member toward a student are more likely to be perceived as harassment than are the same behaviors engaged in by students.

INDIVIDUAL DIFFERENCES IN SEXUAL HARASSMENT

John Pryor (1987) developed the Likelihood to Sexually Harass (LSH) scale which is conceptually similar to Malamuth's (1981) measure of Likelihood to Rape (LR, see Chapter 19). In Pryor's technique, men are asked to imagine themselves in a series of scenarios in which they have power over an attractive woman:

For example, one scenario depicts an interaction between a male college professor and a female student who is seeking to raise her grade in a class. Male subjects are asked to rate the likelihood of their performing an act of quid pro quo sexual harassment in each scenario given that they believe that they could do so with impunity [without punishment]. In the professor/student scenario, for example, how likely is it that the subject would raise the student's grade in exchange

for sexual favors given that his behavior would go unpunished? (Pryor, Giedd, & Williams, 1995, p. 74)

Men who score high on the LSH scale also score high on a number of measures of aggression. They identify with a stereotypic traditional view of masculinity and score high on measures of hypermasculinity (see Chapter 6) (Driscoll, Kelly, & Henderson, 1998). They are also less knowledgeable about sexual harassment than are men with low LSH scores (Perry, Kulik, & Schmidke, 1998).

High LSH scores are associated with a desire to control one's sexual partners, seeking sex as a defense against boredom or as a way to impress others, and seeking sex for sheer physical gratification. It appears that thoughts about social dominance are tightly linked to thoughts about sexuality in the minds of high-LSH men. Thoughts about social dominance may automatically activate thoughts about sexuality in these men.

Laboratory studies have shown that LSH scores can be predictive of sexually harassing behavior. Pryor (1988) asked high- and low-LSH men to teach an attractive woman confederate either how to putt a golf ball or how to play poker. The participants were given a sense of power over the woman by asking them to evaluate her performance and indicating that high performance would qualify her for additional experimental credits. The major dependent variable was sexual touching. In the putting condition, participants were required to touch the confederate as part of the training task. In the poker condition, no touching was required. High-LSH men tended to make verbal sexual overtures and touch the confederate in a sexual way in the putting condition. Low-LSH men did not display either of these behaviors. Neither high- nor low-LSH men exhibited these behaviors in the poker condition. *Reality or Myth* 2

Pryor suggested that the nature of the poker condition provided no situational excuse for men to touch the confederate. Pryor thought his experimental paradigm was analogous to work settings where unsolicited sexual touching sometimes occurs:

Female secretaries who complain about this sort of behavior in the workplace often describe situations where a supervisor leans over them while supposedly peering at a computer screen or the document the secretary is typing.

The same harasser does not lean over the secretary while she is waiting for the elevator. Without the situational excuse, such behavior is more transparently sexual and less socially acceptable. (Pryor et al., 1995, pp. 78–79)

Role models or mentors who demonstrate sexually harassing behaviors contribute to social norms that can encourage such behavior. Sexual harassment can also evolve out of peer interactions when LSH men are in small, cohesive groups.

Some instances of sexual harassment may reflect a lack of social skills in men who have a romantic interest in women they encounter at work. That is, they may sexually harass because of a general insensitivity to interpersonal signals that makes it difficult for them to differentiate circumstances where sexual behavior is inappropriate.

In some cases of sexual harassment, those who abuse their power may deny they were consciously and deliberating misusing their authority. In responding to complaints of harassment, most alleged harassers acknowledge the behavior attributed to them but do not ascribe the same meaning or importance to it. They do not seem to understand that they may be taking advantage of their status and causing another person distress, but attribute their actions to a more acceptable motive—offering a compliment. Some researchers estimate that 75 percent of harassers simply do not consider themselves as such. As Bargh and Raymond put it (p. 87):

One potential reason why men who sexually harass do not seem aware that their power over their female subordinates plays any role in their feelings or behavior toward them is there exists an automatic link between their concepts of power and sex. Automatic mental processes operate so quickly and efficiently that one is not consciously aware of their occurrence.

Men who are likely to harass sexually may have such a strong association between power and sex that when they believe they have authority in a situation, the concept of sex is automatically activated. A man who has an automatic power-sex association would be more likely to harass a woman he perceives as submissive, deferential, or vulnerable because these behaviors would activate his power concept, leading in turn to sexual thoughts.

How are men who differ in their likelihood to harass sexually perceived by others? Denise Driscoll, Janice Kelly, and Wendy Henderson (1998) had college student men and women observe video clips of men being interviewed by a subordinate women. Viewers ranked high-LSH men as higher in LSH, more masculine, less feminine, and more traditional toward women's roles than they ranked men who scored low on the LSH scale. Thus, observers' perceptions of LSH men are very similar to how these individuals describe themselves. These findings have potential implications for trying to prevent sexual harassment. If high-LSH men can be identified, they may be able to be sensitized to aspects of their behavior that leave them at risk for sexual harassment behaviors and charges.

Sexual Harassment in the Workplace

Sexual harassment occurs in a variety of different environments. We first describe harassment in occupational settings.

Sexual harassment may be more likely to occur in situations in which it is perceived as socially permissible (Gutek, 1985). If management is perceived as tolerating or not condemning harassing behavior, some employees may feel freer to engage in such behavior.

Other indicators of a relaxed attitude toward sexual harassment can be the display of sexual material in public places in the work environment, such as erotic calendars, sexually explicit graffiti, or sexually oriented entertainment at office parties. Women more frequently report that they receive uninvited sexual attention in situations in which such sexuality-related behavior is common and implicitly accepted than in workplaces that are free of these conditions (Pryor, Giedd, & Williams, 1995).

SEX-ROLE SPILLOVER

Sex-role spillover refers to "the carryover into the workplace of gender-based roles that are usually irrelevant or inappropriate to work" (Gutek, 1985, pp. 15–16). This can occur in workplaces where men are in a majority and the gender roles that they assume outside work—such as cursing, inappropriate touching, and sexual overtures—carry over to the job. In this context, men are likely to view women in terms of sex-role stereotypes rather than in work roles, and women are more likely to report sexual harassment than are women in more sex-integrated settings (Gutek, 1985).

If a man thinks of women primarily in terms of sexual stereotypes, he is more likely to act toward any particular woman in sexual terms, often inappropriately. A consistent female stereotype revolves around sexuality. In one study, a sexual woman was described as someone who was seductive, flirtatious, and socialized more with men than with women (Noseworthy & Lott, 1984).

When women enter traditionally masculine careers, they are particularly vulnerable to sexual harassment. The introduction of women into male-dominated jobs can be perceived as a threat by men whose self-esteem is heavily based on gender identity. This threat occurs for two reasons. The first has to do with a significant part of male gender identity being work-oriented achievement. The second is that jobs dominated by men are seen as requiring attributes that distinguish men as superior to women (Fiske & Glick, 1995), primarily in strength (blue-collar jobs) or intellect (white-collar jobs). Effective performance by women in these jobs can deflate men's self-esteem and sense of superiority.

Individuals in male-dominated workplaces are more likely to have rigid stereotypes about the general roles of men and women (Gutek, Cohen, & Conrad, 1990). Seeking a career in a male-dominated occupation can put a woman in a double bind. On the one hand, if she displays some typical masculine traits that she needs to get the job, she may be perceived as a "nontraditional" woman and elicit antagonism from some men. On the other hand, if she tries to be accepted by demonstrating more traditional attitudes and characteristics, such as cooking or reading

Sexual harassment may involve physical force, or it may occur in more subtle ways, as in this photo. This man's instrusion into an employee's physical space may go unreported because she fears losing her job.

romance novels, she may be seen as not having the same commitment to her work as do her male colleagues. Before women become accepted as colleagues, they may be exposed to efforts to undermine them through sexual harassment. *Reality or Myth* ❓

Another effect of stereotypes in the workplace is that they emphasize how women and men interact sexually rather than their competence in their work, which encourages sexual harassment. In one study, people who were sexually interested in another person could not distinguish competent from incompetent task performance (Fiske & Glick, 1995).

ROMANCE IN THE WORKPLACE

"I contend that anyone who has ever been in love knows that true power resides in the attraction exerted by the loved one" (Refinetti, 1998, p. 13).

Can love transcend status or power differences? Think of an administrator, manager, officer, or pro-

Workplace flirtations can lead to trouble if there is a power imbalance or if a failed romance makes it uncomfortable to continue working together.

fessor who falls in love with a subordinate. If he or she acts on these feelings, the "superior" risks professional and personal ruin. Who has the power in this type of situation: the person with the higher status or the loved one?

Literature, theater, and film are saturated with themes of love's overcoming differences in class, race, economics, and age. Status or power can be leveled by intense attraction or attachment. It is highly unlikely that sexual harassment policies, no matter how well intentioned, can cast this dynamic out of the workplace or academic environment. Would we want an environment rendered sterile by trying to quash the possibility of amorous intent?

Romantic relationships have always existed in the workplace. The frequency of intimate contact in the workforce has probably increased in the past few decades as the spectrum of employment has become more sexually integrated. For example, about three-fourths of people have reported that they had observed or participated in a romantic relationship at their place of employment (Dillard & Wittleman, 1985). About 80 percent of employees in the United States report different quasi-sexual and sexual experiences on the job, including mutually desired romantic interactions with their coworkers (Gutek, 1985).

Not all sexual intimacy between coworkers constitutes harassment. As Gutek (1992) pointed out, mutual attraction and flirtation commonly occur in the workplace, and men and women alike sometimes seek, and find, relationship partners at work. Mutually consenting adult sexual relations are difficult to attain, however, when there is an imbalance of power between partners in their shared work or educational setting.

▶ **Issues to Consider:** If you found an employee romantically interesting, what would you do?

What happens when a workplace romance dissolves? One or both of the former lovers may develop negative feelings toward the other. Unlike other romances, workplace romances often involve two employees who can interact frequently with one another during daily work routines. This frequent contact can intensify negative feelings, a situation that could lead to accusations of sexual harassment by both former lovers. Charles Pierce and Herman Aquinis (1997, p. 199) provided three possible scenarios that might tend to lead to sexual harassment complaints after a workplace romance between a supervisor and a supervisee dissolves:

> First, out of revenge, a subordinate might accuse his or her supervisor of sexual harassment if the supervisor terminates the romance, especially if the subordinate entered the romance because of a job-related motive such as seeking lighter workloads, a promotion or pay raise, an increase in power, or more vacation time. Second, if a subordinate terminates the romance against the supervisor's wishes, the supervisor may be bitter and attempt to rekindle the romance. The supervisor's coercive attempts to reunite the dyad may be undesired and, hence, considered sexually harassing. Third, a supervisor might try to manage the romantic dissolution by relocating or terminating the subordinate in order to avoid negative feelings from the disengagement.

The perils of becoming intimately involved with someone who has less or more social power than oneself are many. In its most extreme form, this would prohibit most sexual relationships if one sees male-female status as inherently unequal. Radical feminists have proposed that the definition of sexual harassment should include any sexual relationships that involve people with different social status. As Naomi McCormick (1994) pointed out, some feminist authors have argued that all heterosexual intercourse is "rape" because in a patriarchal society, women are not able to give meaningful consent. Sandler (1990, p. 8) asserted, "Another myth is that of the consenting adult. True consent can only occur between equals, and a relationship does not consist of equals when one party has some power over the other." This is a startling oversimplification of the complexity of human relationships. In the real world, people have differing degrees of power in various aspects of their relationship. Who chooses what kind of car to buy, what leisure activities to pursue and what social invitations to accept, and the myriad other decisions we make regularly involve decisions in which one partner may exercise more influence or power than the other partner at some times and less at other times. And as Daphne Patai (1998, p. 228) wrote, "The one kind of power never mentioned, of course, is the power of sexual attraction and attractiveness—a power women have used for millennia, even in historical moments when they were deprived of civic or political rights." Rather than spending time trying to define the trivial, we should reserve our judgment of sexual harassment for cases that result in actual discrimination.

Sexual Harassment in Educational Settings

Sexual harassment in college settings differs in several respects from sexual harassment in the workplace. Although students are highly dependent on faculty members for grades, letters of recommendation, and research opportunities, they may have more options than do employees for finding other faculty with whom they can work if a particular faculty member attempts to harass them. Furthermore, students are in school for only a limited period of time, whereas employees may feel pressured to put up with harassment for prolonged periods because of the need to keep a job or preserve seniority. On the other hand, students tend to be more vulnerable and naive about harassment than are employees. Students who are in their late teens or early 20s may be flattered by the attention of a professor whom they respect. They may not understand the inappropriateness of having sexual relations with a powerful person who is in a position to provide or withhold aid that is important for the student's future career.

A limitation of the study of undergraduates is that they are less likely than other adults to perceive behaviors as harassment. More research is needed with more representative samples and with people who have experienced some of these behaviors. Many people who experience various sexual behaviors do

H I G H L I G H T

Dealing with Sexual Harassment by an Instructor

If you are sexually harassed by an instructor, you should contact authorities on your campus about the incident. Seek out another professor whom you trust or the chairperson of the department. If these people are not supportive, talk with someone at the campus affirmative action or civil rights office. Sometimes students are reluctant to report such incidents for fear that the instructor in question will give them failing grades or will be fired. Affirmative action regulations protect people who file harassment complaints from grade discrimination. If you believe that the instructor who has made advances toward you is not approaching other students and if there have been no other reports of harassment, the instructor generally is put on probation and watched closely. Assuming that there are no further reports of harassment, no career damage occurs. It is common for instructors who engage in such behavior to do so with many students, however. Those who are reluctant to report an incident should place more emphasis on the welfare of their fellow students, who could also become targets, than on the career of the harassing instructor.

not consider them to be harassing (Cortina, Swan, Fitzgerald, and Waldo, 1998; Fitzgerald et al., 1988). Some students do feel sexually harassed, however.

Harassment in educational settings is quite prevalent. In their review of studies conducted at 11 universities, Allen and Okawa (1987) found that, in response to anonymous questionnaires, between 13 percent and 33 percent of students reported experiencing harassment, which ranged from instructors' leering and patting in an offensive manner to threats or bribery to gain sexual intimacy. Although you may think that these students are imagining that their instructors' interest in them is not just academic, Louise Fitzgerald and her colleagues (1988) administered an anonymous survey to male faculty, and 25 percent of them reported having had sexual encounters with students. Only one faculty member described the relationship as harassment.

Somers (1982) found that 8 percent of the women in her sample reported that either they themselves or others whom they knew had dropped a class or avoided a particular instructor or teaching assistant because of his embarrassing sexual language or advances.

Inappropriate sexual contact also occurs between graduate students and their professors. Several surveys have been conducted to determine the preva-lence of sexual contact between female psychologists and their professors during graduate school training. Between 14 percent and 25 percent of the women in these samples reported such intimacy, and almost half reported having been the target of sexual advances by one or more of their professors. Inappropriate sexual contacts with their professors are more likely among younger than older female graduate students, and more likely among those who were divorcing or separating during training (34 percent) than among women who were single or married (22 percent) (Glaser & Thorpe, 1986; Pope, Hammel, Olkin, & Taube, 1996; Levenson & Schover, 1979; Robinson & Reid, 1985). The problem with such student-teacher relationships, of course, is that the students have less power than professors and thus cannot freely give informed consent.

The vulnerability of students to advances by their professors is underscored by findings from Glaser and Thorpe's (1986) survey of female psychologists. Those who had been approached sexually by their professors and/or had sex with them reported that they had perceived the advances as less coercive, unethical, and disruptive of their educational relationships with their professors at the time when they were students than they now perceived them to be. We recommend that you familiarize yourself with the policies at your own school (see "Highlight: Dealing with Sexual Harassment by an Instructor").

Sexual Harassment in Therapeutic Settings

The issue of power differences is particularly stark in the case of the sexual harassment of a patient or client by a physician or psychotherapist. Physicians and psychologists are highly trained, powerful members of society. They usually have more status than their patients or clients who seek their help in dealing with illness or psychological difficulties. For the patient or client, compounding the problem of dealing with sexual harassment is the fact that a client's charge of abuse may be ascribed by the therapist or physician to the client's mental instability.

Occasionally one-sided or mutual attraction may develop between the professional and the patient: 87 percent of the 575 psychotherapists surveyed by Pope, Keith-Spiegel, and Tabachnick (1986) reported feeling sexual attraction toward certain clients. As noted in Chapter 6, such feelings are normal, but professionals who act on their erotic feelings with people who come to them for help are serving their own interests. *Reality or Myth* [?]

To examine whether clinical and counseling psychology graduate students are obtaining training on how to deal with their sexual feelings toward clients, Devine and Allgeier (1998) sampled those who were in at least their fourth year of training in American graduate programs and were applying for clinical internships. Most (78 percent) reported that they had experienced sexual feelings toward at least one client, and almost half (43 percent) described their training for dealing with sexual attraction toward clients as less than adequate.

Studies with different samples indicate that 5 to 10 percent of therapists act on their feelings and become sexually intimate with their clients (Pope et al., 1986). Further, about three-quarters of therapists who have sex with their clients do so with numerous clients. Pope and Bouhoutsos (1987) reported that one therapist had been involved in sexual relations with more than 100 clients. Cases involving physicians and their patients have also been reported. The long-term correlates of such contact for the clients or patients are almost always negative, ranging from hesitation about seeking further professional help to depression, hospitalization, and suicide (Bouhoutsos, Holroyd, Lerman, Forer, & Greenberg, 1983; Grunebaum, 1986; Sonne, Meyer, Borys, & Marshall, 1985; Zelen, 1985).

In addition to the problems attending sexual relationships between people unequal in status, problems arise from the fact that professionals' and clients' motives for sexual intimacy are likely to be quite different. Professionals may perceive themselves as offering therapeutic contact for a brief period of time, but clients, generally dependent while seeking therapeutic or medical help, may believe that they are in love and that their sexual contact is part of a long-term primary relationship, perhaps leading to marriage.

Sexual Harassment in the Military

If there is ever an environment that one could predict would be a bubbling cauldron of sexual problems, it would consist of men and women interacting in a traditional hierarchy in which (some) men reign. Welcome to the U.S. military service or any other military force that has been sex integrated. The military

The military's macho image often attracts men with traditonal values or "sex-role spillover."

TABLE 18.1	Percentage of Service People Reporting Any Type of Unwanted Sexual Attention			
	Percentage of Men		Percentage of Women	
Service	1988	1995	1988	1995
Air Force	14	12	57	49
Army	21	14	68	61
Coast Guard	16	13	62	59
Marine Corps	14	15	75	64
Navy	18	16	66	53

Source: Seppa (1997)

world, by its organization, is more susceptible than many other environments to the infringement of individuals' sexual rights. Rigid, male-dominated power hierarchies have a long history of abusing underlings—both men and women.

Although the number of incidents of sexual harassment in the military declined during the 1990s (see Table 18.1), there are still frequent reports of sexual harassment between officers and enlisted men and women at military bases. Just as in civilian life, most women and men do not report sexual harassment because they fear that it will make matters worse for them.

Military women are more frequent targets of harassment than are military men. Service women are in a male-dominated industry. Although the proportion of women in the military increased from 5 percent in 1973 to 16 percent in 1994, they remain on the lower rungs of the military hierarchy (Seppa, 1997). Women began joining the military after the Vietnam War—long after the influx of women into a variety of other professions that had more

time to deal with trying to regulate sexuality in the workplace.

It is likely that the military, with its macho image, attracts men with traditional values who are more likely to engage in sexual harassment. It is also fertile ground for sex-role spillover as men dominate the work environment and may react to women in terms of sexual stereotypes.

The military has begun to try to address these problems by developing new guidelines for "fraternization." One of the cardinal rules of the military is that there should be no sex, even consensual, between a superior and a subordinate. Military officers are barred from having relationships with troops, regardless of sex, so that friendships do not impinge on combat decisions. However, even that strategy has been inconsistent across the several branches of the military. If an army sergeant dates a higher-ranked air force captain, the sergeant is involved in legal behavior, but the captain is not. In addition, although adultery could still result in a dishonorable discharge, there are more flexible strategies that allow for some judgment as to whether to pursue such a charge.

The military is a harsh taskmaster in creating a force capable of fighting a war. Perhaps as it learns to deal with sexual harassment, it will create a more hospitable environment for its members while retaining its efficiency to conduct warfare.

▶ **Issues to Consider:** To what extent do you agree with the military's policy against fraternization?

Sexual Harassment in Religious Life

Compared to harassment by other professionals, harassment by religious leaders presents a unique problem for the person being harassed: involvement with a power figure who also represents God. It is very difficult to report harassment by a God-like symbol because of the demands, sometimes made, that the persons being harassed keep the events to themselves or they will face spiritual repercussions. The people who are abused have to rethink their religion and consider the idea that God did not protect them. In addition, some churches may view those who file complaints as the enemy and a threat to the faith.

Some of the most well-publicized cases have involved clergy members who sexually approach adolescents, especially Catholic priests who have been accused of abusing adolescent boys. Those clergy who sexually act out with adolescents have underdeveloped or immature sexual coping strategies. They may be unaware of their own sexuality and see teenagers as mirror images of themselves (Loftus & Camargo, 1993). This may be particularly true for "celibate" Catholic clergy. Historically, the Catholic church has done an inadequate job of educating seminarians (students being trained to become clergy) about how to cope with their sexual feelings.

Despite the sensationalized cases in the media, most offending clergy do not molest young people. Most are involved with adult women (Berry, 1992; Loftus & Camargo, 1993). A central psychological issue for those who have been sexually harassed by clergy is low self-esteem that stems from repeated boundary violations. **Reality or Myth**

Most of the media focus has been on the Catholic church, but sexual misconduct by clergy has been found in most denominations. Media coverage of a number of clergy abuse allegations in the early 1990s broke a "conspiracy of silence" by religious and civil authorities. Charges of sexual abuse against clergy before that time were treated as an internal problem by churches, and not reported to police. Image control for the church was always the first mission in these cases. As more abuse by clergy became known, those who had suffered sexual harassment and abuse came forward. By early 1995, more than 600 civil and criminal cases were pending (Sipe, 1995). A number of support groups emerged, including Survivors' Connections and Survivors Network of those Abused by Priests (SNAP).

Richard Sipe (1995) described the framework that guided the response of the Catholic church to this crisis. Many church administrators viewed men as superior to women and blamed women for the crisis. Similarly, some church officials accorded men's needs and pleasure a higher status than those of women, and wished to maintain the traditional power structure.

Recently, some religious authorities have displayed increased urgency in dealing with sexual misconduct by some of the clergy. Administrators of several churches are developing sexual awareness programs for clergy and seminarians. The Episcopal church, for example, has created a risk-management plan to prevent sexual misconduct by Episcopal priests and other church employees. The program stresses training and counseling that teaches clergy how to deal with their own sexual issues.

Reducing Sexual Harassment

Growing public awareness of the problem of sexual harassment has led many to work toward reducing it through changes in individual levels of awareness of the appropriateness of some behavior, changes in corporate policies regarding sexual harassment, and legal rulings discouraging sexual harassment.

INDIVIDUAL RESPONSES AND CHANGES IN SOCIAL NORMS

One of our colleagues, a biologist, wrote to us about an incident that occurred in the 1980s:

We were checking mice for one of the experiments we were doing, and the mouse I was holding bit my finger. I threw my arm up in the air, and the mouse, still attached to my finger, let go and flew into the blouse of my graduate student. Although the mouse had already bitten me, I did not want her to be bitten—especially in her chest region—so I reached in and got the mouse. I'm not sure I would still dare to try to protect my students in this manner given the current climate of sexual harassment claims.

As social norms change, events in the past that had been considered normal may now be labeled as sexual harassment. Individuals may not have interpreted the incidents as sexual harassment before this term became a common part of our language.

Not surprisingly, the increasing awareness of sexual harassment has made many people nervous about their interactions with employees and students. A survey of faculty members at a small university found that two-thirds of the respondents had concerns about false accusations of sexual harassment, and almost half had changed their behavior because of their concern (Nicks, 1996). Specifically, 48 percent left their office doors open while meeting with students, 28 percent never met alone with a student or always met in public, and 20 percent were careful not to touch a student.

CORPORATE AND INSTITUTIONAL RESPONSES

One institutional response to sexual harassment is to mandate sensitivity and awareness training programs for employees to try to reduce the scope of the problem and to avoid litigation. These programs are also used to "rehabilitate" individuals who have violated sexual harassment guidelines.

Such programs have been growing in popularity, in part because they protect organizations from sexual harassment lawsuits by showing their commitment to addressing the problem (Gutek, 1997).

Learning what constitutes sexual harassment is the first step in trying to reduce it.

Those who run these sexual harassment seminars are members of what Daphne Patai (1998) calls the "sexual harassment industry." Most of these counselors appear to be volunteers who attend training workshops taught by other "experts" (cf. Sandler & Shoop, 1997).

Despite the widespread adoption of these programs, there has been very little research on the effectiveness of sexual harassment training. Videotapes are the most widely used instructional method for organizational training. One small study of college students indicated that sexual harassment awareness training videos increased knowledge about harassment and temporarily reduced inappropriate touching behavior of men who had a high propensity to harass (Perry, Kulik, & Schmidtke, 1998). Male participants were videotaped during a 15-minute session with a female confederate in which each man attempted to teach a woman how to put a golf ball. The harassment-training videos had no effect on men who scored low on measures of likelihood to sexually harass. The video also did not influence long-term attitudes associated with the propensity to harass others. Thus, high-LSH men seem to be most affected by this type of training. Perhaps low-LSH men are already sensitized to sexual harassment issues and this training is like preaching to the choir. It also suggests that if attitude change is a goal of this training, video presentations will need to be supplemented by other strategies, such as role playing and small discussion groups, to reduce harassing behaviors.

Some universities have taken forceful steps to counteract this threat to educational freedom. In 1986, for example, the University of Iowa adopted a policy prohibiting any form of sexual advances, requests for sexual favors, or other verbal or physical conduct of a sexual nature toward students by faculty members. The policy also bars faculty members from having romantic relationships with students enrolled in their classes or with students whose academic work they are supervising.

> ► **Issues to Consider:** Do you support the prohibition that exists on some college campuses against instructor-student sexual relations?

Employers who fear lawsuits are taking drastic steps to try to stop sexual harassment before it starts. "Zero tolerance" refers to policies prohibiting just about any speech or conduct with sexual overtones. Many universities and companies, such as General Motors and Wal-Mart, have instituted such policies. This banning movement is perceived by some as a heavy-handed corporate overreaction to legal cases.

LEGAL RESPONSES

Employers are financially liable for employees' sexual misconduct. Two decisions by the U.S. Supreme Court in 1988 made it easier for employees to sue an employer if they claim they have been sexually harassed by a supervisor. In *Firagles* v. *City of Boca Raton*, two municipal lifeguards claimed that a supervisor ignored their complaints of sexual harassment from other supervisors. The city claimed it should not be held liable because no officials in city hall knew about the harassing activities.

In the other case, *Elleith* v. *Burlington Industries,* a marketing employee said her boss's supervisor made constant sexual remarks to her. She claimed that he rubbed her knee and told her that her legs were nice but her breasts were too little. He apparently alluded to having the power to make her job easier or more difficult, which she interpreted to mean that she would have to have sex with him to get ahead. She did not have sex with him and did get a promotion but claimed she was sexually harassed without retribution. In other words, quid pro quo harassment can include mere threats.

In both cases, by identical seven-to-two rulings, the Court ruled that employers are always potentially liable for a supervisor's sexual misconduct toward an employee. To defend themselves, employers must show that they took reasonable care to prevent or promptly correct any sexually harassing behavior. In addition, they would have to demonstrate that the harassing employee did not take advantage of any preventive or corrective opportunities provided by the employer.

If employers are unaware of harassment, they will not necessarily be held liable. In another case, the U.S. Supreme Court protected school systems from lawsuits over teachers' sexual harassment of students. In this case, a Texas school district was not held responsible for the actions of a male teacher who was having sex with an eighth-grade girl. The mother had sued the school system even though school district employees did not know about the sexual relationship.

Men can be sued for harassment of other men. In *Oncale* v. *Sundowner Offshore Services,* the U.S. Supreme Court ruled that male-on-male harassment may be actionable even when it is not sexual in design. In this case, a young man working on an offshore oil rig was physically and verbally harassed by fellow workers and supervisors.

These court rulings will not resolve the confusion about sexual harassment. In an ideal world, company policy would allow employees their privacy and freedom but still punish unwanted, harmful behavior. Unfortunately, no one has yet figured what such a policy should involve, much less how to implement it. In the meantime, lawyers and judges will have to rely on subjective impressions of power, sex, and sensitivity, adding more loops and threads to the complicated maze of sexual harassment law (Dank & Fulda, 1998).

The traditional emphasis on sex in harassment interventions can lead to attempts to eliminate all hints of sexual expression from the workplace, however benign. Instead of viewing harassment law as a tool to promote women's equality as workers, the common understanding of harassment encourages courts and companies to "protect" women's sensibilities. As Camille Paglia wrote in *Time* magazine (March 23, 1998, p. 54):

> *The fanatic overprotection of women is fast making us an infantile nation. We need to treat sex with greater realism and imagination. Women should be taught not that they are passive wards of the state but that sex is a great human comedy where the joke is always on us.*

Title VII of the Civil Rights Act was never meant to police sexuality. It was intended to provide people with the opportunity to conduct their work on equal terms. Sex should be treated like anything else in the environment. When it furthers discrimination, it should be eliminated. When it does not, it should not be in the domain of our civil rights laws.

SUMMARY OF MAJOR POINTS

1. Sexual harassment. Sexual harassment can involve any unwanted verbal or nonverbal sexual behavior. The Equal Employment Opportunity Commission ruled that unwelcome sexual advances, requests for sexual favors, and other verbal or physical contact of a sexual nature constitute sexual harassment in the workplace when (a) submission to such contact is made explicitly or implicitly a term or condition of an individual's employment; (b) submission to, or rejection of, such conduct by an individual is used as the basis for employment decisions affecting the individual; or (c) such conduct has the purpose or effect of unreasonably interfering with a person's work performance or creating an intimidating, hostile, or offensive working environment.

2. Prevalence. The extent of sexual harassment is difficult to estimate because researchers have used different definitions. One overview of studies on sexual harassment in a variety of settings indicated that employees or students have at least a 40 percent chance of encountering sexual harassment in their place of work or study. People have also been harassed by health care professionals, military superiors, and religious leaders.

3. Effects of harassment. Harassment victims report various stress reactions to unwanted sexual approaches. Nervousness, loss of sleep, loss of motivation, and weight loss are just a few of the symptoms that have been reported. Despite these reactions, the violations are seldom reported to employers.

4. Gender differences. Men have higher scores than do women on the Likelihood to Sexually Harass (LSH) scale. Women are more likely than men to rate various behaviors as sexual harassment, but this difference is not large. Male students are more likely to interpret unwanted sexual attention from female professors as relatively benign, compared to female students' interpretation of sexual attention from male professors.

5. Individual differences. Men who score high on the LSH scale tend to identify with a traditional stereotypic view of masculinity. Thoughts about social dominance appear to be tightly linked to thoughts about sexuality in high LSH men.

6. Sexual harassment settings. In addition to the workplace, harassment occurs in a variety of other environments. These include educational, therapeutic, military, and religious settings. Each of these institutions has taken steps to try to reduce the likelihood of harassment.

7. Reducing sexual harassment.   With the publicity associated with some high-profile harassment lawsuits, a number of people appear to have become more aware of potentially harassing behavior and have voluntarily altered their behavior. Many supervisors have attempted to reduce sexual harassment in the workplace by requiring sensitivity and awareness training programs. However, there is little evidence that these programs are effective in the long run. Individuals experiencing sexual harassment now have legal recourse as the result of several recent U.S. Supreme Court decisions.

19

Sexual Assault and Abuse

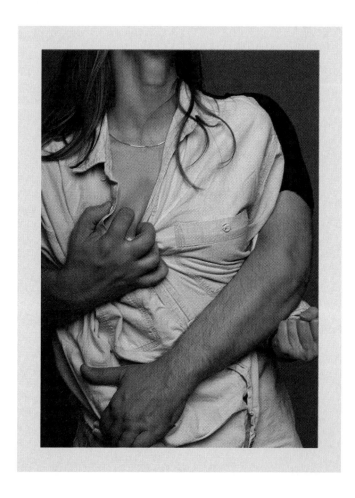

Reality or Myth

1. *About 40 percent of American men report that they have forced a woman to engage in sexual acts against her will.*

2. *Men can be forced by women to have sex against their will.*

3. *Women generally enjoy rape, although they are unlikely to admit it.*

4. *A majority of the sexual crimes against children are committed by adults who are friends or relatives of the victim.*

5. *Sexual contact during childhood almost always leads to emotional problems during adulthood.*

6. *Sexual molestation is the most common form of childhood abuse.*

The ways in which human beings relate to one another sexually reflect the complexity of human emotions and motivations. Sexual activity can be a medium for expressing the deepest and most pleasurable feelings we have, or a vehicle for the degradation and abuse of another. In this chapter we describe sexual interactions that are marked by several forms of coercion. First, we consider sexual assault, in which a person is forced by physical or psychological means into sexual activity. Second, we discuss adult sexual activity with children and adolescents that is against the law in North America—child sexual abuse. We also consider factors that increase the risk of being assaulted or abused and examine the long-term correlates of these experiences.

Sexual Assault

Sexual assault is one of the most exploitative forms of sexual encounter. Often including **rape**, it involves the use of coercion (force) to dominate another person or to obtain sexual contact with another person against that individual's will. In this section, we look at some of the myths that surround rape and sexual assault. Then we survey the characteristics of sexual aggressors and victims, and the factors associated with sexual assault. Finally, we look at the consequences of sexual assault for the victim and the responses by police and the courts to the offense.

THE MAGNITUDE OF THE PROBLEM

In the United States, there was 1 reported rape for every 275 women in 1997 (Federal Bureau of In-

---

sexual assault—Forcing another person to have sexual contact.
rape—Sexual intercourse that occurs without consent under actual or threatened force.

---

vestigation, 1998). The number of sexual assaults reported annually to criminal justice authorities, however, is a vast underestimate of the actual number of assaults committed each year because most assault victims do not report the crime.

Sexual assault is a frightening invasion of personhood. We need, however, to keep this abhorrent act in perspective. The vast majority of men do not rape women. About 3 percent of men and 1.5 percent of women aged 18 to 59 in Laumann et al.'s (1994) nationally representative sample reported having forced a person to do something sexual. Although this is undoubtedly an underestimate because some men and women are reluctant to admit such antisocial activity, it still underlines the fact that most people do not rape, despite the claims of some who contend that all men are rapists or potential rapists.

Most early research on sexual assault was conducted with convicted rapists and with those victims who reported the assault to authorities. More recent research involving surveys of nonreporting victims and nonidentified rapists has challenged a number of common myths about sexual assault. *Reality or Myth* 🔲

RAPE STEREOTYPES

There are many stereotypes about sexual assault. Some of these are supported by evidence; others are utterly false. One of the most common myths about rape is that it occurs because women tempt men beyond men's ability to control themselves. At least two beliefs are reflected in this myth. One is that the victim is at least partially responsible for the attack. This idea is called **victim precipitation.** It has its historical roots in the ancient notion, discussed in Chapter 1, that women are dangerous seductresses and men must be wary of women's power to excite them into a state of uncontrollable lust.

This belief is closely related to the second idea: that after lust has been triggered, men are powerless to prevent themselves from sexually attacking the person who elicited the lust. To evaluate the accuracy of these beliefs, we review what is known about the perpetrators of the crime, the victims of rape, and the circumstances under which rape occurs.

THE SEXUAL ASSAULT OFFENDER

Until recently, information about the characteristics of sexual assault offenders was limited to those who had been arrested for an assault. Only about a third of reported sexual assaults in one year resulted in the arrest of alleged assailants, however (Federal Bureau of Investigation, 1998). In the remaining cases reported to authorities, the assailants could not be found, there was not enough evidence to proceed legally, or police did not believe that a rape had occurred.

Further, recent research suggests that it is inappropriate to generalize from small samples of convicted rapists to the larger population of those who coerce others into sexual contact. Hence we differentiate between *convicted* rapists and *unidentified* rapists, the latter being persons who admit anonymously that they have forced others to have sexual

> **victim precipitation**—The notion that a victim is at least partially responsible for the attack.

contact but whose victims did not report them to authorities, or who were reported but not caught, arrested, or convicted.

Although the ages of those arrested for sexual assault range from 10 to 65, men aged 18 to 24 account for most arrests (Federal Bureau of Investigation, 1998). Women, gay men, and young boys have also been convicted of rape. The majority of convicted rapists use weapons to coerce their victims, and in three-quarters of the cases, physical force is also employed. The majority of offenders are either drinking or drunk at the time of the sexual assault (Abbey, Ross, McDuffie, & McAuslan, 1996).

In contrast to convicted rapists, unidentified rapists rarely use weapons; instead, they rely on verbal coercion, threats, and physical restraint. The deliberate attempt to intoxicate their victims with alcohol or other drugs appears to be a common coercive strategy that both convicted and unidentified assailants use (Abbey et al., 1996; Barbaree, Hudson, & Seto, 1993). Examination of the childhood and adolescence of convicted sex offenders and unidentified assailants has yielded both similarities and differences in the two groups.

Socialization Experiences of Convicted Sex Offenders. First, as noted by William Prendergast (1994), a psychologist who worked with sex offenders in a prison environment for about three decades, many of these men lack self-confidence from an early age. They may compensate for their general sense of inadequacy with exaggerated demonstrations of masculinity, which include assault.

Second, 20 to 30 percent of sex offenders reported being victims of violent sexual abuse during their childhood and adolescent years (Dhawan & Marshall, 1996; Graham, 1996; Groth, 1979; Fedoroff & Moran, 1998). As noted in Chapter 17, this "abuse-to-abuser" hypothesis has been widely accepted among mental health professionals, but there is almost no evidence to support a direct link (cf. Fedoroff & Moran, 1997). One danger of this hypothesis is that victims of child sexual coercion may come to believe that they will inevitably become like their abusers.

Third, it is perhaps not surprising, given the first two findings, that some adult sex offenders report a pattern of having sexually victimized others during their childhood and adolescence (Barbaree et al., 1993). Adolescent sex offenders, similar to their adult counterparts, have lower levels of self-esteem (Monto, Zgourides, & Harris, 1998).

Socialization Experiences of Unidentified Assailants.

In the case of unidentified offenders, the individuals' backgrounds may be more representative of the general population than are those of convicted rapists. Smithyman (1979) obtained a sample of 50 unidentified rapists by soliciting research participants through advertisements. (This method of obtaining the sample limits the generalizability to those men who would be willing to participate in such a study, of course.) Of the men who responded, 72 percent had never been arrested for any crime, and only 6 percent had been arrested for sexual offenses. High school diplomas were obtained by 84 percent, and 58 percent had entered college. Forty-two percent held white-collar jobs, and 26 percent were married. Other researchers comparing uniden-

The attitudes of peers may be more important than class or race in shaping values about sexual coercion.

tified assailants and nonassailants have also found no differences in race, social class, or place of residence between the two groups (Ageton, 1983).

The socialization experiences of unidentified assailants, however, do appear to differ from those of nonassailants. Ageton's (1983) data from unidentified adolescent offenders showed a pattern of estrangement from the values of families and teachers. These boys engaged in various delinquent activities and identified with delinquent peer groups. Compared with their nonassaultive peers, they expected to receive more negative labeling from both their parents and their teachers. In Ageton's five-year study, these differences in assaultive and nonassaultive boys were found before as well as after they had coerced girls to have sex.

Similarly, Kanin's (1985) data indicated that college men who engaged in sexually coercive behavior said that their best friends would "definitely approve" of forcing particular types of women to have sex with them. If the men perceived their potential victims to be "loose," "teasers," "pick-ups," or "economic exploiters," then coercion was justified in their own eyes, and they expected that their peers would approve of their behavior. In the opinion of the men in Kanin's sample, if these women would not consent to sexual contact, then they "deserved" to be forced because they had violated sexual expectations that they raised by "flaunting, advertising, and promising sexual accessibility" (p. 225).

A general portrait emerges from these studies comparing unidentified assailants with nonassailants. The offender tends to be relatively alienated from his family and school system values and to have experienced family violence. Moreover, he identifies with a rape-supportive peer group and a value system that supports his belief that the coercion of some women is justified by the women's behavior, even though the women have not consented to sexual contact.

▶ **Issues to Consider:** How do identified sexual offenders differ from unidentified sexual offenders?

Attitudes and Personality Traits of Assailants.

Studies in which the personality and attitudes of unidentified rapists were compared with those of nonassaultive men have revealed several factors related to high levels of sexual aggression. With a sample of men ranging in age from 18 to 47, Malamuth (1996) found that hostility toward women, acceptance of interpersonal violence, and dominance as a sexual motive were positively related to self-reported sexual aggression. In Rapaport and Burkhart's (1984) research, the more coercion the unidentified assailants reported, the lower their scores were on measures of responsibility and positive socialization. The assailants in Rapaport and Burkhart's research also saw sexual aggression as more acceptable than did the nonassailants.

In an intriguing study of college students, Mahoney, Shively, and Traw (1986) obtained self-reports of coercive behavior and measures of **hypermasculinity**. A man's rating on the hypermasculinity scale (Mosher & Sirkin, 1984) is determined by asking him to indicate which of two statements from 30 pairs better describes him. For example, most hypermasculine men would choose the statement, "You have to screw some women before they know who is boss," in preference to the statement, "You have to love some women before they know you don't want to be boss." Not surprisingly, hypermasculine men reported having engaged in more sexually coercive behavior than did their counterparts, who were more likely to select the less aggressive alternative.

In the light of the Mahoney group's (1986) findings and Kanin's (1985) conclusion that assailants and their peers perceived some types of women as legitimate targets of coercion, it is tempting to speculate that hypermasculine males are most attracted to the **hyperfeminine** women whom they perceive as deserving of assault (Murnen & Byrne, 1991). Other researchers have hypothesized that traditional gender-role identification and gender-role attitudes are related to the likelihood of engaging in sexual coercion. Among both men and women, traditional attitudes toward gender roles are correlated with a belief in rape myths, although the relationship is stronger for men than for women (Christopher, Madura, & Weaver, 1998).

> **hypermasculinity**—Exaggeration of male dominance through an emphasis on male virility, strength, and aggression.
> **hyperfemininity**—Exaggerated adherence to a stereotypic feminine gender role.

Sexual Characteristics of Assailants. It is common to think of rapists as sexually preoccupied people with high sex drives. A rather different picture emerged from the work of Groth and Burgess (1977), who studied men convicted of sexual assault, women who were victims of sexual assault, and victims' descriptions of the assault to the police. Three-quarters of the convicted rapists experienced some kind of problem with erection or ejaculation during the assault. About one-third of the men showed clear evidence of sexual dysfunction of some type.

Ironically, practically none of the convicted rapists reported similar dysfunctions in their sexual relations with consenting partners. Rather, their dysfunctions appeared to be specific to the context of rape. These observations are consistent with the notion that rape is not primarily sexually motivated but instead is an attempt to dominate and subjugate another person. There remains the larger question, however, of why the anger, resentment, and need to control are expressed sexually.

Studies of unidentified rapists are more supportive of the notion that rapists have strong sexual appetites. Compared with nonrapists, the unidentified rapists in Kanin's (1985) sample had had a greater number of sexual partners, as well as considerably more sexual outlets. The average number of orgasms per month from coitus, fellatio, and masturbation was 6.0, compared to 0.8 for the nonassailants. When asked how often they attempted to seduce a new date, 62 percent of the unidentified rapists, compared to 19 percent of the nonrapists, responded "most of the time."

Part of the discrepancy between results of studies of convicted rapists and those of studies of unidentified rapists regarding aggressive versus sexual motivations may stem from the level of relationship between the rapist and the victim. Women who are raped by strangers are far more likely to report the assault, resulting in an overrepresentation of stranger assaults among convicted rapists (McCormick, 1994). It may be that convicted men who rape strangers are using sex to express aggressive, hostile motives, whereas men who rape acquaintances are using aggressiveness to achieve sexual goals, a notion to which we will return when we examine hypotheses about the causes of rape. Before turning to that topic, we consider victims of sexual coercion.

> ▶ **Issues to Consider:** Why do you think that convicted rapists often experience sexual problems during forced sex?

VICTIMS OF SEXUAL COERCION

Victims of sexual assault come from all walks of life. In trying to describe the typical victim of sexual coercion, we face some of the same generalization problems that have plagued research on rapists. We will distinguish among victims who report their assaults to authorities, victims who do not report their assaults but anonymously acknowledge during victimization surveys that they have been assaulted, and victims who do neither and about whom we know nothing.

Many people think of the typical sexual assault as the rape of a young woman by someone whom she does not know. However, about 75 percent of sexual assaults reported to authorities involve people who know each other, and among unidentified victims, the overwhelming majority know their assailants (Federal Bureau of Investigation, 1998; Lonsway, 1996). Sometimes they have just met, sometimes they have been casually dating, and sometimes they are married to each other. Many sexual assaults involve more than one assailant. Further, some of the victims of sexual assault by individuals or gangs are male.

Male Victims of Assault. Popular stereotypes of rape victims do not usually include males. Even when we consider men as rape victims, we think of them as being at risk of sexual assault only when they are in prison and only by male assailants. Indeed, many men are raped in prison. In an ambitious study of prison rape in several prisons in a midwestern state, Struckman-Johnson et al. (1996; see also Struckman-Johnson, 1998) found that 22 percent of imprisoned men anonymously reported having been raped (compared to 7 percent of imprisoned women). A quarter of the rapes of men were gang assaults. Women (staff) were among the perpetrators in 5 percent of the cases, and they were the sole perpetrators in 2 percent of the cases.

Reports of male victims from rape crisis centers and the data from several recent studies demonstrate that nonimprisoned men can also be sexually assaulted by women (Struckman-Johnson & Struckman-Johnson, 1994). In Laumann et al.'s (1994) national study, 3.6 percent of the men reported having been forced into sexual contact, which would generalize to more than 3 million American men.

Perhaps because of the traditional definition of rape as an act committed by a male against a female, most researchers studying acquaintance assault have constructed their measures on the assumption that males are perpetrators and females are victims. Struckman-Johnson (1988) administered a survey to college students that allowed them—regardless of their sex—to respond as assailants, victims, or both. In her sample, 22 percent of the women and 16 percent of the men reported that they had experienced at least one forced-sex episode.

As might be expected, the strategies men and women used to obtain sex differed. In Struckman-Johnson's (1988) study, 53 percent of the female victims, compared to 9 percent of the male victims, reported sexual coercion through physical restraint. In contrast, male victims were more likely to report the use of psychological force (48 percent) than were female victims (16 percent). For 12 percent of the incidents, the force used included physical restraint, physical intimidation, threat of harm, or actual harm (Struckman-Johnson & Struckman-Johnson, 1994). Like victimized women, men who are raped find the event traumatic and the reporting of it difficult (see "Highlight: Male Rape" on page 454).

Later in the chapter, we describe the after-effects of rape on women. Following rape by women, many college men experience the same sorts of disruptions in eating, sleeping, sexual relationships, social relationships, and psychological functioning as college women and women in the general community report (Struckman-Johnson, 1991). The self-reported negative emotional impact was less when the coercion was from female than from male perpetrators. In addition to the fear, anger, and self-blame that is commonly felt by women who have experienced coercion, the men coerced by women felt that their masculinity had been threatened. In contrast, heterosexual men coerced by men were concerned about perceptions of their sexual orientation (Struckman-Johnson et al., 1996). *Reality or Myth* ?

HIGHLIGHT

Male Rape

This account was sent to us by a young convict after he took a human sexuality course in prison:

It was the policy for inmates to shower—all at once—in a large shower room. While showering, I was aware of a hand brushing against my genitals. As I turned and looked around, I observed a young male on his hands and knees as a much larger youth began raping him anally. The cries were loud and scary as the incident continued. I pretended not to notice as another man stepped in front of the youth and began to force his penis into the youth's mouth. I stood there in sheer disbelief as the youth became a sexual "sandwich" for the two larger youths. After they had both ejaculated, they punched and kicked the smaller man until he lay still on the floor—blood and semen running from his anus. . . . It was not a pretty sight. It is a memory which is deeply imbedded in my mind—as vivid as though it was yesterday. Whatever happened to the young man who was victimized? He committed suicide three days later.

Female Victims of Assault. The true incidence of the sexual assault of women is difficult to estimate because the relevant statistics are compiled in different ways by different sources. Further, police reports include only a fraction of incidents because many victims do not report the assault. Even when they do, legal authorities do not always believe the victim. A nationally representative sample of adolescents revealed rates of sexual assaults of females by adolescent males as much as 300 times higher than police reports show (Ageton, 1983).

Studies of adolescents are particularly important because of the consistent finding (among both victims who report to authorities and those who report only anonymously on victimization surveys) that females in their reproductive years, 16–35, are at greatest risk of sexual assault (Maletzky, 1996; McCormick, 1994). Although research on victims who report the assault to authorities has suggested that they come predominantly from lower socioeconomic classes, such studies may overrepresent the poor because victims who can afford to do so may seek treatment from private sources to avoid having to deal with the police and the media. Findings based on representative samples show that a woman's risk of sexual assault is unrelated to her social class (Ageton, 1983).

The overwhelming majority of female victims know their assailants. The level of relationship varies

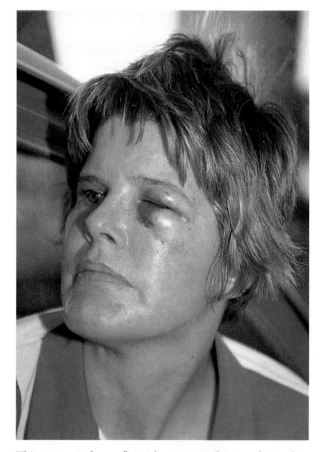

This woman's face reflects the trauma of a sexual assault.

considerably across studies; assailants range from casual acquaintances of the victims to friends, teachers, neighbors, classmates, dates, lovers, fiancés, and spouses. In Laumann et al.'s (1994) national sample, only 4 percent of women who experienced forced sexual activity claimed that the perpetrator was a stranger.

Among samples of college students, between 86 percent and 98 percent of the victims knew their attackers (Koss, Dinero, Seibel, & Cox, 1988; Mynatt & Allgeier, 1990). Acquaintance assault (sometimes called date rape) first received attention when Kirkpatrick and Kanin (1957) found that 62 percent of college women they surveyed reported experiencing at least one episode of offensive force in the year before they entered college, and 56 percent reported experiencing at least one such incident during their first year in college.

Perhaps the most startling statistics emerged from a study of the responses of college men to a questionnaire containing inquiries about the use of offensive sexual aggression (Kanin, 1969). Specifically, the men were asked whether they had personally attempted to have sexual intercourse with a woman by using force that was disagreeable and offensive to her. About 22 percent of these men admitted to the use of force.

The form and the extent of force that female victims experience seem to vary as a function of whether the assailant is a stranger or an acquaintance. As we might expect, acquaintance assaults are less likely to involve either a weapon or physical injury to the victim than are assaults by strangers (Allgeier, 1987; Koss et al., 1988). Among college students, the pattern of assaults sometimes involves a man's attempt to engage in a particular sexual activity with little or no prior sexual play. As Parcell and Kanin (1976) noted:

> These episodes usually consist of males going for the "whole scene" in one relatively simultaneous maneuver, rather than proceeding along some sequential seductive order. In other words, the abrupt aggressive act may include some combination of efforts at kissing, fondling, attempting to remove clothing, maneuvering the female into a coitally advantageous position, male exposure, and so on. (pp. 19–20).

Perpetrators of sexual assault often deliberately attempt to intoxicate victims with drugs or alcohol. As Roiphe (1993) pointed out, a man may give a woman alcohol or drugs, but she chooses whether to consume them, unless drugs are slipped into her drink. Such deceptive behavior has been occurring with the drug Rohypnol, known on the street as "roofies." This odorless, colorless, tasteless tranquilizer is dropped into victims' drinks, causing them to pass out and have little memory of what happens next. In response to highly publicized reports of women being raped after being victimized by this ploy, President Clinton signed a bill in 1996 outlawing Rohypnol and other "date-rape drugs." The bill subjects rapists to an additional 20 years in prison if they use a narcotic to incapacitate their victims.

The majority of assaulted women feel extremely hostile following the attack, with about a third reporting anger or disgust, or both. Other emotional reactions include fear, guilt, and emotional pain. Women with relatively assertive personalities, however, make fewer internal attributions of responsibility; that is, they engage in less self-blame for the assault than do women who are relatively nonassertive (Mynatt & Allgeier, 1990). An interesting finding emerged from Koss et al.'s (1988) study in that 73 percent of the women they categorized as rape victims did not define their experience as rape. These women apparently did not recognize that their self-reported experience met the legal criteria for sexual assault. Further clouding our interpretations of rape, 42 percent of women categorized as rape victims in Koss's study later had consensual sex with the man who had allegedly raped them earlier (Gilbert, 1992).

As with acquaintance rape, sex forced on women by their husbands is seldom defined by the women as rape or sexual assault and is almost never reported to authorities (Russell, 1984). Among the college student sample that Koss et al. (1988) studied, 351 of the women (11 percent) were married. Of these, 13 percent reported having been raped by spouses or family members.

What Provokes Sexual Assault?

Among the current hypotheses used to explain rape are victim precipitation, uncontrollable lust, uncontrollable aggression, exaggerated gender-role identity, and exposure to violent pornography. As we discuss in Chapter 20, exposure to violent pornography has been shown to increase acceptance of rape myths and negative attitudes toward women. We do not know whether exposure to violent pornography sufficiently lowers inhibitions against aggression in the real world to the point that a man who is irritated by a woman and then sees violent pornography would actually seek out that woman to rape her. We now turn to other ideas, starting with the hypothesis that has received the least support: the notion that victims cause assailants to rape them.

Victim Precipitation. The majority of adults—both men and women—blame the victims of sexual assault for provocative behaviors before, during, and after they have been forced to engage in sex. Almost all research on victim blaming for sexual assault has focused on attitudes toward female victims.

The belief that a victim precipitates assault by her behavior comes in a number of guises. About two-thirds of a sample of U.S. citizens agreed that "women provoke rape by their appearance or behavior" (Feild & Bienen, 1980). Teenagers—males and females alike—are less likely to perceive the wearing of an open shirt, tight jeans, or a revealing bathing suit as a signal of sexual interest or availability by a man than by a woman (Zellman & Goodchilds, 1983). In addition to being held responsible for assaults because of the way they dress, women, according to various surveys, are also held accountable if they hitchhike or enter a man's apartment (McCormick, 1994).

At odds with the stereotypes of victims' provoking their own assaults were the results of a study sponsored by the Federal Commission on Crimes of Violence, which concluded that only 4 to 6 percent of rape charges involve victim precipitation (Curtis, 1974). That study was conducted more than two decades ago; the assault rate has risen since that time, but there is no evidence to suggest that rates of victim precipitation have increased.

Uncontrolled Lust or Uncontrolled Aggression?
Belief in victim precipitation may stem in part from the assumption that a rapist attacks a victim out of an intense, overpowering sexual drive unleashed by a sexually provocative woman. During one rape trial observed by the McCahill (1979) group,

The defense argued to the jury that the victim "really isn't very pretty. I'll bet she invented the story of rape to attract attention to herself, or perhaps she even consented out of loneliness." Then dropping his voice and speaking specifically to the men in the jury, he added, "I'm sure you've all heard women lie through their teeth when they're lonely." In the same case, as further proof the defense asked the wife of the defendant, a very attractive young woman, to parade before the jury, while he commented, "She is really more attractive than the complaining witness. Why would he need to rape this homely girl anyway with a wife like this?" (p. 188)

As Feild and Bienen (1980) pointed out, if a relatively unattractive victim charges rape, she may be perceived as lying—"No one would be turned on by her." However, if the victim is attractive, some observers would maintain that the rapist was so overcome with passion that he could not help himself. Clearly, both approaches imply that the rapist's motivation is sexual rather than assaultive. Despite this common belief, most experts have concluded that sexual arousal and aggression fuse into a volatile pathway to rape (Malamuth, 1996; Muehlenhard, Danoff-Burg, & Powch, 1996).

Eugene Kanin (1985) found some evidence that unidentified males who rape acquaintances may have both aggressive and sexual motives, as the male assailants in his sample perceived themselves to be sexually deprived. Although the average number of monthly sexual outlets they reported far exceeded the number reported by nonassailants (6 versus fewer than 1), the number of sexual outlets they desired was 18 compared to 11 for nonassailants. Because nonassailants also reported a desire for greater sexual contact than they were having but did not feel compelled to force women to engage in nonconsensual sex, what is it that motivates the rapist to engage in sexual aggression? Assailants reported receiving considerably more pressure from their peers to engage in sexual activity than did nonassailants. This finding provides some support for the idea that exaggerated gender-role norms and identification may underlie the perpetration of sexual assault, a hypothesis to which we now return.

▶ **Issues to Consider:** To what extent do you believe
that rapists are motivated by sexual arousal versus
needs to dominate and aggress against their victims?
Do you think that rapists from different populations
(e.g., stranger rapists, acquaintance rapists) may differ
in their motives?

Exaggerated Gender-Role Identity. The traditional
socialization of men and women may set the stage for
conflict and sexual assault. Men are trained to believe
that a truly masculine man is aggressive and has intense sexual needs (Byers, 1996; Hall & Barongan,
1997). Many traditional people believe that women
are not particularly interested in sex but can be
"awakened" sexually with enough persuasion and seductive power. Accordingly, some rapists believe that
even though their victims struggled, the woman secretly enjoyed the rapist's sexual prowess. In other
words, the assumption is that just because a woman
says no, she does not necessarily *mean* no. Even if she
means no initially, continues this assumption, the
sexual activity will lead her to change her mind
(McCormick, 1994; Muehlenhard and Rodgers, 1998).

For women, traditional feminine socialization
only increases the barriers to communication between
men and women. Women are encouraged to give conflicting messages. They are taught that the attention
of men is extremely important and that the best way
to obtain such attention is to be sexually attractive
and desirable. According to the conventional wisdom, however, a "good" woman does not agree to
sexual relations readily; even when she is sexually interested in her partner, she is supposed to maintain a
facade of passive disinclination. If she appears to be
too interested in having sex, she risks being labeled as
"easy." As described in Chapter 6, some women have
reported using the token no when they desired closer
sexual intimacy to avoid assignment of such negative
labels. Men are expected to push the issue of sex, and
women are expected to resist. Both men and women
learn about these gender-role expectations at early
ages, which may impede rather than enhance heterosexual communication. Further, some acquaintance
assaults may result from the confusing communication with which young people must cope when they
are attempting to decipher others' desires.

The belief that men ought to—or at least inevitably do—push for sexual intimacy and that

women must therefore set limits is deeply ingrained
in both Eastern and Western cultural traditions (Hall
& Barongan, 1997; Humphreys & Herold, 1996).
Thus it is important that parents and others who
help to shape young people's outlook and behavior
take responsibility for teaching youths to communicate what they do and do not want in their interpersonal interactions, so that they may reduce the
potential conflict arising from traditional male and
female roles. Children and adolescents need to understand that violence is not a solution to anything
and that it is possible to clarify their current interest
or lack of interest in sexual intimacy by discussing
sexual feelings honestly and directly with potential
partners.

We hope that research over the next few years
will yield more information relevant to these hypotheses about the causes of sexual assault. In the
meantime, both research and the efforts of various
advocacy groups have done a great deal to reduce
the pain associated with the aftermath of rape.

THE AFTERMATH OF SEXUAL ASSAULT

The anguish wrought by sexual assault often extends
far beyond the actual experience. For about a third
of victims, the rape episode itself is only the preface
to a series of traumatic events that can last for years
(Kilpatrick, Edmunds, & Seymour, 1992). Further,
the common belief that rape by a stranger is more
traumatic than rape by a boyfriend or husband is not
supported by research on assault (Golding, 1996;
Kilpatrick, Best, Saunders, & Veronen, 1988). The
Kilpatrick group's study found that women assaulted
by spouses or dates were as likely as those attacked
by strangers to be depressed, fearful, obsessive-
compulsive, and sexually dysfunctional years after
the assault.

On the basis of their research with victims of rape
seen at Boston City Hospital, Burgess and Holmstrom
(1974) described a **rape trauma syndrome**. The syndrome consists of two phases. The acute phase, which
can last for several weeks after the rape, generally includes one of two basic reactions. With an *expressive*
reaction, the victim cries frequently and expresses

rape trauma syndrome—Emotional and behavioral consequences that victims experience after being raped.

After a sexual assault, it is important that victims receive counseling and support to help reduce their fears and alleviate inappropriate feelings of guilt over the attack.

feelings of fear, anxiety, tension, and anger. With a *controlled* reaction, the woman is composed, calm, and subdued.

Following the acute phase, women go through a long-term *reorganization* phase. During this period, which can last more than a year, women experience a variety of reactions. Some move repeatedly and switch jobs or even stop going to work. Fears of any situation resembling that in which the rape occurred are common. A rape survivor may experience disruptions in consensual sexual relationships; avoidance of sexual activities that he or she formerly enjoyed; or disturbances related to specific activities that took place during the event, such as swallowing if the assault involved forced oral penetration. Sexual assault can also cause excessive menstrual bleeding, genital burning, missed menstrual periods, and painful intercourse (Golding, 1996).

Finally, some victims have a *silent* rape reaction (Burgess & Holmstrom, 1974). They experience the kinds of reactions described above but do not tell anyone about the assault. They are thereby deprived

of the opportunity to obtain the support and counseling that may help them to resolve their fears and their undeserved feelings of guilt.

In addition to their personal reactions, many assault victims have to contend with a series of painful and humiliating episodes in police stations and in the courts (see "Highlight: Was He Asking for It?"). The aftermath of the mugging described in this Highlight seems ridiculously farfetched. It is not so farfetched, however, when the crime is sexual assault. In fact, by substituting the idea of sex for the idea of money in the questions in the Highlight, you can obtain a fairly realistic picture of the kind of interrogation that many victims of sexual assault have endured. *Reality or Myth* ?

WHAT SHOULD ASSAULT VICTIMS DO?

A victim of sexual assault should call the nearest rape crisis center for help immediately, *before* changing clothes, bathing, or doing anything else. Many crisis centers provide a volunteer to accompany the victim during everything from initial medical treatment to final court appearances. Some centers also offer group counseling sessions to help victims cope with the immediate and long-term effects of the attack. There are many of these centers throughout North America.

In the course of the medical examination and treatment administered after an assault, a victim usually receives a physical examination and an inspection of the genitals or other areas violated during the assault. A sperm sample is collected if possible, and other evidence of assault is documented. Many states have recently passed laws requiring the county or state to pay the cost of such medical examinations.

After undergoing a medical examination and treatment, the victim should report the assault to the police. The majority of victims, however, do not do so. The two factors that significantly increase the likelihood of reporting a sexual assault to the police are (1) if the victim sustained a physical injury during the assault and (2) if the offender used a weapon (Bachman, 1998). Many victims are reluctant to report because they feel guilty and responsible for the assault. Further, some victims fear rejection by their mates, family members, and friends in the event that the assault becomes public knowledge. The small proportion of victims who overcome their fears and

Was He Asking for It?

John Jones walks six blocks from his office to the subway every day after work. Occasionally, he gives some coins to some of the beggars who solicit money along his route.

One evening, he stayed at work later than usual because he had been invited to a dinner party and needed to change his clothes. He brought a nice shirt and a sport coat with him to work and changed in the restroom. It was dark and rainy when he left the office. The other office workers had left for home earlier, and the street was deserted. About halfway to the subway, John noticed one of the beggars to whom he had occasionally given spare change approaching him. The man held out his hand, but John smiled and said, "Sorry, but I'm afraid I don't have any extra today," and continued on his way. He thought that the beggar was following him, so with some apprehension, he began walking more quickly. The next thing he knew, he had been tackled to the ground, and the beggar told him to give him his wallet or "I'll cut you up good!" It had gotten quite dark, so John could not see if the man had a knife or some other weapon; he decided that maybe it would be best if he just gave up the wallet. The beggar grabbed it and ran off.

John staggered home to call the police. When he got home, he still felt upset, so he fixed a drink, took a shower, and changed into dry clothes to try to calm down before making the call. He was told to come to the station to file a report.

Throughout his dealings with the police, and later, in court, John was exposed continuously to statements and questioning that suggested that he had not really been robbed or that he had provoked the beggar into the assault:

"It is six blocks between your office and the subway, so why didn't you take a cab? Aren't you asking for it when you parade the street every night?"

"Have you ever given away money to anyone before?"

"Did you ever give money to the person you *claim* mugged you?"

"You don't look like you've been hurt; how do we know that a mugging occurred?"

"Can you prove your wallet was taken?"

"Why were you so dressed up? Wasn't that just inviting the assault?"

"You've given him a dollar or two before and now you claim he took your wallet containing $50, but in giving him some money, weren't you in effect consenting to give him all your money?"

"You didn't resist the mugger; therefore, you must have really wanted to give him your wallet."

"You said that he threatened you, but you didn't see the knife, and in fact, you handed over your wallet to him, so it doesn't sound like a mugging at all."

"If you really were mugged, why did you wait two hours before calling? Maybe you really wanted to give the man your money at the time but then changed your mind later."

---

inhibitions enough to report the assault have no guarantee that the police will record the charge or that the rapist will be convicted.

SEXUAL ASSAULT AND THE CRIMINAL JUSTICE SYSTEM

Legal authorities may determine that an assault charge is unfounded for many reasons. If there are obvious discrepancies in the victim's story or if the police conclude from their investigation that no offense occurred or was attempted, they will declare the charge unfounded.

Kanin (1994) studied the forcible-rape cases in a small city in a midwestern state over a nine-year period. Of the 109 reported rapes, 41 percent were determined to be false. Revenge, attention seeking, and the need for an alibi (e.g., an unmarried adolescent becomes pregnant and tries to avoid responsibility) were the most common motives for the false allegations. Unfortunately, these cases complicate and detract from the efforts to reduce our high rates of sexual assault.

When a case is determined to be unfounded, it is not included in the crime statistics, and the authorities do not deal with it in any way. Under these conditions, actual victims may find themselves in the unexpected and bewildering predicament of having come to the police for aid (depicted by the media as the courageous and correct course to take), only to have the door slammed in their faces.

The assistance of a female crisis center volunteer is potentially useful in reducing the likelihood that the police will judge an assault charge unfounded. Moreover, McCahill, Meyer, and Fischman's study (1979) of rape reports in Philadelphia showed that the presence of another woman during the report—whether she was the police officer taking the report or the secretary taking notes during the interview—was associated with a reduced proportion of rape charges that are declared unfounded.

About half of all complaints that are declared founded do not result in an arrest. Moreover, of those arrested, only 10 percent are prosecuted. Based on these figures, an alleged rapist's chances of being convicted for assault are only 1 in 100 (Maletzky, 1998). Most of us would be willing to bet quite a bit of money if the probability of losing were only 1 percent.

State Laws on Sexual Assault. In an effort to improve these rather grim statistics, dramatic changes are being made in the legal definition of assault and the treatment of the victim whose case does reach the courtroom. When victims, aided by crisis center volunteers, report assaults to the police and tell their stories in court, they not only diminish their own feelings of helplessness but also have the satisfaction of reducing the likelihood that the rapist will be able to attack others in the future.

Many states no longer employ the term *rape* because of its connotation of forced penile-vaginal penetration. The broader phrase *sexual assault,* which implies coercive sexual contact that does not necessarily involve penile-vaginal intercourse, has become more common.

Also, many states have rewritten their laws in gender-neutral terms so that the victim and the offender can be either male or female. Previously, sexual assaults on males were prosecuted under sodomy laws. The problem with using sodomy laws is that both participants, the perpetrator and the victim, are usually charged.

The issue of consent remains a crucial one in the definition of sexual assault. For example, in **statutory rape,** an older person is charged with having sex with another person who is not considered old enough to give consent to sexual activity, even if the younger person willingly engaged in or even initiated sexual contact. Our statutory rape laws can be traced to England more than 700 years ago, when ravishing a maiden "under the age of 12" became illegal (Donovan, 1997). These laws became part of the American legal system through English common law. Today, the age of consent in the United States varies by state and ranges from 14 to 18 years of age; in more than half the states, the age of consent is 16. In other parts of the world for which we have information, the age of consent ranges from 12 in Spain to 21 in Mexico (Caron, 1998).

Some politicians have called for stricter enforcement of statutory rape laws in an attempt to reduce adolescent pregnancy and birthrates. Recent studies indicate that about half of all babies born to minor women are fathered by adult men (Donovan, 1997). This approach is unlikely to reduce adolescent pregnancy rates, however, because the phenomenon is more complicated than that of young men "seducing" girls. Indeed, stricter enforcement could keep pregnant girls from seeking health care because of fear that their partners may be identified.

Returning to the issue of force, in the hypothetical story presented in the Highlight ("Was He Asking for It?" on page 459), it was implied that the mugged man consented to the mugging because he had earlier given away money to many people, including the mugger. That is, of course, patently absurd. However, the same logic has prevailed in both societal attitudes toward rape victims and the arguments of attorneys who are defending alleged rapists. For example, if a

statutory rape—Sexual intercourse with a person who is under the legal age of consent in a given state.

victim had ever consented to have sex with anyone, or if she and the offender had ever engaged in a sexual interaction—even kissing—then the traditional view was that she must have consented to whatever sexual acts her assailant desired. In response to objections that such assumptions essentially put the victim rather than the assailant on trial, the U.S. Congress passed the Rape Victim's Privacy Act in 1979. This law limits the extent to which evidence of the victim's previous sexual experience with people other than the defendant can be introduced.

Another major change in some states' sexual assault laws is the elimination of the requirement that, to prove a sexual assault, the victim must have resisted. Under some circumstances, passive submission may be the victim's best strategy. Some victims who adopt passivity, however, are later described by defense attorneys as having consented to the sexual contact. To prove nonconsent, victims had to have done everything in their power to resist the assault, even if their actions might have exposed them to further brutality and injury. In part because of the work of rape crisis centers throughout the country, lawmakers and judges are beginning to realize that a woman need not have severe injuries to be a victim of sexual assault.

Clearly, the victims of sexual coercion face ongoing difficulties long after they experience an episode of sexual assault. It would be desirable to find a means of preventing all sexual coercion. Because that goal is unlikely to be met, however, people should take steps themselves to reduce their risk of being sexually assaulted.

> ▶ **Issues to Consider:** At what age do you think a person is capable of giving consent to taking part in sexual activity?

FACTORS ASSOCIATED WITH BEING SEXUALLY ASSAULTED

Marital status is correlated with risk of assault, with single women being at greatest risk, followed by divorced or separated women; married women are at least risk (Russell, 1984). Moreover, women in their adolescence or early 20s are at greater risk than are older women. It is impossible to alter factors such as age or marital status to try to reduce the risk of assault. However, accumulating evidence indicates that there are strategies that can be used to reduce

the likelihood of an assault or to fend off an assault attempt.

Other risk factors have been identified that are somewhat more controllable. The chances of victimization increase as women lead "riskier" (less protected or less "traditional") lives—for example, by being sexually active, living apart from parents and (if in college) outside a dorm, and lacking a visible male partner (Mynatt & Allgeier, 1990). Among adolescent females, those who are alienated from their parents and teachers, identify with a delinquent peer group, and engage in delinquent acts themselves are more likely to become victims of sexual assault than are their nonalienated peers (Ageton, 1983).

The data regarding the relationship of rape with victims' use of alcohol are mixed. After a conference presentation of the results of their research comparing college students' experiences at rural colleges in Australia and the United States, Roberto Hugh Potter and Alban L. Wheeler (1998) reported returning home to be greeted by posters around campus stating, "Friends Don't Let Friends Date Drunk." Although this is good advice, Potter and Wheeler's results did not support the hypothesis that alcohol is the primary risk factor for sexual assaults of students. It is interesting, however, that they found alcohol to be involved in slightly over half (57 percent) of reported sexual assaults at the Australian university, where the legal age for drinking is 18, compared to slightly less than half (43 percent) at the American university, where the legal age for drinking is 21.

In their survey of college students, Antonia Abbey and her colleagues (1996) concluded that neither the man nor the woman had been drinking in 41 percent of attempted or completed rapes, and both had been drinking in 36 percent of the cases. However, in only 3 percent of cases was it only the woman who had consumed alcohol. Abbey and coworkers (1996) recommended combining prevention programs for alcohol consumption and sexual assault. The data do not appear to support that conclusion; further, an important methodological question needs to be answered: What is the baseline for drinking alcohol during consenting sexual activities? We are neither advocating the use or avoidance of alcohol. Instead, we are questioning the assumption that drinking (in moderate amounts) increases a person's risk of being sexually assaulted.

The general sexual climate within the peer groups of victims differs from that within the peer groups of nonvictims. Hall and Flannery (1985) found that girls aged 14 to 17 whose best friends were not sexually active were less likely to have been raped than those whose best friends were sexually active. The authors suggested that if a young woman is part of a peer group known to be sexually active and is sexually active herself, the man who rapes her may perceive her as being interested in sex and as having led him on.

In addition, the consensual sexual experience of sexual assault victims is greater than that of nonvictims (Abbey et al., 1996; Koss & Dinero, 1988). In Koss's research, victims reported an average of 12 sexual partners, whereas nonvictims reported an average of 4 partners. Compared with nonvictims, women who had experienced rape were more likely to have had as their first sexual partners strangers, casual dates, or married men, and they were less likely to have had steady boyfriends or a fiancé as their first sexual partners. Victims in the Koss study were also less likely than nonvictims to report that they believed that their first intercourse experience would lead to marriage.

Reducing Your Risk of Sexual Assault.   Many of these steps are more applicable to acquaintance as-sault than to assault by strangers, but, as we have seen, most assaults involve acquaintances. Much of this discussion also applies to potential male victims.

1. *Determine your sexual policies*. If you have not thought about what you need in a relationship before you would feel comfortable with or de-sirous of sexual contact, you may communicate considerable ambivalence about your wishes to a partner, who may interpret your ambiguity as a desire to "be persuaded." Thus, it may be helpful to make a list of your general sexual policies. What kind of person would you find acceptable as a potential sexual partner? How well would you want to know this person prior to physical intimacy? How much commitment would you need before you found sexual rela-tions acceptable? Where and when would sexual contact be comfortable for you? Add any other factors that you consider important in making a decision about having a sexual relationship. Peo-ple sometimes alter their policies, but it is advan-tageous for you to clarify in your own mind the general conditions under which sexual intimacy is acceptable to you.

2. *Discuss your policies regarding sexual activities*. We commonly negotiate such nonsexual activities

Women can develop a sense of confidence by learning methods of self-protection to prevent sex-ual victimization.

as where to eat dinner and what movie to see. Why not explicitly negotiate the acceptability and timing of sexual activities as well? Although evidence directly demonstrates that such negotiations do not eliminate the risk of assault attempts, the directness and firmness with which a person communicates nonconsent to sexual activity are positively related to resisting successfully an attempt at forced sexual contact (Maletzky, 1998, 1988; Quinsey & Upfold, 1985).

3. *Negotiate in public, and avoid being alone with a person until you believe that you can trust him or her.* Quinsey and Upfold's (1985) analysis of attempted versus completed rapes indicated that rapists were least likely to be deterred when the attempt was made inside a building or car and against someone whom they knew.

4. *Avoid becoming intoxicated if you are with a person with whom you do not wish to become intimate.* Abuse of alcohol or drugs by assailants and victims is common at the time of a sexual assault (Abbey et al., 1996; Barbaree et al., 1993). Although a beer or two over the period of several hours probably won't reduce your ability to fend off an unwanted sexual approach, intoxication lowers the inhibitions of a potential assailant; it may also impede the ability of a potential victim to escape an assault attempt.

5. *Make your feelings known both verbally and nonverbally.* In the event that someone does try to force you to have sex, communicate in every way possible that you do not want sexual contact. Men have cited victim resistance as the primary reason for the failure of an assault attempt. Some self-identified rapists in Kanin's (1985) sample reported surprise that their victims had been so easily intimidated; the assailants described other occasions of assault attempts that clearly had been rebuffed. Victim resistance of any kind tends to deter assault, and screaming is a particularly strong deterrent (Maletzky, 1998; Muehlenhard, Andrews, & Beal, 1996). Most males interpret screaming as strong evidence of nonconsent (Byers & Lewis, 1988; Garcia, 1998). The fact that a scream is more likely to be effective if someone other than the assailant can hear it is another reason to avoid being alone with a person until you believe that you can trust him or her.

One important qualification should be added here. Although the vast majority of assaults are carried out by acquaintances and do not involve the threat of lethal weapons, if someone attempts to assault you using a weapon as the means of coercion, resistance may be ill advised.

In summary, take as much active control of your environment as you can. Remember, however, that following all of these steps will not eliminate the possibility of being sexually assaulted or seriously injured during an assault. There are no absolute rules for dealing with all assaults; ultimately, you must decide which strategy seems most likely to get you out of the particular assault situation with the least amount of harm. We live in a society in which violence is commonplace, and hostility and aggression are often expressed against inappropriate targets. We hope that the information provided in this chapter will help you reduce your risk of being sexually assaulted. In the next section, we consider another form of coercion for which most of the preceding steps may be of little use because the target is below the age of consent and may not have the skills to implement them.

*C*hild-Adult Sexual Contacts

Child-adult sexual interactions by definition involve coercion because children are not legally capable of giving informed consent to sexual activity. An individual who provides informed consent understands both the meaning and the possible consequences of an action, but children and young adolescents often do not have a clear understanding of sexuality. One of the main reasons adults are severely punished for sexual activities with children is that they take advantage of a child's naiveté.

When a sexual relationship involves two people who are related to each other, it is called **incest**.

incest—Sexual activities between family members who are too closely related to be able to marry legally.

In general, incest refers to any sexual interaction between individuals who are so closely related that marriage between them would be illegal. The word *incest* comes from Latin and means "impure" or "soiled." Although incest can occur between two people of any age, it most frequently involves a child and an adult family member or sibling.

Sexual activity between a child and an adult is a crime in every state. Doctors, psychologists, teachers, and health professionals who work with children are legally required to report to legal authorities all suspected cases of the sexual abuse of children. By law, authorities must investigate these reports, and district attorneys must prosecute the cases.

PREVALENCE AND CHARACTERISTICS OF SEXUAL ABUSE OF CHILDREN

In attempting to determine the prevalence of any phenomenon in a country, it is useful to have a nationally representative sample. Until the 1990s, when Finkelhor, Hotaling, Lewis, and Smith (1990) and Laumann et al. (1994) reported their results, no such data were available on the prevalence of the sexual abuse of children. Finkelhor et al. (1990) asked respondents four screening questions by telephone about past experiences (occurring at age 18 or under) with what they might now consider to be sexual abuse: attempts by others to touch them sexually, initiate sexual acts including intercourse, photograph them in the nude, exhibit themselves, or perform sex acts in their presence. Of the respondents, 27 percent of the women and 16 percent of the men answered yes to one of the questions. Detailed follow-up questions were then posed to probe their experience. Using an interview procedure, the Laumann (1994) group found that 17 percent of women and 12 percent of men reported being touched sexually during childhood. An overview of 16 cross-sectional surveys of sexual abuse in North America found a prevalence rate of 14.5 percent for women and 7.9 percent for men (Gorey & Leslie, 1997). These different figures result from methodological variations and differences in how sexual abuse has been defined.

In the United States, the number of allegations of the sexual abuse* of children reported annually to child protective services leaped from an estimated 34,000 in 1976 to 400,000 in 1994 (U.S. Depart-

ment of Health and Human Services, 1996). This huge jump in reported child sexual abuse probably resulted from increased media attention and the enforcement of state laws requiring health professionals to report suspected cases of sexual abuse, rather than from a sudden epidemic in the incidence of the sexual abuse of children. The actual incidence of child abuse is not showing systematic marked increases. In surveys, the experience is reported equally frequently by people of different age **cohorts** (Finkelhor et al., 1990; Gorey & Leslie, 1997; Laumann et al., 1994). If sexual abuse were increasing, we would expect to see higher rates among younger people, but that is not the case.

A review of the research that has focused on children who have been sexually abused, or on adults who remember having been sexually abused as children, indicates that heterosexual men are the perpetrators in 95 percent of the cases of sexual abuse of girls and 80 percent of the cases of sexual abuse of boys (Finkelhor & Russell, 1984). Second, sexual abusers are not generally violent (Okami & Goldberg, 1992). In a national sample, physical force was used in only 19 percent of incidents involving girls and 15 percent of episodes involving boys (Finkelhor et al., 1990). Third, children, like women, are far more likely to be sexually abused by acquaintances—relatives, siblings, family friends, and neighbors—than by strangers (Finkelhor et al., 1990; Laumann et al., 1994). *Reality or Myth* ?

However, particular conditions—more or less prominent at various points in the past few generations—may increase the likelihood of child sexual abuse (and other forms of abuse and violence, such as sexual assault). We look at these next.

---

*We occasionally use the phrase "child abuse" synonymously with the phrase "sexual abuse of children." The kind of child abuse that involves the neglect of children or the nonsexual physical beatings and other abuse of children has not disappeared, but as Paul Okami (1990) pointed out, such destructive behavior has taken a back seat to the sexual abuse of children in the concerns of our society. It is also beyond the scope of this book.

---

cohort—A group from a particular generation; for example, those born from 1970 to 1979 are members of a different cohort from those from 1980 to 1989.

RISK FACTORS FOR SEXUAL ABUSE DURING CHILDHOOD

In general, it appears that children in disrupted, isolated, and economically poor families are at higher risk of sexual abuse than youngsters in more stable and middle-class families, although child sexual abuse occurs at all social levels (Finkelhor et al., 1990; Kinsey et al., 1953). Based on their nationally representative study of adults, Finkelhor et al. (1990) identified two risk factors for males and four primary risk factors for females for sexual abuse during childhood. For males, the risk factors were living with their mothers alone or living with two nonbiological parents. For females, the risk factors were having an unhappy family life, living without a biological parent, having an inadequate sex education, and region of residence.

Based on his earlier sample of college students, Finkelhor (1984) identified some of these factors plus some additional risk variables. Notably, being reared by a sex-punitive mother was correlated with experiencing sexual abuse. By "sex-punitive mother," Finkelhor meant a mother who warned, scolded, and punished her children for asking questions about sexuality, for masturbating, and for looking at sexually suggestive or explicit pictures. Finkelhor found that girls with sex-punitive mothers were 75 percent more vulnerable to sexual victimization than was the typical girl in the sample.

LONG-TERM CORRELATES OF CHILD-ADULT SEXUAL CONTACTS

Although most people vehemently condemn child-adult sexual contacts and claim that such experiences have profound effects on the child that last into adulthood, a few defend such relationships. For example, in 1984 the Dutch psychologist Theodorus Sandfort published a report of his research with 25 boys, aged 10 to 16, who were involved in sexual relationships with adult males. Most of the boys described their sexual relationships as predominantly positive and did not perceive them as representing abuse of authority by adults. It is important to note that these were boys who did not feel coerced. Across a number of studies, a smaller proportion of males than females perceived harm from these encounters (Rind & Tromovitch, 1997).

In contrast to Sandfort, others claim that sex during childhood leads to maladjustment and prostitution. Although a great deal has been written about these "effects" that sexual relations with adults may have on children, most of the literature is either speculative or based on biased samples from which little can be concluded (Rind, 1995; Rind & Tromovitch, 1997). For example, because psychotherapists often uncover child-adult sexual incidents in the backgrounds of their clients, they have sometimes concluded that these experiences underlie the problems that led the person to seek therapy (see "Research Spotlight: Memories of Sexual Abuse During Childhood" on page 466). Similarly, because substantial numbers of prostitutes have backgrounds that include sexual contact with adults during their childhoods, some observers have assumed that early sexual experience leads to prostitution.

Studies of nonclinical populations (people who are not in therapy) are important because they give a better picture of the association of child-adult sexual contact than do clinical reports. If someone who has experienced abuse believes that everyone with such experiences will have problems later in life, they probably will attribute all life difficulties to the childhood abuse rather than looking at factors in their current life circumstances. In contrast, knowing that many people are not necessarily permanently harmed by many types of childhood sexual experiences allows a wider range of options in explaining their current life situations. Depending on the severity and length of their abuse experiences, some children do experience long-term negative effects. But these individual cases tell us little about the general population of children who have been sexually approached by adults.

One review indicated that women who had a history of childhood sexual abuse were more likely than women with no such history to experience depression, sexual dysfunction, anxiety or fear, homosexual experience, and revictimization experiences (Beitchman et al., 1992). Revictimization—also known as victim recidivism—refers to findings that adults who had unwanted childhood sexual experiences are also more likely than adults who did not to report unwanted sexual experiences in adulthood (Possage & Allgeier, 1993; Stevenson & Gajarsky, 1991).

Other systematic surveys of normal populations, however, suggest that child-adult sexual contacts do

RESEARCH SPOTLIGHT   Memories of Sexual Abuse During Childhood

Much publicity has accompanied cases in which men and women recall being sexually abused many years after the event(s) occurred. In some cases, people report the abuse as long as three decades later. Most of these recovered memories occur when the individuals see therapists who help them "remember" past abuse.

One of the more publicized cases involved Cardinal Joseph Bernardin (who died in 1996) in which a man reported recalling, while hypnotized, repeated sexual abuse by the cardinal decades earlier. The "therapist" had no training in hypnosis and had a master's degree from an unaccredited institution (Pendergrast, 1995). The man later retracted his allegation. In 1994, when the man was dying of complications from AIDS, Cardinal Bernardin said mass for him and anointed him in an emotional reconciliation.

Three different patterns are apparent in current cases involving memories of childhood sexual abuse. In one, an adult tells a therapist or other health care professional about having experienced sexual contact with an adult when he or she was a child. The therapist and client explore the current meanings of the event and attempt to resolve the client's feelings so that the event does not intrude on the client's current functioning or relationships.

In a second pattern, a client clearly remembers an episode of having had sexual contact with an adult while he or she was a child, but has sought therapy for current problems and does not perceive the childhood experience as contributing much to these now-pressing issues. The therapist can either accept the client's perception

and work with him or her to resolve current problems or treat the childhood event as if it is the reason for the client's current difficulties.

In a third pattern—one described by Pendergrast (1995) and that we have also seen among our students—some therapists operate on the assumption that any current difficulties (e.g., depression, relationship difficulties, sexual dysfunctions) stem from having been sexually abused as a child. One of our students told us about her sister, who was having some adjustment problems during late adolescence. Her family decided to have her treated in a private psychiatric hospital. The therapist she saw was convinced that her difficulties stemmed from childhood sexual abuse. He asked a series of questions about her relationship with her father. While she was growing up and her father hugged her, where did he put his hands? Did he ever kiss her on the lips? Did he ever enter the bathroom or her bedroom while she was changing her clothes? The therapist's leading questions continued despite the girl's contention that she had never been abused. He had her locked in her room for several days, but she was finally able to contact her family, who obtained her release. In this pattern, the therapist was clearly convinced that adult difficulties must have resulted from sexual contact during childhood.

In another case, described by Elizabeth Loftus (1997), a psychologist who specializes in research on memory, Nadean Cool, a nurse's aide, went to a psychiatrist to help her cope with a traumatic episode Cool's

---

not inevitably lead to long-term problems in adult functioning (Kilpatrick, 1992; Laumann et al., 1994; Rind & Tromovitch, 1997; Rind, Tromovitch, & Bauserman, 1998). In a survey of 501 predominantly middle-class women, the majority (55 percent) reported having had some sexual experience with peers or adults during childhood (Kilpatrick, 1986). The presence or absence of sexual contact during childhood, however, was unrelated to stressful family relations, depression, marital satisfaction, sexual satisfaction, or self-esteem in adulthood.

We might expect that children's sexual experience with a relative—particularly a parent—would have more damaging consequences than sexual abuse by a nonrelative because incest would presumably disrupt the child's sense of stability within the family. In support of this hypothesis, Kilpatrick (1986) found that adults whose childhood sexual experiences involved a parent or other relative who used pressure, force, or

guilt to obtain the sexual contact did show somewhat more impairment in their adult functioning in all of the areas measured except sexual satisfaction. In terms of its impact on adult functioning, however, the crucial issue appears to be the use of invasive force and coercion by a relative rather than the sexual contact. Another study of a random sample of more than 1,000 college student women also indicated that the majority of respondents had unwanted sexual contacts during childhood (Hrabowy & Allgeier, 1987). The more invasive the act was, the more currently troubled the women were by it. Even so, the level of invasiveness was not related to the general measures of psychological adjustment.

Many mental health professionals believe that the reactions of parents, relatives, and adult authorities to sexual incidents are the key factors in determining the effect of these events on children (McCarthy, 1998). Young children have little under-

daughter had experienced. The psychiatrist, apparently convinced that Cool herself had been sexually abused in childhood, used hypnosis and convinced Cool that she had repressed memories of having been raped, eating babies as part of her membership in a satanic cult, having sex with animals, and being forced to watch the murder of her eight-year-old friend. The psychiatrist believed, and temporarily convinced Cool, that she had more than 120 personalities, including people of varying ages, angels, and a duck! Ultimately, Cool questioned the psychiatrist's diagnosis and sued the psychiatrist for malpractice. The case was ultimately settled out of court in 1997, with Cool being awarded $2.4 million. We hasten to add that most mental health professionals do not operate on the assumption that their clients' problems—whatever their reasons for entering therapy during adulthood—stem from repressed memories of sexual abuse during childhood.

Most people, however, think of memory as a recording of all the events they have ever experienced, much like a camcorder records whatever is filmed. However, memory is much more variable than that. It is common for people not to remember many events in their lives. In addition, we constantly add, delete, and reconstruct our past experiences to bring them in line with our current beliefs. Loftus (1997) and her colleagues have conducted more than 200 experiments involving more than 20,000 research participants that demonstrate how exposure to misinformation can induce memory distortion. They also found that the use of hypnosis is not necessary to introduce the distortion of memories—we humans seem to be very suggestible. Although Loftus acknowledges that we need much more research on the topic, she has reached three conclusions about how false memories can develop.

First, humans experience social demands to remember particular events, and when pressured, we tend to comply. Second, memories can be induced when we are asked to imagine events that we are having difficulty remembering. Third, false memories are most likely when we feel these pressures whether we are participating in an experiment, involved in therapy, or just engaging in our everyday activities.

A few years ago, the television program *20/20* showed a segment on research done with children, "Out of the Mouth of Babes." Over a series of many weeks, the children were repeatedly asked questions about events that did not happen. For example, they were asked about getting their finger caught in a mouse trap, or having their genitals examined by a pediatrician. Initially, the children denied that the event had happened. But over the weeks of questioning, gradually the children reported the event and developed elaborate details about the (nonoccurring) event.

Recovered-memory syndrome is not just an academic issue. Families have been broken up and people sentenced to prison because of "recovered memories." A report of a long-repressed memory of abuse from a client should certainly be treated as a possibility that needs further investigation and evidence before it is accepted as "truth."

standing of what is sexual. Therefore, they have difficulty in labeling the incident, if they seek to label it at all. Older children are more aware of sex and thus, depending on what they have learned about sexuality, are more likely to react to abusive incidents with vague feelings of wrongdoing or guilt over their participation, even if they were coerced. Their feelings of guilt can be either reduced or increased by adults' reactions.

Fear is a child's most common reaction to a forced sexual interaction with an adult (Finkelhor, 1979). Fear may also be the primary reason that children avoid telling anyone about the incident. In one study of adults, only 26 percent of women and 15 percent of men reported that they told someone about sexual abuse at the time of the experience (Laumann et al., 1994).

When a child does tell a parent or other authority figure, the adult who receives this information may, for various reasons, cover it up rather than report it. First, he or she may not believe the child. Such nonrecognition of the sexual contact may be the response that is most damaging to the child's self-concept. Even when an adult believes a child, the adult may avoid reporting the incident for fear of entanglement with legal or social welfare authorities. If the offender is a family member or close friend, a parent or adult who learns of the incident is less likely to report it, perhaps because of fears that the child or the adult offender will be removed from the home (Gaines & Allgeier, 1993). This concern is a relatively realistic one: many of our legal and social policies regarding the sexual abuse of children have had the unintended side effect of further disrupting the family rather than aiding the adjustment of children, particularly when the adult-child contact involves relatives.

If adults overreact to incidents of child sexual abuse, children may feel that they are guilty of some

Most who work with the young, such as these Girl Scout leaders, are trustworthy and caring.

unspeakable act and may blame themselves for what occurred. If adults act reasonably, attributing responsibility to the offending adult, where it belongs, children can come away from the experience with minimal distress. It is also important that parents not focus on the sexual nature of the incident. Sexual activity per se, whether it involves exhibitionism, fondling of the genitals, or sexual intercourse, has no relationship to the degree of trauma experienced by children (Bagley, 1996; Finkelhor, 1979; Higgins & McCabe, 1994).

If a child is able to talk with a supportive person, whether a family member or a counselor, about an abusive sexual interaction, residual feelings of shame or fear may subside. It is important for the child or adolescent to vent the emotions and concerns that may stem from such contacts. A supportive person should discuss the situation with the adolescent or child in a matter-of-fact way and use the following guidelines in the conversation:

1. Sexual feelings and the desire for sexual attention are perfectly normal.

2. It is inappropriate for adults to interact sexually with children.

3. Sex is not evil, nor are all adults bad. In fact, the adult with whom the child had sexual contact is not necessarily a "bad" person. The behavior of the adult under these conditions, however, was inappropriate.

It is crucial to stress that the child is not responsible and should not feel guilty. Clearly, the use of children by adults to meet their own needs is exploitative.

▶ **Issues to Consider:** What do you think about the possibility of repressing the memory of traumatic events and then remembering them many years later? If a friend or relative reported such an experience, how would you respond?

PREVENTION OF CHILDHOOD SEXUAL ABUSE

Childhood sexual abuse prevention (CSAP) programs have proliferated in the past two decades, with millions of children in North America taking part in them. Viewed as a first line of defense against child sexual abuse, these programs are designed to enable children to identify and avoid sexual abuse, but they can create undesirable side effects. Psychologist James Krivacska (1991) identified two cornerstones of the CSAP philosophy: the touch continuum and empowerment.

The *touch continuum* defines what is good touch (touch that feels good and is good for the child), bad touch (touch that the child wishes to avoid such as unwanted hugs or touch that hurts), and confusing touch (touch that may start out feeling good but ends up being bad touch). Contact with the genitals is often described as bad touch, although the genitals in these programs are often referred to vaguely as "parts covered by a bathing suit" or "private parts." A child's initial introduction to an adult talking about human genitals may convey the idea that touching the genitals is bad (Krivacska, 1990, 1991).

The second major cornerstone of CSAP programs is the concept of *empowerment*. This refers to children playing an active role in avoiding sexual abuse. It assumes that children can take responsibility for themselves and make choices about how they lead their lives. This assumption is problematic when applied to young children, who do not have an adequate understanding of complex sociosexual interactions. Thus, as Krivacska (1991) noted, children may be placed in a guilt-producing double-bind:

> The programs deny that children are at all responsible or to blame for sexual abuse, yet they teach them that they are responsible for preventing the abuse. This is clearly unreasonable. In their attempts to reduce children's guilt in having been sexually abused, most CSAP programs also unintentionally increase children's feelings of guilt when they find themselves in situations where they are unable to prevent the abuse from happening again after they have been exposed to the program. (p. 4)

It is ironic that school systems that have so persistently avoided sex education at the elementary school level often feel no qualms about exposing children to CSAP programs. Thus, a child's first encounter with a formal presentation about sexuality is in terms of abuse. The implications of this approach will probably be seen in the sexual attitudes of future generations.

We agree with Krivacska that sexual abuse prevention programs need to be included in a larger program of sexuality education for primary school children. This sexuality education needs to be geared toward activity promoting and encouraging the age-appropriate development of their sexuality. For example, Wurtele (1993) reported that a CSAP program for Head Start preschoolers that included teaching children the correct names for their genitals as well as emphasizing that it was acceptable to touch their own genitals in private appeared to affect the preschoolers' attitudes toward their own sexuality positively.

Before ending this section, it may be helpful to put the phenomenon of child sexual abuse into perspective by examining rates of other forms of victimization of children. David Finkelhor, one of the foremost authorities on the topic of sexual abuse, has provided rates of childhood victimization ranging from the least common to the most common per 1,000 U.S. children (Finkelhor & Dziuba-Leatherman, 1994). As may be seen by inspection of Figure 19.1, of the 14 forms of victimization, assault by siblings ranks first, childhood sexual abuse ranks tenth, and homicide ranks fourteenth. It is curious that the more prevalent forms of childhood victimization have received far less publicity than childhood sexual abuse. *Reality or Myth* ☐   *Reality or Myth* ☐

Gender Differences in Sexually Coercive Behavior

We conclude by examining a finding that has cropped up throughout this chapter: most victims of rape, harassment, child sexual abuse, and incest are females, and most perpetrators are males. Some people might use this finding to buttress an argument that males are innately dominating and aggressive and that females are destined to be victims, submissive and masochistic. But for various reasons, this simplistic explanation is unconvincing. First, in all coercive episodes, there are instances in which males are the victims and females the perpetrators. Second, most males do not coerce sexually, and many females experience a lifetime free of sexual victimization. Third, research on cross-cultural differences in the incidence of rape suggests that rape and other forms of sexual coercion may result from social factors (Hall & Barongan, 1997).

One key to reducing the occurrence of sexual coercion of children might be to determine why the overwhelming majority of assailants are males and victims are females. Our informal language is replete with phrases that suggest the sexual stimulus value of young females. Rarely does one hear references to a romantic or erotic relationship between a "woman" and her "boy," but it is difficult to listen to a popular music station for long without hearing an adult male singing about his "girl" or "baby." The common pairing of "man" with "girl," strictly speaking, refers to a pedophilic relationship, although we may not think of it in that way unless sensitized to the issue.

Women in most cultures involve themselves with men who are older and larger than they are, whereas men generally select partners who are younger and smaller (Buss, 1999). Thus erotic arousal in response to children would presumably require less of an alteration of culturally sanctioned sexual preferences for men than for women.

Women are traditionally socialized to expect men to initiate sexual contact, whereas men learn to take the initiative in sexual relations and to overcome any (anticipated) female resistance. This cultural pattern

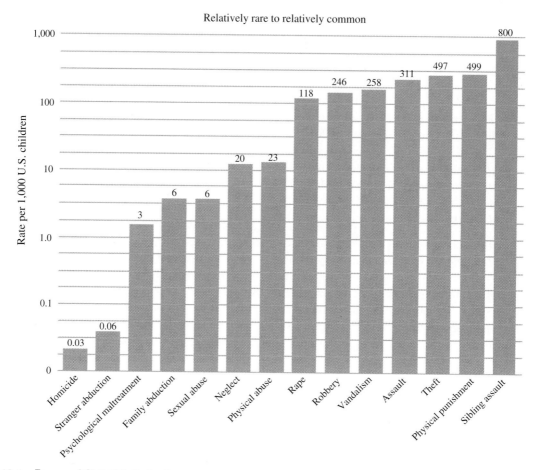

Figure 19.1 Forms of Child Victimization

These rates of various forms of victimization of children demonstrate that many potentially harmful behaviors are far more common than the highly publicized crime of child sexual abuse.

may make men more likely than women to initiate sexual contacts with children.

In the absence of sexual partners, men seem to suffer more of a loss of self-esteem than do women (Buss, 1999). Under these conditions, men may be more likely to use children sexually to regain their self-esteem.

Females are more frequently the recipients of sexual coercion than are males. As a result, they may be more likely to empathize with feelings of exploitation and thus be less likely to express their sexual feelings toward children.

Finally, throughout most of history, women and children have been viewed as the property of men.

Father-initiated sexual activity within the family often has been seen as a right and thus, although not approved of, has usually not been punished. Wives, who have been seen as the property of their husbands, have had few rights, sexual or otherwise.

If differing social experiences of men and women contribute to sexual coercion, then certain trends in North American society may help to reduce the incidence of all forms of coercion. As more egalitarian and less possessive sexual relationships become the norm, the equation of sexuality with dominance and aggression may be lessened.

SUMMARY OF MAJOR POINTS

1. Varieties of sexual assault. A large majority of sexual assaults are carried out by people who are acquainted casually or intimately with the victim. Date rape is prevalent in our culture, and about one-quarter of the college men in one sample reported that they had attempted to force sexual relations. Many college women anonymously report that men have forced or attempted to force them to have sex. Males and spouses also experience sexual coercion. Although the majority of rapists and victims are in their adolescence or early 20s, sexual assault may occur from birth to old age.

2. Characteristics of sexual assailants. Convicted sex offenders tend to be aggressive and lacking in self-esteem. Some report having been sexually and/or physically abused during childhood and adolescence. Moreover, the stereotype of the assailant as a sexually driven male without access to willing partners is not supported by research. Unidentified assailants tend to be alienated from their families and supported by peers, who encourage and approve of both sexual exploits and the victimization of particular categories of women.

3. Victims of sexual coercion. Sexual assault victims come from all walks of life. Females in their adolescence and early 20s are at greatest risk of sexual coercion. Children, older women, and men, however, also experience sexual victimization. One finding that generalizes across victims of sexual assault is that the majority of them knew the offender.

4. Sexual assault stereotypes. Three major hypotheses have been advanced as possible explanations of sexual assault: victim precipitation, uncontrolled lust or uncontrolled aggression, and exaggerated gender-role identity. The notion that victims precipitate sexual assault is completely unsubstantiated in about 95 percent of the cases. There is some support for the theory that offenders are motivated by aggression and general feelings of inadequacy, but little evidence exists in favor of the uncontrolled-lust hypothesis.

5. Reducing vulnerability to sexual assault. Ways to reduce chances of being sexually assaulted include knowing one's own sexual policies, avoiding being alone or intoxicated with a person one does not know well, and communicating one's disinterest in having sex in a clear, firm, and straightforward manner. In the event that a potential assailant persists, multiple strategies (talking, screaming, running away, and so forth) are more effective in dissuading the attack than are single strategies.

6. The sexual coercion of children. Because children do not understand the nature and potential consequences of sexual activity, they are unable to give informed consent to such interaction. The long-term correlates of sexual contacts vary considerably depending on the age difference between the child and the perpetrator, the degree of force, and the level of invasiveness. Despite some psychologists' claims, based on clinical cases, that such experiences always cause adult maladjustment, studies of normal samples indicate no direct causal link between adult psychological adjustment and unwanted sexual experiences during childhood. The responses of other adults in the child's environment to the sexual episode may be related to the extent to which the child can cope with the experience. A child who reports having been sexually victimized by an adult should receive support and counseling to reduce his or her feelings of guilt and responsibility.

7. Sex differences in sexual coercion. Males are far more likely to use sexual coercion than are females, and females are far more likely to be sexually coerced than are males. Several theories have been advanced to explain the reasons for these sex differences. To the extent that differences in the sexual socialization of men and women contribute to the problem, the growing support for equality in personal, educational, and occupational environments may gradually reduce the prevalence of all forms of sexual coercion.

20

Sex for Profit

Reality or Myth?

1. The use of sex to sell magazines and other products is ineffective.

2. X-rated erotic movies contain more violence than PG-13 or R-rated films.

3. North Americans generally agree on what material they consider obscene.

4. Viewing sexually explicit material increases a person's likelihood of committing a sex crime.

5. The depiction of child sexual activity is illegal in North America.

6. Some prostitutes enjoy their work as well as the income that it produces.

The next time you watch television or flip through a magazine, notice how frequently the commercials or advertisements emphasize sex appeal. Attractive and seductive young models promote everything from mouthwash to cars. With the widespread use of sexual messages in advertising and the prevalence of graphic depictions of sexuality in films and in print, it is assumed that using sex to sell a product makes money.

In this chapter we describe the intersection of sexuality and the profit motive. Much of the controversy about sexual products centers on their possible effect on consumers, particularly those who are young and impressionable. We review what is known about the effects of exposure to various types of erotic media and discuss laws concerning sexually explicit material. In addition to viewing and listening to erotic material, consumers can buy sexual services from prostitutes. We consider different kinds of prostitutes, legal constraints on prostitution, and the characteristics associated with prostitutes and with those who purchase their services.

Varieties of Sexual Products

Erotic material may be viewed in magazines, in theaters, or at home on television programs, videocassettes, and the Internet; it is found in nightclubs featuring adult entertainment, adult bookstores, and even advertisements for products that have no readily apparent connection with sexuality. Before discussing the profits generated by these materials, we need to define a few key terms.

The word **erotica** generally refers to sexually oriented material that is acceptable to the viewer. **Pornography** is sexually oriented material that is not acceptable to the viewer. This term comes from the Greek word *pornographos*, which refers to stories about prostitutes. There are, of course, many definitions of pornography, but they tend to reflect the likes and dislikes of the definer. What one person may find appealing, pleasant, and arousing, another may judge disgusting, unpleasant, and unarousing.

Hard-core erotica or pornography is sexual material that explicitly depicts the genitals or sexual acts. X-rated movies and materials displayed in adult bookstores are usually hard core. **Soft-core erotica** or pornography is sexual material that is suggestive, but not explicit, in portraying the genitals or sex acts.

---

erotica—Sexually oriented material that is acceptable to the viewer.
pornography—Sexually oriented material that is not acceptable to the viewer.

hard-core erotica—Erotica that explicitly depicts the genitals and sexual acts.
soft-core erotica—Erotica that is suggestive, but not explicit, in portraying sexual acts.

Magazines that can be purchased from most newsstands, such as *Playboy* and *Penthouse*, are examples of soft-core erotica.

MAGAZINES

In 1953, the same year that Kinsey and his group published their research on women's sexuality, *Playboy* became the first national magazine to display bare breasts and buttocks. In 1970, *Penthouse, Playboy*'s most successful imitator, became the first mass-market magazine to display pubic hair on its models. Prior to that time, the vulvas of models were shaved or air-brushed out. Other similar magazines soon followed, and depiction of the genitals became increasingly common. These magazines reached their peak circulation in the 1970s and then began to lose readership, perhaps because they were less explicit than the hard-core magazines (Kimmel & Linders, 1996).

Nonetheless, the continuing power of sex in selling magazines is reflected in the sales figures for the annual swimsuit issue of *Sports Illustrated*. In 1995 *Sports Illustrated* sold almost twice as many copies of its swimsuit issue than of its other monthly issues. Revenues for the issue and tie-ins (such as videos and calendars) reached about one-third of the magazine's net income for that entire year. ***Reality or Myth*** ?

ADVERTISEMENTS

Advertisers have shown people in various states of undress and intimate poses. Examine the advertisements in Fig. 20.1. The use of sexual images has become overt, and analyses of the content of advertisements during the past two decades support the conclusion that nude or semi-nude models (women much more so than men) are a common element in advertising in the United States and other countries (Wiles, Wiles, & Tjernlund, 1996).

This trend may reflect a belief by the advertising industry that sex sells, but does it? Does sexual content in an advertisement increase the likelihood that consumers will purchase a particular item? The answer appears to be no, unless the product is related to sexuality (Gould, 1994). For products that are unrelated to sexuality, research indicates that overt sexual content in ads is less effective than nonsexual content. Although provocative stimuli may grab attention initially, memory of a brand name and comprehension of an ad's message are reduced when there is irrelevant content, sexual or otherwise, in the advertisement (Severn, Belch, & Belch, 1990). Despite the absence of evidence for the effectiveness of using sex appeal to sell products, the advertising industry nevertheless continues to turn out sexually explicit ads.

This explicitness brings up the question of what limits, if any, should apply to the advertising industry's attempts to sell products by linking them with sexuality. Not surprisingly, data indicate that erotophobic persons report less enjoyment of and less exposure to erotic material compared to erotophilic persons (Kelley, Byrne, Greendlinger, & Murnen, 1997). In addition, erotophobic people generally report higher approval of censoring erotic materials than do erotophilic people (Lopez & George, 1995).

 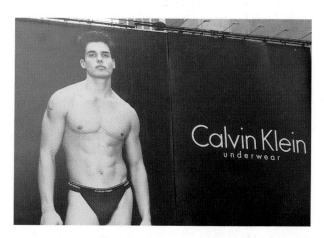

Figure 20.1   The Use of Partial Nudity to Sell Products

(See Chapter 6 for definitions of erotophilic [positive] and erotophobic [negative] emotional responses to sexual feelings and experiences.)

> ▶ **Issues to Consider:** Should erotophobic persons have to tolerate exposure to the sexually suggestive material that permeates contemporary advertising and other media?

TELEVISION PROGRAMS

The use of sex in the electronic and print media is hardly limited to advertisements. One study found an average of 10 incidents of sexual behavior per hour during prime time on the major networks (Lowry & Shidler, 1993). Almost all depictions in this medium are of heterosexual activity that is recreational and mostly between unmarried partners (Brown & Steele, 1996).

As you may know from your own viewing experience, one difficulty with television's presentation of sex is that programs depicting sexual encounters rarely deal with the possible consequences of sexual activity. For example, characters shown engaging in sex with each other seldom discuss potential negative outcomes, such as unwanted pregnancy and STDs, and what they can do to reduce their risks. The absence of modeling responsible sexual decision making may lead viewers into an unrealistic view of the range of consequences for sexual behavior. Brown and Newcomber (1991) found a relationship between the proportion of sexual depictions viewed and adolescents' own sexual behavior. Nonvirgins were more likely than virgins to watch television programs containing sexual content.

Hamburg (1992) and Hechinger (1992) more globally described television viewing patterns and sexual content. Overall, the average 18-year-old has spent only half as much time in school as watching television. U.S. viewers are exposed each year to almost 10,000 scenes of suggested sex or innuendo, and more than 90 percent of sex portrayals on TV involve people who either are unmarried or are married to someone else.

The tendency to exaggerate the glamor of sexuality has led fundamentalist religious groups to advocate the censorship of erotic activity on television. Other organizations, including Planned Parenthood, suggest that when sexual activity is portrayed, the possible unwanted consequences should also be presented. "They did it 20,000 times on television last year. How come nobody got pregnant?" was a slogan used by the Planned Parenthood Federation of America in an adolescent pregnancy prevention program a few years ago (Meischke, 1995). Similar advice could be given to the producers of the numerous explicit sexual scenes featured in many music videos. The controversy about the effects of the commercial portrayal of sex intensifies when we turn to movies and books that directly aim to evoke sexual arousal.

> ▶ **Issues to Consider:** The next time you watch a sex scene in a network show or on M-TV, think about how you would inject information about responsible sexual behavior into the script.

EROTIC MOVIES AND VIDEOS

In the 1970s, the market for sexually explicit films flourished. The market for cinematic erotica took another turn in the 1980s when the video recorder began to chip into the profits of adult theaters and magazines. The steadily climbing sales and rentals of hard-core videocassettes suggest that consumers prefer watching these films in the privacy of the home rather than in a theater (Kimmel & Linders, 1996).

Hard-core or X-rated movies probably contain the most explicit depictions of sexuality that North America has produced, but their plots are typically dull and predictable. Sociologist Ira Reiss characterized most X-rated films as having a thin plot and unimpressive acting:

> *The scenes focus upon oral, anal, and coital acts with extensive closeups of that action. The acts are mostly heterosexual, and when they are homosexual, unless the film is made specifically for male homosexuals, the focus is upon lesbian sexual acts. The absence of male homosexuality is due to the strong attempt to appeal to Western heterosexual males' lustful feelings in these films. Little or no physical violence against women occurs in the vast majority of these films. There may be some status differences in the male and female roles portrayed, but physical force rarely enters in obvious ways into sexual action. I believe that this is the most common form of erotic film today. It is hard-core in that erections and vulvas are shown frequently and usually joined.* (1986, pp. 174–175)

The typical X-rated film is a fantasy about sexually insatiable women who are incapable of resisting any type of male sexual advance. In a matter of seconds, regardless of the man's approach, attractiveness, or relationship with her, the woman is overcome by her sexual passion and willingly participates in all sorts of sexual activities. In a culture in which males are socialized to be sexual initiators—a role in which they are vulnerable to rejection by females who are not sexually interested in them—it is not difficult to see why the insatiable female fantasy is so popular. The female counterpart to this male fantasy can be seen in women's romance novels (see "Highlight: Romance Novels—Erotica for Women?") and, more recently, explicit sexual films and novels from a female perspective that women find more sexually arousing than the typical X-rated film (Pearson & Pollack, 1997) (cf. Candida Royale's Femme Productions).

Historically, most erotica has been aimed at arousing males. Men's seemingly greater interest in obtaining erotic material probably explains this marketing strategy. In one college sample, men reported viewing erotic material an average of about six hours a month, whereas women reported viewing such material only about two and a half hours a month (Padgett, Brislin-Slutz, & Neal, 1989).

Hard-core and X-rated movies are often the targets of groups that advocate censorship. However, these films generally contain less violence than R-rated films or other movies that even children are permitted to see. The highest incidence of violence occurs in PG-13 films, followed by R-rated films, with X-rated films trailing far behind (Scott & Cuvelier, 1993).

In Laumann et al.'s (1994) representative sample of American adults, 23 percent of men and 11 percent of women indicated they had watched X-rated movies. Consumers of X-rated movies do not fit into any easily identifiable category. Reiss (1997) examined a number of surveys of representative groups of Americans 18 and older, conducted between 1973 and 1996 by the National Opinion Research Center. The higher the educational attainment, the more likely the person was to have attended an X-rated movie. Of particular relevance to feminists' concerns ··t X-rated movies may promote gender inequality ··s's finding that people who attended X-rated ere more, not less, egalitarian in their

gender-role attitudes than those who did not. Similarly, patrons of an adult movie theater who responded to questionnaires placed on a counter in the theater had more positive attitudes toward women than did college men and women (Padgett et al., 1989). Furthermore, the frequency of X-rated video rentals is unrelated to a man's attitudes toward feminism and rape (Potter, 1999). Thus, research does not support the idea that erotica fosters positive attitudes toward the subordination of women. *Reality or Myth*

ADULT BOOKSTORES

Paralleling the expanding market for sexually explicit films, adult bookstores have also shown growing profits. These bookstores sell hard-core erotica of a sort not readily available at other retail stores. In addition to printed media and videos, a range of other products is often available, including such sex toys as vibrators, massage oils, dildos, and other sexual aids. Some stores also offer live sex shows featuring everything from nude dancing to simulated live sexual acts.

A study of 26 adult bookstores in the Philadelphia area found a strong overlap between the stores and such forms of vice as drug distribution, gambling, and prostitution (Potter, 1989). All of these establishments had peep-show areas where a customer could enter a booth and insert coins or tokens to

This 17-year-old boy checks out the display in the window of a sex shop in Copenhagen, Denmark. The Scandinavians are generally more tolerant of erotica than are their North American counterparts.

H I G H L I G H T

Romance Novels—Erotica for Women?

Romance novels have been phenomenally successful, selling millions of copies and appearing regularly on best-seller lists. They are female fantasies, written mainly by women. The erotic romance generally features a young woman whose innocence is violated by an older man; his repeated assaults result in pregnancy and marriage. The struggle between the two for dominance, the man's eventual triumph, and his ultimate domestication are consistent plot elements. In one study, readers of these novels reported having sexual relations twice as often as nonreaders of romance; in addition, they often used fantasy as a complement to intercourse, whereas nonreaders did so rarely, if at all (Coles & Shamp, 1984). Romance novels are a kind of soft-core erotica that women find socially acceptable.

Reiss (1986) suggested that in one sense female erotic fantasy may be based on the same principle as male erotic fantasy; that is, it is enhanced by removing the negotiating power of one's sexual partner. In romance novels, the male is depicted as obsessed with romance. His intense love for the heroine renders him helpless to resist; he must pursue her and give her what she desires. Feminine gender-role expectations are compatible with this scenario, and a woman can relax her sexual guard and feel safe (Thompson, 1994).

Women are pressured to be both selective and sexually responsive in North American culture. Men are socialized to become sexual initiators, ready to perform at the drop of an eyelash. Is it any wonder that women and men often prefer different types of erotica?

---

watch a film. Twelve had booths where a viewer could pay for a curtain or blind to be raised. In the booth, a male or female employee behind a glass partition converses with the customer through a telephone or intercom system. The employee gradually undresses and engages in sexual talk with the customer. Eventually, the employee carefully solicits the customer and, for additional payment, goes to the customer's side of the booth (or the two retire to another part of the store) for sex.

Glory holes were provided in 24 of the 26 stores in their peep-show areas (Potter, 1989). A glory hole is a circular opening two to six inches in diameter in the side wall of the booth, through which genitals may be inserted. The booths usually feature homosexual themes, and their purpose is to allow two men in adjacent cubicles to engage in manual or oral stimulation.

In Philadelphia, the retail pornography outlets are intertwined with prostitution and are part of organized criminal networks. Investigations by the Federal Bureau of Investigation have revealed complicated patterns of common ownership of pornography outlets, massage parlors, and after-hours clubs in that city. These patterns are not unique to

Philadelphia. Similar arrangements flourish in many other cities, contributing to an estimated annual gross income of up to $9 billion (Potter, 1989).

TELEPHONE SEX

Those who seek sexual stimulation at a distance can dial a 900 telephone number and listen to explicit sexual talk for a price. The so-called dial-a-porn industry allows a caller to have a conversation with a paid performer at the other end of the line or to listen to a prerecorded message (Glasock & LaRose, 1993). Roughly 1 percent of all men and no women report using this service (Laumann et al., 1994). For fees that range from $3 to $12 a minute, a caller can indulge in sexual fantasies with a telephone worker who will "talk dirty" to the caller and charge the episode to that person's monthly telephone bill or credit card. Advertisements for such services can be found in the personal ad sections of many newspapers and in sexually oriented magazines.

For this illusion of sexual fulfillment, the caller is often treated to a worker's feigned interest in his or her fantasy. Many calls are forwarded to the worker's home, where he or she may try to titillate

The World Wide Web, like other communication modes, has its share of sexual displays and services. Just as they have supported censoring other media, some politicians have advocated censorship for sexually oriented material that finds its way onto computer screens.

the customer while going about such ordinary pursuits as cleaning the kitchen or reading the newspaper (Borna, Chapman, & Menezes, 1993).

THE WORLD WIDE WEB

The computer has combined with modern telephone technology to create a highly efficient means for the transmission of information. It should come as no surprise that one of the oldest human desires has hooked up with the latest technology. By connecting to a particular web site, a computer user can contact individuals in chat rooms or companies with similar interests in the United States or other places in the world. Users can meet through the computer, exchange messages and engage in erotic banter, exchange telephone numbers, arrange dates, and upload and download files.

Adult-oriented sites, with names like ThrobNet and KinkNet, feature libraries of X-rated films and interactive adult games such as "The Interactive Adventures of Seymore Butts." In this game, the wrong answer gets Seymore a refusal or a slap in the face; the right answer lands him in bed, where the viewer gets to see hard-core sex.

Almost every type of conventional and unconventional sexual interest can be accessed via the In-

ternet, including sounds and stories, pictures and movies, and real-time interactions. An example of the rapidly evolving technology involved in on-line "porn" sites was featured in *Time* magazine (Quittner, 1998). One particular site, DoMeLive.com, advertises live sex with the user on one end of the exchange and a live nude on the other. The nude then responds to the requests of the customer at the cost of $5.95 per minute. The company that runs DoMeLive.com reports serving 8,000 peep-show minutes a day, which gross about $300,000 a week.

Some on-line web sites make direct approaches to people with atypical interests (Kim & Bailey, 1997). Sadomasochism, bestiality, or almost anything else imaginable is available. Of particular concern have been highly publicized incidents of individuals' obtaining child erotica and attempting to contact youngsters (usually through deception) to arrange meetings for sexual purposes. Lame (1998) estimated that two-thirds of the visitors to children's sites were adults masquerading as children to engage in cybersex. This has led some legislators in the United States and other countries to propose various types of censorship of sexually oriented material that finds its way to computer screen, just as other media formats have been censored. We will undoubtedly see more attention to the censorship issue in the coming years.

▶ **Issues to Consider:** Do you think the government should censor erotic material on the Internet? If not, why not? If you favor censorship, what guidelines would you propose?

EROTIC DANCING

Erotic dancing—the gradual shedding of clothes to music in bars, restaurants, theaters, clubs, and private shows—has a long history. Depending on the locale, strippers may shed all their clothes or strip down to scanty G-strings (the rule in most U.S. cities). In table topping, the disrobing dancers perform on the tables where the customers are seated.

Erotic dancing, also known as stripteasing, has been primarily an entertainment provided by women. Three factors appear to be associated with women's entrance into this profession: residing in an area where such opportunities for employment are available, being aware of the potential for earning a rea-

Contact between a male dancer and women in the audience is not unusual in the stripping business.

sonable or good living through the profession, and perceiving—based on assessments from others—that one is sufficiently attractive and qualified to succeed in the job. Female strippers usually enter the profession to earn a livelihood, and some take in additional money by engaging in prostitution with customers of the club or theater where they perform (Forsyth & Deshotels, 1997; Thompson & Harred, 1992).

The majority of strip clubs pay the dancers the minimum wage or nothing at all; in fact, the dancers pay the club a fee per shift. For their income, the dancers depend on tips and, in some cases, subsequent paid sex with the customers. Similar to restaurants, the strip clubs vary in their atmosphere and cost to customers. Although only a small proportion of the 1,500 clubs in the United States can be described as "upscale," their numbers are growing in metropolitan areas. Such establishments, known as "gentlemen's clubs," provide additional services, such as exercise rooms, tanning salons, hair salons, and fax machines (Forsyth & Deshotels, 1997).

Craig Forsyth and Tina Deshotels (1997) interviewed erotic dancers about their profession and goals. Many of the women reported taking drugs to reduce their inhibitions about nude or semi-nude dancing, with marijuana being the most commonly used intoxicant. Although their interactions with men at the clubs were typically impersonal, many of the dancers said that the clubs provided good places to meet men and indicated that they would quit dancing to marry the right man. In fact, most dancers saw marriage as a future goal.

More recently, men have increasingly entered this occupation. In contrast to most female strippers, male strippers apparently are motivated frequently by the opportunity to meet women (or men) with whom they may subsequently engage in sex—and not necessarily for money (Dressel & Peterson, 1982). Male strip shows often involve costumed individuals or group performances in various scenarios; members of the audience may approach a dancer while offering a tip, after which physical contact such as kissing or fondling may occur.

Male and female strippers alike believe that society views them in a negative light. Thus they often describe themselves to others as entertainers or dancers in an effort to avoid negative stereotypes (Ronai & Cross, 1998; Thompson & Harred, 1992).

"APHRODISIACS"

Certain foods and drugs have a reputation for heightening sexual arousal or enhancing the pleasure of sexual stimulation and orgasm. A substance believed to have such effects is called an **aphrodisiac** (after Aphrodite, the Greek goddess of love). The interest in aphrodisiacs has proved a profitable business for the purveyors of these purported sexual enhancers.

Humans have quested after aphrodisiacs through the ages. The sexual organs of animals, as well as objects that look like sexual organs, have sometimes been used in love potions. Alleged aphrodisiacs favored by various societies have included powdered rhinoceros horn (one of the reasons that the rhinoceros is an endangered species), bees' wings, elephant tusks, oysters, the blood of bats mixed with donkey milk, radishes, elephant sperm, olives, and sheep or bull testes ("Rocky Mountain oysters"). Interestingly, the chemical composition of rhinoceros horn is similar to the human fingernail, but no claim has ever been made that fingernail biting increases sex drive.

Despite longstanding popular beliefs, however, there is not much reliable scientific evidence that so-called aphrodisiacs can affect sexual desire. Most information about their effects is based on the retrospective reports of drug users, surveys, anecdotal evidence, or uncontrolled studies. Ideally, research in this area should employ a double-blind design, in which neither the volunteers nor the investigators know who receives the substance under investigation and who gets a placebo instead. Nevertheless, there is a brisk market for any substance reputed to enhance sexual drive and functioning.

Some drugs may indirectly affect sexual response by generally stimulating physiological or psychological function. However, many reports of heightened sexual responsiveness following the use of a particular substance may have more to do with a person's beliefs and expectations about the substance than with the substance itself. Table 20.1 lists and describes some of

the more common substances that allegedly affect sexual functioning.

Many of these drugs can have severe side effects. It should be apparent from this information that no drug directly determines the course and intensity of sexual response. Instead, drugs only modulate the experience of sexual activity. Human sexual response is a complicated interaction of psychosocial factors that is subject to many influences beyond chemicals.

OTHER FORMS OF EROTICA

Individuals can employ erotica to arouse themselves or a sexual companion. Used with a partner, erotic materials can enhance lovemaking, and some forms can serve as a substitute for those who lack a partner.

A wide array of products are billed as enhancing sexual proficiency. Vibrators, dildos, creams, pastes, and lubricants are just a few of the tamer items competing for consumers' business. About 2 percent of men and women report using vibrators or dildos (Laumann et al., 1994). Individuals or couples may use such sexual aids to heighten their sensations during masturbation or coitus. For example, a number of companies manufacture scented lubricants, with some variations aimed at women and others at men. There is no evidence that these kinds of stimulants are harmful, and some do, in fact, produce the sensations—warmth, numbing—claimed. For those who prefer human-like playthings, there are various inflatable dolls that can be used as a sexual partner. Consider the following advertisement, typical of those found in contemporary sex-oriented publications:

> *Playgirl*
>
> *Lifesize-like in every detail. June is the only human-like action doll available in America. Let her life-like reproduction female qualities astound you as they have others. Her breasts are human-like in every detail, boasting texture and structure right down to the finest point. Her open mouth is an achievement in design; the human-like action, tight flexible cheeks inside the mouth, work on the principle of air suction. Imagine coming home to your own 21st century playgirl, always ready for action. Dress her up in lingerie, bathing suit, dainty underclothes.*

---

aphrodisiacs—Drugs, foods, or other substances that are popularly believed to heighten sexual desire and performance.

TABLE 20.1   Substances Commonly Perceived As Being Aphrodisiacs

Name	Effects	Hazards
Cantharides (Spanish fly)	Dilates genital blood vessels; irritates the urinary tract	Causes abdominal and urinary tract ulcers; possible severe pain
Yohimbine	Central nervous system (CNS) stimulant; mixed effects, seems to prolong erection	Is poisonous if taken in large doses
Alcohol	CNS depressant; in low doses, effects stem from psychological expectations	In large doses, inhibits sexual function; alcoholism is a major cause of erectile failure in men
Barbiturates and sedatives	CNS stimulant; in low doses, effects stem from psychological expectations	In large doses, inhibit sexual functioning
Cocaine	Stimulant; moderate doses may intensify sexual sensations	With prolonged use, can lead to sexual dysfunction and psychological problems
Amphetamines	Stimulants; moderate doses may intensify sexual sensations	With prolonged use, can inhibit sexual functioning and produce feelings of paranoia
Amyl nitrate	Stimulant	Can cause problems with blood pressure
Marijuana	Affects neurotransmitters in the brain; effects highly dependent on psychological expectations	In some people, can create psychological dependency after prolonged use
Psychedelics (LSD, etc.)	Affect neurotransmitters in the brain	Can cause adverse psychological reactions
Opiates (heroin, etc.)	Depressants	Causes negative psychological reactions, physical addiction; lowers testosterone levels in males; inhibits ovulation
Androgens	Increase hormone levels; enhance sexual functioning for a few hours in some people who are low in androgen production	Have masculinizing effects on females

Sources: Bancroft (1989); Brown & Munson (1987); Crenshaw & Goldberg (1996); Crowe & George (1989); Gay, New-Meyer, Perry, Johnson, & Kurland (1982); George, Gournic, & McAfee (1988); Malatesta, Pollack, Wilbanks, & Adams (1979); Moss, Panzak, & Tarter (1993); Rosen (1991); Rosen & Ashton (1993); Rowland, Kallen, & Slob (1997); Weller & Halikas (1984); Wilson & Lawson (1978).

. . . Think of the fun you'll have dressing June the way you feel a woman should dress.

Other advertised products are of more dubious quality. Several years ago, we received a promotional piece on a so-called sex pill for men, called NSP-270, that purportedly would compensate for certain male "nutritional deficiencies" and promote penis growth. Although the ad contains some remarkable graphs in which penis-shaped bars indicate the length of a man's penis before and after he has taken NSP-270, readers never learn which "famous California medical school" has developed this "nutrient."

Many people condemn erotica and sexual aids, but the trade would not be flourishing if consumers did not support it with their money. In 1998, the state of Alabama banned the sale of vibrators and other sex toys used to stimulate the genitals. A federal judge overturned the ban in 1999, saying the state had no reason to prohibit sale of the devices.

▶ **Issues to Consider:** What forms of erotica have you encountered that we have not mentioned?

Erotica and the Law

The word **obscenity** is often used interchangeably with the word *pornography*, but *obscenity* also has a legal meaning. In U.S. law, obscenity refers to illegal erotica. In the United States, laws regulating erotic material date back to the nineteenth century. The most important one is the Comstock Act, named after its major advocate, Anthony Comstock, the most prominent member of the New York Society for the Suppression of Vice. The Comstock Act, passed in 1873, made mailing obscene, **lascivious,** or **lewd** material a felony. Still in effect, the law is enforced by the Inspection Service of the U.S. Postal Service.

Gradually, however, U.S. courts moved away from the suppression of all depictions of sex-related activities. In a 1933 obscenity trial, federal judge Leonard Woolsey ruled that James Joyce's great novel *Ulysses* was not obscene because the author did not intend the book's "dirty parts" to be sexually arousing; instead, wrote Woolsey, Joyce aimed to portray human consciousness in a new literary mode. When the decision was appealed, Judge Augustus Hand proclaimed the doctrine of "dominant effect": obscenity must be evaluated on the basis of the work as a whole. In other words, a little sex can be diluted by a lot of nonsexual content. In a 1936 case, Judge Learned Hand stressed that the positive effects of the context could counterbalance the negative effects of the embedded sexual descriptions.

Enforcement of the obscenity laws has been uneven because of the difficulty in defining what is obscene. In 1957 the Supreme Court, in *Roth* v. *United States,* attempted to provide a more precise definition of obscenity, and this definition remains the current legal one. In its decision, the Court stated that for material to be considered obscene, it must meet three essential criteria: (1) it must be offensive to contemporary community standards; (2) the dominant theme of the work must appeal to **prurient** interest in sex; and (3) the work must be devoid of serious literary, artistic, political, or scientific value. This ruling did not lead to a clarification of the legal issues. The meaning of "community standards" is vague. A community can encompass both fundamentalist churches and a university with a liberal faculty; Republicans and Democrats; conservatives and liberals; and elderly, middle-aged, and young persons. How does one arrive at the community standard?

In an attempt to determine whether a single "community standard" response to erotic materials could be found, college students participated in a study of "judgments about photographs" (Allgeier, Yachanin, Smith, & Myers, 1984). Students at the university where this research was done are quite conservative, and most regularly attend religious services. They were asked to rate photographs portraying nudity, heterosexual and homosexual activity, group sex, and so on. There was considerable variation in the ratings of how arousing, pornographic, and offensive each photo was. The absence of similarity of responses in this homogeneous group suggests that establishing a community standard would be even more difficult in a population as diverse as that found in U.S. cities.

The Supreme Court attempted to clarify the definition of obscenity again in a 1987 decision. The Court ruled six to three that some sexually explicit works may not be obscene even if most people in a city or state think that the works have no serious literary, artistic, political, or scientific value. According to Justice Byron White, "The proper inquiry is not whether an ordinary member of any given community would find literary, artistic, political, or scientific value but whether a reasonable person would find such value in the material taken as a whole." The question remains, of course, how we define a "reasonable person."

Contemporary social pressure to censor erotic depictions comes from two groups, one of which includes mainly political conservatives and religious fundamentalists. This group generally supports strict regulation of sexual behavior and considers use of erotica a pathway to sexual degeneracy. The second group consists of feminists who object to erotica that they consider degrading to women. They see certain

---

obscenity—The legal term for material that is foul, disgusting, lewd, and offensive to accepted standards of decency.
lascivious—Tending to stimulate sexual desire.
lewd—Sexually unchaste; inciting lust or debauchery.
prurient—Provoking lasciviousness.

forms of erotica as leading to aggression against women. Many feminists also assert that erotica reinforces traditional gender roles by emphasizing the subordination of women and the power of men in sexual relationships.

In 1992 Canada redefined obscenity as sexually explicit material that involves violence or degradation. Adult erotica, no matter how explicit, is not considered obscene. Erotic material that contains violence, degradation, bondage, or children is considered illicit obscenity. In effect, the Canadian court decided that a threat to women's equality is an acceptable ground for some limitation of free speech. As of this writing, Canada is the only nation that has defined obscenity in terms of harm to women rather than as material that offends moral values. It should be noted, however, that not all feminists support censorship of sexually explicit materials (Norton, 1999).

We know of no research exploring judgments of whether certain themes are perceived as degrading to men. In fact, we are not sure how anyone would construct heterosexual erotica that contained elements that would be judged by women—or men—as de-grading to men, short of the rape of men by women, as described in Chapter 19.

Judgments of the themes of sexually explicit material are a separate issue from judgments about whether such material should be censored. National surveys conducted almost every year from 1973 to 1986 in the United States by the National Opinion Research Center indicated that the majority of respondents in every survey agreed that the distribution of pornography to adults should not be illegal (Smith, 1987).

More important than whether people approve of the availability of erotica is whether particular kinds of erotica can be harmful. A choice confronting any society is the degree to which it wants to suppress material that may trigger antisocial behavior in some of its citizens. To protect the First Amendment rights of free expression, the courts have ruled that only those forms of expression that have a "virtual certainty" of producing potential harm can be banned. The conclusions of several national commissions concerning whether certain types of erotica cause harm are presented in "Highlight: Public Policy and Erotica," on page 484. *Reality or Myth*

The Effects of Erotica

There is intense controversy over the effects of exposure to erotica, particularly violent erotica. We now examine what is known about erotica and its effects.

NONVIOLENT EROTICA

In this section, our focus is on erotica that portrays consensual sexual activities. Does erotic material containing no aggression against women stimulate people to engage in sexual acts that they would normally avoid? Or does this material provide a sexual outlet for individuals who might use other means to satisfy their sexual desires if erotica were not available? Is exposure to erotica related to sex crimes and violence?

Since 1970 many studies have exposed research volunteers to nonaggressive sexual material. A review of these studies reveals no support for the belief that exposure to nonviolent erotica affects the rate of sex crimes, attitudes toward rape, or evaluations of rape victims (Davis & Bauserman, 1993; Kimmel & Linders, 1996; Winick & Evans, 1996). This is true for both short-term (less than an hour) and long-term (anything beyond an hour) exposure to nonviolent erotica.

One criticism of experimental research, however, is that the behaviors under study are affected by the artificiality of the laboratory setting and may not appear in real-life settings. To avoid such artificiality, Smith and Hand (1987) took advantage of the fact that a sexually explicit movie was screened once each semester at a private southern university. They conducted a field study on the campus to assess the possible links between nonviolent erotica and aggression. In the semester that the researchers carried out the study, the feature movie was *Up and Coming*, which the authors described as a film

H I G H L I G H T

Public Policy and Erotica

President Lyndon Johnson appointed the U.S. Commission on Obscenity and Pornography in the late 1960s. After funding much research and holding many hearings, the commission released its report in 1970. The commission's efforts were reported in nine technical volumes, two of which were specifically concerned with the effects of erotica.

Essentially, the commission arrived at a "no-harm" conclusion, maintaining that, according to the available evidence, exposure to or use of explicit sexual material does not play a significant role in causing crime, delinquency, sexual deviancy, or severe emotional disturbances (Amoroso, Brown, Pruesse, Ware, & Pithey, 1971). Overall, the commission recommended that federal, state, and local legislation should not interfere with the right of adults who wish to read, obtain, or view explicitly sexual materials. In the 1970s and 1980s, similar committees in Britain and Canada reached similar conclusions.

In 1985 the United States Attorney General's Commission on Pornography was formed. Also known as the Meese Commission (named after Attorney General Edwin Meese III), it delivered its final report in 1986 after hearing testimony from witnesses around the country and reviewing more than five thousand magazines, books, and films. The commission claimed to have found a "causal relationship between sexual violence and exposure to erotica that featured children and/or violence." Its assertion of this causal link has provoked serious criticisms of its conclusions. A number of studies have examined the correlation between exposure to explicit materials containing sexual violence, and attitudes toward women and assault. However, the correlational design of the studies reviewed by the commission did not allow any conclusions about the causes of sexually assaultive behavior on adults or children.

Despite the fact that the Meese Commission's conclusions were not warranted by the data its members reviewed, the commission made 92 specific recommendations aimed at halting the spread of erotica. Many of these recommendations related to more aggressive enforcement of the law with respect to erotic materials.

---

portraying the efforts of a young singer to establish herself in the country and western music industry. Her attempts to reach stardom provided for a number of sexual encounters with and among producers, agents, and fellow performers. In addition to graphic scenes of sexual intercourse, episodes of oral sex, anal sex, lesbianism, and group sex were depicted. Though the plot did include a brief scuffle between the singer and a rival female performer, the movie did not portray behavior that could be characterized as overtly sexually violent or coercive. (Smith & Hand, 1987, pp. 391–392)

On Monday of the week before the film was shown, the authors questioned more than 200 undergraduate women from the campus on whether they had been victims of aggression during the previous weekend. The following Friday night, the film was shown, and the audience included about a third of the undergraduate men at the college. On the next two Mondays following the film's screening, the women were again asked to describe any experiences that they had had with aggression over the previous weekend. There were no significant differences in the percentage of women reporting aggression before the film's showing (20 percent) versus after its screening (19 percent and 16 percent). Furthermore, those women whose male companions attended the movie reported experiencing no more aggression from the men than did the women whose companions had not viewed the film. *Reality or Myth* ？ 4

VIOLENT EROTICA

Exposure to violent pornography has been shown to heighten sexual arousal in some men, promote acceptance of rape-supportive attitudes, and foster negative attitudes toward women (Donnerstein & Linz, 1986; Malamuth, 1984). To examine the effect of exposure to violent pornography, Neil Malamuth and Edward Donnerstein (1984) presented men with a series of slides and corresponding tapes of women reading stories that included either coercive (use of force) or consensual (mutually consenting) sexual interaction. These researchers used self-reported arousal as well as genital measures of erection to assess men's responses to these forms of erotica. Before participating in the studies, volunteers were asked to indicate the likelihood that they would commit rape if they could be sure of not getting caught. Those who revealed that they thought they might engage in coercive sexual acts were classified as force oriented.

Although the designs of these studies varied, the stimuli usually consisted of a story of an attractive woman wandering along a deserted road. A man finds her there, but when he approaches her, she faints. He carries her to his car, and when she awakens, they engage in sex. In one version of this basic story, the woman is tied up and forced to have sex in the car. In other variations, she clearly consents to the act. Regardless of which rendition they saw, male volunteers found this story arousing, as indicated by both self-reports and the extent of their erections. This finding is consistent with others showing that some rape portrayals elicit relatively high sexual arousal in nonrapists (Malamuth, 1984; Malamuth & Check, 1983).

Even a rape portrayal emphasizing the victim's pain and distress may, under certain conditions, stimulate high levels of sexual arousal in viewers. But this effect appears to vary as a function of whether the viewer describes himself as force oriented (Lohr, Adams, & Davis, 1997; Malamuth, 1981). As portrayed in Figure 20.2, force-oriented volunteers reported having more arousal fantasies after exposure to the rape version than after exposure to the mutual-consent version. Non-force-oriented men, however, reported having more arousing fantasies in response to the variations of the story involving mutual consent than in response to the rape variation.

What about the kind of violent pornography that depicts a positive reaction on the part of the vic-

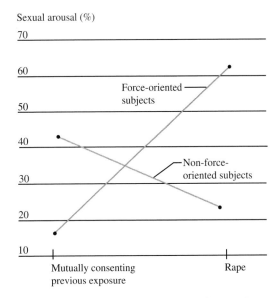

Figure 20.2   Violent Pornography and Sexual Arousal
As this graph illustrates, men who indicate some likelihood that they would commit rape (force-oriented men) are more aroused by violent pornography than are men who indicate they would not (non-force-oriented).

tim? As Donnerstein (1984) pointed out, pornographic media quite often portray victims of assault as responding favorably to a rape. Further, in real life, convicted rapists often fail to perceive their assaults as coercive, believing that their victims desired intercourse and enjoyed their sexual attentions (McCormick, 1994).

Donnerstein (1984) reasoned that exposure to stories in which a woman is depicted as having a positive reaction to sexual assault would increase aggressive behavior against women. To test this hypothesis, each male volunteer was paired with a female confederate, who either angered the man or treated him in a neutral manner. Each man then watched one of four films: a neutral version, a variation that involved consensual interaction, a version in which the victim had a negative reaction to forced sex, or a variation in which the victim's reaction to forced sex was positive. After viewing one of these films, the volunteer was given an opportunity to administer simulated electric shocks to the female confederate. Of the volunteers who had been angered prior to watching the movie, those who had viewed either of the forced-sex films chose to give higher levels of electric shock to the female confederate than did those who viewed either of the other films. Even the nonangered men became more aggressive (as measured by electric shock level) following exposure to the version of the film showing a positive reaction to forced sex. When a male confederate angered a male volunteer prior to his exposure to the film, the versions of the film did not affect aggression toward the male confederate.

To determine if the limited range of responses offered by previous experimenters had affected findings, William Fisher and Guy Grenier (1994) provided a broader range of alternatives for volunteers. That is, after being angered by the female confederate and shown sexual material containing violent content, men in Fisher and Grenier's research could select shock, verbal feedback, or the alternative of simply being debriefed, receiving their experimental credit, and terminating their participation in the study. Almost all participants selected the last alternative. This research is preliminary and needs to be replicated to see if the finding holds up.

To investigate the effect of violent pornography on women's arousal, Wendy Stock (1982) presented college women with variations in rape depictions while measuring their genital responses and their subjective reports of arousal. Based on the women's responses, Stock concluded that women are not aroused by rape when it is described realistically. But she did find heightened arousal as a result of viewing distorted portrayals of rape in which victims do not suffer. This is, of course, not the experience of most victims of rape.

The beliefs of some rapists and members of the general public that women secretly enjoy rape is not supported by Stock's findings. Her work suggests that society should be concerned about rape representations that lead viewers to perceive sexual assault as an erotic experience. Our current knowledge does not permit us to determine whether men who report strong arousal to rape depictions and are aroused by their own rape fantasies will actually commit rape.

The likelihood of a link between arousal in response to violent pornography and the commission of sexual assault was strengthened by research conducted more than two decades ago. The researchers (Abel, Barlow, Blanchard, & Guild, 1977) found that convicted rapists were as aroused by rape depictions as they were by portrayals of sexual interactions involving mutual consent. Nonrapists, in contrast, were more aroused by portrayals of consensual sex than by portrayals of forced sex.

Violent pornography degrades both women and men because it depicts women as wanting to be attacked, harmed, and assaulted and portrays men as wanting to inflict pain on other human beings. Because of the demeaning nature of violent erotica and its possible negative effects, some people favor banning it. Before censorship could be instituted, however, someone would have to determine what kinds of violent material should be prohibited and who should make that determination. Another problem is that the effect of censorship in the past has been to increase the profits of the producers of banned material. If violent pornography is found to pose a danger to women, we believe that the withdrawal of consumer support would be far more effective in stopping the production of aggressive pornography than would attempts at censorship.

▶ **Issues to Consider:** How would you design a message that rape is a frightening, traumatizing experience for its victims for videos that portray sexual assault?

PROLONGED EXPOSURE

The 1970 Commission on Obscenity and Pornography found that continued or repeated exposure to erotic stimuli resulted in a decrease in sexual arousal and interest in such material. But this conclusion has been challenged by the work of Zillmann and Bryant (1984, 1988). They concluded that following long-term exposure (4 hours and 48 minutes over a six-week period) to erotica that did not contain overt violence, men and women became more tolerant of bizarre and violent forms of erotica, less supportive of statements about gender equality, and more lenient in assigning punishment to a rapist whose crime was described in a newspaper account.

Prolonged exposure also produced other effects, such as discontent with the physical appearance and sexual performance of an intimate partner and the questioning of the values of marriage. It deepened men's callousness toward women, as reflected in increased acceptance of such statements as these: "A woman doesn't mean no until she slaps you" and "If they're old enough to bleed, they're old enough to butcher." Long-term exposure to erotica, however, did not increase aggressive behaviors. The material Zillmann and Bryant used commonly depicted women as sexually insatiable. Perhaps short-term exposure is not sufficient to produce changes in attitudes that reflect this unrealistic view of women. On the other hand, prolonged exposure to pornography that portrays violence against women has consistently been linked to negative effects, such as lessened sensitivity toward rape victims and greater acceptance of force in sexual encounters (Davis & Bauserman, 1993; Linz, 1989).

These findings make it difficult to reach any firm conclusions on the effects of prolonged exposure to nonviolent erotica. Moreover, even in cases in which negative effects have been found, we do not know how long these effects last, and this is an issue that researchers need to address. For example, it appears that any changes that occur after short-term exposure to violent erotica are not deeply ingrained and may fade when the participants receive an educational debriefing reminding them that the material is fictional, women do not enjoy sexual coercion, and so forth (Allen, D'Alessio, Emmers, & Gebhardt, 1996; Malamuth & Check, 1984). Such debriefings are required by ethics committees of institutions that receive federal research funds. Research on debriefing after prolonged exposure to erotica should be conducted to determine whether those effects are short-lived.

As we have emphasized in this chapter, there is no scientific consensus on whether serious harm is likely to result from exposure to erotica. We believe that the basic issue is violent images, not erotic images. It is interesting that our culture exposes the young to graphic details of violence on television and movie screens and in magazines without the same intense public concern that attends exposure to erotica or pornography (Brown & Steele, 1996).

CULTURAL VARIATIONS

Cultural practices and value systems may temper the influence of viewing erotica. For example, bondage and rape themes are prominent in novels and films in Japan. In Japanese films, the plot often involves the rape of a high school girl, a theme that is also evident in cheap erotic novels and sexual cartoons. Abramson and Hayashi (1984) pointed out that one of the best ways to ensure the commercial success of a Japanese adult film is to include the bondage and rape of a young woman.

The popularity of this theme might lead one to suspect that Japan would have a high rate of sexual assault. Yet Japan has one of the lowest reported rates (i.e., number of rapes per 100,000 people) among the industrialized countries in the world; the reported rape rate in the United States is more than 14 times higher. The assault laws in the two countries are essentially the same, and Japanese women are as reluctant to report assault as are U.S. women. A possible explanation for Japan's low assault rate is that the message expressed in erotica is mediated by cultural values. In Japan, people are socialized to have a strong sense of personal responsibility, respect, and commitment to society and to experience shame if they behave improperly (Dion & Dion, 1993).

CHILDREN AND EROTICA

The use of children as models for sexually explicit magazine photos and as stars of erotic movies is a major concern of many social agencies and citizens' groups. Both houses of Congress held hearings on child erotica in 1977. Witnesses at the hearings estimated that as many as half a million children were involved in the production of erotica. After these hearings, the federal government and nearly all state governments enacted laws against the production, distribution, and possession of child erotica.

Involvement in the production of erotica is a form of sexual exploitation associated with various adverse emotional, behavioral, and physical reactions in children, as well as in adults who were exploited as children (Finkelhor & Browne, 1985). Evidence of these reactions comes from clinical studies of children who were seeing therapists or other professionals, however, so we need to be careful in generalizing these findings to all children involved in such activity.

Some people oppose prosecuting those who ensnare children in the production of erotica. Their claim is that these products provide viewers with sexual release and that having such an outlet for their sexual tension prevents the consumers from seeking young people for sexual activities. Current law, however, bars children from participating in the production of erotica because they are incapable of giving informed consent.

Adults who pay, entice, or coerce children to engage in this activity can be prosecuted under child abuse laws rather than under obscenity laws. We favor this course of action for three reasons. First, obscenity laws may at times violate First Amendment guarantees of freedom of expression. Second, it is generally accepted that the First Amendment permits the outlawing only of material that is considered of-

fensive to public taste and morality, a judgment that is often difficult to make. Third, children, whether clothed or nude, are not obscene; it is the exploitation of children that is obscene. Adults who abuse their responsibilities toward children by exploiting them are therefore guilty of child abuse.

In 1982 the U.S. Supreme Court ruled unanimously that states may prosecute publishers and sellers of child erotica without having to prove that the materials showing children engaging in sexual acts are legally obscene or appeal to prurient interests. According to the Court, the simple inclusion of children engaging in sexual acts is enough to justify prosecution. *Reality or Myth*

rostitution (Commercial Sex Work)

We have considered how advertisers use sex to sell products and how materials such as erotic magazines and films, as well as sexual aids, are designed to elicit sexual arousal. In this section, we examine the direct sale of sexual services.

THE OLDEST PROFESSION

Prostitution appears to have been practiced at least as far back as we have historical records, and hence it is often called the world's oldest profession. The word *prostitute* comes from the Latin *prostituere*, which means "to expose." Under Roman law, prostitution was defined as the sale of one's body indiscriminately and without pleasure.

Prostitution flourished in ancient Rome; street prostitutes offered their services to patrons of the theater, the circus, and gladiator contests. As a prelude to the contests between gladiators, patrons would view shows featuring a variety of sexual acts. After the contest was over, those patrons interested in having sex were taken by the prostitutes to the arches beneath the public buildings, known as the *cellae fornicae*. This practice was so common that the word **fornication** came to mean "engaging in

---

prostitution—The practice of selling sexual stimulation or interaction.

fornication—Sexual intercourse between people who are not married to each other.

---

nonmarital sexual intercourse" (Bullough & Bullough, 1987).

Through recessions and boom times, prostitution remained a means of employment for poverty-stricken females before and after the Roman Empire. Prostitution was widespread in urban areas of Europe during the Middle Ages. In France, for example, the Paris steam bath, a popular rendezvous spot for prostitutes and customers, was licensed and taxed by the state and closed during Holy Week and Easter. That the prostitutes of Paris had their own patron saint, Mary Magdalene, underscores the Roman Catholic church's tolerance of prostitution during this period. Apparently, the church had adopted the reasoning of St. Thomas Aquinas, who compared prostitution to sewers in a palace: just as the palace would be polluted by sewage if one removed the sewers, the world would be polluted by lust if society removed the prostitutes.

Attitudes toward prostitution shifted in the 1500s. Two factors are related to the decline in the legal toleration of prostitution in the sixteenth century. First, with the Reformation, Protestant and, later, Catholic authorities came to regard open prostitution as a moral outrage. Second, syphilis began to spread rapidly in Europe after 1500. The disease was thought to have been transmitted to the general population by sailors returning from the New World, and civil and church authorities attempted to limit its spread by imposing tight control over sexual contacts (Bullough & Bullough, 1987).

Elisabeth Shue's prostitute in the film **Leaving Las Vegas** falls through the hierarchy from call girl to streetwalker.

In the Victorian era in England, a period noted for its supposed purity and prudery, prostitution flourished. Officially, the prostitute was a social outcast, but implicitly she was tolerated. She provided an outlet through which the proper nineteenth-century man could satisfy his passion. Victorian prostitutes were most often women who had been caught in the squalor and degradation of the urban slums that grew up around the mining and milling industries. Selling sexual favors was their main hope for survival.

Commercial Sex Work in Contemporary Society

Although there is still a strong relationship between poverty and prostitution, in some ways the nature of prostitution has changed markedly in the twentieth century. In the first part of the century, most transactions with prostitutes were conducted in houses where prostitution was the sole business. The employees worked, ate, and slept there. Because small red lights were used to indicate that the houses were

open for business, the areas in which they were clustered became known as red-light districts. In some nations in northern Europe, as well as in some counties in the state of Nevada, houses of prostitution continue to operate legally. For the most part, however, prostitutes in contemporary America operate out of a variety of other settings that reflect the economic status of the prostitute.

Streetwalkers are on the lowest rung of the ladder in the hierarchy of prostitution and at greatest risk of being victimized on the job (Miller & Schwartz, 1995; Vanwesenbeeck, de Graaf, van Zessen, Straver, & Visser, 1995). They solicit on the street and often work for, or are attached to, a **pimp**, who usually has more than one woman working for him. He protects them from outside assaults and generally takes care of them, although by the nature of his business, he is also highly manipulative of the women. The pimp usually takes a considerable share of the prostitute's earnings in exchange for his "protection." Some streetwalkers are recruited from among drug abusers and young runaways. However, most pimps are not interested in substance abusers because of economic reasons. Substance abuse is expensive, and addicted prostitutes are not reliable employees (McCormick, 1994). A growing exception occurs in crack houses where prostitutes exchange sex for drugs, particularly crack cocaine. Crack users and their sex partners are at special risk for HIV transmission (Inciardi, 1995). This greater risk occurs because the crack cocaine tends to lengthen the time spent in sexual stimulation, thus increasing the likelihood of tearing of the vaginal, anal, or penile skin. In addition, crack-using prostitutes tend not to use condoms with their multiple partners.

Streetwalkers have traditionally worked during the night, but daytime solicitation has become common in large cities. Some streetwalkers, for example, solicit by day in X-rated movie houses. After an arrangement has been struck, the streetwalker usually takes her "trick" (customer) to her apartment or to a cheap hotel, where the manager or room clerk typically is fully aware of the situation. A relatively new variation in streetwalking occurs in truck stops and highway rest areas. At truck stops, women

streetwalker—A prostitute who solicits on the street.
pimps—Prostitutes' business managers, some of whom also have sexual relations with their "girls."

known as "commercial beavers" provide sexual services in the drivers' cabs (McCormick, 1994).

Bar and hotel prostitutes are somewhat higher in the hierarchy of prostitutes than are streetwalkers. The bar girl usually enters into an arrangement with the owner or manager of the bar where she works. For example, she may receive a percentage of the drinks that she entices the customer to buy for both of them. More frequently, the bar girl is tolerated by the ownership because of the business she attracts. Unlike the streetwalker, the bar girl sometimes finds herself in competition with amateurs and may have to solicit aggressively. The customer may become quite disgruntled if he at first thinks the bar girl is taking an interest in him because of his lovable personality and then discovers that there is a price attached to any sexual activity. The bar girl's fee for sex is generally higher than that charged by the streetwalker.

Because hotel managers generally frown on open solicitation, hotel prostitutes must be subtle and skilled in sending nonverbal messages to potential clients. After a deal has been made, sexual activity usually takes place in the customer's hotel room or apartment. Many hotel prostitutes work a bar one day and a hotel the next. They generally operate without pimps.

One of the more visible forms of prostitution is the storefront variety. In this version, women are employed by massage parlors or thinly disguised business fronts, such as escort services, to provide sexual services to the customers. Although there are legitimate massage parlors and escort services, many run an operation involving both massage and masturbation (M&M) of customers. For an additional fee, the "hand whores" may also provide oral sex or, less frequently, coitus. Many women employed by massage parlors and escort services are amateurs: college students, homemakers, sales clerks, nurses, secretaries, and women in other occupations who are supplementing their incomes (McCormick, 1994). Women hired through escort services to entertain at conventions are sometimes prostitutes. They may be asked to service delegates, visitors, and convention personnel, as well as to perform before a limited audience. The performances involve dancing, stripping, and lesbian and heterosexual activities. The convention prostitute may have a pimp who acts as a booking agent.

Bar girls often operate with the tacit approval of the bar manager.

At the top of the prostitution hierarchy is the **call girl**. She usually works out of a comfortable apartment, and if she has a pimp, he acts as her business manager. Typically, her prices are high, and her clientele is screened, with solicitation generally occurring by telephone. New customers are located through references and word of mouth. The call girl is likely to provide services other than purely sexual ones, such as serving as an attractive date for dinner or a party. It is widely believed that many corporations and government agencies employ call girls to entertain important customers, agents, and dignitaries. Although the use of call girls by government agencies, particularly intelligence agencies, is probably not as great as espionage novels suggest, prostitutes' involvement in espionage has a long history.

call girl—A high-priced prostitute whose customers are solicited by telephone or by word-of-mouth references.

Male Prostitutes.   It should not be surprising that the possibility of earning money for sexual favors has attracted males as well as females. Like their female counterparts, most male prostitutes often sell their bodies for financial gain as well as sexual pleasure (Calhoun & Weaver, 1996).

Many heterosexual male prostitutes function in a manner similar to that of call girls. These men may be "kept" by an older woman, or they may work for an escort service for single, wealthy women. The **gigolo's** relationship to the client is generally well defined, requiring little or no emotional involvement.

More common are males who sell their sexual favors to other men; in fact, many male prostitutes describe themselves as homosexual or bisexual (Earls & David, 1989). The homosexual prostitute is called a "hustler" or sometimes a "boy," or in England, a "rent boy" (West, 1993). Such men usually ply their trade on the street or in gay bars and baths. Unlike female streetwalkers, male prostitutes usually do not have pimps (Calhoun & Weaver, 1996). In the homosexual culture, prostitutes drift in and out of the occupation; homosexual prostitutes are more likely to be part-timers than are heterosexual prostitutes (Luckenbill, 1985).

Male prostitutes tend to be more suspicious, mistrustful, hopeless, lonely, and isolated than are nonprostitute males (Simon, Morse, Osofsky, Balson, & Gaumer, 1992). These characteristics may be a response to the chaotic and often dangerous environment in which they exist. This environment may intensify the psychological characteristics that led them to "the life" in the first place. More than 80 percent of the 211 men in Simon et al.'s study used multiple drugs, with alcohol, marijuana, and cocaine being the most common; 28 percent reported injecting drugs and sharing needles with their customers. This intravenous drug use is alarming from a public health standpoint because of the possibility of transmitting HIV and other STDs. Condom use was infrequent or never occurred, according to the men and their customers (Morse, Simon, Balson, & Osofsky, 1992).

Streetwalking men in Atlanta, Georgia, were interviewed by Jacqueline Boles and Kirk Elifson

---

gigolo—A man who is paid to be a woman's escort and to provide her with sexual services; a kept man.

(1994). Although you might assume that these men were gay, only 18 percent of their sample self-identified as homosexual, about a third were bisexual, and the rest described themselves as heterosexual. The bisexuals tended to make statements such as, "I have [paid] sex with men and I have a girlfriend; I guess that makes me a bi" (p. 44). HIV infection rates for the men in each sexual identity category were higher for those who frequently engaged in receptive anal sex, had many sexual partners, used drugs frequently, and had a history of other STDs.

Child Prostitutes.   The lure of money for unskilled labor is often difficult to resist. One disturbing statistic is the increase in U.S. arrests for prostitution of those under 18 years of age. Between the 1960s and 1980s, the annual arrests for this age group shot up almost 400 percent (Maguire, Patore, & Flanagan, 1992). It is estimated that there are about 100,000 child prostitutes in the United States, some as young as 12 or 13, who were tempted or coerced into prostitution as a means of supporting themselves (U.S. Department of Labor, 1996).

Although this is a horrendous social problem in the United States, it pales when compared to child prostitution in some countries in Latin America and Southeast Asia. For example, it is estimated that there are 200,000 child and adolescent prostitutes in Brazil (Beyer, 1996). In Colombia, girls as young as 8 years old are performing in many of the major cities in sex clubs as strippers. Poverty, family violence, and, in Latin American countries, "machismo" are the bedrock of child prostitution (Beyer, 1996, p. 33). Machismo is a cultural belief system that views men as superior to women. Men are thought to have intense, uncontrollable sexual drives that are a sign of their strength and power. In contrast, women are seen as passive in their sexual needs and satisfied within the confines of domestic activities. Men seek women other than their wives to meet their sexual needs. This involves visiting prostitutes whose value is often determined by their youth. There is a belief that the younger the females are, the less likely she is to have an STD.

Child prostitution transcends national borders (see "Highlight: Prostitution Across Cultures"). Japanese school girls have found an occupation to increase their ability to buy high-status objects such

H I G H L I G H T

Prostitution Across Cultures

Sexual tourism has received increasing recognition in the news media. Many North American, Australian, European, and Japanese men travel to places such as Thailand to view sex shows, purchase erotic materials, and engage in sex. The promotion of Thailand as a tourist sexual resort has been looked on with tolerance by government officials, who view it as an economic asset (Manderson, 1995). Although there are other countries in which sex tourism is promoted, Thailand has remained a major destination for men seeking sexual adventure. Manderson (1995) described the atmosphere in the Patpong area of Bangkok, the capital of Thailand. This is an area of nightclubs, drinking lounges, and go-go bars. Most of the sex performances are oriented toward heterosexual men, although transvestite, transsexual, and same-sex entertainers are also part of the panorama.

Most sex performances take place in the bars. Customers are expected to buy the "bar girls" a drink. If they negotiate sex, they pay the bar a "fine," and then the sex workers receive a set fee (half of which goes to the brothel keeper) and possibly a tip.

On stage, women engage in a variety of sexually exotic acts. Single acts include using the vagina to smoke cigarettes, open bottles of soft drinks, pick up sushi with chopsticks partially inserted in the vagina, and many other similar demonstrations. Duo acts may be faked but also include heterosexual and lesbian sexual interaction. "Heterosexual acts work through a menu of poses that display penile length, stroke style, female agility, usually without ejaculation because there are often several performances in an evening. Lesbian sex involves caressing, tribadism, and cunnilingus" (Manderson, 1995, p. 313).

In Latin America, vacation packages to such places as the beaches of the Dominican Republic and to San José, the capital of Costa Rica, often include sex with children. In San José, for example, there are more than 2,000 child prostitutes whose customers are almost always from other countries (Beyer, 1996).

There are many harmful aspects to this sex industry, such as young children being sold by poor families to people providing sexual services. In addition, it is estimated that a majority of these commercial sex workers are infected with HIV. Such an environment presents a true health hazard. What has been promoted as a sexual paradise for tourists can become a sexual hell for those who contract incurable STDs.

---

as Chanel perfume and designer clothes. As one 16-year-old girl put it, "Girls in my school tend to be split up into the girls who have such things and those who don't. If you have the brand-name things, you're important" (Stroh, 1996). To acquire these things, girls participate in "telephone clubs," where they can call men and decide after talking with them whether to meet them for sex. The girls can earn up to $1,000 from each liaison with an older man.

These telephone clubs started appearing in the mid-1980s. In the past few years, the number of these clubs across Japan has increased to more than 2,200. A PTA survey indicated that as many as 25 percent of high school girls had called a telephone club at least once (Stroh, 1996). The system works like this: Men pay about $20 to rent small rooms in the clubs, where they can watch television and wait for girls to call them. The girls call toll-free numbers advertised in public telephone booths and on packets of tissues that are distributed on street corners.

In 1995, about 1,500 men were arrested for having sex with teenage girls they met through telephone clubs, and more than 5,000 girls aged 18 and younger were questioned for involvement in sex-related offenses and prostitution (which is illegal in Japan)—a 16 percent increase from the previous year

These streetwalker children are seeking customers in Seattle, Washington. "Tiny Annie" was reported to say, "For a blow-job, it would be $30 on up and for a lay it would be $40 on up. Most of these [veteran] ho's charge more than us little kids do."

(Stroh, 1996). In 1996, a school principal near Tokyo was arrested for running a prostitution ring involving 280 14- to 17-year-old girls.

Prostitution by girls and women will continue to exist in staggering numbers as long as there are people mired in poverty and females are treated as inferior to males.

> ▶ **Issues to Consider:** If a man or a woman engages in sex with another person in exchange for a favor, a promotion, influence, or dinner, is this prostitution?

The Trade. Prostitution is a topic that proper society prefers to avoid contemplating. Perhaps because of societal disdain, not only do stereotypes abound, but knowledge about prostitution is lacking. It is not uncommon to hear laypersons describe female prostitutes as man-hating lesbians or nymphomaniacs.

The research indicates that female prostitutes' attitudes toward their clients, and toward men in general, are varied rather than uniformly negative (Diana, 1985; McCormick, 1994). Contrary to the popular belief that prostitutes are sexually unresponsive during their work, Savitz and Rosen (1988) found in their study of streetwalkers in Philadelphia that 70 percent of the women reported enjoying intercourse all, most, or some of the time; 83 percent reported the same degree of pleasure from receiving oral sex; and 63 percent enjoyed giving oral sex.

Another stereotype about female prostitutes—that most are lesbians—is also not supported by research. Most female prostitutes consider themselves heterosexual or bisexual, not homosexual (Diana, 1985; Savitz & Rosen, 1988). Prostitutes sometimes engage in sex with another woman in response to a customer's desires; for example, a male-female couple may hire a prostitute to have sex with one or both of them.

The financial fortune of prostitutes depends on how many tricks they can turn in a working day. (Call girls are typically an exception to this assembly-line approach because they are often hired for an entire evening by a customer.) The more customers a prostitute can bring to orgasm, the more money he or she makes. Thus, after a client pays for a particular service, the prostitute generally attempts to bring the customer to orgasm as quickly as possible, usually after two to three minutes of sexual contact. The most frequently reported practice to accomplish this goal is oral sex, as cited by both prostitutes (Freund, Leonard, & Lee, 1989) and their customers (Wallace, Beatrice, & Mann, 1988). Most prostitutes prefer oral sex because it takes less effort than coitus, the next most common sexual practice. In third place is "half and half": oral stimulation followed by coitus. These kinds of sexual contacts, along with the manual stimulation of customers' genitals, account for almost all sexual transactions between prostitutes and their clients. Vaginal intercourse is more likely to occur if the customer is a regular client, that is, has frequent sexual contacts with the same prostitute over a long period of time—specifically, one to three times a week over 1 to 14 years (Freund et al., 1989).

The number of customers whom a prostitute services in a working day or night varies greatly, depending on such factors as client availability, the prostitute's mood, and negative characteristics of a potential customer. Published accounts indicate an average of 4 to 12 sexual encounters per workday (Diana, 1985; Freund et al., 1989). The large number of sexual contacts, of course, puts prostitutes (and customers) who do not use condoms at an elevated risk of contracting STDs. The specter of fatal illness has altered the sexual practices of prostitutes, with many now regularly employing condoms and abstaining from high-risk sexual behaviors (Earls & David, 1989; Freund et al., 1989). Condom use in sexual encounters has been reported by 38 percent to 74 percent of prostitutes (Cohen, Hauer, Poole, & Wofsy, 1987; Freund et al., 1989; Wallace et al.,

1988). Condom use varies depending on the sexual activity. Of male clients of female streetwalkers, 72 percent of the clients reported using condoms during vaginal intercourse, and 33 percent reported doing so during oral sex (Freund, Lee, & Leonard, 1991). *Reality or Myth* **6**

Prostitution and the Law.   Prostitution is not an easy activity to define or categorize. For example, if a man or a woman engages in sex with another person to secure a favor, a promotion, or influence, is this prostitution? Consider this account by a former prostitute of her first experience with prostitution:

> *It would have been when I was still back in high school, when I screwed my husband-to-be in the back seat of the car. He bought me coke. A Coca-Cola, and popcorn. At the time I didn't consider it [prostitution]. Now I do. At the time I thought I was having fun.*
> (Goldstein, 1979, p. 23)

Legal definitions of prostitution vary from one time and place to another, but they generally include some notion of indiscriminate sexual activity or promiscuity, as well as barter. State legal codes typically forbid making money from the provision of sexual fulfillment. For example, a 1968 ruling of the supreme court of Oregon stated: "The feature which distinguishes a prostitute from other women who engage in illicit intercourse is the indiscrimination with which she offers herself to men for hire" (Rosenbleet & Pariente, 1973, p. 381). Prostitution and commercialized vice include sex offenses such as (1) prostitution; (2) keeping a **brothel**—a house where prostitutes and customers meet for sexual activity; (3) **pandering** or **procuring**—serving as a go-between in commercial sexual transactions (also called pimping), transporting, or detaining women for immoral purposes; and (4) all attempts to commit any of the preceding (Maguire & Pastore, 1995).

Every state in the United States has laws regulating prostitution, soliciting for prostitution, or loiter-

---

brothel—A house where prostitutes and customers meet for sexual activity.
pandering—Serving as a go-between in commercial sexual transactions; generally pimping or procuring.
procuring—Obtaining customers for a prostitute.

ing for the purpose of prostitution. Nevada is the only state in which counties are given the option to allow prostitution, and several do. These counties, however, confine prostitution to brothels and have laws against soliciting customers in other vicinities.

The frequency of this "criminal" violation, and the numbers of men and women involved in it, are difficult to estimate. Prostitution is not an offense reported by a victim or complainant, and hence the statistics based on arrests are not a clear reflection of the incidence of this activity. Arrests tend to be sporadic, and differences in the number of arrests from one locality to another may reflect the attitude of local law enforcement officials rather than the incidence of prostitution.

Prostitution represents the only sexual offense for which women are prosecuted more often than are men. In 1994 there were more than 95,000 arrests for prostitution and commercialized vice in the United States (Maguire & Pastore, 1995). The fact that a disproportionate number of Blacks were arrested (46 percent) probably reflects prostitution's link to economic factors. Those individuals who are arrested for prostitution are usually streetwalkers, who tend to come from the lower socioeconomic strata of our society.

Enforcement agents often deploy a vice-squad undercover officer to pose as a **john**, a slang term for a prostitute's customer. The prostitute is arrested when she offers a sexual service for a price. To avoid arrest, the experienced prostitute is careful about how she words her proposition to a potential customer. She may ask him whether he wants a good time or some fun. She also approaches the matter of her fees in a roundabout way. If a prostitute is arrested and convicted, she is usually fined but typically does not spend much time in jail. Either her pimp or a friend usually secures bail money. Fines tend to be minimal and jail sentences short.

Patronizing a prostitute is illegal in some states, but there has been little concerted effort to prosecute customers. In some states, however, the patron of prostitution does face a fine of $500 or more and a year or more in jail. A customer is most likely to be arrested when a female police officer poses as a prostitute and entices him into asking for a sexual service and offering money for it. The punishment for pimping is much more severe than that for prostitution, although few pimps are arrested.

It is the working man or woman in the prostitution network who bears the brunt of legal penalties. To protect themselves, many prostitutes have joined the local and national unions that have emerged in North America and Western Europe. The decriminalization of prostitution would have a number of advantages for the prostitute and for society. City and state governments spend a great deal of money trying to control prostitution, with little success (Boles, 1998). If prostitution were legalized, pimps would likely lose much of their influence on the trade. Prostitutes could be licensed, taxed, and regularly examined for STDs. The civil rights of prostitutes and of their consenting adult clients could be protected. Children would also be barred from entering prostitution.

Becoming a Prostitute. A number of scholars have examined the factors or circumstances associated with becoming a prostitute (Boles, 1998; Bullough & Bullough, 1996). Poverty, disenchantment with life prospects, a tedious job, failure in school, a turbulent home life, and physical and sexual abuse are some of the factors associated with entry into prostitution. Although these background conditions may predispose an individual toward prostitution, they are not sufficient to guarantee entry into the trade. If they were, there would be a lot more prostitutes, given the number of people who come from an impoverished background or have experienced physical or sexual abuse.

What is necessary for most females is contact with someone involved in the world of prostitution: a prostitute or pimp, or a bartender or hotel clerk. Through these associations, a female learns about the world of prostitution. If she decides to become part of this world, she typically develops a relationship with a pimp. She is taught the tricks of the trade: how to protect herself from disease, dangerous customers, and police officers, and how to do the least amount of work for the most money. In one study of 200 street prostitutes, almost 80 percent reported having started prostitution as juveniles. About one-third of these women also reported

---

john—A slang term for the customer of a prostitute.

having been involved as juveniles in sexually explicit activity that was photographed. Contrary to the popular notion, "once a prostitute, always a prostitute," the average span of a prostitute's career was about five years in one study (Potterat, Woodhouse, Muth, & Muth, 1990).

Like their female counterparts, male prostitutes often come from a background of poverty, strained parental relations, poor education, and little or no work experience (Boles, 1998). If they seek or are exposed to experienced hustlers or customers, they may choose to enter the trade. Unlike female prostitutes, they are not trained or supervised in the trade. They learn how to hustle by observation and through interaction with other hustlers and customers (Calhoun & Weaver, 1996).

The Prostitute's Clientele. The clients of prostitutes have not been studied thoroughly. Kinsey and his colleagues (1948) found that about 69 percent of the White men in their sample had had some sexual experience with prostitutes. Many of these men reported only one or two experiences. Laumann et al.'s (1994) data indicated that the use of prostitutes' services appears to be on the decline. Only 3 percent of men in the study reported that their first coitus was with a paid partner.

Using peepholes, one-way mirrors, and other observation posts more than two decades ago, Stein (1974) witnessed hundreds of sessions between cooperating prostitutes and their clients. She described the men whom she observed:

> At first I looked for signs of "abnormality" in the clients. I felt that any man who paid for sex must be some kind of "loser." I was disappointed. I saw a few "losers," of course, but most of the clients were agreeable, reasonably attractive, upper-middle-class men, businessmen or professionals. (p. 10)

Studies of massage-parlor patrons on the West Coast (Armstrong, 1978) and in Illinois (Simpson & Schill, 1977) reported that the typical customer appeared to be indistinguishable from the average U.S. man. Interviews with 30 johns who had paid for sex an average of 50 times revealed that almost all were involved in personal relationships that included sexual activity. They purchased sex by choice rather than out of necessity (Holzman & Pines, 1982). In their association with prostitutes, many of these men experienced feelings and displayed behaviors that were typical of regular courtships. For example, before meeting a prostitute, they attempted to make themselves physically appealing by bathing, dressing fashionably, and using cologne. Many were aroused by the potential adventure and danger of associating with a prostitute.

Freund et al.'s (1991) interviewers approached men in their cars, sometimes with introductions by prostitutes, and obtained responses from 101 male clients of prostitutes. These men averaged about 40 years of age (ranging from 21 to 72). Their ethnic background was similar to that of the general population in the area (Camden, New Jersey), and they reported an average of about five years of paying for sex. Most were regular clients, with 93 percent reporting visits monthly or more frequently and 63 percent seeing a prostitute weekly or more frequently. About half had had sex with the same prostitute or the same small group of prostitutes.

These studies paint a picture of prostitutes' customers as middle-class men in search of sexual satisfaction and adventure. But prostitutes are undoubtedly used for many different reasons by a wide range of men, including these:

1. Men with physical or emotional problems that create difficulty in finding a partner.

2. Married men in search of novelty without emotional involvement (Buss, 1999).

3. Men whose work involves considerable absence from home.

4. Men who seek a type of sex they cannot or will not request from a wife or girlfriend.

5. Men who feel that only "bad" girls are truly interested in the pleasures of the flesh.

A Final Note. Prostitution exists because of the market for it. The same statement applies to erotica and other uses of sex for profit by advertisers and movie and video producers. People are often attracted to participation in erotic or pornographic ventures or to prostitution because these enterprises provide more income than they imagine they might be able to obtain through other employment. Their motivation is, of course, the same one that prompts people to offer any service for which there is a societal demand. Viewing or using erotica or sexual aids by oneself or with a steady partner may continue to flourish because these activities do not expose people to AIDS. In contrast, the novelty or adventure asso-

ciated with buying sexual intimacy from prostitutes will likely be tempered by the possibility of contracting a fatal disease.

SUMMARY OF MAJOR POINTS

1. Soft-core and hard-core erotica. Materials designed to elicit sexual arousal can be divided into soft-core and hard-core erotica. Soft-core magazines endured substantial losses in readership in the 1980s. Part of this decline is probably attributable to the greater availability of hard-core or X-rated materials and increased sales of sexually explicit videocassette films that consumers can view in the privacy of the home.

2. Sex and the consumer. Sexuality is a major theme in the U.S. marketplace. It is a staple of television programming and permeates advertising. The images used by advertisers and filmmakers glamorize sex without mentioning the possible consequences of sexual activity. Erotic products, advertisements, and services can be found in magazines, newspapers, theaters, and adult bookstores. Consumers can purchase sexual services through telephone sex, strip shows, theaters, bars, or the Internet.

3. Aphrodisiacs and drugs. Humans' ongoing quest for chemical substances to enhance sexual desire and performance has generally been fruitless. Some substances may affect sexual response indirectly because of the user's belief about their powers or because of their effects on psychological feelings. Caution is advised in taking any so-called aphrodisiacs; some have health-threatening side effects. In small doses, alcohol and some drugs may have indirect effects on sexual expression by reducing inhibitions, but in large doses or when taken over lengthy periods, these substances usually diminish the capacity for satisfying sexual relations.

4. Obscenity. For material to be considered obscene, it must meet three essential criteria: (1) it must be offensive to contemporary community standards,

(2) its dominant theme must appeal to prurient interest in sex, and (3) the work must be devoid of serious literary, artistic, political, or scientific value. In 1987 the Supreme Court ruled that the proper application of community standards is not whether most people in a locality would find literary, artistic, political, or scientific value in allegedly obscene material but whether a reasonable person would find such value in the material taken as a whole.

5. Effects of erotica. The evidence indicates that most forms of erotica do not trigger sexual aggression in or cause harm to observers. Two exceptions may be violent erotica and child pornography.

6. Violent erotica. Researchers have concluded that the majority of college men do not find violent pornography as arousing as depictions of consensual relationships. A sizable minority of men, however, are more aroused by aggressive sexual depictions than by consensual erotica; such responses are also characteristic of convicted rapists.

7. Children and erotica. The Supreme Court ruled in 1982 that states may prosecute the publishers and sellers of child erotica without having to prove that their materials are legally obscene. Because children are not legally capable of informed consent, adults who pay, entice, or coerce them to engage in sexual activity can be prosecuted under child abuse laws.

8. Prostitution. Prostitution has flourished since the beginning of recorded history. Most of its practitioners have come from impoverished backgrounds. Every state in the nation has laws regulating prostitution. Usually the prostitute rather than the customer is prosecuted. Some prostitutes have organized unions that provide services to improve the working conditions of prostitutes.

Afterword

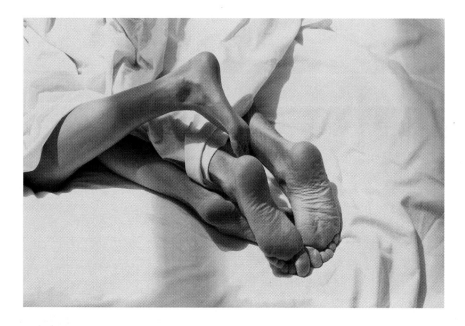

Now that you have come to the end of this text, we would like you to take a moment to reflect with us on the book and the class you are finishing. Throughout this book, we have emphasized a number of important ideas, including the complexity of sexual interactions, the importance of separating sexual myths from reality, and the value of forming your own sexual policies, hopefully as a basis for loving sexual interactions.

We hope you have come to appreciate the complexity of sexual interactions.

Pepper Schwartz (1993) began an address to The Society for the Scientific Study of Sexuality this way:

Sex is messy, passionate, tentative, exultative, anxiety-producing, liberating, frightening, embarrassing, consoling, appetitive, and cerebral—in other words, contradictory, different for different people, different for the same person at different times, operating at three or four different levels at the same time. . . .

And that just covers masturbation! Add another person and it gets really complex.

The factors that contribute to our sexual feelings and responses are numerous, and we are not necessarily conscious of all the variables. Our historical, religious, and family background, as well as cultural norms, can all have an impact on sexual feelings and responses. So can our experiences in both sexual and nonsexual relationships with other people. Further, these variables interact with one another. For example, our experiences can lead us to form expectations about current situations, and those expectations may be enough to exert an influence on our sexual responses. Other factors that come into play include concerns about STDs or unwanted conception. Health or biological factors contribute to sexual interactions, as do psychological factors, such as guilt about sexual feelings. Sexual interactions are further complicated by the fact that each person is unique and relates differently to the same person at different times. Our intention is not to complicate your life unnecessarily. Rather, we hope that increased awareness of how these different variables can influence your sexual feelings and behavior can help you to formulate policies that contribute to more satisfying relationships.

We hope you have sharpened the ability to recognize your sexual assumptions and beliefs.

All of us tend to accept particular sexual (and nonsexual) myths and stereotypes without determining whether they are supported by adequate evidence. We hope we have convinced you to undertake a critical examination of the particular sexual myths and stereotypes that predominate in your environment. As we said at the beginning of the book, unquestioning acceptance of sexual myths and stereotypes is often related to negative consequences of sexual activity, such as rape, STD transmission, or unwanted pregnancy, and unwanted social consequences, such as prejudice against people with STDs or whose sexual behavior is out of the mainstream. We hope that the knowledge that you have gained from reading this book will help you to avoid these risks of sexual interactions.

We hope that you have come to share our belief in the importance of developing clear sexual policies that will improve your chances for satisfying sexual interactions.

Sexuality touches many aspects of our lives. Even those of us who choose to be celibate must still contend with our and others' sexual feelings in our roles as policymakers and voters and when others request advice as they struggle with sexual decisions. Those of us who do want to express our sexual feelings have many decisions to make regarding the conditions under which we will engage in sexual activity, with whom, in what ways, and with what degree of commitment. Although the task of developing sexual guidelines is not necessarily as straightforward as it might seem at first blush, we hope you are convinced that it is a worthwhile effort.

We believe that, ideally, sexual guidelines reflect the fundamental values of honesty, equality, and responsibility. We agree wholeheartedly with the following words of Ira Reiss (1997, p. 223): "All sexual encounters should be negotiated with an honest statement of your feelings, an equal treatment of the other person's feelings, and responsibility for taking measures to avoid unwanted outcomes."

In addition to the themes above, we have written this book on the basis of two values that lay at the core of our beliefs about sexual interactions. We would like to share them with you, in the hope that, if you have come to appreciate these values, they will guide your conduct beyond the end of this term or semester.

We believe it is critically important to provide accurate information about sexuality through the education process.

We believe that education about sexuality is important, not only for the college students for whom we wrote this book, but for younger students as well. Many relatively well-educated politicians, social commentators, school board members, school officials, teachers, and parents support education in the primary and secondary schools about illicit drugs on the assumption that such education will reduce the likelihood that young people will abuse drugs. In a rather astonishing paradox, some of these same people attempt to block the provision of realistic and thorough education for sexuality. They assume that exposure to sex education will lead young people to engage in "precocious" or early sexual relationships with one another. If providing education about sexual feelings and behavior (with the intention of reducing unwanted consequences associated with sexual contacts) encourages young people to engage in early sexual experimentation, wouldn't exposure to drug education lead young people to explore various illicit drugs and ultimately to abuse drugs? As it happens, education about the potential short- and long-term effects of drug abuse discourages young people from initiating or continuing drug use. And as you know from reading this book, the same relationship exists between thorough and accurate sex education and the initiation of early unprotected sexual contact. As a poster currently popular in some circles proclaims, "If you think education is expensive, consider the costs of ignorance."

We believe in the value of sexual pluralism.

One of our underlying values in writing this book is the notion of sexual pluralism—the opposite of sexual dogmatism. Rather than following other people's beliefs or assumptions about what is right and natural, we need to figure out what is right for us among many options. Many people in North America have embraced cultural pluralism, which respects diversity in ethnic background, religious affiliations, occupations, and lifestyles. Sexual pluralism is the recognition that we also vary in our level of responsiveness to particular sexual activities. For example, some people prefer oral stimulation or other sexual activities to penile-vaginal intercourse. Most people are attracted to partners of the other sex, but a significant minority are not aroused by other-sex partners, responding instead to same-sex partners. Still others are not affected by the sex of a potential partner. There is no single standard or right way to engage in sexual intimacy. There is no evidence indicating that reading human sexuality texts and taking human sexuality courses lead to shifts in sexual orientation or adoption of activities that were previously not appealing to particular individuals. However, exposure to the diversity in sexual activities and sexual preferences among consenting adults does appear to lead to greater acceptance of variations in others' consensual sexual behaviors. We see great value in the efforts to minimize the attempts of any one group to impose its beliefs and values on others who are engaging in mutually consenting sexual activity. We hope that you can generalize such increased tolerance for sexual diversity to nonsexual contexts such as nonjudgmental acceptance of others' religious beliefs, ethnic backgrounds, and lifestyles. Tolerance of diversity may initially be a difficult response to develop and maintain, but it is crucial for a more loving and peaceful world.

Glossary

abortions Spontaneous or medical terminations of pregnancies before fetuses can survive outside the uterus.

acquired immunodeficiency syndrome (AIDS) A virally caused condition in which severe suppression of the immune system reduces the body's ability to fight diseases.

alveoli (AL-vee-OH-lee) Milk-secreting cells in the breast.

amebiasis (ah-ME-BYE-uh-sis) A parasitic infection of the colon that results in frequent diarrhea.

amniotic sac The pouch containing a watery fluid that envelops a developing fetus in the uterus.

amygdala (uh-MIG-duh-luh) Brain center involved in the regulation of sexual motivation.

analingus (a-nil-LING-gus) Oral stimulation of the tissues surrounding the anus.

androgen insensitivity syndrome Condition in which males secrete normal levels of androgen but lack a normal androgen receptor gene on the X chromosome and are thus unresponsive to androgen.

androgens Generic term for hormones that promote the development and functioning of the male reproductive system.

androgyny (ann-DRAW-jih-nee) The ability of a person to express both stereotypically masculine and stereotypically feminine traits and behaviors; from the Greek *andro*, meaning "male," and *gyn*, meaning "female."

aphrodisiacs Drugs, foods, or other substances that are popularly believed to heighten sexual desire and performance.

artificiality The extent to which a research setting differs from one's normal living environment.

asphyxiophilia Elevation of carbon dioxide in the blood via reduction of oxygen to the brain by applying pressure to the neck with a rope or belt during arousal and orgasm. Supposedly enhances the intensity of orgasm but sometimes results in accidental death.

asymptomatic (A-symp-toe-MAH-tik) Without recognizable symptoms.

autoeroticism Sexual self-stimulation.

autosomes The 22 pairs of chromosomes that are involved in general body development in humans.

Barr body Condensed, inactive X chromosome that distinguishes female cells from male cells. It appears as a dense clump when it is stained and examined under a microscope.

behaviorism A theoretical approach that emphasizes the importance of studying observable activity.

bias An attitude for or against a particular theory or hypothesis that influences one's judgment.

biphobia Negative attitudes toward bisexuality.

birth control The regulation of conception, pregnancy, or birth with preventive devices or methods.

bisexual The capacity to feel erotic attraction toward or to engage in sexual interaction with both men and women.

body cells All the cells in the body except germ cells. Also called somatic cells.

Braxton-Hicks contractions Irregular contractions of the uterus that are often mistaken for the onset of labor.

brothel A house where prostitutes and customers meet for sexual activity.

call girl A high-priced prostitute whose customers are solicited by telephone or by word-of-mouth references.

candidiasis (KAN-dih-DYE-ah-sis) An infection of the vulva and vagina caused by the excess growth of a fungus that occurs normally in the body.

cannula (CAN-u-luh) A tube inserted into the body through which liquid or tissue may be removed.

castration anxiety Fear of losing the penis, thought by psychoanalysts to result from the child's fear of retaliation for forbidden sexual desire toward one's mother.

cerebrum (sare-REE-brum) The surface layer of cell bodies that constitutes the bulk of the human brain.

cervical cap A contraceptive rubber dome that is fitted to a woman's cervix; spermicide is placed inside the cap before it is pressed onto the cervix.

cervix (SIR-vix) The lower end of the uterus that opens into the vagina.

Cesarean section (C-section) An incision made through the mother's abdomen, under a general or local anesthetic, so that the baby can be removed.

chancre (SHANG-ker) A dull-red, painless, hard, round ulcer with raised edges that forms where the spirochete causing syphilis enters a person's body.

chancroid (CANE-kroid) An STD characterized by soft, painful genital sores.

chlamydia (clah-MID-ee-uh) For the minority of those with symptoms, an STD accompanied by discomfort during urination and in men, a thin, whitish discharge.

chorion The outermost of the two membranes that completely envelop a fetus.

chromatin (CROW-mah-tin) The substance in the nucleus of a cell from which chromosomes form during mitosis.

chromosomes The strands of deoxyribonucleic acid (DNA) and protein in the nucleus of each cell. They contain the genes that provide information vital for the duplication of cells and the transmission of inherited characteristics.

clitoris (CLIH-tor-iss) Small, highly sensitive erectile tissue located just above the point where the minor lips converge at the top of the vulva; the only known function is to provide female sexual pleasure.

cognitive Related to the act or process of engaging in mental activity (thoughts).

cohabitation An arrangement in which an unmarried couple live together.

cohort A group from a particular generation; for example, those born from 1970 to 1979 are members of a different cohort from those from 1980 to 1989.

coitus (KOY-tus) Penetration of the vagina by the penis; also called sexual intercourse.

colostrum (cuh-LAWS-trum) A thin, yellowish fluid secreted from the nipples before and around the time of birth.

concordance rate The likelihood that if one person manifests a certain trait, a relative (twin, sibling, uncle, etc.) will manifest that same trait.

conditioned response (CR) An acquired response to a stimulus that did not originally evoke such a response.

conditioned stimulus (CS) In classical conditioning, a stimulus that is paired with an unconditioned stimulus until it evokes a response that was previously associated with the unconditioned stimulus.

condom A sheath placed over the erect penis for prevention of pregnancy and protection against disease.

congenital adrenal hyperplasia (CAH) Genetic malfunction of the adrenal glands resulting in secretion of too much adrenal androgen during prenatal development, leading to masculinization of genetic females.

contraceptive foams Spermicidal foams that are injected into the vagina prior to coitus.

contraceptive suppositories Solid contraceptive substances containing a spermicide, inserted in the vagina prior to coitus, and that melt in a matter of minutes.

contraceptives Any techniques, drugs, or devices that prevent conception.

control variables Variables that are held constant or controlled to reduce their influence on the dependent variable.

copulation (kop-you-LAY-shun) Sexual intercourse involving insertion of the penis into the vagina.

corona (cor-OH-nah) The sensitive rim of the glans.

corpora cavernosa (COR-por-uh kah-vur-NOH-sah) Two columns within the penis that contain small cavities capable of filling with blood to produce an erection.

corpus luteum (COR-pus LOO-tee-um) The cell mass that remains after a follicle has released an egg; it secretes progesterone and estrogen.

corpus spongiosum (COR-puhs spun-jee-OH-sum) A column of spongy tissue within the penis that surrounds the urethra and is capable of blood engorgement during sexual arousal.

correlational method A research method involving the measurement of two or more variables to determine the extent of their relationship.

couvade (ku-VAHD) Phenomenon in which some men develop symptoms similar to those of their pregnant partner.

Cowper's glands (COW-perz) Two small glands that secrete a clear alkaline fluid into the urethra during sexual arousal.

cremaster muscle (CRE-mah-ster) Muscle that runs from the testes into the spermatic cord and controls the proximity of the testes to the body.

cross-sectional research Comparisons of distinct but similar groups at the same point in time.

cruising Socializing in a variety of locations in the attempt to find a partner.

cunnilingus (KUN-nih-LING-gus) Oral stimulation of the female genitals.

curette (cure-RET) A scooplike instrument used for scraping bodily tissue.

cystitis (sis-TYE-tis) A general term for any inflammation of the urinary bladder marked by frequent urination accompanied by pain.

deoxyribonucleic acid (DNA) (dee-OX-see-RYE-boh-new-KLAY-ik) A chemically complex nucleic acid that is a principal element of genes.

dependent variables Variables that are measured or observed.

Depo-Provera A contraceptive with a long-acting progestin that is injected every three months.

diaphragm (DYE-uh-fram) A dome-shaped rubber contraceptive device inserted into the vagina to block the cervical opening. The diaphragm should always be used with a spermicide.

dihydrotestosterone (DHT) A hormone produced from testosterone that is responsible for the development of the external genitals of the male fetus.

dihydrotestosterone-deficiency (DHT) syndrome Genetic disorder that prevents the prenatal conversion of testosterone into DHT because of the absence of an enzyme (5-alpha reductase) that is necessary for this conversion. At birth, males with DHT-deficiency syndrome do not have identifiably male genitals.

dilation (die-LAY-shun) Expansion or opening up of the cervix prior to birth.

dilation and curettage (D&C) (die-LAY-shun and CURE-eh-taj) Dilation of the cervix followed by scraping of the interior of the uterus with a curette.

dilation and evacuation (D&E) An abortion method, generally used in the second trimester, in which the fetus is crushed within the uterus and then extracted through a vacuum curette.

double blind study A research design in which neither the participants nor the experimenters know which treatment is being applied until the research is over.

dyspareunia (DIS-par OO-nee-ah) Recurrent and persistent pain associated with intercourse for a woman or man.

ectopic pregnancy A pregnancy that occurs when a fertilized egg implants itself outside the uterus, usually in a Fallopian tube.

effacement Flattening and thinning of the cervix that occur before and during childbirth.

ego In psychoanalysis, the rational level of personality.

ejaculation Expulsion of seminal fluid out of the urethra during orgasm.

ejaculatory ducts (ee-JAK-u-la-TOR-ee) Tubelike passageways that carry semen from the prostate gland to the urethra.

Electra complex In Freudian theory, a daughter's sexual desire for her father.

embolism Any foreign matter such as a blood clot or air bubble that causes the obstruction of a blood vessel.

embryo The unborn organism from the second to about the eighth week of pregnancy.

emission Propulsion of sperm and fluid to the base of the urethra during orgasm.

endocrine glands (EN-doe-crin) Ductless glands that discharge their products directly into the bloodstream.

endometrium (en-doe-MEE-tree-um) The lining of the uterus, part of which is shed during menstruation.

engagement Movement of the fetus into a lower position in the mother's abdominal cavity, with its head past her pelvic bone structure.

epididymis (ep-ih-DIH-dih-mis) Tightly coiled tubules, located at the top of the testes, in which sperm are stored.

epinephrine A hormone secreted by the adrenal gland that is involved in emotional excitement; sometimes called adrenaline.

episiotomy (eh-PEE-zee-AW-tuh-mee) A surgical incision made from the bottom of the entrance to the vagina down off to the side of the anus to prevent vaginal and anal tissues from injury during childbirth.

equity In a personal relationship, a perceived balance between the benefits the relationship provides and the personal investment it requires.

erectile dysfunction Recurrent and persistent inability to attain or maintain a firm erection despite adequate stimulation.

erogenous zones Areas of the body that are erotically sensitive to tactile stimulation.

eros Erotic love.

erotica Sexually oriented material that is acceptable to the viewer.

erotophilic Having a positive emotional response to sexual feelings and experiences.

erotophobic Having a negative emotional response to sexual feelings and experiences.

estradiol The major natural estrogen, secreted by the ovaries, testes, and placenta.

estrogens Generic term for hormones that promote development and functioning of the female reproductive system.

exhibitionism Obtaining sexual gratification by exposing one's genitals to an unwilling observer.

experimental method A research method involving the manipulation of one or more independent variables to determine their influence on dependent variables.

Fallopian tubes (fah-LOW-pee-an) Tubes through which eggs (ova) are transported from the ovaries to the uterus.

fantasies Usually pleasant mental images unrestrained by the realities of the external world.

fellatio (fell-LAY-she-oh) Oral stimulation of the male genitals.

female condom A pouch placed inside the vagina to line the vaginal walls for prevention of pregnancy and protection against disease.

fetal alcohol syndrome (FAS) A disorder found in the offspring of heavy drinkers that causes a group of specific symptoms, including mental retardation.

fetishism Obtaining sexual excitement primarily or exclusively from an inanimate object or a particular part of the body.

fetus The unborn organism from the ninth week until birth.

fitness A measure of one's success in transmitting genes to the next generation (reproductive success).

follicle-stimulating hormone (FSH) A gonadotropin that induces maturation of ovarian follicles in females and sperm production in males.

follicles (FALL-ih-kulz) In the ovary, sacs of estrogen-secreting cells that contain an egg.

follicular phase Menstrual-cycle phase during which follicle-stimulating hormone stimulates the growth of the ovarian follicles.

foreplay Term used by some people to refer to sexual behavior occurring before intercourse.

fornication Sexual intercourse between people who are not married to each other.

frenulum (FREN-yu-lum) A small piece of skin on the underside of the male glans where the glans meets the body of the penis.

frotteurism Obtaining sexual arousal by touching or rubbing one's body against the body of an unsuspecting or nonconsenting person.

gardnerella vaginalis Infection producing a thin, smelly discharge; afflicts both men and women.

gender (JEN-der) The social-psychological characteristics associated with being a male or a female in a particular culture.

gender differences Differences in physique, ability, attitude, or behavior found between large groups of males and females. Also called *sex differences*.

gender identity The feeling or conviction that one is a male or a female.

gender roles The traits and behaviors expected of males and females in a particular culture.

gender stereotype A belief about the characteristics of a person based on gender.

gender-role identification The process by which individuals incorporate behaviors and characteristics of a culturally defined gender role into their own personalities.

gender-role socialization The training of children by parents and other caretakers to behave in ways considered appropriate for their sex.

generalizability The extent to which findings from a particular sample can be described as representing wider populations and situations.

genes Part of DNA molecules, found in chromosomes of cells, that are responsible for the transmission of hereditary material from parents to offspring.

genital tubercle A small, protruding bud of fetal tissue that develops into either a penis or a clitoris.

genital warts An STD that can also be contracted nonsexually; caused by the human papilloma virus.

germ cells Sperm or egg cells.

gestation The entire period of prenatal development, from conception to birth.

gigolo A man who is paid to be a woman's escort and to provide her with sexual services; a kept man.

glans The sensitive tip of the penis or clitoris.

gonadotropins (goh-NAH-doe-TROE-pinz) Chemicals produced by the pituitary gland that stimulate the gonads.

gonorrhea For those with symptoms, an STD accompanied by painful urination. In males, smelly, thick, yellow urethral discharge. In females, vaginal discharge and mild pelvic discomfort.

Gräfenberg spot (GRAY-fen-berg) An area of sensitivity accessed through the upper wall of the vagina. Also known as the G-spot.

habituation Responding to someone or something out of habit rather than out of current feelings.

hard-core erotica Erotica that explicitly depicts the genitals and sexual acts.

hepatitis B A virus that attacks the liver; often sexually transmitted.

herpes simplex type II A viral infection contracted through physical contact with an infected person during an active outbreak of the sores.

hominid Family of two-legged primates of which only humans survived.

homophobia Negative attitudes toward homosexuality.

homosociality A period in middle and late childhood in which social and personal activities are centered around members of the same sex.

hormone (HOR-mohn) Internal secretion of an endocrine gland that is distributed via the bloodstream.

human chorionic gonadotropin (HCG) (CORE-ee-ON-ik goh-NAH-doe-TROE-pin) A hormone produced by the placenta.

human immunodeficiency virus (HIV) The retrovirus that causes AIDS.

hymen (HYE-men) Layer of tissue that partially covers the vaginal entrance of most females at birth.

hyperfemininity Exaggerated adherence to a stereotypic feminine gender role.

hypermasculinity Exaggeration of male dominance through an emphasis on male virility, strength, and aggression.

hypoactive sexual desire disorder Deficient or absent sexual fantasies or desire for sexual activity with anyone.

hypospadias (HY-poe-SPAY-dee-us) A condition in which the urethral opening is located somewhere other than at the tip of the penis.

hypothesis (hy-PAW-theh-sis) Statement of a specific relationship between or among two or more variables.

hysterectomy Surgical removal of the uterus.

hysterotomy (HIS-ter-AW-tuh-mee) Surgical incision into the uterus; when used for abortion, the fetus is removed through the incision.

id In psychoanalysis, the source of psychic energy derived from instinctive drives.

immunosuppression The suppression of natural immunologic responses, which produces lowered resistance to disease.

incest Sexual activities between family members who are too closely related to be able to marry legally.

inclusive fitness A measure of the total contribution of genes to the next generation by oneself and those with whom one shares genes, such as siblings and cousins.

independent variables Variables that are manipulated or varied by an experimenter.

infanticide The killing of an infant after its birth.

infatuation Foolish and irrational love.

informed consent The ethical principle of informing potential research participants, before they consent to participate, of any aspects of the research that might be embarrassing or harmful.

inhibin (in-HIB-in) A hormone produced by the testes that regulates sperm production by reducing the pituitary gland's secretion of follicle-stimulating hormone.

instincts As Freud used this term, biological excitations that lead to mental activity.

intersexuality A condition in which a person is born with both male and female characteristics, such as an ovary on one side and a testis on the other, with an ova-testis on each side, or with ambiguous genitals. Also called *hermaphroditism.*

interstitial cells (in-ter-STIH-shul) Cells in the spaces between the seminiferous tubules that secrete hormones.

intra-amniotic injection Replacement of amniotic fluid with either prostaglandins or a salt solution, causing fetal circulatory arrest; occasionally used in second-trimester abortions.

intrauterine device A small plastic device that is inserted into the uterus for contraception.

john A slang term for the customer of a prostitute.

labioscrotal swellings The fetal tissue that develops into either the scrotum in a male or the two outer vaginal lips in a female.

labor The process of childbirth, consisting of contractions, thinning out and expansion of the cervix, delivery of the baby, and expulsion of the placenta.

lanugo (lah-NEW-goh) Fine hair that appears on the developing fetus during the fifth or sixth month.

laparoscope (LAP-ar-oh-SCOPE) A long, hollow instrument inserted into the abdominal cavity through a small incision directly below the navel.

lascivious Tending to stimulate sexual desire.

latency In psychoanalytic theory, a stage lasting from about 6 years of age until puberty, in which there is supposedly little observable interest in sexual activity.

lesbian A woman who is attracted to or has sex with other women.

leukorrhea (LOO-kor-EE-ah) A whitish discharge from the vagina, often caused by a fungus infection.

lewd Sexually unchaste; inciting lust or debauchery.

limbic system The set of structures around the midbrain involved in regulating emotional and motivational behaviors.

limerence (LIH-mer-ence) Love marked by obsession and preoccupation with the loved one.

lochia (LOH-kee-ah) Dark-colored vaginal discharge that follows childbirth for several weeks.

longitudinal research Research carried out with the same sample of people over a period of months or years.

lubricant A shiny, slippery fluid secreted through the walls of the vagina during sexual arousal.

lust Intense sexual desire.

luteal phase Menstrual-cycle stage following ovulation during which growth of the uterine lining is stimulated by secretion of progesterone from the corpus luteum.

luteinizing hormone (LH) A gonadotropin that stimulates female ovulation and male androgen secretion.

lymphadenopathy Condition involving swollen lymph nodes in the neck, armpits, and/or groin.

meiosis (my-OH-sis) Cell division leading to the formation of gametes in which the number of chromosomes is reduced by half.

menarche (MEN-ark) The first menstrual period.

menopause The end of menstruation, ovulation, and a woman's reproductive capacity.

menstruation The sloughing of the uterus's endometrial lining, which is discharged through the vaginal opening.

mitosis (my-TOE-sis) A form of cell division in which the nucleus divides into two daughter cells, each of which receives one nucleus and is an exact duplicate of the parent cell.

modeling Learning through observation of others.

monogamy Having sexual contact with only one partner for a given period of time.

mons pubis In adult females, the cushion of fatty tissue above the labia that is covered by pubic hair.

motile Exhibiting or demonstrating the power of motion.

Müllerian-duct system Fetal tissue that develops into the internal female reproductive structures if the fetus is genetically female.

Müllerian-inhibiting substance (MIS) A hormone secreted by the fetal testes that inhibits the growth and development of the Müllerian-duct system.

muscle tension Involuntary contractions of muscles during sexual response.

myometrium (MY-oh-MEE-tree-um) The smooth muscle layer of the uterine wall.

natural selection The process whereby species evolve genetically as a result of variations in the reproductive success of their ancestors.

necrophilia Sexual arousal and/or activity with a corpse.

nondemand pleasuring Partners' taking turns in exploring and caressing each other's bodies without attempting to arouse their partner sexually.

nongonococcal urethritis (NGU) (non-GON-ohj-KOK-al yur-ree-THRY-tis) A term for urethral infections in men that are usually caused by the chlamydia bacterium.

normative The average or typical response of members of a sample.

Norplant A contraceptive implant, inserted into a woman's upper arm, that slowly releases hormones to inhibit ovulation.

nymphomania Excessive and uncontrollable sexual desire in women.

obscenity The legal term for material that is foul, disgusting, lewd, and offensive to accepted standards of decency.

obsessive-compulsive reaction Engaging in compulsive behaviors in reaction to persistent or obsessive thoughts.

Oedipus complex (EH-dih-pus) In Freudian theory, a son's sexual desire for his mother.

ontogeny (on-TOJ-en-ee) The history of the development of an individual organism.

operational definition Description of a variable in such a way that it can be measured.

opportunistic infections Infections with formerly rare or nonfatal diseases that HIV-infected persons are unable to fight because their immune system is suppressed by AIDS.

oral contraceptives Pills containing hormones that inhibit ovulation.

ovaries (OH-var-rees) Two small organs that produce eggs and hormones, located above and to each side of the uterus.

overlapping distribution A statistical term describing situations in which the levels of a variable for some members of two groups are the same, although a difference exists between the average levels of the particular variable for the two groups.

ovulation The release of a mature egg from an ovary.

pandering Serving as a go-between in commercial sexual transactions; generally pimping or procuring.

paraphilia (par-rah-FIL-ee-ah) Love of the unusual; the term now used to describe sexual activities that were formerly labeled deviance (*para*: "beside or amiss"; *philia*: "love").

participant observation Conducting research while simultaneously engaging in the behavior with the group being studied.

passive immunity A kind of immunity to certain diseases or conditions acquired by a baby when it receives its mother's antibodies through her breast milk.

patriarchy (PAY-tree-ar-kee) A society in which men have supremacy over women, who are legally and socially dependent on them.

peak experience Maslow's term for a personal experience that generates feelings of ecstasy, peace, and unity with the universe.

pediculosis pubis (peh-DIK-you-LOW-sis PYOU-bis) A lice infestation of the pubic hair; commonly referred to as crabs.

pedophilia (PEH-doe-FIL-ee-ah) Preoccupation by an adult with sexual contact with a child.

pelvic inflammatory disease (PID) Swelling and inflammation of the uterine tissues, Fallopian tubes, and sometimes the ovaries.

pelvic nerve The parasympathetic nerve involved in involuntary sexual responses of the genitals.

penis (PEE-nis) The male sexual organ.

penis envy In psychoanalytic theory, a woman's wish to possess a penis.

perfect failure rate The failure rate of a contraceptive method when it is used consistently and correctly.

perimetrium (pehr-ih-MEE-tree-um) The thin connective tissue membrane covering the outside of the uterus.

perversion Deviance from the normal in sexual activities or desires.

phallus The penis.

philia Love involving concern with the well-being of a friend.

phylogeny (fu-LOJ-en-ee) The evolutionary history of a species or group.

pimps Prostitutes' business managers, some of whom also have sexual relations with their "girls."

placebos Usually an inert substance or treatment that exerts an effect because of an individual's psychological beliefs.

placenta (pluh-SEN-tuh) The organ formed by the joining of the uterine wall tissue with that of the developing fetus; a major source of hormones during pregnancy.

platonic love Nonsexual love for another person; often referred to as spiritual love.

polyandry (PAW-lee-ANN-dree) Norm in which it is acceptable for a woman to have more than one husband or partner in the same time period.

polygamy (pul-LIG-uh-mee) Relationship or marital form in which people may have more than one partner during a period of time without violating the culture's norms.

polygyny (puh-LIH-jih-nee) Norm in which it is acceptable for a man to have more than one wife or partner in the same time period.

pornography Sexually oriented material that is not acceptable to the viewer.

postcoital douching (DOO-shing) Insertion of chemical solutions into the vagina after coitus in the usually vain attempt to kill sperm.

postpartum (post-PAR-tum) Relating to the time immediately following birth.

postpartum depression Intense sadness or general letdown some women experience following childbirth.

premature ejaculation Ejaculation before the man wants it to occur.

premenstrual phase The 6 days prior to menstruation, when the corpus luteum begins to disintegrate if the egg has not been fertilized.

priapism (PRE-uh-PIZ-um) Prolonged and painful erection without sexual desire.

primal scene A child's observations of parental coitus.

proceptivity The initiation and escalation of a sexual interaction with another person.

procuring Obtaining customers for a prostitute.

progestagens Generic term for hormones that prepare the female reproductive system for pregnancy.

prostaglandins Hormones that stimulate muscle contractions as well as help regulate ovulation and the release of prolactin from the ovaries.

prostate gland Gland located at the base of the male bladder that supplies most of the seminal fluid.

prostatic acid phosphatase (PAP) A fluid secreted by the prostate gland.

prostatitis (praw-stay-TYE-tis) Inflammation of the prostate gland accompanied by burning pain during and after ejaculation.

prosthesis Artificial replacement for a body part.

prostitution The practice of selling sexual stimulation or interaction.

prurient Provoking lasciviousness.

puberty The onset of reproductive maturity, occurring at age 12–13 for females and, usually, a few years later for males.

pubococcygeus muscle (PC muscle) (pew-bow-cawk-SEE-gee-us) The muscle that surrounds the vaginal entrance and walls.

pudendal nerve (poo-DEN-dal) Nerve that passes from the external genitals through spinal cord segments S2 through S4 and transmits sensations from the genitals.

purdah The practice of secluding women from men.

quickening The first fetal movements felt by the mother.

quid pro quo Requiring something in exchange for something else, for example requiring sex from a student in exchange for a better grade.

rape Sexual intercourse that occurs without consent under actual or threatened force.

rape trauma syndrome Emotional and behavioral consequences that victims experience after being raped.

reactivity The tendency of a measurement instrument (or observer) to influence the behavior under observation.

recessive gene Gene whose characteristics only appear when paired with another recessive gene.

reductionism Explaining complex processes in terms of basic physical and chemical activities (for example, explaining human sexual desire only in terms of hormonal activity without reference to the particular characteristics of a desired partner).

refractory period Period of time following ejaculation during which nerves cannot respond to further stimulation.

reliability The extent to which a measure elicits the same response at different times.

replication The practice of repeating a study with a different group of research participants to determine whether the results of previous research are reliable.

reproductive bias The belief that the only justification for engaging in sexual contact is to reproduce. People who adhere to this belief perceive sexual activities that cannot result in conception (e.g., mutual masturbation, oral-genital stimulation) as sinful.

reproductive success The extent to which organisms are able to produce offspring who survive long enough to pass on their genes to successive generations.

reticular activating system (RAS) The system of nerve paths within the brain that is involved in arousal.

retrograde ejaculation A condition in which the base of the bladder does not contract during ejaculation, resulting in semen discharging into the man's bladder.

retrovirus A form of virus that cannot reproduce inside a host cell until it has made copies of its own structure.

rhogam (ROW-gam) A substance that prevents an Rh-negative woman from developing antibodies to the Rh factor in subsequent embryos.

rhythm method A birth control technique based on avoidance of sexual intercourse during a woman's fertile period each month.

sampling The process of selecting a representative part of a population.

satyriasis (SAH-ter-RYE-uh-sis) Excessive and uncontrollable sexual desire in men.

scabies A contagious skin condition caused by an insect that burrows under the skin.

schemas Cognitive plans or structures that serve as guides for interpreting information and planning behavior. Basically the same as *scripts*.

scripts Largely unconscious, culturally determined mental plans that individuals use to organize and guide their behavior.

scrotum (SCROH-tum) Sac that contains the testes.

self-report bias Bias introduced into the results of a study stemming either from participants' desire to appear "normal" or from memory lapses.

semen (SEE-men) Milky-white alkaline fluid containing sperm; a product of fluids from the epididymis, seminal vesicles, prostate, and Cowper's glands, combined with sperm from the testes.

seminal vesicles (SEM-ih-nal VES-ih-kelz) Two saclike organs lying on either side of the prostate that deposit fluid into the ejaculatory ducts to contribute to semen.

seminiferous tubules (sem-ih-NIF-er-us) Long, thin, tightly coiled tubes, located in the testes, that produce sperm.

sensate focus Concentration on sensations produced by touching.

serial monogamy Having sexual contact with only one partner for a given period, but if and when that relationship ends, beginning a monogamous relationship with a new partner.

sex chromosomes The pair of chromosomes that determines whether an individual is female or male.

sex guilt Sense of guilt resulting from the violation of personal standards of proper sexual behavior.

sex linkage The connection between the sex chromosomes and the genes one inherits. When a person inherits a sex chromosome, he or she also inherits the genes it carries.

sex-typed identification Incorporation into the personality of the behaviors and characteristics expected for one's sex in a particular culture, with avoidance of those characteristics expected of the other sex. Also called *gender-typed identification*.

sexual arousal disorders Failures to attain or maintain erection or vaginal lubrication and swelling despite adequate stimulation.

sexual assault Forcing another person to have sexual contact.

sexual aversion disorder Extreme dislike and avoidance of genital sexual contact with a partner.

sexual double standard The belief that a particular behavior is acceptable for one sex but not for the other.

sexual harassment The use of status and/or power to coerce or attempt to coerce a person into having sex; also, suggestive or lewd comments directed at a person in occupational, educational, or therapeutic settings.

sexual masochism Sexual gratification through experiencing pain and humiliation.

sexual sadism The intentional infliction of pain or humiliation on another person for sexual excitement.

sexual surrogate A member of a sex therapy team whose role is to provide education and direction as well as to have sexual interactions with a client as part of the therapy.

shigellosis (SHIH-geh-LOW-sis) A form of dysentery (diarrhea) that can be transmitted by sexual contact.

social constructionism Theoretical framework that emphasizes the importance of cognitions (thoughts) in creating a shared reality.

socialization The process of developing the skills needed to interact with others in one's culture.

soft-core erotica Erotica that is suggestive, but not explicit, in portraying sexual acts.

spectatoring Evaluating one's own sexual performance rather than involving oneself in the sexual experience with one's partner.

spermatic cord (spur-MAH-tik) Cord that suspends the testes and contains the vas deferens, blood vessels, nerves, and cremaster muscle.

spermicide A chemical that kills or immobilizes sperm.

squeeze technique A treatment for premature ejaculation in which a man signals his partner to apply manual pressure to his penis to delay ejaculation.

statutory rape Sexual intercourse with a person who is under the legal age of consent in a given state.

sterilization A surgical procedure performed to make a person incapable of reproduction.

streetwalker A prostitute who solicits on the street.

stress Physical, emotional, or mental strain or tension.

suction abortion Removal of the contents of the uterus through use of a suction machine.

superego In psychoanalysis, the level of personality corresponding to the conscience.

sympto-thermal method A way of determining the date of ovulation based on changes in a woman's basal body temperature and the stretchability of her cervical mucus.

syphilis An STD that may be accompanied by painless sores called chancres among those with symptoms.

systematic desensitization A behavioral therapy in which deep relaxation is used to reduce anxiety associated with certain situations.

teratogenic (tare-AH-toe-JEN-ik) Causing birth defects.

testes (TES-tees) Two small, oval organs located in the scrotum that produce mature sperm and sex hormones.

testosterone The major natural androgen.

thalamus (THAL-uh-mas) The major brain center involved in the transmission of sensory impulses to the cerebral cortex.

transition A short period of intense and very frequent contractions that complete dilation of the cervix to 10 centimeters.

transsexual A person whose gender identity is different from his or her anatomical sex.

transvestite A person sexually stimulated or gratified by wearing the clothes stereotypic of the other sex.

triangular family system In psychoanalytic theory, the notion that a male homosexual's mother is intimate and controlling and his father is detached and rejecting.

tribadism Sexual activity in which one woman lies on top of another and moves rhythmically for clitoral stimulation.

trichomoniasis (TRIK-uh-muh-NYE-ah-sis) An inflammation of the vagina characterized by a whitish discharge.

triphasic oral contraceptives Low-dose birth control pill in which the levels of hormones are varied over the menstrual cycle.

tubal ligation Cutting or tying the Fallopian tubes to block sperm from reaching the egg.

typical failure rate The failure rate of a contraceptive method that takes into account both failure of the method and human failure to use it correctly.

umbilical cord The connection of the fetus to the placenta, through which the fetus is nourished.

unconditioned response (UCR) A stimulus-evoked response that is not dependent on experience or learning.

unconditioned stimulus (UCS) A stimulus that evokes a response that is not dependent on prior learning.

unrequited love Intense romantic/erotic attraction toward another person who does not have the same feelings toward you.

urethra (ur-REE-thrah) Duct or tube through which urine and ejaculate leave the body.

urogenital folds Folds or strips on each side of the genital tubercle of the fetus that fuse to form the urethral tube in a male or the inner vaginal lips in a female.

uterus (YOU-tur-us) The place where a fertilized egg is implanted and the fetus develops during gestation.

vagina (vah-JYE-nah) The muscular tube that extends from the uterus to the vulva.

vaginismus (VAH-jih-NIS-mus) Involuntary spasms of the pelvic muscles surrounding the outer third of the vagina.

vaginitis (VAH-jih-NYE-tis) A general term for any inflammation of the vagina.

validity The extent to which something measures what it was designed to measure.

variable Any situation or behavior capable of change or variation.

vas deferens (VAS DEH-fur-renz) Slender duct through which sperm are transported from each testis to the ejaculatory duct at the base of the urethra.

vasectomy Male sterilization involving cutting or tying of the vas deferentia.

vasocongestion Engorgement with blood.

vasovasectomy Surgical reversal of vasectomy.

vernix caseosa (VUR-nix kah-see-OH-sah) A greasy substance that protects the skin of the fetus.

viable Able to live and continue normal development outside the uterus.

Viagra (vy-AG-ra) A drug that increases the likelihood of erection by blocking an enzyme that allows blood to flow out of the penis.

victim precipitation The notion that a victim is at least partially responsible for the attack.

volunteer bias Bias introduced into the results of a study stemming from systematic differences between those who volunteer for research and those who avoid participation.

voyeurism (VOY-yer-ism) Obtaining sexual arousal by observing people without their consent when they are undressed or engaging in sexual activity.

vulva (VULL-vah) External female genitals: the mons pubis, outer and inner lips, clitoris, and vaginal opening.

wet dream Slang phrase for orgasm and/or ejaculation while asleep.

withdrawal Removal of the penis from the vagina before ejaculation.

Wolffian-duct system Fetal tissue that develops into the internal male reproductive structures if the fetus is genetically male.

zoophilia (ZOO-oh-FIL-ee-ah) Sexual activity with animals.

zygote (ZYE-goat) The developing organism from fertilization to implantation.

References

Abbey, A. (1987). Misperceptions of friendly behavior as sexual interest: A survey of naturally occurring incidents. *Psychology of Women Quarterly, 11,* 173–194.

Abbey, A., Ross, L. T., McDuffie, D., & McAuslan, P. (1996). Alcohol and dating risk factors for sexual assault among college women. *Psychology of Women Quarterly, 20,* 147–169.

Abbott, S., & Love, B. (1985). *Sappho was a right-on woman: A liberated view of lesbianism.* New York: Stein and Day.

Abel, G. G., Barlow, D. H., Blanchard, E., & Guild, D. (1977). The components of rapists' sexual arousal. *Archives of General Psychiatry, 34,* 895–903.

Abel, G. G., Osborn, C., Anthony, D., & Gardos, P. (1992). Current treatment of paraphiliacs. *Annual Review of Sex Research, 3,* 255–290.

Abel, G. G., & Rouleau, J.-L. (1990). The nature and extent of sexual assault. In W. L. Marshall, D. R. Laws, & H. E. Barbaree (Eds.), *Handbook of sexual assault* (pp. 9–21). New York: Plenum.

Abma, J., Driscoll, A., & Moore, K. (1998). Young women's degree of control over first intercourse: An exploratory analysis. *Family Planning Perspectives, 30,* 12–18.

Abortion's long siege. (1992, April 27). *Newsweek,* 44–47.

Abrams, M. (1985). Birth control use by teenagers: One and two years postabortion. *Journal of Adolescent Health Care, 6,* 196–200.

Abramson, P. R., & Hayashi, H. (1984). Pornography in Japan: Cross-cultural and theoretical considerations. In N. M. Malamuth & E. Donnerstein (Eds.), *Pornography and sexual aggression* (pp. 173–183). Orlando, FL: Academic Press.

Adams, H. E., Motsinger, P., McAnulty, R. D., & Moore, A. L. (1992). Voluntary control of penile tumescence among homosexual and heterosexual subjects. *Archives of Sexual Behavior, 21,* 17–31.

Adams, H. E., Wright, L. W., Jr., & Lohr, B. A. (1996). Is homophobia associated with homosexual arousal? *Journal of Abnormal Psychology,*

Adler, N. E., David, H. P., Major, B. N., & Roth, S. H., Russo, N. F., & Wyatt, G. E. (1990). Psychological responses after abortion. *Science, 248,* 41–44.

Adler, N. E., David, H. P., Major, B. N., Roth, S. H., Russo, N. F., & Wyatt, G. E. (1992). Psychological factors in abortion: A review. *American Psychologist, 47,* 1194–1204.

Adler, N. L., & Hendrick, S. S. (1991). Relationships between contraceptive behavior and love attitudes, sex attitudes, and self-esteem. *Journal of Counseling and Development, 70,* 302–308.

Ageton, S. S. (1983). *Sexual assault among adolescents.* Lexington, MA: Lexington Books.

Ahlburg, D. A., & DeVita, C. J. (1992). New realities of the American family. *Population Bulletin, 47,* 2, 1–42.

Ainsworth, M. D. S. (1989). Attachments beyond infancy. *American Psychologist, 44,* 709–716.

Ainsworth, M. D. S., Blehar, M. C., Waters, E., & Wall, S. (1978). *Patterns of attachment: A psychological study of the strange situation.* Hillsdale, NJ: Erlbaum.

Alary, M. (1997). Gonorrhea: Epidemiology and control strategies. *Canadian Journal of Human Sexuality, 6,* 151–159.

Alfonso, V. C., Allison, D. B., & Dunn, G. M. (1992). Sexual fantasy and satisfaction: A multidimensional analysis of gender differences. *Journal of Psychology and Human Sexuality, 5,* 19–37.

Allen, D., & Okawa, J. B. (1987). A counseling center looks at sexual harassment. *Journal of NAWDAC, 50,* 9–15.

Allen, M., D'Alessio, D., Emmers, T. M., & Gebhardt, L. (1996). The role of educational briefings in mitigating effects of experimental exposure to violent sexually explicit material: A meta-analysis. *The Journal of Sex Research, 33,* 135–141.

Allgeier, A. R., Allgeier, E. R., & Rywick, T. (1981). Orientations toward abortion: Guilt or knowledge? *Adolescence, 16,* 273–280.

Allgeier, A. R., Allgeier, E. R., & Rywick, T. (1982). Response to requests for abortion: The influence of guilt and knowledge. *Journal of Applied Social Psychology, 12,* 282–292.

Allgeier, E. R. (1984). The personal perils of sex researchers: Vern Bullough and William Masters. *SIECUS Report, 12* (4), 16–19.

Allgeier, E. R. (1992). So-so sexuality: Field research on gender roles with a preliterate polygynous tribe. In G. G. Brannigan & M. R. Merrens (Eds.), *The undaunted psychologist: Adventures in research* (pp. 218–234). New York: McGraw Hill.

Allgeier, E. R., Allgeier, A. R., & Rywick, T. (1979). Abortion: Reward for conscientious contraceptive use? *The Journal of Sex Research, 15,* 64–75.

Allgeier, E. R., Travis, S. K., Zeller, R. A., & Royster, B. J. T. (1990, March). *Constructions of consensual versus coercive sex: A survey of student-instructor sexual contacts.* Paper presented at the annual meeting of the Western Region of The Society for the Scientific of Sex, San Francisco.

Allgeier, E. R., & Wiederman, M. M. (1994). How useful is evolutionary psychology for understanding contemporary human sexual behavior? *Annual Review of Sex Research, 5,* 218–256.

Allgeier, E. R., Yachanin, S. A., Smith, K. H., & Myers, J. G. (1984, May). *Are erotic photographs pornographic, offensive, and/or arousing? Correlations among judgments.* Paper presented at the meeting of the Midwestern Psychological Association, Chicago, IL.

Allstetter, B. (1991, May). Compulsory contraception: Does the punishment fit the crime? *American Health,* pp. 32–33.

American Academia of Pediatrics. (1997). Breastfeeding and the use of human milk. *Pediatrics, 100,* 1035–1037.

American Cancer Society. (1993). *Cancer facts and figures—1993.* Atlanta: Author.

American Cancer Society. (1996). *Cancer facts and figures—1996.* Atlanta: Author.

American Cancer Society. (1997). *Cancer facts and figures—1997.* Atlanta, GA: American Cancer Society.

American Cancer Society (1999). *Cancer facts and figures—1999.* Atlanta, GA: Author.

American Psychiatric Association (1980). *Diagnostic and statistical manual of mental disorders* (3rd ed.). Washington, DC: American Psychiatric Association.

American Psychiatric Association (1994). *Diagnostic and statistical manual of mental disorders* (4th ed.). Washington, DC: American Psychiatric Association.

Amoroso, D. M., Brown, M., Pruesse, M., Ware, E. E., & Pithey, D. W. (1971). An investigation of behavioral, psychological, and physical reactions to pornographic stimuli. In *Technical Report of the Commission on Obscenity and Pornography* (Vol. 8, pp. 1–40). Washington, DC: GPO.

Andres, R. L. (1999). Social and illicit drug use in pregnancy. In R. K. Creasy, & M. D. Resnik, (Eds.). *Maternal-fetal medicine* (4th ed.) (pp. 145–164). Philadelphia, PA: W. B. Saunders Company.

Andrews, F. M., Abbey, A., & Halman, L. J. (1991). Stress from infertility, marriage factors, and subjective well-being of wives and husbands. *Journal of Health and Social Behavior, 32,* 238–253.

Ansuini, C., Fiddler-Woite, J., & Woite, R. (1996). The source, accuracy, and impact of initial sexuality information on lifetime wellness. *Adolescence, 31,* 283–289.

Apfelbaum, B. (1984). The ego-analytic approach to body-work sex therapy. *The Journal of Sex Research, 20,* 44–70.

Apfelbaum, B. (1989). Retarded ejaculation: A much-misunderstood syndrome. In S. R. Leiblum & R. C. Rosen (Eds.), *Principles and practices of sex therapy* (2nd ed., pp. 168–206). New York: Guilford.

Aral, S. O., & Holmes, K. K. (1991). Sexually transmitted diseases in the AIDS era. *Scientific American, 264,* 62–69.

Aral, S. O., Mosher, W. D., & Cates, W., Jr., (1992). Vaginal douching among women of reproductive age in the United States: 1988. *American Journal of Public Health, 82,* 210–214.

Armstrong, E. G. (1978). Massage parlors and their customers. *Archives of Sexual Behavior, 7,* 117–125.

Arndt, W. B. (1991). *Gender disorders and the paraphilias.* Madison, CT: International Universities Press.

Arndt, W. B., Foehl, J. C., & Good, F. E. (1985). Specific sexual fantasy themes: A multidimensional study. *Journal of Personality and Social Psychology, 48,* 472–480.

Aron, A., Aron, E. N., & Allen, J. (1998). Motivations for unreciprocated love. *Personality and Social Psychology Bulletin, 24,* 787–796.

Ashcraft, D. M., & Schlueter, D. (1996, May). *Safer-sex practices of rural area college students from 1976 to 1995.* Paper presented at the Eastern and Midcontinent Region Meeting of the Society for the Scientific Study of Sexuality, Pittsburgh, PA.

Asscheman, H., & Gooren, L. J. G. (1992). Hormone treatment in transsexuals. *Journal of Psychology and Human Sexuality, 5,* 39–54.

Bachman, G., Levine, T., Muto, K., & Hatfield, E. (1994). *Love schemas and commitment.* Unpublished manuscript. University of Hawaii, Honolulu.

Bachman, R. (1998). The factors related to rape reporting behavior and arrest: New evidence from the National Crime Victimization Survey. *Criminal Justice and Behavior, 25,* 8–29.

Bagley, C. (1996). A typology of child sexual abuse: The interaction of emotional, physical, and sexual abuse as predictors of adult psychiatric sequelae in women. *Canadian Journal of Human Sexuality, 5,* 101–112.

Bailey, J. M., Gauling, S., Agyei, Y., & Gladue, B. A. (1994). Effects of gender and sexual orientation on evolutionarily relevant aspects of human mating psychology. *Journal of Personality and Social Psychology, 66,* 1081–1093.

Bailey, J. M., Kim, P. Y., Hills, A., & Linsenmeier, J. A. W. (1997). Butch, femme, or straight-acting? Partner preferences of gay men and lesbians. *Journal of Personality and Social Psychology, 73,* 960–973.

Bailey, J. M., Miller, J. S., & Willerman, L. (1993). Maternally related childhood gender nonconformity in homosexuals and heterosexuals. *Archives of Sexual Behavior, 22,* 461–469.

Bailey, J. M., & Pillard, R. C. (1991). A genetic study of male sexual orientation. *Archives of General Psychiatry, 48,* 1089–1096.

Bailey, J. M., Pillard, R. C., Neale, M. C., & Agyei, Y. (1993). Heritable factors influence female sexual orientation. *Archives of General Psychiatry, 50,* 217–223.

Baldwin, J. D., & Baldwin, J. I. (1997). Gender differences in sexual interest. *Archives of Sexual Behavior, 26,* 181–210.

Baldwin, W. (1976). *Adolescent pregnancy and child-bearing: Growing concerns for Americans.* Washington, DC: Population Reference Bureau.

Baldwin, W., & Cain, V. S. (1980). The children of teenage parents. *Family Planning Perspectives, 12,* 34–39, 42–43.

Bancroft, J. (1989). Man and his penis—A relationship under threat. *Journal of Psychology and Human Sexuality, 2,* 7–32.

Bandura, A. (1986). *Social foundations of thought and action.* Englewood Cliffs, NJ: Prentice-Hall.

Banks, A., & Gartrell, N. K. (1995). Hormones and sexual orientation: A questionable link. *Journal of Homosexuality, 28,* 247–268.

Barak, A., Fisher, W. A., & Houston, S. (1992). Individual difference correlates of the experience of sexual harassment among female university students. *Journal of Applied Social Psychology, 22,* 17–37.

Barbach, L. G., & Levine, L. (1980). *Shared intimacies: Women's sexual experiences.* New York: Anchor.

Barbaree, H. E., Hudson, S. M., & Seto, M. C. (1993). Sexual assault in society: The role of the juvenile offender. In H. E. Barbaree, W. L. Marshall, & S. M. Hudson (Eds.), *The juvenile sex offender* (pp. 1–24). New York: Guilford.

Bargh, J. A., & Raymond, P. (1995). The naive misuse of power: Nonconscious sources of sexual harassment. *Journal of Social Issues, 51* (1), 85–96.

Barkow, J. H., Cosmides, L., & Tooby, J. (Eds.) (1992). *The adapted mind: Evolutionary psychology and the generation of culture.* New York: Oxford University Press.

Barlow, D. H., Mills, J. R., Agras, W. S., & Steinman, D. L. (1980). Comparison of sex-typed motor behavior in male-to-female transsexuals and women. *Archives of Sexual Behavior, 9,* 245–253.

Baum, B. (1997, January 24). Congresswoman explains private reason for her pro-abortion stance. *Bowling Green Sentinel Tribune,* p. 8.

Baumeister, F. L., Smart, L., & Boden, J. M. (1996). Relation of threatened egotism to violence and aggression: The dark side of self-esteem. *Psychological Review, 103,* 5–33.

Baumeister, R. F. (1988a). Masochism as escape from self. *The Journal of Sex Research, 25,* 28–59.

Baumeister, R. F. (1988b). Gender differences in masochistic scripts. *The Journal of Sex Research, 25,* 478–499.

Baumeister, R. F., & Leary, M. R. (1995). The need to belong: Desire for interpersonal attachments as a fundamental human motivation. *Psychological Bulletin, 117,* 497–529.

Baumeister, R. F., Wotman, S. R., & Stillwell, A. M. (1993). Unrequited love: On heartbreak, anger, guilt, scriptlessness, and humiliation. *Journal of Personality and Social Psychology, 61,* 377–391.

Beach, F. A. (Ed.). (1976). *Human sexuality in four perspectives.* Baltimore, MD: Johns Hopkins University Press.

Beatrice, J. (1985). A psychological comparison of heterosexuals, transvestites, preoperative transsexuals, and postoperative transsexuals. *Journal of Nervous and Mental Disease, 173,* 358–365.

Beck, J. G. (1993). Vaginismus. In W. O'Donahue & J. H. Geer (Eds.), *Handbook of sexual dysfunctions: Assessment and treatment* (pp. 381–397). Boston: Allyn & Bacon.

Beigel, H. G. (1953). The meaning of coital postures. *International Journal of Sexology, 4,* 136–143.

Beit-Hallahmi, B. (1985). Dangers of the vagina. *British Journal of Medical Psychology, 58,* 351–356.

Beitchman, J. H., Zucker, K. J., Hood, J. E., DaCosta, G. A., Akman, D., & Cassavia, E. (1992). A review of the long-term effects of child sexual abuse. *Child Abuse and Neglect, 16,* 101–118.

Bell, A. R., & Weinberg, M. S. (1978). *Homosexualities.* New York: Simon & Schuster.

Bell, A. R., Weinberg, M. S., & Hammersmith, S. K. (1981). *Sexual preference: Its development in men and women.* Bloomington: Indiana University Press.

Bell, R. R., Turner, S., & Rosen, L. A. (1975). A multivariate analysis of female extramarital coitus. *Journal of Marriage and the Family, 37,* 375–384.

Belsky, J. (1991). Parental and nonparental child care and children's socioemotional development. In A. Booth (Ed.), *Contemporary families: Looking forward, looking back* (pp. 122–140). Minneapolis: National Council on Family Relations.

Belzer, E. G. (1981). Orgasmic expulsions of women: A review and heuristic inquiry. *The Journal of Sex Research, 17,* 1–12.

Bem, D. J. (1998). Is EBE theory supported by the evidence? Is it androcentric? *Psychological Review, 105,* 395–398.

Bem, S. L. (1975). Sex-role adaptability: One consequence of psychological androgyny. *Journal of Personality and Social Psychology, 31,* 634–643.

Bem, S. L., & Lenney, E. (1976). Sex typing and avoidance of cross-sex behavior. *Journal of Personality and Social Psychology, 3,* 48–54.

Bem, S. L., Martyna, W., & Watson, C. (1976). Sex typing and androgyny: Further exploration of the expressive domain. *Journal of Personality and Social Psychology, 34,* 1016–1023.

Benedek, T. (1959). Sexual functions in women and their disturbance. In S. Arieti (Ed.), *American handbook of psychiatry,* Vol. 1 (pp. 727–748). New York: Basic Books.

Bentler, P. M., & Peeler, W. H. (1979). Models of female orgasm. *Archives of Sexual Behavior, 8,* 405–424.

Bentler, P. M., Sherman, R. W., & Prince, V. (1970). Personality characteristics of male transvestites. *Journal of Clinical Psychology, 26,* 287–291.

Benton, J. M., Mintzes, J. L., Kendrick, A. F., & Soloman, R. D. (1993). Alternative conceptions in sexually transmitted diseases: A cross-age study. *Journal of Sex Education and Therapy, 19,* 165–182.

Berdahl, J. L., Magley, V. J., & Waldo, C. R. (1996). The sexual harassment of men: Exploring the concept with theory and data. *Psychology of Women Quarterly, 20,* 527–547.

Berger, G., Hank, L., Rauzi, T., & Simkins, L. (1987). Detection of sexual orientation by heterosexuals and homosexuals. *Journal of Homosexuality, 13,* 83–100.

Berger, R. M. (1996). *Gay and gray: The older homosexual man.* Binghamton, NY: Haworth.

Bermant, G. (1976). Sexual behavior: Hard times with the Coolidge Effect. In M. H. Siegel & H. P. Zeigler (Eds.), *Psychological research: The inside story* (pp. 76–103). New York: Harper & Row.

Berry, J. (1992). *Lead us not into temptation: Catholic priests and the sexual abuse of children.* New York: Doubleday.

Berscheid, E., & Walster, E. (1974). Physical attractiveness. In L. Berkowitz (Ed.), *Advances in experimental social psychology* (pp. 157–215). New York: Academic Press.

Betzig, L. (1989). Causes of conjugal dissolution: A cross-cultural study. *Current Anthropology, 30,* 654–676.

Betzig, L., & Lombardo, L. H. (1992). Who's pro-choice and why. *Ethology and Sociobiology, 13,* 49–71.

Beyer, D. (1996). Child prostitution in Latin America. In U.S. Department of Labor, Bureau of International Labor Affairs (Ed.), *Forced labor: The prostitution of children* (pp. 32–40). Washington, DC: General Printing Office.

Bieber, I., Dain, H. J., & Dince, P. R. (1962). *Homosexuality: A psychoanalytic study.* New York: Basic Books.

Biggar, R. J. (1986). The AIDS problem in Africa. *The Lancet,* January 11, 79–83.

Billy, J. O. G., Tanfer, K., Grady, W. R., & Klepinger, D. H. (1993). The sexual behavior of men in the United States. *Family Planning Perspectives, 25,* 52–60.

Bixler, R. H. (1982). Sibling incest in the royal families of Egypt, Peru, and Hawaii. *The Journal of Sex Research, 18,* 264–281.

Bjorklund, D. F., & Kipp, K. (1996). Parental investment theory and gender differences in the evolution of inhibition mechanisms. *Psychological Bulletin, 120,* 163–188.

Blair, C. D., & Lanyon, R. (1981). Exhibitionism: Etiology and treatment. *Psychological Bulletin, 89,* 439–463.

Blanchard, R. (1989). The classification and labeling of nonhomosexual gender dysphorias. *Archives of Sexual Behavior, 18,* 315–334.

Blanchard, R. (1993). Varieties of autogynephilia and their relationship to gender dysphoria. *Archives of Sexual Behavior, 22,* 241–251.

Blasband, M. A., & Peplau, L. A. (1985). Sexual exclusivity versus openness in gay male couples. *Archives of Sexual Behavior, 14,* 395–412.

Blieszner, R., & Adams, R. G. (1992). *Adult friendship.* Newbury Park, CA: Sage.

Blumstein, P. W., & Schwartz, P. (1976). Bisexuality in men. *Urban Life, 5,* 339–359.

Blumstein, P. W., & Schwartz, P. (1983). *American couples.* New York: Morrow.

Bogaert, A. F. (1996). Volunteer bias in human sexuality research: Evidence for both sexuality and personality differences in males. *Archives of Sexual Behavior, 25,* 125–140.

Bogaert, A. F., & Blanchard, R. (1996). Physical development and sexual orientation in men: Height, weight, and age of puberty differences. *Personality and Individual Differences, 21,* 77–84.

Bogaert, A. F., & Hershberger, S. (1998, June). *The relation between sexual orientation and penile size.* Paper presented at the annual meeting of the International Academy of Sex Research, Sirmione, Italy.

Boles, J., & Elifson, K. W. (1994). Sexual identity and HIV: The male prostitute. *The Journal of Sex Research, 31,* 39–46.

Borna, S., Chapman, J., & Menezes, D. (1993). Deceptive nature of dial-a-porn commercials and public policy alternatives. *Journal of Business Ethics, 12,* 503–509.

Bornstein, R. F., & Masling, J. M. (Eds.) (1998). *Empirical perspectives on the psychoanalytic unconscious.* Washington, DC: American Psychological Association.

Bouhoutsos, J. C. (1981, August). *Sexual intimacy between therapists and patients.* Paper presented at the meeting of the American Psychological Association, Los Angeles.

Bouhoutsos, J. C., Holroyd, J., Lerman, H., Forer, B., & Greenberg, M. (1983). Sexual intimacy between psychotherapists and patients. *Professional Psychology, 14,* 185–196.

Bowers, J. K., & Weaver, H. B. (1979). Development of a dual-form abortion scale. *The Journal of Sex Research, 15,* 158–165.

Bowlby, J. (1973). *Attachment and Loss: Vol. 2. Separation, anxiety, and anger.* New York: Basic Books.

Boxer, A. M., & Cohler, B. J. (1989). The life course of gay and lesbian youth: An immodest proposal for the study of lives. *Journal of Homosexuality, 17,* 315–355.

Bradford, J. M. W., & Greenberg, D. M. (1996). Pharmacological treatment of deviant sexual behavior. *Annual Review of Sex Research, 7,* 283–306.

Brame, G. G., Brame, W. D., & Jacobs, J. (1993). *Different loving: An exploration of the world of sexual dominance and submission.* New York: Villard.

Brannigan, G. G., Allgeier, E. R., & Allgeier, A. R. (Eds.). (1998). *The sex scientists.* New York: Longman.

Breakwell, G. M., & Fife-Schaw, C. (1992). Sexual activities and preferences in a United Kingdom sample of 16- to 20-year-olds. *Archives of Sexual Behavior, 21,* 271–293.

Brecher, E. M., & the Editors of Consumer Reports Books. (1984). *Love, sex, and aging.* Boston: Little, Brown.

Brennan, K. A., & Shaver, P. R. (1995). Dimensions of adult attachment, affect regulation, and romantic relationship functioning. *Personality and Social Psychology Bulletin, 21,* 267–283.

Bretschneider, J. G., & McCoy, N. L. (1988). Sexual interest and behavior in 80- to 102-year-olds. *Archives of Sexual Behavior, 17,* 109–129.

Briere, J., & Runtz, M. (1989). University males' sexual interest in children: Predicting potential indices of "pedophilia" in a nonforensic sample. *Child Abuse and Neglect, 13,* 65–75.

Bringle, R. G., & Buunk, B. P. (1991). Extradyadic relationships and sexual jealousy. In K. McKinney & S. Sprecher (Eds.), *Sexuality in close relationships* (pp. 135–153). Hillsdale, NJ: Erlbaum.

Brody, S. (1997). *Sex at risk.* New Brunswick, NJ: Transaction Publishers.

Brown, G. R., & Collier, Z. (1989). Transvestites' women revisited: A nonpatient sample. *Archives of Sexual Behavior, 18,* 73–83.

Brown, J. D., & Newcomer, S. F. (1991). Television viewing and adolescents' sexual behavior. *Journal of Homosexuality, 21,* 77–91.

Brown, J. D., & Steele, J. R. (1996). Sexuality and the mass media: An overview. *SIECUS Report, 24* (4), 3–9.

Brown, R. (1996). *Against my better judgment: An intimate memoir of an eminent gay psychologist.* New York: Harrington Park Press.

Brown, S. A., & Munson, E. (1987). Extroversion, anxiety and the perceived effects of alcohol. *Journal of Studies on Alcohol, 48,* 272–276.

Brown, S. I., & Booth, A. (1996). Cohabitation vs. marriage: A comparison of relationship quality. *Journal of Marriage and the Family, 58,* 668–678.

Buckle, L., Gallup, Jr., G. G., & Rodd, Z. A. (1996). Marriage as a reproductive contract: Patterns of marriage, divorce, and remarriage. *Ethology and Sociobiology, 17,* 363–377.

Buhrich, N. A. (1976). A heterosexual transvestite club: Psychiatric aspects. *Australian and New Zealand Journal of Psychiatry, 10,* 331–335.

Buhrich, N. A., & McConaghy, N. (1977). The discrete syndromes of transvestism and transsexualism. *Archives of Sexual Behavior, 6,* 483–496.

Buhrich, N. A., Theile, H., Yaw, A., & Crawford, A. (1979). Plasma testosterone, serum FSH, and serum LH levels in transvestites. *Archives of Sexual Behavior, 8,* 49–53.

Bullard—Poe, L., Powell, C., & Mulligan, T. (1994). The importance of intimacy to men living in a nursing home. *Archives of Sexual Behavior, 23,* 231–236.

Bullough, B. (1994). Abortion. In V. Bullough & B. Bullough (Eds.), *Human sexuality: An encyclopedia* (pp. 3–8). New York: Garland.

Bullough, B., & Bullough, V. L. (1996). Female prostitution: Current research and changing interpretations. *Annual Review of Sex Research, 7,* 158–180.

Bullough, V. L. (1983, November). *Presidential address: The problems of doing research in a delicate field.* Presented at the Annual Meeting of The Society for the Scientific Study of Sex, Chicago, IL.

Bullough, V. L. (1994). *Science in the bedroom: A history of sex research.* New York: Basic Books.

Bullough, V. L., & Bullough, B. (1987). *Women and prostitution: A social history.* Buffalo, NY: Prometheus.

Bullough, V. L., & Bullough, B. (1993). *Cross-dressing, sex, and gender.* Philadelphia: University of Pennsylvania Press.

Bullough, V. L., & Weinberg, J. S. (1988). Women married to transvestites: Problems and adjustments. *Journal of Psychology and Human Sexuality, 1,* 83–104.

Bumpass, L. L. (1997). The measurement of public opinion on abortion: The effects of survey design. *Family Planning Perspectives, 29,* 177–180.

Bumpass, L. L., Sweet, J. A., & Cherlin, A. (1991). The role of cohabitation in declining rates of marriage. *Journal of Marriage and the Family, 53,* 913–927.

Burg, B. R. (1988). Nocturnal emission and masturbatory frequency relationships: A nineteenth-century account. *The Journal of Sex Research, 24,* 216–220.

Burgess, A. W., & Holmstrom, L. L. (1974). *Rape: Victims of crisis.* Bowie, MD: Brady.

Burstein, G. R., Gaydos, C. A., Diener-West, M., Howell, M. R., Zenilman, J. M., & Quinn, T. C. (1998). Incident *Chlamydia trachomatis* infections among inner-city adolescent females. *Journal of the American Medical Association, 280* (6), 521–526.

Buss, D. M. (1994). *The evolution of desire: Strategies of human mating.* New York: Basic Books.

Buss, D. M. (1996). Sexual conflict: Evolutionary insights into feminism and the "battle of the sexes." In D. M. Buss & N. M. Malamuth (Eds.), *Sex, power, conflict: Evolutionary and feminist perspectives* (pp. 296–318). New York: Oxford University Press.

Buss, D. M. (1999). Evolutionary psychology: The new science of the mind. Boston, MA: Allyn and Bacon.

Buss, D. M. et al. (1989). Sex differences in human mate preferences: Evolutionary hypotheses tested in thirty-seven cultures. *Behavioral and Brain Sciences, 12,* 1–49.

Buss, D. M., et al. (1990). International preferences in selecting mates: A study of 37 cultures. *Journal of Cross Cultural Psychology, 21,* 5–47.

Buss, D. M., & Schmitt, D. P. (1993). Sexual strategies theory: A contextual evolutionary analysis of human mating. *Psychological Review, 100,* 204–232.

Butler, C. A. (1976). New data about female sexual response. *Journal of Sex and Marital Therapy, 2,* 40–46.

Buunk, B. P. (1991). Jealousy in close relationships: An exchange-theoretical perspective. In P. Palovy (Ed.), *The psychology of jealousy and envy* (pp. 148–177). New York: Guilford Press.

Buunk, B. P., Bakker, A. B., Siero, F. W., van den Eijnden, R. J. J. M. and Yzer, M. C. (1998). Predictors of AIDS-Preventive Behavioral Intentions among adult heterosexuals at risk for HIV-infection: Extending current models and measures. *AIDS education and prevention, 10,* 149–172.

Byers, E. S. (1996). How well does the traditional sexual script explain sexual coercion? Review of a program of research. *Journal of Psychology and Human Sexuality, 8,* 7–25.

Byers, E. S., & Heinlein, L. (1989). Predicting initiation and refusals of sexual activities in married and cohabiting couples. *The Journal of Sex Research, 26,* 210–231.

Byers, E. S., & Lewis, K. (1988). Dating couples' disagreements over the desired level of sexual intimacy. *The Journal of Sex Research, 24,* 15–29.

Byrne, D. (1971). *The attraction paradigm.* New York: Academic Press.

Byrne, D. (1977). Social psychology and the study of sexual behavior. *Personality and Social Psychology Bulletin, 3,* 3–30.

Byrne, D., & Fisher, W. A. (Eds.) (1983). *Adolescents, sex, and contraception.* Hillsdale, NJ: Erlbaum.

Byrne, D., Fisher, W. A., Lamberth, J., & Mitchell, H. E. (1974). Evaluations of erotica: Facts or feelings? *Journal of Personality and Social Psychology, 79,* 111–116.

Byrne, D., & Murnen, S. K. (1988). Maintaining loving relationships. In R. J. Sternberg & M. L. Barnes (Eds.), *The psychology of love* (pp. 293–310). New Haven: Yale University Press.

Byrne, D., & Schulte, L. (1990). Personality dispositions as mediators of sexual responses. *Annual Review of Sex Research 1,* 93–117.

Cadman, D., Gafini, A., & McNamee, J. (1984). Newborn circumcision: An economic perspective. *Canadian Medical Association Journal, 131,* 1353–1355.

Cado, S., & Leitenberg, H. (1990). Guilt reactions to sexual fantasies during intercourse. *Archives of Sexual Behavior, 19,* 49–63.

Cagampang, H. H., Barth, R. P., Korpi, M., & Kirby, D. (1997). Education now and babies later (ENABL): Life history of a campaign to postpone sexual involvement. *Family Planning Perspectives, 29,* 109–114.

Caird, W. K., & Wincze, J. P. (1977). *Sex therapy: A behavioral approach.* New York: Harper & Row.

Calhoun, T. C., & Weaver, G. (1996). Rational decision-making among male street prostitutes. *Deviant Behavior: An Interdisciplinary Journal, 17,* 209–227.

Call, V., Sprecher, S., & Schwartz, P. (1995). Marital sexual intercourse frequency in a national sample. *Journal of Marriage and the Family, 57,* 639–652.

Campbell, M. K., Waller, L., Andolsek, K. M., Huff, P., & Bucci, K. (1990). Infant feeding and nutrition. In K. M. Andolsek (Ed.), *Obstetric care: Standards of prenatal, peripartum, and postpartum management* (pp. 206–221). Philadelphia: Lea & Febiger.

Cancian, F. M. (1986). The feminization of love. *Signs: Journal of Women in Culture and Society, 11,* 692–709.

Cannon, D. (1987, November). *Twenty years of sex guilt: Construct validation of the concept.* Paper presented at the Annual Meeting of The Society for the Scientific Study of Sex, Atlanta, GA.

Caporael, L. R. (1997). The evolution of truly social cognition: The core configurations model. *Personality and Social Psychology Review, 1,* 276–298.

Carey, M. P., & Johnson, B. T. (1996). Effectiveness of yohimbine in the treatment of erectile disorder: Four meta-analytic integrations. *Archives of Sexual Behavior, 25,* 341–360.

Carlson, J., & Hatfield, E. (1992). *The psychology of emotion.* Fort Worth, TX: Holt, Rinehart & Winston.

Carmichael, M. S., Warburton, V. L., Dixen, J., & Davidson, J. M. (1994). Relationships among cardiovascular, muscular, and oxytocin responses during human sexual activity. *Archives of Sexual Behavior, 23,* 59–79.

Carnes, P. (1983). *The sexual addiction.* Minneapolis: CompCare.

Carnes, P. (1991). *Don't call it love: Recovering from sexual addiction.* New York: Bantam.

Caron, S. L. (1998). *Cross-cultural perspectives on human sexuality.* Needham Heights, MA: Allyn & Bacon.

Caron, S. L., Davis, C. M., Wynn, R. L., & Roberts, L. W. (1992). "America responds to AIDS," but did college students? Differences between March 1987 and September 1988. *AIDS Education and Prevention, 4,* 18–28.

Carroll, J. L., Volk, K. D., & Hyde, J. S. (1985). Differences between males and females in motives for engaging in sexual intercourse. *Archives of Sexual Behavior, 14,* 131–139.

Carter, C. S. (1992). Hormonal influences on human sexual behavior. In J. B. Becker, S. M. Breedlove, & D. Crews (Eds.), *Behavioral endocrinology* (pp. 131–142). Cambridge, MA: MIT Press.

Carter, C.S. (1998) Neuroendocrine perspectives on social attachment and love. *Psychoneuroendocrinology, 23,* 779–818.

Casler, L. (1968). Perceptual deprivation in institutional settings. In G. Newton & S. Levine (Eds.), *Early experience and behavior* (pp. 573–626). New York: Springer.

Cassell, C. (1984). *Swept away*. New York: Simon & Schuster.

Catania, A. C. (1992). Reinforcement. In L. R. Squire (Ed.), *Encyclopedia of learning and memory* (pp. 558–562). New York: MacMillan.

Cate, R., Long, E., Angera, A., & Draper, K. K. (1993). Sexual intercourse and relationship development. *Family Relations, 42,* 158–164.

Cates, Jr., W. (1998). Reproductive tract infections. In R. A. Hatcher, J. Trussell, F. Stewart, W. Cates, Jr., G. K. Stewart, F. Guest, & D. Kowal (Eds.), *Contraceptive technology* (17th ed.) (pp. 179–210). New York: Ardent Media.

Cates, Jr., W. and Ellertson, C. (1998). Abortion In. R. A. Hatcher, J. Trussell, F. Stewart, W. Cates, Jr., G. K. Stewart, F. Guest and D. Kowal (Eds.). *Contraceptive Technology* (17th ed.) (pp. 679–700). New York: Ardent Media.

Cates, Jr., W., & Raymond, E. G. (1998). Vaginal spermicides. In R. A. Hatcher, J. Trussell, F. Stewart, W. Cates, Jr., G. K. Stewart, F. Guest, & D. Kowal (Eds.), *Contraceptive technology* (17th ed.) (pp. 357–369). New York: Ardent Media.

Cates, W. C., Jr., & Stone, K. M. (1992a). Family planning, sexually transmitted diseases, and contraceptive choice: A literature update—Part I. *Family Planning Perspectives, 24,* 75–84.

Cates, W. C., Jr., & Stone, K. M. (1992b). Family planning, sexually transmitted diseases, and contraceptive choice: A literature update—Part II. *Family Planning Perspectives, 24,* 122–128.

Catotti, D. N., Clarke, P., & Catoe, K. E. (1993). Herpes revisited. *Sexually Transmitted Diseases, 20,* 77–80.

Centers for Disease Control. (1993, August 6). Recommendations for the prevention and management of chlamydia trachomatis infections. *Morbidity and Mortality Weekly Report, 42,* RR–12.

Centers for Disease Control and Prevention (1995). Trends in sexual risk behavior among high school students—United States, 1990, 1991, and 1993. *Morbidity and Mortality Weekly Report, 44,* 121–123, 131–132.

Centers for Disease Control and Prevention (1996). *HIV/AIDS Surveillance Report, 8* (2), 1–39.

Centers for Disease Control and Prevention (1997) HIV/AIDS Surveillance Report, 9 (2), 1–43.

Centers for Disease Control and Prevention. (1997). *HIV/AIDS Surveillance Report, 9* (2), 5–43.

Cheng, S-T. (1997). Epidemic genital retraction syndrome: Environmental and personal risk factors in southern China. *Journal of Psychology and Human Sexuality, 9* (1), 57–70.

Cherlin, A. (1981). *Marriage, divorce, remarriage*. Cambridge, MA: Harvard University Press.

Chivers, M., & Blanchard, R. (1996). Prostitution advertisements suggest association of transvestism and masochism. *Journal of Sex and Marital Therapy, 22,* 97–102.

Chodorow, N. (1978). *The reproduction of mothering*. Berkeley and Los Angeles: University of California Press.

Choo, P., Levine, T., & Hatfield, E. (1995). *Gender, love schemas, and reactions to romantic break-ups*. Unpublished manuscript, University of Hawaii, Honolulu.

Christopher, F. S., Johnson, D. C., & Roosa, M. W. (1993). Family, individual, and social correlates of early Hispanic adolescent sexual expression. *The Journal of Sex Research, 30,* 54–61.

Christopher, F. S., Madura, M., & Weaver, L. (1998). Premarital sexual aggressors: A multivariate analysis of social, relational, and individual variables. *Journal of Marriage and the Family, 60,* 56–69.

Christopher, F. S., & Roosa, M. W. (1990). An evaluation of an adolescent pregnancy prevention program: Is "just say no" enough? *Family Relations, 39,* 68–72.

Clark, C., & Wiederman, M. W. (1998, June). *Gender and reactions to partner masturbation and use of sexually explicit media*. Presented at the annual meeting of the Midcontinent Region of The Society for the Scientific Study of Sexuality, Indianapolis.

Clark, R. D. (1990). The impact of AIDS on gender differences in willingness to engage in casual sex. *Journal of Applied Social Psychology, 20,* 771–782.

Clark, R. D., & Hatfield, E. (1989). Gender differences in receptivity to sexual offers. *Journal of Psychology and Human Sexuality, 2,* 39–55.

Clarke-Stewart, K. A. (1978). And Daddy makes three. *Child Development, 49,* 466–478.

Clarke-Stewart, K. A., & Bailey, B. L. (1989). Adjusting to divorce: Why do men have it easier? *Journal of Divorce, 13,* 75–94.

Clement, U. (1990). Surveys of heterosexual behavior. *Annual Review of Sex Research, 1,* 45–74.

Clement, U., Schmidt, G., & Kruse, M. (1984). Changes in sex differences in sexual behavior: A replication of a study on West German students (1966–1981). *Archives of Sexual Behavior, 13,* 99–120.

Clements-Schreiber, M. E., Rempel, J. K., & Desmarais, S. (1998). Women's sexual pressure tactics and adherence to related attitudes: A step toward prediction. *The Journal of Sex Research, 35,* 197–205.

Clemmer, D. (1958). *Some aspects of sexual behavior in the prison community*. Proceedings of the Eighty-eighth Annual Congress of Corrections of the American Correctional Institution, Detroit, MI.

Clifford, R. E. (1978). Subjective sexual experience in college women. *Archives of Sexual Behavior, 7,* 183–197.

Cochran, S. D., & Mays, V. M. (1990). Sex, lies, and HIV. *New England Journal of Medicine, 322,* 774–775.

Cohen, J. B., Hauer, L. B., Poole, L. E., & Wofsy, C. B. (1987). *Sexual and other practices and risk of HIV in-*

fection in a cohort of 450 sexually active women in San Francisco. Paper presented at the Third International Conference on AIDS, Washington, DC.

Coleman, E. (1987). Bisexuality: Challenging our understanding of sexual orientation. *Sexuality and Medicine, 1,* 225–242.

Coleman, E. (1990). The married lesbian. *Marriage and Family Review, 13,* 119–135.

Coleman, E. (1991). Compulsive sexual behavior: New concepts and treatments. *Journal of Psychology and Human Sexuality, 4,* 37–52.

Coleman, E., Bockting, W. O., & Gooren, L. (1993). Homosexual and bisexual identity in sex-reassigned female-to-male transsexuals. *Archives of Sexual Behavior, 22,* 37–50.

Coles, C. D., & Shamp, M. J. (1984). Some sexual, personality, and demographic characteristics of women readers of erotic romances. *Archives of Sexual Behavior, 13,* 187–209.

Coley, R. L., & Chase-Lansdale, P. L. (1998). Adolescent pregnancy and parenthood: Recent evidence and future directions. *American Psychologist, 53,* 152–166.

Commons, G. (1994). The drainage ditch. In L. Barbach (Ed.), *Pleasures: Women write erotica* (pp. 186–188). New York: Harper & Row.

Conklin, B. A., & Morgan, L. M. (1996). Babies, bodies, and the production of personhood in North America and a Native Amazonian society. *Ethos, 24,* 657–694.

Cooper, A. J. (1986). Progestogens in the treatment of male sex offenders: A review. *Canadian Journal of Psychiatry, 31,* 73–79.

Cooper, M. L., & Orcutt, H. K. (1997). Drinking and sexual experience on first dates among adolescents. *Journal of Abnormal Psychology, 106,* 191–202.

Corey, L. (1994, March-April). The current trend in genital herpes. *Sexually Transmitted Diseases,* Supplement.

Cortina, L. M., Swan, S., Fitzgerald, L. F. and Woldo, C. (1998) Sexual harassment and assault: Chilling the climate for women in academia. *Psychology of Women Quarterly, 22,* 419–441.

Cox, D. J. (1988). Incidence and nature of male genital exposure behavior as reported by college women. *The Journal of Sex Research, 24,* 227–234.

Cox, S., & Gallois, C. (1996). Gay and lesbian identity development: A social identity perspective. *Journal of Homosexuality, 30,* 1–30.

Cramer, D., & Hewitt, D. (1998). Romantic love and the psychology of sexual behavior: Open and closed secrets. In V. C. de Munck, (Ed.), *Romantic love and sexual behavior* (pp. 113–132). Westport CT: Praeger.

Cramer, D. W., Schiff, I., Schoenbaum, S. C., Gibson, M., Belisle, S., Albrecht, B., Stillman, R. J., Berger, M. J., Wilson, E., & Stabel, B. V. (1985). Tubal infertility and the intrauterine device. *New England Journal of Medicine, 312,* 941–947.

Cranston-Cuebas, M. A., & Barlow, D. H. (1990). Cognitive and affective contributions to sexual functioning. *Annual Review of Sex Research, 1,* 119–161.

Creasy, R. K., & Iams, J. D. (1999). Preterm labor and delivery. In R. K. Creasy, & M. D. Resnik, (Eds.). *Maternal-fetal medicine* (4th ed.) (pp. 498–532). Philadelphia, PA: W. B. Saunders Company.

Creasy, R. K., & Resnik, M. D. (Eds.). (1999). *Maternal-fetal medicine* (4th ed.). Philadelphia, PA: W. B. Saunders Company.

Crenshaw, T. L., & Goldberg, J. P. (1996). *Sexual pharmacology: Drugs that affect sexual function.* New York: Norton.

Crepault, C., Abraham, G., Porto, R., & Couture, M. (1977). Erotic imagery in women. In R. Gemme & C. C. Wheeler (Eds.), *Progress in sexology* (pp. 267–283). New York: Plenum.

Crowe, L. C., & George, W. H. (1989). Alcohol and human sexuality: Review and integration. *Psychological Bulletin, 102,* 374–386.

Cullins, V. E., Remsburg, R. E., Blumenthal, P. D., & Huggins, G. R. (1994). Comparison of adolescent and adult experiences with Norplant levonorgestrel contraceptive implants. *Obstetrics and Gynecology, 83,* 1026–1032.

Cunningham, M., Barbee, A., Pike, C. L., & Chen-Huan, C. (1995). Their ideas of attractiveness are, on the whole, the same as ours: Consistency and variability in the cross-cultural perception of female attractiveness. *Journal of Personality and Social Psychology, 68,* 261–279.

Cutler, W. B., Friedmann, E., & McCoy, N. L. (1998). Pheromonal influences on sociosexual behavior in men. *Archives of Sexual Behavior, 27,* 1–13.

Cutler, W. B., Garcia, C. R., & McCoy, N. (1987). Perimenopausal sexuality. *Archives of Sexual Behavior, 16,* 225–234.

Cutright, P. (1971). Illegitimacy: Myths, causes and cures. *Family Planning Perspectives, 3,* 26–48.

D'Augelli, A. R. (1998). Developmental implications of victimization of lesbian, gay, and bisexual youths. In G. Herek (Ed.), *Stigma and sexual orientation: Understanding prejudice against lesbians, gay men, and bisexuals* (pp. 187–210). Thousand Oaks, CA: Sage.

Daling, J. R., Weiss, N. B., Voight, L. F., McKnight, B., & Moore, D. E. (1992). The intrauterine device and primary tubal infertility. *New England Journal of Medicine, 362,* 203–204.

Dank, B. M., & Fulda, J. S. (1998). Forbidden love: Student-professor romances. *Sexuality and Culture, 1,* 107–130.

Darling, C. A., & Davidson, J. K., Sr. (1986). Enhancing relationships: Understanding the feminine mystique of pretending orgasm. *Journal of Sex and Marital Therapy, 12,* 182–196.

Darling, C. A., Davidson, J. K., Sr., & Cox, R. P. (1991). Female sexual response and the timing of partner orgasm. *Journal of Sex and Marital Therapy, 17,* 3–20.

Darling, C. A., Davidson, J. K., Sr., & Jennings, D. A. (1991). The female sexual response revisited: Understanding the multiorgasmic response in women. *Archives of Sexual Behavior, 20,* 527–540.

Darney, P. D. (1994). Hormonal implants: Contraception for a new century. *American Journal of Obstetrics and Gynecology, 170,* 1536–1543.

Davenport, W. H. (1965). Sexual patterns and their regulation in a society of the Southwest Pacific. In F. A. Beach (Ed.), *Sex and behavior* (pp. 164–207). New York: Wiley.

David, H. P. (1992). Born unwanted: Long-term developmental effects of denied abortion. *Journal of Social Issues, 48* (3), 163–181.

David, H. P., Dytrych, Z., Matejcek, Z., & Schuller, V. (Eds.) (1988). *Born unwanted: Developmental effects of denied abortion.* New York: Springer.

Davidson, A. (1995, August). *Women's decisions to switch from Norplant to other methods.* Paper presented to National Institutes of Child Health and Human Development, Bethesda, MD.

Davidson, J. K., Sr., Darling, C., & Conway-Welch, C. (1989). The role of the Grafenberg spot and female orgasmic response: An empirical analysis. *Journal of Sex and Marital Therapy, 15,* 102–119.

Davidson, J. K., Sr., Hoffman, L. E. (1986). Sexual fantasies and sexual satisfaction: An empiracle analysis of erotic thought. *The Journal of Sex Research, 22,* 184–205

Davies, K. A. (1997). Voluntary exposure to pornography and men's attitudes toward feminism and rape. *The Journal of Sex Research, 34,* 131–137.

Davis, C. M., & Bauserman, R. (1993). Exposure to sexually explicit materials: An attitude change perspective. *Annual Review of Sex Research, 4,* 121–209.

Davis, C. M., Yarber, W. L., Bauserman, R., Schreer, G., & Davis, S. L. (1998). *Handbook of sexuality-related measures.* Thousand Oaks, CA: Sage.

Davis, J. A., & Smith, T. (1984). *General social surveys, 1972–1984: Cumulative data.* New Haven: Yale University, Roper Center for Public Opinion Research.

Davis, S. F., Byers, R. H., Jr., Lindegren, M. L., Caldwell, M. B., Karon, J. M., & Gwinn, M. (1995). Prevalence and incidence of vertically acquired HIV infection in the United States. *Journal of the American Medical Association, 247,* 952–955.

Davison, G. C. (1991). Constuctionism and morality in therapy for homosexuality. In J. C. Gonsiorek & J. D. Weinrich (Eds.), *Homosexuality: Research implications for public policy* (pp. 137–148). Newbury Park, CA: Sage.

Day, R. D. (1992). The transition to first intercourse among racially and culturally diverse youth. *Journal of Marriage and the Family, 54,* 749–762.

de Carvalho, M., Robertson, S., & Klaus, M. H. (1984). Does the duration and frequency of early breast feeding affect nipple pain? *Birth, 11,* 81–84.

de Munck, V. C. (Ed.). (1998). *Romantic love and sexual behavior.* Westport CT: Praeger.

de Waal, F. B. M. (1995). Sex as an alternative to aggression in the bonobo. In P. R. Abramson & S. D. Pinkerton (Eds.), *Sexual nature/sexual culture* (pp. 37–56). Chicago: University of Chicago Press.

Deaux, K. (1995). How basic can you be? The evolution of research on gender stereotypes. *Journal of Social Issues, 51* (1), 11–20.

DeBuono, B. A., Zinner, S. H., Daamen, M., & McCormack, W. M. (1990). Sexual behavior of college women in 1975, 1986, and 1989. *New England Journal of Medicine, 322,* 821–825.

DeCecco, J. P., & Parker, D. A. (1995). The biology of homosexuality: Sexual orientation or sexual preference? *Journal of Homosexuality, 28,* 1–27.

Dekker, J. (1993). Inhibited male orgasm. In W. O'Donahue & J. H. Geer (Eds.), *Handbook of sexual dysfunctions: Assessment and treatment* (pp. 279–301). Boston: Allyn & Bacon.

DeLamater, J. D., & MacCorquodale, P. (1979). *Premarital sexuality: Attitudes, relationships, behavior.* Madison: University of Wisconsin Press.

DeLisle, S. (1997). Preserving reproductive choice: Preventing STD-related infertility in women. *SIECUS Report, 25* (3), 18–21.

DeMaris, A., & Rao, K. V. (1992). Premarital cohabitation and subsequent marital stability in the United States: A reassessment. *Journal of Marriage and the Family, 54,* 178–190.

DePaulo, B. M., & Kashy, D. A. (1998). Everyday lies in close and casual relationships. *Journal of Personality and Social Psychology, 74,* 63–79.

Devine, S. A., & Allgeier, E. R. (1997, November). *Education of student clinicians regarding sexual feelings toward clients.* Paper presented at the Annual Meeting of the Association for the Advancement of Behavior Therapy, Miami.

Devor, H. (1993). Sexual orientation identities, attractions, and practices of female-to-male transsexuals. *The Journal of Sex Research, 30,* 303–315.

Devor, H. (1997). *FTM: Female-to-male transsexuals in society.* Bloomington, IN: Indiana University Press.

Dhawan, S., & Marshall, W. L. (1996). Sexual abuse histories of sexual offenders. *Sexual Abuse: A Journal of Research and Treatment, 8,* 7–15.

Diamond, M. (1982). Sexual identity, monozygotic twins reared in discordant sex roles and a BBC follow-up. *Archives of Sexual Behavior, 11,* 181–185.

Diamond, M. (1993). Homosexuality and bisexuality in different populations. *Archives of Sexual Behavior, 22,* 291–310.

Diamond, M. (1996a). Prenatal predisposition and the clinical management of some pediatric conditions. *Journal of Sex and Marital Therapy, 22,* 139–147.

Diamond, M. (1997). Sexual identity and sexual orientation in children with traumatized or ambiguous genitalia. *The Journal of Sex Research, 34,* 199–211.

Diana, L. (1985). *The prostitute and her clients.* Springfield, IL: Thomas.

Dick-Read, G. (1932/1959). *Childbirth without fear* (2nd rev. ed.). New York: Harper & Row.

DiClemente, R. J. (1989). Adolescents and AIDS: An update. *Multicultural Inquiry and Research on AIDS, 3* (1), 3–4, 7.

DiClemente, R. J., Forrest, K., & Mickler, S. E. (1990). College students' knowledge and attitudes about HIV and changes in HIV-preventive behaviors. *AIDS Education and Prevention, 2,* 201–212.

Dillard, J. P., & Witteman, H. (1985). Romantic relationships at work: Organizational and personal influences. *Human Communication Research, 12,* 99–116.

Dineen, T. (1996). Manufacturing victims: What the psychology industry is doing to people. Montreal, Quebec: Robert Davies Publishing.

Dion, K. K., & Dion, K. L. (1993). Individualistic and collectivistic perspectives on gender and the cultural context of love and intimacy. *Journal of Social Issues, 49* (3), 53–69.

Dion, K. L., & Dion, K. K. (1988). Romantic love: Individual and cultural perspectives. In R. J. Sternberg & M. L. Barnes (Eds.), *The psychology of love* (pp. 264–289). New Haven: Yale University Press.

DiPlacido, J. (1998). Minority stress among lesbians, gay men, and bisexuals: A consequence of heterosexism, homophobia, and stigmatization. In G. Herek (Ed.), *Stigma and sexual orientation: Understanding prejudice against lesbians, gay men, and bisexuals* (pp. 138–159). Thousand Oaks, CA: Sage.

Docter, R. F. (1988). *Transvestites and transsexuals: Towards a theory of gender behavior.* New York: Plenum.

Dodson, B. (1987). *Sex for one: The joy of self-loving.* New York: Harmony.

Doll, L. S., Peterson, L. R., White, C. R., Johnson, E. S., Ward, J. W., & the Blood Donor Study Group. (1992). Homosexually and non-homosexually identified men who have sex with men: A behavioral comparison. *The Journal of Sex Research, 29,* 1–14.

Donnerstein, E. (1984). Pornography: Its effect on violence against women. In N. M. Malamuth & E. Donnerstein (Eds.), *Pornography and sexual aggression* (pp. 53–81). Orlando, FL: Academic Press.

Donnerstein, E., & Linz, D. (1986). Mass media, sexual violence, and media violence. *American Behavioral Scientist, 29,* 601–618.

Donovan, P. (1997). Can statutory rape laws be effective in preventing adolescent pregnancy? *Family Planning Perspectives, 29,* 30–34, 40.

Dornan, W. A., & Malsbury, C. W. (1989). Neuropeptides and male sexual behavior. *Neuroscience and Biobehavioral Reviews, 13,* 1–15.

Douthitt, R. A. (1989). The division of labor within the home: Have gender roles changed? *Sex Roles, 20,* 693–704.

Dreger, A. (1998). *Hermaphrodites and the medical invention of sex.* Cambridge, MA: Harvard University Press.

Dressel, P. L., & Peterson, D. M. (1982). Becoming a male stripper: Recruitment, socialization, and ideological development. *Work and Occupations, 9,* 387–406.

Driscoll, D. M., Kelly, J. R., & Henderson, W. L. (1998). Can perceivers identify likelihood to sexual harass? *Sex Roles, 38,* 557–588.

Dunn, M. E., & Trost, J. E. (1989). Male multiple orgasms: A descriptive study. *Archives of Sexual Behavior, 18,* 377–399.

Dziech, B., & Weiner, L. (1984). *The lecherous professor.* Boston: Beacon Press.

Eakins, P. S. (1989). Free-standing birth centers in California. *Journal of Reproductive Medicine, 34,* 960–970.

Earls, C. M., & David, H. (1989). A psychosocial study of male prostitution. *Archives of Sexual Behavior, 18,* 401–419.

Ecker, N., & Weinstein, S. (1983, April). *The relationship between attributes of sexual competency, physical appearance, and narcissism.* Paper presented at The Conference of the Eastern Region of the Society for the Scientific Study of Sex, Philadelphia, PA.

Ehrhardt, A. A. (1975). Prenatal hormone exposure and psychosexual differentiation. In E. J. Sacher (Ed.), *Topics in psychoendocrinology* (pp. 67–82). New York: Grune & Stratton.

Ehrhardt, A. A., Grisanti, G., & McCauley, E. A. (1979). Female-to-male transsexuals compared to lesbians: Behavioral patterns of childhood and adolescent development. *Archives of Sexual Behavior, 8,* 481–490.

Ehrhardt, A. A., Meyer-Bahlburg, H. F. L., Feldman, J. L., & Ince, S. (1984). Sex-dimorphic behavior in childhood subsequent to prenatal exposure to exogenous progesterones and estrogens. *Archives of Sexual Behavior, 13,* 457–477.

Eliason, M. J. (1997). The prevalence and nature of biphobia in heterosexual undergraduate students. *Archives of Sexual Behavior, 26,* 317–326.

Elicker, J. M., Englund, M., & Sroufe, L. A. (1992). Predicting peer competence and peer relationships in childhood from early parent-child relationships. In R. Parke & G. Ladd (Eds.), Family-peer relations: Modes of linkage (pp. 77–106). Hillsdale, NJ: Erlbaum.

Ellis, H. H. (1933). *Psychology of sex: A manual for students.* New York: Long & Smith.

Ellis, H. H. (1942). *Studies in the psychology of sex.* (2 vols.) New York: Random House (originally published in 7 vols., 1896–1928).

Ellison, P. T. (1991). Reproductive ecology and human fertility. In G. W. Lasker & C. G. N. Mascie-Taylor (Eds.), *Applications of biological anthropology to human affairs* (pp. 14–54). Cambridge: Cambridge University Press.

Elmore, J. G., Barton, M. B., Moceri, V. M., Polk, S., Arena, P. J., & Fletcher, S. W. (1998). Ten-year risk of false positive screening of mammograms and clinical breast examinations. *New England Journal of Medicine, 338*, 1089–1096.

Emory, L. E., Williams, D. H., Cole, C. M., Amparo, E. G., & Meyer, W. J. (1991). Anatomic variation of the corpus callosum in persons with gender dysphoria. *Archives of Sexual Behavior, 20*, 409–417.

Epstein, J. S., Moffitt, A. L., Mayner, R. E. et al. (1985, September). *Antibodies reactive with HTLV-III found in freezer-banked sera from children in West Africa* (abstract 217). Twenty-fifth Interscience Conference on Anti-microbial Agents and Chemotherapy, Minnesota, MN.

Erikson, E. H. (1968b). *Identity, youth, and crisis.* New York: Norton.

Erikson, E. H. (1982). *The life cycle completed: A review.* New York: Norton.

Ernulf, K. E., & Innala, K. E. (1995). Sexual bondage: A review and unobtrusive investigation. *Archives of Sexual Behavior, 24*, 631–654.

Ewald, P. W. (1994). *Evolution of infectious disease.* New York: Oxford University Press.

Fagot, B. I. (1995). Psychosocial and cognitive determinants of early gender-role development. *Annual Review of Sex Research, 5*, 1–31.

Fairchild, H. H. (1991). Scientific racism: The cloak of objectivity. *Journal of Social Issues, 47* (3), 101–115.

Farr, G., Gabelnick, H., Sturgen, K., & Dorflinger, L. (1994). Contraceptive efficacy and acceptability of the female condom. *American Journal of Public Health, 84*, 1960–1964.

Fassinger, R. E., & Morrow, S. L. (1995). Overcome: Repositioning lesbian sexualities. In L. Diamont & R. D. McAnulty, R. D. (Eds.), *The psychology of sexual orientation, behavior, and identity* (pp. 197–219). Westport, CT: Greenwood Press.

Fausto-Sterling, A. (1997). Beyond differences: A biologist's perspective. *Journal of Social Issues, 53* (2), 233–258.

Federal Bureau of Investigation. 1993. *Uniform crime reports for the United States, 1992.* Washington, DC: GPO.

Federal Bureau of Investigation. (1996). *Uniform Crime Reports for the United States, 1995.* Washington, DC: GPO.

Federal Bureau of Investigation (1998). *Uniform Crime Reports for the United States, 1997.* Washington, DC: GPO.

Fedoroff, J. P., & Moran, B. (1997). Myths and misconceptions about sex offenders. *Canadian Journal of Human Sexuality, 6*, 263–276.

Feeney, J. A., & Noller, P. (1990). Attachment style as a predictor of adult romantic relationships. *Journal of Personality and Social Psychology, 58*, 281–291.

Fehr, B. (1993). How do I love thee? Let me consult my prototype. In S. Duck (Ed.), *Individuals in relationships: Understanding relationship processes* (Vol. 1, pp. 87–120). Newbury Park, CA: Sage.

Feild, H. S., & Bienen, L. B. (1980). *Jurors and rape.* Lexington, MA: Heath.

Felty, K. M. (1995). Single parents. In D. Levinson (Ed.), *Encyclopedia of marriage and the family* (pp. 663–670). New York: Simon & Schuster.

Fenichel, O. (1945). *The psychoanalytic theory of neurosis.* New York: Norton.

Fichtner, J., Filipas, D., Mottrie, A. M., Voges, G. E., & Hohenfellner, R. (1995). Analysis of meatal location in 500 men: Wide variation questions need for meatal advancement in all pediatric anterior hypospadias cases. *Journal of Urology, 154*, 833–834.

Field, T. M. (1998). Massage therapy effects. *American Psychologist, 53*, 1270–1281.

Finkelhor, D. (1979). *Sexually victimized children.* New York: Free Press.

Finkelhor, D. (1980). Sex among siblings: A survey on prevalence, variety, and effects. *Archives of Sexual Behavior, 9*, 171–197.

Finkelhor, D., & Browne, A. (1985). The traumatic impact of child sexual abuse. *American Journal of Orthopsychiatry, 55*, 530–541.

Finkelhor, D., & Dziuba-Leatherman, J. (1994). Victimization of children. *American Psychologist, 49*, 173–183.

Finkelhor, D., & Hotaling, G., Lewis, I. A., & Smith, C. (1990). Sexual abuse in a national survey of adult men and women: Prevalence, characteristics, and risk factors. *Child Abuse and Neglect, 14*, 19–28.

Finkelhor, D., & Russell, D. E. H. (1984). The gender gap among perpetrators of child sexual abuse. In D. E. H. Russell (Ed.), *Sexual exploitation: Rape, child sexual abuse, and workplace harassment* (pp. 215–231). Beverly Hills, CA: Sage.

Firestein, B. A. (Ed.). (1996). *Bisexuality: The psychology and politics of an invisible minority.* Thousand Oaks, CA: Sage.

Fishbein, E. G. (1989). Predicting paternal involvement with a newborn by attitude toward women's roles. In P. N. Stern (Ed.), *Pregnancy and parenting* (pp. 91–97). New York: Hemisphere.

Fisher, H. E. (1989). Evolution of human sexual pairbonding. *American Journal of Physical Anthropology, 78*, 331–354.

Fisher, H. E. (1992). *The anatomy of love.* New York: Norton.

Fisher, J. D. (1988). Possible effects of reference group-based social influence on AIDS-risk prevention. *American Psychologist, 43,* 914–920.

Fisher, J. D., & Fisher, W. A. (1992). Changing AIDS-risk behavior. *Psychological Bulletin, 117,* 455–474.

Fisher, S. (1973). *The female orgasm.* New York: Basic Books.

Fisher, T. D. (1986). Parent-child communication about sex and young adolescents' sexual knowledge and attitudes. *Adolescence, 21,* 517–527.

Fisher, T. D. (1989b). Confessions of a closet sex researcher. *The Journal of Sex Research, 26,* 144–147.

Fisher, T. D. (1993). A comparison of various measures of family sexual communication: Psychometric properties, validity, and behavioral correlates. *The Journal of Sex Research, 30,* 229–238.

Fisher, W. A. (1997). Do no harm: On the ethics of testosterone replacement therapy for HIV+ Persons. *The Journal of Sex Research, 34,* 35–36.

Fisher, W. A., Branscombe, N. R., & Lemery, C. R. (1983). The bigger the better? Arousal and attributional responses to erotic stimuli that depict different-size penises. *The Journal of Sex Research, 19,* 377–396.

Fisher, W. A., Byrne, D., White, L. A., & Kelley, K. (1988). Erotophobia-erotophilia as a dimension of personality. *The Journal of Sex Research, 25,* 123–151.

Fisher, W. A., & Grenier, G. (1994). Violent pornography, antiwoman thoughts, and antiwoman acts: In search of reliable effects. *The Journal of Sex Research, 31,* 23–38.

Fiske, S. T., & Glick, P. (1995). Ambivalence and stereotypes cause sexual harassment: A theory with implications for organizational change. *Journal of Social Issues, 51* (1), 97–115.

Fitzgerald, L. F., Drasgow, F., Hulin, C. L., Gelfland, M. J., & Magley, V. J. (1997). Antecedents and consequences of sexual harassment in organizations: A test of an integrated model. *Journal of Applied Psychology, 82,* 578–589.

Fitzgerald, L. F., Gelfland, M. J., & Drasgow, F. (1995). Measuring sexual harassment: Theoretical and psychometric advances. *Basic and Applied Social Psychology, 17,* 425–445.

Fitzgerald, L. F., Shullman, S., Bailey, N., Richards, M., Swecker, J., Gold, Y., Ormerad, M., & Weitzman, L. (1988). The incidence and dimensions of sexual harassment in academia and the workplace. *Journal of Vocational Behavior, 32,* 152–175.

Fitzgerald, L. F., Weitzman, L. M., Gold, Y., & Ormerod, M. (1988). Academic harassment: Sex and denial in scholarly garb. *Psychology of Women Quarterly, 12,* 329–340.

Fleming, D. T., McQuillan, G. M., Johnson, R. E., Nahmias, A. J., Aral, S. O., Lee, F. K., & St. Louis, M. E. (1997). Herpes simplex virus type 2 in the United States, 1976–1994. *The New England Journal of Medicine, 337,* 1105–1111.

Flexner, C. (1998). HIV-protease inhibitors. *New England Journal of Medicine, 338* (18), 1281–1292.

Foa, U. G., Anderson, B., Converse, J., Jr., Urbansky, W. A., Cowley, M. J., III, Muhlhausen, S. M., & Tornbloom, K. Y. (1987). Gender-related sexual attitudes: Some cross-cultural similarities and differences. *Sex Roles, 16,* 511–519.

Ford, C. S., & Beach, F. A. (1951). *Patterns of sexual behavior.* New York: Harper & Row.

Ford, N., & Mathie, E. (1993). The acceptability and experience of the female condom, Femidom®, among family planning clinic attenders. *British Journal of Family Planning, 19,* 187–192.

Forrest, J. D., & Fordyce, R. R. (1993). Women's contraceptive attitudes and use in 1992. *Family Planning Perspectives, 25,* 175–179.

Forrest, J. D., & Kaeser, L. (1993). Questions of balance: Issues emerging from the introduction of the hor-monal implant. *Family Planning Perspectives, 25,* 127–132.

Forsyth, C. J., & Deshotels, T. H. (1997). The occupational milieu of the nude dancer. *Deviant Behavior: An Interdisciplinary Journal, 18,* 125–142.

Fowlkes, M. R. (1994). Single worlds and homosexual lifestyles: Patterns of sexuality and intimacy. In A. S. Rossi (Ed.), *Sexuality across the life course* (pp. 151–184). Chicago: University of Chicago Press.

Frank, A. P., Wandell, M. G., Headings, M. D., Conant, M. A., Wood, G. E., & Michel, C. (1997). Anonymous HIV testing using home collection and telemedicine counseling. A multicenter evaluation. *Archives of Internal Medicine, 157,* 309–314.

Franzoi, S. L., & Herzog, M. E. (1987). Judging physical attractiveness: What body aspects do we use? *Personality and Social Psychology Bulletin, 13,* 19–33.

Frayser, S. G. (1994). Defining normal childhood sexuality: An anthropological approach. *Annual Review of Sex Research, 4,* 173–217.

Frazier, P. A., Cochran, C. C., & Olson, A. M. (1995). Social science research on lay definitions of sexual harassment. *Journal of Social Issues, 51* (1), 21–37.

Freed, R. S., & Freed, S. A. (1989). Beliefs and practices resulting in female deaths and fewer females than males in India. *Population and Environment, 10,* 144–161.

Freeman, D. (1983). *Margaret Mead and Samoa: The making and unmaking of an anthropological myth.* Cambridge, MA: Harvard University Press.

Freud, S. (1955). *Beyond the pleasure principle, group psychology, and other works* (Vol. 18). London: Hogarth.

Freund, K. (1985). Cross-gender identity in a broader context. In B. W. Steiner (Ed.), *Gender dysphoria: Development, research, management* (pp. 259–324). New York: Plenum.

Freund, K., & Blanchard, R. (1986). The concept of courtship disorder. *Journal of Sex and Marital Therapy, 12,* 79–92.

Freund, K., Steiner, B. W., & Chan, S. (1982). Two types of cross-gender identity. *Archives of Sexual Behavior, 11,* 49–63.

Freund, M., Lee, N., & Leonard, T. (1991). Sexual behavior of clients with street prostitutes in Camden, New Jersey. *The Journal of Sex Research, 28,* 579–591.

Freund, M., Leonard, T. I., & Lee, N. (1989). Sexual behavior of resident street prostitutes with their clients in Camden, New Jersey. *The Journal of Sex Research, 26,* 460–478.

Frezieres, R. G., Walsh, T. L., Nelson, A. L., Clark, V. A., & Coulson, A. H. (1998). Breakage and acceptability of a polyurethane condom: A randomized controlled study. *Family Planning Perspectives, 30,* 73–78.

Friedan, B. (1963). *The feminine mystique.* New York: Norton.

Fromm, E. (1956). *The art of loving.* New York: Harper & Row.

Frost, J. J., & Forrest, D. F. (1995). Understanding the impact of effective teenage pregnancy prevention programs. *Family Planning Perspectives, 27,* 188–195.

Furstenberg, F. F. (1976). *Unplanned parenthood: The social consequences of teenage childbearing.* New York: Free Press.

Furstenberg, F. F., Brooks-Gunn, J., & Morgan, S. P. (1987). *Adolescent mothers in later life.* New York: Cambridge University Press.

Futterweit, W. (1998). Endocrine therapy of transsexualism and potential complications of long-term treatment. *Archives of Sexual Behavior, 27,* 209–226.

Fyke, F. E., Kazmier, S. J., & Harms, R. W. (1985). Venous air embolism: Life-threatening complications of orogenital sex during pregnancy. *American Journal of Medicine, 78,* 333–336.

Gabelnick, H. L. (1998). Future methods. In R. A. Hatcher, J. Trussell, F. Stewart, W. Cates, Jr., G. K. Stewart, F. Guest, & D. Kowal (Eds.), *Contraceptive technology* (17th ed.) (pp. 615–622). New York: Ardent Media.

Gagnon, J. H. (1985). Attitudes and responses of parents to preadolescent masturbation. *Archives of Sexual Behavior, 14,* 451–466.

Gagnon, J. H. (1990). The explicit and implicit use of the scripting perspective in sex research. *Annual Review of Sex Research, 1,* 1–43.

Gagnon, J. H., & Simon, W. (1973). *Sexual conduct: The social sources of human sexuality.* Chicago: Aldine.

Gaines, M. E., & Allgeier, E. R. (1993, May). *Parents' knowledge, attitudes, and responses to child sexual abuse.* Paper presented at the Annual Meeting of the Midcontinent Region meeting of The Society for the Scientific Study of Sex, Cincinnati, OH.

Gallo, P. G., & Viviani, F. (1992). The origin of infibulation in Somalia: An ethological hypothesis. *Ethology and Sociobiology, 13,* 253–265.

Gallop, J. (1997). *Feminist accused of sexual harassment.* Durham, NC: Duke University Press.

Gallup Poll Monthly. (1995). Legality, morality of abortion, no. 354, 30–31.

Gallup Poll Monthly (1998). Attitudes toward abortion, Number 357, 12–13.

Gandhy, S. (1988). Crimes against women in India. *Philosophy and Social Action, 14* (4), 22–30.

Gangestad, S. W., & Buss, D. M. (1993). Pathogen prevalence and human mate preferences. *Ethology and Sociobiology, 14,* 89–96.

Gangestad, S. W., & Thornhill, R. (1997). Human sexual selection fn developmental stability. In J. A. Simpson & D. T. Kenrick (Eds.), *Evolutionary social psychology* (pp. 169–195). Mahwah, NJ: Erlbaum.

Gangestad, S. W., Thornhill, R., & Yeo, R. A. (1994). Facial attractiveness, developmental stability, and fluctuating asymmetry. *Ethology and Sociobiology, 15,* 73–85.

Garcia, L. T. (1998). Perceptions of resistance to unwanted sexual advances. *Journal of Psychology and Human Sexuality, 10* (1), 43–52.

Garcia, L. T., & Carrigan, D. (1998). Individual and gender differences in sexual self-perceptions. *Journal of Psychology and Human Sexuality, 10* (2), 59–70.

Gates, C. C. (1988). The "most-significant-other" in the care of breast cancer patient. *Ca—A Cancer Journal for Clinicians, 38,* 146–153.

Gay. G. R., New-Meyer, J. D., Perry, M., Johnson, G., & Kurland, M. (1982). Love and haight: The sensuous hippie revisited. Drug/sex practices in San Francisco, 1980–1981. *Journal of Psychoactive Drugs, 14,* 111–123.

Gebhard, P. H., Gagnon, J. H., Pomeroy, W. B., & Christenson, C. V. (1965). *Sex offenders.* New York: Harper & Row.

Gentry, C. (1991). *J. Edgar Hoover: The man, the secrets.* New York: Norton.

George, L. K., & Weiler, S. J. (1981). Sexuality in middle and late life. The effects of age, cohort, and gender. *Archives of General Psychiatry, 38,* 919–923.

Gerrard, M. (1987). Sex, sex guilt, and contraceptive use revisited: The 1980s. *Journal of Personality and Social Psychology, 53,* 975–980.

Gerrard, M., & Gibbons, F. X. (1982). Sexual experience, sex guilt, and sexual moral reasoning. *Journal of Personality, 50,* 345–359.

Gettelman, T. E., & Thompson, J. K. (1993). Actual differences and stereotypical perceptions in body image and eating disturbance: A comparison of male and female heterosexual and homosexual samples. *Sex Roles, 29,* 545–562.

Giami, A., & Schiltz, M-A. (1996). Representations of sexuality and relations between partners: Sex research in

France in the era of AIDS. *Annual Review of Sex Research, 7*, 125–157.

Gilbert, N. (1992). Realities and mythologies of rape. *Society, 29*, 4–10.

Gilligan, C. (1982). *In a different voice: Psychological theory and women's development.* Cambridge, MA: Harvard University Press.

Glaser, R. D., & Thorpe, J. S. (1986). Unethical intimacy: A survey of sexual contact and advances between psychology educators and female graduate students. *American Psychologist, 41*, 43–51.

Glasock, J., & LaRose, R. (1993). Dial-a-porn recordings: The role of the female participant in male sexual fantasies. *Journal of Broadcaster and Electronic Media, 39*, 313–324.

Glass, S. P., & Wright, T. L. (1992). Justifications for extramarital relationships: The association between attitudes, behaviors, and gender. *The Journal of Sex Research, 29*, 361–387.

Glazener, C. M. A., Abdalla, M., Stroud, P., Naji, S., Templeton, A., & Russell, I. T. (1995). Postnatal maternal morbidity: Extent, causes, prevention, and treatment. *British Journal of Obstetrics and Gynecology, 102*, 282–287.

Gold, S. R., & Gold, R. G. (1991). Gender differences in first sexual fantasies. *Journal of Sex Education and Therapy, 17*, 207–216.

Gold, S. R., & Gold, R. G. (1993). Sexual aversions: A hidden disorder. In W. O'Donahue & J. H. Geer (Eds.), *Handbook of sexual dysfunctions: Assessment and treatment* (pp. 83–102). Boston: Allyn & Bacon.

Golding, J. M. (1996). Sexual assault history and women's reproductive and sexual health. *Psychology of Women Quarterly, 20*, 101–121.

Goldman, R., & Goldman, J. (1982). *Children's sexual thinking: A comparative study of children aged five to fifteen years in Australia, North America, Britain, and Sweden.* London: Routledge & Kegan Paul.

Goldstein, P. J. (1979). *Prostitution and drugs.* Lexington, MA: Lexington Books.

Golombok, S., & Tasker, F. (1996). Do parents influence the sexual orientation of their children? Findings from a longitudinal study of lesbian families. *Developmental Psychology, 32*, 3–11.

Gonsiorek, J. C. (1991). The empirical basis for the demise of the illness model of homosexuality. In J. C. Gonsiorek & J. D. Weinrich (Eds.), *Homosexuality: Research implications for public policy* (pp. 115–136). Newbury Park, CA: Sage.

Gonsiorek, J. G. (1995). (Ed.). *Homosexuality and psychotherapy: A practicioner's handbook of affirmative models.* New York: Haworth.

Goodall, J. (1971). *Tiwi wives.* Seattle: University of Washington Press.

Goodheart, A. (1992). Abstinence ed.: How everything you need to know about sex you won't be allowed to ask. *Playboy, 39*, 42–44.

Goodman, R. E., Anderson, D. C., Bu'lock, D. E., Sheffield, B., Lynch, S. S., & Butt, W. R. (1985). Study of the effect of estradiol on gonadotropin levels in untreated male-to-female transsexuals. *Archives of Sexual Behavior, 14*, 141–146.

Gordon, C. M., & Carey, M. P. (1995). Penile tumescence monitoring during morning naps to assess male erectile functioning: An initial study of healthy men of varied ages. *Archives of Sexual Behavior, 24*, 291–307.

Gorey, K. M., & Leslie, D. R. (1997). The prevalence of child sexual abuse: Integrative review adjustment for potential response and measurement biases. *Child Abuse and Neglect, 21*, 391–398.

Gosselin, C. (1978). Personality attributes of the average rubber fetishist. In M. Cook & G. D. Wilson (Eds), *Love and attraction* (pp. 395–399). Oxford, England: Pergmon.

Gottman, J. M., Coan, J., Carrere, S., & Swanson, C. (1998). Predicting marital happiness and stability from newlywed interactions. *Journal of Marriage in the Family, 60*, 5–22.

Gould, S. J. (1994). Sexuality and ethics in advertising: A research agenda and policy guideline perspective. *Journal of Advertising, 23*, 73–80.

Graber, B. (1993). Medical aspects of sexual arousal disorders. In W. O'Donahue & J. H. Geer (Eds.), *Handbook of sexual dysfunctions: Assessment and treatment* (pp. 103–156). Boston: Allyn & Bacon.

Grady, W. R., Klepinger, D. H., Billy, J. O. G., & Tanfer, K. (1993). Condom characteristics: The perceptions and preferences of men in the United States. *Family Planning Perspectives, 25*, 67–73.

Grafenberg, E. (1950). The role of the urethra in female orgasm. *The International Journal of Sexology, 3*, 145–148.

Graham, K. R. (1996). The childhood victimization of sex offenders: An underestimated issue. *International Journal of Offender Therapy and Comparative Criminology, 40*, 192–203.

Granberg, D. (1985). The United States Senate votes to uphold Roe versus Wade. *Population Research and Policy Review, 4*, 115–131.

Granvold, D. K., Pedler, L. M., & Schellie, S. G. (1979). A study of sex role expectancy and female post-divorce adjustment. *Journal of Divorce, 2*, 383–393.

Green, R. (1987). *The "sissy boy syndrome" and the development of homosexuality: A fifteen-year prospective study.* New Haven: Yale University Press.

Green, R., & Fleming, D. T. (1990). Transsexual surgery follow-up: Status in the 1990s. *Annual Review of Sex Research, 1*, 163–174.

Greenberg, R. P., & Fisher, S. (1996). *Freud scientifically reappraised.* New York: Wiley.

Greer, G. (1971). *The female eunuch.* New York: McGraw-Hill.

Gregor, T. (1985). *Anxious pleasures: The sexual lives of an Amazonian people*. Chicago: University of Chicago Press.

Grenier, G., & Byers, E. S. (1995). Rapid ejaculation: A review of conceptual, etiological, and treatment issues. *Archives of Sexual Behavior, 24,* 447–472.

Grodstein, F., Goldman, M. B., & Cramer, D. W. (1993). Relation of tubal infertility to history of sexually transmitted diseases. *American Journal of Epidemiology, 137,* 577–584.

Groth, A. N. (1979). Sexual trauma in the life histories of rapists and child molesters. *Victimology: An International Journal, 4,* 10–16.

Groth, A. N., & Burgess, A. W. (1977). Sexual dysfunction during rape. *New England Journal of Medicine, 297,* 764–766.

Gruber, J. E. (1990). Methodological problems and policy implications in sexual harassment research. *Population Research and Policy Review, 9,* 235–254.

Grunebaum, H. (1986). Harmful psychotherapy experiences. *American Journal of Psychotherapy, 40,* 165–176.

Gutek, B. A. (1985). *Sex and the workplace*. San Francisco: Jossey-Bass.

Gutek, B. A. (1992). Understanding sexual harassment at work. *Notre Dame Journal of Law, Ethics, and Public Policy, 6,* 335–358.

Gutek, B. A. (1997). Sexual harassment policy initiatives. In W. O'Donohue, (Ed.), *Sexual harassment: Theory, research, treatment* (pp. 185–198). Needham Heights, MA: Allyn and Bacon.

Gutek, B. A., Cohen, A. G., & Konrad, A. M. (1990). Predicting social-sexual behavior at work: A contact hypothesis. *Academy of Management Journal, 33,* 560–577.

Hack, M., Wright, L. L., Shankasan, S., Tyson, J. E., Horbas, J. D., Bauer, C. R., & Younes, N. (1995). Very-low-birth-weight outcomes of National Institute of Child Health and Human Development Neonatal Network, November 1989 to October 1990. *American Journal of Obstetrics and Gynecology, 172,* 457–464.

Hall, E. J., & Ferree, M. M. (1986). Race differences in abortion attitudes. *Public Opinion Quarterly, 50,* 193–207.

Hall, E. R., & Flannery, P. J. (1985). Prevalence and correlates of sexual assault experiences in adolescents. *Victimology: An International Journal, 9,* 398–406.

Hall, G. C. N., & Barongan, C. (1997). Prevention of sexual aggression: Sociocultural risk and protective factors. *American Psychologist, 52,* 5–14.

Hallstrom, T. (1977). Sexuality in the climacteric. *Clinical Obstetrics and Gynecology, 4,* 227–239.

Halpern, C. T., Udry, J. R., & Suchindran, C. (1994). Effects of repeated questionnaire administration in longitudinal studies of adolescent males' sexual behavior. *Archives of Sexual Behavior, 23,* 41–57.

Hamburg, D. A. (1992). *Today's children: Creating a future for a generation in crisis*. New York: Times Books.

Hamer, D. H., Hu, S., Magnuson, V. L., Hu, N., & Pattatucci, A. M. L. (1993). A linkage between DNA markers on the X chromosome and male sexual orientation. *Science, 261,* 321–327.

Hammel, G. A., Olkin, R., & Taube, D. O. (1996). Student-educator sex in clinical and counseling psychology doctoral training. *Professional Psychology: Research and Practice, 27,* 93–97.

Hansson, R. O., Knopf, M. F., Downs, E. A., Monroe, P. R., Stegman, S. E., & Wadley, D. S. (1984). Femininity, masculinity, and adjustment to divorce among women. *Psychology of Women Quarterly, 8,* 248–260.

Hardy, J. B., Duggan, A. K., Masnyk, K., & Pearson, C. (1989). Fathers of children born to young urban mothers. *Family Planning Perspectives, 21,* 159–163, 187.

Harlow, H. F., & Harlow, M. K. (1962). The effect of rearing conditions on behavior. *Bulletin of the Meninger Clinic, 26,* 213–224.

Harlow, H. F., & Mears, C. (1979). *The human model: Primate perspectives*. Washington, DC: Winston.

Harlow, H. F., & Novak, M. A. (1973). Psychopathological perspectives. *Perspectives in Biology and Medicine, 16,* 461–478.

Harry, J. (1993). Being out: A general model. *Journal of Homosexuality, 26,* 25–40.

Hartman, W. E., & Fithian, M. A. (1984). *Any man can*. New York: St. Martin's.

Harvey, S. M., & Scrimshaw, S. C. M. (1988). Coitus-dependent contraceptives: Factors associated with effective use. *The Journal of Sex Research, 25,* 364–378.

Hatcher, R. A. (1998). Depo-Provera, Norplant, and progestin-only pills (minipills). In R. A. Hatcher, J. Trussell, F. Stewart, W. Cates, Jr., G. K. Stewart, F. Guest, & D. Kowal (Eds.), *Contraceptive technology* (17th ed.) (pp. 467–509). New York: Ardent Media.

Hatcher, R. A., & Guillebaud, J. (1998). The pill: Combined oral contraceptives. In R. A. Hatcher, J. Trussell, F. Stewart, W. Cates, Jr., G. K. Stewart, F. Guest, & D. Kowal (Eds.), *Contraceptive technology* (17th ed.) (pp. 405–466). New York: Ardent Media.

Hatcher, R. A., Trussell, J., Stewart, F., Cates, Jr., W., Stewart, G. K., Guest, F., & Kowal, D. (Eds.). (1998). *Contraceptive technology* (17th ed.). New York: Ardent Media.

Hatfield, E., & Rapson, R. L. (1993). *Love, sex, and intimacy: Their psychology, biology, and history*. New York: HarperCollins.

Hatfield, E., & Rapson, R. L. (1996). *Love and sex: Cross-cultural perspectives*. Needham Heights, MA: Allyn & Bacon.

Hatfield, R. W. (1994). Touch and sexuality. In V. L. Bullough & B. Bullough (Eds.), *Human sexuality: An encyclopedia* (pp. 581–587). New York: Garland.

Haub, C. (1992). New U.N. projections show uncertainty of future world. *Population Today, 20,* 6.

Hawton, K. (1992). Sex therapy research: Has it withered on the vine? *Annual Review of Sex Research, 3,* 49–72.

Hazan, C., & Shaver, P. R. (1990). Love and work: An attachment-theoretical perspective. *Journal of Personality and Social Psychology, 52,* 511–524.

Hechinger, F. M. (1992). *Fateful choices: Healthy youth for the twenty-first century.* New York: Hill and Wang.

Heim, N. (1981). Sexual behavior of castrated sex offenders. *Archives of Sexual Behavior, 10,* 11–19.

Heim, N., & Hursch, C. J. (1979). Castration for sex offenders: Treatment or punishment? A review and critique of recent European literature. *Archives of Sexual Behavior, 8,* 281–304.

Heiman, J. R. (1975). The physiology of erotica: Women's sexual arousal. *Psychology Today, 8,* 90–94.

Heiman, J. R. (1977). A psychophysiological exploration of sexual arousal patterns in females and males. *Psychophysiology, 14,* 266–274.

Heiman, J. R., Gladue, B. A., Roberts, C. W., & LoPiccolo, J. (1986). Historical and current factors discriminating sexually functional from sexually dysfunctional married couples. *Journal of Marital and Family Therapy, 12,* 163–174.

Heiman, J. R., & LoPiccolo, J. (1988). *Becoming orgasmic.* New York: Prentice-Hall.

Heiman, J. R., & Meston, C. M. (1997). Empirically validated treatment for sexual dysfunction. *Annual Review of Sex Research, 8,* 148–194.

Heinlein, R. (1961). *Stranger in a strange land.* New York: Putnam.

Henderson, J. S. (1983). Effects of a prenatal teaching program on postpartum regeneration of the pubococcygeal muscle. *Journal of Obstetrics, Gynecology, and Neonatal Nursing, 12,* 403–408.

Hendrick, C., & Hendrick, S. S. (1993). *Romantic love.* Newbury Park, CA: Sage.

Hendrick, S. S., & Hendrick, C. (1992). *Liking, loving, and relating.* Pacific Grove, CA: Brooks/Cole.

Hendrick, S. S., & Hendrick, C. (1995). Gender differences and similarities in sex and love. *Personal Relationships, 2,* 5–65.

Henshaw, S. K. (1993). Teenage abortion, birth, and pregnancy statistics by state, 1988. *Family Planning Perspectives, 25,* 122–126.

Henshaw, S. K. (1997). Teenage abortion and pregnancy statistics by state, 1992. *Family Planning Perspectives, 29,* 115–122.

Henshaw, S. K. (1998). Unintended pregnancy in the United States. *Family Planning Perspectives, 30,* 24–29, 46.

Henshaw, S. K., & Kost, K. (1996). Abortion patients in 1994–1995: Characteristics and contraceptive use. *Family Planning Perspectives, 28,* 140–147, 158.

Henshaw, S. K., & Van Vort, J. (1992). *Abortion factbook, 1992 edition: Readings, trends, and state and local data to 1988.* New York: Alan Guttmacher Institute.

Hensley, W. E. (1996). The effect of ludus love style on sexual experience. *Social Behavior and Personality, 24,* 205–212.

Herbert, J. (1996). Sexuality, stress, and the chemical architecture of the brain. *Annual Review of Sex Research, 7,* 1–43.

Herdt, G. (1994). Mistaken sex: Culture, biology, and the third sex in New Guinea. In G. Herdt & S. Nanda (Eds.), *Third sex: Third gender: Beyond sexual dimorphism in culture and history* (pp. 419–445). New York: Zone Books.

Herdt, G. H. (Ed.) (1984). *Ritualized homosexuality in Melanesia.* Berkeley and Los Angeles: University of California Press.

Herdt, G. H., & Davidson, J. (1988). The Sambia "Turnim Man": Sociocultural and clinical aspects of gender formation in male pseudohermaphrodites with 5-alpha reductase-deficiency in Papua New Guinea. *Archives of Sexual Behavior, 17,* 33–56.

Herek, G. M., & Capitanio, J. P. (1996). "Some of my best friends": Intergroup contact, concealable stigma, and heterosexuals' attitudes toward gay men and lesbians. *Personality and Social Psychology Bulletin, 22,* 412–424.

Herek, G. M., & Glunt, E. K. (1988). An epidemic of stigma: Public reactions to AIDS. *American Psychologist, 43,* 886–891.

Herek, G. M., & Glunt, E. K. (1993). Interpersonal contact and heterosexuals' attitudes toward gay men: Results from a national survey. *The Journal of Sex Research, 30,* 239–244.

Herold, E. E., Mantle, D., & Zemitis, O. (1979). A study of sexual offenses against females. *Adolescence, 14,* 65–72.

Herold, E., Mottin, J., & Sabry, Z. (1979). The effect of vitamin E on human sexuality. *Archives of Sexual Behavior, 8,* 397–403.

Hewlett, B. S. (1991). *Intimate matters.* Ann Arbor, MI: University of Michigan Press.

Higgins, D. J., & McCabe, M. P. (1994). The relationship of child sexual abuse and family violence to adult adjustment: Toward an integrated risk-sequelae model. *The Journal of Sex Research, 31,* 255–266.

Hirsch, M. S., D'Aquila, R. T., & Kaplan, J. C. (1997). Antiretroviral therapy. In V. T. DeVita, Jr., S. Hellman, & S. A. Rosenberg (Eds.), *AIDS: Etiology, diagnosis, treatment, and prevention* (4th ed.) (pp. 495–508). Philadelphia: Lippincott-Raven Publishers.

HIV comes in five family groups. (1995). *Science, 256,* 966.

Hochhauser, M., & Rothenberger, J. H., III. (1992). *AIDS education.* Dubuque, IA: Brown.

Hoenig, J. (1985). Etiology of transsexualism. In B. W. Steiner (Ed.), *Gender dysphoria: Development, research, and management* (pp. 11–32). New York: Plenum.

Hogben, M., & Byrne, D. (1998). Using social learning theory to explain individual differences in human sexuality. *The Journal of Sex Research, 35,* 58–71.

Holzman, H. R., & Pines, S. (1982). Buying sex: The phenomenology of being a john. *Deviant Behavior: An Interdisciplinary Journal, 4,* 89–116.

Honea-Fleming, P., & Blackwell, R. E. (1998). Infertility and pregnancy loss. In B. R. Carr & R. E. Blackwell (Eds.) *Textbook of reproductive medicine* (2nd ed.) (pp. 693–706). Stamford, CT: Appleton and Lange.

Hooker, E. (1969). Parental relations and male homosexuality in patient and nonpatient samples. *Journal of Consulting and Clinical Psychology, 33,* 140–142.

Hoon, R. W., Wincze, J. P., & Hoon, E. F. (1976). Physiological assessment of sexual arousal in women. *Psychophysiology, 13,* 196–204.

Horney, K. (1933). The denial of the vagina. *International Journal of Psychoanalysis, 14,* 57–70.

Horwitz, A. V., & White, H. R. (1998). The relationship of cohabitation and mental health: A study of a young adult cohort. *Journal of Marriage and the Family, 60,* 505–514.

Hostetter, H., & Andolsek, K. M. (1990). Psychosocial issues in pregnancy. In K. M. Andolsek (Ed.), *Obstetric care: Standards of prenatal, intrapartum, and postpartum management* (pp. 95–106). Philadelphia: Lea and Febiger.

Howard, M., & McCabe, J. B. (1990). Helping teenagers postpone sexual involvement. *Family Planning Perspectives, 22,* 21–26.

Hoyenga, K. B., & Hoyenga, K. T. (1993). *Gender-related differences: Origins and outcomes.* Boston: Allyn & Bacon.

Hrabowy, I., & Allgeier, E. R. (1987, May). *Relationship of level of sexual invasiveness of child abuse to psychological functioning among adult women.* Paper presented at the Midwestern Psychological Association Meeting, Chicago, IL.

Humphreys, T. P., & Herold, E. (1996). Date rape: A comparative analysis and integration of theory. *Canadian Journal of Human Sexuality, 5,* 69–82.

Hunt, M. (1974). *Sexual behavior in the 1970s.* Chicago: Playboy Press.

Hunt, S., & Main, T. L. (1997). Sexual orientation confusion among spouses of transvestites and transsexuals following disclosure of spouse's gender dysphoria. *Journal of Psychology and Human Sexuality, 9* (2), 39–51.

Hurlbert, D. F. (1993). A comparative study using orgasm consistency training in the treatment of women reporting hypoactive sexual desire disorder. *Journal of Sex and Marital Therapy, 19,* 45–55.

Hurlbert, D. F., & Whittaker, K. E. (1991). The role of masturbation in marital and sexual satisfaction: A comparative study of female masturbators and nonmasturbators. *Journal of Sex Education and Therapy, 17,* 272–282.

Hyde, J. S., DeLamater, J. D., & Hewitt, E. C. (1998). Sexuality an the dual-earner couple: Multiple roles and sexual functioning. *Journal of Family Psychology, 12,* 354–368.

Hyde, J. S., DeLamater, J. D., Plant, E. A., & Byrd, J. M. (1996). Sexuality during pregnancy and the year postpartum. *The Journal of Sex Research, 33,* 143–151.

Imperato-McGinley, J., Guerrero, L., Gautier, T., & Peterson, R. (1974). Steroid 5 reductase deficiency in man: An inherited form of male pseudohermaphroditism. *Science, 186,* 1213–1215.

Imperato-McGinley, J., Peterson, R. E., Gautier, T., Looper, G., Danner, R., Arthur, A., Morris, P. L., Sweeney, W. J., & Schackleton, C. (1982). Hormonal evaluation of a large kindred with complete androgen insensitivity: Evidence for secondary 5-alpha-reductase deficiency. *Journal of Clinical Endocrinology Metabolism, 54,* 15–22.

Inciardi, J. A. (1995). Crack, crack house sex, and HIV risk. *Archives of Sexual Behavior, 24,* 249–269.

Ingrassia, M., Springen, & Rosenberg, D. (1995, March 13). Still fumbling in the dark. *Time,* pp. 60–62.

Innala, S. M. & Ernulf, K. E. (1989). Asphyxiophilia in Scandinavia. *Archives of Sexual Behavior, 18,* 181–189.

Jacklin, C. N., DiPietro, J. A., & Maccoby, E. E. (1984). Sex-typing behavior and sex-typing pressure in child-parent interaction. *Archives of Sexual Behavior, 13,* 413–425.

Jacobson, N. S., & Christensen, A. (1996). *Integrative couple therapy: Promoting acceptance and change.* New York: W. W. Norton.

Jamison, P. L., & Gebhard, P. H. (1988). Penis size increase between flaccid and erect states: An analysis of the Kinsey data. *The Journal of Sex Research, 24,* 177–183.

Janus, S. S., & Janus, C. L. (1993). *The Janus report on sexual behavior.* New York: Wiley.

Jay, K., & Young, A. (1979). *The gay report.* New York: Summit Books.

Jenks, R. J. (1998). Swinging: A review of the literature. *Archives of Sexual Behavior, 27,* 507–521.

Jennings, V. H., Lamprecht, V. M., & Kowal, D. (1998). Fertility awareness methods. In R. A. Hatcher, J. Trussell, F. Stewart, W. Cates, Jr., G. K. Stewart, F. Guest, & D. Kowal (Eds.), *Contraceptive technology* (17th ed.) (pp. 309–323). New York: Ardent Media.

Johnston, V. S., & Oliver-Rodriguez, J. C. (1997). Facial beauty and the late positive component of event-related potentials. *The Journal of Sex Research, 34,* 188–198.

Jones, E. F., Forrest, J. D., Goldman, N., Henshaw, S., Lincoln, R., Rosoff, J. I., Westoff, C. F., & Wulf, D. (1986). *Teenage pregnancy in industrialized countries.* New Haven: Yale University Press.

Jones, J. H. (1981). *Bad blood: The Tuskegee syphilis experiment.* New York: Free Press.

Jones, J. H. (1998). *Alfred C. Kinsey: A public/private life.* New York: Norton.

Jones, J. R. (1974). Plasma testosterone concentrations in female transsexuals. In D. R. Laub & P. Gandy (Eds.), *Proceedings of the second interdisciplinary symposium on the gender dysphoria syndrome.* Ann Arbor, MI: Edward Brothers.

Jones, K. L. (1999). Effects of therapeutic, diagnostic, and environmental agents. In R. K. Creasy, & M. D. Resnik, (Eds.). *Maternal-fetal medicine* (4th ed.) (pp. 132–144). Philadelphia, PA: W. B. Saunders Company.

Jones, W. H., Chernovetz, M. E., & Hansson, R. O. (1978). The enigma of androgyny: Differential implications for males and females? *Journal of Consulting and Clinical Psychology, 46,* 298–313.

Jorgensen, C. (1967). *Christine Jorgensen: Personal biography.* New York: Ericksson.

Joseph, J. G., Montgomery, S. B., Emmons, C. et al. (1987). Magnitude and determinants of behavioral risk reduction: Longitudinal analysis of a cohort at risk for AIDS. *Psychology and Health, 1* (1), 73–95.

Joshi, V. N., & Money, J. (1995). Dhat syndrome and dream in transcultural sexology. *Journal of Psychology and Human Sexuality, 7* (3), 95–99.

Kafka, M. P. (1997a). Amonoamine hypothesis for the pathophysiology of paraphilic disorders. *Archives of Sexual Behavior, 26,* 343–358.

Kafka, M. P. (1997b). Hypersexual desire in males: An operational definition and clinical implications for paraphilias and paraphilia-related disorders. *Archives of Sexual Behavior, 26,* 505–526.

Kalichman, S. C. (1991). Psychopathology and personality characteristics of criminal sexual offenders as a function of victim age. *Archives of Sexual Behavior, 20,* 187–197.

Kameya, Y., Deguchi, A., & Yokota, Y. (1997). Analysis of measured values of ejaculation time in healthy males. *Journal of Sex and Marital Therapy, 23,* 25–28.

Kanin, E. J. (1985). Date rapists: Differential sexual socialization and relative deprivation. *Archives of Sexual Behavior, 14,* 219–231.

Kanin, E. J. (1994). False rape allegations. *Archives of Sexual Behavior, 23,* 81–92.

Kaplan, H. S. (1974). *The new sex therapy.* New York: Brunner/Mazel.

Kaplan, H. S. (1979). *Disorders of sexual desire.* New York: Brunner/ Mazel.

Karlen, A. (1994). Aging and sexuality. In V. L. Bullough & B. Bullough (Eds.), *Human sexuality: An encyclopedia* (pp. 12–15). New York: Garland Publishing.

Karpman, B. (1954). *The sexual offender and his offenses.* New York: Julian Press.

Katz, J. N. (1995). *The invention of heterosexuality.* New York: Dutton.

Katz, P. A. (1996). Raising feminists. *Psychology of Women Quarterly, 20,* 323–340.

Katz, R. C., Hannon, R., & Whitten, L. (1996). Effects of gender and situation on the perception of sexual harassment. *Sex Roles, 34,* 35–42.

Kegel, A. M. (1952). Sexual functions of the pubococcygeus muscle. *Western Journal of Surgery, Obstetrics, and Gynecology, 60,* 521–524.

Kelley, K., Byrne, D., Greendlinger, V., & Murnen, S. K. (1997). Content, sex of viewer, and dispositional variables as predictors of affective and evaluative responses to sexually explicit files. *Journal of Psychology and Human Sexuality, 9* (2), 53–71.

Kelly, J. A. (1995). *Changing HIV risk behavior: Practical strategies.* New York: Guilford.

Kelly, M. P., Strassberg, D. S., & Kircher, J. R. (1990). Attitudinal and experiential correlates of anorgasmia. *Archives of Sexual Behavior, 19,* 165–177.

Kilpatrick, A. C. (1986). Some correlates of women's childhood sexual experiences: A retrospective study. *The Journal of Sex Research, 22,* 221–242.

Kilpatrick, A. C. (1992). *Long-range effects of childhood and adolescent sexual experiences: Myths, mores, and menaces.* Hillsdale, NJ: Erlbaum.

Kilpatrick, D. G., Best, C. L., Saunders, B. E., & Veronen, L. J. (1988). Rape in marriage and in dating relationships: How bad is it for mental health? In R. A. Prentky & V. L. Quinsey (Eds.), *Human sexual aggression: Current perspectives* (pp. 335–344). New York: New York Academy of Sciences.

Kilpatrick, D. G., Edmunds, C. N., & Seymour, N. K. (1992). *Rape in America: A report to the nation.* Arlington, VA: National Victim Center.

Kim, P. Y., & Bailey, J. M. (1997). Side streets on the information superhighway: Paraphilias and sexual variations on the Internet. *Journal of Sex Education and Therapy, 22,* 35–43.

Kimmel, D. (1978). Adult development and aging: A gay perspective. *Journal of Social Issues, 34* (3), 113–130.

Kimmel, M. S., & Linders, A. (1996). Does censorship make a difference? An aggregate empirical analysis of pornography and rape. *Journal of Psychology and Human Sexuality, 8,* 1–20.

King, A. J. C., Beazley, R. P., Warren, W. K., Hankins, C A., Robertson, A. S., & Radford, J. L. (1988). *Canada youth & aids study.* Ottawa: Federal Centre for AIDS Health Protection Branch, Health and Welfare Canada.

Kirby, D., Barth, R. P., Leland, N., & Fetro, J. V. (1991). Reducing the risk: Impact of a new curriculum on sexual risk-taking. *Family Planning Perspectives, 23,* 253–263.

Kirby, D., Korpi, M., Barth, R. P., & Cagampang, H. H. (1997). The impact of the Postponing Sexual Involvement Curriculum among youths in California. *Family Planning Perspectives, 29,* 100–108.

Kirkpatrick, C., & Kanin, E. (1957). Male sex aggression on a university campus. *American Sociological Review, 22,* 52–58.

Kite, M. E., & Whitley, B. E., Jr. (1998). Do heterosexual women and men differ in their attitudes toward homosexuality? In G. Herek (Ed.), *Stigma and sexual orientation: Understanding prejudice against lesbians, gay men, and bisexuals* (pp. 39–61). Thousand Oaks, CA: Sage.

Kitson, G. C., & Morgan, L. A. (1991). The multiple consequences of divorce. In A. Booth (Ed.), *Contemporary families: Looking forward, looking backward* (pp. 150–161). Minneapolis: National Council on Family Relations.

Klatt, H-J. (1998). Sexual harassment policies as all-purpose tools to settle conflicts. *Sexuality and Culture, 1,* 45–65.

Klitsch, M. (1993). Vasectomy and prostate cancer: More questions than answers. *Family Planning Perspectives, 25,* 133–135.

Klitsch, M. (1995). Still waiting for the contraceptive revolution. *Family Planning Perspectives, 27,* 246–253.

Kochanek, K. D., & Hudson, B. L. (1994, December 8). Advance report of final mortality statistics. *Monthly Vital Statistics Report, 43,* Supplement.

Kockott, G. & Fahrner, E. M. (1988). Male-to-female and female-to-male transsexuals: A comparison. *Archives of Sexual Behavior, 17,* 539–546.

Kohl, J. V., & Francoeur, R. T. (1995). *The scent of eros: Mysteries of odor in human sexuality.* New York: Continuum Publishing Company.

Kolata, G. (1995, May 28). Will the lawyers kill off Norplant? *New York Times,* p. C1.

Komarow, S. (1997, February 27). Gays say military violates "Don't ask, don't tell." *USA Today,* p. 4D.

Koonin, L. M. et al. (1997). Abortion surveillance—United States, 1993 and 1994. *Morbidity and Mortality Weekly Reports, 46,* Special Supplement 4.

Koralewski, M. K., & Conger, J. C. (1992). The assessment of social skills among sexually coercive college males. *The Journal of Sex Research, 29,* 169–188.

Koss, M. P., & Dinero, T. E. (1988). Predictors of sexual aggression among a national sample of male college students. In R. A. Prentky & V. L. Quinsey (Eds.), *Human sexual aggression: Current perspectives* (pp. 133–147). New York: New York Academy of Sciences.

Koss, M. P., Dinero, T. E., Seibel, C. A., & Cox, S. L. (1988). Stranger and acquaintance rape: Are there differences in the victim's experience? *Psychology of Women Quarterly, 12,* 1–24.

Koutsky, L. A., Holmes, K. K., Critchlow, C. W., Stevens, C. E., Paavonen, J., Beckman, A. M., DeRouen, T. A., Galloway, D. A., Vernon, D., & Kiviat, N. B. (1992). A cohort study of the risk of cervical intraepithelial neoplasia grade two or three in relation to papilloma virus infection. *New England Journal of Medicine, 327,* 1272–1278.

Kroon, S. & Whitley, R. J. (1994, November 13–15). *Can we improve management of perinatal HSV infections?* International Herpes Management Forum, Recommendations from the Second Annual Meeting.

Kuiper, H., Miller, S., Martinez, E., Loeb, L., & Darney, P. (1997). Urban adolescent females' views on the implant and contraceptive decision-making: A double paradox. *Family Planning Perspectives, 29,* 167–172.

Kurdek, L. A. (1993). Predicting marital dissolution: A five-year prospective longitudinal study of newlywed couples. *Journal of Personality and Social Psychology, 64,* 221–242.

Kurdek, L. A., & Schmitt, J. P. (1985/1986). Relationship quality of gay men in closed or open relationships. *Journal of Homosexuality, 12,* 85–99.

Kurstin, C., & Oskamp, S. (1979, September). *Contraceptive behavior after abortion.* Paper presented at the American Psychological Association convention, New York.

Kyes, K. B. (1995). Sexuality and sexual orientation: Adjustments to aging. In L. Diamont & R. D. McAnulty (Eds.), *The psychology of sexual orientation, behavior, and identity* (pp. 457–470). Westport, CT: Greenwood Press.

Laan, E., & Everaerd, W. (1995). Determinants of female sexual arousal: Psychophysiology theory and data. *Annual Review of Sex Research, 5,* 32–76.

Ladas, A. K., Whipple, B., & Perry, J. D. (1982). *The G spot and other recent discoveries about human sexuality.* New York: Holt, Rinehart, & Winston.

Lamb, M. (1998). Cybersex: Research notes on the characteristics of the visitors to online chatrooms. *Deviant Behavior: An Interdisciplinary Journal, 19,* 121–135.

Lander, J., Brady-Fryer, B., Metcalfe, J. B., Nazarali, S., & Muttitt, S. (1997). Comparison of ring block, dorsal penile nerve block, and topical anesthesia for neonatal circumcision: A randomized controlled trial. *Journal of the American Medical Association, 278,* 2157–2162.

Langevin, R., Paitich, D. P., Ramsay, G., Anderson, C., Kamrad, J., Pope, S., Geller, G., Pearl, L., & Newman, S. (1979). Experimental studies of the etiology of genital exhibitionism. *Archives of Sexual Behavior, 8,* 307–331.

Langevin, R., Paitich, D. P., & Russon, A. E. (1985). Voyeurism: Does it predict sexual aggression or violence in general? In R. Langevin (Ed.), *Erotic preference, gender identity, and aggression in men* (pp. 77–98). Hillsdale, NJ: Erlbaum.

Langlois, J. H., & Casey, R. J. (1984, April). *Baby beautiful: The relationship between infant physical attractiveness and maternal behavior.* Paper presented at the Fourth Biennial International Conference on Infant Studies, New York, NY.

Langlois, J. H., & Roggman, L. A. (1990). Attractive faces are only average. *Psychological Science, 1,* 115–121.

Langlois, J. H., Roggman, L. A., Casey, R. J., Ritter, J. M., Rieser-Danner, L. A., & Jenkins, V. Y. (1987). Infant preferences for attractive faces: Rudiments of a stereotype? *Developmental Psychology, 23,* 363–369.

Lannon, C. M., Bailey, A. G. D., Fleischman, A. R., Kaplan, G. W., Shoemaker, C. T., Swanson, G. T., & Couston, A. (1999). Circumcision policy statement. *Pediatrics, 103,* 686–693.

Laumann, E. O., Gagnon, J. H., Michael, R. T., & Michaels, S. (1994). *The social organization of sexuality: Sexual practices in the United States.* Chicago: University of Chicago Press.

Lawrence, D. H. (1930). *Lady Chatterly's lover.* New York: W. Faro.

Laws, D. R., & Marshall, W. L. (1991). Masturbatory reconditioning with sexual deviates: An evaluative review. *Advances in Behavior, Research, and Therapy, 13,* 13–25.

Lazarus, A. A. (1989). Dyspareunia: A multimodel psychotherapeutic perspective. In S. R. Leiblum & R. C. Rosen (Eds.), *Principles and practices of sex therapy* (2nd ed., pp. 89–112). New York: Guilford.

Lee, J. A. (1973). *The colors of love: An exploration of the ways of loving.* Don Mills, Ontario, Canada: New Press.

Lee, J. A. (1998). Ideoloies of lovestyle and sexstyle. In V. C. de Munck, (Ed.), *Romantic love and sexual behavior* (pp. 33–76). Westport CT: Praeger.

Lees, R. B. (1975, March). *Men and abortion: Anxiety and social supports.* Paper presented at the conference on New Research on Women and Sex Roles, Ann Arbor, MI.

Leiblum, S. R. (1993). The impact of fertility on sexual and marital satisfaction. *Annual Review of Sex Research, 4,* 99–120.

Leiblum, S. R., & Rosen, R. C. (1989). Introduction: Sex therapy in the age of AIDS. In S. R. Leiblum & R. C. Rosen (Eds.), *Principles and practice of sex therapy* (2nd ed., pp. 1–16). New York: Guilford.

Leigh, B. C. (1989). Reasons for having and avoiding sex: Gender, sexual orientation, and relationship to sexual behavior. *The Journal of Sex Research, 26,* 199–209.

Leitenberg, H., Detzer, M. J., & Srebnik, D. (1993). Gender differences in masturbation and the relationship of masturbation experience in preadolescence and/or early adolescence in sexual behavior and sexual adjustment in young adulthood. *Archives of Sexual Behavior, 22,* 87–98.

Leitenberg, H., Greenwald, E., & Tarran, M. (1989). The relationship between sexual activity among children during preadolescence and/or early adolescence and sexual behavior and sexual adjustment in young adulthood. *Archives of Sexual Behavior, 18,* 299–313.

Leitenberg, H., & Henning, K. (1995). Sexual fantasy. *Psychological Bulletin, 117,* 469–496.

Letourneau, E. J., & O'Donohue, W. (1993). Sexual desire disorders. In W. O'Donahue & J. H. Geer (Eds.), *Handbook of sexual dysfunctions: Assessment and treatment* (pp. 53–81). Boston: Allyn & Bacon.

Letourneau, E. J., & O'Donohue, W. (1997). Classical conditioning of female sexual arousal. *Archives of Sexual Behavior, 26,* 63–78.

LeVay, S. (1991). A difference in hypothalmic structure between heterosexual and homosexual men. *Science, 253,* 1034–1037.

LeVay, S. (1993). *The sexual brain.* Cambridge, MA: MIT Press.

LeVay, S. (1996). *Queer science: The use and abuse of research into homosexuality.* Cambridge, MA: MIT Press.

Lever, J., Kanouse, D. E., Rogers, W. H., Carson, S., & Hertz, R. (1992). Behavior patterns and sexual identity of gay males. *The Journal of Sex Research, 29,* 141–167.

Levin, R. J. (1992). The mechanisms of human female sexual arousal. *Annual Review of Sex Research, 3,* 1–48.

Levin, S. M., & Stava, L. (1987). Personality characteristics of sex offenders: A review. *Archives of Sexual Behavior, 16,* 57–79.

Levine, M. P., & Troiden, R. R. (1988). The myth of sexual compulsivity. *The Journal of Sex Research, 25,* 347–363.

Levitan, M. (1988). *Textbook of human genetics.* New York: Oxford University Press.

Levy, K. N., Blatt, S. J., & Shaver, P. R. (1998). Attachment styles and parental representations. *Journal of Personality and Social Psychology, 74,* 407–419.

Lewes, K. (1988). *The psychoanalytic theory of male homosexuality.* New York: Simon & Schuster.

Lewes, K. (1995). Psychoanalysis and male homosexuality. In L. Diamont & R. D. McAnulty (Eds.), *The psychology of sexual orientation, behavior, and identity* (pp. 140–120). Westport, CT: Greenwood Press.

Lewis, R. J., & Janda, L. H. (1988). The relationship between adult sexual adjustment and childhood experiences regarding nudity, sleeping in parental bed, and parental attitudes toward sexuality. *Archives of Sexual Behavior, 17,* 349–362.

Lewis, W. J. (1997). Factors associated with post-abortion adjustment problems: Implications for triage. *The Canadian Journal of Human Sexuality, 6,* 9–16.

Lief, H. I, & Hubschman, L. (1993). Orgasm in the postoperative transsexual. *Archives of Sexual Behavior, 22,* 145–155.

Lifson, A. R., Darrow, W. W., Hessol, N. A., O'Malley, P. M., Barnhart, J. L., Jaffer, H. W., & Rutherford, G. W. (1990). Kaposi's sarcoma in a cohort of homosexual and bisexual men. *American Journal of Epidemiology, 131,* 221–231.

Lightfoot-Klein, H. (1989). The sexual experience and marital adjustment of genitally circumcised and infibulated females in the Sudan. *The Journal of Sex Research, 26,* 375–392.

Lindberg, L. D., Sonenstein, F. L., Ku, L., & Levine, G. (1997). Young men's experience with condom breakage. *Family Plannng Perspectives, 29,* 128–131, 140.

Linz, D. (1989). Exposure to sexually explicit materials and attitudes toward rape: A comparison of study results. *The Journal of Sex Research, 26,* 50–84.

Lish, J. D., Meyer-Bahlburg, H. F. L., Ehrhardt, A. A., Travis, B. G., & Veridian, N. P. (1992). Prenatal exposure to diethylstilbestrol (DES): Childhood play behavior and adult gender-role behavior in women. *Archives of Sexual Behavior, 21,* 423–441.

Liu, R., Paxton, W. A., Choe, S., Ceradini, D., Martin, S. R., Horuk, R., MacDonald, M. E., Stuhlmann, H., Koup, R. A., & Landau, N. R. (1996). Homozygous defect in HIV-I coreceptor accounts for resistence of some multiply-exposed individuals to HIV-I infection. *Cell, 86,* 367–377.

Loftus, E. F. (1998). Creating false memories. *Scientific American, 277,* 70–75.

Loftus, J. A., & Camargo, R. J. (1993). Treating the clergy. *Annals of Sex Research, 6,* 287–303.

Lohr, B. A., Adams, H. E., & Davis, J. M. (1997). Sexual arousal to erotic and aggressive stimuli in sexually coercive and noncoercive men. *Journal of Abnormal Psychology, 106,* 230–242.

Long, G. T., & Sultan, F. E. (1987). Contributions from social psychology. In L. Diamont (Ed.), *Male and female homosexuality: Psychological approaches* (pp. 221–236). Washington, DC: Hemisphere.

Lonsway, K. A. (1996). Preventing acquaintance rape through education: What do we know? *Psychology of Women Quarterly, 20,* 229–265.

Lopez, P. A., & George, W. H. (1995). Men's enjoyment of explicit erotica: Effects of person-specific attitudes and gender-specific norms. *The Journal of Sex Research, 32,* 275–288.

Lottes, I. L. (1992). The relationship between non-traditional gender roles and sexual coercion. *The Journal of Psychology and Human Sexuality, 4* (2), 89–109.

Lottes, I. L. (1993). Nontraditional gender roles and the sexual experience of heterosexual college students. *Sex Roles, 29,* 645–669.

Louderback, L. A., & Whitley, B. E., Jr. (1997). Perceived erotic value of homosexuality and sex-role attitudes as mediators of sex differences in heterosexual college students' attitudes toward lesbians and gay men. *The Journal of Sex Research, 34,* 175–182.

Lowdermilk, D. L., Perry, S. E., & Bobak, I. M. (1997). *Maternity and women's health care* (6th ed.). St. Louis: Mosby.

Lowry, D. T., & Shidler, J. A. (1993). Prime time TV portrayals of sex, "safe" sex, and AIDS: A longitudinal analysis. *Journalism Quarterly, 70,* 628–637.

Luckenbill, D. F. (1985). Entering male prostitution. *Urban Life, 14,* 131–153.

Lukse, M. P., & Vacc, N. A. (1999). Grief, depression, and coping of women undergoing infertility treatment. *Obstetrics and Gynecology, 93,* 245–251.

Lukusa, T., Fryns, J. P., & van den Berghe, T. (1992). The role of the Y-chromosome in sex determination. *Genetic Counseling, 3,* 1–11.

Lunde, I., Larsen, K. L., Fog, E., & Garde, K. (1991). Sexual desire, orgasm, and fantasies: A study of 625 Danish women born in 1910, 1936, and 1958. *Journal of Sex Education and Therapy, 17,* 111–115.

Luria, Z., & Meade, R. G. (1984). Sexuality and the middle-aged woman. In G. Baruch & J. Brooks-Gunn (Eds.), *Women in midlife* (pp. 391–397). New York: Plenum.

Lytwyn, A., & Sellors, J. W. (1997). Sexually transmitted human papillomaviruses: Current concepts and control issues. *Canadian Journal of Human Sexuality, 6,* 113–126.

Maccoby, E. E. (1998). *The two sexes: Growing up apart, coming together.* Cambridge, MA: Harvard University Press.

MacDonald, J. M. (1973). *Indecent exposure.* Springfield, IL: Thomas.

MacNeil, S., & Byers, E. S. (1997). The relationships between sexual problems, communication, and sexual satisfaction. *Canadian Journal of Human Sexuality, 6,* 277–283.

Magoun, H. W. (1981). John B. Watson and the study of human sexual behavior. *The Journal of Sex Research, 17,* 368–378.

Maguire, K., & Pastore, A. L. (1995). *Sourcebook of criminal justice statistics, 1994.* U.S. Department of Justice, Bureau of Justice Statistics, Washington, DC: GPO.

Maguire, K., Pastore, A. L., & Flanagan, T. J. (1992). *Sourcebook of criminal justice statistics—1992.* Washington, DC: GPO.

Mahoney, E. R., Shively, M. D., & Traw, M. (1986). Sexual coercion and assault: Male socialization and female risk. *Sexual Coercion and Assault, 1,* 2–8.

Main, M., & Hesse, E. (1990). Parents' unresolved traumatic experiences are related to infant disorganized status: Is frightened and/or frightening parental behavior the linking mechanism? In M. T. Greenberg, D. Cicchetti, & E. M. Cummings (Eds.), *Attachment in the preschool years* (pp. 161–184). Chicago: University of Chicago Press.

Main, M., & Soloman, J. (1990). Procedures for identifying infants as disorganized/disoriented during the Ainsworth strange situation. In M. T. Greenberg, D. Cicchetti, & E. M. Cummings (Eds.), *Attachment in the preschool years* (pp. 121–160). Chicago: University of Chicago Press.

Major, B. (1993). Gender, entitlement, and the distribution of family labor. *Journal of Social Issues, 49* (3), 141–159.

Major, B., & Cozzarelli, C. (1992). Psychosocial predictors of adjustment to abortion. *Journal of Social Issues, 48* (3), 121–142.

Malamuth, N. M. (1981). Rape proclivity among males. *Journal of Social Issues, 37* (4), 138–157.

Malamuth, N. M. (1984). Aggression against women: Cultural and individual causes. In N. M. Malamuth & E. Donnerstein (Eds.), *Pornography and sexual aggression* (pp. 19–52). Orlando, FL: Academic Press.

Malamuth, N. M. (1996). The confluence model of sexual aggression: Feminist and evolutionary perspectives. In D. M. Buss & N. M. Malamuth (Eds.), *Sex, power, conflict: Evolutionary and feminist perspectives* (pp. 269–295). New York: Oxford University Press.

Malamuth, N. M., & Check, J. V. P. (1984). Debriefing effectiveness following exposure to pornographic rape depictions. *The Journal of Sex Research, 20,* 1–13.

Malamuth, N. M., & Donnerstein, E. (1984). *Pornography and sexual aggression.* Orlando, FL: Academic Press.

Malatesta, V. J., Pollack, R. H., Wilbanks, W. A., & Adams, H. E. (1979). Alcohol effects on the orgasmic-ejaculatory response of human males. *The Journal of Sex Research, 15,* 101–107.

Maletzky, B. M. (1996). Evolution, psychopathology and sexual offending: Aping our ancestors. *Aggression and violent behavior, 1,* 369–373.

Maletzky, B. M. (1998). On the Offensive. *Sexual Abuse: A Journal of Research and Treatment, 10,* (4) 269–272.

Manderson, L. (1995). The pursuit of pleasure and the sale of sex. In P. R. Abramson & S. D. Pinkerton (Eds.), *Sexual nature/sexual culture* (pp. 305–329). Chicago: University of Chicago Press.

Manlove, J. (1997). Early motherhood in an inter-generational perspective: The experiences of a British cohort. *Journal of Marriage and the Family, 59,* 263–279.

Mann, J. (1977). Retarded ejaculation and treatment. In R. Gemme & C. Wheeler (Eds.), *Progress in sexology* (pp. 197–204). New York: Plenum.

Mansfield, P. K., Koch, P. B., & Voda, A. M. (1998). Qualities midlife women desire in their sexual relationships and their changing sexual response. *Psychology of Women Quarterly, 22,* 285–303.

Marks, M. A., & Nelson, E. S. (1993). Sexual harassment on campus: Effects of professor gender on perception of sexually harassing behaviors. *Sex Roles, 28,* 207–217.

Marmor, J. L. (1954). Some considerations concerning orgasm in the female. *Psychosomatic Medicine, 16,* 240–245.

Marshall, D. (1971). Sexual behavior on Mangaia. In D. Marshall & R. Suggs (Eds.), *Human sexual behavior: Variations in the ethnographic spectrum.* (pp. 103–162). Englewood Cliffs, NJ: Prentice-Hall.

Marshall, P. & Vaillancourt, M. (1993). *Changing the landscape: Ending violence—achieving equality. Final Report of the Canadian Panel on Violence Against Women.* Ottawa, Canada: Minister of Supply and Services.

Marshall, W. L., Eccles, A., & Barbaree, H. E. (1991). The treatment of exhibitionists: A focus on sexual deviance versus cognitive and relationship features. *Behavior Research and Therapy, 29,* 129–135.

Marsiglio, W. (1987). Adolescent fathers in the United States: Their initial living arrangements, marital experience, and educational outcomes. *Family Planning Perspectives, 19,* 240–251.

Marsiglio, W., & Shehan, C. L. (1993). Adolescent males' abortion attitudes: Data from a national survey. *Family Planning Perspectives, 25,* 162–169.

Martin, T. C., & Bumpass, L. L. (1989). Recent trends in marital disruption. *Demography, 26,* 37–51.

Maslow, A. H. (1962). *Toward a psychology of being.* Princeton: Van Nostrand.

Masters, W. H., & Johnson, V. E. (1966). *Human sexual response.* Boston: Little, Brown.

Masters, W. H., & Johnson, V. E. (1970). *Human sexual inadequacy.* Boston: Little, Brown.

Masters, W. H., & Johnson, V. E. (1979). *Homosexuality in perspective.* Boston: Little, Brown.

Matteson, D. P. (1997). Bisexual and homosexual behavior and HIV risk among Chinese-, Filipino-, and Korean-American men. *The Journal of Sex Research, 34,* 93–104.

Mattson, S., & Smith, J. E. (1993). *Core curriculum for maternal-newborn nursing.* Philadelphia: Saunders.

Mauldon, J., & Luker, K. (1996). The effects of contraceptive education on method use at first intercourse. *Family Planning Perspectives, 28,* 19–24, 41.

McAnulty, R. D. (1995). The paraphilias: Classification and theory. In L. Diamont & R. D. McAnulty (Eds.), *The psychology of sexual orientation, behavior, and identity* (pp. 239–255). Westport, CT: Greenwood Press.

McCabe, M. P., & Delaney, S. M. (1992). An evaluation of therapeutic programs for the treatment of secondary inorgasmia in women. *Archives of Sexual Behavior, 21,* 69–89.

McCahill, T. W, Meyer, L. C., & Fischman, A. M. (1979). *The aftermath of rape.* Lexington, MA: Lexington Books.

McCarthy, B. W. (1993). Relapse prevention strategies and techniques in sex therapy. *Journal of Sex and Marital Therapy, 19,* 142–146.

McCarthy, B. W. (1998). Commentary: Effects of sexual trauma on adult sexuality. *Journal of Sex and Marital Therapy, 24,* 91–92.

McCarthy, J., & McMillan, S. (1990). Patient/partner satisfaction with penile implant surgery. *Journal of Sex Education and Therapy, 16,* 25–37.

McCauley, E. A., & Ehrhardt, A. A. (1977). Role expectations and definitions: A comparison of female transsexuals and lesbians. *Journal of Homosexuality, 3,* 137–147.

McClintock, M. K. (1971). Menstrual synchrony and suppression. *Nature, 299,* 244–245.

McClintock, M. K., & Herdt, G. (1996). Rethinking puberty: The development of sexual attraction. *Current Directions in Psychological Science, 5,* 178–183.

McCormick, N. B. (1979). Come-ons and put-offs: Unmarried students' strategies for having and avoiding sexual intercourse. *Psychology of Women Quarterly, 4,* 194–211.

McCormick, N. B. (1994). *Sexual salvation.* Westport, CT: Greenwood.

McDonald, K., & Parke, R. D. (1986). Parent-child physical play: The effects of sex and age of children and parents. *Sex Roles, 15,* 367–378.

McKusick, V. A., & Amberger, J. A. (1993). The morbid anatomy of the human genome: Chromosomal location of the mutations causing disease. *Journal of Medical Genetics, 30,* 1–26.

McLaren, A. (1981). "Barrenness against nature": Recourse to abortion in pre-industrial England. *The Journal of Sex Research, 17,* 224–237.

McVey, T. B. (1997). Depression among women with hypoactive sexual desire: Orgasm consistency training analysis and effect on treatment outcome. *Canadian Journal of Human Sexuality, 6,* 211–220.

McWhirter, D. P, & Mattison, A. M. (1984). *The male couple: How relationships develop.* Englewood Cliffs, NJ: Prentice-Hall.

Mead, M. (1935). *Sex and temperament in three primitive societies.* New York: Morrow.

Meischke, H. (1995). Implicit sexual portrayals in the movies: Interpretations of young women. *The Journal of Sex Research, 32,* 29–36.

Melnick, S. L., Jeffrey, W. R., Burke, G. L., Gilbertson, D. T., Perkins, L. L., Sidney, S., McCreath, H. E., Wagenknecht, L. E., & Hulley, S. B. (1993). Changes in sexual behavior by young urban heterosexual adults in response to the AIDS epidemic. *Public Health Reports, 108,* 582–588.

Metz, M. E., & Miner, M. H. (1995). Male "menopause," aging, and sexual function: A review. *Sexuality and Disability, 13,* 287–307.

Metz, M. E., & Miner, M. H. (1998). Psychosexual and psychosocial aspects of male aging and sexual health. *The Canadian Journal of Human Sexuality, 7,* 245–259.

Meyer, J. K., & Reter, D. J. (1979). Sex reassignment. *Archives of General Psychiatry, 36,* 1010–1015.

Meyer-Bahlburg, H., Gruen, R. S., New, M. I., Bell, J. J., Morishima, A., Shimski, M., Bueno, Y., Vargas, I., &

Baker, S. W. (1996). Gender change from female to male in classical congenital adrenal hyperplasia. *Hormones and Behavior, 30,* 319–322.

Michaud, S. L., & Warner, R. M. (1997). Gender differences in self-reported response to troubles talk. *Sex Roles, 37,* 527–540.

Mickler, S. E. (1993). Perceptions of vulnerability: Impact on AIDS-preventive behavior among college adolescents. *AIDS Education and Prevention, 5,* 43–53.

Milic, J. H., & Crowne, D. P. (1986). Recalled parent-child relations and need for approval of homosexual and heterosexual men. *Archives of Sexual Behavior, 15,* 239–246.

Millar, W. J., Wadhera, S., & Henshaw, S. K. (1997). Repeat abortions in Canada, 1975–1993. *Family Planning Perspectives, 29,* 20–24.

Miller, B. C., Christopherson, C. R., & King, P. K. (1993). Sexual behavior in adolescence. In T. S. Gullotta, G. R. Adams, & R. Montemayor (Eds.), *Adolescent sexuality* (pp. 57–76). Newbury Park, CA: Sage.

Miller, J., & Schwartz, M. D. (1995). Rape myths and violence against street prostitutes. *Deviant Behavior: An Interdisciplinary Journal, 16,* 1–23.

Miller, M. V. (1977). Intimate terrorism. *Psychology Today, 10,* 79–80, 82.

Miller, M. V. (1995). *Intimate terrorism.* New York: Norton.

Miller, W. B. (1986). Why some women fail to use their contraceptive method: A psychological investigation. *Family Planning Perspectives, 18,* 27–32.

Miller, W. B. (1992). An empirical study of the psychological antecedents and consequences of induced abortion. *Journal of Social Issues, 48* (3), 67–93.

Miner, H. (1956). Body ritual among the Nacirema. *American Anthropologist, 58,* 503–507.

Misovich, S. J., Fisher, J. D., & Fisher, W. A. (1996). The perceived AIDS preventive utility of knowing one's sexual partner well: A public health dictum and individuals' risky sexual behavior. *The Canadian Journal of Human Sexuality, 5,* 83–90.

Money, J. (1988). *Gay, straight, and in-between: The sexology of erotic orientation.* New York: Oxford University Press.

Money, J. (1991). *Genes, genitals, hormones, and gender: Selected readings in sexology.* Amsterdam, Holland: Global Academic.

Money, J., & Ehrhardt, A. A. (1972). *Man and woman, boy and girl.* Baltimore, MD: Johns Hopkins University Press.

Money, J., & Tucker, P. (1975). *Sexual signatures: On being a man or woman.* Boston: Little, Brown.

Monsour, M., Harris, B., Kurzweil, N., & Beard, C. (1994). Challenges confronting cross-sex friendships: "Much ado about nothing?" *Sex Roles, 31,* 55–77.

Montagu, A. (1969). *Sex, man, and society.* New York: Tower.

Monto, M., Zgourides, G., & Harris, R. (1998). Empathy, self-esteem, and the adolescent sex offender. *Sexual Abuse: A Journal of Research and Treatment, 10,* 127–140.

Moore, K., & Caldwell, S. B. (1977). *Out-of-wedlock childbearing.* Washington, DC: Urban Institute.

Moore, K. L. (1989). *Before we are born* (3rd ed.). Philadelphia: Saunders.

Moore, M. (1998). The science of sexual signaling. In G. G. Brannigan, E. R. Allgeier, & A. R. Allgeier (Eds.), *The sex scientists* (pp. 61–75). New York: Longman.

Moore, M. M. (1985). Nonverbal courtship patterns in women: Context and consequences. *Ethology and Sociobiology, 6,* 201–212.

Moore, M. M. (1995). Courtship signaling and adolescents: "Girls just wanna have fun"? *The Journal of Sex Research, 32,* 319–328.

Morokoff, P. J., & Gillilland, R. (1993). Stress, sexual functioning, and marital satisfaction. *The Journal of Sex Research, 30,* 43–53.

Morse, E. V., Simon, P. M., Balson, P. M., & Osofsky, H. J. (1992). Sexual behavior patterns of customers of male street prostitutes. *Archives of Sexual Behavior, 21,* 347–357.

Moser, C. (1998) S/M (Sadomasochistic) interactions in semi-public settings. *Journal of Homosexuality, 36* (2), 19–29

Mosher, D. L. (1966). The development and multitrait-multimethod matrix analysis of three measures of three aspects of guilt. *Journal of Consulting and Clinical Psychology, 30,* 25–29.

Mosher, D. L. (1988). Revised Mosher guilt inventory. In C. M. Davis,, W. L. Yarber, & S. Davis (Eds.), *Sexuality-related measures: A compendium* (pp. 152–155). Lake Mills, IA: Authors.

Mosher, D. L., & Sirkin, M. (1984). Measuring a macho personality constellation. *Journal of Research in Personality, 18,* 150–163.

Mosher, W. D., & Bachrach, C. A. (1996). Understanding U.S. fertility: Continuity and change in the National Survey of Family Growth, 1988–1995. *Family Planning Perspectives, 28,* 4–12.

Moskowitz, J. T., Binson, D., & Catania, J. A. (1997). The association between Magic Johnson's HIV serostatus disclosure and condom use in at-risk respondents. *The Journal of Sex Research, 34,* 154–160.

Moss, H. B., Panzak, G. L., & Tarter, R. E. (1993). Sexual functioning of male anabolic steroid abusers. *Archives of Sexual Behavior, 22,* 1–12.

Mott, F. L., Fondell, M. M., Hu, P. N., Kowaleski-Jones, L., & Menaghan, E. G. (1996). The determinants of first sex by age 14 in a high-risk adolescent population. *Family Planning Perspectives, 28,* 13–18.

Muehlenhard, C. L. (1988). "Nice women" don't say yes and "real men" don't say no: How miscommunication and the double standard can cause sexual problems. *Women and Therapy, 7,* 95–108.

Muehlenhard, C. L., Andrews, S. L., & Beal, G. K. (1996). Beyond "just saying no": Dealing with men's unwanted sexual advances in heterosexual dating contexts. *Journal of Psychology and Human Sexuality, 8,* 141–168.

Muehlenhard, C. L., Danoff-Burg, S., & Powch, I. G. (1996). Is rape sex or violence? Conceptual issues and implications. In D. M. Buss & N. M. Malamuth (Eds.), *Sex, power, conflict: Evolutionary and feminist perspectives* (pp. 119–137). New York: Oxford University Press.

Muehlenhard, C. L., & Hollabaugh, L. C. (1988). Do women sometimes say no when they mean yes? The prevalence and correlates of women's token resistance to sex. *Journal of Personality and Social Psychology, 54,* 872–879.

Muehlenhard, C. L. and Rodgers, C. S. (1998). Token resistance to sex: New perspectives on an old stereotype. *Psychology of Women Quarterly, 22,* 443–463.

Munroe, R. L., & Munroe, R. H. (1977). Male transvestism and subsistence economy. *Journal of Social Psychology, 103,* 307–308.

Munroe, R. L., Whiting, J. W. M., & Haley, D. J. (1969). Institutionalized male transvestism and sex distinctions. *American Anthropologist, 71,* 87–91.

Mureau, M. A. M., Slijper, F. M. E., Slob, A. K., & Verhulst, F. C. (1995). Genital perception of children, adolescents, and adults operated on for hypospadias: A comparative study. *The Journal of Sex Research, 32,* 289–298.

Murnen, S. K., & Byrne, D. (1991). Hyperfemininity: Measurement and initial validation of the construct. *The Journal of Sex Research, 28,* 479–489.

Murrell, A. J., Olson, J. E., & Frieze, I. H. (1995). Sexual harassment and gender discrimination: A longitudinal study of women managers. *Journal of Social Issues, 51* (1), 139–149.

Mynatt, C. R., & Allgeier, E. R. (1990). Risk factors, self-attributions, and adjustment problems among victims of sexual coercion. *Journal of Applied Social Psychology, 20,* 130–153.

Nahmias, J., Weis, J., Yao, X., Lee, F., Kodsi, R., Schanfield, M. Matthews, T., Bolognesi, D. Durack, D., Motulsky, A., Kanki, P., & Essex, M. (1986). Evidence for human infection with an HTLV III/LAV-like virus in Central Africa, 1959. *Lancet, 1,* 1279–1280.

Nakagawa, M., Lamb, M. E., & Miaki, K. (1992). Antecedents and correlates of the strange situation behavior of Japanese infants. *Journal of Cross-Cultural Psychology, 23,* 300–310.

Nathanson, B. N. (1979). *Aborting America.* New York: Doubleday.

Neidigh, L., & Krop, H. (1992). Cognitive distortions among child sexual offenders. *Journal of Sex Education and Therapy, 18,* 208–215.

Neinstein, L., Goldering, J., & Carpenter, F. (1984). Non-sexual transmission of sexually transmitted diseases: An infrequent occurrence. *Pediatrics, 74,* 67–76.

Ness, R. B., Grisso, J. A., Hirschinger, N., Morkovic, N., Shaw, L. M., Day, N. L., & Kline, J. (1999). Cocaine and tobacco use and the risk of spontaneous abortion. *New England Journal of Medicine, 340,* 333–339.

Newcomb, M. D. (1985). The role of perceived relative parent personality in the development of heterosexuals, homosexuals, and transvestites. *Archives of Sexual Behavior, 14,* 147–164.

Newcomb, M. D. (1986). Sexual behavior of cohabitors: A comparison of three independent samples. *The Journal of Sex Research, 22,* 492–513.

Newman, G., & Nichols, C. R. (1960). Sexual activities and attitudes in older persons. *Journal of the American Medical Association, 173,* 33–35.

Nicks, S. D. (1996). Fear in academia: Concern over unmerited accusations of sexual harassment. *Journal of Psychology, 130,* 79–82.

Niku, S. D., Stock, J. A., & Kaplan, G. W. (1995). Neonatal circumcision. *Common Problems in Pediatric Urology, 21,* 57–65.

Norman, C. (1986). Sex and needles, not insects and pigs, spread AIDS in Florida town. *Science, 234,* 415–417.

Norton, A. J., & Moorman, J. E. (1987). Current trends in marriage and divorce among American women. *Journal of Marriage and the Family, 49,* 3–14.

Norton, J. (1999). Invisible man: A queer critique of feminist anti-pornography theory. *Sexuality & Culture, 2,* 113–124.

Noseworthy, C. M., & Lott, A. J. (1984). The cognitive organization of gender-stereotypic categories. *Personality and Social Psychology Bulletin, 10,* 474–481.

Novak, M. A., & Harlow, H. F. (1975). Social recovery of monkeys isolated for the first year of life. *Developmental Psychology, 11,* 453–465.

Offir, J. T., Fisher, J. D., Williams, S. S., & Fisher, W. A. (1993). Reasons for inconsistent AIDS-preventative behaviors among gay men. *The Journal of Sex Research, 30,* 62–69.

Okami, P. (1990). Sociopolitical biases in the contemporary scientific literature on adult human sexual behavior with children and adolescents. In J. Feierman (Ed.), *Pedophilia: Bio-social dimensions* (pp. 91–121). New York: Springer-Verlag.

Okami, P. (1995). Childhood exposure to nudity, parent-child co-sleeping, and "primal scenes": A review of clinical opinion and empirical evidence. *The Journal of Sex Research, 32,* 51–64.

Okami, P., & Goldberg, A. (1992). Personality correlates of pedophilia: Are they reliable indicators? *The Journal of Sex Research, 29,* 297–328.

Okami, P., Olmstead, R., & Abramson, P. R. (1997). Sexual experiences in early childhood: 18-year longitudinal data from the UCLA Lifestyles Project. *The Journal of Sex Research, 34,* 339–347.

Okami, P., Olmstead, R., Abramson, P. R., & Pendleton, L. (1998). Early childhood exposure to parental nudity and scenes of parental sexuality ("Primal Scenes"): An 18-year longitudinal study of outcome. *Archives of Sexual Behavior, 27,* 361–384.

Olds, J., & Milner, P. M. (1954). Positive reinforcement produced by electrical stimulation of the septal area and other regions of the rat brain. *Journal of Comparative and Physiological Psychology, 47,* 419–427.

Olds, S. B., London, M. L., & Ladewig, P. W. (1992). *Maternal-newborn nursing* (4th ed.). Redwood City, CA: Addison-Wesley Nursing.

Oliver, M. B., & Hyde, J. S. (1993). Gender differences in sexuality: A meta-analysis. *Psychological Bulletin, 114,* 29–51.

Olson, D. H., & DeFrain, J. (1994). *Marriage and the family: Diversity and strengths.* Mountain View, CA: Mayfield.

O'Sullivan, L. F., & Allgeier, E. R. (1994). Dissembling a stereotype: Gender differences in the use of token resistance. *Journal of Applied Social Psychology, 24,* 1035–1055.

O'Sullivan, L. F., & Allgeier, E. R. (1998). Feigning sexual desire: Consenting to unwanted sexual activity in heterosexual dating relationships. *The Journal of Sex Research, 35,* 234–243.

O'Sullivan, L. F., & Byers, E. S. (1992). Incorporating the roles of initiation and restriction in sexual dating interactions. *The Journal of Sex Research, 29,* 435–446.

Otis, M. D., & Skinner, W. F. (1996). The prevalence of victimization and its effect on mental well-being among lesbian and gay people. *Journal of Homosexuality, 30,* 93–121.

Padgett, V. R., Brislin-Slutz, J. A., & Neal, J. A. (1989). Pornography, erotica, and attitudes toward women: The effects of repeated exposure. *The Journal of Sex Research, 26,* 479–491.

Paglia, C. (1998, March 23). A call for lustiness. *Time,* p. 54.

Paige, K. E. (1978). The ritual of circumcision. *Human Nature, 1,* 40–48.

Palson, C., & Palson, R. (1972). Swinging in wedlock. *Transaction* (formerly *Society*), *9,* 28–37.

Parcell, S. R., & Kanin, E. J. (1976, September). *Male sex aggression: A survey of victimized college women.* Paper presented at the Second International Symposium on Victimology, Boston, MA.

Paris, J. (1992). Dhat: The semen loss anxiety syndrome. *Transcultural Psychiatric Research Review, 29,* 109–118.

Parke, R. D., & O'Leary, S. E. (1976). Father-mother-infant interaction in the newborn period: Some findings, some observations, and some unresolved issues. In K. Riegel & J. Meachem (Eds.), *The developing individual in a changing world: Social and environmental issues*, Vol. 2 (pp. 653–663). The Hague, Holland: Mouton.

Parker, R. (1991). *Bodies, pleasures, and passions: Sexual culture in contemporary Brazil*. Boston: Beacon.

Patai, D. (1998). The making of a social problem: Sexual harassment on campus. *Sexuality and Culture, 1*, 219–256.

Patrick, D. M. (1997). Chlamydia control: Components of an effective control strategy to reduce the incidence of chlamydia trachomatis. *Canadian Journal of Human Sexuality, 6*, 143–150.

Paulozzi, L. J., Erickson, J. D., & Jackson, R. J. (1997). Hypospadias trends in two U.S. surveillance systems. *Pediatrics, 100*, 831–834.

Pauly, I. B. (1974). Female transsexualism: Part II. *Archives of Sexual Behavior, 3*, 509–526.

Pauly, I. B. (1985). Gender identity disorders. In M. Farber (Ed.), *Human sexuality: Psychosexual effects of disease* (pp. 295–316). New York: Macmillan.

Pauly, I. B. (1990). Gender identity disorders: Evaluation and disorders: Evaluation and treatment. *Journal of Sex Education and Therapy, 16*, 2–24.

Pauly, I. B., & Edgerton, M. T. (1986). The gender identity movement: A growing surgical-psychiatric liaison. *Archives of Sexual Behavior, 15*, 315–330.

Pavelka, M. S. M. (1995). Sexual nature: What can we learn from a cross-species perspective? In P. R. Abramson & S. D. Pinkerton (Eds.), *Sexual nature/sexual culture* (pp. 17–36). Chicago: University of Chicago Press.

Pearson, S. E., & Pollack, R. H. (1997). Female response to sexually explicit films. *Journal of Psychology and Human Sexuality, 9* (2), 73–88.

Peele, S., & Brodsky, A. (1975). *Love and addiction*. New York: Maplinger.

Pelletier, L. A., & Herold, E. S. (1988). The relationship of age, sex guilt, and sexual experience with female sexual fantasies. *The Journal of Sex Research, 24*, 250–256.

Pendergrast, M. (1995). *Victims of memory: Incest accusations and shattered lives*. Hinesburg, VT: Upper Access.

Peplau, L. A., Garnets, L. D., Spalding, L. R., Conley, T. D., & Veniegas, R. C. (1998). A critique of Bem's "Exotic Becomes Erotic" theory of sexual orientation. *Psychological Review, 105*, 387–394.

Peplau, L. A., & Gordon, S. L. (1983). The intimate relationships of lesbians and gay men. In E. R. Allgeier & N. B. McCormick (Eds.), *Changing boundaries: Gender roles and sexual behavior* (pp. 226–244). Palo Alto, CA: Mayfield.

Peplau, L. A., Rubin, Z., & Hill, C. T. (1977). Sexual intimacy in dating relationships. *Journal of Social Issues, 33* (2), 86–109.

Perlow, D. L., & Perlow, J. S. (1983). *Herpes: Coping with the new epidemic*. Englewood Cliffs, NJ: Prentice-Hall.

Perper, T. (1985). *Sex signals: The biology of love*. Philadelphia: ISI Press.

Perry, E. L., Kulik, C.T., & Schmidtke, J. M. (1998). Individual differences in the effectiveness of sexual harassment training. *Journal of Applied Social Psychology, 28*, 698–723.

Perry, E. L., Schmidtke, J. M., & Kulik, C. T. (1998). Propensity to sexually harass: An exploration of gender differences. *Sex Roles, 38*, 443–460.

Perry, J. D., & Whipple, B. (1982). Multiple components of female orgasm. In B. Graber (Ed.), *Circumvaginal musculature and sexual function* (pp. 101–114). New York: Karger.

Peterson, H. B., Xia, Z., Hughes, J. M., Wilcox, L. S., Tylor, L. R., & Trussell, J. (1997). The risk of ectopic pregnancy after tubal sterilization. *New England Journal of Medicine, 336*, 762–767.

Pfäfflin, F. (1992). Regrets after sex reassignment surgery. *Journal of Psychology and Human Sexuality, 5*, 69–85.

Pfeiffer, E., Verwoerdt, A., & Wang, H. (1968). Sexual behavior in aged men and women. *Archives of General Psychiatry, 19*, 756–758.

Phillips, G., & Over, R. (1992). Adult sexual orientation in relation to memories of childhood gender-conforming and gender-nonconforming behaviors. *Archives of Sexual Behavior, 21*, 543–558.

Phillips, G., & Over, R. (1995). Differences between heterosexual, bisexual, and lesbian women in recalled childhood experiences. *Archives of Sexual Behavior, 24*, 1–20.

Pierce, C. A., & Aquinis, H. (1997). Bridging the gap between romantic relationships and sexual harassment in organizations. *Journal of Organizational Behavior, 18*, 197–200.

Pierce, C. A., Byrne, D., & Aquinis, H. (1996). Attraction in organizations: A model of workplace romance. *Journal of Organizational Behavior, 17*, 5–32.

Pithers, W. D. (1993). Treatment of rapists: Reinterpretation of early outcome data and exploratory constructs to chance therapeutic efficacy. In G. C. Hall, R. Hirschman, J. R. Graham, & M. S. Zaragosa (Eds.), *Sexual aggression: Issues in etiology, assessment, and treatment* (pp. 167–196). Bristol, PA: Taylor & Francis.

Planned Parenthood Today. (1997, Fall–Winter). New contraceptive in clinical trials. *Planned Parenthood Today*, p. 3.

Pleck, J. (1983). Husband's paid work and family roles. In H. Lopata & J. Pleck (Eds.), *Research in the interweave of social roles, Vol. 3. Families and jobs* (pp. 251–333). Greenwich, CT: JAI Press.

Ploem, C., & Byers, E. S. (1997). The effects of two AIDS risk-reduction strategies on heterosexual college women's AIDS-related knowledge, attitudes, and condom use. *Journal of Psychology and Human Sexuality, 9* (1), 1–24.

Pocket Criminal Code. (1987). Toronto: Carswell.

Pomeroy, W. (1972). *Dr. Kinsey and the Institute for Sex Research*. New York: Nelson.

Pope, K. S., & Bouhoutsos, J. C. (1987). *Sexual intimacy between therapists and patients.* New York: Praeger.

Pope, K. S., Keith-Spiegel, P., & Tabachnick, B. G. (1986). Sexual attraction to clients: The human therapist and the (sometimes) inhuman training system. *American Psychologist, 41,* 147–158.

Pope, K. S., Levenson, H., & Schover, L. (1979). Sexual intimacy in psychology training: Results and implications of a national survey. *American Psychologist, 34,* 682–689.

Pope, K. S., Sonne, J. L., & Holroyd, J. (1993). *Sexual feelings in psychotherapy.* Washington, DC: American Psychological Association.

Popovich, P. M., Gehlauf, N. N., Jolton, J. A., Everton, W. J., Godinho, R. M., Mastrangelo, P. M., & Somers, J. V. (1996). Physical attractiveness and sexual harassment: Does every picture tell a story or every story draw a picture? *Journal of Applied Social Psychology, 26,* 520–542.

Possage, J. C., & Allgeier, E. R. (1992, June). *The relationship between recidivism and child sexual misuse from a learned helplessness perspective.* Paper presented at The Annual Meeting of the Midcontinent Region of The Society for the Scientific Study of Sex, Big Rapids, MI.

Potter, G. (1989). The retail pornography industry and the organization of vice. *Deviant Behavior, 10,* 233–251.

Potter, R. H. (1999). Long-term consumption of "X-rated" materials and attitudes toward women among Australian consumers of X-rated videos. *Sexuality & Culture, 2,* 61–85.

Potterat, J. J., Woodhouse, D. E., Muth, J. B., & Muth, S. Q. (1990). Estimating the prevalence and career longevity of prostitute women. *The Journal of Sex Research, 27,* 233–243.

Powell-Griner, E. (1987). Induce terminations of pregnancy: Reporting states, 1984. *Monthly Vital Statistics Report, 36,* Supplement 2.

Prasad, S. (1993, February 25). India asks moms to abandon babies, not kill them. *Bowling Green Sentinel Tribune,* p. 10.

Prendergast, W. E. (1994). Prisons: Sex in prison. In V. L. Bullough & B. Bullough (Eds.), *Human sexuality: An encyclopedia* (pp. 488–493). New York: Garland.

Prescott, J. W. (1975, April). Body pleasure and the origins of violence. *The Futurist,* 64–74.

Presser, H. B. (1974). Early motherhood: Ignorance or bliss? *Family Planning Perspectives, 6,* 8–14.

Presser, H. B. (1980). *The social and demographic consequences of teenage childbearing for urban woman.* (Final report to NICHD). Washington, DC: National Technical Information Service.

Prince, V. (1977, September). *Sexual identity versus general identity: The real confusion.* Paper presented at the Meeting of the American Psychological Association, Toronto, Canada.

Prins, K. S., Buunk, B. P., & Van Yperen, N. W. (1993). Equity, normative disapproval, and extramarital relationships. *Journal of Social and Personal Relationships, 10,* 39–53.

Pryor, J. B. (1987). Sexual harassment proclivities in men. *Sex Roles, 17,* 269–270.

Pryor, J. B., Giedd, J. L., & Williams, K. R. (1995). A social psychological model for predicting sexual harassment. *Journal of Social Issues, 51* (1), 69–84.

Pryor, J. B., LaVite, C., & Stoller, L. (1993). A social psychological analysis of sexual harassment: The person/situation interaction. *Journal of Vocational Behavior, 42,* 68–83.

Purifoy, F. E., Grodsky, A., & Giambra, L. M. (1992). The relationship of sexual daydreaming to sexual activity, sexual drive, and sexual attitudes for women across the life-span. *Archives of Sexual Behavior, 21,* 369–385.

Quinsey, V. L., & Upfold, D. (1985). Rape completion and victim injury as a function of female resistance strategy. *Canadian Journal of Behavioural Science, 17,* 40–50.

Quittner, J. (1998, May 18). Boogie sites. *Time,* p. 35.

Rachman, S. (1966). Sexual fetishism: An experimental analogue. *Psychological Record, 16,* 293–295.

Rainwater, L., & Weinstein, K. (1960). *And the poor get children.* Chicago: Quadrangle.

Rapaport, K., & Burkhart, B. R. (1984). Personality and attitudinal correlates of sexually coercive college males. *Journal of Abnormal Personality, 93,* 216–221.

Rates of Cesarean delivery—United States, 1993. (1995). *Morbidity and Mortality Weekly Reports, 44,* 303–307.

Read, J. S., & Klebanoff, M. A. for the Vaginal Infections and Prematurity Study Group. (1993). Sexual intercourse during pregnancy and preterm delivery: Effects of vaginal microorganisms. *American Journal of Obstetrics and Gynecology, 168,* 514–519.

Reamy, K. J., & White, S. E. (1987). Sexuality in the puerperium: A review. *Archives of Sexual Behavior, 16,* 165–186.

Reed, J. (1984). *From private vice to public virtue.* New York: Basic Books.

Refinetti, R. (1998). Sexual harassment, sexual consent, and beyond. *Sexuality and Culture, 1,* 5–17.

Regan, P. C. (1996). Rhythms of desire: The association between menstrual cycle phases and female sexual desire. *The Canadian Journal of Human Sexuality, 5,* 145–156.

Regan, P. C., & Berscheid, E. (1995). Gender differences about the causes of male female sexual desire. *Personal Relationships, 2,* 345–358.

Rehman, J., Lazer, S., Benet, A. E., Schaefer, L. C., & Melman, A. (1999). The reported sex and surgery satisfaction of 28 postoperative male-to-female transsexual patients. *Archives of Sexual Behavior, 28,* 71–89.

Reik, T. (1949). *Of love and lust: On the psychoanalysis of romantic and sexual emotions.* New York: Farrar, Straus, & Giroux.

Reiner, W. (1997). Sex assignment in the neonate with intersex or inadequate genitalia. *Archives of Pediatric and Adolescent Medicine, 151,* 1044–1045.

Reinisch, J. M., Ziemba-Davis, M., & Sanders, S. (1991). Hormonal contributions to sexually dimorphic behavioral development in humans. *Psychoneuroendocrinology, 16,* 213–278.

Reiss, I. L. (1986). *Journey into sexuality: An exploratory voyage.* Englewood Cliffs, NJ: Prentice-Hall.

Reiss, I. L., Anderson, R. E., & Sponaugle, G. C. (1980). A multivariate model of the determinants of extramarital sexual permissiveness. *Journal of Marriage and the Family, 42,* 395–411.

Reiss, I. R. (1997). *Solving America's sexual crisis.* Amherst, NY: Prometheus Books.

Resnik, R., & Calder, A. (1999). Post-term pregnancy. In R. K. Creasy, & M. D. Resnik, (Eds.). *Maternal-fetal medicine* (4th ed.) (pp. 532–539). Philadelphia, PA: W. B. Saunders Company.

Riddle, J. M., Estes, J. W., & Russell, J. C. (1994). Ever since Eve . . . Birth control in the ancient world. *Archaeology, 47* (2), 29–35.

Rind, B. (1995). An analysis of human sexuality textbook coverage of the psychological correlates of adult-nonadult sex. *The Journal of Sex Research, 32,* 219–233.

Rind, B., & Tromovitch, P. (1997). A meta-analytic review of findings from national samples on psychological correlates of child sexual abuse. *The Journal of Sex Research, 34,* 237–255.

Rind, B., Tromovitch, P., & Bauserman, R. (1998). A meta-analytic examination of assumed properties of child sexual abuse using college samples. *Psychological Bulletin, 124,* 22–53.

Robbins, M. B., & Jensen, G. G. (1978). Multiple orgasm in males. *The Journal of Sex Research, 14,* 21–26.

Roberts, J. M. (1999). Pregnancy-related hypertension. In R. K. Creasy, & M. D. Resnik, (Eds.). *Maternal-fetal medicine* (4th ed.) (pp. 833–872). Philadelphia, PA: W. B. Saunders Company.

Robinson, P. A. (1976). *The modernization of sex.* New York: Harper & Row.

Robinson, W. L., & Reid, P. T. (1985). Sexual intimacies in psychology revisited. *Professional Psychology: Research and Practice, 16,* 512–550.

Roche, J. P. (1986). Premarital sex: Attitudes and behavior by dating stage. *Adolescence, 21,* 107–121.

Roche, J. P., & Ramsbey, T. W. (1993). Premarital sexuality: A five-year follow-up study of attitudes and behavior by dating stage. *Adolescence, 28,* 67–80.

Roiphe, H., & Galenson, E. (1981). *Infantile origins of sexual identity.* New York: International Universities Press.

Roiphe, K. (1993). *The morning after: Sex, fear, and feminism on campus.* Boston: Little, Brown.

Romanowski, B. (1997). Syphilis: Epidemiology and control. *Canadian Journal of Human Sexuality, 6,* 171–177.

Ronai, C. R., & Cross, R. (1998). Dancing with identity: Narrative resistance strategies of male and female stripteasers. *Deviant Behavior: An Interdisciplinary Journal, 19,* 99–119.

Roosa, M. W., & Christopher, F. S. (1990). Evaluation of an abstinence-only adolescent pregnancy prevention program: A replication. *Family Relations, 39,* 363–367.

Rosario, M., Meyer-Bahlburg, H. F. L., Hunter, J., Exner, T. M., Gwada, M., & Keller, A. M. (1996). The psychosexual development of urban lesbian, gay, and bisexual youth. *The Journal of Sex Research, 33,* 113–126.

Rosen, R. C. (1991). Alcohol and drug effects on sexual response: Human experimental and clinical studies. *Annual Review of Sex Research, 2,* 119–179.

Rosen, R. C. (1996, June). *Pharmacological treatment of male erectile disorder: Palliative or panacea?* Paper presented at the Annual Meeting of the International Academy of Sex Research, Rotterdam, The Netherlands.

Rosen, R. C., & Ashton, A. K. (1993). Prosocial drugs: Empirical status of the "new aphrodisiacs." *Archives of Sexual Behavior, 22,* 521–543.

Rosenberg, L., Palmer, J. R., Zauber, A. G., Warshaver, M. E., Strom, B. L., Harlap, S., & Shapiro, S. (1994). The relation of vasectomy to the risk of cancer. *American Journal of Epidemiology, 140,* 431–448.

Rosenbleet, C., & Pariente, B. (1973). The prostitution of the criminal law. *American Criminal Law Review, 11,* 373–427.

Rosenfeld, D. S., & Elhajjar, A. J. (1998). Sleepsex: A variant of sleepwalking. *Archives of Sexual Behavior, 27,* 269–278.

Rosenwasser, S. M., Wright, L. S., & Barber, R. B. (1987). The rights and responsibilities of men in abortion situations. *The Journal of Sex Research, 23,* 97–105.

Ross, H., & Taylor, H. (1989). Do boys prefer daddy or his physical style of play? *Sex Roles, 20,* 23–33.

Ross, M. W. (1980). Retrospective distortion in homosexual research. *Archives of Sexual Behavior, 9,* 523–531.

Ross, M. W., & Need, J. A. (1989). Effects of adequacy of gender reassignment surgery on psychological adjustment: A follow-up of fourteen male-to-female patients. *Archives of Sexual Behavior, 18,* 145–153.

Rossi, A. S. (1978). The biosocial side of parenthood. *Human Nature, 1,* 72–79.

Rossi, A. S. (1985). Gender and parenthood. In A. S. Rossi (Ed.). *Gender and the life course* (pp. 161–191). Hawthorne, NY: Aldine.

Rossi, W. (1976). *The sex life of the foot and shoe.* New York: Dutton.

Rowland, D. L., Greenleaf, W. J., Dorfman, L. J., & Davidson, J. M. (1993). Aging and sexual function in men. *Archives of Sexual Behavior, 22,* 545–557.

Rowland, D. L., Kallan, K., & Slob, A. K. (1997). Yohimbine, erectile capacity, and sexual response in men.
Archives of Sexual Behavior, 26, 49–62.

Rubin, A. M., & Adams, J. R. (1986). Outcomes of sexually open marriages. *The Journal of Sex Research, 22,*
311-319.

Russell, D. E. H. (1984). *Sexual exploitation: Rape, child
sexual abuse, and workplace harassment.* Beverly Hills,
CA: Sage.

Russo, N. F., & Dabul, A. J. (1997). The relationship of
abortion to well-being: Do race and religion make a difference? *Professional Psychology: Research and Practice, 28,* 23-31.

Russo, N. F., Horn, J. D., & Schwartz, R. (1992). U.S.
abortion in context: Selected characteristics and motivations of women seeking abortions. *Journal of Social Issues, 48* (3), 183–202.

Rust, P. (1995). *Bisexuality and the challenge to lesbian
politics: Sex, loyalty, and revolution.* New York: New
York University Press.

Rust, P. C. (1993a). "Coming out" in the age of social constructionism: Sexual identity formation among lesbian
and bisexual women. *Gender and Society, 7,* 50–77.

Rust, P. C. (1993b). Neutralizing the political threat of the
marginal woman: Lesbians' beliefs about bisexual
women. *The Journal of Sex Research, 30,* 214–228.

Ryan, A. S. (1997). The resurgence of breastfeeding in the
United States, *Pediatrics, 100,* 99.

Sacks, B. P., Kobelin, C., Castro, M. A., & Frigoletto, F.
(1999). The risks of lowering the Cesarean-delivery rate.
New England Journal of Medicine, 340, 54–57.

Sacks, S. L. (1995). Genital HSV infection and treatment.
Clinical Management of Herpes Viruses. IOS Press.

Saluter, A. F. (1992). Marital status and living arrangements: March 1992. *Current Population Reports,* Series
P20–468.

Sandfort, T. G. M. (1984). Sex in pedophiliac relationships: An empirical investigation among a non-represen-
tative group of boys. *The Journal of Sex Research, 20,*
123–142.

Sandler, B. R. (1990). Sexual harassment: A new issue for
institutions. *Initiatives, 52* (4), 5–10.

Sandler, B. R., & Shoop, R. J. (1997). *Sexual harassment
on campus: A guide for administrators, faculty, and students.* Needham Heights, MA: Allyn and Bacon.

Savitz, L., & Rosen, L. (1988). The sexuality of prostitutes: Sexual enjoyment reported by "streetwalkers."
The Journal of Sex Research, 24, 200–208.

Schiavi, R. C. (1990). Sexuality and aging in men. *Annual
Review of Sex Research, 1,* 227–246.

Schiavi, R. C. (1994). Effect of chronic disease and medication on sexual functioning. In A. S. Rossi (Ed.), *Sexuality across the life course* (pp. 313–339). Chicago:
University of Chicago Press.

Schiavi, R. C., White, D., Mandeli, J., & Levine, A. C.
(1997). Effects of testosterone administration on sexual
behavior and mood in men with erectile dysfunction.
Archives of Sexual Behavior, 26, 231–241.

Schlesselman, J. J. (1990). Oral contraception and breast
cancer. *American Journal of Obstetrics & Gynecology,
163,* 1379–1387.

Schneider, K. T., Swann, S., & Fitzgerald, L. L. (1997). Job-
related and psychological effects of sexual harassment in
the workplace: Empirical evidence from two organizations. *Journal of Applied Psychology, 82,* 401–415.

Schoen, E. J., Anderson, G., Bohon, C., Hinman, F.,
Poland, R., & Wakeman, E. M. (1989). Report of the
task force on circumcision. *Pediatrics, 84,* 388–391.

Scholes, D., Daling, J. R., Stergachis, A. S., Weiss, N. S.,
Wang, S. P., & Grayston, J. T. (1993). Vaginal douching
as a risk factor for acute pelvic inflammatory disease.
Obstetrics and Gynecology, 81, 601–606.

Schott, R. L. (1995). The childhood and family dynamics
of transvestites. *Archives of Sexual Behavior, 24,*
309–327.

Schreiner-Engel, P., & Schiavi, R. C. (1986). Lifetime psychopathology in individuals with low sexual desire.
Journal of Nervous and Mental Disease, 174, 646–651.

Schreurs, K. M. G. (1993). Sexuality in lesbian couples:
The importance of gender. *Annual Review of Sex Research, 4,* 49–66.

Schultz, W. C. M. W., Van De Wiel, H. B. M., Hahn, D. E.
E., &Van Driel, M. F. (1992). Sexuality and cancer in
women. *Annual Review of Sex Research, 3,* 151–200.

Schwanberg, S. L. (1993). Attitudes toward gay and lesbian woman: Instrumentation issues. *Journal of Homosexuality, 26,* 99–136.

Schwartz, S. (1973). Effects of sex guilt and sexual arousal
on the retention of birth control information. *Journal of
Consulting and Clinical Psychology, 41,* 61–64.

Scott, J. E., & Cuvelier, S. J. (1993). Violence and sexual
violence in pornography: Is it really increasing? *Archives
of Sexual Behavior, 22,* 357–371.

Segraves, K. A., Segraves, R. T., & Schoenberg, H. W.
(1987). Use of sexual history to differentiate organic
from psychogenic impotence. *Archives of Sexual Behavior, 16,* 125–137.

Segraves, K. B., & Segraves, R. T. (1991). Multiple phase
sexual dysfunction. *Journal of Sex Education and Therapy, 17,* 153–156.

Segraves, R. T. (1988). Drugs and desire. In S. R. Leiblum
& R. C. Rosen (Eds.), *Sexual desire disorders* (pp.
313–347). New York: Guilford.

Sell, R. L., Wells, J. A., & Wypij, D. (1995). The prevalence of homosexual behavior and attraction in the
United States, the United Kingdom, and France: Results
of national population-based samples. *Archives of Sexual Behavior, 24,* 235–248.

Sensibaugh, C. C., & Allgeier, E. R. (1996). Factors considered by Ohio juvenile court judges in juvenile bypass judgments: A policy-capturing approach. *Politics and the Life Sciences, 15,* 35–47.

Sensibaugh, C. C., Yarab, P. E., & Allgeier, E. R. (1996, May). *Back burner relationships: Another stop on the extradyadic continuum?* Paper presented at the Annual Meeting of The Society for the Scientific Study of Sexuality, Pittsburgh, PA.

Seppa, N. (1997, May). Sexual harassment in the military lingers on. *APA Monitor, 28* (5), 41–42.

Sevely, J. L., & Bennett, J. W. (1978). Concerning female ejaculation and the female prostate. *The Journal of Sex Research, 14,* 1–20.

Severn, J., Belch, G. E., & Belch, M. A. (1990). The effects of sexual and non-sexual advertising appeals and information level on cognitive processing and communication effectiveness. *Journal of Advertising, 19,* 14–22.

Shackelford, T. K., & Larsen, R. J. (1997). Facial asymmetry as indicator of psychological, emotional, and physiological distress. *Journal of Personality and Social Psychology, 72,* 456–466.

Shannon, T. W. (1913). *Self-knowledge and guide to sex instruction: Vital facts of life for all ages.* Marietta, OH: Multikin.

Shaver, P. R., & Hazan, C. (1993). Adult attachment: Theory and research. In W. Jones and D. Perlman (Eds.), *Advances in personal relationships* (Vol. 4, pp. 29–70). London: Kingsley.

Shaver, P. R., & Hazan, C. (1994). Attachment. In A. L. Weber & J. H. Harvey (Eds.), *Perspectives on close relationships* (pp. 110–130). Needham Heights, MA: Allyn & Bacon.

Shaver, P. R., Hazan, C., & Bradshaw, D. (1988). Love as attachment. In R. J. Sternberg & M. L. Barnes (Eds.), *The psychology of love* (pp. 68–99). New Haven: Yale University Press.

Sheets, V. L., Fredendall, L. L., & Claypool, H. M. (1997). Jealousy evocation, partner reassurance, and relationship stability: An exploration of the potential benefits of jealousy. *Evolution and Human Behavior, 18,*387–402.

Shepela, S. T., & Levesque, L. L. (1998). Poisoned waters: Sexual harassment and the college climate. *Sex Roles, 38,* 589–611.

Sherfey, J. (1972). *The nature and evolution of female sexuality.* New York: Random House.

Shew, M. L., Remafedi, G. J., Bearinger, L. H., Faulkner, P. L., Taylor, B. A., Potthoff, S. J., & Resnick, M. D. (1997). The validity of self-reported condom use among adolescents. *Sexually Transmitted Diseases, 24,* 503–510.

Shilts, R. (1987). *And the band played on: Politics, people, and the AIDS epidemic.* New York: St. Martin's.

Shilts, R. (1993). *Conduct unbecoming: Lesbians and gays in the military, Vietnam to the Persian Gulf.* New York: St. Martin's.

Shotland, R. L., & Hunter, B. A. (1995). Women's "token resistant" and compliant sexual behaviors are related to uncertain sexual intentions and rape. *Personality and Social Psychology Bulletin, 21,* 226–236.

Shulman, J. J., & Merritt, C. G. (1976). Postpartum contraception: Subsequent pregnancy, delivery, and abortion rates. *Fertility and Sterility, 27,* 97–103.

Shusterman, L. R. (1979). Predicting the psychological consequences of abortion. *Social Science and Medicine, 13,* 683–689.

Siegelman, M. (1972a). Adjustment of homosexual and heterosexual women. *British Journal of Psychiatry, 120,* 477–481.

Siegelman, M. (1972b). Adjustment of homosexuals and heterosexuals. *Archives of Sexual Behavior, 2,* 9–25.

Siegelman, M. (1987). Empirical input. In L. Diamant (Ed.), *Male and female homosexuality: Psychological approaches* (pp. 33–79). Washington, DC: Hemisphere.

Silverstein, L. B. (1996). Fathering is a feminist issue. *Psychology of Women Quarterly, 20,* 3–37.

Silverstone, B., & Wynter, L. (1975). The effect of introducing a heterosexual living space. *The Gerontologist, 15,* 83–87.

Simon, A. (1998). The relationship between stereotypes of and attitudes toward lesbian and gays. In G. Herek (Ed.), *Stigma and sexual orientation: Understanding prejudice against lesbians, gay men, and bisexuals* (pp. 62–81). Thousand Oaks, CA: Sage.

Simon, P. M., Morse, E. V., Osofsky, H. J., Balson, P. M., & Gaumer, R. (1992). Psychological characteristics of a sample of male street prostitutes. *Archives of Sexual Behavior, 21,* 33–44.

Simon, W., & Gagnon, J. H. (1987). Sexual scripts: Permanence and change. *Archives of Sexual Behavior, 15,* 97–120.

Simpson, M., & Schill, T. (1977). Patrons of massage parlors: Some facts and figures. *Archives of Sexual Behavior, 6,* 521–525.

Singelis, T., Choo, P., & Hatfield, E. (1995). Love schemas and romantic love. *Journal of Social Behavior and Personality, 10,* 15–36.

Singelis, T., Levine, T., Hatfield, E., Bachman, G., Muto, K., & Choo, P. (1997). *Love schemas, preferences in romantic partners, and reactions to commitment.* Unpublished manuscript. University of Hawaii, Honolulu.

Singer, J., & Singer, I. (1978). Types of female orgasm. In J. LoPiccolo & L. LoPiccolo (Eds.), *Handbook of sex therapy* (pp. 175–186). New York: Plenum.

Singh, D. (1994). Is thin really beautiful and good? Relationship between waist-to-hip ratio (WHR) and female attractiveness. *Personality and Individual Differences, 16,* 123–132.

Sipe, A. W. R. (1995). *Sex, priests, and power: Anatomy of a crisis.* New York: Brunner/Mazel.

Sly, D. S., Quadagno, D., Harrison, D. F., Eberstein, I. W., Riehman, K., & Bailey, M. (1997). Factors associated with the use of the female condom. *Family Planning Perspectives, 29,* 181–184.

Smith, M. D., & Hand, C. (1987). The pornography/aggression linkage: Results from a field study. *Deviant Behavior, 8,* 389–399.

Smith, M. U., & Katner, H. P. (1995). Quasi-experimental evaluation of three AIDS prevention activities for maintaining knowledge, improving attitudes, and changing risk behaviors of high school seniors. *AIDS Education and Prevention, 7,* 391–402.

Smith, T. W. (1987). The polls—a review: The use of public opinion data by the attorney general's commission on pornography. *Public Opinion Quarterly, 51,* 249–267.

Smith, T. W. (1991). Adult sexual behavior in 1989: Number of partners, frequency of intercourse, and risk of AIDS. *Family Planning Perspectives, 23,* 102–107.

Smithyman, S. D. (1979). Characteristics on "undetected" rapists. In W. H. Parsonage (Ed.), *Perspectives on victimology* (pp. 99–120). Beverly Hills, CA: Sage.

Somers, A. (1982). Sexual harassment in academe: Legal issues and definitions. *Journal of Social Issues, 38* (4), 23–32.

Sonne, J., Meyer, C. B., Borys, D., & Marshall, Y. (1985). Clients' reactions to sexual intimacy in therapy. *American Journal of Orthopsychiatry, 55,* 183–189.

Spector, I. P., & Carey, M. P. (1990). Incidence and prevalence of sexual dysfunctions: A critical review of the empirical literature. *Archives of Sexual Behavior, 19,* 389–408.

Spector, I. P., & Fremeth, S. M. (1996). Sexual behaviors and attitudes of geriatric residents in long-term care facilities. *Journal of Sex and Marital Therapy, 22,* 235–246.

Spengler, A. (1977). Manifest sadomasochism of males: Results of an empirical study. *Archives of Sexual Behavior, 6,* 441–456.

Spitz, R. A. (1947). Hospitalism: A follow-up report. In D. Fenichel, P. Greenacre, & A. Freud (Eds.), *Psychoanalytic studies of the child* (Vol. 2, pp. 113–117). New York: International Universities Press.

Sprague, J., & Quadagno, D. (1989). Gender and sexual motivation: An exploration of two assumptions. *Journal of Psychology and Human Sexuality, 2,* 57–76.

Sprecher, S., Barbee, A., & Schwartz, P. (1995). "Was it good for you, too?": Gender differences in first sexual intercourse experiences. *The Journal of Sex Research, 32,* 3–15.

Sprecher, S., & McKinney, K. (1994). Sexuality in close relationships. In A. L. Weber & J. H. Harvey (Eds.), *Perspectives on close relationships* (pp. 193–216). Boston: Allyn & Bacon.

Springer, N. P., & van Weel, C. (1996). Home birth: Safe in selected women, and with adequate infrastructure support. *British Medical Journal, 313,* 1276–1277.

Stack, S., & Gundlach, J. H. (1992). Divorce and sex. *Archives of Sexual Behavior, 21,* 359–67.

Stake, J. E., & Oliver, J. (1991). Sexual contact and touching between therapist and client: A survey of psychologists' attitudes and behavior. *Professional Psychology: Research and Practice, 22,* 297–307.

Steben, M., & Sacks, S. L. (1997). Genital herpes: The epidemiology and control of a common sexually transmitted disease. *Canadian Journal of Human Sexuality, 6,* 127–134.

Stein, M. L. (1974). *Lovers, friends, slaves . . . : The nine male sexual types, their psycho-sexual transactions with call girls.* New York: Berkley.

Steinem, G. (1994). *Moving beyond words.* New York: Simon & Schuster.

Steiner, B. W. (1985). The management of patients with gender disorders. In B. W. Steiner (Ed.), *Gender dysphoria: Development, research, management* (pp. 325–350). New York: Plenum.

Stern, M., & Karraker, K. H. (1989). Sex stereotyping in infants: A review of gender labeling. *Sex Roles, 20,* 501–522.

Sternberg, K. J., & Lamb, M. L. (1992). Evaluations of attachment relationships by Jewish Israeli day-care providers. *Journal of Cross-Cultural Psychology, 23,* 285–299.

Sternberg, R. J. (1986). A triangular theory of love. *Psychological Review, 93,* 119–135.

Sternberg, R. J. (with C. Whitney). (1991). *Love the way you want it: Using your head in matters of the heart.*

Sternberg, S. (1998, July 23). Scientists disturbed by slow pace. *USA Today,* pp. 1D–2D.

Stevens, C. E., Taylor, P. E., Pindyck, J., Choo, Q. L., Bradley, D. W., Kuo, G., & Houghton, M. (1990). Epidemiology of hepatitis C virus: A preliminary study in volunteer blood donors. *Journal of the American Medical Association, 263,* 49–53.

Stevenson, M. R. (1998). Reconciling sexual orientation. In G. G. Brannigan, E. R. Allgeier, & A. R. Allgeier (Eds.), *The sex scientists* (pp. 100–112). Boston: Addison Wesley Longman.

Stevenson, M. R., & Gajarsky, W. M. (1991). Unwanted childhood sexual experiences relate to later revictimization and male perpetration. *Journal of Psychology and Human Sexuality, 4,* 57–70.

Stewart, F. (1998). Vaginal barriers. In R. A. Hatcher, J. Trussell, F. Stewart, W. Cates, Jr., G. K. Stewart, F. Guest, & D. Kowal (Eds.), *Contraceptive technology* (17th ed.) (pp. 371–404). New York: Ardent Media.

Stewart, G. K. (1998). Intrauterine devices (IUDs). In R. A. Hatcher, J. Trussell, F. Stewart, W. Cates, Jr., G. K. Stewart, F. Guest, & D. Kowal (Eds.), *Contraceptive technology* (17th ed.) (pp. 511–543). New York: Ardent Media.

Stewart, G. K., & Carignan, C. S. (1998). Female and male sterilization. In R. A. Hatcher, J. Trussell, F. Stewart, W. Cates, Jr., G. K. Stewart, F. Guest, & D. Kowal (Eds.), *Contraceptive technology* (17th ed.) (pp. 545–588). New York: Ardent Media.

Stock, W. E. (1982, November). *The effect of violent pornography on women.* Paper presented at the National Meeting of the Society for The Scientific Study of Sex, San Francisco, CA.

Stockdale, M. S., & Vaux, A. (1993). What sexual harassment experiences lead respondents to acknowledge being sexually harassed? A secondary analysis of a university survey. *Journal of Vocational Behavior, 43,* 221–234.

Stokes, J. P., Damon, W., & McKirnan, D. J. (1997). Predictors of movement toward homosexuality: A longitudinal study of bisexual men. *The Journal of Sex Research, 34,* 304–312.

Stokes, J. P., McKirnan, D. J., Doll, L., & Burzette, R. G. (1996). Female partners of bisexual men. *Psychology of Women Quarterly, 20,* 267–284.

Stoller, R. J. (1977). Sexual deviations. In F. A. Beach (Ed.), *Human sexuality in four perspectives* (pp. 190–214). Baltimore, MD: Johns Hopkins University Press.

Storms, M. D. (1980). Theories of sexual orientation. *Journal of Personality and Social Psychology, 38,* 783–792.

Storms, M. D. (1981). A theory of erotic orientation development. *Psychological Review, 88,* 340–353.

Strassberg, D. S., & Lowe, K. (1995). Volunteer bias in sexuality research. *Archives of Sexual Behavior, 24,* 369–382.

Strassberg, D. S., & Lockerd, L. K. (1998). Force in women's sexual fantasies. *Archives of Sexual Behavior, 27,* 403–414.

Strassberg, D. S., & Mahoney, J. M. (1988). Correlates of the contraceptive behavior of adolescents/young adults. *The Journal of Sex Research, 25,* 531–536.

Strassberg, D. S., Mahoney, J. M., Schangaard, M., & Hale, V. E. (1990). The role of anxiety in premature ejaculation: A psychophysiological model. *Archives of Sexual Behavior, 19,* 251–257.

Striegel-Moore, R. H., Goldman, S. L., Garvin, V., & Rodin, J. (1996). A prospective study of somatic and emotional symptoms of pregnancy. *Psychology of Women Quarterly, 20,* 393-408.

Stroh, M. (1996, September 1). Girls who offer sex upset Japan. *Los Angeles Times,* p. 1.

Stroup, A. L., & Pollock, G. E. (1999). Economic consequences of marital dissolution for Hispanics. *Journal of Divorce and Remarriage, 30,* 149–166.

Struckman-Johnson, C. (1988). Forced sex on dates: It happens to men, too. *The Journal of Sex Research, 24,* 234–241.

Struckman-Johnson, C., & Struckman-Johnson, D. (1994). Men pressured and forced into sexual experience. *Archives of Sexual Behavior, 23,* 93–114.

Struckman-Johnson, C., Struckman-Johnson, D., Rucker, L., Bumby, K., & Donaldson, S. (1996). Sexual coercion reported by men and women in prison. *The Journal of Sex Research, 33,* 67–76.

Strum, S. C. (1975). New insights into baboon behavior: Life with the pumphouse game. *National Geographic, 147,* 627–691.

Stuart, F. M., Hammond, D. C., & Pett, M. A. (1987). Psychological characteristics of women with inhibited sexual desire. *Journal of Sex and Marital Therapy, 12,* 108–115.

Suomi, S. J., & Harlow, H. F. (1971). Abnormal social behavior in young monkeys. In J. Hellmuth (Ed.), *Exceptional infant: Studies in abnormality* (Vol. 2, pp. 483–529). New York: Brunner/Mazel.

Suomi, S. J., Harlow, H. F., & McKinney, W. T. (1972). Monkey psychiatrists. *American Journal of Psychiatry, 128,* 41–46.

Swaab, D. F., Gooren, L. J. G., & Hofman, M. A. (1995). Brain research, gender, and sexual orientation. *Journal of Homosexuality, 28,* 283–301.

Sweat, M. D., & Lein, M. (1995). HIV/AIDS knowledge among the U.S. population. *AIDS Education and Prevention, 7,* 355– 372.

Symons, D. (1979). *The evolution of human sexuality.* New York: Oxford University Press.

Szasz, T. (1990). *Sex by prescription.* Syracuse, NY: Syracuse University Press.

Taddio, A., Stevens, B., Craig, K., Rastogi, P., Ben-David, S., Shennan, A., Mulligan, P., & Koran, G. (1997). Efficacy and safety of lidocaine-prilocaine cream during circumcision. *New England Journal of Medicine, 336,* 1197–1201.

Tamminen, J. M. (1994). *Sexual harassment in the workplace: Managing corporate policy.* New York: Wiley.

Tanfer, K., Cubbins, L. A., & Billy, J. O. G. (1995). Gender, race, class, and self-reported sexually transmitted disease incidence. *Family Planning Perspectives, 27,* 196–202.

Tanfer, K., Grady, W. R., Klepinger, D. H., & Billy, J. O. G. (1993). Condom use among U.S. men, 1991. *Family Planning Perspectives, 25,* 61–66.

Tannen, D. (1990). *You just don't understand: Women and men in conversation.* New York: William Morrow.

Tanner, W. M., & Pollack, R. H. (1988). The effect of condom use and erotic instructions on attitudes toward condoms. *The Journal of Sex Research, 25,* 537–541.

Tasker, F. L., & Golombok, S. (1997). *Growing up in a lesbian family.* New York: Guilford Publications, Inc.

Telljohann, S. K., & Price, J. H. (1993). A qualitative examination of adolescent homosexuals' life experiences: Ramification for secondary school personnel. *Journal of Homosexuality, 26,* 41–56.

Tennov, D. (1979). *Love and limerence.* New York: Stein & Day.

Tepper, M. L., & Gully, P. R. (1997). Lovers and liars: Hepatitis B as an STD. *Canadian Journal of Human Sexuality, 6,* 135–142.

Thacker, T. B., & Banta, H. D. (1983). Benefits and risks of episiotomy: Interpretive review of the English literature, 1960–1980. *Obstetrical and Gynecological Survey, 38,* 322–338.

Thayer, S. (1987). History and strategies of research on social touch. *Journal of Nonverbal Behavior, 11,* 12–28.

The Institute of Medicine (1996). *The hidden epidemic: Confronting sexually transmitted diseases.* National Academy Press: Washington, DC.

Thiessen, D., & Young, R. K. (1994). Investigating sexual coercion. *Society, 3,* 60–64.

Thompson, S. (1994). Changing lives, changing genres: Teenage girls' narratives about sex and romance, 1978–1986. In A. S. Rossi (Ed.), *Sexuality across the life course* (pp. 209–232). Chicago: University of Chicago Press.

Thompson, W. E., & Harred, J. L. (1992). Topless dancers: Managing stigma in a deviant occupation. *Deviant Behavior: An Interdisciplinary Journal, 13,* 291–311.

Thornton, A. (1988). Cohabitation and marriage in the 1980s. *Demography, 25,* 497.

Tiefer, L. (1996). The medicalization of sexuality: Conceptual, normative and professional issues. *Annual review of sex research, 7,* 252–282.

Tiefer, L. (1997). Response to testosterone injection study and Fisher's concerns. *The Journal of Sex Research, 34,* 37.

Tiefer, L., & Melman, A. (1989). Comprehensive evaluation of erectile dysfunction and medical treatments. In S. R. Leiblum & R. C. Rosen (Eds.), *Principles and practices of sex therapy* (2nd ed., pp. 207–236). New York: Guilford.

Tietze, C., Forrest, J. D., & Henshaw, S. (1988). United States of America. In P. Sachdev (Ed.), *International handbook on abortion* (pp. 473–494). New York: Greenwood.

Tollison, C. D., & Adams, H. E. (1979). *Sexual disorders: Treatment, theory, research.* New York: Gardner.

Tortora, G. J., & Grabowski, S. R. (1996). *Principles of anatomy and physiology* (8th ed.). New York: Harper-Collins.

Trivedi, N., & Sabini, J. (1998). Volunteer bias, sexuality, and personality. *Archives of Sexual Behavior, 27,* 181–195.

Trivers, R. E. (1972). Parental investment and sexual selection. In B. Campbell (Ed.), *Sexual selection and the descent of man* (pp. 136–179). Chicago: Aldine.

Troll, L. E., & Smith, J. (1976). Attachment through the life span: Some questions about dyadic bonds among adults. *Human Development, 19,* 135–182.

Trussell, J. Contraceptive efficacy. In R. A. Hatcher, J. Trussell, F. Stewart, W. Cates, Jr., G.K. Stewart, F. Guest and D. Kowal (Eds.). *Contraceptive Technology* (17th Ed). Pp. 779–799. New York: Ardent Media.

Trussell, J., & Kowal, D. (1998). The essentials of contraception. In R. A. Hatcher, J. Trussell, F. Stewart, W. Cates, Jr., G. K. Stewart, F. Guest, & D. Kowal (Eds.), *Contraceptive technology* (17th ed.) (pp. 211–247). New York: Ardent Media.

Trussell, J., Strickler, J., & Vaughan, B. (1993). Contraceptive efficacy of the diaphragm, the sponge, and the cervical cap. *Family Planning Perspectives, 25,* 100–105, 135.

Udry, J. R. (1998). Doing sex research on adolescents. In G. G. Brannigan, E. R. Allgeier, & A. R. Allgeier (Eds.), *The sex scientists* (pp. 49–60). New York: Longman.

Umberson, D., Wortman, C. B., & Kessler, R. C. (1992). Widowhood and depression: Explaining long-term gender differences in vulnerability. *Journal of Health and Social Behavior, 33,* 10–24.

Ungvarski, P. J. (1997). Update on HIV infection. *American Journal of Nursing, 97,* 44–51.

U.S. Bureau of the Census. (1996). *Statistical abstracts of the United States* (116th ed.). Washington, DC: GPO.

U.S. Department of Health and Human Services (1996). *Child maltreatment 1994: Reports from the states to the National Center on Child Abuse and Neglect.* Washington, DC: U.S. GPO.

U.S. Department of Health and Human Services (1997). *Child maltreatment 1995: Reports from the states to the National Center on Child Abuse and Neglect.* Washington, DC: U.S. GPO.

U.S. Department of Labor. Bureau of International Labor Affairs. (1996). *Forced labor: The prostitution of children.* Washington, DC: General Printing Office.

U.S. General Accounting Office. (1995). *DOD service academies: Update on extent of sexual harassment.* Washington, DC: National Security and International Affairs Division.

U.S. Merit Systems Protection Board. (1981). *Sexual harassment in the federal workplace: Is it a problem?* Washington, DC: U.S. Government Printing Office.

U.S. Merit Systems Protection Board. (1988). *Sexual harassment in the federal government: An update.* Washington, DC: U.S. Government Printing Office.

U.S. Merit Systems Protection Board. (1995). *Sexual harassment in the federal workplace: Trends, progress, continuing challenges.* Washington, DC: U.S. Government Printing Office.

Uvnas-Moberg, K. (1998). Oxytocin may mediate the effects of positive social interaction and emotions. *Psychoneuroendocrinology, 23,* 819–835.

Uvnas-Moberg, K., & Carter, C. S. (1998). Is there a neurobiology of love? *Psychoneuroendocrinology, 23,* 749–750.

van de Velde, T. H. (1930). *Ideal marriage: Its physiology and technique.* New York: Covici-Friede.

Van Goozen, S. H. M., Wiegant, V. M., Endert, E., Helmand, F. A., & Van de Poll, N. E. (1997). Psychoendocrinological assessment of the menstrual cycle: The relationship between hormones, sexuality, and mood. *Archives of Sexual Behavior, 26,* 359–382.

van Ijzendoorn, M. H. (1995). Adult attachment representations, parental responsiveness, and infant attachment: A meta-analysis on the predictive validity of the Adult Attachment Interview. *Psychological Bulletin, 117,* 387–403.

van Kesteren, P. J., Gooren, L. J., & Megens, J. A. (1996). An epidemiological and demographic study of transsexuals in the Netherlands. *Archives of Sexual Behavior, 25,* 589–600.

Van Wesenbeeck, I., de Graaf, R., van Zessen, G., Straver, C. J., & Visser, J. H. (1995). Professional HIV risk taking, levels of victimization, and well-being in female prostitutes in the Netherlands. *Archives of Sexual Behavior, 24,* 503–515.

Van Wyk, P. H., & Geist, C. S. (1984). Psychosocial development of heterosexual, bisexual, and homosexual behavior. *Archives of Sexual Behavior, 13,* 505–544.

Vance, E. B., & Wagner, N. N. (1976). Written descriptions of orgasm: A study of sex differences. *Archives of Sexual Behavior, 5,* 87–98.

Vermeulen, A. (1986). Leydig cell physiology. In R. J. Santen & R. S. Swerdloff (Eds.), *Male reproductive dysfunction* (pp. 49–76). New York: Dekker.

Verschoor, A. M., & Poortinga, J. (1988). Psychosocial differences between Dutch male and female transsexuals. *Archives of Sexual Behavior, 17,* 173–178.

Verwoerdt, A., Pfeiffer, E., & Wang, H. S. (1969). Sexual behavior in senescence: Patterns of sexual activity and interest. *Geriatrics, 24,* 137–144.

Vogel, D. A., Lake, M. A., Evans, S., & Karraker, K. H. (1991). Children's and adults' sex-stereotyped perceptions of infants. *Sex Roles, 24,* 605–616.

Wagner, G., & Kaplan, H. S. (1993). *The new injection treatment for impotence.* New York: Brunner/Mazel.

Wagner, G., Rabkin, J., & Rabkin, R. (1997a). Effects of testosterone replacement therapy on sexual interest, function, and behavior in HIV+ men. *The Journal of Sex Research, 34,* 27–33.

Wagstaff, D. A., Kelly, J. A., Perry, M. J., Sikkema, L. J., Soloman, L. J., Heckman, T. G., & Anderson, E. S. (1995). Multiple partners, risky partners, and HIV risk among low-income urban women. *Family Planning Perspectives, 27,* 241–245.

Wallace, J. I., Mann, J., & Beatrice, S. (1988, June). *HIV-I exposure among clients of prostitutes.* Paper presented at the IV International Conference on AIDS, Stockholm, Sweden.

Wallen, K., & Parson, S. W. A. (1997). Sexual behavior in same-sexed nonhuman primates: Is it relevant to understanding human homosexuality? *Annual Review of Sex Research, 7,* 195–223.

Walling, W. H. (1904). *Sexology.* Philadelphia: Puritan.

Walster, E., Aronson, V., Abrahams, D., & Rottman, L. (1966). The importance of physical attractiveness in dating behavior. *Journal of Personality and Social Psychology, 4,* 508–516.

Walster, E., Walster, G. W., & Berscheid, E. (1978). *Equity: Theory and research.* Boston: Allyn & Bacon.

Walters, A. S., & Curran, M. C. (1996). "Excuse me sir? May I help you and your boyfriend?" Salespersons' differential treatment of homosexual and straight customers. *Journal of Homosexuality, 31,* 135–152.

Walters, A.S., Hayes, D.M. (1998) Homophobia within schools: Challenging the culturally sanctioned dismissal of gay students and colleagues. *Journal of Homosexuality, 35(2),* 1–23

Warner, D. L., & Hatcher, R. A. (1998). Male condoms. In R. A. Hatcher, J. Trussell, F. Stewart, W. Cates, Jr., G. K. Stewart, F. Guest, & D. Kowal (Eds.), *Contraceptive technology* (17th ed.) (pp. 325–355). New York: Ardent Media.

Watkins, E. S. (1998). *On the pill: A social history of contraceptives, 1950–1970.* Baltimore: Johns Hopkins University Press.

Webster, D. C. (1996). Sex, lies, and stereotypes: Women and interstitial cystitis. *The Journal of Sex Research, 33,* 197–203.

Weinberg, J. S. (1994). Research in sadomasochism: A review of sociological and social psychological literature. *Annual Review of Sex Research, 5,* 257–279.

Weinberg, M. S., & Williams, C. J. (1975). *Male homosexuals: Their problems and adaptations.* New York: Penguin.

Weinberg, M. S., Williams, C. J., & Calhan, C. (1995). "If the shoe fits . . .": Exploring male homosexual foot fetishism. *The Journal of Sex Research, 32,* 17–27.

Weinberg, M. S., Williams, C. J., & Pryor, D. W. (1994). *Dual attraction: Understanding bisexuality.* New York: Oxford University Press.

Weinrich, J. D. (1994). Homosexuality. In V. L. Bullough & B. Bullough (Eds.), *Human sexuality: An encyclopedia* (pp. 277–283). New York: Garland.

Weinrich, J. D., Grant, I., Jacobson, D. L., Robinson, S. R., McCutchan, J. A., and the HNRC Group (1992). Effects of recalled childhood gender nonconformity on adult genitoerotic role and AIDS exposure. *Archives of Sexual Behavior, 21,* 559–585.

Weis, D. L. (1983). Affective reactions of women to their initial experience of coitus. *The Journal of Sex Research, 19,* 209–237.

Weisse, C. S., Turbiasz, A., & Whitney, O. J. (1995). Behavioral training and AIDS risk reduction: Overcoming barriers to condom use. *AIDS Education and Prevention, 7,* 50–59.

Weizman, R., & Hart, J. (1987). Sexual behavior in healthy married elderly men. *Archives of Sexual Behavior, 16,* 39–44.

Welch, M. R., & Kartub, P. (1978). Socio-cultural correlates of incidence of impotence: A cross-cultural study. *The Journal of Sex Research, 14,* 218–230.

Weller, R. A., & Halika, J. (1984). Marijuana use and sexual behavior. *The Journal of Sex Research, 20,* 186–193.

Wellings, K., Field, J., Johnson, A. M., & Wadsworth, J. (1994). *Sexual behavior in Britain: The national survey of sexual attitudes and lifestyles.* New York: Penguin Books.

Wells, B. (1986). Predictors of female nocturnal orgasm. *The Journal of Sex Research, 23,* 421–437.

West, D. J. (1993). *Male prostitution.* New York: Haworth Press.

Weston, D. (1998). The scientific legacy of Sigmund Freud: Toward a psychodynamically informed psychological science. *Psychological Bulletin, 124,* 333–371.

Whipple, B. (1994). G spot and female pleasure. In V. L. Bullough & B. Bullough (Eds.), *Human sexuality: An encyclopedia* (pp. 229– 232). New York: Garland.

Whipple, B., Ogden, G., & Komisaruk, B. R. (1992). Physiological correlates of imagery-induced orgasm in women. *Archives of Sexual Behavior, 21,* 121–133.

Whitam, F. L. (1977). Childhood indicators of male homosexuality. *Archives of Sexual Behavior, 6,* 89–96.

Whitam, F. L., Daskalos, C., Sobolewski, C. G., & Padilla, P. (1998). The emergence of lesbian sexuality and identity cross-culturally: Brazil, Peru, the Philippines, and the United States. *Archives of Sexual Behavior, 27,* 31–56.

Whitam, F. L., Diamond, M., & Martin, J. (1993). Homosexual orientation in twins: A report on sixty-one pairs and three triplet sets. *Archives of Sexual Behavior, 22,* 187–206.

Whitam, F. L., & Mathy, R. M. (1986). *Male homosexuality in four societies: Brazil, Guatemala, the Philippines, and the United States.* New York: Praeger.

White, G. L. (1981). Relative involvement, inadequacy, and jealousy: A test of a causal model. *Alternative Lifestyles, 4,* 291–309.

White, G. L., & Helbick, R. M. (1988). Understanding and treating jealousy. In R. A. Brown & J. F. Fields (Eds.), *Treatment of sexual problems in individuals and couples therapy* (pp. 245–265). Boston: PMA.

White, L. K. (1991). Determinants of divorce: A review of research in the eighties. In A. Booth (Ed.), *Contemporary families: Looking forward, looking back* (pp. 141–149). Minneapolis: National Council on Family Relations.

Whiting, B., & Edwards, C. P. (1988). *Children of different worlds.* Cambridge, MA: Harvard University Press.

Whitley, B. E., Jr. (1989). Correlates of oral-genital experience among college students. *Journal of Psychology and Human Sexuality, 2,* 151–163.

Whitley, B. E., Jr. Wiederman, M. W., & Wryobec, J. M. (1999). Correlates of heterosexual men's eroticization of lesbianism. *Journal of Psychology and Human Sexuality,* [in press]

Wiederman, M. W. (1993). Demographic and sexual characteristics of nonresponders to sexual experience items in a national survey. *The Journal of Sex Research, 30,* 27–35.

Wiederman, M. W. (1997). Pretending orgasm during sexual intercourse: Correlates in a sample of young adult women. *Journal of Sex and Marital Therapy, 23,* 131–139.

Wiederman, M. W. (1998). The state of theory in sex therapy. *The Journal of Sex Research, 35,* 88-99.

Wiederman, M. W. (1999). Extramarital sex in America. *USA Today* (magazine).

Wiederman, M. W. (in press). Sexuality research, IRBs, and subject pools. In G. Chastain & R. E. Landrum (Eds.), *Protecting human subjects: Departmental subject pools and institutional review boards* (pp. 201–219). Washington, DC: American Psychological Association.

Wiederman, M. W., & Allgeier, E. R. (1996). Expectations and attributions regarding extramarital sex among young married individuals. *Journal of Psychology and Human Sexuality, 8* (3), 21–35.

Wiederman, M. W., Allgeier, E. R., & Weiner, A. (1992, June). *People's perceptions of vocalizations made during sexual intercourse.* Paper presented at the Midcontinent Region meeting of The Society for the Scientific Study of Sex, Big Rapids, MI.

Wiederman, M. W., & Hurd, C. (1999). Extradyadic involvement during dating. *Journal of Social and Personal Relationships.*

Wiederman, M. W., Weis, D. L., & Allgeier, E. R. (1994). The effect of question preface on response rates to a telephone survey of sexual experience. *Archives of Sexual Behavior, 23,* 203–215.

Wilcox, A., Weinberg, C., & Baird, D. (1995). Timing of sexual intercourse in relation to ovulation: Effects on the probability of conception, survival of the pregnancy, and sex of the baby. *The New England Journal of Medicine, 333,* 1517–1521.

Wiles, C. R., Wiles, J. A., & Tjernlund, A. (1996). The ideology of advertising: The United States and Sweden. *Journal of Advertising Research, 36* (3), 57–66.

Will, J. A., Self, P. A., & Datan, N. (1976). Maternal behavior and perceived sex of infant. *American Journal of Orthopsychiatry, 49,* 135–139.

Wilson, G. T., & Lawson, D. M. (1978). Expectancies, alcohol, and sexual arousal in women. *Journal of Abnormal Psychology, 87,* 358–367.

Winick, C., & Evans, J. T. (1996). The relationship between nonenforcement of state pornography laws and rates of sex crime arrest. *Archives of Sexual Behavior, 25,* 439–453.

World Health Organization Task Force on Methods for the Regulation of Male Fertility. (1996). Contraceptive efficacy of testosterone-induced asoospermia and oligozoospermia in normal men. *Fertility and Sterility, 65,* 821–829.

World Health Organization Task Force on Psychological Research on Family Planning. (1982). Hormonal contraception for men: Acceptability and effects on sexuality. *Studies in Family Planning, 13,* 328–342.

Wrangham, R. W., & Peterson, D. (1996). *Demonic males: Apes and the origins of human violence.* Boston: Houghton Mifflin.

Wu, F. C. W., Farley, T. M. M., Peregoudov, A., & Waites, G. M. H. (1996). Effects of testosterone enanthate in normal men: Experience from a multicenter contraceptive efficacy study. *Fertility and Sterility, 65,* 626–636.

Wurtele, S. K. (1993). Enhancing children's sexual development through child sexual abuse programs. *Journal of Sex Education and Therapy, 19,* 37–46.

Yarab, P. E., & Allgeier, E. R. (1997, April). "Who" really does matter: Reactions of jealousy and perceived threat based on the characteristics of an interloper. Paper presented at the annual meeting of the Eastern Psychological Association, Washington, DC.

Yarab, P. E., Sensibaugh, C. C., & Allgeier, E. R. (1998). More than just sex: Gender differences in the incidence of self-defined unfaithful behavior in heterosexual dating relationships. *Journal of Psychology and Human Sexuality, 10* (2), 45–57.

Zagumny, M. J., & Brady, D. B. (1998). Development of the AIDS Health Belief Scale (AHBS). *AIDS Education and Prevention, 10,* 173–179.

Zaviacic, M., & Whipple, B. (1993). Update on the female prostate and the phenomenon of female ejaculation. *The Journal of Sex Research, 30,* 148–151.

Zelen, S. L. (1985). Sexualization of therapeutic relationships: The dual vulnerability of patient and therapist. *Psychotherapy, 22,* 178–185.

Zellman, G. L., & Goodchilds, J. D. (1983). Becoming sexual in adolescence. In E. R. Allgeier & N. B. McCormick (Eds.), *Changing boundaries: Gender roles and sexual behavior* (pp. 49–63). Palo Alto, CA: Mayfield.

Zelnik, M., & Kantner, J. F. (1978). Contraceptive patterns and premarital pregnancy among women aged 15–19 in 1976. *Family Planning Perspectives, 10,* 135–142.

Zilbergeld, B., & Evans, M. (1980). The inadequacy of Masters and Johnson. *Psychology Today, 14,* 29–43.

Zillmann, D., & Bryant, J. (1984). Effects of massive exposure to pornography. In N. M. Malamuth & E. Donnerstein (Eds.), *Pornography and sexual aggression* (pp. 115–138). Orlando, FL: Academic Press.

Zillmann, D., & Bryant, J. (1988). Pornography's impact on sexual satisfaction. *Journal of Applied Social Psychology, 18,* 438–453.

Zlokovich, M. S., & Snell, Jr., W. E. (1997). Contraceptive behavior and efficacy: The influence of illusion of fertility control and adult attachment tendencies. *Journal of Psychology and Human Sexuality, 9* (1), 39–55.

Zucker, K., Bradley, S., Oliver, G., Blake, J., Fleming, S., & Head, A. (1996). Psychosexual development of women with congenital adrenal hyperplasia. *Hormones and Behavior, 30,* 300–318.

Zucker, K. J. (1996). Commentary on Diamond's "prenatal predisposition and the clinical management of some pediatric conditions." *Journal of Sex and Marital Therapy, 22,* 148–160.

Zucker, K. J., & Bradley, S. J. (1995). *Gender identity disorder and psychosexual problems in children and adolescents.* New York: Guilford.

Name Index

Subject Index

Aborigines (Australia), 169, 283–284

Abortion, 223, 246–260
adolescents and, 251–252, 253, 261
Catholic church and, 15
contraception following, 253
cultural diversity and, 15
definition of, 247
diethylstilbestrol for, 255, 256
dilation and curettage for, 257–258
dilation and evacuation for, 258
early in pregnancy, 255–256
emergency contraceptive pills for, 255–256
first-trimester, 16, 248, 250, 253, 256–258
health risks with, 227
human chorionic gonadotropin for, 244
hysterotomy for, 258
as individual and family dilemma, 252
intra-amniotic injection for, 258
intrauterine device for, 255
late-pregnancy, 258–259
legal aspects of, 224, 251, 252, 253–255, 256
male role in, 259–260
menstrual extraction for, 255, 256
methods of, 255–259
minors and, 254
moral debate over, 248–251
number of, 247, 253
partial-birth, 258–259
for population control, 15
psychological responses to, 259
reasons for, 251–253
religion and, 248
repeat, 253
RU-486 for, 255, 256

second-trimester, 258
spontaneous (miscarriage), 199, 200, 201
suction, 256–257

Abstinence, 15, 224, 287–288, 297, 397, 398

Abuse, *see* Childhood sexual abuse; Wife abuse

Acne, 192

Acquaintance assault (date rape), 20, 139, 455, 456, 457, 462–463. *See also* Assault, sexual

Acquired immunodeficiency syndrome (AIDS), *see* HIV/AIDS

Acyclovir, 393

Adam and Eve, 7

Addiction
interpersonal, 160–161
sexual, *see* Compulsive sexual behavior; Excessive sexual desire
see also Alcohol; Drug abuse

Adolescence, 289–293
abortion and, 251–252, 253, 261
attachment in infancy and, 149
contraceptive use and, 227–228, 253, 263, 264, 378
fantasies in, 130, 290
gender-role identification in, 289–291
gender-role socialization in, 279
genital stage in, 269, 290
HIV/AIDS and, 377–378
hormonal implant use and, 239
identity vs. role confusion in, 269, 289–290
koro and, 9
marriage in, 309
masturbation in, 97, 287
nocturnal orgasm in, 94
oral-genital sex in, 103

parental attitudes toward sexuality and, 138
parenthood in, 261–264
pregnancy in, 247, 253, 260–264, 288, 289, 460
prostitution and, 491–493, 495
psychosexual development in, 269
psychosocial development in, 32, 269, 289–290
romantic love in, 153
sex education and, 227, 263–264, 287–288, 289
sex offenders and, 451
sex portrayals on TV and, 475
sexual activity in, 287, 291–292
sexual assault and, 454, 456, 461, 462
sexual attitudes and, 130
sexual double standard and, 289–290
smell and, 127
witchcraft and, 9
see also Dating/mating; Puberty

Adolescent Family Life Act (1981), 288

Adoption, 16

Adrenal glands, 68, 82, 274

Adult bookstores, 476

Adultery, *see* Extramarital sexual relationships

Adulthood, attachment in, 150, 156–159. *See also* Long-term relationships; Marriage; Middle age; Old age; Young adulthood

Advertising, 4
attractiveness and, 283
sexual images in, 474–475

African Americans
abortion and, 248, 250
Tuskegee study of untreated syphilis and, 54, 55

Afterbirth, *see* Placenta

Aggression, *see* Assault, sexual; Child sexual abuse; Wife abuse

Aging, double standard on, 311–312. *See also* Middle age; Old age

Agreements, honoring, 143–144, 163

AIDS (acquired immunodeficiency syndrome), *see* HIV/AIDS

AIDS dementia complex, 390

Aids, sexual, 480–481

AIS, *see* Androgen insensitivity syndrome

Aka Pygmy tribe, 274

Alcohol
as an aphrodisiac, 481
prenatal development and, 198, 199–200
sexual assault and, 455, 461, 463
sexual dysfunction and, 356

Alveoli, 202, 215

Amazonian basin, 169–170

Ambition, mate selection and, 20

Amebiasis (amebic dysentery), 395

Amenorrhea, 197

American Association for Sex Educators, Counselors, and Therapists, 371

American Cancer Society, 68

American Civil Liberties Union, 481

American Indians, 105

American Medical Association, 49

American Psychiatric Association, 340–341, 416

Amniocentesis, 200

Amniotic fluid, 176, 209, 210

Amniotic sac, 174, 175

Amphetamines, 481

Amygdala, 89, 90

Amyl nitrate, 481

Analingus, 103, 327. *See also* Oral-genital sex

Credits

p. 280: Myrleen Ferguson/Photo Edit; p. 282: Tony Freeman/Photo Edit; p. 285: SuperStock; p. 286: Joel Gordon; p. 287: Michael Newman/Photo Edit; p. 292: G & M David De Lossy/The Image Bank; p. 294: M. Siluk/The Image Works; p. 296: Nawrocki/Picture Perfect; p. 298: Bob Jacobson/Index Stock; p. 304: Kathleen Ferguson/Photo Edit; p. 305: David R. Frazier Photolibrary; p. 312: left, Kirkland/SYGMA; right, Reuters/Corbis-Bettmann; p. 313: Pacha/Corbis-Bettmann; p. 314: Gender and Life Cycle from *Geschlechtskunde* by Magnum Hirschfield, photo from the New York Public Library; p. 318: David Austen/Stock Boston; p. 320: Joel Gordon; p. 327: Mark Howes; p. 328: *Le sommeil* by Gustave Goubet, Musée du Petit Palais, Paris—photo by Bulloz/Art Resource; p. 329: James Leynse/SABA; p. 330: Ramey/Stock Boston; p. 339: Chris Maynard/Gamma Liaison; p. 343: Joel Gordon; p. 348: S. Oskar/Index Stock; p. 353: Esbin-Anderson/Omni Photo; p. 354: Gabe Palmer/ The Stock Market; p. 356: Comstock; p. 363: Theo Westenberger/Gamma Liaison; p. 374: Joel Gordon; p. 377: James D. Wilson/Gamma Liaison; p. 380: courtesy Massachusetts Dept. of Public Health/Div. of Communicable and Venereal Diseases; p. 381: Atlanta Center for Disease Control; p. 391: George Moore/Custom Medical Stock; p. 392: Phototake; p. 393: Medichrome/The Stock Shop; p. 397: Esbin-Anderson/The Image Works; p. 400: Charlie Varley/Sipa Press; p. 404: left, Evan Agostini/Gamma Liaison; right, John Nordelli/The Picture Cube; pp. 406–408: Dr. Donald Laub; p. 412: Ted Soqui/SYGMA; p. 415: J. Van Hasselt/SYGMA; p. 417: Roswell Angier/Stock Boston; p. 418: Bonnie Kamin/Photo Edit; p. 420: Tom Herde/The Boston Globe; p. 422: *Sculptor with Centaur and Women* by Pablo Picasso, Sotheby Parke Bernet, Art Resource, NY; p. 428: David Oliver/Tony Stone Images; p. 432: left, John Byrum; right, I. Boddenberg/Index Stock; p. 438: Chuck Savage/The Stock Market; p. 442: R. Ellis/SYGMA; p. 444: Jim Davis/The Boston Globe; p. 448: Allen Mcinnis/Gamma Liaison; p. 451: Comstock; p. 454: Michael Newman/Photo Edit; p. 458: Joel Gordon; p. 462: Cindy Charles/Photo Edit; p. 468: Joel Gordon; p. 472: Justin Sutcliffe/Sipa Press; p. 474: left, J. Sohm/The Image Works; right, Joel Gordon; p. 476: Elizabeth Rice Allgeier; p. 478: Joel Gordon; p. 479: Nik Kleinberg/Stock Boston; p. 489: Suzanne Hanover/1995 United Artists Pictures, Inc./Kobal Collection; p. 490: Joel Gordon; p. 493: Mark Ellen Mark Library; p. 498: Regine M./The Image Bank.

ILLUSTRATIONS

By Leslie Evans: pp. 98, 99, 101, 102, 104, 106, 107, 206, 365.

By Sandra Sevigny: pp. 68, 69, 72, 73, 75, 76, 80, 81, 85, 88, 89, 112, 114, 123, 157, 170, 171, 175, 179, 181, 200, 205, 213,230, 231, 232, 234, 237, 242, 243,257, 280, 367, 369, 387, 470, 485.

The following illustrations are from Allgeier, Albert R., and Elizabeth R. Allgeier, *Sexual Interactions: Basic Understandings.* Copyright © 1998 by Houghton Mifflin Company. Used with permission: Figures 4.1, 4.3, 4.4, 4.5, 4.6, 4.7, 4.8, 4.9, 4.10, 4.11, 5.10, 5.11, 6.1, 8.1, 8.2, 8.3, 8.4, 8.5, 9.1, 9.2, 9.4, 10.2, 10.3, 10.4, 10.5, 10.6, 10.7, 11.1, 15.2, 15.3.

Figure 14.3 reprinted with permission from D.H. Hamer, S. Hu, V. Magnuson, N. Hu, A. Pattatucci, "A Linkage Between DNA Markers on the X Chromosome and Male Sexual Orientation," *Science,* Vol. 261 (July 16, 1993): 323. Copyright © 1993 American Association for the Advancement of Science.

Figure 14.4, "Exotic Becomes Erotic: A Developmental Theory of Sexual Orientation," figure 1, p. 321 from *Psychological Review* 1996, 103, 320–325. Copyright © 1996 by the American Psychological Association. Reprinted with permission.

TEXT

The following are from Allgeier, Albert R., and Elizabeth R. Allgeier, *Sexual Interactions: Basic Understandings.* Copyright © 1998 by Houghton Mifflin Company. Used with permission: Highlight, p. 40; Table 2.1; Research Spotlight, p. 54; Highlight, p. 69; Research Spotlight, p. 115; Tables 5.1–5.4; Highlight, p. 142; Research Spotlight, p. 162; Highlight, p. 166; Highlight, p. 180, Highlight, p. 190; Table 9.1; Table 10.2; Research Spotlight, p. 288; Highlight, p. 368; Table 15.2.

Highlight p. 21, "The Valencia Declaration on Sexual Rights," from the close of the 13th World Congress of Sexology. Reprinted by permission.

Excerpts pp. 93 and 121 from *Shared Intimacies: Women's Sexual Experiences* by L.G. Barbach and L. Levine. Copyright © 1980 by Lonnie Barbach and Linda Levine. Used by permission of Doubleday, a division of Bantam Doubleday Dell Publishing Group Inc.

Table 10.2, "Risks Associated with Life and Fertility," from Hatcher et al., *Contraceptive Technology,* Irvington Publishers, 1994. Reprinted with permission of Irvington Publishers, Inc.

Research Spotlight p. 270 from *Children's Sexual Thinking,* 1982, Ronald and Juliette Goldman, pp. 62–63, 73–74. Reprinted by permission of Routledge, London.

Table 12.2, reproduced with the permission of The Alan Guttmacher Institute from Mott, F.L., "The Determinants of First Sex by Age 14 in a High-Risk Adolescent Population," *Family Planning Perspectives,* 1996 28(1): 13–18.

"Letter from Harvey," p. 316, permission granted by Ann Landers/Creators Syndicate.

Highlight p. 340 Copyright © 1972 by Barbara Love and Sidney Abbott from the book *Sappho Was a Right-on Woman.* Reprinted with permission of Stein and Day Publishers.

Table 17.1 based on responses to questionnaires completed by people located through sadomasochistic magazines and clubs, by Breslow, Evans, and Langley (1985). *Archives of Sexual Behavior,* 14, p. 315. Copyright 1985 by Plenum Publishing Company. Reprinted by permission.

Tables 17.2 and 17.3 adapted from Kinsey, A.C., Pomeroy, W., Martin, C., Gebhard, P. , *Sexual Behavior in the Human Female,* pp. 663, 677–678. Philadelphia: Saunders, 1953. Reprinted by permission of The Kinsey Institute for Research in Sex, Gender, and Reproduction, Inc.